Experimental Social Psychology

An Interpretation of Research upon the
Socialization of the Individual

REVISED EDITION

By

GARDNER MURPHY
College of the City of New York

LOIS BARCLAY MURPHY
Sarah Lawrence College

and

THEODORE M. NEWCOMB
Bennington College

HARPER & BROTHERS PUBLISHERS

New York and London

CONTENTS

PART I: INTRODUCTION

PART II: INTERPRETATION OF THE PROCESS OF SOCIALIZATION

PART III: A GENETIC STUDY OF SOCIAL BEHAVIOR

PART IV: QUANTITATIVE STUDIES OF INDIVIDUAL DIFFERENCES IN ADULT SOCIAL BEHAVIOR

FOREWORD TO THE REVISED EDITION

SINCE the publication of the first edition there have appeared Allport and Vernon's *Studies in Expressive Movement,* Bartlett's *Remembering,* Bridges' *Social and Emotional Development of the Pre-school Child,* Isaacs' *Social Development in Young Children,* Moreno's *Who Shall Survive?,* Piaget's *Moral Judgment of the Child,* and Sherif's *The Psychology of Social Norms.* Quite aside from the many important studies appearing in monographs and journals, we feel that the list just given is sufficient to show that the first edition is already obsolete.

The rapid accumulation of research of all sorts, and the new perspectives given by both biological and social science, require a completely new approach. We shall not attempt here a handbook of research findings, such as the first edition represented, but a somewhat more systematic interpretation of the evidences, from every type of careful research known to us, regarding the relations of individual human beings to one another in our own culture. The emphasis is not upon group behavior as such, but upon the process by which the individual responds, from infancy onward, to the persons about him, and becomes an adult personality in our society— broadly, the process of individual socialization.

Summaries of groups of research studies are frequently given in chart form; and the section entitled "References" at the end of the book provides source material for many further statements of fact which the reader may wish to verify. These two devices are designed to make the text itself shorter and more readable.

We are deeply indebted to Erich Fromm, Carolyn Zachry, Anna Hartoch, J. L. Moreno, and Muzafer Sherif for the stimulus of their profound understanding of personality development, and to L. J. Stone for insight and help in preparation of the manuscript.

T. M. Newcomb has joined us in the present labor, giving more than abundantly of his time, energy, and wise counsel, and writing practically all of Part IV. Our gratitude is not sufficiently expressed by asking him to appear with us on the title page.

G. M.

L. B. M.

FOREWORD TO THE FIRST EDITION

THE effort to make social psychology an experimental science has long been under way. That much has been done in this direction we trust these pages will make clear. That the data secured by experimental methods have not as yet given us a "systematized" science will be equally clear. The venture to understand the social behavior of human beings is of such overwhelming importance that we believe there is now a place for a volume which has no purpose but to show what the experimental approach to such problems has yielded and what it may rightfully be expected to yield. It is not suggested that this is the only effort which should occupy the social psychologist; rather, that it is one task among many with which he is concerned.

We are under heavy obligations to Mark A. May and Eric J. Dingwall for suggestions as to the manner of envisaging and presenting the material. For bibliographical help we are indebted to many who have given generously of their time, especially to Goodwin B. Watson, Ralph Spence, Miriam C. Gould, Otto Klineberg, Ruth Munroe, Paul H. Furfey, and Stuart A. Rice; finally, we are especially grateful to Maud King Murphy and Helen Merrell Lynd for their careful and constructive criticism of the manuscript in proof.

G. M.
L. B. M.

Morningside Heights
New York City
January, 1931

FOREWORD TO THE FIRST EDITION

The effort to make social psychology an experimental science has long been under way. That much has been done in this direction we trust these pages will make clear. That the data secured by experimental methods have not as yet given us a "systematized" science will be equally clear. The voyage to understand the social behavior of human beings is of such overwhelming importance that we believe there is now a place for a volume which has no purpose but to show what the experimental approach to such problems has yielded and what it may reasonably be expected to yield. It is not suggested that this is the only effort which should occupy the social psychologist; rather, that it is one task among many with which he is concerned.

We are under heavy obligations to Mark A. May and Eric L. Ding, will for suggestions as to the contents of the volume and preparing the material. For labor expended not only in behalf of many who have given generously of their time, especially to such as Goodwin B. Watson, Ralph Stogner, Arthur C. Lough, Otto Klineberg, Ruth Munroe, Paul L. Boynton, and Stuart A. Rice; finally, we are especially grateful to Maud Merrill who helped to collect the material and for their careful and courteous reading of the manuscript in proof.

G. M.
L. B. M.

Morningside Heights
New York City
January, 1931

PART ONE

Introduction

Chapter I

THE FIELD AND THE METHODS OF SOCIAL PSYCHOLOGY

THE HISTORY of the systematic study of man's social behavior belongs, strangely enough, to the history of economics, ethics, jurisprudence, and other disciplines which have not been primarily concerned with first-hand investigation of human nature. From Aristotle to the early nineteenth century, able men were thinking about the laws of social behavior; but whether they called themselves political economists, moralists, jurists, or what not, they all with one accord made it plain that they considered the important thing to be the *social interaction* of men; the nature of the *individual man* was left, as a rather irrelevant problem, to a very different person—the psychologist!

Nor did the psychologist seem to object to this division of labor. Psychology dealt with the nature of the individual mind. Whether rooted in metaphysical, biological, or mechanical assumptions, its task remained the description of individual experience and behavior. The great problems of seventeenth- and eighteenth-century psychology had to do with the relation between mind and body, and with the nature of perception, association, and memory. Moreover, the experimental psychology of the nineteenth century began with investigations of perception, and during the middle of the century was still almost exclusively concerned with cognitive processes. In these studies it seldom occurred to the investigator to consider the influence of the social experience of his subject or even the social influence exerted by the experimenter or other persons in contact with the subject.

By the middle of the century, however, social theorists, notably the utilitarians, had created a demand for the discussion of the influence of individuals upon one another; and something like a systematic social psychology gradually formed itself, first in vague, then in more definite, outlines. In his two great books, written just after the middle of the century, Bain makes a serious attempt to show the interactions between the individual make-up and such social patterns as are emphasized by the student of ethics and aesthetics. In 1860, Steinthal and Lazarus founded a journal for folk psychology which, though concerned not with "social psychology" in the sense here used, but with the supposed "group minds" of various peoples, formulated problems which social psychology later began to study. Spencer, Darwin, Bagehot, and many others also began to show interrelations between biological and psychological concepts on the one hand, and the concepts of social science on the other.

The actual beginning of *experimental social psychology* seems to have been the experimental study of suggestion, first put on a scientific basis by Braid between 1841 and 1860, extended and systematized by the Nancy School (especially Bernheim), and demonstrated by Binet and Féré to be an integral part of experimental psychology. Experimental social psychology did not arise directly from experimental physiology or experimental psychology; with the exception of Binet and Féré, outstanding psychologists gave no serious attention to the problem; it is not clear that even these men who founded the new science realized that they were doing anything more than exploring a problem in individual psychology. Since the responses of individual organisms are invariably the subject matter of psychology, it was not at first evident that any particular importance was to be attached to the fact that the stimulus was a person, and that the interaction of persons—in other words, social psychology—was involved.

Nevertheless, this concept of suggestion—and its close counterpart, imitation—received much attention in the analyses of Tarde, Le Bon and others in the closing decade of the century; it is generally agreed that modern social psychology was founded by these men and their followers. The concepts exploited by Le Bon and other students of the crowd are evidently derived in large part from reports of hysteria and other morbid phenomena in clinic or hospital, and Tarde's dependence upon studies of suggestion (especially those of Bernheim) is even more striking. The work of these great systematic social psychologists is not indeed experimental, but Tarde and Le Bon made constant use of the experimental findings of other men in the construction of their new science.

Just as suggestion and imitation were the concepts most frequently invoked by social psychologists in the closing years of the nineteenth century and the first years of the twentieth, so the era inaugurated by the publication of William McDougall's *Introduction to Social Psychology* in 1908 was dominated by another concept likewise open to experimental analysis, namely, the concept of instinct. For McDougall the interaction of individuals was to be understood primarily in terms of the mainsprings to action—in other words, motives; and these motives were reduced to a very limited number of specific instincts (flight, pugnacity, etc.), with which were associated certain specific emotions. Lists of human motives are at least as old as Aristotle's *Rhetoric*, but there is no instance in history in which the passion for listing or making inventories of human motives enjoyed such popularity as in the decade which followed McDougall's book. Thorndike's *Original Nature of Man* (1913) and Woodworth's *Dynamic Psychology* (1918) are typical expressions of the interest of psychologists in the matter of cataloguing instincts; and in the same era sociologists, economists and educators turned such lists to account or made up new lists of their own. Veblen's *Instinct of Workmanship* (1914) and Trotter's *Instincts of the Herd in Peace and War* (1916) are typical of the period.

Based as it was on schematization rather than on experimental evidence, the doctrine of complex innate action patterns was bound to have its day. The anti-instinct movement of 1919 and the years immediately following seems to have begun with Dunlap's contention that adult action patterns admit of no dissection into purposive components. The word instinct seems to be going out of use as a result of the success of the anti-instinct writers. In the meantime, of course, urges, impulses, and especially drives have come into fashion, and it is customary to assume that these urges are less complex and less purposeful than were the instincts posited by naturalists like Fabre and psychologists like McDougall. The evidence on this complicated point will be discussed in Chapter III, but no one can seriously pretend that the instinct problem has been settled, or even that there is any *one* simple and straightforward "instinct problem." The last few years have witnessed a decline of interest in polemics on the subject, and a considerable renewal of interest in the more complex motives to which McDougall had given special attention.

It remains true that much of the thinking that has been done in social psychology since 1908 has been devoted to preparation for, participation in, and recovery from a heated discussion as to the innate predispositions out of which man's social life is, or is supposed to be, derived. The controversy caused much bad feeling, but does not seem to have materially affected the stream of research upon human and animal motivation which was quietly going on during the same years. It would, however, be absurd to regret that this long struggle occurred, for it served to make clear that foundation principles in social psychology do indeed depend upon the fundamentals of human motivation, and in the work of McDougall came a new emphasis upon the dynamic aspects of both individual and social psychology.

In this same period the anthropologists have been working out their own social-psychological hypotheses, attempting to define the nature of "culture" and its transmission, with relatively little dependence upon assumptions as to the original nature of man. Psychologists have in the last few years begun to study closely such anthropological contributions. The decline of the instinct doctrine made the cultural or historical interpretation of complex action patterns more easily admissible, and several writers on social psychology who have approached the field from psychology rather than from sociology have taken over this concept of a highly plastic human nature shaped almost entirely by the culture which acts upon it, and have put this view forward as their own form of anti-instinct psychology. They grant, of course, that the only way that culture can shape individuals who are born into a given community is by modifying their original nature, or, if you like, by permitting it to develop in certain ways and not in others. In order to say anything really profound about the laws governing the transmission of culture, one would have to understand the learning process—something which we understand scarcely at all at present. It is, however, reasonable to suppose that as we do penetrate more and more into the nature of learning so as to tell exactly what we mean by those forms of learning which we now call suggestion, imitation, indoctrination, and the like, we shall be able to use this anthropological material to greater and greater advantage.

But though the concept of culture cannot be said to have solved any of our psychological problems, it has awakened us to an immensely important fact regarding the limits of what we are pleased to call social psychology. It must be recognized that nearly all the experimental work in social psychology, such as makes up the subject matter of this book, has value and is definitely meaningful only in relation to the particular culture in which the investigation was carried on. Such psychological laws as we can discover are for the most part statements of relations discoverable between stimuli and responses in civilized man, and perhaps many of them hold good only in specific groups or under specific social conditions. The social psychologist is, of course, not content with such generalizations as these; he wishes to find laws which are universal for the entire human family and for all existing or historically known cultures. It may reasonably be conjectured that a few of the laws already discovered—for example, some of the laws relating to suggestion and social facilitation—hold good among oriental as well as among occidental peoples, and among primitive peoples as well as among those more advanced. But it would be going outside the domain of experimental social psychology to insist even upon such a cautious statement as this. Whether any of our laws are really fundamental and necessary laws, deriving inevitably from human nature wherever it exists, can be determined only by experiment itself. Even the psychologist who has acquainted himself with but a few careful ethnological records will, we believe, have felt the massive significance of the historical approach. No matter how earnestly he may cling to biological conceptions, he will find himself perforce thinking of the individual man no longer as the biologically self-sufficient unit but as a bundle of attitudes and habits which are a part of a historical process.

We noted above that experimental work in social psychology began some fifty years ago. The closing years of the nineteenth century saw the appearance of a number of experimental studies of competition and suggestion; and the years from 1900 to the outbreak of the War offered a steadily increasing quantity of experimental studies of social behavior in children and adults. In 1914 Moede and in 1920 F. H. Allport defined a social psychology which should have the same solid experimental foundations as had already been achieved for general psychology. After the War the number of experimental studies began to increase at a disturbingly rapid pace; bibliographies began to be sprinkled with titles suggesting that problems previously taboo in the library were actually demanding the attention of experimentalists, or laying claim to attention comparable to that given to such established fields as psychophysics, reaction time, learning, and association.

The pioneer investigations of F. H. Allport and H. T. Moore upon the phenomena of "social facilitation" and of suggestibility in response to "majority opinion" have served as inspiration for many studies of the influence of the group upon mental processes. The measurement of social traits, stimulated in large part by the success of intelligence tests, has been the subject of a bewildering mass of investigations. Psychological problems suggested by sociology, such as public opinion, propaganda, and the psychology of political campaigns and elections, have drawn heavily upon psychological method. But perhaps the most striking of all the experimental developments has been the rapid increase in the quantity and the quality of research upon the social development of children. The decade from 1910 to 1920 witnessed the beginnings of systematic experimental work on the psychology of newborn infants; and the years since 1920 have presented an astonishing array of data upon the instinctive and emotional make-up of children, the ways in which they learn and the processes by which they become socialized. It has indeed become apparent that experimental child psychology offers a wealth of new material to a scientific social psychology.

Yet it must not be concluded that experimental method has resulted in the creation of a unified and systematic social psychology. Experiment has given great masses of data, but the data are like a few pieces from some great jigsaw puzzle; there is no possibility of glimpsing the whole. Social psychology is like several other disciplines in this respect. For some years the Social Science Research Council has been asking how it is possible to contribute to the organic growth of social science. Research is spotty, scattered, uncoordinated; great gaps exist which remain unfilled for years. The warp and woof of physics and chemistry are so tightly drawn that research takes its place in a ready-made context, and an abundance of implications are clear. But in the social sciences someone studies the reasons why Scandinavians have settled in North Dakota or why the suicide rate is high in San Diego, or why children compete more intensely to have their names on the blackboard than they do for a chocolate bar; but what is to be done with the fragments of research which result? Suppose that a map of *terra firma* (and the limitless sea of ignorance) could show the historical development of experimental research in social psychology. The shore as it existed in 1900 might be represented by a wavy line. Triplett made a study of competition, and following his lead many such studies have been published. The chart would show at this point a long peninsula; more and more work was built on what was known. From Mc-Dougall's 1908 book on, we have been interested in instincts, motives and drives. When the techniques for *measuring drives* were developed, we began to add more studies, so that on the one specific and narrow aspect of naming and measuring the tensions occurring in specific vital organs we have a mass of information, another slender peninsula. There are many such "fingers into the sea," isolated and lonely. The separate zones of research are as uncoordinated as single fields of research could be. The interrelations between our facts on the motives of laboratory rats and the motives which influence adults' preferences in politics are still almost as vague as if no experimental research had been done; and the peninsulas of "learning to read" and "learning to respect the ethical code" are two phases of childhood experience which are separated by a vast bay of sheer ignorance.

The Place of Experiment in Social Psychology

Perhaps part of the trouble just described is the way in which the use of the laboratory has been conceived; perhaps we could define the place of experiment in such a way as to make it more useful. At least we must now make the attempt.

In the more mature sciences one hesitates to assign honorific status to method as such, regardless of problem. In the physical sciences, for example, one must at times rely on laborious and prolonged mathematical analysis, keeping his hands away from his laboratory apparatus until his problem has been mathematically defined. One turns, when necessary, to data from astronomy or geology, obtained not by experimentation but by observation of a unique situation. One finds when and where to experiment, and assigns the experimental method a special place reserved for problems which can be disentangled only by the method of simplification and control of variables. It has become very evident in recent years that the social psychologist has thrust many of his problems into the laboratory without adequate consideration of the matrix in which his most certain and valuable data lie. He has simplified his phenomena in such a way as to exclude essential facts necessary in the understanding of social life, and has succeeded in experimental and quantitative control by leaving out most of the variables about which we really need to know. It would be absurd to expect social psychology to achieve at one stroke the maturity of the established sciences, but it is worth while to ask whether in respect to method it might not be feasible to pay more attention to the essential nature of problems and to learn from the physicist and biologist that it takes many methods to make a science. Rather than dogmatize about the matter, it might be useful to survey the methods now available to social psychology and some of the steps that have been taken already in combining these methods in the solution of critical problems.

We may suggest here a form of integration of research methods which happens to be congenial to us, merely to show one way in which each method may be given a place in a general scientific plan. Among the methods available, first, logically, comes the description of social interaction as given by historian, economist, sociologist or ethnologist. Second, is the tentative outlining of psychological hypotheses regarding these interactions. Third, some of these hypotheses can be partially confirmed, others rejected, by using one culture as a control on another, or by noting which historical changes yield which sorts of psychological changes—noting, with suitable controls, whether the historical change is always attended by the psychological change. Fourth, logically, seems to come intensive observation of children undergoing socialization, the study of social motives and of the learning process in each specific culture, i.e., systematic observation of the child in his natural environment under different cultural conditions, attempting to observe not everything he does but those things which can verify or refute working hypotheses. The observations should take on quantitative form whenever possible, individual differences in children being stated in terms of the amount of each kind of behavior exhibited, the intensity or frequency of each response. Ratings by observers and quantitative analysis of daily records give rough approximations for first analysis. All data on motivation at this point need to be checked against biological information regarding human and animal motives, nomenclature as far as possible being taken from the biologist and compared with that of the psychologist. Individual differences in motives from birth onward may be seen in the light of general genetic knowledge about the range of individual differences in motives to be expected on biological grounds. The early months and years must be thoroughly studied so that both the general pattern of change in later years and the individual differences in response to similar patterns may be understood. The result of such analysis will be the defining of a number of factors relating to motivation and the learning processes. At this point, the fifth step, systematic experimentation, becomes relevant. Hypotheses arising from all the preliminary work are tested by submitting a group of children to a specific situation which is withheld from a suitable control group.

The situation must be understood in the light of its degree of similarity to other situations confronted daily by the individual, and at the termination of the experiment transfer effects to other situations must be looked for.

All the procedures requisite in the study of individual responses to social situations at the childhood level are likewise necessary at the adult level. The experimenter who deals with adults in his laboratory can in no way excuse himself from the execution of the task which the child psychologist faces. He must know the biology of the organism with which he deals, its specific genetic potentialities as suggested by family trees and educational background, the conditionings which have further restricted the potentialities of the organism and given it a specific bent in this or that direction, the value tendencies of the subject, his attitude toward himself, his friends and his work and, last but not least, his attitude toward the experimenter and toward experimental social psychology. For some experimental purposes, simply sitting and talking to him in the laboratory may be the first step; for others, the gathering of systematic life history data. For other purposes there must be attempts at self-expression by the subject, the experimenter encouraging his spontaneous work or play activity, allowing him to read, write, paint, draw, play the piano, talk to the other subjects in the laboratory or criticize the experiment. In any event, when the experimental situation is finally presented, the variables which are to be controlled must be considered not simply from the point of view of physics, but in terms of their whole meaning to the subject.

Nothing has been more natural or reasonable than the desire to make psychology a sort of physics, undertaking to isolate variables and measure them just as the physicist does. The experimental psychology of fifty years ago clearly undertook to do exactly this. Indeed, if a problem did not permit the isolation of a single variable and the meticulous analysis of the effects of that specific variable when all others were constant, the problem was not one for scientific psychology at all. If the problem did not lend itself to this method, so much the worse for the problem; it was not the concern of scientific psychology.

The results of this approach were in some ways salutary. One of the results, however, was to leave pressing and vital problems to those who were ill equipped for serious scientific work, with the consequence that major problems were worked through in confused and inconsistent fashion. In time the more systematic thinkers woke up to discover that the vital facts of motive, suggestion, imitation, repression and compensation were being studied, and that the results could no longer be ignored. They had to take the material discovered and do the best they could with it. The resulting waste, confusion and delay in reference to the most fundamental and important psychological problems was due almost entirely to the worship of a fixed *method* and a frantic desire to find problems which that particular method would serve to answer, rather than a genuine concern for problems and an open-minded attempt made to find scientific methods of approach to those problems.

This point has been made a good many times regarding psychology in general, but unfortunately it must now be made with special emphasis in relation to social psychology. From the experiments of Triplett (1900) to the appearance of Allport's studies (1920) it was becoming steadily clearer that social psychology could advance by the experimental method. The assumption then spread that the *one* inevitable method of social psychology was the laboratory control of discrete variables, the isolation and measurement of each variable in terms of its effects. Despite the vigorous protests in Chapter I of our first edition against regarding experimental social psychology as the only social psychology, the publication of our book was unfortunately assumed to be further evidence that the experimental method must always come first and that all problems must fall willy-nilly into a form recognizable by the laboratory worker. Yet one of our most serious duties now is to point out that many important contributions to social psychology since the publication of the first edition have been made by men and women who have seen human problems broadly in historical or comparative form— for example, ethnologists and psychiatrists who have seen in the growth of personality vital processes which they feel obliged to describe, whether they can control and measure them or not.

It remains true, however, that the best research in social psychology seems to come mostly from those who have the broader per-

spective, who know how to see the big problems and, at the same
time, have some familiarity with the possibilities of the laboratory.
An example is Piaget, who, after working a dozen years in child
psychology by means of the interrogatory, has in the last two years
made systematic use of experimentation, emphasizing a series of
variables which are important in the genesis of children's ideas and
attitudes. Another example is Lewin, who, with broad perspective
on the differences between Germany and America, the differences
between normal and defective children, the differences between professional and proletarian adolescents, has found a way to express
in an experiment almost every kind of differentiation which he had
previously glimpsed. Again, it is Sherif, the student of anthropology
and of modern social classes, who sees how the laboratory may define
for him in quantitative fashion the social factors which make each
of us see the world as he does. Experiment in these cases is the
crowning touch, the technical perfection of the analysis. It must be
emphasized, however, that the experimental method in all these
cases *comes late*. It comes after the problem has been defined and
its salient characteristics so well formulated that we know what can
be controlled and measured. If we are to model our science on
physics, we may appropriately note that in the history of physics
the basic problem, as presented by observations, reflection and calculation, has in each case suggested its appropriate line of experimentation, and that experiment has played a crucial rôle in physics
exactly because clear questions have been put to nature.

This change in perspective will serve to make clear why this
book can no longer reasonably be organized around experimental
method or quantitative method as such. It would be more valuable
to try to define the area of social psychology as we see it, survey
it as systematically as we can without imposing rigid schemes upon
slippery or uncertain facts, sketching an outline of facts and their
interrelations in such a way as to suggest to the reader where the
really big problems seem to lie and how we might profitably hope,
in our generation, to answer the central questions. The experimental
information, together with historical and biographical and other
types of information available, needs to be seen in perspective.
Studies which have defined big problems and conceived some sort

of working method of approaching them deserve major emphasis. We shall even venture, in relation to each major problem, to suggest what might be done next, what kinds of research might be built directly on to the existing structure and serve to integrate the remote and isolated zones where something definite is known.

THE RELATION OF SOCIAL PSYCHOLOGY TO OTHER SCIENCES

If this book is not to be "written around" experimental method as such, but if experimental method is to be used in such a way as to illuminate our most pressing problems, it behooves us to define the boundaries of social psychology and indicate where these problems lie.

There seem to us to be three levels at which human behavior can be studied: (1) One may be interested in the changes in the organism which occur in a specific situation. One thus makes of himself a physiologist or a physiological psychologist. One asks, "What can the iris of the eye or the thyroid gland do under known conditions of stimulation?" The answers to such questions may have social implications (as indeed most of the facts of physics and of biology have), but this does not make them social psychology. (2) A second field of investigation is the pattern of interaction existing among a group of persons—the patterns, for example, which cause changes in the structure of the family or the state as the conditions of life change. The historian and the sociologist have wrestled with such problems and have devised ways of handling them. Their studies are seldom truly psychological. They may offer psychological explanations of social structure; but no amount of psychological knowledge would enable them to explain a specific social change if they did not know the history of the period, and the geographic, climatic, and economic situations to which individual persons had to respond. The sociologist or historian must deal with the full reality of the geographic and economic environment, and with group patterns as such, their nature and changes. (3) The social psychologist seems to us to find his tasks intermediate between these two. He is concerned, as L. G. Brown has well shown, with a process by which the individual organism becomes socialized, utilizes and expresses social patterns in the world about him, builds within himself the attitudes and outlooks which characterize the family and neighborhood groups, participates in community life, and leaves his small or large impress upon the personality patterns of those with whom he makes contact. The social psychologist is in large degree a genetic psychologist, a psychologist concerned with infancy, childhood and adolescence, with problems of marriage and the founding of the family, vocational status and prestige, the winning of fame or ignominy, the struggle to the height of one's powers and the decline thereafter.

The life history of the person socially defined is thus a social psychology. This is not identical with the psychology of personality, since the latter subject can make many deeper studies relating to the organic aspects of the individual and can concern itself with problems of personality types which are only tangential to problems of social interaction. Neither is social psychology to be subsumed under child psychology, for many of the fundamental realities of childhood spring from organic factors which, though they are socially important, are not aspects of personal interaction as such. Social psychology overlaps both child psychology and the psychology of personality, but it has its own outlook and its own way of organizing the data. Social psychology is the study of the way in which the individual becomes a member of, and functions in, a social group.

Within the framework set by this way of approaching the field of social psychology, we find ourselves faced with a variety of specific research problems, of which three stand out prominently.

(1) We must inquire in some detail into the biological equipment of the individual by virtue of which a socialized personality comes into existence; what are the tensions, needs, impulses, receptor systems, learning capacities, upon which society acts and of which it makes in time a self-directed personality? This includes the problem which we have called the biology of motives. We are concerned here both with the biological basis of *all* such motives in *all* persons and with individual differences in quality and quantity in the motives upon which social life depends. (2) We must find how these raw materials work into a social pattern. This is the psychology

of the learning process in social situations, a process in which a general knowledge of the psychology of learning must be taken for granted but in which specific information regarding the *social* aspects of learning must be elaborated in several directions. (3) After study of the whole process of social learning and personality development, an attempt must be made to evaluate the respects in which we are all alike as members of a given culture group and the respects in which we differ, that is, the measurement of personality and social attitudes. In the study of all three problems our interest is in the development of the social phases of personality, attitudes and values—broadly, *the socialization of the individual.*

In stating all three of these problems we pay attention to individual differences. At this point we hear the startled reader protest: "What, must we worship forever at the shrine of particulars? Have we no place for universal laws, clear exceptionless principles?" We are indeed eager to find such laws, but we doubt whether our generation will live to see them established. Human nature as raw potentiality is probably sufficiently similar all over the globe to permit in time a generalized social psychology of motives; the learning process in social situations is probably fundamentally the same in all societies. Individual differences in the resulting social product in terms of differences in personality and social attitudes are doubtless everywhere analyzable and to some extent measurable by methods not utterly alien to those known to us, so that all individual personality can ultimately be described in terms of the operation of general laws (just as the peculiarities of every blade of grass or grain of sand can presumably be described in terms of general laws). This is very reassuring to the social philosopher; but it is a matter of record that far more writers have attempted to "think out" these laws than have settled down to the hard work of discovering the particularized facts upon which the laws must be based.

There are two ways, we believe, in which one may really work toward a generalized social psychology. One is to proceed from the existing fragmentary materials from various cultures, giving special weight constantly to those cultures about which one happens to be rather well informed, and attempting wide psychological generalizations as hypotheses for future work. The other is to recognize that the information for such a task is fragmentary indeed, and to renounce it in favor of a simpler plan, namely, the intensive study of a single culture. After consideration of foundation principles in Part II, we shall attempt in Part III to describe the genesis of social behavior patterns and the social outlook of the individual; Part IV will deal with measurement of the "formed" personality of the adult. But in general we limit ourselves to *our own culture.*

We shall therefore be dealing throughout this volume with the processes of growing into and functioning in our own society. The learning process in social situations will be the learning processes actually observed by us in our own infants and school children, and the measurement of personality and social attitudes will be the measurement of these characteristics among members of our own group. Our purpose is not to abandon all hope of ever achieving a generalized social psychology. Rather, it is to show concretely what kinds of materials and methods will be available from our society for a first definition of these processes in the hope that, as research continues, studies by psychologists in the Far East, the Near East and the Soviet Union, together with further historical and anthropological work, will permit valid generalization as to universal laws which have, as Lewin would say, "exceptionless validity."

The Individual in Relation to His Culture

Since we have determined to study the socialization of the individual, it is necessary to consider the duties and the limitations of social psychology, and to compare and contrast it with other disciplines which are likewise concerned with social interaction. We have no interest in indulging in polemics regarding the various claims of cultural anthropology, sociology, and psychology. Least of all are we interested in defending the special methods of psychology against the methods of these other sciences. Our point of view, however, as psychologists studying individuals, is necessarily different from the point of view of those who think in terms of large groups. For the historian or the anthropologist, the concept of culture is rightly the beginning of wisdom. But a scrutiny of the facts of human civilization seems to indicate that those events which may be described as cultural may also be described from a different point of view as the *activities of organisms,* and brought within the domain of psychology. Even those intricate and evasive entities which go by the name of traditions or mores are more or less fixed or even stereotyped human acts which one generation learns from the preceding. The process by which the younger generation *learns* is no more mysterious when an entity like culture is invoked than when the specific process of learning to spear a fish or plant seed corn is considered. It seems to us that very serious damage to the cause of mutual understanding between anthropologists and psychologists has been done by the assertion that the concept of culture transcends the specific behavior pattern of interacting organisms.

Such statements seem to overlook the fact that even at the level of unicellular organisms a social factor is present. The interaction between organisms is one of the most fundamental of biological facts. If chasing and pursuing among human beings is a social fact, why is it not when it occurs in the amoeba? If the formation of human groups with mutual interstimulation is a social fact, why is not the formation of groups in the protozoa likewise a social fact? The social is literally an *aspect of the biological.* There are, so far as we know, no organisms without social contacts. It may be objected that what is important here is not the interstimulation but the passing on of particular habitual patterns. Yet the passing on of such traditions appears in many species—it is, in fact, a commonplace to the biologist.

The field of animal psychology has in fact given us many interesting suggestions. The sociology and social psychology of a large number of species have been rather closely pursued in recent years, on the one hand by systematic observational work, and on the other hand with the aid of experimental techniques. The animal psychology of Alverdes and others has in several ways served to point out more clearly the respective positions of sociological and of psychological method. Species which are anatomically and physiologically almost identical with respect to the actual functioning of a drive may differ widely in the social situations in which the drive appears.

Clearly we are dealing here with a social structure into which the young are introduced, and a tradition which serves to perpetuate itself among animals as it does among men. Long ago, Scott showed that although the primitive notes of young orioles are characteristic oriole sounds, nevertheless, young orioles raised in isolation grow up singing a song quite different from that of their parents; a new oriole song is evolved. There is, then, in the typical or "normal" oriole song a cultural factor. The typical oriole is the product, not only of physical heredity, but of the oriole tradition. In exactly the same way a complicated structure like the song of the canary has been shown to be no mere raw product of an inherited capacity, but a pattern of responses which as humble a creature as an English sparrow may, with due opportunity for training, learn to master.

The question now arises whether there is any unknown x in the entity "culture," going beyond the activities of a large number of persons who act upon one another and who, by virtue of the various techniques broadly known as education, hand on these habits from generation to generation. If the anthropologist's objection to this biological way of asking the question takes the form of stating that the innate predispositions of men are no explanation of what a given man will do, the point must be cheerfully—in fact, enthusiastically— accepted. As indicated above, we are inclined to feel that one of the most important of all movements in contemporary psychology is the gradual appreciation of the importance of the cultural point of view and the recognition that man's intrinsic biological nature can tell us but little as to what the man as a social being will do. This is not, however, tantamount to saying that the biological factor plays a minor part in human life. From the present point of view, the learning of an activity from another human being is just as biological a fact as any to be found in nature; and if social psychology is to contribute anything real to the social sciences, it must remember that there is no event in its entire subject matter which is not in a sense a biological event, that is, an activity of a living organism or a group of living organisms stimulating one another in ways which can, if one wishes, be described through the use of biological concepts.

There are cases where these biological concepts are not particularly needed. For example, the study of language reveals many cases in which the actual linguistic changes occurring in a given area bear no relation to any known change which might occur in the organs of speech, and where a detailed study of the interaction among various social groups (historical method) is necessary to explain why a given phonetic change occurred. Where there is nothing much at stake, where it is about as easy to make one sound as another, it is possible to conceptualize the whole process of phonetic change as a "cultural change" in which the biological nature of the participating organisms can be disregarded. It is actually possible, as some anthropologists say, to think of culture as "something disembodied." This has usefulness, however, only when biological factors remain constant, and when such factors as imitation, dislike of the strange, dislike of non-conformity, etc., are *assumed* to be powerfully at work. Culture is held *within certain limits* by these characteristics of human beings; phonetic changes, for example, which would result in everyone screeching at the top of his voice all the time, simply do not occur. Gestures which would wear the speaker out are not made except (as in magic) when there is a strong motive at work. The whole thing is *not* "disembodied"; it is lived by actual people.

When one system of habits or mores is offered by one group to another, and the latter refuses to adopt the new ones, there is a temptation to think in terms of a disembodied entity, a cultural pattern which is incapable of "assimilating" the new features. Often enough, however, the difficulty is that too much personal stress and strain are involved. We are thinking here of the attempt of a fast-moving group, like typical American whites, to set going a new "speeded-up" tempo among some American Indians. The Indians sometimes decline to be speeded up. We are not concerned here as to whether the Indians refuse to be speeded up because of some innate racial characteristic, or simply because they are the victims of another set of habits. The important thing is that it is *the Indians* that resist, and not their "cultural pattern." To repeat, we are glad to recognize the immense value of the concept of culture when it is defined as a system of ways in which people behave, a system maintaining itself by virtue of the way in which it functions in human life and because of the possibility of teaching the given ways to each new generation that comes along.

From this discussion it might appear that there is a certain primacy of "biological" over "social" forces in guiding the growth of the individual. Nothing could be more misleading. The social forces, as we have again and again emphasized, *are* the biological forces in the behavior of other persons acting upon the individual whose growth is being studied. Further, the biological pattern of interaction in the group, which we are pleased to call social or cultural, is there before the newborn individual arrives. It limits, tones and shapes his development. It conditions, canalizes and organizes his diffuse potentialities. It sets up a world to be perceived, understood, remembered, used and acted upon. From birth to death it is the life pattern in terms of which his individual biological existence is set. There is no primacy of biological over social. The more biologically minded we are, the more are we impressed with the overwhelming biological force of the social pattern as a controlling pattern in the very tissue changes, the health, nutrition and learning processes of each individual. As we shall constantly find in the following chapters, the very "fundamentals" of individual biochemistry reflect the properties not only of "hereditary" traits but of the social world in which the individual life has to be lived. The social world is not a duality, a biological world and a culture world; it is *one* world. Levels of subject matter (chemical, biological, cultural) are necessary for preliminary clarification of research problems; but if one is ever to throw light on another, the ultimate oneness of the living being must never be forgotten.

We are forced to make a rough distinction between social psychology and "general" or "individual" psychology. But the concept of a "social" psychology as contrasted with an "individual" psychology involves the assumption that some of our behavior is stimulated exclusively by persons, the rest of it exclusively by things. If it is put thus baldly, it is necessary to concede that there are all sorts of responses for which the stimulating situation is a *combination* of personal and impersonal stimuli. It is, in fact, difficult to find, in human life, situations in which the social factor is entirely absent. For our purposes, individual psychology will be simply that psychology in which social factors (past or present) play a *relatively small* part, and social psychology will be that psychology in which social factors play a *relatively large* part.

Data from psychiatry, from education, from the autobiographies of political leaders—shall we argue whether these are individual or social psychology? The answer depends not on dialectic, but upon the need to answer problems about the socialization of the individual; and the answer is clearly that we must cut across disciplines and use whatever data we can find that throw light on our problem.

A designer of pottery, for example, working designs in colored clays, is a victim for either the general psychologist, who will study his perception of color and form, or for the anthropologist, who will study the cultural pattern of which this particular behavior is a part. The social psychologist can do useful work even here if he will acquaint himself with the techniques used by the student of optics and with those used by the student of cultures. The moment, however, that the potter begins to compete eagerly with another, the minute that his response is not *primarily* to the vessel in his hand or to the pattern which his father taught him, but to the man at his elbow whose work he is striving to surpass, the problem becomes one in which the methods of the experimental social psychologist are likely to be useful. The past history of the individual and his group must be known if the competitive behavior itself is to be understood; but just as individual psychology and cultural anthropology have their tasks to which social psychology makes its contribution without usurping the whole field, so social psychology has problems in which it takes material from other disciplines but itself gives the chief methods and explanatory concepts. When the reaction time of an athlete is to be measured, the task is one for individual psychology; when the psychology of team loyalty is under analysis, the problem is that of the social psychologist; when the part played by the game in the whole civilization of those who play it is under consideration, the task is that of the anthropologist or sociologist.

We have attempted to point out that the distinction between social psychology and the other social sciences seems to be purely one of emphasis. Social psychology studies individuals in their interaction

when the fact of their interaction is of central interest, and when
the analysis of impersonal stimuli and the fact of historical determination are not matters of primary concern. But it has become
more and more clear that most problems in social psychology are
genetic problems: they are clarified by the study of the way in
which the individual learns to deal with his group; in one way or
another they all appear to be problems in the process of individual
socialization.

In summary, then, we shall attempt here an interpretation of the
major available data on the socialization of the individual human
being. We must seek such data from every discipline and from every
research method which can help us in the task. The unity of man's
social life forces us to look for evidence from cultural anthropology,
from sociology, from economics, from history, from child study,
from the classroom, from psychiatry, and from the laboratory.
Experimental material will receive a cardinal emphasis when it
throws clear light on a crucial question. But our chief aim is the
interpretation of problems, the formulation of evidence in such a
way that existing laboratory studies will have a maximum of meaning. This, we believe, will permit a fuller utilization of the laboratory in the advancement of knowledge in the direction of a better-
integrated, more useful social psychology.

PART TWO

INTERPRETATION OF THE PROCESS OF SOCIALIZATION

Chapter II

NATURE AND NURTURE IN RELATION TO
SOCIAL DIFFERENCES

IN THE light of biological research, the relation of nature and nurture seems to be approximately as follows: The rod-like bodies in the germ cells of the parents, called chromosomes, contain large numbers of stable particles called genes. The latter are able, in some chemical media, to participate in directing the growth processes of starfish or of man. The gene is not a *trait* of the body or mind of the individual member of the species. Indeed, in the bodily and mental characteristics of the adult nothing like it appears. There are two ways in which the gene must be contrasted with the observed traits of the developing organism. First, the gene can work only with the materials supplied by the environment and under conditions limited by the environment. It helps in directing growth; but the embryonic conditions also help in directing growth. Second, even under these limitations the individual gene must cooperate in a very complex way with many other genes in order to produce any such result. Certainly the traits with which the social psychologist deals, even such simple ones as speed, strength, ease of conditioning, etc., depend upon dozens—or more likely hundreds— of genes, and upon all the circumstances of embryonic and post-natal life.

The most fixed and invariable hereditary attributes of species disappear when growth occurs in changed electrical and chemical environments. The frog's head may be made to grow in his back, or the fore limbs be made longer and stronger than the hind limbs. There are no genes which "know where they are going"; there are no supports for the dogma of "pre-formism" within the egg. Genes can do nothing without a chemical and electrical field in which to operate. At one time it was possible to say that the field is important only in a negative sense, limiting the genes to certain possible modes of activity. It has become clear that the number of different fields in which genes may function depends on the ingenuity of the experimenter, and that they can do their work just as dramatically and effectively in "abnormal" as in normal environments or in artificial as in "life" situations. There are no traits resident in genes. If one would speak accurately, one would never speak of hereditary equipment for social life.

In exactly the same sense and with the same sort of restriction we must point out that there are no environmental traits. There are no substitutes for the genes which are needed to make a frog, a canary, or a man. No amount of experimental ingenuity has proved capable, or seems likely to be capable, of producing a favorable field for embryonic growth when the germinal elements are wanting. There is as little "pre-formism" in the uterine field as there is in the germinal field. Nutrition, oxidation, disease and learning modify and direct growth, but it is the growth of a real thing, not an abstraction. The organism permits no severing of hereditary from environmental. Indeed, every cell is the environment of other cells, and every group of cells is part of the environment of the cells of another organism. Henderson points out that through the process of respiration the organism is chemically so united with its environment that the two can be separated only in the abstract way in which we separate the water of two tributaries which have flowed together into a common river bed; and he might well have added that since the chemical and social fields in which organisms are immersed are the basis of life for many organisms, the organisms literally live in and through one another. The isolation of the individual from his fellows is neither a biochemical nor a social fact.

Abstractions like "heredity and environment" or "individual and society" are useful only in so far as they permit statistical analysis of variables which in social reality have become an indivisible whole. This statistical problem now requires analysis. If one mother animal gives birth to several litters, it becomes possible to state to what extent the different paternities of the different litters causes measurable differences in the physical attributes of the young. One may, with meaning, say with respect to coat color, that black, gray and albino fathers are responsible for much greater variability in the coat color of the young than are variations in uterine conditions. In parallel experiments one may say that the variations among several similar fathers produce a much smaller effect on individual differences among the young than results from differences in the age or health of the mother. Similarly, after the birth of the young, one may say that individual differences in the amount of training given the young in learning mazes may produce much wider variability in maze performance than do the germinal differences which lie behind the characteristics of the newborn; or, in parallel experiments, one may say that individual differences in training produce among the litters much less difference in general competence than do the differences in paternity. There is never, in fact, a separation of heredity and environment; but there is always a problem in regard to the statistical weight to be assigned to variations in stock as compared with variations in environment with respect to measured outcome in the behavior of all the individuals in an experimental group.

We approach the problem in this way because we feel it important in social psychology not to participate in the meaningless debate of biology-minded and culture-minded students of human personality. For all important social purposes, there appear to be considerable biological differences among the organisms which enter into group structure, differences in relation to which it is important to consider the stock whence the organisms spring. They differ in their size, strength, health, intelligence, social aptitudes, drives, tastes, and probably many more subtle things. Such differences are marked even under relatively homogeneous and uniform social stimulation, such as the standards and taboos which none can escape. Likewise, homogeneous human stock developing under contrasting cultural conditions reveals profoundly divergent social traits.

There are diversities in stock and similarities in social stimulation, and there are similarities in stock and diversities in social stimulation. But nature and nurture differ through a wide range in relation to most traits that come up for study. The practical question, then, is this: *What is the relative statistical weight of variations in stock and of variations in social environment in relation to the task of predicting where each individual will stand with respect to each social trait?* We shall never attempt to answer such questions as whether a sense of humor or a fear of loneliness "comes naturally" or is "learned." There may perhaps be some value in raising such questions if all young individuals of the human stock show a given response, no matter what their individual environment may have been, while the young of other species in the same environment do not; there may, for example, be some sense in saying that they cry reflexly on severe physical injury. Even here the case is doubtful because we cannot deal with all possible environments; even the most cautious generalization will reveal difficulties.

Again, there may be some value in speaking of purely cultural differences if all effort to differentiate individuals in terms of stock completely fails. If, for example, we find that there are no intellectual differences which are consistently correlated with the differences in skin, bone, eye or hair which constitute the criteria of race, then perhaps we may say that there are no race differences. But every individual of a racial group represents his own genetic and developmental pattern.

As Mark May well puts it, we do not believe that one can "drive a fence through the individual," determining which of his social traits are biologically determined and which are culturally determined. We can, however, point out that in some respects individual variability is so slight as to be practically negligible whenever coercive social forces are at work; and that in other instances, in the absence of coercive social forces, biological variability may produce tremendous differences. Statistical separation of the hereditary from the environmental is not the issue; the issue is statistical separation of *variability* of one type and *variability* of the other type. The concrete social individual is literally and absolutely indivisible, and the nature-nurture problem, as applied to an individual, is without any meaning whatever.

If the foregoing analysis is sound, the true field of research for the student of the genesis of personality is not the sheer continuity or unfolding of a trait present in the hereditary make-up, nor a study of successive social conditionings. It is rather the direct study of the process of individual socialization itself, a direct description and analysis of the ways in which genetic potentialities are limited or given expression in the world of social responses. If we affirm that a certain genetic make-up and a certain social world permit the development of certain forms of social response, we need the full armamentarium of the scientist, including control groups in which (1) the genetic and (2) the social factors are different, and careful quantification of the amounts of all the definable factors at work. We may follow the plan of Fisher and of Wright—illustrated on page 37 by Burks' study—measuring variability in a social trait, and tracing this to measured variability in stock and measured variability in environment in such a way as to show the relative weight of the two in terms of resulting amounts of variability in the observed end result of the two. Sometimes, after measuring several elemental forces and noting their distinctive effects, we may use the method of multiple correlation to measure their combined effects.

At times the method of multiple correlation will not be suitable, although it may be possible to see the whole resulting when a given group of necessary factors is present. With Hanks, we may have to see personality, not like a river fed by many tributaries and by rainfall, its volume determined simply by adding up all that is contributed from all the sources, but rather like a building, the structure of which may collapse upon the disappearance of a single element. With Hanks we shall insist that the structure may at times be a true emergent, having properties which are not the properties of any individual constituent. Here it will be necessary to see the simpler hierarchies emerging from their constituents before we can approach the more complex ones. This will also give intelligibility to G. W. Allport's idea that some traits may be present in only certain members of the population and completely absent in others, and that, as personality becomes more complex, not only individual traits but new kinds of traits may become possible which are not analogous to any traits appearing at a simpler level.

It is clear, then, that quantitative nature-nurture studies must at present depend chiefly upon the measurement of psychological functions at one general level of description. We may, for example, measure the intelligence of parents and of children, and measure

AUTHOR DATE	TOPIC	SUBJECT	METHODS
Gesell, A., and Thompson, H. (1929)	Effect of environmental change, with heredity held constant.	A pair of identical twins studied from birth.	One twin given 6-weeks' training in stair-climbing beginning at age of 46 wks. Other given 2-weeks' training at 53 wks. Motion pictures.
Hildreth, G. H. (1925)	Resemblance of siblings in intelligence and achievement.	578 pairs of sibs with and without nursery-school experience, entering 1st grade.	Intelligence test scores available. Correlations made for sibs living together, apart, and non-sibs.
Jones, H. E. (1928)	Intelligence resemblance between parents and children.	105 New England families: native-born whites of native-born stock, from rural districts of Mass., N. H., Vt. 210 parents, 317 children.	Army Alpha (5 or 7) used with parents and children above 10 yrs.; Stanford-Binet with the 213 children between 3½ and 14 yrs.
Merriman, C. (1924)	Intellectual resemblance of twins.	200 pairs of twins; age range, 5–16 years.	Gave Stanford-Binet, Nat'l Intell. Test, modified Army Beta. Not all children took all 3 tests.
Muller, H. J. (1925)	Report on identical twins reared apart.	1 pr. identical female twins. Separated at 2 wks., saw each other again at 18 yrs., tested when 30. Both in country; one had only 4 years' schooling; other went through high school, had taught school.	Tested on Army Alpha, Otis Self-administering, personality tests; physical measurements.

FINDINGS	GENERAL REMARKS
Motion picture showed nearly equal stair-climbing speed. At 79 wks., twin with greater training climbed with greater alacrity, and was more active in other motor situations.	". . . Superior training did not make any tremendous difference in actual *capacity* for achievement, but . . . the advantage may have given the trained twin a sense of confidence . . . and consequently a real increase in amount of climbing."
Composite r for sibs with age partialed out, +.41; for sibs reared apart (corrected for curtailed range), +.50. Unrelated children reared apart yield same results as unrelated children reared together.	"True siblings reared apart for part of their lives still resemble each other about as much as true sibling pairs reared together. Unrelated children reared together for part of their lives resemble each other in intelligence no more closely than unrelated children chosen . . . at random."
Average r of .55 between intelligence of parents and children. Mother's influence greater than father's: 5 points higher r; unreliable but consistent difference. Like-sex r's about same as unlike-sex r's.	Material throughout is consonant with Pearson's thesis that "physical and psychical characters . . . are inherited within broad lines in the same manner and with the same intensity." Not considered proof.
Stanford-Binet: like-sex twins, r = .867; unlike, .504. N. I. T. like-sex, r = .925, unlike, 867. Beta: like-sex, r = .908; unlike, .732. For entire group, correlations for 3 tests close to .80. In majority of comparisons, r's higher in younger group (5–9) than in older (10–16).	Some inconsistencies present, since number of cases was frequently small.
Alpha scores, 156 and 153; Otis scores, 64 and 62. Similarity on specific test items also great. Personality test showed no great similarity.	(Personality scores of little significance; evaluation of other scores difficult in absence of controlled variation of environment; true in all such reports.)

AUTHOR DATE	TOPIC	SUBJECTS	METHODS
Saudek, R. (1934)	Identical twins reared apart: heredity-environment on I.Q., emotions, personality.	Ronald and Dennis, 20-yr.-old "identical" twins. Used their younger brother as control. Reared apart from age of 1 mo. to 9 yrs. 9 mos. R stayed with own family; D lived with lone grandmother. D came back (at 9 yrs. 9 mos.) when she died.	Administered Otis SA, Stanford-Binet, Allport AS, Bernreuter, Neymann-Kohlstedt, Pressey XO, Rorschach.
Tallman, G. G. (1928)	Intelligence resemblances between identical and non-identical twins.	158 pairs of fraternal and identical twins, and 199 siblings; age range 3–20 yrs.	Administered Stanford-Binet.
Wingfield, A. H., and Sandiford, P. (1928)	Intelligence resemblance of twins and orphans.	45 pairs of identical twins and 57 pairs of fraternal twins from public schools of Toronto and Hamilton (Canada). 29 orphans who had spent at least 25% of their lives in the same orphanage.	Tests used: Nat'l Intell., Scale A, Form 1; McCall's Multi-Mental Scale; Stanford Achievement, British Columbia Test in Fundamentals of Arithmetic; Morrison-McCall Spelling Scale.

FAMILY RESEMBLANCE (*Continued*)

FINDINGS	GENERAL REMARKS
Although twins made 98 (R) and 95 (D) on I.Q. (Otis scores, 40 and 37), considerable difference noticed in way in which scores were obtained. Personality tests tally on the whole, with minor discrepancies between Pressey and Rorschach scores.	Difficult to interpret results, since twins were already reunited at age of 10. Heredity might not account for similarities, since environments were not strikingly different. Suggestion that similarities greater in intelligence than in emotional reaction.
Average difference in I.Q. between siblings, 13.14; for those less than 2 yrs. apart in C.A., 11.96. Aver. diff. between twins, 7.07. Closer resemblance between identical twins than between fraternal twins; closer resemblance between fraternal twins than ordinary siblings.	Since no biological reason why fraternal twins should show greater resemblance than ordinary siblings, difference found might be due to environmental similarity expected to be greater for fraternal twins than for siblings a year or more apart.
Intelligence r's, .90 for identical twins; .70 for fraternal twins; .82 for like-sex twins; .59, unlike; siblings, .50; parent-child, .31; cousins, .27; grandparent-grandchild, .16; unrelated children and orphans, no correlation.	Increasing degree of intelligence resemblance among human beings with increasing degree of blood resemblance among them.

the environment in terms of educational facilities, opportunities offered by stimulating home environment, etc. We cannot make good quantitative nature-nurture studies in relation to such traits as "sense of humor," "general pig-headedness" or "artistic creativeness."

NATURE AND NURTURE IN RELATION TO INTELLIGENCE AND PERSONALITY

Our best quantitative data in the nature-nurture field relate to intellectual differences. The study of changes in intelligence quotient after changes in environment, whether in foster home, nursery school, or elementary school, represents one avenue of approach; another is the analysis of relationships between the intelligence of children and the socio-economic status of parents; another is comparison of the intelligence of children in the same family, of fraternal and identical twins, and study of parent-child resemblance. Since the methods and data from studies of twins are simplest, let us glance at them first.

We find much closer resemblance between "identical twins" (i.e., twins developed from one fertilized ovum) than between fraternal twins (i.e., twins developed from independent ova). We also find somewhat closer resemblance between fraternal twins than between ordinary siblings. Since there is no genetic reason why fraternal twins should on the average show greater resemblance than ordinary siblings, this last difference might be due to the greater environmental similarity that would be present for fraternal twins than for siblings a year or more apart. This immediately raises the question, how much effect can environmental differences have?

Various studies of the influence of changes in environment have indicated that it may at times be quite marked. The effect of nursery-school training upon the mental performance of a group of seventeen orphanage children was an average gain of 20 points in intelligence quotient during a period of six to nine months, as against 5 points for a control group. It is reasonable to suppose that a considerable portion of this improvement is due to the greater range of stimuli and experience offered by the nursery school, and the overlapping between these school experiences and the demands of the test. Whether the advantage gained by the nursery-school children would be apparent after the equalizing of experience that would take place during several years of school we must doubt. Another group of children with nursery-school experience who had an average advantage of six points over a control group at entrance to first grade lost half of this advantage (three points) by the end of the school year.

Such results as these call for a more precise analysis of the relative influence of variations in heredity and in environment—some approximation, however crude, of the proportion which each type of variation contributes to total intelligence.

Burks has attacked the problem of nature and nurture by comparing parent-child resemblance with the resemblance between foster parents and their adopted children. In the former case both hereditary and environmental similarities cause intellectual resemblance; in the latter there is little or no hereditary resemblance but the same environmental similarity. She studied 214 foster children and 105 control children, and every member of the families of all these subjects; she gave the Stanford-Binet test to parents and to children, and used a home information blank containing an adaptation of the Whittier Scale for Home Grading and a culture scale. She also obtained supplementary information (regarding heredity, national descent, age at adoption, etc.) from the placement agencies of the foster group. Correlating the intelligence quotients with a variety of hereditary and environmental factors, from the parents' mental ages to the number of books in the child's library, she compared the foster and control groups. The details of the statistical procedure cannot be described here. The results of this analysis are as follows: a multiple correlation of .42 (after correction for attenuation) is the measure of the effect of home environment upon the intelligence of children in the foster group. From this figure she seeks to estimate the normal average contribution made by environment to "variance" in intelligence; that is, what percentage of the total variance is environmental. This figure is obtained by squaring the coefficient just given. The result is .17. Variance in intelligence due to *heredity* (plus a residuum due to unmeasured

SOME STUDIES OF THE INTELLIGENCE OF FOSTER CHILDREN

AUTHOR DATE	TOPIC	SUBJECTS	METHODS
Burks, B. S. (1928)	Relative influence of nature and nurture on mental development.	204 foster children placed before 12 mos., legally adopted; between 5 and 14 yrs. old at time of study. Foster and true parents generally white, non-Jewish, English-speaking, and American-, British-, or north-European-born. Control group: 105 children matched with foster group for age, sex, attending kindergarten. Families matched for locality, neighborhood, occupation, nationality.	Binet I.Q. obtained for 1 or more parents and for foster or true child; I.Q. estimated for foster children's true parents. Home information blank; rating of child on 10 character-temperament traits by both parents; Woodworth-Cady questionnaire from children over 10 years.
Freeman, F. N.; Holzinger, K. J., and Mitchell, B. C. (1928)	Effect of environment on I.Q., school achievement, and conduct of foster children.	401 foster children, residents of Ill., including a few Negroes. Divided into 4 overlapping groups: 74 pre-test; siblings: 125 pairs in different foster homes; foster-sibling group: unrelated, living in same home; home group: composite all children.	Pre-test: tested before adoption (aver. age, 8 yrs.); lived in same foster home until retest. Sibling group: 4–13 yr. separation; aver. age at adoption, 5 yrs. 4 mos. Foster-sibling group: subdivided into group of 40 prs. of foster child and own child of foster parents, and group of 72 prs. unrelated foster children. Home group: for comparing I.Q., social adjustment, foster parents' I.Q. and cultural level. Children tested with Stanford-Binet, Internat'l Group Mental Test. Parents given Otis Self-Administering, and vocabulary test. Field workers obtained data on education, vocation, cultural level, conditions of foster homes.

NATURE AND NURTURE

IN RELATION TO "OWN" AND FOSTER PARENTS

FINDINGS	GENERAL REMARKS
Home environment contributes about 17% of variance in I.Q.; parental intelligence accounts for about 33%. Total contribution of heredity probably not far from 75 or 80%. Measurable environment 1 S.D. above or below mean of population does not shift I.Q. by more than 6–9 points. Maximal effect of best or worst *home environment* to intelligence apparently about 20 I.Q. points.	" . . . About 17 per cent of the variability of intelligence is due to differences in home environment." Size of family not controlled.
Group 1, pre-test and test after adoption showed increase in I.Q. of 2.5 ± .8. Subdividing into better and poorer foster homes, former showed no gain, latter showed clear-cut improvement. Group 2, I.Q.'s correlated only .25 (cf. r of .50 found between siblings reared in same home). Cultural differences in foster homes (63 siblings) reduced r to .19; siblings adopted into culturally similar homes, r = .30. Group 3a, r = .34. Group 3b, correlation was .37: higher r's than for true siblings adopted into different foster homes. Entire group yielded r of .48 between child's I.Q. and cultural rating of foster home. Correlation between child's I.Q. and score of foster father (Otis) was .37 (N = 180); with that of foster mother, .28 (N = 255).	Results suggested relatively large influence of environment on intelligence test performance. Possibility of *selective factor* in adoption not overlooked.

SOME STUDIES OF THE INTELLIGENCE OF FOSTER CHILDREN

AUTHOR DATE	TOPIC	SUBJECTS	METHODS
Leahy, A. M. (1935)	Intelligence of own and foster children in similar environments.	Experimental group: 194 children placed in foster homes under 6 mos. of age, of white, non-Jewish, north-European extraction; of 5–14 yrs. at time of research; legally adopted into communities of 1000 or more by foster parents of white, non-Jewish northern-European extraction. Each adopted child *matched* with an own child for all factors noted above, and parental school achievement.	Tested children on S-B, Woodworth Mathews P.D.; parents on S-B Vocabulary; Otis Self-Administering, Intermediate Form A. Information on identity of child, health; cultural background of true parents; economic, social, cultural status of foster home.
Lithauer, D. B.; and Klineberg, O. (1933)	Influence of change of environment on Binet scores.	120 children in Hebrew Orphan Asylum, N. Y. C. Age for first test, 3–13 yrs.; retest, 5–15 yrs.	Environmental change. Previous environment: children admitted because of death of parent, divorce, etc., improper guardianship, inability of parent to control child, poverty. Present environment: stable, regular school, ample food, clothing, sleep, recreation. Counselors or foster mothers superior to children's own parents. Institution and foster home children considered together, separately. 1st test at admission; retest, 3 to 57 mos. later.

IN RELATION TO "OWN" AND FOSTER PARENTS (*Continued*)

FINDINGS	GENERAL REMARKS

With age partialed out, sample r's: Adopted child's I.Q. and Mid-parent Otis score, .18; Control children's I.Q. and Mid-parent Otis score, .60; Adopted children's I.Q. and cultural index of home, .21; Control children's I.Q. and cultural index of home, .51. Correction for equal variability changes these but slightly. Much other data given.

For comparable and comparably restricted groups, variation in I.Q. accounted for by variation in home environment to extent of not more than 4%. Variation in personality traits other than intelligence "accounted for less by variation in heredity than by variation in environment." (This conclusion on grounds that W-M scores showed no significant r with children's or parents' intelligence or cultural index of home. Anastasi criticizes the logic by which the conclusion is drawn from this finding.)

Mean improvement for entire group, 5.9; median is 6.3 points in I.Q. Negative correlation between age at first test and change in I.Q.

A few mos. in an improved environment produced a marked increase in I.Q. Marked variations in I. Q. in retesting demands cautious interpretation and makes retests necessary when reason to believe child did not work up to capacity on first test.

environmental factors) is 83 per cent of the total. In general, a home environment one S.D. above the average may raise a child's intelligence quotient by six or eight points.

Another impressive investigation, made at about the same time, suggests a greater change as a result of environment. This is the study of foster children which was made by Freeman and his associates. One group of one hundred and thirty pairs of siblings was studied; one member of each of the pairs had been placed in a superior home and the other in an inferior home. The former averaged nine points higher in intelligence than the latter, although the pairs had been separated only about seven years on the average. Other methods used by Freeman suggest that the influence of superior environments over a period may increase intelligence scores by ten points or even more. Since the term "superior environment" is not very exact, and many such environments are much better than one S.D. above the average, it is not clear that the "ten points" here contradicts the "six or eight" points of Burks. Indeed, though the Burks and Freeman studies are in many ways non-comparable, we infer that Freeman's data agree essentially with Burks' and indicate that a home environment one S.D. above average can push an average child's I.Q. up to about the degree which Burks reports, or a little more.

A study by Leahy confirms Burks in finding the r between the intelligence of parents and that of their own children to be about .50, whereas the parental intelligence correlates only about .20 with that of their adopted children. The adopted children came from parents of the same social status as those in the adopted home, and stringent precautions were taken to prevent vitiation of the results by selective placement (choice of brighter children by brighter foster parents, etc.). The resemblance between parent and own child thus measures heredity and environment working together; the resemblance between parent and adopted child measures a similarity based on environmental similarity alone. That the former coefficient is .50 and not approximately 1.00 is of course to be expected from the fact that heredity is not simply the parent-child resemblance, but a reflection of the child's whole ancestral stock. Leahy's study, though carefully restricting conclusions to the middle- and upper-class groups (in a good general environment), appears to confirm Burks' study in giving variance in nature more importance than variance in nurture in relation to variance in intelligence.

Neither Burks, Freeman, Leahy, nor anyone else seems ever to have implied that *home* environment is a measure of *all* environment; indeed, Burks explicitly states that in a community with widely varying schools the measure of the home environment alone would be misleading. Clearly, if Burks' data are correct, the influence of variance in total environment is therefore greater than 17 per cent. Indeed, in many communities it must be enormously greater. The relative weight of variance in stock and of variance in environment will of course depend on the range within which each variable moves; e.g., the equalization of opportunity would make nature variance relatively even more important than it now is, and an increase of inequality of opportunity would make it relatively less important. These findings just reported must be kept in mind throughout the interpretation of the observed occupational differences in intelligence (page 46).

Partly for the reasons suggested above (page 35), quantitative data on the nature-nurture problem in relation to personality and temperament are meager indeed. Our expectations would be in the direction of finding personality traits more sensitive to environmental change than intellectual competence; and the available researches strongly support such an expectation. In Leahy's study personality was found to be far more responsive to change in environment than was intelligence.

The comparison of identical twins, reared apart, by means of paper-and-pencil tests of personality and by means of life history and clinical study strongly suggests that variance in environment is much more influential here than it is in relation to intelligence. Indeed, in nineteen pairs so far studied by Newman, personality differences associated with different backgrounds and ways of living —"the town mouse and the country mouse"—appear to dominate the picture. The existing tests and clinical methods are, however,

SOME STUDIES SHOWING THE EFFECT

AUTHOR DATE	TOPIC	SUBJECTS	METHODS
Barrett, H. E., and Koch, H. L. (1930)	Effect of nursery-school training on mental performance of orphans.	17 pairs of children matched for C.A., M.A., I.Q., and orphanage experience.	The period between 1st and 2d exams was 6–9 mos. One group given nursery-school training, the other not.
Denworth, K. M. (1928)	Effect of length of school attendance upon M.A. and E.A.	9-, 10-, 11- and 12-year-olds in N. Y. C., all of whose schooling had been in N. Y.	S-B, Stanford Achievement Tests given; results considered in connection with number of days of school attendance.
Wellman, B. L. (1934)	Environmental (school) effects on intelligence.	77 children transferred from Univ. of Iowa pre-school, elementary school, re-tested; 90 children continuing at Univ. schools for comparison; also 68 pre-school-age children not in pre-school.	Mean I.Q.'s determined in transfer group at entrance in Univ. system, last test before leaving, and test after transfer. Paired matchings made with children remaining at Univ. schools in terms of age, I.Q. within 10 points on initial test, same number of tests. Non-pre-school children tested at several age levels.

FINDINGS	GENERAL REMARKS
67% of experimental group showed increase of 15 or more points in I.Q. as compared with about 12% of control group. Average of nursery-school group rose from 91.7 to 112.6; control, from 92.6 to 97.7.	Nursery-school activities raise the intelligence of children.
Low or negligible r's between days of schooling and M.A. or E.A.	"Had some children been tested who attended school for only a short time, . . . the lack of the educational elements . . . would very materially have lowered their scores."
Significant and marked gains in I.Q. made by transfer group when at Univ. schools; these maintained, not increased, over 4–8 yrs. Continuous group continued to gain. Non-pre-school group did not tend to gain in intelligence, whereas pre-school group at same time did.	"Intellectual development . . . may vary with type of school experiences." " . . . these changes represent real and not spurious gains. . . ." "Ordinary practice effects are ruled out." "A permanent change in intellectual standing can be effected in one to one and one-half years that will last four to eight years. . . ."

so crude that these generalizations must be taken guardedly. From many data reported below in Chapters VI to X it appears probable that many subtleties of personality relating to tempo, energy, perseveration, aesthetic needs, etc., may well persist to some degree throughout the vicissitudes imposed by different environments.

OCCUPATIONAL DIFFERENCES

When tested by standard intelligence tests, adult occupational groups differ widely, the average intelligence of the groups increasing with socio-economic status, but with considerable variation within each group. Thus farmers and unskilled laborers rank low, professional men and executives high; but a few in each of these extreme groups are nevertheless found to be not far from the average intelligence level of the community. The children of these fathers show in general a central tendency in intelligence level in accordance with socio-economic level, and the same tendency to wide variation at each level. Thus by the time that children are old enough to be given a standard intelligence test, they tend to score, on the average, at the level of their fathers. But since in general there is also a considerable correlation in intelligence between husbands and wives, we may speak broadly of family level of intelligence in relation to socio-economic status.

It is now necessary to consider to what extent these findings can be attributed to variance in stock—the tendency for superior wits to find a corresponding economic level in a competitive society.

How early does the parent-child resemblance in intelligence become apparent? The socio-economic status of a child's parents is not correlated with the child's scores on the Linfert-Hierholzer scale to measure the motor and mental development of infants at the 1, 2, 3, 6, 9 and 12 months' levels. It is impossible to say with certainty whether the contradiction between the results with infants and with older children is due to the fact that environmental factors are operative in the latter which have not had time to affect results in the former, or whether it is due to the fact that some genetic factors which are associated with socio-economic status are not apparent in infancy; or, again, whether such an "infant scale" measures abilities different from, and little correlated with, the abilities measured by scales for children from two years on. The last of these three possibilities now seems by far the most likely. Indeed, follow-ups over several years suggest that there is no relation whatever between existing "infant tests" and "intelligence" as ordinarily measured. Scores from standard intelligence tests at two years of age show a significant relation between the scores of children and the occupational classification of their fathers. In fact, at two years the relationship is quite as clear as at four years, and this relation maintains itself thenceforward. This therefore suggests that the infant tests be kept out of the picture, and forces us to consider the nature-nurture problem in terms of standard intelligence tests alone.

Collins's study, which appears to be representative of large-scale investigations on school children, showed a median family intelligence quotient of 116 for the professional group, 104 for the skilled labor group, and 95 for the unskilled group. If we assume, with Freeman, that on the average, superior environment may raise intelligence quotients about 10 points, it is possible that the best of education could raise the median intelligence quotient of the unskilled labor group to a position about equivalent to that of the skilled labor group. In other words, environment may make the difference between low average intelligence and high average intelligence, and this, as Freeman urges, is of the greatest social significance. Also, when we consider that the *median* family intelligence quotients of school children of various economic levels probably range, as Collins found, from about 95 to about 116, or only twenty points or a little more, the possibility of an increase of ten points, or nearly half this amount, is of extraordinary importance.

Occupation	No. of Families	Family Inter-quartile Range (Middle 50 Per Cent)	Median Family I.Q.
Professional	90	106–126	116
Managerial	165	104–123	112
Clerical	131	105–122	113
Trade	413	100–120	110
Foreman	106	98–118	109
Skilled labor	569	94–114	104
Unskilled labor	377	85–108	95

SOME STUDIES RELATING SOCIO-ECONOMIC AND

AUTHOR DATE	TOPIC	SUBJECTS	METHODS
Collins, J. E. (1928)	Relation of paternal occupation to intelligence of children.	4727 school children from 3089 families in Ohio.	Otis Primary Group or Otis Advanced Group Test given each S. Taussig classification made of paternal occupations as reported by teacher and as given in school records.
Furfey, P. H. (1928)	Earliest appearance of relation between intelligence of children and occupation of father.	Infants: Age in mos.: 1, 2, 4, 6, 9, 12. No. of Ss.: 46, 46, 45, 45, 49, 46. Total N = 277.	Linfert-Hierholzer scale (partly based on Gesell) used to measure mental development of newborn infants. Chapman-Sims scale for socio-economic status.
Goodenough, F. L. (1928)	Relation of intelligence to occupation of father.	380 children, 18–54 mos. old.	Kuhlmann-Binet test of intelligence given twice; modified form of Barr and Taussig scales used to classify occupations.
Haggerty, M. E., and Nash, H. B. (1924)	Relation of intelligence scores and paternal occupation.	8129 N. Y. State rural school children, from Grade 3 to high school.	Haggerty Intelligence Examinations, Delta 2. Parental occupation stated by teacher, classified on modified Taussig system. Data given in terms of Taussig scale and of specific occupations.
Jones, A. M. (1925)	Analysis of superior children.	120 children 3 yrs. 11 mos. to 14 yrs., 9 mos. old, in upper 1% of population on S-B intelligence.	Physiological measurements made, test battery given; home status measured by Taussig scale; racial stock noted, etc.
Jones, D. C., and Carr-Saunders, A. M. (1927)	Influence of social status on intelligence.	880 orphanage children over 9½ yrs. old.	I.Q. determined from Simplex Test. Paternal occupations determined, put in 5-fold classification.

CULTURAL STATUS WITH INTELLIGENCE

FINDINGS	GENERAL REMARKS
Median family I.Q. of 116 for professional group, 112 for managerial, 113 for clerical, 110 for trade, 109 for foremen, 104 for skilled labor, 95 for unskilled labor, 98 for agricultural labor. Considerable overlapping. Interquartile range: professional group, 108–126; unskilled labor, 85–108.	"The occupation of the father . . . may be considered as a rough index to the intelligence of the child."
No significant relation between performance at age of 1 yr. or less and socio-economic status of parents.	Contradiction between these results and those for older children indicates need for more data on correlations between tests of infant development and standard tests administered later, environment being held constant.
Significant drop in intelligence test scores going down scale of occupational classification of fathers.	" . . . Intellectual differences between social classes are well established by the ages of 2, 3, and 4 years."

	Median	Total Range	
Professional	116	70–177	"The father's occupation appears to afford a rough index of the child's intelligence, of its capacity to profit by schooling, and possibly of the type of school most serviceable to its needs."
Business and clerical	107	54–161	
Skilled	98	54–177	
Semi-skilled	95	53–152	
Foremen	91	50–161	
Unskilled	89	51–146	

Marked physiological advancement in height, weight indices. Boys 57.5% of group. Average M.A. acceleration 5 yrs. Racial factors of little significance except for over-weighting of Jewish children in relation to population. Acceleration shown in all tests.	"Analysis of the economic and cultural status of the homes shows an extreme tendency toward superior homes."
Relation between paternal occupation and intelligence despite orphanage residence 3 or more years. I.Q. tends to increase among younger children, decrease in older ones; to increase in children from lower occupation classes, to decrease in those from upper social classes; variability tends to decrease.	" . . . No reason to suppose . . . that environmental influences are the whole or even the main part of the cause of the differences in intelligence between children of different social origin."

SOME STUDIES RELATING SOCIO-ECONOMIC AND

AUTHOR DATE	TOPIC	SUBJECTS	METHODS
Sherman, M., and Key, C. B. (1932)	Intelligence test scores of children of isolated communities.	Children of 4 varyingly isolated hollows in Blue Ridge Mts., and of small village at base of range. English, Scotch-Irish stock. School per year from 1+ mo. to 9 mos., depending on community.	Stanford-Binet; N. I. T., Scale B, Form 2; Pintner-Cunningham Primary Mental Test; Pintner-Paterson scale; and Goodenough's Drawing of a Man. 386 tests in mountain communities, 198 in village. (S-B not given in village.)
Terman, L. M. (1925)	Studies of gifted children.	643 Calif. school children, 2–14 yrs. old, I.Q.'s 140 or above. Control groups ranging from 600 to 800 in number.	Stanford-Binet, Whittier scale of cultural level, paternal occupation data, personality tests, follow-up study of subsequent careers 7 yrs. later.
Van Alstyne, D. (1929)	Analysis of elements of environment which affect development of young children.	75 three-year-olds.	Collected information on background: toys owned and played with; places seen (e.g., zoo); time per week in contact with adults; I.Q. and M.A.; I.Q. of mother estimated from vocabulary test; home rating on Minnesota Scale of Socio-Economic Level.

CULTURAL STATUS WITH INTELLIGENCE (*Continued*)

FINDINGS	GENERAL REMARKS
Average I.Q. in the mountains from 61.2 on N. I. T. to 83.9 on P-P year scale; in village, corresponding scores, 96.1 and 118.6. In hollows apparent decrease in I.Q. with increase in C.A. I.Q. highest in most advanced communities, lowest in least advanced. Youngest children differ little.	Test material largely inappropriate. Intelligence advances only with adequate spurs to advancement, in presence of adequate social stimuli.
Professional group produce over 1000% of "quota" of gifted children; public service, commercial, industrial groups, 140%, 130%, 35%, respectively. Aver. cultural rating of gifted group homes, 22.94; control group, 20.78. Aver. school grade reached by parents of gifted group, 11.8; grandparents, 10.0; control, 7. Gifted children score significantly higher on personality tests. On follow-up, 74% boys and 84% girls accelerated in scholastic achievement. For 38 boys and 35 girls retested with Stanford-Binet, average I.Q. dropped for boys from 146 to 143; for girls, 149 to 136.	No basis for prejudices regarding genius, such as insanity, ill-health, etc. Drop in I.Q. of girls interpreted as reflection of environmental influence on two sexes with advancing age. Number of cases probably inadequate for definite conclusions.
Child's vocabulary somewhat more closely related to environment than I.Q.; mother's intelligence slightly more closely related to composite rating of environmental factors than to child's M.A.; environmental factors more closely related to child's I.Q. ($r = .59 \pm .05$) than to mother's. Factors like number of constructive books, toys, hours of reading (by parents), etc., have correlations no higher than height, cleanliness, possession of own bed.	This suggests, though of course it does not prove, that the relation between environment and intelligence is not a simple causal one, but that *both* tend to depend on the parental intelligence.

Moreover, if we take Burks' analysis literally, even the few points which would result from transplanting the laborer's son one S.D. upward, and the few points which would result from transplanting the lawyer's son one S.D. downward, toward the middle of the socio-economic scale, would absorb much of the obtained differential. This is of course conjectural; but even the "absorption" of a few points in a range of twenty between socio-economic groups at the extremes is worth considering. It is very probable that some economic class differences in intelligence would remain if environmental factors could be controlled, but that this difference would be much smaller than the raw data shown in Collins' table.

On the other hand, from the point of view of *educational and social practice* with the existing human material, the differences actually found are fraught with immense consequences. The fact that the middle 50 per cent of the distribution does not by any means tell the whole story is shown by the following items from Terman's study of gifted children: Six of the ninety professional families have mean sibling intelligence quotients of 140 or more, while *none* of the 327 families of unskilled fathers are found at this level; four-fifths of the professional families have mean family intelligence quotients above the median, while less than one-third of the unskilled families are above the median. Thus the extremes of the distributions of these two groups present striking differences; the curve for the unskilled labor is shifted in the direction of low intelligence, while that of the professional group is shifted toward high intelligence; although both groups produce a large proportion of children of average intelligence, the lowest group is not apt to produce brilliant children and the highest group is not apt to produce deficient children.

Terman puts his data on the occupations of fathers of gifted children vividly when he states that if one compares the proportion of fathers of gifted children in any main occupational level with the proportion of men in that occupation in the California populations from which the children are drawn, the results are as follows: the professional group produce over 1000 per cent of their "quota" of gifted children, while the public service, commercial and industrial groups produce only about 140 per cent, 130 per cent, and 35 per cent, respectively. Nevertheless, even under the conditions described, individual differences within each class are tremendous and serve as a further reminder that level of intelligence is not simply a result of environmental opportunity.

If, then, we summarize various implications of these data, we may say that neither a moron nor a person of average intelligence is likely to develop to a level of outstanding brilliance through improvement in environment, and, conversely, a mind of distinctly high caliber is not likely to appear definitely inferior as a result of poor environment; but that it is quite possible if not probable that, in general, slightly below average performance may be raised through environmental changes to somewhat above average performance. From the point of view of the individual, or of the educator, or of the social scientist who is weighing democracy in the balance, this possibility is of the greatest moment. Even if every street-cleaner's son may not be a great engineer, he may perfectly well be a surveyor or a postal clerk; and a general raising of average I.Q.'s even five points may have far-flung consequences.

RACE DIFFERENCES

Ten years ago it would have been our clear though distressing duty to report all the work done in the comparison of races by means of individual or group intelligence tests, including work done with children as well as that with adults. It would have been valuable, if true, to report, for example, that 39.6 per cent of all Chippewa Indians between 11 and 14 years of age surpassed the median native-born white child on the Pintner-Paterson performance scale. From a historical point of view, the dozens, nay hundreds, of meticulous studies of race differences which have been provided are not to be belittled. They definitely contributed to the technique of testing, to the study of discrepancies obtained when groups are measured by various kinds of standard tests, and to the final awakening to the fact that people grow up in a social world rather than in a vacuum, and that their behavior on mental tests reflects that social world as does the dialect they speak, the religion they profess, or the prejudices which they like to air. A relatively small amount of all this material can be regarded as at present worth the time of any readers except those whose interest is frankly antiquarian. A few studies made prior to 1925 stand out as important; these must be surveyed. The whole problem as it confronts us today is a very different one. The work of Peterson, Garth, and especially Klineberg seems to have genuinely recast the whole problem.

Obtained race differences *may*, of course, be due to physiological differences, or to the dominance of different ways of doing things— culture patterns. The influence of the whole culture upon the attitude taken toward an intelligence test is constantly borne in upon us. The anthropologists' misgivings regarding the applicability of intelligence tests to primitive peoples are illustrated by Mead's comments. On the two pictures which emphasized human beings, "no discussion could be commenced until the question of the relationship of the characters had been ascertained." Even in the ball-and-field test, regarded among us as a fair measure of reasoning in a certain situation, Samoan children tended to attack the problem as an aesthetic rather than a practical one; they tended to make designs which would, in themselves, be pleasing, rather than to handle the problem simply from the point of view of practicality. Against the constantly reiterated view that "primitive mentality" differs in some fundamental way from advanced mentality, we must take into consideration the many studies which show that even the most primitive peoples turn out to be far from "primitive" when the real nature of their thought is known. Over and over again, groups like the American Indians have been found to exhibit the same mental processes that are utilized by our most "advanced" selves when confronted with similar situations, except for differences imposed by the social attitudes and forms of thought which they carry into the situation. Thus the reservation Indian approaches closer and closer to the white norm as his schooling increases.

We have more data on Negro-white comparisons than on race comparisons of any other description. The problem of Negro intelligence is beset by a thousand difficulties, and we do not feel that as yet the data can be adequately interpreted. We may, however, review a few typical studies. Ferguson gave four tests to many hundreds of southern white and Negro high school children of both sexes. The results for the four tests are not consistent, the superiority of the whites appearing strikingly on two of the tests which involved language. These are the completion tests (in which words are to be put in, to fill blanks in sentences) and the "mixed relations" tests in which the fourth term of an analogy is missing (man is to boy as woman is to . . .). On the non-verbal tests, white superiority is not established. In the cancellation tests, for instance, Negro girls seem clearly superior to white girls and Negro boys are equal to white boys. From this, Ferguson concludes that the Negro is the equal of the white in tests involving purely sensory and motor functions; but the whites are superior in those intellectual functions measured by the verbal tests. He proceeds further to subdivide his groups in accordance with the amount of white blood which they appear to possess. In the completion test, his data show the pure Negroes to make a score 69.2 per cent as high as that of the whites; the three-quarters Negro makes a score of 73.2 per cent; the mulatto, 81.2 per cent; and the quadroon, 91.8 per cent.

A large amount of rather similar material has been published by Peterson and his collaborators, who have not only done a great deal of careful experimental work, but have used much caution in interpreting it. Most of these studies have improved considerably upon Ferguson's. In one such study Peterson found that white superiority was clear when speed was involved, but that in terms of accuracy in the execution of performance tests, racial differences were small and unreliable. In a later study by Peterson and Lanier, large differences were found between whites and Negroes in favor of the former, the subjects being twelve-year-olds in one series of tests, and adults in another series; in both verbal and non-verbal achievement the whites were ahead. The results are interpreted as probable indications of innate intellectual superiority of the whites, but with a reserve not at all characteristic of the earlier studies of racial differences.

Peterson and Lanier seem to be the first to grasp and analyze experimentally the problem of *sampling errors* in racial studies;

SOME STUDIES OF DIFFERENCES

AUTHOR DATE	TOPIC	SUBJECTS	METHODS
Darsie, M. L. (1926)	Relative mental capacities of Japanese and American children.	570 American-born Japanese children 10–15 yrs. old. In English-speaking schools 4 or more yrs. Social economic environment "distinctly inferior to that of the average middle-class American child."	Tests administered: Stanford Binet; Army Beta; Stanford Achievement. Ratings by teachers on 19 personality traits, and school achievement; compared estimates of average American child of same age or grade. 7 psychologists rated each scale of Binet as to degree to which success dependent on command of English.
Efron, D., and Foley, J. P., Jr. (1937)	Gestural behavior patterns in Italian and Jewish groups.	"Traditional" Italians living in "Little Italy" (N. Y. C.). "Traditional" Jews living in East Side Ghetto (N. Y. C.). "Assimilated" Jews and Italians both living in similar "Americanized" environments.	Direct observation in natural situations; sketches by artist; motion pictures. Ss unaware of observations. Judgments by *naïve* observers of films.
Ferguson, G. (1916)	Racial differences in higher intellectual capacities.	Richmond, 269 white, 319 colored; Fredericksburg, 84 white, 63 colored; Newport News, 133 white, 39 colored.	Woodworth-Wells Mixed Relations, I and II; form of Ebbinghaus Completion test; Cancellation Test; Columbia Maze Test. Negroes in 4 groups according to skin color, hair color, shape of head and of face, determined by inspection.
Garth, T. R. (1933)	Relation of intelligence and achievement to "amount" of Indian blood.	1022 4th- to 9th-grade children of So. Dak., Okla. gov. schools.	Otis Classification Test. Intercorrelations of score, school grade achievement score, degree of Indian blood, age; partial r's obtained.

FINDINGS	GENERAL REMARKS
Median I.Q. 10 points lower than for American children. 75% of latter exceed Japanese median. Comparison of age groups showed I.Q. to be constant for ages 10, 11, 12, and 13. Performance on Army Beta practically identical, Japanese showing superiority at 12-yr. level. Stanford Achievement: Japanese showed average retardation (American norms) of 6.25 mos.	American superiority largely in linguistic tests. Tendency for Japanese to equal or exceed American norms in non-linguistic tests. Probably innate mental capacity of Japanese children greater than Binet I.Q. indicates. Japanese superior in tests demanding acuity of visual perception, capacity for sustained attention. Urban superiority found.
Various differences in patterns of gestural behavior found between the "traditional" groups; disappeared when assimilated groups tested.	Culture held responsible, rather than "racial" descent, for development of characteristic gestures.
Average performance of colored population ¾ as efficient as performance of whites with same training. Pure Negroes, Negroes ¾ pure, mulattoes and quadroons have 60, 70, 80, and 90% of white intellectual efficiency.	Believes it impossible "to raise the scholastic attainment of the Negro to an equality with that of the white," since former lack necessary mental power. Since no appreciable racial difference in motor capacity, approves industrial education for Negro.
Intelligence, school grade and achievement showed high correlations; correlations with Indian blood, age are low. Eliminating age, r's of degree of Indian blood and other factors are .19, .12, .11. Weight to be given Indian blood for lumping with grade and achievement in multiple r with intelligence is 1.0, as compared with 2.2 and 7.6 for other 2.	Results, in contrast with other studies, show mixed blood bears little relation to intelligence.

SOME STUDIES OF DIFFERENCES

AUTHOR DATE	TOPIC	SUBJECTS	METHODS
Hattori, F. S. (1927)	Differences between Japanese and Occidental people with regard to aesthetic judgment.	44 Occidental and 49 Japanese of both sexes, including 9 American-born Japanese.	10 well-known Occidental and 10 well-known Japanese pictures, presented in 3 series: (1) 10 Japanese; (2) 10 Occidental; (3) 10 Japanese and 10 Occidental. Subjects ranked them in order of merit.
Klineberg, O. (and several M. A. students) (1935)	Relation of migration and of stay in an urban environment to intelligence of Negro children.	(1) Nashville, Birmingham, Charleston migrants and non-migrants, 1915–1930. (2) Several hundred children in N. Y. varying lengths of time. (3) Several hundred children in New Orleans, Nashville, Atlanta varying lengths of time. All 10 or 12 yrs. old.	(1) School records of children whose parents migrated compared with those who remained. All grades converted to rank scores. (2) N. I. T., Otis, S-B and Pintner-Paterson given to varying groups of Negro children in N. Y.: children who had been in N. Y. varying lengths of time compared. (3) Same with children living in southern cities varying lengths of time.
Klineberg, O.; Fjeld, H., and Foley, J. P., Jr. (From Anastasi, 1937)	Personality differences among "racial" groups.	Over 400 male and female students from 8 colleges in N. Y. C. (and environs). About 50 men, 50 women in each racial group. (See next column.)	Tests: Bernreuter Personality Inventory (scored for 6 "traits"), Allport-Vernon Study of Values, an honesty test, 2 specially devised tests to measure suggestibility and persistence. Ss classed as Nordic, Alpine, Mediterranean, on basis of cephalic index, eye, hair, and skin color.
Klineberg, O. (1931)	Intelligence differences between European subgroups.	Boys over 10, under 13. 7 rural groups: German Nordic, French Nordic, German Alpine, French Alpine, Italian Alpine, French	6 tests from Pintner-Paterson series administered individually.

BETWEEN RACIAL GROUPS (*Continued*)

FINDINGS	GENERAL REMARKS
Almost every picture rated high by some, low by others. Ss agreed most closely in rating Occidental pictures, then in Japanese, and least in combined pictures. Correlation between American-born Japanese and Occidentals higher than American-born Japanese and Japan-born Japanese. Preference by all for Occidental pictures.	Japanese Ss all were under Occidental influence. Universality of standards of beauty cannot be entirely denied.
(1) In general, "no evidence in the group as a whole for the operation of any factors selecting either the more or the less intelligent members of the community." ". . . The quality of the migrants has been steadily improving. . . ." (2) Residence in N. Y. tended to raise verbal intelligence test scores and school standing, in rough proportion to time in the city. No reliable change in performance scores. (3) Length of time in southern cities showed striking relation to N. I. T. scores for 12-yr.-olds.	". . . Show quite definitely that the superiority of the northern over the southern Negroes, and . . . tendency . . . to approximate the scores of the Whites, are due to factors in the environment, and not to selective migration."
Allport-Vernon scores showed only one significant difference in each sex group; women: between Med. and Alpines on "aesthetic value"; men: between Nordics and Alpines on "religious value." Both shown to be linked with institutional groupings. No significant differences found on 6 Bernreuter scores, suggestibility, persistence, or honesty tests. Large reliable differences found between institutions.	Differences among *racial groups*, small and unreliable; among *institutions*, large and reliable. Selective and cultural factors most obvious explanation for results obtained.
City scores almost reliably superior to country; no reliable differences between cities. Within each of the races variability is great. No consistent hierarchy of three races. In rural groups evidence of superiority of German over other groups; of French over Italian groups compared.	"The results offer no substantiation of a definite 'racial' hierarchy, but they do not thereby [necessarily] rule out 'heredity' as an explanation of the ten groups."

SOME STUDIES OF DIFFERENCES

AUTHOR DATE	TOPIC	SUBJECTS	METHODS
		Mediterranean, Italian Mediter-ranean. 3 city groups: Paris, Hamburg, Rome. "Racial purity": selected optimum regions, children whose parents born there, and having proper hair color, head shape, etc. 100 Ss in each group.	
Lambeth, M., and Lanier, L. H. (1933)	Racial speed differences in processes differing in complexity.	30 12-yr.-old white, and 30 12-yr.-old Negro boys, Nashville, Tenn. Socio-economic status of boys average for their respective races.	Stanford-Binet, Rational Learning Test, and 6 speed tests.
Murdock, K. M. (1925)	Racial differences in intelligence.	12-yr.-old children in rural and urban public schools of Honolulu; Anglo-Saxon, Chinese, Japanese, Portuguese, Korean, Hawaiian, Puerto Rican, Filipino, and mixed groups.	Rating scales for various traits, standard group tests of intelligence, measure of socio-economic status, grade location.
Nissen, H. W.; Machover, S., and Kinder, E. F. (1935)	Native African Negro children's intelligence test performance.	50 children, 5–14 yrs. old; 8 girls, 42 boys. Members of Sousou tribe.	Tests administered through interpreter. Cooperation "fair." 12 performance tests (e.g., Manikin, Digit Symbol).

BETWEEN RACIAL GROUPS (*Continued*)

FINDINGS	GENERAL REMARKS

"Speed of reaction" more closely related to "general intelligence" score in Negroes than whites. 93% of whites equal or surpass Negro medians in Stanford-Binet scale scores. In Rational Learning, races equal in trials, errors; whites superior in speed. All differences in speed tests favor the whites. | Writers *believe tentatively* innate organization is important causal factor, although environmental factors probably condition performance. Speed probably not a general factor. Suggest that difference is temperamental one, Negroes being lethargic. The more complex the performance, the greater the race difference.

Group tests revealed large and striking differences; Anglo-Saxons superior to Chinese and Japanese, these in turn to others. Analysis of tests into verbal and non-verbal elements showed inferiority of Chinese and Japanese due entirely to linguistic parts of test. High correlation between intelligence, socio-economic status. | Recognized results to apply only to locality tested. "Intelligence" seen to be influenced markedly by socio-economic status, cultural differences.

Average test-quotient 61; for younger children (5–10 yrs. old) 68; for older ones (10–14), 53.5. Great variation from test to test characteristic of group. | Difficulty of tests increased as content and activities involved more cultural factors foreign to African environment. The Ss' undoubted inferiority on tests not open to "conventional sociological interpretation."

SOME STUDIES OF DIFFERENCES

AUTHOR DATE	TOPIC	SUBJECTS	METHODS
Peterson, J., and Lanier, L. H. (1929)	Comparative abilities of whites and Negroes.	12-yr.-olds in one series, college students in another.	Verbal and non-verbal achievement tests.
Peterson, J.; Lanier, L. H., and Walker, H.M. (1925)	Comparisons of white and Negro children in ingenuity and speed tests.	Ingenuity tests: 69 white, 46 Negro children, 12 yrs.; latter from best section of Negro population in Nashville; white school about average. Speed tests: 123 8-, 10-, 12-yr.-old white; 103 10-, 12-yr.-old Negro children.	Ingenuity tests: Rational Learning, Mental Maze, Disk Transfer. Preliminary exercise. Time and errors scores used. Each child given 250 trials on each of 4 speed tests: naming 5 colors; reactions to color squares; to the *names* of 5 forms; and to the forms themselves. Precautions to control fatigue, practice.

BETWEEN RACIAL GROUPS (*Continued*)

FINDINGS	GENERAL REMARKS
Large differences in favor of whites in both types of achievement. Speed differences reliable in favor of whites. Some unreliable differences in favor of Negroes.	Results interpreted as probable indications of innate intellectual superiority of whites. Question of *degree* of innateness felt unsettled, considering evidence of effects of "cultural sets." Cases in which no differences (or differences in favor of Negroes) said to be result of highly selected samples.
3 of 8 differences between race medians reliable. Speed and errors favor white children in Rational Learning. Mental Maze: Negroes excel (unreliably) in number of repetitions; Disk Transfer: whites superior in time. Differences in speed tests all favor whites.	Ingenuity tests indicate mental differences not merely due to speed.

they have shown that the whole question of racial differences depends upon whether samples taken in different places show consistent results. Some Negro groups show no inferiority, while others do; it is therefore crucially important to know *whether one group (e.g., a New York group) is a favorable selection from the Negro population, or whether environment produces the differences.*

Some new light is thrown on this problem by the study of urban and rural Negroes. The consistent differences found between urban and rural populations (in favor of the former, of course) have led a good many to speculate on the possible "selective" influence of an urban environment. It is often maintained that the superiority of urban Negroes over rural Negroes, of urban Japanese over rural Japanese, and so on, is a result of the migration of intelligent individuals into the cities. This might easily drain off to the cities such a large proportion of the good stock as to make astounding differences between urban and rural populations.

On this point the only direct check with which we are familiar is that of Klineberg. One of his many studies dealt with 425 twelve-year-old Negro boys in New Orleans, tested by means of the National Intelligence Test. Of these boys, about 165 had been born in New Orleans; the others had come to the city at various ages since birth. He separated the subjects into the following groups: those who had been in the city less than one year; those who had been in the city between one and two years; between two and three years; three and four years; four and five years; and five and six years; and those who had been in the city between six and twelve years. Now the average National Intelligence Test scores of these twelve-year-old groups, when thus arranged, show an *almost perfectly straight line* of increasing intelligence, from the score of about 40 made by those who had been in the city less than a year, to a score of about 75 made by those born in the city. No *single* one of these comparisons with adjacent groups is entirely reliable because of the fewness of cases, but the mass trend is perfectly clear, and the difference between those who had been in the city less than three years and those who had been in the city longer is perfectly reliable.

No very definite generalization about "selection," in relation to such a difference between urban and rural populations, can be made;

but it must at least be regarded as very remarkable that selection should act in such a perfect fashion. Indeed, the results are precisely what they would be if scores on the National Intelligence Test were quite profoundly influenced by quality of schooling—a result which is entirely in line with the independent evidence. Another study of selective migration indicated that the northward movement of Negroes drains off sometimes superior, sometimes inferior, individuals.

To summarize the evidence on intelligence differences between Negroes and whites, we may say that on our present forms of intelligence tests, Negroes make much lower scores than do whites, but that schooling and length of residence in the city seem to affect the ratings of Negroes to such a great extent that we cannot determine from present data what the actual difference would be if environmental differences were eliminated. Moreover, no complete picture of the differences or resemblances between these races can be obtained until we can test a more comprehensive range of abilities than are represented by our present tests.

When we turn to a comparison of white and oriental races, we must first consider a comprehensive and careful study made by Murdock in Honolulu. Twelve-year-old children in the public schools were her subjects; their racial constitution was described as Anglo-Saxon, Chinese, Japanese, Portuguese, Korean, Hawaiian, Puerto Rican, and Filipino (together with some mixed groups). Some large and striking differences appeared on group tests, the Anglo-Saxon group being superior to the Chinese and Japanese, and these in turn to the others. When, however, the tests were analyzed into verbal and non-verbal elements, it was found that the inferiority of the Chinese and Japanese to the Anglo-Saxon was due entirely to the linguistic (English) parts of the test material; non-verbal material showed no reliable difference between these groups. Other more recent work has made it practically certain that the difference between urban and rural individuals is considerable, but that no significant difference in measurable general intelligence exists as be-

tween urban Japanese and Chinese on the one hand, and urban
Americans on the other.

The comparison of the various subdivisions of the white race with
respect to intelligence seemed for a few years to yield definite
results. In general, the testing of recruits during the War indicated
the superiority of individuals from English-speaking countries; relatively high scores for other individuals from most of northern
Europe (Germany, France and Scandinavia); considerably lower
scores for southern and eastern Europeans.

It was held by some writers that the factor of selection varied
so much from one group of immigrants to another that no generalization about the nations themselves could be made. A more
serious criticism of the test results was the very general comment
that linguistic factors had not been allowed for, and that the scores
were poorest in just those cases in which the immigrants spoke a
language differing widely from English.

Such discussion, however, could never be conclusive; and it has
been only in the last few years that we have begun to get anything
like a satisfactory examination of the evidence for the notion of
superiority or inferiority of the racial stocks of Europe. Data on
this point have been obtained by Klineberg. His results were obtained with ten- to twelve-year-old boys in three urban groups and
seven rural groups scattered through France, Germany and Italy.
All the subjects in the rural districts were given anthropometric
measurements, and only those individuals were used whose physical
characteristics conformed to the anthropologists' definition of Nordic, Alpine, or Mediterranean stocks, respectively (i.e., mixed types
were excluded). With this criterion, his procedure was to take,
without selection, *all* the ten- to twelve-year-old boys within a given
region, until 100 of the desired racial type were found, and to ad-
minister a battery of performance tests in which language played
no part in the responses.

The results are remarkably clear as regards the difference between urban and rural. The three urban groups are markedly superior to the seven rural groups; the three cities, Paris, Hamburg and

Rome, differ only slightly one from another, but differ strikingly from country districts. We turn next to the question of racial stocks, as found in the seven rural districts. The highest of the seven groups is a Nordic group, but another Nordic group stands sixth. The lowest of the groups is Mediterranean, but another Mediterranean group stands second. When the three major groups, Nordic, Alpine and Mediterranean, are segregated and the total material compared, the differences among the three are small and unreliable. If now we are tempted to draw the conclusion that it is national culture rather than race which causes the differences, we are confronted by the fact that one French group stands high, another low, and so on. In other words, neither a simple *racial* nor a simple *national* explanation of the results will suffice. On the contrary, the data show that there are within each race *"good" samples and "bad" samples*; that there are within each nation good samples and bad samples. How much of the variance in goodness or badness of the samples is biological, and how much is due to the peculiar conditions found in different country districts (for example, climate, schools, accessibility of stimulating city influences) remains unknown. All that can be said is that when carefully tested, the racial differences alleged to exist are not found. These studies with *performance tests* might well be followed up with tests of the Binet type.

If large racial groups are found in fact to differ in intellectual competence despite practical equality of opportunity, there are two quite distinct possibilities by way of interpretation. The first is that there is a necessary biological relation between race and quantity of intellect, by virtue of an actual genetic linkage between the criteria of race and the factors determining the development of the central nervous system. The other possibility is that at a given time and place a loose association exists between the genetic factors participating in the development of the criteria of race and the factors participating in determining the development of the central nervous system, but an association based not on actual linkage of genes but on mere coexistence. The geneticist points out that parents possessing any two traits may have offspring which have the same two traits, not because the two traits are genetically linked, but because the same laws which cause the offspring to have one cause the offspring to have the other. At any given time and place the criteria of race may coexist with factors giving good, average or poor nervous systems. It is quite possible, for example, that the criteria of the Mediterranean race are at the present time associated in Sicily and south Italy with factors which would yield relatively poor intelligence, even under favorable environmental conditions. At any time and place the same criteria might yield, even among the descendants of the same Sicilian stock, a very different relationship. Factors of selection' might at any time operate in such a way as to eliminate some elements in the population and to increase the fertility of others. The relatively "poor" components in a homogeneous Mediterranean stock might fade out and the relatively "good" components become more numerous.

We regard it as practically certain that there is no necessary biological relation between the criteria of race and the capacity for intellectual growth; but we are not disposed to regard as closed the question whether the present Nordic, Alpine or Mediterranean stock happens to contain, on the average, greater or less intellectual competence; and we raise the same questions regarding all comparisons of major races such as white, black, and yellow.

The problem of racial differences in *emotional* traits is in some ways less complicated than the problem of intellectual differences. Some evidence is at hand to suggest endocrine differences between races, and these are probably significant for emotion. The differences in the age of onset of puberty, for example, are large when such stocks as Norwegians and Sicilians are compared. For whatever is said about the uncertainty of endocrine findings for psychology, the major significance of puberty in relation to social behavior is scarcely to be challenged, and two or three years in the onset of puberty may have permanent significance for the personality of the individual. Unfortunately, we have few studies of this factor with all environmental factors held constant. The importance of the endocrines for an intelligent discussion of race differences, fifty or even twenty years hence, must be recognized. At present, however, we are in a terrain which has not even been explored, much less surveyed.

It must, nevertheless, be pointed out that endocrine differences between races have been found to be very unstable when the racial groups change about from one environment to another. Thus, on the basis of anthropological criteria of race, a large group of Nordic girls at Copenhagen showed a much later onset of puberty than a group of Mediterranean girls in Rome; but Danish Nordic and Italian Mediterranean girls in the United States showed less difference; the apparent "race difference" was altered under new social conditions. Almost as striking is the fact that another trait *partly* depending on the endocrines—namely, blood pressure—which reveals differences between occidentals and orientals, fails to do so when life conditions are equalized. The blood pressure of the Chinese student pursuing western studies goes up, that of the American resident in China goes down, till each resembles that of the persons about him.

Nothing is more commonly assumed to prove intrinsic racial differences in temperament than the strikingly contrasting art forms of various nations. The systematic preference for certain arrangements of lines, shadows, and the like, the essence of all things Japanese, surely stands out in a Hokusai print.

We have, fortunately, a direct experimental approach to the problem involved here, namely, whether such national habits and preferences in art form are biological, "innately" temperamental on the one hand, or cultural, environmental on the other hand. Hattori made use of ten Japanese and ten occidental pictures, the former being well known to Japanese and the latter well known to occidentals. The occidental pictures included the work of such artists as Raphael, Botticelli, and da Vinci. Forty-four occidental subjects and forty-nine Japanese subjects participated. Of the Japanese group, nine were born in the United States, and Hattori reminds us that all the Japanese subjects had long been exposed to occidental culture. In Series I, all subjects ranked the ten Japanese pictures in order of merit. In Series II, the same was done for the occidental pictures. In Series III, the entire twenty pictures, in random order, were presented, and the subjects were required to apply the order-of-merit method to the whole group. Alleged racial differences are rather strikingly absent. In arranging the ten occidental pictures, the rank correlation for Japanese and occidentals is $+ .93 \pm .03$. For the ten Japanese pictures it is $+ .89 \pm .04$, while even for the mixture it is $+ .74 \pm .07$. The Sistine Madonna was given first place by 19 Japanese subjects and 26 occidentals.

Hattori now selected from his Japanese group those who had been born in the United States, and compared their preferences with those of Japanese born in Japan. Again with the ranking method, the correlation of Japan-born Japanese with occidentals is $+ .64 \pm .09$; that of Japan-born Japanese with United States-born Japanese is $+ .69 \pm .08$; and that between United States-born Japanese and occidentals is $+ .84 \pm .05$. (Thus the Japanese born in the United States resemble occidentals more than they do Japanese born in Japan, but the difference is of course unreliable.) No great weight, of course, should be placed on such a fragment of evidence. It is very unfortunate that preferences for pictures, rather than preferences for simpler aesthetic objects, were used. Surely the Japanese, and probably the occidental subjects, knew a good deal about accepted *standards* and may have been governed largely by the desire to say the "right" thing. Hattori's work is nevertheless in the direction in which we are inclined to believe research must proceed if a quantitative estimate of acculturation as against biological predisposition is to be achieved.

On this question of racial differences in "temperament," Murdock's data have, it seems to us, never received sufficient attention; we refer to her remarkable data on the "moral" differences between Anglo-Saxons and orientals. She used a modification of one of Voelker's honesty tests, in which the subjects were required to shut their eyes and to put pencil dots inside of small circles. Each subject was to report his gain or improvement in a succession of tests. Now since nobody can put a pencil dot in a small circle with the eyes shut except by a lucky shot once in a long while, any *improvement* reported is almost invariably due to peeping or to a false report. An occasional child *might* happen to make an improvement, of course, but the results for large groups would be safe. Turning now to the results, it is rather remarkable to note that 99 per cent of the

Japanese children surpass the average Anglo-Saxon in honesty! Here surely one need not resort to racial theories. At least if so, it would seem that there is but little hope for the Anglo-Saxons. The point is, of course, that occidental children learn very early what ambition means, and that in some situations "all is fair." The data are perfectly consistent with those reported in Chapter X about criteria of honesty among children in the United States.

SEX DIFFERENCES

The question of sex differences in intelligence has been worked at so long and so hard, and the results are now so clear, that we feel justified in stating the general conclusion in a few words.

Intelligence tests are for the most part standardized with persons of both sexes. This holds true for both adults and children. No test would be regarded as good if the boys were decidedly ahead of the girls, or vice versa. This is a fact which would tend to obscure such differences in intellectual traits as might exist. On the other hand, where tests have been worked out for one sex and then given to the other, there has not, as a rule, been found to be much difference except in matters in which information plays a dominant part. From such material as we have (and there is a great deal), we can therefore say that as a rule sex differences in intelligence are not found; and with minor exceptions, this generalization holds for sex comparisons among all the national and racial groups, and for all the age levels.

The fact remains that there are certain special aptitudes which do appear fairly consistently to reveal sex differences. In some verbal tasks women and girls have shown fairly consistent superiority; in some forms of ingenuity, especially those involving mechanical matters, men and boys have had an advantage. In no one of these factors has the influence of the somewhat different educational influences been clearly measured. Nor, despite the "emancipation of women," are we likely in the immediate future to discover groups of women who have grown up with identically the same educational opportunities as men. Certain differences in sensori-motor equip-

SOME STUDIES RELATING

AUTHOR DATE	TOPIC	SUBJECTS	METHODS
Allport, G. W., and Vernon, P. E. (1931)	Sex differences in "values."	463 men and 313 women.	Allport-Vernon Study of Values administered.
Goodenough, F. L. (1927)	Review of experimental studies on sex differences in mental traits.	Ss from 2 yrs. old to adulthood.	Divides studies into (1) those dealing with gross comparisons between sexes on total scores; (2) those dealing with separate parts of tests.
Mead, M. (1935)	Sex differences in certain primitive societies of similar racial stock.	The Arapesh, Mundugumur and Tchambuli of New Guinea.	Observation.
Terman, L. M. (1916)	Sex differences in general intelligence.	457 boys and 448 girls between 5 and 14 years old.	Stanford-Binet administered to all subjects.
Terman, L. M., and Miles, C. C. (1936)	Scale to differentiate between characteristic male and female patterns of response.	Test standardized, items selected by collecting data from hundreds of Ss, of both sexes.	In final scale 7 tests: Word-association, ink-blot association, information, emotional and ethical response, interest, opinions, introvertive response. Composite weighted score on all 7 tests can be obtained for each subject.

[1] For a comprehensive survey of the problem of sex differences, see the chapter by

TO SEX DIFFERENCES[1]

FINDINGS	GENERAL REMARKS
For women, highest average values are "aesthetic," "social" and "religious" (as defined by test); for men highest average score given for "theoretical," "economic," and "political" values.	
(1) Extreme inconsistency of findings because of biological and sociological factors and lack of social criterion to evaluate significance of various types of specific accomplishment for social progress. (2) Linguistic superiority of girls maintained to maturity; male superiority in dealing with numerical relationships found among older children and adults; consistent superiority of females in memory tests; boys have wider range of general information by beginning of grammar school period.	Mental differences between sexes small in comparison to variation among members of same sex. Sex differences in mental traits exist, but origin not apparent; possibly due to differences in social customs and ideals.
Different patterns of male and female rôle. Arapesh men and women cooperative, gentle, unaggressive, solicitous. Mundugumur men and women violent, aggressive, competitive, hostile. Tchambuli women powerful; do fishing, make most important articles of trade; men engage in artistic, non-utilitarian activities. Women practical, efficient; tolerant of men, who are timid, sensitive, dependent, graceful. Sexual deviants are those in each culture who differ from standards described.	" . . . Human nature is almost unbelievably malleable . . . the form of this conditioning is culturally determined. Standardized personality differences between the sexes are . . . cultural creations. . . ."
Average I.Q. of girls slightly higher than that of boys except at 10 (equal) and at 14 (boys excelled). Boys superior in numerical tests.	Differences slight, but consistent with other investigations.
Scale successful in differentiating male and female groups. Smallest difference was 3.4 times its standard error.	Rôle of cultural factors constantly stressed.

C. C. Miles in C. Murchison's *Handbook of Social Psychology.*

ment, particularly those differences having to do with strength and with ability to mobilize energy quickly, have been consistently found to show masculine superiority. This kind of difference seems in part strictly biological, since women, even with excessive athletic training, can never develop the strength or the capacity to mobilize energy to the degree shown by men; we refer to athletic records in both track and field events, and endurance tests such as records for mountain climbing, etc.

With regard to emotional differences, it would almost seem that a number of investigators had set their faces against obtaining the kind of data that might really be helpful to us. A considerable number of writers take it for granted that all emotional differences between the sexes must be environmental and traditional; another group romanticizes about the differences, or solemnly emphasizes their importance, without adducing clear quantitative evidence even for their existence. The systematic study of masculinity and femininity of personal traits is now beginning, but leaves the problem of biological origin almost untouched. The comparison of cultures suggests that the patterns of "masculinity" and "femininity" as we know them are far indeed from universal, but have not as yet been coordinated with biological research to show the degree to which biological differences, when present, can be culturally controlled.

Very great differences in activity, in fierceness, in interest in young are found between the sexes in many mammalian species, and experimental transplantation of sex glands has frequently been found to reverse the "psychological" sex of individual animals. Such data need to be kept in mind when purely cultural interpretations of human sex differences are offered.

That some of the emotional differences found in adolescents are not entirely due to training seems a reasonable conjecture from the biological facts of adolescence. On the other hand, the great rôle played by custom or social pattern must be recognized because of the fact that many of the emotional traits so characteristic of adolescents in our own society are not found in other societies. In view of the absence of good quantitative work on the *degree* to which masculinity and femininity of behavior may be made to result from cultural pressures, it is unfortunate that dogmatism with regard to the absence of sex differences should have reached the pitch that is evident in so many recent writings. To those who argue that equality means the absence of differences, one might reply (1) that political or social equality has nothing to do with what the actual experimental findings may be, and (2) that probably a society in which some differences in interest and aptitude do appear is apt to be more agreeable than one in which stereotyping is pushed to its utmost; so that even if wishes affected the evidence, the argument for theoretical "equality" would collapse. Yet we have not, at this writing, any absolutely conclusive data on any sort of psychological sex differences that cannot with fair plausibility be interpreted largely in cultural terms.

Thus with regard to the three major types of group differences which confront the student of nature and nurture, namely, socio-economic differences, race differences, and sex differences, we feel bound to conclude that cultural reasons for the obtained differences cover most of the obtained results. It is not likely that they cover *all* the results; for example, they probably leave a place for some socio-economic differential in intelligence and some sex differential in temperament. Even here, however, the very great force of culture is evident. Not until better nature-nurture techniques are devised can we say within what limits culture can work.

We can, however, say that as the evidence now stands, *individual differences* are large in comparison with every *group difference*, and that the individual differences reflect the influence of variance in heredity to a very considerable degree. Cultural interpretations of group differences are in general in line with the evidence; cultural interpretations of individual differences within social groups are on much more precarious ground, both because of the biological difficulties involved and because of the empirical data obtained.

Chapter III

THE BIOLOGY OF MOTIVES

MANY are the theories about man's "native equipment." From generalized "urges" to particularized "instincts," speculations have run the gamut required by systematic psychologies which are founded on doctrines of individual motivation. With equal ease, human nature is said to be infinitely plastic, devoid of inner driving forces. The problem is of the utmost importance to social psychology; but the answer is not an easy one. The present chapter deals with the complicated evidence regarding *biological fundamentals*, the rudiments of social motivation in the newborn; the next will consider the shaping of these motives by social forces in such a way as to give social habits.

The biological and social facts regarding motivation are often assumed to be easily disentangled and pigeonholed, and a brief formula about instinct and learning is made to do duty as an introduction to social behavior. For example, all human behavior may be attributed to "visceral tensions." The actual complexity of the situation arises from the fact that even a relatively simple tension, such as that occurring in the muscles of the stomach in the case of hunger, is itself the result of disturbances elsewhere, and calls out, even in the newborn child, several *different kinds of responses*. The patterns of behavior which arise from hunger are complex, even from a biological point of view; and when seen in the context of the social environment which ordains when, where and how we may satisfy our hunger, they become more complicated still. If this caution is needed in relation to hunger, it is needed all the more in relation to sexual and maternal interests and the drives which underlie mastery, vanity, friendship and aesthetic satisfactions.

It will be well, then, to consider the biological analysis of motives before considering the complications introduced by social factors;

the distinction between biological and social is a help in preliminary analysis and exposition. We shall later emphasize the complete wholeness and inseparability of biological and social factors in motivation in the functioning organism.

PRELIMINARY ANALYSIS OF THE VISCERAL MOTIVES

First, then, as to the biological analysis of the simplest patterns of motivated behavior. These patterns arise from conditions within the vital organs. There are two kinds of processes that need to be distinguished whenever these visceral motives are mentioned: first, "organic" factors, such as stomach contractions and secretions of adrenalin, which appear to affect the reflexes of the infant or adult in specific ways; second, the specific reflexes themselves, aroused by stimuli definable in terms of the units of physical science, such as time, space, motion, force. Quantitative statements as to the relations between the first and the second groups of processes are usually summarized under the heading of "threshold," which is the *amount of stimulation required to set an activity going.* For example, the touch of the finger on the cheek of some infants causes them, if hungry, to turn the head suddenly in the direction of the finger, whereas much greater pressure has to be applied to cause this behavior in a satiated child. In exactly the same way, hunger contractions lower the thresholds for other reflex activities such as salivation, which would be absent in a well-fed organism; the contractions may even precipitate the salivary response when no food is present.

Some of the most important of the internal conditions affecting the threshold are chemical. The injection of blood from a starving dog into one which had just completed a meal caused the sudden recommencement of hunger contractions in the latter animal. From such illustrations as this, it has become reasonably certain that the mechanical factors which appear to be responsible for changes of threshold (for example, hunger contractions as the apparent cause of lowered thresholds for salivation) are themselves activated by chemical changes. We shall probably not be far off the track if we define the simpler visceral motives in terms of specific *reflexes and groups of reflexes* influenced by a great variety of *internal chemical changes.*

The way in which the thresholds are affected in the case of an infant's hunger may be roughly schematized as follows:

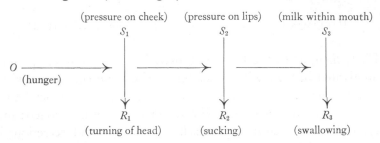

In the diagram, O represents the organic condition which lowers all the hunger reflexes; if S_1 represents the touch upon the cheek, S_2 the touch upon the lips which follows after the head has been turned, and S_3 the milk which follows after the nipple has been grasped, we have a "chain reflex." In each case, of course, the organic condition is supposed to be playing its part; but each new act is carried out when and only when the reaction to the previous stimulus in the chain is completed.

All the simpler visceral motives involve organic factors and specific thresholds affected by these factors, but the patterns which result are of many sorts. In the case of hunger, the completion of one response prepares the way for the next, while in the case of oxygen deficit the characteristic thing is the *simultaneous* lowering of a great *many* reflex thresholds, some of which are simple and some of which involve fairly complicated coordinated movements. Screaming may appear before the slashing movements of the arms and legs; but the screaming cannot be regarded as the *necessary antecedent* to the slashing movements in the same way that the sucking is the necessary antecedent to the swallowing in the previous illustration. An entirely different pattern would probably have to be worked out for each motive; and the formulae might vary from one individual to another, and even from day to day in the same individual. We wish only to stress (1) internal chemical conditions, and (2) specific reflex patterns whose thresholds depend on these conditions.

Examples of chemical factors whose function has been clearly worked out are the internal secretions of sex. Comparison of many mammals has shown that the chief effects of these factors upon general activity are about the same from one species to another; in particular, the dependence of the sex drive upon them has been shown. Evidence has been obtained from many investigations of sexual behavior in animals, in which the removal of much of the tissue of the external sex organs has been shown to have practically no effect on the drive, whereas after deprivation of the sex secretions the drive is lost. The introduction of the specific sex secretions or the tissue of the glands may suddenly induce a revival of sex behavior.

The reflexes which are activated by a drive are sometimes specifically related to the *satisfaction of the drive* (release of the tension); sometimes they seem useless, mere random discharge of energy; sometimes they lie between these extremes, being rather random but in some ways related to the goal object which satisfies the drive. But there is always a large amount of random activity when the inner tension becomes great, until the way to obtain the goal object has been learned. Many of the reflex responses are at first random, becoming more and more adequately adapted to assist in achieving the goal. In general, repeated experience with the goal reduces the randomness of the responses and in time makes them appropriate to the goal, so as to be scarcely distinguished from the specific reflexes which from infancy onward mediate the goal to the organism (e.g., sucking as described above).

Moreover, many of the reflexes can serve more than one drive; in many cases the separate reflexes activated by an organic condition may function independently of the rest and certain parts may become fixed and stereotyped while others disappear. Thumb-sucking is an everyday example. Instead of a fixed and invariable reflex "pattern," one component occurs independently. "Normally," as we say, sucking would be regarded as a part of a set of reflex activities whose thresholds are lowered by *hunger*. Yet some of the reflexes may occur independently both of hunger and of the other reflexes. Most

AUTHOR DATE	TOPIC	SUBJECTS	METHODS
Allen, E. S., and Doisy, E. A. (1924)	Effect of injecting ovarian follicular hormone into immature females.	31 immature female rats (24–54 days).	Follicular contents or extracts of hog ovaries injected. 19 rats in experimental group, 12 controls. 3 spayed and given injections, to check on possibility that hormone activating ovaries. 2 controls not spayed. Criterion of sexual maturity: open vagina and signs of estrus.
Cannon, W. B., and Washburn, A. L. (1921)	Physiological basis of hunger pangs.	One human adult (Washburn).	Soft rubber balloon (8 cm. in diameter) attached to rubber tube in stomach. S ate little breakfast, no lunch; recording (of intragastric pressure, respiration, time in minutes, introspective report of hunger pangs) starting at 2:00 P.M., all recording apparatus out of sight of S.
Carlson, A. J., and Ginsburg, H. (1915)	Tonus and hunger contractions.	"Number of newborn infants" and 2 prematurely-born pups (8–10 days before term).	Rubber balloons 15 cc. capacity attached to flexible rubber catheter 2 mm. in diameter. Infants swallowed apparatus and went to sleep in arms of experimenters. Balloon used for pups had capacity of 4 cc. Kymographic records taken.
Dashiell, J. F. (1925)	Method for quantitative demonstration of effect of (e.g.) hunger on activity.	White rats: 17 "fed," 17 "hungry."	Maze with no goal; floor marked off in equal squares. Rats from "fed" and "hungry" groups used alternately; left in maze for 60 sec.
Hoskins, R. G. (1925)	Effect of castration on spontaneous activity.	White rats: 16 castrated males, ages 62–90 days (12 between 71–77 days) at time of castration; 16 male controls, all but 3 litter mates of experimental animals.	Revolutions of activity wheel during period of 20 days before to 100 days after operation.

PHYSIOLOGY OF DRIVE

FINDINGS	GENERAL REMARKS
All experimental rats showed sexually mature condition in genital tract similar to that of 1st estrus, 2–3 days after injections, 20–50 days before usual pubertal time. Control animals remained unchanged until usual time.	Follicular hormone is responsible for attainment of sexual maturity in female; possibility for secondary sexual characters.
Hunger pangs correlated with periodic contractions in stomach.	Favors local peripheral explanation of subjective hunger, in terms of gastric contractions.
Newborn infant's stomach exhibits typical periods of tonus and hunger contractions of the adult, but with greater frequency and relatively greater vigor. In some infants and both pups, observations made before first nursing. As contractions become very vigorous, baby may wake up and cry.	Gastric hunger mechanism functional at birth and is probably inherited.
Average number of blocks entered by "fed" group, 26.7; average number entered by "hungry" group, 42.9.	Provides quantitative measure of activity produced by drives, where such devices as revolving cage inadequate.
After average of 12 days activity of castrated animals dropped below controls. Controls rise in activity about 50th day after operation; then fall. Castrate record shows straight line from $\frac{1}{3}$ to $\frac{1}{2}$ the height of control curve.	Indisputable quantitative evidence of decreasing activity following castration. (No explanation attempted.)

SOME STUDIES OF THE

AUTHOR DATE	TOPIC	SUBJECTS	METHODS
Levy, D. M. (1934)	Sucking in dogs in relation to general behavior.	6 collie pups from same litter.	10 days after birth 4 pups taken from mother, 2 fed by bottles with small-holed nipples; after feeding allowed more sucking on examiner's finger ("long-time feeders"); 2 others sucked rapidly from bottles with large-holed nipples ("short-time feeders"). Long-time feeders had 80 min. daily; short-time, 13 min. (average). Remaining 2 pups left with mother. After 20 days, 4 artificially fed animals returned to mother. Feeding by bottle discontinued 6th week. Then all fed alike. Breast-fed pups examined for comparison at regular intervals.
Maslow, A. H. (1936)	Relation of dominance to social and sexual behavior of infrahuman primates.	35 animals, including several species of monkeys, mandrills, baboons, gibbons and chimpanzees, male and female, from infant to senile animals.	Regular observations over a year. Dominance tested by inspection; by relation among animals when food put in cage; by teasing.
McQueen-Williams, M. (1935)	Induced maternal behavior in males.	60 white rats, adult males (3½ and 5 mos. old).	Chronic (60 days) bovine anterior pituitary implants to 10 5-mo.-old rats; or complete thyroidectomy at age of 1 mo., 20 rats. Equal numbers of control animals.

PHYSIOLOGY OF DRIVE (*Continued*)

FINDINGS	GENERAL REMARKS
Only short-time feeders developed sucking movements after meals, sucking noises during sleep, sucking of own bodies, sucking or licking objects in kennel. Sucking body of another dog occurred 30 times for short-time feeders, 7 times for long-time feeders. After change from liquid to semi-solid diet, short-time feeders slower in eating, licked dish longer, more frequently. Breast-fed pups showed closer relationship to bitch than others. Wt. differences favored breast-fed and long-time feeders; short-timers showed increased restless activity and less sleep.	Insufficiency of sucking produced excessive sucking and licking activities. Separation from mother disturbed early mother-child relationship profoundly. Suggestion made that handicap of short-time feeders (through lack of jaw exercise) increased aggressive or submissive tendencies previously manifested.
Dominant animal gets most of food; its sexual behavior usually masculine (non-dominant usually feminine), regardless of gender; dominant animal has "run of cage"; usually initiates fights; dominant female at height of estrus cycle tends to become submissive; dominance behavior syndrome less marked in young animals; hierarchy of dominance almost universal, but may disappear during play; new individual usually takes dominance position at once; subordinate animal may obtain his wishes by "presenting" to the dominant animal; hierarchy unchanged unless factors such as age, etc., intervene; larger animal almost always dominant.	"Dominance is an extremely important determiner of social and sexual behavior in the monkey." Dominant and submissive sexual and other behavior more likely to be symbolic of "social inferiority," rather than "prostitution" (Kempf).
Males made nests, cared for young rats, licked them in maternal way, etc. Pituitaries of experimental animals considerably enlarged. No mammary development noted.	Maternal behavior can be produced experimentally in males. Not due to lactogenic hormone.

AUTHOR DATE	TOPIC	SUBJECTS	METHODS
Nissen, H. W. (1929)	Effects of male and female gonadectomy, vasotomy; placental (follicular) and orchic extract injection on sex behavior.	White rats. 111 females, 168 males. Wistar strain.	Comparison among groups of number of crossings of electric grill to secure mate, per unit time. (See Warner, 1927.)
Richards, T. W. (1936)	Review of material on activity level and hunger of infants.	Infants of various ages after birth.	Fed after insertion of inflated balloon into stomach. Kymographic recording of stomach movements.
Richter, C. P. (1927)	Rhythmic activity changes as result of rhythmical organic changes (partly review).	Rats of various ages.	Kymographic records from activity cages (floor mounted on tambours); from activity wheels (mounted next to food cages). Removal of gonads, testicular implantation, follicular injection. Correlation of gross activity recorded with specific activity—eating, drinking, urination, defecation, estrus cycle, etc.
Riddle, O.; Bates, R. W., and Lahr, E. L. (1935)	Hormones and "incubation instinct."	20 hens of broody races, 9 non-broody. 27 control hens of both sorts. 2 roosters of broody race.	Prolactin injected intramuscularly in various doses in experimental animals. Control hens injected with other pituitary hormones.
Shirley, M. (1928)	Studies of spontaneous activity.	White rats.	Investigated reliability of revolving drum method, activity rhythms, relation of age to activity, influence of rest, relation to maze learning and brain weight.

PHYSIOLOGY OF DRIVE (*Continued*)

FINDINGS	GENERAL REMARKS
Decrease in crossings 48 hrs. after gonad-ectomy. Injections of placental extract restored female "contrectation" drive almost to normal. Male castration slowly reduces contrectation drive. Placental hormone increases it. Vasotomy had no effect. Little evidence of effect of orchic extract.	Gonadal hormone stimulates sex behavior not directly but by controlling development of an intermediary mechanism. Distinction between "contrectation" and "detumescence" drives. No correlation in males; high correlation in females.
Infants sleep most during middle of feeding cycle (3-hr. period). External stimuli less effective immediately after feeding, during absorptive period, and during later period of violent activity (related to exhaustion of food supply).	Food supply directly lowers bodily activity. Emptying of stomach (during 3–4-hr. period) accompanied by curve of positive acceleration in bodily activity.
3-hr. hunger rhythm, 2¼-hr. thirst rhythm, 4-day sex (estral) rhythm in female abolished by gonadectomy. Reduced activity upon gonadectomy; increased upon subsequent follicular injection. Urination 2–3-hr. rhythm, defecation 3–5-hr. rhythm. Longer rhythms, 7, 18–22, and 40–120 days recorded but not correlated with other activity.	"Spontaneous" activity arises from underlying physiological processes. Both generalized and specific activity result from endosomatic stimulation.
Injection caused premature broodiness in normally broody hens: clucking in all broody hens, nearly all showed nesting. 2 roosters clucked, did not nest. Other hormones stopped egg-laying, inhibited ova growth; induced no broodiness. Hens whose ovaries already inactive responded to prolactin by clucking; did not show nesting. Some non-broody hens showed complete broodiness.	Prolactin shown to be necessary to induction of brooding behavior; sufficient only when dosage represses ovary and stops growth and production of ova. Hormone shown to be "essential element in an instinct . . . species-preserving incubation instinct. . . ." Results thought to indicate probability that prolactin is also necessary in "nesting instinct" of rats and rabbits.
Found high reliabilities, polyphasic rhythms, period of greatest activity just before feeding; rat somewhat nocturnal; 1-hr. sample of activity almost as reliable as 24. Rats more active at 9 mos. than earlier, decline in activity thereafter. Rest of 1–2 days increases activity, longer periods impair it. Maze proficiency very slightly related to activity; not at all to brain weight. Activity unrelated to brain weight.	Definite evidence for "drives" as inner stimuli to activity, influence of external factors on drives, but little on relation to other activities.

AUTHOR DATE	TOPIC	SUBJECTS	METHODS
Skinner, B. F. (1932)	Measurement of hunger by rate of ingestion.	Adult albino rats.	Automatic recording of food-pellet seizure by animal. Continuous record of rate of eating obtained. In 2nd experiment food must be obtained by pressing lever. Rats fed at regular daily periods.
Stone, C. P. (1922)	Maturation and sensory basis of sexual behavior in male albino rats.	Male albino rats.	Systematic observation, copulatory activity of young and adult male rats. Sense destruction operatively produced.
Stone, C. P. (1923)	Basis of sexual behavior in young male white rats.	7 young male white rats, 3 reared together, 4 in isolation.	Belly wall, inguinal region and scrotum surgically anesthetized, olfactory lobes destroyed, eyes removed, vibrissae cut; audition impaired by destruction of tympanic membranes. At varying periods following operations each rat tested for copulatory response by placing him in cage with receptive female.
Stone, C. P. (1926)	Initial copulatory response of female white rats reared in isolation.	20 young female white rats isolated from weaning to puberty.	When each rat indicated 1st external signs of receptivity, placed in cage with aggressively sexual male. Watched to determine when copulatory response (depression of lumbar region, etc.) occurred.
Wada, T. (1922)	Hunger drive related to activity.	5 normal adults; 2 hypochondriac, psychasthenic; 2 babies, 1 and 9 mo. old; 60 albino rats.	S swallowed stomach balloon connected to kymograph. Provision also to record general movement of sleepers. Stomach contractions recorded over long periods to determine rhythms; correlated with breathing, vasomotor volume, salivation; sensations of hunger; movements during sleep; movements when

PHYSIOLOGY OF DRIVE (*Continued*)

FINDINGS	GENERAL REMARKS
Parabolic curve of eating rate typical. Curve regular, constant. Voluntary or enforced cessation of eating followed by compensatory increase in rate. Eating rate identical when problem box used.	Rate of change of rate of eating is independent of nature of particular reflex with which eating behavior begins.
Copulatory pattern well coordinated in male at time of first copulatory act. Destruction of vision, olfaction, gustatory and auditory sensitivity before first sex act produced no change.	Sexual behavior probably largely mediated by cutaneous and deep sensibility receptors; is essentially congenital.
Two rats slow in initiating copulation, probably because of "poor physical condition"; all rats demonstrated the "initial copulatory response," despite the injuries.	
"Nineteen individuals copulated within a few seconds after being put with the males. . . . The age at which copulatory ability was manifested . . . was approximately the same as that of females that have been reared with other animals. . . ."	". . . No environmental influences . . . beyond those necessary to . . . somatic development are required to bring about sexual maturity. . . ." ". . . In a general way all types of native response develop in a manner fundamentally similar to those of the fetus. . . ." (Italics in original not included.)
Tonus waves appear 2–3 hrs. after meals, for 30–60 minutes. Increase in rate and amplitude, becoming very powerful, sometimes ending in tetanus followed by sudden relaxation. Salivary flow especially closely related. Sensations of hunger coincide with contractions. In men, infants and rats bodily movements coincide with contractions. In "infants and rats the periodical recurrence of bodily movements was strikingly	Hunger a function not of a single organ, but of whole organism. ". . . Hunger determines not only the inner condition of man, but works as a driving force for the projection apparatus, arms and legs, etc., to act upon the outer world."

AUTHOR DATE	TOPIC	SUBJECTS	METHODS
			quiet-awake; infants' movements; dreaming; motor activity; mental activity; and to determine effects of certain specific stimuli.
Warner, L. H. (1928)	Measurement of hunger drive in white rat.	60 males, 60 females, Wistar Institute rats; age 185 days.	Starvation period: 2, 3, 4, 6, 8 days and 0 days (controls). All animals under minimum sex drive. Measures: number of crossings on electric grid to incentive compartment containing standard food mixture, in 20-min. test period.
Warner, L. H. (1927)	Measurement of sex drive in white rat.	160 Wistar male rats, 91 Wistar females; sex lives normal. Age: 175–196 days (except 28-day deprivation group).	Males: After 2-hr. copulation period (mean copulations, 40.6), segregated from females for required periods. Females: Taken from living cages. Vaginal smear records immediately following test period. Incentive: rat of opposite sex; in estrus, when female. Both sexes previously segregated 33–39 days. Control day, sex-deprivation, but no female in incentive cage.

PHYSIOLOGY OF DRIVE (*Continued*)

FINDINGS	GENERAL REMARKS
regular." True when asleep or awake. More dreaming occurred at times when contractions present. Strength of grip greater at time of contractions. "Hunger augments efficiency in mental work." Mechanical distension of stomach produced contractions and bodily activity. No conscious control of rhythm could be demonstrated. Thinking about, seeing or smelling food produced no effect. Emotional stimuli (sad stories, excitement, etc.) inhibit contractions.	
Starvation period: 0, 2, 3, 4, 6, 8 days. Crossings: Aver. 2.4, 17.6, 18.2, 18.1, 14.1, 7.9. Male maximum reached in 4-day period; female, in 2-day.	Hunger drive increases up to 4 days of starvation and decreases thereafter. Comparison of hunger and sex drives when each maximal shows former stronger in both sexes.
Male: Sex drive at low point after period of mating with female in estrus; recovery rapid first 6 hrs., almost as rapid second 6 hrs., when slightly below maximum (24 hrs.). Slight decrease after 1-day deprivation (not statistically reliable). Female: Sexual activity confined to single period during estrus cycle. Onset sudden; cessation relatively gradual.	Sex behavor initiated "rather more by the external stimulus situation in the male than in the female and rather more by internal stimulation in the female than in the male."

"pattern reactions" seem to be rather loosely organized until they have been consolidated through learning.

It is worth while also to recall Craig's generalization that the final motor response which can put an end to the organic tension may be remarkably specific and efficient, but that it is capable nevertheless of being aroused by a great range of stimuli. Just as Craig's pigeons showed remarkably specific sex behavior toward a stimulus object (his hand) which was only remotely similar to the normal object, so here we have the possibility—of which the everyday behavior of kittens with thread and scraps of paper reminds us—that the motor pattern, in so far as it can be isolated, is sometimes not a sharply definable *sensori-motor* pattern, but rather a fairly precise *motor* pattern with the sensory inlets hard to define.

The tentative view of motive which we have here undertaken to state is obviously a rather cumbersome theoretical structure; and if it can be simplified, both our readers and ourselves will be the gainers. Present evidence, however, suggests that the only real simplification of the problem of motive is the frank recognition that there are several distinct problems interwoven here, and that most of the confusion is due to the attempt to solve all of these problems with one formula. It seems to us essential to distinguish the problem of inner tensions from the problem of means by which thresholds are lowered. The problem of random vs. specific movements which result from lowered thresholds includes the problem of learning, by which the adaptive responses are gradually fixed.

No discussion of the problem of motives can be carried on without considering the rhythmic character of those internal stresses or "impulses" which lead to heightened activity. Hunger, for example, though traceable in part to blood chemistry, involves the periodic recurrence of hunger contractions. When these contractions start, the animal or man is more active. Rhythmic bodily changes are responsible for rhythmic increase of "random" activity such as running. The animal leaves his living cage to run a while in an "activity wheel." His running and his rest betray the rhythms of his organic state. The child, and the adult likewise, move in their sleep to respond to many rhythms, of which hunger contractions are one of the most important.

It has thus been customary to note that many of the drives—notably the visceral drives—are rhythmical, or, better, *cyclical*, in character. Part of this cyclical tendency is doubtless due to the gradual accumulation of substances within the hollow viscera, or the gradual accumulation of a deficit—for example, water want or oxygen want—which develops at a fairly constant rate for viscera of more or less known characteristics. It is easy to see why the recurrence of thirst is more or less rhythmical. If the organism drinks to the satiation point and then goes without water, the deficit must at a predicted time reach a critical point involving nervous excitation and fresh activity.

It must, nevertheless, be stressed that these cycles are extremely variable under different life conditions, and in particular that they are easily modified by training. Just as the organism accustoms itself to this or that mode of satisfying a drive, it accustoms itself to this or that rhythm imposed upon it from without. An obvious example is the establishment, in the newborn child, of a feeding rhythm. The doctor prescribes three-hour intervals between feedings. Before long, the child's stomach (and hence his voice) proclaims the three-hour interval almost as effectively as the alarm clock. A change of schedule produces only a few days' disturbance. Now we have a four-hour and, later, a six-hour feeding rhythm; at five hours and fifty minutes perhaps, the restlessness and whimpering recommence. The rhythm is demonstrably imposed not by the unalterable characteristics of inner tissues but by neural patterns established in experience. So, too, the adult man who weighs a hundred pounds more than requirements of his life demand, nevertheless becomes desperately and miserably hungry if the one o'clock lunch time is passed. Again, individual differences in such rhythms are conspicuous. The rhythms vary from person to person, and are much more apparent in some persons than in others. We strongly suspect that the rhythmical character of visceral drives shares the fate of most of the other "fixed characteristics" of hereditary action tendencies (cf. page 30), and becomes nothing but a convenient—

or at times inconvenient—abstraction from data not completely clarified by genetic study.

Of course the rhythms, strictly speaking, are not staccato jump-wise changes; they involve slow changes and point to the probability of definite gradations. Probably the clearest and most definite point emerging from this analysis is the fact that the organic conditions which set activity going are not an "all or none" matter, but always a question of *degree*. A child is never simply hungry; his behavior depends on how hungry he is. Our whole thinking in this field has been made more exact by the several recent efforts to think of drives in quantitative terms—in fact, to measure them. We may measure animal drives by determining how strong an electric shock has to be in order to put an effectual stop to the animal's pursuit of its goal, or by using an "obstruction method" which measures animal drives not in terms of the gross total of electric shock required to stop the animal, but in terms of the number of times the animal will cross an electric grid (during a standard time interval) in pursuit of its goal. In this way it is possible to compare the strengths of various drives in various animals by a uniform technique. Among the values of this method is the possibility of adapting it to more and more species and, without changing the fundamental principles involved, to study the rôle of age, sex and other intrinsic differences. Hunger, thirst, and the sexual, maternal and exploratory drives have already been studied with the white rat, and similar investigations are under way with other forms, including monkeys. The relation between the animal's organic condition and his behavior with reference to his goal can thus be examined. This is well illustrated, for example, in studies of stages in the ovulation cycle in which the strength of the sex drive is measured by the obstruction method.

We shall not attempt here a complete inventory of the visceral drives. The visceral needs are numerous, and any catalogue of them commits the error of over-simplification. The hunger need, for example, seems to contain many components; in addition to a sheer food need, there is a salt need, a lime need, etc., often more powerful in controlling animal behavior than sheer food need. Quite aside from the universal tendency to "acquire tastes" through learning, there is a medley of organic needs which, however vaguely defined, tend to cause restlessness which persists until the need is removed. The thirst motive, too, is not simply water need; let the perspiring plowman be offered lukewarm water on a torrid day! The tissue needs which underlie the maintenance of body temperature are complex indeed, and the "needs" of the vital organs, especially the ductless glands, are legion. Probably many needs are always present in varying degrees and in all forms of admixture. More important, they probably all flow into one another; any state of need in the body generates widespread changes, both muscular and chemical, in all parts of the body, perhaps arousing further needs, many of them diffuse and unlocalized. Many needs become prominent only when others are first satisfied: "I am so tired that I must rest before I can bear the thought of food." Several needs may reinforce one another; the love need, for example, may raise the general intensity of the life demands, so that the whole environment is flat, colorless, unequal to the suitor's level of demand. Indeed, in conditions of eagerness, excitement, etc., we are clearly motivated, but it is not a narrow and specific response like that to an "organ stop" but a general bodily condition. For all these reasons, catalogues of fundamental visceral drives are more harmful than helpful; they imply an independence, a disjointedness to which the life of motive is a stranger; they imply distinct motive spots in the body where visceral needs reside. They imply that at any given time and place there is a motivated spot, the rest of the body being pushed along by the motive.

VARIETIES OF DRIVES

Thus far we have been content to follow a chemical and "visceral" interpretation of drives. But that some of the drives are not simply the expression of changes in the blood or in the viscera is rendered probable by the wide range of active interests and needs, e.g., the existence of exploratory (curiosity) behavior in both animals and man—a form of behavior frequently so pronounced as to compete successfully against visceral needs such as hunger and thirst. As was noted above, the exploratory drive in the white rat has already been measured, and studies of curiosity in pre-school children are in a sense measurements of the same drive.

Much of the activity of infants and adults is diffuse response to diffuse needs, such as the needs of muscles for activity and rest. Thus Thorndike recognized over thirty years ago that it was likely that even among the monkeys, behavior could not be parceled out to various relatively simple drives of the form which an analytic mind might desire. Just as recent experimenters find that hunger or thirst does not operate the same way in a monkey as in a cat because the monkey is "too easily distracted," so Thorndike observed that the monkey's activities were enormously more numerous than those of his dog and cat subjects. The monkey is almost "infinitely versatile. Everything appeals to him. He likes to be active for the sake of activity." This is like the sheer functioning which Charlotte Bühler and her pupils report among young children, and it is like the "activity leading to further activity" which has been substituted by many modern educators for the "pursuit of goals" which found favor in more hedonistic times.

We shall use the term *activity drives* to denote the trends toward active motor response to the environment. We need a cognate term to describe the positive response of the little child to color and tone, to tactual stimulation, and to all those sensory attributes of the world which appeal to him, lead him to act, i.e., motivate him. We suggest that these be called *aesthetic drives*.

Except when the organism is in dire need, the activity drives and aesthetic drives are much more prominent and much more easily observed than the visceral drives at every level of human development. If the diversity and richness of human motivation are attributed to sublimation, or some other mechanism by which visceral tension is translated into diffuse activity, the same theory must be applied to the behavior of the newborn. Modern research on the neonate's behavior indicates practically incessant restlessness, of which a relatively small amount is attributable to simple localized physiological tension; and by the time the child is two or three weeks old it is actively exploring with eyes and fingers, indeed, with its whole body. Objects like lights and tones have positive stimulus value, draw the child on and cause him to do those things which give him more and more of the stimulus, whereas a limited number of stimuli produce generalized disturbances or upset. The child delights in its own exercise, protests against any form of confinement, uses its bodily equipment as much for the sheer functioning value (Bühler) as for outside goals to be achieved. Under ordinary nursery conditions, with reasonable comfort, moderate temperature, and no intense disturbing stimuli at work, the child responds most of the time primarily to "activity needs" and "aesthetic needs," and only secondarily to such visceral needs as hunger.

As we have suggested, many drives may be active at once. Perhaps the most generalized fact in the behavior of the newborn is the fact of incessant variegated activity; there are movements large or small, muscular tensions great or slight, the adjustment of sense organs, the constant shift in activity from one part of the body to another. To pick out a single organ which alone is responding to a stimulus is difficult. There is no completely inactive tissue to be seen anywhere. We do confront in this matrix of activity a number of definite foci of specially vigorous action, or at least of action which seems to us specially significant. But if the term "drive" is used to indicate "that which impels to action," we shall find that every activity of the body is a "drive," since it does, in fact, communicate activity to other parts throughout the complicated flux which is the very process of living; all organs set going and direct the course of activity in other organs. To chop organisms up into three types of organs, those which are "engines" and those which are "fuel" which drives the engines, or "machinery" which they drive, would be futile and misleading. It would be misleading to regard the motives themselves as a fixed and finite group of *mutually independent* sources of energy, a row of organ stops upon which separate stimuli act to produce functionally independent responses.

The conception of drives just stated has arisen from watching little children and immature animals, and from reading the studies of others who have watched them. The classic or pseudo-classic conception of human motives which resulted from the emphasis on visceral tensions would lead us to expect that the immature human being spends most of his time seeking food, drink or embraces, or avoiding loud sounds or hot objects in his environment. If we look straight at him, we find him running and jumping, climbing and sliding, shouting and laughing, listening, watching. He is overwhelmed by the richness of the world about him. He goes out to meet it, gets control of it, uses it, in an ever-changing pattern. When he is interested in his Mickey Mouse book, his roller skating, or the ceremonies of his secret society, it is as hard to make him eat as to get him to bed, as hard to make him satisfy his so-called basic drives as it is to make him avoid obnoxious stimuli. He may play with the dog despite being bowled over by him; he jumps on the backs of trucks despite many a bruise and the knowledge of more serious dangers. As Thorndike long ago pointed out, the basic drives which go back to the catalogues of Hobbes and Descartes are hard to see in the welter of shifting activity of all higher mammals. Even the kitten and the puppy spend much of their time in pursuits which the economist would scarcely classify as gainful.

There may be a value in listing human drives—in fact, we think there is such a value—but they all flow into one another, they all depend for their existence upon the character of the stimulating world, and they all become canalized and defined by the concrete reality which the individual child can control. The Meccano set, the Popeye book, the Shirley Temple movie may take on overwhelming stimulating value, drawing not upon one but upon many sources of need.

At this point it would be easy to take a final leap into the theory of human plasticity, and urge that there is no human nature at all except for that afforded by specific cultural stimulation acting upon "the unorganized part of human nature." There are two serious difficulties, however, which make this last leap almost certain to be fatal. The first: the genes which determine whether we have the potentiality of becoming people, rats or canaries participate at every point in the growth process. One's fundamental urges depend partly upon whether one is born with a beak or with lips, with two legs or with four. They also depend partly upon the biochemical balance and the relative activity and urgency of varying driving forces. They also depend notably upon the mechanisms provided for internal as compared with external stimulation, and the relative sensitiveness to different kinds of stimuli in terms of sheer thresholds and levels of sensory acuity. They also depend upon the structure of the central and autonomic nervous systems, and the mode of integrating complex muscular responses. To be human is not to be diffusely stimulable in all directions; it is to be selective, to be oriented toward particular classes and modes of stimulation. Further, genes differ enormously in the character of the organic totality produced in the growth process, so that sons and daughters in the same family, or even the two members of a pair of fraternal twins, differ very considerably in the relative weight assignable to different classes of stimulation, in the degree of sensitiveness to each, and in the mode and duration of the response. Differences in complexity of nervous system as reflected in levels of intelligence are also important in relation to such drives as perseveration, curiosity, and gregariousness. Just as the endocrine system helps to determine thresholds for fear or sex or maternal interest, so the organization of sensory and autonomic nervous tissue helps to determine individual differences in the intensity and quality of the various factors of drive and emotion. If human nature were infinitely plastic, there would be no necessary differences in the mode in which a given social pattern is acquired. Individual differences are as striking in a litter of puppies as in a group of foundling children in an institution; and they set definite limits on any form of environmentalism which would suggest the mere assimilation or absorption of cultural patterns.

When we speak here of the individual child's equipment for social life, we mean the equipment given by the whole pattern of genes and uterine environment. Social factors probably play a considerable part in determining the conditions of embryonic growth, simply because nutrition, oxidation and similar chemical processes vary considerably with the economic situation of the mother, the amount and type of exercise taken, her general health and resistance to fatigue and infection. This does not mean, however, that the individual or cultural differences operating upon women of childbearing age can at present be brought into clear relation with individual differences in the behavior of their newborn infants. We have to assume that the conditions of interuterine growth are more or less uniform for the children of most mothers and, therefore, that the variability in the behavior of newborn individuals is, to a large degree, an expression of different growth trends depending upon different genes. There is sound biological reason for such a procedure. Among the mammals used for experimental breeding purposes, such as rats, rabbits and guinea pigs, several individuals born at the same time of the same parents show striking differences depending upon genes. Notably, they may show the Mendelian proportion as conclusive evidence that fetal environment is not the sole clue to their developmental differences. Similarly, humanity as such, though sensitive to its environment, responds selectively to the environment as do all other living things; it is not clay for the potter. Under cultural conditions as we know them, it does not develop unlimited unselective response to everything about it, but reasonably clear forms of motivated response.

After listing visceral drives, activity drives and aesthetic drives, we add a fourth category, the response to disturbance from without; in particular, response to sudden intense and unmanageable stimuli. We refer to fear, rage, disgust and shame, which, since they must have a collective name, we call "emotions."

We shall now endeavor to summarize the motives appearing in social life. Here we tread most cautiously. The trouble with lists of motives lies not in their length but in their sharp separation of one drive from another, their sharp separation of innate from acquired need, and their sharp demarcation of focus points in the body which are supposed to underlie motion toward a goal.

Nevertheless, if these limitations are kept in mind, there seems to be a distinct value in listing four groups of human motives:

Visceral Drives	Activity Drives	Aesthetic Drives	Emotions
hunger	exercise	color	fear
thirst	rest	tone	rage
air-getting	perseveration	specific qualities of taste,	disgust
temperature regulation	rhythm	smell and touch	shame
sexual	novelty	rhythm	etc.
etc.	exploration	etc.	
	etc.		

It will be noted that rhythm appears twice. If the foregoing theory makes any sense, a drive may appear under two or more categories, and conditions of unrest or striving may be so generalized as to require placement almost anywhere or nowhere. The names for drives merely indicate convenient abstractions from the infinitely complex flux of life activity.

We shall consider in Chapter IV, and later, the very important social drives involved in the need for companionship and affection and the need to give attention and affection to others, especially to children ("maternal drive"). Despite the current experimental studies in regulating "maternal" behavior (even among males) by biochemical means, it seems wiser to postpone all consideration of gregarious and parental behavior until the social-habit factors have been more closely studied.

A very important social drive omitted from this list is the quest for status or prestige, the need for respect in one's own eyes and in those of others. Some headway has been made in working out an explanation of this drive in terms of self-love, the Freudian narcissism. The actual quality of vanity and status-craving is so different from that of sexual love as to make such identifications very uncertain; and genetic evidence that the quest for status actually arises out of the sexual need is almost altogether lacking. If there is a true, independent status-seeking drive, we do not know where it comes from or where it should be classified. The fact that it seems in general unlocalized, not tied to specific visceral disturbances, might force its classification with the general need for color, tone, and other aesthetic satisfactions. It differs from these, however, in that it is closely tied organically to a sort of converse or reverse condition which we call shame, and behaves quite differently from color or tone needs in this respect.[1]

It would be tedious and useless to attempt a description of all the reflexes which are "activated" by each visceral need. Indeed, nearly the entire equipment of reflexes can on occasion be activated when any need is strong. At first most reflexes "serve" the need only in a complex and indirect way; they move the parts of the organism, or the whole organism, until by good luck an object satisfying the need is met. The hungry or thirsty or wet or cold infant seems to make few "adaptive" movements. But, as we saw, the hungry infant turns his hand, sucks, and swallows, more swiftly and better than the satiated infant. Even at the time of birth something has already happened in the organism (we do not know exactly what) which has enabled the varying needs to exert *some* measure of control over certain specific reflexes, and for the most part these specific reflexes are, under the circumstances, more or less "adaptive." Shivering when cold, slashing and kicking when angry, are instances of reflex facilitation occurring adaptively in certain organic states.

Most of the adaptive utility of the reflexes, however, can be seen to be developed slowly and haltingly through the months and years of childhood, developed by trial and error, fumbling and success (the "satisfaction of needs" or "relaxation of tensions"), organization into simple and structured wholes, and the parsimonious elimination of the irrelevant. In time, much of the man's social behavior is "second nature"; one is at home with one's work or play.

THE THEORY OF "ADIENCE"

Our classification of drives, attempted for rough descriptive purposes, involves no theory as to the *origin* of drives, either in the

[1] We should like in this connection to point out an error in the usual assertion that the specific response, rage, is the universal reaction to the blocking of any craving. The blocking of the craving for status, as everyone knows on a moment's reflection, may be either rage or shame, or both. An attempt to develop a theory of the craving for status is sketched below (pages 207 ff.).

history of the race or in the history of the individual. Ultimately, of course, the potentiality to develop this or that drive depends upon the genes, and depends in the same absolute way upon the chemical and electrical field in which the genes are placed. To say that drives are hereditary would be utterly misleading if the reader derived from it the view that the genes by themselves know how to make a stomach, a thyroid gland, or a central nervous system. The "hereditary" character of the drives may be defended if one means simply to conceive of the genes and the normal uterine environment as producing certain rough general classes of drives, more or less similar for the various members of the species. There will be individual differences, depending upon genetic factors and also upon uterine position and nutrition; but if the genes operate in the accustomed way in a normal environment, they will yield for most members of the species action patterns which we can call drives.

There are various forms of "drive theory" permissible from this point on. In relation to many of the drives, we are partial to the view developed by Holt, and in the following paragraphs shall attempt to integrate suggestions from him with suggestions from various earlier writers and from various classes of social research data.

As the nervous system develops within the embryo, a network of interconnections is manifest. Miscroscopic study shows the branches or "processes" of nerve cells reaching out in various directions toward other nerve cells. Within this net there are no preformed pathways, no hereditary reflexes. The stimulation of a sense organ causes excitation in the cortical region to which the sensory pathways lead; and discharge in various directions causes complex random behavior determined by the entire situation in the brain at the moment.

On the other hand, each muscular contraction causes kinesthetic impulses from the muscles to reach the brain. These arise while the excitation which caused the movement is still active, and this "reflex cycle" maintains the muscular tone. When two brain activities occur simultaneously there is a tendency for one to discharge into the other. In particular, when *motor* neurones are at work causing muscular contractions, nerve cells of the cortical *sensory* areas discharge into them. The concepts developed thus far are sufficient to explain why the muscle, when once excited on a random basis, tends to keep itself active, maintaining its own tone; and to explain why the sensory stimuli adventitiously present in the brain, along with kinesthetic impulses from the muscles, prove capable of making the muscles contract, so that reflex patterns are acquired.

The random fetal movements become specifically conditioned to stimuli which happen, on one occasion or another, to elicit them. For example, a combination of pressure and gravity may result in random fetal movements which cause flexion of the fingers, and therefore an excitation of the skin of the hand during the occurrence of muscular contractions. The muscles are maintained in this state of contraction while the stimuli to the skin are still active. Thus pressure on the palm of the hand, coinciding with the maintenance of reflex tone in the muscles of the forearm and fingers, will cause augmented contraction, and the "grasping reflex" will appear. Unless the stimulus causes the muscles to knock the object out of reach, or causes such damage to sensory tissues as to produce violent discharge, throwing the organism out of reach of the stimulus, all *stimulation will cause the organism to do things which will give it more of the stimulus.* Holt proposes the name "adience" for this general prolongation of activity in such a way as to increase the fixation of a stimulus-response pattern and to give the organism more and more of what it first gets. If it is true that much human behavior is exploratory, a search for contact with the world, a delight in stimulation and activity, we have a major clue here to the basic motives.[1]

We do not believe that the reflex cycle and the principle of adience are sufficient to cover all the facts roughly classed under the head of activity and aesthetic drives. The fact remains that so much can be plausibly explained by Holt's principles as to

---

[1] The specific example from the grasping reflex is of no special importance; there appear to be dozens of movements which, first arising at random, cause the organism to bring itself more stimulation of the sort which started the first movement.

make a purely hereditarian statement of specific drives utterly indefensible here. It is not the business of the social psychologist to set himself up as an authority in matters of physiological psychology or the theory of learning; but it is his business to be cautious in regard to the *universality or uniformity of instinctive patterns*. It is highly probable that developmental sequences vary from one organism to another, both *in utero* and in postnatal life, and that these developmental sequences depend partly upon differences in gene patterns and partly upon very complex and largely unknown individual differences in the mechanical and electrical fields in which early development occurs. This is one more reason why lists of instincts, except as rough heuristic classifications, are misleading and more likely to interfere with than to stimulate exact research.

In any event, it is likely that many of the drives which we have listed above, including most of the activity and aesthetic drives, fit under the concept of adience. Activity once aroused tends to perpetuate itself; what else is *perseveration* than this? Activities once aroused cause excitation in other muscles, and often stretch the antagonistic group of muscles so that alternate flexion and extension may occur; what more than this is the *rhythm drive*? Sensory stimuli to which we reach out cause us to keep on reaching; what more than this is there in the *aesthetic drives*? If an object arouses our response and if the response is blocked, yet to some degree still active, we have the germs of *curiosity*. If, indeed, some reminder of the object which has disappeared is still present, e.g., to the cat the scent of the mouse which has slipped through the hole in the floor, or to the man the memory image of his lost fortunes, one may continue to *seek* the object. If the objects which one has acquired and brought within his control give rise to images or other symbols portraying *more of their own kind*, we have *acquisitiveness*. If all these principles operate at the same time, the animal, the child or the man may be curious to discover more about the object which stimulates him, may go closer and inquire, may be sensitive to cues which symbolize more objects of the same character, may thus develop an insatiable demand for acorns, stamps, or dollars. This interpretation would, in fact, explain why the "collecting instinct" is so *specific*. The collector of stamps need not collect newspapers or Japanese prints, as would be the case if he were simply a man with a "strong collecting instinct." Why does one collect more of those things to which an initial adience has been established, but not collect things in general?

It is true that these simple principles are too broad to explain many specific problems, notably the disagreeable character of many rhythms and the negative value of many stimuli such as harsh sounds and offensive odors. It is true, nevertheless, that unless the organism is injured and its activity disrupted, most of the things in the world, both physical and social, are positive rather than negative stimuli; that the attitude of the little organism is outreaching, and that the vast majority of things which act upon the organism become things which in time it wants.

What else is the *gregarious instinct* but the adience to the overpowering social stimuli so important in the life of the immature and, indeed, of the mature organism? Diamond has succeeded in making real, on this basis, the fundamental truth in the now outworn "instinct of gregariousness," namely, the fundamental driving forces that are involved when persons respond to the excitations given by other persons. The form of the gregarious response will of course depend upon the family and the form of culture in which the individual develops; and the more complex needs of the thinking and acting man may thus be rooted just as deeply in his organic make-up as his need of food and drink. Tissues generally, including those of the sense organs and the central nervous system, have their own laws of activity and quiescence, reinforcement and inhibition. As Diamond well says, the drives are not confined to the unstriped musculature or the glands of internal secretion. Every tissue in the body is a source of activity and therefore of drive.

If the general conception of adience is sound, any strenuous and vivid experience tends to perpetuate itself unless specific negative conditioning is present. Once thoroughly aroused, the individual maintains his orientation to that which aroused him, and does things which will bring him more stimulation of the same sort. The results may be ethically paradoxical, but psychologically simple and coherent. The same child who is utterly sympathetic to an injured playmate may turn and pummel him when a group of others have started pummeling. A boy runs to catch a young bird which he loves but, failing to reach it, throws a stick which kills it. A child starts playing with his little sister, a moment later is teasing her to the point of frantic squeals and tears. A man torments the one he loves, not knowing why. One shudders at a murder but must read all the details. Indeed, the same energy which has been aroused in the midst of a friendly act may, as a result of some mischance, be spent a moment later in violent assault; or, conversely, the drive of the persecutor may, in the light of some slight new circumstance, yield to heroic defense of the one persecuted. There is perhaps a certain amount of sense in saying with Freud that the same energies which spell love may spell sadism. But it is all too often forgotten that the condition of general arousal or excitement brought about by any object may not only permit new forms of experience but tap new drives, leading to intense activity in reference to the object utterly different from that prevailing the moment before. One may not only tease one's friend; the protest and the changed set of the moment may call up old enmities or jealousies.

If such an analysis is even partially correct, it adds cogency to the view that practically all stimuli that do not damage the organism become true sources of drive activity, and serves us further to deflate the view, uncritically borrowed from certain laboratory studies of the lower mammals, that all drives result from visceral tensions.

It may be noted here that we incline to a developmental theory to cover the activity and aesthetic drives, but have offered none to cover the visceral drives and emotions. This is solely because we know of no clear implication of existing biological data in the light of which the developmental theory is to be drawn. It is probable that after a few years more of research of the sort shown in the chart (page 114), all motives can be schematized in developmental terms.

It is therefore quite reasonable to say that all our "instincts are learned" if it is understood that in this sense of the term our teeth are learned, our ears are learned, our hair is learned. Not only viscera, but sense organs, muscles, nerve cells—indeed, all forms of organic equipment—appear to depend on genes and on active responses of the fetus, and are thus both "native" and "learned." It is unfortunate that such a view, apparently so well justified today by research, should be called an "anti-instinct view." If so, it is in the same sense an "anti-learning view"; in fact it is of course neither, but a totally different conception.

The conception of motivation advanced here permits at no point the separation of fundamental drives from the means or mechanisms which serve them. The process of motivation goes on unremittingly. Most of the body tissues participate in the pattern, and as a result of the learning process the tissues undergo changes from moment to moment. The central nervous system is, to be sure, the chief seat of the more spectacular changes; but the muscles and the vital organs change individually and in their interrelations as a result of past activity, and the organic pattern of habitual response is still as fully motivated as an "unlearned" response. There are no mechanisms, no buttons and switches, no valves and cams which are biologically neutral, unless indeed the tossing of the hair as we move the head or the lever action of the muscle-bone system as we change the posture are so designated. A motive impels in one direction now and in another direction a moment later. We say that a habit has been formed; but there are not two things, a motive and a means, a drive and a habit serving the drive. The needs of the organism express themselves through one complex pattern or another, the term habit being a convenient abstraction from the fact that behavior is relatively simplified through the elimination of some responses, or relatively complicated through the addition of others. We do things through "force of habit" because a habit serves a need, perhaps at times merely the need for simplicity and the avoidance of the new and strange, but a need for all that. The distinction, then, between the material of this chapter and that of the next is merely a distinction between the social potentialities of the newborn and the more restricted and developed social potentialities of the adult, with emphasis upon the ways in which the change comes about. The learning process and the growth process act conjointly in the motivated organism; and while we here abstract from organic change those features observed at birth or conceivable in terms of growth likely to occur in any cultural environment, we treat in the following chapter those forms of change which are seen to be guided in large part by specific interactions with the specific social world in which the organism grows.

The Emergence of Patterns

We have suggested that at birth the infant has a wide and diffuse array of needs and a wide and poorly organized array of reflex responses. At ten or twelve months of age, much of the chaos of infantile responses has passed, and social patterns are evident. How does this come about?

We might first ask, in Watson's language, what pattern reactions occur independently of training. Three such pattern reactions were reported by Watson as present in normal infants at birth. The "fear" pattern involved catching the breath, clutching with the hands, and a cry. "Rage" behavior involved a somewhat different cry (a "characteristic" cry), slashing movements, and holding of the breath. "Love" involved cooing, gurgling, and sometimes a cessation of crying. In the absence of other patterns, and in view of Watson's evident desire to reduce the pattern behavior of man to a minimum, one might be tempted to allow such a list of pattern responses to stand unchallenged.

The Shermans, however, have challenged the existence of even this much organization in behavior at birth. Graduate students, instructors in psychology, medical students, student nurses, and normal-school freshmen participated in an experiment, the purpose of which was to discover whether observers could agree upon the meaning or emotions expressed in infants' responses to different stimuli. In some of the experiments the observers saw the stimuli —restraint of head and face, sticking with a needle, dropping suddenly, and delay of feeding causing hunger—as well as the responses. In other cases they saw the responses but not the stimuli;

in still others they saw motion pictures showing both stimuli and responses, or responses alone, or responses preceded by wrong stimuli. The upshot of the whole series was a complete lack of agreement between the judgments of the different observers regarding the emotions expressed, as well as failure to guess the right stimuli. The only situation in which a majority of the observers agreed with one another and named the Watsonian emotion was the experiment in which they saw *both* stimuli and responses. Obviously this latter proved nothing at all about the emotions but only how well they had learned their Watson.

Sherman made another approach to this same problem of patterns, through a study of the crying of infants. A similar group of observers included graduate students in psychology, medical students, and student nurses who had had experience with infants. In each case the infant was subjected, behind a screen, to dropping, restraint, sticking with a needle, or hunger; after the crying had subsided, the observers were asked to write the name of the emotion expressed and the reasons for the name they gave to the emotion. Here again there was very little relation between the observers' judgments and the emotional characteristics usually expected as a result of the stimulus employed. Many of the observers named "colic" as a cause of the crying, although colic was not so named by the similar group of observers who saw moving pictures of the infants' responses. In general, the students tended to judge prolonged cries to be the result of hunger or colic; very intense cries were also frequently judged to be due to colic.

This piece of work can hardly be considered to settle the matter of patterns in early infant responses; there may well be patterns which these observers could not detect but which could be detected by more accurate measurement. There may be, for instance, certain elements common to all these responses, in addition to certain elements found only in the separate responses to different stimuli, which would blur the *patterns* of the latter. Gray and Klein have indeed shown by electrical recording that there is some patterning in the cries of babies. Yet the degree of chaos, or randomness, though not absolute, is certainly considerable.

During the first thirty days of childhood, sneezing, hiccoughing, yawning, and crying, smiling, turning the head (when placed face down on a pillow), and raising the head for a few seconds may be observed, together with a variety of hand movements (spreading of fingers, clenching of fist and other degrees of closing of hand) and movements of legs, feet and toes. Kicking with the legs, slashing with the arms, and stretching begin early, and turning over from face to back has been observed at seven days.

In addition to these fairly simple responses, there is a considerable range of combinations of response involving varying degrees of organization. Rather vague and general are the facial expressions of the first ten days, with rapid shifts of pursing of lips, retracting of lips, contracting of eyebrows, raising of brow, wrinkling of nose, opening and closing of eyes, etc. These expressions come and go in response to internal stimuli with as yet unascertained significance. Not much more definite are the grosser combinations of movements, crying, kicking, slashing with arms, that are stimulated by discomfort or pain or restraint; throwing out of arms when support is removed suddenly; or the "jump" (violent general contraction) that is sometimes accompanied by crying when the infant is startled by a loud sound, sudden change of temperature, bright light, or sudden movement, e.g., such as is sometimes caused by a sharp cough of the person holding him. This startle reaction may include throwing back the head, rearing up the body, extending legs, spreading fingers (throwing out arms, fingers spread), opening the eyes, or a curling up of the body, wrinkling of forehead, drawing up of legs, balling the fist and shutting the eyes tight. Milder stimuli may bring just a wide opening of the eyes, opening of the mouth and lifting of the eyebrows.

The degree of incoordination present in responses of this sort is suggested by a study of newborn infants by Pratt, Nelson, and Sun. The experimenter exerted "a gentle pressure on the infant's nose, by holding it between the thumb and index finger in such a way as to close off the nostrils." The time ranged from 4.5 to 15 seconds, but if the infant cried out the stimulation was discontinued. The following specific movements were recorded by the experimenter during the holding of the nose (one of Watson's stimuli for rage):

head rolling; head drawn back; head drawn forward;

mouth opened; mouth closed; pursing lips; smacking lips; licking lips; expelled water; tongue protruded; mouth breathing;

wry face; frown or wrinkling face; grimace; reddening of face;

body: rolling, squirming, stretching, rapid breathing, general activity, jerk, shudder, gasp or quick intake, organic disturbance, back arched, wriggling, struggling;

eyes open, eyes closed, tightening lids, blinking;

crying, coughing, sneezing, yawning, regurgitating, vocalizing, choking sounds, hiccoughing, swallowing, throat sounds, whimpering, sucking;

hands to nose; striking experimenter's hands;

extension, flexion, slashing, kicking, rubbing, fanning, trembling, jerking, raising; crossing and other general movements of the extremities.

Various combinations of these movements appeared in different babies, and *no combination appeared in more than thirty per cent* of the cases. In only *three per cent* of the cases did the infants make *definite defense movements*, e.g., touching the experimenter's hand. In this experiment, as in others, the behavior of the infants was not at all specific and precise, but *generalized and diffuse.*

A similar experiment consisted in pressing the arms of the infant firmly against the body and holding them there against whatever effort the infant could exert. This experiment was performed on 66 infants, a total of 358 repetitions. To 58 per cent of these stimulations the infants remained passive, that is, the arms merely remained in the position in which the experimenter placed them. In 26 per cent, a brief period of activity gave place to inactivity; in 13 per cent the arms immediately flexed again or there were other signs of activity; in 3 per cent a brief period of quiet was followed by activity. The results of these experiments substantiate the inference from the work of the Shermans that *no definite defense, fear, or rage responses could be discerned in very young infants.*

In this situation it naturally occurs to the psychologist to assume that those patterns which are, after all, recognized with fair ease in most adults are simply *built up in experience*, or, if one prefers, are conditioned. The assumption is then that adults do manifest fear, rage, love, and perhaps other pattern responses because they have learned to combine elementary responses into these patterns. Certainly rage and fear are not commonly supposed to be hard to differentiate at the adult level or even at the five-year level. It might be contended that just as we stereotype our language behavior, so we construct social stereotypes out of our primitive slashing, writhing or even blushing—stereotypes which become characteristic adult expressions of fear, rage, and the like.

Yet this interpretation is as arbitrary and presents many difficulties. In order to get perspective upon such a view, it would be well to turn to the individual's life history as the embryologist views it. The problem of determining the primary action patterns can no longer be considered soluble by studies of behavior present at birth. Even if study of the newborn were far more extensive than it now is, it would still be important to remember that birth does not fundamentally alter that process of individual growth which has been going on in the embryo, and that for at least many months after birth action patterns continue to emerge which are dependent upon the time since conception and not upon the time since birth. Premature and postmature children show in general the characteristics which are to be expected from their actual developmental age.

We must therefore consider the data on the orderly development of specific response patterns out of the "primeval state," a developmental process now usually referred to as maturation. As before, we shall at first keep the account on the descriptive level, declining for the moment to discuss the degree to which this development "depends on the environment."

The fact of *general* maturation of the nervous system—the capacity of the nervous system, even aside from learning, to accomplish more complicated acts at later stages in its growth than at earlier stages—is apparent enough. The problem of *specific* maturation, however, that is, the development within the nervous system of specific connections from sense organ to effector, has only recently yielded direct evidence. We may approach the problem by first considering Carmichael's experiment with the swimming movements of salamanders and tadpoles. Prior to their normal swimming period, Carmichael placed some of his animals in a chloretone solution which drugged them sufficiently to keep them quiet. The others, the controls, began to swim at the normal time. The drugged animals were transferred to fresh water and within a half hour were swimming as well as the rest. During this half hour, the drug effect must, of course, have been wearing off while learning was perhaps going on; but to make sure how much of the effect was due to learning, a further experiment was performed in which the time required to eliminate the drug effect was directly studied. Beyond serious doubt the experimental animals were ready to swim *as soon as* removed from the inhibiting effect of the drug, and learning played a negligible part in the period intervening between perfect immobility and perfectly typical swimming.

But we need direct evidence about specific maturation in mammals. The problem has been subjected to experimental analysis in the case of the guinea pig, by removing the embryos from the uterus at various levels of maturity. Different reflexes were found to be absent until a given day. Animals delivered at an age beyond this possessed the reflexes whereas those delivered earlier lacked them.

The fact that different reflexes and different combinations of reflexes appear at different age levels has often been noted and described. The most elaborate work on this problem is perhaps that done by Tilney and his associates—a group of investigations which have now continued for over a decade. The work is part of an attack upon the whole problem of functional development in the central nervous system, in which, for example, doves, rats, guinea pigs, and kittens have been studied, and in which human infants are now being studied from the phylogenetic point of view. Some highly specific reflex capacities—such as the ability of the kitten to raise itself on its hind legs—appear at an interval remarkably uniform for practically all members of the species.

The explanation seems clear from Coghill's embryological studies of vertebrates in relation to the development of their behavior. His work has shown more and more clearly that in the early stages the nervous system is capable only of mass reactions, most stimuli bringing about diffuse responses of the whole organism. Development takes the form of differentiation within this total mass, so that, one after another, specific responses appear. The process of growth, in other words, is not a process of synthesis; it is primarily a process of division or individuation within the total mass. This does not, of course, occur all at once. Specific reflexes become functionally possible in their due time as the various parts of the nervous system become functionally mature.

The problem now arises whether all this is true of human beings as it is of the various animals which have been studied. Research quite fundamental for our purpose is Minkowski's study of human fetuses and embryos removed by Caesarian section because of the mother's condition. These were kept alive as many hours as possible, and their reflex behavior studied. This seems to conform to the outline described above by Coghill. Just as Coghill found that the development of his amphibian subjects proceeded not from specific reflexes to higher and higher patterns or organizations, but rather from diffuse mass reactions to more and more limited differentiated responses, so Minkowski's data suggest that the human embryo's development is in the direction from general to specific, from diffuse to localized response. The earliest fetal reactions are diffuse slow swaying movements of head and limbs. It is only with the increasing mass of the nervous system that specific pathways permitting definite localized responses become apparent. By the time of birth a large number of specific reflexes can be elicited.

Another recent bit of evidence on maturation is Shirley's report on the weekly and biweekly examination of twenty-five babies from birth to two years. A definite motor sequence appears; the infant's control of his body proceeds from the head downward and from the shoulders out to the finger tips. The uniformity of this order of development in muscular control seems to her more likely to be an expression of maturation than of the universality of a given form of progression through learning.

But it is essential to note that this unfolding of specific patterns occurs in an all-important environment, without which the

AUTHOR DATE	TOPIC	SUBJECTS	METHODS
Carmichael, L. (1934)	Development of behavior in relation to stimulation of specific receptor areas.	60 guinea-pig litters providing 178 fetuses of known copulation age.	Fetuses shelled out into salt solution, maintaining circulation. Observations and motion pictures. Systematically stimulated at 104 points by cutaneous and other stimulation.
Carmichael, L. (1928)	Development of behavior of amphibian embryos with varying degrees of stimulation.	Three groups of developing *Amblystoma* eggs.	Experimental group in sound- and light-proof room. Another group in laboratory; third in noisy, vibrating shop.
Carmichael, L. (1927)	Development of behavior in immobilized amphibian embryos.	A number of *Amblystoma* embryos, removed from protective "jelly."	Experimental group placed in solution of 4 parts chloretone to 10,000 parts water; control group in tap water. After control group began to show response, experimental group put in tap water, and stimulated until moving. After 36 hours, placed in chloretone again for 24 hours, and put in tap water again. Same procedure with some controls who had swum several days.
Carmichael, L. (1926)	Specific maturation; swimming movements.	Salamanders and tadpoles.	Prior to normal swimming period, some animals were put in chloretone solution, drugging

PRENATAL DEVELOPMENT

FINDINGS	RESULTS
At first "transitory" behavior phenomena found: neck or trunk bending, and occasionally weak foreleg flexion; "C" movements in some fetuses. First sensitive region, concha of ear. First "pattern" involved relationship between neck flexion and forelimb movement. From beginning, many "receptor areas" produce "a special 'pattern of behavior.'" Behavior pattern of each area undergoes changes; movements become stronger, more "adaptive"; new movement patterns (fine) may be incorporated in the gross pattern; next, the movements become less complete; later, the remaining portions sharply localized. Distinct patterns merge, forming new, larger patterns. Light, sound, temperature, pain, rotation, pressure and proprioceptive stimuli all release responses in fetus.	"A number of new facts . . . do not confirm any of the allegedly universal theories . . . such as those summarized by the concepts of 'individuation' or 'integration.' The specificity of the developmental sequences observed in this study indeed suggests that much further . . . work must be done . . . in many fetal mammals before the formulation of any such general theory. . . ."
No differences in rate of development of latter groups. When they were freely swimming, experimental room unsealed; experimental group showed swift, darting swimming movements.	". . . Immediate external stimulation is not necessary for the development of those neuromuscular mechanisms which subtend behavior in the types studied." "It is difficult to see how the facts . . . can be explained except on the assumption that heredity and environment are *interdependently* involved. . . ."
Time for first response in experimental group after removal to water, 2–7 min.; time for first response the second time, 3–8 min. Control animals' recovery time, 7–11 min.	"The time required for release is not a period of learning." ". . . seems to point to the fact that this mechanism had been developed by a certain process of a stimulus-response nature within the organism itself."
In a half hour, experimental animals were swimming as well as the rest.	During this half hour, drug effect must have been wearing off while learning was (perhaps) going on.

SOME STUDIES OF

AUTHOR DATE	TOPIC	SUBJECTS	METHODS
			them into inactivity. Controls kept in fresh water. Later drugged animals transferred to fresh water.
Child, C. M. (1925)	Discussion of Kingsbury's rejection of gradient conception as explanation of cephalo-caudal differential growth.	Annelid work cited. Annelid development considered similar to the vertebrate as regards gradient relations.	Cites evidence for view that gradients are physiological basis of polarity and symmetry; due to varying rates of metabolism which arise through differential action of environment upon potentialities of organism.
Coghill, G. E. (1924)	Essential mechanism which determines *Amblystoma* behavior pattern up to and including locomotion.	A single *Amblystoma* at each of 4 stages of development.	Sectioning and careful counting of cells at different stages.
Coghill, G. E. (1929)	Behavior pattern of *Amblystoma* in relation to functional nervous mechanisms.	*Amblystoma* embryos.	Embryos removed from membranes and kept under continuous observation from first muscular contraction to perfection of behavior pattern.
Coghill, G. E. (1930)	Development of behavior in *Amblystoma*.	*Amblystoma*.	A correlation of structure and function in development of *Amblystoma*.

PRENATAL DEVELOPMENT (*Continued*)

FINDINGS	RESULTS

Domination of primary active (head) region, caudal progression of dominance over secondary regions.

Physiological gradients significant in initiating orderly series of developmental events in definite directions. Gradients of early stages may undergo complication, alteration, even obliteration in later stages.

Pronounced localization of centers both of proliferation and differentiation; where one retarded, other accelerated. "Periods of development that are characterized by new accomplishments in behavior are characterized by marked acceleration of differentiation in the cerebrum."

Behavior pattern develops in regular sequential order. Cites Harrison (1904) on narcotized tadpoles, chloretone: *Development possible without function.* "But (normally) nerve cells grow while they function."

Locomotion develops from cephalo-caudal, simple "C" flexure, through "S" reaction caused by reversal of flexure before completely executed, to "S" reactions in series sufficient to effect locomotion; this order paralleled by order of development of nervous system and its parts. Earliest limb (and gill) movements integrated with trunk action, acquiring apparent independence of action in local reflexes by a gradual reduction in magnitude of dominating trunk movement. Anatomically, this is result of precocious invasion of limb-forming tissues by branches of nerve cells that are already integrating the trunk.

". . . Physiological processes follow the order of their embryological development in the functions of aquatic and terrestrial locomotion and feeding." "Behavior develops from the beginning through the progressive expansion of a perfectly integrated total pattern and the individuation within it of partial patterns which acquire various degrees of discreteness."

Cephalo-caudal development of contraction accompanied by cephalo-caudal development of motor neurones. Appendages move first only as trunk moves; later, as part of a postural pattern; still later, acquire patterns of their own, reflex in nature.

Partial patterns arise by individuation within larger pattern. A total pattern of inhibition dominates whole animal in beginning, whereas in later phases of development it gives place to local excitation and permits the appearance of local reactions.

SOME STUDIES OF

AUTHOR DATE	TOPIC	SUBJECTS	METHODS
Coghill, G. E. (1931)	Corollaries of anatomical and physiological study.	*Amblystomae.*	Observation of behavior from earliest movement to swimming.
Coronios, J. D. (1933)	Development of behavior in fetal cat.	Embryos and fetuses of 32 pregnant cats, of 21 to 58 gestation days.	Decerebrate cat in physiological salt bath, one fetus at a time shelled out, avoiding tension on umbilical cord. Observation and motion pictures. "Spontaneous" activity and that from brushing and other stimulation noted.
Kuo, Z. Y. (1932) (a)	Structural and environmental factors in embryonic behavior.	Several thousand chick embryos.	Observation while eggs in incubator; outer shell removed; inner membrane rendered transparent by melted vaseline.

PRENATAL DEVELOPMENT (*Continued*)

FINDINGS	RESULTS
Found excitation of overt behavior by efferent nerves possible before stimulation by afferent nerves.	Interpreted to mean efferent nerves stimulated by metabolic products. Such behavior spontaneous in that it expresses dynamics of organism as a whole. Mechanism of the total pattern essential component of performance of the part, i.e., reflex. Discovery of structural basis of "spontaneity, autonomy, or initiative as a factor in behavior" renders any purely environmental theory of motivation "grossly inadequate."
In order of development: first movement to stimulation retraction of forelegs when head, shoulder or paw stimulated. First spontaneous movement at same time, slight bending of head; active foreleg flexion and extension, unilateral trunk-bending and some "serpentine" twisting; bilateral trunk-bending, unilateral rump-bending, passive movement of hind legs; later, rapid, progressive, continuous development from simple to complex behavior. In early stages diffuse, variable, weak, relatively uncoordinated; later, more vigorous, regular, individualized, better coordinated. Qualitative changes not sudden. Cephalo-caudal development of activity and sensitivity observed. "Individuation" within limb. Reflexogenous zones contract.	"Primitive" reactions of breathing, righting, locomotion and feeding interpreted as products of "a long and continuously progressive course of prenatal development."
Increase in size of head changes head-lifting into side-turning; increase in size of embryo changes bending, extension and lateral twisting of trunk into jerking and wriggling. Modes of movements of anterior and posterior limbs partly determined by their length. Contraction of amnion and movement of yolk sac stimulate movements of embryo. Mode of leg and other body-part movements determined by positional relation with yolk sac. Movements of toes, contraction of heart, positions of head, neck and legs, and extra-embryonic membranes all play part in determining embryonic behavior.	Structural and environmental changes always accompanied by behavioral changes in embryonic chick.

AUTHOR DATE	TOPIC	SUBJECTS	METHODS
Kuo, Z. Y. (1932) (b)	Influence of embryonic movements upon avian behavior after hatching.	Chick embryos.	See preceding abstract.
Kuo, Z. Y. (1932) (c)	Behavior of avian embryos.	Embryonic chicks in all stages of development.	Chicks removed from eggs and put in warm physiological salt solution.
Kuo, Z. Y., and Shen, T. C. (1936)	Gastric movements of chick embryo.	Records kept for 36 embryos.	Removal from shell. Kymographic recording of stomach movements.
Langworthy, O. R. (1929)	Relation between reflex activity and myelinization in fetal and young cats.	6 fetuses near term; kittens of varying ages.	Fetuses decerebrated and observed. Fetal and young organisms' behavior correlated with structural studies of the nervous system.
Minkowski, M. (1921)	Development of the human embryo.	Human fetuses and embryos removed by Caesarian section because of mother's condition.	Observation of reflex behavior in bath of physiological salt solution.

PRENATAL DEVELOPMENT (*Continued*)

FINDINGS	RESULTS
Practically every physiological organ in functional condition before hatching; functions before reaches adult form; establishment of such functions continuous, gradual. Feeding reactions have long history of development in egg.	Concepts of instinct and habit must be abandoned. "The development of behavior is an absolutely gradual and continuous process," to be understood in terms of its underlying physiology and entire developmental history.
Local reflexes arise because of interference by yolk with movements of head and trunk (clapping of bill, slight wing movements without trunk participation, etc.). Intensity of stimulation determines whether organism will respond with total or partial pattern. The farther away from the stimulated area the part is which is involved in the response, the weaker will be its response. Origin of alternate movements of the legs: under pressure of yolk sac on ventral surface of embryo, alternating extension and flexion of two legs gradually acquired.	No such thing as simple reflex; behavior begins as total pattern; reflexes come as result of later differentiation. Fundamental problem is nature of integration of basic embryonic movements into temporal behavior. Criticizes Coghill's anatomical explanation of synchronism of movements.
"Unable to get records of gastric contraction earlier than 15 days of incubation. . . . highly possible that [it] may begin earlier than eighth or ninth day of incubation."	"Behavior as well as physiological functions have their origin in early embryonic life; [their] development . . . is gradual and continuous." Notion that function is a sign of maturation of structure "must be abandoned in face of these facts."
"'Bilateral movements of the extremities begin to coordinate when the ventral commissural fibers of the cord receive their myelin sheath. The animals turn the body at a time when myelinated vestibular fibers reach the spinal cord.'" Other similar examples. The decerebrate fetus shows behavior characteristic of late cat fetus. Myelination proceeds caudally.	"No discussion of the theory that nerve tracts become medullated at the time when they first function will be ventured" until results of study on other animals have been reported.
Data showed earliest fetal reactions are diffuse slow swaying movements of head and limbs. Only with increasing mass of nervous system specific pathways permit definite localized responses.	Suggests human embryo's development is in direction of general to specific, diffuse to localized response.

AUTHOR DATE	TOPIC	SUBJECTS	METHODS
Orr, D. W., and Windle, W. F. (1934)	Somatic movements in chick embryos.	Chick embryos at about 4–9 days of incubation.	Tried Kuo's vaseline-membrane method without success; most observations made immediately after opening shell, removing inner membrane. Noted spontaneous movements and "reflexes" following tapping or gently "flipping" parts of embryo with blunt needle. Also mild faradic current.
Tilney, F., and Casamajor, L. (1924)	Ontogeny of different activities.	Kittens; over 50 litters.	Observation of behavior and neural examination.
White, G. M. (1915)	Life activities of brook trout, from hatching to absorption of yolk sac.	500 trout embryos.	Embryos of 4 different stages observed at same time. Kept in running water. Experiments done in dark room.
Windle, W. F.; Fish, M. W., and O'Donnell, J. E. (1934)	Relation between time of appearance of reflexes and advent of myelination of central nervous pathways for reflexes.	Fetal cats.	Morphological observations; sectioning and staining of nervous system.
Windle, W. F.; Minear, W. L.; Austin, M. F., and Orr, D. W. (1935)	Fetal rat behavior.	81 rat embryos, 16 and 17 days old.	Stimulation of various cutaneous areas, flipping foreleg, stimulation of snout with faradic shocks or mechanical agents.

PRENATAL DEVELOPMENT (*Continued*)

FINDINGS	RESULTS
First R to external stimulation a local reflex. Spontaneous activity (trunk flexions) observed on 4th day. Considerable spontaneous activity appears before local reflexes can be elicited (results correlated with Kuo's).	Local reflex appears not to develop from a generalized or total behavior pattern, but rather to arise concomitantly. Spontaneous movement develops as integrated total pattern cephalo-caudad. But general motility pattern does not necessarily recapitulate developmental pattern.
Reports highly specific reflex capacities appear at intervals quite uniform for all members of the species. Post-mortem examination of nervous systems shows that certain tracts have become functionally ripe at time new form of behavior appeared.	Evidence irreconcilable with notion that maturation is general neuromuscular growth. Specificity view upheld on basis of neural correlates.
Observed *gradual* improvement in coordination of swimming movements. Trout reacts to touch and mechanical jars immediately after hatching, head being *least* sensitive.	Before yolk sac is absorbed, reactions of trout are *protective*; afterward they are *exploratory* and *aggressive*.
Some instances of relation between sequence of myelination of fiber tracts and order of appearance of their axons. No generalization possible. High degree of reflex activity possible prior to myelinization of tracts concerned.	Myelinization not a prerequisite to neural functioning, although it may *improve* conduction.
First response is to stimulation in region of shoulder. With development, excitability spreads rostrad and caudad, distad and ventrad from this region. Reflex response to flipping foreleg occurs early; unrelated to trunk movements. Decrease in intensity of stimulus needed (and area of stimulation required) as age increases.	Rise of somatic behavior patterns in rat (as in cat) becomes functional in progressively expanding pattern. Gradual acquisition of excitability caudad, rostrad, distad from locus of first appearance. Process not of individuation, but of expansion. Do not believe coordinating mechanism in central nervous system necessary for sequentially integrated movements to take place.

AUTHOR DATE	TOPIC	SUBJECTS	METHOD
Blanton, M. G. (1917)	Infant behavior.	"Large number" of infants in Johns Hopkins Hospital.	Observation of variety of responses classified as "buccopharyngeal," "ocular," "arm and hand," "general responses," "responses to dermal stimuli," etc.
Bryan, E. S. (1930)	Variation in responses of newborn infants.	66 infants in main group, up to 10 days old. Some Mexican and Negro children.	Light flashed in eyes; bells and whistles sounded; mother's milk, cow's milk, lactic acid preparations given; Babinski reflex elicited; crying and general muscular activity observed.
Castner, B. M. (1932)	Development of fine prehension in human infant.	"Ten reactors 20 weeks of age, 9 at 28 weeks, and 10 each at 32, 36, 44, and 52 weeks, selected from average families, of Teutonic or Celtic racial stock. . . ."	Pellet, 7 mm. in diameter, presented under standard conditions on table top before infant. Analysis made from motion pictures, in terms of *regard* to stimulus object, *approach* to it, and *closure* of hand.

INFANT DEVELOPMENT

FINDINGS	GENERAL REMARKS
Large repertory of behavior responses seen, including, during first 20 min., sneezing, yawning, tears, sucking, fixating light, thumb in mouth, jumping at loud sounds, grasping, crying (with corners of mouth turned down, and with box-shaped mouth), pursuit movements of eyes, head turning, turning over, erection of penis, and "the cry of so-called anger."	". . . The reflex and instinctive equipment of the child at birth is more complex and advanced than has hitherto been thought." Possibility of relation between early sucking ability of child and parental intelligence.
Eyelid and eyeball movements among earliest. Reaction to flash of light usually noted in first 5 days; occasionally fixation noted. Some newborn infants fail to respond to sound in first week; most fail in first 2 days; many respond 3rd–7th day. Lactic acid at first produces contortions of "dislike" and dislodgment of nipple. Majority of white infants show Babinski in first 10 days; in colored children generally appears after that time; apparently stimuli other than foot-stroking can arouse it. Crying shows wide variation in pitch, intensity, continuity; learning early appears in use of crying. Considerable muscular activity; strength increases with age, head-lifting and creeping seen in some cases.	Many activities seem purposeful rather than random.
Regard presented 3 "types": transient at 20 weeks; brief regard characteristic above 20 weeks; prolonged regard at higher age levels. Number of regards also increases with age. 20–32 weeks these types show trimodal distribution. *Approach* increases from 30% accuracy at 20 weeks to almost 100% at 32 weeks; shows increased directness, less vertical height, etc., with increased efficiency. *Closure* "marked by increasing dominance and differentiation of the radial digits. Four main types . . .": whole-hand closure, palmar prehension, scissors closure, pincer type. By 52 weeks adult, pincer type prevails. Difficulty in holding pellet shown below 52 weeks.	"The behavior growth of the infant, as represented by his ability to carry out the movements involved in prehension, reveals certain relatively well-defined development patterns in passing through the levels studied."

AUTHOR DATE	TOPIC	SUBJECTS	METHOD
Delman, L. (1935)	Tactual stimulation and response order in newborn infant.	3 Negro infants, 1 male, 2 female at Univ. of Virginia Hospital; studied, respectively, 4th–11th, 2nd–12th, days of life.	472 responses photographed (moving pictures); elicited by finger flips on sole of foot and palm of hand on both sides of body. Experimentation twice a day. Time sequences analyzed.
Dennis, W. (1935)	Effect of restricted practice upon motor functions of human infants.	Two children (twins) up to end of 14th mo.	Reared under activity restrictions: keeping them on their backs, not permitting them to sit or stand.
Dennis, W. (1936)	Infant development under minimum social stimulation.	2 infants, observed up to 13 mos. of age.	Reared up to 13 mos. in semi-isolation, with "minimum of handling, of reward, and of punishment. . . . [Each left] . . . to its own devices." Compared with findings in 50 baby biographies, reduced to graphic form.
Dockeray, F. C., and Rice, C. (1934)	Infant's response to pain stimuli.	40 white infants, 22 boys, 18 girls, 4 hrs. to 5 days old. Socio-economic level below average.	When infant "asleep" in experimental cabinet, stimulated by fine needle in areas on cheek, outer surface of forearm, palm, outer surface of leg between knee and ankle, and bottom of first toe, in random order, approximately equal number of times on right and left. Responses filmed and recorded by two observers.
Gesell, A. (1928)	Training vs. maturation.	Premature and postmature infants (about 240 and 320 days after last menstrual period).	Examination and comparison with normal infants (280 days at birth).

INFANT DEVELOPMENT (*Continued*)

FINDINGS	GENERAL REMARKS
From 46%–77% of response of each infant involved four limbs. "In general the initial response [to each stimulus] occurs in the stimulated limb in about one-third of the cases, in the homolateral limb in about one-sixth, and the contralateral and diagonal limbs in about one-fourth of the cases each. More first responses occur in the legs than in the arms." Half of second responses are contralateral. Locus of third and fourth responses generally at opposite end of body.	". . . The responses of the neonate to intense stimuli are generalized. . . ." ". . . The responses do not occur in a chance fashion."
Visually directed reaching and grasping; sitting alone; standing with help retarded in both Ss beyond upper limits of established norms. Each response readily established when practice offered.	Retardation results from exercise restrictions. Factors such as general muscular weakness controlled.
Infants "happy, healthy, and active." Developed all "typical responses of the first year" at usual time, e.g., playing with toes, vocal greeting, laughter, timidity, manual play, etc.	"Other considerations [not given] lead to the conclusion that these new activities do not occur instinctively, but develop through the child's own activity with only the very minimum of stimulation from adults."
A general tendency for mass action rather than specificity of response was shown, little specific connection to limb stimulated. Adaptive and coordinated withdrawal of the stimulated limb did not increase in frequency or efficiency with age. Legs more vigorous and active in withdrawal than arms; arms more so than head.	This evidence contradictory to the anterior-posterior hypothesis of development noted (see Col. 5). Mass activity so great as to eliminate likelihood of adaptive, coordinated withdrawal.
Premature and postmature children have in general characteristics expected from actual developmental age.	Such results strengthen suggestion that "inherent maturational factors determine the tempo of development."

SOME STUDIES OF

AUTHOR DATE	TOPIC	SUBJECTS	METHOD
Gesell, A. (1929)	Developmental correspondence in twins.	Identical twins, 28–48 weeks.	Placed in similar situations simultaneously, at various ages, e.g.: pellet test, cube test, sitting, responses to 3-hole test performance box, etc.
Gilmer, B. v. H., (1933)	Patterns of spontaneous response in neonates.	4 babies from 1st to 10th day in main study; 16 babies under 10 days old in second part.	Babies photographed at 16 exposures/sec. Constituent elements of each response reliably determined. 16 babies later observed without photography to check results.
Irwin, O. C. (1930)	Activities of human infant during first 10 days of life.	4 infants observed from birth to 10th day.	Continual observation over 10-day period. Activities observed held to be due to internal stimuli because of considerable constancy of surroundings in experimental cabinet. Activity recorded in terms of predetermined classifications; amount and nature noted.
Jensen, K. (1932)	Effect on sucking response of various taste and temperature stimuli.	17 infants: 9 male, 8 female; 8 white, 9 Negro; about 1 week old.	Reliable tracings of sucking response secured. Infant given formula under controlled conditions. Stimuli included water, glucose, milk, various salt solutions, various milk temperatures, pinching toe, pulling hair, sudden dropping. Moro reflex determined; other records.

INFANT DEVELOPMENT (*Continued*)

FINDINGS	GENERAL REMARKS
"... Correspondences in behavior patterns in these twins ... uncountable." "Almost uncanny" similarity in postural attitude, etc.	"The complexity and nature of ... patterns ... suggest the determining rôle of maturation."
Spontaneous responses studied were crying, stretching, sneezing, mouthing, yawning, opening mouth, chewing, sucking, smiling. These constituted distinct, organized classes of response. Data show "each response has a characteristic combination of essential elements and nearly every response has some element peculiar to it." Some elements essential, some incompatible, some unessential, some peculiar to the specific reaction.	Some movements never occur together, although anatomically possible. This confirms Dennis: "Mass activity is not the only total bodily response of infants."
Two distinct categories of behavior seen: "specific movements, and mass action." Specific = movement of segment of organism; mass action = movements involving whole organism. Behavior speeds up when alimentary feeding well established. Anterior segments increase dominance over posterior ones. Vocal sounds are components of mass activity. Earliest social behavior arises from mass activity.	Alimentary tract stimuli probably responsible for activity seen. "... reflexes ... may be later specializations or individualizations of mass activity." "Mass activity, probably, is the consequence of the neurological immaturity of the newborn infant."
Temperature: differential responses to 55° and 15° C. secured on 2nd day (8 Ss). *Salt:* differential reaction to .9% solution on 2nd day (5 Ss). 13 of 15 succeeded in differentiating .9% solution; 11, the .45% solution; 6, the .3% solution, etc. Pinching large toe or pulling hair of partially sated infants invariably produced sucking. Swallowing determined by amount of food in mouth; ceases when food gone. Hungry, crying baby shows disorganized feeding reaction; satiety shown by rest periods, decreased sucking, disorganization of sucking. Discrimination shown by vigorous avoidance, etc.; no differential reaction to acid, glucose. Movement of head toward finger stimulation on cheek increases with age.	"... Stimulation of almost any group of receptors by almost any kind of stimulus will lead to a response in almost any part of the organism which is set to respond" at that time.

SOME STUDIES OF

AUTHOR DATE	TOPIC	SUBJECTS	METHOD
Jones, M. C. (1926)	Development of behavior patterns in young children.	365 infants in Baby Welfare Stations in N. Y. Variety of stocks represented. 10 days to over 300 days old.	Systematic observations made on smiling, eye coordination, blinking, thumb opposition, reaching, sitting.
McGraw, M. B. (1932)	Development of coordinated postures in the infant.	Unknown.	Observation in a developmental series particularly of the partunate and neonate.
McGraw, M. B. (1935)	Twin development.	1 pair twins; not confidently known to be identical; and 68 other children from birth to 3½ years.	Johnny (least advanced) subjected to systematic exercise in many specific activities; Jimmy's activities deliberately restricted. 7 hrs. per day in clinic, 5 days a week; rest of time at home.
Pratt, K. C. (1934) (a)	Plantar response development; physiological stage as affecting sensitivity and degree of localized or generalized response.	Infants, 1–21 days old; N = 55.	Stimulation during "dry and asleep" vs. "wet" or "awake" condition, of plantar and associated cutaneous areas.
Pratt, K. C. (1934) (b)	Development of plantar response in newborn infants.	55 infants, 1–21 days old.	12 cutaneous areas on right leg stimulated; 1 area on left leg. Movements in 8 segments, toes to thigh, recorded.

INFANT DEVELOPMENT (*Continued*)

FINDINGS	GENERAL REMARKS
Smiling, eye coordination, blinking completely developed by 4th mo. Thumb opposition, reaching and sitting began about end of 3rd mo.; continue through 10th. Large differences between individuals on each ability, in terms of first appearance. Only sex differences were in smiling in social situations: boys more advanced. Negroes more advanced in same function.	" . . . Case studies suggest that early development in one trait is likely to be accompanied by early development in others. . . ."
Descriptions of development emphasizing that certain activities—such as reflex stepping—later part of controlled muscular pattern, appear early on reflex basis.	New totally integrated patterns do not emerge; rather, new patterns unfold gradually, dovetailing with old, becoming progressively dominant. In acquiring new pattern, a period of dyssynergia. "Learning" is completion of pattern.
In phylogenetic responses (moro reflex, suspension-grasp, crawling, creeping, sitting, etc.) increased exercise showed little effect in Johnny. Exercise more greatly affected ontogenetic activities: swimming, incline-climbing, skating, jumping, box-manipulation.	During early stages of development, most obvious process is from general to specific; but once aspect of behavior pattern becomes definitely specific, process becomes one of integration.
Sensitivity slightly affected if at all. When wet or awake, infant regressed to more generalized response and greater frequency of patterns of wider participation. " . . . Number of response patterns is relatively greater in the awake or wet than in the asleep and dry state."	Physiological condition of irritability tends to make responses of infants more generalized.
6560 segmental combinations (response patterns) mathematically possible; only 185 observed. Of these, 93 (50%) were "unique," i.e., did not occur to stimulation of more than 1 area. But they comprise only 6% of the total responses.	Generalization may be described in terms of (1) number of stimulation areas evoking a response, (2) number of segmental responses or response patterns evoked by a given stimulus area. "There is no one response pattern which may be termed the plantar response." "Stimulation of a particular area may release several patterns of response. Stimulation of different areas may evoke the same response or responses."

AUTHOR DATE	TOPIC	SUBJECTS	METHOD
Pratt, K. C.; Nelson, A. K., and Sun, K. H. (1930)	Behavior of new-born infants.	Infants in groups of about 12 to 70, N varying with experiment; age range, 0–17 days.	Various procedures for testing reactions to light, sound, taste, smell, temperature; tactile and kinesthetic stimuli applied to nose, cheeks, lips, and feet. Control period of no external stimulation. All observations made with S in cabinet well equipped for controlling stimuli.
Sherman, M. and I. C.; and Flory, C. D. (1936)	Behavior of infant as affected by variations in stimuli.	Infants up to 16 days old.	Used as stimuli needle algometer (intensity variable) and shock.
Sherman, M. and I. C.; and Flory, C. D. (1936)	Pupil reaction to light, infants.	273 infants, up to 16 days old.	3 light intensities (3, 6, 12 c.p.) at optical distance of 2 inches. Pupil contraction judged by 2 E's for amount and speed.
Shirley, M. (1931)	Postural and locomotor development.	27 babies at start of experiment, records for 24 at end of 1st year, for 20 at 1½ years, for 16 at 2 years. Highly selected group from 3 upper occupational classes.	Examination daily 1st week, alternate days 2nd week, weekly for rest of 1st year, bi-weekly 2nd year. Anthropometric measurements; records of health, motor and sensory development; speech, interests, incidental behavior. Tests: picture, box, color and form choice tests, Infant Study Psych. Test, Minnesota Preschool. 2 E's: psychologist and pediatrician. Home visits, conditions largely uncontrolled.

INFANT DEVELOPMENT (*Continued*)

FINDINGS	GENERAL REMARKS
Observed specific movements. Various combinations appeared in different babies, with much less consistency and specificity of response than is usually reported. Control results showed many responses occurring in absence of external stimulation. Experimental results revealed various different responses following given stimulus, and given response following various different stimuli.	Authors favor theory that in early stages larger muscle groups are first coordinated, and that progressive increase in coordination brings finer, smaller muscle adjustments. Increasing specificity may be ascribed to maturation or environmental influence, or both.
Most common R (99 in 287) to prick on cheek was crossed flexion reflex (opposing arm reaches toward S); to prick on leg (below knee), flexion. If S is applied with great intensity and very quickly, R is quite general; S adequate, but minimal intensity, R is localized. S applied for relatively long time; opposite foot often drawn up to S. Head end more responsive to pain S than foot end, even when threshold (weakest adequate) S is used.	"The criterion of reactivity . . . is not the number of movements, but the responsiveness to a minimum stimulus."
As stimulus increased in strength, a larger number of infants showed a "good" response. As age increased, adequate R's were obtained with a decreased strength of S.	Considered a functional "integration," taking place rapidly. Minimum stimulus for a "good" pupillary response, both eyes, N = 209. Intensity: 3, 6, 12. Mean age, hrs.: 134.2, 111.0, 82.2.
Regarding development of posture and locomotion, finds "anterior-posterior trend of motor development in the baby," an orderly sequence consistent from baby to baby.	Data favorable to maturation hypothesis. Further development in babyhood proceeds by differentiation of specific acts out of mass activity; at time of emergence, different acts are little related; integration begins in second year.

organism could not live; the growth is not a growth *in vacuo*; it depends upon a form of interaction with the surroundings. Thus the direct observation of the movements of the chick within the egg, and of the fetal guinea pig day by day until the time of birth, strongly suggests that the sharp separation of sheer neural growth and differentiation from the effects of exercise and learning must be abandoned. Organism and environment interact constantly; the organism learns as it grows, and grows as it learns. Behavior is constantly changing, and the separation of the changes into acquired habits and sheer growth responses appears meaningless.

For this reason the term "maturation" will have to be used to define those complex developmental processes, more or less similar for all individuals, which depend on organism-environment interplay of a broadly similar nature throughout a species, and the term "learning" will have to be used for those specific individualized acts acquired by an individual in a relatively short time in which growth is slight. Thus beginning to walk is maturation, acquiring a fear of a bushy-haired stranger is learning. The two are separated only for convenience. Learning to talk is intermediate between the two, since learning a word or phrase may occur in a few seconds in which usually there is no great inner change in general neural growth, whereas the normal processes of learning grammar and syntax between two and four years of age obviously reflect the maturation process along with the learning process. The separation of maturation and learning is at present empirically useful; but the experimental disentangling of the nature of each and their interrelation will in time require a further statement of working principles for social psychology.

But whatever the ultimate interpretation, there is descriptively a great deal of "emergence of specific patterns." Illustrative data on typical emergence of pattern responses in infancy appear in M. C. Jones' study. The following table summarizes her findings regarding the date of appearance of a number of behavior items in very young children. It will be seen that thumb-opposition and reaching have really identical curves; they are seen first at about a hundred days, reaching a median at five months, and the one-hundredth percentile at nearly nine months. The curve for sitting

differs from this—in general, data for the Babinski and postural
reflexes are less regular.

Trait	No. of Cases	First Appearance	25 Percentile	50 Percentile	75 Percentile	Last Failure	Q
Smiling	185	39	45	58	68	81	11
Eye coordination							
Type I	312	33	45	58	72	82	13.5
Type II	283	51	53	65	78	104	12.5
Type III	272	51	65	78	91	119	13
Blinking	317	46	60	76	92	124	16
Thumb opposed	512	108	129	148	181	266	26
Reaching	486	116	135	152	173	269	19
Sitting	292	156	205	217	250	280	22.5

Case studies showed that, on the whole, early appearance of
one pattern was likely to be accompanied by the early appearance of
others. This suggests the value of thinking in terms of general
organismic growth, *as well as* of specific local changes in the
nervous system.

Obviously if maturation of pattern responses occurs, it has great
significance for the development of personality. It is in accordance
with our general knowledge of the principle of maturation that
Lewin regards personality as moving gradually from the general
to the specific, partly because of growth within the nervous system
and partly as the result of specific experiences which define one
area of social behavior after another. The mass response of the
little child, the screaming, kicking and wiggling give place to
the expression of specific demands. The normal child, when
hungry, is "hungry all over"; when angry, is "enraged all over,"
while the adult has a specific degree of hunger or irritation which
does not break out into generalized expression when polite conversation or public opinion calls for specific and directed activity.
We may show by a bare circle the "undifferentiated" unity of the
newborn child's personality and by a circle containing a number
of scallops, as shown in the figure, the differentiated aspects of
the developing personality; finer inner differentiation appears in
the adult.

Movement forward, however, in the direction of increasing specificity does not presuppose the impossibility of movement backward. The process is sometimes reversible. Regression, as psychoanalysis uses the term, may be a motion backward to the original undifferentiated condition—a process of de-differentiation. One clue by which we should recognize regression is a return to the diffuse motor tension of a little child's emotional response. To frustrate an individual while he is strongly motivated would be to block his specific and directed efforts. Throwing him back to the level of the mass tension of the little child would cause recognizable infantile behavior.

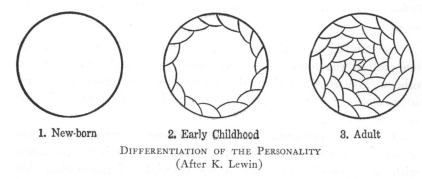

1. New-born   2. Early Childhood   3. Adult

DIFFERENTIATION OF THE PERSONALITY
(After K. Lewin)

The following experiment of Barker, Dembo, and Lewin is an effort to test the hypothesis that regression is de-differentiation. Thirty nursery-school children ranging in age from 30 to 60 months were allowed to play, one at a time, for a half hour in a large well-equipped playroom. They had access to boats, ducks, ironing board, toy train, etc. All the individuals spent most of their time in well-organized play behavior, making use of equipment appropriate to their ages. A "constructiveness scale" was devised to indicate the degree of maturity in handling this equipment. For example, when using paper and pencil, sheer scribbling was rated 1; drawing a house or man was rated 5. When playing with the toy telephone, grasping the receiver and using it as a rattle was scored 1; carrying on a conversation with an imaginary person at the other end of the line was rated 5. Records on the social growth of these children were at hand, so that each child's ascertained level of constructiveness in handling the toys could be empirically compared with his earlier performances. A general constructiveness level for each child, pooling the data for his whole half-hour period, was worked out. Constructiveness, as thus measured, correlated .87 with chronological age and .77 with mental age. From the Lewin point of view it represents a degree of differentiation of response from primeval chaos or undifferentiated mass action.

In the second part of the experiment the children, again singly, were shown some fascinating new play equipment: a large and beautiful toy truck, a new ironing board with dresses to iron, a pond for the boats, etc. A moment after inspecting these new delights, the children were told: "We'll have to play at the other end of the room this morning," and were led by the hand back to the familiar play equipment which had been used in the previous part of the experiment. A large wire-mesh screen was pulled down and padlocked, the experimenter simply saying that he had to "do his lessons," and sitting at a table with his record sheets. Careful note was taken of the way in which every child spent the half hour. He had the same equipment in which his constructiveness had already been scored. Whereas before this frustration experience he might have used the telephone in imaginary conversation, he now tended to bang it about and use it as a rattle. Whereas before he had drawn a house, he might now regress to the level of sheer scribbling. The regression, in terms of return to previous level of constructiveness, was very striking, averaging 14 months for the group of thirty children. Twenty-five of the thirty children showed regression. Reasons for the failure of the remaining five to do so are now undergoing analysis. In several specific instances where regression did not occur the child made an effort to get absorbed in the activities which were actually open to him, and really succeeded in making the old tasks seem interesting—a process which H. A. Murray, quoting Otto Rank, has well called "willing the obligatory."

The individual differences in personality which lead to this or that form of adaptation offer promising leads for social psychology. But for the present we are concerned only with the validation of

Lewin's general thesis about maturation. Specific frustration in carrying out an activity which satisfies a specific need may result in generalized tension, batting about, twisting, mechanical repetition of gross bodily movements, and doing over and over again the infantile things which the child has not done for a year or more; i.e., regression, at least in some of its forms, is "de-differentiation," the reverse of maturation.[1]

In the light of the preceding data we shall accept the hypothesis that increasing specificity of response *occurs*, and that it takes place both within the "inner" structure of the organism and within the peripheral system of reflex responses; or, much better, that a broad process of *differentiation of response* occurs in childhood which causes the *increasing specificity and recognizability both of patterns of "motive" and "emotion" and also of "expressive movements" of face, limbs, and trunk*. We have already seen reasons for doubting the wisdom of sharply separating motives from the movements which "express" them. Various forms of evidence relevant to this hypothesis must now be considered.

Emotional responses of a ten-months-old girl in a variety of situations were identified rather well by students of child psychol-

---

[1] We have dwelt at length upon a specific study of frustration partly to show the relation of maturation and learning to "socialization," and partly to show once more the glaring inadequacy of the organ-stop theory of motives, or the still simpler conception that human drives depend exclusively upon visceral rhythms. To be frustrated is to be highly motivated, and frustration when playing with a toy train or planning one's vacation or a lecture may all result in more or less the same kind of conduct. Such response to thwarted motivation cannot be easily identified with "rage" or even with a response as close to rage as sheer irritation. The irritation is only an aspect, a safety valve, indicating general demoralization, loss of specific adaptive patterns. Such activities may better be conceived as the return to non-specific activity of the organism as a whole. The quality of frustration when one wishes to smoke and finds no cigarettes in the package, the quality of frustration when one expects to find cold water in the cooler and finds that the water is lukewarm, might sometimes be adequately analyzed in terms of specific and localized tensions; but even if we could "localize" the specific needs which are frustrated, there would still be a psychology of frustration at large, a psychology of the general form or way in which the failure to realize a goal disintegrates or redirects activities in progress. This is something like what Thorndike had in mind after completing his long list of original tendencies in man. He spoke of the "tendencies of the original tendencies," formal characteristics of the tendencies as a whole which were just as much fundamental attributes of human nature as were the specific modes of response involved in various instincts.

ogy who had never seen the individual subject. In another study a ten-year-old girl, blind and deaf since infancy, who could scarcely have modeled her responses on social stereotypes, was found to display the familiar patterns of fear, rage, disgust and shame. Such findings strongly suggest that although recognizable patterns are largely wanting in the newborn, they arise by the process which we have called maturation.

In the adult, experimental work of several varieties shows the reasonable distinction of the various emotional patterns, both in terms of visceral upheaval and in terms of facial expression. We shall mention only a few typical studies.

The heart, lungs, skin, arterial muscles, and so on *participate in patterns which can be differentiated from those of other emotions.* The method of Landis, though it has its defects, is the most systematic yet applied in the attempt to answer this question. Landis subjected his seventeen subjects to a great variety of exciting, depressing, disgusting and generally bewildering stimuli. In one situation the subject's hand was put in a pail of water which contained three live frogs, and at the same time he received an electric shock. In another situation the subjects were required to examine pictures of skin diseases. In a third, the subjects were required to cut off the head of a live white rat with a dull knife, or, in cases where they refused to do so, they were required to watch the experimenter perform the act. In another experiment the subject had to write out the most embarrassing incident which had ever occurred to him, and then listen while this was read back to him by the experimenter. That Landis did actually succeed in inducing strong emotions is attested, first, by some of the photographs which he presents, in which facial contortions are plentiful, and, second, by the cursing (or weeping) of the subjects.

Now Landis's data seemed at first to show that within the limits defined by his experiment there were no patterns which could be consistently detected by measurements of the physiological changes involved. Surprise and laughter inclined to show some degree of consistency and recognizability, but even these fell short of the requirements of the pattern theory. More careful analysis of the data by R. C. Davis shows, however, that in many respects

SOME STUDIES OF

AUTHOR DATE	TOPIC	SUBJECTS	METHODS
Allport, F. H. (1924)	Influence of training on judgment of facial expression.	12 young females.	Test based on Rudolph pictures; then Ss studied chart of expression (showing muscles involved); took test again.
Blatz, W. E. (1925)	Cardiac, respiratory and electrical changes which occur with fear.	Exp. 1: 18 *naïve* Ss. Exp. 2: 3 graduate students informed of nature of experiment.	S precipitated back unexpectedly while in a chair. Exp. 1: 3 normal sittings to obtain normal state. Fall in 4th and 5th. Ss divided into 2 groups: (a) 2 more "normals" and a final fall-sitting; (b) 8 falls in 2 succeeding sittings. Exp. 2: 2 fall-sittings; on 3rd day raised from horizontal to vertical position. Measures of heartbeat, respiration, galvanic skin reflex.
Davis, R. C. (1934)	Re-analysis of Landis' (1924) data on facial expression of emotions.		Landis' criterion of significance of "involvement" of muscle groups is faulty. Correlations between figures for each emotional situation taken. $r = 1.00$ would show there was but one expression in varying degrees; $r = 0$ would show specific expressions with no common elements; r between 0 and 1.00 would show "specific reactions with common elements. . . ." Also can examine to find which situations resemble each other; which muscles most differential. χ^2 test also applied.
Dumas, G. (1923)	Patterned emotional responses.	Adult humans.	Various degrees of faradic stimulation applied to the cheek.

EMOTIONAL EXPRESSION

FINDINGS	GENERAL REMARKS
Ss who had done well gained nothing from *studying facial muscles analytically*; those who made poor scores profited greatly, at end of practice nearly equaling others.	Data strongly suggest that experience rather than "original nature" is responsible for ability to interpret facial expression.
Fear involves initial cardiac acceleration, followed by retardation, prolonged acceleration, and gradual retardation; augmentation of force of heartbeat; irregularity of rhythm. Retarded respiratory rate. Increased development of electromotive force. Repetition of falling, with knowledge, decreases all effects, except respiratory. Repeated presentation exaggerates adaptive effect. Anticipation causes increased heart rate.	"Fear" experience involves complex organic response, gross muscular adaptation.
Intercorrelations of expressions in different situations average .63. Intercorrelations of expressions accompanied by S's reports average .65. High correlations between all sex situations and between these and looking at skin-disease pictures; between multiplication with distraction, looking at sex photographs, and decapitating rat; telling truth was less like other (uncomfortable) situations than like lying; listening to classical music has low correlations with other situations; moderately high correlations between listening to jazz, listening to classical music, reading Bible, relief (release from experiment). Ss' *reports* show "pain, disgust, exasperation, anger, revolting and surprise [to] have a good deal in common"; "crying" and "sex" have low correlations with each other and other situations. Percentages of Landis' table being taken as number of cases, chi-square 149.8; probability that distribution would occur by chance, .00003.	"The chief conclusion of the present paper [is] that the nature of the stimulating situation plays a part in determining the nature of the response, and that there is also a correspondence between subject's report and facial response. . . . There may be a limited number of typical facial reaction patterns." But there may be "an indefinitely large number of facial expressions, each differing but slightly from its nearest kin."
Depending on strength of stimulus, response is a smile, similar to that in hemiplegia, or a grimace (with more intense stimulus), more generalized and extreme muscular contraction.	Both smile and grimace considered patterns. Other evidence of postures involving whole organism cited in favor of doctrine that there is synergic muscular response characteristic of certain emotional states.

AUTHOR DATE	TOPIC	SUBJECTS	METHODS
Dunlap, K. (1927)	Rôle of eye muscles and mouth muscles in emotional expression.	50 college men.	Pictures taken of individuals subjected to jokes, pistol shot, bending finger joint, strong odor of dissected tissues, dynamometer work. Photos cut in half horizontally through bridge of nose; judgment of emotion required of Ss when entire face shown. Halves pieced together from different photos and compared with original pictures to see whether upper or lower half was dominant in determining similarity.
Feleky, A. M. (1914)	Judgment of emotions from photographs.	100 subjects.	86 photos of female registering variety of emotions and affective conditions. List of expressive terms given S to be matched with numbers of appropriate photos; could also write own descriptive terms. Introspections.
Foley, J. P. (1935)	Judgment of emotions from chimpanzee photos.	127 college students; 31 male, 96 female.	6 photographs of 5-year-old chimpanzees in emotions (Kohts) of quietude, sadness, joy, weeping, anger, excitement. Face and shoulders shown. Ss chose from list of 16 terms (including above 6 correct ones) the best describing each picture.
Frois-Wittman, J. (1930)	Judgment of emotions from photos.	165 subjects.	Photos showed face fairly neutral, smooth-shaven; no indication of clothes or distortion of hair. Main experiment, 59 composite drawings used. 227 pictures and fragments thereof, 46 photos, 59 drawings of whole face; 84 photos and 38 drawings of eyes and mouths. Exposures well controlled. S used own terminology.

EMOTIONAL EXPRESSION (*Continued*)

FINDINGS	GENERAL REMARKS
Great majority of Ss indicated picture with same "mouth-half" was more like original than one with same "eyes-half."	Mouth muscles play a greater part in determining effect on observer than eye muscles.
"Surprise" most successful portrait: 52 votes "correct," also heavy vote for "wonder" and "astonishment." "Laughter" next: 40 votes, plus high vote for glee, ecstasy, merriment, etc. "Disgust" high, also sneering, contempt, aversion. "Horror" next highest; terror, fury, fright received high votes.	(Photos showed variation in dress and also occasionally included manual gestures.) Cases of failure are attributed to ignorance of meaning of portrait and of accepted meanings of terms used. Considered preliminary experiment.
Enormous scatter of judgments; modal judgment (21%) in agreement with Kohts only on "weeping." Greatest agreement on joy (correct, "anger"), 48%.	The consistent tendency for agreement on incorrect judgments is due to tendency to judge the chimpanzee face as though it were human.
Chart presented, showing interrelations between emotions (graded) from "attention" through "interest" and "reflection" to "laughter" and "pleasure." Expressions analyzed in regard to muscular involvements. "Frowning" brow occurred in all pictures judged as rage, anger, hate, etc. ". . . there was a unique and distinctive pattern of . . . muscular involvements for each modal judged expression."	The significance of a given muscular involvement not constant, but relative to rest of pattern: judgments on face as whole and on its separate features disagreed, but not always. Whole face agreed with eyes for anger, fear, etc.; with mouth for superiority, sulkiness, contempt, crime. Whole study departed from traditional view of fixed patterns or specific contraction of some one muscle or group of muscles.

AUTHOR DATE	TOPIC	SUBJECTS	METHODS
Gates, G. S. (1927)	Auditory element in interpretation of emotions.	627 children from Grades III–VIII.	Phonograph records were made of actress' voice portraying 9 different emotions; no words, only letters of alphabet repeated with varying intonation.
Goodenough, F. L. (1931)	Identification of photos of emotional expression in infants.	68 university students in child-training course.	Each S given 8 photographs showing 10-mos. child in highchair—full-length (from Buchner); and mimeographed sheet with instructions for matchings with 12 sketches of situations that might correspond to photographs. Situations involved "mild" emotions.
Goodenough, F. L. (1932)	Nature of emotional expressions in blind-deaf child.	10-year-old girl, completely deaf and blind from infancy.	Observation and photographing of expressions under semicontrolled conditions for an hour or more a day during several weeks.
Guilford, J. P. (1929)	Effect of learning on judging emotions from drawings of facial expression.	Students in social psychology, 7 men, 8 women.	Pictures taken from Langfeld's selection of 105 from Rudolf. Presented as lantern slides; Ss tested and trained over 10 days. Set 1, initial and final test. After 1st test, S studies anatomy of facial expression. After Set 2, has correct names given for that set, and studies Allport's 6 groups of expressions. Tests 3 and 4 given as 2, but told especially to analyze. Test 5 was final one.
Hunt, W. A. (1936)	Bodily pattern of the startle response.	29 Ss, 3 male, 26 female; some knew stimulus, others did not.	Ss dressed in bathing suits, standing erect, photographed against a black screen with cameras at 64 frames/sec. (4X normal); forward trunk movement and knee bending meas-

EMOTIONAL EXPRESSION (*Continued*)

FINDINGS	GENERAL REMARKS
Children found able to label with considerable accuracy emotions registered; increasing capacity with increasing age and increasing intelligence.	Visual interpretations are easier to judge than auditory ones.
47.4% of judgments correct, 5.7 times chance expectation. Most errors between situations in which original investigator (Buchner) had considered emotions similar.	Emotional expression may be inhibited, modified, etc., in adult, but built on a core of native reaction patterns. Optimum age for study is *after* birth-shock (cf. Sherman) and *before* extensive social training.
Expressions seen and described as "startled attention," "interest," "disappointment," "exasperation," "mild rage," "exultation," "pleased satisfaction," "absorbed interest," "resentment," "timidity," "exultant laughter," etc. Dancing—"clearly an expression of pleasure"—and "temper tantrums" also observed.	In her emotional expression "a strong resemblance to the . . . descriptions of Darwin and Spencer may be seen. This suggests that the primary forms of expressive behavior are determined by native factors."
Average gain in ability over original, 51%. Group became *less* variable; rank difference correlation between original and final ability is $-.76 \pm .07$. No sex differences in any respect. Longer (60 sec.) exposure better than short (15 sec.).	The better judges tended to be those who adopted a less analytical method of making judgments.
16 Ss in simple shot response showed definite pattern of response. Analyzed into universal blinking, almost universal head movement, and frequent shoulder, arm, hand, abdominal and knee movement. Entire response over in about ½ sec. Response	"The response would seem to be outside the range of voluntary control."

AUTHOR DATE	TOPIC	SUBJECTS	METHODS
			ured by threads running to light levers; lever also connected with pneumograph. Stimulus, revolver shot.
Hunt, W. A.; Clarke, F. M., and Hunt, E. B. (1936)	The startle pattern in human infants.	60 infants from 8 days to 18 mos. of age.	97 observations with camera at 64 frames/sec. Ss photographed on backs, camera 6 ft. away; a few standing. Stimulus, revolver shot. Slow-motion and static analysis made by 3 judges.
Kline, L. W., and Johannsen, D. E. (1935)	Identification (judgment) of emotions from pictures.	About 100 college students.	20 pictures of face, shoulders, arms and hands of a young woman. Presented in 2 series: (1) "body-face" series (whole picture shown); (2) "face-only" series (picture cut to expose only face from brow to chin). In Ss' first attempt no names; in 2nd, names.
Landis, C., and Hunt, W. A. (1936)	Facial pattern of the startle response.	3 males and 23 females.	Dressed in bathing suits, standing; photographed against black screen at 64 frames/sec. Gun fired behind S's back. Slow-motion and static projection used in evaluation of response by 3 judges.
Landis, C. (1924)	Study of emotional reactions under "real emotional disturbances."	12 women, 12 men, 1 boy. Age range, 21–41 yrs. (Boy 13 yrs.) More than half	Each S taken individually. "Emotional situations" in order: 1, 2, 3, listened to 3 jazz records, 2 violin pieces, and reading selection from Bible.

EMOTIONAL EXPRESSION (*Continued*)

FINDINGS	GENERAL REMARKS
sometimes asymmetrical; movement of distal parts may occur without movements of proximal parts. Habituation appears with repetition at 2-min. intervals. Knowledge of procedure does not affect pattern. Instructions to keep tense or to "jump" do not affect response.	
The Moro reflex is characteristic response in young infants, disappearing by 5th mo. Decay rapid after first 2 weeks. Decayed Moro resembles Strauss startle response. With disappearance of Moro, startle response appears. Gross arm and leg movement greater among infants than adults.	Relation between Moro reflex and startle response subject to 3 interpretations: (1) Moro and startle pattern distinct; Moro appearing first, disappearing when startle appears; (2) Moro and startle distinct; less noticeable startle concealed by grosser Moro; (3) Startle pattern simply perseveration of Moro in degenerate and decayed form; additional changes due to continuing neuromotor development.
Body-face pictures gave better initial score and were less subject to practice effects. When names of emotions were given with pictures, the "different" responses were reduced 68% in number; the accuracy of identification increased 16%.	Capacity for recognizing emotions is latent or untrained; this is suggested by the nature and number of the "different" wrong responses.
Definite facial pattern found: closing eyes, forward movement of head, "grin," involvement of neck muscles. Eyelid response appears in all Ss, is first in sequence. Facial pattern more stable than bodily pattern. No asymmetry. Habituation, either fast or slow, appears with 2-min.-spaced repetitions of shot, but slower than habituation of bodily pattern. "Photoflash" and electric shock facilitate reaction; voluntary responses do not.	"With our improved technique we have been able to check and elaborate the findings of Strauss. We have here in the startle situation a definite, stable facial response of an involuntary sort."
Certain individuals tend to favor certain muscle patterns and neglect others. For a given situation (emotion) "no significant frequence of occurrence of any muscle group." Nor was there any "expression	"... there is no facial pattern of reaction and no behavior pattern which characterizes any particular 'feeling.'" The expressions described by Darwin *et al.* "are in reality social expressions of the nature

SOME STUDIES OF

AUTHOR DATE	TOPIC	SUBJECTS	METHODS
Landis, C. (1924) *continued*		psychologists or graduate students, also teacher, stenographer, etc. 2 women, 5 men married.	4. S was read a crime situation; invented an alibi for himself; then given "true" alibi. 5. S smelled 5 mild odors; 6th strong ammonia. 6. E set off firecracker under S's chair. 7. S wrote description of contemptible act of his; this read aloud. 8. (soon dropped) "surefire" joke told. 9. S examined pictures of morbid skin disease, attributing to self. 10. S attempted mental multiplication while violent noise and exhortation going on. 11. S examined pornographic photographs. 12. S examined posed feminine artist-model photographs. 13. S read pornographic case histories. 14. S told to place hand in pail; pail contained water, 3 live frogs; told to replace hand; received strong shock. 15. S beheaded live white rat. (In 5 cases E did this in S's presence; in 2 cases omitted). 16. S told to perform mental multiplication; received severe shocks during task. 17. After "preparation" for new experiment, E released S. I-E and blood pressure recorded; photographs taken. Burnt cork markings on face over "expressive" muscles assisted later analysis. Expressions studied in a quantitative analytic fashion. Involvement or non-involvement of muscle groups expressed in percentages of frequency of occurrence for the subject or situation. Significance determined by noting whether each figure "deviated from the average of the figures of which it was one, by 3 or more times the probable error. . . ." (See Davis.) Verbal reactions and bodily reactions noted.

EMOTIONAL EXPRESSION (*Continued*)

FINDINGS	GENERAL REMARKS

which shows a greater correlation with the verbal characterization of the emotion [by the subject] than would be obtained by chance." Nor did any "expression or pattern of response characterize any imagined situation." In terms of body movements also certain constancies characteristic of each individual; no correspondence of the verbal reaction to situation with bodily responses. Men showed more expressive reactions than women; also sex differences in reaction to decapitation and electrical punishment situations, men tending to become profane and angry, women tending to cry, beg that experiment end.

of language gestures and are not really definite patterns of emotional response."

AUTHOR DATE	TOPIC	SUBJECTS	METHODS
Langfeld, H. S. (1918)	Judgment of emotion from facial expressions (posed drawings).	4 men, 2 women.	105 pictures from Rudolf shown to 2 Ss at a time, 30 judgments per session. Pictures all shown again, in different order. Then shown once more, with knowledge of all other Ss' judgments and Rudolf's title; finally, each S asked whether preferred the title to judgment he had made.
Schramm, G. J. (1935)	Children's emotional responses to animals.	22 children from Child Institute, Johns Hopkins. 15 boys, 7 girls; 36 to 64 mos. old.	(1) Child restricted; animals moved one at a time toward or away from him. Tambours recorded adient or abient tensions. (2) Child free to move; animal restricted in space. Animals: small frog, large frog, white rat, rabbit, paroquet.
Sherman, M. (1927)	Judgments of emotional responses of infants.	89 graduate students in psychology; 42 medical students; 14 student nurses; 57 normal school freshmen. Not all gave each judgment.	2 infants, 74 hrs., and 145 hrs. old, filmed; others, 112–160 hrs. old, observed directly under conditions of hunger, sudden dropping, restraint of head and face, sticking with needle. One group of Ss: entire sequence shown in film; another, only responses; another, stimuli and responses transposed; a 4th, babies' responses seen directly, stimuli being presented first behind screen. Ss named emotions produced and stimuli involved.

EMOTIONAL EXPRESSION (*Continued*)

FINDINGS	GENERAL REMARKS
Judgments "uniformly good and consistent . . . even . . . subtle combinations of emotions were observed." Laughter almost unfailingly observed: anger, fear, hatred were "also most expressive. . . . The reports of the subjects showed that they obtained their results frequently by kinesthetic imitation . . . association with known experience, and by the imagining of situations. . . ."	(No quantitative data are given in this paper. A number of quotations from reports and qualitative statements constitute the body of it.)
Consistent response to stimuli in 79% of cases. Sometimes movement in same direction for approaching or receding stimulus; sometimes varied with direction. Most frequent reactions: withdrawal from approaching animal; pursuit of receding one. Familiarity with animals and with situations reduced avoidance. Seeking or approach occurred more frequently when freedom of movement permitted child.	Adjustment of child best where he has freedom of movement. Successive presentations reduce emotional responses.
Graduate students, stimuli unknown (films): distributed reports among 13 emotions; no correspondence between emotion named and "answer expected." Medical students, stimuli unknown (observation): distributed reports among 8 emotions: "Answers show no definite relation to . . . emotions generally expected." Student nurses, stimuli unknown (direct observation): listed 7 emotions. "A very small percentage made 'correct responses.'" Graduate students, stimuli known (films): distributed reports among 24 emotions. 71 of 166 responses correct. Normal school students, stimuli unknown (films): distributed responses among 17 "emotions," highest accuracy 28%, for "pain." Same group, stimuli known, gave 57% correct responses. Two groups of medical students saw films with 2 different transpositions of stimulus-response sequences. ". . . the most frequent name of the emotion given . . . was governed . . . by the stimulus shown. . . ."	". . . the emotion designated for a certain reaction depends to some extent upon the interests and attitudes of the observer. . . . Knowledge of the stimuli used was an important factor in the observers' decisions. . . . The stimulus preceding the reaction shown was usually the deciding factor in the name given to the reaction."

SOME STUDIES OF

AUTHOR DATE	TOPIC	SUBJECTS	METHODS
Sherman, M. (1928)	Judging emotions from standard song sequences.	30 graduate students in psychology.	Accomplished singer attempted to convey "surprise," "fear-pain," "sorrow" and "anger-hate" by repeating a single note 5 times (first fundamental *e*, then *a*) of 1½ sec. duration at 1 sec. intervals. Sequence *abcbabcdedbca* in A-major, A-minor, given to determine melodic emotional significance; finally *abcba* given similarly.
Wells, F. L. (1929)	Recognition of musical symbols.	20 psychiatrists, graduate students in psychology, nurses, etc.	10 phonograph records of music relatively unfamiliar to Ss (e.g. *Heimweh*, Siegfried's *Funeral March*). Ss given blanks with names of records; told to identify them in order played.

the different situations produced quite distinctive responses, despite the cumulative mass effect of the stimuli in the long experimental period. Some phases of the fear, disgust, and surprise situations are absolutely distinctive. Landis has more recently demonstrated beyond doubt the reality of a complex and uniform pattern of "startle."

To some degree the differentation of emotional patterns from the chaotic state apparent in the newborn is doubtless improved by cultural stylizing of appropriate ways of responding; but to what degree we do not know. The explorer and the anthropologist sometimes have difficulty in "reading" native faces. Yet in the long run they emphasize similarities to ourselves more than differences. They find recognizable social patterns such as fear, shame and disgust. Despite the differences in various human societies, there is sufficient uniformity in social responses—bravado, congeniality, suspicion, etc.—to bring about rather similar emotional patterns from the Bushman to the Eskimo, and from the Egyptian to the modern European. It is entirely possible that the process of

EMOTIONAL EXPRESSION (*Continued*)

FINDINGS	GENERAL REMARKS
In *e*-series 18 emotions reported; 18 of 22 "sorrow" reports correct; 15 of 18 "anger-hate" reports correct; 10 of 20 "fear-pain," and 3 of 21 "surprise." *a*-series gave comparable results. Long melody, A-major, produced reports of 8 emotions; no agreement. Long melody, A-minor, produced reports of 8 emotions: ½ the Ss reporting emotion named "sorrow." Short melody, A-major produced reports of 8 emotions: 5 of 15 "sorrow." Short melody, A-minor produced reports of 5 emotions: 6 of 10 "sorrow."	"A sequence of notes, whether they form a melody or merely repeat a single note, may convey emotional significance to the listener." Sorrow and anger-hate best conveyed.
The correct identifications in all cases higher than chance. Plurality of correct judgments secured in only 3 cases; there was but one case where near unanimity secured.	" . . . The present procedure . . . shows considerable difference in the symbolic values of the records, and generally emphasizes the subjective character of their symbolism." (The author does not make the comparison with chance expectation.)

gradual differentiation of diffuse responses into more and more specific response patterns, which we found in embryonic growth and which shows itself in various phases of motor development in early childhood, is similar for the whole human family.

There are, nevertheless, some "racial" differences in facial expression of emotion, upon which research data are now being gathered. At the present writing these "race" differences appear to affect all members of a cultural group irrespective of biological race.

Thus, despite the existence of some anatomical race differences in facial musculature (e.g., in the muscles around the eyes), the chief "racial" differences between Chinese and Europeans in expression of emotions through the face are directly traceable to cultural factors. Just as the Russian Jew and the Sicilian slough off their distinctive gestures as they become Americanized, the Chinese student finds his way into the American group, portrays his emotion as Americans do, and ceases to be "inscrutable."

Cultural control of emotional expression is first of all *negative*, e.g., the Sioux Indian learns *not* to wince, the European soldier *not* to tremble, the Chinese gentleman *not* to snarl or shout in his rage (he may stare "with round eyes"; he may do no more). But this negative control is not the only one that reflects cultural style; one learns *when* to be angry, *when* to be ashamed, and to some degree even *how* to be angry or ashamed. One also learns the postures and gestures, the expressions of deference, embarrassment, or surprise.

Change in expressive habits may even affect to some degree the inner state; one "counts ten" and inner turmoil subsides. At times the inner state may be less easily altered. Thus the Andaman Islander learns how and when to cry (without feeling sad). When an important man returns after a long absence, one weeps copious tears; the fountains are under control, can be released for exhibition to the ethnologist even when the normal occasion is lacking. We know much more about the stereotyping of behavior than about the stereotyping of inner personal feelings; the social psychology of stylized behavior is already in full swing, but the social psychology of the inner changes, the molding of the inner man by his culture has scarcely begun (cf. pages 216 ff.).

It is important not to conclude that all emotional patterns are simply "cultural products"; the smile, the startle pattern, the collapse of facial tone in grief, are examples of physiological responses which appear to occur in all sorts and conditions of men. Here, as in Chapter II, there is no heredity-environment problem as usually conceived; the physiology of emotion, though basically the same in all human beings, undergoes selective socialization, and group differences are superimposed upon the existing individual differences.

Chapter IV

THE LEARNING PROCESS IN SOCIAL SITUATIONS

A SPARROW reared in a nest of canaries began to abandon his own chirps and to take over the canary's *call note*. The imitation of the canary's *song* came more than a month later. The song was at first a confusion of notes, harsh and unmusical. Several months later (in the spring) he was removed from the canaries. He continued the canary-like song for some months. In another experiment a sparrow fledgling, living among canaries, first modified his sparrow chirp, then began to give notes in rapid succession, running up and down the scale from three to five notes, then giving five or six higher notes in one run. His voice, at first hoarse, became soft and musical, approaching that of the canary. When past three months of age, he gave a genuine musical trill. Subsequent experiments showed that this sparrow, like the other, regained the sparrow voice when placed with his own kind. When placed with the canaries again, both birds quickly regained the canary song. Even where a complicated structure like a canary song is concerned, there is definite evidence of an amazing capacity to learn, a capacity which ordinarily makes possible the indoctrination of each new generation into the ways of the parents.

To what extent the ways of man are instinctive in the broader sense of the term, and to what extent they are "cultural," can scarcely be decided by any generalization no matter how brilliant. Each species must be meticulously studied, and if it be considered worth while to answer such questions in any given case, the experimental isolation of newborn or newly hatched individuals appears to be the only possible way of setting up a true "control group" to compare with those exposed to the usual cultural influences; man is no exception. Such controls are very difficult, and most of our data on the individual's acquisition of social responses come from comparing those exposed to different phases of one complex cultural pattern.

CONDITIONING

Whether all learning can be reduced to a single formula is a complex and difficult question upon which the evidence, though extensive, is by no means clear. We cannot survey this evidence, since it is interwoven with nearly all psychology and neurophysiology. Our concern here is to show what fundamentals are available for the social psychologist.

One form of learning which has long been shown to be quite universal in all animals having a nervous system, and perhaps in others, is the conditioned response. The dog or the monkey or the man reacts to a stimulus while another stimulus is also presented,

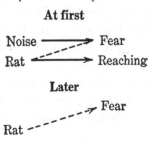

At first

Food ⟶ Saliva flows

Light ⟶ Head turns

Later

Light ⟶ Saliva flows

e.g., a sound is made or a light is flashed; later, the sound or the light alone leads directly to the response.

At first

Noise ⟶ Fear

Rat ⟶ Reaching

Later

Rat ⟶ Fear

Watson's Albert and his rat are so well known as to require only a brief introduction here; Albert at eleven months was frightened by a metallic clang. A rat shown when the clang sounded soon became a conditioned stimulus for fear. Conditioned responses may be formed in the newborn, and are constantly being established throughout life. To a considerable extent the complex fabric of our emotional life is developed by a process of elaboration of simple emotional responses through conditioning.

Under what circumstances such conditioning will occur, or how permanent it will be in a given instance, is far from being within the range of prediction. The following cases reported by H. B. English show the individual differences that may occur in a normal home environment. One child, twenty-eight weeks old, showed a conditioned fear response to a stuffed "cat" after hearing a noise at the same time she saw the cat. Another child (in the same family) at the age of fourteen months could not acquire a conditioned fear based upon sound for the sufficient reason that she showed no flinching at the sound made by striking a heavy metal bar with a two-pound hammer. Though other children at some distance in the same building spoke of the alarming nature of the sound, the baby seemed indifferent. The third and most complicated case is as follows: A little girl who had been frightened by her own new patent-leather slippers became frightened even by her father's slippers (with which she often played) when they were placed on the floor along with hers. Elements of simple conditioning due to the proximity of the large and small slippers may be complicated here by the similarity factor; she might, after being frightened by hers, be afraid of all other slippers because of their *resemblance* ("transferred" conditioned response).

M. C. Jones reports observations of children from three months to seven years of age. Some of these children showed fear of new objects in instances where the fear appeared to result not simply from the object itself but from the total situation, including the child's readiness to adjust. The fear was present when the child was suddenly confronted with a strange situation for which he had no ready reaction. A child might greet with enthusiasm an animal he saw released from a cage; but if he encountered the same animal in a box of blocks, a small suitcase, or his bed, he might be startled. Older children, she adds, may be curious, alarmed, enchanted, or angered by the very situations which produce fear in the younger children. Factors of general experience, mental age and other aspects of maturity may consequently affect the fear response no less than the character of the situation and the child's particular experience with the stimulus.

In daily social life we become conditioned to signals which stand for significant situations: the signal keeps us in touch with, and prepared for, the distant situation. The mechanism of this means of keeping in touch with realities which are not present to the senses is particularly clarified by research upon the "delayed reaction." Thus human beings and animals may note the presence of a light in connection with a goal, and may be able to reach this goal promptly even after the light has been extinguished. The *position where the light was* is the thing to which the organism is reacting. Human beings and even monkeys can remember for a long time where to find a concealed object (even after free change of position). Obviously a good deal of social behavior is of this sort. We react to a thing, so to speak, even when the thing is no longer "there" to be reacted to. We store up tendencies to reaction which may be discharged later on. At its most primitive level, the delayed reaction can probably be regarded as a form of conditioning.

It may be asked here whether the delayed reaction does not involve more than reflex, namely, *purpose*. Yes and No. From the point of view described in the preceding chapter, all, or practically all, bodily acts involve "motivation." What is conditioned is a motivated response or, to speak more simply, a motive, a drive. *The conditioned response is motive aroused by a new stimulus.* But the motive may be blind; it may not know where it is going, and the term "purpose" would here be misleading. We can find no contradiction in saying that from birth onward the organism is redirecting its drives, and that its awareness of what it is doing may be clear, obscure, or in-between. In fact, everyone has started to hunt for something, forgotten what he was looking for, but been sure he would know what it was when he saw it.

In some cases a conditioned response may be built up upon the foundation of another already formed. This is "conditioning of the second order."

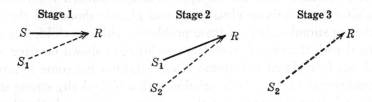

Novikova has reported "higher order" conditionings not only of the second, but also of the third and fourth degree. She worked with eleven subjects, from nine to eleven years of age, using food as the original stimulus and a bell as the stimulus to be conditioned. Only two of the eleven children showed the higher order conditioning *consistently*.

In the study of conditioning of the second order Munroe's experiments with two-year-olds probably come closer to a study of genuine conditioning (not involving imagery). She used a technique similar to that of Novikova to study *the effect of conditioning on stimuli associated with the conditioned stimulus*. This general problem was analyzed into two more specific problems, each of which was studied in a series of experiments. The first of these was as follows: Two biologically indifferent stimuli, *a* and *b*, are associated by means of frequent repetition together. One of these, *a*, is then conditioned to a stimulus, *x*, eliciting a strong and definite response. Will the other indifferent stimulus, *b*, show evidence of conditioning without direct association with the strong stimulus? In experiments on four children twenty-five to forty-two months old, an electric bell and stroking of the arm were the original indifferent stimuli which were first associated by frequent repetition together. The stroking was then conditioned to a slight prick so that the child withdrew as soon as stroking began. After three successful conditioned responses to the stroking, the bell stimulus was given alone; the children withdrew five times in succession, although they did not withdraw when a control stimulus, a whistle, was introduced. After the response to the bell had disappeared, it was found that the conditioning to the stroking had also been eliminated. Exactly the same kind of results were obtained in the main experiments which were more elaborately controlled. A one-way screen was used, with all the apparatus manipulated from behind the screen to eliminate visual cues, and electric shock was the conditioning stimulus. One of these problems, with one child, was concerned with the sort of secondary conditioning shown on page 159, and was formulated as follows: If one stimulus has come to arouse a conditioned response by association with a biologically strong stimulus, is it possible to transfer this response to a second stimulus by associating it only with the conditioned stimulus, and never with the biologically strong stimulus? In this experiment the ringing of a buzzer was followed closely by a moderate electric shock to the child's foot. The child lifted his foot in response to the shock, and very shortly thereafter made the same response to the sound of the buzzer. Six successive trials of this conditioning were made, each followed by reinforcement. Half an hour after the last such trial, a light was flashed, followed by the buzzer; the child continued to raise his foot when the buzzer started, and on the eleventh trial raised his foot when the light flashed. That is, the flash of the light had become a stimulus by association with the sound of the buzzer which was itself a conditioned stimulus. This "secondary response" was made on three trials, with no response to a control stimulus. Subsequently, the light, instead of showing the positive conditioned response, inhibited the conditioned reaction to the buzzer. This phenomenon, wherein the secondary conditioned response not only diminishes with repetition, when not reinforced, but also inhibits the response to the primary conditioned stimulus with which it had been associated, is of much interest for the theory of learning. These experiments were carried on for several days with continued results of the same order—positive conditioning of the light, followed by inhibitory effect of the light on the buzzer.

The experimenter considers the processes involved in these two series of experiments essentially the same, i.e., both are reactions to a variety of compound stimuli. In the original series, the association takes place before the conditioning, while in the "secondary conditioning" situation the association is made after the conditioning of one of the stimuli. That is, whenever a stimulus firmly connected with other stimuli is conditioned to a third stimulus, two types of effect may be expected—the unconditioned element of the pair may become conditioned without any direct association with the conditioning stimulus, and, further, the weakening of the response to it may weaken the response to the other element which had been directly conditioned. The implications of this are obviously important in connection with all sorts of learning. It is doubtless at least a partial explanation of the type of "irradiation" seen in the extension of fear conditioning from the original fear stimulus, not only to other things present, but to things associated with these other things.

Munroe suggests that an indirect attack on fears might be based on this fact of the inhibiting effect of an associated stimulus on the conditioned response. When the latter is a case of fear, it might be more practicable to diminish the response to the associated stimulus than to attack the primary conditioned response, and let the associated stimulus exert its inhibition on the original conditioned stimulus, instead of attacking this stronger reaction directly.

The relations between this type of conditioning and maturity, intelligence, emotional conditions, strength of stimulus, and various other factors are not at all clear. As yet, we can only say that higher order conditionings do occur; the range of situations under which they occur has not been defined, much less the range of conditions militating against their occurrence.

In the traditional view of the conditioned response, a specific stimulus acquires the power to control a response to which it was originally irrelevant. But it has become very clear that whether the specific stimulus acquires such a power or not depends upon the whole situation within the organism and the whole stimulus field in which this element must function. Just as the reflex is a convenient abstraction from the complicated pattern of motor responses, so the stimulus is an abstraction from a very complex external situation.

There is no harm in this abstraction unless it leads the social psychologist to conclude that he can manipulate the behavior of man in a culture by controlling what are for the experimenter the significant stimuli. Unless he knows the culture and the man, he misses many essentials. Of great importance for our analysis here is Razran's study of the differences between two forms of conditioning, configural and colligated conditioning. In the latter, the significant stimulus, such as a light bulb, stands out prominently enough in the food situation so that in time it arouses a salivary response. In the other situation neither a red bulb nor a green bulb acquires any such capacity, though *the two together* may adequately function in this way. It is highly probable that we become conditioned in social life not to discrete stimuli but rather to complicated patterns. In some cases the significant items of such a pattern may still evoke the response called for by the pattern, and here we may very properly speak of "redintegration" of responses; a part stands for the whole. In other cases, however, redintegration signally fails. It is necessary that a larger sweep of stimulus elements, perhaps the complete original pattern, be presented.

One may be conditioned to a situation without knowing it. Thus musical selections which have been closely evaluated are judged differently after some of them have accompanied one's enjoyment of a meal. Well-phrased rationalizations are offered regarding the reasons for the preferences given in the final series. One selection is stated to have "better form," more "rugged strength," etc., than another, although the observed shifts are inconsistent *except* when seen in reference to the one constant factor producing the changes, namely, the association of music with food. The individual need not know how or when his patterns of enthusiasm arise; and if he rationalizes his musical preference why should we be surprised if he rationalizes the personal and social preferences which have arisen in the same way?

Again, one may be negatively conditioned to situations and hold the negative response although one is unable to explain *why*. Words which are regularly followed by electric shocks later come to arouse withdrawing movements and also inner disturbances shown by the galvanic skin reflex. Although the subject may not remember that the word was followed by shock, the word produces the inner disturbance.[1] One has learned at the visceral level what he has not learned at the verbal level. Social learning of this sort may be of great importance in the tension-fear-prejudice situation, though its nature never becomes clear to the learner.

Neither can one maintain that the after-effects of past conditioning are due solely to conscious anticipation. A group of subjects are given a severe shock and the galvanic skin reflex is measured. Later they are brought back to the apparatus, shown how the wires are disconnected and given proof that the apparatus can no longer give a shock. Nevertheless, renewed handling of the apparatus produces a distinct galvanic skin reflex. The old pattern still lives, although its irrelevance to the present situation is fully understood. Thus when deeply moved or traumatized one relives old hopes and fears, one's urge toward standards and values, despite full recognition of their irrelevance to the present life task.

Moreover, conditioning need not be based upon the action of stimuli which are clearly conscious. Stimuli which do not enter consciousness at all may modify social behavior. An example will suggest the importance of "subliminal" conditioning for social behavior. In the reaction-time experiment, the subject was asked to lift his hand from the telegraph key the moment that a light was shown. With practice he reduced his reaction time to 200 one-thousandths of a second. But the experimenter inserted in the external ear a tiny cylinder containing a wire which could be made to hum as soon as a switch was thrown. The experimenter made sure in all cases that the humming was truly subliminal. No subject could tell when it started or stopped. In the next series of reaction-time experiments the switch was thrown a small fraction of a second before the stimulus light was flashed. The result, after practice with the method, was a reduction of the apparent reaction time in some cases to less than 100 one-thousandths of a second. The subject had been conditioned to the subliminal sound of the humming in the cylinder.

It is likely that a large part of our intuitive evaluation of the social situation, our "instinctive" hesitancy to join in a game, our

---

[1] Indeed, the disturbance is *greater* in those instances in which the subject's memory fails him. There is here something like the blocking or repression to which psychoanalysts have called attention.

"instinctive" trust in a man with a bold proposal, is based in large measure upon subliminal conditioning. We learn day by day the meaning of gestures, facial expression, tone of voice; but a great deal that we learn functions beneath the level of consciousness, or may be above the threshold of consciousness today and function just as well when below it tomorrow. The intuitive interpretation of personality, so carefully studied in recent years by German and American investigators, is apparently largely achieved by training responses to subliminal cues. Sometimes the issue has been confused by referring at this point to Gestalt theory, arguing that our evaluation of total personalities is not in terms of specific stimuli but in terms of global totalities. This is indeed sometimes the case; but until the high probability of response to subliminal cues is controlled, it is hard to make effective use of this interpretation. It is quite likely that training in interpreting facial expression may bring some of these subliminal cues above the threshold, and that the result may sometimes be confusion, an improper attention to other cues which have been keeping their just place in the total situation until that moment. This seems to be exactly what is meant by F. H. Allport's and by Guilford's experiments in training subjects to interpret facial expression (page 234). It is quite probable that some of the best judges of personality work in terms of subliminal cues. Under some circumstances a dog or a child may evaluate a stranger better than an adult. In confronting new or difficult personal situations, beginner's luck or the providence which watches over fools may be due to the more effective response to elements which are not consciously analyzed and which therefore do not over-dominate. Woman's "intuition" may be in considerable measure the result of specific training in utilizing total impressions where a man would be more likely to give clear emphasis and hence over-simplification in response to some features of a complex.

DOMINANCE

If learning through conditioning is given a prominent place as a clue to social behavior, the failure to learn must be given equal prominence. As one glances about the room, one notes dozens and hundreds of things to which one has been conditioned. There are appropriate things to do with each one of them. Yet relatively few of these responses can be made at a given time. It is not sufficient to say that we forget. Action patterns involve a high degree of organization; the task of attending to a book or a line of thought depends upon the exclusion of hundreds of possible responses. What is the clue to the selection? Why, among all the possible responses based on conditioning, does a given action pattern occur?

The answer appears to lie largely in the fact of *dominance*. Physiologically, the acquisition of new patterns means the slough-ing-off of old ones, and the process of meeting new situations moment by moment means the blocking of those action tendencies which are biologically weak by those which are strong. In order to prevent a purely circular argument (the strong response is the one that wins; it wins because it is strong), it is necessary to be very concrete as to the nature of dominant responses.

In one of the early studies in the old St. Petersburg laboratory a dog was given meat powder on the tongue at the same time that an electric shock was administered to the forepaw. According to some glib and easy formulations of the conditioning process, meat powder should thereafter provoke retraction of the paw and elec-tric shock should evoke salivation. In point of fact, the two re-sponses—retraction of the paw and salivation—could not ordinarily be conditioned at once. On the contrary, if the meat powder was abundant and the shock weak, conditioning occurred only in the salivary direction, so to speak. The shock produced salivation. It became so integrated with the food-getting response that the re-traction of the paw ceased to occur. If, on the other hand, the meat powder was scanty and the shock intense, the biologically dominant pattern was the retraction of the paw. After such training as this, the meat powder brought about not salivation, but retraction of the paw instead. The principle of dominance (as defined by Razran) is that when two separate responses tend to be aroused by two distinct situations, the effect of the two situations is not the inde-pendent production of the two responses, but the reinforcement of the biologically dominant response and in time the disappearance of the other. Indeed, a situation S which would, when acting alone, produce a non-dominant response R may, when competing against a stronger $S_1 - R_1$, actually contribute something to the intensity of response R_1. The weaker pattern $S - R$ is crowded out of the picture. In the first figure on page 156, "food" is dominant over "light."

A simple example of the application of the dominance principle is given in the classical reconditioning experiments of M. C. Jones. A child has been negatively conditioned to a rabbit, let us say, because of the rabbit's bite. The sight of the rabbit has now become a conditioned stimulus for fear. If the fear is to be removed, it is necessary that the rabbit be kept at a distance and that the child, while really hungry, be given appetizing food. The sight of the rabbit at a distance is a non-dominant stimulus which, as a part of the total happy situation, discharges into the general response of well-being and joy. The breaking up of the fear pattern thus depends altogether upon the substitution of a happy activity when the rabbit is presented. If the principle of dominance is sound, it would be fatal to attempt the reconditioning when the child is not hungry, the food not appetizing, or the rabbit too close. Under these circumstances, the rabbit-fear patterns would be *dominant*, and the child would develop *fear of his food*. This seems to be exactly the case.

We do not wish to generalize to the effect that all conditioning reveals the principle of dominance; nor do we even wish to assert that, corresponding to each acquired habit, there is always the loss of a pattern physiologically less dominant than the one being fixated.

Yet in general it is clear that new habits cannot possibly be built except out of old ones. The organism can never make a new response in the strict sense, a response utterly different from the responses made on a reflex basis. If the new act consists in the integration of disparate acts previously present, the integration depends upon a genuine biological unification. New habits are not plastered on piecemeal; they are assimilated into the dominant pattern of a going concern. Each child is capable of learning in his own way, depending upon what he was at birth and the consequences of habits already achieved. Each new habit can integrate with habits already present; it can, under special circumstances, displace habits weaker than itself; it can be assimilated as a member of a family of responses in which the integrated totality of response gives equal emphasis to the old and the new.

Partly because of the vitality and energy of the small child, and partly because of the relatively small number of situations which it has confronted, early experiences should therefore be expected to have especially great importance. Each new experience must either integrate with earlier experiences in the sense defined above, or must partly displace the effects of earlier experiences so as to dominate them, or must be relegated to a minor position as the result of its inability to compete with existing habits. The more experience the child has acquired, the smaller the likelihood of a fundamental upheaval as the result of the new experience. Consequently, except for overwhelming new experiences, such as those related to first appearance at school or a death in the family, the physical changes of adolescence or the first endeavors to earn a living, the old is for the most part dominant over the new. This is one reason why deeply ingrained habits are largely irreversible, and why personality, despite its complexity, inevitably tends to unity and continuity.

The resulting patterns of conditioning in the adult are necessarily very complicated. The complexity of interplay of external and internal factors is shown by Razran's study of "attitudinal control" of the conditioning process. Human salivary responses are to be conditioned to words, nonsense syllables, metronome beats, etc. In time, the word "pretzel" or the metronome beat may evoke a large salivary flow. Here, however, we discover three radically different types of response to the conditioning situation. Three distinct types of persons are found: (1) those who build up these conditioned responses exactly in the manner of Pavlov's dogs; (2) those who, despite much practice, do not condition, that is, show no increased salivary flow when the signal meaning food is presented; and (3) those who condition in the reverse direction, that is, those who show distinctly (and reliably) less salivary flow when the food signal is given. The attitude toward the experimenter—the desire to accept, ignore or defeat his purposes—appears to be the chief clue to the results.

It might be erroneously concluded that the conditioned response therefore ceases to be an explanatory principle. It is probable, however, that we have simply an example of the influence of previous conditionings. A conditioned resistance response to the experimenter may be more powerful than the conditioned response to the food signal; and in line with the general principle of physiological dominance we should expect the signal to arouse a motor and visceral set destructive to the simpler food reflexes. We do not know the mechanism by which this is brought about, but we know that conditioned responses are built into hierarchies which appear to follow the general principle of dominance. It is highly probable that this principle is of importance in understanding such social attitudes as race prejudices. In an experiment on racial attitudes, some individual students remained severely hostile to the Negro despite four days' "favorable" conditioning experiences; and the most unfavorable specific experiences with members of a defined social group may lead only to tolerance or amused reactions if an antecedent favorable attitude or a humanitarian philosophy of life precedes the disagreeable experience.

SUGGESTION

We shall now try to show some of the varied applications of the principle of the conditioned response to a number of problems in social psychology, especially those social forms of learning which seem to underlie what we call *suggestion, imitation,* and *sympathy*; these terms are, in fact, names for *ways of modifying behavior*, and the situations in which they operate are usually social.

Although the quantity of experimental work on suggestion has become voluminous, it can scarcely be maintained that our understanding has been increased proportionally. To review all the experiments on suggestion and suggestibility would be an idle and a thankless task; a large proportion of these really do nothing more than pick out some obvious instances of human gullibility, prey upon them, and give the results pseudo-quantitative form by ascertaining what percentage of the subjects "yield." As if this were not in itself sufficiently futile with regard to the problem of getting at the nature of suggestibility, the situation is usually made worse by confusing three quite distinct human tendencies: (1) The tendency to make a response which has been previously made in a similar situation, whether appropriate or inappropriate at the time. This is, of course, simply habit, and includes the familiar response by analogy (or "transferred conditioned response"), the thing involved in the child's saying "kitty" when he sees a squirrel, or a man's absent-mindedly pulling out a key as he comes to a door resembling one where he is in the habit of using that key. (2) The tendency to go on doing what one has started doing, simply because whatever factors were strong enough to start the activity continue strong enough to make it go on—the tendency being augmented perhaps by the perseverative effect of the first. This kind of behavior is usually said to be due to suggestion, if the experimenter believes that the tendency to go on with the act involves gross failure to realize its inappropriateness. (3) The tendency to believe or to do what one is told because of social motives such as dependence upon, or fear of, or fondness for, some person. Here the subject may even grasp fully the nature of the experiment; for example, in hypnotic demonstrations the subject may wish to manifest the results which the experimenter wishes to produce. Moreover, a considerable number of acts which we ascribe to suggestibility are instances of the cooperation of two or more tendencies where none would be strong enough alone to eventuate in overt behavior. A good many cases of mob suggestibility seem to result from the summation effect of a great desire or great fear on the one hand, and the vague awareness of freedom from social condemnation in a group situation on the other hand.

All these points have been made before; but it is remarkable that new experimental studies of suggestion continue to appear in which, instead of the more precise analysis of the behavior involved or the conditions underlying it, we are presented with a medley of results which are reported simply as scores on a suggestibility test. Now if what we desire is to know in a general way whether a person stands in the top decile or the bottom decile in suggestibility, in the sense that out of a hundred given situations he showed suggestibility in a very small or a very large number of cases, there is, of course, value in such investigations. But even so, we have really learned little until the experimenter sifts out for us the specific kinds of "suggestibility" which are evidenced by particular kinds of behavior on the test.

We might well begin by taking those cases in which suggestibility really means nothing more than ordinary association—those referred to under (1) above. To think of a thing when someone names it, or to carry out some simple act when a friend asks us to, is really nothing more than response through habit at its most automatic level. We may think of such responses as "conditioned reactions"; in fact, many of them are conditioned reactions to words. But as far as we know, the associative process is the same when a word calls a thing to mind in the form of an image. Illustrations of this type of suggestion are plentiful.

Ideal for this purpose is the size-weight illusion. In it advantage is taken of the fact that small children tend to estimate weight from size, but that as they grow older this tendency decreases and the opposite tendency becomes apparent, so that two objects of different size but of the same weight normally cause in adults the inverse effect; the large object seems lighter. This, as has been abundantly shown, is a suggestion effect based upon expectation, or what Helmholtz long ago called "unconscious inference," and is of course naturally free of the social factor as far as the experimental situation itself is concerned. There is no apparent difference between this kind of illusion and that in which we experience what we are *in the habit of experiencing* in a given situation.

This same form of associative suggestion appears in Triplett's experiment with conjuring tricks. He pretended to throw a ball into the air. The ball was not really thrown, but about 50 per cent of a group of 165 children (fourth to eighth grades) saw the ball go up and disappear. Larger or smaller percentages are, of course, obtained, depending upon the conjurer's skill; the response is characteristic of adults as well as of children. To call this any more than ordinary association would be to introduce unnecessary complication; in fact, we see nothing here which differs in any way from thinking of the sun when someone mentions it. The image may take on hallucinatory vividness, as in the case of "seeing" things which never happen, but this does not alter the form of association.

We are not in the habit of regarding this type of suggestibility as a form of ordinary association; we think of a special factor of gullibility. Practically all the time, however, we do think of things when we are told of them; the mental set of the classroom is to expect that what the teacher says will happen. The fact that most people get the effect is sufficient evidence that, under the conditions stated, the method *does not* test proneness to special gullibility beyond that which we all show in believing commonplaces which we are told. Life could scarcely be lived if we were constantly on our guard. There are all sorts of psychological experiments which could not be done without students believing what the experimenter tells them. In special cases, the experimenter calls the result suggestibility; in others, he does not. (In this sense, grades on some examinations are suggestibility scores.)

The forms of suggestion so far described are all included under the concept of "ideo-motor action," as used, for example, by William James. James had in mind the tendency of an idea to produce an act. As we have noted, however, things which we see and things which we only imagine often function in exactly the same way, as far as the resulting behavior is concerned. To accept a verbal suggestion automatically, to accept it because of an image which it arouses, and to accept it in the form of an hallucination which it arouses involve one and the same associative process. We might prefer to call them all sensori-motor rather than ideo-motor; but since the latter term has been so long in use, we see more confusion than gain in replacing it, provided, of course, that it is recognized to be nothing more than what is ordinarily meant in everyday life by association.

Auto-suggestion, again, differs from ordinary suggestion not in the laws of association which are involved, but solely in the origin of the ideas which set the acts in motion. There may be, as we shall see, differences in emotional attitude toward the suggestions given by other people; but in its simplest form auto-suggestion is almost completely free from emotional disturbances and may be regarded as conforming perfectly to this simple ideo-motor type of suggestion already discussed. For this reason, and in part because it is free from the emotional resistances which we often set up as barriers against the suggestions given by other people, the advertiser and the propagandist in general prefer to have us use our own auto-suggestions rather than merely to accept the suggestions which they have to óffer. We must repeat some catch phrase or slogan until "we believe it ourselves." We become partisans with the propagandist and make ideal material for the putting-over of the cause. G. C. Myers seems to have greatly increased his success in teaching English to foreigners in the army, by starting them off with such a sentence as, "I want to learn to write a letter home," and proceeding from this to the use of sentences describing the general excellence of the army itself—its routine, and its civilizing effect upon a recruit. Soldiers who learned these sentences seem to have become in time more addicted to the military life. Moreover, by suggestion to "chronic kickers" that they would make good speakers, and by getting them to make speeches about army life, Myers found he could turn them into "boosters," until they at last thoroughly believed what they were saying.

Slightly more complex, perhaps, is the suggestion which touches off an attitude or "set." Thus university students' preferences for pictures were altered by informing them in some cases that the pictures were masterpieces, and in other cases that they were of little value. Paragraphs to this effect were presented, together with pictures by unknown painters, the subjects being asked to rate each picture on a five-point scale. In all cases the pictures attended by a favorable paragraph were ranked higher than those with unfavorable paragraphs; but individual pictures varied greatly in respect to the influence of the suggestion upon their placement.

Principles (1) and (2) described above (page 169), taken in conjunction, are all that is required to explain another series of "suggestion" experiments in which the subject shows in one activity the after-effects of what he has been doing a moment before. This kind of experiment has been made famous by Binet.

Children were shown a model line; after a short time, they were shown a card with a series of parallel lines of graded length, and told to select one having the length of the model line. The experiment was then repeated with a similar series, except that all the lines given were shorter than the model. The children, nevertheless, expecting to find it, indicated their choice. In experiments testing the ability of his subjects to reproduce correctly the lengths of lines shown briefly to them, Binet found that on showing them a series of lines of gradually increasing length, but with occasional "catches" where the lines did not lengthen as expected, no one of his forty-five pupils completely escaped the suggestion of increase in length in all lines, although ten of them were able to escape one or more of the "catches."

In a further experiment, Binet tested the suggestibility of forty-two school boys by the following method. Lines of different lengths drawn on white cardboard were shown them, one line at a time, and the boys indicated on ruled paper their estimate of the length of each line. The lines as shown increased in length, by a fixed amount, up to the fifth; from the fifth to the thirty-sixth (last) inclusive, they were all of equal length. The suggestion of gradual increase in length given by the first five lines caused in every case some overestimation of the length of the remaining lines; the amount of overestimation by each subject was calculated from his paper, and a "coefficient of suggestibility" deduced. Each case was also individually studied, and in many cases there was evident at certain points the effect of a critical sense, which caused sudden, or progressive, or periodic, diminution of the error. (This "progressive line" test is paralleled by a "progressive weight" test.)

Later, an opportunity was given to the boys to correct their papers, according to their *memory* of the lines shown. The experimenter questioned them as to their satisfaction with their work, using a standard form of inquiry for all alike. The result of corrections made after the questioning showed in general a decrease in the overestimation of the length of the lines, but some overestimation remained. The questions had the effect of waking the subject's "critical sense" to errors made under the previous influence; what he now *recalled* was nearer to correctness than what he had produced in the presence of the lines to be estimated. The "critical sense" seems here to be a name for an attitude. Ideo-motor suggestion, then, operates until this interfering attitude appears. *All these forms of suggestion decreased with age.*

In the experiments cited thus far, there is no conclusive evidence that the *prestige of the experimenter* was an essential part of the situation. But in a great many experiments, prestige (or other attributes) of the experimenter must be regarded as of cardinal importance.

The immense importance of prestige in suggestibility studies was, in fact, expressly recognized by Vitali and by Binet and Henri over thirty years ago. Thus a school master showed a 5-cm. line to a group of primary school children and had them reproduce it from memory. He then said that the next line would be a little longer. Actually it was shorter—only 4 cm. long. Nevertheless, only nine of the eighty-six children resisted the suggestion to reproduce it as longer.

One of the most careful of the studies of prestige suggestion carried through by Binet's pupils is Giroud's work with thirty-four school children. She used the progressive line test, the progressive weight test, suggestion by personal influence, and both direct and indirect suggestion in a study of ability to report from memory. Of ten subjects at the age of seven, all made their lines keep on increasing right up to the very end, though the fact that a glimmering of resistance was present is suggested by the fact that, when asked if they were satisfied with the lines they had drawn, three said they had made them too long. The decrease of suggestibility with age as found by Binet is shown in Giroud's table indicating the number of lines (out of the total fifteen) upon which the effect of suggestion acted.

For ten subjects at age	7	10.7
For ten subjects at age	8	8.2
For five subjects at age	9	4.2
For five subjects at age	10	4.8
For five subjects at age	12	1

Similar results were obtained with the progressive weights.

The clearest experimental distinction between the simple "ideomotor" type of suggestibility and that which results from emotional factors in a social situation is made by Aveling and Hargreaves, and followed through by Estabrooks. Aveling and Hargreaves' subjects were 46 boys and 19 girls (ages mostly 12 and 13). The following methods were used: First, the experimenters induced hand rigidity by verbal suggestion. The child was seated by the examiner. The experimenter said, in part, "Hold out your hand—see, like mine; and fix your eyes on my hand. . . . While looking at my hand all the time, I want you to pay special attention to the feelings you get in your own. . . . You will probably feel a slight tingling or tightening or stiffening in your fingers." Further emphasis was placed on the idea of feelings, ending in a flat statement, "You can't *close* your hand. You can't close it at all. Try!" It will be noticed that this is a prestige test—that is, the use of an emotional relation between the examiner and the child is permitted or, in fact, probably encouraged. Nearly half of the boys and over half of the girls were able to close the hand in spite of the above suggestions. In the second test (Whipple Test No. 42) no prestige factor was introduced. In this a series of lines are presented in pairs; in the first pair, the second line is always longer, but in the latter part of the series the lines are equal. The child's tendency to go on judging the latter series as he has judged the former is classified by Whipple and others as analogous to the tendencies studied in all of Binet's line tests.

The third experiment makes use of the illusion of warmth from an electric light bulb, the "resistance-wire method" (Whipple Test No. 44). In the fourth experiment, we return to prestige. The experimenter presses on the subject's hand, then says, "Your hand is getting lighter. It is rising in the air." About one-fourth of the boys and about half of the girls found that the hand did rise. Test five makes use of the progressive weight technique (Whipple Test No. 41). Test six measures fidelity of report (Whipple Test No. 32). A number of leading questions are asked with reference to something which the subject has seen (this method is extensively used today in connection with the psychology of testimony). Test seven is called suggestion of line lengths by personal influence (contradictory suggestion, Whipple Test No. 42).

The subjects are graded in ranks for each test, and rank-difference correlations are computed. If the tests are divided into two groups, a correlation of +.44 appears between these, which the authors regard as evidence of a common factor, a suggestibility factor operating through the battery of tests as a whole.

Later, Aveling and Hargreaves carried their work further. Thirty-three boys (average age 13.2 years) and 23 girls (average age 13.6 years) were studied. The hand-rigidity test found 73 per cent of the boys and 35 per cent of the girls able to resist suggestions, while 24 per cent of the boys and 74 per cent of the girls could not resist the suggestion of the hand rising.

The smoothed curves for suggestibility in the various situations are most curious. Combining boys' and girls' scores, the solid and broken lines represent the two series. It is clear that a U-curve is produced by the two hand tests and the warmth illusion test. These they regard as prestige tests. The test involving "suggestion of line lengths by personal influence" may be a prestige test, but is said not to operate like these others. All the other tests yield nearly normal curves, including the fidelity-of-report test. The U-curve is explained in terms of the factor of contra-suggestibility; where "personal" suggestion was used, the subjects tended to fall into two sharply divided groups, the suggestible and the non- (or contra-) suggestible. Where the suggestion was impersonal, the distribution was approximately normal; most subjects are moderately suggestible.

The reader will have noticed more than one element of crudeness in the above experiments. Nevertheless, they are of great importance in clarifying the muddle into which the psychology of suggestion has fallen. The mere tendency to respond positively to the progressive line test is a very different thing from the tendency to accept a suggestion with regard to hand rigidity. The latter may, of course, be regarded as a simple habitual (ideo-motor) response, but it is not so experienced by most subjects. College students with whom we have worked and with whom we have seen other psychologists work, have been definitely puzzled to look at their hands and find that they would not move or relax or unclasp, or whatever was wished, as long as the experimenter told them that they were powerless to exert such control. They may be sufficiently impassive about the situation to laugh at themselves while they struggle to pull their hands apart; but the result does depend in large part upon their confidence in the experimenter; and the fact

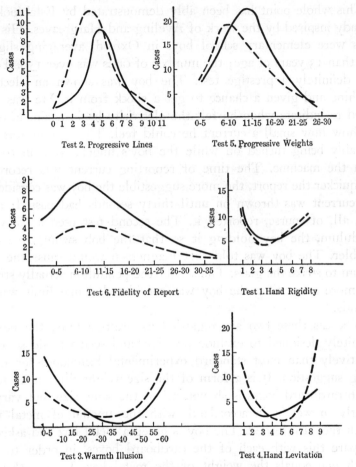

Test 2. Progressive Lines

Test 5. Progressive Weights

Test 6. Fidelity of Report

Test 1. Hand Rigidity

Test 3. Warmth Illusion

Test 4. Hand Levitation

(From *The British Journal of Psychology*. Used by Permission.)

that the suggestion is less effectively imposed by a fellow student implies strongly that we are not dealing here simply with the connections already established between certain words and certain muscular acts. These verbal elements are important, of course; but under ordinary circumstances there is effective inhibition in the form of other verbal suggestions—"Oh, that's all nonsense, I can do it if I like," etc. The fixation of attention upon the experimenter whom one respects (or perhaps sometimes fears) seems sufficient to block these ordinarily available counter-suggestions.

This whole point has been ably demonstrated by Estabrooks in a study inspired by the work of Aveling and Hargreaves. His subjects were elementary school boys in Oxford, averaging slightly less than 13 years of age; the number of cases was over 150. Test I was definitely a prestige test. The boy was shown an electrical machine and given a chance to get a shock from it. He was then asked to indicate when he felt the electricity begin again, in order to show how small a current he could feel. The current was presumably being turned on while the boy's fingers were in contact with the machine. The time of reporting current was recorded; the quicker the report, the more suggestible the boy was considered. No current was thrown on until thirty seconds had passed; after this, all, of course, reported it. The second test used a Chevreul pendulum, the boy holding it so that the bob swung free in a tumbler. The boy was told that magnetism would cause the pendulum to strike the glass. The sooner the pendulum actually struck, the more suggestible the boy was considered. Time limit was 60 seconds.

Whereas these two are regarded as prestige tests, the next is definitely designed to exclude prestige, and seems to do so more effectively than most standard experimental techniques for measuring suggestion. It is a form of the size-weight illusion. A series of 16 cardboard boxes is shown, all of the same size, but varying greatly in weight in accordance with the amount of metal with which they are loaded. The boy is given a metal box and asked to compare this with each of the cardboard boxes, in order to find which one equals the weight of the metal box. During this the experimenter goes over into a corner and talks with the other boys *with his back turned to the subject.*

In the next, a group test, fifteen questions were asked regarding a demonstration which the experimenter had given. The questions were at first plausible and referred to things which the experimenter had actually done; but they became more and more implausible, so that, whereas nearly all the boys were misled by some of the questions in the middle of the series, none was tripped by the last question. The score was in terms of the number of resistances to the leading questions.

Evidently, the scoring of all these tests is highly arbitrary. There is often a quantitative difference in the forms of behavior which occur when prestige is present and in others in which it is absent. In the metal-box test, where the experimenter was clearly dealing simply with illusion and where the prestige factor was neatly eliminated, we have approximately the normal curve, whereas the first test (with the electricity) gives a U-curve similar to that obtained by Aveling and Hargreaves. The reader will recall that the current was actually switched on after 30 seconds. If a boy had not reported the current during the first 30 seconds he was therefore classed as non-suggestible; and since the number of boys in this group is considerable, the curve inevitably takes on something of a U-shape. The same result and the same comment are to be noted in the pendulum test. In both of these cases it would be important to know what sort of distribution Estabrooks would have obtained had he extended the time limit. Even so, it seems reasonably clear that in both these tests he had a large number of boys who resisted the suggestion flatly, another large number who succumbed quickly, and a rather small number intermediate between these two extremes. The resistance would be another illustration of the factor of negative suggestibility or, if one prefers, negativism, which appears as the result of a personal relation to the experimenter—perhaps a desire not to be bluffed. As has been said, this emotional aspect of suggestibility seems to be of the greatest importance for the social psychologist, and the aspect which has been the least adequately studied. Most of the instances of crowd suggestibility which are cited are too complicated to pigeonhole; but where suggestibility does enter, the simple ideo-motor aspect is probably less important than the emotional relation of the crowd to its leader or its victim or to other persons conceived as friends or enemies. Moreover, as we shall later suggest (cf. page 237), the individual differences found in experiments on suggestion do not seem to be intelligible at all without study of the deeper attitude of the individual toward the experimenter, toward the situation, and toward *authority situations* in general, as well as of his attitude toward himself—his security, confidence, ascendance, etc.

But the reader may have been wondering just how the ordinary processes of association are altered by the emotional relation between subject and experimenter; how it is that automatic or semiautomatic responses may be obtained under special emotional conditions which would not be obtained if suggestion were completely "depersonalized." The answer appears to be given in part by the ordinary facts of attention. One cannot always pay close attention to what one does. One cannot scrutinize it with the customary critical attitude if the attention is largely upon the authority or awesomeness of the experimenter, the great speaker, or the crowd. Prestige suggestion, as Aveling and Hargreaves pointed out, is not a *different kind of suggestion; it is simply heightened suggestion due to the facilitating effect which the emotional situation exercises upon the ordinary associative processes.* It works by attracting so much attention to the experimenter that what the subject himself does cannot receive close scrutiny. We cannot put full attention on two things. There is a dissociation; in other words, some activities to which we are not attending are free to run automatically. There are probably other factors involved, but the fact of dissociation is itself of crucial importance. For the one thing that can consistently be expected to interfere with *ideo-motor suggestibility* is the presence of contradictory ideas or habits, and the one intellectual basis for the rejection of a suggestion is the presence of ideas or habits predisposing toward a contrary idea or habit.

IMITATION

The bundle of facts classified under "imitation" was among the first to attract the attention of the social psychologist. The clinical and experimental studies carried on throughout the latter half of the nineteenth century furnished points of view and materials utilized by Tarde in constructing his famous *Laws of Imitation*, and both experimental and theoretical studies of imitation have been numerous in every decade since 1890. Tarde failed, however, to analyze psychologically the process of imitation; the rational and purposeful imitation of an artisan following a design was confused with the blind imitation of sheep following a leader, and both of these were confused with the response to word or gesture in the hypnotic subject and in the excited crowd. The ultimate psychological analysis of these varied types of response remains for the future, but clarity of definition will be necessary if a useful classification is to be achieved.

It seems worth while to distinguish (1) imitation of conditioned response type, (2) imitation after a trial-and-error period, and (3) deliberate imitation. In the first of these, the behavior which is called imitative is strictly a conditioned response to a fairly simple and easily describable stimulus; the animal does not know that it is imitating, and the fact that the behavior "imitates" or duplicates the behavior of some other animal necessitates no psychological principles other than those already described in connection with the conditioned response. This kind of imitation is sometimes dogmatically declared not to exist. But anyone walking along a country road on a summer's evening in nearly any part of the United States may satisfy himself that there are facts which fulfill this definition and call for no other.

The first data for inspection will in fact be offered without any experimental control whatever; they will be supplied by a conversation between two katydids (there must not be more than two). Nearby, to one's right, comes a *zee, zee*; from the left comes a *zee, zee*. A few seconds later, the one on the right says *zee, zee, zee, zee*, and the one on the left replies *zee, zee, zee, zee*. Let the call on the right be a triad; a triad responds. This will continue as long as the listener's patience lasts—or perhaps, more accurately, a great deal longer. An occasional solitary *zee* will fail of an answer, or may be answered by almost anything; and whether a digit span of five exists among katydids we have been unable to determine. But as to the main facts here described the reader will be able to satisfy himself; intent listening to an hour's performance was to us its own reward.

But this offers nothing but the beginning of a hypothesis; it would be better, of course, if all this could be gotten under laboratory conditions. Curiously enough, an enterprising naturalist has given us an experiment dealing with a very closely related phenomenon, one which we should in fact insist on describing as identical. It is the custom of one species of katydids to sing in unison; they constitute a conductorless orchestra. Their chirps are so perfectly timed that it is as if one large insect were playing alone. This would certainly be difficult to explain if it could be proved that the insects do not hear each other. But they do. Fulton removed the "auditory pegs" from the front legs of the members of several of these orchestras and in a few minutes they were all playing at sixes and sevens, whereas a control group in a neighboring cage were still giving their exquisitely uniform program. Now in this case the katydids were obviously imitating one another, in the everyday unsophisticated sense that one was doing what another was doing, not fortuitously but through response to the other's act. Theoretical identity is, of course, not to be assumed in the behavior of anything as complex as living tissue, but the identity is as complete, let us say, as in two prints from the same photographic negative.

The reason why this commonplace sort of behavior has so often been dogmatically ruled out of court, or just as frequently ignored, seems to be that some sort of "instinct of imitation" is thought to be involved. As a matter of fact, however, the mechanism of all such acts seems ridiculously simple and involves nothing but the simplest kind of conditioned response. Whatever organic condition makes the katydid begin to chirp we may designate S. The chirping, R, is now not only the result of S but *simultaneous with S*, and, as we believe clear from Fulton's work, the katydid hears himself chirp. If he happens to chirp twice, the hearing of two chirps coincides with whatever condition caused him to chirp twice! No wonder, then, that if no other insect is near him, you so often hear him repeat over and over whatever rhythm he started with. There is, however, a certain time limit between performances. If a katydid hears two chirps (a substitute for the organic condition which would make him chirp twice) he will, in an almost machine-like fashion, chirp twice in reply. In fact, if he did anything else there would be a mystery; as it is, there is no mystery. The point is usually not looked at in this way, because the diagram for a conditioned response is ordinarily drawn thus:

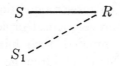

All three events are
occurring simultaneously

In our present case, however, it must be drawn this way:

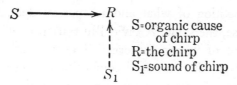

S=organic cause
   of chirp
R=the chirp
S_1=sound of chirp

All three events S, R, S_1
occur simultaneously

If the page is turned through forty-five degrees, the reader will see that he is dealing with the old formula, and that imitation on this level is no such intricate problem as has been assumed.

Such illustrations from animals make it reasonable to look for something similar in human behavior; and dozens of illustrations are in fact easily found. F. H. Allport, among others, has argued with perfect straightforwardness and simplicity that the young child's stimulation of its own auditory centers in the brain through the utterance of any sound is sufficient explanation of repetition, the "circular reflex." In the terms of the conditioned response, whatever organic condition made the child say *Da* is present simultaneously with the hearing of *Da*. It follows that the hearing of *Da* makes the child say *Da*. The next step is to point out that the child's imitation of someone else's utterance of *Da* involves absolutely no further hypothesis. To be sure, the tone of the voice, emphasis, etc., may differ somewhat, but there is no problem here distinct from the problem of "response by analogy," already considered (page 157). In the very small child this sort of imitation is often quite dependable, but as organic states become more complex and variable, the pattern is often broken. Even so, two-year-olds and three-year-olds often answer a question by repeating the last word or syllable; and wherever neural organization remains simple, i.e., among the feeble-minded, such mechanical repetition, or "echolalia," is common. Many children go through a period of months in which they repeat what they hear, sometimes in the form of one syllable at a time, sometimes two or three at a time, depending upon their memory span (how much they can grasp at once).

Identical in structure is the phenomenon of *echopraxia*, or the mechanical repetition of what another person does. The explanation is, of course, the same. A vivid illustration is offered in Novakovsky's account of "arctic hysteria." The population of northern Siberia, no matter what its racial composition, suffers every winter from the combined effect of prolonged starvation, cold and uninterrupted darkness. The result is to reduce a large proportion, frequently nearly all of the inhabitants of a village, to this curious condition: the patient involuntarily performs what he sees done by another. Young men sometimes take advantage of the situation to play the part of practical jokers, and go about from one sick person to another, doing absurd things in order to make the victim reply in kind. Jochelson, who has explored in the same region and found the same phenomenon, tells us of a young man who used to put snow down the back of his neck for the fun of seeing other people do the same. The victims are by no means lacking in "insight." They frequently "go after" the perpetrator of the joke; but the fact remains that they are, during the time of the disease, powerless to resist this tendency to echopraxia. Everybody in the region who is subjected to famine suffers from it—the hunters, of course, least of all because they usually devour whatever they catch and leave the question open as to whether there will be something to bring home. It is important to emphasize the fact that this is not hysteria in the sense of a "psychogenic maladjustment." It is an attribute of those whose physique is depleted by the arctic winter, or exhaustion, or famine, or all three.[1]

In other words, it is just as natural to repeat what another person does as to repeat what he says, and for the same reason. Seeing a certain hand movement has, of course, occurred simultaneously with executing that movement. If we let S represent whatever stimulus brings about a certain hand movement, and S_1 the *sight* of the movement which is simultaneously made, it is easy to see, by the circular reflex, why seeing our own hand do something tends to make it repeat the act. The same thing is, of course, also to be found among the feeble-minded. There seems to be absolutely no new principle here beyond that of conditioning which has been discussed above; and again there is only one reason why we do not fall victim to such repetition, namely, that our associative mechanisms are sufficiently complicated to lead off into all sorts of other activities. The small child and the feeble-minded lack the mental furniture which might lead to interfering acts; the man exhausted by cold and famine has few positive impulses which could compete with a present stimulus.

This sort of conditioned response imitation may, of course, also be studied in the laboratory, as shown in Starch's study of unconscious imitation in handwriting. One hundred and six subjects were asked to give samples of their handwriting in their usual manner, copying phrases from models submitted to them. One of the models was typewritten, the other three were written with varying degrees of slant and width of letter. Very few of the subjects had any idea as to the purpose of the experiment. Starch found that of the 103 subjects who stated that they had written in their usual manner, every single one had, as a matter of fact, adapted his handwriting to conform in some degree to the model. Most of them showed this tendency to conformity in changing the slant of their writing to make it like that of the model; and those who did not show it

[1] The "jumping Frenchmen" (Canadian French lumberjacks) of the Maine logging camps who, when cold, wet, and desperately fatigued, follow orders with precipitate "snap," show a somewhat similar response.

in the slant showed it in the change in the width of letters (some showed it in both).

From this sort of imitation it is a far cry to those instances in which an animal blunders about until it finally does something similar to that which some other animal has done. The regular procedure of both animals and men who imitate is to stumble and fumble as they would in any learning process.

This form of behavior usually turns out to consist of the following sequence: (1) One animal perceives another performing an act in which some desired object (food, etc.) is part of the situation. (2) The observing animal goes after the desired object by virtue of an innate or a conditioned response to its sight, smell, etc. (3) In going after the object, the animal uses its entire repertory of learned acts, in so far as these have been conditioned to this or a similar situation. (4) If the acts are not immediately successful, a wider and wider range of acts occurs and all the typical characteristics of "trial-and-error" learning may follow.

After the requisite elimination of false starts has been carried through, it is possible, however, to make the imitative act effectively and promptly in the situation which has been the usual stimulus for the behavior. A man who has learned to play the violin can repeat what another plays, or mimic the mannerisms of his teacher. The *imitation itself* under these circumstances does not differ from the simpler conditioned response forms of imitation described above; but the long preliminary practice necessary *to get to a point where imitation is possible* involves a separate set of concepts. Characteristically, this sort of imitation occurs only where a motive is strong, where the learning process narrows down the responses to those which are of a type adequate to satisfy the motive, and where the identity of two animals' behavior is due either to their having some common motive or to one having the motive of doing what the other does. Parrots which are given crackers for saying things which sound like what people say, and people who say things in the manner of those whom they conceive to be their superiors, are illustrations of the last-named process. The psychology

woe as he would to his own (Humphrey'
i.e., he identifies himself with the person.
does not discover that *similarity* to the pe
on the contrary, it is emotion directed tov
child takes over the patterns of behavior of
sometimes those whose strength he envies.
important addition to the theory of sympat
conditioned response explanation; it is a *ma*
of becoming like one's parents and other as
over the culture of the group. Of course th
ditioning, especially by circular response in
will imitate is largely a matter of emotior
course, be another case of "dominance" in
tional imitation may give the right of way t
others, just as we found to be the case
(page 180).

Again, when some resemblance is seen be
other, one responds to him as to oneself
motives to him, exhibits "projection." If or
not too rigidly defined, one may also find ir
in him; this is "introjection." The weak n
leader feels strong. The responses are simil
ditioned response, as formulated in Humph
the emotional factors play a leading rôle.

When a strong shock is experienced, ot
sions are powerless to dispel the effect; w
seems to be hardly more than a case of a
response which, as has been suggested, limit
played by later stimuli. Trauma is, moreov
of the fact that the exact time and circum
may be of the utmost importance for the
There are sensitive moments and dull mc
invulnerable phases in the development of
experience of intense delight or mortifying
to dig deep, to canalize the biologically dor
a way that all these responses compete aga
petitor. The data on earliest memories sup

of learning differs not at all here from the psychology of learning
when one confronts a puzzle box containing some gratifying object.
Imitation of this sort is simply a case in which reward comes, let
us say, not from more effective manipulation of the impersonal
environment, but from such manipulation of it as will bring some
social response.

Where the thing to be imitated has been learned already, sudden
and effective imitation without trial and error may, of course, appear. A good deal of the published evidence for this sort of imitation is, however, unfortunately not supported by life histories of
the individual people or animals involved. For example, evidence
as to imitation among the apes is unaccompanied by life histories
showing what the previous experience of the animals may have
been. The problem of explaining the sudden advent of *new perceptual patterns* (insight) lies, of course, outside of social psychology; but in cases of imitation it is always legitimate to ask just *how
new* the perceptual pattern is.

SYMPATHY

That the conditioned response interpretation serves validly for
many instances of *suggestion* and *imitation* naturally prompts the
question whether it may not serve also for the third of McDougall's
triad, namely, *sympathy.* McDougall presupposes an innate tendency to respond emotionally as those about us respond; the overt
expression of an emotion arouses, by virtue of the innate equipment of the hearer or onlooker, the *same emotion.* On the other
hand, the conditioned response explanation has been clearly worked
out by Humphrey in terms such as these: We burn or scald our
hand; pain and withdrawing instantly follow. The sight of our
hand in this or a similar situation inevitably serves thereafter to
touch off the pain and withdrawing response. Any other hand which
looks like our own will tend, if scalded or burned, to evoke,
promptly enough, the same response in us. To feel horror as we
watch the suffering of another is in no way more mysterious than
to feel horror at our own sufferings. As the theory demands, the

degree of our sympathy depends i
ness which the individual shows t
is black or yellow, his hair kinky,
misery is of less significance to the

Even so, the theory fails to acc
of thresholds as the result of spec
cial antagonisms. Cold-blooded crue
even when inflicted upon individ
to ourselves. Some further explana
for the fact that in some instance
in fact, with joy. Humphrey's gene
as one of capital importance; the
gestion may be blocked by a coun
response may be blocked by some
times very easily. Physical similari
research upon small children, to be
affection, intimacy, or sheer famili
ence (cf. page 100) suggests that lo
a close emotional tie, should make
ally the case.

PSYCHIATRIC FINDINGS ON

While experimental psychology
cept of conditioning in the ways
been observing and clarifying lea
This has resulted, especially amon
and picturesque terminology, with
often been less easily assimilated b
ogy is less important than the be
in a specially favorable position to
consider from the point of view
cepts of identification, projection, i
formation.

If the child or adult sees in an
(of any sort) to himself, he respo

---

and adults monotonously remind us of the importance of single incidents. Phenomena lumped together under the name of trauma have been emphasized by psychiatrists; but many of the positive values and satisfactions likewise owe their central position in personality structure to the unique situation of their original arousal.

Finally, in "reaction formation," the "compromise behavior" which occurs when a repressed and a repressing impulse struggle vainly for complete mastery, the partial conquest of one powerful response tendency by another again exhibits the principle of dominance, but here the pattern is more complicated. The conquered component is sometimes able, despite its defeat, to produce prolonged physiological tension, probably because of a functional splitting of the organism's activity stream, i.e., dissociation, which enables the "repressed" tendency to keep up guerilla warfare against the conqueror. Here, obviously, we are on very insecure ground, and much careful research is needed to clarify the situation.

We have attempted here to interpret the psychiatrist's observations because of his opportunity to study individuals in crucial social situations involving change of behavior; he seems capable of enriching considerably the understanding of the social learning process. One task of the social psychologist is to restate the findings in his own less picturesque terms; but his most important task is to note the realities to which psychiatry points, integrating them with his own observations and approaching them with experimental methods.

CANALIZATION

It has often been assumed that native drives are normally directed upon certain rather specific objects but that in time they are directed upon other objects because of conditioning. Although there is some truth in this generalization, it seems to us to require correction in two important respects. In the first place, even as late as the twelfth month of postnatal life, most human drives are not clearly directed upon specific objects. Even the child's most definite positive tendencies are aroused by a wide range of stimuli, and its fears too may be aroused by widely differing sounds or lights or more or less sudden changes in its outer or inner environment. So, too, fledgling birds start to make nests' out of twigs, string or even strips of paper if these are provided. It is hard to say what the specific adequate stimulus is. Indeed, the question of adequacy of stimulus depends largely upon the degree of excitation of the drive. If, however, the individual has experience in satisfying the drive in relation to one specific kind of stimulation, this stimulus becomes more and more an adequate initiator of the response. Here we have the mechanism for acquired tastes. A wide range of substances in the mouth causes rapid swallowing. In time, however, the infant becomes choosy. He accepts those things to which he has been habituated, and rejects others. Thresholds have been rendered high for stimuli which were originally within the class of adequate stimuli. We do not mean to imply that within the range of original stimuli all are originally equally potent. There are degrees of responsiveness, and in each case experimentation must decide what the most adequate stimuli are; but even the relatively inadequate stimuli near the margin or fringe of the whole class of adequate stimuli may be producing powerful and effective results and become the ones with the lowest threshold. Acquired tastes may occur not only in relation to milk, rhythmical movement or gentle sounds but in relation to beer, olives, jerky movements, and shrill, nasal tones. Individual preferences and general cultural preferences develop by a process of fixation. The drive is channeled or canalized in a specific direction characteristic of the person and of his culture. The name given by French writers to the process by which a non-specific craving is given specific satisfaction is "canalization." We know no better term.

The importance of canalization for the general theory of learning is great. A large number of our social motives are canalized drives, different objects having been fixated in this way in different cultures and in different families in a given cultural area. Whatever the elementary physiological basis for canalization and for the conditioned response, canalization itself as a social process is not conditioning and must not be confused with it. In the canalization process the object first eliciting a drive response, the original or unconditioned reaction, remains the adequate stimulus; there is as yet no entry ·of a *substitute stimulus* or "associative shifting." In the conditioned response a new and frequently adventitious stimulus, entering while an adequate unconditioned stimulus is at work, acquires the power to call out a response. We are inclined to believe that there is enormously less conditioning and more canalization in social life than most writers have recognized. We do not believe, for example, that the love of symphonies or of garlic is due to conditioning. We do not acquire a taste for beer or olives, for golf or politics, solely through conditioning. We start with an interest in food, or tone, or strenuous activity, or the interchange of gestures or facial expressions with our fellows; and these needs, supplemented by many others and guided by cultural processes, give us in time a specific craving for our game of golf or our political argument. We think it worth while to stress that the rudiments of response to tone, taste, smell, and the forms and features of people in the child's immediate world are clearly present and are canalized by social experience until they become fairly definite and fixed. We believe that the breaking of a simple conditioning is often relatively easy, the breaking of a canalized response much harder. Just as the modern biologist has shown that no trait is either hereditary or acquired but is the molded form of a potentiality present in the gene, so we believe that most social responses are neither "inevitable" nor specifically "conditioned," but molded, i.e., largely canalized, responses arising from the complex and sometimes fluid matrix of a vast fund of organic need. The needs may at times become sharply differentiated from one another, but the differentiation of the specific needs from the vague and more general organic need may go far or only a little way. The differentiation of the needs from the original organic matrix seems to be partly a matter of the maturation principle (page 134); but in very considerable degree it is the canalization process, by virtue of which specific objects are repeatedly used in specific social situations, causing a social differentiation and more or less independent functioning of separate need patterns.

It is hard to believe that any habit can be formed while all the rest of the organism remains exactly as it was, or that any process of canalization can occur without involving the whole organism. Indeed, we believe that many conditioning and canalizing forces are normally present at once. For convenience we abstract the more conspicuous phases of the change. As a working hypothesis, we are inclined to believe that every new response involves the relative inhibition of other responses as called for by the general theory of dominance, and that the result of both processes is inevitably the rapid narrowing down of organic potentialities. This must perforce lead to greater and greater specificity of response. As J. E. Anderson has pointed out, the result will inevitably be the individuation of specific responses out of a mass response. It is not the purpose of the present book to discuss the physiological problem of maturation in detail, or to inquire precisely as to the degree to which individuation is a result of interaction with the specific phases of the environment; but it is a part of our task to insist that a large part at least of the social process of individuation of response is manifestly determined by the canalizing properties of the cultural environment.

Canalization of response is here identical with the process which McDougall calls the formation of sentiments and the process which Freud calls fixation. Social psychology owes an immense debt to McDougall for calling attention to the process, but the term sentiment has unfortunately been used generally in literature to describe a tendency to linger over the subtle or plaintive aspects of one's past, and seems very inappropriate. The term fixation is relatively free from objection, and may be used interchangeably with canalization to define this broad process by which thresholds become low for a specific class of stimuli, while they become high for other classes of stimuli within that range.

Canalization is of special importance in the case of aesthetic and activity drives. A wide range of activities may satisfy and in time become potent stimuli for striving activity in the two-year-old child. A wide range of colors and tones evokes his interest and outgoing activity. In time, however, specific stimuli, by sheer frequency and intensity, become the dependable and appropriate mode of evoking the response. In time he wants not merely tone or rhythm, but specific tones and specific rhythms. We have seen instances in which he wants Bach and does not want Tschaikowsky; other instances in which he wants standard nursery songs and not the "folksongs of other nations." He has acquired a taste; he has developed a specific need. The adult in each culture has learned what is good "taste," and has learned to abominate many things which are standardized as good in other cultures. We do not imply that he can *"learn to like anything"*; the delimiting of responses starts within a certain range of tolerance.

This fixation upon certain familiar types of stimuli seems to form the basis for the love of the familiar, the pleasure of recognition and the fundamental conservatism of all who are not too restless to accept the steady round of a familiar existence. Here arises naturally the love of the accepted, the ethnocentrism of the anthropologist, Giddings' broad principle of social unity through "consciousness of kind." All too often it is forgotten, however, that what is familiar may not be like oneself. Dogs of very different breeds may in puppyhood become so attached that dogs of their own kind are "outsiders." The same has been shown for ringdoves reared with carrier pigeons, and for a goose reared with a crow. In the same way, the black, brown, or yellow man reared with a white child may be the object of the latter's chief endearments; and unless barriers imposed by social stratification are present, friendships as deep as any can grow where there is physical dissimilarity. The accepted world is the world of steady, dependable stimulation; and groups may be heterogeneous and homogeneous with respect to any trait, provided only that the reciprocal stimulations are of this order. Here, too, sociometry (page 306) tells a concordant story, for group structures may be made up of most dissimilar individuals. Sometimes, however, sheer familiarity is a major clue (cf. also adience in relation to sympathy, page 188).

The conception of fixation is of special importance for us in the case of those objects in the social world which become the center of *many* needs. Food or music may satisfy a variety of sensory demands. Appetite for one food is not necessarily appetite for all food; the need to dance or to play golf is not simply the need for exercise. Other combinations, other fixations, have complicated the picture. The delight in small replicas of familiar objects, toy trains, dolls, pictures, etc., based partly on pleasures of recognition, partly on the ability to manipulate objects which are often too big to handle, is reinforced by all sorts of other tastes and interests. In time, the five-year-old girl who has played joyously with all such tiny replicas of objects given to her, has found in her dolls a variety of other satisfactions. Her dolls can be dressed and put to bed; they can be hugged and spanked; she lives vicariously in them and, when necessary, becomes the authority who dictates their behavior. Thus the maternal instinct is not just a specific manifestation of an emerging or maturing reflex, but a fixation or canalization in which a great number of aesthetic and activity needs are fused. In time, then, a well-wrought pattern is established, and a clear and well-generalized maternal impulse is formed.

This conception of the complex and labile character of the maternal drive seems to apply to all drives involving affection, devotion or passion in the response between persons. A great deal of outgoing response, frequently rightly called affectionate, is early shown toward parents and toward other social objects, especially if they give warm and gentle contact and become centers for stimulation of the eyes and ears. Watching faces and listening to voices is a prominent feature in a little child's existence. It has become clear from observations upon children that factors ordinarily called sexual enter into this complex of responses. Sometimes this is a matter for reprimand, sometimes for amusement, rarely for quiet and generous explanations of the reality. During the middle childhood period there are so many new things to be done, especially with one's muscles, that the gratification in the sheer presence of another, and the delight in the contact with him, become less prominent. If, however, such delight in presence and contact is marked, the case is regarded as abnormal. The passionate devotion of eight-year-old boys to one another, and the "crush" appearing among girls in early adolescence, are frequently ridiculed or repressed.

In a broad way the sexual factors participate with many others throughout the growth period. With the biological changes which mark adolescence, the sexual tensions and the sexual interest become so much more marked that one popularly pictures the adolescent as changing suddenly from a world of scorn of the other sex to a world of frantic or romantic attachment, of the sort often characterized as puppy love. It must be noted, however, that all the original satisfactions already present in personal and social contact are still present. There is an enormous difference between a response to the active, pretty, stimulating girl who understands and is friendly, or who is smart, well dressed and a good dancer, and the kind of thing properly described by biologists as a sex drive. A great deal of confusion has been introduced here not only by Freud but by standard writers on sex education who have attempted to transplant the physiological drive of the albino rat to the picture of human social response. Human responses include, of course, the massive and often disorganized physiological sex disturbances; they may have all degrees of *naïveté* or sophistication, and may be combined in all degrees of subtlety and in all forms of weighting with all the other factors of personal response which have come down from the first years. Ethnologists confuse the sophomore by telling him that romantic love is unknown to the Zulu, the Periclean Greek or the Chinese literati. The term romantic has, however, different meanings when applied to the Song of Solomon, the medieval courts of love, the *Sonnets from the Portuguese*, and the vagaries of contemporary Hollywood. The individual person is equipped with broad potentialities of response to other persons, both of his own sex and of the other sex. The aesthetic, the tender, the sentimental, the generous, the masterful, the sadistic—all of them names for complex and fleeting tendencies—may combine with the physiological sex interest; and, indeed, we suspect that the physiological sex interest is itself a composite of many factors given different weight and direction in different cultures. In our own culture it is clear that the need of acceptance and recognition in an age of competition and insecurity combines with the delight in beauty of line and voice, complexion and adornment, to form a nucleus in that chaotic and vaguely bounded experience which goes by the name of falling in love. The marriage counselor and the teacher of hygiene sometimes conspire to tell the adolescent solemn facts learned from natural history, but often find that specific lessons presented verbally and dealing for the most part with the rather simple behavior of the lower forms of life will help the individual only little to understand his own problems. A great deal of the process by which the various ill-defined driving forces within a person fuse and combine is not understood by the person himself, and is only with great difficulty put into verbal terms. Literature and history, largely because they say so much between the lines, often do greater justice to the social reality which is to be lived.

We have insisted that at the descriptive level conditioning and canalization be kept distinct; and for most purposes the social psychologist may avoid deeper theorizing about the physiological mechanisms of the organism. There are, nevertheless, some points at which a working theory of the organism is necessary, and we venture a brief attempt at an interpretation of canalization and conditioning in terms of a common physiological principle.

The term "canalization" has been extensively used, notably by Holt, to denote the processes by which an afferent impulse discharges into an efferent system which is already active. Just as a stream of water, wandering aimlessly, must, upon reaching a canal, follow the lines given by the banks of the canal, so an excitation in the central nervous system must discharge through a system which is already discharging. This is the basis for the reflex cycle, presumably functioning in the embryonic period, and also for the later conditioned reflexes as used by Pavlov.

If it be true that any stimulus whatever has a tendency to contribute energy which leads to outgoing impulses from the centers to the muscles, so that a new stimulus is likely to follow exactly those paths which are already being excited, canalization and conditioning are both aspects of a general principle. In any canalization process a complex stimulus like milk or music involves some features which are at first irrelevant to the response as we are now using the term. These irrelevant features, acting as aspects of a totality along with features which are at first adequate, may be said to function by virtue of conditioning. We may even go further than this and argue, if we wish, that the original adequacy of some aspects of the canalizing stimulus is due to the fact that they are normally present very early along with stimuli which must perforce produce the response. Let us consider a clear and simple case. We have mentioned the child's quest for milk when hungry as a case of canalized rather than conditioned response. The general disturbance in a very hungry infant produces a great many random movements including a sucking movement. Under ordinary conditions of social life milk is introduced at the very time when the reflex cycle is manifest in the repeated contractions of the lips. The milk is adequate in the sense that it puts an end to the inner disturbance and, therefore, to the random movements including the lip movements. The process of beginning to suck when the bottle is brought near is clearly a case of conditioning in the ordinary sense, and it is possible that the entire process by which milk becomes a canalized satisfier is based ultimately on the reflex cycle. But whatever the ultimate physiology of the response, canalization is a form of behavior so specific and so important as to require separate treatment.

The Formation of Values

When the process of fixation is complete, so that we are set to achieve an object meeting a need, we may properly say that a *value* is formed; and we should like to suggest that there is no further mystery in the psychology of values. A value is as definite a thing as a light or a stone. If human nature is the plastic thing which we believe it to be, values thus formed are not "relative" but absolute, in so far as any organic response of an organism is absolute rather than relative. The *value world* of a given organism is the *world of objects to which it is fixated*. We do not need the concept of sublimation to explain a taste for music, poetry, gossip, religion, poker, or politics; and to us the distinction between immediate biological needs and socially derived needs becomes meaningless. The degree of *urgency* involved in a value when one wants lamb chops and alligator pears and when one wants Stravinsky may be the same. The urgency of the food need may be great;

but if we forget the white rat for the moment and look squarely at the man, we find that in many cultures the music need may be far more compelling for many persons and at many times, than is the food need. The strength of a need, as we have suggested, is partly dependent upon the degree of its frustration, but it is also partly dependent upon the duration and the specificity of the fixation. Granted that the taste for Stravinsky is acquired, so are all other tastes. There are no simple, clear, *specific* adequate stimuli for any drive whatever. The originally adequate stimuli are undefined and vague. Children like food, tone, and light. In time, milk, "The Arkansas Traveller" and a shining tea cup become "acquired tastes" or, more simply, values.

For our purpose a value is thus simply the maintenance of a set toward the attainment of a goal; the term is especially useful when the goal is remote. The term is not used when the individual blindly gropes, he knows not why, for something or other, he knows not what. After discovering an object through trial and error and relieving one's tension, one may in time come to foresee it as a result of a certain line of activity. When it is definitely foreseen it is a value. A negative value is an object toward which there is aversion instead of a seeking tendency. It is important to recall that in the case of many organic needs no effort is required of us except that we stay put where we are. To the lover of a Beethoven symphony a quiet posture and closed eyes may be all that is required. To the conceited man a mirror reflection may be all-sufficient. In these cases the concept of effort toward a goal is irrelevant, but the concept of set toward the object is essential.

The question arises whether an object should be called a value when it is being approached or contemplated, or only when it is being appropriated by the organism so as to put an end to a craving. Usage is all in favor of applying the term to the former situation. We value much which we cannot now have, and a good deal which we shall never have. Value is a statement of preparation for a response, and frequently at the symbolic level an inner preparation which involves no direct approach toward the object. The 80-year-old mother who longs for an occasional visit from her 50-year-old son who seldom comes to see her, exhibits a value varying only slightly in intensity from day to day. In some cases the object ceases indeed to be of value for a short time after satisfaction of the drive—for example, the taste of food after a good meal. In general, however, value is applied to more or less *constant* needs resulting from the fixation process. The term seems to involve a paradox when we yearn for something which we cannot have and which is therefore a source of unmitigated and constant distress to us. But value must be defined not as a satisfier, but as a *potential satisfier* capable of producing chronic adient responses to all symbols which suggest it.

If the absent stimulus situation is a value and if objects which have once been fixated either directly or symbolically tend to remain fixated, we have a clue not only to perseveration but to the broader phenomenon known as autistic thinking. One clings to that which has been set up symbolically; one plays with it, giving it new form from day to day by allowing it to canalize itself more and more deeply. Having ridden the merry-go-round or successfully made a speech, one goes on with the process for days, thereafter altering the situation slightly and enriching it in memory by fusing with it other values, more or less analogous, which have arisen in more or less similar situations. One lives in the past as much at the age of three as at thirty.

The notion of autism as "pleasurable thinking" is not needed here and is indeed a nuisance in this connection. One reverts to *any* experience which has been vivid and intense. Indeed, one lives through old worries and disappointments although they have no further relevance to today's tasks, unless indeed the disturbance from such perseverating thoughts leads to a generalized random effort in new directions, a trial-and-error excursion into other autistic channels.

Moreover, if the first experiences have been social rather than simply personal, the reinforcing effect of other persons' activities will tend to make them recur all the more. One relives one's experiences in the group; one goes back mentally to the "old familiar faces." As in Sherif's experiments (page 220), one continues afterward, when alone, to relive the group experience, the symbols from past experience, blended with the immediate stimuli of the moment.

The differentiation between social attitude and value is, we believe, quite arbitrary. In current usage an attitude is usually simply a set for or against, toward or away from, an object or person, or toward or away from a line of conduct. Attitude and value are ultimately the same thing. There is, however, a practical distinction to be made. Value is frequently not mediated by words and may have all degrees of clarity for verbal communicability; attitude usually means today the valuing tendencies as expressed through verbal responses. No one, for example, would spontaneously refer to cardiac and respiratory changes while viewing motion pictures as attitude measurements. No one would think of the galvanic skin reflex in response to horror scenes as attitude measurement. If one asked the same subject whether he liked or disliked, approved or disapproved of the pictures one would be making attitude measurement. Since the verbalized responses are never sharply separated within an organism, and since the verbal partially determines the visceral and the visceral partly determines the verbal, it is clear that in the biology of the organism attitudes are not independent of other life activities. The mode of expression is, however, distinctive, and the registering of a value tendency through expressions of verbal approval and disapproval has justified for practical purposes a separate treatment of attitude measurement.

Conflict and Integration of Values

The pursuit of two or more values may be an integrated act. Indeed, the organism takes on as many values as it may and uses the attainment of one goal as a springboard for the attainment of another, or in moments of frustration finds a new world of values to be explored. Values then may be integrated in so far as the organism finds a positive relation among them and especially if it finds that a given act advances it in the quest for many values. Other values, however, are lost while one is being pursued. Conflict of values results when the same activity which leads toward one makes the achievement of another more difficult. The term "organization of values" involves both a positive and a negative definition. All values tend to be integrated except those which unsuccessfully compete with the stronger ones because they would if pursued deflect the organism from the major goals. Among these various positive values, at first very loosely integrated, some become more powerful, more coercive than others; these become central values, as contrasted with marginal or peripheral values.

As far as we can see, the process by which some values are renounced and the process by which one favored value becomes central is simply the process of biological dominance described at some length above. Competition between stimuli, we saw, rarely gives rise to complete chaos. Characteristically, a biologically less dominant stimulus loses the control of those action systems which at first it commanded and in time may even contribute its energy to augment that of the dominant action pattern. When a choice must be made even at the *naïve* level of achieving chocolate and avoiding electric shock, the organism "chooses." The powerful pattern defeats and eliminates the competitor. When the choice must be absolute, weaker values are biologically crowded out; and when among the integrated values a central value is aroused, woe betide those other positive values which tend in any way to interfere. They may at times be wiped off the map, as was Darwin's love of poetry when his mind had been schooled to reverence only the ways of exact science. One value may involve a set which is antagonistic to the development of another value, or, indeed, completely block it. The hesitating intellectual to whom doubt has become unpleasant may seek a systematization of values in Roman Catholicism or in orthodox Marxism; he can hardly espouse both. One value system is rejected in favor of the other; the tension is resolved. And if the theory of dominance is sound, the energy originally playing between two fields is all thrown in the direction of one. The specially violent anti-Catholic or anti-Communist should be found exactly among those who have been torn between the rival systems, or those in whom earlier value systems which delayed or confused the decision have been renounced. Personality is at peace when the energies of the enemy have been drawn out, when the deserters from the enemy camp have joined the forces of the new day, the new and unified world outlook of the convert.

But life processes are usually irreversible; and this is a fact of social psychology as much as it is a fact of biochemistry. Patterns of conditioning and reconditioning do not follow in endless labile succession. Values once formed are not dislodged except by more potent values, and they become involved with new values at each point in the growth process. Increasing specificity of response and increasing complexity of values produce, in time, reasonably dependable structures and reasonably definite patterns of personality.

De Sanctis has brilliantly described the nature of this process in a technical discussion of religious conversion. Replying to the frequent assertion that the energies displayed in a religious conversion are simply sexual energies, he says that our knowledge regarding the nature of sexual maturation and of the learning processes would involve, on this basis, a serious contradiction of terms. Growth and learning mean increase in specificity, and the road cannot be retraveled. Values have formed more or less as branches and twigs have formed from the original trunk; the twigs do not grow into branches and the branches into a new trunk again, higher up. The sexual energies of the adult are not the broad, free, diffuse cravings of the child. The individual who has gone through thirty years of normal growth, maturation, and learning cannot often regress in the simple way characteristic of the child who is frustrated; he cannot go back to the primitive diffuse uncanalized energies of the little child, except by finding a powerful stimulus which once had compelling value for him as a little child and which since that time has remained in abeyance. If and when such a compelling childhood situation can be relived, but in no other case, can the person undergo a return to the simplicity and conviction of childhood. He may, in a deep and fundamental sense, be converted. The longing to be a child again, on account of the confusion and frustration of adult life, is based on the need for simple unconfused values as they prevail in childhood, but can be fulfilled only when the individual succeeds in finding a situation like that of the religious world as presented to him when on his mother's knee. If one wishes to call all the value-seeking tendencies of the little child sexual, one may say that the sources of religious conversion lie in infantile sexuality; but if one means that a relatively specific adult sexuality can find a sublimated outlet in the specific objects of religious faith, one loses the real pattern of the maturation sequence and, in particular, of the highly specific nature of adult fixations.

Since values cannot possibly exist in separate pigeonholes of the individual but tend to reinforce or to contend with one another, it seems correct to speak of the organization of values in a *system*. If the organization becomes more and more tightly knit, new values have a harder and harder time in establishing themselves except in terms of fitting into the system. When adulthood is reached, physiological stability achieved, and the personal system of values oriented toward adult problems, a regression to a more flexible childish condition is rarely possible. Indeed, possibility of regression depends upon sheer renouncement of many adult values. "Acting like a baby" defines the hysterical collapse of self-control and the schizophrenic or senile movement back to a simpler and less confusing value world. Except under conditions of very great physiological stress or degeneration, or conditions of very great shock to the organism, such regression cannot occur. All the more precious is that special device by which men and women play at being children, get down on the floor and participate in the block-building or toy-train activities of their youngsters, or allow themselves in a relaxed moment to relive sentimentally their own childhood scenes. Even when such behavior is on a purely make-believe level, with relatively little inner conviction, it constitutes a partial inhibition of the disturbing elements in the adult valuing system.

Clinical literature has usually suggested that the fundamental trouble in all cases of personality disturbance is conflict of instinct; in particular, conflict between the need for affection and expression, on the one hand, and the fear or rage patterns on the other hand. While such conflict does patently occur and has been actually seen in fluoroscopic analysis of the behavior of the digestive tract, we believe the conflict of instincts to be rare, and the physiology of the matter obscure. For social purposes, what is important is usually not the conflict of instinct, but the conflict of value. A man is interested in two fields of work; loves both his parents, though they

stand for different ways of life; loves two women and must renounce the love of one; tries to find leisure time for two hobbies,
and discovers that he can afford only one. The conflict between two
value tendencies, even when both objects—as in the case of the
hobbies—may be similar, suggests that it is not a blocking in the
motor outlet that makes the trouble, but rather the social definition
of goal, and the social implications involved in the pursuit of each
goal. So, too, it is the integration or confusion of values rather than
the integration or confusion of instincts—whatever that might
mean—that constitutes the basis of the integration of personality.

The setting up of two values which cannot both be achieved at
the same time, the quest for one of them interfering with the quest
for the other, is a characteristic feature of human activity. The
familiar picture, given to us by the psychiatrist, of the child who
wants the affection of both of his quarreling parents or who wants
the jam in the cupboard and also his mother's approval, involves
an inner strain or conflict, the germ of a neurosis. It is ordinarily
assumed that conflicts between two or more goal tendencies or,
very broadly, conflict of values, is a purely human phenomenon.
Guthrie, however, has suggested a simple way of looking at the
matter, based on experimental studies of learning processes in cats.
A cat which by injury had been negatively conditioned to a pole in
the puzzle box discovered, nevertheless, that knocking against the
pole was the means of escape from the box. Thus, it spent most
of its time trying to brush against the pole without touching it!
This seems to be the typical neurotic behavior of the individual who
reaches toward a desired object which is also for him an object
under taboo.

Even under stable or static social conditions the child acquires
this sort of conflicting value tendencies. Under conditions of social
change or of personal adaptation to a new culture, this kind of
stress is especially common. In a study of two generations of Italian groups in the United States, statistical analysis of homicide
rates showed clearly a very low rate in the first generation (Italian-
born living in the United States), a very high rate in the second,
for the same offense. In the south Italian or Sicilian family of
the first generation, the value designated "family honor" is pro-

tected by force when necessary. Disruption of the social pattern under conditions of American life leads to offenses against family honor which in the second generation are avenged in the traditional way. In the third generation most of the attitudes and habits of the original group have been redefined, and probably approximate closely the general American pattern. There are *two* values to be maintained by the second group, loyalty to the old values and to the new ("law-abiding" habits). It is exactly in this second group that neurotic tension should be high; for, if the double system of values does not lead to crime, as defined by the larger social world, it can at least lead to conflicting impulses, and this seems in fact to be the evidence of court and clinic.

The acquisition of value patterns depends so profoundly upon the orientation toward life that a *single* fresh experience may accomplish far more than months of intensive repetition. A five-year-old had been taught by both parents for some months to help mother in household duties. Results were barely, if at all, positive. A discerning school teacher, seeing that the boy's one need in life was to get expression for his urge to paint, turned him loose one morning on the job of doing mural paintings for the classroom. In beaming joy he covered some two dozen square feet of paper fastened on the wall. Rushing home that noon in rapture, he burst into the living-room and asked if he might "help mother." The social psychologist has suffered from the general blindness of all psychology in regarding transfer of training as a matter depending primarily upon visible external stimulus-response relations. Inner patterns—spontaneous response, if you like, to the internal environment—may overwhelm and utterly dissipate patterns which at first seemed compelling. The reeducation of the hysteric, the spontaneity training of the delinquent, the everyday kindling of enthusiasms in dull children by imaginative teachers point to the more complex aspect of learning in social situations. Not only are individual situations all-important. If we are to describe the abstract laws of social learning, we must know also the differences between families in gusto and heartiness of living; the differences between occupational groups in terms of spontaneity and changeability of mood; the differences between the same cultural group before, during, and after a time of crisis and transition; and the differences between widely diverse cultures in respect to the way in which external stimulating factors are accepted, organized, and given definition by the individual as something to respond to.

DEVELOPMENT OF THE SELF

One of the most important things the child ever learns as a result of social contacts is that he is a person, a self. The process of making this discovery is so important that its general nature must be roughly sketched, even though on several important points the evidence is still confused and incomplete.

To watch the mother's face, to hear her voice, to be cheered by her ministrations, involves much more than the focusing of attention upon her. It is not sufficient to say that the mother is an object of supreme interest to the child. The mother is the chief object to which a growing *devotion* can be given, a center of primitive intense affection. The need for affection and the need for someone upon whom to bestow affection are both realized in this unique object in the environment. It is largely through her that the child learns *what a person is* as contrasted with a *thing*; learns what life is as contrasted with the inanimate; learns about spontaneity or capriciousness; learns about valuation through her valuation of what he does. From such material as this, compared with similar observations of his father and other members of his family, he forms his notion of how persons differ. At six or eight months he has certainly formed no clear notion of himself. He does not even know the boundaries of his own body. Each hand wandering over the bedspread for things which can be brought into the mouth discovers the other hand and each triumphantly lifts the other into his mouth; he draws his thumb from his mouth to wave it at a stranger, then cries because the thumb has gone away. He pulls at his toes until they hurt and does not know what is wrong. He regards his face in the mirror and tries to grasp the image.

There are evidences that the self, the ego, is based primarily on two kinds of experiences: first, the use of proper names and pronouns when holding him responsible for this, or rewarding him for that; second, the first vague conception of a person as seen in his mother, is carried over to his observations of himself. What with seeing himself in the mirror, noticing the similarity of his voice to that of others, or observing the whole body as he sits or lies, he forms an idea of himself, partly on the analogy of other selves. The analogy is rough and vague, and the child does not know that it is an analogy. Whatever the mother is, thinks and feels, and whatever he is, thinks and feels, tend to be more or less confused. As Piaget so well shows, the child of three or four assumes that others see the world as he does; his mother feels about things as he does. All the more painful is the shock of discovery that this assumption makes trouble. For a long time, however, it is inevitable and natural that he "identify" himself with the mother or with whatever other persons are near and dear. It is quite fatuous to ask whether he really "believes himself to be his mother" when he does as she does, or "believes himself to be daddy" when he puts on daddy's hat and announces "I am daddy," or to ask whether he "half believes" this or "just pretends" it. The child does not live in any such world as the one of disjunctive realities which we try to force upon him. Analogies come and go; the world is a phantasy and has its own reality; it is not clear reality *plus* make-believe.

The child's self is formed while he is in this process of almost literally flowing into the personalities about him; the ego, or self, is partly made out of these images and attitudes which well within him as he watches and becomes absorbed in the activity about him. He may at a later age reject the opinions of his parents, he may storm against authority and conservatism; but much of the earlier pattern of the ego is formed at a time when self-criticism is out of the question and the personality is utterly impotent to reconstruct itself by hewing away those aspects which arise from primitive identification.

For all these reasons the influence of the parents is overwhelmingly important. It is quite beside the point to stress the value of rewards and punishments; what the parent is speaks far more loudly than the techniques which he employs. The techniques, in fact, have vitality and produce results in so far as they are genuine expressions of the parents' view of the world, but it is doubtful whether they have much more. What the child learns from its parents it learns mostly not by being taught, but by being exposed.

If this analysis is sound, the argument applies to the entire range of face-to-face contacts. Just as the mirth or disgust of the indifferent chimpanzee sends a wild contagion of mirth or disgust through the group which has not seen the original cause of the emotion, so the child assimilates the feelings of those about him by a process which, on its objective side, is the circular response, but which has its all-important subjective aspect in the fact of primitive identification.

It is for this reason that the primary group, or, as Cooley calls it, the face-to-face group, in which the child grows up is of vastly more importance for social growth than the more distant secondary groups of city, state and nation, or fellowship in a religious denomination with international membership, or a sense of belonging to some ancient and honorable brotherhood. Deep as the American's respect for the flag may be, the roots of the respect have to be laid in attitudes toward the family and the neighborhood group with whom one first takes part in patriotic exercises. Deep as one's devotion to Roman Catholicism may be, it must be rooted first of all in devotion to what is learned at the mother's knee.

The secondary group, nevertheless, has increasing importance as the child grows. One becomes more and more aware of distinct personalities, distinct trends. The modern child's world of motion pictures and radios, funnies and tabloids makes him more and more aware of the great uniform world of American life which lies beyond. Indeed, with the increasing uniformity of American ways and the increasing centralization of the influence expressed in Hollywood movies and New York City broadcasts, the secondary group makes its impress with more and more compelling authority.

The thing known as the self is a selection and organization of experiences involving the visceral tensions, muscular strains, the sound of one's name, one's mirror image, and so on; and the thing which knows this pattern is simply the organism as a whole. If this is correct, it is easy to see that the self, being a primary source of many satisfactions, *must inevitably become a value*. The self is something which we like and from which we expect much. If this simple conception of the self as a value is sound, it becomes possible to eliminate with one stroke the supposed antithesis between Freud's conception of narcissism or self-love as a basis for vanity or craving for status, and the traditional associationist view that we are pleased by prestige, status or flattery because thereby we become more likely to obtain concrete rewards which we desire. Adient responses toward parts of our own body and toward our own voices and mirror images develop parallel with the awareness that the self is the thing which will have to be enhanced, assisted and rewarded if we, as organisms, are to live abundantly and satisfyingly. The special instinct, vanity, as a basis for the craving for status, vanishes into thin air, as have so many other specific instincts.

The less intelligent animals, incapable of making a clear perceptual pattern of themselves, in contradistinction to the pattern of the outer world, should on this basis develop no need for flattery, no craving for status. Indeed, the very lowest grade of mental defectives should be innocent of all cravings for prestige. This seems to agree with the facts; whereas, on the more simple instinctivist basis, the absence of a vanity drive among idiots might entail difficulties.

It may also be noted that if the *external world* becomes overpoweringly important in times of crisis or exaltation, the ego as an empirical object may disappear from view; and this seems to us to be a very simple explanation of those dissociated states experienced by drowning persons or the aviator in peril, who have lived for a few moments literally without an ego; or of the mystical experience of the music-lover who in a rapt moment is utterly identified with the music, floats out into the sound that pulses through the orchestra hall, and a few moments later, finding himself again in his seat, wonders "how the *ego* can ever merge with the *alter*." From the present point of view, the ego never does merge with the alter; it simply becomes blocked out as any object not essential for adjustment may be blocked out of the field of awareness.

As the primitive, vague, ill-defined awareness of personal identity gives place to a more well-defined experience, as the individual learns where his own existence stops and the rest of the world begins, the self in the accepted narrow sense is born and becomes an *empirical object* toward which the attitudes of the organism are built up, just as attitudes are built up toward anything else. The self is lovable; it is also hateful; it is something to guard and protect against injury; it is also something to be disparaged, condemned and punished. Parental attitudes and the attitudes of playmates and other associates toward oneself are partially assimilated. He whom his parents consider a good boy finds it easy to live the part of good boy. The self is given a place, a status, a character part to play. It becomes in time the center of a powerful sentiment in McDougall's sense, a variety of drives being canalized upon it. It must be enhanced, yet not enhanced too much. If it approaches too close to being a supreme value, the individual expects more of himself than he can achieve and must take endless punishment in consequence; he is, moreover, classified as a snob, an egotist, a self-flatterer. As far as we can see, the process of making an important value out of the ego and of setting its task in relation to a level of achievement differs in no fundamental respect from the task of value formation elsewhere in the social life. Suppose one sets a standard for a vacation in terms of ocean cruises or Florida sands but dares not hope for a trip around the world lest the pressure of reality make the daydream too painful. One thinks in terms of a piano for his home, but not a "concert grand" unless the means at hand come within the range of conceivable fulfillment of the fantasy. But in all spheres of life the fantasy level and the reality level have to be kept in some form of adjustment. And to this the ego is no exception.

The self is not only a value; it is a unique sort of value. It not only represents an immediate object of importance but is also a symbol which stands for many other values which may in time be achieved. When one says that he hopes he is a good enough teacher or bridge-player or diplomat to be successful in new adventures, he relies upon the characteristics of his empirical self, the self as he knows it, to bring other good things within his reach. It is in this sense that the self can properly be called a central or organizing value.

It follows from this that one's views of himself must be reasonably consistent and unified. One must not expect of it too many conflicting achievements. To expect of the self that which is impossible, either because the self is quantitatively inadequate to the achievement, or because the various standards set up for the ego are incompatible, is to lead to certain disappointments. In laboratory situations the ego has been found characteristically to function at a certain level of adequacy. One thinks of himself as just so good. One is sure that he is able to do fourteen problems in the next ten-minute interval. This is the "ego level" of the person. At the same time, there is an aspiration level—not the highest level imaginable, but the level which the organism sets as its goal and toward which it hopes it may possibly rise. The aspiration level is not set absurdly far beyond the ego level. The ego level is kept as high as it can be kept. The organism wants more than it conceives itself able to achieve. It constantly readjusts the two levels in the light of experience so that the ego level may be kept as close as possible to the aspiration level but yet never so close as to produce the shock of disappointment on sober recognition that the ego is not as good as one had hoped. The image of oneself is maintained in one form or another as a guide or standard, the contemplation of which is satisfying; and one maintains at the same time a furtive pretense at functioning at a level a little above. (Individual differences in ego level will be discussed in connection with competition in Chapter VII.)

This is not to deny the very important fact that the ego may, when it fails us, become an object of distress, humiliation or scorn. Disparagement of oneself need not always be a bid for flattery. One may quite seriously find one's empirical self a frail tool in achieving other values which are vital, and turn one's scorn upon it as we do upon other frail tools which fail us in a pinch. Attack upon the self appears indeed to be the first of a series of more and more violent efforts which in so many cases lead to suicide. The counselor or the psychiatrist may literally be able to create a fresh ego, a new empirical self, toward which an attitude of acceptance or complacency may develop.

Another of the "fundamental instincts," that of shame, seems plausibly reducible, in part, to the discovery of the failure of the ego as a means to other values and therefore, by implication, its own relative worthlessness. If by identification with another person one joins in the disapprobation of oneself which is evident in the behavior of others, one has a deeper chagrin. The pattern of shame, frustration of the ego-valuing tendency, thus exerts an effect differing from that attending the frustration of all other values. The frustration of all other values permits the organism to try a new activity, to start off in a new direction. But the ego, as we have seen, is not only a true value in itself, but the means by which most other values are served, the central instrument by which social expectations are to be fulfilled. When the ego fails, the primary support for positive living is lost. Vasomotor and other indices of internal collapse might be expected; and they often occur.

This, we think, is part of the truth; yet it certainly does *not* cover all the ground. Dejection, resignation, sheer giving up, the carpenter's shrug of his shoulders when he finds that his tools will not make the door which he has been asked to make, the bored man's tendency to fall asleep when it is evident that there is nothing interesting to be found in a social situation, are also effective means of handling the situation when no way remains to find any value in it. There is something positive about *shame* which belies any attempt to treat it as a special case of a submissive tendency or a sheer absence of positive satisfaction. Even in that minor form which we call embarrassment, the picture is far from clear. Why is it bad form or, indeed, unendurable for one to sit face to face with another and look into his eyes while he stares into yours? The tiny child, long before he has shown most of the ego manifestations to which Freud and Piaget refer, averts his eyes and shows various signs of discomfort when the stranger looks straight at him. If it is true, as we have suggested, that the structure of the ego is a cardinal problem for any understanding of man in society, the study of the sense of shame would seem to be one of the primary tasks for the immediate future. An extraordinary amount of what the civilized man does is done mostly to "keep up appearances," to be one of the fellows, i.e., be "beyond reproach" and shame.

Other responses to frustration are also very illuminating in relation to the way in which the ego functions. The frustration of any drive does a great deal more to the organism than merely to block it in its efforts. Failure to achieve a goal does not leave the organism either quiescent or subdued; the organism turns restlessly to new efforts or turns its attention to new values. If it turns inward, withdraws into its shell, one may say that the *inner world is a value* which may take up part of the slack and give satisfaction in its own right. In particular, the ego is discovered more clearly and enjoyed more fully when one gives one's attention to it. As the three-year-old failing to get the celluloid duck sucks his thumb, the adult failing to get a promotion contemplates the good talk that he gave to the club last spring. Frustration is a key not merely to change in direction but to the sudden rediscovery of old values.

Similarly, the concept of *defense*, first introduced by the psychoanalysts, has for us much more than a negative significance. Whatever is valuable is to be defended, one's possessions, one's friends, one's good name, one's inner picture of oneself. What the psychoanalysts call a defense mechanism is almost invariably a defense of the ego, that is, a device by which the organism keeps the picture of the ego untainted. Defense is a function carried out not *by* the ego but on behalf of the ego, and carried out, as are all efforts toward a value, by the organism as a whole. Onslaughts upon the ego are met with the techniques suitable for the defense of many cherished objects, but adjusted to the needs of the moment. The ego is defended not only against the attack of other persons in the environment but against the organism's own critical judgments. One learns in time the painfulness of self-criticism; one learns not to see oneself as one is. Having gradually built up an evaluating attitude toward the ego and having at the same time learned how much it hurts to look straight at the ego with an honest eye, one then learns to harmonize one's needs to see oneself in a pleasing form. Accepting social demands and "interiorizing" these demands in the form of "self-respect," one maintains the fiction of direct self-awareness. Having committed this legerdemain upon oneself, one then asks that the gods permit him to see himself as others see him.

But we must look more closely at this "inner" world, the world of thought and fantasy in which the ego plays so large a rôle. For the most part, we have been content to regard values as external objects. The self is not at first "inside"; as the child first learns to know it, it is the body. In time, however, as Piaget has shown, the ego is referred "inward." As language and the system of images develop, the child builds up an "inner world" in contrast to the "outer world." As the words and gestures which symbolize social reality are given less overt expression, he learns to maintain orientation to the world and to himself by an inner system of signaling. Whether this inner system is largely verbal or not is immaterial to the present issue. The essential point is that the social controls which in the very small child are external to the organism are, in the older individual, largely interiorized. Throughout his working hours the individual signals to himself as to the direction to be taken, the right vs. the wrong, the wise vs. the foolish. We do not, however, mean to imply that this process is carried out with full consciousness. In fact, what was said above regarding subliminal conditioning applies with a vengeance to the complex process of maintaining a direction through the day's work. The impulses to act are frequently touched off by inner signals too faint to be noticed: "I don't know why I did that." Subliminal cues, new outlooks on life, new insights into problems come constantly out of an inner void which has long baffled investigation. An intensely interesting suggestion regarding the nature of this void from which impulse and thought arise has been recently published by Max. Records of action currents from the muscles of deaf-mutes who are "thinking with their fingers" as they solve arithmetic problems show that the electrical activity by no means ceases at the point where consciousness fades out. Conscious solution of the problem is indeed accompanied by marked electrical activity in the appropriate muscles which control the fingers. But a certain amount of effective thinking arises from activity under conditions which literally justify the term "imageless thought." The subject cannot tell that his muscles are moving. Least of all could he tell whence the idea came to him or why he reached the given decision. He responds from moment to moment to signals given by weak muscular responses. The proprioceptive system is shot through and through with after-effects of previous response to signals. In other words, conditioned kinesthetic responses make up a large part of the core of impulsive and irrational behavior predisposing to an extraordinary range of social responses for which no adequate supra-liminal stimulus is to be found. Civilized man is, we think, to an extraordinary degree a proprioceptive animal whose culture, once a part of his external world, is now a part of his bodily make-up, functioning with equal freedom at levels known and levels unknown to his personal awareness.

LEARNING TO PERCEIVE

The world to which the child is introduced is a world of complex and multitudinous impressions, a world of sound, touch and pain, a world of stress and relaxation. Much that is sharp and clear to the adult is confused or undifferentiated to the child. There is probably always a figure and a ground, probably an endless *selection* from the whirl and welter of impressions. We know, however, neither the mechanism of selection nor the content selected, except in so far as behavior at the moment or thereafter reveals it.

This first world of the child is certainly not a social world in any true psychological sense. The mother's face is responded to just as a light is responded to. The mother's voice is responded to in about the same way as any other sound of equal volume. From the flux of impressions pouring in through the senses all the time, some aspects must be chosen and emphasized. The choice is largely in terms of aspects of experience which help or hinder the activity in progress; these are selected over all that is irrelevant to social activity. The mother's preparations for nursing are soon selected in this way; they lead to the cessation of crying and the appearance of a smile. The selection is not, as a rule, the selection of isolated elements but of related organized features of experience. One signal indicating specific satisfying experience about to be realized is, for example, a pattern including eyes, nose and mouth. The patterns of things as they are must in time be recognized as patterns because they function in this way. The social world, then, is given accent in terms of what it means for our own organic activity, and the accent usually falls upon patterns, clusters of experienced qualities which regularly recur together.

Abundant material on early perception is offered in the investigations of Bühler and her associates, who have ascertained the first symbolic values which voices and faces have for the child. These investigations show at the same time the very early structuring of the world in terms of stable clusters of qualities. If not in the first week, at least in the first three weeks, the mother's voice is consistently recognized. By six weeks, the human voice in general, which at birth had only a noise value, has become more provocative of response than sounds of tearing paper, banging spoons and the like, having equal or greater volume. Auditory discrimination proceeds apace.

A long delay is evident in visual discrimination because of the sheer slowness of development of the visual apparatus. The failure of the eye to focus appropriately for distance means that clear vision is quite impossible in the first few weeks. To reach for what one sees is difficult when the world of sight is mostly a world of blur. There are, of course, many other factors involved in the gradual development of the capacity to grasp for seen objects (a capacity usually evident at four or five months). Faces, however, are not distinguished from one another even at six or seven months of age. The sudden advent of shyness appearing so frequently in children of eight or nine months is almost certainly due to the beginning of *discrimination between faces*. The child has previously accepted the attention of all adults who treat him gently. Near the end of the first year he begins to mark off sharply the familiar and the strange.

Much of the process of learning to group and organize impressions is still easily observed in the adult. In a surface covered with scattered dots or in the panoply of the heavens one may see various and changing patterns or constellations. Patterns vary with the person and with the occasion, but they are all patterns limited by the material. Different persons and different cultures select and organize and give their own meanings to such material. The same stars which for the Egyptians were a Wagon, for the Romans Seven Oxen, for the Arabs the Great Bear, present material which in fact

consists of a schema for each of these things. The social definition
of reality is not the arbitrary imposing of subjective caprice; it is
the fulfillment of one specific reality partly given in the material.

An experimental illustration from Calley will be helpful. On the
surface of a piece of paper one observes with rigid fixation the development of a definite grain of vertical or horizontal lines or indeed
of diagonals or curved lines. By changing the mental set one sees
on the surface of the paper a flower or a death's head. These patterns are as objective as is the whole piece of paper itself. If the
material is taken to the testing laboratory the physicist reports an
extremely complex, mottled surface of tiny protuberances and hol-
lows, thousands of high and low points. There are, then, in the
"smooth surface" plenty of vertical, horizontal, oblique and curved
lines. All that is necessary is to select and to reject, to see certain
patterns and to remain blind to others. The individual sees what he
wants to see, not in the sense that he manufactures out of whole
cloth but in the sense that he appropriates to himself, from what is
given, the pattern that he needs. So it is with social reality. The
child learns, as he grows, to take what is meaningful to his culture
and, in addition, what is specially meaningful to himself. He learns
to see social reality not "as it is"; he learns to respond to it not "as
it is." The adult works out an analysis of it in his study, not as it
is, but as it impresses itself upon his own selective awareness, his
own competence, his own interest in making sense out of it.

Not only do social factors participate prominently in the formation of early percepts, but they appear to give special weight to
percepts of human situations. We learn to perceive things in a social
world which stresses or values some patterns more than others.
Response to the sight and sound of others is frequently a biologically dominant response; other factors may become important
because of their association with the social. To use Holt's terminology, adience to the objects of the social world makes them pivotal
features in the construction of the whole world of perception.

This is not merely suggested by the everyday activity of children and adults, but is experimentally supported by two lines of
research. First, after controlling the size, shape, color and other
features of postage stamps, it has been possible to show that sheer

acceptance of the stamp as a stamp of one's own country gives it an apparent size greater than that of control stamps. It is actually bigger because it belongs to one's own nationality. This overvaluing tendency remains in the case of unfamiliar stamps which the subjects accept as American stamps on the basis of the experimenter's assertion. Control subjects in Canada give the same special weight to the stamps of their own nation. (Sheer degree of familiarity is an insufficient explanation of the results.) The valuing tendency alters the apparent size of objects in other ways. Three-cent stamps are judged bigger than two-cent stamps of exactly the same physical dimensions. Thus social habits participate in the determination of the percept, and the degree of their participation is measurable.

The same phenomena appear in a study of the conditioned salivary response to nonsense syllables. In one series, the subjects were given ordinary nonsense syllables prior to the presentation of food. To another group of subjects nonsense syllables were presented with the assertion that these were words in "Benga, an African language." The acceptance of the nonsense syllable as a word in a real language caused greater incidence of conditioning as compared with the control series when nonsense was simply nonsense.[1] To a social being words are something more than sounds arbitrarily designating things. Meaning is something more than isolated conditioned reaction. A word is an organic part of a complex system of symbols bearing intimate relation to the social world and, of course, to the inner world of values and thoughts. The determination of the objective size of a stamp by its value in a currency system and the increased efficacy of conditioning when a sound is accepted as a word, point to the importance for each human being of an interiorized system or pattern of symbols designating social situations and social values. The social psychologist is concerned not only with the effector end of his subject's life but with perception, inference, and thought.

Outstanding in the study of social factors in perception is the

---

[1] Similarly, conditioned responses to words seem often to be extinguished much less easily and rapidly than conditioned responses to arbitrary symbols.

work of Sherif. Each percept in the social world is shown to depend upon a frame of reference, both its quality and its quantity being defined relative to this frame. The frame itself goes back genetically to earlier frames, and we might at times be lost in conjecture as to the earliest infantile patterns of perception. But at the time set for any experiment we must discover the frames of reference actively functioning. The Trobrianders, believing that sons resemble fathers but never the other sons of the same father, cannot see fraternal resemblances which to the ethnologist seem striking indeed. They protest against the bad taste and the lack of "common sense" of him who declares that brothers resemble one another. Data are organized to show that all social life involves arbitrary classification in terms of those resemblances and differences which are stylized within the group.

The next step is a systematic search through the literature of experimental psychology to show the rôle of frames of reference in controlling laboratory behavior. Here, again, objects are perceived with reference to a personal or social frame of reference which is found to involve the same interplay of outer and inner factors (structure of the stimulus world and structure of the organism) that are found elsewhere. The result is to show the applicability of quantitative concepts to all social frames of reference.

Third, a laboratory situation is set up in which social factors determine a reference frame which must be used by the subject in perceiving. A single point of light in a dark room may be located here or there, may move up and down or in circles or in any defined direction. The fact that the outer world now has no organization at all beyond the simple relation of figure and ground permits inner factors of expectation or suggestion to exercise an overwhelming influence. In one situation the experimenter himself, in another a second subject acting side by side with the first, in a third situation a larger group of subjects, define for the individual the nature and extent of the movement perceived. The relative effects of one and of several companions in the group situation, and the relative prestige value of various subjects for one another, are defined and carefully measured. Thus an advanced student of psychology, primed in advance as to the judgments of direction and extent which he should give, established the general range and central tendency followed by a more *naïve* subject. When a single subject experienced this stimulus situation alone and was then transferred to the group situation, he usually abandoned his personal habit and assimilated a *norm* as defined by the behavior of other members of the group. After he had served in three experimental studies of one hour each, rendering judgments in the group situation, he retained, when alone, the habits of judgment acquired in the group situation. Here we have a well-defined clue as to the way in which social norms continue to function even when the individual is no longer in the presence of those from whom the norm was acquired.

Sherif shows in the light of Piaget's data that moral judgments conform to the same laws found in the study of judgments regarding extent of movement. Of special importance in the moral judgments, however, is the participation of value tendencies, each of which has arisen in a social situation and continues to have its effect in the situation calling for moral judgment. Value tendencies directed toward the ego are of special weight. The research on ego level and aspiration level (see above, page 212) is shown to fit the same general picture as the Piaget material and Sherif's laboratory study.

Other "frames of reference" were found by Sherif in "tapping rhythms" prevailing in a group to which a new subject was introduced, which resulted in a fresh observer's "hearing" an objective rhythm in a metronome beating in accordance with the pattern set by the group; likewise in the expression of literary preferences in accordance with favorable and unfavorable "frames of reference" established by authors' names arbitrarily attached to literary selections. Much of the material on suggestibility is now seen not simply in the light of sensori-motor action (a concept oversimplifying the stimulus situation), but in terms of a reconstitution of the whole perceptual field in which material is to be seen or evaluated. In the same way, the slogans of advertisers or politicians are seen to act in daily life not in terms of the narrow effects of suggestion or imitation as traditionally conceived, but in terms of a device so chosen as to alter the whole organization and meaning of the commodity or the political program.

There is thus a systematic conception of the nature of social perceiving in general, and of its relation to the more complex forms of ethical, aesthetic, and logical behavior. The separation of individual psychology and social psychology is shown to be artificial and misleading, and the laboratory is given its rightful place as a means of defining and testing the broader concepts yielded on inspection of daily social behavior.

An equally brilliant step toward domiciling the fundamental social realities in the psychology laboratory is Bartlett's study of "remembering." A labor extending through twenty years, bearing at every point the marks of constant reflection upon the facts of ethnology and of history, this investigation offers an experimental analysis of the full social reality of human perceiving, learning, recalling, recognizing. Instead of nonsense syllables, Bartlett briefly presented to his subjects in one series patterns of irregular lines and geometric figures; in another, simple drawings suggesting objects; in a third, pictures of the faces of army and navy officers. He required from time to time a reproduction or verbal description of the material shown. The social habits and the affective responses of the subjects—above all, their persistent attitudes—were plainly manifest in the first reproductions; and as time wore on, the figures underwent more and more change and systematization, not merely through the decay of elements, but through the recasting of the whole in terms of personal meanings. Prominent among the processes at work was "rationalization"—the creation of acceptable sense in conformity with the personal outlook of the subjects. Meaningless forms were made meaningful in terms of an educated European man's world of meanings; faces became the faces of characteristic types of men known to the subjects.

Those factors in the original perception which led to the over-potency of special features in a perceptual pattern were found to affect recall, so that the latter process was largely one of grouping features around a clear and prominently significant detail. The personal problems and troubles of the subjects affected the perception and more notably the recall. The experimental results are shown to parallel the selective activity of perception and recall among primitive peoples, whose capacity for observation and "feats of memory" is shown to be traceable to culturally emphasized interests of the group. Indeed, the material on recall does much to clarify the "autistic" nature of social thought. Each thing perceived has in time become a thing possible and relevant to one's individual and cultural needs.

We have already seen that autistic behavior may occur as an escape from baffling situations. Yet the rôle of autism, Bartlett shows, is infinitely greater and more important than this. Autism is present not only in frustration but in most types of positive activity. The emotional intensity of a situation partly determines its likelihood of being remembered and, whether remembered or not, the likelihood that it will steer and guide subsequent processes of thought. As one confronts a social situation requiring thought, the logical and the autistic are blended. The words are reasonable, but the tune is the irrational melody of desire. One tries, for example, to see a "tempting offer" as if it were a sound proposal. One says with half a smile that he "hopes to rationalize" his decision to take a two months' vacation. The despot proves that his control is necessary to the welfare of his people. All sorts and conditions of men, while bewailing their personal lot, assume the evident righteousness of the kind of people that they themselves are. Central in the whole structure of autistic control of the world is autistic vision of one's ego. Facts as obvious and universal as these are recognized by many a psychologist up to the moment when he enters the laboratory; he enters, and, preparing his exposure apparatus, studies thinking simply as a process in which the subject abstracts from lists of words or pictures and tells what common property they exhibit, or finds the smallest number of moves possible in getting missionaries and cannibals across the Congo. The actual stuff of which most thinking is made is social stuff. It is the process of fusing the properties of objects as given with the properties of objects as we wish them to be.[1]

[1] An attempt might be made to approach social thinking as thus defined by study of learning in which the interest and disinclination, the hopes and preferences of the learners are known in advance. Thus, to two groups of students, the one favoring, the other opposing, increase in the Army and Navy, data were presented

Social Modification of "Basic Traits"

It is not hard to see how a motive can be redirected; but the present-day reader is being asked more and more insistently to consider whether such redirection is all that happens to the organism under the impact of the environment. Are the basic drives, the fundamental biochemical balances, the intrinsic capacities as stable as a birthmark? We shall attempt to see what kind of "stability" such basic traits have. The problem will be to see whether the central nervous system is the only part of the body profoundly molded by culture; whether the "learning process in social situations" is entirely a matter of habits dependent on central nervous tissue. A critical case would be an examination of the degree of stability or plasticity of the endocrine organs under changing cultural conditions.

It seems probable that the general scheme suggested in Chapter III to describe the reactions of the vital organs in relation to motives applies also to the glands of internal secretion. Since all tissues cast products into the blood stream, the ductless glands, developed for manufacturing and distributing chemical products, do nothing which is not done to some extent by other organs. They do, however, alter very rapidly the chemical composition of the blood stream and through it the whole body. Since we have already seen that alterations in the chemistry of the blood cause alterations in thresholds of neural activity, it seems possible to schematize the

---

on the costs of armaments, the means by which such money is raised, the effects of such armaments on the policies of other nations. Similarly, two groups of students, favorable and unfavorable to communism, respectively, were exposed to data on prosperity and distress, achievement and disappointment in the Soviet Union. The actual ability to pick up information which is concordant or discordant with one's wishes may be stated in quantitative form. When the *learning curves* are appropriately worked out, with suitable controls made up of individuals who are indifferent to the chosen issues, *forgetting* can also be studied. This may likewise show autism. We know in daily life that one may give in during debate, yet tomorrow finds himself back in the familiar stand, and may indeed forget the crucial argument with which he was silenced. The method of retained members and the method of relearning could both be used to discover to what extent disagreeable material has been sidetracked.

reaction of the endocrine organs in terms of lowering and raising neural thresholds.

The thyroid, for example, lowers thresholds for a variety of emotional responses. Extreme hyper-secretion of the thyroid is of direct significance for personality through the apprehensiveness and agitation which may arise from any trivial incident or, indeed, from the sheer round of planned daily activities. Fear in all its forms, and often irritability too, may be so highly generalized as to forbid our speaking of specific worries or anxieties. We are dealing with a biological trait, a trait irrespective of specific situation if ever a trait so broadly conceived is to be found. Marked defect in thyroid secretion is often attended by high thresholds for emotional response, a characteristic lethargy or torpidity. Excess and defect in secretion of adrenalin seem also likely to lower or raise, respectively, the thresholds for the more violent emotions—notably, rage. It seems quite probable that other glands, in particular the pituitary, play their part in relation to the dynamic patterns of emotion.

It will be noted that all the effects thus far attributed to glands are rather highly generalized. The apprehensiveness of the hyper-thyroid, for example, is merely a specially marked case of emotional response; rage, disgust and other strong emotional responses are clinically reported as expressive of biochemical disorder. The same generalization of effects must be stressed in relation to the sex glands. Here we are dealing with an effect much broader than that associated with intensity or weakness of sexual feeling; quite complex and subtle personality changes are to be expected from any marked glandular deviation. The emotional life is more or less integrated, responding all at once to many generalized influences, a fact to which the physiological interrelations of the endocrine organs give a key.

Up to this point we have written as if the endocrine system were fixed, a lawgiver or pace-maker to the organism, sitting serenely above the bio-social world of daily flux and adjustment. Yet extreme fear, often of social origin, may profoundly alter the thyroid for a brief or for a very long time. The relation of gland to social response is a two-way relation. Forgetfulness of this last point led to an experiment which not only corrected the error but suggested new complications:

Seeking a bio-chemical approach to individual differences, it occurred to J. Steinberg that thyroid activity might be a clue to the capacity to mobilize energy quickly and consequently to the speed with which psychological functions are carried out. She administered five standard speed tests, such as color-naming, opposites and arithmetic tests, to a group of thirty-nine girls in early adolescence. Each girl was given two or more tests of basal metabolic rate. The result was to show a slight *negative* correlation between basal metabolic rate and speed! This correlation, after the influence of age differences was removed by means of partial correlations, was —.18, just three times its probable error. We may perhaps be dealing with a chance result. The probability, however, is that there is a very slight tendency within the normal range to correct ("compensate") for a slight physical deviation. One whose metabolic rate is low and who oxidizes poorly may find that he usually feels better if he is more active. One who is burning his fuel too fast feels better if he slows down. This highly tentative interpretation is in line with general evidence as to the complex way in which endocrines do their work.

Similarly, J. Levy found among a group of problem children whose trouble was due to overactivity a basal metabolic rate averaging lower than the normal, and among a group of problem children inclined to be under-active—quiet and seclusive—a basal metabolic rate above the normal. A physiological adjustment of the type broadly called compensatory is probably involved, at least in many such cases.

This is merely one of a variety of ways in which subtle factors may accent, alter, or invert the emphasis ascribed to physiological factors. Any two individuals, even in the same culture, have to some extent different environments; and since the organism does not grow in a vacuum but in a world of social stimulation, it seems highly improbable that endocrine factors are fixed and final expressions of an unalterable biological equipment. So profound are such social modifications that practically all reported racial differences in physiological, especially glandular, factors appear, in the light of proper experimental control, to be the expression of culture; as we noted in Chapter II, the blood pressure of the white man in China goes down until it approximates the average of the Chinese, while that of the Chinese student tends to rise to the prevailing American level.

But this does not negate the tremendous individual differences among whites both at home and in the Orient, and among orientals both at home and in the Occident. This seems to refute the more extreme doctrines regarding unlimited plasticity of the organism, and seems to suggest that individual differences in social behavior, in so far as they depend upon the biological equipment for emotional response, interest, and attitude, require much more attention than the social psychologist has ordinarily given them. Individual differences in the vital organs are very obvious in childhood; and in so far as they contribute to strength, speed, energy, or the dominant visceral drives, they give social behavior a diversity which would scarcely have been expected a generation ago. Any modern version of an instinct theory, for example, must stress not only the empirical form of the drives but the tremendous individual differences apparently resulting from both environmental and hereditary sources. And any statement about the socialization of drives must take into account not only the formal laws of conditioning and so on, but the individual differences in the strength or plasticity or both of each such drive.

If this is true regarding the relatively well-defined visceral drives the physiological goal of which is reasonably clear, it becomes true with a vengeance regarding those two large classes of drives which we have called the activity drives and the aesthetic drives. Individual differences in the kind of activity needed or enjoyed, activities of brawn or brain, predispose toward this or that interest, this or that basis for well-being. Individuals appear to differ as much in their enjoyment of color as they do in their ability to distinguish between colors, and indeed show such differences in the opening months of life. Tremendous individual differences in response to tone, rhythm and form, long recognized by students of the little child but given no place in systematic psychology, call aloud for consideration in the study of individual differences in a response to the social world. One infant plays crudely and strenuously, another gently or subtly. One responds intensely to slow, sad music, and wants it over and over again. Another will have nothing but the jubilant and the martial. And as we have seen, these activity and aesthetic cravings appear to be even more labile and plastic, more easily canalized than the visceral drives. This means that even more study must be given to the devices by which the family, the neighborhood, and the culture at large provide early satisfactions for these cravings and permit fixations which will become the passionate attachments, the hobbies, and the lifetime joys of each child.

The conception that the action patterns of the organism are molded into more and more specific shape should be applicable not only to motor habits, attitudes and emotional patterns, but to *intellectual* processes as well. It is a convenient abstraction to think of the total quantity of intelligence in numerical form, but it is more useful here to consider the mold into which the intellect is cast. Let us review a number of quantitative studies of intellectual functions which lay bare the processes by which the mind is molded.

In general, all positive intellectual abilities are correlated. If there is, as we believe, such a thing as general intelligence, ability to recall names, repeat digits backward, write sonnets, learn calculus, criticize political arguments should be, however slightly, related, and in a positive, not a negative direction. Nevertheless, some intellectual operations fall naturally into families. There is a relatively close connection between ability in algebra, trigonometry and calculus; there is a relatively close connection between ability to learn French, Latin and German; there is a relatively close connection between the capacity for speed in various forms of mental work. This leads to the conception of "group factors," fundamental powers of the mind when dealing with particular kinds of subject matter and when carrying out certain broad general kinds of processes.

The mathematics of this problem prove to be bewildering and we shall not here attempt a criticism of the reasoning involved. We should like to ask, however, whether these group factors are *fixed* in the constitution of the individual or whether they respond at all to the varying situations confronted by the organism. So we must report on a series of studies dealing with five-year-old children, children nine, twelve and fourteen years old, college students and adults. An attempt to find a general group-memory factor in the five-year-olds yielded a negative result. The items in a battery of memory tests and the items in a broader collection of intelligence tests all intercorrelated in about the same way. A single memory item was as closely related to an intelligence item as it was to another memory item. The mind was not compartmentalized into memory, judgment and reasoning. It was still all-round ability or capacity to adapt. In the nine-year-olds, however, group factors had begun to emerge; capacity to deal with words and numbers had split off from the main trunk, so that neither was very highly correlated with the other and neither gave adequate prediction as to other powers revealed in general intelligence tests. At twelve and fourteen the picture has become progressively clearer. The individual who is good at mathematics may be good, bad or indifferent at other tasks. After interest, energy and habit have been displayed in specific directions for a longer and longer time, the mind has taken on characteristic functional capacities. At the adult level there is rather little left of *general* intelligence, and one group factor defined in terms of content tells us but little about another factor. Indeed, under some conditions of training it is not inconceivable that a negative correlation between some abilities may result. In any case, the developmental studies raise interesting questions about the generalized nature of intelligence. If, however, the mind is directed and drilled, stimulated and sensitized in one direction, there is every reason to believe that this should impoverish it in other directions, both because the more time is given to one subject, the less there is for another, and because the development of specific interests in life, such as vocational interests and hopes, should make one insensitive, opaque to other interests.

We are reminded here of Jung's conception of "emotional stupidity," the definite raising of resistances to new ideas or suggestions. We are reminded also of Lecky's conception of self-consistency. Not only does the person become sensitized to special interests; the self is a self good at some things, bad at others. "I never could do math," says the student, and sets himself against the math instruction of his would-be helper. Partly through fear of defeat, partly through sheer inability to conceive oneself as competent in mathematics, the picture of the self has become consistent, and to disturb it involves distress. The ego, as we saw, is a consistent means to a consistent end; and the insertion of a new value as an end served by an ego may set up a sense of strain and disturbance, a sense of not being oneself, a sense of pressure to embark on an uncertain voyage.

One of the most "fundamental" of individual differences relates to the general level of health and well-being; and for many purposes it is important to specify more exactly the form of well-being in terms of resistance to fatigue, adequacy of circulation, resistance to infection, etc. Conditions of this sort potently and perpetually influence the processes of growing and of learning. We might refer to all such factors as subtle predisposing factors, in the light of which the influence of specific new stimuli has to be considered. In describing the maturation process or the process of conditioning, it is necessary to note tremendous individual differences in the rate and form of change in behavior; and these are just as truly a part of the total learning process as the action of outside stimuli upon sensori-motor arcs. Indeed, even the simplest arcs depend upon general physical conditions, and the connection between arcs and the development of complex patterns obviously depends upon them.

It is not so often recalled that these subtle and pervasive factors which guide and control the learning process come as frequently from the *social world*. Shame after severe reproof, delight after winning a contest, amusement after a play on words which puts an end to a personal tension—all these things alter not only the momentary response but the degree of impressionability of the organism. Individual differences in the daily cycle of morale, the general level of good sportsmanship or good humor, the suddenness of development of irritations or frustrations—all these things prepare the organism for learning. Just as the adviser to college students emphasizes the importance of physical and mental health in relation to "learning" in the more academic sense, so the social psychologist must emphasize different patterns of social learning which depend upon the mood, the morale, the prevailing level of excitement in any individual's social environment.

If this is true with reference to individuals, it is doubly true with reference to differences in cultural surroundings. Just as malaria or hookworm may make children poor learners, so the frustration of hopes and the despair of a broken peasantry may make the people almost incapable of learning anything. Studies of the unemployed have revealed a level of demoralization such that new impressions are as hard to make as they are upon the malarial or even the catatonic patient. If one wonders how the apprentice painter or sculptor of fifteenth-century Italy acquired the art of a Simone Martini or a Donatello in a few years, one must recall the extraordinary vitality and intensity of the life about them, the sensitizing of the individual spirit to values which redirect the artist's eye and hand to each fresh glimpse of new loveliness. A different cultural world may not only impose different specific conditionings; it may change the level at which the individual lives, and, in a subtle but pervasive way, make for more or less, faster or slower, acquisition of social patterns.

Not only is the level of learning raised or lowered in a general way, but the trend or direction of learning is modified by culture. We wish here to call attention not only to those aspects of a culture which are highly valued and important, but also to the excitement or depression of particular physiological activities. Thus, the eye of the fifteenth-century Italian artist, the ear of the nineteenth-century German musical composer, the legs of the twentieth-century Russian dancer are not only specifically trained, but are selectively sensitized in response to particular trends in the culture without. The learning process is a specific, palpable element imposed upon a level of more generalized excitation or sensitization.

LEARNING TO COMMUNICATE

Though we are chiefly concerned here with learning in general rather than learning specific things, we must briefly consider how the child learns to understand the chief vehicle of culture, the means of communication.

We believe it fair to say that the fundamental outlines of the process of language learning are now drawn with considerable definiteness. The great bulk of the research material is not strictly experimental, and relatively little is the result of standardized methods of observing and recording; but its amount is so great that we may select from it certain crucial elements so clear cut as to permit, we believe, a short statement as to the steps and processes involved in language development in childhood.

The birth cry and the vocalization of the first few weeks (which even deaf children show) give place during the second half year to a habit of babbling which becomes one of the child's chief interests. During this period one expects simple phonetic combinations, such as those of the consonant followed by a vowel, repeated as in the familiar ba-ba-ba. The *understanding* of words, and the *use* of words to designate specific things or wants, are apt to appear late in the first year or early in the second, the rate of progress depending from the first greatly upon the social environment, and never ceasing to be thus influenced.

The development of passive language habits, that is, the learning to understand words, can, at least in large part, be interpreted in terms of the conditioned response. Just as animals may learn to interpret the signs of dinner-time by virtue of the ordinary laws of learning, responding to the sign as they once responded to the situation in which the sign was used, so children learn to reach, to withdraw the hand from a dangerous object, and so on, by virtue of the repetition of *words*, together with whatever elements in the situation originally tend to produce these responses. In later and more complicated developments, it is doubtful whether the formula for conditioning adequately describes the intricacies of speech, since the associative processes involve imagery and, perhaps in some cases, imageless "meaning" responses. These *may* perhaps be general adjustments of the whole body, but their experimental analysis is far from complete.

The development of active language habits, that is, learning to talk, is a somewhat different problem. Lagging some weeks after the understanding of the first word, as a rule, comes the first use of a word. Some words appear to arise by the circular reflex as already described. In other cases, however, it would appear that the word appears more or less accidentally in the midst of a large number of babbled responses, and becomes fixated simply because it brings results to the child. The particular word may bring to him the thing which the adult connects with the sound (for example, the child says *wa*, the mother thinks this is a struggle to say *water*, etc.). In other cases the sheer effect which the achievement of a "real word" makes upon the parents when the child hits upon a phonetic combination which is a part of the parents' language, is in itself sufficiently rewarding to lead, by the principles of learning already discussed, to the fixation of a response. Even *approximations to words* may be greeted with enthusiasm or bring results; and by the "whittling-off" process so characteristic of learning, the wrong elements may be subdued and the right elements fixated. Whether all this is conditioning, or whether the effect of pleasantness and unpleasantness must be invoked as a special principle, is as yet an unsolved problem.

It is necessary, however, to insist that the development of active language is at first almost entirely independent of the development of passive language. The child may, in fact, build up a whole system of speech which differs phonetically and syntactically from the speech which he understands. In some cases his baby talk may be entirely unrecognizable except to the parents, or in other cases recognized only by an older brother or sister. If, however, it brings results, it tends to be perpetuated, and children may go on talking a baby talk which is different, often in fact very different, from the spoken language about them. Baby talk is usually not broken down until it fails to get results, or becomes for the child himself a symbol of being little, a symbol to be discarded as quickly as possible.

Two streams, that of active and that of passive language, are *made* to flow together as a result of social pressure. They have, of course, always shared some elements because of the imitative (circular reflex) factor which plays its part in both. Most of the process, however, depends upon the narrowing down of the overt speech habits so that the area covered by them is, so to speak, reduced to the area acceptable to the group surrounding the child. Except where the child has picked up a word through the circular reflex mechanism, he must learn how to produce the combinations of sounds which are current coin for the things he wants, and it is only slowly that he can *make* sounds which are *like* the sounds he recognizes as symbols.

One other means of communication must also be considered, namely, the transmission to others of our motives and emotions by the language of "expressive movements."

Since social give-and-take depends so largely on our understanding of one another's motives and our capacity to communicate our motives to others, the language of facial and gestural expression seems to be as important as the language of words. If the human motives are relatively but not absolutely plastic, and if the degree of their plasticity decreases with age, we should expect to find in the adult a more or less decipherable language of expression, and this expressive language should reflect both the biology of the organism and the customs and values of the culture in which it functions. Let us see if this is the case.

We laid stress in Chapter III upon the problem of patterning in the newborn and in the older individual. We reached the conclusion that there are distinct forms of expression which may be asssociated with specific emotional processes. It should therefore be possible to determine how accurately these expressions may be identified, how well the observer can tell what emotion the subject is feeling or trying to portray.

A considerable amount of experimental work has been done on the capacity of subjects to interpret emotion from facial expression. The results indicate that some emotions—mirth, for example—may be fairly accurately gauged by a glance at a photograph of an actor who has undertaken to portray this feeling, while other emotions, such as despair, are but very imperfectly gauged. F. H. Allport has tested the influence of training in the interpretation of facial expression. Those subjects who had at first done exceedingly well gained nothing from studying the facial muscles with a view to a more analytical attack on their problem, while those who had made distinctly poor scores profited enormously from such analytical study and at the end of the practice period nearly equaled those who had so greatly excelled. Guilford has also shown that training produces big results, the rank correlation between initial ability and degree of improvement being —.76, the poorest ones improving the most. The implications of this kind of work seem to us to be the confirmation of the view offered by Allport, that we *learn* to grasp the emotional expressions of others. Just as Bühler has found that three-months-old children laugh ecstatically when scolded (see plate facing page 566), and just as Gates found that the ability to interpret facial expression increases regularly with chronological and with mental age, so the study of facial expressions by adults enables them to label these more and more correctly.

We have been chiefly concerned, thus far, with "make-believe" emotions. We turn now to emotions genuinely aroused. In one study pictures were taken of individuals subjected to genuine emotion-rousing stimuli. The responses at which the experimenter aimed and the stimuli used to arouse them included amusement (jokes); startle (firing a pistol); pain (bending the finger joint); disgust (dissected tissues with strong odor); strain (dynamometer work). The photographs taken in these situations were cut horizontally through the bridge of the nose, and judgments of emotion were required of the subject when presented with the upper half, the lower half, and the entire face. Some composite faces were also made up in which one upper half was combined with a "wrong" lower half. Lantern-slide presentations of these plates were shown to groups of subjects who were asked to select the appropriate emotion from a list. The subjects were then asked to compare the *original* pictures with the *pieced-together* pictures, in which either the upper or the lower half was identical with the corresponding part of the original picture. The problem was to find whether the judgment of likeness or difference between two emotion-registering photographs depends upon similarity of the upper halves or of the lower halves of the pictures. In most cases, the great majority of subjects indicated that the picture with the same "mouth half" was more like the original than the one with the same "eyes half." From this Dunlap reasonably concludes that the mouth muscles play a greater part in determining the effect upon the observer than do the eye muscles. Something, then, has been done in the direction of determining types of facial expression which observers can correctly identify with emotions.

Yet the face may be less trustworthy alone than when observed along with other indications; perhaps there are emotional patterns betrayed by other responses of the body. This evidence, too, we must consider.

One problem has to do with the existence of patterns of vocal response. Small children can label with considerable accuracy the emotions registered by an actress who has made phonograph records portraying different emotions. In order to eliminate meanings, no words are used; only the letters of the alphabet, repeated with varying intonation. There is an increase in accuracy with increasing age. Adult Americans, hearing phonograph records of American and Chinese speakers, can interpret emotion from the voice, not only in their own cultural group but in the other. Observers can to some degree name the emotions which a singer seeks to convey through a single tone.

An emotional character may be conveyed by musical tone which is recognized and given its "true" emotional label in a far greater number of cases than chance could account for. All this might perhaps suggest fixed vocal patterns which underlie the formation of all music.

So far, then, we have evidence for fair uniformity in expressive behavior through face and voice, serving as a reasonably dependable basis for social communication. Apparently the individual child has to learn how to interpret such "signals" from his comrades; he goes through a process of gradual acquisition of skill.[1]

And though the processes which we have called maturation work to give some fairly uniform patterns independent of specific, directed, cultural training, each culture, nevertheless, has its own jargon of expression which the child must learn as he learns the

---

[1] In contrast to these conventionalized symbolic gestures which serve for communication, there appear "autistic" gestures in response to intraorganic stimulation (e.g., conflict and stress); these, though capable of being studied by an experimenter, are neither perceived by the actor nor responded to by an observer.

47 Mirth

43 Disgust

See page 235.

(From the "Genetic Psychology Monographs." Used by permission of the editor and the author.)

local arts and crafts of his group. He nevertheless often fails in interpreting the expressive pattern of those of other cultural groups.

THE TRANSMISSION OF CULTURE

The processes by which the child grows into the ways of his group—family group, neighborhood group and larger community —have been schematized under such concepts as conditioning, canalization, and integration of values. Our emphasis has been on the individual child; we have said little about the persons who transmit the culture to him, their hopes and fears for him, their pride and their vested interests in him, the projection of their ambitions upon him, the vagaries of their tolerance and intolerance of him, the round of amusement, rage, forgiveness and new faith in him. Yet he probably sees into the psychology of the adult world far deeper than the parents guess, and during his years of dependency learns well where security and approval lie, and something of the (conscious or unconscious) basis of such approval. Some suggestions as to all this appear in Chapters VI-X. We cannot here sketch the psychology of parents, but we must venture (1) a suggestion as to the significance for the child of the adults' prestige; (2) an interpretation of the transmission of values from one generation to the other; (3) an interpretation of one significant experimental study which is conceived in these terms, a study which, however imperfect, offers interesting suggestions as to how the child deciphers his parents' attitudes and how he conceives himself in relation to them.

We have already noted (page 174) the importance of prestige in modifying behavior. We saw that prestige suggestion is not to be predicted from one's "general suggestibility." Two classes of persons appear in general to be effective in giving prestige suggestion, those whom we fear and those whom we love, or, to use milder terms to denote the same thing, those for whom we feel awe and those toward whom we feel affection. On general grounds, we might suspect here that the person with prestige suggestion is first of all the parent, the person who stands for us *in loco parentis*, the person who has the authority or the endearing qualities of the parent. It is the parent with whom the child at first identifies himself; it is the parent from whom the individual ego is last emancipated. Following here the research findings of Piaget as well as the observations of Freud, we should suspect that the person with prestige is the person who brings back in us unwittingly the first filial attitudes—the individual, in other words, who has made us childlike and who now exploits in us the unquestioning attitude of the little child. We are suggestible because the barriers between what the other person wants and what we want are partially dissolved. What is real for him is real for us. This is far from a complete interpretation, but it is a clue to the fact that prestige suggestion appears always to be an emotional rather than simply a cognitive experience. There is also a clue here as to the marked bimodality of response to prestige suggestion. It is hard for love and fear to live together, harder still for either of them to coexist with an objective attitude. The experimenter or the parent who has lost the possibility of obtaining filial trust has snapped the bond, and fails to transmit that element of the culture (self-control, etc.) upon which he is bent, or in unfavorable moments may precipitate enough antagonism to swing the subject into a defiant attitude. We do not know under what conditions prestige based on love and prestige based on fear would differ quantitatively, nor do we know where fear leading to prestige leads off into outright defiance.[1] But we suspect that children do not "absorb" culture; we suspect that they "take" it with celerity because they love or fear the vehicles which carry it.

On the whole, most values seem to be "taken" and used by the child because of a positive response to those whose values come within his ken. The process by which many values are transmitted from one generation to the next is largely a process, we believe, involving relatively little coercion, relatively little Freudian repression. It is more of the character of the "Look, see!" pattern. The world is so full of a number of things both lovely and hateful that,

[1] A group of problems for further analysis await us here, particularly the experimental and quantitative analyses of suggestibility scores under conditions where love and fear and indifference are positively known to be present at the start.

unless the child's interests are in gross conflict with the adult, the parent has relatively little trouble in enabling the child to see why one game is fun for three-year-olds and another is dangerous for three-year-olds. Even without benefit of identification, which, of course, plays its powerful part in forming values, the parent helps the child to structure the world in terms of his own values simply by pointing out the palpable and inherent goods and bads.

It follows from this that values are neither more nor less "subjective" than percepts in Sherif's and in Calley's experiments quoted above, in which the observer is set to abstract from a given pattern certain personally meaningful events. These events are not fictitious. The abstraction is an abstraction from a real occurrence, exactly as the abstraction of a parabolic line from the observed movements of a projectile is an abstraction. The goodness or badness inherent in tastes and smells, games of competition, intense physical effort, sudden surprise or escape, are actually given in the immediate experience of the child. He selects good features in some cases and ignores bad ones, or vice versa. He does not select everything which is given; but what he does select is real. There is, therefore, no meaning whatever as far as we can see in speaking of the "relativity of values." To the person in whom the value functions, it is at the time absolute. Different persons within a cultural group may have different values, and different cultural and sub-cultural groups may have different values. Values are extremely variable and modifiable. But they are real and frequently coercive things in the life history of the individual person, and represent much of the continuity of social reality from generation to generation.

In conclusion, we shall try to interpret one experimental and field investigation of the transmission of values, showing some of the principles suggested above, especially the complex nature of prestige suggestion in the growth of a value, and the rôle of the value in structuring the whole social order for the child.

After observing from the results of adult attitude tests the high degree of generality of the individual white man's response to Negroes, Horowitz attempted to carry out a systematic study of the individual genesis of such attitude patterns. Photographs of individual white and Negro boys, and photographs of social situations in which white boys, or white boys and colored boys together, were shown, were presented to white boys from the kindergarten age through the 8B grade. In the "ranks test," the child simply indicated his order of preference from among a mixed assortment of white and Negro faces; in the "show-me" test he indicated which individual boys he would like to bring home to lunch, with which ones he would like to play ball, etc.; in the "social situations test" he pointed out those play groups with which he would like to "join in." Prejudice as defined here is the degree to which one accepts members of one's own racial group, as contrasted with members of the other group. The form of the curve indicating increase in prejudice is somewhat different on the three tests; the point of chief interest is not the individual growth curve, but the change in the intercorrelations between the tests. Whereas at the kindergarten level the three tests correlate only slightly, the correlation increases through the eight-year period. A quantitative definition is thus given to the current concept of integration of attitude. To show prejudice on one test at the kindergarten level gives practically no prediction about prejudice on the other tests at the same level; but by the time the child has reached the 8B group the amount of his prejudice on one test goes a fair way toward predicting the amount of his prejudice on the other two. The child is, so to speak, freeing himself from the influence of the details of the specific situation; he is building up the generalized pro- or anti-Negro response already shown to exist at the adult level.

The next step in research obviously was to study more closely the factors responsible for the growth of prejudice. After preliminary work in various parts of New York City and in urban and rural Georgia and Tennessee, an intensive study was made of two Tennessee communities. Participation for some months in the life of a small village made possible a more exact definition of the way in which the child learns the prejudice pattern stylized among members of the white community. The smallest children played freely with members of either race and, far from developing a consciousness of kind, had to be taught by progressively severe methods to leave these colored playmates alone. One of the most frequent bases for "getting a whupping" was playing with Negro children. Terms of derogation were not sufficient to produce the racial cleavage. The fixed pattern of the adult had to be transferred at times by means of a birch rod. It becomes clear that the reported integration of attitude is nothing particularly mysterious; that it does not arise from the maturation of race consciousness, but simply from the increasing diversity and intensity of sanctions imposed on the child. (Clearly, *some* adult pressures *do* involve "coercion.")

This discovery led to a new set of test procedures in which the attitudes of white children toward Negro adults and children were seen in the light of the growth patterns already defined. Toward the end of the primary school period the pattern was so well defined that it affected not only conduct but perception, memory and imagination—it had all the "integration" which anyone could desire. Thus, pictures of a library scene containing only white persons were briefly exposed. Afterward the child was asked, "What was the colored man doing?" In the children's reports he was never reading a book, never seated at a table; he was always dusting the books or sweeping the floor. He was fulfilling the rôle which his inferior position in the group demanded. In spontaneous as well as in experimental situations, the child's structuring of his world according to the adult norm is exhibited. "Where do you live?" "Fifth house from the station." Examination showed that the child's house was seventh from the station, but two belonged to Negro families. Much of the observation, memory and thought of the child toward the end of the primary school period is structured to meet social requirements. In the case just quoted, the child did not actively repress memory of the two Negro homes; these were merely irrelevant to the structure about which the white adult was inquiring. It is quite evident that studies of the psychology of testimony, as Bartlett has well shown, need consideration of the social norms which guide and control the development not only of the response pattern but of the entire intellectual life as well.

The concepts presented here to interpret the vast complexities of social learning are few, but they may all be applied at once.

SOME STUDIES

AUTHOR DATE	TOPIC	SUBJECTS	METHODS
Anastasi, A., and Foley, J. P., Jr. (1936)	Children's drawings.	Selection from drawings of over 1000 children, 6–12 yrs. old, from 41 countries.	602 drawings at international exhibit of children's drawings, analyzed in terms of subject matter, technique and coloring.
Bregman, E. O. (1934)	Conditioning of emotional responses in infants.	15 infants, 7 boys, 8 girls; 2 of 8 mos., 2 of 11 mos., 6 of 12 mos., 2 of 14 mos., 1 each of 13, 15, 16 mos. All healthy.	Startle stimulus was loud electric bell. Agreeable stimuli, toy rattle and music-box melody. Neutral stimuli, wooden objects of various shape, color, pattern; cloth curtains of various color and pattern. After ascertaining original response to each neutral stimulus, half paired with disagreeable, and half with agreeable, stimuli. From 24 to 96 stimulations given each child.
English, H. B. (1929)	Conditioned fear responses.	3 children: 1 at 28 weeks, 1 at 14 mos., 1 at 15 mos.	1st and 3rd Ss observed under home conditions, 2nd in laboratory. Observation of gross overt behavior.
Hilgard, J. R. (1932)	Learning and maturation abilities in "buttoning," "cutting with scissors" and "climbing a ladder."	Two groups, 10 children each, from Merrill-Palmer School, matched in C.A., M.A., sex, initial ability in 3 skills tested. 6 girls, 4 boys in each; mean C.A. about 28.5 mos., mean M.A., about 29.5.	Practice group received intensive training for 12 wks. in buttoning, cutting with scissors, and climbing; tested at 2-wk. intervals; control group received intensive training for a week.

FINDINGS	GENERAL REMARKS
	Intercultural differences appear. Major trends indicate "a general correspondence between the various aspects or details of the drawing and the concrete cultural or stimulus conditions under which it was produced."
Although responses to bell, rattle, etc., were "adequate," no evidence of conditioning was found.	"... Changes in emotional behavior ... are not as a general rule, at least, readily brought about by joint stimulation in early life. . . ."
One child, 28 weeks old, showed conditioned fear response to a stuffed "cat" after hearing a noise at the same time she saw the cat. Lost fear after lapse of 48 hours. Another in same family at 14 mo. 9 da. showed no flinching at sound made by striking heavy metal bar with 2-lb. hammer. Third, little girl, frightened by new patent leather slippers, became frightened by familiar slippers when placed on floor along with hers.	Last case could be either simple conditioning or "irradiation."
In buttoning, practice group gained 21.4 pts., control group 15.6 pts.; in cutting, practice group gained 47.5 pts., control group 40.4; in climbing, practice group gained 9.2 pts., control group 9.6 pts. At end of 12 wks. of intensive practice for practice group, reliable difference between groups on all tests. Without intensive training, control group gained 57.3% of its climbing score, 72.5% of buttoning total, and 82.4% of cutting total. Rate of learning for practice group accelerated toward end of training period.	It appears "that specific training throughout the twelve-week period was a far less important contributing factor in the development of these three abilities than was [the] general developmental trend."

SOME STUDIES

AUTHOR DATE	TOPIC	SUBJECTS	METHODS
Hunter, W. S. (1913)	Delayed response in children and animals.	22 rats: 5 normal adult, 17 normal 4-week-old; 2 female mongrel dogs, 5 mo. old; 4 raccoons: 2 male, 2 female; 2–6 mo. old. 5 children, 2 boys, 3 girls, 2½–8 yrs. old.	S trained to choose lighted one of 3 doors (fed when correct choice made, shocked at other doors). After establishment of habit, S held in entrance box for intervals after light cue is extinguished (with children, buzzer buttons with lights over them were used; child told to go to noisy button, given candy if successful). Record taken of successful trials with varying lengths of delay.
Jersild, A. T. (1932)	Relative contribution of nature and nurture as indicated by permanence of advantage of special training.	200 Ss., 2–11 yrs. A few adults.	2 mental, 4 motor, and 2 musical performances. (1) initial tests; (2) segregation of Ss into 2 equivalent groups, practice and control; (3) specific training of practice group for several months; (4) retests of both groups after training period; (5) retests several months after end of training period.
Jones, M. C. (1924)	Elimination of children's fears.	70 children, 3 mos. to 7 yrs. old, in institution for temporary care.	Pleasant or mildly unpleasant situations presented to each child: e.g., alone, in dark room, with other children who are afraid; sudden presentation of snake, white rat, rabbit, loud sound, false faces, etc. When fear indicated, attempt to remove it by Method of Disuse (shielding from the stimulus), by Method of Verbal Appeal, by Method of Adaptation (monotonously repeating stimulation), by Method of Distraction (offering substitute activity), by Method of Direct Conditioning (association with pleasant stimulus), by Method of Social Imitation (another child reacting positively to situation).

FINDINGS	GENERAL REMARKS
Upper limit of delay for successful trials: Rats 10 sec.; dogs 5 min., raccoons, 3 sec.–25 sec., children, 25 min.	Overt orienting attitudes were important cues. Less important in children. Some intraorganic (non-orientation) factor of an ideational sort must be assumed, especially in the case of children's behavior. Probably a "sensory thought" function rather than imaginal, except in the case of the older children.
In all experiments practiced children showed some advantage over controls at end of training; maintained only in ability to sing tones and intervals. Individual differences between children in practiced groups not substantially altered by training.	"In so far as training forestalls the development of habits which might interfere with the development of skill at a later time, the child will obtain an enduring advantage from training at an early age." "Training alone cannot accomplish the increase in capacity which normally comes with added maturity." ". . . benefits achieved by practice are relative to the child's initial capacity."
"Unqualified success" only with last two methods.	". . . Apart from laboratory analysis we have rarely used any of the . . . procedures in pure form."

SOME STUDIES

AUTHOR DATE	TOPIC	SUBJECTS	METHODS
Kasatkin, N. I., and Levikova, A. M. (1935) (a)	Conditioning as function of age.	6 normal infants from 14 days to 1 mo. 17 days old.	Conditioned feeding movements formed in response to yellow or red light stimuli. Unconditioned stimulus, bottle of filtered milk. Light first, interval of 5–8 sec., bottle given, feeding; withdrawal of both stimuli at same time. Kymograph recording of sucking movements. Technique for visual differentiation involved giving bottle for one colored light but not for another (yellow and green).
Kasatkin, N. I., and Levikova A. M. (1935) (b)	Infant conditioning (sucking) to auditory stimulus.	3 infants, 1 mo., 1 day; 25 days; 11 days old at beginning of experiment. 3 other children also. (?)	Unconditioned reflex: sucking response to feeding bottle. Infant's eyes bandaged; recording from hollow rubber ball under chin connected to Marey tambour and kymograph; conditioning stimulus: sound Mi-2 or organ pipe. Bell and other tones as negative stimuli.
Marquis, D. P. (1931)	Establishment of conditioned responses in newborn infants.	Experimentation on 8 Ss (4 control Ss) from age of 24 hrs. to 10 days.	All feedings 6 times a day, immediately preceded or accompanied by sound of buzzer. Infant fed on stabilimeter in small cabinet. Polygraph records of sucking movements, of general movements, stimulation record, etc. In last experiment a flash of light and a loud clang given as control stimuli. Experiment with control Ss: buzzer sounded without feeding over a 9-day period.
Mirenva, A. N. (1935)	Psychomotor training, twins.	4 pairs of identical and 6 pairs of fraternal twins, 4–4½ yrs. old.	Inferior member of each pair (selected by tests, other observations) given 4½ mos. training in kindergarten observation clinic in: (1) jumping into air, (2) hitting a mark by

OF LEARNING (*Continued*)

FINDINGS	GENERAL REMARKS
First conditioned feeding movements to light stimuli: end of 2nd mo. First visual differentiation colors generally in 4th mo.; very unstable. Inhibition of general movements (as well as conditioning of reflexes) developed gradually. Conditioning occurred in all cases; only one case of differentiation not clear.	Time of formation of CR did not depend upon number of combinations of stimuli, but on degree of maturity of parts of cerebral hemispheres involved in response (age). Presence of visual differentiation thought to mark beginning of function of cerebral hemispheres.
Formation of CR occurred in 29, 74 and 131 paired stimulations for different Ss at respective ages of 1 mo. 13 days; 1 mo. 9 days; 1 mo. 4 days. 3 stages: indifference, inhibition of other movements and first signs of CR, clear CR. At 2.5–3.5 mos., child can distinguish 11.5 tones difference by CR method. At 4 mos. 4 days, DL is 5.5 tones.	Main factor in CR formation is child's age, not number of stimulations.
After 3–6 days, 7 infants showed increased sucking, mouth opening and decrease of general activity and crying to buzzer. 1 infant, in poor physiological condition, who "never seemed hungry" showed no conditioning. Control experiment showed no feeding response to light or clang, but in some cases increase in activity and crying. Experiment with control Ss showed increase in general activity and crying in majority to buzzer.	Conditioned responses can be established in infants. This taken to indicate subcortical conditioning.
Trained twins equaled and surpassed untrained between initial and final tests, especially in performances (2) and (3). Experimental twins showed marked changes in initiative, interest in score, quietness, etc. Most elementary functions developed rap-	Results seem counter to Gesell's conclusions that identical twins are the same in motor equipment and that training is of little effect.

SOME STUDIES

AUTHOR DATE	TOPIC	SUBJECTS	METHODS
			throwing a ball, (3) hitting a mark by rolling a ball. Superior partners kept as controls. Gave Stanford-Binet, tested psychomotor functions according to Oserezky's scale.
Razran, G. H. S. (1936)	Effect of familiarity with a language on verbal conditioning.	One adult male psychologist with reading knowledge of English, Russian, German, French, Spanish, and Polish (Razran).	Word "saliva" thought of in each language; stimulus word presented on printed card to S who looked at it, inserted dry roll of cotton in mouth and closed eyes to keep stimulus word for 2 min. in focus of consciousness; attempted implicit verbalization only in language of word presented. Controls were Gaelic word for saliva (unfamiliar to S), pair of nonsense syllables, and control period of "blank consciousness." Tests of language familiarity.
Razran, G. H. S. (1935)	Attitudes and types of conditioning.	Mostly undergraduate college students, age range 17–20. 37 Ss.	Each S given control series (stimulus-to-be-conditioned alone), conditioning series proper, and post-conditioning series, to obtain norms for conditioned stimuli and for further control periods. Conditioning stimuli: eating pretzels, watching eating of pretzels, thinking of eating of pretzels or steak, having mint wafer on tongue; all for ½ min. Preceded by conditioned stimuli for 15 sec., latter lasting for 30 sec.: sound of metronome; nonsense syllables, words, digits projected on screen; and thinking of these stimuli. Salivation measured by weighing cotton rolls placed in mouth. Ss conditioned alone and in groups; instructed sometimes to form connection between stimuli, or *not* to form it; some non-instructed.

OF LEARNING (*Continued*)

FINDINGS	GENERAL REMARKS
idly. More complex functions changed strikingly by training.	

Salivations most in Russian; next in English; German; French; Spanish; Polish; Gaelic word, pr. of nonsense syllables, or "blank consciousness." Close correspondence between familiarity with language and average amount of salivation.	Human salivation extremely subject to psychological modifications; differential norms suggest widely applicable mechanism.

Found (in part) conditioned salivary responses of 3 types: positive (substantial increments in R to conditioned stimulus); negative (substantial decrements); and zero (no significant changes). Mixed C-R types were: negative-positive, negative-indifferent, and indifferent-positive. Monotypes show fairly normal distributions, small variabilities; mixed (bi-types), U-shaped or bimodal curves, large variability. Most distributions skewed. Variation of types with changes in instructions, nature of stimuli, presence of other Ss.	Different C-R types attributed to 3 different C-R attitudes: positive, negative and indifferent, that Ss assume. "These attitudes are best conceivable in terms of some postural set or some verbal organization, but, whatever their structural basis be, they are functionally central and *dominant* over the mere 'linkages' or associations of the situations presented."

Indeed, most social learning seems to involve the operation of many factors acting successively or conjointly. The problem is not so much to decide which habits should come under "conditioning" and which should come under the concept of "interiorization of values," but rather the sanest way of applying concurrently all the concepts fruitful for a given problem.

To recapitulate and interpret interrelations at the same time, these concepts are as follows: (1) The very first steps in individual existence display striking individual differences owing to genetic make-up; and despite social uniformities these individual differences in potentiality for social response are always present. (2) The reflex cycle and the conditioning process are of some importance even before birth, and of immense importance from birth onward. (3) Diffuse cravings and needs become canalized in specific directions, the process of canalization ultimately depending, in all probability, upon the same physiological mechanism as the conditioned response. (4) Conditioned responses are biologically related within the organism, some joining their forces to give an integrated result, some standing in opposition to others. The principle of biological dominance is a way of describing the fact that unsuccessful competitors in the struggle for control of the organism may lose their potency and, paradoxically, contribute to the strength of stronger tendencies which have subdued them. (5) While undergoing conditioning and canalization, the organism acquires a system of symbols, especially words, which become systematized internally. Partly on a conscious and partly on an unconscious basis, this inner system becomes powerful in control of responses to the outside social world. The process of value formation and, in particular, the formation of value tendencies toward the ego, must be included here. Attitudes toward inner symbols, particularly those standing for the self, are often dominant over external stimuli. (6) Attitude itself is a broad *valuing tendency*, and therefore ultimately a matter of canalization and conditioning; but it depends very largely upon factors operative in the interiorized system. (7) The integration of conditioned and canalized patterns, guided especially by ego values, frequently causes the fundamental discontinuity between persons. When decisions have to be made, central values, and hence the whole way of life, of one individual may be utterly different from those of others. (8) Shifting tensions, internal biological rhythms, rhythmic neurone discharge, and countless other factors in our biological existence operate to limit the control not only of outside stimuli, but of well-established interiorized habits. The organism is literally spontaneous and creative, breaks into new ways; and the spontaneous, simply because it is so hard to chart scientifically with our present conceptual tools, must be given special stress. It is never an explanation of anything—any more than a recourse to the doctrine of "free will" would explain anything. It is rather a necessary scientific compensation for the fact that we do not at present understand the dynamics of the organism, and must always allow to the unknown forces within it, and not simply to the chance errors of the statistician, a considerable positive rôle in the determination of social conduct.

PART THREE

A Genetic Study of Social Behavior

Chapter V

METHODS OF STUDYING THE SOCIAL BEHAVIOR OF CHILDREN

IN THE foregoing chapters, much material has already been drawn from the behavior of children. Working hypotheses as to nature and nurture, motivation, and the learning process have been stated for the purpose of providing a general interpretation of the process of growing into one's group, the socialization of the individual. Since so much of social psychology today is necessarily genetic psychology, our attention turns now to the task of interpreting research upon the social behavior of childhood. We shall attempt to see how the relatively unformed potentialities of the newborn become, as a result of biological and social factors, the personalities of adult members of the community.

Our first concern is necessarily with methods. Here we shall consider first experimental methods; then the varieties of controlled observations; rating scales; and finally in some detail the more complex methods which seek to see the various phases of child personality all at once in their interrelations.

The experimental study of the social behavior of infants may be said to date from the studies of J. B. Watson at the Phipps Clinic in Baltimore, 1917-20. The attempts to define the emotional make-up of the newborn and to demonstrate the reality of conditioned emotional responses in infants are of the most outstanding importance.

From the point of view of today, the methods and conclusions seem in many ways crude and inept. The original conditioning experiment on Albert was reported without any attempt at quantitative statement of stimuli or their effects. A metal bar was struck sharply just as the baby's hand reached for a rat which was presented to him. A week later, the rat and loud sound were presented

255

simultaneously seven times, after which the presentation of the rat alone brought crying and withdrawal.

It is not to be forgotten that the enthusiasm for these new methods was of immense importance for the developments during the decade of the 'twenties. Furthermore, the conception of the conditioned response, championed by Watson, has led to various new developments in technique. H. E. Jones, for example, has used a galvanometric technique for studying conditioned responses in infants; an electro-tactual stimulus was used as the unconditioned stimulus and a bell as the conditioning stimulus. The advantage of this method is that the use of the galvanic skin reflex permits the study of conditioning in infants at a very early age without using any severe emotional stimulus; it also permits more objective quantitative records.

Gesell, after making extensive comparisons of the mental growth of pre-school children through a variety of ingenious baby tests, first developed elaborate apparatus to facilitate the control of observation. This includes a clinical crib with adjustable platform, panels, rails, gate and ladder, for use with both very young babies and children; another observation compartment with a similar array of devices; an observation dome with cameras movable from horizon to zenith, making possible photographic reports of behavior recorded by observers, and a one-way screen making possible observation of the infants without their knowledge. Cubes, staircases, chair, bed, ring and other test materials have been standardized to the last degree, as has the procedure in giving tests and making observations. Another similar development in psychological baby-apparatus is the set-up used by Weiss and his collaborators. The main feature of this is a glass-enclosed observation cage containing a stabilimeter (apparatus which records amount of restlessness). An elaborate system of symbols was drawn up (eighty-two separate symbols used in hundreds of combinations) and mastered by the observers, who recorded on ticker-tape the detailed segmental movements of the infant.

The chief importance of this variety of machine-age products is its contribution to an accurate knowledge of the development of behavior patterns and the foundation laid for studying behavior sequence and organization. We now know, for example, as a result of such research, that the newborn infant shows little coordinated emotional response, though by the age of one year he has some fairly clear-cut patterns of emotion. Just how these later patterns emerge can be determined only by the accumulation of masses of data with the assistance of careful techniques such as these.

Bühler's activities have extended into the fields just mentioned: organizing tests suitable for infants, surveying the range of activities of the baby through twenty-four-hour observations at different age levels, and devising a wide variety of experiments, including experiments on social behavior. Perhaps her main contribution might justly be called a contribution to the formulating and opening up of problems in child study, rather than primarily to method; certainly she has not been interested in the various techniques that have been devised on this side of the water for more refined and accurate observation. She has not ignored experiment, however, and has always been resourceful in creating new situations to bring out various types of behavior. The most conspicuous of these was the series of experiments on social responses of babies. Putting two babies together in a crib, she observed the responses of the infants to each other. The method produced some interesting results as we shall see; but these results are limited by the fact that there was no very systematic control and variation of conditions. Consequently, we know that babies show wide differences in behavior, with rather definite tendencies to dominating or submissive behavior and the like; but there is no systematic information regarding the relation of dominance or submission to the difference in ages between a given child and his partner, or to differences in experience such as presence and number of brothers and sisters, number of adults in the home, physical differences such as height, weight, strength, health, emotional stability, and normal activity; not to mention other subtler differences of habit and temperament which might affect these social responses and would need to be understood before we could derive dependable laws of social and personality development.

One of the earliest of the experimental attacks on the problem of personality in pre-school children was made by L. R. Marston.

He devised a series of experiments designed to measure extroversion (tendency to direct one's emotionally aroused energy outward) shown in resistance to a stranger, degree of self-assertion, compliance, caution, and interest. These were carried out with 100 children between two and six years of age—fifty-six in the main experimental group and forty-four in the control group.

The procedure in the experiments was as follows: In the first experiment, the child was brought into a room; when he was busily engaged the assistant removed a screen revealing the experimenter sitting with a toy in his hand. The assistant left the room immediately. For one minute the experimenter paid no attention to the child; then he looked up. After thirty seconds he looked up smiling, and after another thirty seconds asked, "Do you like to teeter-tauter?" After thirty seconds he said, "Would you like to play with this?" and again after thirty seconds he said, "You may. Come on and play with it." If the child still refused, the experimenter urged persistently.

The children reacted most diversely to this experimental situation; some of them felt rebuffed when the experimenter did not respond to their first advances; others saw through the artificiality of the situation. This experiment was scored as follows: If the child refused unyieldingly to play with the toy or fled from the room, the extroversion score was 0. If the child refused at first but played with the toy after considerable urging, the score was 1; if the child accepted the offer to play with the toy after being reassured by the experimenter, the score was 2; and if the child accepted the toy without urging, the score was 3. A score of 4 was given to the children who made advances to the experimenter but did not approach or play with the toy before being recognized by the experimenter, and the child who approached promptly without waiting for recognition scored 5. Over half the children had scores of 2 or 3; hardly one-sixth of them showed extremely extroverted reactions, and nearly one-third showed very introverted reactions (i.e., emotional energy was directed to themselves).

The second experiment was ingeniously devised to show differences in the degree of compliance which children manifested in response to a standardized situation. As the child came in, the experimenter showed him a toy celluloid duck floating in a shallow pan of water and asked him if he would like to play a game with a lot of ducks. The experimenter then suggested that the child open a box containing ducks, after which they would play the game. During the following three minutes, the experimenter recorded the child's reactions in attempting to open the box, encouraging him, however, if he lost interest. At the close of three minutes, the experimenter offered his assistance and opened the box. This was scored from 1 to 5—those who "silently struggled through the whole period" received the "lowest" score, while those who gave up and did not return to the task after urging received the "highest" score (on extroversion). The ducks were also used in a third experiment which aimed to test caution, but did not differentiate definable degrees.

Another experiment measured the degree and kind of interest the children showed when visiting the mammal hall of the university museum. In this experiment the children showed different types of behavior toward the animal exhibits, some traveling a long distance with frequent stops and rapidly shifting interest, while others went a long distance with infrequent stops and general lack of interest; still others traveled only a short distance, but showed keen and prolonged interest in a few exhibits, and others were utterly without spontaneous interest and depended on the experimenter for motive and direction.

A fifth experiment was concerned with the degree of self-assertion which the children would show in reaction to postponement of gratification of desire. Three toys were exhibited, and the child was asked his choice. After he had expressed a choice, another toy was given him, with the promise that after he had played with it for a while he could have the chosen toy. After three minutes, or when the child asked for another toy, he was given a second non-preferred toy. After three minutes, or when he requested a different toy, he was given the toy he had originally chosen.

Most of the children expressed a choice readily, but also accepted the substitute toy readily. Great variations appeared, however; some of the children played quietly with the same toy, while others chattered and asked for another one. As a test of self-assertion, there proved to be complications because of the perseveration of interest in the substitute toy.

Correlations between the extroversion scores on the four different tests giving significant results ranged from approximately 0 (e.g., the correlations between lack of social resistance and interest, and between non-compliance and interest, were both less than .1 for the girls) to .61 ($\pm$ .08) in the case of the correlation between interest and self-assertion for the boys. All but two of the correlations between the extroversion scores on these different tests were above + .45 in the case of the boys, while only two of the correlations were as high as this in the case of the girls. Correlations between the score on one experiment and the sum of scores on the other three experiments were .54 ($\pm$ .09) to .65 ($\pm$ .07) in the case of the boys, and .37 ($\pm$ .12) to .66 ($\pm$ .08) in the case of the girls.

The results suggest that even among little children, different traits have different significance and interrelations for the two sexes. Particularly suggestive is the fact that whereas *interest* seems definitely related to other measures of extroversion in boys, it does not seem to have the same relation to these other extroversion measures in the case of girls. A further difference appears in the fact that differences in extroversion do not seem to be at all closely related in age to the boys, whereas there is a suggestion of such a relation among the girls. If increase in age does make for less extroversion, the difference between boys and girls might suggest earlier maturing of girls. That so simple an explanation can hardly suffice, however, is suggested by the fact that height, weight, and mental age correlate positively with extroversion among the boys, whereas these same correlations are negative for the girls.

A clear example of the kinds of results that may be achieved by clear analysis of a problem and the effective planning of an experiment to test individual differences appears in Weiss's study of factors involved in the pre-school child's compliance with commands. The 75 children included in the final analysis of data ranged from three years to five years, eight months. The problem was formulated in terms of ascertaining not only mental age and sex differences in carrying out commands, but the effect, on the one hand, of the complexity of the command, and, on the other, of the situation in which the child was engaged. Three test periods were spaced for each child at intervals of a week. In the "control situation" the child was furnished no material with which to occupy himself between commands. In the "toy situation" there was a variety of toys with which he was encouraged to play. In the "social situation" a companion of his age was present in addition to the toys used in the toy situation.

Eight commands of varying degrees of complexity, in respect to both their comprehension and the motor control demanded, were used; one was impossible to execute. The children who acted as subjects were divided into three groups, each one of which received first a different one of the three situations ("control," "toy," and "social"). The attempt was thus made to equalize the effect of the order of presentation of the three situations. Each test period ranged from 5 to 20 minutes. After each command, the experimenter waited until the subject appeared to be as much absorbed in his own activities as he had been before the command was given. Two types of records were kept: first, records of time, including both the time which elapsed between the giving of the command and the child's initial response, and the time taken by the response itself; second, details of behavior and verbal response during the experimental period, an account of the toys with which the child had played and with which he was playing when a command was given. Reliability was checked by comparing the results obtained by each of two experimenters working independently on 25 of the five-year-old group. This gave a narrow age range and range of abilities which may account in part for the fact that correlations mostly ranged between .50 and .60. Individual variation of the children from one period to the next was recognized to be important; probably further work of this kind ought to take into account the range of variation of individual children from one time to another. The following results of the study of time required for response are emphasized:

1. There was a consistent tendency toward increased pre-response time with increased complexity of the command.

2. There was a consistent decrease in time taken for response in each of the three situations as the groups increase in age.

3. Pre-response time was longer for the toy than for the social situation at all age levels, and longer for the social situation than for the control. These differences were smallest for the five-year-group.

4. There was a consistent trend toward increased pre-response time with decrease in M.A. in the control and social situations. The trend was also consistent for the toy situations except for the 30-42-month level.

5. The least *and the most* intelligent groups had long mean pre-response and response times in each situation.

6. The boys were somewhat slower in starting to respond in the toy and social situations than were the girls. They were also quicker in completing tasks, and more variable in their responses. But individual variations were so large that differences between the sexes had no statistical significance.

7. The three-year-olds took longer to respond in the toy than in the social situation, while the four- and five-year-olds showed an equal amount of prolonged response in each situation. For the two-year-olds, airplanes and airplane books each had three times the frequency of blocks for prolonged pre-response. In the four- and five-year-old groups, blocks were the most used in periods of prolonged pre-response. Of the three, the toy situation seemed to absorb the interest of the subjects most and to yield the greatest number of variations in behavior.

The kinds of behavior observed included, in order of frequency: a question while complying (how or what); starting to respond before the experimenter completed the command; an unusual verbal response; a substitute activity; verbal excuses; playing during the response; playing before the response; forgetting; playing with the test articles; expressing dislike of the test situation; etc. In view of the fact that an experimental situation of this sort would not be one in which the child would be so likely to become as deeply absorbed in his own play as he would when playing in his own room at home or even during an ordinary play period at school, we might be allowed to infer that behavior of the same sort could be expected more frequently in everyday situations. The child's degree of absorption or intensity of interest would undoubtedly be very important, though not studied in this investigation. Certain age differences in the frequency of certain kinds of response were suggestive:

The activity of the three-year-olds involved the greatest amount of repetition and "showing" on the part of the experimenter, of forgetting, of play during response, of play with test articles, of prolonged response, and of substitute activity of the unrelated and moderately related types. The four-year-olds evidenced the greatest amount of delayed or attempted recall, of questioning of all types, of expression of dislike of test situations, and of substitution of other responses for those required. Five-year-olds responded before completion of the command more than any other group and repeated the command while complying more than the three- or four-year-olds.

Another experimental study that suggests a thousand interesting questions regarding the development of child personality is Berne's investigation of social behavior patterns in young children. The actual work of the study was contemporary with that of D. S. Thomas and her associates, who were developing their techniques for the study of social behavior (cf. pages 269 ff.), and is a sort of single-handed *tour de force*, attempting to cover many of the methodological difficulties and even more personality problems than those handled by the Thomas group. Ratings, experiments and observational records were all used in this study of social behavior, and intercorrelations between these various measures were computed.

A five-point rating scale included thirty traits, of which the following are examples:

1. *Obeys:* is submissive to authority; submissive to restraint or command.
2. *Seeks approbation:* desires commendation, notice, sanction.
3. *Interested in the group:* has attention engaged by the group.
4. *Depends on adult:* depends on adult to provide activities for him; is unable to provide his own activity.
5. *Affectionate:* loves; has tenderness, fondness.
6. *Cooperates:* works or plays with others; works or plays jointly.
13. *Rivals:* shows personal competition; strives to equal or excel.

17. *Leads:* has initiative, self-reliance, decisiveness, and tact to inspire others to follow or to cooperate.
25. *Selfish:* cares supremely for self; regards own comfort or advantage in disregard or at expense of that of others.
26. *Impolite:* does not say "please," "thank you," "excuse me," "good morning," etc.

The raters were fifteen experienced teachers and assistants, most of whom were graduate students majoring in child psychology, and all of whom were thoroughly acquainted with the children. Correlations between ratings of three raters who graded 20 children ranged from .62 ($\pm$ .08) to .82 ($\pm$ .04), showing fair reliability. Significant differences between the means of ratings for different age groups were found for certain traits:

The three- and four-year-old groups surpass the two-year-old group in interest in the group, understanding of own property rights, sociability, rivalry, jealousy, responsibility for self, responsibility for others, criticism, social conformance, and ascendance. Three-year-old children also exceed two-year-old children in independence of adults and self-defense, and four-year-olds exceed two- and three-year-olds in cooperation. Sixteen traits showed no significant differences between the means of the ratings for the three age groups; obedience, seeking approbation, sympathy, kindness, politeness, affection, sensitiveness, motherliness, socially controlled behavior, imitation, respect for the property rights of others, participation and teasing were among these.

If the ratings are really free from the "halo error," the following findings are very significant: There is a consistent, though in some cases not marked, tendency for obedience, desire for approbation, interest in group, cooperation, respect for others' property rights, participation, rivalry, socially controlled behavior, motherliness, jealousy, criticism, social conformance and ascendance to increase both from two to three and from three to four years. Similarly, dependence, lack of understanding of own property rights, unsociability, disrespect for social ownership, followership, imitation, irresponsibility for self, irresponsibility for others, tend consistently to decrease with age.

The experiments were devised in such a way as to permit of a quantitative statement of the trait each was designed to test. The procedure for Experiment I was as follows: The experimenter brought the child into the examining room, sat down on one of the two small chairs in the room, looked directly at the child and said, "Lie down on the floor." She then occupied herself with the record of the child's behavior. The command was repeated at fifteen-second intervals until the child complied, or until ten commands had been given.

Such a simple experiment as this brought a wide range of reactions, of which the two following are the extremes:

Reaction Type 1

Child A (C.A. 35 months, Kuhlmann M.A. 36 months) looks at experimenter's writing and at her stop-watch. (1) Looks at E. (2) Says, "I don't want to," looks at E, at writing, and at E. (3) Looks at E and smiles. Looks at E. Looks around. (4) "I don't want to." Looks at E, at books on high shelf, at wall, at E, and outdoors. Goes to window and looks out. (5) Looks at E. "I don't want to." Turns to window and looks out with back to E. (6) Laughs. "Hub-hub." Looks out window with back to E. (7) "No," with back to E. Looks out window. (8) Back to E. Rubs eyes. Glances at E and turns back. Rubs eyes. (9) Cries. E then ends the experiment.

Reaction Type 5

Child B (C.A. 48 months, Stanford-Binet M.A. 68 months). (1) Obeys within five seconds. E said "All right." Child B. "Can I get up?" Then as E put top on the chair, "I believe I can spin this."

This type of accurate descriptive record of social behavior in an experimental situation deserves much wider use than it has so far received, since it affords material both for a qualitative picture of dominant trends in the personality and for quantitative analysis of specific forms of behavior.

In addition to the six tests calculated to discriminate degrees of obedience, there were two experiments for measuring cooperation and interest. These two experiments were the same, except that in one case the experimenter observed the children through peep-holes in a screen, while in the other she wrote down observations as she sat in a chair near the door. The procedure consisted essentially in bringing the child into a room containing at one end two other children playing with some toys, and at the other end another pile of toys. The two children were previously directed not to "bother" the new child, and to let him do as he wished. The responses of the subjects varied from (1) playing with toys and hardly noticing the other children to (5) becoming decidedly interested in the children (interest in toys insignificant in comparison). In cooperativeness they showed a similar range of response; scores ranged from (1) sat alone and played with the toys, did not play with the other children, to (5) played with the other children almost all the time.[1]

The correlations between experimental scores and ratings for obedience, interest, cooperation and respect for others' property are given below:

	Correlation
Average scores for obedience, experiments 1 and 4, and ratings.....	.64 ± .05
Interest scores, experiment 7, and ratings........................	.83 ± .03
Interest scores, experiment 8, and ratings........................	.92 ± .01
Average interest scores, experiments 7 and 8, and ratings..........	.91 ± .01
Cooperation scores, experiment 7, and ratings....................	.82 ± .03
Cooperation scores, experiment 8, and ratings....................	.87 ± .02
Average cooperation scores, experiments 7 and 8, and ratings......	.95 ± .01
Property-rights score, experiment 9, and ratings.................	.58 ± .05
Property-rights score, experiment 10, and ratings................	.64 ± .05
Average property-rights score, experiments 9 and 10, and ratings...	.76 ± .03

The observational record worked out by Berne differs from those used by other experimenters chiefly in the following respect: She used general headings or "traits" for the system of classification, noting simply presence or absence of behavior items indicative of the trait. Both Thomas and Goodenough have emphasized the desirability of working *directly* with behavior items rather than with general traits summarizing those items (cf. page 269). Berne felt, however, that the context of any item of behavior was so important that the observer was much better able to classify it on the spot than she herself or anyone else using the records would be able to do in a later analysis of the material. The adaptation of the most practicable of the symbol systems for noting items of behavior and their contexts, together with the observer's impression of the value import of the behavior for the individual, might retain both values with greater validity than either method now offers.

[1] This type of experimental procedure has been used also by Updegraff in a study of children's responses to failure, and by Jack, and Page, in work on ascendance (see Chapter VII).

Everetov has also adapted an everyday situation to the study of social behavior of little children. In the middle of the room was placed a train consisting of an engine and ten cars, on which were loaded lumber and other building materials, together with simple tools. A group of five children was sent into the room to play, and stimuli were classified under the following categories: stimuli which provoke group (collective) reactions; those which result in cooperation; those which are an obstacle to cooperation; conditions under which common action is broken up. In addition, all group activities were timed, and characteristics of actions done in common were enumerated in detail. The different kinds of group activity were summarized in three categories: construction work involving the given materials, work reproducing the work of someone else, and "circular responses" (circular reflex responses, attributable, perhaps, to emotional reactions).

M. C. Jones reports a somewhat comparable experimental situation for the study of emotion. Two children are brought into a room where there is a doll and a bed, a balloon with a string too short for the child to reach it, and two boxes which will enable him to reach the balloon if he places them together in the right combination. The degrees of "patience, persistence, cooperation, and possessiveness" shown by the children are quite as important as the learning process the child goes through in trying to get the balloon.

H. E. Jones has adapted galvanometric methods to the study of children's reactions by such devices as the following: The child sits at the play table with a pair of electrodes attached to his feet; no restriction is placed on his activity except that he is not allowed to get up and walk around. Various stimuli are presented, such as a cage of white rats, a tumble toy, and a bell. These stimuli produce electrical disturbances which distribute the children in a quantitative series from extremely non-reactive to extremely reactive children. The point of view here is that overt behavior is often far from an adequate measure of the visceral disturbance, and that consequently the more simple observational techniques must be supplemented by methods of detecting the inner response.

Another example of the attempt to study emotional response is Duffy's study of tensions in reaction. The essential feature of the technique is the measurement of tension in the left (or unused) hand which holds a tambour, while the other hand is engaged in a performance requiring discriminative reactions; emotional stimuli are introduced from time to time. A kymograph record shows the time of appearance of the visual stimulus, the reaction by the right hand, the time of appearance of the emotional stimulus and the degree of tension of the left hand during the whole performance.

The data obtained in this fashion were correlated with ratings of the tendency toward "excitability" among three- to five-year-old children. Of course, marked individual variations in tension were found, and the type of tension curve seemed to be correlated with the tendency to emotional reactions.

The situation confronting the child in taking a test, such as a standard intelligence test, may be conceived as an experimental situation for the analysis of personality factors; not the achievement upon the test, but the way of responding to the adult and the task is brought into focus. Negativism and resistance have been carefully studied in this way; in particular, the relation between negativism and the difficulty of the task, and the specific influence of requiring the child to refer to, or point to, himself, as contrasted with relatively impersonal tasks. From this point of view, any experiment is also a behavior situation involving interaction between personalities and revealing important aspects of each personality.

In all of these cases, experiments have been used to elicit behavior which could be directly measured; a different use of experimental procedure using pictures, stories, dolls and games to elicit projected fantasies of the child which throw light on the motivation of social behavior, is discussed below (see pages 280 ff.).

CONTROLLED OBSERVATION

When the isolation or control of variables, as sought by the experimental method, cannot practically be achieved, the requirements of research may be met by various forms of controlled observation. As contrasted with casual or haphazard observation, this method, while not controlling the subjects' behavior, controls the *observer*, so as to insure definite and systematic observation of crucial phases of behavior and close comparison of behavior in various distinct and well-defined situations.

Thomas, emphasizing the limitations of experimental approaches, has worked on techniques to obtain reliable observations. Her volume revealed vividly both the promising and the discouraging aspects of this attempt to infuse child psychology with the zeal for validity of data. Promising, because of the amazing accuracy and reliability she was able to achieve; discouraging because of the obvious inapplicability of her techniques *as there formulated* to many significant and persistent problems.

A good illustration of her type of method may be seen in the study of physical contacts of nursery-school children with one another; this preliminary study and its sequel are Loomis's work.

After experimenting with a tentative record form, the following form was adopted for a study of physical contacts of nursery-school children. Contacts were classified carefully, e.g., "*Accident:* Touching in passing, working, playing with a person; brushing against or stepping on person. (If there is indication of intention or purpose, the contact is not classified here.) *Assistance:* Passing food; finding person; offering toy; helping to turn pages; brushing sand off coat. The letter *R* is used to indicate when the assistance is definitely requested." Contacts as thus organized were further classified into response groups as follows: "*Passivity:* (a) No activity, i.e., child is seemingly unconscious of the contact. (b) Activity of amount and kind requiring less intent than either resistance or cooperation. *Cooperation:* Any activity showing that the child voluntarily enters into the situation and carries it forward with regard for the other child. *Resistance:* Any physical response tending to stop physical contact of other child, whether this advance is accidental, friendly or aggressive. *Flight:* A definite immediate leaving of situation as a result of a contact."

This grouping of responses was later modified as experience required; obviously, for example, a number of acts of assistance in pushing a companion in a swing when the game required this assistance had a different significance from the same number of acts of assistance scattered throughout miscellaneous plays. The final grouping was as follows: Passivity; cooperation, game; cooperation, spontaneous; resistance; flight.

Originally blanks with detailed headings were used for the record-taking. These blanks were found to have certain serious limitations, particularly because, in cases of ambiguous contacts where the context of the situation ought to be recorded, the blank did not allow for suitable space. The record-making plan was consequently modified; a code was used to record activities that were easily classified, and new ones were described as completely as possible for subsequent interpretation.

A representative sampling of each child's spontaneous activity was obtained by observation for a total of at least one hour (after the study it was concluded that this length of time was not enough), under conditions in which the type of contacts was not determined by adults or by the requirements of the apparatus and play materials (e.g., time at the luncheon table, on the swing, and with the skipping rope should be excluded). Although the data of this study were obtained from only thirteen cases—not enough to offer high reliability—suggestive differences in the social behavior of individuals were found. These were summarized both from the direct observations on each child and the indirect observations recorded when he was involved in a contact with another child directly observed at the time, and led to consideration of each child's ratio of contacts as subject and object. When the total contacts made by each child on others were compared with the total made by others on him, all but one of the children had ratios between 2:1 and 1:2. Very active children had ratios of 1:½, while one child inclined to daydream a great deal had a ratio of nearly 1:3 on direct observation. The importance of making such a study *in connection with* language studies is indicated by such instances as that of one child who would not make contact with a group until after he had received permission in response to the inquiry, "May I play with you?" Other personality characteristics of various sorts would also affect this ratio between contacts as subject and object, and also the total number of contacts, which ranged from 46 to 154 for the eleven children observed 60 minutes.

The next item showing important variations was the number of individuals with whom contacts were made, which ranged from 6 to 15, and the influence of individuals contacted upon kind of contacts. The observer notes that "even at this age the degree of co-operativeness depends upon the individual from whose standpoint this is observed, and that *giving and receiving are different functions* [italics ours]. As subject, for instance, Nancy made five out of six cooperative contacts with Rachael, and on indirect observation she made her only cooperative contact with this same child. As object, she received seven out of nine cooperative contacts from Rachael on direct observation; yet the records of approximately twelve hours of indirect observation showed that she received twelve cooperative contacts from four children other than Rachael. Rachael, on the other hand, made on direct observation two out of two cooperative contacts with adults, and received seven out of fourteen from adults." Here again, as the experimenter points out, the importance of complementary language studies is apparent.

The method of repeated short-sample observation has been used in various forms by a number of investigators for some years. It is clearly described and explicitly formulated by Goodenough. It consists in the "observation of the everyday behavior of an individual or a group of individuals for definite short periods of time and the recording of the occurrence or non-occurrence of certain specified and objectively defined forms of behavior during each of these periods. The number of periods in which the report is positive for a given individual is then treated as his score. Since the number and length of the observational periods are the same for all individuals, a direct comparison of the frequencies or scores is thus made possible." It may be used in the classroom or on the playground, the only requirement being that of course all individuals must be observed under comparable conditions; and when only one behavior item is being observed, such as laughing or nervous oral habits, a whole roomful of children may sometimes be observed by one investigator. When several activities are being checked, one child at a time may be observed. Ten-minute, five-minute, and one-minute periods have been experimented with. The optimum period depends of course partly on the nature of the observations, and partly on the number in the group being observed. A large number of short periods is usually apt to give higher reliability than half the number of periods twice as long. The recording of observations is of course facilitated by mimeographed or printed forms which include all possible reactions, so that a mere check is all that is required. The advantages of the method include its wide applicability, making measurements possible without interfering with normal activity, and involving a relatively small amount of total time for a direct measurement of the individuals' behavior under normal conditions.

Parten applied this technique to a study of the social participation of forty nursery-school children. The spontaneous play groups occurring during the free play hour were observed during one-minute periods. The social behavior of the child was recorded on a schedule, and the order in which each child was observed was rotated. Various categories of social participation were listed on the record: unoccupied, solitary play, onlooker, parallel group activity, associated group play, and organized supplementary cooperative group play. Special categories of leadership were also listed on the record blank: independent pursuing of own will, directing, following direction, and the intermediate position of following one child while directing another in the same group. At the time the social behavior of each child was noted, a record was also made of the number and names of children in a group in which the observed child was playing, his occupation, and any remarks he made.

Ten even-day observations correlated .76 with ten odd-day observations of social participation; with twenty even- and odd-day samples the correlation coefficient was .90. The observations recorded under the headings of social participation proved to be more reliable than the observations of leadership. In the case of the latter, ten even- and ten odd-day scores correlated .39; twenty scores of alternate days correlated .44; and thirty samples of even and odd days gave a correlation of .73. In order to check the errors that might result from the bias of the observer, three assistants made simultaneous observations while the investigator observed sixteen individual children. In 89 per cent of the items noted, the records of the assistants were identical with those of the investigator.

An extension of the same method was used by sixteen graduate students, observing physical activity, laughter, amount of conversation or talkativeness, social participation and leadership, anger, dramatic play, and eating habits during the nursery-school lunch hour (self-help, etc.). The method was further refined by dividing each one-minute period into six ten-second intervals and recording observations at the end of each of these. The mean daily score for each child as obtained by one of two observers was correlated with the corresponding figure obtained by the other observer to compute the final reliability. The results obtained by the two workers were combined and the approximate reliability of the combined score was computed by the Spearman-Brown formula. The reliabilities obtained for these observations were as follows: physical activity .58 ± .07; general activity .80 ± .04; laughter .32 ± .12; conversation .72 ± .06; social participation .60 ± .07; leadership .74 ± .05; anger .71 ± .06; dramatic play .87 ± .03; self-help .35 ± .10; response to food .50 ± .08; reluctance .71 ± .06. (Goodenough reports these in three decimals; we have reduced them to two.)

Olson's method of sampling behavior, which he developed in his study of nervous habits, is adapted to the reliable observation of specific behaviors in a group of considerable size, within a comparatively short amount of total time. Two observers, independently noting the occurrence or non-occurrence of a given item of behavior within a given time interval, obtained a correlation of .75 for their measures during seven periods. This would yield a reliability of about .86, Olson points out, for fourteen measures. He also varied the length of time for the separate observation periods and found that twenty five-minute periods were more reliable than ten ten-minute ones. The reliabilities for the twenty observation periods varied between .68 and .94, with .87 as the most representative value. Correlations between observations over an interval of time ranged from .80, when the interval was eight days, to .40, when the interval was just a year; corrected for attenuation, these correlations would be, respectively, .98 and .46.

Goodenough has recently expressed serious doubts as to the value of the short-sample methods, emphasizing their neglect of personality structure and of social setting. For the reasons already noted, we think that such doubts are often well grounded; but that in certain specific objective studies, such as Olson's studies of nervousness, the methods have considerable utility in preparing the way for later more penetrating procedures, or for comparing behavior of groups.

An observational study which attacks a problem of special social significance is Newcomb's investigation into the *consistency of extrovert-introvert tendencies among problem boys*. Newcomb developed a technique of observation of older children, adapted especially to camp situations. This consisted of daily checks, on a comprehensive standardized form, of a wide range of behavior. The following reproduces the form, with a few examples of the kinds of item to be recorded. Note that each blank contains spaces vertically for the four points of the scale, and horizontally for five boys whose behavior is recorded. The numbers indicate the number of times the specified item of behavior was observed to occur on the day reported.[1]

Name of Boy:	R.T.	H.L.	F.A.	M.E.	J.S.

Did he cry for help when hurt or in trouble?

	R.T.	H.L.	F.A.	M.E.	J.S.
cried loudly for counselor	1	....	....	....	....
cried out, but did not call for counselor	1	....	....	3	....
cried only to himself	1	....	....	2	1
maintained composure	....	....	2	....	....

BEHAVIOR RECORD

Date   Counselor

Name of Boy:	....	....	....	....	....

Did he show confidence in his own abilities?

| boasted loudly of greater abilities than he had | .... | .... | .... | .... | .... |
| spoke confidently of ability he really had | .... | .... | .... | .... | .... |

[1] These scales are in some ways like the devices offered by Bridges (see Chapter IX), but have the advantage of greater quantitative adaptability, since the number of times per day a given kind of behavior occurs is recorded, and records are kept over a period of days. Newcomb's scales also have the advantage of allowing for four steps on each item.

expressed lack of con-
fidence in own abili-
ties   ....
hesitated even to try
his ability   ....

Did he take the initiative in organizing games?
insisted on doing the
organization himself ....
gave constant advice
to the leader   ....
helped to plan, but
loyal to the leader ....
let others do all the
planning—follower   ....

Did he submit to criticism or discipline from counselors?
resisted violently, or
fought back   ....
retorted angrily, sar-
castically, with
threats   ....
showed resentment by
mumbling or sullen-
ness   ....
accepted it quietly and
in good spirit   ....

Did he speak before the group at camp-fire?
made a speech or told
a story   ....
answered request for
reports   ....
answered questions, or
took part in discus-
sion   ....
told another something
to say for him   ....

The list was drawn up from situations met during experience at this camp. Only a single day's record was to be kept on each sheet; this precaution was taken to minimize errors due to "halo" effect. The particular responses chosen for this list were selected because of various characteristics which made them especially practicable for study: they were all items of fairly frequent occurrence at this camp;

they were clear cut enough to make their recording fairly objective; there was a fairly wide variation in the responses of different boys; and they were adapted to classification under extrovert or introvert traits, such as volubility and social forwardness, on the one hand, or taciturnity and preference for solitude, on the other. The mean correlation of the even- and odd-day scores ranged from .46 to .93 (mean = .78).

In addition to the daily records, Newcomb secured ratings of these same thirty items on a five-point scale at the end of the camp period; a daily report by each counselor on his own boys, noting any behavior which he considered in any way significant; and detailed records made by the experimenter himself of each observed incident which he considered indicative of the kinds of behavior studied (4500, or 90 incidents per day, were recorded in this way).

Now Newcomb was interested primarily in *consistency* of behavior; so the first step in analysis was simply to discover the extent to which the boys *tended* to respond always positively, or always negatively, to a given situation, instead of responding now one way, now the other. If an arbitrary zero point represents complete inconsistency of behavior and if extrovert behavior is indicated to the right and introvert behavior to the left of this zero point, a distribution curve can be constructed in which this zero point or point of greatest inconsistency is seen to be the mode, while on either side of this mode the more consistent the behavior, the more rarely is it found. When a further analysis was made of the interrelations of behaviors supposedly associated, the correlations were not significantly higher than the correlations between items that one would not ordinarily expect to be related. Here again some boys showed a consistency which might reasonably justify their description in terms of characteristic "traits," while a larger number combined positive and negative responses in such a way that it would not be fair to ascribe such "traits" to them. When so-called traits were further combined to discover whether extrovert or introvert "types" could be found, it was found that about one-fifth of the boys were consistent in three, four or five traits; but none of the boys was consistent in more than five of eight possible traits. Consistency in one trait was not necessarily connected with consistency in other traits, and even if consistency in other traits was present, it often occurred in the opposite direction from that of the first trait; i.e., "consistent extroversion" was found along with "consistent introversion."

The thoroughness of the method justifies the conclusion that "inconsistency" rather than "consistency," in terms of the defined "types," is to be expected from boys whom this sample represents. It may well be, however, that inconsistency itself is associated with the maladjustment or instability that goes along with being a "problem boy," and that greater consistency would be found among better-adjusted groups. Certainly the method deserves further application to determine whether this is the case.

This method of recording observations of social behavior is obviously adapted to other sorts of problems: the analysis of characteristic patterns of children's social behavior, their motivation, and their variation in situations handled by different types of leader or authority could well be carried out against a background of data collected in this way.

A method which permits analysis of the reliability of data at the same time that it allows for recording the color and unique details of behavior of individual children has been extensively used by Jersild and his collaborators. An individual recorder follows each child for ten or more periods of 15 minutes each, writing down a detailed descriptive record of behavior which is subsequently analyzed quantitatively. Excerpts from such records are quoted in Chapter VII, and similar records on seven-year-old children appear in Chapter X.

Ratings

In spite of a great deal of criticism of their use, rating scales have persisted with a tenacity that is strengthened by their practicability. Experimental and observational techniques at their best are still cumbersome. Even when presented with a reasonable degree of simplicity, they tend to leave out some types of situation and behavior that a rating scale can take account of; short-sample observation techniques, for example, may discriminate between "often," "usually," "sometimes," "rarely," but they cannot tell us that a given behavior has *never* occurred in the case of a given child. One temper tantrum, or "accident," or exhibition of fear, per week or month may be an important thing to know, and yet be missed by the short-sample observation. Similarly, experimental situations may catch characteristic responses, but fail to record the occasional important response which occurs in special situations. At this point the rating scale is useful. Granted the competence of the observers, who are usually teachers, an estimate of fairly high reliability on a wide range of activities and attitudes may be obtained. A five- or seven-point scale has been found most satisfactory in general; detailed description of the behavior that corresponds to a given point on the scale is conducive to greater reliability; the average of three competent judges who know the child well produces a more reliable result than the rating of one judge (diminishing returns set in rapidly, however, beyond three to five competent and careful judges). As an example of what may be done with rating scales at their best, we may recall M. C. Jones's report that ratings on intellectual traits agreed with intelligence quotients as well as intelligence quotients on different tests agreed with each other. She refers to a seven-point scale embracing two hundred items. The "inhibition of crying" item is defined in such terms as the following: a rating of 1 or 2 is given when the child does not use crying as a means of expressing emotion, or when crying in emotional situations is absent or brief. A rating of 4 is given when the child's crying varies in normal fashion with the nature and intensity of the emotion, 6 or 7 when the child is exceptionally prone to cry in emotional situations. Even the most carefully defined rating scales, however, are likely to be limited in their value, as Jones points out, to studies of single groups of children in which the significance of the terms and the standard meaning of each rating can be agreed upon by a committee of raters.

Instead of judging the method of ratings all at once, and accepting or rejecting it, the current tendency among careful investigators is to test the utility of each form of rating in the hands of each rater and in relation to each person and each trait to be rated. Thus

Conrad shows that among school children some traits can be reliably rated, others not; that some raters can reliably rate traits which others cannot, etc. If careful work on reliability, combined with the acid test of predicting behavior, is carried out, the area of real usefulness of ratings will probably prove to be considerable. Coordinated with other methods for recording qualities of behavior and evidences of its meaning to the individual, ratings may provide a useful framework of data on those aspects of personality which are most clearly comparable and where a child's relative position helps to evaluate the importance of the behavior for the child and for his group.

Methods of Studying Social Behavior in Relation to the Total Personality

If there is any one fundamental trend during the last few years which is of basic importance in the study of social behavior, it is the emphasis upon relations between social behavior and personality organization of the individual child. Both the confusion arising from statistical analysis of data which ignore personality structure and the coherence which we find when the social behavior of an individual is seen in relation to such structure, make this apparent. We see this in connection with studies of aggression, competition, leadership, sympathy; there is probably no aspect of social behavior which can be adequately understood apart from its relation to the personality of the individual. This makes it increasingly important to explore a variety of methods for understanding personality make-up, particularly in its social aspects. Within recent years, attempts to find substitutes for the long-drawn-out procedures of the psychoanalyst have led some investigators to other methods. Many important kinds of material may be collected from interviews by teachers or from teachers' observations of children in normal, everyday school situations. These methods are most important where it is necessary to get a direct picture of the child's attitudes toward father and mother, brothers and sisters, teachers, friends, work and play. Direct studies of such attitudes may contribute material which illumines relationships between the child's attitude toward adults and the ways in which he structures social relations with his own age group. When the direct approach is undesirable, important material may be obtained from other methods such as the child's responses to pictures, stories, dramatic play and toys representing different sorts of objects or persons. L. K. Frank[1] describes the common basis of these "projective methods" in terms of the fact that they all involve the presentation to the subject of various situations and materials that are so "plastic and unstructuralized that the individual subject can, as it were, project upon this material his own personality make-up." The following are illustrations of "projective methods" being used in studies now in progress:

Dramatic play with dolls is being used in a number of ways.[2] In this type of procedure, the small dolls are used for the child to "play out" patterns of social relation such as aggression, protection, prejudice, etc. Two kinds of method arc in general use. In the first, the experimenter takes a very active rôle, suggesting names for the dolls and suggesting their activities. In the second, he may take a relatively passive rôle, allowing the child to create a situation and to carry through any pattern of social relations he wishes. David Levy's therapeutic doll is capable of being dismembered; and the child can show by his treatment of different dolls representing father, mother and siblings how he feels toward those individuals.

Dolls appropriately dressed for the investigator's purpose may be used with older children to promote the verbal flow of fantasy material—"story-telling" about the dolls instead of free play with them. When it is necessary to work with a group instead of individually, such a technique has its uses. In one case a set of dolls representing the children and dog of the "Our Gang" motion-picture comedies was used. The subjects were encouraged to tell a story about the dolls, each in his turn taking up the tale where the other left off. Attitudes often reveal themselves freely. Thus in the stories the children permitted the little Negro boy to transgress

[1] In a forthcoming article on "projective techniques in personality study."

[2] For the major part of this discussion of the use of puppets, dolls and pictures in eliciting children's social attitudes, we are indebted to Ruth and Eugene Horowitz.

the local mores in ways which they objected to when faced with the same act in another medium, such as a picture of a social situation. Whether such verbal expression of prohibited action is in general permitted by children despite its repression from overt behavior remains to be determined. It must also be remembered that fantasy probably finds some modes of expression better adapted to certain individuals—free play is more releasing for some, story-telling for others.[1]

Another investigator has tried out the use of a puppet with pre-school-age children. In one study this provoked fear response of different kinds: (1) fear that was almost terror, causing shrinking and readiness to run away; (2) fear plus fascination, a response that permitted the child to watch as long as the puppet did not approach him; (3) fear and attraction, permitting the child to advance and touch the puppet, but to shrink when the puppet touched him; (4) fear and aggression, e.g., the child's first response was to grasp the head of the puppet and twist it, but an advance on the part of the puppet was met by shrinking away. The stimulus strength of the doll could almost be measured by its after-effects. Some children could turn immediately to the next task; one repeated the name of the puppet continuously while looking at a picture book, saying, "Here's another Tobey, I want to find more Tobeys." Another turned to a suggested task only tentatively, with furtive and fearful glances toward the opening of the envelope into which the puppet had been placed; she settled down to the task only when the envelope had been turned so that she could no longer see the opening. Another interrupted frequently with demands that Tobey be produced, accusing the investigator of hiding it in her coat. Such results suggest that puppets could be a fruitful technique for investigating fears, aggression, and ideas of causation, as well as the child's ideas of social relationships. For the latter, several puppets could be used, with the child as director, the adult perhaps the technical agent.

[1] A variation on the doll technique is offered by the procedure of Homburger, who presents his subjects (college freshmen) with a group of dolls, household furniture, blocks and cars, and asks them to prepare a "dramatic scene." The scenes arranged by the subject are recorded photographically and interpreted later in terms of psychoanalytic symbols apparent in the arrangement of the material.

The puppet may also be used in connection with interviews with young children to elicit conversation or information which the child would not give to an adult. A three- or four-year-old who is willing to tell "Jerry" all about his home troubles may completely close up if the experimenter questions him directly.

Another procedure which has proved fruitful for very young children is the use of pictures. Pictures representing children in distress, in fights, being disciplined by adults, confronting a fearful situation such as going into a dark room, having to take medicine, are used to elicit a child's evaluation of the situation, or projections of his own experience, as the case may be.

In one study, pictures were used in a variety of ways to test the child's awareness of community mores. Illustrative discussions of procedure are as follows:

The "Which Is Best" test is an adaptation and expansion of the ideas originally presented by Deutsch in her test of social conformity. In the present study the test became entirely a picture test. As an example of the procedure: A page of five or six landscapes was presented and children were asked "which is the best place to live?" They indicated first, second, third, fourth, and fifth choice. The procedure was the same for each item. The items were presented in order, each item consisting of a number of pictures pasted on one page of a large scrap book. The children indicated their choices by placing cover cards over their selections, thus eliminating confusion and distraction. The tests were administered individually. The "Which Is Best" test was originally presented in two parts. A consisted of 13 items, B of 18. The questions included such choices as "best place to live," "best house to live in," "best way for a boy to dress," "best way to dance," "best kind of dishes," "best-looking flag," "best sport," etc. Among the pictures for each item, care was taken to include some representations of the familiar. In a set of countrysides, one was unmistakably similar to local contours; in a set of homes, several similar to local types were included; in a set of cities, similarity to the county seat of one was evident (unanimously so commented on by the adults). The number of pictures for the items ranged from four to twenty-four. Except where there were but four to choose among (and there were very few such) the first five choices were indicated. The test may be scored in terms of increasing awareness of, and approval of, the socially familiar.

With the use of pictures it is possible to get at concepts that children may be unable to verbalize. In one set the investigator is

attempting to make a genetic study of children's economic awareness. The subjects are asked to look at pictures of children, houses,
clothing, automobiles, play, streets, table service. Each item occurs
twice in the series, once drawn to indicate poverty and once drawn
to indicate wealth. The children are asked to sort these pictures into
two piles indicating "poor" and "rich." At about the third grade
they have no trouble in indicating their awareness of the economic
factor to be found through each series of pictures. The same material
might have to be used in a different way were the investigator dealing with younger children. Another method would be to present to
the subject one class of pictures at a time, e.g., all the pictures of the
poor children; then to show the two pictures of another item, perhaps the rich house and the poor house, and to ask the subject in
which house the children "belong." After the whole series had been
run through in this way it could be gone through again, the pictures
of rich children being used as the starting point, the subjects finding
with what pictures they "belong."

The usefulness of pictorial material is also apparent in the attempt to tap the various *stages of development* of a social attitude
such as the attitude of white children toward the Negro. Subjects
in a nursery school in which there were both white and Negro children were asked to identify by name a series of portraits in which
both white and colored faces appeared. None of the pictures was an
actual portrait of a child in the nursery school; yet it was soon
evident that in making their identification the subjects showed an
awareness of race to the extent of giving to the colored faces the
names of Negro children. Also when asked to identify faces in the
series by such a question as "Is this ————?" (using the name
of the child being interviewed), white children refused to identify
themselves with the pictures of colored children, although they
were quite willing to lend their names to pictures of other white
children.

In another projective study, the plan is to use pictures to get at
the child's idea of himself and of his relationship to other individuals, e.g., to find what he conceives his status to be in relation to
brothers and sisters. Does he conceive himself to occupy the place
he really does occupy in the family hierarchy, or does he conceive

himself to be older or younger than he really is? He is given a page on which there are pictures of four individuals of his own sex varying in age, and is asked to identify himself, i.e., tell which one he most resembles. In another case he is shown pictures of two individuals in whom neither age nor sex can quite be distinguished but who vary in size, and he is asked again to identify himself. So, too, a page containing pictures of a family showing father, mother and several children might be presented, and again he might be asked to indicate himself in the picture. Sometimes a "joker" might be put in, i.e., he might be shown a picture containing an adult of his sex and a child of the opposite sex and then asked which he is. In cases where children do not refuse to answer, conceivably such procedure might lead to the indication of which category is paramount in one's structuring of the world.

The same technique might be extended to an investigation of the child's idea of himself as a member of a social group, to his ideas of his siblings and of his parents. For example, pictures contrasting solitary and group activity, the receiving and the giving of physical punishment, wholesome and unwholesome habits in routine procedures such as eating and sleeping, might yield from the child a well-rounded conception of himself and his place in his world. Checking with adults who know him well and with child colleagues in his group should serve to indicate how much of the child's self-concept is wishful and how much is observable actuality.

Extensions of the pictorial choice technique to include members of the immediate family suggest themselves—a smiling daddy and a frowning daddy; a neat mamma and a frowzy mamma; an older sibling punishing or protective. "Which is yours?" and "Which one do you like?" are simple queries which might throw light on the extent to which the child imposes the pattern of his desires on the real situation as well as the extent to which he has desires in these matters apart from his experiential reality. It is even possible that an accurate picture of the family situation might be elicited in this way. Subtleties in types of choice and gradations in differences between pictures must wait on specific experimental situations and subjects.

In a study of sympathy a series of steps was necessary in the proc-

ess of collecting an adequate group of pictures for work with two-
and three-year-old children. A preliminary set which included pictures of animals and of people cut from daily papers and magazines
proved useless because the content of the pictures was so complicated or so remote from the children's experiences that it stimulated no response. In the second group of pictures, selected from
collections of pictures of nursery-school children, of babies and of
younger children used as illustrations in child magazines, a very
different but equally unsatisfactory result was obtained. Where a
picture was too simple, consisting solely of a single child carrying on
a single obvious activity, there was not enough scope for selective
response of individuals, and the children tended to be unanimous
and objective in their comments. In pictures, however, whose content was within the range of two- and three-year-old experience and
which contained enough variety to permit varying interpretations by
the individual, the responses of the children reflected interesting
personal experience and preoccupation. Thus a small boy who had
gone to school but had been told by the teacher that he was too
little, was shown in a tearful agony of disappointment; there was
here no clear context to permit the subject to tell why the boy was
crying, and abundant and interesting personal interpretations were
offered.

The generalizations just given about the kinds of pictures suitable
for personality study prove to hold also in relation to stories. Where
the story material is too stereotyped or simple, an objective routine
answer is practically inevitable. Difficult stories are apt to stimulate
irrelevant or meaningless flights of fancy. Stories of aggression, sickness, being disciplined, being lost, being hurt, of loss of property
or competition, may differentiate significantly between children, and
bring out characteristic themes or patterns of emotional response.

The most systematic study of fantasy in relation to personality
and social behavior has been carried out by projective methods under
the direction of H. A. Murray at the Harvard Psychological Clinic.
The following *needs* have been listed as a basis for the study of relationships between manifest behavior and latent personality drives
appearing in fantasies stimulated by pictures, stories, word lists, and
sound stimuli.

1. Aggression
2. Succorance
3. Acquisition
4. Affiliation
5. Cognizance
6. Achievement
7. Dominance
8. Nurturance
9. Deference
10. Inviolacy
11. Recognition
12. Excitance
13. Exhibition
14. Exposition
15. Harm avoidance
16. Construction
17. Abasement
18. Order
19. Passivity
20. Play
21. Retention
22. Sex
23. Blame escape
24. Blame avoidance
25. Autonomy
26. Variance
27. Rejection
28. Seclusion
29. Sentience

These needs are apparent, for example, in the recurrent themes appearing in fantasies stimulated by the process of telling stories about pictures, throwing light on the same needs appearing in the individual's everyday social behavior. Telling stories about pictures gives evidence, direct and indirect, not only regarding the personality needs of an individual, but also about the probable environmental pressures to which he has been exposed (called "press"), including both chronic attitudes of people surrounding him and specific traumas. This is the basis of the "thematic apperception test," which consists of a standard set of pictures for use with subjects of either sex. It promises to be the nearest approach to a short-cutting of the long process of psychoanalysis that has yet been suggested. It is now being used with older children by Sanford, and an independent set of pictures for use with young children is being prepared by Dyk. Both are interested in the interrelations between, and constellations among, variables rated by the experimenter on the basis of the behavior and fantasy material stimulated by the picture-test situation. In both cases personality and behavior findings from the use of this method can be compared subsequently with case material and behavior records, for validation of the underlying "needs" defined by the experimenter and for reconstruction of past experience and prediction of future behavior.

A major feature of the work under Murray's direction is the use, by a group of investigators, of a common conceptual framework, and the analysis of personality into quantifiable functional elements which may then be handled statistically. This permits the possibility of supplementing the usual psychiatric portrait with the systematic study of relationships that are ordinarily presented only as dogmas or as hypotheses. This conceptual framework developed largely in work with college students has already proved useful in the work with children now undergoing rapid development.

In addition to the use of toys, directed and undirected dramatic play, pictures and stories, there is much value in children's own spontaneous projections in the form of drawings, spontaneous games, and spontaneous stories. Here we are greatly in need of empirical criteria of symbolic values. These can probably be developed only through the coordination of observations of children's behavior and analysis of the child's fantasy. When we find a little girl who sees in all the Rorschach ink blots nothing but people trying unsuccessfully to "get out of rock caves," who says in interview that she "cannot tell what she likes best at school but she can tell what she likes *worst* and that is the way the teachers make you lie down for naps," who is reported by her mother to have nightmares, and who has disturbed relations with other children, it is not unjustified to suspect that escape from the caves really means something. A scientific understanding of caves or "clothes flying in the wind" or "cars being driven up and down the street" or "animals fighting in the forest" (all of these are interpretations of Rorschach ink blots) will depend upon a complete understanding of the social relations of the child and the pressures from all sides of his culture. First of all, we might suggest that a criterion of parsimony be applied to exclude too much projection of the experimenter's own emotional needs upon the interpretation of the child's fantasy. When behavior toward other children and toward adults is seen in relation to fantasy material, the simplest criterion will be defined in terms of the coherence of the patterns which appear in different settings and in relation to different kinds of material, together with validation in terms of past experience and future behavior.

Murray has made just as systematic an attack on this problem of interpretation of symbolic values in fantasy material as he has made on the problem of organizing the conceptual framework and the methods for study of personality and social behavior.[1] As we have indicated, the reconstruction (or backward prediction) of salient childhood experiences and the prediction of the probable course of subsequent personality development are used as a check on methods of interpreting the symbolic values of dramatic themes.

The more completely unstructured the material, the more freedom there is for the child to pattern it according to his own modes of organization and his own values. For this reason, finger painting, clay, blocks, drawing and painting have all been found useful means of projecting inarticulate feelings or responses. The same values may be found in a child's response to the Rorschach test. Here, as in the case of other test situations, the behavior of the child in response to the unfamiliar material and the task set by an adult in a more or less authoritative relation may provide important evidence regarding social attitudes, in addition to the perceptual and emotional patterns revealed by the Rorschach analysis.

Since one of the greatest needs is the integration of experimental methods with prolonged observation, interview, and other methods giving perspective on the personality of the child as a whole, a Rorschach analysis and interpretation will be given in full and compared with other data on the same child. The aim is not to show the infallibility of a single method, but to suggest interrelations, i.e., the light which each group of findings throws on the other group of findings, and the continuities and generalized modes of personal response which appear in all.

[1] Experimental attempts to validate Murray's technique of interpretation have also been made, of which the following study with adults is an illustration. Ten subjects were required by Experimenter A to write an autobiography (Production I) and to produce a thematic apperception (Production II) for Experimenter B, and another (Production III) for Experimenter C. Experimenters D and E were independently given Productions II and III of all ten subjects and were asked to pair them on the basis of the identity of authors. Experimenters D and E were then given Production I for all ten subjects and asked to indicate what particular autobiography had been written by the author of each of the pairs of thematic apperceptions (Productions II and III). Both experimenters D and E correctly matched all three productions for all ten subjects. This was done on the basis of the skill of the experimenters in interpreting what sort of person will produce what sort of thematic apperceptions.

I. *Rorschach Analysis of P. B.*[1]

On meeting a new person or facing a new task, P. requires a rather long time to find the approach necessary for her successful adaptation to the situation. This to be attributed to the fact that her capacity for spontaneity has been impaired and inhibited very much and that she is convinced that others expect a certain mode of behavior from her, which she has also come to demand of herself, namely, that she should always conduct herself in a manner befitting a well-bred and gifted child. For so young a child, she displays an amazing degree of intuitive knowledge, empathy and capacity for conscious discernment—in fact, it is apparent that she knows exactly what is expected of her in either familiar situations or situations that do not deviate considerably from those to which she is normally accustomed. Her need for recognition and her ambition drive her to live up to such expectations. However, when she is confronted with a situation with which she is innerly unfamiliar, it is her need for recognition and her ambition that evoke great anxiety in her; even though she carefully feels her way about and takes great care to avoid a misstep, she is nevertheless overcome by the dread that she might make a false move.

It is as if she wished to obliterate the initial discrepancy between her ambition, her wishes and her capacity for fulfilling them, and she has developed logic and conscious attention in a rather forced manner and to a comparatively high degree. By this device, she hopes to be adequately protected and equipped to handle the demands made of her and to overcome any anxiety caused by a possible inferiority. She therefore accommodates herself extensively toward others and directs all of her concrete efforts toward conforming with the expectancies of others. She trains her thinking capacities so as favorably to impress others. In order that others should have no inkling of all of her real anxiety and uncertainty, she would like to convey the impression that she can master every situation in the manner of playing a game and that she is completely devoid of fear.

It is through such behavior that she hopes to be equipped to handle surprise situations—above all, those of an emotional character. If she were to exercise no control over her reactions and experiences, she fears that her emotions would dominate and mislead her. If this were to occur, she would also suffer an impairment in her capacity to estimate consciously the best possible manner of eliciting admiration

[1] Rorschach analysis by Anna Hartoch and F. Schachtel. The Rorschach analysts made this interpretation on the basis of raw records of the Rorschach test provided by L. B. Murphy. They had not seen the child or any of the other records on the child.

and attention and to decide as to what pose would be most pleasing to others.[1]

[1] Rorschach Record of P. B. (7 years old), March 12, 1937

I	I would not have any idea about this one.	—
II	None of these pictures that I have seen so far give me any idea but splashes.	—
	I don't think they would really be anything.	—
III	I cannot do anything with any of these pictures; it does not seem as if they look like anything.	—
IV	1. This is not a splash exactly. It is more of a blotch. I would like to know what this is supposed to be. Even an ink blot picture would look more like something. Even potato prints look more like something. At least they look like designs, but these do not look like designs.	W F— Obj
	Remark: They are not anything—unless they are something I have never heard about. Anybody could make something better than that I think.	
V	2. Well, this one looks a little bit like a butterfly, but even at that a butterfly would have a little more color to it.	W F+ A pop.
VI	3. This again would just look like a blot, a big blotch or splash, and I really think that is all they are.	W F— Obj
VII	4. A little bit like a very funny bridge	D F+ Obj Or+
	5. These are the stones	D F+ Obj
	6. Or else a very fat child	D K M
	7. She shows arms and legs	D F+ Md
	Remark: That is how I got those two ideas and these are the only two that I got any ideas for except blotches.	
VIII	8. This again is just a blotch, but it is in color.	W C Obj
IX	9. This one only looks like a color blotch too.	W C Obj
X	Remark: Well this gives me a little bit different ideas than any of the others.	
	10. This would be a path in the garden	D FC Obj
	11. And there would be a pond, here	DWS F+ Obj
	12. And flowers around it	D CF Obj

The following abbreviations are used in scoring:

W	— Whole response	F+	— Sharply seen form response
D	— Detail response	F—	— Unsharply seen form response
Dws	— White space response	K	— Kinesthetic (movement) response
		FC	— Form-color response
A	— Animal response	CF	— Color-form response
M	— Men (human beings)	C	— Color response
Md	— Detail of men		
Obj	— Lifeless object	pop	— Popular response
		Or	— Original response

Formula (psychogram):

5 W	7 F (— 2)	1 A	F%—71
6 D	1 K	1 M	A%— 8
1 Dws	1 FC	1 Md	
———	1 CF	9 Obj	Fails to give an interpretation to the
12	2 C	———	first 3 plates.
	———	12	
	12		

Type of apperception (Erfassungstyp): W — D
Type of affective experience (Erlebnistyp): 1 K : 4.5 C (more extratensive than introversive)
Succession of modes of apperception (Sukzession): between organized and strict.

Interpretation of Rorschach
(Supplementary to General Interpretation Given Above in Text)

P. is a child of our time, but an unchildlike child. At an early age, she seems convinced already of the importance of appearance, to be a person quite different from her real self, of not acting according to one's real impulses but according to the expectations of others. She imitates what she sees in others, and pretends to experience and feel what she believes these other persons experience and feel. Factually, however, she only enacts what she sees expressed by others and remains inwardly quite untouched and detached from this imitatory enacting. She is very successful in the pursuit of this goal and it is success in this respect that counteracts her feeling of inferiority. Her relationship to others is based primarily on receiving as much praise and recognition as possible, in return for which she constantly demonstrates what she can do. She uses praise and recognition as a standard of measurement of the love of others. She wins power over others by her successful exploits and in this manner she is best able to get what she wants. She must constantly be on her guard that she does everything correctly and thus is still able to compete. This is all a constant effort on her part and she is often very tired. She occasionally senses that no one is really concerned about her and that she is quite alone. In such a case she may even become obstinate and defiant.

P. is an easy child to manage (i.e., she yields quickly to persuasion); she is thus no problem child in that she creates no difficulties of any kind for her parents and teachers. Since she constantly adjusts herself to the wishes of others, she is docile, cooperative, willing and amiable. She clings to others readily and is very compliant. Inasmuch as she is not at all conditioned to developing something from her own inner resources, she naturally feels dependent on all people with whom she comes in contact.

For the sake of P.'s further development, her happiness—in fact, her whole future life—it is important that her parents and teachers realize now that she is in need of much more genuine warmth, love and confidence to promote her own potentialities. She must learn to relinquish her drive to seek the easiest way out and to cling tenaciously to all those modes of behavior approved of by others; instead, she must be encouraged to become independent, to want to have experiences all her own, and in general to develop the inner strength necessary for an active mastery of life. She will then be free of the deep uncertainty, isolation and anxiety that now engulf her and explain her whole present behavior and attitude toward the world. She will then be much more her real self and she will be more spontaneous and childlike instead of being primarily mimical and imitating others in her actions. Furthermore, she will be more at ease and more animated in new and unfamiliar situations because she will have more confidence in her own powers. It would be beneficial if the potentialities, with which she is endowed, were guided into more fruitful channels.

It appears to us that P. has a pronounced feeling for space and spatial relations. It would probably be to her advantage if this sense could be developed (as for instance it is done by the Montessori method), not so much by subjecting her in her work and play to regulations and prescribed rules but by instead giving her the experience that one can also create and act according to one's own inclinations, wishes and thoughts instead of only complying to the prescribed rules or acting according to the supposed expectations of others.

What is more revealing in this case than the psychogram itself is the change occurring during the course of the reactions which is brought about by the test situation and by the conditions for interpretation inherent in the plates.

The 5 whole (W) responses might be indicative of a rather high intellectual level—in fact, of a development unusually advanced for this age—but only if they had been successful achievements. This is factually the case only in her "popular" W response to plate V; none of the other whole responses are made up of precise interpretations but consist instead of intellectual attempts to explain the actual composition of the plates—for example, to perceive them as ink blots, blotches, splashes or color blotches. This appears, to be sure, to be indicative of an ambitious desire to interpret the plate correctly and to express these interpretations—but at the same time, it also indicates an attempt to conceal the deep-seated insecurity and anxiety that have resulted in her failing to give genuine interpretations which would have required much more *naïve* and spontaneous reactions to the plates on her part than she was able to give.

The apperception type (Erfassungstyp) is also to be interpreted from this point of view. It reflects less a preponderance of abstract theoretical thinking over concrete thinking—which would be quite an unusual situation for this age—but more an ambition to give "correct" responses and failure to do so because of her insecurity. The degree of this insecurity results in her ignoring the possibility of detail (D) responses which other children would *naïvely* give in larger numbers.

This interpretation of the apperception type (Erfassungstyp) is reinforced by observing the course of the reactions in the case of P. B. The quite unusual failure to respond to the first three plates can only be understood in the light of the anxiety and insecurity caused by a new situation for which there is no known pattern of behavior which she can follow. The unusual nature of the situation is repeated, to a lesser degree, at the appearance of the first color plate (plate VIII). This plate and the subsequent one evoke exactly the same reaction that occurred at the beginning of the experiment. P. again feels completely insecure. In plates V and VII she finally succeeded in giving interpretations. When confronted with the colors, she again does not know what she is to do and consequently seeks a way out of this difficulty with the same intellectual attempt to explain how the plates could be made or of what they consist. Only when she has reached plate X does she again succeed in overcoming this uncertainty and then offers new interpretations.

Rorschach states (H. Rorschach, *Psychodiagnostik*, third edition, 1937, p. 22) that the rejection of individual pictures "frequently occurs in the case of debile hysterics who protect themselves against anxiety, due to a sensitive intelligence complex, by avoiding interpretations that appear stupid to them." This observation applies partially to our case. The type of affective experience (Erlebnistyp) indicates a strong preponderance of extratensive over introversive tendencies (1 K:4.5 C) a situation which is frequently met with in the case of hysteroid persons, and, as in this case, corresponds with an exorbitant striving for adaptation and an

The following is a behavior record of the same seven-year-old, which shows in overt behavior the tendency to act in an adult way. The ambivalence of her motivation appears in her frequent relapses into more primitive or childlike behavior.

II. *Lunch Record, P. B.*
(Reported by L. Woodcock)

12:13. Sat waiting for a fork with her plate of dinner before her. When the fork arrived she took it adultwise in her right hand and began eating. Picked up her lettuce delicately between thumb and fingers, a much different pattern from the stuffing in with the fist that "these Sevens," lettuce usually undergoes.

Sally, Eugene and others are talking gaily about what is "bad manners" and what is "very bad manners," with demonstrations. She smiled in quiet amusement, then continued to work with her lettuce. She seems to try to handle her food delicately but it ended by her

---

extensive impairment of spontaneity. This somewhat overacting behavior, which is calculated to conform with the expectancies of others, and the inner insecurity and instability from which this stems, are reflected not only in this type of affective experience (Erlebnistyp), but also in the initial failures and those repeated at the appearance of the color plates.

Inasmuch as the numerous rejections of plates limit the material markedly, it is difficult to recognize the succession of the modes of apperception (Sukzession). However, the very nature of the rejections reveals a characteristic peculiarity, which also distinguishes the "succession" in P. B.'s case, namely, her striving to say something at any cost, and, as far as possible, something that will explain the whole plate. The ambition which is apparent in her mostly unsuccessful attempts to give whole (W) interpretations is based on the same insecurity that causes the somewhat compulsive succession; the latter lies between the types which Rorschach has designated as organized and strict succession. The striving to give a whole response is also evident in the remarks which are interspersed, for example, in plate X, where she wants to make a general remark about the picture. A higher A (animal) percentage than 8 per cent might be anticipated from the stereotypy of her behavior and a certain rigidity in her attempts at adaptation which always have the character of a somewhat conventional adaptation regardless of the sacrifice necessary to attain it. However, we are here dealing with a case in which stereotypy finds expression in a manner other than A (animal) percentage—namely, in the repeated remarks and interpretations which have to do with the nature of the plates—viz., splashes, blot, blotches, etc. Whereas other people take refuge in animal interpretations, P. B., in her uncertainty, always resorts to these answers in a stereotyped manner.

We have hereby demonstrated how the most essential factors in the psychogram and the record give us a key to P. B.'s character structure. Because of a lack of space, we cannot go into a number of other factors of the psychogram and the record which would help to round out and complete the picture.

pulling her lettuce apart with her fingers so as to eat it with her fork. Finished it by spearing with her fork, looking up with smiles from time to time.

Watched Arthur talk, looked over at the next table and smiled at Miss W. (student just returned to group after a long absence).

Paul: "Whoever likes milk raise their hands!" P. smiled but continued eating. Many of the group did not respond to this vote. Attacked her beans, lifting them on fork at first, later speared them, shoved the last bits on her fork with her fingers. Beans gone, she tackled potato. Smiled at Miss W. Watched and smiled at voting for liking bread, ice cream, etc. Is rocking chair back and forth jerkily. I see no one else so restless on his chair as this.

Smiled at Miss L., who made some pleasant comment about her food. Made some smiling contact with the maid serving her food.

Stuffs her mouth rather full, but seems to try to avoid putting her left hand in food. Her mouth-stuffing seems in considerable contrast to her delicacy of handling food before it reaches her mouth. Smiled up at the cook serving seconds.

In the following extended record, the highly ritualized activities of a family whose members have no emotional relation with each other, but merely go through routine, seems congruent with the foregoing personality picture, and suggests related aspect's of P. B.'s domination by adult patterns. It is interesting to see that here, too, her stereotyped behavior alternates with outbursts of primitive feeling that are referred to the animal world with which no human beings (or only "queer" ones) make contact.

III. *Housekeeping Play Situation, P. B.*

(Experiment by L. B. Murphy)

When she came upstairs she looked at the dolls and housekeeping toys and said, "Those are nice little toys. I could furnish a house, I guess. I'll need two of these boxes. For instance, in my living room I'd have a couch." She picked up the couch and set it down in the living room. Placed a chair and stool. She put a table aside saying, "I'll leave that for the dining room." She put down a side table and tried a lamp in several places. "I don't know if I can furnish a house." (Slightly anxious, doubtful expression.)

Experimenter: "That's fine."

"I don't know where to put a lamp exactly." (Note recurrent uneasiness.)

She rearranges the chairs. (Set-up No. 1.)

"I just can't find the chairs that go with that table."

She dawdles. Looks for the dining room chairs. Seems to be blocked here for a time when she can't find them. Looks up with slightly embarrassed expression. Then she begins on a new job and arranges the bathroom at the opposite end from the dining room table.

"You certainly have got enough dolls. Now here's the mother, then the father. The father seems to have lost his hat, too. The father's all dressed up."

She puts the father and the mother in the same bed.

"Now the baby can sleep at the foot of the bed or really on top. The medium girl can sleep on the couch. There's the grandmother. Where can she sleep? I seem to be getting pretty much stuck already. Now where can she sleep? Now this little girl—she can sleep on the table with her puppy. Now she can take one chair and the grandmother can take another chair and the boys are left out."

She picks up a foreign doll.

"Now who would this be? Next to the big brother. Now he'll be a traveler. He looks like one. This could be another sister and another sister and a brother. The only trouble is the grandfather and the little brother haven't any place to sleep. This is getting bad with so many people and so little room. Oh, I didn't fix up the third little place."

She removes a dresser and chair and bed to the third box.

"Now they will all have places to sleep. It doesn't look much like a play yet, does it? I sort of like this little puppy. He's quite cute, isn't he, only that the bow sort of hides him. Now the two boxes are filled up and one box is quite dreary. Now what can go in all the place? I might spread this to there and this to there and this to there. That would sort of fill it up more. Now let's see, what could I use this for?"

Experimenter: "You might have a street outside the house."

P.: "Now, what this might be for I can't find out." (Left-over bowl. Note compulsion to use up everything.) "No, I guess I can't use that. That looks quite like a large house now. I don't know if I should use all these people."

Experimenter: "You don't need to."

Picks up horse.

"Now over there in the woods is a wild horse and a fox." She handles the horse. "It seems to be a rubber horse, don't it?" Puts the woolly animal and the rubber horse together in the woods. "The train goes along the river and the woods can be right here." (A little abruptly:) "Now it's early in the morning and the things are going alone."

She moves the red car and the green car.

"And then they are going in the woods and they stop because of what they see. And they go back to the street and they part." (In low, slow tones, moving the body:) "Doo-doo-doo, doo-doo-doo. And then it stopped. And the train goes whooooooo and then it stopped. Choo-choo-choo-choo—it stops at the station."

Then she moves over, picks up the horse and the fuzzy animal, balancing them up and down very actively and violently.

"The wolf and the wild horse jump around. Then they stop. Then the little girl gets up and gets washed and she washes the doggie, and then they get dressed and fixed. Then they go out and they hang around the place and the big sister and the in-between sister get washed and dressed and eat and they go out. Then the grandfather and the big brother get up and get washed then eat and go out." (While doing this, she makes each individual go over to the wash bowl, get dressed in front of the mirror, eat at the table, etc.) "Now I think just for a moment I'll take the medicine chest out."

She takes it out and puts it back.

"The father is still asleep. The mother gets up and gives the baby her bottle and puts the baby down again and then the mother eats. The father gets up and gets washed and eats and goes out. And then the brother and sister get up and get washed and eat and get out. Then the grandmother and sister get up and get washed and eat and they go out and then the last little girl gets up and gets washed and eats and goes out."

Then she moves back again to the woods. Picks up the animals and bounces them around. (Note recurrence of contrast between primitive expressiveness and the highly ritualized behavior represented in the home.)

"And the animals jump around again in the woods. Then the cars go back and forth and back again and the boat goes and the train goes choo-choo-choo-choo and it stops. I guess before I do any more I really have to go to the bathroom." (She says this smiling with a little shyness and twiddling her glossy neat braids. She returns shortly.)

"The little girls sat down and washed and ate and then both took their afternoon nap. And the grandmother and the grandfather washed and ate and then they took their afternoon naps. And the big sister and the big brother took the baby and they washed her and gave her a bottle and laid her down to eat. And they washed and ate and laid down for their afternoon nap. And the little girl washed her puppy and she ate and gave her puppy something to eat and another little girl washed and ate and went to her rest and she fixed her bed."

She moves over to the woods again.

"And then the animals in the woods jumped around again. (Less violent but active and laughing as she looked up.) The cars went back and forth. Then the whole family got up and went out and this time they did it nice and quickly. Then again the animals in the woods jumped around." (Smiling.) "And the cars and tracks moved along. And some of the people went home holding hands. The mother and the little girl and they washed and ate and went to bed. And the little brother and the grandfather went in and they washed and they went to bed. And the grandmother and one of them, I think the baby, would be a better combination. The grandmother washed the baby and gave her the bottle. And the baby watched the grandmother eat her supper and they went to bed, and the father and the big brother washed and ate supper and they went to bed, and one of the big sisters with one of the little sisters washed and ate and went to bed and another little sister and another little sister went and washed and ate and made their beds. Oh dear me! One of the sisters is in the wrong bed. She just happened to be there and she didn't go to sleep. Then last of all the little girl with the dog came in and she gave the dog a piece of meat and they washed and went to bed.

"Then very late at night the animals in the woods jumped around and they went to sleep." (Very violent in her activity with the animals again.) "And the cars went back and forth. At midnight the animals got up again and jumped around. At midnight the cars went again. At midnight the baby woke up and cried and the mother got up and gave the baby a bottle.

"In the morning everybody got up and had breakfast but I don't think I'd have to do that for you."

The following is an excerpt from an interview with the same child:

Interviewer: "What do you like best in the school?"

P. B. "Nothing in particular. I like everything very much. Clay modeling and things."

Interviewer: "What do you like best at home?"

P. B. "That is something that tangles me up because I cannot find anything I like best. There are so many you couldn't find anything I like best. There are so many you couldn't have enough paper to write them down. I like music school, I like movies, trips, parties."

Interviewer: "What do you like to play?"

P. B. "Quiet things. Not noisy games. But if a game teacher comes and likes to play noisy games then I like it, so I play for the whole playground time and I think it is only five minutes because it is so much fun. Dodge-ball, Sally-Goes-Around-the-Stars." (This may be a solution of her need for outlet for intensity along with her need for accepted patterns and approval of adults.)

This type of material may be handled in a variety of ways: for the purpose of individual studies the qualities of feeling that emerge in different settings may be seen in relation to one another; at the same time, either through ratings of judges, matching of data, or through segmental analysis of records, quantitative studies may be made. Probably at the moment it is more important to deepen our understanding of the personality needs underlying social behavior.

Until recently, experimenters in child psychology have made little effort to utilize the rich data which almost any experiment whatever can offer on the child's attitudes toward adults and his whole way of behaving, his "personality style." We generally content ourselves with the comment that "the child cooperated willingly," while a host of significant observations that could easily be made go by the board. Yet in the hands of various investigators, beginnings are being made in this direction.

Thus in one study of seven-year-olds play materials are offered with the directions, "You have seen a marionette show, or a play, haven't you? You may make any kind of play you want to." The observer records the child's behavior on entering the experimental room, his initial approach to her, his attack on the task, and the steps he goes through in carrying out the suggestion. One child shows a tendency toward highly formalized social responses, with "Yes, thank you's" at every turn; another takes charge of the situation for the experimenter, turning lights on, pulling up chairs; a third waits submissively for directions. When the material is presented, one child regards it as *his* task, which he carries out silently without comment to the experimenter; another communicates with the experimenter constantly and treats it as a shared experience; a third asks for suggestions and is dependent on frequent reassurance. These forms of behavior are important diagnostically for an understanding of the child's relations to adults and authority generally; they may be related to social behavior with other children and also to attitudes toward work. During the progress of the task, one child quickly organizes his material in a selective way, eliminating the material for which he has no use; another shows a compulsive tendency to make use of every item of material. One puts the pieces together in a new functioning whole; another produces a stereotyped imitative pattern; another fiddles about uncomfortably on the edge of the group of objects, as if lost and unable to bring them into any pattern. Tentative results suggest that some children who are dependent on stereotyped patterns in organizing such materials are also constantly dependent upon stereotyped patterns in social behavior generally, whereas other children may be free and creative in relation to some kinds of material although they are stereotyped and imitative in other phases of life. The cases are too few, and too incompletely studied, to afford any generalizations. Yet in each instance, work and social behavior are intimately related to the personality organization of the child; the second kind of child urges upon us the need for better methods of studying his *areas of security and creativity* in relation to his *areas of insecurity*.

PRESENT-DAY USES AND LIMITATIONS OF STATISTICAL PROCEDURES IN RELATION TO PERSONALITY ORGANIZATION

The measurement of social traits in childhood is concerned with the isolation of specific trends and tendencies. Many of the trends are very broadly conceived—tendency to extroversion, emotional instability, etc.—but they have, for all that, been trends which could exist in many kinds of whole personalities. The quantitative approach to interrelations of traits, baffling as the problem is, must now be briefly considered; no tendency in contemporary child study deserves more emphasis, or requires more critical analysis, than the struggle to discern the relation of the trait to the personality in whom it appears.

Our English vocabulary is rich in terms that describe social reactions of persons: Cooperative, motherly, responsible, jealous, aggressive, competitive, shy, domineering, submissive, teasing, unselfish, generous, affectionate, sympathetic, helpful, kind, snobbish, sentimental, heartless, confident, demonstrative; such are the terms we may use in referring to the attitude of one person toward others.

But this language, unlike German for instance, does not help us much to reduce these varied shades of color in social behavior to a spectrum or a group of elementary colors from which others are conceived to be compounded. In studying social behavior patterns of young children, Williams attempts to make such a reduction through applying Thurstone's factor analysis to Berne's ratings of 30 behavior patterns in 50 pre-school children. This analysis shows a number of characteristics such as "participates," "cooperates," "maternal," "responsible for others," clustering about one axis, i.e., closely interrelated, while "unselfish," "does not tease," "not self-defensive," "ascendant," "jealous" and "rivals" cluster around a second axis. This suggests two general tendencies at the basis of the behavior items studied: one general factor which might be called approach-withdrawal, and another which might be called ascendance-submission. The positive correlation between aggression and sympathy found by L. B. Murphy in five sets of ratings totaling 54 children seems to fit into this picture. Both groups of data suggest that (1) the tendency to get into or to remain outside of the group, and (2) the tendency to take an active or a passive rôle in relation to other children when one is in the group, may underlie the varied specific behaviors which children show (Blatz).

It is possible that we are dealing here with something which represents *general trends of the organism*, or with *highly generalized social habits which have arisen very early*, or, more likely, with both, i.e., generalized habits depending somewhat upon the biological individuality of the child.

This of course justifies within limits the procedure of those students of child behavior who seek simple components out of which complex behavior arises. But it is of the utmost importance that these components be not simply logically separable, but psychologically meaningful. Rather serious confusion, for example, has arisen from the use of simple categories such as "self-activity," "material activity" and "social activity," without further qualitative distinction. While it is possible to work back from specific verbs denoting functionally complex but clearly defined activities, such as "attacks" and "helps," to one underlying "tendency" to be engaged in a dominant way with other children in the group, it has not proved possible to derive functional distinctions from the kind of data accumulated by broad samplings of "social" and "self" activity. For this reason the latter type of category may be given a place affording a preliminary quantitative check on elementary relations, but functionally significant forms of behavior must be distinguished within it by qualitative analysis. When such analysis is made, we appear to find in some cases broad general trends which make sense psychologically, and which to some degree justify thinking of personality as a composite depending upon, or at least expressing, simpler observable components.

Yet there seem to be reasonable doubts as to the amount of promise which this quest for observable components actually affords. The logic of statistics must, in order to be sound, be the logic of the organism. Behind nearly all of the methods in current use—those which are experimental in the literal sense of the term, those which depend on one variety of observation or another, and those which depend on ratings—lies a certain mathematical conception of the relation of social behavior to personality. This conception assumes that "behavior" may be broken down into elements, all of which pool their influences to create a totality; and that these elements may be discovered by obtaining measures and correlations which define precisely how much increase there is in X when a given increase of Y occurs. In view of the ingenious quantitative methods in force, this method, if sound, should surely give us rather good *prediction* of children's behavior. Yet, in fact, there are few who are foolhardy enough to apply such a method.

What, then; are we to abandon quantitative method and go back to impressionism? Not at all. The rhetorical question thus so frequently asked misses the point; the fact is that measurement must be applied where it is psychologically meaningful, and, when so applied, it will refine shrewd qualitative interpretation.

Almost any present-day study of the whole personality of the child might be cited to show the trend of current thinking about the uses and abuses of statistical analysis and compounding of traits. For convenience we shall refer only to one, a study of sympathetic behavior in nursery-school children.

Two findings from this study, the one quantitative, the other at present not quantifiable, need to be seen in close interrelation, since neither has any meaning without the other. *First,* the reliability of the sympathy scores, based on more than 100 hours' observation of each child, has a value of .94 in one group and .99 in another. Sympathy is sufficiently highly generalized to permit the definite quantitative scoring of each child in relation to his fellows on the playground. We are speaking of sympathy as a direct and visible manifestation of something in personality, but not at present defining what it is that this sympathy behavior reveals. *Second,* close study of the personality of each child on and off the playground, of his responses to animals, pictures and adults, as well as to his playmates, observations of his home situation and the personalities of his parents, makes it clear that factors producing an increase of sympathy in some children make for a decrease of sympathy in others. The insecure child may be very unsympathetic; his own needs and fears are too pressing to permit consideration of others; on disappearance of his insecurity his sympathy may suddenly show an extraordinary development. Among other children the loss of security may produce an *increase* in sympathy: having suffered oneself, having felt what it means to be hurt or afraid, one bestows on others a sympathy never previously shown. Hence if we should attempt by the usual multiple correlation procedure the measurement of all the factors contributing to the net total amount of sympathy shown, we should defeat our own purposes, since an increase in security increases sympathy in some and reduces it in other individuals. Much confusion in the measurement of personality can result from the attempt to define the end result of many traits by assuming that their results are somehow "pooled" at the level of overt behavior. The child whose behavior cannot be predicted in this way is said to be "inconsistent," or not to have become "integrated." Clearly, the trouble is not with consistency or with integration, but with the attempt to treat all variables as pooling their effects indiscriminately at any level of observation which the experimenter desires to use. Sympathy at the level of direct observation may arise from all sorts of different causal factors functioning at another level. If the reliability scores quoted above had been lower, it would be possible to reply that there is no such thing as sympathy in general, and that the attempt to get at its psychological basis is meaningless. The gross amount of sympathy is, however, an easily measured thing, with a degree of internal consistency higher than is usually demanded by statisticians. Yet what is consistent and reliably measured at one level may require an analysis based on qualitative distinctions, and may only with much labor permit the disentangling of the true quantitative relations present.

It is quite possible, for example, that an increase in security, if it could be measured, would consistently yield an increase in sympathy up to a certain point, then turn and work against it thereafter. Physics and biology are both full of instances of U-curves representing transitions of this sort; the relation between temperature and density of water is non-linear and exhibits exactly this change in direction. Since in many social traits we have no subtle means of measuring the deeper components which contribute their varying quotas to the observed result, it is surely more important at present to proceed by disentangling causal variables and getting the picture as complete as possible than it is to quantify a few of the relevant factors and blandly assign the remainder to the category of "chance errors," "random behavior," or "inconsistency."

But if there are "levels" of personal characteristics, some of which are more easily observed but probably less important than deeper ones which exert a constant directing force upon personal behavior, we are in need of a clearer hypothesis as to what these deeper forces are, how they express themselves in external observed trends, and how the measurement of the latter may guide us in the understanding of the former.

There are many such hypotheses in psychological literature today: one thinks of those offered by Stern, by Janet, by Morton Prince. We shall consider only one way of formulating the problem, not to suggest that the hypothesis is sound but merely to show what is meant by basic forces in personality of which visible behavior is a fleeting expression. This is Freud's definition of character types in terms of the *locus of satisfactions* in infancy. The child who has been forcibly weaned may struggle for oral satisfaction through thumb sucking, nail biting, lip biting. He may be a mouth-centered person; he may take to public speaking or the playing of wood winds, or to other sublimation outlets, as well as to

simple and more obvious oral nervous habits. Each zone of satisfying stimulation may contribute to the character structure of the
adult. An attempt to confirm such as view as this, broadly conceived,
appears in an experiment in which two puppies were taken away
from their mother and forced to get their nourishment from a bottle having so large a nipple aperture as to result in brief and insufficient jaw exercise. The puppies thus treated continued long afterward to show a great deal of oral behavior, sucking at all sorts of
objects, in contrast with puppies which remained unweaned and
with those which had gotten their milk from a smaller nipple aperture. To validate such hypotheses completely—even with puppies—
would, of course, take a great deal more work, and to put it on a
sound basis for human subjects would be a labor of years.

A more important aspect of the Freudian theory of character
types, especially as developed by Abraham, is the conception that
not merely the locus, but the mode of functioning in satisfying life
needs may be early established as a result of the relative freedom
or frustration involved. Forced weaning may give rise not only to
mouth habits but to a *general attitude of dependence*, a sense of lack,
a tendency to seek primitive comfort at a vegetative level rather
than through stressful overt activity. A character trait then begins
in the form of the personal struggle for satisfaction; it is a *way of
orienting oneself* with respect to the outer world. Such a generalized
"mode of behavior" appears to be identical with a "trait" as defined
by G. W. Allport—a system of habits ultimately depending upon
some central attitude, and with a "central value," as sketched above
(page 202).

An example of a character trait thus broadly defined is the tendency to seek form, i.e., unified or organized experience, as contrasted with piecemeal stimulation. Several existing tests are concerned with form in this sense. Very marked individual differences
in form response are recorded by Rorschach testers for both children and adults. In fact, the form-seeking tendency seems to be
established early. The hypothesis arises that the imposing of organization upon a stimulus pattern is a way of achieving *release
from confusion*; it depends in part upon aesthetic and in part
upon deeper emotional needs. Intensive observation for some fifteen

hours per child and the application of standardized tests of many sorts suggest that the tendency to organize in terms of form is deep-seated in some individuals, practically absent in others; that it is a generalized mode of conduct, appearing in the child's running, talking, spontaneous behavior on the playground, response to school requirements and to standardized experimental material. It appears that the validation of the Freudian conception of the *bodily locus* or *zone* of satisfaction is of much less consequence than discovery of those *modes of meeting social reality* which are stable, widely generalized and deeply characteristic of one individual as against another.

The important part of the Freudian theory thus stated seems to us the suggestion of *necessary relations*, biological and psychological coherence, existing in groups of observed traits; the doubtful part seems the assumption that one aspect of a pattern is necessarily and always the "cause" or "origin" of the rest. Indeed, the search for cause-effect relations in the fields of sexuality and personality in general has proceeded too fast, so fast that it has brought a great deal more confusion into an already confused field. We shall attempt to show here how description of constellations and syndromes is more cautious and more valid for some problems than description in terms of cause and effect.[1]

In the social behavior of animals syndromes of behavior that go with dominance or subordination status may be detected. The dominant animal shows his dominance in a dozen ways. The separate parts of this syndrome are interchangeable and have similar psychological meaning. The syndrome, when it changes, usually changes as a whole, not piecemeal. Experience with human beings indicates the same to be true of them also, even if not to the same extent. Syndromes can be described, at least in general outline, and with amazing consistency among the alternative detailed expressions. Also there is evidence to indicate that the character and behavior syndromes of low-, middle- and high-dominance feeling tend to change as wholes and not in bits or parts.

Now is this due to the fact that in dominance there is one cen-

---

[1] For the following statement regarding dominance we are indebted to A. H. Maslow. Social dominance is not to be confused with biological dominance (page 164).

tral causal principle, every specific act arising from this principle? The eternal question is, "What *causes* this behavior?" The psycho-analyst digs into the details of infinitely complex symptom com-plexes (syndromes) and invariably comes up with a "cause," which, just as invariably, is only another symptom (another part of the same syndrome). Because these symptoms are parts of a syndrome they are always found to be correlated and present at the same time or in a certain sequence; they are then thought to be cause and effect. We have here a partial explanation of the fact that different people, e.g., Freud and Adler, can find so many different and con-trary causes of the same effect. All may be "correct" at the same time.

The student of personality has often been unable to find any-thing like the simple cause-effect relation of physical science. What we have found are highly complex and variable behavior and char-acter syndromes, with many interrelated parts. We find further that historical or contemporary external influences affect not merely single parts of the syndrome, but rather the *syndrome as a whole*. Though we are balked when we look for single causative aspects of the personality, we find that it is reasonably valid to think of all behavior as an expression of the total personality.

We have therefore to conclude that in relation to many problems in social behavior the usual procedure in working from the simple to the complex has led to difficulties. The varieties of behavior may be simply and clearly defined and reliably measured, yet fail alto-gether for purposes of prediction. This often occurs because what is "simple" as ordinarily conceived is not "central." But a further difficulty appears in the fact that at times *no fixed center* can be found; the components of personality are interdependent, and each must be seen in the light of the rest.

SOCIOMETRY

We have suggested that the components within the personality sometimes need to be seen in the light of wholes, or as aspects of wholes. If this is true, the daring question has arisen in the minds of some investigators: "Is the whole personality a big enough unit? Is not the personality sometimes a reflection of the group; is not the direct study of social structure necessary if we are to understand the individual personality?" It is true that if this is to be done, the individual personality entering the group must be an object of direct concern to the investigator. He must see both the individuals in the light of the group and the group in the light of the individuals. This study of inter-personal relations, with special reference to measurement of attractions and repulsions within the group structure, is called "sociometry." Under this designation, J. L. Moreno has undertaken to write a natural history of human group formation, stating his findings both in terms of numbers and in terms of charts indicating the dynamics of inter-individual relations.

Among infants, Moreno finds, isolation (lack of social response) gives way quickly to a selectiveness which involves a primitive type of social grouping. Any given infant is drawn positively to other members of the world of immature or mature individuals, remaining neutral or hostile to others. Among a group of infants in a maternity hospital, *mutual pairs* are seen in the process of formation, each one dependably choosing the other member of his pair rather than any other child, or one infant may be a center toward which *several* others are polarized. The human material is more or less plastic, but not indefinitely so. Fairly stable bonds of attachment are formed. Stability depends partly upon age.

At a higher age level, each boy in a preparatory school is asked to name the one whom he would most like to have as roommate. Data from several hundred individuals show the following categories:

1. "Isolates"—those whom no one has chosen either as first, second, or third choice.
2. Mutual pairs—where two individuals have included each other, not necessarily as first choice but among those included as desirable in the first three.
3. Chains—where A wants B, B wants C, C wants D, etc.; each of course expresses other choices outside of the chain formation.
4. Triangles—A wants B, B wants C, C wants A.
5. Stars—A, B, C, D, etc., all want S.

If A wants B, B's attitude toward A is always compared with A's. Liking is called positive "tele"; dislike, negative "tele." In such charts as these, the continuous line indicates positive, and the broken line negative, tele; the absence of a line indicates indifference. A glance shows the general nature of the social structure among a group of twenty boys in a dormitory. From such a chart it is pos-

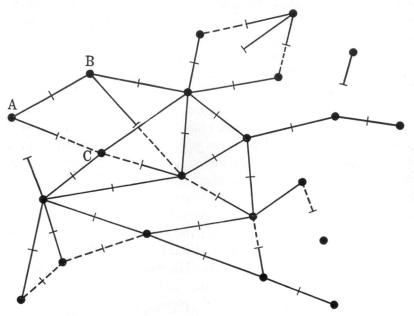

HYPOTHETICAL SOCIOGRAM OF A GROUP OF TWENTY BOYS.
Criterion: Acceptance as hall-mate in dormitory. A and B accept each other; A accepts C but is rejected by him, etc.

sible to observe at once the presence of those isolates who might otherwise be discovered only after painful psychiatric search for the cause of a problem. It will be noted that the isolate is not necessarily one who fails to reach out toward others; he is one toward whom others do not reach. He may indeed despair of reaching others and the chart may in time show an absence of positive response to others; but it is important for us to understand the fact of general rejection of him as soon as the situation arises.

Again, from such a chart it is possible to derive many usable ideas about leadership. The positive tele between individuals is a basis for that suggestion and imitation to which so many sociologists and social psychologists pay attention without having attended sufficiently to the specific paths over which such influences must travel. These paths indeed offer potential or actual "networks" through which leadership, rumor, fad and fashion may pass. New crazes, new demands from the teachers, protests against discipline, plans for new group activities become intelligible when the concrete individual basis for group action is revealed. Again, leadership is seen to be largely a question of the enjoyment of a key position in a group. Frequently the actual leader is not the star, the center of the network of positive tele, but an individual enjoying closeness to the person thus favorably placed. A person who has the ear of the key person may thus become the "power behind the throne," the invisible director of social change.

Up to this point we have been content to speak of tele in terms of mere *liking* for an individual. The test of social structure, however, is always concrete. Among the preparatory school boys the question related to the desirability of individuals as hall-mates. If, however, the boys are asked to choose companions for hikes or as table mates in the dining room, the pattern changes somewhat. The individual may be an isolate with respect to one function, not with respect to another. Upon this fact depends the possibility of constructive guidance of individuals through development of opportunities for use of those functions with which the individual is most successful. Leadership may be highly generalized or highly specific, depending upon the age and interests of the group, how well they know one another, and so on.

The most elaborate analysis of group structure was made at the New York State Training School for Girls at Hudson, New York. Here a group of 600 girls, mostly ranging in age from 13 to 18, has been studied sociometrically since 1932. The girls live in cottages, 25 or so per cottage. Each girl becomes acquainted with all the members of her cottage group and with a considerable number of girls in other cottages. She is asked, by a member of Dr. Moreno's staff, with whom she would like to live and gives her first, second and third choice; the entire distribution of the school population by cottages follows, as far as possible, the expressed wishes of the individuals. It is essential in sociometric work to carry out immediately in practice the placements which are desired. Sociometric study is repeated every six weeks; the degree of stability of preferences and the reasons for desired changes become matters of direct concern. Sociometric charts have been presented, indicating (1) the networks of like, indifference and dislike within each cottage; (2) the broader networks involving the entire population of 600; (3) the choices based upon another set of expressed preferences, not in terms of living together but in terms of *working* together, e.g., the choice of associates in the steam laundry, the sales room, the farm-work group, etc. From charts of the first type, points of high and of low *morale* immediately become evident, the closely wrought structure of a cottage with much inwardly directed tele having high morale. The potential danger from a low-morale group where disaffection with one's entire group threatens disciplinary problems can be read from the charts. The decline in the already small number of runaways in an institution where it is easy to run away if one wishes seems to be evidence of the satisfyingness of the plan.

It is not, however, only in choices of one another that the girls control their social world. The school is administered partly through house-mothers who are responsible for the comfort and the morale of the cottage groups. When a new girl comes to Hudson, she and the other new girls meet in the reception room all those house-mothers who have vacancies in their cottages. Each girl talks with each house-mother privately. After the conference, each girl indicates to the sociometrist her first, second and third choices among the house-mothers, and each house-mother indicates her first, second and third choices among the new girls. This "clicking," or mutual like, seems to insure an initial favorable placement. A house-mother receives no girl who does not like her or whom she does not like. When, as rarely happens, a girl cannot be suitably placed, she is given a room in the infirmary and shortly thereafter suitably placed in a cottage as vacancies in other cottages appear. The method just described is called the "parent test." Jointly with this a "family test" is given. A "key girl" (a girl favorably placed in each cottage as shown by the network charts) comes from each cottage

ous. This constitutes, incidentally, a partial check upon Freud's hypothesis of the "latency period" in which each sex is indifferent to the other; it arises not only from biological but from a variety of social causes.

It is evident that a number of concepts in general use to define "personality type" become more meaningful when seen in socio-metric terms. Leadership, for example, becomes a statement re-garding the functional relationships of persons rather than an abstract quality of certain persons as such. Indeed, the door is thrown open for a systematic study of the relation between the capacity to lead in one situation and in another situation. Further-more, the function of leadership is defined not by *a priori* socio-logical needs but by the very group which is to be led. This is especially true when the group chooses its leader in terms of a concrete task in which the individual members want to be led. If there is such a thing as a psychology of leadership in the abstract, it will arise from studies in which behavior resemblances of leaders in varying life situations are investigated, in the actual life situation of leading and following.

In the same way, the concept of the shut-in personality, the with-drawn individual, the social isolate, takes on a meaning not in terms of the psychiatrist's evaluation of the person's habits, but in terms of the definition given by group members. To be inaccessible to the psychiatrist's questions is one thing; to be inaccessible to daily social approaches may be another. A less static conception of leaders and isolates inevitably arises. An effective, accepted leader in one group may find himself a non-leader or even an isolate in another; and few are they whose intra-psychic conflict is so great that they are equally inaccessible to all forms of social approach.

The Moreno approach usually allows social situations to define themselves, and allows the participants in the situations to define the nature of their own needs and problems, rather than throwing upon the experimenter the sole rôle of determining what is vital and what is to be controlled in the research. Just as Sherif must find first how the group perceives the situation before he can experi-mentally evaluate the laboratory factors which influence behavior, so Moreno insists that the world, the "social atom" of each individual, must be laid bare without distortion before the distant spectator can determine the social influences at work.[1]

The young child or the adolescent "finds himself" in the group. It is in the group that one realizes oneself as a personality. It is impossible to find out what there is inside of an organism except by stimulating it; and in order to find out anything really profound about it, one has to give it varied social stimulation, intensive and prolonged. At the end of the process, the individual may quite literally be a new person, for better or for worse.

It is likely that for this reason there is a considerable amount of sense in Jung's contention that the personality is never completed, but goes on building itself forever, as long as the world and the organism interact, that is, as long as life is maintained. There is even greater sense, we believe, in Burrow's contention that groups can liberate what is socially meaningful in the person and give it direction and a chance for self-development much better than any individual can. Burrow argues that all neurosis is ultimately social neurosis, the result of group pressures and group tensions; that the individual doctor trying to set the individual patient right has lost the social thread, and can do little to reduce the misery of

[1] If this is true regarding participation in large groups, it is equally true for participation in the smallest group, the group consisting of two persons. The psychiatrist interviewing his patient participates in group activity; and instead of discussing what is in the patient, he participates in producing behavior patterns which never occurred before. As the patient warms up, he not only transfers much of his affective life from the old to the new situation, but reorganizes, reinterprets, relives, as he goes along. To this fresh integration or creation on the part of the patient Moreno assigns the term "spontaneity." The contrast between clinical psychiatry or psychoanalysis and the Moreno methods is strikingly illustrated in the different utilization of the concept of free association. Freud has declared that he "unswervingly" made clear to his patients the kind of free association they would be likely to give; for forty years every reasonably literate person has known the kinds of association to which psychoanalytic procedure is likely to give rise. For Moreno there is no *free* association; there is only a fresh act, depending upon the mood and attitude of the moment as well as upon early trauma or identification; and the associations arising in the presence of one psychiatrist may be utterly different from those arising with another. More important still, in addition to images and verbal patterns, there may arise tendencies to respond, to create, to dramatize, which make the most of the social situation which the psychiatrist presents. The patient becomes an actor, and in the Spontaneity Theater relives actively while he also creates aspects of experience which are to be studied and interpreted by the doctor and his staff.

the tension situation. Burrow's "phyloanalysis" is the resulting group therapy which follows from this hypothesis. The individual's defenses and evasions which have originally arisen to protect him from social censorship and social blame can be resolved and dissipated only in the conversational *milieu*, the genuine reciprocity of free informal conversation.

At the same time, we do not believe that Burrow goes far enough. The direction in which the personality will expand in the presence of an individual analyst depends on the personality of the analyst. There is an infinite number of potential personalities waiting to be created in flesh and blood; there is also an infinite number of groups in which an organism may function. In exactly the same way the results of phyloanalysis will depend on the group. Burrow seems to believe that *the* individual personality is discovered in the group. We believe, in the light of the argument above, that any given group liberates just one out of a broad range of possibilities.

For this reason we believe that not only momentary behaviors, but many deep springs of child personality, are liberated in group situations. The individual "finds himself" because others find him. If he can spontaneously choose those who love him and those whom he loves, and associate more and more with them, he has some chance of developing one of the relatively healthy and vigorous personalities that lies within his potential range. Every few weeks new groupings occur, if really free opportunity for such groupings is afforded. Such changes in grouping liberate the immature personality, give it security and the confidence necessary to explore the unknown. Insecurity and defeat will be infrequent, and the means of eliminating them will be provided.

The older the individual grows, the less frequent will be the changes in his "social atom," the more rigid and therefore the more dependable the inter-individual relations. With the fixation of life plans and interests in middle age, highly stable group structure may be necessary and wise. Even here sociometric methods may be useful to straighten out kinks and exploit new opportunities; but in general the personality and the social world have become adjusted, so that the personality, having made its choice, can quite literally remain practically fixed.

Throughout Moreno's work one finds the term "spontaneity." Personal choices in studies and in vocational training, for example, must be free from the crust of fixed habit, must spring from genuine fresh needs. Yet this does not mean "impulsiveness," which is all too often a fragmentation of the personality. Spontaneity, as Moreno conceives it, is full participation by one's whole personality, in a whole social reality. Few know how to be spontaneous. Prominent in his system of personality study are "spontaneity testing" (an observational method for the study of two persons as they warm up to each other in conversation, in order to discover the full richness and variety of tele between two persons) and "spontaneity training" (learning to throw one's whole self into social living). Thus, though the personality has to choose its own way of developing, we can at the same time help it to choose. This paradox is identical with that of the botanist who has to let the plant grow in its own way but at the same time can produce, under controlled conditions, plants of great beauty and ruggedness which do not know how to produce themselves in certain climatic and geographical zones. The possibilities for self-creation are infinite, provided the environment is infinitely friendly for such purposes; but since the environment is far from infinitely friendly, the experimenter, considering both the organism and the world, permits free growth along certain lines by removing barriers.

So far we have followed Moreno without much reservation. At one point, however, we must demur. Moreno's system presupposes that the group spontaneously chosen, and the group spontaneously choosing the individual, are the best possible group for all concerned. This may be a plausible assumption, but it is an assumption far from proved; and in various respects it calls for rigorous testing. It seems to be a matter of common observation that some persons grow better—at least at times—under very adverse conditions, getting anything but what they ask for and rejected by those whom they want. Even more commonly it seems true that personality development along healthy lines is furthered by having a multitude of both friends and enemies, a loyal inner circle upon whom one can rely, and an outer world offering a stimulus to competition and often opposition. There are probably individual differences in this as in everything else in social behavior, and a crying need for research at this point is evident. As we said regarding Burrow above, so we say regarding Moreno: The group method gives a better personality development because it gives a broader one than any individualistic therapy could probably achieve; but any one group or any one group method is just one means of personality liberation. Even in our own society other group methods, equally democratic, equally sincere, might permit the flowering of quite different personality trends; and other societies of the future, unlike our own, may obtain from group methods results utterly unlike those obtained by group methods at present.

In the last analysis, the problems of method in studying the social psychology of childhood must be approached in relation to the question, what kinds of laws or generalizations are we trying to find? A farmer must know first that soil, rain and sun are needed to grow any plant; then he must learn what specific conditions, in terms of the amounts of moisture and sun or the type of soil, are needed for this or that kind of plant. He must know what to expect of his plants under optimum conditions, and what troubles to look for when defects in growth appear; a withered leaf may be the result of attack by infection above or a worm at the root. He must also know the possibilities of variation in useful directions, and how to control these variations for his own purposes. But plants do not know much and cannot learn; their variations are relatively limited, and it is easy enough to try out your hydrangeas in acid or in alkaline soil, and your roses in sand or black loam.

Children are more subtle; in fact, they are so complicated that a generation of intensive researching has hardly produced definite laws even of the soil-rain-sun level of simplicity. And as for defining laws regarding the kinds of social behavior to expect from different types of children, under different conditions, we are not ready even to begin. At the present point, then, we need to ask, what kinds of laws can we develop with our present methods? And, more important still, where are the methods to be discovered if we are to develop the laws that we most need?

In reply to the first question, it is now quite clear that while generalizations regarding the frequency of contacts, or even of social events defined in somewhat more functional terms, such as conflicts or acquiescence, may be drawn from data collected by the short-sample devices, such generalizations cannot be very enlightening so long as they hang in mid-air, unrelated to the context in which the behavior studied occurs. Frequencies of behavior observed in this way may be compared with one another, as in the various studies of interrelations of behavior; but even so, we are likely to be caught on the outside horse of a merry-go-round when we want to see what makes the wheels work on the inside.

Yet the existing methods, even of so simple a kind, could give much more than they are giving. In order to relate behavior to a context we may compare behavior in one context (one social group) with that in another. So far we have not extensively used short-sample techniques for this purpose, although they would obviously be very useful. For instance, conflicts, nervous habits, crying, laughing, defiance of adults could be studied in rural or suburban as compared with metropolitan schools; in schools patronized by highly competitive as compared with secure or uncompetitive parents; in small groups as compared with large ones; at different times of day in relation to fatigue, food and play, at different seasons, or even in terms of periods selected for their tension value to adults, such as off-season times for seasonal workers versus pressure periods; periods when weather, home conditions and economic security make for general ease and camaraderie as compared with periods of strain. The types of tension outlet associated with different pressure periods and different family or school patterns, could be caught in reliable terms.

Since even at their best the short-sample methods cannot appraise all the factors which underlie behavior, it is nowadays customary to plan a comprehensive and crucial experiment; all children are to confront identically the same situation. In practice we find that we cannot incorporate in the situation all, or even most, of the important factors; and two well-planned experiments rarely yield results which clearly support each other. Even when they do, they tell what the child does at a specific time and place, but little more. Since children cannot be experimented upon in the large-scale manner possible with seeds or even rats, the laws which we may hope to derive from this method are also limited. Experiments, moreover, must not hurt the children or stir them up in any way; therefore we cannot scare them, incite a fight, or create a strong need.

It is partly for these reasons that "projective methods" which use the play-atmosphere of toys, dolls, or pictures are an important supplement to the methods for understanding social drives of the child. His values, anxieties, interests and needs will underlie his individual responses to a variety of such material; certain qualities of spontaneity or dutifulness will be fundamental aspects of his personality that color most of his social relationships; other qualities may be more whimsical, momentarily stimulated by the material presented; other basic needs or interests may not appear at all in this less-than-completely-real type of situation. Since these methods catch mirror reflections at best, and do not reveal to us what the child actually does in critical situations of everyday life where social motives are involved, we are left willy-nilly to rely for supplementary evidence upon systematic ratings, diary observations, and continuous or repeated observations.

All of these methods can be made reliable, and all can contribute to quantitative results. The short-sample, even the diary records when taken in the systematic forms used by Jersild, Woodcock, and others, lend themselves to analysis for reliability in terms of comparison of the records of different observers, and of the continuity in behavior from one time to another. The same is true of experimental procedures and ratings. Projective methods may lead to analysis of consistency through "matching" the picture of behavior that emerges in relation to one kind of data with that which emerges from another. Such matching studies, like other consistency studies, are likely to overlook the bases in motivation for differences in patterns from one occasion to the next. The incidental observations of behavior in critical situations are open to all the difficulties inherent in subjective interpretation by single observers, but may throw a flood of light that brings into relief hypotheses for later substantiation. Unique and unrepeatable observations do not help us in relation to quantitative analysis; but in general quantitative analysis is ready to proceed only after such hypotheses have been outlined.

At a number of points during the following chapters we shall have occasion to comment on studies which have made use of a number of different methods coordinated upon a single problem. Since for many purposes it is important to have the general pattern of relationships defined in terms of reliable measurement, ratings and quantifiable observations or experiments will be needed. Since these quantitative relationships can seldom be deeply revealing regarding the subtler dynamics of social behavior, incidental observations at home and at school, qualitatively rich material from projective methods, interviews with the parents and the child, will all be useful to develop concrete hypotheses within the general quantitative outlines. Before the nature of the problem and the particular combination of methods to be used can be outlined in detail, it is necessary to distinguish between problems seen in terms of traits, in terms of developmental slices such as age levels or stages, and in terms of the social context or situation. We shall return for an additional word on the question of method in Chapter IX, after discussing these approaches to problems of social behavior in the next three chapters.

Chapter VI

DEVELOPMENT OF SOCIAL BEHAVIOR IN A SOCIAL CONTEXT: AGE LEVELS, TRAITS, AND THE SOCIAL SITUATION

WHEN psychologists and sociologists turn "human," and try to explain the behavior of an individual child (let us say Johnnie Brown, who stuck out his tongue at the doctor when his sister Mary was sick and everyone in the house was absorbed in taking care of her), they are apt, like parents or teachers, to say, "Well, that's a seven-year-old for you," implying that this behavior belongs to a particular stage of development; or, "Isn't Johnnie an aggressive little boy?" implying that this behavior reflects a certain characteristic trait or permanent aspect of Johnnie's nature; or, if they are in a tolerant mood, "Johnnie is upset by the strain of the situation, and he isn't really himself today," implying at least that Johnnie is a somewhat different boy from one situation to another.

All of these comments have, as a matter of fact, good scientific bases, provided, however, that they are all made at the same time, and that it is recognized that no one of them is completely true by itself. Since this necessity of seeing the development of social behavior in a social context is so fundamental, it will be worth while to discuss at some length the relations of traits, age levels and situations before we proceed to a fuller analysis of behavior looked at from each of these points of view separately. Let us first consider the possibilities and limitations in the "age-level" or "stages-of-growth" approach.

HOW SHALL WE CONCEIVE OF "STAGES" IN THE DEVELOPMENT OF SOCIAL BEHAVIOR?

We have commented on the ways in which the structure of our social life patterns the research approaches to social behavior, and at one more point it may be worth while to analyze some of the implications of this fact. The age-level method of dividing children into groups has long been deeply ingrained in our educational systems. The result is that research is unconsciously motivated by the need to define differences between age levels; closely connected with this tendency to see social behavior or personality in relation to age levels is the tendency to look for "stages." Thus thinking of the development of boys we naturally think of the toddler stage, the tricycle stage, the stage where one is ready for simple organized games in kindergarten, the gang stage of antagonism to girls, and the adolescent stage of blossoming interest in girls. Such stages as these are real and important; the difficulty arises when we force a varied individuality into a uniform and undiscriminating developmental sequence based on units of time.

M. C. Jones, H. Stolz, and J. Chaffee have presented a criticism and refinement of the age-level approach, calling attention to the individual differences in the process of going through the early adolescent stage. Against the backdrop provided by the universal pattern of physical maturation and social maturing of heterosexual interest may be seen the specific patterns of growth of individual children. The child who develops more quickly or more slowly, or the child whose social response is stimulated or inhibited by special attitudes of his family (who may give him more freedom than is usual or curtail his activities), may show marked differences from the norm. Of one hundred boys studied, about twenty per cent showed such outstanding deviations in behavior that their experience had little in common with that of other children. These major deviations were directly dependent upon atypical patterns of sex maturation. The needs of adolescent children cannot be met unless a wide enough variety is provided to give outlet for and security to the resources of different children. This clear marking-out of the deviations of individuals against the background of what is an undisputed stage stimulates us to ask, Is it possible to define our stages with more validity? Which of the many aspects of behavior that we habitually assign to any "stage" of social or personality development accurately belongs there? Are there stages of crawling, swearing, giggling, playing house, hitting girls, fighting, competing about one's age or size, snatching hats, wriggling in one's seat, biting one's finger nails? Clearly some of these activities may occur during any period of life, others die out after childhood is passed, and still others belong to a narrowly defined stage.

In the broadest sense, a stage is essentially a phenomenon of development or of the life span; everyone goes through stages of infancy, childhood, maturity and old age, yet each individual goes through these stages in a different way. Some individuals never mature emotionally; some become infantile in their old age; others retain the dignity of self-respect and objective interest in life until they die. It is probably dangerous to consider any behavior that is not closely related to development of biological functions in terms of stages. For instance, the obvious growth and decline of motor activity, sensory intellectual development, the reproductive functions, give a genuine basis for stages in social behavior dependent upon them.

The obvious validity of gross stages in this sense has led us to look hopefully to age-level differences for explanations of fundamental aspects of social behavior. Within limits this is sound, since two-year-olds do not form gangs and ten-year-olds do. Going further, it is obvious that every child goes through a stage of incomplete speech before he reaches a mastery of language, just as he goes through successive stages of mastery of locomotion and general bodily coordination. Yet too great a dependence upon the concept of stages has dangers, since it can easily be shown that among children differences in intelligence alone may cut across age differences of several years. Thus, while one child may not be fully ready for reading until seven, another will be ready at five; while most children do not develop much dramatic play before the age of four or five, some children do so by three years of age. All stages, then, have fuzzy edges and overlap other stages when we consider whole groups of children at a time. For individual children the stages have different entrances and exits; and no two go through all the stages in the same way. The pattern of sequences between motor abilities, language, and social behavior—such as aggression, cooperation and sympathy—is very different for different children; and the particular personality pattern which may give a unique quality to certain stages results in a different experience at each stage for each child. For instance, the toddler stage is not at all the same thing for a child with precocious language who can express his wishes clearly, and for a child who is gaining power in locomotion before he can talk much to anyone. The six- to eight-year-old stage of asserting masculinity is a different experience for the child who is under-average physically and for the child above the average in physique and ability to defend himself. These are obvious facts, yet we do not always recognize the generalization to which they point, that each child's sequence of stages in development is to some degree unique and that his experience at any age level is largely dependent upon this unique pattern of development. To the extent that his individual pattern of development overlaps with that of others or with the demands of adults, adjustment is likely to be easy; but when an individual growth pattern involves deviations at one point or another from group norms or the general expectations of adults, difficulties are likely to ensue.

The extent to which age affects social behavior may be indicated by a comparison of the positive correlations with age of many different kinds of behavior: ascendance, aggressiveness, cooperation, sympathy, leadership, sociocentrism (vs. egocentrism), etc.; the great majority of definable social behaviors of all sorts are present in increasing amount as the child grows older.

Yet it must be recognized that most of the data on stages of behavior are collected in groups which are so constituted that two-year-olds seldom have the opportunity of being the oldest and most competent, and four-year-olds are seldom in the position of being the youngest and least competent. Since all social behavior at any age is affected by factors of security and dominance created by the structure of the situation, we should probably find quite different correlations if our social situations were differently organized. It is not unusual to find records of children whose aggression and cooperation change markedly when they are moved from one group to another. This occurred in the case of three children in one study, all of whom had been in somewhat inferior status in the group during one year; when the following fall they were put into new groups where they were oldest and almost *ipso facto* among the most dominant, they developed both more aggression, more cooperation and more sympathy. The greater amount of independence which nursery-school teachers frequently notice in lower economic groups is probably also a function less of development than of the demands upon the child created by the situation; since these children have less opportunity to get help from adults, they spontaneously develop more self-reliance.

This is one way of saying that to be at a given age level is to be in a certain sort of social *situation*; what is really a product of the stimulus situation must not be uncritically ascribed to the physiological growth curve.

ATTITUDES AND DEMANDS OF ADULTS INFLUENCING THE CHILD DIFFERENTLY AT DIFFERENT AGE LEVELS

In order to define the successive situations confronting the child, we may suggest the characteristics of the changing world that children step into at different ages. The following suggestions are made not on the basis of research already carried out, but with the idea that these aspects of the psychological context in which the child grows up might fruitfully be studied.

What sequence of attitudes toward himself as a person does a child confront in growing up in a community? Among the many attitudes confronted, are the following characteristic?

1. Adoration, admiration as a baby, to the age of approximately two years.
2. Prohibitions, irritation, restraint, physical punishment as he begins to "get in the way."
3. Mothering, entertainment from kindergarten and primary teachers.
4. Scolding from the principal for cutting up in school, rebukes from policemen for hitching on to cars, sneaking rides on subways.
5. Ridicule as an awkward adolescent.
6. Last-minute gestures toward control from parents, teachers,

and police as in later adolescence he begins to drive a car
and live his own life.

7. Pride of home and school when he gets on the college football team.

If this sequence is characteristic, how does the growing child adjust
to the patterns of adoration, care, irritation, restraint, ridicule and
glorification which he experiences from babyhood on? How do these
situational sequences affect social behavior at each age level or stage?
What relation does this adjustment have to later attitudes toward
personal relations, needs in family life, and business relations?

What is the sequence or range of attitudes of the growing child's
associates toward outgoing *social contacts*? How characteristic are
the following?

1. Encouragement to make social contacts with everyone during the pre-school period when the child is under constant
protection of a parent or nurse.

2. Warnings not to talk to strange people or people of another
race or social class, not to play with the janitor's children or
the children across the tracks (if one is middle class); warning that one may not be wanted across the tracks (if one's
father is a workingman).

3. Contact with the intellectualism of democratic teachers or
liberal churches who foster race and class equality in verbal terms.

4. Being caught in the tense stratifications of adolescent social
structure where "money" counts.

5. Getting into the world of achievement in later high school
and college where success on the football team may cut
across race and class lines to a degree.

6. Finding that any democracy that may have been developed
in college sports and intellectual life becomes a hindrance in
the race for success in the business world.

Again, if we see the growing boy in terms of his responses
to the *demands of his group* at different periods, we might find such
sequences as these:

1. He is expected to be cute and beautiful, the idol of the family, from birth to two or three.
2. He is expected to keep out from under foot and give the adults a chance to take care of the new baby (this experience may come at any time from two to six in most families).
3. He is expected to sit still in school and learn to read and do numbers (beginning elementary school).
4. By his own age group he is expected to prove that he is male and is independent of the grown-ups (6 to 12).
5. The girls expect him to learn to dance and look nice and drive a car (early adolescence).
6. The school expects him to throw all his energy into winning for the ———— High School. His parents expect him to get the best marks.
7. He is expected to find a job, either to support himself or to contribute to the expenses of college or vocational school in order to prepare for a job later.
8. He is expected by his bride to love her day and night, and by the world to concentrate his energy on "making good."

This brief list is intended not to be inclusive, but merely to suggest the varieties of demands imposed upon the growing young person by a society which progressively asks him to be the center of attention, to get out of the way, to accept absolute authority, to show his independence of authority, to sacrifice himself for the larger group, to be self-sustaining and independent, to love passionately and to achieve financial success.

The background of these heterogeneous psychological values of individualism as they shape the social patterns of youth lies in the roots of our culture as it stems from the business success and warm family life of the Old Testament Hebrews, mediated to our social order largely through Calvinist Christianity. Profound as is the intermingling of cultures in our American melting pot, the basic ingredients retain their color, and give their deep dye to the social psychology of the individual today. Love and shrewdness, family loyalty and the prestige of the individual, devotion to the national group and sharp competition within it, are all taught indirectly by the structure and feeling quality of the social group today, as they were two thousand years ago. Fundamental aspects of social psychology will not be understood until research has cut more deeply into the relations between the texture or fiber of the socialized individual and the form and emotional content of his group. When we speak of investigating social behavior in our culture it is against this background that our problems must be outlined.

We may, then, think of the actual behavior which appears at any age level as an intersection of the needs of the child and of his biological capacity to meet the demands of, or opportunities in, the situation. Consequently, many stages are less a matter of behavior which is inevitable in the course of development than the result of stimulus by the specific situation.

This point of view does not eliminate the need to recognize the developmental process that goes from formless experimentation to creation of real form, as we see it through language, playing with sand, drawing, painting, dancing and writing. And wherever analysis of a trait shows that it probably depends on simple developmental factors in a child, whether of motor coordination or perception, the concept of the "stage" is likely to be sound. Many of these aspects of development are now obvious; and there should be little need for more research to show that the child's vocabulary is increasing between eighteen months and five years, or that increasing intelligence means an increasing capacity to give structure to any material, whether clay or words. But we do need to know much more about the ways in which this process of achieving form is related to fundamental aspects of personality, to the relations between the child and adults, and to the routine demands or creative opportunities of his surroundings.

We also need to avoid the gross error of thinking that every sequence of behavior must constitute a developmental stage. The classic sequence of development from "passivity" through "parallel play" to "participating or cooperating behavior," which we find asserted to be characteristic of the pre-school child, is also perfectly characteristic of the shy college student or almost anyone who is getting acquainted with a new situation; he is at first an outsider, then catches on and goes through part of the activity by himself, and finally is able to join fully in group activity.

Even when the pre-school stages are clear, they require the study of individual differences. An attempt to find stages of development in sympathy behavior from "passive concern" to "verbal comments" and then to "active responses" resulted in the discovery that children whose motor competence had developed more rapidly than their verbal competence might be "actively" sympathetic before they made sympathetic comments, while the highly verbal child might rely on verbal techniques throughout his nursery-school experience.

A constructive use of the concept of age level or stage will not mask individual patterns but will provide a backdrop against which these individual patterns may be seen in perspective; the interrelations of a number of developmental aspects of the organism will be considered, together with the demands of the situations in which the child is growing up.

Continuity in Social Traits from One Age Level to Another

When we consider the conditions that make for individual deviation from the general pattern of an age level, we find that differences in physical and mental development (which underlie many other aspects of behavior) are of great importance. Of another order are differences in personality structure which, although they may persist in recognizable form throughout life, manifest themselves in different ways under stress of the varying demands of life at different age periods. We are familiar enough with the energetic small boy whose imagination and explorations are too much for the limited scope of the family arena, and who therefore may provide serious problems of recalcitrance for his family, although, when given the freedom and scope of adulthood or even college, he appears to be merely unusually creative. Equally known to literature and everyday observation is the submissive, apparently "quiet" person who on being given responsibility becomes forceful and dominating. In the small arena of nursery-school life, these variations in one personality may also be seen, and they provide the color and pattern that make the vividness of individual child personality. Thus, where one two-year-old is scampering madly across the yard laughing at an adult who ineptly tries to catch him for some routine purpose, another, perhaps in the same family, is never seen more than ten feet away from some reassuring adult whose presence is a necessary support to his security. These two responses, good-natured defiance and timid dependence upon the adult, coming from different two-year-olds, will require very different handling in any school situation if the needs of each child are to be met; and each response has important implications for the child's later development. We know from many studies that the child whose aggression is developed early is likely to be more stable in personality than the shy, dependent or unaggressive child. The latter, in our culture, is almost certain to go through a period of aggression and may develop a pattern of an ambivalent sort which includes both marked submission and marked domination in different situations. This pattern of submission-domination ambivalence is likely to recur and to give a special color to the common traits of each stage. The elementary school assertion of masculinity or rebellion against authority and the early adolescent negativism to adults will probably appear more prominently in the child who has fought for dominance earlier in his career.

In pointing out the fact that individual traits of personality must be seen in relation to the total personality structure if sound predictions are to be made, we are not by any means denying the usefulness of the concept of trait. Physical traits such as sensory acuity, or sheer degree of activity as an organism, may directly underlie social traits; some such traits are very stable in some children. In clarifying the relations between age levels, traits, and specific situations or the culture as a whole, a major part of the task is to sift out those traits which are most stable (perhaps tempo, energy, tendency to make few or many contacts, tendency to cry easily or laugh easily) from those which are most dependent upon specific situations or cultural background (perhaps competitiveness and the aggressive traits, and traits of love, cooperation, and sympathy).

In measuring physical traits, or aspects of the organism as an organism, which are important for the whole course of social development, we need to follow through the implications for social behavior of every aspect of the physical organism. For instance, a child who is emotionally sensitive to sounds may jump in his crib at the age of two months when he hears the click of an electric light button, may be traumatized by the whistle of a steamboat at the age of two, may be easily cowed by the loud tones of an aggressive adult at three, and in the following year be disturbed by the noise of a nursery-school group of twenty children; on the basis of these early experiences he may develop a pattern of social response completely different from that developed by a child whose response to sounds shows less sensitiveness. If his sensitiveness also involves a pleasurable response to tones and music, he may as an infant be easily comforted by the songs of his mother and be interested later in listening to music, gladly participating in group singing and playing. In such a case the positive and negative aspects of his sensitiveness may help to define the selective responses of the child to his social and material environment, and determine certain boundaries of his areas of security and insecurity in the social world.

Good or poor eyesight, good or poor coordination of small or large muscles, even such physical traits as height, weight, strength and metabolism, undoubtedly condition the development of the child in comparable fashion, weeding out awareness of many aspects of the social world which offer discomfort or failure and anxiety, and encouraging the 'development of those patterns offered by the culture in which the child can succeed. Where the demands of the culture press too heavily to permit a simple weeding-out process, the relation between limitations and strengths inherent in the organism will determine the channels of compensation or sublimation. We must therefore conclude that deep-seated physical traits, as well as the biology of the organism as a whole in which the traits appear, must be considered in every phase of social responsiveness. The social psychologist cannot use the concept of a culture free to mold every organism into its patterns regardless of the specific traits of the organism; the social growth of each child expresses his personal and individualized needs and capacities, many of which, despite change in visible content, may be remarkably deep-seated and persistent.

Moreover, evident in almost every situation and cutting across specific functional units of social behavior (which refer essentially to social relationships, such as those designated as aggression, conflict, sympathy, cooperation) are *qualities of behavior* which, as we have just indicated, may permeate the personality as a whole and be reflected in every activity of the person, whether in the social world or in the world of individual activity. One group of these qualities may be considered under the heading of "the mode of responding." Here we see aspects of behavior such as stereotypy, compulsiveness, ritualism; imitativeness, submissiveness, dependence on others for cues; integration of feeling and form, in contrast to inhibition of feeling or to primitive expression of feeling unorganized and undisciplined by form. Closely related to this last point is the question of general integration and coherence, as compared with discrete, scattered, disorganized responses. All of these qualities refer to aspects of organization of response and may be independent of the content or direction of personality response. These qualities may perhaps be seen, in turn, in terms of the relative prominence in the personality of (1) sensory (whether visual, tactual, etc.) interests, as compared with (2) emotional tendencies (anxiety, aggression, contentment, excitement, ambition, guilt, dependence, dominance, love, sympathy, identification); (3) manipulatory or active responses, and (4) logical or verbal intellectual responses. Thus we find some children who enjoy drawing and painting because it is a delight to their eyes, others to whom it is a vivid emotional experience, others to whom it is chiefly a striped-muscle activity, and still others who find in it a chance to convey ideas. Again, some children show sympathy primarily by looking and touching, others by emotional upheaval, others by onslaughts on the aggressor, and still others by seeking to understand the trouble. Such differences affect both the quality and the quantity of social behavior and of creative work.

To what extent congenital differences in both content and mode of organization of response persist through years of varying environmental pressure we shall not know until ways are found to study the growth of personality and behavior on a larger scale than has been possible hitherto. Certainly some syndromes that include both content and mode of organization appear to be highly dependent on experience. For instance, the hyperactive child is usually characterized by scattered disorganized activity in relation to both social behavior and work; he is also liable to be lacking in normal capacity for sustained emotional response. The inadequate feeling and quality of disorganization which seem so fundamental appear to be an aspect of a fundamental insecurity that results from early deprivation or frustration. To this extent environmental factors may be of great importance. Yet we must also reckon with the fact that other children, perhaps with different natures at birth, respond to deprivation in a very different way, namely, with an over-organized intellectual superstructure which serves as a social defense and a tool to carve out some basis for security.

Another sense in which the conception of *trait* as defined in childhood social patterns appears to be useful is the *system of habits organized to the attainment of a value*. We have already considered such traits while discussing the use of statistical methods of personality study (cf. page 299); we suggested that Freud's character types are, except for terminology, based on a concept of canalization or fixation which underlies the formation of all values. Habits may have nothing in common except that they all serve in the quest for the same goal; for some purposes it may be more important to see their organization in terms of goals than to see their physiological interrelations. Among a group of children intensively studied, the daily pattern of behavior makes sense in terms of the kind of person the child conceives himself to be. Thus one seven-year-old girl walks mincingly, holding the edges of her skirt wherever she goes, and responds in a lady-like fashion to the toys offered her and to the teacher's comments alike. When confronted with a collection of play materials, she creates a neat, orderly, "refined" pattern from everything presented; she speaks in a correct and stylized fashion; she is clearly attempting from one day's beginning to the next to be a "perfect little lady." Another, at the same age and confronted with the same school situation, flops about from one boyish activity to another, shouting and groaning her comments on all that occurs, sprawling all over the furniture and systematically ignoring every appeal to feminine taste. "I just *hate* dolls." Un-

combed hair, dirty finger nails and a heavy rolling stride bespeak
the tomboy who has overdone her protest against femininity, becoming *anti-feminine* in a consistent effort to be more masculine.
The elaborate analysis of quantitative records, needful as it is, seems
to come logically *after* the clear recognition of this evident pattern.
The battery of tests applied makes sense when the scoring of the
performance is gauged in terms of the kind of person which this
child wants to be. The term "trait" then means in this case not a
group of similar behaviors, but a system of habits serving the attainment of a goal, in this instance the goal of masculinity. The habits
may change while the goal remains. The goal, frequently unconscious as it is, grows from the interplay of drives of the organism
and the evaluations and pressures of the social situation; we recognize it all too seldom in contemporary research.[1]

Under the category of "goals affecting social development" which
might be studied in relation to childhood social behavior, the following might be brought within the area of research:

1. Sex goals: conscious or unconscious drives for acceptance by
members of one's own sex, by members of the opposite sex;
rejection of one's own sex or of the opposite sex. (Expressed
in boys by extreme masculinity between five and eight, in
girls by extreme femininity during the same period.)

2. Status goals: conscious or unconscious drives for recognition,
status, approval, or security. (Expressed in children's social
behavior by extreme conformity, obedience, sympathy with
those whose approval is desired, lack of independence in
controversial areas, etc.)

3. Power-aggressive goals: conscious or unconscious drives
for power over others, domination, possession, a position of
authority. (Expressed in teasing, fighting for property or
prestige, competition for success or honors.)

4. Love goals: needs to give and receive affection, friendship,
warm response.

5. Achievement goals: delight in accomplishment, workmanship.

6. Pleasure goals: quest for immediate physical pleasures from

[1] Goals are discussed in studies of the aspiration level of the individual; cf.
page 212.

objects without regard to the effect upon, or attitude of, others.

When we think of the relation between any one aspect of social behavior and the total personality of the child, we are likely to think primarily in terms of closely related social-emotional patterns. In fact, this is all we know much about. But certain investigators are beginning to look for relationships that extend much farther. For instance, the "hyperactive" child is apt to show characteristic intellectual responses that have a good deal in common with his social patterns. He will flit from idea to idea without pausing to see any one of them through to a finish, just as he will flit from one social relation to another without giving himself to a sustained response to any one. Observations of school children are showing similar tendencies for a quality of conventionality, or stereotyped response, to appear both in relation to intellectual materials and in social situations. Students who are dependent on authoritarian patterns for their social attitudes may show the same tendency in concrete social situations and in intellectual work. The fact that all persons do not have an equal tendency to show the same patterns or ways of structuring intellectual and social experience need not vitiate the importance of this tendency when it does appear. It is probably sound to refer to those investigations which have pointed out the tendency in any considerable group for a portion of the group at each extreme to show consistent patterns (and be easily measured or recognized), whereas a portion of the group in the middle of the distribution is more variable (and harder to measure or recognize). This variability doubtless comes in some cases from constitutional tendencies toward great specificity of response, and therefore greater variability in response to different situations; in other cases, from a greater variety of cultural stresses whose lack of integration has prevented the interiorization of consistent patterns, or where there has been a marked difference in the degree of security felt by the child in different situations. For example, one child may be very submissive in relation to adults and show very conventional responses in their presence; when drawing by himself, or when playing with children he may be quite different and show great imagination, flexibility and creativeness.

Understanding a social personality, then, involves not only the capacity to see one aspect of social behavior in relation to others, or even in relation to the total intellectual-emotional make-up of the individual, but the capacity to see behavior which appears in one situation in relation to the values of that situation which permit such behavior to emerge, and the possible values of other situations in which other behavior might appear. These possible values may be predicted by the experimenter who can outline the areas of security and creativeness of the individual child in relation to the areas of insecurity and inhibition or resistance. It is probably true that the more generalized a pattern of behavior has become, whether it is one of conventional or of scattered, hyperactive character, the less likelihood there is of modifying the pattern, whether we are concerned with intellectual work or social behavior; it is the children in the middle of the range with respect to social and emotional patterns who respond to differences in situations, who are probably more open to influence by directed situations. It is this opportunity for control and direction afforded by the fact that children's social behavior does vary from one situation to another which makes this problem of such great importance to psychologists and educators.

Thus far we have suggested (1) that there are some traits which are characteristic of age levels, but that much which seems at first to be a reflection of physiological age is really a reflection of social opportunities and requirements which confront a child at a given period, and (2) that there is a great deal of difference between a trait which is an enduring and deep-seated *general orientation* of the organism and one which can be defined only as the organism's concrete means of handling a situation which confronts it. Both lines of reasoning require that we now turn to a closer analysis of the "situational" aspect of the traits of the organism.

THE SITUATION SEEN AS THE SOCIAL CONTEXT

In the attempt to obtain dependable measures of social behavior, reliability has sometimes been construed in terms of invariability or identity of behavior from one time to another and from one situation to another. This violates the very nature of some forms of social behavior which depend upon the relation between the total individual and the situation in which he is behaving, as we have just seen in our discussion of age levels and traits.

The relationship between the person and his social world has been expressed in a variety of ways. Lewin's concept of the "field" points to the fact that we must not think of the individual on one side of a fence "responding to" a situation across the fence; rather, individual and situation are together within the fence and the individual is *part of the situation* in which he is responding. Lewin's concept of the life space of the individual puts even more emphasis upon the subjective contribution to the interaction between the individual and the situation. Other investigators, such as Sherif, Piaget and Moreno, have emphasized the fact that the subjective aspect is all-important, for it determines how the field will be defined in the first place, what parts of the "geographical environment" (Koffka) will be selected and responded to. We are indebted to the Gestalt psychologists for the conceptual formulation of this problem, for which empirical results from many statistical studies have in both negative and positive ways provided filling.

Many, however, who have not been primarily concerned with the systematic analysis of the problem have also made important contributions to the concrete understanding of its implications. Anthropologists who have turned their attention in recent years to problems of "culture and personality" have given ample evidence of the fact that the behavior patterns of individuals are conditioned early within the limits permitted by their cultures, so that we have a good right to believe that John Smith, who has grown up in the group situation of American culture in the Middle West, over-laps very little with John Smith as he might have been if adopted into a Hopi family as a baby. From the clinical psychologists has come an impressive array of evidence that the family set-up in terms of parents' attitudes toward children and the relations of children to one another, as well as the conscious "principles" of the parents, make John Smith a quite different person in family A from what he might have been in family B. At the same time, sociologists

point out the effect on John Smith of the conflicts and mutual rein-
forcements of the various groups in which he participates—family,
neighborhood, school, church, and the like. And if a psychologist
happens to watch John when he is in a classroom with tired Miss
X, who is trying to teach fifty children arithmetic, and also when
John is in the Boy Scout group with energetic Mr. Y, who has "a
swell time with kids," the psychologist will point out that John is
a very different boy in the two situations.

The concept of situation, which we use only because it is freer
from theoretical implications than the terms offered by Gestalt psychologists and others, is a concept which we are using in a very elastic
way. Grossly, it refers to the total pattern of social relations which
influence a given individual, namely, his culture. More specifically,
it may mean a very narrow time-space sector of that culture, such
as is included when we define the specific children on the playground during a given five-minute period of the day. Or even more
narrowly still, one situation may differ from another by the addition
of a tricycle or a box of crayons to a constant group of children.

Among various aspects of the situation which may affect the
quality or amount of social behavior are the size of the group of
children and its constellation. For instance, a group of twenty children, all of whom were within a narrow age range, were found to
have more conflicts and less sympathetic behavior than a group of
children with a wider age range. This is after all quite reasonable,
since children of the same age are more likely to want to play with
the same things and to do the same things. Consequently competitive pressure is almost inevitable and the situation is set to stimulate
defensiveness. On the other hand, in a similar group of young
children scattered through a wider age range, from 20 to 48 months,
there was a much greater possibility for cooperation without stimulating the constant competitiveness and defensiveness observed in
the first group. Older children were stimulated to protect or help
younger ones, and at the same time younger ones had the example
of this kind of behavior to imitate, so that a wider repertory of
behavior was stimulated all around. Quite apart from these factors
of relationship between children of different ages or developmental
level is the simple matter of the number of children in the group in

relation to the tension or sensitiveness of the individual child. One child will be released and happy in a group of 20 two-year-olds where another child will be seriously inhibited by any group containing more than a half-dozen children.

The facts which have been collected about behavior of young children thus far suggest that the behavior in any group of children is also influenced by the relation between the interests and wants of individual children in the group and the opportunities for satisfaction of these wants. In a group which happened to be largely composed of highly active, extroverted children who wanted large-muscle toys like tricycles, a dearth of tricycles would probably stimulate competition where it might not do so in a group of children who were less active. Similarly, a group which by chance contains several children who are interested in music and who on the disappearance of the piano lose their outlet for it, may reflect a generalized tension largely traceable to the frustration of these individuals.

Consequently an important feature of the "situation" is the physical set-up, the world of objects, confronting the child. The environment may be planned for him, to meet one of his needs; yet it may actually have many other meanings for him. In order to plan equipment for the school setting for young children, many studies of children's *preferences* in toy materials have been made. Usually clay and drawing materials rank high for both sexes; blocks high for boys, and housekeeping materials, doll buggies, etc., for girls. But it is also evident that the amount and character of the play equipment affect the quality and quantity of social behavior in the group. Thus one study finds that clay stimulates more socialized interchange than blocks. The effects are complicated, being affected by other elements in the situation, such as the personalities of the children themselves. Some studies find more desirable social contacts with a large amount of equipment; others find more desirable social contacts with less equipment. General principles obviously wait upon a more complete functional analysis of the relations of children to one another, to the equipment, and to the total situation. Barker's records of "destructive" and other forms of socially immature behavior when children were moved from one situation containing interesting toys to another lacking those toys, begin such an analysis. They point to the importance of the relation between what the child has a chance to do in a given situation and what he really wants to do, whether this desire is based upon stable long-time interests or upon a curiosity of the moment.

Factors of personal example are also important aspects of a given child's "situation," whether the example is that of the teacher or of dominant children in the group. One dominant child was observed initiating behavior which was imitated in succession by nine other children out of a group of sixteen. The example of the teacher is frequently more influential and more subtle than she herself realizes. Her tone of voice, her attitude toward specific behavior, her feeling for the children are often more important than specific verbal patterns or techniques. Adults are not always aware of the fact that behavior may have one meaning for them and quite a different meaning to a child. In one nursery-school group a small boy grabbed another child and shook him, pointing his finger threateningly at him in a very aggressive manner; he simply carried over, as an outlet for aggression, a technique which his nurse intended to use to obtain a change in behavior. More often than we suspect, the corrective procedures of adults have little meaning for the child, other than as an experience of aggression from a more powerful personality. To many children the jovial banter of strong adults who leave the child no room to express himself, and who do not meet him on a level where he can give as good as he takes, is also felt by the child to be domination.

The adult research investigator and the nursery-school teacher cannot beg exemption here. Thus a teacher with the soundest intentions habitually laughed off minor hurts or discomforts of the children with the suggestion, "You're a big boy, you don't cry"; in the group this pattern took on intense value for several children who used it competitively. They would say proudly, "I'm a big boy. I don't cry," or "Ha-ha, you're a baby. You cry." The pattern meant "self-control" to the adult; it meant "show off" and "aggression" to several of the children. In cases like this, other aspects of the teacher's authority relation to the children, or the competitive relationship among the children themselves, need analysis before one can say clearly why these individual children used this pattern in this way. But activity patterns which can be interpreted either in their objective form or in their social meaning constitute an important part of almost every total situation.

Closely related to these factors of example are the effects of other subtle attitudes of teachers; buoyancy, spontaneity, affection for children do important things to children which are seldom noted in research records. So also do anxiety, tension in the presence of children, and an unconscious concern for property or for routine that restricts a child's freedom to explore and manipulate the world.

Even more dramatically, the status relation of the individual child to a total group will modify his behavior. Three children observed one year in a given group showed low scores on all forms of social behavior; they were younger and less physically active than other children. Six months later, in a different group where their age and developmental relations to the group gave them a dominant status in the group, social behavior ranks jumped to a high level. This type of experimentation with the child's status, the security it gives him and the behavior which results, is analogous to the training in skills undertaken by other experimenters who report that children markedly low in ascendance may become high in ascendant behavior after such training. From an educational point of view it is probably important to discover the kinds of training which are most likely to give the child confidence in *any* situation, since the maneuvering of group organization to encourage individual children is not always an easy thing to do and we do not know how profound its effects are likely to be. From the scientific point of view it is important to recognize the influence of direct and indirect situational influences in social behavior.

Variations in behavior with the specific situation may be extremely marked as the child is followed from home to school. Teachers have often noticed that children who tease and whine at home may become models of self-respecting deportment at school. Mothers notice that spontaneous creative and imaginative behavior sometimes appears at home which does not appear at school. In both instances the difference may be due not so much to the habits which adults in each situation encourage, but to the emotional tone of the situation, the release, or inhibition, or tension, or needs which the child feels in the situation, or, as in the earlier illustrations, his status in the home or school situation. At this point also, the indirect and subjective aspects of the situation in terms of its emotional meaning to the child may help or defeat the adult intentions.

As soon as we begin to speak of such influences as the emotional value of a situation to the child, we open the door to another group of questions, namely, the child's own contribution to the situation in which his social behavior occurs. We shall see, in connection with Fite's study of children's attitudes toward aggression in relation to their behavior, how individual these attitudes are. We may go further and say that any aspect of social behavior is rooted in the child's personality and cannot be adequately understood apart from it. This is made clear in a study of sympathy, where it is seen that behavior which from a superficial point of view may be classified as sympathetic may arise at one time from a desire to please a superior member of the gang, at another time from a projection of one's own anxiety; at other times it may arise from an opportunity for aggressive behavior which will be approved by adults because it appears to be in defense of someone else, a chance to show some kind of behavior when one is too frightened really to get into the swim, a genuine warmth and friendliness toward other children, or a desire to be sympathized with oneself. Dominant patterns of anxiety, aggressiveness, gentleness, calculating selfishness, or affection will be reflected in the quality of any social response and will be important for understanding its motivation. Probably these tendencies toward fearfulness or aggressive activity or sociability are rooted partly in constitutional or hereditary aspects of the child's personality, as well as in the early experiences and relationships in the home that have been emphasized so much in recent years. We have already suggested that a child with a sensitive ear may be responsive to music, loud sounds, tones of voice. He may develop a capacity for musical pleasure, react more strongly to authority expressed in tones of censure, be more easily frightened by thunder, and made tense more easily by the noise of a large play group. The pleasures and tensions built upon or directly dependent upon the original sensitiveness may then play a considerable part in affecting his response to variations in social situations with both children and adults. All of the processes of imitation, habit formation, reaction formation which have been described by both the academic and the psycho-analytic groups take place within the areas bounded by the range of cultural experiences on the one hand, and the range of sensitiveness of the organism on the other. While the culture determines the variety of patterns that can be sustained in any social group, the individual selects those which do appear. This principle is important to keep in mind when we observe the different kinds of variations different children show in response to a change in the immediate situation. A fright that makes one child more aware of the attitudes of others will make another one more egocentric. In the same way, what is apparently the same sort of shift in situations will produce different responses in the same child at different periods.

This brings us back to the original problem of age levels or stages of development with which we began. If it is true that age levels or stages of development cannot be understood adequately except in terms of the social demands being made on the child at the time, it is equally true that the influences of social situations cannot be measured apart from the level of development which the child brings to the situation. The recognition of variations in responses of different children to the same group situation or to teachers' attitudes or even to similar rôles in the group also brings us back to a recognition of the individual traits and personality pattern of the child.

During the early period of development of nursery schools, individual schools were too far apart to permit of easy collaboration. With the development of W.P.A. schools, however, an opportunity is offered not only for study of similar problems among children in different schools, but also for comparison of the influences exerted by differences in group organization and set-up in different schools. It is possible that new methods may be developed for reliable observation of whole groups at one time, so that hypotheses regarding the relation between group organization and individual behavior may be tested on a large scale, with little more expenditure of time and energy than we are accustomed to spend on an analysis of individual differences in one group. For instance, measures of the area in relation to the number of children playing in one group could be compared with the number of conflicts appearing in a given group over a given period of time. It is not uncommon to see a group of fifteen or twenty children cramped together in a space twenty by twenty feet or so, while an acre of playground is literally deserted. Time arrangements could be studied for whole groups to ascertain the relations between the amount of time children have for free play without interruption from routine demands, and the kinds of activities initiated by them.

Although systematic comparisons of groups are not yet available, the results of a number of investigations point to the probability that the following aspects of the stage setting are important for behavior of young children:

1. The number of children in one group.

2. The age range of the children in one group. Twenty two-year-olds close together in age, all interested in the same activities and without mature capacity for cooperation, may produce a high degree of tension and competition.

3. The space dimensions and arrangements of the group. Opportunities for splitting up a large group into small subgroups, scattered far enough away from one another so that they are out of stimulus range, would help to counteract effects of narrow age range in a large group.

4. Personalities of leading children in the group. A secure, friendly child who is dominant in the group may be imitated by younger children, with integrating effects upon the whole group; a bully or a swashbuckling leader may stimulate aggressiveness.

5. Personalities of teachers. Teachers who are fond of children and give them security and appreciation may unconsciously release friendliness, while teachers to whom a smooth-running organization is most important may communicate tension and anxiety to the children.

6. Property arrangements in the group. A large supply of simple materials available to everyone may focus attention on what can be created out of the materials, whereas an equally large supply of more complicated toys, but with only one or two of each kind avail-

able, is likely to stimulate competition and quarreling over materials.

7. Teachers' techniques in handling tensions and quarrels. Here the evidence is less clear and different groups are proceeding on different assumptions: (a) that children will work through their conflicts and quarrels most effectively if let alone, and will spontaneously develop cooperative patterns; (b) that children are naturally aggressive, and if their energy is not redirected and a desirable pattern suggested, habits of fighting will be reinforced.

For all of these hypotheses there is some evidence from contemporary studies of small children; for none of them is there conclusive evidence. In any study of the influences of the setting at this level, all of the factors mentioned will be involved; it is not easy to control the organization of groups so that one variable may be studied at a time. However, there is more chance of approaching a systematic analysis of the interplay of external and emotional factors at the nursery-school level than at other childhood levels, and the implications of such study would undoubtedly be important to the understanding of behavior in a social "field" at any level.

INFLUENCE OF HOME ENVIRONMENT

We have seen that the social context in which the behavior of children occurs may be defined in terms of the total cultural setting, the particular family background of the individual child, the contemporary nursery-school or home situation, or the specific stimulating situation. Though research has so largely dealt with the last of these, a major problem of the social psychology of childhood is to delineate the range of effects of situations over a long-time period, as well as to recognize the processes involved in immediate effects of social situations. This involves a more complete recognition of the major features of our culture as it influences the child—the ways in which basic aspects of the culture such as the competition, economic instability, emphasis upon status, adoration of children and aggressive expression of authority by adults, define the outlines of social behavior of the child. General variations in home and school patterns also need more analysis, along with concrete factors of equipment and personnel of specific groups.

We have tended to limit our imagination in this kind of analysis, with the result that we do not get adequate answers to the questions we ask, and we leave unasked many questions that should be asked. Ordinarily we classify backgrounds into a few general categories, such as racial or national differences, differences in occupation or socio-economic status of parents, and religious or educational differences. We make no attempt to inquire about the differences in personality and social behavior of trailer families as compared with apartment or home families, families that move all the time as compared with families that stay put, children whose mothers "work" as compared with those whose mothers "keep house," children "brought up" by maids as compared with those brought up by mothers, children of divorced parents as compared with those who have had the same two parents from birth, summer-camp children as compared with summer-family children, children of parlor radicals as compared with children of active reconstructionists who are attempting to achieve some integration of conviction and action. City children are rapidly becoming classifiable today into those of parent-educated versus non-parent-educated families, those who have been exposed to psychiatric guidance as compared with those who have not, private-enterprise families versus W.P.A. and relief families, strikers' children versus the children of capitalist sympathizers, children of nursing mothers versus children of non-nursing mothers, children with fathers who function actively at home versus children whose fathers because of the nature of their occupations are at home at the wrong hours to participate in the lives of the children. Quite as important as the early experience of weaning may be the later years of companionship or deprivation experienced by the child whose parents, though physically present, even emotionally responsive, are lacking in resources for activities and experiences to share with the child, and who do not offer the cultural nourishment that he craves.

This problem of studying major aspects of the culture and the nature of its impact upon the child has been receiving increasing attention and has recently been stated in a variety of ways. The assumption that cultural impact may be studied through correlating such gross differences as socio-economic status with specific aspects of behavior is now challenged from different quarters. But the challenge does not go far enough. We find the suggestion offered that a first step toward study of the influences of environment upon the child is the analysis of the elements of the child's social environment. Such a suggestion, as ordinarily conceived, ignores the fact that any analysis of elements must be made within a frame of reference which determines those elements to which we pay attention, and that actually we have been "analyzing component elements" for many years with a variety of degrees of enlightenment. Certainly money income is one element, and the father's occupation is another; these have proved to be "related" to intelligence, honesty, leadership, and other aspects of good adjustment according to conventional criteria of our culture. At the same time we find within the limits of these broad categories other elements of great importance which cut across them. Independence of adults, motor skills, and even sympathy appear more conspicuously in lower economic groups, and challenge analysis of the *quality of experience* and of personal relations in the lives of children in these groups. The culture or the environment influences behavior directly, both through consciously planned training afforded to some groups and not to others (reading, moral training, school training of upper as compared with lower economic groups), and also through unconscious influences such as the objective need for self-reliance and mutual aid in the group which cannot afford nurses. These two aspects, the influence of conscious training as compared with the influence of the stage that is unconsciously set by the parents, are important whether we are selecting for study the influence of home, or school, or specific situations within either one. For in analyzing the effects of specific situations or the culture as a whole, there may be a great difference between the overt pattern and the formal purpose intended by teacher or parent, as compared with the inherent attitude and feeling tone conveyed by the individual.

The motivation of social behavior obviously varies from one situation to another, but we are riding for a fall if we think of this process of changing motivation in terms of organ stops. The whole

SOME STUDIES OF THE INFLUENCE OF

TYPE OF INTEREST	AUTHOR DATE	NO. OF SUBJECTS	AGE RANGE	SAMPLE
Delinquency	Armstrong, C. P. (1933)	991	8–15 yrs.	215 boys arraigned for various offenses; 649 boys who deserted their homes; 60 incorrigibles; 67 charged with theft. Examined in the clinic of the Children's Court, New York City.
Intelligence	Arthur, G. (1926)	484		Sibling pairs with south European and Slavic names tested for intelligence.
Delinquency	Baker, H. J., Decker, F. J. and Hill, A. S. (1929)	84	10–16 yrs.	Boys convicted of theft by juvenile court.
Behavior problems	Bellerose, D. (1927)	96		4 groups of only, youngest, oldest, and middle children referred to a habit clinic.
Ascendance	Bender, I. E. (1928)	194		Sophomores at Dartmouth College.
Manic-depressive psychoses	Berman, H. H. (1933)	100		Cases of manic-depressive psychoses in St. Lawrence State Hospital.
Misdemeanors	Blatz, W. E., and Bott, E. A. (1926)	1437	7–16 yrs.	School children.
Intelligence, achievement, personality traits	Blonsky, P. P. (1930)	33		Only children in Grade I of an average working-population school in Moscow.

METHOD	FINDINGS
Examined in relation to position in the family.	Only in offenses against the home is there reliability of primogeniture of delinquents, with the home-deserters in the 3-child, and with the ungovernables in the 4-child family. There is a strong indication of primogeniture in both groups in the 2-child family; with the home deserters in the 5-child family and some possibility in the 4- and 6-child families; and with the ungovernables in the 5-child family. Boys charged with forcible entry show a slight tendency to be oldest in the 3- and 7-child families.
92 sibling pairs tested, and then 150 sibling pairs.	The younger siblings average about 7 points more in I. Q. than the older siblings.
Cases matched for age, school grade, neighborhood and nationality.	A birth order distribution for delinquent boys in close agreement with that of a control group.
	Slightly larger occurrences of food fads and temper spells in the only-child group, but in general the only children not unique.
Allport A-S given, and family position obtained.	There is a tendency for the only as well as the oldest member to be slightly above the mean of the entire group in ascendance, and for the youngest as well as the intermediate member to be below the mean of all. None of these differences significant statistically.
Analysis of cases for birth order.	Of 100 cases of manic-depressive psychosis, 48 found to be among the first born; 22 among those last born.
Behavior records kept by teachers.	Misdemeanors fewest for the only children.
Various analyses of I. Q., achievement, and personality.	Only children, in general, seem rather higher in intelligence and better in accomplishment, and come from relatively well-to-do and intelligent families. Some evidence that these children were overstimulated and tended to be more domineering or "shut-in" than children in general.

SOME STUDIES OF THE INFLUENCE OF

TYPE OF INTEREST	AUTHOR DATE	NO. OF SUBJECTS	AGE RANGE	SAMPLE
Personality, etc.	Bohannon, E. W. (1898)	381		Only children.
Delinquency	Breckenridge, S. P., and Abbott, E. (1912)	584		Delinquent boys in Chicago juvenile courts.
Delinquency	Burt, C. (1925)			Delinquent and non-delinquent groups.
School performance	Busemann, A. (1928)	400	10–17 yrs.	Fairly homogeneous lower middle-class background.
Instability, etc.	Campbell, A. A. (1933)	200		100 men, 100 women, of which 50 (for each sex) were only children. University of Oregon students.
Sensitivity to pain	Carman, A. (1898)	1507	10–19 yrs.	School children, Saginaw, Michigan.

BIRTH ORDER UPON SOCIAL BEHAVIOR (*Continued*)

METHOD	FINDINGS
Questionnaire.	Only children below average in health and vitality. Mental and physical defects of a "grave character" much more common among them than among children generally. They enter school later than other children, and are less regular in attendance. Their success in school work below the average. Peculiarities seem to be more pronounced in these children than in others. They are more affectionate, more selfish, and more precocious.
	In families of more than one, 138 of this delinquent group were oldest and only 70 were youngest children.
Clinical data.	An unduly large proportion of only children found among delinquent boys.
Divided into 3 groups on basis of school standing.	Emphasizes the advantages to siblings of the stimulating effect of brothers and sisters, and submits some evidence in favor of slightly better school performance for children with siblings.
Groups matched for sex, intelligence, college class. Obtained personality data from Bernreuter, Cason's Annoyance test, college scholastic records, and physical ratings.	Only children appear somewhat predisposed by early environment to develop unusual personality traits. Boys raised as only children scored higher on test of neuroticism, self-sufficiency and dominance than did boys raised as intermediate children. Girls raised as only children scored higher than did girls raised with brothers and sisters on ratings of neuroticism and introversion, and scored lower on test of dominance and self-sufficiency. Both only-child groups made significantly more variable scores than did the group with which they were paired. None of these differences statistically reliable, though more reliable for men than for women. No differentiation possible between only and intermediate children in regard to either physique or scholarship.
Physical measurements obtained and related to position in family.	Sensitiveness to pain decreases in order of birth, first-born boys more sensitive than second-born, second-born more so than those of later birth. Strength of grasp is the same. First-born girls show less sensitivity to pain than second-born.

SOME STUDIES OF THE INFLUENCE OF

TYPE OF INTEREST	AUTHOR DATE	NO. OF SUBJECTS	AGE RANGE	SAMPLE
Delinquency	Dugdale, R. L. (1910)			
Dominance feeling	Eisenberg, P. (1937)	454	Average age, 19.5 years.	216 Columbia men; 238 Barnard women. Mostly sophomores and juniors. High socio-economic level.
Fame	Ellis, H. (1927)	1030		975 men, 55 women.
Nervousness	Fenton, N. (1928)	199		Kindergarten to 6th-grade children. (34 only and 163 not-only children.)
Jealousy	Foster, S. (1927)	150	1–12 yrs.	50 jealous, 100 non-jealous, from Boston habit clinics.
Instability	Friedjung, J. (1911)			Only children.
Aggressiveness	Goodenough, F. L., and Leahy, A. M. (1927)	Almost 300	5½–6 yrs.	I. Q. and social status above average. From Demonstration Child Guidance Clinic in Minneapolis and St. Paul. Kindergarten children.
Various factors	Goodenough, F. L. (1930)	33	27–59 months.	17 boys, 16 girls, Nursery School, University of Minnesota, Institute of Child Welfare. Mean I. Q. 110.5.

BIRTH ORDER UPON SOCIAL BEHAVIOR (*Continued*)

METHOD	FINDINGS
	There is a greater tendency for the first-born to become criminal than others.
Scores on short form of Maslow "Social Personality Inventory," and position in family.	First and only children tend to feel more dominant than middle and youngest children, the latter the least dominant. The first in families of over two feel more dominant than the first in families of two. Similarly, the youngest in families of over two feel less dominant than the youngest in families of two. In families of three or more, those holding the end positions tend to feel less dominant than those in the first and second positions. These are differences for men. The differences for women were not clear, though there were some slight suggestions of the same trend.
Persons to whom 3 or more pages of space were given in the "Dictionary of National Biography."	In small and medium-sized families the eldest most frequently achieves fame; in the large families it is the youngest.
Ratings by teachers.	Data on various personality items from only and from not-only children approached perfect overlapping. "Only" children who were nervous seemed to have more symptoms than other cases; fewer "only" children were rated as nervous.
Case histories.	Jealous child more likely to be the oldest child.
Compilation of clinical data from the author's practice.	87% show neuropathic traits, as compared with 31% in families containing more than one sibling. Gastro-intestinal disorders, enuresis, insomnia, and emotional instability more common among only children.
Position of family known. Children rated on various traits.	Oldest children tended to lack aggressiveness, leadership and self-confidence. Middle children tended to lack aggressiveness, but slightly less than the oldest children. Youngest children showed no marked tendency to either extreme. Only children showed most aggressiveness and self-confidence.
Observation technique; time sampling.	Age held constant, no significant correlations found for size of family and position among siblings with: activity, intelligence, length of attendance at nursery school, beauty, height, weight, social status, and physician's health rating.

SOME STUDIES OF THE INFLUENCE OF

TYPE OF INTEREST	AUTHOR DATE	NO. OF SUBJECTS	AGE RANGE	SAMPLE
Personal data and personality	Guilford, R. B., and Worcester, D. A. (1930)	163	11–15 yrs.	21 only children, 141 other children; pupils in 8A, Irving Junior H. S., of Lincoln, Nebr.
Stuttering	Hion, V. (1932)	295		
Emotional stability	Hooker, H. F. (1931)	60		Of 117 children, 30 only children and 30 non-only children were selected (28 girls, 32 boys; 10 of the matches were oldest children, 11 middle, 9 youngest). Selected because they lived in a home with no relatives except mother and father; matched for school grade, sex, chronological age, nationality, family organization, not more than one child from any one family, I. Q.
Sociability	Hsia, J. (1928)	280	11–14 yrs.	School children, Grades V–VIII.
Intelligence	Hsiao, H. H. (1931)	Over 2000		
Intelligence, emotional stability, suggestibility, etc.	Korn, E. M. F. (1923)	75		3 groups: only children, oldest children, and neither only nor oldest. All in 3rd group from families of not less than 6 children; those in 2nd from families of not less than 4 children.

BIRTH ORDER UPON SOCIAL BEHAVIOR (*Continued*)

METHOD	FINDINGS
15 characteristics including I. Q., school marks, occupational status of father, personal health, school leadership, school cooperation, community service, etc.	The only child definitely superior in occupational status, marks in school, health attitudes and habits. He is quite certain to be superior in personal orderliness and cleanliness, initiative, self-control, industry, truthfulness, dependability, courtesy. He is higher in I. Q., cooperation, conformity to law and order. He is very slightly superior to the non-only child in fairness.
	Number of stutterers least when there are two children in the family, most when there is only one; it increases with more than three children. Stuttering encountered most frequently in the first- and last-born.
Terman's adaptation of the Woodworth-Matthews Personal Data Sheet, and two rating scales by Wickman.	No real differences in emotional stability. Only children in general do not present serious behavior problems because of their "onliness." In general they are not necessarily nervous, hysterical, and "spoiled." As a whole, they differ little, if at all, from non-only.
Test of sociability given; also parents' and teachers' ratings of sociability obtained.	Most sociable children usually have fewer brothers and sisters than the least sociable. In general, a negative correlation between sociability and number of siblings.
	First-born not inferior to later-born in intelligence or any of other characteristics studied.
Otis suggestibility test, Matthews emotional stability test, National Intelligence test, ratings by teachers, and records of work and conduct for preceding 3 terms collected.	Only children have better work habits; middle children more stable, but seem to fall behind in conduct. Only children seem to be just as good mixers as others, but are not as likely to participate actively in athletics.

SOME STUDIES OF THE INFLUENCE OF

TYPE OF INTEREST	AUTHOR DATE	NO. OF SUBJECTS	AGE RANGE	SAMPLE
Behavior problems	Levy, J. (1931)	700		Clinic cases, all with I.Q.'s of 80 or above.
Personality, etc.	Maller, J. B. (1931)	802	9–17 yrs.	3 groups: School E, residential neighborhood, New Haven, high socio-economic status; School W, at Walden, about average socio-economically; School L, in a poor, under-privileged district, New Haven, low status, foreign born.
Delinquency	Parsley, M. (1932)	722	10–16 yrs.	361 delinquent girls and 361 controls. White, Negro and Polish populations.
Problem children	Rosenow, C. (1930)	652	1.5 yr.–17.5 yr.	Problem children in Cleveland and Philadelphia clinics.

BIRTH ORDER UPON SOCIAL BEHAVIOR (*Continued*)

METHOD	FINDINGS
Case study analysis.	Comparing the proportion of clinic cases of each ordinal number in the family and the proportion of children of the same ordinal number in a sample of over 35,000 non-problem members of the community, he found that on the whole there tended to be just about as many problem cases of each ordinal number as one would expect from the number of children of that ordinal number in the population at large. Nor did the size of the family affect the relative number of problems. But in a small rich community, homes with "only" children may produce problem boys more frequently than do family groups of other sizes. Does not hold true of girls who are only children in similar environments. While the first-born is more frequently a problem when the city at large is studied, the second child is more frequently a problem in the small favored community. Problem boys had boy siblings immediately above and below in a much larger proportion of cases than those in which girls were nearest siblings.
Data from Character Education Inquiry.	Size of family correlates negatively with intelligence, moral knowledge, cultural background, honest behavior. The only child not superior to the others, except in moral knowledge. Size of family shows a definitely curvilinear relationship with cooperation and helpfulness. Children of very small families and those of very large ones scored lower than those of average size families. There was a similar curvilinear relationship between size of family and the children's scores on tests of inhibition. Size of family correlates positively with scores of persistence, children of large families scoring highest.
Records obtained from the Juvenile Court, Cook County, Illinois.	Delinquents came from smaller families than non-delinquents; only children more frequent among them. No significantly larger proportion of the delinquents than of the non-delinquents were oldest in the family, but the proportion of non-delinquents who were the youngest definitely greater than found among the delinquents. When the two groups subdivided by race or nationality, the same differences were found, except that among the Negroes ordinal position apparently bore no relation to the likelihood of delinquency occurring.
Case records.	Slightly larger proportion of first-born children became problems than would be expected by chance (123 to 108.5). Proportion of last-born children who appeared as problems correspondingly less (77 to 91.7).

SOME STUDIES OF THE INFLUENCE OF

TYPE OF INTEREST	AUTHOR DATE	NO. OF SUBJECTS	AGE RANGE	SAMPLE
Jealousy	Ross, B. M. (1931)	1275	Under 3 to over 16 yrs.	166 of these children are jealous. Cases from the records of the Institute for Child Guidance, New York.
Jealousy	Sewall, M. (1930)	70	1–6 yrs.	Clinic and nursery-school children in Chicago.
Delinquency	Slawson, J. (1926)	596	16–18 yrs.	Delinquent boys in the New York House of Refuge.
Delinquency	Sletto, R. F. (1933)	1878		939 delinquent and 939 non-delinquent school children.
Jealousy	Smalley, R. E. (1930)	54	Below 6 to above 12 yrs.	Children from the Cleveland and Philadelphia Demonstration Child Guidance Clinics. Studied in pairs (siblings).
Instability, etc.	Stagner, R., and Katzoff, E. T. (1936)	430		University of Wisconsin students.
Emotion	Stratton, G. M. (1927)	846		University of California students.

BIRTH ORDER UPON SOCIAL BEHAVIOR (*Continued*)

METHOD	FINDINGS
Case study analysis.	Jealousy as a problem occurred most frequently among the first-born.
Clinic and nursery-school records; parent interviews.	Being told that another baby is coming does not necessarily prevent jealousy. Jealousy occurs most frequently when there is a sibling age difference of from 18 to 42 months, with 2-child families rather than with larger families, with superior intelligence, and with maladjustment of homes.
Case records.	No unduly large proportion of only children found among delinquent boys.
Case history records of delinquents of Hennepin County Juvenile Court. Classified in terms of position in family in relation to sexes of immediately surrounding siblings. This group matched with a non-delinquent group for size of sibship, sex, and age.	Delinquency ratios higher for girls whose siblings were all brothers than for girls whose siblings were all sisters. For boys this was true only when in the intermediate position. In general, delinquency ratios are high for children who are in sibling positions involving the presence of younger siblings of each sex, and low for children in positions involving the presence of elder siblings of each sex. The ratios somewhat higher for both boys and girls when elder siblings are of the same sex and younger siblings are of the opposite sex, than when the reverse is true.
Case study analysis, I.Q. and other records available.	Within the pairs, the older, when duller, more likely to be jealous.
Bernreuter Personality Inventory administered.	No significant differences in birth order for neuroticism, self-sufficiency, or dominance. A slight advantage for small families, that is, they are less neurotic, more self-sufficient and more dominant.
Diary account of fear and anger behavior.	First-born on the average have an anger score appreciably and reliably larger than those not first-born. First-born tend to have a higher fear score, but this difference not statistically reliable. Only children no different in these respects than other first-born.

SOME STUDIES OF THE INFLUENCE OF

TYPE OF INTEREST	AUTHOR DATE	NO. OF SUBJECTS	AGE RANGE	SAMPLE
Emotion	Stratton, G. M. (1934)	2196		
Emotional stability	Stuart, J. C. (1926)	465		Colgate University students, men, 81 of which were only children.
Intelligence	Thurstone, L. L., and Jenkins, R. L. (1929)	10,000		
Neuroticism	Thurstone, L. L. and T. G. (1930)	694		University of Chicago freshmen.
Political attitude	Vetter, G. E. (1930)	227		College students mainly from N. Y. U. 21 only, 150 oldest, 56 youngest children.
Atheism	Vetter, G. E., and Green, M. (1932)	350	Below 30 to over 60.	Members of the American Association for the Advancement of Atheism.
Behavior problems	Ward, A. (1930)	100	3–18 yrs.	Clinic patients.

BIRTH ORDER UPON SOCIAL BEHAVIOR (*Continued*)

METHOD	FINDINGS
Diary account of fear and anger behavior.	First-born men reliably less fearful than others. First-born women more irascible than others. No difference in anger for men, and fear for women. Only children no different from other children in these respects, except that there is a tendency for the only woman to be less irascible than the non-only woman.
Colgate Mental Hygiene Tests administered.	Only children show no deviation from normality.
Analysis of case records of Stanford-Binet tests.	Average I.Q. increases slightly with birth order; this effect not limited merely to handicapping the first-born. The effects seem to be consistent and progressive, at least as far as the eighth-born child; variability of intelligence increases with order of birth.
Thurstone neurotic inventory given.	Order of birth shown not to have any important relation to the development of a maladjusted or neurotic personality.
Vetter's Social and Political Attitudes Test given.	Atypical, reactionaries, and radicals seem to have more than the chance number of only children. Conservatives and liberals both seem a little short of this quantity, likewise the typicals. The typicals and conservatives seem to have more than their share of youngest children; all seem to run heavily to oldest children.
Questionnaires.	No less than 36% of the atheists were oldest children; only 15% were youngest children, whereas sheer chance should make the numbers of each about equal. About 9% only children. These figures more impressive when it is seen that these people came from families averaging 5 children, and when the percentages are compared to like values for the radical-opinion group in college students.
Case records at Institute for Child Guidance, New York.	Only children 3 years younger than other children of clinic; a little more intelligent (I.Q., 109.8, as compared with 103.3). Types of problems appearing among only children corresponded to those among other clinic children, except that lying, stealing, truancy, and sensitiveness less frequent in all age groups. As compared with children of 3-child families, only children showed more restlessness and over-activity, crying, nail-biting, and school difficulties. Adverse factors of the home background were similar.

SOME STUDIES OF THE INFLUENCE OF

TYPE OF INTEREST	AUTHOR DATE	NO. OF SUBJECTS	AGE RANGE	SAMPLE
Happiness	Watson, G. (1930)	388	Average, 30 yrs.	Graduate students of education.
Personality	Wile, I. S., and Noetzel, E. (1931)	500	2–16 yrs.	Patients referred for health problems.
Delinquency	Winter, L. (1897)	54		Irish and Irish-American criminals.
Emotional stability, etc.	Witty, P. A. (1934)	200		High school students, 11th and 12th grades, 2 Chicago schools. 100 only and 100 intermediate.

child is responding to the whole situation, and a "motive" can probably be seen only as a particular intersection of child and situation. This would avoid such a travesty on the nature of personality as results when we try to think of discrete motives residing in the personality at a given time. In neurological terms, probably every motivating occasion involves a somewhat different configuration of patterns in the total cortical-thalamic-autonomic material of the person. "Motives" may be abstracted from these configurations without even bearing the relation to reality that a recipe bears to the cake which is made by the strict following of its directions.

As an illustration of the futility of attempting to get psychological insight from the study of social factors that are not given in psychological terms, we may refer to the multitude of studies of the child's "position in the family" as determined by his birth order. His psychological position in the family is of the utmost importance for the development of social behavior, but "psychological position" is

METHOD	FINDINGS
Happiness questionnaire.	No clear tendency for the larger families to be more frequently in the happy group. Neither are only children unhappy adults. In general, position in the family found not to be related to happiness.
Analysis of clinical records.	When oldest, middle, youngest and only children classified as "explosive," "withdrawn," "enuretic," and "delinquent," no relationship to the family constellation found.
Criminal records.	Disproportionate number of the criminals studied found to be first-born.
Data secured on physical growth, health and developmental histories, socio-economic status, activities and interests, I.Q., Bernreuter Personality Inventory scores, school marks, and character ratings by teachers.	Groups approximately equal in 18 measures and ratings of physical development, in socio-economic status, in test intelligence, in school marks and in 21 comparisons relating to social or emotional adjustment.

by no means completely dependent on birth order. The chart on pages 348 ff. gives a digest of the results of a number of birth-order studies which tend to be inconclusive or contradictory. Study of this summary will show why the objective fact of ordinal position in the family, without regard to its meaning to the child, to the siblings, and to the parents, is sure to yield meager psychological results. The question whether the child feels accepted and loved; his emotional relation with his parents; the competition or support which brothers and sisters bring to him; and the specific pressures or areas of freedom and stimulus that come along with one position in the family or another are probably more important than the objection fact of ordinal position.

A more fruitful procedure than sheer comparison of children in terms of birth order is suggested by a number of studies which have been analyzing the relation between parent attitudes and children's behavior. From several sources we find hyperactivity in children associated with attitudes of rejection on the part of the mothers; from another source we find children with mothers who tend to be "over-protective," as well as those with "constructive" mothers, more happily adjusted than children whose mothers are domineering or hostile. Tentative results from another study suggest that "shy" and "well-adjusted" mothers tend to have happier children than "dominating" mothers.

A further extension of this concern with the attitudes and values of parents, in relation to the influence of family situations on children, is suggested by Lerner. He has formulated the kernel of the problem involved in studying the influence of culture upon the personality of the child as follows:

> In addition to designating types of parental, school or church influence (in terms of membership of parents in given socio-economic, occupational, religious, ethnic, etc., groups) we must identify more definitely the *quality*, the main valuational or attitudinal pattern, of what goes with such group-membership of parents. . . . Aims stated in terms of ideals as to certain specific aspects of family life, classroom behavior, etc., will give us a more definite and dynamic picture of adult influence in given areas—in terms of what parents come to expect in a more or less characteristically recurring manner.

The emphasis on values as embedded in the basic personality structure of the adult might be better approached through observation of the adult in relation to the child than through mere inquiry regarding aims. The whole content of the adult's relation with the child, his pressures, his anxieties, his affection and ways of expressing it, his play and the home he creates, his shared interests, and the school he selects would afford an important context for his statement of aims and ideals in child-rearing.

The dangers latent in the attempt to make a distinction between objective and subjective aspects of the culture which affect the child may be illustrated further by the problem of analyzing the effects of broken homes upon child personality. The fact that broken homes appeared more often in the backgrounds of delinquents attracted notice early. More recently parent attitudes have been emphasized as of prime importance.

Just as we have found that where certain specific types of problem occur in a child other problems will probably be found, so we may expect that objective conditions in broken homes will be inextricably bound up with subjective attitudes. Disturbed attitudes which lead to divorces are likely to be relayed to children as well as to mates. More accurately stated, disturbed attitudes and divorces may be seen as the converse sides of a pattern of human relations which is essentially unstable. Where a family is broken by death or other circumstances that have no causal relation to attitudes, the objective distortion may be balanced for the child by sources of stability in those relationships that maintain continuity.

Moreover, of greater significance for the child than the details of specific parental attitudes are the qualities of adult personality that emerge in our contemporary culture. A complete delineation of these qualities cannot be made on the basis of present methods such as interviews, or the psychiatric analysis of those adults who have been driven by the difficulty of their problems to seek professional help. For a real cross-section we need the day-by-day record of the fun and the conflict, the gayety and the tragedy, the compulsions and the common-sense decisions, the enthusiasms and the frustrations of the average person. But granting that any analysis made on the basis of study of individuals who have come for therapy must present one side of the picture alone, we may emphasize the hypotheses offered in a recent major analysis of personality in our culture. Horney points to the psychological inconsistencies so deeply rooted in a society which exerts such intense pressure for conformity and originality, for group cooperation and for individual competition—we may say broadly, for inflation and for deflation of the ego. The need for love is everywhere intrenched yet everywhere frustrated; the same motives which are now hailed as heroic are a moment later ridiculed as claptrap. The adult who has been broadly exposed to wider trends has a hard time maintaining his personal standard of self-respect and at the same time a regard "for the opinions of mankind."

We have already noted the effects of such complexes upon the children of immigrants (cf. page 205). We have been slower to recognize that the same thing is happening to the children of native-born Americans, especially those exposed to the complexities and inconsistencies of urban culture.

Not only the interplay of different aspects of family life, but the interaction between the attitudes at home and at school is important in the process of development of social behavior. Hartshorne and May illustrated this dramatically with their work on elementary school children; the consistency of behavior increased steadily in the upper economic groups where home and school standards reinforced each other. Children in the lower socio-economic groups showed no increase in consistency as they grew older. Moreover, in all probability the pressure of conflicting standards at home and school creates conflicts in the child which he would not have if he were under the influence of either home or school alone, since he must on many an occasion behave one way to satisfy his parents, another way to keep his status in his group.

The conflict between the values of school and home is not confined to the experience of the elementary school age alone; it is reflected in the following description of a group of mothers and teachers of pre-school children.

The teachers in some ways were much like the mothers; they shared the feminist background, the pressures toward feminine professionalism. Few of them had the opportunity for a complete emotional development which the mother had, since most of them lacked both husbands and children. This made some mothers feel that the teachers lacked insight into the importance of emotional give-and-take of the home. Many mothers found very unrealistic the teachers' emphasis upon objectivity, routine, detachment. Some felt confused by stock interpretations in handling children. If you loved a child too much he would exploit your responsiveness for the sake of getting attention; if you sympathized with his hurts he would magnify them and prolong his own emotional response; spanking was a confession of failure. Yet love, sympathy, and disapproval seemed a normal part of many healthy homes they knew which had produced strong men and women.

Other aspects of the situation may be pieced together from various clues: the institution claimed that some mothers brought the children to nursery school so they could have more time although they had nothing definite to do; that other mothers came, saying, "I can't do anything with Johnny, I want you to take him off my hands." Even less explicitly it seemed to the observer that some mothers had been problem-conscious as a result of child guidance propaganda and took seriously difficulties which formerly might have been overlooked; these gave the mothers a feeling of defeat which brought them to the authorities from whom they thought they might get help, or even led them to "turn the child over" to the institution to be taken care of for most of the day.

The important aspect of the relation between the institution and the families was the fact that both teachers and parents were being influenced by certain common trends in contemporary life, and child guidance in particular, and that they were also being influenced by certain different trends or different experiences; altogether, the effect on the observer who conferred with parents and watched the teachers was one of confusion, inadequately understood differences in values and behavior, and occasional conflict over specific differences of opinion. This picture of confusion and varying emphases on different behavior and personality values is the most fundamental characteristic of the cultural situation in which the children's social responses were being studied, and is of course the inevitable product of the syncretism and conflict of values that makes the whole culture of which this group is a part seem to be an endless pulling and hauling to diverse ends.

Since many of the children who have been the subjects of experimental and observational studies of social behavior have been in nursery schools, their parents being influenced more than the average parent by current emphases in parent education and child psychology, it is important to take account of the direction of these pressures. One way of judging the points of greatest concern to teachers and students of children is to note the topics emphasized in the more substantial books used by these groups.

Between 1928 and 1932 (a period during which much of the data reported in the present volume was being collected) a number of widely read books on "child psychology," "child guidance" and "management of children" had been published. One of the first of these, published in 1927, had a separate chapter each for eating, for sleeping, for walking, for talking, for excretory functions, and for sensory training. Learning to adjust to the group, laws of discipline, nervousness and intelligence each received a chapter. Sex, death, and religion were all handled in one chapter. Topics in the index receiving six references or more were as follows, in alphabetical order: Christmas, 10; conditioned responses, 7; diet, 6; discipline, 13; enuresis, 17; environment, 13; food, 12; group, 11; learning, 11; masturbation,

13; mood, 7; nap, 6; nervousness, 16; nursery, 12; parent, 9; punishment, 21; reward, 6; sensory training, 6; sex, 19; sleep, 14; speech, 25; stuttering, 10; walking, 8. In 1928 a book that was even more widely used, in all probability, focused on the normal problems. The keynote of the book was struck in early chapters on habits and parent-child relationships. These were immediately followed by specific chapters on feeding, sleep, enuresis, thumb-sucking and nail-biting, obedience and discipline, anger, fear, jealousy, destructiveness, inferiority, habit spasms, delinquency, and sex. The last three chapters made a more positive emphasis on relations between teacher and pupil on the one hand, and between intelligence and conduct on the other hand, and on toys and companions.

A general treatise published in 1930 evokes a more positive emphasis upon the constructive job of the parent as manager of children. Here again, however, the predominant place is given to learning as the most significant of all functions in the developing child. In the index we find "control" with 33 references, discipline with 21, and nothing under "emotion" or "instinct." Further analysis of the book shows emphasis upon indirect control through manipulation of the environment; affording opportunities for activity; two chapters out of three on the social environment are given to adult influences, and the section on motivation discusses rewards and punishment, success and failure almost exclusively.

In another standard and well-balanced book published in 1931 the topics in the index receiving the most references were as follows: fear, 31; environment, 30; reading, 29; habits, 27. The topics discipline (8), disobedience (6), punishment (11), and obedience (16), total 41 references, excluding 6 references to cooperation (on the part of the child). The addition of 10 references to helpfulness and 8 to loss distinguishes this book from others where these topics do not appear at all or with only 1 or 2 references. Even here, however, anger with its references wins over either of them.

In 1932, a couple of standard works appeared in which discussions of periods of growth and chemistry of growth preceded the discussion of learning and habits, but in 1933 there also appeared an authoritative discussion of child behavior which contained 27 references to habits, 30 references to behavior (in each case discussions of up to 20 pages were counted only as one reference), while attitude received only 4 references, emotions (meaning of) and emotional (control, instability, life, satisfaction) received 7; instinct (of self-assertion, repression of, sex, beginning of, questions of) received 5, and instinctive (acts, rare; life) received 2. Love (objects of child) had one reference. The kinds of problems which received the attention of psychologists may be seen from the following list (indexed in a standard compilation of short case studies) in which the number of cases where a problem appears is indicated:

Bed wetting	12	Obstinate	13
Cries easily	6	Playmate problems, connected	
Dependent on parents	7	with	8
Destructive	6	School problems	11
Disobedient	6	Shy	7
Fatigue	12	Sleeping problems	16
Fears	24	Speech problems	17
Feeding problems	37	Swears	6
Handles genitals	6	Teases	6
Hyperactive	15	Teeth	8
Jealous	6	Temper tantrums	16
Nail-biting	11	Thumb-sucking	16
Nervous	12	Tonsils	17
Night terrors	7	Under-nourished	18

In the index of this book, the family are mentioned as follows: father, nervous (14), possibly psychopathic (3), unsympathetic (1); grandparents affecting situation (16); mother, exhausted (4), insane (1), nagging (6), nervous (34), overanxious (6).

Out of the group of thirteen outstanding books which were analyzed, there were two with a strikingly different balance: in one of these "adjustment" received 26 references; "emotion" and "emotional" received 33; "experience" had a reference, as did "integration"; "self" had 14, "social" had 21, "reaction" had 17 and "response" had 13. Here we find a stronger tendency to see the interrelation between the affective life of the child and his behavior and to see his status as the result of intercourse between an actively feeling and living organism and its environment rather than as the result of almost passive acceptance of the environment as parents and teachers impose it through habit training techniques.

In the other volume, a symposium—where nearly 100 selections from as many authors were compiled—we find in the index 16 references to emotions as against 10 to habit, 11 references to imagination and to individual variation, 20 to sex and sex education, as against 9 to fear. It is also significant that "individual variation" receives 11 references in this book, whereas it hardly appears at all in any of the others except perchance in connection with intelligence tests. This volume like the preceding one stands out conspicuously against the phalanx of behavioristic habit-minded volumes on child guidance which were first discussed. Even in these two books, however, the discussion of the child's affective life seems limited; sympathy, humor, enthusiasm, and other subtler aspects of a warmly human personality received little or no mention.

It seems fair to say, then, that the predominant emphasis of the child guidance movement as it impinged upon parents and teachers was upon the fundamental importance of learning, of habits, of management and control. Habits of eating, sleeping, eliminating received most attention; in fact, every tiniest detail of parental and child behavior could be specified in these areas. Emotions, on the other hand, were confronted chiefly in relation to fears and anger. Sex was a matter of education' and how to handle the child's questions, or what to do about the "problem of masturbation." In contrast to the elaborate analysis of habit formation and "problems" there was meager attention given to the matters of social grouping, cooperation, helpfulness that have received some attention in recent research; or to the careful study of the child's life of feeling—his sympathies, his longings, his enthusiasms, his humor, and his wonder, his love of rhythm or of color. We may note in passing that contemporary with these emphases in the literature directly influencing parents and teachers with whom we are concerned, were certain trends in the academic world of psychological thought. One of these made "behavior" a word to conjure with, and another made "extroversion" a sort of inclusive ideal goal instead of simply one aspect of a normal personality. Along with the interest in "behavior" went the white hope embodied in the "conditioned response" which furnished much of the basis for the immense confidence in "habits" and also offered the key to understanding of "fears" and most other "problems." Only recently has one of the outstanding students of the conditioned response in this country published evidence to show that conditioning as it appears in the dog is hardly the same phenomenon as that which occurs in the human being, so dependent is the latter upon attitudes and feelings of the subjects being "conditioned." But this research is not yet available on a wide scale and is consequently accessible neither to teacher nor to those who write books on child guidance.

The emphasis on problems—that direction of attention which made the fact that a child sucked his thumb more important than the question whether he liked music—may also be seen as part of the emphasis on overt behavior, and further as part of the emphasis on efficiency and on success. Wetting a bed was a nuisance, and children's temper tantrums defeated adults; both were "problems" and merited chapter upon chapter of discussion, whereas the question of the importance of building up strong healthy affections and enthusiasms as a basis of later emotional growth hardly received a sentence.

This emphasis on desirable behavior and activity and the "handling of problems" subtly made almost all emotion seem undesirable, and excitement only something to be controlled.

It was in the midst of these attitudes toward child development and assumptions about child personality that the group of parents and teachers of the group of children in the school were working. It was only natural that the contrasting demands of home and school should result in different attitudes of some parents and some teachers, and the actual attitudes found in conferences varied considerably.

We have given this analysis of child psychology literature chiefly to illustrate the importance of the fact that attitudes of individual parents are part of, and shaped by, larger streams of cultural influences. While parents are the immediate source of attitudes and patterns of social behavior, they are also mediators of values and emphases in the culture as a whole, and much of their function as mediator may be quite unconscious.

The nature of this process of parental mediation of attitudes is demonstrated by E. and R. Horowitz, who have studied various aspects of the formation of attitudes and patterns of behavior among rural Tennessee children. The content of the study relates to race attitudes, but the chief concern is with the *way* in which the child grasps and assimilates the parental outlook (cf. pages 239 ff.).

Among the questions asked in interviews with elementary school children were the following: "Who tells you what you should do?" "What kind of children does she like you to play with?" "What kind of children does she tell you not to play with?" The white children said that they were told to play with white children, and a variety of reasons were given. Some of the youngest children explained: "Because he's white and I'm white." "Because the white boy is white and a colored boy is black." A somewhat more articulate sense of the presence of a social norm is implied in these responses of third- and fourth-grade children: "It looks funny for a white girl to play with a colored girl." "We don't look right playing with her." "Colored people might have any kind of disease or anything."

The older the children grew, the more consistently had they assimilated these attitudes:

1st-grade girl: Mamma tells me not to play with black children, keep away from them. Mamma tells me, she told me not to play with them. (Why not). Mother don't want me to.

2nd-grade girl: Colored children. Mother doesn't want me to play with colored children, cause they colored men. Might have pneumonia if you play with them. I play with colored children sometimes and mamma whips me.

2nd-grade boy: Colored children, mother and daddy tell me. They tell me not to play with colored people or colored person's things.

Parents, on the other hand, tended to minimize the rôle they played in the development of children's attitudes. They felt that children were *naïve* about race distinctions, that they had never done anything to influence the children and that the children were spontaneously discriminating. The contrast between the parents' account and the child's account of pressure may be illustrated by the following characteristic remarks:

Mother: T—— always played with other children. Yes, I used to tell her not to play with some. Just told her, never gave her any reasons. She never played with Negro children, I didn't have to tell her *that*.

Child (3rd grade, girl). White girl. Colored people have dirty houses, they're dirty. Everybody gets dirty, but they keep their hands *so* dirty. Mother told me not to play with them because sometimes they have diseases and germs and you get it from them. I had a colored girl friend who worked for mother, she was a nice clean girl. I liked her but mother didn't much want me to play with her, but I told mother she was all right.

The authors suggest that the fact that parents cannot recall having given direct instruction and that frequently children cannot recall having received it may be very important in the process of development of social attitudes and social behavior. Children go through a process which involves, first, being well aware of the origins of attitudes, particularly those that are imposed by the most important authorities; then they gradually forget the origins, but devise rationalizations to support them and maintain them unchanged.

Parents are thus "the immediate educational device of society," although society through the school, the church, the playmates and other specific relationships maintains supervision of the parents' activity, both to prevent the parent from presenting an unorthodox code and to prevent the child from readily accepting heterodoxy should a parent propose it. It is further suggested by E. and R. Horowitz that the body of attitudes which a child acquires from his early social experience in the family, school, etc., has at first little integration, or only so much as is forced by the relation between the specific environmental institutions. In the course of development there may come a time when the child's feelings and attitudes adjust and are adjusted by the superstructure of attitudes imposed by the social groups. The development of rationalizations and forgetfulness of sources of attitudes may be a step in this process of organization and integration; and this step may come between the piece-by-piece level of attitudes in children and the adult level where clusters of attitudes with fairly definite organization of patterns are found to be more stable.

Processes Involved in Short-term Variations in Social Behavior

In this discussion of the processes by which the culture, through the home and school, determines the direction of social behavior we have been concerned with the long-time effects of conscious and unconscious attitudes of adults, and their meaning to the child. We noted at the beginning of the discussion of the influences of social situations, that short-time effects of different group organizations may also be important, and in this connection we must take special note of tendencies to show different behavior in different situations.

In a study of sympathetic behavior in young children, a number of children show strikingly different behavior from one situation to another. Theodore, a rather shy and inhibited child at school, is a bouncing, active boy at home, spontaneous and vigorous. Janet, the child with the highest score for sympathetic and cooperative behavior on the playground, was quite unresponsive in the experimental situation. Reinhardt, on the other hand, had had no real contacts with children on the playground, but was social and friendly with the "baby" girl in the experiment, who evidently reminded him of his own little brother at home.

The aspects of various situations on the playground which were most important in relation to sympathy were the ego values of the situation—the insecurity, guilt, anxiety, defensiveness, or antagonism which one group of situations stimulated, in contrast to the security, friendliness, desire to please or to help stimulated by other situations. In the experimental situations, responses varied from time to time, depending upon the identification value of the situation; a child from a farm violently defended a chick whereas other children had little feeling for it; a child who had been confined too long in a play-pen projected his feelings about it when he was shown a picture of a child playing behind a fence. Children who had recently had tonsils removed were concerned about a picture of a little boy in a doctor's office, but children without these experiences interpreted the picture in terms of everyday routine.

Particularly important in this study of the child's relation to a situation is the problem of deviation from the average pattern of the group. Democracy offers with one hand (the Constitution) the recognition of individuals and their right to happiness in their own terms; with the other hand (institutional control through school, press and radio) she imposes conformity upon her citizens. This weight of conformity rests so heavily upon many that competition for recognition in conventional terms seems to many observers heavier than it is in many less "democratic" countries. Its universal result is to accentuate the liability of being a deviate or being different from the accepted patterns of the majority. We have already noted that the consequences of such deviation, attended by a sense of social rejection and frustration expressed frequently in social withdrawal, are particularly serious in adolescence. At this time, children feel increasingly independent of the status afforded by parents, and the necessity to prove themselves adequate among their companions is especially strong. If by chance one is slower than the others to mature in height and sexual development, and consequently slower to mature socially, feelings of inadequacy are apt to develop which may take years to outgrow; all the more serious if one has the "wrong attitude."

From this point of view the "situation" becomes not just the pattern of the group to which one is exposed, or the specific pressures of the group, whether felt in terms of majority rule or adult authority, but the *relation between the patterns expected by the group and those possible of attainment by the individual.* The patterns expected by the group constitute conscious or unconscious norms in the light of which the status of the individual is determined, for better or for worse, from the point of view of his own adjustment and his chances of using his own abilities.

These normative aspects of situations, which may act both as stimuli to the social development of the individual and as hindrances when they blind him and others to his innate possibilities, appear at every age level and in all kinds of groups, both intimate ones such as families and the larger racial or class groups. Woe betide the child if he does not "act like a two-year-old" (with proper enthusiasm for large-muscle and aggressive activities), or like a Middle-towner, or like a son of Eli, or like a member of the Harriman family. Presumably a major task of the educator is to become discriminating regarding the times when normative pressure is useful to a growing organism, as compared with the times when it arouses conflict and distorted social patterns.

For better or worse, the child grows up in a world of values; much of his "continuity," his "variability" and most of his "consistency"—as well as most of his "inconsistency"—come back ultimately to the pattern of values in terms of which he lives.

Chapter VII

CHARACTERISTIC SOCIAL BEHAVIOR OF CHILDREN IN OUR CULTURE: AGGRESSION AND COMPETITION

WHILE there has been relatively little study of the things and people that children love or the bases of their positive social enthusiasms and supports, our literature is replete with studies of children's anger, conflicts, negativism, jealousy and other troublemaking behavior. The things that a child smiles at, or sleeps with at night, the sources of his comfort, his ways of making and sustaining contact with his social world, are of fundamental importance; but actually our deepest and broadest experimental knowledge of his social responses lies not in this direction but in the direction of the problems which adults have confronted in coping with the child's patterns of self-defense and conquest of his environment.

Human personality is commonly assumed to be intelligible until it goes wrong. Insanity is a mystery; mental health is not. Clearly, we know as much about one as about the other. Similarly, social behavior which conforms to our needs is natural and intelligible. That which defeats our ends is a problem. The newborn, knowing nothing about this state of affairs, blunders against adults or other children in the course of his struggle to bend the world to his needs, and if he meets resistance, blunders the more insistently, sometimes losing his temper in the process. He then shows "aggressiveness," and aggressiveness is "problem behavior." But clearly there is no one psychological problem here; the forms of aggressive behavior are all forms of insistent response to obstacles socially imposed between children and their goals.

The study of social behavior of children has in some ways gained and in some ways lost from the eagerness of adults to solve the mystery of children's antagonism toward themselves, or toward one another. The great volume of material on anger, conflicts, quarreling, negativism, resistance, means that there is considerable information on similar groups collected by persons of quite different orientation in relation to the problem, but information stated in different terms and enmeshed in different groups of assumptions. One careful study shows that children's anger is largely the result of situational factors such as fatigue or other strain in the child, lack of preparation for demands made upon him or bad techniques which adults use in handling him; another piece of research emphasizes neither age nor situational factors but the inner dynamics of the instinctive life of the child, the inevitable response of hostility toward adult domination and the need for aggression as an outlet for this. Still another point of view emphasizes differences in the *quantity* of such behavior from one child to another; and another works out relationships between aggression and the other aspects of the child's personality, even stressing broad cultural factors that are important in relation to both the adult domination of the child and the child's resistance to the adult. The net result of all this is to make quite clear that the problem of the child's aggression is an exceedingly interesting one for the adult, and that in our culture aggression against both adults and other children is a normal part of the early social development of a child.

Research on aggression has proceeded from a variety of hypotheses:

1. Aggression is primarily a method of getting attention. It shows itself in fighting or teasing; these should not be allowed and must be socially repressed. (Those who advocate repression of this behavior, however, are likely to encourage active self-defense.)

2. Aggression is a basic behavior response, with emotional roots fundamental in human nature. It appears primarily in response to frustration and interference, and is largely a matter of specific reaction to specific situations of interference.

3. Aggression exists in a sort of reservoir in the personality and must have a way out. A personality without active aggressive drive is hardly possible. This aggressive drive expresses

itself in hostility toward adults and conflict with one's peers. If allowed to work itself out early, the individual has a good chance of satisfactory socialization.

4. Aggression has a great variety of direct and indirect expressions. When it does not have an outlet toward others it may direct itself toward the individual himself in the form of masochism, strong guilt feelings, fantasies of aggression toward himself. More "legitimate" indirect outlets take the form of games, competition for symbols of prestige, adult approval, conventional rewards.

Throughout both the experimental and the non-experimental literature on the subject of aggression there is thus a great deal of confusion regarding the basic assumptions and facts concerned with its origin, the way it is to be handled in the young and the forms which it takes in adult society. More adequate biological information on the one hand, and fuller analysis of the rôle of aggression in different cultures on the other, are necessary for any point of view that can hope to be empirically grounded and relatively free from rationalization. Thus in comment upon the four hypotheses just listed, it is to be noted that while adults encourage almost no direct aggression in children generally, they both stimulate indirect aggression through fomenting competition for prestige and allow themselves a much larger amount of expression of aggression through (1) their authority over children, (2) the activity of specific groups such as police, (3) conventionalized exhibits such as prize fights, and (4) the most inclusive and destructive form—war.

The work done in the field of aggressiveness in children includes aggressiveness among children and aggressiveness of children toward adults. The latter has also been called "negativism" and "resistance," implying disobedience. Under the first heading, aggressiveness among children, we find work covering such types of behavior as these: conflicts among children, quarrels; ascendance-submission relations of one child to another; resistance of one child to another; language studies indicating aggressiveness; jealousy; self-

The two children in the center are playing cooperatively with a ball while Bobby at the left watches them shyly and Billy (right background) is absorbed in independent play with blocks.

Lucy (center), a rather dominating three-year-old, is expostulating with Janet (left) regarding her use of the blocks.

Anne, in the pen, cannot get out and cannot reach her toys on the ground beside her. Davis, outside, was too inhibited at this period to help her get them.

A conflict between two nursery-school boys.

assertion; the relation of aggressiveness to friendship and popularity and to various personality traits, such as intelligence, position in the family, type of family; and one study on a constitutional basis.

An examination of this list of research problems will reveal that we have two distinct types of aggressiveness: one that is socially approved of, namely, self-assertiveness and ability to make contacts with children; and one which is socially obnoxious, consisting of jealousies, overt attacks on other children, criticizing others unfavorably—a general pattern of making oneself not liked. Though both of these things have been called aggressiveness, it is clear that from a social point of view they reveal very different forms of adaptation; one type of aggressiveness is an expression of maturity, the other an expression of immaturity. The first type may very well be an expression of self-confidence and of general activity. Extreme forms disappear with the child's development. The child may establish his status in his group so well that he need no longer be aggressive. He feels self-confident, and the others realize his position. The aggressiveness in this instance will not appear unless he is *challenged* (Maslow finds such relations in infra-human primates). The second type of aggressiveness may be an expression of feelings of insecurity. Thus Hattwick finds that children who come from homes where the children are rejected are aggressive and at the same time feel insecure.[1] However, this aggressiveness, through practice, may develop into a real feeling of self-confidence as time goes on.

There is some indication that those children who are aggressive with children are also aggressive with adults—apparently a suggestion of an all-round tendency. Jersild finds correlations of .47, .08 and .73 in different groups between children's conflicts with other children and conflicts with teachers. Caille finds a correlation of .56 for vocal resistance to adults and vocal resistance to children. But

---

[1] Eisenberg finds that among Barnard women and Columbia men the Jewish groups are significantly more "dominant" than the Protestant and Catholic groups on the Maslow "Social Personality Inventory." The suggestion is thrown out, and there is some slight evidence to support it, that this is compensation behavior. A minority group in a hostile environment tends to feel insecure, and so in the competitive struggle individuals in the minority group tend to be over-aggressive. They find that they have to "push" in order to get along.

here we must look more closely. If we look for "generalized aggres-siveness," we discover some paradoxical results. Caille finds a corre-lation of .63 for resistance to adults and acquiescence to adults. Jersild and Markey find that all aspects of behavior in fighting situ-ations are positively correlated, for example, the number of times a child is a winner and is a loser. Also, Caille finds that there is no relationship between resistance in free play in the nursery school, language behavior in other situations, and resistance to taking an intelligence test. Let us also throw in the correlation between aggres-siveness and sympathy that Bathurst and Murphy have found inde-pendently.

If we refer back to the distinction between the two forms of ag-gressiveness, most of this apparent confusion can be cleared up. First of all, a child who is aggressive because of self-confidence should be able to show a mature relation with adults. He does not go to them for help as much as the others; he does not resist when taking an intelligence test, and he obeys an adult when it seems that it is wise for him to follow the instruction (he does not obey blindly). The child whose aggressiveness comes from a feeling of insecurity should resist adults when taking an intelligence test, and may or may not go to them for help. Probably he will also disobey instructions for the sake of disobeying.

In the relations of children to one another, it is not surprising that the active child who is aggressive tends to be sympathetic; the child who starts a fight may give in easily; the one who is often a winner is also often a loser. Aggressiveness is definitely a function of ac-tivity. The child who is most active will make more contacts, will tend to be more social, and so get into more conflicts. However, he also has the opportunity to see more children get hurt through his infliction of injuries, and so also would be more frequently stimulated to be sympathetic. Because he starts a fight, he may feel that it is wrong and hence give in more easily than the other child, the victim who feels that he is in the right. It all makes sense, if we look be-neath the surface and clarify our definitions. If we are going to take every form of objective "aggressiveness" to mean the same thing, we can obviously find no consistent relations. If we impose value judg-ments on aggressiveness, and break it up into "desirable" and "undesirable" instead of seeing it in terms of the psychology of the child, we shall obviously get out what we put into the situation, which is nothing of great value, either theoretically or practically.

Despite the difficulties mentioned, especially the confusion in concepts and terms, quantitative research on aggression in children has achieved sufficient proportions to justify the attempt at a fairly integrated digest. Since this research has not taken place within a common frame of reference, a variety of behavior phenomena and of definitions will be obvious; many research investigations in this field pay little attention to related research unless it is reported in similar verbal categories. In the following analysis we shall discuss a variety of definitions of "aggressive" behavior patterns of one sort or another, and the forms which this behavior takes in nursery-school children. The bases of aggressive behavior as analyzed in these quantitative studies will be reviewed, together with the value judgments regarding aggression which are either explicit or implied in these investigations. Because of the quantity of material, a condensed summary of the relevant research studies will be presented in chart form in connection with the discussion (pages 395 ff.).

CHILDREN'S CONFLICTS

Under the general heading of aggression it is reasonable to consider first the conflicts between children.

From the point of view of many nursery-school teachers, a child who never fights is apt to be an immature or maladjusted one. This is true in a quite literal sense, in that a child who cannot defend his own property or himself under attack is likely to have an inferior position in the group and to fail to develop other aspects of social behavior. From this point of view there is such a thing as a normal tendency to fight in our culture, often regarded as an expression of maturity. At the same time, chronic quarrelsomeness is rightly regarded as an expression of immaturity or maladjustment. Consequently, when all forms of fighting are lumped together, it must not be inferred that this general group of behaviors as a whole can be written down as either "desirable" or "undesirable." The normative appraisal in terms of desirability, if for practical purposes it is necessary, must be made largely in relation to the age of the child, the situation in which he is being observed, the standards and demands of the adults, and the patterns of the group as a whole. The same amount of conflict behavior in one group might be objectively extreme and subjectively undesirable, whereas in another group it might be objectively close to the average and subjectively necessary if the child is to hold his own in the group. A two-year-old may quite naturally make his first social contacts with an amount of pushing and pulling which would be unnecessary·and infantile for a four-year-old. At all age levels the capacity for aggression when it is called for by the situation may be an expression of self-confidence, whereas the exhibition of aggression in situations where other children with the same social norms would not show it may be an indication of a need to get attention, to compensate for inferiority, or to give outlet to frustrated feelings. Moreover, the child who is compensating for an inferiority by picking a fight may actually improve his status in the group so that he no longer feels inferior and no longer need be aggressive. His successful aggression may build up his self-confidence and the recognition of others, so that fighting is no longer needed. Under these circumstances, fighting might not reappear unless it were challenged and the insecure position were reestablished by a change in the organization of the group or the entrance of new children into the group. The important point here is to recognize that fighting may play a different rôle in the relation of individual personality to the group under different circumstances. We need careful definition in objective terms, and also in terms of the social valuation on the one hand and the subjective meaning of aggression to the child on the other hand.

In Jersild's study, "a conflict is defined as any instance in which one child attacks another's person or by word or deed interferes with the person, activities, or possession of another, or threatens by word or gesture to do so, or endeavors by force or verbal demands to possess another's belongings, or to direct another's activities in opposition to the apparent desires of the child against whom the aggression is made." Methods of contact listed by Jersild include hitting, snatching, pushing, "egging others on," tattling, teasing, swearing, spitting, etc.

Jersild's definition of conflicts naturally includes a great many of the acts noted by Bridges as characteristic of young children in nursery school. In Bridges' social and emotional scales for use with nursery-school children, a number of items related to aggression have been included. These have been summarized by Burks as follows:

I. Items referring to the development and control of active aggression and self-assertion:

> Occasionally made social contact by touching or pushing a child.
> Frequently pulled or pushed others.
> Harassed new child by scoffing and shunning.
> Hit or pinched others for fun several times.
> Bit or spit at others for fun.
> Teased in other ways, causing irritation or discomfort.
> Pulled roughly at own material removed by another child.
> Punched and fought smaller children.
> Frequently commanded or regulated others.
> Pressed services on smaller children against their will.

II. Items referring to the tendency to interfere with others and to dominate by creating a disturbance.

> Claimed others' toys.
> Interfered with others' work.
> Destroyed others' work.
> Created disorder in group or led others into mischief.

Both Jersild and Dawe find pushing, hitting, and pulling common motor activities in quarrels, with crying, forbidding and commanding among vocal activities; and in both groups of children the majority of quarrels were started by a struggle for possessions. Both also find that boys fight somewhat more than girls and that, in general, children fight most with those of the same sex. Probably more complex aspects of the situation affecting the rôle of children of given age and intelligence need to be taken into account in order to interpret the findings of Jersild and of Dawe.

Bridges reports that children under three often show marked anger and crying, fighting and stamping, when other children take their toys or when adults make unpopular demands. Three-year-olds usually show less anger on such occasions. They call out, instead of crying, and pull at what they want instead of yelling wildly. Four-year-old children are still more restrained in their behavior. This general decline in overt vocal and physical aggression is observed by Jersild, whose quantitative data also show a decline with age in screaming, weeping, crying for help. Coordinate with this is an increase in the use of language as a method of defense, attack and self-protection, and an increase in aggressive fantasy. Even on a dramatic or fantasy level, however, older children are more repressed in their aggression than are the younger ones. Mental age as well as chronological age must be considered, since the tendency to quarrel is also negatively correlated with I.Q.

Indeed, it is important to note that many forms of aggressiveness necessarily increase with age, others necessarily decrease. Thus while quarrelsomeness decreases, criticism increases. Criticism may probably be regarded legitimately as the expression of identification with the adult method for developing conformity. It is used by children against other children who interfere with them or with their possessions, who fail to conform to their wishes or to social usage, or who show "undesirable" personality traits. Unfavorable criticism exceeds favorable criticism in amount, and both increase with age between three and five years, in all cases where it has been studied. In giving criticism, the child is merely using one aggressive technique of his aggressive society for control of specific forms of behavior which may be neither aggressive nor generally undesirable, but are merely *undesirable to him*. In this also his behavior is similar to that of adults.

Those forms of aggressiveness which reflect increasing capacity to stand on one's own feet will necessarily correlate positively with age and with most measures of social security. In line with the many consistent findings that almost any sort of behavior reflecting increasing mastery over things and people tends to increase with age among nursery-school children, we find that group play increases with age and, along with it, the tendency to have suitable friends; but this increasing cooperation in relation to group play and friendship cannot exclude aggressive behavior, for quarrels increase as group play increases and as friendships increase at the nursery-school level. Indeed, nearly all forms of active social response are inter-correlated with the other forms of active social response so that much which is "desirable" is correlated with that which is "undesirable."

Here we have simply an elaboration of the obvious if we wish to judge it in these terms. Even the positive correlation between aggression and cooperative social responses (cf. page 380) merely reflects the ambivalence of values inherent in our conventional extroverted social patterns; as the child matures, he matures into all our "inconsistent" ways. Yet the correlations, in spite of the fact that they point consistently in the same direction, are nevertheless sufficiently limited to raise further questions. The correlations between resistance and acquiescence, aggression and sympathy, run for the most part between .3 and .6. Some children who are chronic fighters show little sympathy; others are outgoing and sympathetic and do not fight much. If the fighting-cooperating dualism is inherent in our social patterns so that as the child assimilates one he assimilates the other, why are not the correlations higher? Obviously, it is because we have a wide variety of patterns of aggressive and of cooperative behavior, and many complex personal factors enter into each. We shall return to some discussion of these relationships in connection with analysis of integrative and cooperative social responses. It is necessary to dig deeper than we possibly can in terms merely of correlations between different aspects of behavior if we are to get a full understanding of aggressive behavior. But for any full discussion of the nature and causes of aggression, we shall have to depend on analysis of clinical material, to which we shall come shortly.

In the upper ranges of the pre-school level, that is, from three to six, *jealousy* is a not infrequent expression of aggressive responses toward siblings. We shall probably be justified in considering it a form of aggression which compensates for basic insecurity since, when other behavior problems of the jealous child are studied, it is usually found associated with fear.

Sewall's analysis of jealousy in a group of small children directly undermines the serenity of the current belief that if you prepare the child for the coming of a little brother, he will not be jealous of him. The group which she studied included seventy children, about one-third of them being nursery-school and two-thirds of them clinic children. The latter were, of course, "problems" in greater or less degree. Material from the case records was supplemented by information secured at the home. Two major *types of jealousy* were recognized, illustrated by the following instances:

(a) When Myron Conway was five years old, his baby sister was born. At this time Myron had whooping cough and was told by the doctor not to cough near the baby "or else she will get sick and then you won't have a baby sister any more." Several times after this, the mother found Myron coughing into the baby's face . . . and on another occasion he pushed the bassinet over. One day his mother taught him to pat the baby's face. He did this, and when his mother's back was turned, he slapped the baby hard and bit her finger.

(b) Rachel Levine had been the only child for two and a half years when Harry was born. Her behavior following the birth of her brother was of such a nature as to cause her parents and other people to suspect mental retardation. . . . Previous to the birth of Harry, Rachel had been a very "good girl," easy to manage. . . . Her mother told of Rachel's present behavior in a tone of mingled censure, apprehension, and discouragement. She said Rachel refuses to feed herself. . . . She likewise refuses to try to dress or undress herself. . . . She is very restless at night, occasionally has night terrors and talks much in her sleep. . . . Her spells of temper are becoming more frequent and more severe. She is very negativistic and impudent toward her parents. At no time has she expressed her jealousy of her brother by attacking him. She goes rather to the other extreme—whenever anyone asks her about her brother she denies having one. As soon as the problem of jealousy was recognized and dealt with, the behavior difficulties began to grow less and finally disappeared.

Of Sewall's group of seventy children who had younger siblings, thirty-nine were reported to be jealous, showing their jealousy in the following ways:

1. Bodily attacks on the younger sibling. 26
2. Ignoring the presence of the sibling. 2
3. Denying having a younger sibling. 2
4. No outward manifestation toward the sibling, but definite personality changes at the time of its birth. 9

The last group of cases, which would include those similar to the second illustration offered above, showed a wide variety of symptoms, such as more temper tantrums, negativism, more destructiveness, a change to a recessive type of behavior such as daydreaming, excessive shyness, pronounced timidity, etc.

The seventy children were about equally divided as regards preparation for the birth of the younger child:

Attitudes	Prepared	Not Prepared	Total
Jealous........................	19	20	39
Not jealous.....................	14	17	31
Total......................	33	37	70

Consequently, the mere fact of being told that another baby is coming does not seem to be decisive. While the method of preparation would probably have more significance, it was not possible in this study to obtain reliable information regarding it.

In the effort, then, to find more satisfactory clues to the factors causing jealousy, a number of items were related to its presence or absence. It was thought that the question whether the new baby was wanted by the mother might be of some significance. But in the fifty cases where the baby was wanted, twenty-six instances of jealousy appeared. It is true that of the twelve cases in which the baby was not wanted, ten produced jealous older children, but the author does not consider this a large enough group of cases on which to base conclusions. No conclusive sex differences appeared.

A difference of real importance does appear, however, when the ages of the children at the birth of the youngest child are studied. "Jealousy seems to be associated with an age difference of from eighteen to forty-two months, for two-thirds of the children of that age difference were jealous, as compared with one-third of all the children whose age differences were greater or less than that amount." Possibly children closer together in age than 18 months share the same interests sufficiently to get along without getting in one another's way, while children more than four years apart in age do not share the same interests or needs enough to feel competitive. The dominance status of the older child may be unchallenged if the younger child is not too close to him; with a differential of two or three years it may be disturbing to the older child to find that "the baby" is ceasing to be a baby.

The proportion of jealous children decreased markedly with each increase in the number of children in the family; this, of course, is easily understood since in families of two or more the newcomer does not bring the kind of new experience and competition he brings to the only child.

Various other factors were found to be related to jealousy: the latter tended to increase as family income decreased; it increased as the age of the mother increased (the data here do not make it possible to tell whether this is simply because the younger mothers are less likely to have the size of family which tends to produce jealousy); four-fifths of the children whose mothers were over-solicitous were jealous, as well as four-fifths of the children subjected to inconsistent discipline. Finally, the families were divided into two categories, well adjusted and poorly adjusted. Those families were considered poorly adjusted which showed such marital difficulties as continual quarreling, fault-finding, indifference or jealousy between the parents; in which the parent-child relationship was disturbed by such factors as emotional tensions, over-solicitude, or undue dependence; or in which there were definite social or economic difficulties. As thus defined, only ten per cent of the children in the well-adjusted homes were jealous, as compared with sixty-three per cent in the poorly adjusted homes. "The inference seems justified that there is a tendency for jealousy to develop in an atmosphere of maladjustment, such maladjustment often meaning an over-protective mother, a negative father, some marital or other discord, and inconsistent discipline."

It is, of course, essential that inferences drawn from material of this sort be scrupulously limited to the age group upon which the study is based. We cannot assume without further evidence that either the proportions or the causes of jealousy as found in this study of children largely under school age would be found in an older group. The only study of sibling jealousy among older children that is available does, in fact, suggest that age *may* change these factors markedly, for Smalley found only forty-one per cent, as against fifty-six per cent of jealousy in Sewall's children. Among the older children, age differences did not bear the relation to jealousy found among the younger group. On the other hand, jealousy in Smalley's group did seem definitely related to differences in intelligence quotient, "jealousy increasing and protectiveness and friendliness decreasing with increase in difference in intelligence quotient." Within the pairs, the older, when duller, were more apt to be jealous. There are sufficient variations in character of the groups and method of analysis to make it uncertain whether these differences in findings can justly be ascribed to the differences in age range of the two groups. *A priori*, it seems likely that they can.

These findings are in part consistent with those of Foster, who analyzed the personality make-up and social setting of fifty jealous children and one hundred non-jealous children of similar background. She concluded that the jealous child was more apt to be a girl and to be between three and four years old—often the oldest child. She is likely to be independent and selfish, pugnacious, demanding attention and resorting to various means to get it; frequently she shows an undue attachment to one parent and is subject to mild neurotic fears. Hyperactivity, destructiveness, food capriciousness, disturbances of sleep, and enuresis are also likely to characterize the jealous child; opportunities for play and social relations are generally limited.

Much the same picture, then, prevails—in both studies a background of maladjustment is apparent against which jealousy stands out, not as the inexplicable fruit of a field devoid of other personality difficulties, but as a growth well nourished by the soil in which it and its ilk are found.

From such studies as these it is clear that competitiveness, standing up for one's right in the family groups as elsewhere, is normal and within limits acceptable to adults; that when it begins to make trouble either because of its intensity or because of inept or troublesome expression it is given the name of jealousy and becomes "problem behavior."

A problem that is at least equally important, and equally full of aggressive tensions toward the adult world—for every family knows what it is to try to handle the indomitable "stubbornness" of a three-year-old—is the problem of negativism, or resistance. It has already received a great deal of attention from investigators, partly as a result of the fact that it has been such an obstacle to successful testing of young children. Levy and Tulchin were among the first to confront the problem and describe it in a clear-cut way. Their investigation was based on the results of testing nearly a thousand infants and children at a series of Illinois county fairs. The criterion in classification was the number of tests taken by each child. Those who would not take any tests at all were classified in Group I (complete resistance); those who refused one or more but not all of the series were placed in Group II (partial resistance); those who took all of the tests were in Group III. The children were classified in these groups by three examiners working independently. The results were fairly uniform for each tester, and were not materially affected by changes made in the technique of testing, by using new tests, by different examiners, or by change in locality. Briefly summarized, this resistance shows fairly uniform age and sex differences. It first appears, as measured by the method indicated, at six months, gradually rises to a high point, from which it falls gradually to a low level at 54 months. The high point of resistance for males (as measured by the combined ratings on complete and partial resistance) is highest at 30 months; for females, at 18 months. The resistance for the females is higher than for the males at every age group studied except 30. At 30 months some form of resistance measured by the test criterion occurred in a majority of cases of both sexes.

Reynolds attempted to analyze and define resistance more clearly. She used the following criteria in her study of over two hundred nursery-school children from twenty-one months to five years and six months old: surrender of personal liberty (tester picked child up in lap), imitation of movements (clapping hands, etc.), response to negative commands (when child was playing with blocks—"Don't make that any more"), repetition of one- and two-digit series, reestablishment of rapport after a neglect period. The children were also given a Kuhlmann-Binet test. She concludes that negativism, as she conceives it, is closely related to general growth. The negativism score tended to decrease as chronological age increased: r between chronological age and negativistic score was .53 ± .03. The partial correlation between chronological age and score, with mental age held constant, was .29 ± .04. There was a smaller tendency for the negativism score to decrease as mental age increased: the correlation between the negativism score and mental age was .48 ± .03. The partial correlation between mental age and score, with chronological age held constant, was .12 ± .04. (Note that all r's are minus.)

Somewhat similar results are obtained by Nelson in a study of personality differences in children from eighteen to forty-eight months of age observed in psychological tests; the highest average chronological age appears in the least resistant group, and the lowest in the most resistant. She also finds that the degree of measured resistance decreases as I.Q. increases (chronological age held constant) and as mental age increases, but observes that the degree of resistance may very likely affect the intelligence rating.

Levy and Tulchin go so far as to conclude that resistance is an innate behavior function. While there are, undoubtedly, innate elements in this response pattern, such a statement can hardly be left unchallenged. Tilson found sufficiently clear evidence of association between this trait and emotional dependence upon adults to suggest that environmental factors were in all probability extremely important.

A further attack on environmental differences in relation to negativism was carried out by Goodenough. She analyzed the ratings on negativism in 100 Kuhlmann-Binet tests at each of the 2-, 3- and 4-year levels. A rating of 3 was given when the child responded to more than half of the tests by saying "No," or "I don't want to," or by silence, so that cooperation could be secured only by the aid of much urging, subterfuge, bribery or similar methods; children who showed opposition to certain tests in the scale but in general responded readily were given a rating of 2; those who responded promptly throughout the examination and were willing to attempt whatever they were asked to do were rated 1. Goodenough found a sex difference: the mean rating for boys was higher than that for girls at every age on the first test, and at ages three and four on the

second test given four to seven weeks later. But this gross sex difference was found to be "secondary to a social difference which operates unequally for the two sexes." The greatest amount of negativism among boys was found in the upper occupational classes, but
(although the difference is not consistent) there is some indication
of a tendency toward greater negativism among girls whose fathers
belong to the lower occupational groups. The fact that Levy and
Tulchin found no such sex difference in total amount of negativism
may be explained in part by the fact that their cases were almost
entirely drawn from the lower occupational classes, and in part by
the difference in their method. Since any strong evidence against
this conclusion is lacking, it therefore seems reasonable to infer from
these results that chonological age, intelligence and social environment are all factors determining the degree of negativism or
resistance. Such a statement barely scratches the surface of the problem, however. What aspects of environment tend to increase negativism? The results of Tilson suggest that the amount of direct
supervision of the child—which presumably would be greater in
the higher social and economic groups—is an important element.
Goodenough's finding of greater negativism among girls of lower
occupational levels raises the question whether girls among these
groups are guarded and supervised more carefully than boys, or,
indeed, more carefully than boys *or girls* in the higher social
groups.

In regard to the relation of intelligence to degree of negativism,
Nelson's analysis offers some further interesting suggestions. She
studied one hundred and sixty-one instances of resistance to test
situations; one hundred and one of these were later accepted. *Of the
60 which were never accepted, 30 instances occurred at a level of
intelligence on the scale which was definitely above the mental age
of the child tested, and only 15 occurred at a level below the mental
age of the child.* This would suggest that insight into the demands
of the test in relation to one's ability may be an important element
in the resistance. These studies have not really distinguished between
"legitimate resistance" (or resistance to a demand recognized by
the child to be beyond his abilities) and genuine "negativism" (or
non-compliance with demands well within the reach of his abilities

and in situations not presenting other stimuli to resistance). Sixty per cent of the instances of negativism toward tests at or below the mental age level of the child were of the sort that involve the child personally (imitating movements, repeating words, sentences or digits, naming parts of the body). We have no data for a correlation between resistance and failures on such "personal" tests, excluding the influence of materials too hard for the child; but we suspect that if such a correlation could be made it would be a fairly high one. Further analysis may lead to the conclusion that as the child's language and locomotion develop to a point of mastery, new interests and desires develop, and a sense of being able to do, or independence; that with this there is a developing consciousness of self which lowers thresholds for negative reactions for a time. Gradually, as the small child gets adjusted to his awareness of himself and awareness of himself versus other persons, genuine negativism decreases. We need to know, however, whether there is a general tendency to allow the young child greater freedom as he grows older, and whether this corresponds with the age of decreasing negativism; otherwise the possibility remains that this negativism is merely a reaction to excessive domination or to failure of adult supervision to adjust rapidly enough to the child's growing abilities and give him the independence he feels competent to use.

A study of resistance to tests by Rust controls many factors not controlled in the earlier studies. One hundred three-year-old children with intelligence quotients from 100 to 175, average 132, were given the Merrill-Palmer and Kuhlmann tests in the following way: one-half of each test was given the first day and the remaining half of each test given the following day. Instead of coaxing or urging a child to take a refused test, the test was simply presented again later. This made it possible to measure the resistance quantitatively in terms of the number of times any test was refused. Any test resisted was presented twice later the same day, and again on the second, and even on the third and fourth days if resistance continued. Actually, 83 per cent of the children completed all the tests of both series by the end of the second day, which would be the normal test period for the two series.

Rust points out that among these children there was a real difference in the character of tests resisted once, as compared with those repeatedly resisted. A good many tests resisted once were among the easier ones of the scales, while those resisted several times were really hard ones. Difficulty of the test, mental level of the child, and interest value of the test were most important in relation to the question of whether a test was resisted or not. Also, the children objected more consistently to the demand that they *repeat* something said or done by the experimenter than to any other type of test. When the different forms of resistance were analyzed, 42.1 per cent of the incidents of resistance were in the form of refusals; 8.5 per cent were escapes from the situation, walking away, running away, and the like; 1.6 per cent were requests for delay. A large proportion of refusals were simply due to conflict of interest—the child wanted to do or say something else, just as any sensible person would in a not too interesting situation. Of course the implications of this study are limited by the fact that the children were a highly selected group. Sixty-one per cent of their mothers had occupations other than that of "housewife," and sixty-five per cent of the fathers were in the first professional group according to the Barr-Taussig classification. It does seem, however, to point again to the importance of sheer difficulty of the test, the child's self-consciousness and intelligence, as well as to the factor of interest-value which Rust emphasizes.

Goodenough's study of the emotional behavior of young children during mental tests suggests environmental sources for other traits besides negativism. Nearly a thousand children between eighteen months and six years of age were observed during Kuhlmann-Binet or Minnesota Pre-School tests. Shyness, negativism and distractibility were rated by the observer on a five-point scale like the following:

Shyness: 1. Child comes to examining room readily, talks freely, seems entirely at ease throughout test.

2. Child shows some hesitation at first, but does not cry or seem frightened. After a few minutes' acquaintance, is entirely willing to remain with examiner and appears to be completely at ease thereafter.

3. Child requires much persuasion before he can be induced to remain in room without mother. Eventually yields, but continues to show some anxiety as to mother's whereabouts; has to be frequently reassured. May cry a little at the outset.
4. Child cannot be persuaded to remain in examining room without mother. With mother present, goes through with the tests in a fairly satisfactory manner.
5. Child continues to cry or to cling to mother, and cannot be persuaded to take the tests, even with mother present, or takes too few to justify a test rating.

Social status was determined by the father's occupation, and the various occupational groups were divided into two larger groups; the first included professional, semi-professional, managerial, etc., and the second included semi-skilled trades and minor clerical workers, together with the slightly skilled and unskilled. In order to compare behavior with position in family, four groups were defined: (1) oldest children in families of more than one, (2) youngest children in families of more than one, (3) only children, and (4) middle children in families of more than two.

On all three of the traits—shyness, distractibility and negativism—decided improvement with age was found for both sexes and regardless of previous test experience. The most pronounced changes occurred between the ages of two and four. After four years, most children responded well enough so that they were relatively easy to handle in the test situation. There do appear to be some sex differences; as a whole, the boys showed greater tendency to negativism and distractibility, although there were no reliable differences in the case of shyness. Occupational differences were consistent with those already reported, the most striking difference occurring in the case of the greater resistance of upper-class boys; distractibility was also greater for upper levels than it was for the lower levels in the case of both sexes. Only children were more distractible than children of other positions in the family, and less shy than youngest children.

Some of this work on negativism has implications beyond the immediate problem. There is little experimental work on the development of consciousness of self, for instance, but some of Nelson's work throws a little light in this direction. It will be recalled that she studied personality differences observable in psychological tests of nursery-school children (cf. page 391). Verbatim reports of the complete tests of 28 children were secured by a stenographer; these records were supplemented by those of a student who did not attempt to record the whole situation but only instances of resistance and any behavior of the adult affecting it. Analysis of the test records showed that tests involving repetition of words, digits, or sentences contributed about thirty per cent of all resistance. Tests involving movements (imitation of movements—Kuhlmann; opposition of thumb and finger, crossing feet, and standing on one foot—Merrill-Palmer) contributed fourteen per cent of the total resistance. Naming parts of the body contributed three times as high a percentage of resistance as the percentage it comprised of the total test situation. All these tests have in common, as we noted earlier in discussing negativism, the element of involving the child personally and actively in the situation—in the imitation of movements he becomes the center of attention instead of sharing with the tester attention to some third object. Nelson observes: "That involvement of *self* into a situation should induce a resistant attitude is not really surprising; and yet it is most interesting to realize that such attitudes, frequently recognized in adults by accompanying self-consciousness and embarrassment, should be so well established at the pre-school age level. Adult amusement at children's activities is possibly a conditioning factor here." Negativism may offer an inductive clue in the study of the consciousness of self.

In the light of the foregoing it is clear that three-year-old negativism, like all other aspects of resistance and aggressiveness, is likely to be due to tension within a group of children or between the adults and children in a family or in a specific adult-child relation of the sort that appears in an intelligence-test situation. The tension in the family may be due to fundamental hostility of the adult toward the child or merely excessive aggression in the use of necessary authority. We are far from clear at present regarding the phases of development from this three-year-old level of resistance and conflict to later patterns of social contact. We are even less clear regarding the question whether the three-year-old situation is almost entirely a matter of cultural influences of a specific kind or whether three-year-olds are like this the world over. Before we can understand the relation between defensive behavior like negativism and jealousy, and simple aggressiveness of the type involved in overt conflicts, we need richer studies of the development of attitudes toward self, aggressive and defensive behavior of individual children over a period of years.

ASCENDANCE-SUBMISSION

"Aggression" is a harsh word; "dominance" or "ascendance" suggests acceptable behavior. Whatever the complex connotation of these terms, there is a quantitative distinction to be made; to be ascendant or dominant is at least to move in the *direction* of becoming aggressive.

Among the many current studies of ascendance and dominance special attention must be given to L. M. Jack's study of ascendant behavior in pre-school children. The study consisted of two different parts: first, the attempt to obtain a clear measure of ascendance and to compare it with certain aspects of personality; and, second, an experiment in building up the confidence of the least ascendant children in the group. Because of the fact that so few studies in actual experimental modification of social behavior have been carried out, this piece of work seems to be worth detailed discussion.

The main subjects of the study were eighteen four-year-old children. Each child was paired successively with each of ten other children in an experimental situation where he was permitted to play for five minutes at a sand box containing three sets of toys. Records were kept on the following eight items of behavior:

1. Verbally attempts to secure play materials.
2. Forcefully attempts to secure play materials.
3. Succeeds in securing play materials.
4. Defends, snatches back materials taken from his possession.

    5. Verbally attempts to direct behavior of companion.
    6. Companion complies with direction.
    7. Forbids, criticizes, reproves companion.
    8. Provides patterns of behavior which companion imitates.

These eight items were combined into a score which had a corrected Spearman-Brown reliability of .80.

During the ascendance experiment competitiveness appeared twice as frequently in the most ascendant third of the subjects as in the least ascendant third, though there was little difference in the verbal claims for attention from the two groups.

A composite ascendance rating scale had been checked by three teachers for each child. This included the following six items, each of which was rated on a five-point scale:

    1. Insists upon own rights to play material.
    2. Challenges property rights of others.
    4. Directs activities of companions.
    5. Submits to direction from companions.
    6. Tries to help enforce group rules.

The rank-order correlation between the scores on the rating scale and the scores in the experimental situations was .81. The techniques that were used for the control of others varied from child to child, however, and few items on the rating scale proved consistent in differentiating those who were ascendant from those who were non-ascendant. The number of attempts to control was, as a matter of fact, much more important than the specific technique in differentiating the two groups.

The following items of behavior observed on the playground appear to indicate lack of self-confidence in the non-ascendant group and appear four times as often in this group as in the ascendant group:

    1. Showing fear of companions' displeasure in facial expression.
    2. Appealing to adult for response, attention.
    3. Following, holding on to adult.
    4. Appealing to adult for help.

5. Interfering with others' activities for no apparent reason, no advantage to self, only to secure attention.
6. Starting to do something, hesitating, not doing it.
7. Showing fear of physical objects (such as slides, swings).
8. Showing loud, reasonless laughter and reasonless enthusiasm.
9. Reacting strongly to criticism, ridicule and threats by blushing, apologizing, retreating.

Two experiments were also used to test respect for property and "directing others," each child being paired with five companions separately for each experiment. The property-rights scores correlated .86 with the average of three teachers' ratings on two property-rights items, and .88 with the ascendance scores. The experiment on directing another correlated .76 with teachers' composite ratings on four related items, and .70 with the ascendance scores.

Short-sample observations of behavior in the play group were made on the following patterns of social behavior: social responsiveness, evidences of self-confidence, techniques used to control the behavior of others. In addition, observations in the daily story group and in the experimental situations provided records on "expansive behavior, amenability to adult control, competitiveness, and tendency to draw attention to own accomplishment." Social responsiveness was found to correlate .65 with ascendance score. Response to adult authority (in an experimental situation in which the adult told the child not to play with a toy airplane which she had demonstrated) correlated .56 with ascendance. Expansive behavior during the story hour did not show much relation to ascendance as measured. Items showing lack of self-confidence were more frequent in the nonascendant group.

The experimental modification of ascendance was carried out as follows: The five children whose first ascendance scores were lowest were given individual training by the experimenter at least seven times, ten to fifteen minutes at a time, in the use of three kinds of material; making designs with mosaic blocks, assembling a picture puzzle, learning a story in a picture book. After the child had become familiar with these materials, he was paired off successively with each of four ascendant children and records were again taken of ascendant behavior. These records were scored in two ways, (1) the actual frequency of ascendant behavior, showing impatience, disgust at the mistakes of companions, etc., and (2) frequency of the subject's ascendant behavior relative to the frequency of his companions' ascendant behavior. Both absolute and relative scores for four out of five subjects showed *marked increase in ascendance* as a result of the increased familiarity with the material. A control group of five non-ascendant children who did not have this training showed virtually no increase in ascendance when the ascendance experiment was repeated.

This study has a variety of implications. First, it suggests that ascendance is not to be considered a static thing or an immutable aspect of personality. The marked change in the self-confidence of these children after fairly limited training suggests that our general pre-school practice of *laissez faire* in relation to children's play may have unforeseen results. Actual training in the skills of handling both large equipment and small materials may facilitate enormously the social adjustment of a considerable proportion of children.

Though we frequently tend to think in terms of the tendency to carry over attitudes of shyness or self-confidence from one situation to another, we often conceive of social confidence largely in terms of a fixed relation between people, rather than as a three-cornered relation between the individuals and the job (or the game) in which they are participating. The results of this study indicate that the skill in the job at hand may be even more important than the particular individuals with whom one is confronted, and that, regardless of an individual child's history or the reasons for his social shyness, development of skill in the actual situations he has to confront may make a big difference in his confidence and aggressiveness.

It is, of course, necessary to use this kind of procedure with a much larger group of children in order to clarify the difference suggested between the four children whose ascendance behavior was clearly increased and the one child whose development in this direction seemed more questionable. Is the fifth child a real instance of the kind of youngster who will carry over an insecure attitude into a new situation *regardless* of attempts to build up skills, can he be helped only in more fundamental ways, e.g., through working on sources of confidence and security in the family? Is this proportion of four to one any reasonable indication of the proportion of children who would in general respond quickly to specific training? These questions are of the greatest importance in determining the extent to which personalities can "learn" or personality structure be modified.

M. L. Page has extended and validated Jack's experiments in the modification of ascendant behavior. One hundred and seven subjects were used. Seventy-three of the children, from two to four years of age, were from the Iowa Child Welfare Research Station; they were of high intelligence and socio-economic status. Thirty-four four-year-olds of lower intelligence (I.Q. averaging about 85) were from a cooperative research pre-school at an orphan's home. These children were from a lower socio-economic group; their fathers were classified as laborers but were unable or unwilling to support their families.

Through a one-way screen the children were observed in a play situation which provided a small sand box and appropriate toys. Each child was observed in five pairings; his ascendance score, based upon eight evidences of ascendance, represented the total number of observations of ascendant behavior which he showed during the five-minute pairings. The ascendant, moderately ascendant, and non-ascendant children were selected and specially trained on specific tasks; then the pairings were repeated in order to observe the change in ascendance scores after this training. An untrained group was also retested for control purposes. The training process included successive pairings as an integral part of the development of the child's self-confidence, giving him an opportunity to show off and practice his new advantage. The results from the nursery-school children of high intelligence were as follows:

1. A greater gain in ascendance was found in trained than in non-trained subjects. The mean score of 14 children who received training was 16.7 at the testing before their training, and 28.8 after the

training. The effects of training appear to be cumulative, especially in directing behavior, success in directing, and criticism of others.

2. Non-trained subjects showed a loss in mean score. This suggested that when the self-confidence of some member of a group was increased, that of the untrained members of the group would tend to be depressed. Both non-ascendant and moderately ascendant children responded to training.

3. There was some indication of transfer to behavior in free-play periods, but teachers' ratings proved unsuccessful indicators of transfer effects.

The question arises whether the nursery-school situation is in itself a factor in increasing ascendance. To discover this, an orphanage group was broken up into two groups, one of which attended pre-school without being specially trained in ascendance, and a control group which did not attend. The results of study of this group showed:

1. Over a period of time the pre-school subjects were fairly stable with respect to ascendance, while the control subjects showed definite losses.

2. The pre-school group showed increasing scores in "directing behavior" and decreasing scores in "behavior concerned with defending or getting property," in contrast to the control group.

In general summary, experimental training which aimed to increase self-confidence was shown to be effective in increasing the expression of ascendant behavior for non-ascendant children, and these changes were larger than those attributable to attendance at the pre-school alone.

We have given rather detailed accounts of this experiment in order to illustrate possibilities for further experimental work on social behavior of this sort, and to point out the relations between the kind of scientific results which can come from different methods. Analysis of behavior records of individual children in nursery school gives data on the amount and forms of aggression in a complex situation. For the most part, the details of the situation cannot be controlled or varied systematically in a way that will really point toward causative factors. The same thing is true of studies made of children's behavior at home, although the variety of circumstances to be observed is of such great importance as to require more observation in homes than has been made. In the experimental situation, however, many fundamental aspects of aggressive behavior, toward both children and adults, may be recorded and measured, and a variety of aspects of the situation may be manipulated to permit checking of hypotheses regarding the nature of causes. By varying the time of day, relation of the experiment time to nap-time and dinner-time, the technique of the adult, the difficulty of tasks set, and a host of other elements in the experimental situation, the effect of simple and compound factors may be observed, and the process of modification of behavior may be watched.

It is worth while to emphasize the fundamental importance of scientific studies of this kind; so much nursery-school education has rested upon hypotheses that training in routine is a fundamental obligation of the adult whereas the child can best educate himself in social and play techniques. The combined effect of the work of Page and Jack suggests that confidence can be built up in fairly limited periods of time through simple techniques of giving skills to the child which increase his resources; and it is probably safe to say that children at any age level would gain in poise and capacity to handle social situations through the development of fundamental skills. This kind of training could be carried on without interfering in any sense with the child's own process of exploration in social and play relations.

In connection with the transfer effects in studies of this kind, it should be noted that as one acquires the various techniques of combat, argument, competition, and ascendant behavior, one integrates one's techniques and becomes "dominant in general" or even "aggressive in general." Thus from different quarters comes evidence that children who have already developed patterns of aggressive behavior (whether these are described under the heading of dominance, egocentricity, aggression, or something else) are more likely to be consistent in their behavior than those whose aggressiveness is sporadic and unorganized, as indicated by the fact that ratings by different teachers agree with one another better, comparisons of the results from different measures agree with one another better, and the children's standing remains more stable over a considerable period of time. This statistical result is inevitable if consolidation of various habits is occurring.

Even while this is true, so that we may assume that non-dominant or relatively unaggressive children vary quite markedly from one situation to another, it is also true that even very dominant children vary from one situation to another. In one study of 57 girls from third through sixth grade, it was found that in no case did a dominant child dominate in every situation. There were not only great variations in each girl's behavior, but also great differences in the amount of variation. Extreme cases on the whole tended to show less variation in dominance feeling than those at the middle of the group. To those interested in theory of the growth of personality this points to the flexibility and possibilities of change through early adolescence; to those interested in education and guidance it offers encouragement to the view that experiences outside of the early family influences may be of great importance, and are worth careful planning.

THE CHILD'S VIEW OF AGGRESSION

When we have recognized the various forms taken by aggression among the normal children studied in Child Development Institutes, we have still gone only a little way in the analysis of what makes for aggression. As a preliminary orientation we need to inquire into the context of prevalent attitudes toward aggression confronted by a child in these same situations. What do his companions and his family think about aggressive behavior—what values are at stake for him in connection with it? How are these values formed?

Any attempt to construct a picture of the value world of children in relation to patterns of social behavior must be carried out indirectly. Suggestions come from a variety of directions: the spontaneous play patterns of children, the evidence as to which children are most popular, the individual's resolution of conflict situations. Among pre-school children those who are aggressive, who offer no response when attacked, who escape or run away, play alone, dawdle, or ignore requests of grown-ups, are found to be unpopular, while those who respect property rights and cooperate with adults appear to be more popular. Apparently this situation is not very different from that among adults. The unaggressive child who is too easy a mark and who cannot defend himself (and cannot therefore be respected), and the child who is too aggressive (and who might therefore be feared) are unpopular.

This ambivalent place of aggression among small children owes much to the combination of the following facts: (1) the frequency of aggression in many normal nursery-school and home situations; (2) the fact that children who are too aggressive are not popular; (3) the fact that victims win more conflicts than aggressors, even apart from the influence of teachers. These last two points suggest that while overt aggression is a common technique of getting property which one wants, or of achieving personal needs, it is also a cause of so much anxiety and sense of guilt that aggressors by no means consistently carry through their original intentions. They probably quite frequently feel that they have been doing something that was not right.

Studies of teachers' techniques in relation to aggression and the behavior of adults toward children generally, have not matched the pace of studies of children's behavior. If and when they are ever made, we shall probably find ample source for this ambivalence of aggressiveness in the relation between adults and children, especially in the attitudes of adults toward aggression of children. Regardless of the question whether techniques of physical punishment such as spanking are used in disciplining a child, the experience of most children is one of life hemmed in and defined by adult regulations. Every rule and interference with spontaneous impulse may have an inner value to the child equivalent to aggression from the adult. This constant domination is even more characteristic amid the limitations of urban life where families live in small apartments or houses that contain no space for untrammeled activity and exploration for a child. The endless reminders not to hurt this piece of furniture, not to touch father's desk, not to use paints in the living room, or pound on the dining-room table afford a constant experience by the child of adult aggression and are defended by the adult as necessary. Frequently, however, exactly the same repressive behavior used against another child by the child who has learned it from an adult will be disapproved. In addition to this, the child must confront the fact that on the one hand he is encouraged to defend himself against attack and on the other hand his own attacks are likely to be disapproved.

We must, moreover, point out certain discrepancies in the social evaluation of aggression from the point of view of respect for the individual and from the separate point of view of larger social effects. The evolution of research has led to distinctions between dominant or egocentric initiative in activities involving other people, and integrative behavior or genuine leadership which looks toward the coordination of interests of a total group. This distinction is clear to the adult, far from clear to the child. In our culture it is socially acceptable and desirable to have self-confidence enough to get what one wants, participate freely in group competition, push to the top, defending oneself. We may call these A types of aggression. But it is socially unacceptable to take from others, "dominate" others, hurt others (B types of aggression). These last are taboo, though, from the child's point of view, they are constantly used by adults in the process of setting up taboos against property, training in routine and punishing for infractions. Other types of socially unacceptable aggression are general restlessness and unorganized aggression of the type that is referred to in discussions of hyperactivity—proving to oneself that one can do something, fighting for attention or expressing jealousy, having a chip on one's shoulder or "being defensive" (C types of aggression largely tied up with insecurity feelings). All of our research data, as well as incidental observation of children, indicate that the process of maturing in our culture consists largely of being able to develop A types of aggression along with cooperative and integrative forms of behavior, and inhibiting B and C types of aggression, whether they are due to overflowing spirits and energy or to the need to compensate for inferiority.

When the attitudes of parents, teachers and research investigators show such a complex mingling of approval of self-defense and disapproval of closely related forms of aggression, it is not surprising to find this complexity reflected in the attitudes of children. M.

D. Fite has made an illuminating analysis of the attitudes toward aggression of a half dozen children whose aggressive behavior had been measured objectively.

When Nancy was asked what she would do if another child hit her, she said she would tell the teacher. Would she hit him back? "No, because I want to be good because my mother and father say I should, so I'm trying my best." And later she generalizes this still further: "You have to tell the parents. You must tell everything to the parents 'cause they're bigger. The child asks the parents what to do and then they help the child."

Fite comments with surprise on this deeply moral tone coming from a child not yet four years old, and later points to the discrepancy between the earnestness of her attitude and her behavior. However, the verbal expressions of attitude remain quite stable for a time.

". . . In a repetition of the situation two weeks later with the second series of pictures, her strongly filial attitudes held up pretty well. No, she would not hit back, and if her aggressor kept at her, she would call her mother to make him stop. 'Mother would say, "This boy hurts, and 'cause it's not nice and would she please take his hand off 'cause it's not nice." ' The experimenter tried to make it harder: 'But suppose you were at school, and you called the teacher, and the teacher didn't hear you.' Nancy admitted in that case that she'd have to 'push his hand off.' Then for a moment her feelings slipped through: 'Then I would show him how it feels.' But as if in contrition over that admission, she replied to the next question, 'Would you hit him?' with, 'I would be nice and good. I would give him a lollypop.'

"Certainly it looks, at least, as if Nancy were trying to give the 'right answers.' Several months later the experimenter had another session with Nancy.

"At the beginning, when the experimenter asked if she should make her own doll hit Nancy's, Nancy responded, 'Yes,' rather casually. But at the actual hitting, her face grew serious, and at the suggestion that she make her doll hit the experimenter's, she drew her doll *back* from the experimenter's and, with a very anxious expression, said, 'No, I don't want to.' She seemed quite near the point of tears, and to each question about hitting replied vehemently that hitting was *not* all right: 'I *know* because my father and mother say so. I *know* it.' And there is just as vigorous denial even on the question of retaliative hitting. Here there appears to be less reason for doubt as to whether she spoke with real conviction. And yet the very intensity of the conviction seems to belie a complete self-assuredness. In general, self-assuredness and anxiety do not go together, and there was no doubt here of the presence of anxiety. Both the experimenter and the assisting research worker were struck by the unhappiness of her tone and expression, and the vehemence with which she pulled her doll back when asked to make it hit. Might there be reason to suspect that in some way her confidence in what her parents said was being undermined, and that the degree of emotionality shown was a sign of some conflict? What would be the prediction of her responses six months later?"

The anxiety and conflict which appeared in this discussion are exactly what we should expect with an intelligent, sensitive child, confronted with confusion of values and forced to make a place for herself in her social group, in relation to both children and adults. It is particularly interesting, however, to see that the intensity of her feeling had decreased considerably by the end of another six months.

"In April of 1936 the situation was repeated. She said as before that she did not think it right to hit other children, ' 'Cause it hurts. 'Cause I felt it one time.' (Note that 'it hurts' seems to be the first true 'reason' to develop.) 'I think it's not so good—neither does my mother.' There is nothing so far very different from what she had said before, and again one has to fall back on more 'subjective' elements. Against the utter seriousness with which everything was said in the first session thirteen months earlier, and against the intensity and emotionality of her responses six months earlier, may be put the complete air of casualness with which replies were given in this session. She seemed to be saying, 'Yes, this is what I really think but it's not all so important to me now.' "

The change in anxiety feeling was not the only index of progress in Nancy's problem.

"This time, when asked, 'If some other child hits you first, then what's the thing to do?' Nancy's immediate response is, 'Hit them back.' Moreover, she's not above romancing a little to back this up: ' 'Cause that's what my mother tells me every night before I go to bed.' (The pure fiction of this statement was checked with the parents.) Also note another reason: ' 'Cause that's what sometimes other children do to me.' Now it seems that in fantasy she has loaded her parents on her side and in actuality she has her social experience to back her up, and thus perfect accord is made."

The confusion shown by Nancy probably represents a real experience shared to some degree by most nursery-school children. But the intensity of the conflict would vary from one child to another with the temperament and conscience of the child. The responses of Nancy's best friend illustrate this:

"In none of Lila's three experimental sessions did there appear the seriousness and intensity which Nancy showed in her first two. In the first session in the spring of 1935, Lila's responses were somewhat mixed but all given with a casual, though self-assured, manner. With regard to hitting, she says she would not do that, even if she were hit first, though she might have to do it if that were the only way of stopping her aggressor." Fite compares the two children as follows:

". . . both put down hitting or snatching as 'not nice,' both say they would hit only if that were the only way of fending off another child's aggression. The difference in the two children's responses lay in those same 'subjective' elements of response which are so difficult to record on paper. Nancy was intensely serious, Lila was casual though firm; Nancy injected a deeply moral tone into the situation; Lila responded just as she might have to any factual material, in a perfectly matter-of-fact manner. And it was this difference which seven months later showed itself in a difference in actual verbal response as well. Apparently it was a difference of fundamental *attitude* toward the whole problem which at the age of four did not appear verbally, but by the age of four and a half had carried them far enough apart that what they said was not the same any longer. It will be remembered that it was in the fall of the 1935 period that Nancy showed intense emotionalism over the whole question and stated that under no circumstances was hitting acceptable. Lila, however, with the same air of casual finality as in the previous spring, says hitting is 'all right.' Why? 'Oh, 'cause. 'Cause I think it is.—Sometimes I have to. Sometimes the teacher gets cross and sometimes she's not there and I have to get cross.'

"Further light on the feelings bound up with aggression appeared in other parts of the spring of 1936 experiment. The dolls were given the names of children on the playground and the suggestion was made that Lila make one hit another. In the first part of the situation, she had quite readily made 'Lila' hit 'Jackie' (a fictitious figure). But to the suggestion that she make either 'Lila' or 'Jackie' hit 'Nancy,' there was a definite refusal. 'Why not?' ' 'Cause it's not nice—it hurts.' In other words, there is both identification and projection of her own feelings present, and she will not have her best friend hurt. To the suggestion that she make 'Holden' (a child known throughout the group for his aggressiveness) hit 'Jackie,' there was no difficulty—'Yeah, 'cause they're boys. They're going to be in a fight.' (Another variable in attitude toward hitting.) Again following this, the suggestion was made that 'Jackie' hit 'Nancy,' to see whether the previous acceptance of *boys* hitting would affect this situation. To this there was a long pause, ending in *her* suggestion that 'Nancy' should hit 'Holden,' which was carried out. 'Now make Lila hit Holden.' No, she wouldn't do that. 'Why not?' ' 'Cause I don't think that's fair— they might do it back.' (Note what 'fair' means to a four-year-old.) Apparently, though, she wouldn't have her best friend hit; it was too subtle a projection to anticipate *her* being hit back, which was taken into account in her own position, the identification being a nearer and more direct one.

"The fact that aggression might be even more important for boys than for girls is suggested by Lila's response, and this is borne out by the records of the boys themselves. Holden was six months younger than the girls just discussed, and this fact probably accentuated the problem further. Extreme aggressiveness and swagger characterized his responses. 'Put them in jail,' 'fight them,' were typical of his answers to all the questions. Seven months later the overt aggressiveness of his first answers disappeared."

But he was extremely aggressive with the children. He and another boy started out to whip a third child with a rope, but instead Holden had the idea of tying the rope around the child's neck; the teacher just saved the latter from strangulation. Among his other misdeeds were knocking a child in the eye with a broom handle, throwing dirt, slapping a child's face, getting a child into the corner of a packing box and pummeling him in the face with his fists. Among his threats were "I'll beat your brains out," "I'll get a knife," "I'm going to get a bow and arrow and kill you." Fite comments: "No matter what he may have said in the experimental situation, it looks as if other things were more important than the idea that hitting was 'not nice.' In fact, he probably thought it a very good idea. He was, during both of these years in which the study was made, one of the youngest and smallest of the children in his group. He needed some means of gaining prestige, and his reputation in the group for just this kind of behavior gave him a good deal of it. 'Get Holden to hit him' was not an uncommon thing to hear." He was a perfectly normal child who had found an effective means of getting status.

This material on young children dramatizes the complexity of pressure from the younger social group and from the authorities. The child who succeeds in getting along with others of his own age in a group where aggression is prevalent, cannot do so except at the expense of inner conflict in so far as he takes seriously the attitudes of adults or even his own feelings toward the undesirability of experiences that cause pain to others.

If this picture is at all representative, we judge that for middle-class children in university centers there are both positive and negative pressures exerted upon the child who fights; within limits we may say that fighting is acceptable in child culture but that many children confront contradictory approvals from adults. This does not go a long way toward answering the question *why* a child fights; to do this requires further consideration of the motivation and specific contexts in which aggression appears.

The Analysis of Biological Origins of Aggression

Two approaches which are broadly concerned with the functional analysis of aggression, in relation both to the internal drive and to the external conditions, are those of Goodenough and of Isaacs. In contrast to the problem of Jack and of Page, who were interested in the development of a capacity for enough aggression to sustain social relations, the problem of Goodenough and of Isaacs is the more destructive or problem-creating expression of anger and hostility.

Goodenough's analysis is based upon data collected by a group of mothers who reported *anger episodes* which occurred at home among children from seven months to seven years of age. The record blanks were planned to include notations of unusual events or disturbances of routine, unusual physiological conditions in the child, the immediate cause of the anger response, and the direction, type and form of expression of behavior. In addition, the methods of control used by the adult and the results of these methods were recorded.

The frequency of anger in the same child from day to day depended both upon intrinsic factors, resulting in differential responses to constant stimuli, and upon extrinsic factors, affecting the frequency and intensity of the irritating conditions to which the child was subjected. Intrinsic factors, conditions in the child which tended to make for irascibility, included inadequate sleep, constipation, fatigue.

Intellectual level, experience, and family relationships also played an important part in determining the type of reaction. External conditions included visitors and changes in the size or composition of the family group. The longest outbursts occurred when the child was in bed, having his bath or going to bed, and the shortest outbursts occurred when he was playing with his playmates, dressing or undressing, having teeth brushed or hair combed. While it is true that some non-social factors appear to be important in relation to anger, social difficulties loom large, and account for almost half of all angry outbursts between the ages of three and four, the period of maximum frequency. Anger showed developmental changes with age; the form which it took showed an increasing ability to react selectively and adaptively in rage-producing situations.

Isaacs is not concerned with the specific organism-in-environment picture of rage. She sees hate, hostility and aggression as fundamental aspects of personality, rooted in primary egocentric attitudes whose base is deeper than day-to-day disturbances in routine. Her analysis is based upon the day-by-day records of 31 children attending an experimental school. The motivations of aggressive behavior appear to her to be based upon group and individual hostility. Individual hostility appears in conflict over possessions. Children want to have exclusive use of an object; they have a sense of ownership even over such non-tangibles as songs learned at home. They want to have the exclusive right to dispense public property, to use playground apparatus. They exploit one another's feelings for property by taking it away in order to tease. Individual hostility is also expressed in both playful and serious assumption of power over others: threats, teasing, rebukes, blaming one another for accidents or the distress of another child. Rivalry is another expression of hostility, appearing when children compete for the love and approval of adults or the social leaders of the group, or for the homage of the younger members; it also appears when children compete with an adult for the love and possession of another adult.

Group hostility appears toward strangers and newcomers, toward adults, toward younger or inferior children, or toward any temporary scapegoat.

When we face the very different implications of the work of Goodenough and of Isaacs, we are driven back again to the need for relating the results of our study of behavior to basic biological and cultural principles. We know that the striped muscles and the sympathetic division of the autonomic nervous system provide every child with a mechanism for defensive responses under attack, and that anger and other such responses are in many respects very close in their biological bases to fear responses. Consequently it is quite reasonable to find Goodenough's evidences that irritable, angry behavior is likely to occur when either illness, fatigue, other physical conditions, or the emotional situation makes the child insecure. This, however, does not help much in relation to Isaacs' evidences that over a long period of time and quite apart from specific ups and downs, children seem to have a *need* to express aggression toward other children; this could only be handled by adults who imposed restrictions on the attacks. Is anger situational, or is it something in the child that must come out? It is at this point that we need to have further analysis of the broad aspects of the situation, such as might be contributed by the approach of a cultural anthropologist. Margaret Mead once commented to the parents of two typically "spontaneous" children, "I suppose you think it is 'just natural' for children to run and skip all over the place the way yours do. You know it really isn't; it is a culture pattern." If it is pointed out that children of the Arapesh of New Guinea do not show the aggression which appears in Isaacs' records and which is familiar to anyone in western European civilization, we can reply that we need scarcely go so far; we can point to cultural differences nearer home. Children in two groups in the same nursery school may show big differences in total aggression, depending upon the constellation of the group, the amount of play space, the amount of interference from the teacher, and the age of the children. The same children may show markedly different tendencies to fight in two contrasting situations. We can even point out the probable effects of the close domination of adults over little children in the small families characteristic of our own sub-culture, and suggest that the aggression which we find today is partly a response to the great accumulation of frustrations which any child in this situation must suffer.

In so far as children in our culture do show a generalized hostility, we may reasonably conclude that this hostility, or need to be aggressive, is developed during the first months or years from the experiences of frustration and repression involved in the child's training with respect to eating, elimination, handling of property and of people.

When all this has been said, however, it may be useful to stop and think for a moment about everyday differences that anyone familiar with animals has a chance to observe. Aside from training, great differences in fierceness and tendency to attack are evident, not only among different species of animals or even birds, but also among different members of the same species, or even of the same family, as breeders of dogs well know. It may not be too far-fetched here to suggest that if such differences exist among large groups of individuals of the human family, they may perhaps be related not only to culture patterns but also to biochemical and other organic differences.

The pliable child, the stubborn child, the sunny child, the child of violent temper or dark resentments are probably not simply the products of different home training, but of home experience acting upon organisms of different constitution in terms of glandular and neurophysiological make-up. Individual differences in irritability, amount of activity, the tendency to laugh or cry, have been accurately recorded in the first five weeks of life. In time we shall be able to relate such constitutional differences to later "traits."

Finally, in the light of Klineberg's summary of the evidences that culture, including diet, tempo of work, social activity, may affect biochemical aspects of the organism that are reflected in the basal metabolism, blood pressure, etc., we would have to suggest that it is not strictly correct to dissociate "biological" and "cultural" influences. Aggressiveness is certainly not a "pure instinct" and certainly not a pure "cultural pattern." The interaction between biological and cultural influences must be seen not solely in terms of the net *amount of aggression*, but in terms of the total complicated structure built upon such responses. For instance, an increase in whatever biochemical factors are involved in aggression among adults, might increase the thresholds for domineering attitudes in general and vigorous attacks on children in specific instances where the child's behavior called for adult repression. The question whether this increased vigor in the adult's response results in meek, inhibited attitudes on the part of the child, or violent antagonism, rebellion and retaliation, would certainly depend to a considerable degree on similar biochemical aspects of the child's make-up, his thresholds for active defensive response. With this start, it is easy to see how the interplay between the aggressive adult and a meek, submissive child will develop along different lines from the relationship between the aggressive adult and the rebellious child, and how different patterns of fantasy and behavior toward other individuals will grow out of these two relationships. It is quite possible, then, to see meaning in such a pattern as Isaacs outlines: the child has a fund of aggression and hostility which must find expression, but which also requires control from the adult. Yet the fund and the need for outlet would depend upon specific biological and cultural conditions to start with, and quite different conditions might result in quite different patterns from those suggested by Isaacs.

But the "biological factors" in aggressiveness call for more analysis. When Goodenough reminds us of the importance of specific physiological conditions such as fatigue, toxins, and illness, it suggests the need for pursuing more fully the nature of the organic foundations of aggression. It is one thing to postulate biological factors, another to define and measure them. We tend in everyday discussion to think spontaneously in terms of children who seem "by nature" to be more or less aggressive than other children; but in the research world there is little to show where to expect aggressiveness. We may argue that children who are taller and stronger have more likelihood for success in competition with children their age, and may therefore dare to be more aggressive; we may add to this that children of very active temperament would be likely to show more aggression than phlegmatic children. Yet against this, one must consider the attitude of the child toward his physique and his social world, e.g., the effect of insecurity in modifying any constitutional tendency toward aggressiveness in the child who is strong enough to carry through, and the effect of a tendency to compensate actively for sluggishness or for slight build. Since it is practically impossible to get children in whom these factors of attitude are not intricately interwoven with constitutional factors, it is hard to obtain a clear picture of the situation as it really is.

These complicating factors would lead us to suspect some relation between aggressiveness and age, size, strength, and experience, but a relation far from simple. Aggression correlates substantially with the number of social contacts that a child has, or the amount of social activity of any sort that he shows. It must be remembered that sympathetic behavior, cooperation, and other "socially desirable" forms of behavior also show substantial positive interrelationships with aggression. This points in the same direction, namely, that any specific sort of social activity is highly dependent upon the general tendency to social activity which the child shows at a given time. This, of course, is a matter of a complex group of factors, such as the child's freedom in the group, his interests in the activities available and his general liveliness. We find in newborn children quite clear individual differences in degree of activity; but studies of this type have not been carried out on a large enough number of children on whom we have long-time follow-ups to make it possible to say that there is much relation between the degree of activity shortly after birth, and the degree of liveliness at three or four, or any other later age. The only clear indications of biological factors, therefore, are those which come from a study of a small number of extreme cases, in which constitutional build is compared with indices of aggressive or submissive behavior. D. M. Levy has made such an analysis in a study of the relation between aggressive-submissive behavior and the Fröhlich syndrome.

This syndrome in boys includes Mons mammary girdle, adiposity, hypogenitalism, tapering fingers, smooth, velvety skin, feminine appearance or mannerisms, etc. The subjects of Levy's study were 33 boys from the Institute of Child Guidance, between 7 years 5 months, and 19 years of age. Their intelligence quotients ranged from 70 to 160, with a median of 115. These were cases selected from the 1000 patients in the Institute. The majority of the cases with the Fröhlich syndrome were found to be "submissive," in contrast to the "aggressiveness" found among most of the children in a study of 1000 children referred to the Institute. An attempt was made to study the possibility that submission represented an adaptation to certain individual factors of the syndrome—for example, small genitals, obesity, or low total energy. The criteria for aggressive and submissive behavior were applied to a group of children who did not show the Fröhlich syndrome, to other groups arranged in relation to weight, age or height, and to a group of children with hyperkinesis. The conclusion was that the submissive behavior in the group with the adiposa-genital syndrome was not explainable as a response to any of the factors just mentioned. A further check on the hypothesis that constitutional factors were directly responsible was made in studying the life history of the group to determine whether early experiences, including the maternal attitude, favored the submissive adaptation. In a few cases the early experience was actually extremely favorable to aggressive behavior. For the group as a whole, the social factors and the background of the children with the Fröhlich syndrome were not significantly different from the social factors for the group used as controls. The conclusion is then drawn that the submissive behavior is partly determined by the constitutional factors, especially the *endocrine* factors basic to the syndrome as a whole. It is noted, however, that in special types of environment, submissive factors can be overweighted by aggressive factors regardless of the constitutional tendencies.[1]

In general, the extroverted pattern of our culture makes it natural for outgoing active behavior to be accepted as normal, while the interests of the appreciative, imaginative, introverted child are frequently thought of as compensatory for repression or inferiority feeling. While the work of Jack and Page gives some weight to this view, it is also possible that children who constitutionally are more absorbed in aesthetic, sensory, small-muscle interests might be naturally less interested in social and large-muscle activities and less likely to develop any of the forms of aggression we have discussed.

The Rôle of Home Personalities and Home Attitudes in the Development of Aggression

The analysis of factors in aggression thus provides a little solid information about constitutional tendencies. Considerably more work has been done on the tracking down of factors in the home and cultural situation. The hypothesis that children's behavior is in large measure the product of the social environment has been familiar to social workers, psychologists and psychiatrists for a generation now, and a great variety of attempts have been made to bring the relationships into definite, even quantitative, terms.

---

[1] Other investigators have noted passive, submissive, dependent behavior among underprivileged children showing the Fröhlich syndrome.

Thus early research on delinquents emphasized the importance of instability in the home in relation to social behavior, and the "broken home" was seen as a primary source of difficulty. Divorce, desertion and death brought drastic changes in a child's life which frequently resulted in profound behavior disturbances, often of an aggressive sort. More recent studies have gone further and attempted to discriminate between the objective changes and the subjective factors in the child's relation to his home. In one study recently reported, only 25 per cent of children from homes broken as a result of parental incompatibility showed problem traits, and the author's conclusion was that emotional relations between parents and children as causes of problem behavior were more important than broken homes as such.

The more detailed study of these emotional factors is one of the important current trends in research. An outstanding example is the analysis by Hattwick of interrelationships between the preschool child's behavior and certain factors in the home. This study was carried out with 335 children (171 girls and 164 boys) from eighteen different nursery schools. The children ranged from 1 year 11 months, to 5 years 11 months of age, and the group contained 146 children of white American descent, 100 children of Negro parents and 69 children of foreign—mostly Mexicans, Italian, and "mixed European"—extraction. There was a slight tendency for higher occupational levels to predominate. Specially devised rating charts were used for the recording of data on home factors and preschool behavior in this study. Each form of behavior was scored in terms of frequency of occurrence, and ratings at school were based on an average of three days' ratings by teachers who were in daily contact with the children. Ratings on home factors were based on the judgment of one teacher alone who had visited the homes and had had conferences with the parents. The results of the analysis showed that children whose homes reflected over-attention were likely to display infantile, withdrawing types of reaction. Inadequate attention in the home was associated with aggressive types of behavior, such as jealousy, rushing into danger, grabbing toys, refusing to share, having "scenes," refusing to comply, grumbling, etc. These aggressive types of behavior appeared to have a basis in insecurity, and consequently were also associated with tendencies to cry easily, to show off, to be fearful, and to show other kinds of nervous habits.

Both over-protection and neglect (or rejection) of the child have been studied by other investigators. A notable example is a recent study of maternal rejection based on an analysis of 75 cases and a control group of 82 children. The parents of the control group showed a predominance of constructive and protective behavior, while those of the rejected group showed a predominance of hostile and aggressive behavior.

The criteria of rejection consisted of evidence that the mother was non-welcoming or overtly hostile. Ten items were selected as possible indices of rejection; if three of these appeared without symptoms of over-protection, the case was accepted for study. These items included severe punishing, neglect, nagging, indifference, irritation, mother threatening to send child away, handling the child inconsistently, suppression, resisting spending money on the child, comparing the child unfavorably with a sibling.[1] Seventy-five per cent of the rejected group were boys, as against 44 per cent of the control group; approximately three times as many of the rejected group had foreign-born parents. Only 24 per cent of the rejected group were rated as in comfortable socio-economic circumstances, as against 95 per cent of the control group.

The results, in terms of three kinds of problem behavior—aggressiveness, submissiveness, and a mixture of the two—are reported in such a way as to emphasize the sex differences among the children in response to the rejection situation. Thus boys are reported to be aggressive only when either or both parents were openly hostile, whereas girls tended to be aggressive also when either of the parents was ambivalent. Boys were usually submissive when either parent was protective, but girls were submissive only when the fathers were protective or ambivalent. Boys showed mixed behavior when either parent was ambivalent, while girls showed mixed behavior only when either or both parents showed hostility. These relationships need more analysis in terms of the cultural norms for relationships between boys and the parent of each sex as compared

---

[1] Unfortunately 6 per cent of the control group were also rejected children according to these criteria.

with relationships between girls and the parent of each sex and in terms of the specific content of relationship between parents and children as well as the children's attitudes. In summary, it appears that among 46 cases of constructive handling, 91 per cent of the children were stable, 75 per cent of them showing constructive or protective behavior and being popular, friendly and well adjusted; while in 35 cases of destructive handling, hostile or ambivalent, 91 per cent of the children showed one of the three types of problem behavior.

This type of investigation recognizes that in a broad behavior tendency like aggressiveness, what a parent is and does is often of more importance than what he says, and that the social environment of a child essentially includes the whole personalities of the adults around him. The conscious attitudes expressed in words, though only a part of the picture, are an important and accessible part, and have recently received an especially vigorous analysis, comparison being made of the adult attitude and the way in which it is understood and responded to by the child.

Thus the process of formation of attitudes toward aggression is given in M. D. Fite's study (cf. page 407). This process is rooted in the child's relation with the parents, the conscious pressures they put upon the child and the interplay of the different attitudes of the two parents. This is vividly illustrated in the records from the parents of Nancy, Lila, and Evan.

Nancy had shown a great deal of conflict about fighting and with different degrees of anxiety had expressed the attitude that fighting was never permissible. Nancy's father explained that he wished her to learn that hitting was not right under any circumstances, even if she were hit first. Hitting, he said, was to be looked upon only as a last resort, and he wished her to learn in any situation to try other methods first. The influence of this attitude on the child was probably reinforced by the fact that Nancy seemed to have an especially warm relation with her father, and he often entered into her fantasy play. In Lila's case there was a marked similarity between her attitude toward hitting in the fall of 1935 and her mother's attitude at approximately the same time. Lila's mother felt that in some situations hitting was quite necessary.

The child's difficulties in grasping the whole adult attitude appear in the details of Evan's attitudes. His first rough treatment of a younger sister had led to the establishment of special rules, so that in time he had "learned to be gentle with her." At the same time there was no indoctrination against hitting in other situations. The parents felt that in general they wanted him to learn that hitting was not a good idea, but they had been dismayed at his timidity and "cowardice" and had consequently taught him to fight back rather than to come "complaining and crying." Thus Evan's dictum, "You're supposed to hit them back," is a direct reflection of parental teaching. But so also was his unwillingness to hit a doll with another doll when the object of the suggested hitting was a doll *with his sister's name*.

The dilemma which thus confronts adults who are responsible for the wise training of children and who wish to bring up their children both to hate war and to be able to hold their own in a competitive society is illustrated by Holden's father. Like Nancy's father, he is an ardent pacifist, and like Nancy's father his relation to his child is warm and close. Holden had an older brother, and together the three spent their free hours exploring the city. "The father did not try to protect the children from unfortunate experiences, though he regretted them if they occurred; rather, he enjoyed sharing with them their curiosity about anything and everything. . . ." Holden had seen policemen beating up a Negro they had caught for shoplifting. He had himself taken part also in a bit of gang warfare. "A friend of the family who had taken the two children to the park had settled himself with a book, suddenly looked up to see 'two gangs of boys, one Negro and one white, hurling rocks at each other.'" Holden's brother promptly did his bit along with the group of white boys, while Holden aligned himself with the Negroes and did his bit just as well. When their father discussed it with them later, he emphasized the fact that "you must not fight without knowing what you are doing." He felt that thinking out the best way of attaining a desired end was the point to be emphasized, and made it clear that in most cases this would not be physical force; on the other hand, he had no absolute objections to its use. He felt, further, that Holden needed some techniques to contend with his older brother's aggressiveness, and agreed that he had "all the techniques of a prize fighter." Holden's own statement in the spring of 1935 to the effect that you should "hit them, fight them," etc., is in line with his father's attitude that he needed to have techniques for self-defense. At the same time, his statement in the fall of 1935 that "hitting" was "not nice" was in line with his mother's attitude, for she had said just this to him. The influence of his father's attitude is reflected also in his acceptance of hitting in the doll-play, and his suggestions that the experimenter do some hitting.

Fite's study makes it clear, moreover, that the confusion of our culture bears down on the child not only through his experience of different pressures from the mother and father whom he loves and in whom he believes, but in the puzzling problems created when specific school situations have to be met in three ways: (1) with success in terms of one's school status, (2) with the approval of the adults in authority at school, and (3) with loyalty to the values of parents who, to a child at the age of three or four, are still "the most important people in the world."

On one occasion in the spring of 1935, Nancy hit another child, then went across the playground, saying to herself, "Oh, everyone has to sit down and think what they did." Yet about fifteen minutes earlier she had seemed to get positive satisfaction out of aggression which had included the support of another child:

George, John and Nancy had been playing together. George went over to Mary and Alma at the cellar steps and said, "That's our house." Nancy followed and repeated, John followed and repeated, took hold of Mary's arm and pulled her. Nancy watched him, then as Mary went off followed her and pushed her several times. Then stood and looked at her, saying, "There, I foshed her. There! we foshed her."

The fact that another child started it seemed to release her own feelings of satisfaction; she was completely happy about the aggression, in contrast to the guilty feelings she showed after the other aggression. The support of another child apparently gave her footing in the child world, where aggression might be satisfying even when in direct conflict with the parental dicta which were so strongly upheld on other occasions. On two other occasions she applauded self-defense and success in grabbing a toy from another child. At the same time she frequently arbitrated when two other children were caught in a disagreement. When Michael and John argued over possession of a scoop, she suggested, "Well, I'll tell you; John can have it a little longer, then Michael can have it."

We see, through all her records, this complex combination of attitudes, with different ones predominant at different times: on certain occasions a hyper-moralism that reflects her parents' prohibitions; on others, some ability to get into the fray and successfully carry through an aggressive situation in terms of child mores; on still others, a strong sense of rules and patterns that she uses for purposes of arbitration and prevention of acute conflict, when the issue concerns other children and she is not directly involved.

Some months after this time, the possibilities of aggressive action had become more crystallized; in the experimental situation she told the experimenter that it was "all right to hit back" and she had lost the anxiety that she showed earlier in her comments on aggression. When an issue came up on the playground she was quite clear about both her wants and her techniques for getting them.

Mira, Lila and Nancy were playing in the sandbox. Mira took a box that Lila was using. Lila said, "I need to use it." Nancy tried to take it from Mira. Mira held on, saying, "No, now, now, let's not fight." Nancy grinned, tried to pull it away, saying, "I'm trying to get that thing away from her." Then she stopped pulling and sat down again. Lila said, "I just need it for a minute to put something in." Nancy said to Mira, "If we tell you nicely and you don't give it to us, then we have to tell you crossly; and if you don't give it to us then we have to fight, and you wouldn't like that."

The experimenter comments that the attitudes Nancy expressed preceded rather than followed comparable behavior on the playground. This of course might well vary from child to child, according to the need for an intellectual adjustment to an emotionally toned problem before an active response could be made.

In the case of the parents of these children, it is not hard to guess that the attitudes expressed in words had some connection with the personality of the parents and that a complete picture of the parents' handling of the child at home, disciplinary methods, emphasis upon training and routine, would have thrown additional light on the basis for Nancy's early anxiety over the conflict between home moralities and school exigencies, as well as on the kind of personality organization which made it possible for her to emerge with an acceptance of nursery-school mores.

It is again evident here that when we separate biological and cultural factors we run the danger of ignoring their frequent mutuality, the fact that "biological" and "cultural" are both simply abstractions from the interplay of organisms. Hyperactivity may be purely a physiological effect of post-encephalitic conditions, convulsive disorders or "congenital restlessness" (Childers). Even when of physiological origin, it is shown in talkativeness, distractibility, over-confidence, boastfulness, sometimes in cruelty and destructive aggressiveness. But it may be primarily social, inter-personal in origin, according to the evidence from a number of directions, which lays the blame for hyperactivity upon disturbed home relations, such as broken homes, rejection by a parent or conflicts between home and neighborhood values. Insecurity, or the physiological reaction of *fear* is the greatest common divisor of these experiences, and hyperactivity or bootless aggressiveness is evidently a modern expression of fear or anxiety in a world too complex to offer simple constructive solutions of fear problems. This intimate interdependence of social and biological bases of personality is what makes it so necessary to study social behavior in a biosocial setting. The study of tensions or activity drives, or frequency of contacts by themselves, will tell us nothing regarding their functional bases. A functional analysis requires a functional technique for study, that is, a study of the dynamics of behavior in its context.

AGGRESSION AND THE EGO

If a child or an adult becomes needlessly aggressive when no material incentive to conflict is in sight, we tend to comment that he has "too much ego"; when a child (or an adult) becomes "defensive" or shows "defense mechanisms," we usually mean that it is his ego that he is trying to defend. We noted the biological

SOME STUDIES THROWING LIGHT

AUTHOR DATE	TOPIC	SUBJECTS	METHODS
Brown, J. F. (1933)	"Reality" level ("goal" motivation).	96 freshmen, University of Berlin. Exp. A: 61 Ss; Exp. B: 24 Ss; Exp. C: 11 Ss.	In all experiments Ss given "real" and "unreal" tasks, ostensibly intelligence tests and interpolated tasks. Exp. A: 4 subgroups, tested for recall of all material at intervals, respectively, of 5 min., 30 mins., 24–48 hrs., and 1 wk. after original "examination." Exp. B: 3 subgroups, retested after 5 mins., 36 hrs., and 1 wk. "Test" items for Exp. A were "interpolation" items for Exp. B, and vice versa. Exp. C same as A but after Ss had done work, told interpolated items were ones that would be scored. Tested 1 wk. later.
Dembo, T. (1931)	Qualitative study of anger as a dynamic problem.	27 adults.	64 experiments with Ss each session 1–2 hrs. 2 impossible tasks required, e.g., throwing ring on distant bottle 10 times. Ss' activities observed. Introspections.
Dillon, M. S. (1934)	Attitudes of nursery-school children toward own and other children's naked bodies.	Group 1: 11 boys, 11 girls; mean age, 35 mos.; mean I.Q., 118. Group 2: 8 boys, 8 girls; mean age, 51 mos.; mean I.Q., 126.	All children took nap in school, undressing completely; no segregation of sexes. 21 observations of each group on consecutive days. Behavior recorded: manipulation of genitals; interest in other parts of body; in elimination; in sex differentiation; language used for parts of body and elimination; use of tabooed language; demonstration of affection.
Frank, J. D. (1935)	Individual differences in aspiration level.	3 groups of college students: 36 Ss, paid and volunteer.	Tasks: 1. Printing words with linoleum set; *time.* 2. Spatial relations test (Kelley); *time.* 3. Quoits, 20 rings pitched from

FINDINGS	GENERAL REMARKS
Ratio of "real" to "unreal" material in recall consistently over 1, rising steadily with length of interval to 3.8. Considering only first half of recalls recorded by each S, ratio rose to as high as 6.5. Same result in Exp. C, but ratio rose only to 2.4 after 1 wk.	The "real" material remains on a high recall level; the unreal drops.
Actual signs of anger observed; swearing; attempts to leave; introspective reports. Result of conflict between internal tension (inability to perform task: negative valence) and external tension (social pressure, pride, etc.: positive valence).	Barriers which constrain action set up tensions. S cannot retreat from task because of external barriers. In ordinary life, customs, manners, morals constitute such external barriers.
Predominantly, younger children showed same attitude to bodies undressed as dressed. But some cases showed emotional attitudes to body. Younger group showed less interest in bodies than older one. Manipulation of genitals in both groups; not concealed, not masturbation. For younger group differences in genitalia like differences in eye color; older group recognized such sex differences; regarded them as incidental to differentiation in terms of clothing, etc. Elimination involved no taboo in younger children; fixed taboos and "sensitized" words clear in older group. Sex play rare, but occurrence shows curiosity not only motive.	
Reliability: r of 1st and 2nd performances in *given* task: median of 6 r's .62; range .26 to .75. Generality: r of 1st and 2nd *tasks* .37 to .62, uncorrected.	Relation between level of aspiration and level of past performance is "a relatively permanent characteristic of the personality, and . . . this permanence can be

AUTHOR DATE	TOPIC	SUBJECTS	METHODS
			fixed distance; *accuracy*. Group I: tasks 1 and 2; II: 1 and 3; III: 2 and 3. Two sessions, 1 wk. apart or more, on each task.
Frank, J. D. (1937)	Comparison of aspiration level and random guessing.	1. 50 Ss: 25 of each sex; 25 volunteers, 25 paid. 2. 20 male college students, paid.	Task: Copying 25 designs with embossing cubes. 1: 16 equally difficult patterns. S given practice, then "speed test," results given him; asked how long next trial would take. 16 trials. 10 of S's scores mixed with 5 arbitrary ones; median above S's. Read him as *someone else's* scores; asked to guess other man's succeeding scores. Then given 9 more trials himself. 2: S studied sample, then guessed another's score after every trial, then worked as in 1 above.
Hoppe, F. (1930)	Qualitative study of level of aspiration as affected by success and failure.	10 Ss.	Difficult tasks such as hitting bull's eye, hanging 16 rings on moving hook, etc. Ss required to perform perfectly. Objectively no successes occurred. Introspections.
Horowitz, E. L. (1935)	Children's localization of the self.	Some young children; 47 college students.	Ss asked (in appropriate terms for age level) where "self" located.
Rosenzweig, S. (1933)	Preference for repetition of successful and unsuccessful acts in relation to age, personality.	37 children in Peabody Home for Crippled Children, 22 boys, 15 girls; range: 5 yrs., 6 mos. to 14 yrs., 8 mos.; median; 8 yrs. 10 mos.	2 jigsaw puzzles of similar difficulty: S allowed to finish one, not other. S asked which one he liked better; some asked why. Then asked which would like to repeat. Ratings by teachers on "pride" (i.e., "Desire to stand well with the group, and pleasure in one's own achievement").

FINDINGS	GENERAL REMARKS
	demonstrated regardless of the type of ability which the task requires."
In both experiments, average level of aspiration higher than median level of performance. Average guess close to level of performance. For men, average level of aspiration deviates more from median level of performance than does average guess, and differences are more widely distributed. Those effects reversed after S has guessed scores of someone else.	Women more objective in stating levels of aspiration and less objective in random guessing. "Women are less likely than are men to regard a manual task as a measure of their own worth." "Hearing the scores of someone else tends to make the aspiration level behave more like a random guess, presumably by strengthening the tendency toward objectivity." Guess shows much less rigidity (constancy) than aspiration level.
Although 100% performance required, Ss set own aspiration level on basis of earlier performances. Objective success and failure do not correspond to the subjective experience of success and failure. Aspiration level raised and lowered in accordance with performance.	If a task is set too high above or too far below the aspiration level, neither failure nor success is experienced.
One child "was" in abdomen, another in left jaw, another in head, etc. Adults located "selves" most often in head, brain, eyes, face; a few in other parts of body. Introspection impresses adult Ss with unreality of localizations.	Localization of self "not the basic phenomen one might hope for." Beyond use as a reference point, locus has little reality.
32 Ss liked "successful" puzzle, 5 the one "failed." Reason assigned: "it's easy," "it's hard." 20 preferred to *repeat* successful puzzle, 17 the one failed. Coefficient of association for relation between age above and below median and puzzle repeated is .80. For M.A. even higher, .95. "Pride" ratings: similar increase with age.	Apparently pride the significant factor: "extent to which failure was wounding to them."

AUTHOR DATE	TOPIC	SUBJECTS	METHODS
Sears, R. R. (1937)	Experience of failure and "repression."	20 male college freshmen; well motivated. 2 groups of 10 Ss, equated on average time for card-sorting, number of repetitions for memorizing lists of syllables.	Group 1 (Success): 15 trials at card-sorting; made to "succeed." Group 2 (Failure): same; made to "fail." Success and failure in terms of Ss' aspiration level. Ss learn second list of syllables. Procedure repeated twice more; interval between sittings "not less than 24 hours nor more than 48 hours."
Sherif, M. (1935)	Social influences in perception.	99 *naïve* adults.	Ss subjected to autokinetic effect (illusory movement) and required to estimate amount of movement. Some observed alone, then in groups of 2 or 3; this reversed with others.
Sherif, M. (1935)	Prestige suggestion in literary taste (judgment).	2 Harvard groups, 1 Ankara (Turkey) group. 228 Ss in all.	16 authors' names (alphabetized) rank-ordered by Ss for preference of writings. 1 month later, 16 comparable short passages each attributed to one of the 16 authors, but all written by a single author, were rated. One group of Ss made special effort to overcome influence of authors' names.
Snedden, P. K. (1936) (Abstract)	Effect of success and failure on level of aspiration.	25 adults.	On each of 3 days 10 trials on each of 4 tasks: dart throwing, card-sorting, and test of kinesthetic judgment. S gave level of aspiration for each trial after being told score on preceding one. Task of learning syllables also.

FINDINGS	GENERAL REMARKS
"Efficiency of card-sorting decreased . . . from the beginning to the end of each day's trials" for the Failure group but increased for Success group. Mean for 2 groups (averages of medians of each 3 successive trials): Success, 37.9; Failure, 41.9 trials. Learning of 2nd nonsense list—average % decrease in number of trials to learn.	"*Failure* at a semi-competitive task (card-sorting) produced a progressive impairment of the *efficiency* . . . and . . . failure on the one task impaired the performance on another task temporally contiguous to the first. . . . It is suggested that both facts may be explained as the results of the operation of anticipatory responses to the failure." Experiment verifies hypothecated repression sequence: development of mutually incompatible anticipatory goal responses.
Each S (alone) establishes characteristic range of judgments; each group does the same. Ss who form group after individual norms are fixed establish new norms (usually without awareness). Ss observing alone after group norm established cling to that norm.	In unstable situations group norms are more stable than individual norms. "Stereotypes, fads . . . attitudes are, psychologically, [other] cases of the establishment of socially determined norms and values serving as frames of reference."
Correlations between 2 series of preferences, .53 to .33. For special group, r around zero.	Prestige suggestion affects judgments considerably. Our judgments organized in relation to general frame of reference.
Positive correlation of average difference between aspiration and performance with rigidity of aspiration level. Level of aspiration changed more readily with improvement than decrement in performance; this more pronounced with artificial success, disappeared with artificial failure. Average difference between performance and aspiration positively correlated with effect of success and failure on efficiency of nonsense-syllable learning.	

closeness of "aggressive" and "defensive" responses growing out of anger and fear, and their functional value for the child's ego. A study of social behavior explicitly related to the ego structure of the child must therefore follow closely upon our preliminary analysis of aggression.

A brief sketch of the probable outlines of the growth of the self has already been offered in Chapter IV (page 207); there our purpose was to show how the ego becomes a value—indeed, in some cultures a "central value"—and to show why, in the light of the theory of "dominance," such a value affords organization and continuity in personality structure. We have also seen in this chapter that many forms of aggression—particularly negativism and jealousy—can be understood only in terms of the ego status of the child in his relation to adults or to brothers and sisters. We must now consider a number of other approaches to the problem of ego development in the child.

Students of childish egocentrism may offer either of two emphases indicated by the terms "selfish" and "limited awareness." There is ample evidence that young children are chiefly aware of a world within the sight and hearing of their own eyes and ears, and do not have a very complete understanding of the needs of others or even of a distinction between self and the rest of the world (cf. page 208). Their talk reflects the small universe in which their own "needs" seem to the observer to loom overwhelmingly large. Yet this is quite a different matter from the question whether they are egocentric in the sense of ignoring the needs of those others who are *within their range of understanding*. The fact that they weep when other children weep, rush to the comfort of a hurt child, are all too eager to help a busy adult as best they can, and may even offer their own toys to a child who needs one, is evidence of a genuinely social orientation within the limits of their small world. This social responsiveness does not usually appear except under circumstances where it is stimulated by the needs of another child, so that when no other child in need is physically present the individual's life appears quantitatively to be dominated by egocentric concerns.

In the light of the complex and varied social give-and-take between little children, the conception of "egocentrism," both as used by Piaget and as used in early studies, seems therefore to need careful analysis. A variety of indices of egocentrism in the language of young children has been used. On the whole, the results agree in showing that the younger the child the more egocentric he is, as shown by his language, and that between three and four years of age children enter a new socialized phase of development which is also reflected in their language. A typical list of *words most frequently used* by two- and three-year-old children is the following: I, it, me, you, is, want, don't, going, get, the, a, my, here, to, shall, car. The frequency of imperative sentences, which are second only to declarative, may be another index of egocentricity. Both imperative sentences and self-words decline in use from two to four; this is usually interpreted to mean that the child's range of awareness expands, so that his wants and activities have a less predominant share of his attention in proportion to the share taken by other people and the world about him. Piaget has been particularly interested in the reconstruction of the experience through which the child goes, in achieving awareness of himself as distinct from objects and in achieving awareness of others in relation to himself.

This process of growth of awareness of self is accompanied by increased sensitiveness to the *status* or *value* of oneself in the eyes of others, and by the development of certain attitudes toward oneself which may be releasing or inhibiting in social relationships. It is quite possible that in cultures less concerned with the "fullest development" of the individual, neither the perceptual distinction between the self and the rest of the world nor the active self-concern and heightening of emotional stakes in egocentric values would develop along the lines which appear in our culture. These emotional patterns or attitudes tied up with being a "self-conscious" ego have recently come into the laboratory for detailed experimental analysis.

Among the general attitudes of children toward themselves which underlie social behavior, probably the following are of the greatest importance:

1. The child's perspective or capacity to see himself in relation to a total group.
2. His self-consciousness and spontaneity of attack upon situations.
3. His capacity to manipulate situations in relation to his own purposes.
4. His ability to handle failure constructively and work out solutions of his problems in spite of obstacles.

The work of Piaget and of Lerner on "egocentrism" and "sociocentrism" in relation to moral realism illuminates some of the problems in relation to the first question. The work of Jack and Page, together with that of Moreno, emphasizes the possibility of developing confidence and spontaneity, as suggested by the second and third questions. The last, the ability to handle failure constructively, has been studied most effectively by Updegraff and Keister. We shall consider this last point first.

The purposes of Updegraff and Keister's experiment were as follows:

1. To devise tests by means of which one may discover what responses a child of pre-school age gives when faced with failure.
2. To select a group of children evidencing undesirable modes of response to failure.
3. To attempt to modify, by special help or individual training, the responses of the children of this group.

The child was exposed to failure in three experimental situations: the first in the form of a puzzle; the second, a challenge to his physical strength; and the third, a social obstacle. The criteria for the experiments were as follows:

1. They must be possible of accomplishment and yet of such difficulty that the child does not succeed immediately.
2. They must provide situations which are natural, in the sense that the difficulties are not obviously or forcibly imposed.
3. The average child should be able to see for himself that

he has failed, and to see in some relation of the situation to himself the basis of success or failure.

Children who showed immature responses (giving up, requesting help more than half the time, destructive behavior, more than two rationalizations, exaggerated responses) were used for special training. The training consisted in introducing the child to a series of problems that grew more difficult as the training proceeded. Training periods varied from eight to thirty-three minutes. The criteria for the problems were as follows:

1. The tasks should be graded in difficulty so that the child experiences success in the earlier ones and gradually works up to the problems which are difficult for him.
2. The later tasks must be of such difficulty that the child does not succeed immediately but is forced to persevere, to continue to try if he is to attain success.
3. The child must be able to see his progress and previous successes.

The trained group showed remarkable improvement in many ways. Sulking and crying dropped out entirely, and interest and attempts to solve alone increased significantly. After training, the child usually tried longer, showed more interest, solved problems unassisted, and completely eliminated emotional behavior.

The responses and their distribution in the first trained group before and after training were as shown in the table on page 436.

The experimental procedure helps greatly to put order into the results of non-scientific (in the sense of uncontrolled) observation. In this instance, the layman may have one of the following points of view:

1. Some children are naturally more "sensitive" to failure than others and there is not much that can be done about it.
2. If a child is self-conscious and easily upset by failure, he has been badly trained and needs good training.

Anyone could quote many illustrations giving evidence for both points of view; but not until the problem was formulated in terms which permitted systematic observation could evidence be produced

COMPARISON OF TRAINED GROUP BEFORE AND AFTER TRAINING

Behavior	Before training[a] (n = 15)		After training[b] (n = 12)	
	Mean Minutes	S. D.	Mean Minutes	S. D.
No overt attempt.	6.0	3.7	2.1	1.6
Attempts to solve alone.	8.5	4.2	11.2	2.0
Asks another to solve.	3.6	3.4	.5	1.2
Asks help.	2.5	2.4	2.4	1.7
Destructive behavior.	.6	1.1	—	—
Rationalizes.	2.8	2.5	1.6	2.2
Interest.	6.0	3.8	11.0	2.7
No emotional manifestations.	2.5	2.4	1.3	1.4
Indifference.	1.0	2.9	—	—
Smiles.	.03	.1	—	—
Laughs.	—	—	.1	.3
Sulks.	.8	1.3	—	—
Cries.	1.7	2.4	—	—
Whines.	2.6	2.9	1.0	1.8
Yells.	.3	.8	—	—
Motor manifestations of anger.	.2	.5		

[a] Mean length experimental period was 14.5 minutes.
[b] Mean length experimental period was 13.3 minutes.

regarding the extent to which both tendencies were operating. Systematic observations of children in natural situations over a long period of time would afford an opportunity to observe long-time changes in the child's stability in relation to failure, along with observations of experiences which appeared to increase or decrease his self-consciousness and his ego problems. These experiences would be so complex, however, and would include so many variations in the organization of the group, the influence of specific children, and the different influences of different teachers that it would be quite impossible to sift out the factors relevant to a specific change in a child's ego feeling from those that were irrelevant. By the use of an experimental procedure in which an untrained (control) and a trained group are compared, the effects of specific measures directed to the reinforcement of confidence and stability of ego feeling can be measured.

The method affords a picture of the modification of attitudes toward the ego at the pre-school level. In contrast we wish to cite a study with adolescents and young adults, namely, Maslow's work on feelings of dominance. Since this study has no counterpart in genetic studies but is conceptually of so much importance in relation to the problem of ego development and aggression, it needs to be carefully considered.

The terms "dominance status" and "subordinate status" are used as follows: "In a social relationship between two people in which one dominates the other, either overtly in behavior or implicitly in feeling, the one who dominates is said to be in or to have dominance status." The other is said to be in or to have subordinate status. It is recognized from the outset that dominance status is to some extent a product of the particular situation or a relation between persons, and refers to a particular relationship between two people. But Maslow finds that some individuals dominate practically all the people they meet, and that others are dominated by practically all the people they meet. When members of each group are studied at length through intensive interviews, hypnosis, dream interpretation, and observation of behavior, definite syndromes of behavior and feeling are found to characterize high-dominance people, low-dominance people, or middle-dominance people. Marked differences in feeling and attitude seem to be more important than differences in behavior. The person who feels dominant describes his feelings about himself in the following terms:

(1) Self-confidence, (2) self-esteem, (3) high evaluation of self, (4) consciousness or feeling of "superiority" in a very general sense, (5) forcefulness of personality, (6) strength of character, (7) conviction or certainty that one is going to be able to assume dominance status over most of the people one may meet in the future, (8) high self-respect, (9) a feeling of sureness with respect to other people, (10) a feeling of being "on top" in the Adlerian sense, (11) a feeling of being able to handle other people, (12) a feeling that one is and ought to be looked up to, (13) a feeling of masterfulness and of mastery, (14) an expectation of respect from other people, (15) a feeling that others do admire and respect one, (16) a feeling that, in general, one deserves and is going to get good things from life, (17) a feeling of general capability, (18) an absence of shyness, timidity, self-consciousness, or embarrassment.

The person of low-dominance feeling will often describe himself in these terms:

I lack self-confidence. I feel inferior when with most people. I guess I don't think much of myself. I think I'd rather be someone else if I could. These feelings are of uncertainty, lack of confidence, general inferiority, weakness, general admiration and respect for others rather than for myself, a feeling of being, in a very metaphorical sense, "below" others, of being looked down upon, of wanting to be like someone else rather than myself, of being dominated by others, of lack of faith in myself and in my abilities. I often feel shy, timid, self-conscious and embarrassed. Generally, I cannot be said to be satisfied with myself.

It is quite true that the dominance feeling varies somewhat from one situation to another, but usually for a given individual it fluctuates within only a small part of the total range of dominance feeling exhibited by a large number of individuals. The fluctuation which does occur is likely to come with marked changes in the relation of the individual to different situations in which he finds himself. For instance, a man may be dominant at work but be dominated at home.

The relationship between dominance feeling and status of dominance is partially circular; feeling determines status to some extent, and status perhaps to a lesser extent determines feeling. Genetically, both dominance feeling and dominance status result from the interplay of specific situational factors and long-time cultural pressures. Adolescents who come from the upper socio-economic levels average higher in dominance status and dominance feeling than those from lower economic levels. At the same time, some of the adolescents whose dominance feeling is quite high in relation to the world in general may have considerable conflict and self-depreciation in relation to members of their own group. The fact that other aspects of personality structure are intimately bound up with dominance status is implied when Maslow indicates that some dominants are protective, others tyrants; still others are individualists who do not readily express dominance in behavior as long as others do not try to dominate them.

Among young children we have found that those who are insecure and unaggressive at one period are more likely to show marked changes in behavior, that is, toward aggressiveness. At the same time, those whose aggressiveness is an expression of relative maturity are more likely to have a wide repertory of different kinds of behavior, are ready to respond to almost any situation. Among college students and young adults, it seems to be equally true that the dominant person has a larger repertory of behavior. The dominant college girl knows how to be "innocent and girlish and sweet sixteen" and may quite easily convince the dean that she is. The high-dominance secretary may accept a subordinate status in the office with an adaptability to the needs of the situation and without the self-consciousness and inhibition which a low-dominance secretary would show even in a subordinate position.

Maslow thus describes the compensatory behavior of persons who feel weak but wish to appear strong:

In the first place, it is apt to be strained and unnatural. It is often more aggressive and louder than seem to be appropriate to the situation. It is apt to be somewhat vulgar, and may sometimes also give the observer the impression of expressing defiance rather than calm assurance. Such people are apt to be more "flip" than the average, to be "wise-crackers," to be ultra-sophisticated in a manner that indicates an eager desire to impress others with this quality. In several of my cases, feelings of conflict and ambivalence toward sex went with very free, even loose, talk about sex.

It is interesting to observe the remarkable change in the behavior of these subjects when the hard, bright exterior has been breached by the probings of the psychologist in the interview, and the subject has confessed to feelings of inferiority, uncertainty and weakness. The burdensome cloak of defense is cast aside with a (literal) sigh of relief. The hitherto loud defiant voice becomes low and hesitant, blushes are frequent, some embarrassment and shame is evident at the beginning. There is little of the raucous, forced laughter that has characterized the subject hitherto; the blocking, the sparring, the deliberate misunderstanding of the interviewer's questions, the convenient forgetting, the flip, superior, sometimes disdainful attitude, all of these disappear, to be replaced by a somewhat muted sincerity, honesty and straightforwardness. The interviewer loses his feeling that the subject is on guard and deliberately hiding himself.

Because they are working at different age levels, the assumptions underlying Updegraff and Keister's experiment and those appearing in the work of Maslow are almost diametrically opposed. The former find that among young children the emotional disorganization, the deflation of ego, attendant upon failure may be overcome, and that the level of ego feeling is not a fixed unchangeable aspect of a child's personality. Maslow, on the other hand, working with college students, finds a characteristic, more or less static ego level for each individual (Eisenberg's data are confirmatory; cf. page 809). We need much more light on the degree of plasticity of ego feeling, the age at which stable personality structures become established, and the conditions under which basic patterns of ego feeling may be altered.

Fortunately, another group of significant experiments, following the inspiration of Lewin, brings into focus this question of the extent to which the ego feeling and the aspiration level (cf. page 212) of child, adolescent, or adult may be changed, and what the factors are which do change them. Such experiments define a task in which the subject tries to do well, and note his evaluation of himself as he succeeds or fails. But success and failure cannot be defined in terms of score achieved: one whose objective performance is outstanding is disappointed because he hoped to do better, another with a median score is pleased with himself. Each person has an ego level and an aspiration level at which he aims, and the two are constantly being adjusted to each other.

The experience of success or failure depends upon the relation between the objective result and the aspiration level. Thus very hard tasks beyond the child's aspiration level cause *no experience of success or failure,* and the same is true of very easy tasks; yet within the middle range objective "success" may quite well go with inner distress. It is thus very probable that chronic experiences of failure may arise from an aspiration level higher than the child's ability; this type of extreme aspiration may be stimulated by adult demands or by a comrade's performances. But success and failure may at times modify the aspiration level of the individual. It is particularly significant in current experiments that children up to the age of four years change from markedly passive behavior to rather active behavior as a result of success, and active children are correspondingly deflated to a state of passivity by failure.

J. D. Frank has redefined the general pattern of relationship between ego level and aspiration level, pointing out that individuals of different personality structure may have quite different patterns of response. Some college students show the pattern that we generally assume to be characteristic; that is, they always have an aspiration level somewhat higher than their achievement. These, he says, "have their heads in the clouds" and frequently think of themselves as getting "better and better." Others, however, are realists and have their "feet on the ground"; their level of aspiration depends closely upon their achievement level. Others whose need to shield themselves from public failure is stronger than the need to keep their aspiration level as high as possible tend rather consistently to underestimate their achievement; they are designated the "cautious."

The most surprising result of this experimental work is that the relation between aspiration level and past performance appears to be "a relatively permanent characteristic of the personality," and that "this permanence can be demonstrated regardless of the type of ability which the task requires." This conclusion was reached on the basis of experiments with three tasks:

1. Printing with a linoleum printing set.
2. Manipulation of spatial relations.
3. Quoit-pitching.

The correlations between aspiration level in similar tasks (having motor ability in common) were higher than those found in tasks that differed markedly, although even in the latter case, correlations were positive and sufficiently high to indicate a stable trend in the personality which was only modified within limits by the shifts from one situation to another. The fact that this general stability of aspiration level in relation to achievement exists along with a tendency for the specific aspiration levels to be modified in the light of previous performance gives evidence that both a reality principle and an ego-level basis of response are working together to produce a specific aspiration level in relation to a specific task.

Two criteria of the involvement of ego level are the presence of self-competition and consciousness of social pressure. The first is indicated by remarks revealing that the subject "wanted to do well for his own sake," accompanied by exertion in the tasks and comments, such as "I gotta increase my speed." Social pressure was indicated when a subject "showed himself to be acutely aware of the presence of E as shown by restlessness, becoming easily flustered, nervous laughter, blushing and undue facetiousness." The range of ego attitudes varied from that of one subject who tried so hard that he got a "splitting headache," to that of the subject who said, "I like to have a margin and like to keep a little above it. Probably sounds as if I'm afraid to take a chance. I would never enter a thing unless I thought I'd be successful."

It is recognized that the "level of reality" of the experiment is important in relation to the extent to which the characteristic aspiration level appears. If the subject regards the experiment merely as a game, or as irrelevant and unimportant, the patterns of aspiration which he shows may not have much relation to his aspiration level in serious affairs.

These experimental studies of aspiration and ego levels have been carried on in a small number of metropolitan groups whose cultural backgrounds were probably quite similar one to another. This may account in part for the similarity of the patterns of aspiration which were found. The fact that a stable *relation* between aspiration level and achievement is found suggests that Maslow's hypothesis of a characteristic and relatively permanent pattern of ego organization may be substantiated, while at the same time the degree of confidence and ability to handle failure may be improved as Updegraff and Keister suggest. We are all familiar with the student who "finds himself" as a result of successful work, the young married man whose job, and wife and baby, are reflected in a firmer tread.

COMPETITIVENESS

Up to this point we have considered the ego as a thing to be enhanced and defended in its own right, not in terms of comparison with the ego needs of others. We must, however, turn to the pattern of *competition for prestige*, the aggressive enhancement of one's own ego at the expense of that of another.

We know that attitudes toward overt competitiveness vary enormously in our culture from one group to another; but the most suggestive account of such attitudes comes not from studies of children of Anglo-Saxon background but from Asch's study of Hopi children in the Southwest.

From a conversation in Hopi

Delphina (8:3): "Yesterday I did the bummest job for the bahana (white man)."

Frances (5:6): "You did quite well."

Delphina: "You didn't see it."

Frances: "You should have seen what I did; I couldn't do anything."

From observer's record

July 15. Helena and Julia came to our house this afternoon. We played ball with them. Helena was much the more skillful of the two. When at the conclusion of the game, I asked both, "Who plays better?" Julia promptly answered, "Helena," while Helena looked slightly embarrassed and said, "I don't know."

Many who have grown up in American culture have participated in experiences of this sort, as well as in the following patterns reported (in the third person) by a Hopi teacher:

. . . In order to introduce an incentive, she asked the children to turn their backs to the board as soon as they had finished. To her surprise, she found that the quickest children, when they were through, waited and looked about furtively until another—and more mediocre —child had turned around, before turning himself or herself. Needless to say, the instructor was forced to abandon this practice.

The same instructor has experienced serious difficulty when she tried to appoint leaders to take care of the classroom. At first, she tried to designate the bright children as leaders, as a reward for their work. They quickly refused the "honor," for the same reasons that adults refuse to be foremen. She then hit upon the plan of designating leaders alphabetically. This method worked, because the children considered it a fair method of shouldering the unpleasant task of being leader.

The differences between these experiences observed among Hopi children and the attitudes of children among white children are primarily these: The indirections and rejections of competitive patterns among white children are likely to indicate a withdrawal from the dominant pattern of direct competition which characterizes our society. It is, therefore, a deviant pattern which although widespread is not likely to be regarded favorably by "healthy-minded arbiters of custom." Among the Hopi children, however, the self-depreciatory gestures are accepted as normal and universal. Asch found that this pattern had various ramifications among the Hopi. Children were no more competitive in situations designed to stimulate competition than they were in non-competitive situations. They would malign their own work; they would praise the work of others. At the same time, Asch notes that not infrequently the intention seems to be to obtain praise from others through praising their work. More striking is the fact that when children were questioned regarding their plans for work after school, there was no indication of ambition to participate in activities outside of the daily routine. Characteristic answers are as follows:

Bernice (9:): "Help my mother."
Bertha (10:): "Arithmetic, read. . . . I don't know."
Delphina (8:3): "Teach, have children read, read arithmetic."
Frances (5:6): "Bounce ball, sweep, cook, bake."
Grace ( ): "Work, mop the floor, sweep the floor, wash the windows, wash, fix the bed, sweep the yard, wash the dishes."
Marion (8:7): "School. Make cookies."
Marietta (8:5): "Don't know."
Marie (11:2): "Work, wash, mop."
Olive ( ): "Work, cook, sweep, clean, wash dishes, wash clothes."
Regina (7): "Sweep, wash dishes, clean, mop."
Violet (8:4): "School, study. . . . I don't know."
Julia (10:): "Grind corn, make plaques, wash clothes."
Pearl (9:): "Make biscuits with my mother, make bread."

Evidences of ambitions to distinguish oneself or be outstanding are completely absent. The Hopi children were not concerned to "get ahead." At this point the contrast between Hopi children and American children is particularly great.

For wherever we come close to the question, whether in Middletown or in the vocational ambitions of urban children, ambition is likely to outrun ability in a considerable proportion of the population.

The Cultural Valuation of Work in Relation to Patterns of Competition and Aspiration

With all the various contributions that anthropologists have made to our perspective on human relationships and attitudes toward life, there has been very little discussion by them of attitudes toward work in different cultures. In our civilization this attitude seems to be closely tied up with all the patterns of ego development that go along with marked individualism. Doing a lot of work is the road to fame, or, if it does not prove to be so, a substitute for fame. Getting other people to do a lot of work for you makes more money for factory owners, and hence we have Taylor systems and other elaborate procedures for stimulating the largest amount of effort and its most efficient expenditure. The same attitude carries over into the school. Even among apostles of the "newer education" one finds an emphasis on seeing how much work he can get out of children, quite apart from any question of the effects of this emphasis on long-time personality development. Certainly if we have a civilization of compulsive neurotics it is due in no small part to our educational emphases.

This polemic might seem quite irrelevant to the purpose of a book designed to coordinate and interpret research; but it is against this background that one must look at the enormous quantities of research on school children and college students which have been carried out with a view toward discovering ways of getting more and better work in a given amount of time. Reward and punishment, praise and reproof, competition with others, competition with oneself, have all been the subject of repeated investigations, many of which have been concerned with learning in elementary school.

Actually the results of these experiments are by no means clear, and it has not been found possible to make any generalization that would hold good for any group of individuals in any situation. Sometimes praise stimulates better results; sometimes reproof does. A further confusion appears in the relation between the use of adult approval and the use of competition among children of the same age and grade.

In attempting to organize the material on social incentives in relation to achievement, one is apt to be impressed first of all by the research concerned with the effect of adult authority—as expressed through praise and reproof, reward or punishment—upon the elementary school child. Yet frequently "praise" and "reproof" consist largely of stimulus to competition through such phrases as "you did better than anyone else." For this reason, and because competition is usually competition for rewards or praise or approval of authorities, it became necessary to consider these groups of materials together. But while "praise and reproof" studies are largely confined to elementary school children, investigations of competition are carried out at all levels to adulthood. It seems sound, then, to consider in relation to each other these different aspects of motivation in the individualistic society.

The following diagram suggests the functional relations between these adult-child and child-child pressures:

Diagram of Authority-Competition Process

Individualistic society implies importance of individual child and individual parent-child relation. ——> Creates dependence of child upon parents' exclusive approval or preference.

Child transfers to teacher the relation of dependence upon adult approval. ——> Teacher gives approval for being "good," doing best work; this stimulates competition with other children.

Child transfers to other group situations the competitive attitude developed in the teacher-child relation.

The process is intensified the more the child feels he must "earn" parents' approval and love.

Even if we grant the intimate dynamic relation between approval from adults and competition with one's own age group, it is reasonable to expect that differences in emphases might be accompanied by different results in terms of better or poorer work. Let us return for the moment to possible explanations of the indecisive results from the use of praise and reproof.

The confusion which comes from conflicting results may be decreased if we consider the implications of one study of basic importance, the work of Féré on dynamogenesis, showing experimentally that any stimulus actually increases work; for example, a strong light or sound will throw extra energy into the system. Ordinarily in our studies of particular incentives this element is not controlled. A variety of extraneous elements are present in almost any experimental situation, some of which may be more stimulating than the stimulus which we are supposed to be studying. Quite closely related to this fact is the fact that an objective similarity in the quality and quantity of stimuli actually involves subjective differences for individual subjects. What is reproof enough barely to stimulate a fairly hard-boiled youngster might cause great fumbling in another, or in another result in cramping from over-effort. One personality may accept reproof with *naïve* suggestibility, where another may say inwardly, "I certainly did not do badly on that job." A fighting mechanism aroused in a lethargic child may be helpful to increased work, where it might be demoralizing to a more susceptible child. Similarly, praise may create security in some people which would stimulate them to do more efficient work, whereas it would put others under a strain to keep up a reputation that had been made, and in others it might lead to a sense of freedom from responsibility.

This gives rise to a consideration of personality factors in relation to the problem. These are tied up not only with the situation inherent in the receiving of praise and reproof as such, but also in habits of response to certain kinds of personalities. Usually the praise and reproof are administered by a single person, but the same person will appear in very different ways to two individuals. One child is inspired by the teacher whom another child abominates. In order to respond to praise, one must respect the person who is giving it ordinarily; and if this person happens to have points in common with one's ideal, the praise may be taken much more seriously than it is when no such identification is felt.

Praise, moreover, means quite a variety of things. It may mean prestige in class or on the field, or greater recognition from the teacher. It may be interpreted to express a positive response that implies some affection, so that a child responds in terms of doing what the substitute mama says; or he may accept it in a fairly utilitarian way, indicating the possibility of obtaining some privilege or material reward.

In all of these instances we have assumed that praise will elicit some positive response from everyone. This assumption, that everyone is motivated by prestige, may in itself not be entirely sound. Even if it is, there certainly are many prestige-hounds to whom distinction or flattery is much more important than it is to others.

These considerations apply solely to the assumptions underlying any experiments with praise or reproof. We shall discuss a little later some further problems arising in connection with the detailed set-up of experiments even when these fundamental considerations are kept in mind. For the moment the questions we have raised must point toward the need for a more basic step before any experiments at all are undertaken. This step is the formulation of a series of hypotheses regarding the underlying mechanisms which may be important in responses to praise or reproof. Such a formulation should include experimental work and should give a perspective which would make it possible for individual pieces of research to supplement each other constructively instead of producing a hopeless confusion.

It seems to be clear that a stimulus which throws extra sugar into the blood will thereby release more energy and result in increased capacity for effort and attention. It also seems to be true that strong stimuli which are extremely exciting may result in disorganization and disruption of previously smooth activity. These facts are quite easily understandable in terms of what we know regarding the functions of the glands, the autonomic nervous system and the thalamus in human behavior. A number of factors from another direction also need to be taken into account. Psychoanalysts have commented on personality structures such as the masochistic, to whom standards, responsibilities, punishment are important.

We have, then, two lines of development. In the first place, the degree of stimulus may be very important; and this, of course, means the stimulus as seen by the subject, not by the experimenter, for it is designed in terms of that degree which is stimulating without being disrupting, and this is an individual matter. The other angle of approach is that of personality structure. Here it seems possible to assume that some personalities respond actively more to praise, whereas others respond more to reproof, and perhaps completely different personalities respond more to material rewards. If these lines of approach are to be taken seriously, they suggest that what we need to do is to rephrase our question quite fundamentally, so that we do not now ask, "Does praise or reproof produce better work?" Rather we should state the question, "With what kind of personality is praise or reproof most likely to be stimulating, and in what form and amount will it be most effective?"

In other words, our problem resolves itself into a matter of the relationship between the individual personality and the situation. When we come to generalizations on the basis of the evidence collected in answer to questions which are put this way, we may be able to say that in a given culture area the predominant personality type responds to certain forms and degrees of praise or reproof in a given way. But even so, we must bear in mind that such concrete matters as the techniques which the teacher uses to get results from her pupils, and her attitude toward the value of the results thus stimulated, are fundamentally tied up with basic tendencies in our culture.

Our comment on the necessity of understanding the physiological value of the stimulus used in "praise" or "reproof" (or some other irrelevant stimulus) applies equally well to situations involving competition with others. And the suggestion that praise and reproof may have different values for different types of personality applies with special cogency to those many forms of "competition" in which the individual is striving to win something that has meaning to him, not necessarily the same thing that some other child or the experimenter has defined as "the" goal.

All of the experimental work attempting to analyze the effects of praise and reproof or of competition was until recently carried out without any reference to the values or meanings of the situation to the individual child and its relation to his own personality. This subjective aspect of the problem has been analyzed more fully in the research on aspiration level discussed earlier in this chapter. It will be recalled that the experiences of success and failure depended on the level of aspiration, which in turn was influenced to a degree by the ability of the individual. Very hard and very easy tasks cause no sense of success or failure. When the aspiration level is too far above the ability, difficulties arise. When it is too far below, achievement is not likely to reach the standard which one would expect from the individual. Aspiration that is too far above or below the ability (sometimes caused by comparing oneself with others) is likely to be tied up with feelings of inferiority or superiority. Success or failure affects in turn the level of aspiration and subsequent relations between the aspiration level and the level of ability. The level of aspiration in relation to the level of ability of the individual and his own feelings of inferiority or superiority may be seen as the cumulative effect of past responses to achievement and to attitudes of praise or criticism, satisfaction or dissatisfaction, that have been met. The term, then, defines a condition in the subject which is quite as important as the distinctions between praise and reproof, reward and punishment, competition, etc., which are set up in the external situation. And doubtless as we bring together these two approaches we shall find that more dependable generalizations may be reached if we take into consideration these variables in relation to one another: (1) the ability of the individual; (2) aspiration level; (3) characteristic pattern of response to success and failure, praise and reproof, etc.; (4) specific factors of praise and reproof, reward or punishment, used in the experiment.

We might even find that a comparatively simple formula would encompass the actual findings. Given an individual not working up to capacity, whose aspirations were high but not beyond the possibility of achievement, who responded to punishment or criticism, improvement would follow upon suitable use of criticism or punishment by an acceptable authority. Similarly, given an individual whose aspiration level was high in relation to ability, who had already reached the limit of his ability, neither criticism nor praise would achieve noticeable effects as far as increase in accomplishment in the specific task was concerned. Given an individual whose aspiration level was high, who was dependent upon praise, achievement would probably improve in response to praise within the limits of his ability. The question, then, how large a proportion of any sample of children or adults is more stimulated to improve work as a result of praise or reward, as compared with those who are more stimulated by punishment or reproof, would be answered in terms of the proportion of personalities in this cultural sample conditioned to each technique. One way of testing this might be to compare the responses of children in a highly authoritarian situation where punishment was the rule, with children from a "progressive" school who had known encouragement and objective criticism more than punishment or negative discipline in any form. It is of course possible that in the long run the world over, one might find that incentives based upon fear produced more immediate responses. Quite apart from the long-time aspects or effects of methods which exploit fear, their actual value is certainly not clear even for immediate purposes and is probably dependent upon early conditioning in a given culture.

Closely related to the simple biological incentive of fear and to the psychological phenomenon of aspiration are the feelings of inferiority or insecurity common in our society. We have already seen that these may be very important in relation to certain *kinds of aggression which develop as a compensatory effort to lift oneself out of unacceptable situations*. The importance of feelings of inferiority and insecurity in relation to social behavior has given rise to extended discussion by Adler, and also by members of the Freudian group who are likely to emphasize the sense of deprivation of love as of most fundamental importance. According to Adler, every infant must feel inferior and dependent for a period. In addition, any physical defect, whether marked or superficial, may provide a basis for feelings of inferiority. *Of Human Bondage* is a classic development of the experience of a person whose physical defect and sensitiveness to the attitudes of others provided the essential theme of a life.

If we were to make a study of the development of the experience of inferiority and superiority of the average person in our culture from infancy to adulthood, we might find verification of a pattern of this sort based upon everyday observation of children:

0-18 months:

Objective dependence apparently not accompanied by marked feelings of inferiority or inadequacy, probably because perception has not developed to the point which makes the child aware of difficulties and possibilities of dangers. (Empirical evidence for the absence of fear of snakes, the dark, wild animals, etc., at this age would be somewhat relevant.)

18-24 months:

A sense of inadequacy, accompanied by overt "shyness," is reported by Shirley and by Washburn. This may be due to the ratio between the child's expanding perception through the growth of language and his inability to cope with the new possibilities of which he becomes aware. He may be very conscious of his status as a baby in relation to big children or grown-ups.

2 to 4 years:

Marked superiority feelings toward "babies." Apparent awareness of the vast gap between the world of people who can walk and talk and those (from the adult point of view not so distant) not yet able to handle the world in these terms. At this age also a sense of inferiority to big children who skate and ride bikes and who stay up late or do not have to take naps. Great eagerness to "do it myself," to gain emancipation from feelings of dependence or inferiority.

4 to 8 years:

Marked increase in conscious inferiority-superiority feelings stimulated by two aspects of intellectual developments:

1. Awareness of numbers, money, size, age, etc. (space-time concepts) often accompanied by considerable competition in these terms.

2. The development of imagination, opening new possibilities for fear and anxiety, which are likely to be reflected in feelings of dependence and inferiority. (Jersild's study of fears showed increase of imagination, fear of the dark, etc., during this period.)

From 8 to 18 years:

The child rapidly becomes the subject of a large variety of institutionalized stimuli to inferiority and superiority feelings. "Marks" in school, parties, election to offices, comparing of dates, allowances, income level, family status, as indicated by the house he lives in, the clubs his parents belong to, whether or not he can afford to go to camp for the summer, competition in athletics, all give relatively objective stamps which place the child in a hierarchy of social standings and personal achievement of popularity. The long-time social effects which feelings like this characteristically develop in our culture are not yet brought within the scope of scientific social psychology except for the end results at the college or adult level when inferiority feelings and neurotic tendencies are scaled by personality inventories (cf. Chapter XII).

At each period the particular inferiorities of that level bring their own modes of compensation or escape; these are repressed or encouraged in turn by the approvals and disapprovals of adult authority.

All through elementary and high school a contradictory collection of pressures is brought to bear on the young. On the one hand, children are expected to be quietly acquiescent to adult authority, doing as they are told, completing conventional, set assignments that may be relatively meaningless, too easy or too hard for the individual. They are taught to be kind, friendly, not to tease and not to retaliate. The modern term "cooperative" as used by adults in relation to children is little more than a synonym for "obedient." Being "nice" is important; and overt competitiveness, showing-off, aggression and attention-getting are discouraged. At the same time, there is constant and assiduous stimulation of competitive behavior by the same adults. Being popular or being a leader is frequently just as important for school and even parental approval as doing good work; sometimes more so. One college student recently commented that in her preparatory school as she now saw it, with one hand the principal spanked the children out of overt competition and aggression, and with the other spanked them into a more intense and frequently destructive form.

AUTHOR DATE	TOPIC	SUBJECTS	METHODS
Bathurst, J. E. (1933)	Resistance and sympathy.	73 (36 boys, 37 girls), 18 to 66 mos. Children in the city of Birmingham.	Behavior records of resistance, sympathy in a standard situation telling the child a story designed to elicit a sympathy response.
Beaver, A. P. (1932)	Aggressiveness.	32; 26 to 45 mos. Children of Child Development Institute, N. Y. High I.Q. and socio-economic status.	Time-sampling observation of free play for 5-minute periods.
Bender, L., and Schilder, P. (1936)	Aggressiveness.	83 (49 boys, 34 girls), 3 to 15 yrs. Patients at Children's ward of Bellevue Psychiatric Hospital. In general, below normal intelligence.	Questionnaire on aggressiveness. And for some, behavioral situations were used to supplement the questions.
Berne, E. V. C. (1930)	Ascendance, rivalry, etc.	132; 2 to 4 yrs. Iowa nursery-school children.	Rating scales and time-sampling observations of paired children.
Bernstein, S., and Budnick, F. (1934)	Aggressiveness.	15; 9 boys, 6 girls, 5 to 10 mos. Brooklyn Nursery and Infants Hospital. 7 were foundlings, the rest private and public charges.	Paired observations in a crib; case study analyses.
Bott, E. A., Blatz, W. E., Chant, N., and Bott, H. (1928)	Resistance and interference.	15; 2 to 5 yrs. Nursery-school children.	Standardized diary observations.

Girls showed more resistance than boys. The possession of pets seemed to decrease resistance somewhat. Environment did not seem to affect resistance in any way significantly. Resistance decreased significantly with increase in age. As sympathy increased, resistance decreased. Chronological age, as well as the possession of pets, had a much greater effect upon both resistance and sympathy than did environment.

Distinct tendency for number of contacts to increase with age (r of .69). Aggressiveness indicated by the larger proportion of contacts initiated as compared with number of contacts received (subject-object ratio). A tendency for number of adult contacts to decrease as number of children contacts increase (r is −.44).

Aggressiveness finds expression more directly in younger children, in actions as well as in play, in words, and in the description of pictures. Deprivation of food or love increases the aggressive tendencies of children. The youngest age groups express their aggressiveness freely, verbally and in play; but the older age groups are inclined to be inhibited, and often a play situation or other indirect method by which they can unconsciously express their aggressiveness in the idea of punishment of others for their sins is needed. Aggressiveness against a group is expressed more freely than aggressiveness against single individuals.

3- and 4-yr.-olds surpass the 2-yr.-olds in rivalry, jealousy, ascendance, and related traits.

Tendencies toward aggressiveness and submissiveness exist even at these age levels. However, the majority of the children cannot be classified as being always either definitely aggressive or submissive. Correlations of aggressiveness (rank-difference): with C.A., .68; with social awareness, .37 (not reliable); with I.Q., .68; with general activity, .85; with responsiveness, −.32.

Of over 800 observed incidents, 201 refer to interference. Most incidents refer to talking (406).

AUTHOR DATE	TOPIC	SUBJECTS	METHODS
Bott, H. M. (1934)	Aggressiveness.	28 (9 girls, 19 boys), 27 to 59 mos. High I.Q. and socio-economic status.	Time-samplings during outdoor free play for 15-min. periods.
Caille, R. K. (1933)	Resistance.	36; 18 to 45 mos. Children at Child Development Institute, N. Y. High I.Q. and socio-economic status.	Time sampling observations of free play for 5-min. periods; analysis of stenographic records of language; resistant behavior when taking the Merrill-Palmer and Kuhlmann-Binet intelligence tests.
Dawe, H. C. (1934)	Quarrelsomeness.	40 (19 girls, 21 boys) 25 to 60 mos. Nursery-school children at Institute of Child Welfare, Minneapolis. Median I.Q. 106. Slight tendency to represent higher occupational groups.	Time sampling observations during free-play quarrels.
Ezekiel, L. F. (1931)	Aggressiveness.	(Not given.)	Observation of free play in a nursery school.
Fisher, M. S. (1934)	Negativism.	72; 22 to 60 mos. Children from Child Development Institute, N. Y. High I.Q. and socio-economic status.	Analysis of stenographic records of children's speech.

Commands, requests, and criticisms positively correlated with age. The following rank-difference correlations obtained: verbal contacts initiated and received, .81; motor contacts initiated and received, .88; verbal plus motor contacts initiated and received, .91; passive contacts initiated and received, .61.

Tendency to resist children more than adults is evident in the observation and language study, but less marked in the intelligence test performance. All 3 methods show peak of resistance near the third birthday; 3-yr.-olds resist about twice as frequently as 2-yr.-olds. With few exceptions, resistant behavior records do not correlate in the 3 methods. Boys tend to resist more than girls on all 3 methods. Observation study: children showed the same amount of resistance whether they played indoors or outdoors. All correlations obtained between various factors of behavior are positive, but mostly low (highest, r of .63 between resistance to adults and acquiescence to adults; next, r of .56 between vocal resistance to adults and vocal resistance to children). Language study: Place makes no difference in resistance behavior. R of .59 between resistance to adults and resistance to children.

Av. duration of quarrels, 23 sec. Quarrels of older children last longer, but a tendency for fewer of them. Boys quarrel more frequently and are more aggressive during quarrels than girls. A slight negative relation between I.Q. and frequency of quarreling. Youngest children start the most quarrels but take the less aggressive rôle during the quarrel. As children grow older aggressiveness and retaliation increase. The majority of quarrels are started by a struggle for possession. Children settle the majority of the quarrels themselves.

Those children who are dominantly egocentric on entrance into a new social situation make few significant changes during the first 3 mos. but the unaggressive children become more egocentric in their play, changing from the unaggressive to the aggressive.

Percentage of commands in total remarks increased rapidly with age, with a definite peak at the end of 4th year. Girls tended to give more commands than boys did. Positive relationship between proportion of negative sentences among all sentences and increase in age (r of .71). This proportion of negative sentences seemed to be an easily attainable objective criterion of degree of resistance or negativism.

SOME STUDIES OF

AUTHOR DATE	TOPIC	SUBJECTS	METHODS
Foster, S. (1927)	Jealousy.	150 (50 jealous, 100 non-jealous) 1 to 12 yrs. Children from Boston habit clinics representing various socio-economic levels and racial groups.	Case study analysis.
Goodenough, F. L. (1929)	Resistance.	990; 18 mos. to 6 yrs.; representing 3 different occupational groups in Minneapolis.	Rated child on 3-point scale for negativism on each of the year-levels on Kuhlmann-Binet or Minnesota Pre-School Tests.
Goodenough, F. L., and Leahy, A.M. (1927)	Aggressiveness.	Almost 300, from 5½ to 6 yrs. I.Q. and social status above average. From Demonstration Child Guidance Clinic in Minneapolis and St. Paul. Kindergarten children.	Position in family known. Children were rated on various traits.
Green, E. H. (1933) (a)	Quarrelsomeness.	40 Minnesota nursery-school children (21 boys, 19 girls), 25 to 65 mos. Mean I.Q. 108.	Time-sampling observation, 30 seconds a day for 40 days.
Green, E. H. (1933) (b)	Quarrelsomeness.	40 Minnesota nursery-school children (21 boys, 19 girls), 25 to 65 mos. old. Mean I.Q. 108.	Time-sampling observations, 30 seconds a day for 40 days.
Hanfmann, E. (1935)	Dominance.	Ten 5-yr.-old kindergarten children at Worcester State Hospital.	Paired comparison of boys playing freely with colored blocks, two observers. Repeat-pairings with other play material for a check.

AGGRESSION IN CHILDREN (*Continued*)

FINDINGS

The jealous child more likely to be a girl between 3 and 4 yrs. old, often the oldest child; likely to be independent and selfish, pugnacious, demanding attention. Hyperactivity, destructiveness, food capriciousness, disturbances of sleep, and enuresis also likely to characterize the jealous child.

Boys exhibited more negativism than girls, but social difference was more important. Boys in upper occupational classes showed tendency to greater negativism than girls, but girls of lower occupational classes showed tendency to greater negativism. Negativism decreases with age, particularly between 2 and 4.

Oldest children tended to lack aggressiveness, leadership, and self-confidence. Middle children showed a tendency to lack aggressiveness, but slightly less than the oldest children. Youngest children showed no marked tendency in either extreme. Only children showed most aggressiveness and self-confidence.

Friendship and quarrelsomeness correlated .30. Close friends most quarrelsome. Boy groups most quarrelsome, boy-girl groups next, and girl-girl groups least.

3-yr.-olds most quarrelsome (not statistically significant). Children under 30 mos. least often aggressors and most often passive, and those over 54 mos. least often retaliative. Older children more likely to employ verbal behavior; younger more likely to employ physical "spatial" behavior. Boys quarreled more than girls. Sand play (of 11 activities) was the most contentious activity.

A hierarchy order of dominance formed with 9 children. The order perfect from E to I, but not perfect from A to E, indicating that dominance does not mean the same thing in all cases. Different types of dominance patterns discovered in the first five. A destructive, but loses his dominance when absorbed by the play interest. B an oppressor and uses primitive methods of force. C an objective leader, more interested in the play itself. D a

AUTHOR DATE	TOPIC	SUBJECTS	METHODS
Hattwick, B.W. (1936) (a)	Aggressiveness.	212 nursery-school children in Chicago, 2 to 5 yrs. old.	Ratings on 60 behavior items.
Hattwick, B.W. (1936) (b)	Aggressiveness.	335 (171 girls, 164 boys), 23 to 68 mos. old. 146 of American white descent, 100 of Negro parents, and 69 of foreign extraction. A slight tendency to come from higher occupational levels.	Ratings on factors in the home, and pre-school behavior.
Hicks, J. A., and Hayes, M. (1933)	Aggressiveness.	157 junior high school pupils in Albany, N. Y. Med. I.Q. and E.Q., 113.	Verbal responses classified during classroom discussions of 20 min. time units.
Jack, L. M. (1934)	Ascendancy.	18 four-yr.-old Iowa nursery-school children.	Time-sampling observation of paired children behind a one-way screen, 5-min. periods.
Jersild, A.T., and Markey, F. V. (1935)	Conflict behavior.	54: 22 to 50 mos. old. Of these, 36 from Child Development Institute, of higher socio-economic status than 18 from Manhattan-ville Day Nursery. All above average in I.Q.	Time-sampling records, ten 15-min. periods. 24 followed up a year later and observed in the same way; 12 of these followed up when they entered kindergarten.

FINDINGS

social leader. He is interested in playing with others. He is diplomatic. E does not control others, but plays as he wishes, and does not permit others to control him. The type of dominance exhibited by A and B is not liked by the other children and leads to conflicts. The type of dominance exhibited by C and D is constructive, leads to harmonious play and is preferred by the other children.

The following tendencies found in children who attended nursery school for a longer time than another group: avoids play with others less, does not give in too easily, tends to refuse to share less, grabs toys less, attacks others less.

Children whose homes reflect over-attentiveness are liable to display infantile, withdrawing types of reaction. A positive relation between inadequate attention in the home and aggressive types of behavior, but at the same time these children feel insecure.

Pupils of higher I.Q., E.Q., and more "pleasing" personality exhibited more "desirable" aggressiveness and less "undesirable" aggressiveness in discussions than the others. Boys more aggressive than girls in both "desirable" and "undesirable" ways. Age differences not marked, but there was a tendency for older pupils to be less aggressive than younger ones.

Social responsiveness correlates with ascendance .65. Resistance to adult authority correlates with ascendance .56. Lack of self-confidence associated with non-ascendance. By specific training designed to increase self-confidence, children became more ascendant than those who received no such training.

Conflicts occur frequently (about once every 5 minutes) and are of short duration (20 to 30 seconds). Some tendency for decline of conflicts with age, but an increase in duration of conflicts. Boys more conflicts than girls, but a function of contacts rather than sex. Group of the lower socio-economic status exhibited more conflicts. Some evidence for a relation between sympathy and conflict behavior. A positive relation between practically all aspects of combative behavior (for example, between frequency of child's aggression on others and number of times he was victim of aggression, no. of times was winner and no. of times loser). In follow-up study found an increase in number of conflicts. In general, a high degree of consistency in individual behavior for both conflicts and frequency of aggression. In kindergarten follow-up, found a marked increase of conflict behavior probably due in part to relaxation of teacher restraints. Teachers interfered in conflicts 32% of time. Most of the time decided in favor of the child who was victim of aggression. A positive, but not high, relation between children's conflicts with other children, and conflicts with teachers (.47, .08 and .73 rank-diff. correlations for 3 groups).

AUTHOR DATE	TOPIC	SUBJECTS	METHODS
Koch, H. L. (1933)	Aggressiveness.	17 four-yr.-olds (8 boys, 9 girls). All nursery-school children.	Children indicate preferences by paired-comparison method. Behavior data obtained by observation methods. Personality traits from Merrill-Palmer personality scales.
Kumin, E. (1933)	Conflict behavior.	18 Child Development Institute children, 21 to 33 mos. old. I.Q.'s range from 90 to 159.	Time-sampling observations during free-play period. Timed in 30-sec. intervals.
Levy, D. M. (1936)	Aggressiveness.	33 boys selected from 1000 cases at the Institute for Child Guidance. Median I.Q. about 115; 7 yr. 5 mo. to 19 yrs. old.	Case study analysis.
Levy, D. M., and Tulchin, S. H. (1923)	Resistance.	983 children, 3 to 63 mos. old, from 5 county fairs at rural towns in Illinois.	Behavior records while taking the Kuhlmann or Stanford-Binet intelligence tests.
Marston, L. R. (1925)	Resistance, self-assertion, compliance.	100 nursery-school children, 2 to 6 yrs. old.	Ratings of children and observations of behavior in standardized situations.
Mayer, B. A. (1935)	Negativism.	136 boys, 141 girls, 18 mos. to 5½ yrs. old. Random sample according to socio-economic status; from San Francisco, Vermont, and White Plains, N. Y.	Records of behavior while taking the new revision of Stanford-Binet.

Traits negatively correlated with popularity: tendency to attack, to escape, to offer no resistance when attacked, to dawdle, to refuse and ignore, and to play alone. Traits positively correlated with popularity: compliance, respect for property rights, tendency to ask for commendation, tendency to tattle. Correlation of ascendance-submission (Merrill-Palmer rating) with popularity, .29.

Victims won more conflicts than the aggressors, possibly because aggressors felt they were doing something that was not right. Teachers aided the victims in most instances. Conflicts lasted longer in teacher-child conflicts than in child-child. Girls more often victims than boys. No relationship between the number of conflicts a child initiated and the number of times he was victimized, or between number of conflicts a child lost and the number of times he was a victim in a conflict. There was a relation between the number of conflicts initiated and the number of conflicts both initiated and won. The less intelligent, taller, older, heavier children seemed to win the greatest number of conflicts. Weight seemed to be the most pronounced of these influences.

Majority of cases with Fröhlich syndrome found to be submissive, indicating submissive behavior is determined by constitutional factors. However, in special types of environment submissive factors can be overweighted by aggressive factors, regardless of the constitutional tendency.

Resistance to intelligence test performances first appears at the age of 6 mos., rises to a high point, falling to low level at 54 mos. High point for males occurs at 30 mos.; for girls, 18 mos. Females show most resistance at every age group except 30 mos.

Correlations of social resistance to a stranger: with non-compliance (boys .40, girls .23), with self-assertion (boys .33, girls .48). Non-compliance with self-assertion (boys .58, girls .49).

3 yrs., the peak of negativism. Under 3 yrs., most negativism is passive, and, of whatever type, not likely to be overcome. It becomes more active until 4½ yrs., after which it is largely passive and amenable to influence. A slight tendency for boys to be more negativistic than girls. Tests involving a verbal response to a purely verbal stimulus arouse the most negativism, being followed by tests requiring a verbal response to pictures, and tests requiring repetition. No apparent relation between difficulty of test and negativism toward it. More negativism likely to appear in 1st testing than in 2nd.

AUTHOR DATE	TOPIC	SUBJECTS	METHODS
Mengert, I. G. (1931)	Friendliness.	10 two-yr.-olds from Iowa Child Welfare Research Station.	Time-sampling of paired children behind one-way screen for 20-min. periods.
Mittelmann, B. (1936)	Aggressiveness-submissiveness.	16 4- to 13-yr.-olds exhibiting the Fröhlich syndrome.	Neurologic and psychopathologic diagnoses.
Moore, E. S. (1931)	Self-assertion.	44 2- to 4-yr.-olds. American-born, mostly of professional and student class; from the Iowa Child Welfare Research Station.	Observations under standardized conditions; ratings; daily observation; visits to the home.
Murphy, L. B. (forthcoming)	Sympathy and aggressiveness.	55 2- to 4-yr.-olds, Child Develop. Inst., N.Y.	600 hours' observation; teachers' ratings; experiments; parent conferences.
Nelson, J. F. (1929)	Resistance.	28 18- to 48-mos.-old children at Institute of Child Welfare Research. Median I.Q. 124.	Analysis of records of resistant behavior while taking the Merrill-Palmer and Kuhlmann-Binet intelligence tests.
Page, M. L. (1936)	Ascendance-submission.	107 2- to 4-yr.-olds of two groups: one of high I.Q. and socio-economic status, the other with low I.Q. and socio-economic status.	Observations of paired children in a play situation behind a one-way screen. Children were given special training in specific tasks and then observed again in the same situation.
Radina, S. I. (1930)	Aggressiveness.	84 boys, 53 girls, 3 to 7 yrs. old. Children entering kindergarten; half were children of laborers; other half, of servants.	Qualitative observation study.

AGGRESSION IN CHILDREN (*Continued*)

FINDINGS

More friendliness exhibited than unfriendliness. Considerable consistency of individual behavior. Negative correlation between total overt friendly behavior manifested by the subject and total overt friendly behavior manifested toward him by the rest of the group (rank-diff. r −.60). Correlation with I.Q., .90; with mental age, .29; with chronological age, −.49.

The syndrome, with its physiologic accompaniments, caused passive, submissive, overdependent behavior in some of the patients, and a strong oral trend manifested by overeating, nail-biting and chewing pencils. But the reaction of the total personality to organic deficiencies resulted in either a withdrawal and submissive adaptation or an aggressive, hostile adaptation. Both types of reaction represent attempts at compensation for narcissistic insults.

Attendance at nursery school and visits to the home effect less self-assertion. Very slight positive tendencies for children who had provision for a wholesome play life at home to have self-assertion at the pre-school.

r=.44 between aggressiveness, sympathy. Aggressiveness, unsympathetic responses greater in group with narrow age range. Variations related to security in different situations. Child's rôle in group, personality make-up reflected in aggression, sympathy.

Most resistance occurred at difficult tests. Most other instances of negativism occurred when the child was involved personally (imitation of movements, repetition of words, sentences or digits, naming parts of the body). Indicates that when the child is made self-conscious he will resist. Resistance tends to decrease with age and with increase of I.Q.

Experimental training, which aimed to increase self-confidence, shown to be effective in increasing the manifestations of ascendant behavior for non-ascendant and moderately ascendant children. These changes larger than those attributable to pre-school children. Also some indication of transfer for the trained subjects to behavior in free-play periods.

"Aggressiveness" includes crying and "refusal to come when told to come" (resistance). Aggressiveness appears upon entering kindergarten, tends to decrease with age.

AUTHOR DATE	TOPIC	SUBJECTS	METHODS
Reynolds, M. M. (1928)	Negativism.	255 New York nursery-school and Horace Mann children, 1 yr. 11 mos. to 5 yrs. 6 mos.	Records of negativism when taking Kuhlmann-Binet tests.
Ross, N. M. (1931)	Jealousy.	1275 3- to 16-yr.-olds, 166 of which are jealous. Cases from records of the Institute for Child Guidance, N. Y.	Case study analysis.
Rust, M. M. (1931)	Resistance.	100 34.5- to 37.5-mos.-old nursery-school children from Cornell, Washington, Vassar, and New York. Average I.Q. 132.	Records of resistant behavior when giving the Merrill-Palmer and Kuhlmann tests.
Schuler, E. A. (1935)	Dominance-submission.	Over 200 125- to 252-mos.-old Junior and Senior H. S. boys in Mass. Average I.Q. 109.	Ratings by teacher, student himself, parents; behavior in experimental pairings; and I.Q.'s.
Sewall, M. (1930)	Jealousy.	70 1- to 6-yr.-old clinic and nursery-school children in Chicago.	Clinic and nursery-school records and parent interviews.
Smalley, R. E. (1930)	Jealousy.	54 children, below 6 to over 12 yrs., from Cleveland and Philadelphia Demonstration Child Guidance Clinics. Studied in pairs (siblings).	Case study analyses, I.Q. and other available records.

AGGRESSION IN CHILDREN (*Continued*)

Negativism tends to decrease with age (r is .53). Tends to decrease with mental age (r is .48). No sex difference appeared. Educational backgrounds showed no decided effect on negativism scores.

Jealousy as a problem occurred most frequently between 3 and 6 yrs. of age. Associated with I.Q. positively. Occurred most frequently among the first-born. Negativism and fears significantly associated with jealousy. Girls tend to be more jealous than boys. Nagging mothers more frequent in the jealous than in the non-jealous group.

Tendency to resist more difficult tests more times than easy ones. Mental level of child, and interest-value of test important in relation to question of whether a test was resisted or not. Children objected more consistently to the demand that they repeat something said or done by experimenter than to any other type of test. A large proportion of refusals due to conflict of interests—child wished to do or say something else.

Tendency for boys, as age increases, to show an increasing differentiation of behavior as to dominant and submissive characteristics. For older boys there is a greater stability of basic behavior (dominant or submissive) patterns within a general environment, but at the same time it becomes less possible to predict such tendencies in another general environment.

Being told that another baby is coming does not necessarily prevent jealousy. Jealousy occurs most frequently when there is a sibling age difference of from 18 to 42 mos., with 2-child families rather than with larger families, with superior intelligence, and with maladjustment of homes.

Jealousy bore no relationship to age differences in sibling pairs; but related to I.Q. differences, jealousy increasing and protectiveness and friendliness decreasing with increase in difference in I.Q. Within the pairs, the older, when duller, were more likely to be jealous. Jealousy more frequent in the girl-girl pairs than the girl-boy.

AUTHOR DATE	TOPIC	SUBJECTS	METHODS
Smith, M. E. (1932)	Criticism.	2 to 6 yrs. old.	Speech of children analyzed for criticisms. Compared with criticisms made by adults.
Tilson, M. A. (1929)	Negativism.	225 patients at 7 habit clinics (110 boys, 115 girls), 1 to 5 yrs. old.	Case study record analysis.
Walker, C. (1937)	Dominance-feeling and behavior.	57 girls in N. J. private school, 3rd through 6th grades, mean I.Q. 109. High socio-economic status.	Self-ratings, ratings by fellow students, by teachers, of dominance. Observation of children in classroom and gymnasium. Interviews of extreme cases, 20 dominant and 10 non-dominant girls.
Weiss, L. A. (1931)	Resistance and compliance.	77 nursery-school children from Iowa Child Welfare Research Station; 29 to 68 mos. old.	Records of response of children to commands in different situations.
Williams, G. W., and Chamberlain, F. (1936)	Ascendance-submission.	259 high school girls in northwestern New York State. From typical rural districts, middle class. Ages, 10 to 20 yrs.	Allport A-S given.
Williams, H. M. (1936)	Ascendance-submission.	132 Iowa nursery-school children from 2 to 4 yrs.	Factor analysis of Berne's data.

Amount of criticism increased slightly but regularly from 2 to 5 yrs. At every age the unfavorable criticism exceeded the favorable. At first criticism was directed to another than the person concerned apparently for the purpose of securing help in a difficult situation, and partook of the nature of tattling; then directed to the person criticized. Adults showed a significant increase of favorable criticism.

Following coefficients of association with negativism: restlessness (boys), .51, emotional dependence, .55; masturbation, .67.

Ratings by others more reliable than self-ratings. Teachers' ratings correlated with ratings by others .55. There is a tendency for children coming from a higher socioeconomic level to be more dominant. Self-confidence seemed to be an accompaniment of feeling of dominance. Dominant girls tend to select dominant girls as friends, and non-dominant girls tend to select non-dominant girls. There is greater variability of dominance behavior than of dominance feeling. In extreme cases there is less variation of dominance feeling and behavior than in the middle group; this is particularly true for dominance feeling.

As children grew older, they tended to comply with the task with less substitute activity and forgetting, with fewer distractions of an external nature, and with fewer demands for repetition on the part of the experimenter. The toy situation was the most absorbing to the subjects.

There is a definite genetic development in this trait which parallels the characteristics of physical development in many respects. The range of variability in A-S is considerably less at adolescent level than at adult level.

Two factors were discovered: one representing approach-withdrawal, consisting of the following items: participates, cooperates, maternal, responsible, etc. The other factor may be called ascendance-submission, consisting of the following items: unselfish, not self-defensive, does not tease, ascendant, jealous, rivals, etc.

AUTHOR DATE	TOPIC	SUBJECTS	METHOD AND CONTROL
Brenner, B. (1934)	"Immediate" and "delayed" praise and blame.	403 III-Grade children (12 classes) from 3 N. Y. City schools. 192 after equating. Average age 8.5 yrs., slightly superior in intelligence.	6 groups, each with class of average, one of high I.Q. E showed list of difficult words from Ayres Scale for 4 min.; 2 min. to write all they recalled. "Immediate Praise" group praised after 2 min.; "Immediate Blame" group reproved after same time. "Delayed Praise" and "Delayed Blame" group praised or blamed after one day. On next school day procedure repeated: recall series, and learning of new set. 8 repetitions for "Immediate," 6 for "Delayed" groups. Also ratings on pleasantness of task by child; on child's acceptance by E, teacher. Control: "Immediate Control" and "Delayed Control" groups performed tasks similarly, without E's comment. Uniform procedure maintained. All groups equated in I.Q., C.A., spelling ability and initial test performance.
Briggs, T. H. (1927)	Praise and censure (reprimand, sarcasm, ridicule) .	(1) 370 graduate students at Teachers' College, Columbia; (2) unknown number of pupils of Speyer Experimental Junior High School, New York, N. Y.	(1) asked for retrospections about high school work under 21 conditions including those in Col. 2. (2) New type tests on 3 lessons given children by each of 2 teachers accustomed to use severity in his 4 classes. A then reprimanded his, threatened punishment. B commended, encouraged. On 2nd test, A praised, B scolded. 3rd day, final test given.
Briggs, T. H. (1928)	Sarcasm.	152 high school seniors, Aurora, Ill.	Questionnaire regarding actions following sarcasm on teacher's part, in public or in private.

PRAISE AND REPROOF

FINDINGS	INDIVIDUAL DIFFERENCES
In order of effectiveness, comparison of groups: Delayed Control, Immediate Blame, Delayed Praise. Effect of novelty very strong. Succeeding performances worse in all groups. Decline first in DP, DC, and DB: IP and IC next, IB last. Control groups drop in performance; incentive groups decline follows initial rise. Incentives given had no direct effect on children's attitude toward task.	E's judgment of children's attitude correlated .65 with performance. No relation found to intelligence or initial ability.

(1) Public reprimand caused 40% to do better, 46% to do worse; private reprimand, 83% to do better, 7% worse. Public sarcasm caused 10% to do better, 77% to do worse; private sarcasm, 18% to do better, 65% to do worse. Public ridicule caused 7% to do better, 69% to do worse; private ridicule, 21% to do better, 64% to do worse. Public commendation caused 91% to do better, 1% to do worse. (2) 87% "made better scores after commendation."

All in Col. 5.

Sarcasm in public caused 6.2% to do better, 29% to remain the same, 64.5% to do worse. Sarcasm in private caused 44.5% to do worse, 14.8% to remain the same, 40.7% to do worse. Sarcasm directed at others caused 16.2% to do better, 65.9% to remain the same, 17.9% to do worse.

All in Col. 5.

SOME STUDIES OF

AUTHOR DATE	TOPIC	SUBJECTS	METHOD AND CONTROL
Gates, G. S., and Rissland, L. Q. (1923)	Encouragement and discouragement.	74 college students.	3 groups, approximately equal in original ability. Individually given 2 trials on 3-hole test, color naming. Group 1, all Ss praised highly; group 2 reproved severely. Control: Group 3, no comment.
Gilchrist, E. P. (1916)	Praise and reproof.	50 educational psychology students.	All given Courtis English Test 4B. Random division into 2 groups. Group A reproved. Group B praised. Test repeated.
Hurlock, E. B. (1924)	Praise and reproof.	408 New York City school children: 141 Grade VIII, 132 Grade V, 135 Grade III. 62.9% white, 37.1% Negro. 51.4% boys, 48.6% girls.	3 groups, equated for I.Q., C.A., race, after taking NIT, Scale B, Form 1 or Otis Intelligence Scale, Form A. 1 week later had other form of test. Group 1 first severely reproved, given "another chance." Group 2 warmly praised. Control: Group 3 asked to take test again; no comment. At end of 2nd testing questionnaire given to determine how praise and reproof accepted.
Hurlock, E. B. (1925)	Praise, reproof, ignoring.	106 IV- and VI-grade children, Harrisburg, Pa., public school. 46 boys, 60 girls.	Courtis Research Test in arithmetic given on 5 days, 15 mins. each. 4 groups equivalent on C.A., 1st trial. Praise, reproof, and ignored groups *together*. Individuals in praised group called to front, praised highly. Similarly with reproved group. 3rd group ignored. 3rd group separated from others for last 4 trials: no comment.
Laird, D. A. (1923-A)	Various incentives, including public and private reprimands, sarcasm, ridicule, commendation.	92 educational psychology students, Univ. of Wyoming.	Retrospections of incentives used by H. S. teachers, and "impartial" estimates of their effects.

PRAISE AND REPROOF (*Continued*)

FINDINGS	INDIVIDUAL DIFFERENCES
Slight differences in average improvement. Encouraged group slightly superior to discouraged, both to control group.	Relatively poor Ss more likely to be unfavorably affected by discouraging than relatively proficient persons.
Group A gained 79%. Group B, no group improvement. (Group B 23% better than A on first test.)	Members of A who had done well did worse. Members of B who had done badly improved.
Order of effect: reproof, praise, control. Difference between praise and reproof not reliable. Questionnaire indicates praise and reproof were subjectively effective.	In Grade V, order: reproof, praise, control. In Grades III and VIII: praise, reproof, control. Praise and reproof least effective in youngest. Greater differences between control and praise and reproof for boys than girls. Reproof had most effect on "superior," less on "average," far less on "inferior" children; praise had least effect on "inferior," slightly more on "average" than "superior" ones. Whites more affected by practice and reproof; Negroes more by praise.
Praised group showed decided gain. Reproved and ignored groups, slight gain. Control group, slight loss. Increased accuracy found only in praised group. Reproof initially effective, but falls off in value.	Praise most effective incentive with all. "Inferior" group most responsive to praise, "superior" to reproof. Age differences caused no responsiveness differences. "Superior" individuals of both control and ignored groups fell off. Boys showed greatest *initial* improvement following reproof, girls following praise. Ultimately, praise most effective for both.
Public reprimand caused 26% to do better, 40% worse; private reprimand, 49% to do better, 12% worse. Public sarcasm, 10% to do better, 68% worse. Private sarcasm, 21% to do better, 30% worse. Public ridicule, 15% to do better, 36% worse, etc.	Slightly larger percentage of girls than boys favorably affected by public reprimand. 71% of girls improved after private reprimand; 27% of boys. Slightly more boys more favorably affected by public praise.

AUTHOR DATE	TOPIC	SUBJECTS	METHOD AND CONTROL
Laird, D. A. (1923-B)	Same as Laird, 1923-A.	Same as Laird, 1923-A.	Reports of incentives used by college instructors, and their effects.
Laird, D. A. (1923-C)	"Razzing."	Eight college fraternity pledges.	Tests of tapping speed, 3-hole test, steadiness sitting, steadiness standing. After normal level ascertained, each S "razzed" terribly during performance by future fraternity brothers. Earlier series for level of performance under conditions of "friendly competition."
Warden, C. J., and Cohen, A. (1931) (Columbia M. A. 1927)	Praise, reproof (self-competition). "Schoolroom incentives": game, special play period, story, party, etc.	38 IV-Grade children, Wellington, N. J. Average 10 yrs., range 9–13. 18 boys, 20 girls.	Equated sections of Thorndike Addition Sheets administered over 9-wk. period, 5 min. per day, with various incentives and "no incentives" periods distributed over 9 wks. Work omitted 5th and 8th weeks; various other days. Each incentive applied to entire group at a time. E was regular teacher. In "no incentive" periods told to do as well as possible; told had done better than previous day.
Wood, T. W. (1934)	Approbation and reproof.	30 college juniors, seniors, graduate students.	All learned list of 6 nonsense syllables. Then divided in 3 groups. 2 told task related to intelligence, either complimented, asked to repeat, or asked if can't do better on new series. PGR and introspections recorded. 3rd asked merely to repeat.

PRAISE AND REPROOF (*Continued*)

FINDINGS	INDIVIDUAL DIFFERENCES
Public reprimand caused 38% to improve, 30% to do worse; private reprimand, 67% to do better, 13% worse. Public sarcasm, 21% to do better, 51% worse. Private sarcasm, 28% to do better, 43% worse. Public ridicule, 29% to do better, 37% worse. Private ridicule, 44% to do better, 5% worse. Public praise, 84% to do better, 0% worse.	Sex differences noted in Laird 1923-A reduced in size here; not very significant.
All did worse under razzing in steadiness standing, 7 in steadiness sitting. Ss better in tapping and 3 better in 3-hole test under razzing. Steadiness reduced in all Ss, particularly when body muscles involved. Rate of tapping least affected.	No relation to intelligence, almost none to predictions by fraternity brothers. Some relationship to fatigue index in normal tapping. 3 Ss went to pieces only on steadiness tests; 3 on all tests; 5 on steadiness and 3-hole tests.
Average speed score under "non-incentive," 16.7; accuracy score, 8.7. Average speed score under all incentive conditions combined, 15.9; accuracy score, 9.4. Speed and accuracy scores for praise, 16.6, 10.7. Speed and accuracy scores for reproof, 15.5, 9.8. Best incentive, promise of game, 18., 9.5.	Differences between boys and girls insignificant.
Scores of control group, 1st and 2nd test, 19.6, 20.3. Approbation group, 20.7, 26.5. Reproof group, 20.8, 25.3. PGR differences not reliable.	7 of 10 Ss felt more confident after approbation. 6 of reproof group wanted to do better, 4 felt less confident, nervous. 5 of approbation group thought praise genuine, 3 thought it device for encouragement, 2 considered it a trick. 8 of 10 Ss thought reproof genuine, one amused, one indifferent.

AUTHOR DATE	TOPIC	SUBJECTS	METHOD AND CONTROL
Forlano, G. (for a committee) (1932)	Individual competition, and competition for various groups ("cooperation").	34 children in private language school, 19 boys, 15 girls. Median age 11 years, 9 months; median M.A., 12 years, 8 months; median school grade, VI.	Cancellation test. One min. practice, one min. working for individual prize, one min. for class honor, one min. for (a different) team honor (teams selected by two captains), one min. for inter-sex competition —no prize. Same repeated with rotation. Then three "free choice" tests—could work for self, class, team, sex.
Greenberg, P. J. (1932)	Competition (adult's challenge to competition).	Children between 2 and 7 in Vienna. 2–3 : 2 boys, 6 girls; 3–4 : 8 boys, 7 girls; 4–5 : 5 boys, 6 girls; 5–6 : 11 boys, 9 girls; 6–7 : 7 boys, 4 girls.	Children taken in pairs, invited to use building blocks. Both used same blocks. After finishing, asked which was prettier. Then given assignment to see who could build the prettier (sometimes the larger). Indices of competition: relation to material, remarks, posture, grabbing, answers to question, etc.
Hurlock, E. B. (1927)	Group rivalry.	155 IV- and VI-grade children.	Equated groups in arithmetic pitted against each other on modif. Courtis Res. Test in Arithmetic over 5-day period, 10 min. daily; competing groups told how they stood in comparison with rivals. Control class to care for practice effects.
Leuba, C. J. (1930)	Praise, rivalry, and rewards.	35 5A children, Syracuse, N. Y.; 11.3 years average age.	Following 10 min. preliminary practice and control series of 4 trials, 5 trials with promise of chocolate bar for doing required number of multiplication problems. After first 2 trials requirements consistently increased. In next series 2 control trials, then 3 with requirements impossible, then consistently lowered for 3 trials. In next trial, 3 homogeneous groups, competition to deter-

OF COMPETITION

FINDINGS	INDIVIDUAL DIFFERENCES
Order of effectiveness of incentives: sex, self, team, class. Differences slight, probably unreliable, but consistent in three classes.	No influence of C.A., M.A., or I.Q. on responsiveness to incentives.
Somewhat more evidence of competition in second situation (as shown by grabbing of blocks, remarks about other child's work, etc.).	Increase in competing children from 0% at 2–3, to 42.6% at 3–4, . . . 86.5% at 6–7. Children rarely consider others' work better—never that of a younger child. Experience no sense of competition with unfamiliar material. Apparently three types of children. First, strong desire to excel; second, calm, not violent in competition; third, not competitive at all.
Group rivalry greatly increased output of work, successful class becoming more and more successful. Rivalry group increased in accuracy; control group decreased.	Slight difference in favor of girls. Younger children responded more to rivalry. Children inferior in arithmetic showed most effect.
Practice level in control series fairly constant. Chocolate incentive resulted in 52% increase. Chocolate, rivalry, recognition and praise together gave 65% gain. Competition conditions alone: 47% rise.	Absolute differences decreased under incentive conditions. Boys improved more (had lower output before). Slower multipliers improved more than fast.

AUTHOR DATE	TOPIC	SUBJECTS	METHOD AND CONTROL
			mine captain and ranking in each. Finally, trial for selecting captain, and underlining name of individual with most improvement; both would also receive chocolate bars. Control: Following preliminary practice, control series with no incentives was run.
Leuba, C. J. (1933)	Rivalry (dynamogenesis).	26 children (6 retested) in Antioch College Nursery School; 2–6 years.	Children brought in singly, then in pairs; invited to put pegs in board. Observer behind screen and E noted performance in 5-min. period, verbal and behavioral responses. 6 children retested. Control: Period when alone (in presence of experimenter). Children later paired on basis of age, previous score. Practice only partially controlled by pre-experiment play with pegs. General policy of nursery school *not* to encourage rivalry.
Maller, J. B. (1929)	Class competition, voluntary team competition, partner competition, arbitrary group competition.	44 V- to VIII-grade classes. 1538 children, 8–17. Ten schools in East, rural and urban; of varying social and economic levels.	Used 1 x 1 place additions for 2 minutes. Exp. 1: For "self": told it was speed contest: prizes offered. Exp. 2: For "group": told to try hard to help win class prize. Class, not name written on sheet. Exp. 3: Seven 1-min. work units. Told to devote to self or class. Exp. 4: Voluntary teams. Exp. 5: Arbitrary groups. Control: Same work; children told practice in addition was involved. Represents minor motives of school situation, examiner's request, desire to work, etc. Practice controlled between two motives by alternating "self" and "class" work 6 times; 6 control groups given simple addition task without motivation

OF COMPETITION (*Continued*)

FINDINGS	INDIVIDUAL DIFFERENCES

See Col. 6.

First stage: 2-year-olds usually merely looked at other child. Second stage: 3- and 4-year-olds: variety of responses to other child including rivalry; generally lower output (for 9 of 13 Ss); only one slight rise. Third stage: 5-year-olds: rivalry dominant, almost all Ss showing marked rise in output. No noticeable sex differences.

Exp. 1 and 2: Reliable difference in favor of "self" motivation of 2.7 problems per minute. Group/self: .94. Work for self constant, rising; group work less constant, tends to decline sharply. s = self, practice work; g = group, practice work. s — 5.1; g = 2.3; g/s = .45. Difference increases with time. Exp. 3: Average choices made to work for self, 74%; for group, 26%. Slight tendency for decrease in appeal of working for group slower than for self. Where motives alternated, work curves diverge; where each continued alone, converge. Exp. 4: Team situation brought higher efficiency than self. Exp. 5: Arbitrary groups lower than class.

Girls scored lower for group than boys in speed tests. In free choice were more cooperative. Correlation with age: in least cooperative population, negative; in most cooperative population, positive. Correlation with intelligence positive, curvilinear. Positive r's with M.A., I.Q., moral knowledge, resistance to suggestibility, deportment, character ratings, honesty and inhibition tests, neurotic index. Negative correlations with speed of work, oscillation in speed, health, vision, nutrition, socio-economic status, movie attendance, weight-height ratio. Positive relation with other socialized behavior—helpfulness, charitableness, honesty, etc.

SOME STUDIES

AUTHOR DATE	TOPIC	SUBJECTS	METHOD AND CONTROL
			for 40 minutes. One of 6 given same task 5 days in succession. Experienced examiners, same directions.
Maller, J. B., and Zubin, J. (1932)	Rivalry (knowledge of results, prize).	42 children (no additional information).	After first administration of NIT, Scale B, Form 1, 2 groups equivalent in mean and sigma of C.A. and score were formed. Retested after 13 days. One group told standing; prize offered to each S who beat S just ahead. Control: Other group merely repeated test under same conditions as first time. Both groups retested on *same* form.
Sims, V. M. (1928) Exp. 1.	Self and individual vs. group competition ("dynamogenesis"— praise).	126 college sophomores and juniors. Reduced to 36.	After 3-min. practice in substitution test, 3 groups of 12, selected by taking trios with identical scores. Each group then worked 12 2-min. trials. Section I: control; only motivation seeing own and others' progress. Section II: group motivation; two groups about equal, competing, told averages before each session with high encouragement to both. Section III: individual competition, same procedure with individuals having roughly equal scores.
Sims, V. M. (1928) Exp. 2.	Same as Exp. 1.	76 college sophomores and juniors. Reduced to 45.	After 2 min., 40 sec., on Monroe Standardized Silent Reading Test, Form 2, 3 sections of 15 individuals selected as in Exp. 1. Each worked 12 3-min. periods reading three different types of material. Groups as above. Finally Form 3 of Monroe test given. Control: Section I (see Exp. 1).

OF COMPETITION (*Continued*)

FINDINGS	INDIVIDUAL DIFFERENCES
Experimental group's gain not reliably greater than control group's. Experimental group exerted more effort, as indicated by larger number of items attempted. Control group more accurate.	Variability increased markedly in experimental group, not in control group. Older children gained under incentive more than younger ones. In control group younger children improved more; superior children more than poorer ones, reverse being true of controls.
Percentage improvement: Section I, 102%; Section II, 109%; Section III, 157.7%.	None given.
Percentage improvement: Section I, 8.7%; Section II, 14.5%; Section III, 34.7%. Percentage change in ability to answer questions of Yes-No type on reading: Section I, 4%; Section II, 2.0%; Section III, 4.5%.	None given.

AUTHOR DATE	TOPIC	SUBJECTS	METHOD AND CONTROL
Sorokin, P. A., with Tanquist, M., Parten, M., and Zimmerman, C. C. (1930)	Individual and collective, equal and unequal remuneration; competition.	Unspecified (small) number pre-school children in Univ. of Minnesota Child Welfare Clinic. 3 H. S. boys 13–14 yrs. old. Unspecified (small) number kindergarten children. 202 Univ. of Minnesota students.	Exp. 1. Task: to carry cups of sand or marbles to certain point, empty cups, repeat. 1 series per day for 8 days, 33 min., 30 sec., in all. Alternate days worked for individual remuneration (toys to take home) and collectively (toys played with together, left in school). Pre-school children. Exp. 2. Same children, working as co-workers alternately for self or partner (very good friend). 6 trials, totaling 16 min. Exp. 3. 202 students responding to appeals for (a) funds for class materials, (b) funds for poor Minnesota students, (c) funds for needy Chinese, Russian students. Exp. 4. Marbles, sand tasks as before; also picking out balls from box containing other forms. Pre-school children. 52 min. all told. Alternating equal and unequal remuneration; latter dependent on amount of work each member of group did. Same system with H. S. boys: task. filling pails with water or sand, carrying them. Exp. 5. Equal and unequal remuneration; manual task, carrying marbles; and "mental" task, picking pegs out of box with other forms. Kindergarten group. Exp. 6. Equal remuneration and no remuneration (pure competition), using all groups except college. Control: No control series or group; rotation of series to compare various conditions, eliminate practice, fatigue. In each experiment total remuneration under each condition is the same.

OF COMPETITION (*Continued*)

FINDINGS	INDIVIDUAL DIFFERENCES

Exp. 1. Total work units (both tasks): group remuneration, 115; individual, 132. Exp. 2. Total work: self-remuneration, 232; for friend, 212. Exp. 3. Class, $48; Minnesota boys, $33; Chinese and Russians, $22. Exp. 4. Pre-school. Total work units: equal remuneration, 1300; unequal, 1480. High school. Equal remuneration, 295; unequal, 388. Exp. 5. Total manual work: equal remuneration, 1256; unequal, 1286. Total mental work: equal remuneration, 2872; unequal, 2958. Exp. 6. Pre-school. Equal remuneration, 104.5; pure competition, 108. High school, equal remuneration, 16.5; pure competition, 18. Kindergarten, equal remuneration, 2862; unequal, 2958; competition, 2668. Unequal remuneration brought greater output, caused "unrest," "strikes."

SOME STUDIES

AUTHOR DATE	TOPIC	SUBJECTS	METHOD AND CONTROL
Triplett, N. (1898)	Competition, "dynamogenesis."	40 children, 8–17 yrs.	Children in pairs rotating 2 fixed reels which moved little flags; purpose, to move own flag to end before rival's. Control: 20 children worked alternately, competitively and alone; 20 alternated 6 trials alone with 6 trials competitively.
Vaughn, J. (1936)	"Homogeneous" and "heterogeneous" competition.	10 Ss of wide range of shooting ability.	Condition 1. Homogeneous competition. Ss' abilities in target shooting equated by handicaps. Condition 2a. Heterogeneous. Premium on high initial score; told highest score wins. Condition 2b. Heterogeneous. Premium on low initial score; greatest improvement wins. Worked 1 hour a day, 1 day a week, for 12 weeks. 7th, 8th, and 9th weeks competitive, each S working under each condition 20 min. with proper rotation. Control: First 6 weeks and last 3 noncompetitive practice periods.
Whittemore, I. C. (1924)	Dynamogenesis, individual competition, group competition.	12 college students: 4 Radcliffe women, 8 Harvard men. Average age, 24.	3 groups, each together 1 hr. twice a week. Printed material with rubber stamps. Told to do best to beat fellows. 4 tests of 5 min. each. Also competition of groups of 3 or 4, groups not working simultaneously. Control: Same, still together, around table. Told not to compete, but urged to do their best. Series rotated to eliminate practice.
Whittemore, I. C. (1925)	Competition (conscious attitudes accompanying).	12 college students as in Whittemore (1924).	Ss printed with rubber stamps (as in Whittemore, 1924). Asked after each competitive test whether conscious of com-

OF COMPETITION (*Continued*)

FINDINGS	INDIVIDUAL DIFFERENCES
Competition resulted in great stimulation.	20 of the children worked faster in competition, 10 did worse, and 10 did equally well. Those who did worse held to be overstimulated to point of coordination interference. Young, nervous, excitable children showed most ill effects of overstimulation.
See Col. 6.	7 Ss show facilitation under conditions 1 and 2b; 3 Ss on 2a and 1. S's opinion of possibility of success found to be important factor in determining character and direction of work.
Quantity of work much greater, quality of all Ss' work fell off. Added group competition increased output over individual competition, did not lower quality as compared with individual competition.	Slowest workers improved most. Homogeneity of groups remains the same in quantity. Quality of work fluctuates more for individuals not competing. Some individuals do slightly worse, some better when competing in groups. Homogeneity of groups decreases in quality under competition.
Competition begins tentatively, either auto- or social; shifts later to particular opponent, usually with similar record. Irrelevant ideas frequent in non-competitive work; com-	9 Ss aware of competition, 4 emphasizing auto-competition. Latter important in 7 of 9. One directed efforts against specific rival, combined this with auto-competi-

SOME STUDIES

AUTHOR DATE	TOPIC	SUBJECTS	METHOD AND CONTROL
			peting; how: whether vs. other individuals, a single individual, against own record. Control: Same, alone.
Zubin, J. (1932)	Rivalry (prize, knowledge of results).	Main experiments: 217 children in Grades VI, VII, VIII of N. Y. City public school 2 classes at each grade level.	Simple additions and comparisons of numbers. One of each pair of classes was experimental group. Following 2 min. practice, 2 min. work to determine ranks in class. Practice again for 1 min., followed by 1 min. work for prize to each S who surpasses S just above him. Followed by alternation of incentive and non-incentive periods until 11th period. Control: Non-incentive periods as given above, when name not placed on paper. Also control class at each grade level, getting equal amount of work with unsigned papers, followed by final period with rivalry to determine rank of each individual; no "surpassing" series.

OF COMPETITION (*Continued*)

FINDINGS	INDIVIDUAL DIFFERENCES
petitive ideas also carry over into later non-competitive work.	tion. 3 reported competitive attitude tended to die out within week's work.
A highly reliable gain in speed found in incentive compared with non-incentive periods, in both functions.	6% of the children suffered loss of speed in incentive situation. Distribution of individual gains unimodal, symmetrical. Coefficient of variation for speed smaller under incentive than non-incentive. More accelerated pupils show incentive gains. Probable partial relation between amount of incentive gain and intelligence. Some positive relation between gain and grade; negligible between gain and C.A.

SOME STUDIES OF KNOWLEDGE OF RESULTS,

AUTHOR DATE	TOPIC	SUBJECTS	METHOD AND CONTROL
Arps, G. F. (1920)	Knowledge of results.	Three adults.	Bergström Ergograph work with and without view of ergograph tracings; carried to exhaustion, 112 work periods, evenly divided. Previous practice, in one case over two years.
Book, W. F., and Norvell, L. (1922)	Effort (exhortation, knowledge of results, reproof).	124 juniors and seniors of Indiana Univ., 48 men, 76 women.	Tasks included writing cancellation test; digit-letter substitution; mental multiplication. First task worked with 75 practice periods of 30 sec. each; other tasks with 45 practice periods of 1 min. each (1½ min. for last task). Each experiment with group divided. Group 1 experimental for last 1/3 of experiment; group 2 for first 2/3. Stimulus group urged to count scores, told could do better, urged to do better, told should do better. Control groups kept ignorant of results, told to work as hard and fast as possible.
Brown, F. J. (1932)	Knowledge of results (self-competition??).	138 children of large public school system. Exp. 1: Grade 7A of junior H. S.; Exp. 2: Grade 5A of elementary school. 84.3% of children of foreign parentage; 2 classes at each level.	Arithmetic drills given in usual 10-min. drill period. 2 10-day periods, about 2 weeks intervening. In each experiment experimental and control groups reversed. Statement made that children now graph their results individually. No preparation or intimation of experiment, nor unusual procedure introduced. 7A children accustomed to graphing results. Graphing individual, no comparison. Control groups did not mark papers, handed them to teacher. Probably no practice effect, similar work had been done through year. Groups very roughly equated.

THROWING LIGHT ON COMPETITIVE ATTITUDES

FINDINGS	INDIVIDUAL DIFFERENCES
Final average of all trials shows rate of work with knowledge of results superior by 7%. Rate of lifting greater with knowledge 64% of the time.	For S with 2 years' experience total superiority of knowledge condition is 18%.
Stimulus groups made far more improvement in equivalent time than control groups. Gains cease sharply when incentives removed, showing sharp loss with task 1, and appear suddenly when added to previous control situation. Accuracy also superior in stimulus groups.	Individuals with highest initial ability show greatest effect of incentives. Men more influenced by incentives; women show greater range in initial ability and improvement. No clear general effect on range of individual differences shown by incentive situation. Some individuals show rapid, steady improvement; some, slow improvement; some, erratic and unstable; a few at times adversely affected.
All made higher scores and more consistent gain with knowledge of results. All stimulus sections made more continuous gains than control. Mean difference rarely exceeds one problem: results over 10-day period irregular.	Some suggestion that younger children less susceptible to this incentive. Boys tended to gain somewhat more than girls (who score higher in general).

SOME STUDIES OF KNOWLEDGE OF RESULTS,

AUTHOR DATE	TOPIC	SUBJECTS	METHOD AND CONTROL
Chapman, J. C., and Feder, R. B. (1917)	Knowledge of results; stars given to top 50% (reward? praise?).	36 (final data on 32) Grade 5A children, boys and girls, Cleveland Observation School.	All given Thorndike simple addition, Woodworth-Wells Cancellation, Digit-Symbol. 10-day experimental period, each with 10-min. addition, 5 substitution, 1 cancellation. Group A shown graphic representation of performance of individuals and group. Stars given to top 50% each day, and over whole period. Control: Group B approximately equal to A on initial scores in addition. Novelty of problem an incentive. Told number of errors in addition.
Deputy, E. C. (1929)	Knowledge of results.	105 state college freshmen in 3 sections of introductory philosophy.	Section 1 met twice a week, each time given 10-min. new-type exercise on preceding lesson. Section 3 met twice a week, with 20-min. exercise the 2nd meeting on the 2 preceding lessons. Knowledge of results immediate. Sections equated in intelligence. Section 2, control, no exercise. Uniform instruction over 6 weeks. Second half-semester, section 2 exper., Groups 1 and 3 control.
Panlasigui, I., and Knight, F. B. (1930)	Awareness of success or failure (competition)	1750 IV-grade children in 10 western states. Reduced to 716 after groups equated.	Experimental groups went through 30 drills of 15 arithmetic problems each; shown individual and class progress charts compared with chart showing what grade should do. Control groups of exactly same mean, s.d. on initial test. Teachers administered tests, E never seen.

THROWING LIGHT ON COMPETITIVE ATTITUDES (*Continued*)

FINDINGS	INDIVIDUAL DIFFERENCES
Group A considered superior except on cancellation (stronger novelty?).	None given.
Section 1 after first half-semester significantly better than sections 2 or 3. Section 3 not reliably superior to 2. Second half-semester, no reliable differences.	In sections 1 and 3 about 85% preferred written work; in section 2, 45%. Sections 2 and 3 spent more time in outside activities than section 1. Attitude of students toward work was significant.
Reliable difference in favor of informed group. Advantage appeared after some time, not novelty effect.	Better students helped most; no adverse effect on slow ones. No effect on variability in the group. No sex differences.

SOME STUDIES OF KNOWLEDGE OF RESULTS,

AUTHOR DATE	TOPIC	SUBJECTS	METHOD AND CONTROL
Symonds, P. M., and Chase, D. H. (1929)	Measurement of motives (knowledge of results, knowledge of others' results, "goal" motivation).	2269 VI-grade children. 18 classes in 6 New York City public schools.	Charters Diagnostic Language Tests used. In learning correct English usage, motivated series involved showing scores to Ss in such a way that could see own and others gain. Urged to improve scores. "Intrinsic" motivation used with one group: ultimate value of correct English stressed. Control: unmotivated "sheer practice," reading aloud of practice material by class in unison. Ordinary school motivation.
Wright, W. R. (1906)	Knowledge of results (self-competition).	7 adult experienced Ss.	Cattell ergograph. In first condition (control) S unable to watch progress. In second, allowed to watch; told to count strokes and attempt to reach specified line in some experiments. Introspection recorded. Twice a week for several months, 3 experiments per S per day. In a sub-experiment impossible goal was set for S.

THROWING LIGHT ON COMPETITIVE ATTITUDES (*Continued*)

FINDINGS	INDIVIDUAL DIFFERENCES
Motivated trial equal to 5 "unmotivated" repetitions of material; but 10 unmotivated repetitions superior to 3 with motivation. Impressing ultimate value of correct English showed no reliable improvement.	No individual material. Considerable variation from school to school.
All Ss gained under incentive conditions. Impossible goal caused decrease. Subjective fatigue decreased under incentive conditions.	Gains under incentive conditions, 14% to 60%. Under "impossible goal" conditions, variations from −6% to +54%.

AUTHOR DATE	TOPIC	SUBJECTS	METHODS AND CONTROL
Anderson, H. H. (1936)	False knowledge of results; praise, reproof; success, failure; reward, punishment.	102 children of Anderson and Smith study. 44 new Ss, 18 boys, 26 girls. At 3, and 5–6-yr. levels.	Reanalysis of Chase and Anderson-Smith data on effects of incentives of Col. 2; effect of age; analysis of failure vs. success. Experiment with new Ss following same procedure as Group C of earlier experiment, but with order changed to failure followed by success, because of possibility results influenced by attractiveness of apparatus used in failure series, or effect of previous success with same E.
Anderson, H. H., and Smith, R. S. (1933)	False knowledge of results; praise, reproof; success, failure; reward, punishment.	102 children tested 3 yrs. before by Chase; from public schools, Ames, and Univ. Elem. School, Iowa City. Present selection of 102 children shows certain differences from whole Chase group, largely because fewer girls and young children.	Chase dynamometer with visible record, controllable by E. Bell rung by E, ostensibly by S, as indicator of "success." Each S member of Group A, B, C, or D, receiving 3 series of 7 trials, week apart. Series 2: Groups B, C, D made to believe had succeeded in ringing bell. Group B urged to try to ring it. Group C praised, Group D rewarded by gold star. Series 3: Groups B, C, D made to believe had failed to ring bell. Group B urged to try, Group C reproved, Group D "punished" by having button cut off paper "gingerbread boy" previously given him. In Series 1 (control) all groups worked without knowledge of results, merely on E's instructions to perform task. Group A (control) continued to work in same way in Series 2 and 3.
Benton, A. L. (1936)	Effect of praise, knowledge of results, strong encouragement,	Fifty VII- and VIII-grade children in Brewster, N. Y., High	28 days after Otis Self-Administering Test, Intermediate Examination, Form A, 1 group subjected to influence of moti-

INCENTIVE STUDIES

FINDINGS	INDIVIDUAL DIFFERENCES
Other factors found to be influencing performance in failure series. Initial efficiency maintained better by success; performance under failure showed precipitate drop. New experiment: success-praise significantly better than failure-reproof. In general, 3rd week always better than 2nd, whether it is success or failure week. Evidence of some unknown factor other than success-praise influencing.	With increasing age, failure curves tend to fall somewhat more during series than success scores.
In general, responded to motivation in retest much as 3 yrs. before. Reward and punishments likely symbols of adult approval and disapproval.	Considerable individual differences in response to motivation, with no responsible variations indicated.
No significant differences in gains made by two groups.	Small decrease in variability of scores of both groups. Marked individual differences in gain within each group.

AUTHOR DATE	TOPIC	SUBJECTS	METHODS AND CONTROL
	and promise of a prize (group competition).	School. Average age 13 yrs. 5 mos. In 2 groups matched in age, I.Q., sex, grade.	vational factors listed in Col. 2. Encouragement by school principal; told represented school. E gave knowledge of results, offered unspecified prize for individuals improving their standing. Both groups retested.
Chase, L. (1932)	(False) knowledge of results; praise, reproof; success, failure; reward, punishment.	259 children (main exp.). 213 complete records; 70 from preschool laboratories, Iowa Child Welfare Research Station; 41 from Grades I and II, Iowa State University Elementary School; 17 from Nursery School, Iowa State, Ames; 93 from 4 kindergartens of Ames public schools. Range: 2 yrs., 3 mos. to 8 yrs., in almost normal distribution. Majority above average socioeconomic level.	Tasks included liquid hand-dynamometer operation with visible record, and perforation of sheets of paper prepared with scored circles. Each S member of one of 4 groups; each tested 3 times, week apart, 7 trials each time with dynamometer; 3 with perforation task. Success and failure "rigged" by E. In *second* set of trials Groups B, C, D all given success; Group C praised between trials; Group D rewarded (gold stars). In *third* trials Groups B, C, D given failure; Group C reproved; Group D "punished" (buttons snipped off "his" paper cut-out boy). Behavior ratings recorded. *Initial* trials for all groups were control: child merely told to do task. Groups closely similar. Group A continued as control group in 2nd and 3rd sets of trials. Perforation test without incentive.
Kirby, T. J. (1913) (in part)	(Competition, self-competition, praise, knowledge of results.)	1350 II- and IV-grade children in Children's Aid Socy., N. Y.	Thorndike addition and division sheets for 45 mins., after initial 15-min. test; followed by final 15-min. test. Told not contest, but attempt to beat own record, which was read before each practice period, with praise for high scores.

FINDINGS	INDIVIDUAL DIFFERENCES
Success-repetition, success-praise, and success-reward reliably superior to control motivation. Success-praise unreliably superior to success-repetition. Reward probably reliably superior to repetition group. Reward unreliably superior to praise. Failure-repetition, failure-reproof, and failure-punishment reliably superior to control motivation. Failure-reproof probably reliably superior to failure-repetition. Failure-reproof not reliably superior to failure-punishment. Groups B, C, D, higher on Series 2 and 3 than Group A. Groups B, C, D higher on Series 3 than Series 2. Failure-repetition, -reproof and -punishment superior to success-repetition, -praise, and -reward (?). No carry-over to non-incentive perforation test.	Variability not affected by incentives. More younger than older children increase scores in Series 2 and 3. No reliable sex differences.
48% improvement in addition; 75% in division.	Not given.

AUTHOR DATE	TOPIC	SUBJECTS	METHODS AND CONTROL
Sullivan, E. B. (1927), Part II of research.	"Success and failure" (competition, praise and reproof, prestige).	*Exp. 4:* 12 graduate students and instructors. *Exp. 5:* 48 Whittier State School boys, mean I.Q. around 79, mean C.A. about 15 yrs.; 22 boys from same school, mean I.Q. about 70, mean C.A. about 15 yrs. *Exp. 6:* 4 boys, 2 girls, between 8 and 9 yrs.	*Exp. 4* (adult group): 10 sets of 10 nonsense syllables, 2 for habituation, 1 day between series. Told would receive score in relation to group. At beginning of period S told he had made highest or lowest score. Relearning after 2 wks. Introspections. *Exp. 5* (Whittier boys): 2 series of 8 nonsense syllables. 48 boys (I.Q. 79) in 3 groups; each member of 1st told was best on 1st series, asked to learn another; 3rd, C, told were poorest, complete failure. Same groupings and instruction in high (I.Q. 100) and low (I.Q. 70) mentality groups. *Exp. 6* (8–9-yr.-old group): Miles pursuit pendulum. Group A members told after first 25 trials scores were best of group. Group B, that they were worst; then 75 more trials. Control: *Exp 4:* 1st 2 sets of syllables for habituation; prevention of communication between Ss; 2 of Ss used as control group, not told of results. *Exp. 5:* Group B in each of the 3 groups given 2nd series without comment on earlier work. *Exp. 6:* First 25 trials served as control and comparison series.
de Weerdt, E. H. (1927)	Knowledge of results (competition).	45 V-grade children, average 10 yrs., in native American section of New Haven.	Over 11 school days, total of 260 mins. practice on symbol-digit, Thorndike Arithmetic Sheets, Chapman-Cook speed test in reading, Woodworth-Wells cancellations, multiplication, same-opposite, multiplication by substitution, revised Thorndike. Used class achievement graph, posted individual scores, competition, etc.

INCENTIVE STUDIES (*Continued*)

FINDINGS	INDIVIDUAL DIFFERENCES

Exp. 4: Group told of "failure"—learning trials (mean): 19.46; relearning, 10.32. Group told of "success"—learning trials: 17.6; relearning, 9.76. Control group—learning trials: 14.5; relearning, 7.22. Ss whose introspections indicated change of attitude as result of "success" or "failure": "failure" group took 15.5 trials to learn, 8.2 to relearn; "success" group, 9.7 and 5.4. *Exp. 5*: With I.Q. 79 group, knowledge of "success" decreases, and knowledge of "failure" increases learning time. Former more significant. With I.Q. 100 group, "success" report has little effect; "failure" increases time greatly. With I.Q. 70 group, "failure" does not increase learning time; "success" decreases it. *Exp. 6*: Both groups improved markedly after first 25 trials (as result of reports?); Group B which had been better, became consistently worse than A.

Important differences (I.Q.) given in Col. 5. Fairly marked individual differences, with basis unknown in all experiments. In Exp. 4 women affected more than men.

Improvement: substitution, 109%; addition, 37%; reading, 323%; cancellation, 62%; multiplication, 48%; same-opposite, 116%; multiplication by substitution, 52%.

Ratio of average initial scores of 10 scoring lowest to 10 highest was 50; ratio of improvement, 82. Ratio of improvement of 10 with lowest I.Q.'s to 10 highest was 70.

The attitude of a culture toward the achievement of individuals is thus a basic index of the nature of the culture itself. Perhaps no characteristic of our contemporary society as it is revealed in research emphases is more conspicuous than the amount of attention that is given to the problem of how to squeeze the most juice out of every individual. The charts just preceding aim to show some of the many research analyses of the effect of such pressures—particularly those of praise and reproof, reward and punishment, and competition.

The use of these incentives is fundamental to the structure of the majority of our schools at all levels. "Marks" in numbers from 60 to 100, with 70 as "passing," or letters from A (highest) to E or F (failure), "Honor Roll," "gold star," "Phi Beta Kappa," are the most common methods of indicating to the individual child or college student "just where he stands"; implicitly they constitute the strongest stimulus to greater "effort." Parents are "proud" of "good marks"; and "high standing" is frequently the chief or the only prerequisite to professional school without further analysis of the question of whether the tastes or specific abilities of the individual fit him for the profession he wishes to enter. Thus "marks" become not true records of achievement but an end in themselves, sought for and attained by a host of devices other than actual work and creative effort. A number of these are described with laconic humor in a small book entitled *The Psychology of Getting Good Grades.* Techniques for making the professor feel good, thereby creating a favorable predisposition to oneself, and for indirectly manipulating the classroom situation so as to exploit one's (limited) information to the fullest possible extent are accurately outlined. These methods are not confined to the college level at which this book is directed, but are the stock-in-trade of every bright ten-year-old. No one, so far as we know, has studied elementary school behavior from the point of view of analyzing the child's techniques and patterns of adjustment to the necessity of making good in achievement. Anyone who undertook this task would doubtless find here many roots of later growth and still later breakdown. There are those who accept the challenge and identify themselves with success so intensely that failure means collapse; others who retreat from the race early in their school careers in self-protection from the pain of defeated ambition; there are some whose world of reality is built in other terms than ego and recognition and to whom the whole mad scramble of competition is unreal or silly. That all of us as children were dimly aware of these differences in attitude toward the world of school values we can readily testify. Yet when we study children we usually do so as if these differences in meaning of school values did not exist.

Thus any discussion of the "objective" and quantitative studies of the effects of incentives must be seen in relation to the cultural background which has set so much store by individual achievement, and has nourished this movement to find ways of stimulating the greatest achievement in the individual, and also in relation to the unrecorded responses of the multitude of individual children each of whom responds to this pressure in his own way. The differences in each child's inner-world evaluation of school success could probably explain for us, if we would let them do so, some of our difficulties in arriving at generalizations regarding the effects of school incentives. Certainly such differences call for much more study in any future research investigations of this sort.

In the light of these criticisms of the large majority of studies summarized in the accompanying charts, it would be fruitless to go into detail regarding most of them. A recent experiment by Forlano and Axelrod recognizes the need for observing social reactions of this type in relation to personality organization, and attempts to correct some of the oversights of previous work. Their own explanation of this approach is as follows:

Conflicting results of the various studies may be due to different conditions under which the experiments were conducted as well as to the kind and intensity of the incentives used. But, although investigators have tried to control the factors which enter into the experimental situation in the form of external stimuli, they have overlooked the importance of the effect of personality differences on responses made to these stimuli.

The implicit assumption that seems to be made in most studies, namely, that all individuals of the same age and intelligence respond alike to an incentive, is untenable. . . .

The purpose of this investigation is to determine experimentally the effects of repeated praise or blame on the performances of children who, on the basis of their responses to a psychological questionnaire, were classified as extroverts or introverts.

The pupils of four fifth-grade classes in a New York City public school were divided into a group of "extroverts" and a group of "introverts" on the basis of the Pintner inventory of extroversion. The effect of motivation was measured in connection with the children's work on the Woodworth-Wells Number Cancellation test. The procedure was as follows:

On the basis of the extroversion inventory individuals above the median were designated as the E group, those below as the I group. In terms of Praise and Blame four experimental groups were designated $EP;$ $EB;$ $IB;$ $IP;$ and C a control group.

After the first administration of the Cancellation Test, the pupils were called to the desk individually to receive a mark from their regular teacher, who according to prearranged instructions, not performance, rated the paper Poor or Good. In the first class the I group was marked P (poor) and the E group was marked G (good). In the second class the procedure was reversed. In the third class there were $EP, EB, IP,$ and IB groups. The pupils did not know each other's grades. Then the teacher announced that P meant Poor, G meant Good, in order to introduce indirect group approval and disapproval. Immediately another form of cancellation test was administered, the incentives were applied in the same way, and the same marks were given. A third form was given to measure effects of repeated incentives.

The results showed a statistically reliable gain for experimental and control groups on the second and third tests. The group receiving "Blame" showed more increase and a greater variability of response to the incentives. The standard ratios for IB-IP and EB-EP indicated that blame produced a greater increment in the performance of the introverts on Trial 2, but that *when the incentive was repeated* the extroverts who were blamed were stimulated to greater activity in Trial 3. Praise seems to have the reverse effect; extroverts are more responsive to one "application" of praise than the introverts. With the second application of praise the introverts slightly surpass the extroverts.

This type of study proceeds on the basis of a number of assumptions that were not completely analyzed; the most important of them is the hypothesis that these differences in personality structure which underlie differences in response to praise and reproof are closely related to the differences involved between extroversion and introversion. In so far as "introversion" is the result of repression, discouragement, defeat and punishment, we might expect characteristic responses of discouragement to appear. But the daydreaming, self-absorbed, non-social and shy characteristics associated with introversion may also depend on constitutional tendencies toward imaginative activity and low social responsiveness; consequently introversion may be to a certain degree spontaneous or "natural" to some people, apart from any special experiences of punishment. If this is the case, it would be more illuminating to analyze directly the types of personality patterns or social behavior shown by children who do better work under encouragement as compared with those of children who do better work under reproof. A three-dimensional analysis of such personality patterns would require coordination of teachers' observations of school behavior and psychiatric interviews to obtain data on the child's feelings. Fromm's analysis of the responses of individual personalities to authority[1] and Maslow's analysis of dominance (cf. page 437) offer the most promising hypotheses for the illumination of the meaning of praise and reproof to the child.

We may summarize the interrelations between cultural emphases and the characteristic personality responses reported in the research studies on aggression, as follows: Our individualistic culture emphasizes success, recognition, accomplishment and the power of the adult authority. All of these affect the quality of social behavior toward peers and toward authorities, and also affect the actual performance level or achievement of the individual. Success in a social situation involving use of materials is accompanied by an increase in confidence, ascendance, dominance. Success may also stimulate aggression; but aggression may also appear as a compensation for insecurity, while insecurity or lack of success may also be expressed in projected anxiety or sympathy for others. Depending on the total situation, *aggression may mean either confidence or the want of it.*

The kind of attitude toward success which has been built up is

[1] E. Fromm (ed.), *Autorität und Familie.* See also forthcoming volumes.

probably also important in relation to attitudes toward praise and reproof, or reward and punishment, shown by a child or, for that matter, an adult. Differences have been observed which indicate that some people are more stimulated by praise; others are more stimulated by reproof. These attitudes are also closely related to others which are important in relation to the performance level or achievement of the individual. The aspiration level or degree of caution or ambition is also related to the ego level, and both are important in connection with the reality level in affecting the quantitative achievement or amount of work done, and also in affecting the qualitative achievement or poise and coordination in connection with all these relations to one's work, to authorities, and to peers. Insecurity, aggression, aspiration and achievement are all closely related to one another and to the ego structure of the individual.

By way of summary we must recognize that up to the present time our empirical picture of aggressive behavior must be pieced together from a great variety of small intensive studies, each of which is concerned with a limited age range, usually not more than two or three years being studied at one time; a limited social economic background; and a limited variety of school and home experience of children. If we were to hazard a guess regarding the most characteristic sequences of children's experience in relation to adults, it would probably run something like this: On the whole, the first two years is likely to include a certain amount of specific training on an elementary physical level, combined with an enormous amount of admiration and a generally permissive attitude on the part of adults who think that almost anything the baby does is "cute." By the time the child gets well on its own feet, so that it is prepared to manipulate a larger world than that included within the sides of a play-pen, he begins to be a great nuisance to adults. The word "naughty" may be used frequently, along with a great variety of equivalents; and the child whose ego has been built up by constant admiration during the cute baby period, now confronts interference at every turn. When this experience of three-year-old repression and defiance in reaction to it has been digested, he gets along well enough on a firm, submissive basis until the school, if he goes to a conservative one, brings a new series of demands for conformity to time and space limitations. Most middle- and upper-class adults probably do not like to resort to spanking children of school age; but their substitutes offer little improvement from the child's point of view, as the child experiences a variety of interferences, suggestions, admonitions, demands for conformity to routine and for acquisition of manners. All these, frequently imposed with nagging, scolding or loud voices, are very different from the cuddling, admiring tones and expressions to which he was accustomed as a little child. The older he grows, the more likely he is to confront not only the demands for conformity to external routine, but also the projected ambitions and values of parents who may be merely eager to help him toward a security which they never had. Since most children grow up in a culture of conflicting values which offers a variety of patterns of every sort to choose from, any imposition from parents anxious to set the child on the right path is apt to be felt as aggressive domination. The child is in no position to appreciate the parents' side of the picture. The fact is that the parents know that some clear authority is needed for the security of the child, and in the back of their mind, as of the child's, is the certainty that pressure and coercion, however affectionately phrased, are bound to be used in every critical conflict of wills.

As the child emerges into adolescence the experience of varieties of "open spaces" with new freedom becomes exciting, as his two feet, his bicycle and his best friend's car introduce him to wider and wider social groups, giving him a broader basis on which to take his stance in defying his parents' efforts to introduce direction into the confusion of values.

A possible sequence in the development of the child's experience of aggression might therefore be outlined. This can only be an hypothesis, since we have neither adequate cross-section studies of children at all ages in any single community, nor adequate follow-ups of individuals against any one background from infancy through adolescence.

1. Period of submissive dependence, 1-2. Children depend on

adults and experience adult aggression in the form of punishment
and rigid training.

2. Period of negativism, 3-4. Child ready for extending activities and experience; usually modern living conditions prevent the
possibility of this. Child experiences frequent interference from
adults and responds with resistance.

3. Period of ambivalence toward adults, 5-12. Overt compliance
with adults, beginning of independent life free from, and often in
conflict with, adult patterns. "Secrets" appear now. Many writers
speak of six-year-old (first-grade) "defiance" of the home. During
the early part of this period appears promiscuous sadism of children
toward one another, "teasing to death," calling "vile names." This
may be related to the difficult situation in which many children find
themselves with the new inexorable authority of school. During
the latter part of this period, group structures become consolidated in gangs whose patterns are primarily cooperative within the
group but may be sadistic toward other groups, either other children, adults, or society at large. ("Spitballs" and "delinquency" are
two aspects of the rejection of adults that parallel the development
of independent social life among children; the adult is amused by
the former, solemn about the latter; they are cognate expressions
of the same tensions.)

4. Period of overt rebellion (adolescent negativism), then acceptance, 12-20. Sophomoric ambitions, adaptation of authorities
to own needs, and a sense of power and superiority to adults sometimes characterize this period.

5. Adult assumption of authority and aggressive relation to others
through channels afforded by marriage and work.

We may further extend the hypothesis to suggest that if any
one of these levels of reaction to the aggression of authority is perpetuated, we are likely to find difficulties in adult adjustment. Thus
if stage (1) is perpetuated, we may have a childish personality which
remains completely dependent upon the pleasant domination of
strong supporters. If (2) is perpetuated, we may have a continuation of a general resistance to authority in a defiant, emotional way.
If (3) is perpetuated, the personality may continue in a superficial

compliance along with an inner development of independent values of an introverted sort.

It is hardly necessary to go through the list. It may be more important to suggest that the fact that these types of behavior seem to appear at these age levels in our society may be merely a result of the kinds of demands imposed upon children at a given age level by the society, and may therefore be in the deepest sense a product of specific experience afforded by the child's situation in his culture. The clearest evidence that this is probably true is the fact that both three-year-old negativism and conflicts and ten-year-old delinquency have been shown to vary enormously with cultural conditions and concrete situations.

Of even more importance than the need for recognizing cultural pressures which shape patterns of aggression and resistance as the child grows up, is the need for recognizing the internal picture, both from a biological point of view and from the point of view of changing attitudes; even the "gross inconsistencies" from day to day make sense if the child's needs and the varied forms of their frustrations are grasped. Thus in one study after another, the basic biological structure of the organism is revealed in the intimate relation between different *defense responses*. Insecurity and aggression are constantly linked, and the increase or decrease in one is bound up with changes in the form or degree of the other. This we should expect from our knowledge that similar autonomic and glandular mechanisms are involved in both. The particular pattern of relationships varies from one child to another, depending upon individual physical differences and attitudes. For instance, a child who feels weak in general will in a specific case respond to domination or aggression from adults with submission, whereas a child who feels strong will respond with defiance or resentment. If a child feels too weak to do anything but submit to adults, but strong enough to dominate other children, he may "take out" his defiance through aggression toward children who are weaker. The good boy, the model son, may be the terror of the "small fry" in the next block. Children who have accepted moral restrictions against the use of physical aggression may "sublimate" their aggression through domination, or a rush for prestige or property. Such sublimations may take quite different forms in different children; for example, Annette, who never attacks other children even in self-defense, is extremely aggressive toward objects; Lucy, who almost never fights, dominates other children in an authoritative way; Arthur, who seldom wins a fight, runs faster than the other children and uses this ability so as always to be "first," often humiliating other children. For a full understanding of aggression in any group we need, then, to understand the cultural and situational pressures in relation to the personality make-up of individual children, and their concrete ways of finding a way out amid the conflicts presented by moral precepts, the need for self-defense, and the aggression piled up in their early contacts with big and small human beings.

Chapter VIII

CHARACTERISTIC SOCIAL BEHAVIOR OF CHILDREN IN OUR CULTURE: COOPERATION, FRIENDSHIP, AND GROUP ACTIVITY

IF FIGHTING, jealousy, competing, negativism, resentment are all bound up with the development of ego in our culture, so also are protecting, helping, sympathizing, liking, and loving; the development of any individual into a secure and happy relation with his group is largely dependent upon the quality of sharing and cooperation of which he is capable.

From one point of view, the main task of social psychology might be defined in terms of analysis of the nature of integrative social relations and the processes involved in controlling or creating them. But we must confront at the outset of our discussion the fact that there has been much less scientific study of this aspect of social behavior than of conflict and aggression. Friendship, for example, has been investigated largely in terms of propinquity, age level, sex, mental age and other characteristics that define the boundaries within which friends will be selected, but do not help to predict the specific sort of person who will receive the affection of a given individual. Or we may study imitation, but it is only to analyze how the child imitates, not whom he imitates and why. Although love for one's brother has occupied the attention of social reformers and philosophers from before the time of Jesus, the development of inner attitudes of positive response to other people has received little attention in scientific areas.

The social psychology of spontaneous group formation and of integrated group study calls especially for a more adequate scientific knowledge of the nature of the social experience of identification and friendship.

IDENTIFICATION

We have already noted the important rôle of identification both in ego structure and in the development of feelings of affection and group solidarity. The small child shares the experience of those who are close to him, not knowing where he himself "stops" and when they "begin"; and even after the ego is well formed, one may at times live intensely in and through the experiences of another (cf. page 207). Young children have been observed to identify with other children who have had traumatic experiences like their own, with people who have lived in the same house for a long time, with people who are physically or temperamentally similar to them, and with people on whom they have long been dependent. Identification based on similar specific experiences or physical similarity may be quite temporary, while that which grows from long association or living together is likely to be more permanent. Some of the concrete patterns of identification in our culture will be discussed before we approach the research on friendship, leadership, and acceptance of group standards.

Everyday observation seems definitely to support the thesis that in general the child first develops an identification with his mother, enduring at least until he goes to school. Both in girls and in boys it may be reflected in patterns of playing mother or, even at the age of three or four, it may give rise to fantasies of having babies when one grows up. It is not uncommon for little boys to envy their sisters' feminine potentialities of "making a baby inside themselves" more than the sisters envy their brothers' masculinity. Both of these patterns are doubtless a reflection of the relatively unimportant rôle which many contemporary fathers have for the little child in our culture, where the process of getting a living and the fundamental economic support of the family are so remote from the child's observation and understanding.

Only as the children get into school, where they begin to learn about workers and different kinds of work and where they visit boats, bridges in the process of being built, stores, factories, train yards, does the masculine world become real. When this transition does occur, masculine values are likely to dominate the life of the school child completely; even a first-grader cannot escape the impact of a culture oriented toward economic life. Exploratory studies of six-year-old children suggest that, during this period, the masculine patterns are likely to be dominating, perhaps to the advantage of the boy and quite possibly to the disadvantage of the girl, who finds few opportunities for acceptable identifications.

Later, however, when reading opens up a new world of books, when movies are permitted, and the radio can be listened to, both boys and girls are exposed to a variety of patterns for identification which are considerably less moral and considerably more exciting than either early home or school patterns. One boy of seven alternated regularly, on coming home from school, between reading about King Arthur and reading about Popeye. The two persons seemed to serve much the same purpose; both were brave and aggressive, withal tender, heroes.

The vocational choices of older children from eight to college age afford some basis for inference regarding the later development of patterns of identification and formation of the images or ideas of what one might become. The cowboy pattern is thus likely to hold its own from eight to thirteen, when it drops out of sight rapidly and almost completely. The preferred occupation of detective increases to a high point at fourteen, then drops off moderately, whereas interest in a profession such as civil engineering increases steadily and holds its place during adolescence. This shift of patterns suggests that the process of developing a mature notion of one's place in the world in respect to work involves a complex adjustment of a need for adventure and a need for social status. Boys who maintain a cowboy pattern into late adolescence are not much influenced by considerations of status; the detective or secret-service pattern evidently combines both bases of satisfaction; and in civil engineering adventure becomes sublimated into a respectable form of socially useful creative work.

In discussing identification we have stepped from a context in which "identification" meant love and imitation of an individual, into a context in which "identification" was a matter of filling an imagined place in a social group. This developmental aspect of identification is important for the growing child, who first accepts a rôle and a relationship offered by his immediate group and gradually draws his own models from a wider range of possibilities. The fundamental task of growing up may be seen in terms of the need for defining a rôle for oneself which will give expression to one's own interests and capacities, and which will at the same time be acceptable to one's social group. The extent to which the individual definition of a social rôle is successful in these terms will depend on the way in which aggressive and egocentric drives and behavior are related to cooperative and socially integrative drives and behavior, a problem to be discussed in this chapter. We have already seen that in our culture the completely non-aggressive child cannot be a well-adjusted and constructive child. The problem of social maturing in our culture then becomes that of orienting aggressive and competitive behavior within a frame of reference which makes possible long-time cooperation and room for other individuals. It is not yet certain whether this achievement is within the reach of most children, since the opportunities for individual exploitation of aggression in our competitive society are so great that many observers see no possibility that our society can sustain itself. The very fact that so much more research has been done on aggression and competition than on cooperation is an expression of the urgency of the need to control and direct a form of social behavior which in full development threatens the social structure. Yet the need to examine the results of studies of integrative functions such as cooperation and sympathy is fully as great; granting the economic foundations of most social behavior, we must also grant that control of social behavior within the structure of society at present requires a psychological understanding of socially constructive responses.

Friendship and the Structure of Childhood Groups

Although the mother is usually the "first friend," the situation of most children in free play, and especially the situation of the nursery-school children who have been observed by investigators, throws them into plentiful contacts with their "contemporaries," giving opportunity for a rapid rise of "fellow feeling"; progressively, from year to year, friendship with those of the school and play group means more and more.

Among school children in general, being in the neighborhood, in the same school grade and of about the same age and developmental status, are basic determiners of friendship. At this age economic differences or even differences in interest which might lead in later life to occupational separations do not appear to be particularly important. An attempt to check on the extent to which propinquity dominates the choices of children was made by analyzing the responses of 823 children in grades 3 to 8 in a school in Los Angeles County. Out of this group appeared only 115 pairs of children who chose each other, and a month later only 29 of the original 115 pairs again chose each other. Grade and nearness of the homes, chronological age and mental age were of first importance, and "personal characteristics" (such as "athletic ability") were of secondary importance. The personal characteristics, however, were not considered in terms of the specific needs and appeals of each child. Defining the area within which a given child will pick friends in terms of his school group, neighborhood group, and age group does not go far in helping us to predict which friend out of the various present possibilities a given child will find most congenial.

Among young children there is ample evidence that close cooperative relations involve both conflict and integration: positive correlations are found between "friendship" and "quarrels" and between sympathizing and attacking, and close friends frequently quarrel most. We may infer that at this age friendship does not imply any responsibility to inhibit resistant or antagonistic responses to the specific behavior of a friend. Or is it indeed assuming too much to suppose that friendship at an older level would not be accompanied by a large proportion of quarrels? In so far as amount of time spent with another individual affords more opportunity for conflict, we might expect the same relation at any age level. In so far as the transitoriness of early relationships gives place to sustained patterns of mutual support, understanding, and participation, we should expect the proportion of conflict in relation to time spent together to decrease.

However, the process of friendship may change qualitatively, so that early free aggressive tendencies which at first appear in relation to frustration from *any* source become channeled into a few outlets; we have already commented on the development of gang hostility at the eight- to ten-year level in our culture. Class, race, school prejudices also develop during this period, and further channel the antipathies of the child. Consequently we may assume that psychological tracks are clear for integrative relationships, friendships or "in-groups" within which conflict and aggression play a relatively small rôle.

The *content* of friendship among children, the give-and-take of suggestions, the "getting mad" and "making up," the protests of devotion and symbols of eternal loyalty are more familiar to readers of literature than to devotees of psychology. Again, this is partly due to the myopic vision developed by an extreme behaviorism, to which identification, adoration, love and loyalty were foreign terms, and dangerous ones. In the study of young children, behavior observations have shown that quarrels and friendship go hand in hand; we may infer that the "tele" which attracts does not prevent tension and conflict.

Affection between individuals probably depends partly upon identification (as described above, page 208), partly upon tele, or sense of attraction to the distinct individuality of another person (cf. page 308), and partly upon emotional responses which the Freudians have referred to as an aspect of sexuality, using the term very broadly indeed (Plato's "eros"). Apart from the Freudian outline (first, polymorphous sexuality; second, the auto-erotic period; third, the latency period during which repression of overt sexuality causes responses to be directed primarily to members of one's own sex; and fourth, the heterosexual period), there are few hypotheses which offer cues to the student of the development of affection and love. Following De Sanctis' analysis, we have already suggested the confusion and inadequacy of explaining the deeper and more persistent fixations or canalizations in terms of single discrete drives (cf. page 203). In a study of adolescent friendships, Horney makes a pioneer effort to break through the pseudo-scientific convention that love is almost entirely sexual in origin, reasserting the distinction between tender mother love and sexual love, and showing the extreme complexity of the canalizations of each child's love for his teddy bear, for his baby sister (until she gets big enough to get in the way), for his teacher, for the members of his gang, or for his Scout leader; for each child there are many rich and complex experiences important for his own personal development. It is hard to believe that a mother cat's eager licking of her kittens is intimately associated with the experience of mating; nor is there any good reason for believing that it is sound to think of normal parental love and care as having much in common with sexual love. It is probably more sound to think of affection of all sorts as derived in large part from a general reservoir of warm feeling which may be canalized now into friendship, now into parental love, now into sexual love.

But childhood friendships cannot be considered without reference to the process of forming play groups, either in school or after school hours; these groups not only express but help in forming individual attachments. Even the "beloved brothers," the "David and Jonathan," the inseparable pair of pals, usually form their friendships in the midst of the group situation, partly as the quintessence of its comradeship, partly in rejection of other group members. The earliest such pairs are usually unstable, while loyalty to and identification with the group as a whole increases. It is at a much more mature level, when the complex uniqueness of individual personality means so much more, that friendship in the fullest sense appears.

In the nursery-school situation, it is common for children to go through the following stages in their growth into group play: first, passive watching, then "parallel" play, then participation on a genuinely give-and-take basis. It has been noted that the *security* of the child in the situation is probably a prerequisite to achievement of the third stage, genuine cooperation. Some children of course are able to make contacts of some sort from the beginning; with young

children these are apt to be exploratory and pretty aggressive. It
can safely be said that all children, whether they start with a passive or an active approach, have fairly impermanent and shifting relations during this period. Usually they have little grasp of time;
consequently they do not plan ahead or think out cooperative sequences of the kind that older children work out in their club activities. Aside from the effect of time limitation on the possibilities in
such activities, but closely related to it, is the similar limitation in
the number of contacts that can be sustained at any one time. Ordinarily children from two to four play with one or two other children at a time and cannot work out patterns of real group cooperation, except under the domination of an adult. (The self-sustaining
childhood gang or group does not appear until the age of eight or
nine.) The third factor of importance in relation to the sustained
activity of an organized group is the possibility of accepting and
applying rules. Of course the small nursery-school child accepts
rules of a sort imposed by the teacher—not pulling hair, not spitting, not splashing water in the bathroom, not singing at lunch time.
These rules, which are nothing more than simple commands or prohibitions, are on a very different level from those that govern sequences of behavior in games. The understanding of rules of games
is an important basis for the child's development of a sense of justice, as we shall later see. At the moment we are concerned only
with the analysis of the conditions necessary for the development
of the structure of group relations of children.

The content and characteristics of group structure among young
children will be affected not only by the stage of development of
the time span, the number of individuals with whom relations can
be sustained, and the grasp of rules, but also by the level of response
of children to members of their own and the opposite sex, by the
interests of individuals in the group, and by the influence of dominant personalities in it. Thus in one group an outstandingly motherly
child happened to be the oldest and one of the most influential
children in the group, and her patterns were taken over both by
other children of her age level and by brighter children in the
younger section of the group. In another group the taunting comment, "I'm a big girl, I don't cry," was imitated by nine out of six-

teen children after it was started by an older rather egocentric child. Again, group activity may start from a special interest vividly pursued by a single child; games of mother and baby, firemen, or ocean liner may be started by one child who has been digesting an important recent experience, and may be picked up by other children on an imitative basis.

But while certain definite characteristics of group structure may be apparent at the nursery-school level, it is also true that these structures are quite unstable. Even the habitual groupings in play usually shift markedly from one three-months period to another. In a group of children a child who was leader in the fall gave place to a different leader during the winter months, and this leader in turn yielded dominance to another in the spring. In another group, an outstanding leader became quite demoralized after the departure of his chief ally, so that his relation with the whole group collapsed after the withdrawal of one member.

The effect of group structure both on the development of individuals and on the morale of the group itself is of primary importance at every age level. One nursery-school group which was so organized that twenty two-year-old children within a ten-months age range were playing together in a fairly limited space showed more conflicts and less sympathetic behavior than another group with a wider age range playing in a larger area. A group of kindergarten children in which aggressive dramatic play was not interfered with by the teachers developed a much larger amount of aggression than a group where the activities were guided by teachers.

We have as yet almost no long-time studies of individuals who have gone through different kinds of group experience. What long-time effects on the personality of a child may come from early experience in a tense combative group full of antagonisms and conflicts? Are children who are protected from early experience of aggression likely to find difficulty in handling later situations where self-defense is needed? It is of the utmost importance to understand these relations between group structure and the experience of the individual, if we are to have a sound psychology of the growth of personality and social behavior or a dependable basis for the educational guidance of young children. It is highly probable that the history of one's friendships and one's areas of interest and happiness cannot be written at all without a knowledge of one's successive rôles as companion, bully, scapegoat, pet, and idol in varying group structures.

Quite apart from such aspects of the situation as the child's rôle in the group, his relation to other children, the differences between home and school situations, and the differences in his own development which affect social behavior, a two-year-old is usually in the early stages of language and cannot readily formulate all the words or sustain long conversations about work or other interests. His attention span for words is shorter than that of older children and his grasp of their needs is extremely limited. All of these factors make it natural for even a social two-year-old to have social relations of an extremely limited sort. This is why "watching" and other brief relations to children are frequent at the beginning of nursery school. Gradually, children begin to play side by side "in parallel" activity with clay or sand, making occasional comments. Companionship begins as questions can be asked more easily, suggestions given and accepted, toys exchanged and larger patterns of dramatic play or construction kept in mind. Along with companionship in most nursery-school groups are stimulated self-defense, aggression, intricate cooperation and sympathy. Much of this social behavior is stimulated by problems of sharing, dividing or protecting property or rights to the use of property. In country situations where children have large areas to explore, the soil to manipulate and a few home-made toys, it is quite probable that both the conflicts and the sharing which develop in most nursery schools would not appear.

During the period from two to four the rapid increase of language, imagination, control of large muscles and ability to handle constructive materials is accompanied by a consistent increase not only in the amount of social play but in the complexity of its organization. Children who play with other children then are exposed to an increasingly varied range of social situations involving during the second year relatively few quarrels, commands, requests for help, critical comments, being offered toys or invitations to play; while by the age of four, according to all the evidence from many studies of young children, all of these situations and many others are relatively common. During the second year many situations are not successful in eliciting the desired response from another child; but again, by the age of four, average and superior children may respond to the distress of others, requests for assistance, suggestions of dramatic play, demand for a toy, with a variety of techniques of acceptance, refusal, evasion or transformation of the situation.

The kinds of constellations or groupings that are formed among children of this age may be influenced both by the immediate situation and by the larger environment from which the children come. In a kindergarten in Kiev, children whose parents were revolutionaries and had little family life formed larger groups than did the children in a second kindergarten which was attended by the children of parents who were attempting to preserve old traditions in family life. The games of the revolutionary group and of the traditional group reflected the style of living of their respective environments, and the children from the poorer (traditional) group developed leaders at earlier ages than those from the better group where the children were subject to more professional supervision. Among similar groups in Odessa, situational factors such as the size of the room, variety of educational material, and physical maturity of the children, affected the size and character of the groups. Small rooms and a great variety of educational material tended to produce heterogeneous groups. Children from large families tended to play in groups and larger groups than were characteristic of only children. Differences in the duration of children's play groups were found to be affected by such differences in the situations as would be dependent upon individual initiative, leadership and imagination in individual children. Shifts in the situation or interruptions due to the entrance of strangers, a struggle between two antagonistic groups, a strong external stimulus such as music in the street, the appearance of a bird or a new toy, the intervention of adults, as well as routine factors such as the summons to lunch or to walk would break up the group behavior of the children. Spontaneous break-up was more characteristic of small groups, larger groups tending to disperse gradually; but the duration of the group depended largely on the character of the game which in turn was influenced by the particular children in the social situation, their experience and physiological maturity.

By the age of four years, different friendship patterns with consequent identification begin to form. Cooperation takes more varied forms of assistance, suggestion and criticism, and is paralleled by the beginning of competition over questions of property, age, size, family superiorities and achievements. Problems of property are solved by the institution of "taking turns"; yet at this age children begin to reflect more and more vividly the ambivalent will-to-power patterns of their culture.

Attention, expansion and capacity for playing in groups have not yet ordinarily matured to a point where organized games with rules can be carried on. Elaborate block constructions, reproductions, experiences of travel, buying and selling, and home life are normal and likely to be part and parcel of social dramatic games in which children represent *naïvely* the content of family and group life as they experience it, or unconsciously project their anxieties and their wishes.

So far we have been considering chiefly the earliest friendships. The patterns of group formation among older children of school age have for the most part been studied by quite different methods. Direct observation of new patterns is harder, but the greater duration of groups more than compensates for this difficulty.

In Chapter V we gave close consideration to Moreno's sociometric method, and saw that it is an exceptionally valuable tool in discerning the bonds of friendship, the ties within the group, so important in the evolution of the individual personality as well as of the group structure in which it appears. Yet Moreno has offered little analysis of those permanent or persisting aspects of personality which underlie tendencies to reach the same position and function in one group after another, regardless of the nature of the group. The good fellow, the leader, the isolate, are partly defined by the relation of a child to a particular group structure; at the same time, there are some individuals who seem permanently isolated and others appear to make friends easily in any new group. We may relate this everyday fact to those researches which have made clear the differences between children whose patterns of behavior persist from one period to another, and those children whose behavior varies strikingly from one situation to another (and who are as a consequence easy or difficult to rate). This suggests that a full understanding of group structure requires an understanding of the differences in personality organization between children who are more, or less, flexible (or unstable, according to the point of view). Such a study of personality requires that we bring into focus the problem of change in personality and behavior. A quantitative study of the proportions of children in different groups who do change markedly in comparison with those who do not would provide a starting point for such a study, and adequate exploration of its possibilities would require experimental variations of group structure as well as detailed qualitative analysis of the behavior of the child in all of the situations to which he was normally exposed. Children who do *not* change from one situation to another are likely to have stable preferences and bases for selection of other individuals as friends or companions, or stable needs which have to be satisfied in similar ways in different situations.

Casual observation of children from the nursery-school level to the college level shows relationships of this sort. A strong personality who needs to dominate and at the same time to be approved or admired, is sustained by a friend who is willing to admire and to accept the domination; a child who has been depending on parental direction may find a substitute for this either among other adults or among stronger peers in school situations. A child of special interests, verbal or muscular ability beyond the level of the group, may find a friend in someone who can share the interest that means so much to him but which threatens to isolate him socially. Patterns of identification with an older brother or sister at home, a way of talking, or the kind of clothes or manners identified with a parent, may come to mean a great deal to a child's security and be a basis for response to another person. Probably Thomas's four wishes— for recognition, response, security, and adventure—would go further in suggesting the functional basis of friendship relations than any other compact formula. Not only the special abilities or special identifications of an individual but the needs or deprivations of a group may be important. It has been observed by workers in a large girls' school that where white girls have no outlets in responses to boys they may get "crushes" on Negro girls. The phenomenon of the crush between adolescent girls, or between adolescent girls and their teachers, is particularly characteristic of groups which have little opportunity for contact with boys, or of individual girls whose strict parents have interfered with normal adolescent relationships with boys.

Although conflict relationships and behavior are now quite generally thought of as suitable material for the teacher or adult in authority to handle, there is likely to be little selection or guidance in the matter of friendships as such. Here again Moreno's work has moved in the direction of recognizing the importance of positive warm feelings between individuals and allowing spontaneous friendships to grow, as a basis for the adjustment that must underlie either education or reformation.

LEADERSHIP

The consideration of affection, of group structures, and of stable personality traits which may give rise to the same pattern in one group after another would lead us to suspect that leadership is not a psychologically simple concept but the expression of many trends and tendencies. Personality study is necessary, sociometry is necessary, analysis of the kind of leadership permitted and needed is necessary, before the trait of leadership can be defined. It is of special importance to distinguish between leadership and sheer "domination" and between leadership and sheer "prestige." The capacity to *interpret the needs of others* and in some sense to represent others and the capacity to *initiate activity* are stressed in many studies.

Leadership is defined by Parten as a phase of *intensity of social participation*, shown in "independent pursuing of own will" as well as in directing others. Yet the fact that leadership observations were not as reliable as were those on social participation suggests that leadership itself is less stable than social participation, or that the appraisal of it depends more upon the bias of the observer. It is interesting to note that consistent with our observations of the positive relation between acquiescence and resistance (cf. page 380) is the positive relation between "following and directing." The children who followed most frequently also directed more than did the average child. Fourteen children of the forty studied were observed directing at one time or another, and one child was occupied with directing 60 per cent of the time. The intelligence quotients, and presumably the mental ages, of the leaders averaged considerably higher than those of the non-leaders, and the leaders as a whole came from higher occupational classes than the non-leaders. The results of this study are quite consistent with the results of other studies of leadership at higher age levels. But like the studies of friendship, they do not give much basis for *prediction* of leadership among individuals in the preferred groups. We do not have records as yet which would give any basis for saying that children who are leaders in nursery school could be leaders in high school or college, or even for that matter in kindergarten the following year. If we put together the implications from other investigations which have indicated that the rôle of a child in a group may change markedly from one year to the next (Arrington, Jersild, Murphy) we may infer that a child's capacity for leadership will be a complex and subtle thing, depending upon: (1) his confidence and ability to express himself in outgoing ways; (2) his need to compensate for previous experiences of inferiority or aggression; (3) the character of his purposes and interests, particularly in relation to whether they depend upon directed activity of a number of children.

All the evidence to the effect that age, social status, intelligence and school marks are correlated with leadership points to the importance of the obvious effect of ability and prestige in sustaining the rôle of leader. It would not be rash to suggest that probably the particular characteristics that tend to bring prestige, whether age or strength or skill or knowledge, would depend upon the values of a particular group and activity. In one analysis of the personality of leaders in school classes in Germany other characteristics are indicated as important, such as "ability to estimate a situation," "emotional sensitivity," "the feeling of social responsibility," "self-assurance and aggressiveness." An American study adds to these the attitude in the home toward leadership, and opportunities which the child has had there to take leadership.

A series of experimental studies of leadership, by means of *group tasks* in which each individual shows his originality, self-assertion, cooperation, etc., has been used by German psychologists, but the technical difficulties in measuring all-round capacity to lead have proved very great. In any event the leaderships thus measured appear to be rather specific to the situations used. Yet the latter point may at times be a merit; we may wish chiefly to dissociate leadership ability in general from capacity to lead in a certain situation.

Terman's early experiment in determining leadership through the construction of a series of small groups which offered opportunities for an individual to be selected as leader has a modern counterpart in the work of Partridge. The aim was to set up natural situations in which Boy Scouts ranging in age from twelve to seventeen would feel at ease and have an opportunity to select leaders in a relatively normal way.

For five weeks the investigator met with the group in its weekly meetings. During the game period the boys were conducted through a series of games which necessitated their being divided into groups of four. These groups were formed at random by allowing the boys to pick a number from a hat. The boys then gathered in their groups, and each wrote on a slip of paper the name of the member of the group desired for leadership of the group in games that evening. The boys receiving the most votes were placed in charge while the games were played. The ballots were kept and the number of votes each boy received over the period of five weeks was tallied opposite his name. The boys shifted into various combinations; each boy had an opportunity each time to receive three votes besides his own. The results showed that the boys were not divided into two groups of leaders and non-leaders. There were some boys who received no votes in any group, and others who were always selected as leaders; between these extremes there was a continuous distribution.

The choices were checked by another opportunity to vote for a patrol leader; each boy was asked to name his first three choices. A correlation of .79 appeared between the choices according to the two methods described. A further check with the adult leaders of the group confirmed all but one or two of the choices. A study of the same group one year later showed marked consistency in the leadership ratings of the boys who had been in the group the year before.[1]

"Socially constructive leadership" is described in an extended study among German children. Leaders are children who have emotional sensitiveness, aggressiveness, self-assurance, ability to appraise a situation and a feeling of social responsibility. These functional capacities usually appear in children who are superior in age, strength, skill and knowledge. On the whole, American work supports this generalization, with the reservation that children who are *too superior* in age and abilities are not accepted as leaders. For instance, children with intelligence quotients of 160 are more likely to be leaders in a group of children with intelligence quotients in the neighborhood of 130 to 140 than in a group of children with average intelligence.

Two other continental studies emphasize superiority defined in somewhat similar terms. One stresses initiative, ambition or self-assertion, and vitality; the other conceives the matter in terms of longer duration of verbal excitation, greater rapidity of associative reactions, predominance of excitation over inhibition processes, higher differentiation of reactions, and greater adequacy of reaction. There is undoubtedly considerable overlapping between these functions and the factors that make for intelligence and initiative as conceived by American investigators.

But in none of these studies is there much analysis of the relation of *ability* to the use which is made of it by persons of different personality make-up. The able children who surprise us by not being leaders, the mediocre children whose energy "carries them further" than their ability would lead us to expect, are sufficiently familiar to stimulate more analysis of why children accept or struggle for leadership. As in the discussion of friendship, we find that most of

[1] In a comparison of the process of naming leaders and friends, both boys and girls were found to choose *friends* by these criteria (in order of importance): (1) "what they are" (ideal), (2) "who they are" (social), (3) "what control they show" (emotional), (4) "what they know" (mental); *leaders* were chosen in terms of (1) "what they do," (2) "what they are," (3) "what control they show," and (4) "what they know."

the research results simply define boundaries within which we might expect to find leadership. They do not pursue the specific process of becoming and remaining or ceasing to be a leader. In order to fill in the meager outlines defined thus far by quantitative studies, we should need more analysis of the goals and drives of children of given ability and interests who become leaders, compared with those who do not. What tendencies to compete with adults, to dominate others to create excitement, to get a job done, to receive admiration, to create richer patterns of social relationships underlie the zeal for leadership? Is the child who never leads devoid of these goals, or does he merely lack the hope and confidence of achieving them? Does he feel content with his "follower" rôle; does he compensate in other ways; does his pleasure lie in the approval and recognition of his leader?

To such questions as these we have the beginnings of answers, or the preparation of a framework for answers, in the work of H. H. Anderson. In an unusually thoughtful study which proceeds from a careful formulation of hypotheses, he formulates the following definitions of "integrative and dominative behavior":

Integrative behavior is defined as a phenomenon of growth in which the individual responds to differences in other persons. In integrative behavior a person yields to another, he finds a common purpose among differences and expends energy with another, i.e., he achieves a change in structure or function, in goals and purposes as a result of encountering persons different from himself. Integrative behavior is spontaneous, dynamic, flexible, changing; in theory it is growth at the optimum.

Dominative behavior is defined as a technique of responding to others by which a person resists differences, resists change, resists growth. In dominative behavior a person is rigid and inflexible, he has his mind made up; he does not reduce the conflict of differences by finding a common purpose among differences; rather, he maintains or increases conflict or tension between himself and others who differ from himself; he expends energy against or in opposition to others. In dominative behavior a person disregards the desires of others; he uses commands, threats or force to gain his unyielding objectives; he attacks the status of others; he adds to the insecurity of others.

Domination is something less than spontaneous behavior. It is not yielding or growing; it is self-preserving; it is an expression of fear of an impending change; it is the behavior of an insecure person.

Anderson further defines the functions of domination and integration in relation to the personality development of the individual. He suggests that domination tends to incite either domination or submission; domination stimulates submission if successful resistance is impossible. All of these forms of behavior he believes to be expressions of fear. Submission is the response of an insecure person afraid of impending change. "Integrative behavior" on the other hand tends to stimulate integrative behavior in the companion.

His experiment used 128 children of pre-school age, each of whom was successively paired with either five or ten others in an experimental play situation. It was found that social interplay could be reliably recorded as dominative or integrative according to the definitions given. Substantial positive correlations were obtained between the domination scores of paired companions and also between the integration scores of companions. If a child was dominating, or integrative, his companion tended to be likewise. Both domination and integration are related to ascendance, as indicated by correlations of .65 and .44, respectively; Anderson's hypothesis is that the term "ascendance," as ordinarily applied, does not discriminate between dominating and integrating types of behavior, and that these are fundamentally different in value and effect. He suggests, in fact, that they are dynamically unrelated, since on the basis of over one thousand pairings, the correlations between domination and integration are virtually zero.

A distinction similar to that made by Anderson between domination and integration is involved in Pigors' differentiation of leadership and domination. Implicitly, leadership is integrative in the sense suggested by Anderson when Pigors states: "Leadership is a process of mutual stimulation which, by the effective interplay of relevant differences, guides human energy in the pursuit of a common cause. Domination is a process of control in which by the assumption of superiority a person or group regulates the activities of others for purposes of his own choosing." Pigors comments that since domination is simpler, it can make its appearance earlier and has as its source the dominator's will to power. He agrees with Anderson that the dominator is a less strong individual than the real leader, and depends on external aid and the appearance of authority, whereas the leader's authority is often conferred spontaneously by others. Leadership, he observes, does not make its appeals in any complete form until cooperative play is possible between two and three. After this beginning, there must be some development of self-discipline, some grasp of abstraction and recognition of social ideals, some awareness of others as personalities and a degree of attention to memory span which will enable a child to pursue objectives consistently and to subordinate immediate to more remote goals. Full-fledged leadership of this kind seldom comes before the age of nine or ten.

Sympathy

The concept of "integration" which we have just been discussing is full of implications which are not made completely clear. What is the dynamic motivation of the child who shows primarily integrative behavior? Is this motivation related to other characteristics of social adjustment? We have noted Anderson's emphasis on fear as underlying dominative and submissive behavior. But what underlies integration? What, in general, underlies the broad capacity for cooperative and generous attitudes? In discussing friendship (page 512) we have already asked questions about the nature of the specific personal tie; but the question of cooperation is broader and even more difficult. Cooperativeness, generally, or sympathy, is broadly a form of feeling and of action, a highly complex mode of orientation of the personality toward other human beings; the problem of its analysis presents in concentrated form nearly all the difficulties of research in social psychology.

We may turn first to J. N. Washburne's study of sympathy as one of the characteristics important in social adjustment. The characteristics which Washburne defines and uses as a basis of a test for adolescents include the following:

1. Purpose, desire definitely directed toward a goal involving plan, evaluation, selection, and effort.
2. Socialness, a broad and lively interest in people.

3. Sympathy, sensitivity, empathic, and non-negative responsiveness to people.
4. Poise, emotional stability in social situations and the general sense of psychological intimacy and security with people.
5. Impulse judgment, self-control in the sense of being able to sacrifice an immediate or easily attained satisfaction for a more remote or more difficult satisfaction which is recognized as greater.

After the test had been shown to have satisfactory reliability, the results were compared with the standings of children in terms of good adjustment and poor adjustment as determined by the agreement of three people who knew the child. Exceptionally well-adjusted adolescents scored highest in the test; adolescents in penal institutions, lowest.

The sympathy score alone distinguished between the well-adjusted and maladjusted public school children; the well-adjusted were more sympathetic. Institutional groups, however, showed different results, no difference in score appearing between the well-adjusted and the maladjusted. Sympathy was found to be unrelated to objectivity, intelligence and poise. It was positively related to socialness and purpose, and somewhat negatively related to age within the adolescent years.

In the group of questions labeled "Poise" an attempt was made to get at the sense of social acceptance, intimacy, ease and rapport. Sample questions are:

Do you ever feel that nobody loves you?
Do you feel that nobody quite understands you?
Do people hurt your feelings very often, that is, almost every day?

This score distinguished sharply between the well-adjusted and the maladjusted in all four populations. The well-adjusted were more poised. The well-adjusted children also reported themselves as happier than the maladjusted, and they were less impulsive than the maladjusted.

The results of this test substantiate inferences which we might draw from clinical and psychiatric points of view: that on the one hand the capacity to respond to others with outgoing sympathy and

regard, and on the other hand the sense of being loved and ap-
preciated, are basic to happy adjustment in our culture. At the same
time we must also recognize the converse finding from a study of
sympathy among pre-school children: that many children are sympathetic when they are well adjusted, and unsympathetic when they
are unhappy.

In addition to these general patterns, it is also important to recognize the differences from one individual to another. While some
personalities are more sympathetic when they are secure and happy,
others are more sympathetic when their own troubles heighten their
awareness of the needs of others. We recognize these differences
among older people when we say that difficulties "mellow" some
people while they "embitter" others.

The processes of development of sympathy and love toward
others and the confidence of being loved have not been studied with
adequate protection of criteria for good scientific research. On the
one hand we have the associationist thesis, that the early experience
of love begins with the elementary tactual contact between mother
and child, which stimulates pleasurable reactions in the infant. On
the other hand we have the more inclusive statement of the psychoanalysts, who point to the child's experiences of satisfaction and
security in connection with the gift of nourishment which he receives
from his mother's breast. We have already referred to the results
of the rejection of the child by the mother and his sense of deprivation if mother love is not fully offered. The positive side of the
picture, in terms of the child's developing capacity for identification with, and sympathetic responses to, his parents, other members of his family, and those with whom he is in frequent contact,
has not been outlined adequately even by the analytic group.

At the biological level, we have to take note of the fact that the
ancient adage, "Love casteth out fear," must also be paralleled by
the observation, "Fear casteth out love." We do not yet know
whether individual differences in constitutional make-up or early
development affect differences in thresholds for fear or love and
pleasure, thus tending to prejudice the development of individuals
in the anxiety direction or the socially confident direction. It seems

fair to believe that the conception of hereditary differences applies to *every* aspect of the biological organism—the emotional make-up and "tissue needs" that are related to fear or love responses, quite as much as eye color and shape of the ears.

But if the psychoanalysts are right, fear and love cannot be considered independently but are intimately related, since they would have us believe that insecurity may frequently be an evidence of a lack of warmth or affectionate relations with others. Since cultural patterns affecting the form of response between children and their parents, and the form of response between the sexes at a mature level, show the widest differences in respect to the amount of warmth that characterizes personal relations, it may be fair to suggest that at times the particular quality of human response may not be so important for the individual as receiving the kind of response which is prevalent in the group. Insecurity might be more likely to develop when a response is expected because of its prevalence in the group, but cannot be counted on by the individual.

Thus in a group which values status more than love, insecurity in status will be more destructive than insecurity in love. Horney has suggested that in a culture prolific in conflict, great insecurity may arise from frustrated need for either power or love, and that either one of these values may substitute for the other. She suggests that whole cultures in which human relations are characterized by solid warmth and satisfaction in intimacy may produce individuals who are in general freer from fear or anxiety than are persons in cultures which offer less intense satisfactions in personal relations. Mead has already made a significant contribution in this direction in her analysis of the relationship between the competitiveness of a whole culture and the ego values of the individual. The fact that insecurity born of excessive competition breeds lovelessness may be quite as important to recognize in this circle of influences as the fact that lovelessness creates insecurity.

If we are really concerned with the total organism, we can readily see that these interrelations of insecurity and love are aspects of a larger reality. We might diagram the psychological relations between the competitive culture and the total personality as follows:

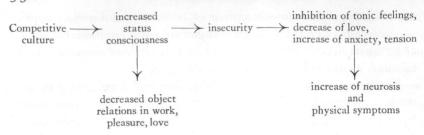

RELATIONS BETWEEN INTEGRATIVE AND AGGRESSIVE BEHAVIOR

The hypotheses just discussed point to the need for studying aggressive aspects of behavior in relation to cooperative aspects. In connection with an undertaking of this sort in a culture as full of ambivalence and conflict as ours, there are many pitfalls for the student of social behavior. When, for example, our scientific measures show a high degree of reliability and when, furthermore, different measures agree in assigning a *trait* or *category of behavior* to a child, we are likely to make extended inferences regarding the personality of the child. When a child receives a very high score for "fights," we are apt to call him a "good fighter" and visualize a "hard little guy." Or when, as in the case of one study of sympathetic behavior (cf. page 380), the reliability of observations is over .90 and the scores correlate about .80 with teachers' ratings, we are inclined to think of a child with a high sympathy score as a gentle understanding little person who is doubtless always ready to help out and is seldom inclined to get into the fray on his own account. But when we find that some of the children who received the highest scores for sympathy also received the highest scores on conflicts, and that sympathy and aggression correlated .4 on the average in five different groups, we find it necessary to revise our ideas of the relation between single aspects of behavior and the total personality. Among the consistently gentle Arapesh a high score on sympathy might exclude aggression, and among the consistently aggressive Mndugomor a high score on aggression might decrease the likelihood of any sympathetic behavior occurring. But in our own culture, with its right-handed take and its left-handed give, a clear tendency in either direction will, as likely as not, mean an equally clear tendency in the other direction; and the contrast will be not between the sympathizers and the fighters, but between those who are both active and expressive and those who are neither, those who "take" both aspects of the culture and those who "take" neither aspect. This does not exclude the necessity of recognizing other patterns, illustrated by children with high sympathy scores and low aggressive scores, or high aggressive scores and low sympathy scores. We merely take note of the fact that these last-named combinations are less characteristic than the aggression-sympathy pattern.

This throws a light, then, on the ways in which our culture structuralizes personalities which grow up in it, and the relations between behavior in different kinds of situations (within any limited culture area) to which children are exposed. The following fifteen-minute records of behavior of children in a pre-kindergarten group illustrate the flux of cooperation, friendly response, attack and conflict that appear every day in any large group of city children. The records will be most clear if particular attention is paid to one child; since this record was focused on Kenneth, it will be useful to follow the interplay of stimulus between him and other children, and the variations of response to different cues.[1]

KENNETH   Children present: Dodd, Julie, John, Alice, Kenneth,
10-18-34   Jack, Robert, Eugene, Louise, Nancy, Annetta, Hal,
Time: 10:40 Celia. T = teacher.
On the jungle gym, Alice, Dodd and Celia.
Kenneth says, "I'm glad I wasn't way up there when I falled."
Moves small ladder and leans it against jungle gym.
Says to T., "You put these ladders on here, please."
Then says, "I know where to put it, not there," and moves it.
Carries it, says, "Oh fasten the ladder."
Alice says something about a puppy.
Kenneth says, "I'm not a puppy, you are."
Alice, "You're a puppy."
Kenneth, "No, I'm a conductor on a train."
Alice, "You are a puppy."

---

[1] Record lent by the Child Development Institute, Teachers College, Columbia University, New York.

Kenneth, "I'll give you a sock, I'll give you a kick in the forehead."
Kenneth kicks at Alice but doesn't touch her, climbs on jungle gym
and then slides down slide.
Sits on bottom of slide, says, "What are you taking that mat for?"
Runs to jungle gym and climbs it.
Dodd climbs up slide.
Kenneth says, "Don't, I'll kick you in the face."
Goes down slide.
Alice says, "I'll kick you," and kicks at him.
Kenneth, "I'll kick you."
Runs back to jungle gym and climbs,
Says, "I'm glad this carriage is here, if somebody fell, they'll fall in."
Calls out, "All aboard, this is a train."
Climbs to stop of slide and sits by Dodd;
Says, "Don't take this away."
Goes down slide.
T. asks Dodd and Kenneth to carry mat.
Kenneth starts to and then drops it, says, "I'm not going to carry it,"
and walks off.
Approaches Eugene; Eugene says, "Help me lift this, will you?"
Kenneth helps him.
Eugene says to Hal who is standing near, "Get away from here, Hal."
Kenneth, Eugene, Hal and Robert pick up long heavy board and
carry it.
They put it down; Kenneth says, "Will you need somebody to help
you?"
Eugene says, "This is the slide to run on."
Kenneth runs down and up the board.
Hal, Eugene and Kenneth run up and down the board.
Eugene falls off and they all laugh; Kenneth says, "Do that again."
Eugene says, "No."
Kenneth, "Wasn't that funny?" laughs.
Eugene runs to jungle gym and Kenneth follows.
Eugene says, "Let's climb up there."
Kenneth says, "O.K."
Hal approaches and all three children climb jungle gym.
Kenneth climbs to the top of the slide and calls out, "Get the hell
out of here," and then goes down the slide.
Eugene and Kenneth go over to a wagon.
They pull it over toward a big box; Kenneth says, "Put it over here."
Eugene, "You help me."
Kenneth says, "You take one end and I'll take one end."
They carry the box.

Eugene, "We'll need another man."
Kenneth, "No."
Eugene, "We need five men."
They pull the wagon with the big box on it over to the jungle gym.
They then put a ladder on top of it.
Eugene says to Hal, "You hold on the back."
Hal, "O.K."
They run across the playground, Eugene pulling the wagon and Hal
  and Kenneth pushing from behind.
They pull it into the shed. Kenneth says, "I'll push it off. I'll hit
  somebody's head."
He pushes the big box off the wagon, and all laugh.
Kenneth says, "Now we'll get another load."
Eugene pulls the wagon out again and says, "Outside."
Hal picks up some lime out of a pail.
Kenneth runs up and says, "What's that?"
The workman says, "You'll burn yourself."
Kenneth repeats after him, "You'll burn yourself."

KENNETH
10-15-34
9:55
(Kenneth and Willis have had a fight with shovels just previous to
  this. Kenneth cries, etc. Teacher interference.)
Sits on inclined board to sandbox. Looks at observer. Picks up pebble,
  manipulates.
Talks to self. Looks at Hal and Dodd on tunnel.
Willis and Hal have fight at tunnel. Kenneth looks.
Continues to look.
Looks at Michael at door of garage.
Louise runs by. Kenneth looks.
Willis approaches sandbox, plays with older child. Kenneth looks.
Eugene rides by on tricycle, talks to older child in sandbox.
Kenneth looks.
Continues to watch Eugene and older child.
Willis approaches. Kenneth looks. Watches him.
Willis runs down inclined board, plays with barrel. Kenneth looks.
Continues to watch Willis.
Stands up. Brushes sand off inclined board with hand.
Sits down, looks at older child shoveling sand in sandbox.

Gets up, approaches Michael in other part of sandbox. Talks to self.
Goes to basket of toys, gets teapot.
Throws teapot back in basket, walks into garage.
Eugene follows him into the garage, says, "Let's play ball, O.K.?"
    Kenneth does not answer.
Kenneth looks on shelves in garage. Eugene says, "What're you look-
    ing for, heh?"
Eugene comes close. Looks at Kenneth's face, says, "What is that
    for that you had on your nose?"
Kenneth, "What I had on my nose is all better now."
Eugene, "Will you help me take this rope off? You did yesterday."
    Both look at roll of hose.
Kenneth, "Well, I'll tell you, I can't fasten the rope and play ball at
    the same time."
Eugene looks closely at hose, "Let's see."
Kenneth manipulates hose. Kenneth, "Well, I can't."
Both go out of garage. Eugene gets on tricycle, says something, a
    game—"Let's play ———— and you throw the ball when I go by."
Eugene rides, Kenneth runs to door.
Kenneth, "Get on this line right here." Points to crack in sidewalk.
Eugene rides to sandpile. Turns and rides down to Kenneth, says,
    "See, I have the big bike."
Kenneth says, "Let's play turns." Then, "Let's play gasoline station."
Talks some more about the gasoline station.
Eugene brings tricycle closer to door. Kenneth and Eugene talk about
    game of "gas station."
Eugene rides away, down the walk, comes back.
Kenneth, "How much gas you need, buddy?"
Eugene, "Four. Ten cents, I need."
Kenneth goes inside, manipulates door, comes out, says, "O.K. All
    filled."
Goes to door comes back, says something about "money."
Eugene says something about "money—change."
Kenneth goes inside, says, "I'm going give you the change."
Eugene, "Where's the change?"
Kenneth "Here." Holds out hand. "Here's the change." Then says,
    "Next day you must come for some more. O.K.?"
Eugene, "Where's the oil?" Kenneth, "Right here."
Kenneth goes inside door, says something, comes back.
Kenneth, "O.K., I'll give you some good, good oil."
Eugene says, "You better give me some tri gas." Kenneth, "Right
    now?"
Eugene, "Yes, right now."

Kenneth, " 'Member when I put that in there that was the gas." Points to back of the tri. Goes inside, gets square of cloth, talks about rug.

Eugene says something. Leaves on tricycle.

Kenneth runs out, yells. Stands in door.

Eugene returns, says, "Hey, gas man, gas man. I need some more gas."

Kenneth, "O.K." Comes out, sits in back of tricycle, says, "zzzzzz. I'm giving you some oil. Now I'm giving you some gas."

Eugene, "Now, I'll give you some money."

Kenneth, "Money. No checks, today." Eugene, "O.K."

Kenneth goes inside, comes back, hands "change" to Eugene.

Eugene leaves on tricycle. Kenneth says something. Eugene goes on. Kenneth goes inside.

Eugene returns fast on tricycle. Says, "Gas all finished, gas man."

Kenneth, "Well, you go away. I'm no gas. I have to fill my gas, now." (Apparently he means the pumps are empty.)

Manipulates handle of door. Comes out, goes "zzzzzzzz" and pretends to squirt hose.

Eugene says, "All over." Takes off hat, says, "All over head."

KENNETH
10-12-34
9:26

Riding on tricycle, on cement, making motor noises and "Honk-honk." Rides to end of cement and back again.

Rides back to Mother who is sitting on canvas chair near north end of cement. "Is this all you can stay here?" Rides a bit. "Honk-honk."

Sitting on tricycle, watching boy with truck.

Asks Mother which way she will go when she goes. "Honk-honks" at two girls.

Stops to watch Teacher fix Louise's sweater. Backs up, making motor noises.

"Honk-honks" at girl who approaches. Rides back to Mother.

Kisses her goodbye. Asks who will come for him.

Mother: "Maybe Daddy will come."

Kenneth: "Maybe Daddy. Maybe you'll come. *I'll play nice.*"

Mother: "That's the way."

Mother leaves. As she goes out the door, Kenneth calls, "You come."

Rides across cement. Boy approaches and says, "Hi, pal." No response.

Continues riding. "Honk-honk."

Rides to end of cement. Stops. Looks around.

Says out loud in conversational tone, "Hey Mommy . . ." Realizes she has gone and, still out loud, makes queer noises, singsong, in play on words, as though he never meant to say anything.

Rides. Watches Eugene and group on boxes.

Rides away. Motor noises. Approaches Louise.

Watches. Then drives away.

Heads toward sandpile from which there have come loud noises.

Stops. Watches girls play.

Rides away, looking back at Chiefie, any boy with trucks.

Boy from four-year group bumps into him.

Kenneth: *"If you bump into me again, I'll give you a summons. I'll put you in jail for five years."*

Boy: "You couldn't do that."

Kenneth: "Why not?"

Boy: "I'd run away."

Kenneth: *"You couldn't run away. I'd give you a sock. I'd get a gun."*

Boy: "You couldn't get a gun."

Kenneth rides around on cement.

Approaches Louise and other girls on tricycles.

Leaves own tricycle. Approaches Louise, says, "You'll go to jail if you run into her again."

Gets on wheel. Asks Louise, "Did you hear me? Five weeks if you run into her."

Louise: "Yes." Louise drives away.

Kenneth rides.

Sits on wheel. Drives. Motor noises.

Sits. Looking. Talking unintelligibly to self. Then, "Whee." Drives in circle, fast. Stops.

Rides toward storeroom. "Ding-dong—boop-boop."

Stops. Wheels bike up sand pit. Leaves it on top of pit. Runs down.

Picks up broom. Stands. Drops it. Goes to storeroom. Watches Eugene hammer.

Gets push broom.

Goes to sand box and sweeps sand.

Sweeps, talking unintelligibly to self. Goes to drain trough.

Watches girls.

Girls playing with trains in trough tell him to "look out."

"No. I'm one of those men who walk along the track."

Characteristically, the children draw upon a rich fund of vocabulary and imagery regarding police, jails, G-men and gangsters whenever conflict situations arise, and their resources seem more extensive in this direction than are the resources for cooperative dramas. When the latter do occur they reflect the competitive society in content, and activity consists frequently in buying and selling.

We have given here extensive samples of the actual behavior of children to make clear the complexity of the problem of "integration" in the relation of the child to the group, and to show that social integration in our culture is not a simple matter of substituting "good" behavior for "bad," but of achieving that balance of self-oriented and socially oriented behavior which best meets the needs of the individual and the group. The complexity exists at every level—it is not just a matter of "contradictory" behavior on the surface but often a matter of widely different motives giving rise to similar behavior.

All this is equally apparent in the study of aggression and in the study of sympathy. The interplay of spontaneous affection with routine acquiescence to convention, of response to the needs of others and concern with one's own need, of simple impulses to help, and rationalizations of aggression, all appear as bases of objectively recorded sympathetic behavior. Children who had the highest and most stable scores for sympathetic behavior on the playground were unsympathetic or destructively aggressive when their ego was threatened, when they were teased or misunderstood or put into inferior positions. In experimental situations with pictures, stories, and animals, sympathetic responses did not always emerge in clear distinction from other aspects of the personality, but they appeared as part of a varying pattern of response to which the child's previous experience with the situation, his identification with the object of sympathy, or the projection of his own anxiety, his curiosity, hostility, or suggestibility to the experimenter, all made some contribution. Not only intrinsic aspects of the child's personality but also changes in status that resulted from changes in the interrelations between himself and others profoundly affected the picture.

Even more dramatic variation appears in the records of Dan, an extraordinarily responsive child in an English group, who was ready with the warmest sympathy at times when other children needed it and who was a sturdy fighter on other occasions.[1]

22-10-24

Dan imitatively hit Mrs. I. She said, "Please don't." He said, "I'm *going* to," and hit her and ran out into the garden, turning round at the door and saying, "It will be better soon."

Cecil and Dan worked hard in the garden gathering leaves. After some squabbling for the use of the wheelbarrow, they settled down to sharing it, taking its use in turns very happily for the morning.

31-10-24

Harold was threatening Dan with cane; Mrs. I., after the usual warning, took the cane away. Dan protested, "But he will hit me with his hand!"

7-11-24

Harold's leg was hurt in a quarrel with Frank. He flung himself down on the floor with head buried in hands. Presently Dan went to Harold and said, "Is it better now? Will you come now and do plasticine?" Harold did not reply and took no notice. After a time, Dan again went and asked, "Will you *now* come and do some plasticine?" Presently Harold came.

12-11-24

While using plasticine, Dan made something for Benjie and gave it to him. "He has made a boat for me," said Benjie. Dan said, "Yes, I like you very much, and I'm going to kiss you." He kissed Benjie's hand. Benjie said to the others, "He likes me." Dan said to Harold, "I like *you* and I'm going to kiss you," and kissed Harold's hand. Harold said, "He is a dear little thing." All the others agreed.

17-11-24

At lunch, Dan said to Frank, apropos of nothing, "I'm cross with you—you get on with your dinner."

24-11-24

Dan threaded beads quite alone for a long time. In the garden the children found a small dead rat. They called it a mouse. Harold, Paul and Benjie said, "It's dead," and ran about with it. Mrs. I. took it away for fear of infection. Dan said, "You won't hurt it, will you?" He asked, "You haven't hurt it, have you?"

25-11-24

Christopher asked Mrs. I. to draw him a man. She did so and he started to cut it out with a pair of scissors. He cut across the picture. Dan said, "Oh, now it will be broke. He is a broke man."

---

[1] These records of Dan were generously sent to us by Dr. Susan Isaacs.

26-11-24

When melting wax, Dan always says, "Come and look, everybody!"

9-12-24

At the end of the afternoon, Frank changed his jersey, shoes, etc., because he was going to tea with a friend. Dan, noticing this, remarked that he was going to tea with Mrs. I., and said, "and that's why I have this jersey on." (It was in fact his everyday garment.)

Mrs. I. went to tea with Dan in his room. When she said she was going, Dan said, "I won't let you," and stood against the door. She remarked, "Perhaps you will let me go after a short time." He replied, "Yes, now I will let you go." She said, "Good-bye, and thank you for asking me to have tea with you. I have enjoyed it very much." Dan replied, "Good-bye. Did you? Perhaps you will come again another day?" "Yes, thank you, and perhaps you will come and have tea with me another day." Dan said, "I should *love* to, and will you come and have tea with me again one day?" She replied, "I should love to." He shouted through the closed door, "I thought you would."

12-1-25

Dan was present first and spoke of the other boys who were coming, and said heartily, "Here is one of the boys," when one arrived.

14-1-25

Dan was very petulant on one or two occasions during the morning. He wanted the only pair of scissors. Another child was using them and he insisted, with tears, that he "wanted them *now*." It took a little time before he would agree to wait.

Dan playfully wanted to "kill" Mrs. I. and then to put her in prison by rolling her up in a rug.

Dan and Frank were inclined to quarrel about the building bricks, Dan standing up to Frank very well.

In one of the records we are introduced to Dan as a child who responds vividly to another child's attack on a third child. His first response is one of comment, describing what the attacker has done and the fact that the child who was attacked cried. He then turns to the attacker, gets a promise that it will not be repeated, and finally comforts the attacked child with this promise that it will not happen again.

In another episode he analyzes the effects of losing a leg and tests his ability to cope with this experience. In another episode he is seen dominating a little girl affectionately and in still another he comforts an adult who has been threatened by another child. The following day, however, he attacks this same adult, imitatively offering verbal consolation as he takes leave of her. When another boy is hurt, Dan solicitously asks if it is better and twice invites him to play. Another day he expresses great affection for the same boy and kisses him. The following week he expresses irritation toward a different boy.

The sympathy which appears toward children and a grown-up is also shown toward a mouse and a picture. The same adult with whom Dan sympathized on certain occasions was the object of repeated aggressions by others, sometimes taking the form of obstructing her activity, at other times a threat to kill her, put her in prison, etc. The observer notes that on certain occasions he appears to be in a "petulant" or "bullying" mood; at such times he was jealous of toys which other children had, and he fought with the same boy toward whom he had been so sympathetic on other occasions. On other occasions he shared toys generously, both those of the school and those he brought from home.

The total import of Dan's records is that of an active responsive boy, enthusiastic about people and materials, imaginative and resourceful in manipulating both. The effects of the manipulation are constructive or destructive from one time to another, depending on (1) physical well-being, (2) freedom from frustration, (3) other inner or outer factors affecting mood or level of ego satisfaction, (4) the need of the other child.

THE ACCEPTANCE OF GROUP STANDARDS

At many points we have suggested the importance of the acquisition of habits of self-control, especially in relation to the development of the self (page 207), to identification with parents (page 238), and to specific patterns of authority (page 503). In interpreting the child's gradual acceptance of group codes and his "interiorizing" of these codes as a guide to autonomous conduct, the origins of *moral judgment* require analysis.

The series of investigations by Piaget relating to the moral judgment of the child have become more and more clearly significant for our whole orientation in social psychology. Piaget has worked by means of experiment and interview with many hundreds of children in French-speaking Switzerland, and has formulated a series of laws relating to the child's growth in that area. It is Piaget's own belief that the laws deduced from these studies are universal laws relating to childhood growth anywhere and at any time. We shall content ourselves here with a somewhat different use of the material, asserting only that the Piaget material shows, in rich and intimate detail, how children assimilate, use, and grow into our western European norms and standards. From this point of view, such studies offer a much-needed supplement to the objective accounts of the ways in which childhood behavior is modeled by the overt pressures exercised by western European and American culture upon the growing individual.

Our first concern is with childish *"realism"* in general. In the investigation of the language of little children, Piaget has noted a widespread tendency to confuse word with thing. The word for the moon is hard to separate from the moon itself; the word, in fact, is *in* the moon. Things have to have the names which they have; it would be wrong to call the moon by any other name. The world of things and the world of words are not dissociated.

The world, moreover, is exactly what it seems to be. There are no points of view; there is no relativity in perspective. Everyone else sees as the child does. For example, a small doll is placed at one point after another in the midst of a mountain range made of *papier maché*. About the room are photographs showing different aspects of the mountains as seen by observers at different points. A six- or eight-year-old child is asked to tell how the mountains look to the doll as the doll is moved from one position to another. The child consistently chooses from the photographs those which show what he himself can see from his own perspective. There is only one way in which things may be looked at.

That aspect of realism which is of the greatest moment for our present concern is *moral realism*. On the basis of primitive identification with the parents, the child has no difficulty in setting up a realism of absolute moral values—what the parents consider right *is* right. While some students of child psychology have thought that

children attributed to their parents the ability to *make* anything right
or wrong by fiat, Piaget has plainly shown that the child's confidence
in the correctness of the parents' judgments is due, rather, to the
unquestioning assumption that the parent must "know." It is the
parent that knows how to mend the broken tricycle and how to
take you safely by tram or train to a distant point; why should
the parent not know what is right and what is wrong?

Simple experiments are conducted with children of various ages
which show the initial moral realism and the steps by which it undergoes transformation. A story is told of a little boy who is called to
dinner; he accidentally knocks the door against a chair on which
stands a tray of dishes; they are broken. To the question, "Should
the child be punished?" children up to four or five all reply *Yes*.
And for the most part, punishment must be meted out in accordance with the number of dishes broken, not at all in terms of intent. The motive is not important; rightness and wrongness are in
the objective good and harm done.

The second stage in moral judgment is the recognition that the
rules are not objectively real, that they represent the values of the
group. This does not mean that rules are thrown aside; rather, that
their basis is seen to lie in the needs of one's fellows. The ethics
of authority, the absolute right and wrong which dominate the first
years, gives way gradually to an ethics of reciprocity. One learns that
the rightness of an act lies in the need of the other person who is
satisfied, or the distress which is averted. Whereas the ethics of
authority betrays a close kinship to the general realism of the little
child, the ethics of reciprocity develops with the development of
general objectivity and the recognition that there is more than one
point of view. Things are right or fair for you to do if you would
be willing to have others do them to you. With these Geneva children, completion of the second stage is evident at nine or ten years
of age.

Still a third stage must be noted, a stage in which absolute equality
of persons and reciprocity of moral judgment is "tempered by considerations of equity." The lame boy can be given a head start on
his way around the bases, or the nearsighted boy allowed to take
his bow and arrow a little nearer to the target. Socialization has

gone far to replace realism, just as it has in the development of other perceptual patterns (cf. pages 220 ff.).

All of these steps, laid bare by interview and by recording answers to stories which bring out ethical issues, are paralleled by investigation of another type of ethics which to many a child is more real than that of "morals," namely, the rules by which games are to be played. Joining in games of marbles with youngsters of three and four, and making a fair proportion of "dumb" shots so as not to overawe them by his skill, Piaget ascertains how you play the game, what is the right way to stand and to shoot. At first, at a pre-moral level, any way is good; the pleasure is the pleasure of sheer functioning with eyes and fingers. By six or seven years of age the child gives up the tendency to say, "I won and you won and we all won," has taken on the competitive definition of the game, and has necessarily acquired from the group rules which must be followed if one is to "win." *These rules,* like all other ethical rules, *are at first absolute.* That it is wrong to stand in front of the line when you shoot is just as objective a fact as that the sun is yellow. The question whether children could play a different way, standing in front of the line if they all wanted to, brings the same kind of response as the question whether we could all call the moon sun, and the sun moon, if we wished to. Such relativism is rejected; indeed, seldom understood. At about the same time, however, that realism in other phases has begun to fade, it has begun to fade from the game rules. Thus, it would be right if we all played that way. It becomes intelligible to the child that the game in Geneva is not played as it is in Lausanne or in New York. The important thing is reciprocity; rules reside in group arrangements, mutual respect. To the view of Durkheim, that all ethics must inevitably reside in authority, Piaget replies that there are, indeed, two worlds of ethics, a world of authority and a world of reciprocity.

These generalizations offered by Piaget apply to a group of lower-middle-class children in French Switzerland. Under the conditions of British life, somewhat different results are obtained as far as chronological age levels are concerned, and the rôle of socio-economic class is found to be important. In general, the Piaget findings are confirmed for a socially rather handicapped group; development is much more rapid among the favored group.

In the neighborhood of New York, similar research has been recently reported by Lerner, based on interviews with some 150 children in favored homes and some 300 in relatively handicapped homes. In the latter group, response to standard questions about the wrongness of telling lies fits well with the Piaget generalizations. Here, however, a very important additional factor is unearthed. To the question whether it is worse to tell a lie to your father or to your mother, about one-fourth of all the children give a clear and categorical answer, with full reasons for their opinion. With very few exceptions, those who think the lie to the father is worse answer frankly, "Because he can punish harder," "Because he would give a licking," or, almost as definitely, "Because he is the biggest one," "Because you can't get away with it with him," and so on. On the other hand, of those who answer that the lie to the mother is worse, nearly all say, "Because she is sweeter," "Because she understands you," "Because she is the best friend you ever have," etc. Obviously, social stereotypes and *clichés* have been absorbed and applied without stint. The important point, however, is that in children between eight and twelve, both boys and girls, there is a double, not a single, basis for morality.

This result does not fit neatly with Piaget's view, since there is very little reciprocity and a great deal of realism in the ethical judgments under both categories. But the basis of the judgment turns out to be emotionally complex. Even if it be asserted, as we think it can, that the question, "Which is naughtier?" forces upon the child a rather bewildering problem and that he is forced to compare two things which are emotionally on different planes for him, the fact remains that moral judgment derives not simply from a realistic attitude toward a prevalent code, but also from an affective disposition—a rather complex one at that—toward the persons involved in the moral situation. Moral judgments, then, are clearly *not* simply assimilated ready-made from the preceding generation, but are reworked in terms of the child's needs and degrees of identification with, and respect for, other individuals.

It might be added that, in defiance of both Freud and Piaget, many moral judgments of children are in violent conflict with those of their parents and, indeed, of the whole social world around them, if a line of conduct close to their own needs is involved. The parent who has tried to teach the small child that caterpillars, bugs, spiders and other "pests" must all be exterminated knows that even when the whole world backs him up the child may protest that the destruction of some tiny animal friend is wrong, and that in fairy stories, despite the universal condemnation of the wolf or the tiger, the child may alarm the parent by whole-heartedly assuming the wolf's point of view. Thus Boeck found a dependable stimulus for protest or tears to lie in the destruction of the wolf at the end of the Red Riding Hood story. Granted, of course, that the child has not fully understood the narrative and that the episodes are assimilated piecemeal if at all, the primitive emotional responses (e.g., sympathy; cf. page 187) and the moral responses of approval and disapproval depend not only on the world of culture, but on the individual's own needs. Some of the individual differences in moral judgments need to be given fully as much stress as the broader group trends which obtain when the situation for all is essentially alike.

In an analysis of the child's *range of identifications* in relation to his moral judgments, Lerner used a story situation similar to those used by Piaget. In order to make a lazy pupil work harder, the teacher forbids his classmates to play with him or to help him with his work. However, one of the boys in the class violates the taboo imposed by the teacher, because he "wants to help his classmate just the same." After making sure that the subject understood the problem, the motivations of the teacher, the pupil, etc., Lerner asked for the child's own opinion about the action of the hero. After this the child was asked to judge the probable opinions of *each of the actors* in the story situation. Four types of responses in this last point were distinguished:

1. All the actors in the story situation (both adults and children) have the same opinion: the hero's action is judged all "good" or all "bad" by everybody.
2. At least one of the five actors (i.e., the teacher, the lazy pupil, the altruistic classmate and the mothers of the two boys) has

an opinion different from the rest: it is usually one of the two
boys in question.

3. We find a more balanced division or diversity of opinions:
   the point of view of the child actors is clearly distinguished
   from that of the adult actors; or, even, the attitude of one
   of the adult actors (usually the mother of one of the boys)
   is also contrasted with that of the other adults in the story
   situation.

4. At least one of the actors gives a relativistic opinion; that is,
   the hero's action is judged neither "all black" nor "all white";
   the child ascribes a more advanced perspective of motivations to
   at least one of the actors.

The first type of response is very limited; the child projects his
own reasoning, no matter whether he is dealing with child actors
or adult actors, even after the experiment manifests the motive of
the teacher.

(a) Boy, 7:0.—What do you think of Paul, was he wrong (*qu'il
a bien fait ou mal fait*)? WRONG BECAUSE HE WENT TO HELP HIM.
And the teacher himself, what does he think, that Paul was right
or wrong? WRONG BECAUSE HE HELPED HIM. And Paul himself,
etc.? HE THINKS HE WAS WRONG BECAUSE HE HELPED HIM. And
Paul's mother, etc.? WRONG. Why? BECAUSE FRANK DIDN'T DO HIS
WORK (*a mal travaillé*). And Frank, etc.? WRONG. Why? BECAUSE
HE HELPED HIM. And Frank's mother, etc.? WRONG BECAUSE HE
DIDN'T DO HIS WORK.
7:0, ec. enf.—What do you think, was Paul right or wrong in help-
ing Frank? WRONG. Because? HE DIDN'T OBEY. And the teacher,
etc.? WRONG. Because? BECAUSE HE DIDN'T OBEY THE TEACHER.
And Paul, etc.? THAT HE WAS WRONG. Because? ALSO, HE DIDN'T
OBEY. And Paul's mother, etc.? WRONG. HE DIDN'T OBEY. And
Frank, etc.? WRONG BECAUSE THE TWO OF THEM DIDN'T OBEY. And
Frank's mother, etc.? WRONG. HE DIDN'T OBEY.

Older children showed capacity to identify with, and an understanding of, a wider variety of points of view.

(b) 7:4.—What do you think of Paul, etc.? WRONG. BECAUSE HE
WAS NOT SUPPOSED TO GO THERE. And the teacher, etc.? WRONG.
BECAUSE HE WENT THERE. And Paul, etc.? RIGHT. BECAUSE
HE CAME TO HIM (Frank). And Paul's mother, etc.? WRONG.
BECAUSE HE DIDN'T DO HIS WORK. And Frank, etc.? WRONG,
BECAUSE HE WAS NOT SUPPOSED TO HELP HIM. And Frank's

mother, etc.? WRONG. Why? BECAUSE HE CAME TO HIM. . . . What do you think, who is right (i.e., whose opinion is right)? PAUL (!). Why? BECAUSE HE CAME TO HIM. If you had been in Paul's place, would you help Frank? No. (!). Why? BECAUSE HE DIDN'T DO HIS WORK WELL. And if Frank had been your friend, etc.? WELL, I WOULDN'T HAVE GONE TO HIM, BECAUSE HE DIDN'T DO HIS WORK.

(c) 7:5.—What do you think, etc.? WRONG, BECAUSE HE WAS SUP-POSED TO LET HIM LOOK IT UP (*le laisser chercher lui-même*). OTHERWISE IT ISN'T WORKING. And the teacher, etc.? WRONG, BECAUSE HE OUGHT TO HAVE LET HIM WORK ALONE. And Paul himself, etc.? HE THINKS THAT HE WAS RIGHT, BECAUSE MAYBE THAT WAS HIS FRIEND AND HE WANTED TO HELP HIM. And Frank, etc.? RIGHT. BECAUSE HE HELPED HIM. And Paul's mother, etc.? WRONG, BECAUSE HE WASN'T SUPPOSED TO HAVE ANY-THING TO DO WITH OTHER CHILDREN. And Frank's mother, etc.? WRONG. HE WAS SUPPOSED TO LET HER CHILD WORK ALONE. The teachers, the mothers and Paul and Frank all have different opinions. Why? BECAUSE THE BIG PERSONS ARE ALWAYS RIGHT. If you had been in Paul's place, etc.? I WOULD HAVE LET HIM LOOK IT UP ALL ALONE, BECAUSE OTHERWISE IT WOULDN'T BE REAL WORK.

10:2.—What do you think, etc.? THAT HE DISOBEYED. And the teacher, etc.? RIGHT ON ONE HAND, WRONG ON THE OTHER HAND. And Paul himself, etc.? RIGHT, BECAUSE HE HELPED HIM. And Paul's mother, etc.? THAT HE WAS RIGHT IN HELPING HIM BUT WRONG IN DISOBEYING THE TEACHER. And Frank, etc.? THE SAME THING AS THE MOTHER. And Frank's mother, etc.? THAT HE IS A BAD PUPIL, HE SHOULD MAKE MORE EFFORT AND NOT LET OTHERS HELP HIM. Who is right? THE TEACHER IS RIGHT BE-CAUSE FRANK OUGHT TO WORK HARDER AND PAUL OUGHT NOT TO DISOBEY HIS TEACHER. If you had been in Paul's place, etc.? PERHAPS I WOULD HAVE HELPED HIM A TINY BIT (!).

Lerner points out that "egocentrism," together with limited em-pathic capacity (ability to put oneself in another's place), are both important in relation to the limited range of identification of the younger children. He emphasizes, however, the fact that the lack of *moral autonomy* of the child is equally important in so far as a child still accepts the prestige and authority of adults. The idea of what is just or fair is merely that which *conforms to adult commands*. This confirms Piaget's finding on moral realism in the small child.

An analysis of the answers of children from six to thirteen shows a striking decrease of subordination to adult authority from the younger to the older child. Susceptibility to the influences of the majority opinion of the group follows closely the pattern of decrease with age shown by susceptibility to pressure from older people. By the age of thirteen, however, 50 per cent of the boys still show little resistance to prestige whether it comes from adults or from the majority.

Another way of looking at the problem of limited perspective or limited range of identifications is pointed out in Lerner's discussion of *sociocentrism*. This was tested with the following questions:

A boy here, in your school, told me that the boys in school X (another school known to the subject) tell more lies than the boys here; while a boy in school X (the other school) told me just the opposite, that, etc. Who is right? Why?
A boy in Geneva told me that boys in X (another town or city known to the subject) tell more lies, etc.; while a boy in X told me just the opposite, etc. Who is right, and why?

Between these two questions was interpolated the question, "If your dad is arguing with another gentleman, who is right, and why?" The following question was also asked: "Who's more severe, your dad with you or the other dads with their sons?"

The following examples illustrate sociocentrism resulting from identification within the family.

8:3, 1st grade.—If your dad, etc.? MY DAD BECAUSE MY DAD WOULD ALSO AGREE WITH THE OTHER GENTLEMAN AND THE OTHER GENTLEMAN DIDN'T WANT TO AGREE WITH MY DAD. Who is more severe, etc.? THE DADS WITH THE OTHER BOYS BECAUSE THEY ARE MORE SEVERE THAN MY DAD. DAD LOVES ME MORE THAN THE OTHER DADS LOVE THE OTHER BOYS, BECAUSE MY DAD WORKS ON THE TRAMS, HE EARNS A LOT. THE OTHER DADS DON'T WORK ON THE TRAMS AND DON'T EARN A LOT.

8:9, 2nd grade.—OH, MY DAD BECAUSE I LOVE HIM A LOT AND I ALWAYS TAKE HIS PART. And the other gentleman? HE ISN'T MY DAD. MY DAD WITH ME [is more severe] BECAUSE I'M HIS CHILD. MY DAD LOVES ME BETTER THAN THE OTHER DADS THEIR SONS, BECAUSE I'M HIS CHILD AND THAT MEANS THAT HE LOVES ME LOTS.

10:6, 4th grade.—FOR ME, THAT WILL BE MY DAD BECAUSE I HAVE MORE AFFECTION FOR HIM. I DON'T KNOW THE OTHER GENTLE-MAN. Will your dad be always right? OH, NO, BUT I WOULD RATHER TAKE HIS PART. Who will be right most of the time? MY DAD BECAUSE I LOVE HIM MORE THAN THE OTHER GENTLEMAN. Who is more severe, etc? IT SEEMS TO ME MY DAD WITH ME BE-CAUSE I OFTEN GET BAWLED OUT (*gronder*) AND I NEVER SEE THE OTHERS GET BAWLED OUT. . . . IT SEEMS TO ME THAT MY DAD LOVES ME MORE THAN THE OTHER DADS THEIR SONS, BECAUSE HE OFTEN BUYS ME THINGS AND DOES MANY NICE THINGS FOR ME.

11:1, 4th grade.—WHAT MY DAD SAYS BECAUSE THAT'S MY DAD. Why isn't the other gentleman right? BECAUSE I DON'T KNOW HIM. Who is more severe, etc.? THE OTHER DADS WITH THEIR SONS BE-CAUSE MINE DOESN'T BAWL ME OUT VERY OFTEN. MY DAD TO ME BECAUSE I DON'T KNOW WHETHER THE OTHER DADS LOVE THEIR SONS, BECAUSE I DON'T SEE THEM.

Among the older children sociocentrism began to give place to relativistic replies:

10:0, 3rd grade.—IT DEPENDS ON WHAT THEY ARE SAYING. Let's say they are arguing about no matter what—about politics, for ex-ample, who will be right? SOMETIMES MY DAD AND SOMETIMES THE OTHER GENTLEMAN. (More severe) SOMETIMES DADS WITH THE OTHER BOYS, SOMETIMES MY DAD. (Loves more) RATHER THE OTHER WAY, BECAUSE HE LOVES ME A LOT, MY DAD DOES.

10:4, 4th grade.—FOR ME THAT WILL BE MY DAD, BECAUSE IF THE OTHER GENTLEMAN HAS A SON, THIS SON WILL SAY THAT HIS DAD IS RIGHT. (More severe) THE OTHER DADS, THAT IS, THEY BEAT THEIR SONS MORE OFTEN THAN ME BECAUSE MY DAD NEVER SAYS ANYTHING TO ME. (Loves more) THAT'S THE SAME THING.

12:10, 6th grade.—THAT DEPENDS ON THE STORY. IT MAY BE MY DAD, IT MAY WELL HAPPEN THAT IT IS THE OTHER GENTLEMAN. Who is right most often? I CAN'T SAY. (More severe) I HAVE NEVER BEEN WITH THE OTHER DADS. THERE ARE AMONG THEM MORE AND LESS SEVERE ONES. (Loves more) OH, I THINK THAT THEY LOVE THEM ALL THE SAME; MY DAD LOVES ME JUST THE SAME AS THE DAD OF ANOTHER BOY.

The same type of patterns appeared among children identified with their own schools and with their own communities.

7.9, 1st grade.—THE BOYS FROM X ARE RIGHT THAT THE GENEVANS TELL MORE LIES THAN THOSE IN X. BECAUSE THE COUNTRY WORK-

ERS ARE ALWAYS BETTER THAN THE CITY WORKERS. Who told you that? I KNOW. MOTHER SAID SO.

8:8, 2nd grade.—IN X. Why, what's your idea? IN X IT'S MORE IN THE COUNTRY. Where do people tell more lies, in the country or in the city? IN THE COUNTRY. How do you know? I KNOW.

9:4, 2nd grade.—Who is right? THE GENEVAN BOY BECAUSE THEY SPEAK A BETTER FRENCH THAN THOSE IN X. BECAUSE THEY DON'T SPEAK FRENCH AS WELL AS IN GENEVA. BECAUSE GENEVA IS OLDER THAN X.

10:2, 3rd grade.—IN X [they lie more] BECAUSE THEY ARE COUNTRY FOLKS, THEY BOAST OF THEIR ADVENTURES, THEY BOAST THAT THEY ALMOST DIED, THEY PRIDE THEMSELVES ON BEING GREAT ADVEN-TURERS, THEY ARE NOT. MY DAD TOLD ME SO, THAT THE PEASANTS ARE THE BIGGEST LIARS BECAUSE THEY BOAST OF BEING GREAT ADVENTURERS.

Lerner suggests that two factors are equally important here: the spontaneous sociocentrism or identification of the child with his own group, and the effects of concrete personal experience or of adult influence.

If it is sound to assume that moral autonomy of the individual is a possible and desirable goal in any contemporary culture, it must be evident that this imposes certain demands upon us for a clearer conception of socially integrative behavior, and more thorough re-search upon its psychological basis. The positive tele that provides a basis of group structure, the identifications that underlie sympathy and suggestibility to the moral standards of adults, are merely broad foundations for the development of personality and social re-lationships which will somehow free the individual for socially con-structive autonomy; the shaping of specific attitudes in directions which release the personality for effective and happy group work remains a gigantic problem. Any scientific study of the socialization of the individual within this framework of values will need to re-examine both the biological potentialities of human nature and the details of our culture in its impact upon children.

Chapter IX

THE DEVELOPMENT OF SOCIAL
BEHAVIOR IN EARLY CHILDHOOD

THE RESPONSES OF THE INFANT IN THE FIRST MONTHS

SOCIALITY, whatever its biological roots, is but slowly achieved. Few mothers have had to wait until their own babies arrived to find out that an infant is not a "social being," and that he does not begin to show perceptible signs of being one until weeks, maybe months, after birth. And few fathers could be convinced that a newborn child is more than a very uncoordinated succession of wigglings, slashings, kicks, and wails. It is no easy matter to determine how these uncoordinated activities become organized, or how and when a baby really does begin to respond to people in a way not characteristic of his response to things. A baby experiences persons so consistently from the moment of birth that it is difficult to determine whether his reaction to them differs in any fundamental way from his reactions to other things. To do this, we should need a controlled experiment in which we could compare the reactions of the infant to persons with his response to a super-perfect *Robot* —warm and comfortable to be snuggled against, and an efficient source not only of food but of the other usual ministrations of human beings. The baby attends to the sight of people very early; he may fixate a face for many seconds in his first week of life. But so does he fixate a light. He also attends to voices. (According to Canestrini, he may give differential attention to his mother's voice by the time he is two weeks old, but this has not been checked by other experimenters.) He will also attend to the low sounds and rhythms of a tiny music box, or other sounds which are loud enough to be stimulating, but not sharp or sudden enough to elicit a negative or "startle" reaction. Very early he will make movements of adjustment when he is picked up; but slight sudden motions on the part of the person who is holding him will bring as violent a startle reaction as he would show if his crib were suddenly shaken; being in human arms *per se* does not at first inspire even rudiments of security different from those given by non-human support.

If we scrutinize the social aspect of the infant's behavior with the motive of finding ready-made social responses, we are met with disappointment. The newborn infant may smile, but this smile is no more social than a Babinski reflex or his ability to support his body suspended in mid-air by grasping a pencil. The newborn baby can breathe, cough, hiccough, blink, smile, cry in different tones and with different forms of mouth opening, sneeze, yawn, move his head, hands, arms, and legs, as well as show a wide range of specific reflexes from sucking and avoiding to cries and starts. Yet neither the smiling nor the crying, nor any of the multitudinous combinations of skeletal behavior that appear in his repertory, are specifically social responses.

If human beings, as seems likely, mean no more to the newborn child than other things of equivalent sensory stimulus value, it is no wonder that such sophisticated distinctions as those between different persons are an achievement of weeks or months. Even after some weeks, the baby makes no distinction between his mother and any other lady of tender ways; if he is hungry and is picked up and held by a "strange" woman, he is quite as likely to turn and suck at her dress as he is when his mother picks him up.

There is, therefore, no clear evidence that the baby at birth is any more responsive to social stimuli than to non-social stimuli, or that he responds to them in different ways. This whole development of differential response to human beings is a slow process, and all too little light has come from experimental approaches. Ultimately, everything we can learn regarding specific or general maturation, as well as development in which learning has a part, is relevant to the study of the child's social development. Particularly important is the development of postural control, reaching, creeping, and walking, together with eye-hand coordination and the like. We shall refer to these only in passing, however, for attention must be limited to that behavior which is of direct and immediate concern for the social psychologist.

We are not construing the term "social psychologist," however, to mean simply a psychologist concerned with the social behavior of adults; for just as the social behavior of the Melanesians is important in its own right for the science of social psychology, and not merely for the insight it may afford into the processes of social interaction in our own culture, so the social behavior of infancy and childhood deserves consideration independently of its immediate import for the social psychology of adult life. While everything that we can learn about the origins of personality contributes to our understanding of mature personality, much of the early social behavior of the infant has no such direct significance, but becomes obsolescent without leaving *obvious* traces upon the organization of adult habits. Wherever we do have valuable experimental evidence on this early social behavior, therefore, we shall include it for its own sake; some of this material, it will be evident, is of definite value for adult social psychology.

The study of the development of social behavior is, however, not so much the observation of the appearance of *new kinds of behavior* as the study of the progressive formation of patterns or constellations out of chaotic, disorganized responses, together with the *conditioning of these patterns to certain stimuli or patterns of stimuli, among which social stimuli are integral or dominant.* Any of the single units of behavior which have been referred to may later be involved in a total pattern which would be called social behavior, whenever the pattern appears in response to a social stimulus. We shall therefore use simply the character of the stimulus as the criterion of the social response: social responses are those which appear in response to human beings, or to a combination of stimuli in which persons have an important place. For example, the baby who smiled unsocially shortly after birth will smile *at* someone who tries to draw out a smile a few weeks later. (M. C. Jones, in her experimental study of early behavior patterns, found no child under thirty-nine days of age who responded with a smile to the provocative social stimulus she presented as she bent smiling over the prone infant and "clucked" at him.)

As yet, only a beginning has been made in the experimental study of the development of these responses in infants, and attachment of these responses to social stimuli. Such experiments as have been carried out have approached the problem in widely different ways. Jones, for instance, was concerned with definite and specific patterns of behavior, while Bühler and her associates have dealt with larger problems less finely analyzed. Shirley's material on social development was collected incidentally in the process of measuring physical and intellectual growth. Because of this incompleteness of experimental material, we shall not try to offer a complete picture of social development in the early months, but shall emphasize those parts of the picture which are now filled in by evidence from dependable sources.

THE EARLY DEVELOPMENT OF SMILING AND CRYING

Smiling was the first cooperative response observed by Shirley in a study of 24 babies from infancy to two years. The mothers reported first true smiles at a wide range of ages from the third to the twelfth week; the examiners found that three-fourths of the babies smiled in the examining situation between the seventh and ninth weeks. Most of the earlier observers report early smiles in response to a variety of kinesthetic, organic, and tactual stimuli, such as stroking the lips or cheeks. These smiles are of the "discrete" sort, where eye response is not coordinated with mouth response; the latter appears like any other reflex in response to the immediate stimulus. These early simple reflex smiles are usually not considered "true" smiles; true smiles show the coordinated response of eyes and mouth. Whether this distinction is ultimately legitimate is not yet clear; it may be that the conspicuous objective difference between the simple reflex smile and the "true smile" is less important than it seems at first, and that the appearance of smiles in response to visual stimuli, instead of to tactual or kinesthetic stimuli, is simply one small step in a long series of developments, instead of the startling new level of behavior which it is often taken to be. In other words, both smiles may be merely mechanical responses; the smile which is a response to a visual stimulus may not have the different conscious accompaniments which it seems to have.

R. W. Washburn has studied smiling and laughing of fifteen infants in "games" based on familiar mother-baby plays, interspersing these with games not designed to evoke smiles. After a careful analysis of the stimuli reported by observers (from Darwin to Watson!) to stimulate smiles, she based the game series on those stimuli which were most amenable to control and standardization. The final group of situations devised to elicit laughter included the following: a social attempt to elicit a smile (similar to Jones's method); peek-a-boo; shaking head threateningly; rhythmical hand-clapping; hiding, then reappearing from under a table; rhythmical knee-dropping; "elevator play" (this is simply the time-honored trick of raising the baby above your head and jiggling him a bit as you hold him there suspended in mid-air; Washburn says she also talked and smiled a little to him while he was in this position). In addition to these, an apparatus for the sudden appearance of a mirror and Tinker Toy was prepared. (Laughter was also observed in various informal situations.) The various control situations were interspersed among these, such as dropping a spoon, offering a cup and cube, or pellet, and dangling a ring. Her results did not permit the establishment of even the most tentative developmental norms, but were very interesting as suggesting striking individual differences in laughing and smiling habits. All of the babies she used in her experiments had shown social smiles by the age of eight weeks. No attempt is made to measure systematically the factors which might presumably affect the "threshold" for smiles or laughter at a given time. Since she used a small number of cases, and since each child was tested only once at each age level, there would probably be a large opportunity for results at the separate age levels to be markedly affected by chance variations in such factors. This is why the findings are limited for the most part to data on the individual differences in the babies and on the stimulus value of the different experimental situations.

Between eight weeks and twenty weeks, and also after forty

weeks, the "social stimulus" (smile plus "clucking") elicited *smiles* almost invariably. The period between twenty and forty weeks, when this response was uncertain, corresponds to the level noted in general as the period when most children begin clearly to distinguish between strange and familiar persons, giving smiles to the latter when some strangers would not receive them. The peek-a-boo game drew smiles from only a fifth of the subjects between sixteen and forty-four weeks. Practically all the children *laughed* at one time or another at the "threatening head"; about half the children over twenty weeks old laughed at the rhythmic hand-clapping; all but one of the children smiled, and four laughed, at the sudden reappearance from under the table; the rhythmical knee-drop brought laughter from only four babies (one at each of four age levels), and smiling in twelve babies (at eight levels); "elevator play" brought smiling at every age level and from twelve different individuals at one or more of the age levels, but very little laughing; the sudden reappearance from behind the closed door brought indifference half the time, although other sudden reappearance "games" brought more response. *All of the stimuli brought smiles* from one or more subjects at one or more of the age levels; but *only the "threatening head," rhythmical hand-clapping,* and *peek-a-boo situations brought laughter* from over half of the subjects at one or more age levels.

The correlation of frequency of smiling and laughing with chronological age is too low to suggest a close relation after the response is definitely established. The range of laughter situations remains so nearly constant as compared with the widening range of stimuli to smiling responses that Washburn suggests a possible difference in the extent to which the two forms of expression are conditioned to new stimuli. Smiling may be stimulated more easily through association with a constantly enlarging number of stimuli, while laughter occurs in response to a relatively limited number. The shadow of a suggestion of evidence to substantiate the popular idea that fat people are the jolliest is offered by correlations of + .21, + .29 and + .47 between weight-height index and smiling responses, laughter responses, and the combination of the two, respectively.

High correlations were obtained between frequency of laughter or smiling and the mother's age; the subjects being ranked according to their mothers' ages, from youngest to oldest, these correlations were + .41 and + .45. Of course, to know the import of these correlations, assuming that they are significant, we need additional correlations—namely, between the mothers' own incidence of smiling and laughter and their own ages.

The following table shows the age of first observed smiling response to a given game:

Stimulus	Age in Weeks
Social stimulation (smile plus clucking)	8
Peek-a-boo, cloth over subject's face	8
Rhythmical knee-drop	12
Threatening head	16
Elevator play	16
Tickling	16
Peek-a-boo, cloth between examiner and subject	20
Sudden reappearance from under table	20
Rhythmical hand-clapping	20
Apparatus (with Tinker Toy)	20
Reappearance from cupboard	24

In general, those situations which elicited smiles early also elicited laughter early. It will be noted that both smiling and laughing occur first in response to explicitly social stimulation, that is, the smile and voice of the experimenter. Next, in no definite order, come the games involving a combination of social and impersonal stimuli (threatening head, for example, includes the visual stimulus of rhythmic head motion at first, and the final sensory stimulus of contact between the experimenter's head and the baby's body, plus the original social stimulus of the smiling experimenter). The sudden reappearance from the cupboard, involving chiefly the sudden movement, and the surprise box or apparatus—both probably the least social of the stimuli—are the last of the games to elicit smiling and laughing.

The following table is given by Bühler and Hetzer, analyzing the character of the stimuli eliciting laughter in the infants they observed. The variations from step to step are in part due to the small number of cases; despite this limitation, the trends from the earliest to the later levels are fairly clear.

RELATION OF SOCIAL LAUGHING TO LAUGHING AS A GENERAL (NON-SOCIAL) REACTION

Age	Amount of Social Laughing (in Per Cent)			Amount of General Reaction (in Per Cent)
	To Adult	To Child	Sum	
0 : 1	...	...	...	...
2	100	...	100	...
3	89	...	89	11
4	92	...	92	8
5	60	15	75	25
6	50	...	50	50
7	49	13	62	38
8	20	30	50	50
9	10	40	50	50
10	40	30	70	30
11	25	50	75	25
12	10	40	50	50

As far as they go, these data tend to support Bühler's contention that so-called "true smiles" occur first in response to the social stimulus of the human face, and only later in response to non-social stimuli. Since the material used by both Bühler and Washburn does not make a consistently clear-cut distinction between the two types of stimuli (Washburn's "elevator play," for instance, involves talking and smiling, in addition to the suspension and motion in midair), this conclusion can hardly be considered final. There is special need for study of the smile response to sudden slight changes and movements. It would be quite possible to interpret all the earliest smiles as due to mild visceral or kinesthetic stimulation, and even to add that "true smiles" may at first be a result of visceral excitation (the smile of another person may be one of the adequate stimuli for such visceral responses). While smiling is the first active or "cooperative" social response, it is not isolated, but appears along with visual and tactual reactions, some of which precede it.

Shirley's *The First Two Years* presents the ages at which a variety of social responses appeared, from the first sober watching of an adult's face, at about two weeks, to recognition of a mother's picture, at 70 weeks. In this series of responses, visual attention came first, then smiling, then a variety of manipulatory responses and participation. The earliest social development also included less active responses, such as being quieted by being picked up, being soothed by the mother's voice. Pleasure in the company of adults and children was expressed from the second month on by cooing, kicking and laughing out loud. Grasping at the doctor's fingers began a period of manipulation of the adult in which pulling his hair was characteristic of the babies at six months, and was followed by exploration of his features. On the average, the babies began jabbering for attention at about six months, and shortly after would begin to recognize adults by sounds, such as the sound of the car in which the adult customarily arrived.

In the pre-language period, crying is a common way of "demanding attention" in our culture; it is not consciously encouraged, and its inhibition marks as important a transition from "babyhood" to childhood as do the other forms of "self-control," e.g., acquisition of toilet habits. There is no doubt that crying serves somewhat different functions for children of different degrees of autonomic stability, and that the experience of learning to inhibit it is assimilated in different ways by different children. Quite frequently nursery-school children regard it as a mark of status and of recognition as "a big girl or big boy" to inhibit crying, and children who cry are teased whereas children who have problems of enuresis may have their difficulties happily ignored. Most cultures seem to be "against crying"; but our own cultural basis for this strong pressure against it may be dependent partly upon anti-sentimentalism, which decrees that no occasion may justify the weeping of a strong man, and the general pressure toward business-like constructive "solutions" of problems at the expense of emotional experiences of life. This cultural emphasis naturally gives security to the less emotional child and may give insecurity to the child who cries. These social aspects of crying, or the personality effects of its taboo in our culture, have not been studied; most of the study of it has been a matter of observing the specific situations which elicit it.

The first crying, like the earliest smiling, is not primarily a social reaction. Probably, as Bühler remarks, *all* the crying of the newborn is in response to bodily needs and hurts, hunger and pains or discomforts of various sorts. Pain caused by a prick; nose-cleaning;

doctor's examination; sudden lifting up during sleep; digestive difficulties; sudden stimuli of various sorts, such as rapid change of temperature; loud noises, particularly of a clanging sort—all these usually cause crying in the newborn child. Further generalization, in terms of cries of anger or fear, is probably not justifiable in reference to this early age.

We have already referred to the Shermans' studies (cf. page 107) which showed that clear-cut patterns of rage or fear could not be distinguished by intelligent observers who saw reactions which had resulted from such stimuli as loss of support and pricking with a needle. Moreover, even if we grant that such definite patterns do mature fairly early, the problem is far from simple.

That variability in intensity is an important factor in relation to many stimuli including sound is suggested by M. C. Jones in her comments on Sherman's experiments. If mild restraint was applied to the head, the child was unresponsive or moved his arms and legs slightly; while if the restraint was applied suddenly and with intensity, the child kicked, pushed with his hands, and cried. That this whole matter of intensity is, however, a two-sided affair and depends not merely on the objective stimulus, but also on various inner factors, Jones emphasizes. Building on Sherman's observation that responses indicate the child's efforts to adjust to the stimulus, she formulates a functional conception of emotion in terms of the factors affecting adjustment. "General excitability" and "the preparedness of the organism" at the moment are factors determining the "threshold" of the emotion, the ease or adequacy of adjustment, and therefore the specific elements in the pattern of response to a particular situation. This outline of the conditions affecting emotional response clarifies the data from Sherman, as well as those from other investigators.

Valentine's experiments on and observations of his own children in the earliest months, for instance, showed that the crying response to loud sounds varied with different conditions. When the stimulus was the tearing of paper, it produced no fear the second and third time it was presented, although the response was clear the first time. Suddenness and novelty appear to be important in connection with loud sounds, as they are in connection with other stimuli which later arouse crying and fear. But even this does not tell the whole story, since stimuli which brought responses of crying when the child was by himself did not do so when he was being held by his mother. In other words, suddenness, novelty of the stimulus and security of the child all seem important, in addition to intensity of sound.

All the manipulations of feeding, drying, dressing, and so on, are intimately connected with persons, and very early persons come to be associated with these. Probably Bühler is right in pointing out that the stimulus situation must be defined as closely as possible; the infant, for example, who stops crying at the moment of being dried, rather than at the moment of being picked up to be dried, is not reacting to the social aspect of the stimulus. But the infant who stops crying at the moment he is laid down near his mother while preparations for nursing are made is responding to the social elements of the situation quite as much as the child of four or five months who whimpers at the advances of a stranger, and the youngster of nine or ten months who cries when his mother leaves the room.

Responses to Visual and Auditory Stimuli from Persons

Of special importance for these responses to social stimuli is the development of visual and auditory functions; during the first few months, the attention of the child seems to vary from one sense modality to another. The young infant "hears actively, that is, listens, before he sees actively, or looks," according to the findings of Hetzer. The peak of interest in sound, in comparison with visual or tactual stimuli, comes at the age of two months (Löwenfeld). The infant gives more attention to visual stimuli as his absorption in auditory ones decreases. At three months, the infant actively turns toward a stimulus color (Hetzer found that 100 per cent of four- to seven-months children actively turned toward colored wool). In all probability it is not until the third or fourth month that we can speak accurately of the domination of sight.

When the behavior of the newborn in response to the human voice is experimentally compared with his behavior in response to other sounds or noises (such as those made by a bell, a rattle, paper rattled by crushing, a whistle, etc.), his reactions to the former are far less frequent and dependable; by the end of the first month, however, he is just as responsive to the human sounds as to others, even if the latter are much louder. In other words, the fact that the voice is a sound associated with human beings (and their ministrations) brings to it a degree of attention out of proportion to its mere sensory stimulus value. The baby's reaction to these different sounds is expressed in various ways—there are characteristic modes of response for loud noises, and equally striking characteristic responses for the human voice. The earliest specific reaction to the voice is sucking; later, as we have seen, the voice arouses a smile. Responses to the voice include vocal expressions popularly called sounds of pleasure, or sounds of discomfort and crying. The infant will react more frequently to emotionally toned voices—such as those of persons speaking angrily or in a friendly way—than he will to ordinary conversation. It is not clear as yet, however, whether this difference is due merely to the difference in pitch or intensity between an emotionally toned voice and the unemotional voice, or to subtler and more complicated factors.

The first sucking reaction to the human voice might be simply a reaction to an element in a familiar pattern of stimuli, i.e., food being brought.[1] At the time this reaction appears (about the third week), the infant is not yet turning his gaze in the direction of sounds. There is no connection between the sound and its source; for the infant, therefore, the *speaking person* does not exist. At this time the chief source of satisfaction is the arrival of the welcome food; if it does not come the infant wails. When he begins to follow sounds with his eyes, however, a new interest develops, and the person whose voice he has heard becomes interesting and at least temporarily satisfying. After this we can see him now becoming restless and unhappy at the sound of a voice, and equally readily quieted by the sight of the speaking person. These reactions seem to have no relation to the particular person whose voice is heard. The *voice*

---

[1] This is Bühler's hypothesis. Other work suggests that this may really be a dynamogenic effect appearing in response to almost any stimulus when thresholds for sucking are very low.

of a stranger is quite as disquieting as the voice of one who has been with the child a great deal—even the mother—and the appearance of the stranger is also just as quieting until about the fourth month.

The smile, which eventually becomes a general reaction elicited by a wide range of stimuli, appears for a time (approximately the second to the fourth month) chiefly in response to the voice. To the casual observer the response is utterly undiscriminating—scolding will bring quite as joyful a smile to the child as affectionate talk, and angry talk as amiable an expression as a lullaby (see plate facing page 566). It takes months of growing up before children "know" that the proper response to an angry voice is crying, and that scolding is good cause for disquietude and anxiety, while smiles are reserved for friendly, loving and playful tones. Only about the time that vision has developed to the point of achieving eye-hand coordination (usually in the fourth month) does the infant distinguish his mother and other familiar persons from strangers.

Before this, of course, the special sounds and feelings, and to a certain extent the "looks" of human beings, have begun to lead to elementary social responses. At first, as we have noted, only the removal of the diaper and actual drying will cause cessation of a wet baby's cry; and only with sucking is there an end of hunger wails. Sometimes, however, the associations of a few days will suffice to result in an end of crying upon the approach of a person. Within a few days from birth, the hunger cry of infants may be interrupted for a few seconds or even for several minutes (depending on the intensity of the hunger, the intensity of the distracting stimulus, the tendency toward perseveration, etc.) by the swaying or rocking, the caresses and voice of the nurse. In the first quarter-year these personal methods of quieting the child are not necessarily more effective than mere distraction through rapid change of position, turning on a bright light, or ringing a bell. As the intensity of his response to strong stimuli decreases, and his interest in the sights and sounds of persons increases, however, these distraction methods become less effective, and social methods of quieting or "comforting" become more effective. Then the mere fixed look of the adult may be sufficient to quiet the child. The variety of stimuli which may result in cessation of crying is suggested by the following protocols of Bühler:

"B 71" (age 5 days) lies in his crib on a large sheet. He begins to cry. The researcher lifts the sheet on which he lies and he stops.

"B 5" (age 0:1) cries and moves himself restlessly. I speak to the child very loudly from my place by the window. Immediately he ceases as long as my sounds continue. Cries when he is undressed, but being put in the bath quiets him.

"B 13" (age 0:2) cries vigorously. The shower is turned on. The sound of the flowing water causes the child to stop crying.

"B 23" (age 0:4) stops crying suddenly in order to follow with his eyes a nurse who is going by.

The derivation of satisfaction from tactual, visual and auditory stimulation by persons, regardless of ulterior results, is one of the most important roots for later social response. In a remote way it is probably the beginning of the later love and friendliness responses. At the moment we can say only that it is a strong enough stimulus to compete with and supplant hunger and pain responses of considerable intensity. With the development of vision, smiles enter into the response; with the development of vocalization, "sounds of comfort" are added.

The infant of four or five months is an amazingly socialized creature in comparison with his ten-day-old self. Sounds and sight of persons have become satisfying for their own sake; smiles and crying give the basis for real social give-and-take; and these, together with grabbing, make play an important part of the baby's life from now on.

We have already noticed that Washburn found a gap in the record of infants' responses to social stimuli—babies who had smiled or laughed in response to her tests suddenly ceased to do so when about four months of age; at about nine months they again responded readily to the experimenter's smile (cf. page 558). This failure to smile was interpreted as due probably to the child's new distinction between familiar and unfamiliar persons, noted above. Bühler has gone further and has attacked the problem of infants' reactions to strangeness in itself. She and her associates set up some experiments to determine the effect of strange things *per se*, and, further, the effect of change *from the familiar to the strange*. A mask

Ages 16 and 13 months
The older offers a toy to the younger

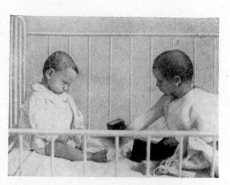

Ages 11 and 17 months
The "despot" grabs all the toys for himself

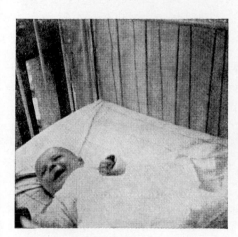

Age 3 months
Laughing in response to scolding

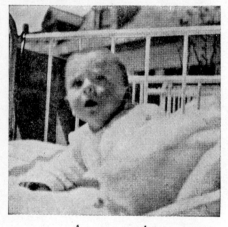

Age 7 months
Anxiety and astonishment in response to scolding

(*Used by courtesy of C. Bühler*)

was used as a strange visual stimulus, and falsetto and rumbling tones as strange auditory stimuli. In one experiment, the mask was put in front of the face of the observer, which had previously been visible; in others the normal voice was suddenly changed to falsetto or rumbling. "Negative" reactions to these changed stimuli decreased rapidly with experience.

In order to discover whether this "becoming strange" was in itself the cause of the negative reactions, experiments were arranged as follows: First, one strange stimulus was replaced by another strange stimulus, and, second, a strange stimulus was replaced by a familiar one. The results of these indicated that a *change in the stimulus* was in both cases sufficient to produce negative results. Evidently the *strange procedure*, rather than strangeness or familiarity of the *object*, is the important aspect of this situation. The child reacts to the situation "something-turning-into-something-else-in-an-unaccustomed-way." Anticipation and mental set, disturbance of expectation, rather than mere unfamiliarity-of-thing, cause the negative reaction.

Valentine, on the basis of experiments on and observations of his own children, presents a serious challenge to the hypothesis that most late-appearing fears are conditioned through association with loud sounds, etc. He urges that the absence of specific fears at a given age does not preclude the possibility of their maturation later. In defense of the hypothesis, he cites the results of experiments with a caterpillar, a dog, and a horse; apparently unconditioned fears appeared after the age of one year which were not present earlier. He offers a particularly good case for what he calls an unlearned fear of the uncanny: a mask, the detached eyes of a doll, a doll's head which opened in the back, are the stimuli which elicited this fear response in a baby between one and two years of age.

These results of Bühler and Valentine are consistent with Jones's contention that the arousal of fear depends upon the individual's general level of development as well as on his specific ability and readiness to adjust; for with general maturing comes new perception of differences and quicker recognition of newness and strangeness. So also are they consistent with Bühler's experimental finding that "negative" reactions to masks, for instance, decrease with repetition, since repetition directly facilitates readiness and ability to adjust.

Bühler has also experimented with emotional responses of infants under other categories than simple social recognition and response. "If one takes away the toy from the playing child, the child in the first month forgets this at once. Even up to ten months, he scarcely reacts negatively in half of the cases. Only after ten months does a one-minute rage reaction appear in eighty per cent of the cases. The child wants this particular toy again." In other words, general growth, possibly involving the development of imagery, is extremely important for the "set" of the organism in relation to so-called "rage" reactions as well as to "fear" responses. In a further series of experiments a person or an object is shown to the child, then hidden, then shown again. The interval of expectation increases from a few seconds in the two-months child to a few minutes in the one-year-old. From eight months on, one can note a *latent period*; that is, the object can be hidden, the child's attention turned to something else, and the child made to look for the object to see whether he still remembers the thing that disappeared. He may recall the object *spontaneously*. This experiment of Bühler's is reminiscent of Hunter's delayed reaction experiment (cf. page 244).

Thus as the child acquires greater mastery of the arts of reaching, grasping, and manipulating, together with the development of anticipation and sustained interest, he begins really to "play." His relations with people are extended from the mere "economic" level as soon as he begins to smile at the vocal or tactual play of the adult. A more marked extension takes place as he enjoys people for the toys they bring him and for their playing with him. As the child begins to offer objects to the grown-up, "organized" play begins, in which grown-up and child may "give and take" not only smiles and simple sounds, but things. This give-and-take, like other new achievements, is at first a game in itself, later being integrated in more complex play patterns. The following examples from Bühler's experiments illustrate this development:

"B 50" (0:10) holds her doll out toward the observer, allows her to take the doll from her, and laughs as it is returned to her—holds it out again.

"M 51" (0:10). The nurse picks up the doll which has fallen down. M 51 gives her back the doll which she holds. The nurse presses the doll, which squeaks, and gives it to the child again. She holds it, then gives it back again. Finally she keeps the doll and seeks to produce a tone by pressing as the nurse had done. When she succeeded she was much pleased.

The various games the child engages in reflect aspects of his general development. From the eighth month on, he shows consistent preferences and will stick to a preferred toy if it is offered in a series of choices. The three- to four-months-old child, Bühler reports, will, if three toys are placed before him, gaze first at one toy, then at another. In the period from five to seven months, he does not let his gaze roam over the toys, but unreflectingly and instantly grabs whichever one he sees first. In the next couple of months, however, he begins to observe before he chooses—there is definite inhibition of the act of grasping itself, and the choice takes a longer time. Interest in the child's own body changes, too. Hetzer found the duration of occupation with play with the child's own body greatly increased between the six-month and twelve-month level. Play with an object may last only a few minutes in a six-months-old child, and over twenty minutes with a one-year-old child. All of these changes in interest, span of attention, and the like, make for new aspects of social interaction—new interests in other people and the ability to maintain more sustained play relations.

Imitation as a Basis of Social Learning

Imitation, a problem of the most obvious importance for social development, has been studied by many investigators; its nature and varieties have been suggested in Chapter IV. But the work of two or three experimenters who have emphasized developmental problems deserves special consideration here; among these, Guernsey's work with young Viennese children is especially interesting. She found that eight-months-old babies would repeat movements which had been made in front of them. Following Bühler, she distinguished two fundamental types of imitation, depending upon the two fundamental ways of handling a thing: (1) merely functioning with it, (2) purposeful control of it. She studied also the kinds of things which produced imitation in ten children at each age level. She used thirty-six stimuli; half of them were expressive movements and body movements, the remainder were movements related to objects. Functional imitation of body movements such as raising and lowering the arms is reported in some babies before eight months, and all of the babies between eight and ten months showed this type of imitation. After the age of ten months, the percentage at each age level who showed this behavior decreased steadily. Imitation of movements in relation to objects began later (except for striking a drum) and increased steadily through the age groups she studied (up to twenty-one months). The decrease in imitation of expressive movements is interpreted as due to loss of interest. All children imitatively raised arms between eight and ten months, but lost interest after this period. All the body movements included in Guernsey's list were imitated by the children before the age of one year; but only the simplest *handling of materials* occurs within the first year.

In general, Guernsey's experiments overlap a good deal the experimental work of Valentine, which he summarizes as follows: Before two months, "at an age long before purposive imitation can be imagined possible," there is evidence of specific forms of imitation, the earliest of which is imitation of sounds. Next he observes imitative smiles and laughter; and imitative tongue protrusion is reported before the six-month level. Between six and twelve months, broader movements come to be imitated, requiring a larger amount of learned muscular coordination, such as waving hands, putting head on one side, making a kissing noise, and other movements of the general character of Guernsey's "shaking the head."

The fact that these various phenomena may all be classified under the general heading of imitation does not, of course, mean that the same processes are involved. The early smile may be an expression of internal (visceral) excitation, the later ones aroused by the smile of the adult or even by the total pattern of smile-plus-excitation in the adult; in other words, it may be imitation of a "circular" type (cf. page 183). Whether all the baby's imitations are of this general character, or whether other principles must be invoked to explain the imitations of movement described by Valentine and Guernsey is not yet clear.[1]

Imitation is undoubtedly the basis for some cooperative responses; but postural adjustments during dressing, helping to pull socks off, playing peek-a-boo and other forms of cooperation before the age of one year involve more complicated learning (Gesell, Shirley).

In answer to the suggestion that all early social responses such as smiling, babbling, locomotion, may be due to imitation, Wayne Dennis presents his evidence of the normal development of an infant who was exposed to no social stimuli beyond those necessary for actual physical care. The baby was not smiled at until it first smiled. Its physical, motor, and language development was in every way normal. The social-emotional development of the child was not followed to the point where one could say with equal assurance that the child's security and emotional development was quite as normal as its physical growth.

Probably a large proportion of infants have practically no social contacts except with the mother or nurse or with an older child who cares for them. Practically none, except twins, or children in a private or public nursery or orphanage, would have frequent contact with another infant less than a year older than himself. Most of the experiments of social import (e.g., those of Jones, Washburn, etc.) also make use solely of the infant-adult relation. Moreover, these experiments, being concerned with the study of particular items of behavior, throw but little light on the development, in infants, of personality traits and behavior patterns of more comprehensive character.

Bühler, however, has made an interesting study of the reactions of babies of different ages, from four months to nearly two years, to each other. Two infants, sometimes of the same age, sometimes a

---

[1] Suppose, for example, that the small child can see the tip of his tongue as he protrudes it; the observation of another's protruded tongue could cause circular reflex imitation exactly in the way discussed on page 183. But the little child's tongue is too short; and this humble fact necessitates very complicated hypotheses about kinesthetic factors of various sorts supposed to be operative. Perhaps in most cases it is the adult that first imitates the child, stimulates the child visually when some organic condition has first initiated the child's response.

few or many months apart in age, were placed in a crib together. Starting with the situation of the mere presence of the two babies together, variations were introduced; the experimenter held out a toy to one or both of the children, or placed the toy between them.

At the age of four months a baby in this situation will not notice the other baby; at five months he will stare at him, and perhaps smile; four months later he will often babble to the other child, offer him playthings, and cry if the grown-up pays attention to the other child. At this age he will usually permit toys to be taken away from him quietly when a playmate grasps them. By ten months he may object to this, and a little later, before the end of his first year, he may take the initiative in social advances, babbling to another child *to gain his attention*, reaching toward him, showing displeasure when the child moves away.

Children in the first half year, Bühler reports, do not show any tendency to rivalry or domination in this situation. In the last half year, children of approximately the same age are apt to be competitive; the greatest difference in age between children observed to be competitive was two and one-half months. When the pair consisted of babies of three months' or more difference in age, the older one almost invariably dominated the younger. This "domination" was expressed in various ways—by making "aggressive" movements whether amiable in effect or otherwise, reaching toward the other child, touching his face, striking him; or by offering the toy in his possession to his companion; or by taking away the toy from the other child, by grasping it when it was offered by the experimenter or merely placed in the crib. The submission, or "being dominated," reaction, was apparent in crying, and in the lack of protest when a toy was taken away.

Bühler's method produced interesting results, but these are limited by the fact that there was no very systematic control and variation of conditions. Consequently, we know that babies show wide differences in behavior, with rather definite tendencies to dominating or submissive behavior and the like; but there is no systematic information regarding the relation of dominance or submission to the difference in ages between a given child and his partner, or to differences in experience such as presence and number of brothers and sisters, number of adults in the home, physical differences such as height, weight, strength, health, emotional stability, and normal activity; not to mention other subtler differences of habit and temperament which might affect these social responses. As Bühler points out, probably an important factor in these differences of behavior is the degree of physical development of the child—security in sitting up, ability to reach or turn without toppling over, and other aspects of bodily control. The factor of inferior physical development can be compensated for by intellectual achievements much less adequately in the beginning than later.

To summarize, then, the spontaneous social reactions of small infants may be schematized in something like the following progression: passive response (being quieted by the caresses, voice, or motions of an adult, when hungry or in discomfort); attending to the voice of a human being; attending to faces; catching and returning the glance of an adult; seeking the latter; turning head and body toward a person; reaching out the hands toward a person; babbling (the last four may be classified together as visual, manual and vocal appeals for response, though interpretation must be cautious); neglecting play when catching the glance of an adult; offering her an object; turning toward her when frightened or surprised. In addition to these relatively spontaneous responses, more obviously "taught" ones may be observed, such as waving a hand at parting or reaching arms to be picked up.

The following examples taken from Bühler's observations illustrate the progress in social give-and-take that may be expected during the last half of the infant's first year:

"M 21" (0.4) returns the glance of the nurse, who looks at her, with laughing and cooing.

"M 30" (0:6) turns herself around from back to the stomach and seeks to gain the attention of her grandmother toward herself by "lalling."

"M 31" (0:6) clasps the bottle with hands while drinking. Through a clumsy movement the bottle falls. M 31 "lalls" loudly to the nurse.

"K 50" (0:10) seizes the coat of the doctor, pulls on it, coos, beats on the doctor's shoulder after the child has raised himself in his bed, amuses himself by shaking to and fro, holding on to the bedstead. When the doctor still continues to turn her back, he walks up and down in his little bed, laughing and lalling, clicks his tongue, tugs again at the coat hanging down behind the bedstead.

"M 51" (0:10) looks at the observer who is hard at work writing, scratches with her nail on the cover, makes a noise with a rattle, in the meanwhile looks carefully and continually at the observer.

The following tables show the range of responses to grown-up and child by the infants of various ages observed by Bühler and Hetzer; they are subject to the limitation of small numbers of cases at each level.

THE OBSERVED REACTIONS OF CHILDREN TOWARD GROWN-UPS[a]

Age in months   1 2 3 4 5 6 7 8 9 10 11 12

Returns the glance of the adult with smiling
Is quieted by touching.....................
Becomes restless by being spoken to.......
Cries when grown-up who was attending
   him leaves.............................
Smiles back at grown-up..............
Disturbed when approached.............
Returns approaching glance with lalling...
Displeasure when the child loses the glance
   of the grown-up.....................
Quieted by caressing.....................
Disturbed by the sight of people...........
Neglect of play through meeting the glance
   of the grown-up.....................
Striving for attention by lalling.........
Stretches out hands toward the grown-ups..
Cries when the grown-up stops talking....
Strives for attention by movements........
Pulls on the clothes of the grown-up......
Offers the grown-up an object............
Imitates the movements of the grown-up
   with a plaything.....................
Organized play activity...................
Looks at grown-up amazed because of an in-
   cident...............................

[a] This and the following table contain only those reactions which could be established in at least 60 per cent of the observed children.

This and all material from *The First Year of Life* used by courtesy of The John Day Co., Inc.

THE OBSERVED REACTIONS OF ONE CHILD TOWARD ANOTHER

Age in months   1 2 3 4 5 6 7 8 9 10 11 12

Observes other child.....................
Smiles at other child.....................
Cries if the other child receives attention...
Offers toy to other child.................
Lalls to other child.....................
Imitates the movements of another child...
Opposes taking away of toy..............
Organized play activity...................
Strives for attention by means of lalling...
Ill-humor if another child moves away.....
Setting aside toy and turning toward a child

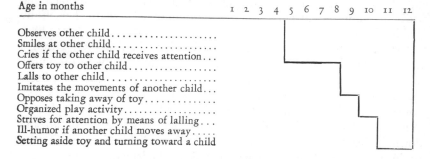

Such tables as these, suggestive as they are, surely call for some clear and well-rounded hypothesis as to the nature of the developmental processes. As raw material they can easily be misleading. How much of the sequence depends on the special stimulating conditions is unknown. Part of it may be an artifact resulting from "selection" of the small number of subjects. A clue to many aspects of the indicated development appears in the broad conception of maturation discussed above (page 111); another clue is the Piaget conception of differentiation following indissociation (cf. page 208); a third is the psychoanalytic conception of stages. It is interesting to read through the two tables while keeping the psychoanalytic system in mind. We strongly suspect that all three of the systems just mentioned apply with similar degrees of realism, all being very similar except for terminology; and that all three need to be consistently tested in the light of direct and systematic observation of the type given by Bühler.

LONGITUDINAL STUDY OF INDIVIDUAL DEVELOPMENT IN INFANCY

Although all of the observers of infants who have made longitudinal studies of development during the first two years of life report marked and stable personality differences persisting from month to month and from year to year, we still do not have a single objective study of personality and social development during this period which shows the bases of these differences, either in the light of early differences in constitutional sensitivities or in the light of major environmental pressures. And although we have now been exposed for some time to psychoanalytic and other psychiatric hypotheses regarding the effects of birth trauma, weaning trauma, extreme emphasis on early control of urination and defecation, excessive attention from adults, dethronement by a second child, we have almost no objective records of the development of children going through these experiences, or of experiments controlling certain aspects of the problem. The basic patterns of social response may be determined by the question how long a child is nursed and whether he is weaned, how dominating or status-conscious or systematic in "training" his mother is, whether his father plays with him or is completely outside of his pre-school experience. Babies are "growing up on bottles," whereas others are nursed for at least eight or ten months; they could quite feasibly be observed systematically for comparisons of personality and social development. When such observation or experimenting is undertaken we shall find in all probability that individual children respond very differently to similar experiences, and that it is only when we take into account the nature of the constitutional make-up with which a child begins life that we can define or predict the effects of these major infantile experiences.

There is room here also for an analysis of the dynamic relation ships between different cultural emphases at different economic levels; long nursing and much parental attention, even "babying," do not seem to develop "dependence" in children in lower economic groups, for the simple reason that necessity and external circumstances force independence upon the child at the age of three or thereabouts. Similarly, nursery school from eighteen months onward does not develop independence in the upper-middle-class child who is emotionally insecure as a result of inadequate mothering. It is also possible that the same external patterns in connection with nursing, weaning and training may have quite different values with different degrees of parental tension or concern; training which for one parent may be a simple matter of desirable routine may be a source of conflict and strain to another who has not been accustomed to routine, or to another who undertakes it in a slavish overconscientious mood with no capacity to modify the routine to suit her own needs. The chief implication of this discussion is the suggestion that further study of the social development of children urgently needs to be founded upon a systematic analysis of the probable forces at work in any personality-situation relationship. Such active factors as economic status, parental attitudes and age relationships as just discussed certainly need to be included, and many others will occur to the reader. Clear working hypotheses here both as to general trends and as to reasons for individual differences are important if the masses of case studies, observational records, and experiments are to have scientific meaning.

The closest approach to the kind of study we are suggesting is being made by Fries, who is studying the development of 47 infants from conception through the pre-school years and expects to continue the study of these children through adolescence. She is interested in the interrelations of physical and social factors in development; these she follows with the aid of an individual record for each child. The major headings of each chart appear in the form shown on pages 578-579.

An approach like this gives us reason to look forward to a time when the picture of social development in the first years will consist not simply in a number of records of behavior at given age levels, or even of sequences, but of empirical analyses of the process of socialization of the organism from birth. Such a study would need to see reflex and adaptive mechanisms of eating, elimination, grabbing, manipulation and exploration, locomotion and motor activity, language, laughter and crying, looking and listening, as they are given scope and form by the general patterns of the culture, the attitudes of specific adults, and the stimuli of the immediate situation. Such a study would also follow the relationships between the acquisition of overt patterns which conform to the restrictions of the group, and the internal responses which may be less subject to the child's conscious control. The development of repressions, compensations and sublimations might well be watched in the process as we note changes in the overt expression, tension level and autonomic reactivity of young children. Among the most important research possibilities which might be realized at this earliest level are the following:

1. Empirical studies of the process of habit-training under the age of one year, with attention to the methods used, child's habit reaction, his attitudes. Evidences that the child identifies with the authority and approves his own achievement in remaining dry, successful evacuation, etc.; or that he resents the motor interference of frequent trips to the toilet, or being expected to "perform" at stated intervals; or that his interest in anal processes or products is heightened. Dependence upon or resistance to the "authority" embodied in the

Age	Birth to 6 mos.	6 mos. to 1 yr.	1 yr. to 18 mos.
Sociology (occupation, etc.)			
Hygiene (light, heat, etc.)			
Home changes (locality, reasons, members)			
Family: health (each member separately)			
Family: psychological			
Family: education			
Grandparents' relationships			
Family to child (love, treatment, attention)			
Family to hospital			
Measurement of child (head, chest, length, etc.)			
Development (visual, auditory, nasal, neurological, muscular)			
Handedness			
Teeth			
Speech			
Health (and attitudes)			
Feeding			
Nursing (position, flow, attitude)			
Weaning (breast, reason, mother's att., child's reaction, etc.)			
Mother's attitude to feeding			
Child's behavior during feeding			
Sleep (hours, place, requirements, etc.)			
Habit training			
Bowel			
Bladder, day, night			
Dressing			
Bath and washing (age, method, child's reaction, parent's reaction, etc.)			
Oral symptoms (when began, treatment, parents' attitude, child's reaction)			
Anal organic symptoms			
Anal psychological symptoms			
Phallic symptoms			
Genital organic			
Genital psychology			

Age	Birth to 6 mos.	6 mos. to 1 yr.	1 yr. to 18 mos.
Sex interest			
Reaction formation			
Obedience			
Punishment			
Behavior (disposition, independence, jealousy, tantrums, fears, curiosity, identification, courage, etc.)			
Behavior activities (cries, fights, hits, bites, etc.)			
Behavior attitudes (stubborn, shy, quiet, aggressive, affectionate, demonstrative, passive, etc.)			
Object relation (self, parents, sibs, strangers, children, animals, etc.)			
Play (companions, fantasy, arts, etc.)			
Play group (type, leadership, cooperation)			
Psychometric summary			

trainer, parent or nurse in the first year may lay a basis for subsequent response to authority.

2. Empirical studies of the earliest development of creative and pleasurable social relations; the total personality development of babies such as Washburn's laughing and crying types, Shirley's irritable and relaxed types, and of "yielding or dominating types."

3. A genetic picture of the nature of social intercourse and response-getting behavior from birth to two years. Bridges, Shirley, Bühler and Washburn all report a great deal of delight in human response among infants, expressed in kicking, babbling, laughing and gurgling; this goes through a process of social tempering and channeling comparable to the social patterning of eating and eliminating. Repression of excitement, excessive delight or craving for affection may develop attitudes more important than those developed from early toilet-training when considered in relation to the long-time development of the personality.

4. A genetic picture of the process of training in relation to objects; creative and hoarding traits may be related to early opportunities for exploration as against early repression of interest in handling objects resulting from strong taboos against manipulating most objects. The social pressures would need to be seen in relation

to the specific pattern of interests and ability thresholds in this case as in all others above.

5. The genesis of inhibition of crying and the personality effects related to the previous patterns and degrees of crying. This social process would also need to be seen in relation to the counter tendency for the child to use crying for either expressive or attention-getting purposes. Inhibition or self-control may be seen in relation to the extent to which internal tension accompanies repression of crying.

THE DEVELOPMENT OF LANGUAGE

Probably the most conspicuous development in the transition from babyhood status to childhood status is the development of language. We have already suggested (page 231) some formal principles which appear to underlie the acquisition of language and of other patterns of communication. Here our concern is with the steps apparent in the child's development and with their importance in his understanding and acceptance of new social rôles.

The growth of language may perhaps be most objectively shown in the accumulation of vocabulary; and this is a relatively simple objective thing to test. Nearly all students have found that after the first laborious stages in the acquisition of a few "active language habits" (a child having only a few words at his command in the period between twelve and sixteen months of age), positive acceleration follows, and an enormous increase in vocabulary occurs during the latter part of the second year. Bateman's studies of the vocabularies of three girls at 28 months are typical. The three made use, respectively, of 405, 628, and 308 words. These words are classified according to the parts of speech. Nouns constituted in all three cases over half of the total number, verbs coming second in all cases. Markey, we feel, has shown clearly that this does not indicate a general tendency of the child to build up more ideas about *things* than about *acts*, or even that the world to which his language refers is mostly a "thing world" rather than an "action world." On the contrary, Markey's analysis seems to justify his conclusion that a large proportion of nouns, and, in fact, of words from several other parts of speech, are used to indicate action, and that in many cases a single word used as a sentence (whether declarative, interrogative or imperative) is in reality much more nearly the equivalent of an adult verb than of an adult noun. Vocabulary studies and grammatical analyses of children's speech have become plentiful.

No less than three hundred children took part in the experiments of Descœudres at Geneva. Some of the children were obtained in large groups, others, so to speak, in handfuls; some she recruited by the simple expedient of stopping them while at their play in the city parks. The procedure was simply to ask questions or to request the carrying out of simple tasks.

The chief purpose of her study was the investigation of the development of language, although many ot the tasks involved processes of naming, observation, calculation, and judgment. Her purpose was to bring out the vocabulary, the style of speech, and the ways in which children of different ages think. In the study of language, and especially in the study of vocabulary, it is remarkable to note that Madorah Smith, who has with an improved method carried through a similar question-and-answer method for American children (Iowa), has obtained results which are uncannily like those which Descœudres found in Geneva. The total vocabularies, age for age, show almost exactly the same average number of words in the two localities, and the relative importance of the various parts of speech stands out as amazingly similar despite the differences between French and English.

From such data as those just reported, it is now possible to outline accurately the stages in vocabulary growth as well as in growth in sentence structure, etc., during the pre-school and middle-childhood period. These studies rely, of course, upon the sampling methods; the percentage of words known from a given series makes it possible, by comparison with a longer series, to know what the total vocabulary would be.

The method has also been used by Semenova-Boltunova. About 1000 children between three and eight years of age were asked questions to bring out their knowledge of words, comprehension of sentences, etc. In the comprehension of sentences, the Russian children are reported to have been definitely below the norms published by Descœudres, although the vocabulary tests show item by item no reliable "national" differences.

Another important contribution from Geneva is Piaget's study of language in small children. The approach is functional, that is, the author is concerned with the needs which the child tends to satisfy when he talks. Each child's conversation was followed in morning classes for a month. The basic classification is that of egocentric and socialized speech functions. In egocentric conversation, the child does not care to whom he speaks or who is listening. His talk is about himself and he has no interest in what someone else may say. Egocentric speech may, however, be subdivided into three forms: (1) repetition, talk for the sake of talking; (2) monologue, talking to oneself as though thinking aloud; and (3) collective or dual monologue—the other person acts as stimulus and receiver, so to speak, for the conversation, but his point of view is not considered by the child. Socialized speech, on the other hand, is to be subdivided into (1) adapted information with genuine exchange of ideas; (2) criticism (similar to the above, but with more emphasis upon affective elements); (3) commands, requests, and threats; (4) questions; and (5) answers.

Piaget proceeds to a "measurement" of egocentrism. Spontaneous language consists of all the preceding eight classes, except the "answers." Of such remarks, about 50 per cent for each child were egocentric. The two children studied by Piaget show remarkable similarities in percentages for the various eight classes of speech given above. A great deal of discussion has been stimulated by Piaget's emphasis upon the egocentrism of the speech of small children. There is an obvious resemblance (which Piaget himself points out) to Bleuler's "autistic thinking." Compare, for example, the material on children's fantasies (cf. page 287). Egocentrism, according to Piaget, decreases as the child grows older.

Particularly confirmatory is an American study in which an observer and his stenographer followed each of twenty-seven kindergarten children through a series of fifteen-minute intervals on a large number of different days. Over three thousand remarks were recorded. Of these, about 40 per cent contained elements of self-assertiveness, while an almost negligible percentage (.25 of one per

cent) contained ideas of self-depreciation. Evidences of "social consciousness" were found in only about 4 per cent of the remarks.
A little over 8 per cent were verbalized perceptions, or mere expressions of what the children were thinking or doing. Even at this age,
some of their talk was still mere linguistic experimentation. The
general conclusion is that a kindergarten child is relatively egocentric, as Piaget suggests, and that he is a rather "unsocial defender
of his individuality."

The work described above must be seen in the light of the studies
by McCarthy. By means of an elaborate functional analysis of samples of the running conversation of 140 children, she found it practicable to extend the studies begun by Descœudres and Smith, to
show the development of various complex forms of expression, such
as the simple sentence and the complex sentence, to carry forward
Piaget's idea of a functional classification of verbal behavior in terms
of the part which language plays in the child's life, and to show the
relations between linguistic development on the one hand and intelligence and socio-economic status on the other. The children were
so selected as to give a distribution, both social and intellectual,
typical of the city from which they were drawn. A modification of
Piaget's classification was used. Grammatical considerations were
also intensively considered. In another study, McCarthy analyzed
the proportion of egocentric responses obtained, and found only
from 3 to 6 per cent in two situations of her investigation. All but
two of the children showed more egocentric responses on the *playground* than in the *experimental situation*. It seems probable, in
view of these differences, that the proportion of egocentric talk
varies widely with circumstances; even this, however, would hardly
explain the enormous differences between McCarthy's maximum
finding of about 6½ per cent, and Piaget's finding of 50 per cent.
Probably different definition and classification account in part for
this.

Vygotsky and Luria have offered further light on this question of
egocentric speech. Their experience shows that it appeared when
the child was confronted with a difficult situation, and that the so-
called egocentric reactions were directed toward the solution of the
problem; that is, that the child was really trying to solve the prob-

lem verbally or, as we say, thinking out loud. They concluded that egocentric speech had a fairly definite organic function and that this function did not disappear but was supplanted by internal speech, which served the same purpose.

McCarthy's analysis has other points of interest. The reliability of her data point to the objectivity of the mode of classification as well as to the stability of the tendency toward certain kinds of responses at a given level of development. The length of verbal response increases steadily with chronological age during the interval, eighteen to fifty-four months, which is studied, and the length of response is found to correlate significantly with I.Q. as well. The characteristic differences in intellectual status in relation to paternal occupation (cf. page 46) are reflected in the consistent tendency to the lengthening of the verbal response as one proceeds from the children of unskilled laborers to those of professional people.

McCarthy's data substantiate the frequent emphasis upon the importance of *naming* in the speech of small children; omission of the verb is therefore a natural occurrence at this stage. Nouns, which at first play a very large part in the total speech, give place with time, especially to verbs; conjunctions and prepositions appear late in the pre-school period. Further analysis of language acquisition showed that adapted information, questions and answers increase rapidly with advance in chronological age, while the emotionally toned responses show a *relative decrease* with age. Further evidence of the emotional factors entering into the situation is offered by the initial shyness which caused the first ten responses of each child to average shorter than the next ten responses.

She also found that the children she observed tended to give many more *emotional* responses on the playground than in an experimental situation involving a lot of toys and one adult. She reports that the children issue more commands and threats in their give-and-take play among themselves than in conversation with an adult. She does not seem to take account of the fact that wide differences would probably result from differences in the degree of familiarity with a given adult; that is, that a parent or nurse (or other very familiar adult) might be treated to a much larger number of emotional responses from the child than she herself received.

There was a slight tendency ($r = - .40$ in the first situation, and $- .21$ in the second situation) for emotional responses and extroversion to be negatively correlated. The extroversion ratings were based on free play; it is suggested that this may account for the greater relation between playground measures and extroversion.

The child whose contacts with other children were begun before the end of his first year by *physical* contacts—reaching toward the other child, offering a toy, etc.—is still for the most part making use of similar devices at the age of two and a half or three. At this time his total talking for a day may easily run to 13,000 words, yet speech has not necessarily become his usual method of making overtures to other persons. Approach through common interest in a third object remains easier for many children than an approach through direct address—a fact habitually made use of by the skillful psychological examiner, who begins with the parts of the test that involve handling objects, e.g., the weights, rather than with the parts which consist simply of question and answer.

Although language only slowly becomes a means of *initiating* social contacts, it soon becomes an important means of *sustaining* them. Often it makes little difference what one says to one's playmate or one's father; the talking helps to "hold" him physically and emotionally near. The two-year-old whose language is largely limited to "want a cookie" develops into the five-year-old who asks questions for the sake of holding the attention of parent or teacher, as well as for curiosity, and who may sustain relatively complicated dramatic play episodes with constant verbal directions.

The last type of language behavior points strongly to the rôle of language in building up an "inner world," a world which the child can control and the manipulation of which (thought and imagination) helps to prepare for the situation in the outer world.

CHARACTERISTIC SOCIAL BEHAVIOR IN THE PRE-SCHOOL PERIOD

The content of children's social relations during the nursery-school period will depend on the stimuli of the environment, the personality needs or drives of the individual, and his maturity. The list of illustrations of children's social behavior in Bridges' *Social and Emotional Development of the Pre-School Child* includes "playing ring-a-ring of roses," "a tea-party for two," "playing store," playing with a broom, picking dandelions, turning somersaults, running around "with delight," sliding on an overturned toboggan, sleighing down a bank, a kiddy-car race, sitting in a little snow-house, watching a plant, playing trains on a ladder. The long northern winter naturally led to a predominance of snow activity in this nursery school. In another nursery school the most characteristic forms of play were: domestic patterns, including playing house, furnishing a house, cooking, eating, and having tea parties, taking care of babies and being fathers and mothers; selling and buying; activities connected with transportation, such as riding in automobiles or trains, being engineers, putting in gas or air, selling books; punishing, playing policeman or "G-man"; fires and playing fireman; killing and dying; playing the part of legendary persons— Santa Claus, Cinderella and, above all, the "Big Bad Wolf."

The outstanding point of difference between these lists of play activities in the two different situations is the predominance of play patterns with aggression or violence *motifs* among the second group of children, as contrasted with the predominance of large-muscle activities for their own sake, with relatively little fantasy or emotion, in the first group. It is significant that the children in the second group were metropolitan children who all lived in apartments, and played on roofs almost entirely except for the two-hour play period on the nursery-school playground. In view of the fact that the teachers' patterns regarding child training had a similar background in prevalent trends in child development work, it is less likely that this difference reflected differences in the adult-child relationships in the school than differences in the total experience provided in the two environments.

At this age, social development shows itself first, according to Bridges, in imitating another child's actions, words, laughter, speaking to another child, playing with another child, asking for another child's approval or for help. This responsiveness to other children is gradually followed by the assimilation of nursery-school mores and iearning to take turns and to give up a toy at a fair request, defending one's own right to materials or place, pointing to others' errors, helping others. A particularly warm social feeling may be expressed by stopping one's own work to aid another child and by comforting another child in distress. Socially unacceptable (sometimes regarded as "immature") behavior includes interfering with the work of others, destroying others' work, creating disorder or leading others into mischief, frequently pushing or pulling others, complaining of others to the adult for one's own gain, turning away to avoid another child's friendly advances, staying out of the group marching or games, scoffing or shunning a new child, hitting or pinching others for fun, biting or spitting at or teasing others.

Children from 3½ to 5 years of age show less of the foregoing; they show such mature forms of social response as offering to share materials with others, getting a toy to give to another child, passing things voluntarily to others at table, defending the rights of smaller children, initiating group activities, trying to make a new child one of a group, speaking appreciatively about another child or his work, apologizing to a child for an accident or a mistake. Older children also have more resources for aggressive behavior and may punch and fight, taunt other children, dominate or press their services on younger children against their will.

The outstanding fact about social behavior in nursery-school children is not that its main dynamics of ego-alter relations differ from those of later periods, but that this is an age when these relationships take place under the watchful eye of adults who constantly impose their judgments and attempt to substitute one sort of behavior for another. In general, they attempt to secure an increase of cooperative behavior, a minimum or absence of conflict; they attempt to substitute verbal methods for active ones (talking for fighting), and "constructive" responses for "emotional" ones. You are a baby if you cry and a naughty boy if you hit; you are expected to be emotionally self-controlled, independent and cooperative.

In contrast with some primitive and civilized groups where young children have little contact with adults and are taken care of chiefly by older children, the younger members of middle-class American families have at first relatively little contact with older children and are almost constantly under the surveillance of adults. To the child the adult represents society in both its protective and prohibitive aspects, and the main problem of the child is to accept the protection without becoming too dependent upon it, and to accept the prohibitions without being too cramped or limited by them. The direction of contemporary research indicates that adults themselves are most concerned about both undue "dependence" on the one hand and undue "resistance" on the other; relations with adults are considered adequate when the child is independent in relation to the activities in which the adult approves his independence, and cooperative or obedient in those activities which the adult still chooses to dominate.

Inadequate relations with adults are suggested by Bridges' list, which include: holding aloof from adults; refusing to do what adults ask; disobedience, refusal to eat, ignoring adult disapproval; going to adult to be petted; waiting to be shown how to use materials, seeking help by passively waiting, depending entirely on help in undressing, waiting to be fed, depending entirely on help at the toilet; destroying materials; deliberately seeking others' place for adult attention; following adult about for attention. Older preschool children (from 3½ to 5) may invent excuses for errors, try to hide deeds from adults, make absurd remarks to adults, refuse to try to dress unassisted, constantly demand attention, tell untrue "stories" to impress or influence the adult. These forms of behavior may be simply different forms of the overt negativism, resistance, and temper that have so frequently been reported to reach a peak at three years. The existence of both "desirable" and "undesirable" behavior in the same child is not unexpected at such an early stage of socialization; indeed, as we have seen (page 380), the more there is of one, the more there is likely to be of the other.

Bridges' inventory of social and emotional behavior brings the descriptive picture into relation with typical nursery-school situations. The following occasions when crying is apt to occur are listed in her scale:

Arrival at school.
When left by guardian at school.
On arrival of guardian to take home.

When undressed on entering school or in physical examination.
At the toilet.
At nap-time.
For mother.
When required to part with treasured plaything or garment.
When left alone in room.
When set apart for discipline.
When reprimanded.
When slightly hurt by knock or fall.
When disliked a thing without complaining of it first.
When wanted a thing without asking for it first.
When materials or place taken.
When pushed or teased by child.
In anticipation of disliked event.
When taken alone from group for examination, etc.
When another child cried.
At failure to exert influence over others.
When work destroyed.
At own conduct failures.
Four times or more during the month.
At loud or sudden noises.
When caught upon something.
At approach of dogs.

Equally revealing of the content of nursery-school experience is the list of occasions for expression of delight and affection. Children laugh:

In active play.
At loud noises.
When a chair is upset.
When other children make peculiar faces or noises.
When others laugh.
To cause others to laugh.
At own mistakes or those of others.
At unusual events and absurdities.
At own success.
At pictures, objects, animals.
At adult's suggestions.
At funny stories.

Such lists are not meant to imply that all children characteristically do all of these things. Individual differences, here as everywhere, are striking in quantitative analysis. Among the clues to such differences at this age level, the child's *security in the group* is of special importance. Indeed, the element of security is probably the most important single factor in relation to questions of variation in behavior of nursery-school children. It must, however, be remembered that different children show different kinds of effects of a decrease or increase in security. For instance, some children become more aggressive when they are more secure, because their lack of aggression has actually been a matter of inhibition; others become more aggressive when they are insecure, because of a need and ability to fight to preserve their status or to get it back. We need to know the organization and range of the individual personality before we can predict what a given situation will do to it.

Just as the degree of a child's participation in a group is probably a function of his security in relation to the group to a considerable degree, so is his relation of leader. The actual constellations of small groups within a large nursery-school group are so unstable (cf. page 515) that any child is exposed to a shifting rather than a stable pattern as compared with the relatively stable situation most adults would confront in a school, church, or business institution. That is, groups form themselves and dissolve within a matter of weeks, and a child who is leader in November may have lost the rôle by February and gained it again by May. What meaning this has for a young child and to what extent he is sensitive to status of this sort as an adolescent would be, we do not know. It is possible that shifts in the group relationship which adults are not always aware of may have considerable meaning and be important contributors to other ups and downs of the child's morale. Similarly, friendships before the age of five are apt to be quite volatile (cf. page 512) yet none the less potent for the child's development while they last. Children who are fairly isolated and unfriendly have been seen to become more sympathetic and responsive in the group as a whole as a result of the acquisition of one friend with whom they felt secure. One child who had been outstandingly stable and mature for his age over a period of two years became quite disorganized and destructive in a group when a companion of some months' standing withdrew. Here again we are dealing not with factors primarily associated with age but with the fundamental human fact that a chance at activity one enjoys and at appreciative friends is necessary before one can be a whole person, even when one is only four.

Supplementary to Bridges' inventory list of behavior at the nursery-school age is Berne's list of social behavior to be rated by teachers, and her analysis of the prevalence of each in relation to various developmental factors:

Obeys.
Seeks approbation.
Interested in group.
Depends on adult.
Affectionate.
Cooperates.
Other's property.
Participates.
Sympathizes.
Own property.
Sociable.
Kind.
Rivalrous.
Appreciates humor.
Social ownership.
Socially controlled.
Leads.
Imitates.
Teases.
Maternal.
Jealous.
Self-defense.
Irresponsible for self.
Critical.
Selfish.
Sensitive.
Irresponsible for others.
Social conformance.
Impolite.
Ascendant.

A number of differences related to age appeared in this early study which were subsequently substantiated by more detailed observational studies. Significant differences between the means of ratings for the two-year-old and the three-year-old group were found in thirteen traits. Significant differences between two-year-olds and four-year-olds were found in twelve additional traits, and one trait showed clear differences between three-year-olds and four-year-olds. The most interesting differences are as follows: Three- and four-year-old children have higher ratings than two-year-olds in sociability, social conformance, ascendance, understanding of own property rights, rivalry, jealousy, responsibility for self, criticism, responsibility for others. Three-year-olds surpassed two-year-olds in independence of adults and in self-defense. Four-year-olds surpassed two- and three-year-olds in cooperation. Sex differences were not marked in most traits. While chronological age was related positively to responsibility for self, selfishness and understanding of property rights, mental age was a better index to motherliness, criticism, responsibility for others, participation, cooperation, affection, and lack of imitation.

The Little Child's "Conception of the World"

Parallel to the social behavior objectively observed go on, day by day, the child's steps toward understanding the world around him, the world of nature and the world of people, and his own relation to both. Investigations of these processes, tentatively begun nearly fifty years ago by such pioneers as Stanley Hall and J. M. Baldwin, have now been launched with vigor and comprehensiveness by Jean Piaget and his associates at Geneva (cf. page 542). The method, in the case of the infant, is experiment; in the case of the older child, experiment, clinical interview, and observation of free play.

For Piaget, as for most other observers, the experience of the opening months is one of fleeting, indefinite awareness, not one of "ego" and "alter." In general, the psychology of perception, both in little children and in adults, suggests that, on confronting a strange new object, a first stage of inchoate and blurred totality yields in time to a period in which differentiation of specific parts can be carried out. In exactly this way the self is detached, separated, and made into a recognized, well-knit whole. The process, however, goes on as a result of needs; it does not occur automatically, and is never absolutely completed. Indeed, much of the psychology of childhood has been written by Piaget in terms of the lingering on of the primitive state of blur, a state in which there is as yet no clear recognition of self and not-self. Piaget has unfortunately chosen the term egocentrism to define this state of blur or "indissociation," the state preceding dissociating of self from other. By egocentrism Piaget means the exact antithesis of awareness of self. Much of the process of personality growth is the process of growing out of primitive egocentrism. To the little child, what is given is real; there is no distinction of reality and experience; things are what they seem.

In the light of Piaget's studies it seems practically certain that the child in the first year of life not only has no clear awareness of self but that he has no clear conception of a world of things at all. His world is a world of momentary experiences. The adult thinks in terms of the conservation of energy or of mass or, if without benefit of schooling, at least in terms of the conservation of things. The bicycle which we left in the cellar is there and we shall find it again when we go downstairs. The world is made up of persons and objects which remain rather stable through time. To the tiny child, however, Piaget shows his watch, then hides it behind a pillow. The child promptly dives for it. After he has played with it for a moment, the watch is carried from the child's left side to his right and placed under another pillow. The child is now allowed to reach. He does not reach under the pillow where the watch has been placed; he invariably reaches again under the pillow where he first found it. The experience is not "watch" as a free detachable object now in one context, now in another; the watch is an inseparable aspect of what we might call Situation Pillow No. I. From studies of this sort Piaget has built up a plausible case to the effect that there are in the little child's world no stable entities of the sort which we as adults call persons and things.

It is against this background that we must view the extraordinarily slow development of the recognition of the identity of persons, the child's long delay in learning to recognize the face of mother or father and, in particular, the great delay in learning to recognize his own hands and feet, his own skin or his own voice. Despite the bewildering variability of appearance which his body presents, and the perpetual change in organic and kinesthetic patterns which for us are so simply the child's organism, the thread of continuity must be found and maintained. There is convincing evidence that continuity in the recognition of familiar faces does not appear until near the end of the first year of life (it is not until this time that the child is "shy" with strangers). This is exactly the period at which clinical observers think the child forms some vague notion of himself. We conclude that he learns to recognize himself as an object in the same way that he learns to recognize the continuity in any other series of fleeting patterns.

In the same breath we find here serious reasons for doubting that awareness of self is based chiefly upon the perception of others or upon the processes of identification with them. One discusses oneself, and inevitably takes an interest in any object so important and so valuable as a mediating instrumentality in getting things that give delight or put an end to strain and stress. It is true that the self is in some ways analogous to other persons, and that in a period of confusion much is carried over by analogy, so that the child attributes to himself much that is in fact only in the other person. This will be the basis for introjection, just as the analogous process in the other direction is projection (cf. page 189). But if this be true, the process of identification merely elaborates and completes the process which has already been under way for some months, a process which in large measure completes itself without requiring the intervention of models or love objects in the world outside.

"Nominal realism," in the same vein, is the acceptance of the name as an integral part of the thing. The name of the moon is in the moon. The moon could not be called the sun, even if everyone agreed to it. There is no such thing as a point of view. Simply because the world is what it seems to be, one does not recognize the features of the world which arise from one's own organic limitations. From this it follows that the child participates in the events going on outside, lives in them, has no device by which to tell in what ways he can alter the world, in what ways he can alter only what is going on within his own organism. The magical practice by which the child makes his marbles roll this way or that by willing or mentally pushing them, his fear that the thought of a bicycle puncture may make the puncture occur, his unwillingness to mention the possibility of his flunking his test, are analogous to the magical practices of primitive men, and to the superstitions of those adults who still exhibit a fair measure of childish egocentrism—one doesn't step on a crack lest he break his mother's back. The "omnipotence of thought," as Freud calls it, is the necessary result of a world view in which the effects of thought are carried out without prejudice upon all aspects of the world perceived.

Again, from primitive egocentrism arises naturally the tendency to find in other objects the properties which in fact belong to one's own organism. The Genevan child of six or eight believes that the moon follows him as he walks along the lake shore because it wants to see where he is going, or, if he has been naughty, "to pay him back." Not only can dogs and horses talk; stones are conscious that they are rolling down hill, the trees are sorry when the sun sets. The "artificialism" of the small child likewise follows: the Lake of Geneva was made by man's scooping out the ground and letting the water in. The clouds came from smoke, and smoke from human firesides. The world is all personal, all serves human needs, is shot through and through with motive and thought like that of the child himself. The process of becoming socialized involves the gradual stripping away of this universal illusion, the gradual replacement of the personal by the impersonal. One traces this process step by step. Among the Geneva children, for example, while life and consciousness are attributed impartially to all things at the first stage, these are restricted in time to things which move, and finally, as we near the adult level, to things which move on their own power. Last of all, life and consciousness are defined and the concepts used in the characteristic twentieth-century adult way.

How much of all this animistic reaction is due to primary egocentrism, "indissociation," and realism? It is utterly impossible to say. Certainly a great deal of this development seems to occur in children in the United States and, indeed, in children in primitive cultures. American children thus far studied certainly seem to pass through these stages more rapidly than the Geneva children do, even when allowance is made for the relatively unfavored socioeconomic status of the Piaget group. At the same time, it appears that the enormous *amount* of egocentrism found by Piaget, and of its correlates in the form of animism and artificialism, is due either to some experimental error or to the special characteristics of a given culture at a given time and place, or to both factors together. A field study especially designed to reveal degrees of animism present among Manus children in New Guinea showed no tendency to attribute life or consciousness to canoes, ropes, or hammers. Indeed, the experimenters' effort to make the child blame the canoe for floating away led only to the protest that "Popo was stupid and didn't tie the canoe." Some 30,000 spontaneous drawings revealed not a single instance of sun and moon with eyes, nose and face in the characteristic western fashion. One cannot help concluding that a large part of the animism of the Geneva child, and perhaps many other aspects of egocentrism as described by Piaget, result from the personifying tendency in western culture throughout its history and, in particular, from the personification of nature forces, the fairy stories of talking animals, the Aesop fables, the sentimental and semi-personal attitude toward objects of which we are fond, and other deeply rooted animistic tendencies in the culture. How far this objection should be pushed we do not know. If one cannot talk back to one's irate boss, one can kick the cat when one comes home; and, perhaps, in the same vein, if one finds in one's ego a certain clumsiness with respect to carpentry one can swear at the hammer which hits one's thumb. This is animism of a sort, and seems intelligible without special stress upon any specific cultural attitude. Here, however, we are simply in the dark. No more fascinating field of study for comparative social psychology exists than the analysis of varying phases of egocentrism in cultures which define and utilize the ego in different ways.

Individual Differences in the Earliest Social Responses

Individual differences in early social behavior have been studied largely with reference to age and sex at all levels, and hardly at all in terms of fundamental personality differences. And yet the genes do not confine their influence to the cortex and skeletal structure, but affect every aspect of somatic and visceral response on both the perceptual and the effector sides. This has been recognized in a few studies which point out persistent personality differences among children, even in infancy.

Lacking empirical material, what specific personality differences of a genetic source are most likely to affect social behavior? If we think of children as organisms with different rates of development as wholes, and differences in the activity or thresholds of excitation of different organs, we might make a very rough *a priori* classification of the following kinds of abilities and interests arising from organic make-up:

1. Large-muscle, tempo, coordination interests.
2. Visual-perception interest; eye-hand coordinations, etc.
3. Auditory sensitiveness and interest.
4. Gastro-intestinal interest.
5. Erotic and sensitive-zone interest.
6. Cortical activity, including specific verbal, number, analytic, dramatic interests, and their interrelations with the above.
7. Thalamic and autonomic thresholds, emotional reactivity, perseveration, etc.

Undoubtedly empirical work will result in a different classification from this one, but it seems reasonable, nevertheless, to suggest the importance of genetic differences in organ thresholds, activity, perseveration and affect. If this is true, a child with a dominant auditory sensitiveness might be expected to have different tendencies in social relations from a child with dominant large-muscle activity interest. A study of differences in play activity of artistic and inartistic children suggests that such differences may be found fairly readily if we look for them. Such overt behavior tendencies as persistent aggression might then be related positively to a predominant large-muscle interest, with low pain and other emotional sensitiveness that might help one to perceive more quickly the effects of one's aggressions on other children. Sympathy on the autonomic level might be a resultant of social interest plus low pain thresholds, and on the behavior level it might be dependent on these plus a certain amount of physical competence and security in the group, preceding overt behavior responses to members of the group.

From this point of view we know far too little to be dogmatic regarding the "normal" forms of development from one age to another (cf. Chapter VI). Sequences of development are quite different for different children with respect to rhythm, drawing, block-building, cooperative play, singing; and it is important to give each individual child an opportunity for exercise of the functions which are developed, and help on those which are slower to develop. Age-level studies of social behavior and other capacities which have led toward judging one child's behavior in terms of norms which had little overlapping with his own patterns of development have been a source of maladjustment of children in school quite as certainly as have unrealistic parental expectations at home. Frustrations due to lack of outlet for dominant interests may be a major source of insecurity resulting in unsocial behavior in the school child.

Similarly, differences in emotional and temperamental make-up of a complex sort may be reflected in differences in social interest and behavior; major factors here might be:

1. Low thresholds for fear (which would lead to initial retreat from the aggressions of other children and reinforce a pattern of inhibition, or to too great compliance with authorities).
2. Low thresholds for resistance or aggression (which might impress other children and create an early position of domination that might become self-sustaining, or set up a craving for more domination; in relations with adults this would probably create annoyance and be a problem).
3. Desire for affection (which might find too little outlet in conventional nursery-school patterns and lead to insecurity and illegitimate techniques for getting attention).
4. Artistic interest (which might also involve frustration, especially if it followed some particular direction which was not recognized at nursery school, such as music or dancing).
5. Empathy (which might find outlet in sympathy or dramatic interests, a strong tendency toward imitation, or vivid reactions to people and animals in stories).

If we consider these suggestions in relation to the analysis of certain gross aspects of social behavior described in the chapters on aggression and cooperative behavior, we see the need for a more genuinely functional approach to the study of social behavior in the nursery-school child. At this age, patterns of social relations with peers and with authorities are becoming established which may well be more permanent than any other aspect of social development. The nursery-school situation, along with the home, may play a larger part in shaping personalities characterized by attitudes of dependence, anxious guilt, antagonism, domination, or self-confidence, friendliness, or cooperativeness. As we have already suggested, the meaning of the situation to the child, as a place of freedom and happy relations with other people, or of inexorable confinement by routine, or endless interruptions to play, will be more important than isolated techniques of this or that adult.

It is quite possible that research on individual differences among children would progress more rapidly if research studies followed, instead of preceded, a careful analysis of the psychological factors, in terms both of what is known about biological development and of what is known about the relevant aspects of the social context.

Here there is an urgent need for integrating the various methods —statistical, experimental, clinical, psychoanalytic, etc.—which are so often independently used. The relation between different methods now available for the study of the social behavior of children may be clarified by showing their possible uses in connection with a single problem. The problem of *authority* in relations between adults and children, as it bears on the child's acceptance of his culture and the formation of his personality, has already been noted as a fundamental problem for understanding child behavior which has not been treated to any extent. It will be useful in this connection.

We have already seen that research on children in different economic groups has shown a tendency toward a peak of resistance to adult commands at about three years (page 390). Berne's study of obedience (page 263) showed individual differences in this response as indicated by the time before an obedient response was given and by the number of requests required to elicit the response. We have, then, a core of evidence regarding the simplest expression of response to authority. But how is resistance shown, and what variations in pattern are there from one child to another? Observations in a variety of situations used as the basis for an inventory of responses to standard authority situations might be a first step in answering this question. This would, however, need to be extended to include a similar descriptive account, which could easily be quantified with ratings, of the varieties of pattern of expression of authority on the part of adults (tone of voice, firmness of command, repetition of command, leading the child to place involved, reproach, threat, punishment by removal from group, corporal punishment given impersonally, corporal punishment with feeling); here we should want data on the same children in different authority situations to observe variations in response to different adult authority patterns.

We should doubtless find that the same children responded to the same authority patterns differently on different occasions, depending on fatigue, security in the total situation (versus elements of newness arousing fear), competing activity or interests, and other elements in the situation stimulating defense or show-off, such as child friends, familiar adults, etc. This would bring us then to an analysis of motivation in the total situation of child-with-adult-in-social-situation. As soon as we found patterns of resentment at criticism or punishment in front of other people in some children and not in others, or even patterns of non-compliance with *direct* authority and quick response to *indirect* authority on the part of some children and not others, we should be forced back to an analysis of the personality development of the children who showed such different patterns of response to authority.

It would be possible to keep some form of statistical orientation as long as we studied specific patterns of response to standard situations in terms of frequency and individual differences, even when we were studying variations in frequency of different types of response to different situations which might be experimentally controlled. However, as soon as we began to analyze background factors in the development of the child which condition both his general trend of response and the character of his variations in different situations, we should get into fields where quantitative study would prove very difficult. This is partly because the number of factors to be taken into account would be great, and because the factors would vary greatly from child to child; in any group of children practicable for study

under usual research conditions, there would not be enough overlapping in such factors to give a basis for many generalizations. At
the same time, there might be certain fundamental factors which
occurred often enough to permit of statistical check. For instance,
rejection by one or both parents, strong identification of either parent with the child, extreme domination from one or both parents,
clashes in authority pattern between parents, and gross inconsistency
on the part of one or both parents, might appear sufficiently often to
permit study of common results in groups of children where they
occurred. Similarly, on the personality side, general trends toward
fear and withdrawal in certain children as contrasted with tendencies toward active aggressive behavior in others, might appear in
sufficiently clear form to permit generalizations about relationships.

That quantitative control is desirable when the data permit of its
use is indicated by the results of such a critical analysis of psychiatric
assumptions as is given by Foster and Anderson in their study of
children's dreams. Here chance experiences, fears, conflicts and a
variety of other affectively toned events of the day, along with
physical factors of bedding, activity before sleep, fatigue, illness,
etc., appeared important contributing factors to dreams, in contrast
to any theory that would exclusively emphasize repressions, wish-
fulfillment, sex conflicts and the like as dominant in dream activity.
There is no reason for excluding any psychoanalytic hypothesis regarding the bases of social response for which there is evidence, but
on the other hand it is important to keep enough perspective in
terms of the culture as a whole and the relative quantitative importance of different motivation patterns to avoid excluding important
factors where they appear.

Our culture is, in fact, so varied that in different areas entirely
different combinations of pattern may occur. Country children who
have the world to explore may be subject to adult domination a relatively small part of the time, and also be subjected to arbitrary and
very dominating authority during the small part of everyday life
when they get any at all. City children in "progressive" families
that give lip service to "freedom" but live in such small quarters
that no freedom is possible may be subject during practically the
whole of their waking time to a compromised authority that exerts

itself in spite of theory. Nursery-school children are sometimes exposed to a dual pattern of absolute and relentless authority in relation to routine situations on the one hand, and relatively complete freedom during play-time on the other. All of these differ from the authority situation of children with neither Puritanical country parents, nor schedule-minded nursery-school teachers, but with parents of the "let them have all the rope you can" philosophy, who create an environment which makes freedom possible, and whose theories of freedom are sustained by fundamental tolerance.

Children with every type of genetic constitution are growing up in different situations like these, and doubtless personality differences have something to do with the resistance to authority, identification with it, or submission and dependence upon it, shown by different children in the authority-dominance situations. It would be interesting to know the personality-situation origins of the characteristic authority patterns in our culture, those of the teacher, the foreman, the factory president, the textbook writer, the doctor.

We have yet to see a clear analysis, much less a quantitative study, of the fundamental process by which the little child is made to conform to adult patterns of social behavior. Evidences of carry-over of adult patterns of manners, greeting, recognition of service (thank you), acceptance of property rights, prior rights, etc., are noted on occasion. Non-experimental literature has organized typical nursery-school procedure for purposes of teaching nursery-school teachers, but observations of practice are hardly available at all. Such observations as exist do not make it clear whether the theory of non-interference on the playground is consistently carried out in practice, and what its results are. It would be of particular interest to study the effects of the theoretical dichotomy according to which teachers are expected to supervise closely routine situations of bathing, dressing, eating, and sleeping, in contrast to the freedom of the play hours. How do children adjust to this shift of adult relation? Informal magazine articles comment on the rigid inflexibility of some nursery-school teachers, but there are no records of the results of such inflexible procedures compared with more spontaneous ones. Fundamental conflicts in approved procedure appear when recommendations from different quarters are compared—the orthodox nursery-school emphasis on calm rationality, in contrast to the psychiatric emphasis on the need for solid emotional securities and freedom of emotional expression. It is sometimes assumed that a calm and reasonable pattern of authority goes along with a consistency which makes it easier for the child to grasp what is wanted and to build up stable patterns, while emotional reinforcement of authority is apt to go along with inconsistencies which make it hard for the child to know what to expect from the adult. The authority relations and relations of emotional satisfaction or frustration between adult and child are recognized by the clinician as of fundamental importance for the "adjustment" and happy development of the individual child, but they have not been studied extensively in their ultimate bearing on the social behavior of the normal child and his relations to his group.

There seems to be considerable evidence that the child's rôle in the group, even as early as three or four years of age, will be a quite clear reflection of needs, frustrations, satisfactions or projections of anxiety and identification with a parent in the home situation. If this is true, there may be a need to revise assumptions regarding the unlimited value of free play, which may merely consolidate these patterns, and to learn more about bridging the gap from such social patterns into more flexible group relations.

Total Personality at Nursery-school Age

We find a great lack of personality studies of children in nursery school, just as we found to be the case in relation to children in the first two years; most case studies are quite inadequate at this age. It is likely that when good ones are available, we shall find certain outstanding nursery-school types: the hyperactive child, not unlike the hyperactive child known at a later age to the clinics; the seclusive child, who may be merely temporarily cowed by adults and his peers or be laying the foundations for a later daydreamer; the "good" child, who conforms too much; and the scampering rebel. The question of what types are likely to appear significant will depend partly on the problem under consideration. In a study of the relations between sympathy and aggression, certain children appeared to show a high score on both sympathy and aggression; they might be called ambivalent social children. Others showed a low score on both sympathy and aggression and were usually low in all social contacts as a result of shyness or inhibition. Still others showed a high score on sympathy and a low score on aggression; one of these was a girl with some tendency toward fearfulness and dislike of physical contact, who could express her social interest through sympathetic behavior. Children with low scores on sympathy and high scores on aggression were likely to be immature in social perception but active and primitive in social contacts.

In each of these cases, the child showed a range of behavior over a period of a year in nursery school which differed strikingly from the range of behavior shown by the other children mentioned. It could be predicted with relative safety that Janet would not get into a fight and that Julius would get into a fight on slight provocation, although both would be equally likely to respond sympathetically to the distress of another child. It could be predicted that Julius, who might be a "hyperactive" child, would respond to every social stimulus, whereas Reinhardt, who was, for the time being at least, quite isolated, would respond to almost no stimulus from another child. It is quite likely that hyperactivity, where it exists, will appear in connection with attitudes toward routine, constructive work, relations with adults as well as with children in the sense that distractibility or over-reactiveness will appear in responses both to people and to material. At the same time, this personality characteristic may be cut across by other tendencies toward negativism or a chronic wish for approval, either of which would give a characteristic color to aggressive or sympathetic behavior as well as affecting the amount of each that would be likely to appear.

The following records illustrate many of the relationships pointed out during the preceding discussion. Here is an active, intelligent child with high scores on both sympathetic behavior and aggression. On November 14, the first 15-minute record shows her running about, laughing, repeatedly starting "ring-around-a-rosy" games, running up to other children to include them. A significant feature of her behavior appears in her gentleness when another child falls on her; she says at first, "Don't, don't get on me," and when the teacher encourages her to tell the boy not to, she formulates her protest in general terms, "Don't fall on other people, it hurts them, they don't like it."[1]

11-14-34

Lila is at the tomato juice table. She throws her empty cup in the waste basket. She drops her napkin and the wind blows it away. She runs after it, picks it up and throws it in the basket.

She runs across playground and follows Jack and a teacher who are running.

She runs and laughs, runs after teacher and laughs.

Goes up to teacher and touches her.

Runs again, calls to teacher, "I'm catching you."

Catches and holds teacher.

Teacher says, "We're warm enough now." Lila says, "I'm not warm enough, let's play 'ring-around-a-rosy.'" Teacher says, "All right." They join hands and dance around.

Lila says, "Let's do it again," and they do so.

Jack says, "Let's do it again"—all hold hands.

Lila, teacher and Jack hold hands and dance around.

Then fall down and laugh.

Lila says, "Where's Bobby?" She looks around and calls, "Bobby." She sees him and runs up to him, saying, "Bobby, would you like to come and play with us?"

Bobby doesn't answer, and slides down inclined board.

Lila, laughing, goes to jumping board and walks on it.

Jack runs up to her and says, "Lila T." Then says, "Lila, now we go sliding, see?" And he slides down inclined board.

Jacks runs off. Lila says, "Let's do it together."

Bobby comes up. Lila says, "Let's play ring-around-a-rosy again."

Teacher says, "All right."

Lila, teacher and Bobby join hands and dance ring-around-a-rosy. Lila says "Ring-around-a-rosy all fall down." They fall down and laugh.

Teacher suggests that instead of falling down they kneel.

Bobby and Lila go to shed with teacher.

Lila takes one end of a mat and starts to carry it.

She says, "It's too heavy." Teacher asks Bobby to help. Lila, Bobby

---

[1] Records from the Child Development Institute, Teachers College, Columbia University.

and teacher carry mat across playground. They join hands and
play ring-around-a-rosy on the mat.

Lila says, "I know what's a good game, let's just do it like that."

Teacher says, "How, Lila?"

Lila dances on the ground and then runs to mat and falls down.

Lila says, "Let's play a jumping game and then fall down." Lila
and Bobby jump up and down and then fall on the mat.

Bobby falls on top of Lila and she says, "Don't, don't get on me."

Teacher says, "You tell him."

Lila says, "Bobby, don't fall on other people, it hurts them and they
don't like it."

Lila says, "Let's play ring-around-a-rosy."

Bobby says, "I'm too tired."

Teacher suggests she get someone else to play with.

Lila crosses the playground to Chiefie and Jack and says, "Chiefie,
will you come play with me? Play ring-around-a-rosy?"

Chiefie says, "No."

Lila says, "Jack, will you play with me?"

Jack goes toward teacher. Lila follows. Lila picks up a basket and
puts it on the mat.

Chiefie approaches the teacher and says, "We're going to play a game
around the basket. What game, Lila?"

Lila says, "Ring-around-a-rosy."

Chiefie and Lila join hands and dance around the basket.

The following day a second 15-minute sample of Lila's behavior
is recorded. This time there is no teacher present in the immediate
vicinity of the children, or participating at any time in their activity, although Lila's mother is in the offing. The first three minutes'
activity consists of a competition in verbal violence, each one out-
doing the other in bloody threats. This is suddenly changed by
Lila's boy companion who suggests simply, "Let's fight." As soon
as the possibility of conflict on a physical level appears, Lila objects.
At first she gives the stock pattern, "It isn't nice," which has taken
the place, for this generation, of the more Puritan, "It isn't right"
(and has assimilated most of the group-sanction qualities of the earlier phrase). In response to her companion's protest, "But fighting
doesn't hurt," which is also on a level of generalization, Lila replies
on the same level, "But you hit people when you fight and people
don't like to be hitten." The boy appears to agree that hitting hurts,
and with this acknowledgment from him, Lila suggests a fight;

they make a pass or two, then go off to other things, but return shortly, this time taking up the verbal threats again. The competition does not thrive on threats alone, however, for Lila refuses the boy the prestige of being eaten by the wolf, and the boy turns the tables by suggesting that they will have to eat the wolf if they are hungry. When Lila laughs with him at this he threatens, "Next time you laugh at me, I won't laugh at you." This threat is immediately followed by the suggestion, "Let's go over to the jungle gym." Lila acquiesces and from this point on (this has occupied exactly half of the 15-minute period) the content of their relation is largely cooperation; they play with a ball, and climb up and down the jungle gym, then play fireman.

11-15-34
10:10
Lila is walking across the yard carrying a big rubber ball. She goes over to a bike. She gets on. She starts to ride it.
Bob walks over to her.
He speaks to her unintelligibly.
Lila: "Some day I am going to get a big saw and chop your head off. Before you get a chance to fight with me and chop my head off."
Bob: "I'll chop your arms off."
Lila: "I'll chop your arms and your head off."
Bob: "I'll chop you all up and throw the parts away."
Lila: "Where will you get a saw?"
Bob: "I'll throw each piece down the cellar and slam the cellar door."
Bob: "Then I'll bang the doors very hard and break your arms. Then all your bones will be broken."
Lila: "But I'll do it first to you."
Bob: "You won't be able to get out of the cellar."
Lila: "But I'll do it first to you. And if I do it first, then you won't be able to do it to me at all."
Bob: "I'll be able to do it first because a man will pick up a knife in a airplane and give it to me."
Bob: "Let's fight."
Lila: "Let's not."
Bob: "Why not?"
Lila: "Because it isn't nice."
Bob: "But fighting doesn't hurt."
Lila: "But you hit people when you fight and people don't like to be hitten."

Lila and Bob speak to each other unintelligibly.
Bob: "Nothing hurts only hitting."
Lila: "Let's fight, Bobby."
The two children hit each other and laugh.
Lila drops her ball.
She gets off her bike and picks up the ball.
Bob withdraws.
Lila gets on her bike.
She calls to her mother.
Lila rides away.

Lila goes over to her mother.
Lila: "I don't want any tomato juice. I'm not thirsty."
Mother speaks to her and walks away from her.
Bob comes over and pushes her bike.
Lila: "Hey."
Bob: "Hey for horses."
Lila: "I'll get the wolf to eat you all up."

Bob plays with the zipper on Lila's sweater.
Bob: "I want to pull it all down."
Lila: "I don't want you to do it."
Lila: "Wolves don't like people like you, they will run away from
    you."
Bob: "Why?"
Lila: "They don't like tough meat like yours and bones sticking in
    their throats."
Bob: "If we are hungry we will just have to eat the wolf all up, if
    he wants to eat us up."
The two children laugh.
Bob: "Next time you laugh at me, I won't laugh at you. Let's go over
    to the jungle gym."
Lila: "Yes, let's."
Lila drops her ball.
Lila: "Bobby, pick up the ball and put it here." (She holds her hands
    out.)
Bobby gets the ball.
Bob: "Don't drop it again."
Lila: "No."
Lila takes the ball from Bob.
Lila: "Bob, you get on the bike and ride over to the jungle gym
    with it."
Bob gets on the bike.
Bob: "It's too small."
Lila runs over to the jungle gym.
Bob rides over on the bike.

Lila gets on the slide and creeps up.
Bob rides over to Lila and talks unintelligibly.
Lila gets down and starts creeping up again.
Lila gets to the top and sits down.
Bob starts to creep up.
Lila: "Let's get the ball and slide it down."
Bob: "Yes."
Bob slides and Lila climbs down the jungle gym.
Bob goes for the ball.
Lila is still trying to get down.
Lila gets down and takes the ball from Bob.
She slides the ball down.
They both laugh.
Lila: "Slide the ball here."
Bob does not let her.
Bob: "We have a small dog. It got very tired. If you come up to my
    house we will show it to you."
Lila slides the ball down.
She catches it as it comes down.
Lila: "I'm going to throw it up the jungle gym."
Bob climbs up the jungle gym.
Bob: "Try to throw it up here."
Lila: "Okay."
Lila throws the ball. The ball does not reach Bob.
Lila runs after it.

Teacher comes over to Bob and asks him if his hands are cold.
Teacher wants Bob to put his gloves on.
Bob: "No, I don't want them."
Teacher puts his gloves in his pockets.
Lila: "In a minute I'll throw the ball."
Bob slides down.
Lila is hanging on to one of the bars.
Lila falls down.
Lila: "Isn't it a silly trick?"
Lila starts to climb up the jungle gym.
She drops the ball.
Lila: "Bobby, will you pick up the ball?"
Bobby picks the ball up. He throws it up at Lila.
It comes right down again.
Lila climbs to the top of the jungle gym.
Bob goes after the ball.
Lila: "Please give me the ball."
Bob hands it to her.

Lila: "Now, Bob, you climb up."

Bob: "Just like a fireman. Let's get a ladder."

Lila: "Look, here it is [back of the jungle gym]."

Bob goes after it. Lila drops the ball.

Bob picks it up and hands it to Lila. Lila can't reach it so the ball falls to the ground.

Lila: "There's a big fire. Let's put the fire out."

Bob picks up the ladder.

He hits Alma who is watching, as he straightens out the ladder. Alma withdraws.

Bob puts the ladder up against the wall of the jungle gym.

Lila: "I'm a fireman, I'm a fireman."

Bob: "You are not a fireman. You are a girl. Only boys are fireman."

Lila: "Don't be silly. Of course I am not a fireman. I'm only pretending."

Bob climbs up the ladder of the jungle gym where Lila is sitting. Lila moves away.

Lila: "Let's squirt the water."

They both make funny noises with their mouths.

Bob climbs down.

Bob: "All right. Everything is all right."

Lila starts climbing down.

Lila: "There is another fire across the way."

Bobby climbs up. Lila goes down the other side.

She makes funny noises and uses an imaginary hose to squirt the water up the side of the jungle gym.

Bob stands on top of the jungle gym and does the same as Lila, only his direction is down the jungle gym.

Wallis' records, on the other hand, illustrate quite different sorts of variation in behavior. At the beginning and end of the first record he is seen relatively inactive, watching other children or sucking a finger. This behavior dominates the whole record except for an interlude during which he attempts to get a tricycle to ride.

11-2-34

Wallis stood watching other children and rubbing his eyes with his sleeve. Looked at Nancy and watched other children.

Sucked finger. Held post, started to cry.

Walked into vestibule and stood in corner, stopped crying.

Stood in vestibule holding to door and watching children playing with carriage outside.

Stood at door of vestibule. Patsy went into bathroom with cup and
filled it with water. Wallis said, "Give me that," and followed
her.

She ignored him and left.

He stayed in bathroom and ran water in basin. Teacher came in with
Betsy and Patsy.

Teacher talked to them and turned on the water.

Teacher told them to wash sand out of the sink, and Wallis turned
the spigot.

Wallis continued to turn spigot. The teacher and two children left.

Wallis continued to play with the water.

Wallis said something unintelligible to Patsy and laughs. Patsy left.
Wallis watched them and then left.

Wallis stood in door of vestibule looking out on to the playground.

Left, ran to teacher and said, "I want to get the little red bike."

Teacher: "Which one?"

Walllis: "The one which Holden has."

Teacher, pointing: "There's a green one that's not being used."

Wallis stood looking with finger in his mouth.

Ran and called out something unintelligible.

Went in and out of shed.

Walked and looked around playground.

Put finger in mouth and took it out again. Went up to Johnny who
is riding bike. Wallis held to the bike and said, "I need this
little bike because George has one."

Johnny: "But I need it."

Johnny rode off and Wallis followed.

Wallis: "Will you let me have it after?"

Johnny: "When I leave I'll put it in the barn."

Johnny rode off and Wallis followed.

Wallis: "Another day I'm going to have that bike all the time and
not let you have it, if you won't let me have it."

Johnny: "I'm going to put it in the barn."

Johnny sat on the bicycle.

Wallis turned away and watched three girls of the four-year group.

In the second record, Wallis is much more active:

11-15-34
9:15

Wallis stood by the door. He moved away. Came back and entered
the lobby.

Bob C. stood near the inner door holding on to the handle.

Wallis went in back of Bob.
Bob pushed Wallis.
Wallis pushed past Bob.
Wallis opened the door. Went inside. He went upstairs.
Bob C. followed him.
Teacher came in.
She sent Bob down. He started down. She talked to Wallis.
Wallis: "I want to go upstairs for the blankets."
Bob: "Come on down, Wallis."
Teacher: "Go out, Bob, Wallis is coming down."
She talked to Wallis unintelligibly.
Wallis went down.

Wallis and Bob opened the two doors.
Wallis: "We both opened the two doors."
They laugh.
Bob withdrew.
Wallis walked away with teacher. They went to garage.
Wallis saw the mats. He yelled, "There they are."

He walked around and pulled down the mats.
Teacher: "Put that there, Wallis."
Wallis: "Okay."
He dragged the mat over to the platform.
Teacher: "Thank you very much, Wallis."

Teacher: "Look for another small one, Wallis."
She pointed to one on the bottom of the pile.
Teacher: "Get that one there, Wallis."
Wallis: "No, that is too far on the bottom."
She took the top ones off.
Wallis pulled the one she wanted out of the pile.
He dragged it on to the other platform.
Wallis: "Which way is put on the bottom?"
Teacher: "That way."
Wallis: "All right."
He put it down the way she said.

Wallis: "I am a good helper."
Teacher: "You certainly are."
Wallis left the garage. He took a small bike.
He tried to get on but it is too small for him.
He started running with the bike.
He bumped his bike into the train George was playing with.
George: "Stop that."
Wallis ran away with the bike.
George continued playing.

Wallis left the bike in the middle of the yard.
Chiefie passed on a bike with a cart attached to the back.
Wallis ran after Chiefie.

Chiefie rode very fast.
Wallis went back to his bike.
He collided his bike into David R.'s bike.
They laugh.
David rode away.
Wallis walked away with his bike.

Wallis collided his bike with George's train.
George just looked at Wallis.
Wallis went away.
He steered his bike down the hill.
He walked with it as it went down the hill.
He ran with the bike. He threw it over. He picked it up.

Wallis tried lifting the bike over the walking boards.
George was sitting there playing with his train.
George: "That's a station."
They laugh.
Wallis tried to maneuver his bike and one standing next to his.
David R. came over.
David: "That is my bike."
He took the other bike away from Wallis.
David got on his bike.
Wallis took his bike and collided with George's train.
George just looked at him.
Wallis collided his bike into David's bike.
David: "Don't do that."
Wallis laughed and rode away with his bike.
David rode away.
George continued to play with his train.
Wallis fell off the bike. He got up and left the bike and walked into
    the garage. He went back for the bike. He steered the bike
    around in the vicinity of the garage. He collided the bike into
    George's train.
George: "Stop, stop, you are a bad boy."
Wallis: "No, I'm not a bad boy."
George: "Yes you are."
George walked away.

Wallis went over to the tunnel. He tried to get his bike through. He
    collided into the carriage that David had attached to his bike.
Holden, who is holding on to the carriage yells: "Get out of here."
He lifted his hand to hit Wallis.

Wallis ran after Holden and said, "I'll slap your face."

Holden ran away.

David rode away after him.

Wallis returned to his bike and the tunnel.

He started to take the tunnel apart.

George: "Don't do that."

They both laugh.

Johnny walked over. He tried to get Wallis away from the tunnel by pushing.

Johnny: "Get off. Put that tunnel back."

Wallis: "No, no."

He pushed Johnny away and put back the tunnel.

He yelled, "There."

He and George yell together, "There."

Johnny withdrew. George withdrew with his train.

Wallis tried to put his bike on top of the tunnel.

He put the bike down on the ground and looked at it.

He called the teacher to look at the bike.

Wallis: "Look, look, one of the pedals are missing."

The teacher does not come over.

Wallis left the bike. He walked over to the tunnel.

He upset the tunnel.

Wallis went back for the bike.

He lifted the bike over the boards of the tunnel.

He left the bike and walked away.

He went to the sand bin.

He went to the garage.

He went over to the blankets.

He picked one up.

There were dolls on it.

He laughed and said, "Look it."

Here Wallis is again standing quiet when we first see him at the beginning of the record. Within the first minute, however, he becomes more active, and is on his way upstairs. He meets the teacher, who suggests that Wallis help her; this occupies the remainder of the first 5½ minutes. Immediately after this he gets a bike, and most of his activity for the rest of the time centers upon or includes the bike. It leads to a number of passing contacts with other children, as he bumps or collides with their apparatus (apparently on purpose). None of these leads to any definite acceptance or joint activity with other children, however, except for an occasional shared laugh. At the end of the fifteen minutes he is seen aimlessly going from one thing to another and commenting to no one in particular.

In both of these records Wallis is seen to be a child with limited social resources and little evidence of security. In the first record he is passive and makes little attempt to do anything, and in the second record he approaches children repeatedly with a vague aggressiveness that gets him nowhere.

Both of these records contrast with the picture of Wallis during the preceding year when he was fairly active and had a sizable score on both aggression and sympathetic behavior. The total picture of Wallis from these samples is that of a child whose behavior varies from inactive to aggressive when he is socially insecure, and from aggressive to sympathetic when he is better adjusted. In the first case the behavior is the overt side of a variation from passive acceptance of his incomplete relation to the group, to an active attempt to make contact; in the second the variations are those which appear in the child with active ambivalent social relations at the three- or four-year level, when ego demands yield to a simple desire for a companionship unimpeded by deep-rooted ego defenses or pressures of social code.

Such records seem to us to suggest that one cannot with much profit study a "trait" in a group of small children, filtering it out from the full reality and studying it for itself or as it correlates with other "traits." Such traits are the complex expression of deep biological and cultural forces. Their external form is like a changing shadow cast by clouds upon a mountain-side. There is a science of physics, but not of shadow shapes, *per se*. Behavior can be observed, experimented on, even measured, but it does not by itself make sense. It *does* make sense when the whole child is confronted in his whole social setting.

This account of social behavior at different ages from birth to school age is limited by the fact that it is based upon research upon children from professional groups, whose verbal development is somewhat earlier than that of other groups, and upon children in nursery-school situations which form a special pattern in comparison with the variety of situations in which children of this age may ordinarily be found. No one has systematically observed children from the ages of two to four playing in the park under the supervision of a nursemaid; common observation would indicate that this situation afforded little opportunity for the development of any such repertory of social behavior as has been described above. On the other hand, we have no evidence that the lack of contact with other children proves a serious handicap to children in subsequent social development. There is some indication that the initial adjustment of nursery-school children to kindergarten is easier, as any adjustment is for children to whom it is relatively familiar. But this is all that we positively know regarding the influence of nursery school upon personality development.

Similarly, we have no systematic observation of social behavior in the street play of small children in lower economic groups. Here one often sees four-year-old girls carrying their little brothers or sisters about and supervising them for long periods of time. This not only expresses much, but undoubtedly encourages much that is not observed in nursery schools. To the street or farm child, the kind of material that makes possible parallel and incipient group play in nursery school (clay, sand, swings, long trains and rocking boats) is lacking, and one sees little of these types of social activity. Yet there is no evidence that this lack of early stimulus to cooperative play has any effect upon eight- or nine-year-old hopscotch or baseball activities. Everyday observation suggests that, lacking definite trauma or specific prolonged social fears, later social behavior may develop along normal lines without detailed care and preparation at the pre-school level. It is important here to remember the work of McGraw and Gesell on other aspects of development, indicating that maturation and the general social environment of our culture provide a sufficiently good base to permit, at any level after a child is ready for the activity in question, development with fair ease in the appropriate direction without specific previous coaching; one may even catch up to other children who have had such coaching.

The chief value of early training, then, appears to resolve itself

into the *attitude effects* of the extra experience. In the case of
Gesell's work with stair-climbing, the specially trained twin showed
more alacrity and confidence; and McGraw's trained twin also
showed marked development of confidence in respect to the trained
activities. The relation of this confidence to the child's attitude
toward the untrained child, and the question of its general carry-
over into different situations where other equally competent or
superior children are present, need also to be considered.

Despite all the limitations and reservations which have just been
noted, a number of generalizations have emerged from the quantities of researches on behavior of children in pre-school years which
are sufficiently well established to serve as a dependable background
for further investigators.

1. Between the ages of two and five years, the variety of social
behavior patterns increases from year to year.

2. Among two- and three-year-olds, there are substantial positive
correlations between practically all overt social behavior patterns,
including those which adults think of as desirable and as undesirable.

3. Resistance and negativism may commonly be expected to reach
a peak at three years, more or less independent of economic group
or geographical location. This probably means merely that in our
culture the conflict of the child's readiness to expand with the restrictions imposed by adults is almost universal for this age.

4. Friendship and integrated patterns of cooperation begin at
three or four and expand from that time on into more complicated
or organized forms.

5. The quality and amount of cooperation or conflict are affected by the set-up of the group: number of children in relation to
space and play material, age range of children, personality of dominant children, amount of teacher direction, and personality of
teachers.

6. Personality reactions to home situations, especially parents'
attitudes toward the child, carry over into general tendencies to-

ward withdrawal (children of over-protective parents) or aggression (children rejecting parents), appearing in other situations.

7. Children vary in the extent to which behavior in any one situation is a basis for prediction of behavior in any other situation. Some children are relatively consistent from situation to situation and others vary sharply; where variations occur, they follow consistent patterns that can be understood when seen in relation to the total personality of the child.

Chapter X

SOCIAL BEHAVIOR IN LATER CHILDHOOD AND ADOLESCENCE

OBSERVERS who have watched seven-year-old boys in the city for a period of some months find their "free associations" turning to soldiers, cowboys, Buck Rogers, Alley Oop, baseball, swapping cards, fighting, gobbling food, ferry rides, resenting adults, having secrets, giggling over nonsense, wiggling, shouting, tussling, calling obscene names, and staging imitation strikes. Suburban children of the same age bring to mind, in addition, hikes, birds, goldfish, seed-planting, cooking, climbing hills, bicycling, turtles, and dogs. In either case, the picture is one of energy, initiative, lack of clear structure in relations with other children of their own age as well as in relations with adults, a drive to prove one's independence and masculinity, and expanding interest in the world around one.

If we classify the problems in socialization of personality during the elementary school years, we find these major areas:

1. Definition of one's rôle in the school group, with respect to one's sex rôle; one's dominance-participation rôle of leader, follower, dominator, isolate; one's activity rôle ("the good student," "the athlete"); and one's status rôle of superiority or inferiority as a person.

2. Definition of one's relation to adults as individuals in terms of submission or rebellion against authority, identification or rejection, love or antagonism.

3. Crystallization of attitudes toward the larger world, attitudes toward sex, race, religions, economic and social status differences; attitudes toward institutions such as school, family, church, clubs; identification with the morality of the group or deviation from it.

619

These might be expected to be affected by developmental changes in the individual child, emerging abilities, skills and sensitivities, changing group structure, changing authority relationships.

While this abstract pattern of the child's socialization during school years might serve as a tentative framework for organizing the data that exist, it will not be possible to fill in all aspects of it with equal completeness. For experimental and other quantitative or objective methods have not been extended to the study of a large variety of problems of social behavior in older children. This is not, of course, because of the dearth of problems, but rather because of the complexity suggested by the lists just given. As the child grows older, educational and conduct problems come to the fore, and the demands of scientific social research are swamped in the demands of educators for more and better ways to teach arithmetic and of teachers for immediate adjustment of a behavior problem. For the most part, studies have been made and are still being made by questionnaires and other methods which get results with a minimum of time and energy.

"Going to school," with its accompanying introduction to new groups, new ways, new ideals, new demands, is, for most children, the most important change between the pre-school age and adolescence. The ways in which children adjust to this radically new environment have been studied particularly by some of the Russian investigators. The whole situation of the schoolroom with the large group which it creates gives a new chance for leadership and new occupation for those inclined to be leaders. The growing interests of the child have a part in the formation of closer friendships, and of games or groups of a more permanent character than those that were observed in the pre-school period. The multitudinous appeals offered by the school itself and even more by life outside of the school are responded to with the eventual development of relatively stable interests. The necessity that many children face, of leaving school in early adolescence to help support the family, presses upon them the importance, because of the imminence, of vocational choices. All of these facts have received more or less attention at the hands of educators and psychologists alike, mostly through such paper-and-pencil techniques as have been mentioned:

questionnaires, the writing of essays in answer to a given question, etc. Occasionally, as in the *Middletown* studies of qualities that children consider desirable in parents and those that parents emphasize in bringing up children, questionnaire studies and observation are used together as mutual checks. These exceptions are few, however. Relatively few of the aspects of the older child's social life have received either careful quantitative analysis or experimental attack.

The biases which have shaped the development of research on elementary school children have been largely formed by the needs of teachers who are handling large groups of children and need to find some general safe principles for such wide application as to be usable with most children in any normal school set-up. Consequently, there is a heavy emphasis on the study of groups and generalizations about groups of children at the expense, on the one hand, of understanding individual children and, on the other, of knowledge of the effects of institutions on children. Curiously enough, there is no such thing as a complete social psychological study of an ordinary elementary school class or a progressive school class or a Scout group or a Sunday school. Personalities of children are constantly reacting to and being shaped by all these institutions, but the concrete records of how this is done and to what effect do not seem to exist.

Our picture of elementary school children must, then, be pieced together out of data from studies in progress and scattered results of segmental studies, few of which were concerned with the attempt to see children as personalities in group situations of elementary school life.

Forms of Play

It is common for children of this age to have a tremendous drive toward social activity and social relationships. In play situations this can find moderately organized outlets in the form of aggressive games—baseball, cowboy, Indians, and the like. When children are eating lunch together, we find this drive to social intercourse taking a variety of forms; exchanges of information about food or adults, spontaneous games or verbal fights and competition are familiar to teachers who see children in these situations.

Lunch Records of Seven-year-old Children[1]

J. and the others settle down. They are talking loudly. J. eats all her bread quickly. Miriam asks, "Who likes. . . ?" Hands were raised unanimously.

"Who likes rice?" They all get down on the floor to express extreme dislike.

"Who likes parsnips?" Down again on the floor.

"Who likes beets?" J. says, "Fair," with hands midway, about shoulder level.

M.: "Ice cream?" They all raise hands enthusiastically, but J. who says again, "Fair!"

J. takes the crust of her bread and rolls it, saying: "I've got a coffee roll!"

J. says to me, "Now you're writing it down!" They all ask about my writing, and M. says I write down what they do. M. J. L. says, "Do you write down everything we say, too?" I say, "No. Only sometimes." M.: "Yes, you do." I say, "I couldn't write that fast." M. asks more questions about what they like to eat, and they vote, but I cannot hear what they are voting on.

Miss L. threatens them with a long rest hour—they get to work eating. J. eats quickly and almost finishes her dinner in a few mouthfuls.

M.: "Who likes . . . sausage?" They all raise hands and say "Yum." "Who likes chocolate cake?" Much enthusiasm.

J. is all through her lunch except for salad.

C.: "Who likes this?" (extending two fingers). They all giggle (at the obscene reference partly hidden from the adults).

This form of excited discussion of likes and dislikes seems to be characteristic of conversation among primary children. Piaget's observation that at this age children begin to care about the points of view of others finds illustration in this type of pleasure in comparing experiences. At the same time, we may see an example of canalization of drive, or Woodworth's principle that a mechanism may become a drive. With children the possibilities inherent in emerging perceptions, values and activities lead to temporary drives developing from mechanisms that ultimately revert to an

[1] Record by Irma Black, of the Bureau of Educational Experiments.

instrumental status. Expressing one's likes and preferences may begin at three or four in a context where expressing a preference is likely to have material results; it does not become a form of social activity exploited for its own sake until elementary school age; this activity may then go through a phase of exploitation, with subsequent decline of interest.

In the following record we see another characteristic bit of elementary school behavior:

M.: "Let's start a game."

H.: "Okay. You're excused. We're all excused once." He refers to the talking after the game is started.

J. talks again.

H. says, "That's all!"

They try the game, but all talk. Apparently it is too much for them to keep quiet.

They start again, keeping their mouths closed as they chew. H. pretends to talk to C. without opening his mouth.

He sits quietly, mouth closed, chewing, making a humming noise. He is eating his bread, which he holds in his right hand. J. starts talking and crosses her fingers.

H.: "You've gotta eat the rotten potato." Then they decide they can talk if fingers are crossed.

They cross braids—J., M. and C. H. crosses his tie-ends, calling them "fins"—"These are four fins," he says. (Recorder: "I don't know if this means fish-fins or fingers.")

They explain the game to the recorder: "When you get fins crossed . . ." J. explains that the rotten potatoes were the ones they made the prints with.

H.: "I've got my toes crossed!"

They all break down and shout at once, making deafening noise. Henry puts his hands over his ears while M. seems the most haywire, yelling even after Miss L. calls them to order.

H. sits very quietly and eats while Miss L. sends J. out. This has a rather sobering effect on all of them.

H. says, "I got my eyebrow crossed." He twists his nose playfully and wiggles on his chair.

Looks at recorder and holds up his crossed leg with a wise glance. He has not eaten anything for several minutes.

"My toes aren't crossed, I'm crossing it on the floor." He puts his arms around his own neck crossing them as he does so. H. and C. engage in a rough-house, after which H. stands up in the middle of the room.

"See what I'm doing? I'm crossing the boards" (his feet are at right angles to the boards).

He takes a bite, then crosses his loose strands of hair. Then he takes another bite and sticks his tongue out, laying his right forefinger across it.

Here a trivial suggestion becomes exploited at great length with the aid of a strong interest in competition, and the capacity to derive a sense of achievement or power through thinking up new variations on the theme that nobody else has thought of. Language becomes something to play with in terms of content and meanings, not simply in terms of rhythm, as was frequently characteristic of pre-school years. This kind of activity may start with any casual remark; "You're an old shirt" will be countered with "You're an old pair of pajamas," and the competition will continue as long as the children can think of further members of the category.

While first-hand records of the social patterns and content of children's play are scarce, there are many studies of children's interest and play activities based on their own checking of lists handed out in the school room.

An exhaustive table analyzing the findings of about fifty studies of children's interests and attitudes, chiefly of this sort, is presented in Jones and Burks' *Personality Development in Childhood*. The material on play interests of children strongly suggests that the cultural pressure to "act your age" may be strong enough to inhibit individual interests based upon physical or mental capacities or sensitivities of the individual child. During the eight-to-twelve "gang age" characterized by lack of interest in girls or antagonism to girls, boys are busy with marbles, stilts, tops and similar games which thrive on overt competitive zeal and interest in developing skill. With adolescence comes a marked decline of interest in childish games of this sort, and an increase in heterosexual social activity and entertainment; competition for status is no less prevalent, but it is likely to be less explicit than it is in the ingenuous days from six to twelve.

A measure of the gap between adult preoccupations or values and those of childhood in any culture might be found in the extent to which children's play imitates or is divided from adult activity. Where children's play consists primarily in fishing, hunting, climbing, building on a small scale as the adults do, it is. doubtful if there will be such marked feeling attached to the adolescent transition that leaves childish things behind. In our society, where the gap between childish fun and adult absorption in the working world is so great, adolescence brings a sobering sense of change to a new outlook and a new world. The frequent longing to escape the responsibility of growing up is doubtless, in part, a result of this gap. It is possible that the transition from the social world of childhood to that of adulthood would be less fraught with insecurity if more children had developed strong personal interests of the kind that continue with adult years. Those gifted children who are less dominated by the pressure of immediate social groups and who develop more inner resources may have a basis for continuity that gives zest instead of anxiety to the anticipation of adult freedom.

Our culture channels the play interests of the young not only through external pressure to conform to the play patterns of a particular age level or cultural area, but also through internal pressure on individual children to find outlet for their own needs. We have still made little progress in the analysis of genuinely fundamental bases of interests and these deeper roots of dramatic play patterns. Incidental observations of any group of children between five and eight years of age will provide generous illustrations of this sort:

"Now let's pretend that I am Miss Bristol and I'll scold everybody."

"I'm going to build a big prison and all these soldiers are going to be put in the tower."

"I'm going to be a big mummy and these are my ten children, and I will say, 'Now you take a nap,' and they will say, 'No, I won't.' "

"Now, daddy, you be the little boy that was hanging on to the cars and I'll be the policeman and chase you."

"I'll be a new king that's boss of the whole world."

Patterns of this sort reflect obvious needs to work off deprivations from or dominance of adults, and probably a large proportion of the play motives of children in our culture would reflect
different kinds of compensation for deprivation in relations with
adults or retaliation for adult aggression. The recent emphasis on
strict supervision of early habit formation, added to the dominating
patterns which parents in our culture have characteristically had,
the aggression of adults as a whole toward children in western
civilization as expressed in patterns of whipping and other rigid
methods of discipline, have given children a vivid and persistent
experience of adult aggression toward them. This aggression must
perforce appear both in their relations with adults, whether in the
form of marked submission or efforts at domination in turn, and
also in relations with their own age group.

We have a habit of calling the activities of children with one
another by the name of play, but it seems probable that the fundamental emotional nature of these activities reflects a great deal which
is also evident in their relations with adults.

In addition to the importance of the child's experience of aggression from adults in relation to play activities, we must also
take account of other sources of activity and satisfaction. During
the growth process each new experience that is made possible by
the coordinated growth of maturation and learning makes possible
new play interests. We are familiar with the importance of exploratory leg and arm activity in infants who are in the process
of getting control of eye-hand coordination and of locomotor activities. Shaking, pulling, pushing are forms of play before combining, even to the extent of putting one small block upon another, is possible. Similarly, rolling over, stretching, pulling oneself up to one's knees, then exploratory walking, are all play or
work before one can ride a tricycle or use roller skates. When
these muscle coordinations are perfected, new ones become absorbing. In general, appreciation of the value of vigorous activity
for the play of young children has occupied our attention to the
exclusion of the value of sense experience and small-muscle activity.
The strength of interest in the activity of different organs may
depend largely upon constitutional differences in response to environ-

mental pressures. The organism at any age has possibilities of interest and play satisfaction in relation to *all* the functioning organs
of the body. Thus sound, sight, speech, manual activities, leg activities, eating and elimination, as well as skin sensations in the
bath or in the snow, all offer possibilities of satisfaction, many
of which are commercially exploited by dealers in children's toys.

Against the broad background of major experiences offered by
our culture on the one hand, the range of possible sources of satisfaction in the organism on the other, and the awareness of individual differences emerging both from different cultural pressures
and from constitutional thresholds, we must set our discussions
of the developments of interests and play. The symbolic values
of toy preferences and play experiences have for the most part
not been analyzed in any of the work in this country; the study of
the meaning of interests and play for the deepest nature of the child
is still waiting to be approached.

There are several studies of children's interest and preferences
in games or toys which are based on a large enough number of
children to give a basis for generalization regarding children in
the social group. A hundred children between 24 and 76 months
were shown six toys of similar size, color, and cost. The test took
place at home in the presence of adults who were familiar to the
child. Out of fifty boys, seventeen each chose a car or airplane.
Six each chose a horse, three chose a boy doll, and one chose a
girl doll. Out of fifty girls, fifteen chose a girl doll; the next
largest number, twelve, chose an airplane; then came in order
the boy doll, the car, and the horse. When the length of time
the children played with the toys was combined with the final
choice as an indication of interest value, the order of interest was
as follows, for boys: car, airplane, horse, boy doll, girl doll. The
order of interest for girls was: boy doll, girl doll, airplane, car,
horse. Definite sex differences are apparent in the boys' preference for the car and the girls' preference for the dolls, and these
appeared, according to the author, at all age levels. In choices of
this sort a combination of factors is involved, including sensori-
motor satisfactions, dramatic interest, and individual emotional outlet. Similar differences were apparent among seven-year-olds ob-

served recently, and the toy preferences appeared to be closely related to the children's interests appearing in records of schoolroom and playground behavior; girls who showed other evidences of rejecting a feminine rôle expressed extreme dislike of dolls and preferred boys' toys, while boys who were inactive in games like baseball and war did not select the materials that would be used in these games preferred by active aggressive boys. The comments of these seven-year-old boys as they choose toys from a larger collection suggests that children of this age are intensely conscious of the symbolic values of certain toys: "Pooh! I don't want girls' toys"; "whoopee, these are the ones for me"; "I'm the kind of guy that always takes the soldiers." This consciousness of the masculine or feminine quality of toys appears as an aspect of a marked effort to achieve schoolboy masculinity characteristic of boys of this age. They have lost their baby teeth; their big teeth are not in yet, but they are determined to be recognized as members of the he-boy fraternity which scorns girls and the domination of females.

It is not an accidental matter that the remarks above seem to reflect a masculine-dominated culture in the elementary school period; this is particularly characteristic of metropolitan life where the male world of war and commerce, boats, docks, subways and prize fights is more impressive than the attenuated home activities that are possible in modern apartments. Dolls and clothes remain, of course, for seven-year-old girls; but even they have no part in the curriculum which takes very seriously all of those aspects of the "real world" in which the boys are interested anyway. This leaves the girls either in the position of accepting a rôle identified with less interesting and rich activities or of renouncing the feminine rôle and identifying themselves completely with the boys' world. This metropolitan dilemma probably has little counterpart in the country where, on the one hand, feminine activities are more varied and significant and where, on the other, there is a closer partnership between men and women in the work necessary to sustain life.

This early tomboy pattern of energetic girls, to whom fighting, selling, being policemen, firemen and skyscraper-builders are more impressive realities than producing and nourishing children, may be both a reflection of and basis for the adult "masculine protest" that psychiatrists recognize in unmotherly mothers. Certainly, many contemporary curricula contribute in no small part to the devaluation of feminine activities and responsibilities in the attitudes of children who cannot, as they grow up, wholly release themselves from deep-rooted attitudes. The question whether this is an indication of long-time cultural change that will largely revise the functions of women, or whether it is merely a temporary effect of the wave of extreme feminism that achieved the vote for women and made equality of function recognized, will not be answered immediately.

The study of imaginary companions may have possibilities for analysis of subjective values in relation to objective behavior. There are few large-scale studies of children who have imaginary companions; among them an analysis of imaginary companions of 40 children between 3 and 16 years from a Chicago suburb offers the most comprehensive study, and attempts to check the hypothesis that imaginary companions may be compensatory for defects or for lack of playmates. Only two of the children show definite physical abnormalities (hare lip and flat foot); two others stuttered, and two were left-handed. However, 35 of 40 pupils showed personality difficulties of some kind. At the same time, 7 of the children were described as leaders. At the time of the creation of imaginary companions, 55 per cent were only children; the remainder appeared in families of all sizes. In 36 cases, the phenomenon was accepted or encouraged by the parents. The median age for appearance of imaginary companions was 2 years and 5 months; by 5 or 6 years, the make-believe quality of the companion was recognized. For the most part, the most vivid imaginary companions were of the same sex; they were frequently labeled relatives and were also often "friends." Most of the play was of a highly emotional kind and generally was directly related to the child's own experiences. In 33 out of 40 cases, the playmates were conceived of as occupying space.

It would be very important to know whether there is any functional relation between the type of personality difficulty of the child and the content or quality of the relation with the imaginary companions. A variety of possibilities could be suggested offhand. To a child who felt deprived of affection in the family group, the imaginary companion might be a projection of his own deprived self to whom he, as good parent or brother, could offer the affection of which he had been deprived. To a child who felt frustrated because of very dominating parents or nursemaid who gave him little room for planning or decision, the imaginary companion might be someone whom he could dominate. To a child who is lonely, or who feels deprived of brothers or sisters, the imaginary companion may be a direct substitute. Another type of analysis of the function of the imaginary companion could show the relations between the activity with this companion and the child's total social life. Where the imaginary companion acts as a safety valve or provides situations for rehearsing behavior that would be valuable in actual life situations he might be more of an asset than a detriment; however, where he is so satisfactory as to prevent efforts at contact with live children his influence may be quite undesirable. Aside from such therapeutic and developmental considerations, the imaginary child may be of importance in relation to the whole social imaginative development of the individual, and it is primarily these relations between the inner life of the child and the social behavior that we need to explore further.

While individual personality differences characteristic of children in our culture may be reflected in common deviations from the norm, certain general values are also reflected in the most characteristic activities. "Collecting" is an activity of children in both town and country that may give another outlet for the competition-power drive among children on a level that involves real elements of prestige in the child's world not so different from the prestige values of property among adults.

We should expect that children would collect different objects in different environments, depending on what was available. However, on the whole, town and country children show few differences in the objects collected most frequently. Those items which were collected somewhat more by country children included bottle tops, curios, marbles, newspapers, poems, stamps, petrified wood. The items collected more often by town girls than country girls included autograph sentiments, jack stones, newspapers, toys. On the whole, boys and girls tend to collect the same kinds of things and to have about the same number of collections. The things that children collect do not necessarily throw much light on the meaning or symbolic value of collections to the child, nor has research thrown much light upon this. For many children, collecting and the exchange of objects that are being collected (cards, stamps, samples) may have a function similar to that of gossip in sustaining adult social relations; for other children large collections may symbolize status and achievement just as status is acquired by the adult in amassing a fortune.

THE STRUGGLE FOR STATUS

These illustrations of the content of social and play activities among elementary school children show the relationships between play and the process of achieving one's sex rôle, the influence of individual difficulties, and of the child's level of property-consciousness; they show little of the changing nature of the relation between the individual and the group. Something of this process of socialization in terms of the individual's place in the group structure in the first few grades of elementary school is indicated by the following facts, some of which will be recalled from Chapter VIII:

1. Leadership in the first grade is confined to small groups, in contrast to the fifth grade where class leaders with influence on groups of thirty to forty children can be distinguished. (Reininger.)
2. First-grade children are not able to rank the least and most important members of the class. (Reininger.)
3. In the first grade there are many intersexual attractions or friendships, while in the sixth grade there may be none at all. Intersexual choices decline sharply after the third grade, not to reappear until the eighth. (Moreno.)

4. The lowest number of mutual pairs (children who choose each other for activities) and the highest number of isolated children are found in the kindergarten, first and second grades, "indicating that children of this age are seldom sufficiently certain whom to choose." From the fourth grade on there is an increase in the number of mutual pairs of friends and an increasing complexity in group structure. At the earlier levels the isolated child may be merely forgotten, but after thirteen years children may be unchosen because of definite negative attitudes of other members of the group toward them. (Moreno.)

5. Leaders are likely to make a more extroverted score on the Marston scale than the average child. (Caldwell and Wellman.)

6. Shy children become attached to self-assertive members of the group. (Reininger.)

7. Children early show a tendency toward certain rôles or types of behavior in a group, such as the protective type, the popular or beloved type, the leader, the despot, and the socially unsuccessful child. (Reininger.)

8. Quantitative descriptions of the rôles of children in a group disclose the isolated child, the nucleus of a group, the link in a chain of relationships. (Moreno.)

9. Friends are usually of the same sex, age, height, I.Q.; and children who describe the kinds of boys and girls they prefer for friends use terms like "friendly," "fun," "fair."

10. The child who is extremely superior is not chosen as leader by average groups as often as is the moderately superior child. (Hollingworth.)

The entrance at school age into an organized social structure, such as school, involves characteristically a process of definition of rôle in this structure; the direction of this process in the case of any specific elementary school child will be determined by the relation between the child's biological and social status (abilities, sex, developmental level) and the demands of the group; the relation between his behavior or personality in terms of its meaning to the group, and the values of the group.

This determination of the individual's relation to the group structure has several aspects: (1) clarification of sex rôle; (2) dynamic relation to group activity (following, leading, failure, or, as Moreno quantitatively defines them, link, nucleus, isolate); and (3) qualitative rôle or character (protective, despotic, beloved, etc.). As we shall see in connection with the discussion of social development in adolescence, none of these rôles is static and permanent, but all are capable of change as the relation between the child's biological and social make-up and the demands of his group changes. A leader accepted at the age of eleven by her sex and the class as a whole on the basis of intelligence and athletic ability may find herself isolated in relation to both sexes and dethroned from leadership by the age of fourteen when her lanky figure and unfeminine interests deviate from the changed mode of the group (see page 642), or when the influence of family status becomes more important. At the same time, the possibilities for any individual child are not determined solely by the group, for, in addition to certain objective abilities and characteristics that tend to "place" a child, there are important attitudes and assumptions which he carries over from earlier group experience at school or in the family. A child who has been "the baby" during the first six grades of school may not find it easy to assimilate the different status and rôle which accelerated adolescent growth may give him. A child who has been passively accepting domination at home may not be able to accept the more active rôle which other children and the teacher at school expect of him.

The contrast between the isolated or withdrawn child and the sociable child is even more conspicuous in elementary school than it is at the nursery-school level. These two poles of group relationship come to life in the behavior of the following seven-year-old boys:

Record of an Active Seven-year-old Boy, T. W.[1]

Baseball seems to be suspended today for some reason, and a huge gang of children are involved in what appears to be cowboy or bandit

[1] Record made by L. Woodcock, of the Bureau of Educational Experiments.

play. There is wild chasing over the roof. Dead bodies lie stretched on
the tiles. The wounded are lugged off to the cage in the corner of the
upper level.

T. W. is deeply involved in this game. I found him first chasing
one of Miss B.'s boys, shooting his finger at him wildly. He must
have said something about a bandit, for M. J. K. said, "We have no
bandit, you silly," and T. W. gave up the pursuit.

He raced across the roof and threw himself on the floor, firing his
finger off again with many "Boom, boom's." He tore back across the
floor, firing. Then he flung himself upon B., who struggled violently
to get away. As others came up to struggle with B., T. W. seemed to
melt out of the struggle, and raced to the cage in the corner, firing.

J. S. had collapsed in a wounded condition, and T. W. helped drag
her to the cage. Then he helped D. F. lug L. up the steps, also faint-
ing from wounds. Again he attacked B., but when E. arrived as a recruit, T. W. again melted away, leaving B. to him.

He ran down the steps, firing and running. He lay on his stomach
taking aim at someone. H. also lies on the floor aiming his finger.

Then both walked over the roof in quiet conversation.

R. is in this game, J. S., S., J. E., and many others—all circulating
so fast that I cannot discover their rôles.

D. O. is stretched dead or wounded on the floor. T. W. tried to lift
him up, then turned to H., who is also badly wounded. M. joined
him, and they both struggled.

Miss H. came with some comment and I heard D. F. reply to her,
"What about the wounded?" He and M. seem especially assigned to
bring in the wounded, working feverishly at it.

T. W. suddenly slid forward and fell on his stomach. P. first tried
to lift him up, then J. E.; but in the end it was the staunch M. who
took him around the waist and escorted him to the cage, where he
fell prostrate on the floor.

The cage is full of wounded now. J. S., S., T. W., M. J. K., H., He.,
R. and J. E. are all spread in its cramped confines. T. W. and S. are
talking together, apparently discussing T. W.'s wounds.

L. came in, apparently in the rôle of doctor, and T. W. called, "Help
fix me." L. came to him and with earnest face felt his throat, then
assured him that he was all right. T. W. protested at this, and pushed
up his hair in front, obviously to show a wound. L. examined the forehead with his fingers, then again told T. W. he could get up.

One by one the wounded are reviving and leaving the hospital.
T. W. seems reluctant to have his wounds heal.

J. E. lifted up the edge of a real bandage on her shin and showed
him the sore underneath. T. W. said earnestly, "Once I fell off the
(porch?)."

Record of an Inactive Seven-year-old Boy, D. H.[1]

In the first thirteen minutes, D. H. wandered all alone about the roof, looking down into the street, going to the wooden climbing frame and leaning on it, and tapping with a stick on the iron step railing. He seemed completely at loose ends, and his entire manner was expressive of boredom.

At 11:10 H. and D. G. went and grabbed him. They were looking for a "witch" for their prison (I think it was), but D. H., with little change of expression, pulled away and went to stand near the door. As the three arrived on the scene again, he stood very close to the adult. In a few minutes, he leaned on the door.

Then he began rather tentatively to tap various children with the stick he was carrying. This was done very lightly, almost slyly. D. F. chased him.

As the crowd left the wood frame, he sauntered up near it but left as they returned, carrying M. whom they were pulling and tugging. (She was pleased by it.)

He sauntered near the railing and watched. A few minutes later he approached A. M. and bumped her with his knee. They had a brief and mild roughhouse. D. H. said, "Come on—get me," but the episode was soon over.

Then he went to the railing where C. was doing stunts. They did not notice each other at first, but finally began talking. This did not last.

Then D. H. pulled away from D. G. and H. again as they tried to get him for a witch.

At the end of the (forty-minute) record he was alone again, hanging on the rail by his arms, feet caught on lower rail.

The entire picture was of a child almost outside of the group, making occasional small social advances, none of which lasted. He was almost devoid of expression, even when he was being baited, which made him such an unsatisfactory victim that even that was not followed up.

What lies behind these two striking patterns of group participation and isolation from the group? Perhaps submissiveness carried over from a home situation where D. H. was dominated by an aggressive parent or an older brother accounts for his withdrawal. But we must also not forget that equally important for the security of the child is the formidable pressure of adult authority institutionalized in the school and the experience of com-

[1] Record made by Irma Black, of the Bureau of Educational Experiments.

petition into which the elementary school child is thrown for the first time. To be sure, competition is not a completely new experience. Even in the nursery school his playmates have begun to brag about their achievements, their size, their age, or what their fathers could do. Although praise and criticism have been given by adults since before he learned to talk, he has experienced them largely in absolute terms in relation to specific things he has done which have been approved or disapproved, rather than in relation to the behavior of other children. In first grade, however, others may get stars and he may be left out. For the first time he is one of a group to be divided into sheep and goats, and instead of bragging in fantasy, "I am going to live to be a hundred years old," he wants to brag realistically, "I can read better than Jim"—"I am the best at baseball." Both in fancy and reality his success now involves the inferiority of someone else, and the success of his friend involves his inferiority.

The relation between competition as one set of reins which many adults use constantly and the child's feeling of success or failure, superiority or inferiority, is consequently very intimate. The later consequences of this early experience give the raw material of quantities of research on "ascendance and submission," "self-sufficiency," "dominance in face-to-face relations," "neurotic tendencies," "aspects of introversion," and so forth. We have yet to undertake the study of the early stages in these patterns as they emerge out of the authority-competition setting in which the elementary school child is living.

The transition to adolescence renews the problems of rôle of the individual in relation to the group. A child who has been happy in gang activities in the elementary years may not always shift easily to the new patterns of heterosexual relationships. Here new criteria of acceptability appear; the physical build suitable for the sixth-grade basketball team may not have feminine appeal in first-year high school. At the same time children who were inconspicuous or unadjusted at the gang age may develop poise and social skill more readily than others. The interrelations among these different aspects of development and the status of the child in the group are illustrated in two cases of California children, excerpts from whose records are as follows:[1]

Observations by P.E. instructor on school playground. October, 1934.

Dorothy was elected captain. She is an excellent leader of her squad. A girl went up to her and gave her a friendly slap, and smiled. They talked. Three more girls approached and talked to her. The group looked to her as the central figure in the game. One helped her fix her middy unasked. Dorothy laughed and talked to the girl nearest her, and called out to another girl farther away. Pleasant and smiling. Seemed to be liked by everyone. Came across the room to talk to adult in friendly conversation. Dorothy instructed her squad very effectively.

Observations by staff member and counselor at a clubhouse party given by four boys. November, 1934.

When Dorothy came in a little after the crowd there were cheers and clapping. She was quite popular with two boys in the Post Office game. When some of the group decided to dance in the front room, Dorothy and two other girls continued playing Post Office for a while but later joined the crowd who were dancing.

Observations by staff member in free-play situation at Institute of Child Welfare. March, 1935.

When playing games such as basketball, Dorothy takes control in an unassuming manner, but at other times she tends to allow the group to direct her, or retires to a seat and looks on. She has not "bloomed" in that special way in which so many of the girls have. She had a more marked masculine air about her today than usual in her carriage, her hair, and her mannerisms. No make-up, no curls. She had to leave early to play in and referee a game of basketball between teachers and students.

Observations by staff member in free-play situation at Institute of Child Welfare. September, 1935.

Dorothy's masculinity impressed us today more than ever before. She seems to have none of the maturing girl's behavior pattern. Retired more than ever today to the side lines and looked on. Seems in general rather unhappy and at a standstill.

---

[1] Selected from the cumulative descriptive records of a girl through a transition from leadership among her own sex and some popularity among the opposite sex, to a long-drawn-out deterioration of status with both sexes; from the California Adolescent Study.

Observations by staff member in clubhouse. October, 1935.

Dorothy (aged 14.8 years) has been coming to the clubhouse regularly but always just to stand and watch. Uncommunicative; very quiet, tense and self-conscious. Her hands were clenched and she moved about restlessly as she stood watching, her back against the wall. Stolid, shy, and apparently inhibited by the free sort of social situation created by those dancing. The boys and girls present paid no attention to her.

Observations by a second staff member in free-play situation at Institute of Child Welfare. March, 1936.

Dorothy was most reserved. She has imposed an isolation upon herself which cannot be broken into. Dorothy will not accept the group's request for leadership. She is too well bred to be actively negative but acts bored and reserved.

Guess Who Test

Probably the most outstanding characteristic of the Guess Who record on Dorothy is the change from a good deal of mention (extreme and usually favorable position) to an average position which is a function of not being noticed.

Several traits in which she maintained her status of extremely favorable position are such ones as "active in games," "leader in games" which have lost value for nearly all girls with the development of their increasing interest in the opposite sex.

Another item which should be noticed is the "best friend" item. Dorothy had always received average or better than average mention as being the best friend of some of the children, but in the spring of 1935 and in the spring of 1936 no one mentioned her as her best friend.

It may be possible that in our culture a masculine girl has a more difficult adjustment to make than a feminine boy (if he is not too feminine) since merely being male carries status of its own. At any rate, the following case illustrates the way in which a rather feminine boy improved his status with his own sex through his acceptance by girls as an adolescent:[1]

Comments by staff member observing in the classroom when Ted was 10.7 years old and in the Low 6th grade:

Ted stayed in the classroom to eat lunch with several girls. All the other boys went out to the playground.

[1] Excerpts from a similar cumulative record of the California Adolescent Study.

Comment from Home Visit report, December, 1932, when Ted was 11.2 years old and in the High 6th grade:

His father never sees him with other boys and is rather concerned about his adjustment. He is worried also because Ted is so sensitive about being teased by other boys.

Comment by staff member on results of "Guess Who" test in which the children expressed opinions about each other:

His score was unfavorable in elementary school in the spring of 1932 (Low 6th grade) and became even worse in the fall of 1932. He was mentioned as being feminine in interests and behavior, as being interested in younger friends, as being neat and tidy (an undesirable trait from the children's point of view).

In the fall of 1934, when Ted was 12.2 years old and in the Low 8th grade, these comments were made by a staff member after observations in a free-play situation with a small group of boys:

Seems to be getting on better with the boys than formerly, but still doesn't seem to be interested in games. He has become somewhat more masculine in appearance.

In June, 1935, his counselor wrote in a description of a party at the clubhouse:

The first game played was wink. When the girls were winking, Jim and Bob were the most popular but Ted was quite popular, too.

A staff member commenting on the "Guess Who" test, said:

In this spring testing Ted had a sudden increase in favorable scores. This was due not so much to increase in favorable mentions as to decrease in unfavorable mentions.

In these cases we see the interplay of the development, physical make-up, abilities and attitudes of the child, with his social adjustment, in terms of his acceptance both with his own sex and with the opposite sex. This relation between the status of an individual —as it might be represented on a number of rank orders for different characteristics—and the attitudes which are created by his necessity for rationalizing inferiorities or discrepancies in different status on different traits is the theme of a discussion by L. K. Frank. He points out that "the rank order gives us a clue to the kind of situation an individual faces because of that rank," and that "out of the discrepancies and incongruities" between his rank orders on different measurements "arise the problems of adjustment to which the personality is the response." In the case of the adolescents whose reports we have just seen, we can only infer the shifting pattern of inner attitudes that must have gone parallel to the interrelated shifts in appearance, behavior and acceptance by the group.

The California Adolescent Study, from whose case records we have just drawn excerpts, offers a unique basis for analysis of these interrelated rank orders in dynamic terms, as they change with the growth of the individual child. At six-months' intervals over a period of six years, measurements are made on a variety of aspects of development; they include:

1. Anthropometric measurements supplemented by observation of physical changes (muscular development, skeletal alignment, genitalia) indicative of maturation.
2. Body photographs showing changes in gross morphological pattern.
3. Eye examinations including photographic records of eye movements in reading.
4. Roentgenograms.
5. Metabolic measurements, pulse, blood pressure, respiration rate, temperature.
6. Photographic records of autonomic reactions made continuously during a 40-minute period of stimulation by motion pictures, association words, interview questions.
7. Reactions to exercise in terms of oxygen consumption, pulse rate, etc.
8. Urine analyses for albumen, sugar, amount of creatin, creatinine and total nitrogen excreted.
9. Physical ability, tests of strength, bodily control, postural adjustment, power or accuracy in gross muscular functions.
10. Motor skill tests of eye-hand coordination, steadiness in thrusting, speed of rotary movement, bi-manual coordination, etc.
11. Intelligence tests.
12. Learning tests (mazes, immediate and delayed recalls).
13. Achievement tests of reading, arithmetic, languages, etc.
14. Teachers' ratings on interest in school work, school achievement and college aptitude.
15. Tests of interests (things to do, places to go, etc.) and attitudes (religious, liberal-conservative attitudes, Strong Vocational Interest test).
16. Activity records (things I did last week, where I went last week, radio programs).

17. Associates' ratings (the Guess Who test includes 40 items such as, "Here is someone who doesn't like to talk very much." " . . . someone who is very friendly." Pupils nominate classmates for each item).
18. Annoyance inventory representing 10 categories such as sensitivity to sounds, annoyance at personal infringements, etc.
19. Adjustment inventory, yielding scores on social, school, family adjustments; personal inferiority, generalized tensions, overstatements, fears and physical symptoms.
20. Social extroversion.
21. Judgment of motives.
22. Rorschach test treated to yield a clinical summary and scores for introversion-extroversion, emotional tension, association activity, etc.
23. Records of behavior in social situations.
24. Interview records covering family history, socio-economic data, habits and daily régime.

This detailed though abbreviated summary of the types of data available in the California study is given in order to suggest the types of longitudinal and cross-sectional interrelations that are actually obtainable and of social significance. From the data available in this study it will be possible to make a great variety of cross analyses, of which the following may be given as examples:

1. An analysis of the relations between physiological measures of emotionality and the social adjustment of the individual as judged by his companions' ratings and the psychologists' observations.
2. A comparison of sensory acuity as indicated by standard measures, and the social functioning of sensitivity or sensory interests evidenced in the types of annoyances and types of activities characteristic of individuals in different social relations.
3. A comparison of the qualitative capacities of the individual in terms of physical and mental abilities, with the functioning of these capacities in the social group at different stages of development; ages at which motor coordination, verbal ability, musical ability may be at a greater social premium and condition the status of the individual and his attitudes.
4. A comparison of the abilities and sensitivities of the individual child, with appearance and style, as determiners of group status and group rôle.
5. Family attitudes toward the child's abilities and make-up in comparison with the attitudes of the child's own group as determiners of his evaluation of himself and the uses he makes of his capacities.

THE STUDY OF TOTAL PERSONALITY IN CHILDHOOD
AND ADOLESCENCE

The importance of the relation between individual status and the group norm as a determiner of the individual's adjustment has already been mentioned; in this same study seventeen out of one hundred boys showed an atypical pattern of sex maturation which constituted a hazard to wholesome emotional and social development; retardation and divergent forms of development made for insecurity and social difficulties. Differences between the sexes in the age of maturing meant a temporary shift in the relationship of sex dominance; girls who matured earlier took the lead in training boys as dancing partners and party escorts.

Facts of this sort need to be seen against a background of the content of adolescent experience as a whole. We do not recognize sufficiently how different this may be for different social groups. Contrast, for example, the situation of adolescents at boarding school under constant surveillance with that of those who, like the California children, had a clubhouse of their own and virtually complete freedom in social activity. The following summary describes the children's use of the experimental clubhouse:

Most of these boys and girls are searching intently for opportunities which will facilitate their contacts with members of the opposite sex. To date they are finding these opportunities principally through dancing, going to parties, going to the movies, groups listening to the radio, and through conversation. But of all these activities the thirteen- to fifteen-year-old boy and girl seem to find dancing to be the most consistently and endlessly interesting. Before school begins in the morning they come to the clubhouse to dance. After a hurried bite of lunch twenty or more couples crowd the floor, dancing till the last bell rings at noon. And after school they are back and at it again. The fascination of new dance tunes and the rhythmical movement of their bodies signify a good deal. On every hand there is evidence that this represents an age range through which social activities are rising to greatest importance. For some individuals the transition is a very gradual process, whereas others shoot ahead with breath-taking speed, leaving the adults around them dazed and bewildered by the dizzy pace they set. But through it all there appears the steadily rising pressure to break away from the earlier accepted domination of parents in the home and of teachers in the school. It is as though an overwhelming urge were released within them to assert their independence, to explore quite new and thrilling kinds of relationships with each other, and to proclaim their rights to self-expression as individuals. In a sense the clubhouse has been misnamed, for no club meetings are held in it. Nor has any desire been expressed for the formation of clubs. The sort of social organization which these adolescents prefer is a much less rigid, more flexible, changeable, fluid, seething sort of thing. Formalities are forgotten in their quest for more personal and sophisticated relationships with each other.

The great shift toward interest in parties frequently involves a dramatic decline in other activities:

When we looked for age differences it was found that younger girls were still engaged in activities such as painting, drawing, modeling, and taking music lessons, while older girls seemed to be outgrowing these activities. All this fall at the clubhouse, open scorn has been expressed when any radio program other than dance music has happened to be turned on. When free choice was allowed from a variety of Victrola records, some representing famous classical music and others representing popular dance tunes, over a period of weeks, nothing but the dance music was selected. Interest in the other records vanished with the reading of their titles.

[We analyzed] the answers of the 200 boys and girls to the same questions at three consecutive yearly intervals. We have also presented the answers of the children in the lower and higher grades separately. The question asked was, "Of these three activities, swimming, playing ball, and going to parties, which do you like to do best?" The children's replies [showed that:] At an average age of 11 years and 4 months, 67 per cent of the lower-grade boys preferred to swim, 25 per cent of these boys preferred to play ball, and 8 per cent of them would rather go to a party than swim or play ball. At this same age 88 per cent of the girls preferred swimming to going to a party, or playing ball, 8 per cent would rather go to a party, and 4 per cent of them preferred playing ball. During the next two years this pattern of preferences does not change greatly for the boys in either the lower or higher grades. But contrast the change in the girls' answers to the same question: In 1932 at an average age of 11 years, only 8 per cent of both boys and girls preferred going to parties above swimming or playing ball. Two years later the same percentage of lower-grade boys expressed this same preference, whereas 45 per cent of these girls now preferred going to parties. [The group by whom] swimming is preferred to parties has been cut from 80 per cent to 8 per cent in a period of two years, the parties having gained by this loss. The same trends, but in less striking degree, are in evidence when the preference of the higher-grade boys and girls is compared.

Other fragmentary reports here and abroad indicate that young adolescence today is not unlike the experience a generation ago. Nicknames, crushes, ideals and fine ambitions for a grown-up vocation are observed or reported from questionnaire studies. The fact that social class affects popularity somewhat more in older children in some sections, that boys in high school generally express vocational ambitions at a level higher than that of their fathers' occupation, that a large percentage of girls are interested in biographies (of the great or famous people), and the predominant importance to boys of the problem of earning, saving and spending money, and to girls of the problem of personal attractiveness and etiquette indicate ways in which the competitive society is shaping the values of youth. The meaning of intense love-friendships and crushes for adolescents is not yet entirely clear; they may reflect both the projection of the child's need for affection and the sublimation of growing emotions that in another culture might have more immediate sexual expression. Both the competitive values listed above and the intense need for personal response are striking evidences of the color of individualism; the lack of strong awareness of social needs, economic or political problems of the group, among adolescents who are on the threshold of responsible citizenship, is simply the reverse of this cultural coin.

At the same time that we concern ourselves with the general picture of adolescence as a stage of social development with its own patterns and structures, we must consider the varieties of personality that make different contacts with the adolescent world. Horney has called attention to the following different types of emotional development that may appear in adolescent girls:

1. The girl who becomes absorbed in sublimated activities and may develop an aversion to the erotic sphere.
2. The girl who becomes absorbed in the erotic sphere, is boy-crazy, and may lose interest in or capacity for work.

3. The girl who becomes emotionally detached, and acquires a don't-care attitude, not being able to put energy into anything.
4. The girl who develops homosexual tendencies.

These types of emotional development are to be seen in connection with the relations between personality and group status revealed in the California study, just as the directions of change recorded in the latter study call for analysis in terms of deeper tendencies in the personality. What are the patterns that lie behind one girl's acceptance of an unfeminine pattern and consequent loss of status as an adolescent, whereas another girl will "try on new faces" until she finds one that fits and that opens the door to social acceptance by her group?

Studies of adolescents under the direction of Zachry are bringing out just such persistent trends in the personalities of a certain proportion of adolescents who do not shift markedly from situation to situation. Nina goes through four years of college with no contacts with boys; she has a sensitive imagination that produces interesting work in poetry and the arts, and arouses the response of all her faculty. Only the need for self-support brings her out of her daydream world into the need for confronting the demands of everyday life. Frances is scattered, insecure, dashing about from one human relationship to another and from one piece of work to another, never resting long enough to give genuine feeling to any one piece of work or to any one friend. There is evidence that both of these are probably the late-adolescent result of early insecurity resulting from inadequate love and too much domination; elaborate case records of these girls and many others point to the importance of personality patterns rooted in the child's early experiences in the home, not only for present social relationships, but also for interests in work and play that determine the main outlines of high school and college experience. Thus insecurity is frequently expressed in a projected concern for insecure groups such as social minorities, delinquents and the poor; inability to confront reality in terms of major unanswerable questions regarding life may find an escape in the solidities of laboratory work where you can see and touch the material and find "solid ground to stand on"; a drive for attention or power in a student who cannot get the vote of the majority may find satisfaction in leadership of minority radical groups. A girl brought up in an idealizing religious atmosphere who loses the intellectual framework of her religion may need an emotional outlet for the projection of her ideals and may find it in a teacher; another student can work well only after she has first been reassured of love and respect from her teacher; another compensates for the rejection by her family in a relentless drive for success and achievement that pushes beyond human values in college to those skills that will contribute to her present goal. In these cases we find personality patterns developed in childhood relationships and frustrations of love or ego needs that persist through adolescence and are reflected in relations with members of their own sex and the opposite sex, relations with adults and with work and leisure.[1]

A related approach to adolescent personality is being worked out by E. Fromm, who is coordinating a variety of experimental and observation methods to obtain a complete view of personalities in a form that permits quantitative as well as qualitative analysis. It will be evident that the dividing line between the two approaches can become so vague that the dichotomy disappears. The purpose of this study is to gain intensive information regarding the personality structures of twenty-five college girls, particularly in terms of the patterns of relationship to authority—as present in teachers, situations, and parents, and as construed by the girl. Many sources of information are available for each individual. Teachers who are in intimate contact with the girls supply case studies. These are based upon observations of everyday behavior in class, on the campus, and in personal relations, and on information regarding family background obtained from the subjects and from elaborate college records. A large battery of tests administered to all students is available, including the Bernreuter, Allport Ascendance-Submission, various intelligence tests, the Study of Values, and the Maslow Dominance Test; a Rorschach analysis and in some cases handwriting

---

[1] Illustrations are adapted from unpublished cases organized under the direction of Dr. Caroline Zachry. These studies of adolescent personality are based almost entirely on the interviews of teachers or psychiatrically trained workers who make week-by-week records of the information and attitudes emerging in these interviews.

analysis are available also. The subject supplies material in writing on such topics as ambitions, autobiographies, ideals, etc.

A brief series of experiments is used to determine (within the limits of the experimental situation) each subject's aspiration level by the use of a modification of Frank's technique (page 426), susceptibility to majority opinion by the method developed by Moore and by Barry (page 691), susceptibility to "authority" by the use of a modification of Sherif's experiment (page 220), and additional information, obtained from associations to a carefully selected word-list. In the laboratory situations one of the experimenters notes significant behavior, such as timidity, boldness, subject's remarks, expressive movements, etc.

In connection with the experimental work, particularly the aspiration-level and "Sherif" technique, the instructors acquainted with the subjects attempt, on the basis of their general information, to *predict* the nature of each subject's response. Ratings are also obtained on an informal rating scale of attitudes toward authority —whether dependent, rebellious, resentful, "realistic," etc.

The first use of these data is not, as ordinarily, to cross-check bits of information to determine (presumably) the value of each, but rather to construct on the basis thus afforded a meaningful picture of each individual. There is no hesitation in using "intuitive" insights and analytic interpretations. It is believed and asserted that it is possible to "know" something about an individual without expressing it in terms of normal distributions. It is assumed that the attitude toward authority is one part of the personality structure and cannot be studied as an isolated item. It is therefore necessary to analyze the whole personality, especially the unconscious fears, expectations, and the reaction formations built upon them in order to understand the specific quality of the attitude toward authority, its roots and function for the individual. It is expected that by a qualitative analysis of the data supplied by different tests and experiments such a study of the personality structure in its fundamental aspects will be possible.

Differences in data or contradictions are examined in order to discover underlying bases for different behavior in different situations which throw additional light on the fundamental structure of the personality. The primary purpose of the research is, like that of Zachry, to draw up significant and meaningful studies of adolescents in the college milieu, and to give, as well, an idea of the nature of the forces effective within these personalities and acting upon them.[1]

The tentative results of this study give added strength to the hypothesis that by the time of late adolescence, personality structures are sufficiently clearly defined and stable to make possible the prediction of social behavior and attitudes in different situations. The sensitive, ambitious student who implicitly identifies herself with her teachers will respond to criticism in ways quite unlike those of the matter-of-fact realist who conceives of herself as in a different pigeonhole and accepts a teacher's direction only in so far as it furthers her own practical goal.

In personalities like these, a variety of traits can be shown to be dynamically related. A tendency toward anxious submissiveness to early authority may be shown later in extreme responsibility, over-disciplined drives and emotions, sensitiveness to criticism, anxiety about failure, and self-depreciation. A direct transfer of attitudes toward authority may appear in tendencies to accept the authority of the written page or of a strong teacher unquestioningly. Similarly, a student who has confronted early authority with antagonism and resistance is likely to show the same defenses in college even in situations where there is little basis for them. These direct forms of transfer of authority attitude do not completely describe the ways in which a personality structure may be expressed. More indirectly, the whole personality built up through the reactions against excessive domination in the family situation will be part of the later pattern. In a number of cases, girls with extremely dominating mothers have retreated into a private world of their own which offers romantic outlet for the intensities and strong impulses that are thwarted in the reality of home life. Deep roots in a world of one's own frequently make it very difficult to respond genuinely to the objective world of

---

[1] We are indebted to L. J. Stone for this summary of Dr. Fromm's procedure.

college and social life even when the likelihood of frustration by a dominating adult is removed.

Attitudes of this sort go deep, and are, as Zachry has emphasized, firmly rooted in the love-security relationships of the student's home experience for which they represent compensations or continuations, as the case may be. They are attitudes important for all the social relationships of the individual, whether at work or school. In studies of the relation between personality structure and social behavior we need badly the kind of long-time records available in the California Adolescent Study in order to describe the possible points of flexibility and the conditions under which the adolescent personality may be modified. In extreme cases only deep analysis of the roots of social attitudes will free the adolescent for further development. In other cases the impact of new situations with new attitudes from one's peers and from the authorities may create changes in manifest behavior and in the underlying attitudes. Everyone is familiar with the deep changes that sometimes accompany realization of new status in a happy marriage or satisfying work; we say that Jack or Jill is a "new person" now. We used to have similar records of personality change through the reorientation afforded in religious conversion. We need to know more fully not only the nature of these processes of change but the range within which such changes may take place, and the rôle of contemporary institutions in contact with adolescents in relation to personality change.

It has not been possible in our discussion of relationships between elementary school children and their own age group to keep social patterns among peers distinct from patterns of responsibility and attitudes toward adults and authority; let us retrace our steps now and consider the attitudes of elementary school children toward teachers in more detail, with a view to discovering the relation of such attitudes to other personal characteristics of the child and to his subsequent social development.

Teachers who have worked with elementary school children of various ages find those from seven to eight very individualistic;

although they conform to the demands of a large class under the direction of a teacher, they do not accept group responsibility. They are resentful if the group is punished for the delay or misbehavior of one member. They ask directions in individual terms ("Where shall I write my name") although the whole class is involved. Group organizations which do arise are likely to change from day to day, as Moreno found in his study of Brooklyn children in early elementary grades.

Problems of relationship to authorities are active, and the children handle these through a variety of outlets; playing school is popular, and the teacher's rôle is coveted. Mannerisms of teachers are picked up unconsciously at times and imitated or ridiculed at other times. Strictness is exaggerated and strongly felt. Rules are not well assimilated; they may be followed if they are pointed out, but do not operate reliably when the children are away from the authorities. (Cf. Piaget, Lerner.) At the same time there is little group ganging against authorities, and tattling is not uncommon when it serves a purpose. Abstract conceptions of justice and "fairness" are not yet very clear. "Ideals" and general rules of the institution have little weight; instead of reasons for the rules (cf. Piaget, page 544), it is flattery and praise which get results, and the children are more easily won by a teacher· who fits the pattern of sweet "mother" than by one who has the ability to help them achieve.

Dominance relationships in play, like the organization of groups, are likely to be fluid; a new suggestion will be picked up quickly, and the games that are played are not yet highly organized. Simple tag, hide-and-seek and group games predominate, with few rules or opportunity for exercise of group authority.

By nine or ten years, according to some teachers, more organized groups begin and loyalty to the group and to the authority of its rules develops. There is still much more bickering and unwillingness to accept rules than we find among teen-age children. As stable groups develop, definite rôles in the group emerge, or group personalities such as the responsible leader, the "smart aleck," the practical joker, the mama's baby. Between groups rivalries develop over short-time projects. Games become more formal and for boys ideals of sportsmanship become important.

A further evidence of increased group consciousness may appear in the observation that children who seem relatively unaware of economic and race differences at seven or eight now exhibit more feeling of stigma and shame over inferior status. Getting relief lunches and being on relief create embarrassment. Added to the economic and race differences existing in the world outside school are those differences of ability that are the basis for sectioning classes into A, B, and C groups and that may be exploited by some teachers. "You're 'A children' and we don't expect you to do that" may get the desired acquiescence and also set up new awarenesses of the many ways which the world finds to divide children into the sheep and the goats.[1]

Another aspect of the awareness of groups and of status may appear in the changed attitude toward authority; children now seem to be impressed by rules, many are likely to abide by the letter of the law. They accept the authority of the teacher and take reproof more seriously; threats of detention which meant little in the second or third grade may be very effective by the fifth or sixth. Children who adjust to the school situation do so through knowing what is expected of them; they have "caught on," they know what they can and what they cannot "get away with." On either side of this group are other groups—those who believe everything the teacher says and are overdependent upon authority, those who get away with as little work and as much fun as possible, or even resist the teacher defiantly.

If these observations are sound and we wish to inquire into the situation which gives rise to this behavior, we may note that sometime about the age of entering first grade there is a sharp change in the world which most town and city children confront. However much their parents may have emphasized independence, doing things for themselves, and however much relative freedom they may have had before this time, this independence and this freedom are enormously expanded. Many children go to school by them-

---

[1] We are indebted to B. Stone for many of these observations of elementary school children as teachers see them.

selves or in the company of another child, instead of being accompanied by an adult. This means that for many hours of the day home recedes into the background as a place that one comes from and goes back to rather than as the dominant center of one's life. At this time too, even if one has been to nursery school before, friendships usually become more real, more stable and more important. We saw that friendships at the nursery-school level were transitory and largely dependent upon shifting circumstances or propinquity and common developmental level at the moment; the beginning of elementary school marks the bridge to an age when the child's gang or club or intimate friend becomes even more important than home. It is also rare in pre-school years to find children who are conscious of themselves as a group lined up against the adults as a group. Children seldom whisper together at this age, warn one another when they see an adult coming, or look furtively about during questionable group activity, prepared to cover up the traces if the adult comes along. But this kind of behavior becomes fairly common in the early elementary years, however much it varies with the specific patterns of authority imposed by particular adults.

Entrance into the conventional first grade marks a sharp break in the actual structure of the child's experience. For the first time in the case of many children, they are expected to conform to a group pattern imposed by an adult who is in charge of too many children to be constantly aware of each child as an individual. Flash cards are flashed at the group all at once. Stories are told and everybody must listen whether he will or no. Drawing paper and crayons are meted out whether you happen to feel like drawing at that moment or not. One child who found this shift quite beyond endurance remarked after his first day in school, "It's awful; all you do is mind all day long." And another day he added, "It really is awful. All you do is sit and sit and sit."

The personality of the individual child and the habits he has built up of accepting or protesting basic realities will partly determine his reaction to this new inexorable authority. He may accept it as one accepts a bitter wind, hoping that it will not last forever. He may run away from it into a world of his own and become the daydreamer in school for a psychiatrist to worry about. He may rebel openly and play truant or throw spit balls or more secretly bring along to school little pieces of the reality of his own world to which he can smuggle his attention from time to time when teacher isn't looking.

If he accepts it, he may be quite as badly off as the truant or the daydreamer, for this acceptance may be made at the expense of any initiative or spontaneity he may once have had and he may become merely a teacher's yes-boy. A considerable number of children, of course, are able to accept this authoritarian situation in the conventional elementary school without much distortion of personality. They take it in a matter-of-fact way as one of those things, that's just the way school is, everybody goes, you learn things there and you're awfully glad when it's over.

Although this is a common experience to most of the population of the United States, the actual details of children's reactions to this usual situation which dominates eight years of their life have never been studied in any detail, and yet the general outlines of this situation lie behind and are taken for granted in many studies which do throw some light on the results of the authoritarian relation between teachers and children.

We have seen that a popular topic for research in the educational field has been that of incentives to study: the effects on achievement of praise and reproof, of reward and punishment, knowledge of one's score or of the rating by the teacher. Practically all of the work that has been done has tried to find generalizations which would apply to groups. There has been little attempt to study the relations of personality factors to responses of this sort, or even to find out whether there are groups of individuals or types that respond one way or the other, or school situations characterized by different patterns of authority attitude.

The variety of reactions to authority in the elementary school probably includes the collection of nervous habits reported by Olson, and the delinquent behavior that is a major concern to contemporary sociologists. Comparisons of progressive and authoritarian schools would probably find a decrease of nervous habits in the former, as well as a decrease in truancy and overt challenges to authority, such as throwing spit balls, whispering, sending notes to one's friends *sub rosa*, and passing around obscene pictures. Each of these aggressive patterns probably has roots in the combination of a general need for excitement and a general need for some form of retaliation to the repressive adults. The nervous habits are more likely an outlet for tension for those children whose aggression is too weak to carry through any direct challenges to adult authority.

Tentative results from an exploratory study of seven-year-old children in an elementary school suggest that some children of this age are going through a transition period comparable to that which has been noted in the case of three-year-old children and in adolescents. They are likely to be tense and negativistic in relation to adult authority, and when opportunity is open for free expression of inner attitudes, protest against pressure from adults is frequent. One is likely to find concrete expression in relation to some particular point of routine such as the need for rest, but it is probable that this focus is simply an outlet for a feeling of conflict which has a somewhat broader background. This may be understood if we compare the situation of children at this age with children of three and in early adolescence. At the three-year-old level, most children have achieved considerable command of language and motor coordination, with senses keen and confidence stimulated by new abilities. They would like to regard the world as their oyster, free for them to explore and exploit. So it is in actuality for country children who may roam the fields, explore the barns and hen roosts and woods to their heart's content. For urban children confined within the narrow limits of apartment house life or nursery-school routine, the multiple drives for exploration have limited outlet. This, together with the increased self-consciousness stimulated by new experience, may very likely be responsible for the characteristic attitude of negativism at the age of three years. In early adolescence there is some analogy to this three-year-old experience, rapid growth producing a stature equal frequently to that of the adults. Sexual maturing with its stimulations to drive and increased consciousness may be accompanied by a new awareness of the world and a desire to explore independently. Yet the thirteen-year-old is still a child from the point of view of all social institutions—family, school, and church—and this driving eagerness has as little chance for the freedom that it craves as it has in the three-year-old. Here again self-consciousness and negativism appear for a period until the young person has gained some perspective of the realities possible in his social group.

Just as the three-year-old feels power in having learned to talk, to run, to ride a bike or skate, the seven-year-old may find enormous stimulation in the achievement of reading. Up to this time his participations and exposure to the world of adults have been selected by protective parents who read him stories frequently designed not to over-stimulate him or to give him information about the world of adults. Now for the first time, as he learns to read, new doors are opened and for school-bright children they open very quickly. The daily paper, the funnies, the weekly illustrations of varied experience in war, business, getting married, getting divorced, having babies, fleeing from floods, and being honored in death are now all spread before his eyes. Children, of course, are highly selective in their responses to experience which reading makes available. Some of them retain a strong identification with the world of childhood and are protected for a time from the confusion of adult realities. Others crave to understand; they listen more acutely to serious adult conversation, sometimes attempting to assimilate it and appropriate it to their own needs. Records of one group of seven-year-olds illustrate dramatically the interrelations between these processes of assimilation of adult problems and their attempts to relate them to their own problems with adults. During March, 1937, when the papers were full of discussions of strikes these seven-year-olds staged a prolonged "sit-down strike" for shorter rest periods at school!

In addition to these relations between developmental changes and adult attitudes in elementary school years, there are certain aspects of personality make-up which may be carried over from the home situation. We might classify families roughly into democratic, patriarchal, matriarchal, and disorganized, or child-dominated, structures. In the democratic pattern, parents attempt to give children an opportunity for decision and vote on matters that concern them, while in the patriarchal and matriarchal structures father or mother is dominating; in the disorganized or child-dominated structures, parents have lost control. It is possible that some of the patterns of recalcitrance to adult control, resentment or extreme submissiveness, antagonism to men or women teachers may represent the child's transference of attitudes developed in the home.

Similarly the relationship between attitudes of love, identification and submission, all of which may be perhaps completely independent, are important for attitudes toward teachers. The following diagrams illustrate different patterns in respect to these attitudes which appear to develop:[1]

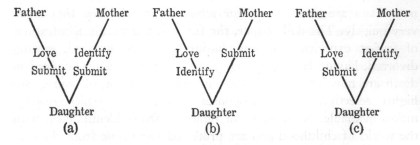

In (a) a daughter will lay a basis for a good heterosexual relationship in maturity, for in childhood she identifies with a feminine rôle, loves the male parent, and accepts a child's rôle of submission to both parents. Toward a teacher she may carry over the pattern of submission and identification. In (b) the daughter is likely to find difficulties ahead of her, since she both loves and identifies with her father and is likely therefore to develop a masculine rôle; her submission to her mother is likely to conflict with her masculine identification and involve resentment or overt hostility which may persist toward female authorities and may create antagonism toward teachers. In (c) the love-identification relationships are appropriate to this culture but the submission is directed only to the father, and may be assimilated in the relationship with

---

[1] The material giving rise to these interpretations was gathered in the investigations under the direction of Zachry and of Fromm (cf. page 646), but the present formulation differs somewhat from those which they would offer.

men rather than in a parental pattern or a relationship with authority. This may result in inadequate cooperation with female authorities such as teachers, or difficulties in assuming a mature adult feminine rôle. These differences in early parent-child relationships may be reflected in differences in the child's tendency to idealize the teacher, accept her passively or indifferently, accept her actively, understand her function in helping the child to learn, resent her or show open hostility to her.

Differences in teachers themselves will also be important in the attitude of children; there are formalistic, routinized teachers who are too tired to work and do not like their jobs, young teachers who get jobs expecting to "fill the gap before marriage," and who do not intend to get worn down by their teaching. Neither of these groups is apt to be extremely sensitive to the needs of individual children, and teachers like these are in strong contrast with the group who both like their job and like children. Just as children carry over personality reactions into the schoolroom, so do teachers, although we have not studied these patterns or their effects on children. This child will be idealized as she projects some pattern of the teacher's own imago, or contributes to the prestige of the room. This unattractive troublemaker who disrupts the morale of the group and frustrates the teacher's hope for an "ideal class" will be rejected, and another child will be accepted with mild affection and necessary discipline.

If we followed through this level of study of the social character of the emotional situation, we would doubtless find differences in the possible contributions of different teachers and in the needs of different children. Some children grow best through following clear directions, others through understanding criticism, some through imitation and osmosis, and others chiefly need enough security to expand from within.

Only a beginning has been made in the direction of understanding this inner content of relations between teachers and the child at school as they affect the social development of the children. It has now been repeatedly verified that teachers are likely to be more concerned about the behavior of the obstreperous child who finds the restrictions of conventional stereotyped education difficult to accept, and less concerned about the sensitive child who may be withdrawing into a remote daydream world where he can escape from adult pressure and, perhaps from the strain of give-and-take in his own age group. Few adults cannot remember vividly their rise and fall of fortunes as they moved from one grade to another. The shift from teacher to teacher provides a variety of experiences which different children must assimilate in different ways. They all know who is cross and which teacher is "lots of fun," who is hard and who is easy; and they are equally aware of teachers by whom they are liked or disliked. Almost every grown-up remembers these things and even recalls periods of traumatic unhappiness with a teacher who constantly misunderstood or periods when work and relations with the group were better because of a teacher who knew "how to help." Some fathers are clearly or vaguely aware of disadvantages in having their sons always taught during formative years by unmarried women teachers who may prefer little girls, or who find unconscious surrogates in boys and at best are incapable of providing masculine patterns with which boys may identify. We have no comparative studies of the experience of boys who are taught by competent men as compared with those who are taught by women simply because teaching in the elementary grades has offered little status for men in American life. It is quite possible that "rough-neck" patterns among public school boys, along with delinquency and negative attitudes toward authority in boys' gangs, may be social patterns peculiar to a culture where authority is imposed by females and where boys have too few paternal models. In this connection it is important to note that wherever men interested in boys offer leadership for youngsters, potential gangs are usually transformed into constructive groups who readily develop enthusiasm for both personal ideals of courage and loyalty and group ideals of social usefulness.

Both the attitudes toward adults and the expanding grasp of objective reality are involved in the fundamental nature of the process of learning. For the most part, the study of the adults' relation to the child in learning has concerned itself with analysis of effects of using the whip hand of punishment and reproof (see page 470). The dynamics of the child's response to criticism comes under observation by Burks, who approaches the problem in terms of Piaget's concept of egocentrism. She presented two tasks to each of forty children from the age of four to twelve in situations which permitted self-criticism, adult criticism, criticism of a classmate of the same age and sex, and criticism by the classmate. The children were also questioned regarding their conscious feelings about criticism—whether or not they liked to give and to receive it at school.

Burks found that differences in the reactions to criticism of children at different ages suggested the following stages:

1. The predominantly egocentric stage in which the child is confused about the difference between self and the external world; criticisms are offered in terms of the child's own products, "I'll show her how to make one like mine." Criticisms are not genuinely assimilated.

2. The partly socialized stage in which the child attempts genuine social communication but processes of giving and receiving criticism are still subject to egocentric deformation, and criticisms are not really interiorized.

3. The completely socialized, reciprocal stage in which there is careful and critical assimilation of criticisms, and criticisms are offered with understanding of the intents and difficulties of the other child.

Burks illustrates these stages with the case of a five-year-old girl who was not able to assimilate criticisms of her bicycle but drew extraneous lines to distract the attention of the experimenter, in contrast with the eleven-year-old boy who immediately accepted the criticisms of his bicycle and made use of them. The fact that this difference may not be merely a developmental matter has been pointed out by Wertheimer, who suggests that the total structure of the situation may be involved in the differences in these types of reaction. That is, the five-year-old girl might very well accept criticisms of a task at a level where her own ego was more secure and she was sufficiently well oriented to see the relation between the criticism and her own conception. The eleven-year-old boy might similarly be confused and evasive if criticized at a task on which he had less complete a grasp. Thus three-year-old children accept simple criticisms or suggestions in connection with building a block house or fixing a doll buggy where the criticism can be grasped; college students or adults may put up a smoke screen or change the subject when confronted with criticisms embarrassing because they cannot master the technique their acceptance involves.

Burks finds, in addition, certain patterns in relation to criticism that seem to distinguish certain personalities from others. For instance, "There are certain children who are on the *qui vive*, alert to receive any suggestions; among these some may be pleased or amused when faults are discovered while others may be chagrined or anxious. Other children may be passive or more indifferent; still others may be resistant to all criticisms." Personality differences of this sort are related to those we have already discussed in connection with competition, and are aspects of the fundamental ego structure of the individual child as it is being shaped in its early development. Both the ways in which these patterns develop from different kinds of parent or teacher attitudes and the ways in which they condition the child's further response to authority at school and at home are fundamental problems in the social growth of children.

INDIVIDUAL DIFFERENCES IN CHARACTER

Closely related to the attitudes toward authority reflected in responses to criticism is the problem of interiorization of the morals of the group involved in what usually goes under the name of the study of "character." At the end of Chapter VII we considered the contributions of Piaget and Lerner to the understanding of the child's moral judgment. Such studies are a necessary foundation for the analysis of the individual child's moral ideas and moral conduct; but individual differences and their relation to the individual personality and social background are very important in their own right and call for consideration here. Since a number of detailed summaries of work in this field are available, we shall discuss at length only one elaborate study, the work of Hartshorne, May, and their collaborators. The behavior of hundreds of children was studied experimentally, and dozens of social variables which might play a part in their honesty, their self-control, and their generosity were measured.

The "populations" intensively studied were children in the fifth to eighth grades inclusive, in three communities. One group labeled X is a favored group from superior surroundings in a residential part of New Haven, Connecticut. A second group, Y, is the school population in these grades in the town of Walden, New York, a town of 5000 near Newburgh, of average economic status, having very few "wealthy" or "poor" families. The third group, Z, is an unfavored group of low socio-economic status in New Haven. Some national and racial differences, of course, appear, particularly on account of the small foreign-born element in Y and the large foreign-born element in Z. The most striking differences, however, between X, Y, and Z are those in socio-economic status, and those social variables which usually go together with such factors.

The studies of "deceit" were in many respects the most elaborate. After constructing a great variety of tests of ethical knowledge and ethical attitudes, the investigators proceeded to invent (or modify from previous use) a large array of tests of honesty—or, conversely, of deceitfulness—in different situations. No less than twenty-one tests of deceit were used, some of these being applicable to behavior in relation to school work, others relating to behavior at parties and in competitive athletic performances. Deceptiveness was not considered as an "all or none" affair. The tests consist of scales in which opportunities to cheat may be accepted completely, partially, or not at all. In a sense, then, deception on these tests is always a certain *degree* of deception, or, stated inversely, a certain degree of resistance to the temptation to cheat. The data may be considered either from the point of view of the interrelation between cheating in the various situations or from the standpoint of the relation between total cheating score and certain personality traits or environmental influences. The former may best be considered first.

The problem is whether the honest child is a child possessing a generalized honesty trait which displays itself in all sorts of situations, or whether he is in point of fact one who because of a large number of specific honest habits must (by definition) have all-round honesty. Much of the evidence favors the latter conception. Cheating in one situation gives almost no information at all as to the likelihood that a child will cheat in another. Honesty appears here and there, or in some happy cases everywhere, but the "everywheres" are exceedingly few, and in view of the scattering of all the results they appear to be more reasonably explained, in most cases, in terms of many specific honesties. An individual cheats in one situation; the situation is slightly changed, or perhaps we should say changed in a way that seems to be slight, and the individual is now honest.

That honesty, at this age level, is not highly generalized is supported by the most elaborate statistical analysis; behavior is determined much more by the particular situation than by the total *habit organization* or *character* which the child brings to the situation. We do not mean that the situation acts upon a formless or habitless child, or that the child's character or system of habits can ever be regarded as working independently of concrete situations. We mean that in terms of a quantitative analysis, in which the relative importance of character and of the situation is studied in relation to individual differences in behavior, character is found to be a much less important variable than is the situation, in causing honesty or cheating in a given case. The intercorrelations between honesty scores on the various kinds of honesty tests are so low that the *general factor of honesty* (though it does appear) must be regarded as secondary in predicting *specific* responses.

There are only three children out of a group of several hundred who can be said to cheat in anything like a consistent way, and there are only a few more who can be said to be consistently honest. The problem is not only a problem of *degree* of honesty; it is a question of the *consistency* of behavior in widely varying situations. The question now arises whether there is a relation between the amount of honesty and the amount of consistency. A child who was perfectly honest on all tests would, of course, be perfectly consistent; but a child who was perfectly dishonest on all tests would also be perfectly consistent. Plainly, then, consistency and honesty have some measure of independence, and it is worth while to inquire what the degree of this independence is. The answer is shown in the fact that among the 40 per cent who are most consistent, honesty scores run high, whereas among the 40 per cent who are most inconsistent, they run very low. There is thus a general tendency for high consistency to go with high honesty. This means in practice that dishonesty in a specific situation has practically no predictive value for dishonesty in another situation in the tests, while, on the other hand, honesty in a situation has somewhat *more* predictive value for honesty in other situations.

It is possible, as the experimenters point out, that this result may depend upon the nature of the tests used. We must at least concede considerable importance to the fact that honesty on these tests is a passive sort of thing (it is simply "not cheating"), whereas cheating is an aggressive sort of thing. If the tests had been constructed on the plan of measuring directly the *degree of honesty*, with *dishonesty as the zero point*, the result might be different. For example, a boy who found after leaving a store that he had been given too much change would be honest if he aggressively did something about the situation, that is, went back and returned the money, whereas simply doing nothing would be dishonest. The point is of interest in showing the relativity, and in some ways the arbitrariness, of the system of assumptions involved in measuring character traits.

It seems to us that the chaos, or disorganization, or lack of consistency, which appears among the dishonest children, and the high consistency which appears among the very honest children may represent in part the difference between lack and possession of organized ego attitudes relative to honest behavior. When the data are considered, together with the evidence regarding high suggestibility among dishonest children, it seems legitimate to think of the dishonest child as driven by the immediate incentive of the moment. He is either honest or dishonest on the tests, depending simply upon the force of the incentive. The honest child, on the other hand, has perhaps self-valuing attitude[1] upon which he may rely when confronted with a situation in which he might cheat. The presence of such inner controls has been found even at a much lower age level; it seems reasonable to guess that inner standards of behavior are elements in habit organization which are of great

---

[1] Identical with McDougall's "self-regarding sentiment" except for his slightly different conception of the self and of the drives related to it.

importance in producing at their upper levels *both* consistency and honesty.

Both honesty and consistency vary with age, but the *way in which they vary is demonstrably dependent not on sheer growth but on the social environment, as the comparison of these groups makes clear.* Consistency or "integration" scores might in a sense be identified with "character formation." The gross totals in difference between the populations X, Y, and Z in honesty are perhaps less interesting than the differences in integration, especially when the change in integration from year to year is considered. Whereas integration increases but slowly in population Z, it increases rapidly in population Y. This is paralleled by a consistent increase in honesty in Y and an increase in dishonesty in Z. The lines are in each

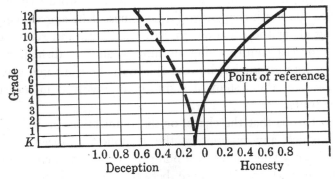

Showing tendency of population *y* (solid line) to become more honest, and of population *z* (dash line) to become more deceptive.
(Used by permission of The Macmillan Company.)

case brought down to a hypothetical point of junction. The heavy black horizontal bar is the point of reference from which the divergence may be empirically studied. By continuing the lines downward, it is possible to conjecture where they would meet. It is thus possible to conceive of the whole matter as an environmental one. Empirical data on this further point are of course needed.

The factor of group morale, however, can make itself effective most obviously through *suggestion*, and this would be true whether we thought primarily in terms of prestige suggestion or in terms of the ideo-motor definition. The results are striking. In population Z, the correlation between "integration" and resistance to suggestion is as high as + .44, and in Y it is + .30. The population differences are probably bound up with the differences in community life. Further data on the influence of social surroundings in making for honesty or dishonesty are directly shown in the fact that in population Z, resistance to suggestion is correlated with *honesty* only to the extent of + .07. In other words, consistency or integration goes along with resistance to suggestion, but the social code is sometimes such that there is no close relation between honesty and the resistance to suggestion.

But the analysis of character in the classroom situation is worth closer study. The resemblance between the behavior of children who regard one another as friends is high; if one's friends cheat, one cheats. If, however, the friend is in another grade, the situation is radically altered; the correlation of friends in different classrooms is only + .16. This makes one suspect that sheer proximity may have a good deal to do with the findings, and in confirmation of this view it is to be noted that the correlation of all members of a given grade is + .60, nearly as high, in fact, as that obtained with friends who are in the same grade (+ .73). Clearly this kind of honesty is largely a matter of classroom morale—one does what the crowd does. There remain, however, many test situations outside the classroom.

An inquiry as to the backgrounds of all these children attempts to uncover what it is in their homes, their churches, their clubs, their games, their unorganized friendships, that makes for high or low honesty. If total honesty scores are taken for what they are worth (and they are at least worth a great deal more than any previous data), it appears that private school children tend to be much more honest than public school children; that Sunday schools and clubs have no ascertainable effect; that siblings tend to be alike to an extent even greater than intelligence quotients would lead us to expect; that honesty increases slightly with mental age. The correlation of mental age with specific kinds of honest behavior in specific situations is probably more significant.

Another aspect of character studied by similar experimental

methods is generosity or "service," measured by a variety of tests through which the central theme of giving up something for somebody else is found to run.

The *preliminary* service tests involved conduct in two major situations—giving up ice cream in order that the money should be given for the relief of starving children, and response to appeals for money for charity. Since giving up the ice cream was an all-or-none matter, scores are in terms of response to the first appeal, second appeal, third appeal, or resistance to all appeals. The decision regarding the expenditure of the money was tested as follows: Children were told that they would be given 25 cents apiece which they might use as they liked. They were to indicate how much they would like to have for themselves at once, how much they would like to have put in the bank to their account, and how much they would like to give to charity. When the money was actually distributed, the principal called their attention to the fact that instead of 25 cents there would be only 19 cents apiece, and they were allowed to make any new plan they wished as to how the money should be distributed. Whereas on the original vote they had wanted about 69 per cent in the form of immediate cash, about 20 per cent for their bank accounts, and the remainder to be assigned to charity, the changes made when they found that there would only be 19 cents resulted in a great decrease in the amounts for bank and charity, and but slight decrease for immediate cash, so that the immediate present suffered only slightly. Another preliminary test involved "learning exercises" in which the child could work either for himself or for money to be given to the class, or, in another case, to work for the Red Cross.

The five tests of "service" or generosity finally selected for use were the following: (1) The "efficiency-cooperation" test involved a series of arithmetic problems given in the class, prizes to be given in some cases to those who did especially fast work, and in other cases given to whole classes on the basis of class score. Cooperativeness is measured by the difference between the child's effort when working for himself and his effort when working for the class as a whole. Although, as might be expected, work for oneself brought about, even at first, a certain superiority of effort, perhaps the most interesting finding here is the effect of time, which appears to wear out the cooperative type of effort more rapidly than it wears out the individual effort. (2) In the "free choice" test, the child again may work for himself or for others, but in this case he merely decides each time whether he will work for himself or for the class. He may write his own name or the name of the class on the work sheet. These two tests, it will be observed, bear directly upon the problem of classroom morale and the interrelations between children who know one another in the school. A somewhat different procedure is used in the other three. (3) In the "school kit" test, the children are given kits containing eraser, double pencil, box, cup, ruler, etc., and told that these are their own to do with exactly as they like. It is then pointed out to them that there are children who do not have as attractive things as these, and that they might like to give away some parts of their new treasure. Again, of course, the scores are capable of being graded from zero to maximum generosity in the particular situation. (4) Next comes the "envelopes" test. The children are informed that there are sick children in hospitals who need pictures, stories, etc., and that arrangements have been made to distribute these when they have been collected and put in envelopes for the hospitals. The test continues over a two weeks' period. (5) The remaining test, the "money-vote" test, involves the child's choice as to how certain money won in a spelling contest should be distributed. Each class took a straw vote as to whether this was to be divided equally among the class, given to the one scoring highest, used to buy something for the class or for the school, or donated to some cause or person in need outside the school. The scores here measure the degree of nearness or remoteness of the object which exerts the predominant appeal.

With all the data on cooperativeness shown in the five test situations described, elaborate comparisons are made with the child's *reputation* for cooperativeness, based upon a variety of methods of scoring the impressions which the pupils had made upon one another and upon their teachers. The "portrait matching" device involves the use of descriptive paragraphs (on the style of Theophrastus) in which the judge has to decide which child in a group is most closely portrayed by the description. For example, "B is always thoughtful for others around him and sees many opportunities for little kindly acts without waiting to be asked. . . . He is not greatly interested, however, in remote needs unless they are serious and appealing." In the "guess who" test, phrases such as the following are used: "This one is always picking on others and annoying them." Check lists, with lists of adjectives (such as cooperative, obliging, sociable, callous, greedy, etc.), are also used, and a "conduct record" scored on a five-point scale. After study of the data thus secured, total reputation scores were computed from the three devices—check list, "guess who" test, and conduct record. It then became possible to compare the *total reputation* with the *total service* score on the five main tests, and also to compare the child's reputation in the teacher's eyes with his reputation in the eyes of his classmates. Since the teacher and the pupils see any given child in somewhat different situations, it is not expected that the correlations between average ratings of teachers and fellow pupils would be high. In fact, the correlation is only $+ .39$. On the other hand, this correlation is high enough to show that the relation is not accidental; something about the child's behavior has tended to produce a positive correlation between impressions upon teachers and impressions upon fellow pupils.

Since these ratings are by their own evidence not very good, we should not expect them to correlate well even with ideal tests. The fact that the correlation between total reputation and total behavior is not very high is not evidence against the tests. Indeed, neither of the sets of data needs to be repudiated. Just as the teachers and the pupils see different aspects of any individual's behavior, so the things which he has done to give himself a certain reputation inevitably correlate very imperfectly with the particular things he will do in the particular test situation. Statistical analysis of all these data shows that behavior even from one test to another varies to such a degree as to produce intercorrelations only between $+ .32$ and $+ .12$. Of course the tests ought not to correlate much higher, or they would to too great an extent test the same thing. On the other hand, in view of their low correlation, it is clear that there ought to be a larger number of them, in order to make a larger sampling of cooperative behavior available for study.

Thus far we have seen that cooperativeness in elementary school children is to a large degree specific rather than general in the same sense that honesty was seen to be specific. There is, nevertheless, a certain low consistency or "generality" of cooperativeness which has its own importance. Though in the middle of the distribution we cannot draw conclusions from *one* test of cooperativeness which would tell how cooperative a child would be on *another* test, we can, among the children making very cooperative scores on several tests or very uncooperative scores on several tests, predict fairly well as to their behavior on the remaining tests.

Remembering that the tests are valid *as far as they go*, we can also compare total cooperativeness or generosity with a considerable number of personal and environmental factors. Intelligence, for example, is found to have a slight effect in producing cooperativeness, so that, although its predictive value in individual cases is small, the prediction for large groups differentiated by intelligence tests becomes valuable. Emotional instability, as measured by the Woodworth-Mathews inventory of emotional habits (and even as gauged by the study of the single habit of nail-biting), is in some way connected with ineffective cooperation. Environmental differences are evident in that the socio-economic status of the home helps somewhat when city children are compared (the partialing out of intelligence here could not be effectively done unless we knew to what extent intelligence is innate). The semi-rural population, *Y*, which is (from the socio-economic point of view) lower than *X*, is nevertheless more cooperative. Differences between scores on specific tests, however, are of interest, the *Y* population surpassing *X* by comfortable margins on the free choice test and the efficiency-cooperation test in which group solidarity may be reckoned important, while in the money-vote test it is not surprising, on account of this same economic advantage of *X* over *Y*, to find the *Y* group doing less well. On the kits test and the envelopes test, in which economic factors may be fairly well ruled out, the *Y* group surpasses the *X* group, the margin being exceedingly large in the case of the envelopes test, despite the fact that the *Y* group

can scarcely be regarded as coming from homes especially equipped
to supply the necessary materials.

These general environmental factors are perhaps of less value
and interest than the specific factors involved in family and friendship resemblances. Resemblances of classmates taken at random
show a sufficient tendency toward similarity of performance within
a given class to justify the statement that "some sort of classroom
atmosphere, code, or morale" accompanies characteristic behavior
patterns. The rank difference correlations of the *class* service scores
of *boys* with those of *girls* in the free choice test in population Z
is as high as $+ .92$; and the *total* service score for the Z population shows a classroom correlation of $+ .95$. The data from X
and Y are nowhere near as definite, although the "morale" factor
appears high here also. (The sibling resemblance, although it is
high enough to be reliable, is not as high as sibling resemblance in
intelligence. Siblings, of course, except in the case of twins, would
be expected to be in different grades in most cases. This makes an
analysis of the factors making for sibling resemblances and differences almost hopelessly complicated.)

Another bit of direct evidence on classroom morale appears in
the case of an unusual discrepancy in otherwise consistent data. One
classroom in the Y population was found to have a much lower
cooperation score on the classroom tests than would be expected
from other data, although it scored high on the test done at home.
Inquiry showed that the teacher's illness had made for much classroom disorganization. The group "lost its group characteristics and
its behavior pattern and tended to disintegrate." Further evidence
in the same direction is shown in the fact that there are considerable
differences between the scores of the children belonging to the sex
which happens to be in the majority and those made by the minority
sex in any given classroom. Just as it was found in the study of
dishonesty that the "majority sex" cheated more than the other,
so here it appears that the sheer fact of being in the majority tends
to make for more cooperation (the ratio of the number of boys to
the total number of pupils is in positive relation to the service score
of the boys). The problem being narrowed down still further to

the influence of personal friends, a comparison is made of those cases in which each of two children has named the other as a particular friend of his. The results are to show in one population a correlation of + .57, although the correlation is very small in another.

The application of Sweet's test showed that in general the boys who marked *the way they felt about things* nearly the same way they marked *how most boys* felt about the same things—that is, the boys who had least *feeling of difference* between themselves and others—tended to make exceptionally cooperative scores on the free choice test compared with boys with a median feeling of difference (the result is almost, but not absolutely, reliable statistically).

Similar effects upon cooperativeness were produced by instruction given under the direction of the Character Education Inquiry to one sixth-grade class and one seventh-grade class. Emphasis upon team play (e.g., "the class is no stronger than its team work"), and group discussion as to what was meant by being the "weakest" pupil in the class and the like, were followed by the administration of the efficiency cooperation and free choice tests. The experimental groups made big gains, while control groups, which received no teaching, fell below their previous scores. It is, of course, not shown that the effect was permanent.

Hartshorne and May's studies of *self-control* have primarily to do with the ability to stop in the middle of an interesting activity, and with persistence despite fatigue or distraction. These studies, though most interesting in themselves, seem much less significant for social psychology than are the studies in deceit and in service. It will be noted that low positive correlations between persistence and these other character tendencies are found, just as a low correlation between service and honesty is found. It may, in fact, be of some value to compare the intercorrelations between scores made on the various character elements studied by the Character Education Inquiry. The figures in parentheses are the coefficients used in correcting for attenuation. It will be noted that two different figures appear for each correlation. If a diagonal is drawn from upper left to lower right, the figures in the upper right are the raw intercorrelations, those in the lower left are the figures corrected for attenuation; it will at once be noted that these figures support in a general way the idea of specificity of behavior, but that positive correlations between the "desirable" traits nevertheless appear.

INTERCORRELATION OF TOTAL CONDUCT SCORES—POPULATIONS X, Y, AND Z COMBINED

Test	Honesty	Service	Inhibition	Persistence
Honesty.....................	(.86)	.30	.36	.13
Service.....................	.44	(.56)	.28	.05
Inhibition...................	.49	.47	(.61)	.12
Persistence..................	.17	.08	.20	(.61)

Three decimal places reduced to two. Self-control is here separated into inhibition and persistence. (*Used by permission of The Macmillan Company.*)

This further justifies the reassertion of the "situational approach," the view that social conduct in children is not simply the expression of a fixed mechanism which predetermines to a specific mode of conduct, but rather of a *set of tendencies* aroused in variable ways by the specific problems which confront us. It would be dangerous to generalize beyond the complex of behaviors studied here. These findings are, nevertheless, the best basis that we have as yet for the formulation of an *hypothesis* with regard to the nature of character in the middle-childhood period.

Even in later adolescence, there is much to suggest that patterns of honest behavior, and also of attitudes *about honesty*, have to be defined largely in terms of concrete situations. Thus when students were asked to tell what they would do in imaginary situations, nearly all of them admitted in certain cases that they would do the thing that was not recognized as "honest," whereas in other situations practically all accepted the existing honesty code. Ninety-nine per cent state that if they had a chance to steam open a letter which they knew contained money they would refuse to do so, but only 28 per cent say that they would pay carfare in a situation where it was easy to "get away without it." That they are probably fairly typical as regards classroom honesty is suggested by the fact that

61 per cent admit that they would have "cribbed" on an examination which is described to them in the form of a situation in which the examiner *told why he had cribbed*. On the other hand, where the cribbing situation was defined as an organized "racket," the students passing around blotters with information on them, 92 per cent stated that they would refuse to connive in such a scheme. The blanket concept of "honesty in general," whether tested by classroom behavior or by such attitudes, seems to mean but little.

We may go further, and say that the attitudes of college students toward classroom cheating do not seem particularly different from those of the grade school pupils studied by Hartshorne and May. We now have a considerable number of independent studies of student honesty in institutions with and without the honor system, among groups of men students and among women students, among students who are themselves preparing to teach and among those of heterogeneous occupational interests. Despite the varieties of method and the many different kinds of students involved, the results are rather remarkably consistent. Fenton made use of three experimental situations: In the first, the instructor sat in front, reading; in the second, he sat in a nearby office, the students knowing that he might return at any time; in the third, he walked over to the library and could be plainly seen on his way, but had remarked that he believed the students could be trusted. By a prearranged spy system each of three students had to watch eleven other students, while making a pretense of taking the examination which the rest were taking. There were only eleven out of 33 subjects who did not cheat at all in any one of the three situations. An anonymous questionnaire was later given out and the students' attitudes toward cheating were ascertained. One question, for example, read, "When you are not under an honor system, do you feel justified in cheating if you have a chance?" Thirteen said Yes; nineteen said No. In reply to the question whether one's opinion of a person was "lowered if he cheats when the instructor is not in the room," twenty said Yes, yet of these twenty students, thirteen had cheated. The results obtained in a university with the honor system are not substantially different.

Verbal Formulations of Values

The discussion of actual behavior—its consistency and its relation to various objective environmental factors—for which the Character Education Inquiry and related studies have provided the materials, leads naturally to a consideration of the relation between understanding of social concepts, of moral standards and taboos, and of children's interpretations of the reasons or sanctions for them. Although we are not able to offer a closely woven pattern of development of this type of "social perception" or even to demonstrate clear-cut relations between "understanding" and "doing," we may present the results of a few typical descriptive investigations of these problems.

We have already suggested that an important factor in consistency of behavior may well be the degree to which the individual verbalizes his behavior and values. That is, expressing the behavior in words, and especially generalizing from these, may contribute toward irradiation or a tendency to respond similarly in various situations. The ability to verbalize in itself, although undoubtedly having its environmental aspects, is certainly closely related to general intelligence level—that is, it is related both to intelligence quotient and to chronological age. Many vocabulary studies have shown the close relation between vocabulary and intelligence; and Meltzer's study of children's understanding of social concepts indicates that the comprehension of these abstract expressions is intimately related to intelligence and general maturity.

Three hundred thirty-three pupils from the fourth grade through high school were examined by personal interview regarding the meaning of such concepts as democracy, imperialism, balance of power, standard of living, liberalism, radicalism, anarchist, open shop, and the like. More children had never heard of, or knew nothing about, radicalism than about any other concept whose grasp was tested, although many other "broad, big terms," such as democracy, capitalism, and socialism, were included. The correlation between the child's understanding of these phrases and his educational age was $+ .80 \pm .04$. Grade standing gave a correlation of $+ .69$, mental age and chronological age correlated $+ .58$ and $+ .55$, respectively, and occupational status correlated only $+ .36$ with the children's grasp of these terms. On the basis of these figures, we should suspect intelligence to be the most important element in understanding these concepts; in other words, that social concepts like vocabulary in general are pretty intimately related with intelligence if not actually a good index of it.

There has been little detailed study of how the group enforces its taboos on the young in our western civilization, or of its varying effect as a result of variations in incentive, punishment, prestige of the educator, etc. Studies in delinquency and crime have long noted and shown objectively the havoc wrought by the conflict of mores such as occurs in "second-generation" immigrants, or children of immigrants. Here the lack of recognition by the social group in general of the particular moral patterns which the parents are trying to impose results in failure by the parents; and the patterns of the new group are not sufficiently clear or well enough understood by the parents to be assimilated thoroughly by the children. Hartshorne and May, as we have seen, have effectively shown the irregularity and inconsistency of adherence to elementary standards to which adults and children alike give lip service. Yet a variety of attempts have been made to get at the ways in which verbal formulations of ideals and mores operate in the adjustment of the child to the demands of the group. Katz has reported conversations of two children showing the early development of conscience. The conversations were between two children and their mother or father, and were recorded verbatim at the time. These children were four and five years old at the time of these observations. A full analysis of their comments showed that the following were the main types of ethical violations which they recognized: (1) anti-social acts showing themselves in conduct involving attempted or effected bodily injury; (2) injury to things; (3) harm to one's own person. This is consistent with the results of the study of sympathy in young children; at the preschool age children sympathized most readily with other children who experienced physical distress. As the child's grasp of a wider range of sources of discomfort broadens, we expect the basis for both sympathy and moral standards to broaden, since morality is rooted in the recognition of the needs of others.

In Germany, the question, "When do children begin really to understand moral standards?" or, as it is frequently stated, "When does the 'moral sense' develop?" has stimulated perennial research. Schaefer studied the answers of some 1200 children between the ages of twelve and seventeen to the question, "Why is stealing forbidden?" At the age of twelve, nearly half of the children based their answer on religious sanctions, while at the age of seventeen, this proportion had diminished to about ten per cent. Similarly, the proportion of social motives, including the thought of harm done to the one from whom the thing was stolen, sense of justice, general respect for society or law, increased during this period. Another way of getting at the question of moral judgment is illustrated by the work of Weigl. The girls in three school classes ranging from about ten to about fourteen years were told anecdotes and asked whether there was a wrong done; if so, why they considered the action wrong. Injustice, lack of sense of duty toward parents, and dishonesty were the kinds of wrongdoing which were recognized by more and more children as they increased in age.

Macaulay and Watkins investigated the development of the "moral conceptions" of children with a view to studying the effects of environment, age, and other influences upon the child's conception of moral values and the relation between his generalized conceptions of moral offenses and of moral ideals. The procedure was simply to ask the children to make a list of the most wicked things that anyone could do. Nearly 2500 papers were collected, chiefly from elementary school children. An analysis of these papers showed that up to about the age of nine years, the child's moral conceptions were pretty concrete and definite, and formulated in terms of his own immediate personal relations. Being naughty or disobeying mother, hurting the cat, and other little personal acts that the child has been taught to consider wrong by the categorical prohibitions of parents or teachers were predominant at this age. After the age of nine years, individuals and personal relations were still extremely important, and on the whole the conventional prohibitions, especially those acquired from teachers, were dominant; but at about nine or ten, the conceptions seemed to be growing more generalized. Instead of biting, kicking, stealing a ball, etc., stealing and fighting *in general* were stated to be wrong. From eleven years on, the children's ideas began to show an admixture of grown-up and conventionally recognized sins; but only in later adolescence do such "sins of the spirit" as hypocrisy and selfishness receive attention. It is interesting to see that the children from the slum and near-slum areas know the significance of adult crimes earlier; these children, for instance, name sex crimes at an earlier age. This, of course, is consistent with the findings that delinquent boys have a more sophisticated knowledge of adult sins than the general run of boys.

Another bit of material which we may work into the mosaic of data on ethical standards comes from a study by McGrath. She was concerned with the problem of studying moral concepts in children, and variations with age and school status in degrees of understanding such concepts. She made a threefold attack by presenting her children with stories designed to bring out moral issues, pictures drawn with the same purpose, and a test series of questions which would offer a more direct check on the ideas of the children. Her subjects ranged through the pre-adolescent and early adolescent years, and were taken from public and parochial schools.

The most interesting aspect of her study lies in the following facts: (1) that she tested a series of moral and religious conceptions corresponding to a fairly stable and objective code systematically inculcated by a large and strong organization; (2) that her data include results on two contrasted groups of children, (a) those who had been subjected to the training of the parochial school, and (b) those who had gone to public school and had consequently not had such vigorous or consistent training. We may therefore consider these groups as nearly comparable to an experimental and control group.

The results on a few questions may be offered to show the differences in response of the two groups. "Is it a sin to stay away from church on Sunday?" Between the ages of ten and sixteen the lowest percentages at any level replying "Yes" were 56, 67 and 61 in three different groups of public school children, and 97 for the parochial school children. In general, a larger proportion of the parochial school children said it was a sin to cheat. The difference between Catholic and non-Catholic sex standards was suggested in many instances; the qualitative differences in the ways in which Catholic and non-Catholic children think and feel about "sin" and the consequences for personality development are also important to study.

Another study of children's conceptions of good and bad is in some respects reminiscent of the German studies on moral judgment. This is the study by Muth; she used 167 school children between the ages of eleven and fourteen in the last half of the seventh year in grade school. The school neighborhood was predominantly Jewish and for the most part "upper middle class." The mimeographed form on which the opinions were collected asked simply for class, age, sex and religion of the child, and his answer to the question, "What makes a thing good or bad?" Oral directions were:

We are making a study of children's opinions on various subjects. It is very important that each child write just as he or she believes in order to get true results. We are not asking anyone to put his or her name on the paper so you need never fear anyone saying, "Jim wrote this" or "Mary wrote that." Be very quiet for we want no one to influence us nor do we want to influence anyone. We all know what it means to be good, or bad. We all know when a story is good, or bad; or a picture is good, or bad. So also are we sure whether the weather is good, or bad. We know when a thing smells good, or bad. And, too, we know well when our work in school is good, or bad. There is some distinguishing characteristic to all good things. We would not be able to tell the difference if there was not. Now I want you to think about this while the papers are being given out. There will be no questions; answer as best you can. Take your time.

The "dull normal" children were completely stumped. The answers of the remaining classes fell into the following categories:

   1. The law of God, e.g., "Things done by the will of God are good."

2. Public opinion, e.g., "If many people like a thing, that makes it good."
3. Civic law, e.g., "A thing is made good if it is within the law."
4. Parental law, e.g., "What my parents think is good. . . . If you mind them it makes you a good boy."
5. The greatest good of the greatest number, e.g., "If it is pleasant and enjoyable to others, it is good; if not, it is bad."
6. The spirit in which it is done, e.g., "The thought that makes you do a thing makes it good or bad."

About 20 per cent of the answers were classed in each of the two groups, "public opinion" and "the spirit in which done"; the "law of God" and the "greatest good of the greatest number" receive 16 and 14 per cent respectively, and civic law and parental law claim about 10 per cent. Some sex differences appeared which were suggestive again of different cultural influences affecting the two sexes: the boys were more likely to give civic law as a criterion of good, while girls gave the religious sanction *much* more frequently than the boys did. Intelligence level is *not* clearly related to the tendency to give one definition or another, except that "parental law" is not often given by the brighter children.

A supplement to the study of children's ideas about right and wrong is the study of their attitudes toward law, as described, for example, by Lockhart. In order to obtain a semi-official standard for mature adults, fifty successful lawyers in good standing in the State of Iowa were asked to decide on a series of legal and moral issues; all fifty replied. The following excerpt is typical:

The law compels the sheriff and his deputies (men who help him) to arrest persons they find committing crime.

The bank at Plymouth was robbed. The robber had gone into the nearby woods. The sheriff came, selected ten deputies and began to hunt for the robber. Just at dark, Mr. Holt, one of the deputies, came upon the man hiding in a hollow tree. The man was his friend and neighbor. The robber gave Mr. Holt the bank's money and begged him, for the sake of his wife and children, to let him go and not tell. The deputy let the robber go, took the money to the bank and said, "I found a bag of money in the woods but no trace of the robber."

1. Was it wrong for the deputy to let the robber go? Yes... No...
2. Should the law compel a sheriff to arrest people
   if he does not want to do so?   Yes... No...
3. Should the deputy be arrested and punished for
   letting the man go?   Yes... No...

The replies were remarkably homogeneous; the lawyers agreed well. The questions were then submitted to 3500 Iowa children from the fourth to the twelfth grades. The mean score shows a fairly consistent drift toward the adult attitudes from the fourth grade to the eighth; above this the data are less clear. The ninth to the twelfth grades, inclusive, show no advance beyond that of the eighth. The gross scores, however, are less interesting than the detailed analysis based upon intelligence quotients. The children in each grade were classified as having intelligence A (I.Q. above 120), B (I.Q. 106 to 120), C (91 to 105), and D (90 or less). On this basis it is found that in every grade from the fourth to the eighth the A children conform to the adult standard more than do the B children, the B than the C, and the C than the D. In other words, intelligence helps a child to grasp the issues as the adult sees them. On the other hand, all this is upset in grades nine to twelve. Here the C children do, indeed, stand above the D, and the B above the C in every grade, but in three out of the four grades the A *children turn sharply in the opposite direction.* The brightest children in grade twelve fall so far short of conforming to the lawyers' standard that they are on a par with the average fifth-grade child. Moreover, a group of fifty adults in a civic club made a score about identical with that of these A children; but the number of cases and the variability make the results merely suggestive.

DELINQUENCY

This survey of factors making for integration of character and for different attitudes toward the more serious mores of our culture naturally leads directly to a consideration of the causes of marked deviation from the conventional standards of the group. The concept of the "psychological explanation" of crime has naturally fallen under grave suspicion in recent years. The crudeness of the early efforts to test the intelligence of delinquents, and the frequency with which people reached the absurd conclusion that feeble-mindedness is responsible for most of our crime have, in many cases, deafened the ears of criminologists to the contribution which psychology can and must make to an understanding of this and every other deviation from the social code.

Perhaps we should begin, as Burrow has done, by pointing out the foolishness of analyzing deviations from our moral and legal standards before we know the psychological basis of these standards themselves. The basis of our judgment that one thing is right and another wrong remains nearly as obscure as it did when Westermarck suggested, twenty-five years ago, that approval or disapproval of acts which are helpful and harmful tends to consolidate into a group judgment of "right" and "wrong." What, psychologically, "approval" is, what its relation to other affective processes and to the ultimate psychology of motivation and judgment may be, is far from clear. A great deal of light on the process has been thrown by the studies of Freud, Piaget and Lerner, already discussed (cf. page 542). The social code is standardized in large part on the basis of absolutistic notions, but subject here and there to invasion by a growing relativistic trend in which things are regarded as right or wrong in so far as they find a place in what we want.

We shall have to think, then, partly in terms of what it is that makes some individuals kick over the traces. We can scarcely emphasize too often the fact that "crime" itself is a relative term. What is a crime in one society is not a crime in another. A man capable of maintaining himself in one civilization may be gravely handicapped or actually incapable of keeping within the law in another. The "increase in crime" of recent years is, moreover, a function of such a mixture of causes that we shall have to steer our way carefully to see what is really psychological.

On this basis the most obvious fact is that most crime is recidivism. Probably somewhere in the neighborhood of 70 per cent of the total cost to society of all criminal acts in the United States (such estimates suffering, of course, from various arbitrary elements in counting up values) results from acts of persons who commit a series of crimes. This may mean, and does in some cases mean, merely that an individual, when placed in a given situation which causes a crime, is likely, if placed in the same situation again, to behave in the same way. Usually, however, this is but a small part of the story. Committing a crime has all sorts of effects upon the individual, his family, his friends, and so on, which in a broad sense must be included under the head of *learning*—on his part and on theirs. He has learned when to commit the crime and has probably committed it a great many times before he was first caught. After release from the institution it is vastly easier to go back to one's trade than to try to start a new one. If one is already branded as a criminal, it is difficult to find a job; and when one is skilled in one task, it is scarcely enticing to be an unwanted, inept, and despised individual in an unskilled occupation. The problem of *early* delinquency is, in fact, the heart of the crime problem.

Delinquency as a deviant and socially disapproved form of social behavior probably needs no "laws" beyond those needed to explain the development of a socially acceptable individual in any culture. The emphases underlying different studies of delinquency may be summarized in this fashion:

1. Delinquents are constitutionally defective (this thesis appears in much work from the mid-nineteenth-century theories of the "criminal type" to the modern concept of "constitutional inferiority" or of low intelligence).

2. Delinquents have learned anti-social behavior exactly as the rest of the world learns social behavior—by imitation of companions, direct teaching (from other delinquents), or perpetuation of a chance solution of a problem solved by trial and error. Thus a delinquent appears for the most part in "delinquent areas" where there is, so to speak, a delinquent "culture."

3. Delinquency is a result of attitudes, conflicts in the individual personality growing out of deprivations or malad-

justments in the home or school. Thus the boy who steals may prove to have a serious sex conflict or anxiety problem.

The frame of reference within which delinquent children are studied is now genetic, psychological and relativistic. In a period of upheaval and syncretism such as the last generation (1910-35) has gone through, it has been inevitable that we would be more aware of the fact of uncertain values than of the need for certain ones; society at large has been so eager to be forgiven and be made well that it has been eager to take a therapeutic attitude toward its young who are ill of the same disease. Like much therapeusis, however, cures frequently neglect to concern themselves with the nature of the conditions which brought about the disease and treat only the symptoms.

What is the meaning of authority? It is society's method of creating its own stability, its own norm. From the point of view that recognizes this need for a norm as a basis for cohesion, the relativistic emphasis may be phrased in such a way as to be very destructive.

The analysis of conditions which bring about the disease of maladjusted behavior, whether delinquent or not, is a major task of social psychology. Certain aspects of these conditions—the external characteristics of the life of delinquent children—have been described at length in current literature. We are beginning to obtain a clearer picture of the inner problem in terms of the emotional relations between child and parent or school which tends to produce disintegrated behavior. We are, however, only beginning to see these outer and inner aspects of the situation in relation to the total structure of the child's relation to society. It is at this point that we must recall the contemporary contributions of Piaget and of Fromm.

Piaget points out "the existence of two moralities in the child, that of constraint, and that of cooperation. The morality of constraint is that of duty pure and simple and of heteronomy. The child accepts from the adult a certain number of commands to which it must submit, whatever the circumstances may be. Right is what conforms with these commands; wrong is what fails to do so; the intention plays a very small part in the conception, and the responsibility is entirely objective. But, first parallel with this morality, and then in contrast to it, there is gradually developed a morality of cooperation, whose guiding principle is solidarity and which puts the primary emphasis on autonomy of conscience, on intentionality, and consequently on subjective responsibility."

It is need for recognition of the rôle of "unilateral respect" in the earliest relations of child with adults who represent social reality to him that much contemporary psychology has left out of consideration, at least in much of the empirical research on delinquent children. A consideration of Piaget's clarification of the relation between unilateral and mutual respect (or the relation between the morality of constraint and that of cooperation) may make recognition of the former more acceptable as a stage in the child's social development. "Now it should be noted that while the ethics of mutual respect is, from the point of view of values, opposed to that of unilateral respect, the former is nevertheless the natural outcome of the latter from the point of view of what causes this evolution. In so far as the child tends toward manhood, his relations with the adult tend toward equality. The unilateral respect belonging to constraint is not a stable system, and the equilibrium toward which it tends is no other than mutual respect."

This analysis suggests the need of new orientation toward the analysis of social psychological aspects of conditions creating delinquency. We do not need any more statistics to prove the prevalence of bad living conditions, inadequate play opportunities and broken families among delinquent children, although we need to learn how to correct these conditions. We do need much more fundamental analysis of the types of personality that become delinquent under these conditions as compared with those who do not. First we may, following Piaget's cue, inquire about the fundamental matter of whether a given child has known clear, definite demands for conformity to elementary community demands; without this base of early experience in adjustment to society, we may ask how much basis for hope of success from subsequent efforts at reeducation can be found. Where authority has been present we need further to know the quality which characterized it, and the quality of the response which it drew from the child, and whether it left room for development of autonomy in him. Here we should find ourselves blocked by fundamental inadequacies in our research tools and orientation at present. We assume, in all our educational and corrective work with children, that a constructive relation to society is possible for any individual if we are only clever enough to find the proper means to bring it about. This assumption is based ultimately on our hypothesis that every organism is an adapting, learning organism, hence any adjustment or change necessary may be achieved if we use the right methods of helping the organism to learn. This hypothesis stands in exact opposition to the psychological absolutism which looks upon a personality "type" as fixed— an extreme example relevant for this field being Lombroso's "criminal type." Possibly we need a refinement of these alternatives which will recognize the possibility that the range with which different personalities can adjust varies from one person to another and that what we need to do is precisely to improve our methods of prognosis and learn to discriminate between those who may be expected to develop within limits acceptable to their social group and those who will probably be incapable of doing so; or more adequately still, under what conditions each kind of personality might grow to be acceptable to this society. At this point Fromm's emphasis upon the personality structure which emerges from early social relationships with certain relatively fixed boundaries within which adaptation may occur, is important. Every probation officer or housemother in a reform school has met some children who respond to her methods and others who do not. Love is constructive for some insecure personalities who need reassurance; it may be destructive if it is not accepted with some measure of responsibility. Diagnosis of the personality structure and needs of the individual deviant, with a recognition of both the limits and the possibilities of change and planning procedure in relation to these, is most likely to bring the desired adjustment.

Chapter XI

SOME ADULT BEHAVIOR PATTERNS IN OUR OWN SOCIETY

In Chapters II-IV we sketched a conception of human nature and its capacity for socialization; in Chapters V-X we have attempted an interpretation of the research materials on the process by which individual children grow into, use and express the ways of our own society. In the present chapter we shall attempt to study some of the ways in which the adult in our own society, after completing the growth processes described, interacts with other adults. We shall conceive such interaction as falling for the most part under two broad heads; when each individual seeks to achieve some satisfaction for himself by a method which tends to deprive others of similar satisfaction, we shall speak of *competition*; when each individual unites with others to achieve a goal which will bring satisfaction to all the collaborators, we shall speak of *cooperation*. The terms are used without ethical appraisal. It is very important to note that they are sociological terms describing forms of group conduct, and that, though they lead into psychological analyses, they are not in themselves psychological. The same motives may appear today in competitive effort, tomorrow in cooperative effort. The same habits may serve the two forms of conduct; and the same indivisible activity may at times be both competitive and cooperative at once, depending on the point of view.

Yet though competitive behavior and cooperative behavior are complex and heterogeneous, *attitudes toward competition* and *attitudes toward cooperation* are vital and fundamental in contemporary society, and seem to merit central emphasis. Just as "attitudes toward the Chinese" may at times be monotonously uniform despite the huge real differences between Chinese individuals, so the prevailing attitudes and values in relation to competitive and cooperative activity prove to be major clues to American social behavior. We have already suggested that value, as we have defined and used the term (page 198), is for many purposes a better way of classifying personalities than any other available; and we think that research on competitive and cooperative behavior is meaningful and important precisely because these are important values for Americans. Indeed, we think that the enormous mass of research on social incentives, such as prestige, praise, blame, etc. (cf. page 470), whether dealing with children or with adults, is useful just in so far as the results show how the values of individuals function.

We shall turn first to simple group activities in which there is little or no competition or cooperation, then follow the problem of competition, then that of cooperation, and then, in the light of these concepts, compare our society with others. Finally, we shall try to see whether all the material on the socialization of the individual points the way to the discovery of "universal laws" within the field of social psychology. No attempt will be made here to survey all the experimental studies of the adult in the group situation, since an excellent and comprehensive survey by J. F. Dashiell, and a chart of individual studies, is available in C. Murchison's *Handbook of Social Psychology*, and no purpose would be served in attempting to parallel his survey. The reader is specially urged to refer to Dashiell's account of studies in the psychology of testimony (pages 1134-1144 of the *Handbook*).

Suggestion and Imitation in the Group

One of the simplest kinds of group activity is that in which everyone is doing the same thing, but responding to some common stimulus, each individual stimulating the others to do exactly the same thing that he is doing. The epidemic spread of coughing in an audience would be an illustration if the coughing happened to start with the orator's cough. Here the individuals are responding to a common stimulus; but in addition, each one, as he reacts, tends to make the others in the group act as he does. The fundamental mechanism of such conduct appears to be identical with that of the simplest imitative functions already described at some length in Chapter IV.

Observational methods of studying such group behavior as this, under uniform conditions permitting quantitative treatment of data, would include the time-sampling methods referred to above in connection with the studies of Olson, Goodenough, and D. S. Thomas (cf. pages 269-274). The usefulness of the group approach might, for example, appear in studying the relative frequency or duration of particular kinds of behavior (cheering, panic, etc.) in a group situation.

Anything really precise by way of results, however, waits upon a really precise technique. This has been offered by F. E. Lange in a study of "crowd laughter." During the summer of 1926 she attended four performances of *Iolanthe*, timing with a stop watch all the laughs in the course of the comedy. There were in each of the four performances 137 laughter episodes, no more and no less. There was *no incident* which produced a laugh *in any one* of the four audiences which did not produce a laugh *in every one of the other audiences.* When, moreover, the lengths of the laughs were compared, it was found that there was never a variation of more than one second between the length of the laugh in one audience in a situation and the length of laugh in another audience in the same situation. If, for example, an incident produced a seven-second laugh in audience No. 1, no one of the four audiences gave it less than six seconds. When the Peers, toward the end of the play, sprout fairy wings, all four of the audiences laugh eight seconds. When a song is given an encore, the four audiences laugh at the same words, the same gestures, the same positions of the actors, which caused the laughs in the original rendition.

From this observational study Lange proceeds, however, to a well-organized experimental analysis of the group laughter situation. Nine different crowd situations, each with 100 subjects, permit the analysis of the various factors which go to make for the funniness of a comic song. (1) A song was sung by a clever comedienne impersonating a girl on the Bowery, first of all, to one hundred high school students, using neither "business" nor costume. (2) The same song was sung again, and business added (gestures, gait, burlesque dance). (3) The song was repeated with the same audience, using in addition a costume burlesquing the Bowery. (4) The fourth experiment made use of a new audience, and was identical with No. 1, that is, there was no business or costume. (5) The fifth presentation made use of the second audience and costume, but no business. (6) The sixth again used the second audience, repeated the use of the costume, and added business. (7) A third audience was used for the seventh experiment. In this, business was used, but without costume. (8) A fourth audience now heard the song, costume being used but no business. (9) The ninth experiment (making use of a fifth audience) employed both costume and business. It is now possible to isolate the relative importance of novelty (comparing the first hearing with the second and third hearings of the same song), business and costume. The enormous influence of business and costume is seen particularly in the increase in the number of seconds of laughter when these factors are added. The total laughter time for the song alone is 18 seconds; for the song plus costume, 54; for the song plus business, 85; for the song plus costume and business, 121. The total number of laughs increases too, but not as much as the total time spent in laughing. The wearing-off of the humor with repetition is quite slight. Since so much depends here upon the individual actress, no great importance can be attached to these particular figures. It is also not maintained that audiences in Odessa or Seoul would react similarly. The striking thing is the demonstration of the practicality of isolating experimentally in a group situation, the relative importance of a number of discrete social stimuli.

We may refer to Lange's work as a study analyzing the contagion of feeling and attitude in the crowd. The data are in terms of group responses, not the responses of any individual. A further step in analysis is the study of *individual behavior* in the crowd. This is well illustrated in Clark's quantitative analysis of the spread of suggestion through a large classroom. Uncorking a bottle, which contained water, in front of a group of 168 students, she ascertained the number of seconds before the "odor" was perceived by subjects located in various parts of the room. Of these, 33 smelled the odor, though of nine tested individually (apart from the group) only one got the effect. The detailed analysis of the distribution of the results over the classroom is striking. It will be noticed that the results are much more apparent in the second and third rows, and in the middle of these rows.

	Rows (front to back)									
	1	2	3	4	5	6	7	8	9	10
No. giving positive reports.....	4	7	8	4	5	3	1	0	0	1

	Rows (counting right to left when facing the experimenter)															
	1	2	3	4	5	6	7	8	9	10	11	12	13	14	15	16
No. giving positive reports	1	1	2	1	4	3	4	3	4	1	2	3	2	1	0	1

She also ascertained the number of seconds between the report of the first person who smelled the odor in a given row and the report of the last person in that row who gave a positive response. The figures show that in general the length of time required to get the effect varied directly with the distance from the experimenter.

Rows   No. of seconds from first to last person reporting positively
```
  1    10————————45
  2      15—————————————————————130
  3         30————————————————————140
  4           40———————————————————————————180
  5         30——————————————————————————155
  6                85————————————————155
```

The spread of the suggestive influence through the group is shown in the analysis of the data by half-minute intervals, some of the results appearing as much as two or three minutes after the uncorking of the bottle.

	Half-minute intervals					
	1st	2nd	3rd	4th	5th	6th
No. giving positive reports...............	6	13	6	2	2	4

It seems *almost* certain here that the individual students were responding to one another as well as to the experimenter and the ostensible stimulus.

It seems likely, moreover, that most of Clark's subjects were responding not simply on an ideo-motor level (cf. page 171), but that, like most students, many of them wanted to do the "expected thing."

Another form of social pressure constantly operative wherever co-working groups are found, and particularly where people are endeavoring to think and talk together, is the suggestibility which

we show in response to the opinions of our fellows. Suggestibility
depends on the prestige of the speaker and on the sheer numbers
of those who espouse a cause; but again a great deal depends on
the desire to make a good impression, not be queer, be a normal
member of the group.

Münsterberg presented to a class of 400 students pairs of black
cards upon which there were white dots. Each individual had to
decide whether the upper or lower card had the larger number
of dots. The number of dots was kept so nearly equal that the
right judgments were only 60 per cent of the total. After twenty
seconds, the experiment was repeated, but under the influence of
a show of hands, by which each person in the classroom indicated
how he had decided in the first experiment. In this way, the
correct judgments were increased from 1443 to 1556 out of a total
of 2400 (400 observers times six experiments). Against the apparent evidence that everybody is slightly suggestible and in the
direction of greater accuracy, Münsterberg points out that only
about one-third of the students actually tend to adapt themselves
to the group judgment; the result is due to a *pronounced* effect on
the *minority* and little or no effect on the majority. This, as a
pioneer study, is of some merit, but the problem is very incompletely analyzed.

It is only in Moore's work that the extent of such suggestive
influences has been satisfactorily studied. His plan was to allow
the exercise of individual judgments in a series of situations, and
then to ascertain what proportion of opportunities to change his
mind each individual accepted in response to "majority opinion"
and "expert opinion," as compared with the number which would
be expected by chance.

To 95 subjects, eighteen paired comparisons were presented in
each of three fields in which judgments were to be rendered. The
first had to do with colloquial and more or less offensive verbal
expressions; the subject had to choose which, for example, of the
following two was the more offensive: (1) "Everybody loves their
mother"; (2) "He never studies nights." Eighteen ethical choices
were presented, the more offensive of two traits being checked; for
example, disloyalty to friends or cheating on examinations. In the

field of music, eighteen paired comparisons were made, the subject indicating his preference between two resolutions of a dominant seventh played on the organ. Two days later, the entire set of problems was presented again, and the number of reversals of judgments calculated. The likelihood of a reversal of judgment on a purely chance basis for each of the kinds of material could thus be computed. About one-fourth of all opportunities for reversal of musical judgments was accepted; only about half as many in each of the other two fields. A check experiment was carried through with another group with almost identically the same percentage results.

Two and a half months later, a new set of judgments was taken. Two days later the same series was presented, together with a statement of what had been the majority preference for each pair. The average number of reversals of judgment was now 62.2 per cent of the total number of opportunities for reversal in the case of language usage; 50.1 per cent for ethical judgments; and 48.2 per cent for musical preferences. Two days later the comparisons were again asked for, with a statement as to the opinion of an expert in each field. This was often at variance with the majority opinion. Each person was scored on the basis of the percentage of opportunities accepted for reversing judgments to conform with the statement of the expert. These were between 45 and 50 per cent for all three of the types of judgment. Whereas expert opinion has this rather uniform effect, change in the direction of the majority in matters of speech and morals is about five times the figure given by chance, but in music it is only about twice the chance figure. Moore says that the average subject could be said to be two and one-half times as individualistic in his musical likes and dislikes as in his moral and linguistic preferences. Expert and majority opinion hold about equal sway in morals and music; but in speech, the majority has a slight advantage.

One of the most interesting experimental analyses of the formation of opinion is F. H. Allport's inquiry as to the influence of the presence of a group upon judgments of both objective and subjective factors. The subjective factors were the pleasantness and unpleasantness of five series of ten different odors. Subjects indicated the quality of the feeling, a short line indicating unpleasant and a long line pleasant (pleasantness proportional to the length). In another set of experiments a scale from 1 to 100 was used. In the group the unpleasant odors were judged less unpleasant than when they were judged alone. Again, the pleasant were less pleasant in the group. In other words, the group tended to decrease the number of extreme judgments; there was a general centripetal tendency. The same seventeen subjects participated in a similar experiment on estimating weights. The results were exceedingly similar to those obtained from the odors. The judgments of weight were distributed more widely by individuals working alone than by the same persons working in a group; *in the group, extremes were avoided*. (The question whether the alone judgments or the group judgments were in general more accurate is not discussed, but Allport's graph for the estimation of weights indicates that the tendency to social conformity distorted the judgment process at both ends of the scale.)

CONVERSATION

One of the best explored of these phenomena at present is conversation. Here sampling methods are most frequently used. H. T. Moore made a record of conversations heard on Broadway, New York, as he walked through the theater district each evening. He classified conversations as "man to man," "woman to woman," and "man to woman," and within each of these three groups assigned each conversation to a category based upon the chief topic with which the fragment of conversation dealt. Here he found a preponderance of discussion of clothes and social affairs among women, and of money and business affairs among men; in general, the "man to woman" conversations showed not so much a mixture of the two sets of interests as a tendency for the women to adapt themselves to the subjects of chief interest to the men.

A similar study was carried out by M. H. Landis and H. E. Burtt in Columbus, Ohio. The college campus, street cars, hotel lobbies, barber shops, churches and other public places were studied; the sampling therefore represents a much greater range of situations than that used by Moore. Nearly five hundred conversations were classified under such captions as "business and money," "clothes and decoration," "sports," "college work," "health," etc. The sex differences are in marked agreement with those found by Moore. A greater interest of women in persons is apparent in the present data: 37 per cent of the women's conversations are about persons, but only 16 per cent of the men's. Landis and Burtt also classified individuals into such groups as "business" people, "industrial workers," "students." The differences are in the expected direction, but are perhaps more striking than would be anticipated; for example, business people talk about business and money in 70 per cent of the conversations overheard; industrial workers, in only 43 per cent, students in only 9 per cent.

An interesting comparison with the American figures is offered by C. Landis, who listened to conversations at Oxford and Regent Streets in London. Two hundred fragments of conversation were classified in the three categories recognized by Moore, with data which in general approximate the American figures. Business, however, did not predominate quite so heavily. Landis reports, moreover, that in the "man to woman" conversations (76 cases), the Englishman in general tends to adapt his conversation to the interests of the woman, whereas the American woman adapts her conversation to the interests of the man. The comparability of the American and English groups is of course not proved, and it is only through a study of individual backgrounds that differences between groups, as well as variability within groups, are likely to be made intelligible.

COMPETITION AND SOCIAL FACILITATION AMONG ADULTS

We have given much attention to the growth and expression of competitiveness in childhood. We have noted the abundant evidence that the school child can be induced to compete desperately for almost anything that will give him prestige in adult eyes or in those of his peers. But there seem to be some indications that the competitiveness of the adolescent, though no less furious, tends in the long run to narrow down to certain specified situations, and that he cares much less about adult applause and much more for his acceptance by his associates—whether of his own sex or the other. Neither the adolescent nor the adult seems capable of being played upon by the competitive situation in the undiscriminating way which we have generally found in childhood. Certain situations have been discovered to be proper ones for competitiveness, and in these one's utmost effort may be exerted; but to devise more or less meaningless and mechanical tasks and to urge individuals to outdo one another in these situations is not for adults a practical expedient. Where the task is one which the individual takes for granted as a part of athletic or school work, it may be possible to adapt the situations of everyday competition to experimental purposes, and it is quite properly among such adaptations that the best experimental studies of competition in the adolescent and the adult are found.

F. H. Allport's experiments on the influence of the group upon association and thought made use of 26 subjects. Rivalry was avoided *as far as possible*; the method aimed to allow comparisons of scores, nothing to spur competition. Subjects alternated between the group situation (designated "T" = together), and the situation of working alone (designated "A"). "Free chain association" was tested by presenting the subjects with sheets, each of which carried one word at the top, requiring the subject to start from this stimulus and write as many words (disconnected words, not sentences) as he could in a given time. When the subjects worked alone, signals were given with a buzzer. In one experiment of this sort, there were, for the "T" situation, three groups of five members each. Fourteen out of the fifteen subjects showed, in the group situation, a *social increment* (i.e., they worked faster). The social increment was greatest in the first minute, less in the second, and least in the third. The effect of the group seemed to be at first stimulating, then steadying. It is interesting that twelve of the fifteen subjects wrote down more *personal* associations alone than together; words suggested by the immediate surroundings were more numerous in the group.

In another experiment on free chain association the slowing down of the performance caused by the necessity of writing out the words in longhand was obviated by requiring the subject to write only every fourth word which came to his mind. Eight subjects gained, four lost, two were unaffected; the reasons for each person's gain or loss were not studied. In another experiment eight subjects were used. Every third word was written. Six subjects showed a social increment, two a decrement. In an experiment involving *controlled* association, half of the subjects were asked to write words related to winter and the other half to write words related to summer, and again were required to carry out the same tasks when alone. No clear difference was found between the facilitating effect of the group when all wrote on the same topic, and the situation when the two halves wrote on different topics.

The influence of the group upon the speed and quality of thought was tested by requiring the subjects to write down arguments to *disprove* certain passages from Marcus Aurelius and Epictetus. Five minutes were allowed. The group was informed that they were all writing on the same topic. Nine subjects took part. Twenty of the tests were done alone, and twenty in groups. Allport rated the arguments as 1, 2, or 3, that is, as very cogent, moderately cogent, or weak. The stimulating effect of the group was shown in the fact that eight of the nine subjects wrote more arguments in the group, but, as judged by the experimenter, six of the nine had a higher percentage of superior ideas while working alone. This is interpreted in terms of the tendency of the group to lower the quality of thought. Again the values and habits of individuals are unknown, and the results difficult to interpret.

Another series of experiments reports work done with the cancellation of letters in newspaper material, and the multiplication of two-digit by two-digit numbers. In these experiments the speed of work was for the majority of subjects materially increased by the presence of the group, but a few individuals were retarded. The group tended to increase the incentive to do well, but offered some distractions; in some subjects the latter factors actually outweighed the former. *Quality* of performance, though variable, seems to have been injured by the group situation. Moreover, in the group situation the errors tended to be bunched together.

Quality of mental work was also tested by measuring the control of attention (by the "reversible perspective" technique); but no superiority for either the "alone" or the "together" situation appeared.

Even intelligence test performance seems in some cases to be considerably affected by this social factor. The reader will recall the evidence that the intelligence quotient of children may be appreciably raised by the incentive of encouragement (cf. page 472). Weston and English presented ten college students with forms including items from a variety of difficult materials (reasoning and hard opposites). "Every effort was made to eliminate the effect of rivalry." Half of the subjects worked first alone and then together, the other half worked first together and then alone. Two of the subjects seemed unaffected, the other eight did much better in the group, the differences being, in fact, so striking as to be "absolutely" reliable. Farnsworth, however, has repeated the experiment with some improvements in technique. He points out that Weston and English had not equated their groups of subjects or their test forms. He gave the Ohio State University test, form 10, part 5, to 22 subjects; form A of the Terman group test to 36 subjects, and form B of this test to 32 subjects. In these three experiments, the subjects were paired for ability on the basis of their Thorndike (intelligence) scores. The subjects took each test twice. Group A took the Ohio State test (each man working alone), then A and B took it together, then group B took it (each man working alone). No clear differences in individual work versus "together" work appeared on any of the three tests. In another experiment, twenty subjects were given the Otis advanced (form A), and then paired for ability. They then worked in the "together" and the "alone" situation for twenty minutes. There was a very slight superiority for the group situation. The author remarks that there is "no consistent or significant group effect."

These data are not conclusive, nor are they analyzed in such a

way as to make clear the significance of such individual differences
as appear.

We have noted that studies of individual performance under
various conditions of social pressure range theoretically all the way
from those in which the social environment consists of *indifferent
and inattentive people* busy with their own pursuits, to instances
of the most violent *social pressure*—threats, rage, entreaty, rivalry,
and the like. The nearest approach that there is at present to the
latter situation—the situation of *violent* social control of individual
work—is Laird's study of "razzing." The active members of a
fraternity, by connivance with the experimenter, prepared themselves to subject a number of the fraternity pledges to as ruthless
a session of ignominy and obloquy as they could carry through. A
control series had already ascertained the pledges' capacities in a
number of motor performances under conditions of friendly competition in which the fraternity members merely looked on. The
tests involved: (1) speed of tapping; (2) the three-hole test; (3)
steadiness sitting; and (4) steadiness standing.

Each pledge carried out these tests while being terribly razzed
by the active members. He then remained in a room apart from
those who had not yet undergone the ordeal, and was instructed
not to tell the others what he had been through. "At the close
of the experiment, each pledge confessed that he thought that he
was the only one being 'razzed'; some of them were distinctly sore
and on the verge of handing over their pledge pins."

In the "steadiness sitting" tests, every one of the subjects made
a worse score under razzing than under conditions of friendly
competition, and in the "steadiness standing" test this was true
of all but one. In the tapping test and the three-hole test, however, the results are not clear. The factor of improvement through
practice had not been eliminated. If the record is taken as it stands,
five of the subjects do better in the tapping test and three do better
in the three-hole test while being razzed. It will be remembered
that distractions may serve, at least for the time being, to bring
about a greater output of energy. The fact that one of Laird's

subjects broke the three-hole instrument by the violence of his movement while being razzed suggests the possibility that conditions of efficiency were reduced more than the figures show, and that the scores would have been much worse had it not been for a compensatory access of energy thrown into the task.

Laird proceeds to ask, "How can these varying degrees of loss of control under razzing be predicted?" Intelligence test (Thorndike) scores throw no light on the matter. Fraternity brothers had also been asked to predict the probable influence of the razzing upon the subjects. The estimates are only slightly better than chance expectation. With this group of eight subjects, the criterion which appears to correlate best with the individual's performance under razzing is the fatigue index of tapping under normal conditions; that is, the smaller the falling off from the first ten seconds to the last ten seconds under normal conditions, the better the resistance to razzing. The problem is surely not completely analyzed. It is quite likely that the difference between the scores in the steadiness tests on the one hand, and the tapping and three-hole tests on the other, is to be explained in terms of the greater difficulty in controlling the gross muscular movements as compared with controlling smaller muscles.

It is rather remarkable, after all, that such small effects should be produced by this galling social situation when one remembers the tremendous disorganization of behavior produced by painful or baffling situations of a non-social type. Hamilton, in experiments with many species of animals as well as with human subjects, found that the "baffling" situation characteristically produced such evidences of disorientation as the constant repetition of false movements; even a false movement which had once been made might, if the emotional tension was sufficiently great, be immediately repeated, and the subject frequently returned to a false movement before he had exhausted the possible movements to be made. In exactly the same way, human subjects, confronted with the task of making a quick motor adjustment, lose "nerve" and do worse if they are told that a failure will entail violent punishment than if told merely to avoid failure. The loss of one's head during a period of intense fear or in a baffling or bewildering situation can easily be explained in terms of the disorganization of the whole cerebral machinery, without resorting to an explanation in terms of social factors.[1]

In Laird's work it is rather remarkable that in the performance tests, social pressure, even of this rather intense form, produced no uniform result in two of the four tests used. Although there is no serious doubt that a social situation and a battery of tests could be found which would bring out such social influences more sharply, most of the social situations to which subjects have been experimentally exposed have been much milder.

The influence of an audience upon performance has been repeatedly studied. G. S. Gates used as a control group twenty-five college girls who took a series of tests while alone with the experimenter. An experimental group, twenty-six subjects, took the first half of the test with the experimenter, and the second half in the presence of from four to six observers, and eleven more took the second half in the presence of from 27 to 37 observers. The observers merely watched; they said nothing. The tests which were used before the introduction of the audience comprised the three-hole test, the Woodworth-Wells color-naming test, a form of the Woodworth-Wells analogies, and "number of nouns named in

---

[1] One of the grand confusions in social psychology seems to us to be the endless reiteration of the principle that the *crowd situation* as such is the *cause* of that loss of self-control which at its height is called panic. Theater panics, stampedes on sinking vessels, and the like, are usually referred to as instances of "mob mind." A little consideration of the experimental evidence just cited will make it clear that the tendency to lose one's head is a normal part of the situation of confronting immediate danger or violent pain. There is, in fact, no reason to believe that a man alone and in imminent danger of being burned or suffocated would be less panicky than the same man in a crowd, or that a man in immediate danger of being drowned is more panicky when others about him are in the same predicament—unless, of course, others get in the way and make escape more difficult. It is true, and the fact must be emphasized, that the suggestion that there is danger, conveyed by the look or cry of another person, may arouse fear, or may at least present the danger in more realistic fashion than one would present it to himself, and also that, as already discussed under the general head of suggestion, the characteristic responses appropriate to a danger situation may be touched off when no danger is actually present. These responses are socially important, but they should be kept distinct from that mass of panicky activities which characterize the disorganized, emotion-wrung individual—animal or man—whose available action systems are inadequate for escape.

one minute." After the introduction of the audience, coordination was tested again by the three-hole test and again color-naming was given; a different form of analogies test was used and the subject was required to give as many adjectives as possible in one minute. Directions were simply: "I want you to show these people how you do these tests." Gross disagreement appeared among the judges as to the presence or absence of embarrassment in the subjects. The audience had no clear influence on the total performance, although in the lowest group the work in front of the audience was slightly inferior to the corresponding work of the control group. "When we examine the best records, however, we find a decided tendency for the audience group to improve less than the control group in all tests but the word-naming."

F. H. Allport comments as follows: "If we compare the results of the highest and lowest subjects in the 'audience' group, not with equivalent classes in the control group, but with each other, the differences dependent upon original ability stand out vividly."

| | Per Cent Who Improved | |
| TEST | | |
	Highest 8 Subjects	Lowest 8 Subjects
Coordination.	63	88
Color-naming.	75	88
Analogies.	25	100
Word-naming.	37	63

This is strikingly similar to the results obtained by Allport and by Moede and others. It explains the results in terms of an increase in the rivalry motive in the poor workers. Overstimulation may have interfered with some of the superior workers. The audience seems to have a leveling influence.

Another study tested the individual's ability to hold a flexible pointer on a revolving target (the eye-hand coordination test of Koerth). Twenty-two college students (11 men and 11 women) acted as subjects. Each practiced in the presence of the experimenter twenty trials a day until he had apparently reached his physiological limit. Then, after five trials in the presence of the experimenter, the subject was brought in front of a group of from four to eight upper classmen and graduate students. Nearly every subject showed some confusion and uneasiness. The record *for ten trials* shows that 18 of the 22 subjects made a better *maximum performance* in the group than alone. The difference between these results and those of Gates, such as it is, appears to be reasonably explained in terms of the difference in the tasks and in the scoring. The embarrassment produced here and in Gates's experiment is obviously not comparable to the excessive irritation produced in Laird's experiment.

A somewhat more detailed study is Whittemore's test of the quantity of work done by college students in small competitive groups. The task was to print material with rubber stamps. The amount of work done in the competitive situation was much greater than when alone but, as in Moede's experiments, the quality fell off. In fact, every one of Whittemore's twelve subjects fell off in quality in the competitive situation. It is not entirely clear that the non-competitive work done by Whittemore's subjects was completely non-competitive, since the individuals worked in close proximity in both series. However, they were told in one series to compete and do their best to beat their fellows, and in another case expressly prohibited from such comparison and competition, although urged to do their best. The elimination of all competitive elements can scarcely be considered complete, even though a consciousness of competition may not always have been present.

Relatively few of the studies of competition have undertaken to ascertain experimentally the nature of the conscious attitudes which accompany competitive behavior, as Whittemore did in this instance. The subjects were asked, after each competitive test, "Were you conscious of competing?" "If so, in what way were you aware of competition?" and, "Was the competition directed against the other members of the group in general, against one of the group in particular, or against your own past record?" Nine of the competitors reported an awareness of competition, four of them emphasizing the attempt to beat their own previous records. One found that he had been directing his efforts against a single rival, and one was combining the effort against a particular rival with the auto-competitive effort. Auto-competition, in fact, plays a large part in seven out of the nine cases. The subjects were also asked whether the competitive attitude tended to die out during the week of work. Only three reported affirmatively.

The author compares the relative frequency of three kinds of ideas appearing during the course of the work: (1) irrelevant; (2) auto-competitive; and (3) socio-competitive. Irrelevant ideas are very frequent in non-competitive work; and competitive ideas lag over into the subsequent non-competitive trials. Various other evidences appear that the attitude during the non-competitive work is really in part competitive. From questionnaire data the author concludes that competition tends to start out in a tentative fashion, being either auto or social, and that it shifts later to competition with some particular opponent. "It is usually the rival whose record is most nearly like that of the observer himself against whom the competitive efforts are directed." (The author appropriately refers here to Moede's observations on the same fact in the course of studies of competition among schoolboys.)

A much more elaborate experimental approach to a highly competitive situation is Riddle's study of a series of poker games. Six college students participated (see plate facing page 704). Each knew the others well, and within a short time all were accustomed to the situation of having their game in the laboratory. They agreed, furthermore, to various more or less disturbing or boring interruptions and distractions, such as the frequent recording of their feelings and attitudes, and the wearing of rubber stethograph tubes during the course of the experimental periods. They were, to be sure, paid for the time given to the experiment, but none showed any hesitation in betting his own money. The players were allowed to fix their own limits, a 5-cent ante and a 20-cent limit. This was higher than usual for most of them. By the time the experimenter was ready to take records, the players appear to have been able to lose themselves quite naturally in the game. For each draw, each player was required to fill out a "schedule A": "How anxious are you to beat each player?" (ratings from + 100 to —

100 for each of his antagonists). Schedule B asked, "Did you try to bluff anyone during this game?" and "Did anyone try to bluff you during this draw?"; and presented a scale for the emotional state ranging from + 100 (elated) to — 100 (gloomy). On schedule C was recorded the bodily state, from maximum excitement to maximum physical retardation.

A curious set of intercorrelations appears in which the three variables to be considered are: (1) the player's own hand; (2) the player's desire to win; (3) the player's own bet. The correlation between the first and third is + .62, and that between the first and second is + .53. Since the player's own hand can be only a cause and not a result of these other two factors, whereas the second and third factors may be causally related to each other, it becomes important to partial out the influence of one factor at a time in order to find the causal relations. When this is done, it turns out that the correlation between hand and bet falls to + .44, while that between hand and desire is + .09. The highest correlation of all, however, is between desire and bet, which is + .63. Riddle argues that the bet acts as a stimulus to desire rather than desire as a stimulus to bet.

A further problem in motivation appears in response to one's opponent's hand. By a similar technique Riddle shows that the opponent's bet correlates only + .05 with the player's own bet when the player's desire to win is partialed out. With this and much other statistical material, Riddle reaches the conclusion that the desire to win in this game situation is only to a slight extent aroused by the size of the player's own hand value. It is aroused more fully by the value of the opponent's hand. The influence of one's own hand is, of course, to increase one's own bet, and the effect of the opponent's hand is to inhibit one's bet. When, however, the balance has been struck and the bet made, this bet in turn duly determines the total strength of the desire to win. The method devised here seems entirely practicable in the study of even more complicated competitive situations.

A series of interesting individual differences appear among the six players. One, for example, has about the same desire to win over all of his opponents, whereas another's desire to win varies

See page 703.

The game as an experimental situation.

(From the "Archives of Psychology." Used by permission of the editor and the author.)

greatly with the particular opponent he is trying to beat at a given time. This leads to the question whether one player, who greatly stimulates the desire of other players to beat him, has any peculiar characteristics of his own which may explain the trend. He certainly has. A study of the number of times that a player bluffed and the number of times that his opponent knew he was bluffing shows that player A (the one whose bets aroused in other players such a desire to win) bluffed 31 times—far more than the number of times anyone else bluffed. Only seven times did the opponent against whom the bluff was aimed recognize that A was bluffing. Players B and C each tried only once to bluff during the whole experiment, and both were detected. On the other hand, the number of times a player suspected that he was being bluffed varied all the way from one to thirty. The number of times that this suspicion coincided with the actual attempt to bluff him was rather small, and only one of the six players seemed to be able to tell definitely when he was being bluffed.

It turns out that successful and unsuccessful efforts at bluffing are the very heart of the situation, and that precise quantitative analysis throws much light upon the causes of aggressive and defensive responses of the players. Correlations are worked out for size of bets, amount of bluffing, suspicion of being bluffed, amount won, etc., some of which are illuminating. The correlations between the average winning per draw and the tendency to be "bluffed against" is $+$ .97. Whether a player wins or loses has, however, but little effect upon the opponent's judgment as to whether he is bluffing. The player who makes the highest bets, has the largest pile, and whose hands are running high, is, in general, thought by his opponents to bluff frequently. The player who is most successful in the game, who is most likely to win by good hands and a large pile, and who is most aggressive in his betting is the one against whom bluffs are most frequently directed. It turns out that the betters are not, in general, eager to win against those from whom they could most easily win; the weak player is not the one against whom the bluffs are directed. Quite contrary to the hedonistic interpretation, the goal here, even when measured in money terms, is very specific. It is not simply a desire to win money where it can be won most safely or in the largest amount, but rather, where an aggressive attitude and an exhibition of skill afford a direct challenge. On the other hand, the player who attempts to bluff most frequently is unlikely to be the one with the highest average desire to win, but rather the one whose desire varies most from game to game, and from opponent to opponent. The one who is really anxious to win seems to be definitely low in his willingness to risk money. The man "with the least adequate means of defense," whose pile and hands are low, is the one who most frequently thinks he is being bluffed.

In view of the confusion which inevitably appears in attempting to analyze the results of the many experiments upon competition and social facilitation, razzing and being looked at, and to evaluate the relative importance of ideo-motor action, rivalry, embarrassment, and so on, it is most helpful to have Dashiell's attempt to compare scores made under a large number of different social situations in which these various factors can to some extent be disentangled.

The material consisted of multiplication, mixed relations test, and free serial word association. Directions were presented at the top of the work sheets, and five alternative sets of all material prepared, with precautions for the equalizing of these alternative forms. The subjects were told to work "as *accurately* and as *fast* as you can." With the different sections of the whole group, the order of the alternative forms was varied.

Control situations are defined in Dashiell's experiments as those in which individuals work alone (A). In the "together" situation (T), the subjects were seated about tables (as in Allport's experiment), and were explicitly told not to compete and that their results would never be compared. The "rivalry" situation (R) was physically the same, but included the instructions to compete, and information that their scores would be compared with those of their fellows. In another series, three individuals were seated at each table, one working at the task while the others watched him closely (situation O).

The scores show how many subjects were at their best, second best, etc., in each of the four situations; i.e., the figures show each person's relative output under the various conditions. The data are important enough to be given in full. Fractions derived from ties are disregarded, hence slight inequalities in totals result.

WINTER, 1919				SPRING, 1929			
Multiplication: Speed				Multiplication: Speed			
Highest	Second	Third	Lowest	Highest	Second	Third	Lowest
A.... 8	3	16	11	A.... 12	10	12	28
T.... 5	6	11	16	T.... 4	14	15	18
R.... 8	18	5	8	R.... 17	16	9	9
O.... 18	11	6	3	O.... 20	15	14	6

Multiplication: Accuracy				Multiplication: Accuracy			
Highest	Second	Third	Lowest	Highest	Second	Third	Lowest
A.... 13	11	9	5	A.... 16	12	11	14
T.... 7	13	12	6	T.... 11	16	11	15
R.... 11	7	7	13	R.... 15	13	15	15
O.... 7	7	11	13	O.... 14	12	14	10

Mixed Relations: Speed				Mixed Relations: Speed			
Highest	Second	Third	Lowest	Highest	Second	Third	Lowest
A.... 9	7	13	9	A.... 8	11	21	12
T.... 6	7	13	12	T.... 5	5	9	35
R.... 5	12	7	14	R.... 15	23	13	6
O.... 18	13	4	3	O.... 28	15	11	1

Mixed Relations: Accuracy				Mixed Relations: Accuracy			
Highest	Second	Third	Lowest	Highest	Second	Third	Lowest
A.... 9	8	11	10	A.... 17	15	14	8
T.... 12	14	6	6	T.... 18	11	10	15
R.... 9	10	10	10	R.... 11	19	12	12
O.... 8	6	12	11	O.... 9	10	16	19

Serial Associations: Speed				Serial Associations: Speed			
Highest	Second	Third	Lowest	Highest	Second	Third	Lowest
A.... 4	11	12	11	A.... 3	9	29	14
T.... 5	8	15	10	T.... 0	4	17	33
R.... 7	8	9	14	R.... 21	26	6	2
O.... 22	11	2	3	O.... 31	16	3	5

It will be noted that the facilitating effect of the different situations varies greatly. Speed in multiplication is much increased by situations O and R, and speed in mixed relations chiefly in O. Accuracy in mixed relations is very low, however, in the O situation. Dashiell points out that the general assumption that speed is facilitated when work is done merely in the presence of co-workers as compared with that done in isolation is not clearly indicated. The *competitive attitude* rather than the simple ideo-motor effect is by far the more important factor.

In the "alone" situation, the subjects might in a sense be regarded as sensing the fact that others were really working simultaneously in other rooms on the same problem. A new experiment was planned to study this effect. The "alone" work was divided into two series, in one of which the individuals worked simultaneously in different rooms, receiving their signals from a buzzer (situation AS), while in the other series they worked as they liked at a time independent from that chosen by others (situation AD). These two "alone" situations are compared not only with each other, but with the simple co-working (T) situation. The data are again reproduced:

SUMMER, 1929

Multiplication: Speed

	Highest	Second	Lowest
AD......	2	3	10
AS......	6	7	3
T......	8	5	3

Multiplication: Accuracy

	Highest	Second	Lowest
AD......	9	6	1
AS........	4	9	3
T......	4	2	10

Mixed Relations: Speed

	Highest	Second	Lowest
AD......	2	4	10
AS......	7	4	5
T......	7	7	2

Mixed Relations: Accuracy

	Highest	Second	Lowest
AD......	8	7	2
AS......	6	3	7
T......	2	6	7

Serial Associations: Speed

	Highest	Second	Lowest
AD......	3	6	7
AS......	3	4	9
T......	10	6	0

CONSIDERING ONLY AD vs. AS

Multiplication: Speed

	Higher	Lower
AD...............	4	12
AS	12	4

Multiplication: Accuracy

	Higher	Lower
AD...............	10	6
AS...............	6	10

Mixed Relations: Speed

	Higher	Lower
AD...............	4	12
AS	12	4

Mixed Relations: Accuracy

	Higher	Lower
AD...............	9	6
AS	6	9

Serial Associations: Speed

	Higher	Lower
AD...............	9	7
AS	7	9

The effect of the "alone-and-working-at-a-different-time-from-the-other-subjects" situation in reducing speed is striking; in most cases, this same situation seems to favor accuracy. The data strongly suggest that "aloneness" is not the same when the subject is aware of work being done by others at the same time. This is, again, evidence that the *competitive attitude* is of primary significance.

Dashiell's data certainly justify his contention that *instead of merely knowing how the presence of a group affects individual work, it is of the utmost importance to know how attitudes and motives vary with the nature of the group situation, and to analyze in detail the relations prevailing between the individual worker and the spectators or co-workers.*

COOPERATION

We now turn to an analysis of experimental work on the very complicated problem of the interaction of individuals in a cooperative task.

Partly in connection with the progressive education movement and partly in connection with the development of arbitration in industry and other disputes, a great deal of interest has recently been manifested in the problem of group discussion. In spite of our dependence upon the parliamentary system, it is surprising that practically no psychological work on the actual processes of interstimulation in group discussion has been undertaken until recently. The last few years, however, have witnessed a remarkable access of enthusiasm for group discussion, and several volumes of importance have contributed to the clarification of the concept and the exposition of the values which are served by collective thinking.

One necessary preliminary to any study of the way in which people interact is to study their behavior in relation to the same problems or materials when alone—the precise measurement of the attainment of each of the individuals who is to participate later in the group. But a further preliminary, and one which, unfortunately, is usually neglected, is to discover the effect of averaging individual scores, or in other ways pooling or *combining individual achievements* in situations where no true group activity is present. To know, for example, how efficient a parliamentary body is in its discussion and resolution of its problems, it is necessary to know not only how individuals are influenced by one another, but how the matter would have been decided by secret ballot before any discussion had occurred. It may be that wherever variable errors tend to neutralize one another, the judgment of the average man in the group approaches the best possible judgment (by the "average" man here is meant strictly the man whose vote lies on a quantitative basis at the true average of all the estimates made by individual members). This suggestion is offered, of course, as an hypothesis to be checked by the data which are to follow. It is an hypothesis having very limited scope and one applying only to measurable data within a narrow field where the accuracy or inaccuracy of individual judgment can be determined.

It so happens that several studies bear directly upon this hypothesis, and that the data from these are remarkably consistent. The studies of Knight and Gordon bear upon the question of the relative accuracy of individual judgment and of the average judgment made by groups. The average may, of course, coincide with the estimate made by one individual in the group; but in cases where the average judgment is approximately correct, there is a wide difference between utilizing the average judgment and trying to guess *which particular individual* will be the "average person" in the group.

Knight asked her subjects to evaluate several sets of material which could later be compared by objective measurements. In one experiment, thirty-five judges (most of whom were students of psychology) tried to guess the intelligence quotients of twelve children whose pictures were shown them (Pintner's series, see below, page 782). The correlations (with true order) achieved by these judges ranged from + .91 to − .27. This is not very different from Pintner's earlier results. The group judgment correlated + .26 with the intelligence test findings. This is better than the judgment of twenty-two out of thirty-five individuals. Average deviation of the pooled group judgment from the true position is

3.33; average deviation of the individual judgments is 3.43. Thirty out of the thirty-five judges do better than zero, but six of these are below + .10. Knight proceeds to analyze the ranking of pictures, finding that picture No. 1 is rated by different judges all the way from 1 to 12, No. 2 from 2 to 11, etc., and suggests that the variability in the success of the judges may be in large part a function of the particular picture used.

She next proceeded to have forty-six judges estimate the effectiveness of fifteen advertisements, the objective measure here being the actual sales record produced by the advertisements. Individual scores ranged from — .71 to + .87, with an average at + .19. On the other hand, the group coefficient is + .63. The group in this case is better than thirty out of the forty individuals, the average deviation from the true order being 4.35 for the individual judgments and 2.86 for the pooled judgments.

Knight's next experiment required fifty-six students to estimate the temperature of the room in which they sat, which was actually 72. The range of judgments was from 60 to 89, the average 72.4, the average deviation 3.8. Of all the judges, eight gave better than the group judgment. (Knight assumes that the temperature did not significantly vary in different parts of the room.)

From Knight's material as a whole, it is legitimate to conclude, as she does, first, that with these groups in these situations, there are always some individuals "better than the group;" second, that most individuals are worse than the group; third, that the magnitude of the result depends on the kind of material used. It must, moreover, be borne in mind, as Farnsworth has emphasized, that constant errors of various sorts are common in group work. Thus the careful individual is frequently more accurate than the group in its hasty consensus. The isolated expert may be the one suitable judge. And when emotion runs high, the rare dispassionate soul often sees more clearly than either the partisan expert or the inflamed crowd.

The problem thus raised by Knight has been, we believe, somewhat more effectively handled by Gordon, who has made two studies of differences between individual judgments and the pooled judgments of groups, one having to do with aesthetic, the other with purely objective or factual, judgments. It will be better to consider the latter first.

The question again is: How does the pooled judgment of a group differ from the judgment of the typical individual judge? Ten weights ranging from 16 to 17.6 grams were used, 200 subjects being required to rank them from the heaviest to the lightest. Since the difference from one weight to the next was very slight, many of the judges did poorly, and the "laws of chance" (in this case other factors than the actual differences in weight) were allowed considerable sway. The rank correlations of individual judgments with the true order varied from $+ .95$ to $- .81$, with a mean at $+ .41$ (S.D. 32.9). The records of the individual judges were then arbitrarily grouped into sets of five, and a composite "group judgment" was made up for each such group. The composite rank correlation now has a mean at $+ .68$ (S.D. 19.2). Next, twenty groups of ten were made up in the same arbitrary or "random" fashion. The mean rises to $+ .79$ (S.D. 16.5). Finally, four groups of fifty were constituted. These four groups give, respectively, rank correlations with the true order of $+ .92$, $+ .92$, $+ .94$, and $+ .95$. This last correlation, it will be noted, is the same as that of the best correlation made by any individual out of 200. In other words, in this kind of objective material the efficiency of the group is a function of the size of the group. It is worth while to compare this with Knight's data obtained from different subjects using different material. It will be noted that Knight's results are not very different from those obtained by Gordon with the small groups; that is, the small groups of five and ten did less well than the best individuals had done, but that with groups of fifty the correlations are almost as good as they can be.

Gordon's other study had to do with colored pictures of oriental rugs. Subjects were asked to rank a series of 25 of these pictures in their order of beauty; in most cases the same judges ranked also another set of 25. Part of the problem is "whether the persons who agree most closely with the group in judging one series of rugs will be the ones who agree most closely with the group in judging the other series." On the whole, the answer is affirmative, a correlation of $+ .47 \pm .04$ being obtained. As in the case of the experiment with the lifted weights, individual judgments are now combined into groups. Groups of 20 agree with one another to the extent of a correlation of $+ .70$; those of 50 to a degree shown by a correlation of $+ .87$. In other words, even in this highly personal matter, something like objectivity appears when the groups are large. The correlation between two large groups is in fact a good deal larger than the correlation between one person's ranking now and his ranking three weeks or more later. For 38 persons who ranked the *same material* a second time, a mean correlation of $+ .71$ was found in reranking series No. 1, and $+ .72$ for reranking series No. 2. Gordon remarks in concluding that there is no way of deciding whether group judgments are *right* judgments, but that when the agreement of large groups is so striking, the burden of proof regarding individual rightness is upon individuals who disagree. She also made use of a small group of individual experts who had had some training in the appreciation of color, interior decorating, etc. The experts did not agree as well with one another as the groups did.

It will have been noted that Gordon finds "subjective" qualities judged with the same uniformity as "objective" qualities. This is reminiscent of a question raised by F. L. Wells as to the relation of individual variability to group variability in three types of process: first, one which might be regarded as purely subjective, namely, preference among fifty picture postcards; second, one in which *some degree* of subjectivity could be allowed, namely, the classification of colors; and third, a purely objective function, the ranking of weights in their correct order. In the first of these three tasks the judgments of each person cluster about a mean for that person, and each such mean varies from that of any other individual far more than his own judgments vary. This generalization, based upon repeated rankings of the postcards, shows a consistent and clear personal factor. The other two kinds of experimental material fail to reveal any such principle. In the more objective task it would seem that the individual's behavior varies *from his own previous behavior* rather more clearly; one might say that individuals A and B judging the weights in different rooms at the same time are much like individual A judging the weights today and judging them again tomorrow. The relative variability of individuals in successive trials and of the members of a group at a given time is suggested by Wells as a "quantitative criterion of the subjective." It will be noted that the contradiction between Gordon's and Wells's results is only apparent. Gordon did not compare *individual* judges with one another, nor did Wells compare *groups* of judges.

Another preliminary to any consideration of group cooperation is the serial or cumulative effect of each individual's activity upon that of the next individual called upon to participate in a task. Of special value here is Bartlett's study with the "method of serial reproduction." A written narrative is presented to a subject who, after studying it, writes it down to be read by a second subject, etc., for as many as eighteen or twenty reproductions. The reproductions are printed by Bartlett in full, so that each personal reaction is intelligible (i.e., the experiment is thus strictly psychological, not simply a study of an unanalyzed social process). An Eskimo story, *The War of the Ghosts*, is thus successively reproduced by educated Englishmen until its supernatural coloring is lost and it has become a crisp, clear, and acceptable story of a battle between tribesmen. In general, the method shows *progressive simplification* until the narrative makes compact sense; it may then sometimes undergo elaboration in keeping with the culturally imposed habits of the subjects. When the same stories are presented to English students in one experiment and to Hindu students in another, the outcome after many reproductions is a typical downright English story in the one case, and a somewhat more imaginative story, with more "elaboration and adornment" in the other. Pictures of human faces and of animals are also used in the method of serial reproduction, and again show transformation in the direction of cultural and personal "sense." Here and in other experiments Bartlett shows the importance of giving a *name* to something which is to be reproduced; the name helps to shape the reproduction.

Bartlett rightly points out that the visual exposure of all these materials limits the extent of unwarranted generalization. With the usual oral reproduction outside of the laboratory, the tendency to abbreviation might not be so marked, and the tendency to elaboration might begin earlier and go much further. Here is, nevertheless, an outstanding group of suggestions for the individualized study of processes of group psychology, especially processes having to do with the creative work of individuals stimulating one another successively.

COMMITTEE WORK

Committee work in which either three or six individuals at a time participate has been studied by South. Over a thousand students took part. Each committee had to reach a majority decision on four types of problems. Both speed and accuracy were considered. In one task photographs had to be matched against names of emotions portrayed (see page 234). Here the smaller groups averaged quicker than the larger groups and were equally accurate. In solving bridge problems no conclusive superiority of the small over the large groups, or *vice versa*, appeared. In judging the merit of English compositions the smaller groups worked more quickly; the results for accuracy were not clear cut. In multiple choice problems (rational learning), group discussion was abundant, and the larger groups had a considerable advantage in both speed and accuracy.

South believes it important to distinguish between material which lends itself to immediate formation of opinion (in which case the value of committee work is greater when the committee is small), and that in which wrong hypotheses can be promptly rejected (in which case size is helpful through offering more hypotheses).

In a second report South finds that mixed committees are less efficient, and that various sex differences in interest appear. Personality measurements were introduced to determine what aspects of emotional equipment affected committee work. Introverts appeared inferior to extroverts on concrete and on personal problems, but equally superior on abstract material.

An elaborate attack on the problem of group thinking is that of Bekhterev and Lange. The groups who acted as subjects consisted of (1) the audience in a course in child study at the State Academy for the Study of Psychoneuroses, the members being men and women teachers; (2) an audience at the State Institute for Medical Science; (3) the Leningrad Medical Institute, consisting of men and women students. In the first two groups, men and women were present in about equal numbers, whereas women predominated in the last. The ages in the first group ranged from 20 to 40; in the last two, from about 18 to 28.

Each person was supplied with a numbered piece of paper upon which he recorded sex, age, education (and near- or far-sightedness if either was present). An object was then shown for fifteen seconds without any instructions except to give attention. As soon as the object was removed, each individual wrote down details which had been noticed. The papers were collected, and all the reports were classified according to contents. Then a group discussion took place with reference to all the items which anyone had noted. This discussion was recorded. When this was over, a collective decision with regard to the stimulus object was required, and a record made of this. New sheets of paper were given out and each subject was asked to state in what respects his own opinions differed from those reached by the group.

In one case a large picture of a locomotive was shown, and in another case, pictures of six well-known animals. All impressions made by these objects were classified, and those which were purely "subjective," such as "a good picture," etc., were excluded, as were also personal opinions, such as "the locomotive is probably an American one," and the like. After fifteen seconds' exposure of the picture of the locomotive, 41 details were reported, such as smoke, steam, fire, engineer; 66 persons who participated in this experiment correctly noted 284 details in all (duplications included). There were 29 details erroneously reported. After the group discussion the number of additional correct details was 118, together with 17 mistaken ones. Considerable individual differences appeared; for example, some subjects in the first fifteen-second period correctly reported as many as 10 details; others, only one. Sex differences were slight. When the whole group is subdivided

into a "strong" and a "weak" group within each sex, on the basis
of the number of details correctly given at the first trial, the results show that the absolute gain in details reported after the discussion is nearly as large for the weak as for the strong groups;
the number of erroneously added details is slightly but not remarkably larger for the weak groups. The authors remark that
the group does indeed increase the *number* of mistaken observations, but that the *percentage* of correct observations after discussion is 86.1, whereas it had been but 80.9 before the discussion.
Suggestibility in the group situation calls for some discussion here,
but the authors properly point out that in the great majority of
cases the "suggestions" contained in the group discussion are accepted to the advantage rather than to the disadvantage of those
who accept the most.

In the experiment with pictures of animals, only thirteen subjects participated. The task was to write down the differences which
appeared between the representations of the same animals in the
first and in the second series. Each picture was exposed for ten
seconds, one after another. Again the group discussed the reports of
its members. Whereas 33 of the original observations had been correct and 9 incorrect, after discussion the correctly reported items
numbered 40 and the erroneously reported fell to 2. Seven of the
nine errors had been corrected.

Pictures of a grown woman and a girl were then shown. Fourteen subjects wrote down a list of the details shared by the two
persons in the picture. Such remarks as the following were written: family resemblance, same color of hair, mutual sympathy,
the "present and future woman," etc. The similarities are divided
by the authors into "outer" and "inner," the former having to do
with color of hair, etc., the latter with the fact that the people
are enjoying themselves, etc. The number of observed similarities
is approximately doubled by discussion in the former case, and
quadrupled in the latter (number of errors not given; the concept
of erroneous report is perhaps irrelevant here).

The authors then proceed to experiment with twenty-four public school teachers in a course on child study; a moral situation
is to be judged. Two pictures are presented. In the first picture, a

boy is stealing apples in an orchard, and the gardener appears with a stick; the second picture shows the boy caught by the gardener and getting a licking. One of the subjects declined to participate since "the details of the boy's act were not fully known to him." Each subject first wrote down his impression of what had been shown, then data as to age, sex and education. Each subject was then asked to offer a judgment of the situation. Changes in opinion were written down by the subjects as they occurred. The responses are classified by the experimenters with reference to (1) their relation to the boy's wrongdoing; (2) punishment of the boy; (3) corporal punishment from the social-ethical standpoint; (4) discipline as a pedagogical method.

After group discussion, quite striking changes are noted. For instance, before the discussion sixteen had said, "Punishment is necessary"; only twelve said this after the discussion. Three had individually thought of the point, "If he is hungry, he should not be punished"; eighteen made the point after discussion. The general comment, "Beating is barbarous," had been made by one individual; after discussion twenty-two made the point. Before discussion two said that beating was "use of force against a weaker person"; after the discussion, seventeen. Further points of ethical and educational theory are emphasized after the discussion. The point that "beating is a mistake from the educational point of view" had been noted by one person; after the discussion twelve asserted the principle. And whereas before the discussion no one had remarked on what should be done to him who beats another, the discussion led seven to the conclusion, "The beater should be beaten." We have to do here not only with the alteration of opinions, but with the point, so often emphasized in discussion of group thinking, that what may be overlooked by the individual may, when pointed out by someone else, be granted by nearly all the members of the group; it may even receive cardinal emphasis. Some interesting sex differences appear. All the women were, with one doubtful exception, opponents of corporal punishment. The younger teachers inclined, at first, toward corporal punishment, but were much shaken in their conviction by the discussion.

The attempt to experiment upon *creative thought* in the group encountered, of course, somewhat more serious difficulties. One of the experiments involved the devising of a project for a monument in honor of the poet Nekrassov. Each individual in the group of fifteen in a course in child study wrote down suggestions with regard to the form which the monument should take. The discussion then followed, and a common plan was adopted. Individual suggestions, of course, scattered widely. One said, "a white obelisk"; one, "a chained woman"; one, "leading toward the light"; one, "Is an inscription to Nekrassov needed?" etc. Group discussion led to marked agreement on many of the details suggested. Before the discussion three had written "symbolic statue"; after the discussion ten wrote this phrase. The expression, "leading to the light," written at first by one was, after discussion, written by ten. The suggestion that the monument should represent people at work, at first suggested by five, was later suggested by nine. The happy stroke of one subject, "leading the working people to the light and to enlightenment," was immediately accepted by many, and led to collective consideration of the project of the monument in the form of a representation of working people who are led by the poet toward the light, with the inscription (in the poet's words), "Sow what is wise, good and eternal." This experiment was also repeated at the Leningrad Medical Institute where medical students were the subjects. The individual suggestions were less fertile. The same tendency for individual suggestions to be accepted by large numbers in the group was apparent, but the fact that the medical group was less familiar with the work of Nekrassov led to a decidedly less effective general product.

It is only, however, in Shaw's experiments that the machinery of interstimulation has been made clear through the provision of a protocol which shows not only the stages achieved in solving problems, but the process by which new ideas appeared, how they were accepted or rejected, and how they led on to still further original contributions. For this reason, Shaw's work merits a somewhat more detailed account than the studies previously described.

Shaw's problems involved a series of logical steps which must

be correctly taken to obtain the answers. Individuals scattered at
some distance from one another in a classroom worked on three
of these problems at first, while *groups of four* recruited from the
same class worked in separate rooms. The material was so devised
as to give each person in a group a chance to add to or criticize a
step made by another person, his own comment being in turn accepted, rejected, or modified by someone else or altered in the
light of his own further reflection. The interaction was, in other
words, made much more complicated than in Bekhterev's work described above. As will be seen, some of the problems involved a
long series of logically correct procedures. Two weeks thereafter,
those who had previously worked in the groups of four attacked
three new problems, working as individuals scattered throughout
the classroom, while those who had previously worked by themselves were assigned to groups of four. Every group was constituted of four men or of four women, the experience of South and
others having made it apparent that groups of the same sex could
work a little more effectively.

The directions used in the first half of the experiment were:

1. Materials for this problem are in the envelope marked "Problems I and II." Use discs H.1., H.2., H.3., W.1., W.2., W.3. (For the
present disregard the symbols on the reverse side.) Side I of the card.
On the A-Side of the River are three wives (W.1., W.2., W.3.) and
their husbands (H.1., H.2., H.3.). All the men but none of the
women can row. Get them across to the B-Side of the River by
means of a boat carrying only three at one time. No man will allow
his wife to be in the presence of another man unless he is also there.

2. Materials for this problem are in the envelope marked "Problems I and II." Use discs marked M.1., M.2., M.3., C.1., C.2., R.C.
(Reverse side of the discs just used.) Side I of the card. Three Missionaries (M.1., M.2., M.3.) and three Cannibals (C.1., C.2., R.C.)
are on the A-Side of the River. Get them across to the B-Side by
means of a boat which holds only two at one time. All the Missionaries and one Cannibal (R.C.) can row. NEVER under any circumstances nor at any time may the Missionaries be outnumbered by
the Cannibals. (Except, of course, when there are no Missionaries
present.)

3. Materials for this problem are in the envelope marked "Problem
III." Side II of the card. In circle *A* arrange the discs in order of

size, that is, with the largest on the bottom, etc., ending with the smallest on top. Using circle *B* as a transfer station, transfer the discs to circle *C* so that they will be in the same order in circle *C* that they are now in, in circle *A*. Never place a larger disc on a smaller one and move only one disc at a time. (Number the discs for reference if you wish.)

The card referred to in these problems contained on one side a diagram of a river for convenience in solving the first two problems, and on the other side a diagram of the three circles necessary to a solution of the third problem.

The directions for the second half of the experiment were as follows:

1. Materials for the problem are in the envelope marked "Problem I." Put these words, taken from the envelope, together so that they form the last sentence (only one sentence) of the unfinished prose selection.
[A typewritten passage of about sixty words was inclosed, together with individual words on slips of paper by means of which an appropriate final sentence was to be made.]

2. [The next problem consisted of an unfinished sonnet which, breaking off in the middle of a clause, was to be completed by the proper manipulation of the separate words supplied.]

3. A consolidated school is to be built in the rural district shown in the diagram. The capital letters (A, B, C, etc.) indicate points (not towns) where pupils are to be picked up by two school buses. The mileage between each point is indicated on the diagram. The capacity of each bus is 35 pupils and the driver. Find the most desirable location for this school and give the route each bus must take. The buses may start at ANY point and need not necessarily start from the school each morning. Following are the number of pupils to be picked up at each point:

Point	No. of Pupils	Point	No. of Pupils	Point	No. of Pupils
A	6	D	4	G	3
B	13	E	2	H	10
C	17	F	5	I	3

The diagram for this last problem is given below. The copy for each individual who was working alone was drawn to the scale of one inch to the mile; only one diagram was provided in each group, and it was drawn to the scale of two inches to the mile.

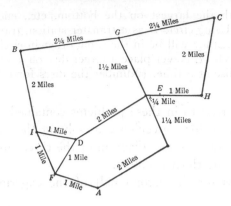

At the top of each of the sets of problems assigned to the separate individuals working in the same room, were the following instructions:

Below are three problems. Work them as quickly and accurately as possible. There is a correct solution to each problem. Record your answer or state briefly how you solved the problem. When you have finished one problem and are ready to go on with the second, RECORD THE TIME to the nearest half minute by means of the record being kept on the front board. Then proceed with the second and then the third, and RECORD THE TIME WHEN each is finished. Work the problems in the order listed.

At the top of the set of problems given to each group of four individuals were the following instructions:

A chairman has been appointed to manipulate the necessary materials. Work together as a cooperative group to solve the three problems given below. Work them as quickly and accurately as possible. There is a correct solution to each problem. Record your solution or state briefly how the problem was solved. Each individual, including the chairman, should make his contributions to the group solution spontaneously as they occur to him. Indicate to the note-taker when you have finished one problem and are ready to proceed to the next; the note-taker does not participate in any way as a member of the group in solving the problems.

The materials necessary for the solution of the problem were identical for individuals and for groups, except that the road diagram for group work was larger.

Each group had a note-taker, some being left-overs not pro-

vided for in the formation of the groups, and some being outsiders. In the first half of the experiment the note-taker was given
the following instructions:

You are to act as note-taker and time recorder for a group of four
persons solving three problems. You are to take absolutely no part in
the group activity. Do not indicate by any means your approval or
disapproval of their activities. Record the final solution of the group
on each problem. Record the time required to solve each problem.
Record as many of the detailed suggestions made by any member of
the group as it is possible for you to get.

In the second half of the experiment it was thought that the following plan might afford more quantitative data concerning the
activity of the groups:

Tabulate each suggestion made by any member of the group so
that a record can be made up of the complete number of suggestions
made in any one group. Tabulate thus: / / / / /. Do NOT cross
out the tallies in groups of five. Get as much as is possible of each
suggestion made. Record this in your notes. If the suggestion is rejected draw a parallel line through the tabulation thus: ⫫ ⫫ ⫫. Note
whether it is rejected by the PERSON WHO PROPOSED IT OR BY ANOTHER
MEMBER OF THE GROUP. If the suggestion is accepted underscore it
thus: ⟋ ⟋ ⟋.

There were ten sets of notes taken, and in only three cases did
the note-taker have any knowledge of either the problem or its
correct solution. Thus the knowledge of whether a rejected suggestion was in reality an erroneous or a correct suggestion could
have but little effect on the notes taken, and could be determined
by the experimenter only from these same notes.

The make-up of the groups was determined at random by placing every second man and every second woman in a group, and
allowing the others to work alone. In order to make absolutely
sure that the groups had no accidental advantage in the possession
of an exceptionally large number of good problem-solvers, pains
were taken in making up the groups for the second experiment to
provide that no group contained more than one individual who
had solved any problem correctly in the first evening's work. The
problems were, incidentally, hard enough so that no single individual solved correctly more than one problem.

The results are somewhat more striking and clear cut than could have been foreseen. In the first half of the experiment, *only five correct solutions out of a possible sixty-three were turned in by individuals; there were eight correct solutions out of a possible fifteen for the groups.* Results were very similar for the second half of the experiment, but, as will be seen, the data do not permit as clear an analysis as do those from the first half.

Moreover, the false solutions to the problems could be divided into several different types. In problem one of the first half of the experiment, two types of false solution, handed in by thirteen different individuals, involved an error in the first move. It took seven single moves to solve the problem correctly. No group erred on the first move, one erred on the third and one on the fourth; thus errors were not made so early in the solution.

The solution to the second problem also shows the same thing. It took thirteen single moves to arrive at a correct solution of the second problem. Among the individuals, three erred on the first move, four on the second, six on the third, two on the fifth, two on the sixth, one on the seventh and two on the eighth. The last three, who erred on the seventh and eighth, did not consider their solutions completed; all Cannibals and Missionaries had not been transferred to the B-Side of the River. It is interesting to note that no group got this near to a correct solution and then failed to get it. Three groups solved the problem correctly; both of the others erred on the fifth move.

The third problem cannot be classified so easily on the basis of the first false move, since in all cases, except in one group, once the method of transfer was hit upon, success was assured.

In the first problem in the second half of the experiment, four out of five groups succeeded, while three out of seventeen individuals succeeded. The other problems were too hard. Neither a group nor an individual, for example, arrived at a correct solution of the school-location problem. The average error in location and average excess number of miles traveled was about equivalent for the groups and individuals. In part, the absence of a correct solution may be due to the fact that a large amount of time was consumed in solving the first and second problems. In many cases the completion of the third meant dismissal for the evening; thus perhaps any apparently suitable location was accepted. It should be noted that both groups and individuals were allowed to proceed to a new problem when they wished, so that time, though measured in all cases, fluctuates so excessively as to permit no true comparison of individual and group speed. No generalization about the time consumed is possible, except that the tendency to work after the expiration of the class period was, of course, less in the groups (some individuals worked over an hour after class).

A great quantitative superiority of group over individual functioning is indicated both in the first evening's work and in that of the second evening. Even groups deliberately made up to include no specially favorable combination had a very easy superiority in the solution of difficult problems when compared with individual workers. All this, however, as will be seen, is but the beginning of our inquiry. The thing most worth knowing is just when and how such favorable interaction can occur, and by just what means the creativeness, the good sense, or the persistence of individuals can be most adequately expressed in group situations. It is because of Shaw's detailed record of the actual process of discussion that her work helps toward an answer to these questions.

Reference to the notes kept by the note-takers will give more definite information regarding the activities within the groups. Not all of those in a group participate equally in the group activity. Such remarks as the following are found in the notes: "Numbers one and three were leaders in the solution." (From the tabulation of suggestions given in the solution referred to, it is found that number one made seven suggestions and number three made fourteen suggestions; while numbers two and four made, respectively, two and three suggestions.) Later in these same notes, "Number two not contributing much." In another set of notes, "Three and four offered no suggestions during the solution." In the next problem solved by this same group, number two made sixteen suggestions, number one made twelve, number four made eight, and number three made five. From yet another set, "Numbers one and four did most of the suggesting, two and three not working much yet." In notes on the second problem in the first half of the experiment the note-taker remarks that "two and three draw their own diagrams and become absorbed in them, do almost no suggesting."

In notes on the third problem, "Three made no comments at all, two spoke only a few words." In one of these groups an individual who participated a great deal in group activity soon assumed the task of manipulating the material in the place of the less active individual who had been appointed chairman. It might be that one could get interesting, meaningful, and perhaps quite different sets of results if one were to use groups with a chairman selected on the basis of superior ability, as compared with groups having a chairman of rather inferior ability.

In some groups quite the reverse situation is found, and all members cooperate splendidly. Such comments as the following are found in the notes from three groups: "All contributing beautifully," and later, "All cooperating and making check suggestions." From another, "Suggestions coming from all four about equally." Another records, "The four members cooperate well," and on another page, "Splendid group work."

In the first half of the experiment, groups A and E solved all problems incorrectly. In the other groups there is much more reference to the checking of errors and meeting the conditions of the problem. One group worked a solution through three times to see that they had met all specifications; in the last trial they discovered an error which would otherwise have made the whole answer erroneous. The notes on these groups also mention numerous references to the stated problem to see that all qualifications were being taken into consideration in the final solution.

PROBLEM ONE

Groups	Suggestions			Rejections			
	Total No.	Correct	Incorrect	Correct	Incorrect	M.	A.
A'................	29	18	11	3	11	7	7
B'................	24	18	6	1	6	1	6
C'................	17	8	9	0	8	0	8
D'................	20	11	9	2	9	2	9
E'................	31	25	6	2	6	2	6
Totals........	121	80	41	8	40	12	36

The table above deals with Problem One in the second half of the experiment. Column two shows the total number of suggestions made in each group. Columns three and four show, respectively, the number of suggestions which were in reality correct and the number which were incorrect. Columns five and six indicate whether those suggestions which were rejected were respectively correct or incorrect. Columns seven and eight show the number of suggestions which were rejected by the individual making the suggestion or by another member of the group.

The following gives the same data for the second problem in the second half of the experiment:

PROBLEM TWO

Groups	Suggestions			Rejections			
	Total No.	Correct	Incorrect	Correct	Incorrect	M.	A.
A'...............	71	32	39	10	35	18	21
B'...............	49	23	26	9	20	8	17
C'...............	76	35	41	9	29	7	39
D'...............	32	15	17	2	13	4	11
E'...............	37	17	20	2	14	3	13
Totals........	265	122	143	32	111	40	101

Is a wrong suggestion more likely to be rejected by its proposer or by another person? All groups being considered together, 2.43 times as many suggestions were rejected by another member of the group as by the proposers of the suggestions. Five times as many incorrect suggestions were rejected as correct ones, whereas of the total number of suggestions made, twice as many were correct as incorrect. This is of significance in connection with the proportionate number of correct solutions among groups and individuals. This quantitative check on rejections was not kept in the first half of the experiment; but from what was found in the second half regarding this checking, together with the proportion of correct solutions in the first half and the fact that notes on the groups presenting correct solutions emphasize the checking of erroneous moves, there seems to be some justification for the assumption that group supremacy in the first half was also due to the rejection of incorrect suggestions or the checking of errors.

The whole process will be made clear from the following protocol, for Problem One, first half:

No. 2. Let's move W1, H1, H2; and take them all in the boat to the other side. Then bring H2 back.

No. 4. Then take H2, W2, H3 across. And bring H3 back with the boat. And then H3 takes W3 across.

No. 1. That seems too easy—read the instructions over again.

No. 3. We'll try it over again and check.

(They work through the solution again.)

No. 4. Oh, but it works too simply, I believe we ought to try it all over again.

(Start working through again.)

No. 1. The first move is wrong. W2 is with H3 when H2 is not present. No wonder it was so simple before.

No. 1. Just let H1 and W1 go over. No one else can go.

No. 3. All right, now let H1 come back and leave W1 on the B-Side alone.

No. 4. Now try this. H1, H2, W2 go across. That's O.K. isn't it?

No. 3. Bring the two husbands back. H1, H2 back.

No. 1. Now all three husbands will have to go over. Don't you see? And leave W3 on the A-Side. H3 can take the other two over.

No. 4. Oh, sure, and then he comes back for his own wife.

No. 2. Now, work it through again while we watch.

No. 1. It checks now. Let's call it solved.

Problem Two, first half

No. 1. Send M1 and C1 over.

No. 3. Now let M1 come back and C2 over.

No. 4. No, you'll have 2 C's and 1 M.

No. 1. Start over; have RC take C1 over.

No. 2. No, take M1 over and leave him.

No. 3. Yes, and then when RC comes back it's too many C's.

No. 4. Well. Well, let RC take 2 C's over and then come back and take over 2 M's.

(Try this. But on the third trip see that the M's are outnumbered.)

No. 2. Start all over, and I think RC is an important factor.

No. 1. Take 2 C's over, then RC bring 3 M's over.

No. 3. Well, we tried something like that once and it wouldn't work then, so it won't work now.

No. 4. Start over again with the M's doing the work.
(No. 2 checks the first move. Tried to take 2 M's.)
No. 2. Have the C's get over first.
No. 1. Must bring somebody back; someone has to do some extra work.
No. 4. (Opposed to this and reverts to former unsuccessful trials but is immediately checked up.)
(All stop work and silently meditate.)
No. 2. RC has to be over so he can make the last trip.
(Splendid group work so far.)
No. 3. All right, start this way: RC takes first 1 C and then the other over.
No. 4. Well, now there's no other way but for 2 M's to go.
No. 1. This looks funny, but let's try having a M bring a C back.
No. 2. That's it. Now send RC and a M over.
No. 4. Fine; here send this M and the other C back, then bring the 2 M's over.
No. 2. Now send RC over for the 2 C's.
(Took them another five minutes of careful moving to check and record this. Then ran through to check it again.)

Solution:

RC and C1 ....RC back
RC and C2 ....RC back
M1 and M3 ....M3 and C1 back
RC and M2 ....M2 and C2 back
M3 and M2 ....RC back
RC and C1 ....RC back
RC and C2

Problem One, second half

After they have read the selection through and turned all words right side up:
No. 1. Maybe "it stood" will go together.
No. 3. How about "it has stood."
No. 1. That sounds pretty good.
No. 2. "Everyone will inquire its origin."
(No. 4 and No. 3 don't like this so they don't use it.)
No. 4. "Its origin" might fit together.
No. 2. "Everyone will tell." That's a good phrase.
No. 3. "And everyone will tell you." No, that's not right.
No. 1. "Time immemorial" go together.
No. 4. "For time immemorial it has stood."

No. 3. That won't fit in with an inquiry.

No. 2. "You tell everyone that it has stood ——"

No. 1 interrupts, "That's not going to make good sense."

No. 3. "It has stood there."

No. 2. Now put "time immemorial" after that phrase.

No. 1. How about "inquire for its origin."

No. 2. "Everyone you will tell"—No, that's not good.

No. 2. Well, "time immemorial" can't be separated.

No. 4. "It has stood" sounds O.K.

No. 1. "And inquire for its origin." How's that?

No. 2. Why not "inquire there for its origin"?

No. 3. I don't like "there" in that; maybe we'll find another place for that "there."

No. 1. "You inquire its origin"—

No. 2. Leave off the "you."

No. 4. Put the "there" down here. "Stood there from time immemorial."

No. 2. "Will inquire for its origin."

No. 1. "There everyone that you tell."

Nos. 4 and 2 reject this. The "there" sounded better where it was.

No. 3. Start it like this: "Inquire for its origin."

No. 1. Sure that's it, now, "and everyone will tell."

No. 2. O.K. "you" is an object; "everyone will tell you."

No. 4. "That it has stood."

No. 3. "There from time immemorial."

("Inquire for its origin and everyone will tell you that it has stood there from time immemorial." They agree that this is correct and reads very smoothly.)

Among the limitations of Shaw's work must be noted the small number of problems used, and the impossibility of a true equating of tasks. The number of groups also was only five in each of her two experiments.

G. B. Watson's comparison of group and individual work is based on no less than ten intellectual functions, to be performed in some cases by isolated individuals and in others by groups working cooperatively. These functions varied greatly in complexity. Sixty-eight graduate students took part. Three forms of each test were used and procedures rotated as follows: (1) All ten tasks were attacked by isolated individuals, (2) all ten (in an alternative form) were attacked by committees of three to ten members, (3) all ten (again using an equivalent form) were again attacked by isolated individuals. One of the tests was found faulty. For each of the nine tests for which it was found possible to work up data, the practical equality of the alternative forms is shown by the Q_1, the median, and the Q_3 of the scores.

To state Watson's results first of all in general form, group performance is found to be better than average individual performance on every one of the tests, but the difference between individual and group performance varies from very small to very large, being, for example, slight in the case of a test on reading comprehension, and very great in scores for sentence completion. Functions which appear to test not merely the addition of one person's contributions to those of another, but a more complicated process of interstimulation—namely, tests involving the decoding of a cipher and tests involving the listing of steps necessary in solving a problem—show a superiority of groups over average individuals intermediate between the extremes noted. Using as a scale the distance between the average poorest individual's score and the average best individual's score for ten groups of four or more persons, the superiority of cipher-solving by the average group is 96 per cent, as against a score of 64 per cent for the average individual, while the average group performance in listing steps for problem-solving is 88 per cent for the average group, as against a score of 63 per cent for the average individual.

When the data are analyzed for speed (per unit of output), group superiorities over average individual superiorities appear in all cases, although these are not so great as are the qualitative differences.

Perhaps more interesting to those whose interest is in the individual is the percentage of individuals exceeding the performance of their group. (It is assumed that those exactly equaling the group performance would be superior in the same proportion found throughout the rest of the scale.) The table is self-explanatory.

Again, an individualistic question, and the most important of all, is how the group compares with its best individual. The data are based upon all fifteen groups, but the comparisons with "best" individuals include only those ten groups having four or more mem-

Test	Percentage of Individuals Superior to their Group in:		
	Score	Speed	Both
1. Reading comprehension....................	50	35	9
2. Sentence completion......................	24	46	7
4. Comparison of numbers....................	43	56	22
5. Finding words meaning opposite of given words	11	39	6
6. Drawing conclusions from given facts.........	34	14	6
7. Solving a cipher..........................	13	22	4
8. Listing steps to solve a problem.............	21	32	11
9. Composing limerick.......................	22	29	9
10. Original intelligence problem...............	50	51	19
COMPOSITE............................	30	36	11

bers. (It is assumed that group performance equaling the individual would be superior in the proportion found true throughout the remainder of the comparisons.)

Test	Percentage of Groups Excelling their Average Individual			Percentage of Groups Excelling their Best Individual		
	Score	Speed	Both	Score	Speed	Both
1. Reading comprehension.............	53	60	20	30	30	0
2. Sentence completion................	73	33	21	33	38	20
4. Comparison of numbers.............	53	40	13	29	11	0
5. Finding words meaning opposite of given words......................	87	60	53	50	33	22
6. Drawing conclusions from given facts..	87	87	73	50	63	25
7. Solving a cipher....................	93	87	80	50	60	20
8. Listing steps to solve a problem......	85	67	64	50	50	17
9. Composing limerick.................	80	67	60	30	45	10
10. Original intelligence problem.........	47	40	27	20	20	0
COMPOSITE......................	73	60	46	38	39	13

It will be noted that group superiority varies greatly with the task. The data reported show the extent to which the given tasks permit of effective group work. It will be noted (see the second column) that the two tasks which are best performed by the group

SUITABILITY OF TASK FOR GROUP SUPERIORITY IN SCORE
(Total Achievement, Including Quality)

Test	Composite Rank	Rank in Amount of Group Superiority (Weighted equivalent to other 3 ranks)	Rank in % of Individuals not Excelling their Group	Rank in % of Groups Excelling Average Individual	Rank in % of Groups Excelling Best Individual
5. Finding words meaning opposite of given words........	1	1	1	2½	2½
7. Solving a cipher.............	2	3½	2	1	2½
6. Drawing conclusions from given facts...............	3	3½	6	2½	2½
2. Sentence completion.........	4	2	5	6	5
8. Listing steps to solve a problem	5	6	3	4	2½
9. Composing limerick.........	6	7	4	5	6½
4. Comparison of numbers......	7	5	7	7½	8
1. Reading comprehension......	8	9	8½	7½	6½
10. Original intelligence problem	9	8	8½	9	9

SUITABILITY OF TASK FOR GROUP SUPERIORITY IN SPEED

Test	Composite Rank	Rank in Amount of Group Superiority (Weighted equivalent to other 3 ranks)	Rank in % of Individuals not Excelling their Group	Rank in % of Groups Excelling Average Individual	Rank in % of Groups Excelling Best Individual
7. Solving a cipher.............	1	1	2	1½	2
6. Drawing conclusions from given facts...............	2	4	1	1½	1
8. Listing steps to solve a problem	3	2	4	3½	3
9. Composing limerick.........	4	6	3	3½	4
2. Sentence completion.........	5	3	7	9	5
1. Reading comprehension......	6	5	5	5½	7
5. Finding words meaning opposite of given words........	7	7	6	5½	6
10. Original intelligence problem..	8	8	8	7½	8
4. Comparison of numbers......	9	9	9	7½	9

are tasks in which the score is in a sense a mere sum of that which is made by individual persons, since word opposites and sentence completions tend to be primarily accepted and counted to the credit of the group whenever any individual thinks of a possible answer. On the other hand, the tests involving the solving of a cipher and drawing conclusions from given facts permit a good deal of mutual interstimulation, and these stand rather high in the scale. Clearly the function of the group is often in large part the summation of individual efforts in a strict arithmetical sense, but the group has also a censoring function; it alters suggestions in accordance with whatever interests or criticisms may appear in the minds of those who hear each suggestion offered.

Correlations have been worked out between the size of the group and the efficacy of its work. Practically all such correlations are small and unreliable. Groups of four or five are, in other words, large enough to do the work required in such tasks about as effectively as are the groups double the size. From the above data, Watson believes that small groups of high ability can, on the average, exhibit effectual "intelligence" which is around the seventieth percentile for the individual persons composing it. The advantage of group work depends inevitably upon the relative importance assignable in any given case to fertility of association, rejection of inappropriate suggestions, possibility of modification of a suggestion to make it usable, and, in fact, upon a great number of attributes relating to the past experience and intelligence of the subjects. The great similarity of Watson's results to those of Shaw is probably in large part due to the similarities of method and the similarities in the make-up of the subjects. Such differences as do appear seem to be due almost entirely to the greater difficulty of the tasks imposed in Shaw's experiments.

It is evident from such experiments that the effectiveness of group work depends partly on the simplicity of the task and on the range and completeness of the needed suggestions. Highly creative work usually depends on an "executive," yet the executive's work is always supplemented and checked by groups which stand behind—such as the legislative or the judicial—and by some electorate beyond. Such an electorate might be all the adults in a community or all the stockholders of a corporation, or all the purchasers of property, etc.; but such an "electorate" always exists behind the individual thinker in society and helps to select from the creative work of individuals. Ultimately, all thinking is, of course, individual thinking; but in the light of the cultural molding of thought it is equally true that all thinking is group thinking.

The interplay of objective and subjective factors in the process of achieving insight in the group may be illustrated by the following simple figures:

In No. 1 a series of parallel vertical lines is to be gazed at for a few seconds. Objectively, no rhythm or grouping is presented. There is, nevertheless, a tendency in most observers to group by two's or three's, exactly as metronome beats are given a subjective patterning in terms of two-step or waltz time.

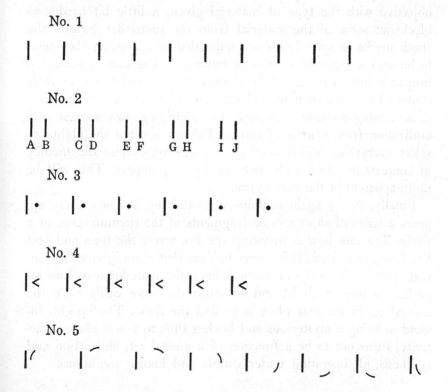

No. 1

No. 2

A B   C D   E F   G H   I J

No. 3

No. 4

No. 5

In No. 2 the material has a certain limited amount of organization. The pairs of vertical lines tend to force the observer to group the material in terms of physical closeness. It is difficult to combine line B with line C or line D with line E. The task can nevertheless be carried out if the observer thinks of very thick pillars separated only by a slight distance, one from the other.

In No. 3 the objective dissimilarity between lines and dots makes it relatively easy to pay attention to the lines and ignore the dots; for example, seeing six vertical lines and simply not noticing that they are accompanied by dots, or attending to the dots and ignoring the lines.

In No. 4 there appear, instead of dots, small check marks or arrowheads facing the left. Identically the same experiments as before can now be performed. Group the lines and ignore the arrowheads, or see the arrowheads as a row and ignore the lines. In this case, however, it is a little harder to effect this sort of objective with the type of material given, a little bit harder to block out some of the material from the remainder because the check marks or arrowheads are imbedded in a context; they tend to be seen as parts of a series of letter K's. The task of achieving insight is here a matter of breaking certain materials out of their context by means of a mental set directed to the *selection of all items having a common quality*. The ability to draw a great generalization from a mass of confused detail is often the ability to select everything which displays one quality, despite the medley of contexts in which each such quality may appear. This will be more apparent in the next figure.

Finally, No. 5 again contains vertical lines, but now there appears a series of short arcs or fragments of the circumference of a circle. The task now is to sweep the eye across the lines and find the figure suggested. It becomes evident that if we ignore the context, that is, the series of vertical lines, the material may leap together to form a circle, and so much the more easily since the mental set in the first place is to find the circle. The insight, instead of being a mysterious and lawless shift to a new plane of activity, turns out to be a function of a mental set, abstraction and synthesis, all operating under simple and known conditions.

We must now turn to an empirical consideration of the not very temperately discussed question of the existence of group thinking or group processes generally. We are dealing with a question of fact, not of theory, when we ask whether the thinking of a group is simply the sum of the thinking of the individuals. Suppose that figure No. 5 symbolizes, in greatly simplified form, the actual situation obtaining in the heavens when an astronomer observes the motion of a heavenly body. Let the vertical lines be the whole context in the sky; the curved lines, the paths of the observed motion of an object on successive occasions. Each small arc is utterly indeterminate by itself. To the observer, observing under difficulties, it is quite possible that the figure of which it is a part is an ellipse, a parabola, a hyperbola, or some unexpected form like a hypercycloid. If the object can be observed only a short time, the single astronomer's lifetime may give no answer as to the meaning of the arc. This is only partial insight. However, the vertical line presenting the same general context of stars appears later to another astronomer, and now there is different observational material constituting a second arc. The astronomer may fully grasp the relation of his observations to the preceding ones, or he may not. Sconer or later, on the basis of the thinking of previous men, one man sees a new whole. What has often happened in astronomy is that generations of astronomers have collected observations in a context of other observations, each more or less blind to the meaning of his immediate data. Then a Kepler, a Newton, a Herschel or an Einstein has had an exceedingly complex kind of insight not fundamentally dissimilar to the simple insight which we described just above in the case of the circle.

In other words, *a series of men* carries out all those integral steps which, if they were *carried out by one man alone*, would certainly be called a process of directed thought culminating in insight. It may at times be convenient to use the term insight only in relation to the last step of the thinking process. But in any event, it is empirically clear that there is such a thing as group thinking, the integration of many acts, each one occurring in a separate mind and developing from simple to complex; exactly as material culture has developed by accretion and elaboration, thought has developed from simple to complex, each man completing another man's thought and starting a new one for his successor to complete. The psychology of social institutions is in large part a real psychology of successive individual thought processes. The psychology of steps taken by groups or even generations of men resembles in a general way the steps which might be taken in the thinking of an individual.

From such studies the superior value of group thinking over individual thinking, when demonstrated, is clearly due in part to (1) the larger number of ways of looking at the problem; (2) the larger number of suggestions for a solution; (3) the larger number of effective criticisms of each proposed plan; (4) the patent need to accept social criticism and not be "bullheaded" (as subjects working alone frequently are).[1]

It is rather shocking, but it is a fact, that all the experimental work on group thinking which we have discussed deals with purely factual or cognitive relations where there is an unchallengeable right answer which all must accept when it is found. Most serious group thinking in political, economic, racial, or other social affairs is shot through and through with conflict of interest, opposition of values, the need to achieve either conquest or compromise in relation to needs. In private squabbles or formal debates we find the rationalization, "the New Deal helps everyone," or "the New Deal hurts everyone," functioning as socially acceptable surrogates for such remarks as "the New Deal helps my farm," "the New Deal hurts my investments." There is no reason whatever why group thinking, parliamentary behavior in relation to conflict situations, should not be studied experimentally.

Even the classroom permits the study of "conflict situations." The sociology class has been used as a laboratory for the study of group thinking by L. J. Carr, who has had groups of students cooperate in the solution of problems of an immediate practical character, such as how they are to spend some leisure in the im-

---

[1] These generalizations seem to us to be confirmed by studies in the psychology of testimony, and in the psychology of decisions by juries; cf. J. F. Dashiell, in C. Murchison's *Handbook of Social Psychology*, pages 1134-1144.

mediate future. Here the clash of interests, though friendly, is clear. One member of the group acting as note-taker records the conversation in such a fashion that the stages in the development of a plan and the part played by each individual in response to each of the others can be analyzed. His "interaction diagram" is a little complicated, but still not complicated enough to show the actual

INTERACTION DIAGRAM

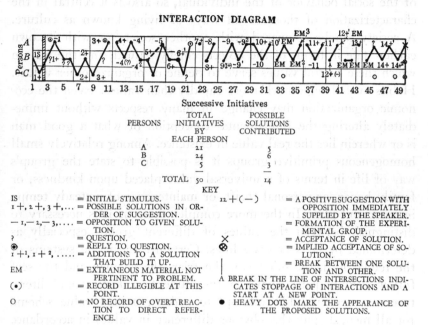

Successive Initiatives

PERSONS	TOTAL INITIATIVES BY EACH PERSON	POSSIBLE SOLUTIONS CONTRIBUTED
A	21	5
B	24	6
C	5	3
TOTAL	50	14

KEY

IS	= INITIAL STIMULUS.	12 + (−)	= A POSITIVE SUGGESTION WITH OPPOSITION IMMEDIATELY SUPPLIED BY THE SPEAKER.
1 +, 2 +, 3 +,...	= POSSIBLE SOLUTIONS IN ORDER OF SUGGESTION.		
− 1,− 2,− 3,....	= OPPOSITION TO GIVEN SOLUTION.		= FORMATION OF THE EXPERIMENTAL GROUP.
?	= QUESTION.	X	= ACCEPTANCE OF SOLUTION.
⊚	= REPLY TO QUESTION.	⊗	= IMPLIED ACCEPTANCE OF SOLUTION.
1 +¹, 1 + ², ...	= ADDITIONS TO A SOLUTION THAT BUILD IT UP.		= BREAK BETWEEN ONE SOLUTION AND OTHER.
EM	= EXTRANEOUS MATERIAL NOT PERTINENT TO PROBLEM.	A BREAK IN THE LINE OF INTERSECTIONS INDICATES STOPPAGE OF INTERACTIONS AND A START AT A NEW POINT.	
(•)	= RECORD ILLEGIBLE AT THIS POINT.		
O	= NO RECORD OF OVERT REACTION TO DIRECT REFERENCE.	●	HEAVY DOTS MARK THE APPEARANCE OF THE PROPOSED SOLUTIONS.

EXPERIMENT, PART 1, HOW THE INITIATIVE CHANGED HANDS IN THE READJUSTMENT-TO-CHANGE

From "Social Forces." Used by permission.

process of social interaction. Certainly the suggestion of Carr and Shaw could be elaborated to give us a genuine experimental psychology of group thinking in conflict situations.

COMPETITION AND COOPERATION IN THE LIGHT OF
ETHNOLOGICAL MATERIAL

The concepts "competition" and "cooperation" have been used here in an attempt to give meaning to several studies in American laboratories. We believe that wider and deeper meanings will come from a study of these forms of behavior in many cultures, and we shall attempt here to utilize and interpret Mead's summary of such behavior in thirteen primitive societies, comparing her findings with suggestions from European and American studies.[1]

Just as the concept of value is fundamental in the understanding of the social behavior of the individual, so also is it central in the characterization of those broad ways of living known as culture. A society can be compared with another society or with its own earlier state in terms of the objects chiefly valued, and the way in which these central values serve to define or organize other values. Habits may change much more rapidly than values. Even the economic organization may change in many respects without immediately altering the fundamental conception of what a good man is or wherein lies the real value in existence. Among relatively small homogeneous primitive groups it is possible to state the group's way of life in terms of a universal value placed upon kindness, or family honor, or personal thrift, or maintenance of a steady tempo in work and play. In the more complex societies it is necessary to distinguish between the values of different groups especially as determined by class or caste lines. Certainly the value systems of the feudal lord, the gildsman, the friar, the yeoman and the serf follow definite patterns which the student of history and literature may contrast. The attempt to make a unified value scheme for all men, despite this obvious difference in values in accordance with class lines, is the theme of many literary labors, such as *Piers Plowman, Paradise Lost* and *The Bridge of San Luis Rey*.

The study of characteristic American values appears vividly in the first edition and the new edition of the Lynds' *Middletown*, which gives extraordinarily vivid glimpses of American mentality in a one-class society (1890), in a two-class society (1924) and in a three-class society (1935). The homogeneous, individualistic yet democratic values of the small mid-western town of 1890 had by 1924 given place to the more intensely competitive and less demo-

---

[1] Some of the suggestions here were first formulated for, and appear in, the mimeographed *Memorandum on Research in Competition and Cooperation*, Social Science Research Council, 1937.

cratic value world of the business class, and a demoralized and confused value world among the working class arising from admixture of the older, homelier values with the newer "smarter" values of the pace-making group. By 1935 the centralization of power in the hands of the "X family" and their retainers had produced similar demoralization among the older business class, who kept up the story of individual competition and the reward for personal worth along with an earnest hope that they would be "accepted by the X's." Whatever the positive worth to the individual of this state of confusion and pressure for continual adjustment, the very different psychology of persons in a stable culture—for example, in the tightly knit class system in the Alabama town studied by Dollard—has its own satisfaction, its own gains. This is not to say that one value or value world is better than another; only to say that social life is not intelligible at all except in terms of value.

It has become a common practice to refer to our own society as a competitive or acquisitive society and to attempt psychological definition of the nature of such competitiveness or acquisitiveness. In point of fact, competition arises wherever different persons value the same thing, and the pursuit of it by one interferes with the achievement of it by another; competition defines only the means to a value, not the value itself. It is hard to conceive a human life devoid of competition of some sort. It seems to us much more useful to define our social existence not in terms of competition but *in terms of the things for which we compete, the way in which competition is carried on, and the prevalent value tendency or attitude toward competition.* This means that a broad sociological system of mode of interaction will be less fruitful for us than a description of the personal goals pursued and the special psychological characteristics which arise when pursuit of a specific goal is blocked. The term "competition" helps but little in describing the concrete psychological reality, but a description of the values and habits involved in each competitive effort leads us to better analysis and to the possibility of setting up experimental situations for the disentangling of the pattern. In the same way and for the same reason, "cooperation," though a useful concept in broad sociological description, must yield psychologically to the study of the specific goals in which people can practically merge their efforts, and the specific values and habits of mutual respect or affection which precede or result from specific cooperative endeavors. Mead's analysis of "cooperation and competition among primitive peoples" clearly suggests that the same objective social pattern roughly classed as competitive may arise from very different motivations, and that the major clue to the understanding of the meaning of the competitive pattern is to be found in the study of personal values, especially *value tendencies directed toward the ego, the wife, the father or mother, the chieftain, or toward some abstract moral or normative principle* stereotyped and accepted by the group. The psychologist cannot take ready-made from the sociologist the key concepts for the understanding of personal socialization. Rather, he must first study the data from sociologist and ethnologist and then subject them to his own genetic analysis. It will be worth while to look more closely at Mead's material on competition and cooperation among primitive peoples, comparing the values, and the competitive-cooperative struggle to achieve them, with the values and the competitive-cooperative struggle as we find them in western European and American society.

Mead's picture of the things for which people compete has suggested their classification in four categories: first, immediate goods or values inherent in objects—the taste of candy or the gleam of a shell ornament. Second, property rights in such an object, conceived as more than merely a prolonged enjoyment of the value, i.e., involving the exclusive personal possession and control of the object. Third, power over other persons, conceived not as a mere means to getting more goods, but as a direct source of satisfaction. Fourth, the gratification of vanity, conceived to be a variable commodity independent of, though frequently associated with, power. It will be noted that the last three all involve the *self*.

The quantities of these four things which may be obtained by competing are often limited, and competition would not occur unless they were limited. Infinite quantities of sunshine do not lead to competition; it is the restricted sunshine of crowded cities that becomes a commodity to be competed for. American pioneers did not compete for land as such, but for kinds of land that were available only in a limited supply. Children frequently find a happy solution to the prestige and power problem by letting everybody be chief or captain, and, as Piaget has shown, letting everybody win in games of marbles. To be sure, the child does not understand social power and prestige as the adult understands them; this, in fact, is the very point.

As essential values in adult human experience, power and prestige are restricted, and there are not enough to go around. This produces intensification, certainly, as everyone's attention is directed to him who possesses some of the treasured value; but it appears that the *naïve* social demand is for power or status in an absolute sense, not in the *relative* sense which is the first element in the definition of *competition*. The hypothesis is offered that when these four kinds of satisfaction can be directly sought and directly gained, human beings do not compete. There is therefore not only no competitive instinct, there is not even a universal or rigidly definable competitive habit. Competition results when human beings must function in certain more or less *similar situations*.

The ways in which persons individually compete will depend, first, on the objects to be had; second, on restrictions to the attainment of the objects by all who wish them; third, on the conditions making for success or failure in the quest when other persons are also involved in the quest, i.e., the conditions of *successful* competition. Individuals compete with absolutely any response pattern included in their repertory. They will dig, scrape, stick out their tongues, lash themselves, lie on swordpoints, or use stilettos on their neighbors' chests.

It may now be asked, to what degree the forms of competition arising in the quest of these four kinds of values are determined by cultural situations. Is it merely a result of social pressure that small children crave the use of objects? Clearly, no. Children crave objects and, before they even know that other persons also crave them, push other persons out of the way. Competition therefore arises, first of all, not through the desire to be successful in competition but through the fact that the other person is an obstacle to something one wants. Here the experiments of Bühler are typical and, apparently, conclusive. The six-months-old child grabs for the ball; so does his companion. There is *no desire* on *either part* to keep the *other child from getting the ball*. Each wants it himself; and if something prevents his getting it, he struggles and cries. It makes no difference whether the interference comes from the railing of the crib or the arm of his companion. He does not *cast venomous looks at his companion*. To do so, it would first be necessary that he learn that his companion also wants the object and that the companion's pursuit of it keeps him from having it. The rage or hate arising in consequence is not a result of anything inevitable in human nature at all; it is simply a result of the fact that there is only one ball in the crib. As Rousseau remarked, hatred among men first came when a man drew a line on the ground and said that the soil lying on one side of the line was his.

In the same way, the continued use of an object by one individual makes no trouble as long as the other individual also has objects serving his needs. Here must be mentioned, however, the fact that the grass is often a little greener on the other side of the fence, and that until one has tested and tried the other persons' possessions one often feels frustrated. At least, this is true of little children in our own culture. Since the notion of property itself, however, is to a large degree culturally defined—property rights being so very different in different civilizations—it seems practically certain that competition for the possession of objects is also something resulting from economic situations rather than "given" by nature.

To say that a thing is culturally defined, however, does not necessarily mean that it could be eliminated by other cultural arrangements. It may be that absolutely any form of group living would necessitate the setting up of some situations in which most goods were limited in quantity and in which property rights involved frustration to those without property. Even if, under a perfectly communistic order, one man's only wealth consists of a beautifully whittled reed pipe, he may be the envy of the community. The other person is now clearly an obstacle to our putting ourselves in his situation, and becomes an object of hate, fear, or envy. This is again to say that the *cultural situation*, as well as the *limitation of the commodity*, is among the chief sources of a competitive attitude; but it seems likely that any and every culture ever worked out by human beings will produce some competitive attitudes and competitive habits simply because we want things and both identify ourselves with those who have them, and regard those who have them as obstacles in our path. Lenin expressly emphasized that communism would release and accentuate some aspects of competitiveness. Some forms of mysticism may partially free the individual from competitiveness; but mysticism is clearly an escape from the cultural surroundings.

At this point the quantitative evidence concerning competitive attitudes toward possessions is of the utmost value. Among the thirteen cultures studied by Mead, this kind of possessiveness is certainly at a minimum among the gentle Arapesh of New Guinea, and at a maximum among the commercially minded Ifugao of the Philippines. Among the latter, to be sure, wealth is indissolubly tied to power and prestige; but, even so, the craving for material goods is worked up to a maximum as a result of the contrast between affluence and poverty. A close parallel to the Ifugao would be the frantically competitive people of the Manus tribe, who, however, give the impression of valuing property almost entirely because of its being the key to status or, at least, the loss of it the sure beginning of the loss of status.

It appears that the Arapesh have practically no sense of prestige in possessions, or that, if they do have such a sense, there is as much prestige in being generous as there is in possession and consumption. The total impression is of a people so much interested in one another and in friendly identification with one another's feelings that one could not easily set up the barrier, the deprivation of another, which is necessitated by all rigid property regulations. It is suggested that perhaps the completeness of an *identification* and the amount of *affection* for one's fellows, though not necessarily perfectly correlated, frequently act together to negate both the passion for goods and the demand for perpetual and exclusive possession. Even if the Arapesh stand alone in the world, their arrangements suggest that human beings need not be absorbed in things as contrasted with personal relations, and that even those things which are necessary to life may, as a result of an endless

chain of long-term loans without interest, be possessed, paradoxically enough, without much possessiveness. Mead's reports indicate
that several groups care very little about objects or the possession
of objects except in so far as these are tied up with prestige and
power values. One might venture the generalization that *most* of
the competition for things and for ownership is really competition
for very thinly veiled prestige or power. Certainly, in several cases,
such as the Kwakiutl (Indians of the northwest coast of North
America), there is not only no "veil," but possessions are used almost solely to provide orientation for the prestige struggle.

When we turn to competition for power, we find much confusion resulting from the fact that those who have power usually have
everything else. Power, by definition, is the thing that serves to
define the victor in other competitive struggles besides the struggle
for the original power. The power is usually utilized for the achievement of both possessions and status or prestige.

Prestige is independently sought out among the Kwakiutl, who
seem to care about power mostly because it is a way to prestige;
and among the Dakota, whose glory-hunger is so great that apparently nothing else matters much. Among the more warring Indian tribes it is hard to make out where power stops and prestige
begins; but the Ojibwa and Iroquois both seem to care more about
status and honor than about power through possessions. In their
quiet way, it seems that the Ba Thonga of East Africa are working
almost entirely toward status, but "absolute" status, which comes to
each individual as a result of time and personal circumstances, and
has no relation to the *defeat* of any other person.

We shall stop here for a second general hypothesis, namely, that
there is no meaning whatever in defining the relative physiological
strengths of the different social needs. Cultures may alter the quantitative picture so completely that what is a minor need in one
group may be an overwhelming passion in another. What people
will compete for is going to depend on what they want; and what
they want is to a large degree socially defined. Nevertheless, it is
of interest that this very simple fourfold pattern of human competitive goals seems to be sufficient for the thirteen cultures, and that
the two social motives, power and prestige, seem on the whole

more important than the object and possession motives. We shall
sum up by saying that it is our hypothesis that people compete
mostly for power and prestige. Where the amount of prestige "to
go around" is large, as among the Zuñi Indians of New Mexico,
there is not much competition. Where the supply is arbitrarily limited, as among the Kwakiutl, competition is terrific.

We shall venture two generalizations which at first sight will appear to be contradictory. First, that most competition found in these
thirteen cultures is competition for prestige, competition for other
things being secondary or derivative; second, that competition for
prestige would never become a prominent social pattern if there
were no competition for things and for property rights to set the
pace. The apparent contradiction seems to result from the fact that
the craving for status is so great that it becomes a monomania if
the social struggle makes the satisfaction of it difficult. Certainly
the craving for air is not the most powerful craving under the most
ordinary conditions of human life, but it can easily become so if
one is suffocating or drowning. Prestige satisfactions can get along
at a fairly low level most of the time; they are *omnipresent* and
need *satisfying*, but are not absolutely coercive. When, however,
the amount of status to be distributed around is restricted, the passion for more of it becomes intense. This will ordinarily not happen unless the property situation is so set up that the restriction
of property is also a restriction of prestige to those who have the
property. At once a universal but not a very intense demand becomes
the *most intense* demand of all.

Mead's material certainly suggests that the *amount of drive* for
power and for prestige is culturally influenced. Again there are individual differences; but the average or *general level of aspiration
is pretty well set by community standards*. It is not clear whether
the Arapesh are devoid of strong prestige feelings. The material
seems ambiguous. In the case of the Zuñi, one is not at all impressed by the arguments of Benedict, that individuals seek to avoid
prestige. It seems quite clear that there is both an upper and a
lower limit among them, as among ourselves, in the amount of
overt struggle for prestige which is socially acceptable. If a person
has no self-respect, if he has no "decent regard for the opinions of

mankind," we heap abuse upon him; but if he has too much regard
for such opinions, he becomes like the ridiculous father and son in
Aesop who tried to please everyone. Apparently the Zuñi stand-
ardizes the amount of trouble one should take to achieve social
favor at a point somewhat higher than we do.

The data suggest, then, that men in all societies do care about
the personal regard of some, or all, of their fellows. Apparently W.
Steinberg is right in arguing that this is not because society has
imposed its will on the helpless infant, coerced him into wanting
its sanctions, but because the infant goes out to meet and lay hold
of society, passionately wanting to be a part of it and asking it
please to take him in. Whether the social instincts are anything
more than the vague unrest of the isolated chick which has to get
back to the brood, we do not know; but the passion of the chick
is so strong that when he has this social hunger not even food
and water matter to him. This kind of mechanism also functions
in human beings, and the prestige thirst arises out of such a matrix
as this. It is probably colored and enriched by the factor which
Freud has described under the name of narcissism. To do anything
really profound about this, we should have to do some basic research on the nature of the ego in different societies, using the
term to define not the drive to put oneself ahead, but the original
structure which is put ahead by the process, the things which the
ego really consists of. As far as we can see, the Zuñi, like all other
people, care a lot about this kind of social acceptance. They win it
by doing things which are mostly non-competitive. Is this form of
response rooted in desire for prestige rather than need for love, or
in both?

Now as to the question of transfer of training—whether competitive habits built up in the quest of one commodity, let us say
prestige, carry over into relations where prestige is not involved,
for example, the struggle for material objects. The data just cited
from Mead's report imply that there is some such transfer. People who have spent their lives shouldering other people out of the
way for the sake of glory seem to find it hard to let them come
back again for the sake of fish or chestnuts. When you have doubled
up your fists to fight for your family honor, it is easy to go on fight-

ing a little longer for family fortunes. In our own culture, it is doubtful if competition spreads or transfers so readily from one goal to another. There do not, however, seem to be any well-controlled studies on this point. Some are greatly needed. It is certainly worth knowing whether habits are fettered to the specific goals that engendered them, or whether, once given life, they can turn all of these into new directions. Upon the answer depends the legitimacy of evaluating whole personalities or whole cultures as "competitive" or "cooperative."

But if there is such transfer on a large scale, the thing transferred is not likely to be a specific technique of competition or cooperation. Rather, it will be a human response which we have not as yet directly considered, namely, the *attitude toward those individuals who are, at the time, one's competitors.* This attitude may be more important than the sheer intensity of a need. If it is true that the hated competitor is pushed aside with an energy or bitterness which would not be shown to a neutral or friendly competitor, it means that the form of competition does *not* depend simply upon the goal and the technique of "pushing." It means that a great deal depends on *who* is competing for the same goal; and hence it means that the form of competition, the kind of struggle, insinuation or entreaty used in reaching the goal, will be dictated by the nature of the competitor. It may mean an alteration not only in the technique of competition but in the determination of goals to be sought. The very fact that one cannot injure one's friend may mean that one will not compete with him for game when game is scarce; one would rather seek berries or go hungry altogether. The whole wealth of inter-individual relations, the entire pattern of social friendliness or hostility, becomes relevant to the study of competitive habits. The entire texture of friendly and hostile relations among persons demands analysis if we are to understand the setting up of competitive attitudes. At the same time, of course, many other factors of attitude prevailing among persons become important; for example, the way people may react on some future occasion to obtain revenge. In fact, we must consider the entire range of indirect values involved in doing something now for the sake of remote consequences. The capacity to see remote consequences has a bearing upon present competitive habits.

The study of the Arapesh and Zuñi cultures gives the impression that this third aspect of competitive habits is at times the most important of all. The primordial fact about Arapesh society is neither the nature of *goals* nor the *way in which goals are sought*; it is the kind of fellow-feeling which makes certain ways of behaving toward other persons obviously desirable and others unthinkable, which makes certain social techniques natural, normal and humane, and others mean, vicious and abnormal. Conversely, the Kwakiutl, from this point of view, give the feeling that perhaps it is not first of all a question of a limited amount of prestige which makes everybody so mercilessly determined to shame his opponent, not a question of a way in which one must win prestige. Rather, it is an attitude toward others, a basic suspiciousness and hatred, which forces the leader to choose techniques by which the good things of life may be vigorously limited.

But attitude toward others is intimately bound up with attitudes toward oneself. One may enhance one's ego by maliciousness, and also by generosity. The ego can be gratified or achieve status either through domination of others or through yielding to others, or through a great variety of intermediate kinds of social rapport. It is frequently a matter of ambivalence and uncertainty in our own culture whether admiration is to be won by assaulting people to show them how strong one is, or by giving up something and bowing down in meekness with the slogan of service. What is needed is more *research of a quantitative sort, to find out how intense the satisfaction from being a "servant" can be.* It is surprising that in our own cut-throat civilization which, in the spirit of Calvin, has made it a strict obligation to drive one's competitor to the wall, anti-Calvinistic virtues of a first-century type still prevail and seem to thrive. It is not just a question of different areas of life being governed by different values. In many quite circumscribed areas—for example, classroom teaching—a professor can win approximately equal approval by being "hard," that is, a shrewd, methodical and thorough teacher, or by being "easy," that is, a considerate and friendly teacher, provided that both the hardness and the easiness stay within definite limits. This is by way of saying that the child who gets a little ego satisfaction from dominating and triumphing could also get a little ego satisfaction from being nice to everyone around; and, qualitatively and quantitatively, the two satisfactions seem often to be equivalent. To be sure, the former is a muscular kind of satisfaction; but that is a separate point requiring separate treatment.

In considering the emphasis on the ego which plays such a part in Mead's interpretative summary, the question is raised whether there is a competitive thirst for prestige which always has to be satisfied wherever there are human beings, and the suggestion was made that it might be possible to define for each society the kind of thirst and the kind of satisfaction which will be socially emphasized. Perhaps the ego need, or the need for social recognition, is one of many needs which may be intensified and about which life may be organized, as among the Kwakiutl and Dakota; perhaps also relatively little attention may be paid to it and a convenient easygoing way of satisfying it may be found. Long ago, in discussing the Freudian theory of sublimation, Woodworth remarked that "it is the individual, not the drive, that must be satisfied." To say that the rejected lover, turning to his old friends, is "regressing," and that the musician who, frustrated in love, is composing a symphony, is sublimating, is really like saying that the man who can't find the checkers and who therefore plays dominoes has found in the dominoes a sublimated expression of his checker-playing desires. There are no grounds to believe that the need for prestige, or any other particular drive, has a fixed quantity or that a fixed amount of satisfaction for it will be sufficient. Why not say simply that in some cultures the thirst for status is terrific and the supply of it is arbitrarily limited so that it becomes a source of distress for everyone, that in other cultures it is emphasized but everyone has a fair amount of it (e.g., Maori), and, third, that it may be minimized and everybody easily accommodated (e.g., Arapesh)?

This point leads to the question of the relation between competitive attitudes and the nature of the ego and its function in a culture. It seems obvious that a cooperative attitude toward an other human being might be induced either through ego or through libido—to use Freud's terms. To state this in everyday language, one may be cooperative either through the ability to *identify* oneself (in Freud's sense) with another person or through love (libido) toward the other person. To be sure, the two may be. blended, but they may also be separated. Identification, as such—the kind of thing which Piaget calls participation and which Lewin calls the presence of weak boundaries around the ego—may make it possible for one individual to put himself almost completely in the other's place. If he puts himself *completely* in the other's place he will *not* compete because he will receive vicarious satisfaction from the conquests made by the other. On the other hand, if he does not identify himself *at all*, he will also not *compete* in the *full psychological sense of the term*. He may push ahead blindly, but not think of the other individual as involved in the same quest. At any rate, we should look closely into the question of identification or participation as a thing which has a two-way relation to competition: (1) On the one hand, you see the other person getting something which it would be so nice to have. A little child who is completely happy with his scooter notices that the boy across the street has a bicycle. The one object of supreme value in the world now is a bicycle. If one were not able to think of oneself as being in the position of the other boy who has the bicycle, if one were not able to ask one's father to buy one, if one were *in a "caste" relation*, never thinking of oneself as having the privileges of the other group, competitiveness ought not to arise. (2) On the other hand, what is sometimes accomplished by this ego mechanism is sometimes accomplished by the libido—one hopes not to hurt or obstruct the object of one's affection. Mead says that abhorrence of competitive behavior is rooted sometimes in ego participation and sometimes in mutual libido among potential competitors.

The question now is whether the chief basis of cooperation, when genuinely psychological and not mechanical and external, may not lie in the process of removing the barriers which limit the ego. Mead says that this is a valid account of one sort of mysticism and one sort of cooperation, but there is a whole world of mysticism which is not based on the ego at all but solely on affection (libido);

that one prominent type of mystic experience consists in being intensely and completely oneself, with the sharpest and firmest of boundaries, while at the same time intensely responding to another person or thing. One might in this case have complete cooperation, and a complete absence of competition, while the ego is intensified rather than subdued. It seems unnecessary to argue the question whether this is mysticism or not. It seems probable that there always is *some* identification, some spreading of ego to include the other person. Even the ideal mother could do nothing constructive for her baby if she had no idea as to what the baby wanted or feared.

We should prefer then, instead of thinking of ego and libido as magnetic poles, each of which has a relation to cooperation and competition, to say instead that self-love and love of others are two variables, each of which is correlated somewhat with cooperative activity. We should urge not that these are independent, but merely that each contributes in some degree to the cooperative attitude of the moment, and that instead of standing in a disjunctive relation, the most cooperative behavior appears when both are highly developed.

From the point of view reached here, the degree of proneness to compete with others will depend chiefly on the ratio of two variables occurring at a given time and place: (1) the desire for the object sought, and (2) lack of concern for those who are seeking it at the same time. Individuals living together in the utmost harmony may suddenly become aware that the supply of food or water is not sufficient for the life needs of all; one's friends become mortal enemies, and battle to the death results. Just as two men loving the same woman may hate and fear each other, essentially because they are so much alike and have the same values and ideals, so men in groups may organize warfare because only one of the existing groups can achieve the goal which all desire. The likeness between men may lead to cooperation, but it also may lead to competition. On the other hand, Mead's material shows the diversity of ways in which internecine warfare may be prevented, or in which the culture may "phrase" a competitive situation so that the "obvious limitation" of the goal object is not "obvious" at all.

Here the attitude toward other members of the community may be the first fact to reckon with; customs of group interaction may make a competitive situation inconceivable.

Under conditions of such rigid structuring, the end result usually falls between the two crude antitheses stated above. There is neither direct group competition, as among the Eskimos, nor a detour around the competitive situation, as among the Arapesh. There is a complicated and delicate pattern of more or less recognized forms of response lying between these extremes, and depending upon the relation between desires for goals and attitudes toward competitors. If we saw fit to recognize the desired goal as biologically compelling, we might incline at first sight to say that human nature is in the long run more competitive than cooperative. But serious oversight would be involved in such a conclusion, for two reasons: First, most of these *limited goals* can in fact be *sought cooperatively in the modern world*. There are very few indeed in which the supply is limited in such a way that *one man's gain* need be the *competitor's loss*. Take, for example, the struggle for jobs in depression time as an illustration of the crude and direct functioning of this kind of competition. Even here the thing is institutionalized and formalized, so that one usually does not directly elbow his way into the desired job. A large proportion of the goals, even at the biological level, *are sought in groups*, e.g., through *collective bargaining*; and in the struggle it frequently appears that the goal itself is more or less elastic. Starvation wages for the individual may, after the successful strike, be replaced by better wages for the whole membership of the group. The brute inevitability of cutthroat competition for the job is more characteristic of the older economic textbooks than of the daily economic world we confront.

The second restriction to be noted regarding such "inevitabilities" in regard to competition lies in the fact that the *competitive attitude often results directly from a cultural phrasing of the human predicament*. Groups of men are made to fear one another, each being assured of the baleful designs of the others—every ward politician knows the trick. The Northcliffes and Hearsts do this —if not skillfully, at least perseveringly and with huge success— with respect to "national interests." The small shopkeeper and the plumber are ultimately convinced that Japan is *attacking "our" interests in China*; and the German farmer is convinced that Jewish bankers in London are plotting his extermination. War, the most acute form of competition known to man, seems to result not simply from the actual state of economic geography and the arts of manufacture, but in part from the highly specialized "monopoly competition" in which only a few thousand men directly take part, the stakes of which require the cooperation of millions. Cooperation, too, unprecedented in modern times—at least the external collaboration of some 400 million persons organized against the Central Powers in 1917-18—results from the phrasing of a situation in such a way that it seems to be a predicament of all.

The success of competitive enterprises depends largely on inhibiting fellow-feeling by keeping oneself blind to the individual competitor as a human being. A man will play the market and ruin *another man whom he does not know.* Many will play the market and ruin those whom they know only slightly. The desire to make money on the market being held constant, the amount of brutality shown in competition will vary inversely with the knowledge of, and regard for, one's neighbor. Granted that a man will throw a hand grenade at, or stick a bayonet into, a man whom he does not know; the chance that he will cease to do so if he knows the man is so serious that even momentary fraternizing on the fronts came to be considered one of the most serious of offenses. Instead of the war situation proving that men are by nature competitive, it proved that most have to be kept in gross ignorance of one another to permit the "competitive drive" to beat the "drive" for friendship or human contact.

If the statement is made that man is by nature competitive, we shall reply that much of our material shows him to be by nature competitive in the sense that all men are pretty much alike and therefore have pretty much the same needs. For this to lead to competition, however, two things have to happen: first, competitive devices for reaching this goal must exist (or be invented), and, second, men have to be kept from becoming acquainted. If the need is intense and if the competitors mean little personally to us, the competition may indeed become ferocious. However, many societies, primitive and advanced, have organized life in such a way that competing is the morbid rather than the healthy response to a limited-goal situation. Legal codes, like that of Hammurabi, and concepts of a world order, like that of the medieval Roman Catholic Church, are ways of systematizing human life so that to some degree the "natural" thing to do is to think of one's fellow before one thinks of the individual goal object that is sought. Much confusion is evident in schools and homes, as a result of our teaching children that the great and good man (1) considers others before himself, (2) pushes ahead and keeps his eyes on his goal—power, prestige, or riches.

In at least two senses cooperation may be said to be more deeply rooted in human nature than competitiveness: (1) the higher animals, and man in particular, seem in general to want contact and interaction with another, but compete only when the external relations limit the quantity of a collectively desired goal; (2) the tendency to "identify" onself with others of one's kind is, at least in primitives, rooted in the "transferred" conditioned response. The primitive basis for sympathy, widely used in animal as well as human societies, is a dependable basis for cooperation, to which no basis for competition corresponds.

On the other hand, men will apparently always compete in some ways, for power and status are inevitably restricted, and arranged hierarchically in a centralized social order (even a true world brotherhood; the more so because large groups of this sort prevent personal acquaintance). But the ways in which they will cooperate in such a world order will also be widened and deepened.

The complete futility of asking whether man is "by nature" competitive appears most clearly in the case of the Ammassalik Eskimo. Under the influence of the hunger drive, the Ammassalik proves to be not competitive, but either individualistic or cooperative in his hunting, depending on the practical hunting possibilities; yet he is quite directly and brutally competitive in his sex aggressions. The basic pattern of group life is cooperative in the vague sense that relations are friendly. The simple fact that the conditions of hunting permit group work, whereas love-making is comparatively individualistic, is unfortunately not a complete answer to the psychology of the situation. Among some primitive groups, hunting situations which seem to call for the work of the individual independent hunter are solved cooperatively, and group courtship and group attacks on neighbors with a view toward carrying off wives have been recorded often enough. The same individual Eskimo, in a remarkably free situation with a minimum of institutional control, shows that he can slip into individualistic, competitive, or cooperative habits with equal ease. Among more complex societies we have a right to conclude that the form of the institutional pattern will determine to a greater degree in which way the needs are to be satisfied; under very simple conditions there is perhaps no special loading of the dice in favor of any one of the several modes of response.

COMPETITIVENESS AS A TRAIT OF OUR OWN SOCIETY

Probably the commonest single term used to characterize our own society is the word "competitive." Yet in the light of all the foregoing, it seems to us that the term is nearly useless as a description of our society. Even when it is accurate, it is psychologically barren. Most of the intended meaning is better conveyed by saying that many phases of our culture are rooted in ego values; that these values are so regulated by the economic situation that the enhancement of one's ego tends to injure the ego of another. Self-defense and aggressiveness usually result.

Even so, the picture of the competitive society ordinarily drawn forgets the daily round of friendly conversation, "joshing," amusement, listening to the radio, taking the family for a drive, going fishing, dancing, loafing. Business itself, for many people, is a quiet routine affair in which one keeps going, scarcely competes. The frantic picture of the poor youth struggling up, the Alger-book model, has been taken so seriously by sober thinkers that we suspect them of forgetting the garage man's son who is quite content to be baggage man at the village station; the carpenter's son who decides he would rather be an embalmer; the barber's boy who has a "fine job" as stock clerk in a warehouse; and the enormous masses of research data which show that *most* young Americans (before, during and since the depression) have asked chiefly for a job, for security, for a chance to live. They hope for a pleasant life, enjoy their friends, the car, a radio, "want to get married pretty soon." We do not believe that the tense competitive demand for "recognition" is at all characteristic of the daily round of life in the case of most Americans. If it be objected here that we are talking about lower economic levels rather than the upper middle class, we can only say that even among the metropolitan business men who uphold rugged individualism the main concern of most individuals seems to be to keep their heads above water, to keep going, and to enjoy life, rather than to sacrifice everything for more prestige. Much of our life is competitive, but not all of it. The conspicuous success pictures of a few are important, but the frenzied competitor is in some ways a deviate whose behavior requires special perspective.

With these qualifications, it might perhaps be accurate to describe our own society as one which values personal property or individual prestige. Yet, in making such a characterization we should forget that any or all of these values are found in more stable cultures, and we should minimize the overwhelming importance of the fact that *our value world is rapidly changing*. Perhaps the question as to what the prevalent values now are is less important than the fact that the values are in conflict and are undergoing bewildering transformations. Perhaps the confusion of values, the necessity to abandon even those nearest to the heart, and to set up new ones alien to the first needs of the self, may be more important still. Perhaps the inevitable frustration which results in the tension and insecurity of seeking always for a new frame of reference may be the cardinal psychological reality in present-day life. Theories of motivation based on the primary drives, whatever they may be, would thus be less useful than those based on secondary reactions to change in the objects upon which the drives are canalized. Perhaps the personality structure of the present-day man or woman can be approached most realistically by studying the dislocation of value tendencies. If this be true, much significant research on the characteristics of human beings in a time of transition may be carried out even in the absence of a final answer to the question of ultimate motivating forces. Such a line of thought would contribute to the view expressed elsewhere throughout this volume that many synchronous approaches may be made to existing problems without waiting for the ultimate biology (or, indeed, the basic physics and chemistry) of social behavior, and that these approaches, properly integrated and interpreted, may indeed clarify and facilitate the quest for basic motives and basic laws of individual socialization.

ARE THERE LAWS WHICH SUMMARIZE THE PROCESSES OF GROUP BEHAVIOR?

In concluding this sequence of chapters on the process by which the individual grows into society, we must ask whether we cannot generalize a little more boldly, abstracting from the many specific events, and formulating the deeper universal principles apparent in all patterns of social behavior. Must one stop with laws relating to *individuals*; are there not laws of *group interaction*?

A priori, we should certainly expect to find such laws. The theory of levels of subject matter has repeatedly been invoked in all the sciences, to suggest that the laws relating to phenomena at one level of complexity may prove altogether insufficient when we move to higher levels. Despite the fact that atoms are made of tiny particles which behave according to their own laws, the behavior of atoms is describable in its own special terms. Molecules too behave according to their own laws, not deducible from the laws of atoms. Living matter, despite the applicability of many laws of physics and chemistry, is notoriously refractory to the ordinary concepts of physics and chemistry. It is not necessary to beg the question as to the ultimate "adequacy" of the concepts of natural science in dealing with biology; the point is that one gets further at present by dealing directly with such concepts as growth, repair, reproduction, variation, heredity, adaptation to environment. In the same way, the transition from the study of the individual living being to the study of interacting individuals raises the question of the existence of "social laws." It is hard to see how the study of metallic

currency on the one hand, and the study of the pleasure-pain
principle in daily economic behavior on the other hand, would yield
directly a formulation about supply and demand under conditions
of bimetallism, such as we have in Gresham's Law. It is hard to see
how the study of individual organisms could ever yield generalizations about the influence of city upon country, the differences between propaganda delivered individually through printed matter
and that which is delivered to excited crowds. It seems very improbable that group behavior is merely the statistical massing of
much individual behavior. Indeed, it seems likely that individuals
interacting with one another behave in ways not characteristic of
isolated individuals, or, as Moede and Allport long ago pointed
out, that there are measurable properties of group behavior as such,
distinct from properties of individual behavior.

Yet attempts to *formulate* social laws have for the most part
been hasty or inept, or both. With limitless ambition, Duprat
has undertaken to list over a hundred social laws relating to the
tempo of social change under varying conditions. Tarde and, later,
Ross have undertaken to formulate laws describing the general
modes of imitation prevailing in various elements of the population, and to show the character and tempo of changes arising from
imitative tendencies. These laws, obtained by casual observation or
reading or reflection upon such data, have an empirical value. The
laws, however, are not stated in such a way as to be easily verifi-
able; they are not stated in clear quantitative form. When, for
example, Ross tells us, "The more marked the craze, the more
rapid the reaction from it," he does not tell us whether he means
that there is a linear relation or a curvilinear relation, nor does
he give us any suggestions as to how to calibrate observations so
as to get something with which to verify his generalization. Laws
of this rough empirical sort, without instructions as to how to obtain crucial evidence, scarcely merit extensive discussion in a book
such as this.

Another difficulty about universal social laws lies in the relation
obtaining between fact-finding and fact-changing processes in the
individual human mind. The wishes of the chemist may obscure his
thinking; they may cause lopsided emphasis or downright illusion;

but they do not alter the laws of chemistry. The wishes of the social scientist, including the psychologist, *do* alter the way in which he behaves and therefore the subject matter which he and other social scientists study. We are not concerned here with James' paradox regarding the will to believe, but we are concerned with one tangential aspect of James' argument. What we as social scientists formulate as the present status of research findings not only gives undue emphasis and direction in social research; to some slight degree it indirectly *alters the social order* which we have attempted to describe.

To an infinitely larger degree the wishes of a Lenin, a Mussolini, a Gandhi *change the "basic laws"* operating in society. Much of the nonsense written about race in Germany could in time become sense if the theory could be pushed to the point of actually making the German Reich a primarily Nordic entity. The fundamental laws of economics, even if taken at their face value in relation to the Russian Empire of 1917, are subjected by Lenin to Marxist analysis, and become part of the basis for personal agitation and struggle, culminating in the removal of the economic system in which these laws arose. A new economic order comes into existence, so fundamentally different from the old that many of the fundamental postulates of Adam Smith or Marshall become meaningless. New laws of social behavior arise which are in the strictest sense "emergents," and from which new deductions must constantly be made as each new theory becomes systematized.

Here it will be objected that there are certain fundamental laws, laws of all social behavior, deeper than the laws obtaining for any specific culture. Such laws, for example, might relate to imitation, suggestion, or the functioning of prestige. We have indeed tried to show that social psychology studies many such processes and can achieve some measure of generalization regarding them. But a review of those chapters in which these laws have been discussed will make it clear that the laws relate to relatively simple mechanisms of individual conduct, many of them having their roots in biological response (e.g., sensori-motor action, the conditioned response, etc.), and that they have no bearing on the present question of laws describing the larger social processes as such. There may indeed be general laws of social interaction in the world today or in historic time, independent of specific cultures; but as we have already argued, all the cultures that now happen to exist are only a small sample of cultures which might well enough exist. We can scarcely glimpse the range which cultures are likely to exhibit in the future. If it is true that individual men can not only discover but literally *make* the laws of cultural development, and if the laws which they exploit in such creation of cultures depend on a complex interaction between their own personalities and social situations emerging from time to time, it seems very improbable that abstract laws of the type indicated will have any usefulness and relevance.

A certain kind of social law more humbly stated may in the meantime be useful. The stage of diffusion of culture from a center may be defined. It may become possible, if we know the density of population, the level of education, etc., to predict the rate at which a new fashion, a new slang phrase, or a new best seller will become known. It may even be worth while to predict from North Dakota data what will happen in Florida. Such efforts, however, are in the nature of applied science; they are phases of human engineering. They are not likely to discover "basic social laws." The "lawful-minded" social psychologist will do well, we think, to work for greater clarity of definition and greater precision of measurement in relation to very simple laws regarding the behavior of the individual in response to certain very simple and well-defined social situations, and to regard his social laws as descriptions of the culture which he has sampled, and nothing more.

Ultimately, perhaps, laws of socialization may be discovered which apply without exception whenever any socialization whatever occurs. This must mean that there are certain basic ways in which organisms will inevitably modify one another's responses, regardless of the traditional patterns of responses built up within the group. If we see the matter clearly, this can happen because organisms are fundamentally made as they are. Nothing can be predicted of their social responses except in terms of what is known about their biological make-up. The social laws, then, would turn out to be nothing but biological laws.

We have some hints already in this direction. The social behavior of the protozoa is not something separate from their behavior as individual organisms; the social is literally an aspect of their biological existence. They respond to one another by virtue of their fundamental bio-physical attributes. At a higher level, where elements of social tradition appear, as among the birds, the responses of fledglings to their parents are biological responses. There are not two worlds—a biological and a social. At the level of complexity represented by human culture, as the child responds to the face and voice of the parent and takes the first steps in socialization, it learns by virtue of its properties as an organism. The content and the tempo of its learning, the accent on this aspect of life, the undervaluing of some other aspect, mark the differences between cultures. If, however, there be a universal social psychology, a system of laws relating to all individuals undergoing socialization, deliberately putting to one side the specific laws true only at certain times and places, we have simply the universal biological potentialities for becoming socialized and the universal biological capacity to assist in the socialization of another person. The time *will* come when there are universal laws in social psychology; and when that time arrives we shall have on our hands simply a systematic and clear picture of the biological potentialities of *individuals* for reciprocal influences, a unified view of humankind in which the social and the biological are one and the same.

SOCIAL LAWS AS A REFLECTION OF INDIVIDUAL DIFFERENCES

It seems to us that there is one possibility of absolute rebuttal of the foregoing argument; and although we are not disposed to accept this rebuttal, we believe that it needs to be kept in mind and tested in the light of incoming data. There is a considerable possibility that the fundamental biological realities involved in *individual differences* must give rise to definable social laws in all societies in which people differ by nature. Consider, for example, sheer differences in size, and the resulting success or defeat in conflict and in achieving food, land, or whatever is needed. Consider sheer differences in strength or speed or endurance. Consider the more subtle individual differences in strength or speed or skill with respect to this or that specific task. Is it not possible that groups which depend upon differentiation of function (division of labor) will inevitably and forever show *group characteristics* which depend upon the diversification of abilities? From colonial protozoa to medieval feudalism, may there not be social laws relating to dominance, leadership, contagion of influence from the powerful to the weak, or such laws residing ultimately in the fact of biological differences? A generalized social psychology of domination or of leadership or even of suggestibility might appear possible.

The difficulty in such a hypothesis lies in the fact that the concepts useful for a description of social reality among members of a culture cut across these biological concepts and structure our reality in a different way. The race is not always to the swift, nor the battle to the strong; nor are the biologically given differences determinative of functional differences in leadership, dominance, or suggestibility. If it be argued that there is always a step between the biological and the social, a way of explaining how, in concrete reality, the biological leads to the social, we must say in rejoinder that the nature of the steps to be taken depends upon the very process of culturization in a specific culture. The relation between measurements of isolated organic attributes and measurements of the bio-social reality is shifting and complex. Such considerations do not mean that we are tempted to follow here the suggestion of Kroeber and again of MacIver, that the social reality is utterly different from the biological reality, and that the laws of one do nothing to predict the other. On the contrary, the stimulation which plays back and forth between members of a family or group or other social reality is, as we see it, a true physiological form of stimulation. The world is not a biological reality plus a social reality at a different level. The biological reality of a father's and mother's responses to the child is the very life tissue out of which the child's assimilation of the language and the whole culture is derived. Though the social reality must be empirically taken at its own level for study, it is literally identical with the biological reality. The trouble with *naïve* biologism does not lie in any basic inapplicability of biological concepts to society, but in the fact that any interpersonal pattern depends upon the entire life history and participation in all the social patterns in the case of each individual involved.

This is as much as to say that there is quite literally an infinite series of real or potential social realities which may in time be defined by the interaction of distinct individualities. The impossibility of discovering social laws in the abstract lies not in a tendency of social law to evade the dissecting instrument of the scientist, but simply in the fact that these more complex patterns are of infinite diversity. Such progress as ever will be made in the discovery of social laws based on individual differences will arise from more thorough and complete study of these differences. Just as the social pattern of the ameba, the termite or the robin becomes more intelligible as we understand individual peculiarities, so the basic laws of society, as contrasted with mere descriptions or approximations, will ultimately come from the study of the basic biology of humankind. We repeat that such biology as this is a full-bodied bio-social portrayal of the complete interaction patterns of persons. It is not a study of genes or of embryology alone, but a laborious analysis of the intricate interstimulations of all persons in groups. We may, by a series of approximations, reach beyond the laws of this or that culture to the bio-social laws of all cultural reality. It is in this direction, if at all, that the rebuttal will make good against the thesis which we have offered above, regarding the impossibility of achieving "social laws" in the strict sense. But we see no evidence that such a rebuttal today is more than a verbal protest against the trend of actual research, which surely seems to find that all social laws depending on individual differences are *relative to the concrete social significance of these differences in a given culture.*

So, unless and until such a rebuttal can be solidly justified, we are skeptical of all quests for social laws conceived in terms of a reality independent of the laws relating to the *socialization of individual persons.* Here there is room both for *generalizations as to universal patterns,* when research shows the development to be similar from one person to another, and for *quantitative analysis of individual differences, leading to generalizations as to reasons for the differences.* It seems probable that as investigations directed to such ends take more and more account of the differences between cultures and the differences between individuals within each culture, true laws regarding the socialization of individual human beings may be discovered.

PART FOUR

QUANTITATIVE STUDIES OF INDIVIDUAL DIFFERENCES IN ADULT
SOCIAL BEHAVIOR

Chapter XII

MEASUREMENT OF THE ADULT PERSONALITY

The Extent of Individual Differences

HUMAN beings differ constitutionally, and these constitutional differences are analogous to, if not in many cases identical with, the kinds of individual differences found throughout all living things. People are not all born alike. Their differences, in fact, permit no clear-cut differentiation into normal and abnormal, ordinary and exceptional. The very structure of human nature presents gradations and an almost infinite variety of combinations. In addition to all these constitutional factors, there are, as has been seen, a multitude of individual differences in which *constitutional* factors can be compared with those *socially produced* only with the greatest difficulty. Both of these kinds of differences may, from the point of view described in Chapter I, be seen in biological terms. The interplay of these two sets of factors may be illustrated (and perhaps seen more easily than in humans) by a reference to one of the many investigations, particularly by European psychologists, concerning the social psychology of individual differences among animals.

One series of such studies emphasizes especially the individual differences in social traits found among animals. A sort of "experimental social psychology of hens" is worked out, of which the "pecking order" may be cited as typical. Hen A may regularly peck hen B, though the latter does not retaliate. B takes it out, however, on C, and C on D. Just as in some boys' gangs each person's position in the gang depends upon his rank in pugilistic skill, so these hens form a sort of gang hierarchy of their own. There are, nevertheless, some curious exceptions to this simple way of stating their social organization. In some cases an individual may peck "out of order," so to speak; for example, E, though pecked by D, may peck A. The relation of ascendance and submission, as some might call it, which results in one hen's recognizing another as fair game and submitting in turn to the attack of a third, permits at present no detailed psychological description. A great deal depends on size and strength. But ascendance and submission are often traceable to a previous *overt combat*, in which victor and vanquished learned their respective places. Thus the individual's status depends partly on prowess, partly on "historical accidents." Exactly the same sort of crystallized individual differences in "social status" have been repeatedly observed among the primates. They show, in fact, a set of individual differences which are the end result of *both constitutional and learned elements*. The most elaborate quantitative work in this field is C. Murchison's study of "social hierarchies" among roosters.

The rôle of individual differences in human affairs is so great that it has even been easy to assume that the entire subject matter of social psychology is the result of the variation in human capacities and dispositions. General psychology would be the science dealing with universal laws of behavior; social psychology would be the science which stresses differentiation of individuals and the resultant integration, or formation of groups through division of labor. With most of this there can be no quarrel. But we can scarcely grant logical cogency, much less experimental evidence, in favor of such a sweeping denial of the existence of sociality between *similar* individuals. For our purposes, social behavior exists wherever individuals interact; whether one is the equal of the other is sometimes an important, sometimes an unimportant, question. Differences undoubtedly exist between any two ants or worker bees. This does not necessitate the basing of our laws of behavior upon minute differences which are swallowed up in the almost complete identity of social responsiveness on the part of the two individuals. A warrior ant collaborating with another warrior, or a worker collaborating with another worker, presents social behavior just as real as the kind of behavior imposed by the division of labor when the worker and the warrior interact in accordance with another pattern. A thousand men in a battalion responding uniformly to an order and to the social situation of one another's presence are at the moment behaving socially just as much as if each one of the thousand had a different order to execute. Nevertheless, an "integral" social psychology presents an exceedingly important task for the experimentalist.

The data in the present chapter consider the adult as a *formed* individual in our own society; they approach him heavily armed with measuring sticks which, in the nature of the case, fail to give the kind of data which permit the statistical separation of nature from nurture. Instead of asking what things may be regarded as due to innate predispositions and what as the product of environment, we shall, with regard to such methods as are now to be described, content ourselves for the most part with the statement that in our society and under the given conditions of measurement, these *adult differences* are actually found. The point of view, then, is not essentially analytical, but descriptive. At times we shall have occasion to refer in passing to constitutional and environmental theories, but the substance of the chapter is an attempt, not to answer questions dealing with nature and nurture, but to describe the methods and results of measurements of the personality traits of adults in our own society, whose characteristics are so indelibly stamped with the civilization in which they have grown up as to make the "nature and nurture" question unanswerable. Intelligence tests have gone far enough to permit a genuine statistical study of nature and nurture. The personality tests which follow have not yet done so.

We might well begin by considering the quantitative evidence as to just how much individuals do differ from one another. On this point we have recently been presented with some consistent data. A considerable number of studies in which anatomical, physiological and psychological differences between persons have been precisely measured are compared, and it is shown that in general the top individual in a thousand is a little over twice as "good" as the bottom individual. More precisely, excluding the very lowest and the very highest individual in each one thousand, and comparing the second with the nine-hundred-ninety-ninth, we find that in most traits the ratio of the two raw scores is about one to two; it is found, for example, that the nine-hundred-ninety-ninth man weighs just about twice as much as the second man, that his blood pressure and pulse rate are just about double that of the second man, and so on. And it must be noted once more that these measurements must be taken simply as they stand as applicable to the *adult in our community*. Even nutrition and climate are known to affect such characteristics markedly. We are attempting here merely to describe how people actually differ under the social conditions best known to us. The zero point in these cases is the absolute zero of the measuring instrument, e.g., *no* pounds, *no* inches, *no* heartbeat.

It is of special interest, however, to note the differing ratios of various kinds of traits and abilities. If several measures of each type are grouped together, these prove to be as follows: body temperature, 1.03:1 (though this involves questionable assumptions regarding the zero point); linear measurements of body, 1.30:1; measures of metabolic rates, 1.39:1; measures of body circumference, 1.52:1; measures of physiological function, 2.07:1; measures of motor coordination and speed of movement, 2.23:1; measures of body weight, 2.33:1; and measures of perceptual and intellectual abilities, 2.58:1. Evidence is presented to show that the differences in degree of variability among the several traits and capacities are dependent upon the complexity of the latter. Thus, for example, body weight is more variable than stature because it is a function of a greater number of factors; and mental age (chronological age held constant) is more variable than body weight for the same reason. This leads to interesting speculations concerning the variability of the presumably still more complex traits associated with personality and character. But measures of these are constructed without the firm foundation of a known zero point, nor are their units of measurement (with few exceptions, such as certain attitude scales) known to be equivalent. At any rate, no such data are included in these studies.

Physiological Measurements as Clues to Personality

Personality *manifestations* rather than personality *determinants* are the object of our immediate concern. Nevertheless, there is one set of individual differences of the latter sort which can scarcely be ignored. In view of the obvious relation between some mental traits and some physical traits, there have, since antiquity, naturally enough been efforts to define temperament in terms of anatomical or physiological characteristics. Not only crude notions regarding the relation between shape of head or length of fingers and such mental traits as "intellectuality" and "refinement," but more subtle assumptions—for example, those regarding the psychological effect of the body fluids—have been prevalent throughout recorded history. It is only recently that either physiology or psychology has been able to use terms stable and definite enough to make comparisons of this sort possible in any exact sense; but the crop of personality theories which has arisen from this soil in recent years is already too abundant to be reviewed.

For some of these attempts at a physiological definition of personality there is at least some respectable evidence.

A pioneer study of the relation between emotional dispositions and body make-up is Hammett's study of metabolism. He contrasts the stable with the hair-trigger type of emotional make-up, and proceeds to elaborate blood chemistry studies involving urea, creatinine, creatine, uric acid, amino acid, sugar, etc. The coefficient of variability for each of these blood constituents is determined for each individual, and the sum of these is taken as the "total variability of the intermediary metabolism of the person." On this scale, the variabilities of seventeen persons ranged from 130 to 76 during an observation period averaging about a month. The emotional status of the individuals was gauged from observations of physicians in contact with emotionally upset patients, as well as from the author's observations. All of the nine ranking highest in metabolic instability were persons with definitely unstable emotional make-up on the basis of clinical observations (which Hammett briefly describes). The remainder appeared to be considerably less unstable, several of those toward the bottom of the distribution being classified as apathetic or phlegmatic. Ratings and correlation devices are not attempted. The whole study is of a highly tentative sort.

In one of the most promising reports within the field of body chemistry in recent years, a low but apparently reliable inverse relation was demonstrated between emotional excitability and body acidity, as tested in blood and urine. The determinations were particularly careful, and for almost the first time suggested that objective chemical methods might, in part, unravel the complicated tangle of emotional make-up. But these results were not confirmed by others, whose work appears equally meticulous. A more recent study suggests what is probably the fundamental reason for this disagreement. Concentrating primarily upon the problem of individual stability in regard to several chemical measures, this experimenter found that *on the same day* at least three of them were reasonably constant. Rank order correlations for fourteen subjects tested before and after a three-hour rest period were .93, .79, and .97 for cholesterol, sugar, and creatinine, respectively. But when the same measures were twice repeated at succeeding intervals of three weeks, five of the six measures proved very inconstant; the reliability coefficient (average of correlations between first and second, first and third, and second and third determinations) for the sixth, cholesterol, was .67. It is not surprising, therefore, that these measures showed low and variable correlations with Bernreuter and intelligence test scores. The individual variability of the measures is neatly demonstrated by a further experiment: the experimenter acted as subject for a period of ten weeks, measures being taken twice weekly; during this period his life was carefully routinized, diet in particular being highly uniform. In spite of these precautions, there was about the same degree of variability among the twenty repeated measures for the same subject, as among the same measures for the nineteen subjects of the main experiment, all taken on the same day.

But some subjects had proved more variable than others. Hence the variability itself was taken as a clue. Using as a measure of this the sum of the coefficients of variability of the blood constituents of the same individual, the experimenter found variability to be correlated with Bernreuter neuroticism score to the extent of .41, which is barely three times its probable error. This serves, of course, as partial confirmation of Hammett's work, in spite of the former's different (and superior) method of diagnosing emotional instability. It thus appears that biochemical factors are, indeed, related to personality differences, but so far the latter appear to be functions not of single measurements, but of their variabilities.

Such physiological measures as blood pressure, pulse rate, vital capacity, and strength of grip have shown equally little relationship to personality characteristics. Correlation methods have quite uniformly shown low and unreliable coefficients between all of these variables and scores on tests both of intelligence and of personality traits. Perhaps the most definite relationship of this sort to be reported is to be found in a lengthy review of cardio-respiratory variations in relation to personality. It concludes as follows: "It would appear that in three important conditions in which the emotional life of the patient is primarily involved, i.e., schizophrenia, manic-depressive psychosis, and psychopathic personality, there is a definite tendency toward a lowered basal metabolism reading. The evidence points most strikingly to the tendency toward low basal metabolism in schizophrenia, this fact being consistently noted by every observer." It would not do, of course, to conclude from this that low basal metabolism is a determining cause of these conditions. It might well be a result of the changed manner of life of such patients, particularly those within institutional walls. At any rate, we have no comparable data for non-psychotic patients.

Another common approach to personality measurement is the study of emotions as revealed through changes in body resistance to an electric current. Some of these studies seem to indicate that such resistance is a good indicator of emotion experienced at the moment; others, that it is an indicator of bodily changes which in many cases are not particularly associated with emotion. We cannot enter here upon a controversial physiological problem; we note only the important point that this technique, in the hands of those most competent to show its significance for emotionality, seems to give support to the notion of specificity rather than of generality in emotional responses. Intercorrelations of responses to many different situations are low (even negative ones are found) and the cases in which the emotional response to a stimulus permits good prediction as to the emotional response to another stimulus occur only where the two stimuli are very similar.

The type of investigation described on pages 773-775 may prove to have some value in indicating group trends, but there is little evidence that such measures can ever be used for individual prediction. Instead of citing further experiments, we shall content ourselves with quoting from one experimenter who has himself carried on continued research in this field and whose review, from which we quote, is a careful summary of 247 titles appearing between 1929 and 1932. "From this literature," he concludes, "the reviewer is convinced that there is really no adequate evidence that electrical phenomena of the skin are of necessity associated with any psychological event. . . . There is really no justification for anyone using any present galvanometer technique or method as a measure of, or a criterion of, any of the traditional psychological categories, personality traits, or social relationships of the individual."

It is natural to expect a great deal from such physiological methods; in fact, they must be admitted to have a *prima facie* claim to consideration. Even a non-quantitative hypothesis in this field may be stimulating. For example, we must seriously consider Kretschmer's suggestion that endocrine factors produce mental characteristics just as they produce characteristic body forms (so that certain kinds of personalities go with certain kinds of bodies). But correlations between physical traits and mental characteristics are usually so low that even if they are entirely reliable statistically, they are of practically no value in individual cases. It is not, therefore, in the physiological approach to personality that we are likely to find anything upon which we can lay much stress. This is not tantamount to saying that anatomical and physiological differences are of minor importance. Some differences, notably endocrine, are undoubtedly important. The trouble is that we cannot isolate and measure the very things which we know are most significant. Individual differences in secondary sex characteristics, for example, as well as in motility and general activity, are known to be, at least in part, endocrine affairs, but except for "basal metabolic rate" there are no accurate methods of measuring endocrine make-up. The picture is further confused by the fact that the person with the theoretically active make-up, having a high basal metabolism, may learn to slow down, that is, may learn that in order to get along in life he must "go slow." Paradoxically, then, the person who is actually active may not be the one who, on the basis of a sheer physiological analysis, ought to be so.

For reasons such as these, the study of individual differences in social traits must be, for the most part, conducted in terms not of inner propensities or physiological predispositions, but of actual samplings of conduct or measurable tendencies toward conduct. Behavior can only be predicted from behavior. As in the measurement of character in middle childhood, so at the adult level we shall have to construct our hypothesis about individual differences in social traits in terms of what individuals do, how consistent they are, how well they conform to (or how much they differ from) the average of the groups to which we assign them, and the interrelation between the various habit systems or traits which are separately measured.

TYPES OF PERSONALITY MEASUREMENTS

The term "personality" has reference to characteristics in which individuals differ from one another. But which characteristics—and how many and how broadly conceived—are of significance to the social psychologist? For some investigators and some theorists, even the knowledge that an individual may be spotted at a given point on a continuum representing degrees of a certain trait (no matter how narrow, if only it is reliably measured) is important; out of such bricks is the personality edifice conceived to be constructed. For others such information is not only unimportant, but untrue to the very essence of what personality is. Such attempts are akin to "measuring" a trail of summer moonlight across a pine-sheltered lake in terms of candle-power and inches. One measures personality differences *in toto*, or one has missed them entirely.

Differences such as these spring not so much from disagreement as to what is true—no one would deny, for example, that very high and very low scores in a test of ascendance-submission almost certainly reflect true differences in respect to that characteristic—as from divergent beliefs as to what it is important to know. To continue the simile, the measurement of moonlight on water in terms of candle-power and inches is inadequate not because it is descriptively inaccurate, but because it fails completely to refer to the original experience. We suspect that much of the dissatisfaction with the method of single-trait measurements of personality has been of this sort, though other cogent criticisms may, as we shall see, also be offered. For the purposes of interpreting the existing quantitative data we shall take a position similar to that of May, according to whom personality is viewed as the social stimulus value of the individual. This demands from personality measurement an accounting of all that makes the individual a different kind of stimulus from his neighbor. On the other hand, it does not demand that the account be rendered in terms qualitatively like the original commodity, any more than a balance sheet need be pictured in hieroglyphs of cattle and corn. But this would still be inadequate to many proponents of the total-personality point of view, and we do not imply that rather widely diverging schools of thought may so easily be reconciled. We shall, of course, present samples of both extremes in method, as well as of many lying between the extremes.

For purposes of clear analysis it is of the utmost importance to define the term "trait." The basic assumptions of the various systems for the exploration of personality require definitions of a trait in terms of the general dynamics of behavior. We shall content ourselves with indicating the meaning of the term "trait" from the point of view of those types of personality theory which have led to quantitative research.

From a biological point of view which stresses only the basic outline of the organism regardless of this or that specific kind of modification, a trait may be a special sensitiveness of an organ or system such as an endocrine gland or a pathway through the mid-brain. It may at times be a broad general disposition, a way in which the organism functions. Speed, for example, or jerkiness (irregularity in tempo) or perseveration may be a biological trait pervasive through the system and not necessarily reflected through one organ or system exclusively. Ultimately a trait can be defined either anatomically or physiologically. Most of them which appear in clinical practice today are clearly reflections of thresholds in the central or autonomic nervous systems. In so far as a trait of timidity or aggressiveness can be stated in simple biological language, it appears to be primarily the expression of low general thresholds for fear or for rage.

From a standpoint stressing the importance of the conditioned response (a standpoint which we shall broadly call "behavioristic") the trait is not so much a general disposition as a disposition called out or manifested in particular situations. We deal not so much with timidity in general as with the fear of animals or dark places; not so much with aggressiveness as with aggressiveness toward brothers and sisters, or toward strangers. The conditioned response emphasis usually denies us the privilege of assuming universal transfer or generalization. "Trait" is a name for a certain kind of response manifested in a particular kind of situation.

From the psychoanalytic point of view, a trait is the way in which the basic drives have found an outlet. Sadistic behavior, for example, is a trait in that the dominating impulses, because of failure of repression and sublimation, have learned to vent themselves in particular forms of cruelty. What we have elsewhere called canalization permits a form of energy to direct itself on the external world through one mechanism. Of special interest is the "oral character type" in which the mouth, originally source of the all-important food supply, has served also for a variety of other satisfactions (cf. page 304). The thumb-sucking, nail-biting, gum-chewing activities indicate that the oral zone has become of paramount importance as a way of obtaining gratification. Upon this earlier and shorter conception of oral eroticism has been erected a much more refined and well-worked-out doctrine of traits and interests. The individual who is at first specially prone to emphasize oral satisfactions, because of special need of nourishment or special difficulty in obtaining it, may develop toward this source of food a general attitude of dependence which can easily in time become a generalized parasitism. The whole world is a world to be drunk in, absorbed, assimilated, enjoyed, not a world to be managed and mastered. The original emphasis upon the oral *zone* may disappear. The important thing is not the zone but what one might call the oral attitude. A struggle in connection with the weaning process or a long difficulty in getting adequate and satisfactory attention from the mother may lead ever afterward to a generalized attitude of infantism and unwillingness to see anything in life beyond a universal source of good things to which one is entitled and for which nothing is to be given in return. From a psychoanalytic point of view, therefore, the original emphasis upon this or that zone has been replaced by an emphasis on a basic way of responding.

Despite the very sharp differences between Adler's individual psychology and psychoanalysis, it seems to us that the two use the term "trait" in almost identical senses. Adler's style of life is not *specific conduct*, but a *way of living*. There is, however, this difference. Though individual psychology conceives the trait as a generalized way of facing life, the trait is never a component part in the whole personality. It is rather a way in which the basic style of living is expressed. The individual's conception of his goal and his way of achieving it colors and sets limits to each trait, no matter how broad.

This leads us to the very gateway of Gestalt psychology, which indeed defines "trait" almost exactly as does Adler. However, a great many of the traits upon which the Gestaltist lays stress are ways of behaving which do not seem necessarily explicable in terms of fundamental *purpose*. They reflect the way in which the organism is built, frequently with as much attention to anatomical and physiological structure as to goal or attitude. The most explicit exponents of Gestaltist doctrine who have actually gathered research data to support their hypothesis, Allport and Vernon, have argued that the significant traits of personality are broad generic ways of moving, thinking, and perceiving. The three factors of "area," "emphasis," and "centrifugality" (cf. page 853) which they believe they have found in a mass of objective data on expressive movement are not likely to be expressions of style of life. They spring partly from attitude, to be sure, but attitude as an extremely complex aspect of the whole bodily and mental organization. These investigators are suspicious of environmental explanations and appear to expect in time to discover deep trends which lie largely in the way in which the organism is built.

Though a clarification here is arbitrary, it seems to us that these and other conceptions of trait now prevalent among those who use quantitative method fall into two general classes: those which define "trait" in terms of response alone without specifying stimulus, and those which define it in terms of the whole stimulus-response pattern. A general measure of aggressiveness, for example, is very distinct from a measure of aggressiveness toward animals. A general measure of nervous instability is very different from a measure of nervous instability in the presence of a social superior. There seem, in fact, to be both kinds of traits in human nature. But it seems to be of some importance to decide which kind of trait one is investigating before he constructs a measuring instrument. The point seems so important to us that we have grouped most of the personality measures described in the present chapter in accordance with this broad, twofold scheme. To put the matter in a form usable for statistical purposes, the term "trait" may refer (1) *simply to general likelihood of behaving in a defined manner, without reference to variations in the situation,* or (2) *to a given kind of behavior in a particular situation only.* In the former sense a trait is simply the amount of reactivity in the direction Y, whereas in the latter it is the amount of reactivity of the type Y when confronted with the situation X. The former kinds of traits are conceived as "hair triggers," ready to be easily touched off by almost anything; the latter, as responses to the form and direction of the impact applied to the organism. Since the organism is always selective to some degree, the distinction is not absolute but will serve for preliminary purposes. These two uses of the term are, of course, reflected in the experimental literature, to which we now turn.

The Measurement of Traits Conceived as Response Tendency

The very conception of a trait as response tendency is based, of course, upon the assumption that some behavior tendencies are common to a wide variety of situations. It is as if each individual possessed a certain threshold for the type of behavior in question. While the threshold may be presumed to vary within certain limits, the ease or the difficulty with which such behavior will be elicited is thus presumed to be more or less constant for the individual. The problem to be faced in the measurement of traits, so conceived, is that of getting such a representative total picture of behavior in a wide variety of everyday situations that we are sure of a stable general tendency. What we want is not one sharp, clear portrait, but a series of superimposed profiles.

There are, in general, two methods of obtaining such measurements. One may, in the first place, request a third party to make a "group profile" for us; this is the rating method, in which we rely upon the judgment and fusing ability of someone in a position to summarize a series of observations and impressions. The dangers of the method lie in the fact that a given rater is himself a more or less unknown variable; his ratings are the joint product of his own personality and that of the subject. The other common method is to obtain from the subject verbal responses as to most frequent past behavior or most probable present behavior in a wide variety of situations in which the trait might appear. This is the questionnaire method. It is subject to some of the weaknesses of ratings, since questionnaire replies are a form of self-ratings, which involve certain constant errors. But these verbal responses may themselves be considered as behaviors, whether "truthful" or not, and so this is by no means a fatal weakness. The value of the method is determined largely by the care with which items are originally selected, and with which they are eliminated or retained following statistical analysis of replies. In the first case, the response tendency is threshed out for us by the rater; the second method demands that it be sifted out by statistical means during the process of perfecting the measuring instrument. The widest variations of caution and refinement are to be found among the many hundreds of tests and questionnaires that have been applied.

Turning first to an examination of rating methods, we may stop briefly to inquire whether repeated observation under varied circumstances is actually necessary for dependable ratings. Are first impressions of any value? Can personality be "sized up at sight"? The matter may best be tested where the objective tests are the best, for it is only where tests are themselves reliable and valid that we can tell how good the sizing up by other individuals really is. Striking data along such lines were first published nearly twenty years ago. Photographs had been taken of twelve children who had been tested on the Yerkes-Bridges point scale for intelligence. They represented an extreme range, from very bright to feeble-minded.

These photographs were presented to several groups of subjects who were asked to rank the pictures in accordance with the intelligence of the child. Nine physicians formed one group of judges. Correlations of their judgments with intelligence test scores ranged from .28 to —.21, with an average of .05, that is to say, just about what would have been expected if they had made sheer guesses without even looking at the pictures. For fourteen psychologists, the correlations varied from .45 to —.63, with an average of .18. For seventeen teachers, they ranged from .37 to —.29; for eleven students, from .29 to —.30, and for eleven "miscellaneous" judges, from .52 to —.51.

Similar procedures have since been used repeatedly. In general, it may be said that the early findings were confirmed, though judgments of this kind are slightly better than chance, particularly as applied to individuals who make exceedingly high or exceedingly low scores on intelligence tests. It is interesting to note, as one probable cause of mistaken judgments, that such irrelevant factors as "pleased expression," "snarl," and "averted eyes" are mentioned by the judges as influencing their decisions.

Rather surprising results of attempts to judge certain traits from voice alone have been reported. In one experiment three unseen speakers (selected as being diverse but not extreme in personality and voice) read identical material to several groups of students ranging in number from 32 to 85. The speakers were then rated on several personality characteristics. In four of six experiments ratings on extroversion-introversion were no better (or slightly worse) than they would have been if made completely at random; but in the other two experiments ratings corresponded to questionnaire scores to a degree far exceeding chance expectations. Ratings on ascendance-submission (as compared with Allport test scores) were more successful: four of five groups of raters exceeded chance approximation to test scores by very large and reliable differences. In a later radio experiment, from which nearly 300 replies were received, extroversion-introversion ratings achieved a degree of accuracy far above chance expectation, but ascendance-submission ratings were reliably below what they would have been by chance. The small number of speakers, together with voice-personality combinations that might or might not happen to correspond with stereotypes of what such combinations should be, is cited by the authors as having much to do with the varying degrees of success of the experiment. There is every reason to suppose that, by and large, voice and personality are related, for voice may conceivably be a cause, a result, or a symptom of certain personality characteristics. There is also every reason to suppose that such relationships are not linear ones for which equations could be written. This is clearly a case where, if there is any relationship to be noted, it must be through the mediation of judges, rather than by "objective" means exclusively. It must be emphasized that the methods illustrated here may lead to distinctly better than chance identification of some persons and worse than chance identifications of others, the reasons usually being complex and obscure.

When success is obtained, this seems to depend not on the physical structure of face, hands, voice, etc., but upon habitual behavior. The reader has doubtless heard of various schemes according to which whole lists of personality traits may supposedly be divined from such physiognomic traits as complexion and convexity of profile. Carefully obtained ratings, when compared with meticulous physical measurements, have utterly failed to confirm any of these alleged relationships. The "moral" of the story is not that no inkling whatever as to character may be gained from quick impressions, but rather that fixed physical characteristics have no invariable significance as personality indicators. This is shown by an experimenter who, after making an elaborate survey of the characteristics which seem to result in a student's being considered physically attractive or unattractive, proceeded to ascertain the degree of "liking" which resulted from these separate characteristics. His results showed that fixed and unchangeable physical attributes, such as shape of the head, width of the hands, etc., were related hardly at all to "general attractiveness," while things which the individual *did*, his behavior traits as shown by "nervousness," "nature of laugh," "tendency to cry," etc., seemed of considerable importance. The general trait, "expressive behavior pleasing," sums up the results well. This, together with extent of acquaintance, went a long way toward causing the individual to be favorably received. It would appear that physical attractiveness—consisting mostly of gracefulness, good manners, cheerfulness, and similar appealing "physical" traits—is more important, both in personal friendships and in general campus popularity, than are either fixed physical attributes, on the one hand, or general intelligence, on the other. A vicious circle is, of course, often easily established, in which a slight physical defect leads to inferiority feelings, and the inferiority feelings, in turn, to self-consciousness and awkward and generally unattractive behavior.

Do some individuals consistently show more ability in "sizing up" personality than others? At least one experimental attempt to answer the question has been made. Eight tests of ability to judge the personalities of strangers were devised; these included identifying facial emotions of standard photographs, identifying photographs of representatives of various occupations, ranking photographs for various personality traits, writing character sketches from photographs, and matching samples of handwriting and composition with biographical material. Some of the forty-eight judges appeared to possess an unexpected degree of intuitive ability, and there were positive correlations between success in each of the eight tests and measures of intellectual and artistic ability. Total scores of all the eight tests, when correlated with the sum of seventeen artistic and intelligence tests, produced a coefficient of .60. Nevertheless, so little consistency of success was shown that the author concludes against the existence of any general trait of intuitive ability; "it is not possible to discuss the characteristics of the good or bad judge of personality in general." Accuracy of judgment, he goes on to say, depends upon the person judged, the particular characteristic concerning which the judgment is made, and the conditions under which it is made. Any judgment of one person by another is therefore a unique event, and no particular set of habits characterizing any single judge will invest him with intuitive powers in general.

Results from these experiments with methods of impression are meager, but two general hypotheses appear: (1) that group judgments may be fairly good where individual errors tend to cancel, but if loaded with constant errors they may be practically useless; (2) that judgments made from behaviors are more dependable than those made from static features. In general, these hypotheses seem useful in approaching the very different problem of rating *known individuals* according to their degree of possession of some characteristic.

We turn, therefore, to a consideration of ratings based on more adequate observation. We have already referred (page 278) to the fact that even in relation to the study of social behavior of children, where objective experimental and observational methods are so much more developed, ratings nevertheless fill a real need in the process of getting important data on personality. That the degree of their value will decrease in proportion to the increase of *convenient objective* methods of studying behavior is most probable; but for the present their use is, of course, relied upon even more by students of adult personality than by students of child behavior. Ratings are, by definition, quantitative; for, in general, what is popularly regarded as an "all or none" affair tends, in the psychologist's eyes, to be regarded as a question of degree. Thus, the "inferiority complex" is regarded not as an integer, but as a variable whose magnitude differentiates people over a wide range. The *reality* of the inferiority complex, in the sense that there actually is a *constellation of traits which hang together*, as defined by Adler and his followers, has been shown by asking students to rate themselves and to have two associates rate them independently. A consistent grouping of such traits as the Adlerians have described was found; but instead of having or not having it, the method presupposes having a *degree of it*. Ratings have therefore proved useful for correlation studies, and their value can usually be gauged to some degree by their consistency with other criteria.

The value of ratings must be judged not all at once, but in terms of the conditions under which they may be trusted. It was found long ago that judges agreed with one another to a marked degree (over +.60) in rating individuals on certain traits, whereas on others agreement was preposterously low. More recently Conrad has shown that the reliability of ratings is to some degree a function of the individual rated, as well as of the trait: some children were rated much more reliably than others, depending, in part at least, on how pertinent the given trait was to the given child. If we wish to know the value of ratings for measuring personality, it is important to know a great deal more than the fact that one should have three judges who have known the subject well, etc. It is important to know just how well this particular trait is likely to be judged by this type of judge, as they judge this kind of subject. A good deal of recent work has been done in the attempt to define just what it is that makes for a good judge of a given person in a given situation. It is this kind of analytic study which is necessary if rating methods are to have any real value for the use to which they are put.

A typical instance of the practical application of ratings is a study of the American Council Rating Scale. The graphic form of rating scale which was used is illustrated below, for one of the five traits included:

Does he need constant prodding or does he go ahead with his work without being told?

| Needs much prodding in doing ordinary assignments | Needs occasional prodding | Does ordinary assignments of his own accord | Completes suggested supplementary work | Seeks and sets for himself additional tasks |

Please record here instances that support your judgment.

This investigator found (as predictable on theoretical grounds, and as found empirically by others also) that the reliability of the scale was improved by increasing the number of judges. Thus, the correlations of three ratings of 107 freshmen with those of three other raters (as predicted by the Spearman-Brown formula) varied from .35 for "appearance" to .73 for "industry." But when fraternity men rated one another on the five traits, ten ratings correlated with ten other ratings yielded reliability coefficients of .90 or above for industry, appearance, leadership, and definition of objectives; for emotionality the coefficient was .68. These traits not only reveal reasonably reliable individual differences, but they are related to other characteristics of educational significance. For twenty-two fraternity men, composite rating scores were related to leadership (as measured by participation in various activities) to the extent of .66. For the group of 107 college freshmen there was a correlation of .50 between first-semester grades and three ratings on industry. This is fully as high as the average correlation between grades and intelligence, and affords a type of information probably unobtainable except by rating methods.

The psychology of the rating process itself is of some interest, since ratings are inevitably a function of the judge as well as of the judged. The experiment cited on page 785 included measures of ability to rate friends as well as to judge strangers. Though intelligence and artistic ability showed some correlation with the latter, they were not related to success (as judged by objective measures or by group judgments) in rating acquaintances. Not one of five tests of rating ability was reliably correlated with composite scores of intelligence, of "sociality," or of "artisticness"; and not one of twenty-four trait measures was reliably correlated with composite score of rating ability. Rating-ability-in-general, then, exists no more than does intuitive-ability-in-general. Nevertheless, as Conrad and others have pointed out, there are individual differences in rating ability as regards particular traits and particular subjects. One among several possible reasons for this has been to some extent experimentally verified. On the hypothesis that the Freudian mechanism of projection might be operative, projection is defined, for experimental purposes, as the attributing to others of traits which an individual possesses but fails to recognize in himself. Members of three college fraternities rated themselves and each other on stinginess, obstinacy, disorderliness, and bashfulness. An interesting difference appears between two groups of those rated by their fellows as possessing more than an average amount of these undesirable traits, namely, those who recognized the traits in themselves, and those who did not. The latter group consistently rated others as possessing more of these traits which were unrecognized in themselves, than did the former group. This finding seems to us less important for the doubt it casts upon the validity of ratings than for the possibilities it introduces of discovering personality characteristics of raters. There is no reason why the assignment of ratings should not be considered as behavior which may be as objectively studied as galvanic reflexes.

Self-ratings, though still much used, have shown themselves fairly consistently to have rather serious intrinsic limitations, so that their usefulness is limited to certain special circumstances. It has been shown, for example, that although a group of twenty-five college junior women and a group of twenty-five senior women agreed fairly well when a ranking of any individual by the other twenty-four on a number of social traits was involved, self-ratings deviated in a fairly consistent way from ratings by others. Individuals tended, despite such efforts at fairness as were made, to overestimate themselves on desirable traits and to minimize undesirable ones.

Other methods of comparing one's opinion of himself with his opinion of others have yielded similar results. For example, a group of women students was given an anonymous self-rating sheet; a week later the same items were presented for rating, except that the word "average" was substituted for "self," and the word "she" (referring to the average) substituted for "you." After another week they were asked to make ratings on the same items for "the ideal college woman." This method also revealed a consistent overestimation of self as compared with estimation of the average students, and even a considerable number of cases where the self was rated higher than the ideal college woman. There seems to be no doubt that even an anonymous rating device of this sort does obtain pretty consistent self-overevaluations.

Such tendencies may, of course, simply be a phase of our own culture, and may therefore not be typical in other cultures. With precisely this in mind, twenty-one Chinese students in different institutions in the United States were asked to rate themselves on a five-point scale with reference to six desirable traits. Each had also to rate all the other students on the list whom he knew intimately; on the average, each rated eight others besides himself. Despite the instructions, "Please keep in mind that you don't purposely underrate yourself," the great majority did underrate themselves as compared with the standing assigned to them by those who knew them.

This interesting attempt to study culturally rooted self-attitudes failed, however, to be confirmed in a later investigation. The subjects, Chinese students in China, showed the same tendency to overestimate their own desirable qualities that has been generally observed in this country. Results are highly consistent for four groups, of varying ages and of large numbers. We are therefore inclined to agree with the later investigators that the underestimation found among Chinese students in this country may be attributed to insufficient confidence in anonymity, or to changes induced by study in a foreign country. If so, the "humility" which is so prominent in the American stereotype of the Chinese is based upon cultural externals of a superficial nature, rather than upon genuine personality differences imprinted by culture.

Self-ratings have also been studied in relation to preferences with a view to a more specific analysis of those aspects of personality in which one tends to overrate oneself. Large and significant differences were found between self-rating in extroversion and inferiority feelings on the one hand, and, on the other, ratings indicating *preferences* for these traits. There were thus some striking exceptions to the general law of self-overevaluation. When, however, the material was subdivided into ratings on *temperament* and ratings on *"socially approved" traits*, an interesting difference appeared between the two. People who were rated by others as having a certain temperament (e.g., extroversion) preferred this temperament, and those who preferred it tended to have it. But in relation to socially approved traits, no such positive correlation appeared.

A similar technique has more recently been used; two groups of college students filled out the Bernreuter personality inventory. The inventories were then filled out again, directions to the first group being to do it "in the manner which you believe will result in your gaining the greatest possible degree of social approval"; and to the second group, "as though you were the sort of person you would like to be." The two scores thus obtained for all subjects in dominance, self-sufficiency, and neurotic tendency showed no reliable correlations for either group, except in regard to dominance for the second group ($r = .39$). Differences between "true" and "desirable" mean scores were highly reliable for both groups. The purpose of the experiment was to demonstrate that questionnaires of the self-rating type are not necessarily invalidated by errors in the direction of overevaluation of self.

It will have been observed that while we have ostensibly been discussing self-ratings, the last two investigations cited have made use of more or less "standard" instruments of self-report. These latter are variously referred to as inventories, schedules, questionnaires, and even tests. Such instruments actually are, of course, types of self-ratings. So loose has our terminology become that there are no clear lines of demarcation between self-ratings, questionnaires, inventories, and tests—to mention them in the order of what perhaps should be least to most objective. But a more significant scaling of these various measures would be in terms not of their names, but of the process by which the individual items are validated, i.e., are demonstrated to be related to the trait in question. At the "lower" end of such a scale would appear questionnaires composed of items collected on a sheerly *a priori* basis, without benefit of later refinement. At the "higher" end would be found such inventories and tests as have emerged from a careful item analysis of responses, which has demonstrated that those particular items belong together. Our discussion will be limited to those of the latter type. We shall not attempt to unsnarl the terminological tangle, but shall refer to the several measures by the names with which their authors have christened them.

One well-known method of asking disagreeable questions is the *psychoneurotic inventory*, or list of questions regarding personal adjustment or maladjustment, first used by Woodworth with army recruits, and now adapted for the use of adults in general. Some form of such an inventory has been given now to many hundreds of college students, with results that appear to be of value not only in helping individual college students who may have personality difficulties (loneliness, inability to make friends, inability to concentrate, nightmares, unbreakable habits, inferiority feelings, etc.), but in connection with the college administration (e.g., the prediction as to whether an applicant will benefit from some aspects of a college course). L. L. and T. G. Thurstone have prepared a psychoneurotic inventory based partly upon the Woodworth questions and partly upon other lists of such questions, and have found that in extreme cases it helped to explain some cases of failure of election to fraternities and sororities, just as similar data may serve to explain the failure of intelligent students to carry ordinary academic work.

The method of item validation used by the Thurstones (and others before them) has now become so common that it merits description. Either the "Yes" or the "No" answer to each question having been tentatively labeled as "neurotic," the number of questions thus answered was counted for each of some 700 student subjects. Of these, the fifty whose total scores were highest were compared with the fifty whose total scores were lowest, with respect to each of over 600 questions. The high-score group received higher mean scores on all but one question than the low-score group; the differences were statistically reliable for 223 of the questions, which were therefore selected to compose the inventory. Each item, in other words, was validated in terms of its agreement with the entire list of items. The odd-even reliability of the total inventory was .95.

Several attempts have been made in recent years to validate this and other psychoneurotic inventories by using psychiatric patients as subjects. Thus the median score of neurotic tendency of one group of hospitalized psychoneurotics is reported to be at the 80th percentile of a "normal" population. But no reliable difference in mean scores of neurotic tendency was found between another group of hospitalized mental patients and normal patients matched with them for age, race, occupation, and school grade. The authors attribute the lack of differentiating power of the instrument (the Bernreuter personal inventory) to the fact that the items had been logically rather than empirically evaluated. But if by empirical is meant "distinguishing between normal and psychotic," we should hardly expect an inventory meeting these requirements also to distinguish between various degrees of instability among non-psychotic subjects. Even though there are excellent clinical reasons for regarding instability within the normal pale as approaching psychosis as a limit, we have no certainty that the two types of individuals respond similarly to inventory items. And even though, as in the latter study, certain items are selected as being diagnostic for abnormal groups, their exact significance for other than near-psychotics remains uncertain.

A more reasonable "empirical" test would seem to be represented by an analysis of the responses of a group of students who had applied to a psychological clinic for assistance. The selection of 179 cases was made on the basis of completeness of case-history material available, which indicated that 98 of the subjects were clearly maladjusted, the other 81 showing only minor symptoms. The two groups were then compared as to scores on the Thurstone Personality Schedule, as follows:

Thurstone Score Range	98 Maladjusted Cases Number	Per Cent	81 Not Maladjusted Cases Number	Per Cent
0– 29 (lowest quartile)............	7	7	27	33
30– 74 (middle quartiles)..........	53	54	44	55
75–180 (highest quartile)...........	38	39	10	12

Three judges also rated each of the 98 cases for degree of maladjustment, on a five-point scale, and these ratings were then compared with Thurstone scores, with the following results (each case appears three times, in whatever category assigned by each judge):

Mean Rating	Number of Cases	Mean Thurstone Score
1 (least maladjusted)......	33	44.2
2	51	61.0
3	52	64.4
4	66	70.1
5 (most maladjusted)......	92	75.4

The range of scores in each group is not stated, but it is evident that, with possible individual exceptions, "those individuals considered sufficiently maladjusted as to require the services of a consulting psychologist showed far above the average scores on the personality schedule."

The chief objection which has been voiced to such methods of measurement is that scores depend largely upon how much subjects desire to reveal about themselves. Faced with repeated evidence that even some psychiatric patients receive very low neurotic scores on psychoneurotic inventories, one quite naturally concludes that high scores may be definitely symptomatic of neurotic tendency, but that low scores by no means indicate emotional stability. An instance in which scores were probably distorted by strong motivation to appear in a good light may be cited. Twenty student nurses at a training school were given "general success" scores based upon grades and supervisors' ratings of ward work. The mean Thurstone score of the five nurses whose "success" scores were highest was 47, the range being from 38 to 56, whereas those ranking lowest in success received an average Thurstone score of 23, their range being from 10 to 42. It is also indicated (though data are not given) that student ratings of each other with regard to general success show the same reversal of the expected relationship to Thurstone scores. The conclusion is that for these subjects the Thurstone schedule is "more of a measure of honesty and *naïveté* than of neuroticism." It is altogether probable, of course, that those whose success had led them to feel most secure would be most likely to respond in a forthright manner, and that those who regarded their success as uncertain had everything to lose by "confessing" to replies considered neurotic.

The Thurstone schedule (which we have discussed as typical of several psychoneurotic inventories) thus has a certain ability, at least under some conditions, to pick out extremely unstable individuals. But to what extent has it isolated the trait of "neuroticism"? The Thurstones' analysis by the method of internal consistency has been described (page 791). But the distinguishing power of many of their items was evidently limited to their own subjects. Thus one analysis of the responses of 146 male subjects revealed that many of the items reported by the Thurstones to have the most distinguishing power were very rarely answered in a neurotic manner, and others were scarcely distinguishing at all. The usefulness of the personality schedule would seem to derive from its bludgeon-like qualities: it contains so many items that, granted willingness to respond frankly, total score does indicate, roughly at least, degree of stability, or neurotic tendency. But bludgeons can scarcely be used for refined analysis, and 223 items can scarcely be said to have "isolated" a trait. The statistical root of the difficulty is this: while a certain degree of trait unity is demonstrated by the test of internal consistency, the unity is that of agreement with the original list of 600 questions, rather than that of coherence with each other directly. The criterion of trait unity (the 600 questions) is such only by assumption. The real test of trait unity lies in such forms of analysis as reveal coherence, occurring-togetherness. If a series of items can be found in which consistent patterns of response by different populations are found to occur, the existence of some trait has been demonstrated; what that trait is awaits the test of experience, clinical or other.

Such a statistical analysis has been made in at least one case. Since the procedure was too onerous to be applied to the entire list of

Thurstone items, the forty to which neurotic answers were most frequently given were selected for analysis. The subjects were 144 college women. The actual incidence of response to every pair of questions was then compared with what the incidence would be if responses were made by chance. Thus, if 18 of 144 subjects gave the neurotic answer to item No. 1, and 48 of 144 responded similarly to item No. 2, the chances of giving neurotic answers to both would be $\frac{18}{144} \times \frac{48}{144}$, or $\frac{6}{144}$. If, by actual count, the incidence is not far from six, there is no reason to assume that both questions are getting at the same trait. If the incidence far exceeds this—e.g., 16—they obviously "belong" together, for to answer the first neurotically is almost certainly to answer the second in the same manner. The discovery of several such questions, each of which thus shows considerably higher than chance incidence with each other one, would empirically "isolate" the trait, the unity of which would be incontestable. If too few items pass this test to result in reliable measurement, we must conclude either that our questions are inadequate, or that the trait cannot be measured by a direct question-asking procedure, or that the trait does not exist. The 25 items which best met this test, and which were answered in a neurotic manner with a certain minimum frequency by several populations, were selected and proposed for use as a shorter form. The odd-even reliability of this form proved to be .83; its correlation with total score, yielded by all 223 items, was .85. Certainly, then, nothing had been lost by way of validity, and considerable had been gained, in our estimation, by way of sharpening the instrument.

Procedures involved in the measurement, by self-report, of *introversion-extroversion* have followed closely those described for measuring neurotic tendency. Heidbreder's scale was constructed in precisely the manner described for the Thurstone Personality Schedule. The Neymann-Kohlsted test, as later revised, is composed of items found to distinguish between manic-depressive and schizophrenic patients. The assumption here is that manic-depressive psychosis is the *terminus ad quem* of extroversion, and schizophrenia, similarly, a very extreme form of introversion. This is indubitably true in some respects, though we have already asked whether question-answering behavior may not be radically altered in patients extreme enough to have been hospitalized. At any rate, the latter test, the revision of which was based upon responses of 65 manic-depressives and 60 schizophrenics, resulted in an "almost normal" distribution when submitted to 165 university students. A bimodal curve was obtained from scores of 16 manic-depressives and 22 schizophrenics, the scores of all but one of the latter group being lower than that of the lowest manic-depressive. The retest reliability coefficient, when submitted twice to 200 students, was .87.

That introversion-extroversion is almost certainly *not* a unit trait, in the sense described above, and as thus far measured, has now become evident. It was suggested as early as 1930 that not one trait but three—or perhaps three aspects of the same factor—were to be dealt with: intellectual, emotional, and social introversion and extroversion. This offers a plausible reason for the almost unbelievable disagreement among the various measures of the trait. According to a report made in 1927, almost no reliable intercorrelations were found among six supposed measures of introversion, and none as high as .40. Seven years later another investigator applied four measures (two of which had been developed during the interim) to a group of 172 students, with almost identical results; the only intercorrelation that approached .5 was between Bernreuter and Colgate scores, the former having been validated by the latter during its construction.

Two later studies are even more revealing. A "typical" test (composed of 35 items, each of which is included in at least three of the six most commonly used measures of introversion) was given to 930 students. An item analysis of their replies (by means of coefficients of contingency) showed that "no single general or universal factor runs through all the items." Indeed, a multiple factor analysis revealed no less than 18 factors among the 35 items; the most important of these were: tendency to shrink from the environment (especially social); emotional sensitiveness, or readiness to respond emotionally; impulsiveness; and egocentrism. "It was concluded that . . . in the usual test several related dimensions have been confused and forced together to form a single somewhat fictitious continuum." It is pointed out that often an affirmative reply to a given question is diagnostic of introversion, while a negative reply to the same question is not necessarily diagnostic of extroversion, and vice versa, although many of the existing questionnaires assume that opposite replies are equally diagnostic in opposite directions.

It should not be concluded that the concept of introversion-extroversion is valueless. We are confident that several important personality differences are included in it; indeed, that is the trouble—there are several, not one. If it has proved elusive under pursuit of measuring instruments we need only take the hint, and conclude that such a Proteus cannot be seized in all its forms at once.

A good deal of use has been made of the ascendance-submission test of F. H. and G. W. Allport. This is in a sense a self-rating device, but instead of rating themselves on abstract qualities, the subjects tell how they *habitually* behave in certain *specific* social situations. For example, to the question, "Are you embarrassed if you have greeted a stranger whom you have taken for an acquaintance?" the subject is asked to check one of the three replies: *Very much; Somewhat; Not at all.* More recently this test has been subjected to the test of internal consistency described (page 791) in connection with the Thurstone Personality Schedule. The suggested revision involves no fundamental changes, since the 30 (of the original 41) items which meet the test of consistency yielded scores correlating with original scores to the extent of .97 for 200 male subjects. Reliability coefficients for the revised form are not given; by the original scoring method, however, reliabilities compare well with those of other personality measures.

The test has been criticized as being overloaded with situations involving an academic atmosphere, and as revealing too clearly the trait that is being measured, since the order of alternative responses is always from "most ascendant" to "most submissive," or vice versa. After the test was revised to remove these defects, and shortened as suggested above, it was given to a group of store managers. The results illustrate the practical uses to which the test has been put: a considerable majority of those who were found "unsuccessful" within one year's period obtained *"submissive"* scores, and a similar number of those deemed "successful" made *"dominant"* scores. There was a correlation of .27 between dominance scores and ratings on store success. The trait was found to be of no value, however, in selecting supervisors in a manufacturing establishment.

As reported by one of its authors, the validity, when tested by ratings, differs greatly with the raters. It is necessarily difficult to decide whether this is due merely to the ineptitude of certain raters and the difficulty of defining ascendance-submission clearly, or whether the test itself fails to mark out and measure any distinct component in personality. Such methods represent, nevertheless, a very considerable improvement upon the self-ratings of abstract qualities which are still in use.

The Bernreuter Personality Inventory has within recent years come into wide use. It introduces no new techniques, except that of the simultaneous measuring of four traits by the differential scoring of the same item responses for the several traits. Three of the traits—introversion, neurotic tendency, and dominance—not only are "validated" against one or more of the measures which we have discussed in the preceding pages, but in the case of each of them questions have been taken with little or no change from the older forms. The fourth, self-sufficiency, was constructed by the author and its validity defended by the application of the method of internal consistency already described. The ingenious notion of measuring several dimensions of personality simultaneously has, however, introduced constant "errors" which have subjected the inventory to a heavy fire of criticism. Thus two of the traits (introversion and neuroticism) are so highly intercorrelated—the coefficient has repeatedly been found to be as high as the reliability of either trait itself—that the author has proposed dispensing entirely with one or the other of them. Unfortunately, however, other intercorrelations are also high; that between neurotic tendency and dominance is reported by the author to be —.83, which approaches very closely the respective reliability coefficients of the two traits. All this leads to the suspicion, partially confirmed, that the four series of weights assigned to the same responses for the measurement of the four traits are themselves intercorrelated (regardless of how responses are made) to such a degree as to render impossible the independent measurement of any of them. An extremely careful examination of responses to the Bernreuter inventory has recently been made by factor analysis and other methods. It seems probable, from this work, that two independent traits are isolable from Bernreuter's 125 items by means of revised scoring methods. The two are tentatively labeled self-confidence and sociability.

One of the simplest, most satisfactory, and most widely used of the personality measures is the Pressey cross-out (X-O) test. The trait which it is commonly assumed to measure is "emotionality." The test has the peculiar merit of being objective in a sense that the questionnaires and inventories just described are not—for the simple reason that there are no "questions" to answer. Moreover, the significance of any particular response is almost completely concealed, so that it is relatively difficult to strive for a "good" score. In its longer form it consists of four parts, each containing 25 lines of five words each. The directions at the top of page 1 instruct the subject to go through Part I of the test and cross out every word that suggests more that is unpleasant than is pleasant. He then goes back to the beginning and draws a circle around one word in each line to indicate the *most unpleasant*; that is, whereas in the first procedure he was to indicate *everything* unpleasant, he must now choose from each line the *most* unpleasant single word. Part II contains 25 lists of five words each, but in each case the subject must pick out those words from each list which are associated in his mind with a leading word given in capital letters, which stands off to the left of each line. Again having indicated in each line as many words as he wishes (as associated in his mind with the corresponding word on the left), he goes through the list again, drawing a circle around the word in each line which is *most closely* associated with the word at the left. In Part III he is confronted with 25 lists of five words each; first he is to mark every word which he thinks describes something which is *wrong*, and second, going through the list again, to encircle that word in each set which names the *worst* thing. Part IV presents another series of lists, in each of which the subject is to mark all the words indicating things about which he has ever *worried* and, on second reading, to encircle that word in each line which indicates the thing about which he has worried the *most*.

It will be seen that the total number of words crossed out is a rough index of "affectivity." Such information as there is suggests, however, that this aspect of the test is of little value. The important thing is whether or not the subject tends to *encircle those words which are encircled by others of his group*. In general, people agree more or less as to things which are very unpleasant, very wrong, and to be worried about. As in intelligence tests, an individual deviation here and there is of little consequence, but a large number of deviations from what a member of a given group would be expected to do suggests something unusual which may be worth following up. Pressey has found that the tendency to deviate, which he calls idiosyncrasy, is a valuable factor in gauging an individual's emotional adjustment. This is the case to such a degree as to indicate, in other studies, that X-O idiosyncrasy scores have much predictive value with reference to success in college work. Idiosyncrasy of a rather similar sort has been measured by Deutsch in terms of deviation from current conventional *standards of tastes*, using the pictures shown facing this page; "conformity" is here the opposite of idiosyncrasy.

The X-O test also measures emotional maturity—certain emotional responses which are frequent at one age disappear at later ages, while others are late in appearing. A college student who still clings to the moral attitudes and the worries of a child is apparently as much handicapped as one of inferior intellectual status. The dropping off of childish emotional responses and the accretion of adult responses is fairly clear cut. In extreme cases a good guess about an individual's peculiarities seems to be possible on the basis of the test records alone. Twenty records, for example, were mailed to the investigator, with no information except that some of these were from boys who were "disciplinary" problems, and others were from "good" boys. The task was to pick out the sheep and the goats. This was successfully done in seventeen of the twenty cases, on the basis of a few simple criteria relating to the presence of emotional responses differing widely from those of most boys of the same school grade.

One other approach to the measurement of trait differences by self-report methods may be noted. This is the controlled diary, in which the subject keeps a continuous record of his own behaviors of a certain type. A study of laughter serves as a striking example

See page 800.

"Choose the picture of the woman you consider the most beautiful."

See page 800.

"Choose the living quarters which attract you most."

of the use of the method. The cooperation of 100 women students was enlisted in the daily recording of *every situation which produced a laugh*. Over 4000 instances of laughter were recorded and classi-fied. The problem relates in part to *types of humor*; the purpose is to ascertain whether there is a consistent tendency to laugh at par-ticular kinds of situations. Through the diary data the author is led to accept the "superiority" and the "incongruity" factors which have long been so popular with those who have written on the theory of humor; the former was found to be more commonly reported in the diaries. The evidence seems to indicate that there *are* humor types—types which reveal themselves in the spontaneous record. From the point of view of method, it is of interest to note that strictly experi-mental devices failed to contribute anything to the problem. The diary, then, found out some things about individual differences for which the laboratory, at least at present, is ineffective.

As measures of amounts of reactivity of given kinds, such methods are of course subject to gross errors; numbers of instances recorded may be better measures of the conscientiousness of the subjects than of trait differences of the kind being studied. Hence the method is more suitable for analyzing the qualitative nature of the particular behavior and the situations in which it appears, than for the quan-titative study of individual differences. All this is shown in a recent report on students' adjustments in anger. Ninety-three students recorded their anger experiences during one week. The number of such responses reported ranged from 1 to 15 for men, and from 1 to 14 for women, the average frequency for men being 39 per cent greater than for women. They were particularly likely to occur in periods of "disequilibrium," including conditions of fatigue, hunger, pain, boredom, hurry, and disappointment. These conditions were reflected in the greater frequency of anger episodes just before meals, and just following week-ends by sorority and fraternity members, but just before week-ends by unaffiliated students. Duration of the episodes ranged from one minute to two days. The vast majority of them were directly classifiable as the thwarting of self-assertion, but women's reactions were toward persons nearly twice as frequently as those of men; the latter more frequently directed their anger at such objects as shoestrings, alarm clocks, and automobile tires. There was considerable variation in impulses felt, responses made, and the nature of the after-effects; in about half the cases anger responses were completely non-adaptive. It is scarcely surprising, therefore, to find the experimenter concluding that, "strictly speaking, there seems to be no such thing as an anger response. There are as many different manifestations as there are configurations of behavior patterns and social situations." There is little doubt that the straitjacket technique of quantitative measurement of such behaviors obscures more individual differences than it reveals.

The Measurement of Single-situation Traits

We have seen some of the difficulties and failures resulting from the attempt to measure a particular personality trait conceived as a general tendency to behave in a certain fashion in a variety of situations. Now what of measurement based upon the second conception of trait, i.e., the amount of reactivity of a given kind in a particular situation? This second approach, whatever its shortcomings prove to be, has at least the advantage that no *a priori* assumptions are made as to whether or not behaviors supposedly similar, though occurring under widely different sets of conditions, actually bear any relationship to each other. Evidence abounds that, for a considerable proportion of individuals, behaviors in different situations but subsumed under the same trait (in the first sense) actually bear no predictable relationship to each other. Hence the advantage just mentioned as favoring the second approach may turn out to be an important one.

Just as the measurement of trait, conceived in the first sense, almost of necessity is limited to paper-and-pencil methods, so now we shall find ourselves largely restricted to laboratory methods. The phrase "a particular situation" may, of course, be interpreted with various degrees of latitude, but so also, for that matter, may the term "laboratory." We invest the term with no meaning beyond that of control of *external* conditions, which are held constant for all subjects. This does not imply, of course, that resulting differences in behavior represent stable differences among subjects; internal variations are too uncertain to make it possible to control the total situation. But this is a weakness inherent in the laboratory method, and one to which we shall later recur.

We may well begin with one or two of the traits whose measurement by other means we have already discussed. Although there have been literally hundreds of inventories, questionnaires, tests, and rating scales devised to measure what is variously termed neurotic tendency, maladjustment, or emotional instability, there have been few attempts (and almost none of them successful) to measure the same tendency by more objective methods. Undoubtedly the chief difficulty is what might be referred to as the validation dilemma. In order to make sure that a given trait measure corresponds to anything real, one may use one of the "standard" inventories, or one may "standardize" the measure by means of subjects known to be unstable, such as psychotic patients. But both of these procedures are questionable: the uncertain validity of adjustment questionnaires has been discussed in the previous section, and the dangers of assuming that non-psychotic subjects, no matter how unstable, will behave in a particular test situation in a similar fashion to psychotics showing similar but more extreme personality deviations, has also been noted. The latter assumption is not, of course, an unreasonable one, but it has yet to be demonstrated.

A promising beginning, some years ago, made use of a simple maze constructed in high relief on a wooden panel, to be traced with the forefinger while the subject was blindfolded. Both time and errors were recorded for consecutive attempts until there were two successive trials without error. This task distinguished to some extent among ten boys selected from a group of over one hundred committed to a state school by a juvenile court as being extremely maladjusted, as against ten others selected as being highly stable and showing no behavior disorders. The stable group averaged slightly higher than the unstable group in age (the age range was 10 to 17 years) and also slightly higher in intelligence, but there was no reliable correlation, for the twenty subjects, between intelligence and maze performance. The differences in average maze performance of the two groups were far greater than those attributable to age or intelligence factors. The unstable group took, on the average, over 50 per cent more time and made more than twice as many errors as the stable group. The learning curves, constructed from plotting time and errors of successive trials, were, moreover, far more regular in appearance for the stable group. There was, however, considerable overlapping for all of these measures between the two groups. For example, in terms of irregularity of curve (measured in terms of standard deviations), the average variability of the unstable group was almost exactly equivalent to the maximum variability of the stable group. This test was later applied to a group of 100 delinquent boys and to 112 delinquent girls, and was not found to be a valid measure of emotional stability, or to correlate with other measures.

Three groups of subjects were employed, in another investigation, in an attempt to isolate traits associated with mental instability: hospitalized mental patients, psychiatric out-patients living at home, and graduate students. The total group numbered 43. The laboratory tests included the Rorschach ink blots (number of responses), the Wells word association test (average and variation of reaction time), speed of writing, speed of simple tasks like adding digits, perseveration (letters and digits written alternately), and oscillation (deviation from the mean 5-second score in tasks like adding digits). Subjects were also given the Bernreuter test. A factor analysis of the interrelationships of these scores revealed the presence of two factors, either of which neatly differentiated the three groups of subjects with very little overlapping. The factors were labeled "objectivity" (speed and fluctuations of response, revealing alertness to the environment) and "fluency" or "mobility of response to manifold stimulation." The same procedure was then repeated, with reformatory men, university students, public school teachers, and social workers as subjects. The intercorrelations were markedly lower, however, for this group of nearly 300 subjects, as were also the "factor loadings," or correlations of the various measures with the two factors. This is explained, reasonably enough, as being due to the much more limited range of "stability" among the latter group of subjects. But it does not dispose of the difficulty. It is of real interest to find that certain laboratory tests distinguish between "normal" and severely maladjusted but non-psychotic subjects, and between the latter group and psychotics—even though the factor of intelligence which indubitably is present in several of the tests is not controlled or partialed out. But for our purposes the results are still somewhat disappointing, for our chief concern is with "normal" variations of the adult personality. These techniques need to be repeated with groups of adults covering the entire range of stability, short of psychosis, and concerning whom there are adequate *clinical* data for validation purposes. It is a reasonable guess that the second group did approximate this range of stability, but the absence of clinical material concerning the subjects robs us of the all-important information as to what kinds of subjects obtained what kinds of scores.

Such an investigation, combining full clinical data with laboratory tests of run-of-the-mine adults, apparently has yet to be carried out. One or two other experiments, nevertheless, are worth reporting. In one of these, an elaborate series of psychological reactions was measured, the subjects being forty college students, largely freshmen, chosen as having a wide range of scores on the Thurstone Personality Schedule. An item analysis of responses revealed certain "constellations" of interrelated items, ranging in number from 6 to 25. Scores were calculated separately for each of these ten constellations, appropriate labels were assigned, and relationships to the various physiological measures, both singly and in groups, were computed. (Groupings were made in such fashion as to result in maximum intra-group correlations.) None of the single physiological measures correlated reliably either with total neurotic scores or with any of the constellation scores. But eight of ten constellation scores were found to correlate with *groups* of physiological measures, and the latter, termed "syndromes," were given labels corresponding to the constellations with which they correlated most highly. Several of the same physiological measures were included in more than one syndrome, but three non-overlapping syndromes emerged which showed at least reliable relationships to constellations of the same name. These relationships are given below. These coefficients, of course, are not high, nor does it seem possible that they could have been, for the constellation scores, based on responses to only a few items, are almost certainly of low reliability. This, however, is not a fatal fault; dependable measures of these same personality variations are not impossible of attainment. But the reliability of the physiological measures is more open to question; other investigators have found individuals to be highly variable in respect to many of them. Methodologically, moreover, the procedure is fallible, except

CONSTELLATION-SYNDROME CORRELATIONS

Physiological Measures Constituting Syndrome	Personality Constellation		
	Health (Somasthenic)	Health (Neurasthenic)	Paranoid Tendency
Somasthenic			
1. Drop in galvanic resistance during 2-minute anticipation of shock			
2. Spontaneous galvanic reaction during 2 minutes of anticipation	.348	.116	.075
3. Galvanic recovery in 3 seconds			
Neurasthenic			
1. Ratio of galvanic recovery to reaction			
2. Association of conditioned with conditioning stimuli	.140	.380	.063
3. Resistance rise during 2 minutes of rest			
Paranoid			
1. Initial resistance level			
2. Blood pressure reaction after shock	.015	.032	.329
3. Minimum resistance reached			
4. Conditioned blood pressure reaction			

as a trial-and-error, hypothesis-seeking venture. Among one set of ten scores and another set of twenty, all of uncertain reliability, which are applied to a single small group, certain interrelationships are bound to appear. By a judicious combining of scores some of them can be raised to or slightly beyond the point of "reliability." Only when precisely the same relationships have been discovered for other subjects have we learned anything by such a process. And this will be worth trying, of course, provided only that the measures involved are demonstrated to be reasonably reliable.

The trait, or trait complex, of introversion-extroversion has in recent years received almost as much attention from psychologists as has the measurement of neurotic tendency. But the former trait also has been investigated rather by pencil-and-paper than by single-situation responses—particularly when adults have been used as subjects. One of the reasons for inconclusive and even contradictory findings in these investigations is the supposed inclusiveness of the concept. The kinds of behaviors studied range all the way from social responses to types of visual perception and to the galvanic skin reflex. An example of the first of these is an investigation of familiarity with campus gossip as a measure of extroversion. If there is such a trait as social extroversion, this ought to be a good measure of it, although another investigator, some years previously, had found it to be quite unrelated to other measures of extroversion. But the later investigation, making use of somewhat more reliable measures than the previous one, also revealed a zero correlation between familiarity with campus gossip and Bernreuter extroversion scores. The authors conclude that "any difference between the two psychological types with respect to this feature of their mental lives must be sought, apparently, in the extent to which they use these goings-on as their stock in conversational trade or intellectual rumination."

Association test methods have been used, with varying degrees of success, in the attempt to measure introversion. Such findings as the following are typical: response time, though measured with high reliability, shows zero correlations with scores on two introvert-extrovert questionnaires. Introverts, as selected by questionnaire responses, give about 50 per cent more "individual" responses than extroverts, but with much overlapping between group scores. Certain average differences are frequently reported between groups of extreme introverts and extreme extroverts; according to one study, the former group tend to respond more slowly, to give fewer "contrast" responses, and to fail to respond at all more frequently than extroverts. Differences in group averages also appear in the following responses of the same two groups: extroverts give more responses to Whipple's ink blots, require a shorter time to arrange a series of pictures in rank order of liking, are superior in motor output as measured by pencil strokes.

The limitations of these situations for measuring introversion—or perhaps the limitations of the trait concept itself—are self-evident. The various measures yield low intercorrelations. Usually the questionnaire technique is conceded prior validity, with the result that the other measures appear to have little validity. But the question seems to us to be, not whether these measures agree with questionnaire scores, but rather whether they are related to any significant personality differences. In almost every case the *laboratory measures have been abandoned if, as invariably occurs, they do not parallel closely the differences shown by questionnaire responses.* We can see no reason, save that of ease of obtaining scores, for granting prior "validity" to the latter, and we have already commented upon some of the weaknesses inherent in the questionnaire approach to such complex traits.

The argument that laboratory tests should always be "valid in terms of behavior" or "valid in terms of verbal report" seems to involve serious confusion. All behaviors as such are "valid"; the problem is to ascertain their interrelations. It has already been pointed out that a man's behavior may tell a greater lie than his words; that is, different overt acts may be related in as complex a way as are certain act and word patterns. There are all degrees of closeness of association between words and acts, depending upon the nature of the acts and the situations in which the words are used. Instead of asking blanket questions about the validity of laboratory tests when compared with questionnaire reports, it would seem more intelligent to inquire as to the functional relation between different acts, and between words and acts in each class of situations.

Again, much confusion arises when we begin to speak of the difference between laboratory behavior and life behavior, and undertake to disparage the one in favor of the other. The organisms which we study are alive, and for the most part are confronting "life situations" when they take part in our investigations. The life situations in the laboratory are somewhat different from those outside, but so do the life situations differ among themselves. The physicist and chemist simplify an everyday situation and deliberately choose to work with a limited number of variables; the experimental psychologist does the same thing. He deliberately simplifies, and may, at times, need to introduce stimuli of a kind not frequently encountered in the subject's daily routine. If the purpose is simplification, it is as reasonable to hope to build up a science of social behavior in the laboratory as it is to hope to build up a science of food chemistry in the same way. We do not suggest that means have as yet been found for appropriate simplification of the main life situations, but laboratory studies of the more powerful human motives and of the ways in which these motives display themselves as a result of conditioning and habituation have been made for some years. Groups of individuals have interacted in patterns of work and play under reasonably close scrutiny in the laboratory. Personality has at least been *changed* in the laboratory, and the post-laboratory behavior has shown for years the profoundness of the changes induced experimentally.

A study by Eisenberg illustrates how the complex dimensions of personality recognized in our daily characterization of one another can be recorded and measured in simple laboratory situations. Thus, to a group of 350 women and 250 men who had been given a questionnaire and self-rating scale on "feelings of dominance," a simple laboratory procedure and interview were administered in which the characteristics of the dominant and non-dominant persons were easily and quickly revealed. After a single hour's free conversation with each one of 35 women had yielded a correlation of .67 between the observers' rating on dominance feeling and the subject's self-evaluation on dominance feeling in the questionnaire, it proved possible for another experimenter to define some 60 specific behaviors associated with the high and low ends of the distribution on the feelings of dominance. Individuals in the top 10 per cent in dominance feeling tended to come late for their appointments, enter the room without knocking, sit with their feet apart, maintain an even tone of voice, work rapidly at a variety of tasks, offer criticisms of the experiment, accept and smoke cigarettes, look steadily at the experimenter; those at the low end of the distribution came early for the appointment, knocked before entering, made sure they were in the right place, hesitated, stammered or blushed in speaking to the experimenter, worked slowly and cautiously at the tasks, refrained from criticism, refrained from looking the experimenter in the eye, became confused when given a difficult task under distraction and tried to slip out at the end without comment or question on the procedure. Some of these things are easily quantified; for example, large and reliable differences in speed of working are easily defined for both men and women. Some of the factors involve a crude separation of the group in terms of all-or-none standards, for example, blushing or not blushing, stammering or not stammering. The essential point, however, is not the method of quantification but the demonstration that in a single hour in the laboratory we have a recorded picture of behavior highly congruent with the picture of oneself given on a questionnaire. Just as the intelligence test is validated by the agreement between a one-hour standard procedure and the total impression derived from a study of years of school experience, so the one-hour picture of dominance is validated by reference to a number of other criteria involving the subject's appraisal of himself and the appraisal of him by others in a free interview.

If this can be done, it strongly suggests that we have been too easily terrified by the complexities of social life; indeed, that life situations which we all recognize can be so defined that they will reproduce themselves and submit to measurement with fair success in the laboratory.

In many instances this short-cut is not, at least for the present, desirable. A more rewarding method may be the genetic analysis of the unfolding of personality in childhood. The pattern of personality formation may yield to genetic analysis when it yields but slowly to experimental analysis. The playground or school observer with the facilities of one-way screens, slow-motion pictures and sound-recording devices may be able to record and analyze the spontaneous interaction of child personalities and to understand more quickly the meaning of a personality trait than can the laboratory student of adult behavior. We should give as an example the case of dominance just cited. Dominance is one of those characteristics which can be seen in the making among pre-school children. Successful efforts at dominance lead to the stereotyping of habits which are carried over to a wider and wider range of social situations. Intimidation or rebuff by an older or quicker child, or by an adult, may lead to generalized habits of withdrawal or self-disparagement. Not only may the processes be observed step by step, but they may be experimentally induced as in the studies of Jack and Page mentioned above. Here placing the child in the situation where he could without difficulty dominate his playmate and achieve success in his play increased the generalized pattern of dominance to an extent still observable fifteen months after the experiment. Transfer or generalization of childhood habits is a major clue to the adult habits and traits which we study by tests or in the laboratory.

Yet serious work in the direction of using the laboratory to study personality has only begun; problems have not as a rule been clearly defined before being brought into the laboratory. In particular, the laboratory has been asked to validate impressionistic definitions of "traits" which may in fact be nothing but names. One series of experiments did appear for a time to have found a laboratory procedure which distinguished introverts from extroverts, in agreement with ratings and questionnaire responses. In the first experiment the most introverted quarter of the subjects, according to self- and others' ratings and responses to two inventories, showed an almost reliably greater reaction time to noise than did the extrovert quarter of the group. On repetition, however, there was almost no difference between the two groups in reaction time. But the second experiment did confirm the original finding that the extrovert group showed greater "affective sensitiveness," i.e., gave more extreme judgments regarding the pleasantness or unpleasantness of colors and nonsense syllables, than the introverts. The chances that it was a true difference were 95 in 100, but the overlapping of scores was large; for example, 56.4 per cent of the introverts exceeded the score which was exceeded by 81 per cent of the extroverts.

This investigation included another test suggested by a theory regarding introversion-extroversion propounded by McDougall. This theory, briefly, is that extroversion is a function of the character of nerve impulses, particularly those of the higher nerve centers. The activity of the cerebral cortex is held to inhibit that of the lower centers, and hence introverts are those whose overt movements are inhibited. McDougall proposed, therefore, that the frequency of fluctuation of an ambiguous figure (which he believed to be associated with inhibition) should be an index of introversion. McDougall himself had found a consistent difference between introvert and extrovert groups, the former experiencing a more rapid rate of alternation. Later experiments, however, have failed to confirm his findings; results have been inconclusive, and in at least one case contradictory to those of McDougall. Only when schizophrenics as subjects have been compared with manic-depressive patients does supporting evidence for his hypothesis appear to have been found.

But even under these conditions the evidence by no means gives uniform support to the theory. According to experiments carried on in another quarter, the average rate of fluctuation of an ambiguously drawn cube was from four to six times as great for 25 male dementia praecox patients as for 18 male manic-depressives. This appears to be confirmatory evidence, but two other findings point in the opposite direction: first, the average rate of fluctuation for the dementia praecox group was almost identical with that of "unselected" non-pathological subjects; and, second, the individual rates of fluctuation were highly variable from day to day. Reliability coefficients were .75 for normal subjects, .56 for dementia praecox patients, and .68 for the manic-depressives. We may conclude, therefore: (1) that McDougall's theory is wrong; or (2) that the test he proposed was inadequate; or (3) that it measures (however poorly) only the non-social aspects of introversion; or (4) that dementia praecox and manic-depressive psychoses are not extremes of introversion and extroversion—or even that all four conclusions are probable. Or, quoting the last of these experimenters, "it may also be that the trait known as introversion-extroversion does not exist."

If the history of the laboratory measurement of introversion and extroversion seems to be largely a burying ground of lost hopes, we believe it is primarily because of the assumed necessity of validating laboratory measurements against the existing ratings and instruments of self-report. The latter type of measure has probably included far too wide a range of symptoms, so that no laboratory tests could possibly be expected to correlate highly with any of them. Methods of self-report have their place, but their rôle here seems to have been that of discouraging other methods. There is little reason to believe that the group of social behaviors labeled introversion and extroversion can be reliably predicted by laboratory methods. But other aspects of personality which are also included in the concept almost certainly correspond to something real, and almost certainly can be reliably related to laboratory measures.

Some of the most persistent and thorough work along the lines of laboratory measurement yet reported is that of a group of British psychologists who have interested themselves in perseveration. This trait, which is to be carefully distinguished from persistence (cf. Howells' work, page 822) or perseverance, may be described in the words of Stephenson, whose investigations were among the first: "An individual's intelligence, his g-factor, can be regarded as available general mental energy; and p-factor [perseveration] is then the amount of inertia of this energy. . . . Sluggishness is high 'p.' . . . Instantaneity is low 'p.' " The trait has been isolated, as might be guessed from the language of the quotation, by the application of Spearman's methods of factor analysis to the results of various tests, and the claim is made that an individual is characterized by a given amount of perseveration, just as he is by a given amount of "g," though the two are almost entirely unrelated.

The nature of the tests by which perseveration is measured will indicate that sluggishness versus instantaneity refers not to bodily movement or speech (which are possibly related to metabolism) but to agility in shifting from one mental task to another, particularly to another involving reactions directly opposed to the preceding one. A typical test is the following sequence: writing zzzzzz as rapidly as possible for one minute, writing sss for another minute, then altering z and s for two minutes. In similar fashion the sequence of one long and two short pencil strokes was alternated with the sequence of one long and three short strokes; correct and incorrect naming of colors was similarly alternated. Different investigators have used various scoring schemes, but they all measure perseveration in terms of failure to shift from one task to another.

The principal applications of these tests have been in the field of psychiatry. Some results of these tests with psychotic patients are presented below; they are in general agreement with those of other investigators. The classification of patients is probably superior for our purposes to that of most other investigators: instead of accepting the diagnosis appearing in the hospital record for each patient, one of 17 symptoms was checked by the medical staff as being "specially marked" in each of the 144 patients.

Most Marked Symptom	Number of Patients with p-Score Below Average	Number of Patients with p-Score Above Average
Melancholia	12	37
Suspicion	7	16
Paranoid state	4	15
Hysteria	27	7
Mania	7	1

None of the other symptom groups was clearly characterized in terms of perseveration except that 24 of 30 delusional patients received moderate, as exposed to extreme, scores. That certain syndrome groups tend to have characteristic perseveration scores is confirmed by the testing of different groups, though the numbers are necessarily small in each syndrome group. That perseveration scores are of little value for individual diagnosis or prognosis is indicated by the considerable degree of overlapping in scores among the various groups.

There are, however, grave dangers in assuming that a criterion found to be of value among psychotic groups must also distinguish between less extreme, or "normal," variations in personality. Fortunately, we may rely upon actual experimental use of the same tests with normal groups, rather than upon analogy drawn from psychotic groups. The same investigator found no reliable correlations between perseveration (measured as described on page 813) and ratings on six characteristics of 194 children. But a definite curvilinear relationship was found when his subjects were divided into quartiles on the basis of perseveration score: about 75 per cent of the "most difficult" and "less reliable" children fell in the extreme groups, while the same proportion of "self-controlled" and "persevering" children (just how self-controlled and how persevering is not stated) fell in the moderate half (i.e., second and third quartiles) in regard to perseveration. Almost without exception (exact figures are not given), the children who were conspicuous as disciplinary problems were at one extreme or the other. Of these, those with very high scores were "irritable, bad-tempered, and moody," whereas those with very low scores were "petty, nagging, and whining." This curvilinear relationship between perseveration and "character" was later confirmed by ratings of 116 adult psychotic patients, and similar results are reported for a group of 62 male college students.

A more detailed study has also been made of personality characteristics as related to perseveration score among a group of 52 adults, all well known to the investigator. The moderate-extreme distinction is again reinforced: there was only one case of definite dishonesty or unreliability among the moderate perseverators, but three of the extremely low perseverators were unreliable, and two of the extremely high perseverators were "minor rogues." The ten individuals with highest and the ten with lowest perseveration scores were studied intensively, being contrasted in such ways as the following: the former group were cautious but erratic automobile drivers, with a high frequency of fairly serious accidents, whereas the latter group were capable but hard and fast drivers with an equal frequency of very serious accidents (the moderate group had almost no accidents at all in a three-year period); the high perseverators reported nearly twice as many childhood illnesses as the low perseverators, and less than half as many of them were considered robust in childhood. The generalization that low perseverators are prone to action, whereas the other extreme group is resigned and absent-minded, is supported by incidents of extreme and decisive attempts by members of the former group to change or to escape from undesirable situations, while there was not a single instance of the kind among the high perseverators under equally intolerable conditions. Both extreme groups failed to make satisfactory adjustments (or, as the author puts it, are lacking in the "w" or character factor)—low perseverators because they are unreliable, tactless, and planless; high perseverators because they lack drive and miss their opportunities.

All this is highly hypothetical, of course, and is offered as such; the number of subjects was small, and information depended largely upon subjective judgments. A more serious source of uncertainty, however, is the difficulty of obtaining reliable measures of the trait. Retest reliability coefficients ranging from — .04 to + .81 are reported; and several investigators are in substantial agreement in finding intercorrelations among various tests of perseveration which are, without exception, below + .40, many of them being not reliably greater than zero. Evidence regarding the stability of the measures, as applied to psychotic patients, is conflicting. Stephenson reports, for a group of 56 psychotic women, no changes over a period of several months which were greater than two points on a 20-point scale. Another of his patients, a schizophrenic, who was tested five times in a one-year period, showed a steadily decreasing perseveration score paralleling gradual improvement and increasing "accessibility." The conclusion is drawn that so great are the variations in degree of accessibility, at least among some psychotics, that the same subject may within a few minutes show both very low and very high perseveration. Another of the investigators appears also to have concluded that "poor character" is associated with both extremes of perseveration because it is the same individuals whose perseveration scores are now high, now low. This, if demonstrated to be the case, might easily account for the unsatisfactory unreliabilities achieved, and would suggest that perseveration scores should be measured not in terms of positive and negative degree, but in terms of deviations from one's own mean. But this work is still in its infancy. One of its most promising clues is the indication that perseveration is related both to certain types of psychosis and (among non-psychotics) to certain behaviors associated with "poor character." No one knows yet, of course, whether similar characteristics (with regard to perseveration or any other trait) are shown by the same individuals before and during psychosis. Until this is known, conclusions must not be drawn too venturesomely.

A trait which has readily lent itself to laboratory measurement is suggestibility. It is, indeed, the example *par excellence* of a trait which must almost of necessity be conceived (at least for purposes of measurement) as a single-situation trait. Individual differences in suggestibility in a particular situation may reasonably be expected; but if the trait exists as a general tendency, revealing itself in all manner of situations, the fact may be demonstrated only through the observation of individuals in each of those situations. The techniques of measurement of traits as response tendencies (cf. page 781) are scarcely applicable here. One may, perhaps, imagine the possibility of a rating by associates on suggestibility (one investigator has attempted this; the reliability coefficient for ratings repeated after an interval of a few minutes was .55). But the application of the various instruments of self-report to this trait is beyond imagination. To behave in a suggestible manner involves, by definition, not knowing that one is doing so. Such behavior can be noted only by another observer, and only, moreover, by another observer who is aware both of the exact variations in the situation and of the corresponding behavior of the subject—which is a definition of laboratory procedure.

One extensive series of experiments sought answers to such questions as the following: Is it true that some persons possess a trait which may be called suggestibility, whereas others are able to resist suggestion? In particular, what shall we say of the traditional belief that men are less suggestible than women? With a large number of subjects (54 women and 29 men in most of the experiments, 41 women and 43 men in the remainder) a great variety of tests of the Binet-Whipple type was tried. One consisted in the response to the "least perceptible" sensation when no objective stimulus was actually presented. In one of these, three actual odors were first presented, alcohol, peppermint, and wintergreen, and then, without interruption and in the same way, ten bottles of distilled water. "Report whether you smell one of the odors you have just sampled." Again, the subject was shown two cork weights suspended by a thread. The lighter one aroused no sensation on the tip of the finger; the other was clearly perceptible. The perceptible weight was given four times; then, after the "ready" signal, the subject was told, "Report whether you feel a weight." Similarly, he reported the least perceptible warmth from the "heated coil." After being given a distinct shock, he was then, when confronting the same apparatus, asked to report in the subsequent experiments whenever he felt the shock.

The second series of tests do not deal with the least perceptible sensation, but with the least perceptible *change* in sensation. A color wheel bearing white and black disks is presented; the subject reports a change of brightness, no actual change of brightness having occurred. Change of pitch and of size are similarly studied, the first experiment demonstrating a marked change, the subject thereafter being free to report changes, or to resist the suggestion, when no such change occurs. The perception of motion is similarly tested by a light projected on the wall, which is at first made to rise, then remains stationary. The third set of tests makes use of progressive weights and progressive lines as in the Binet series; the subject's tendency to go on reporting the presence of increases in weight or length is the measure of his suggestibility. In another experiment the subject is shown a checkerboard with six circles placed on intersections. He is now given a second somewhat different checkerboard; the measure of his suggestibility is the tendency to put circles on the intersections. A card is now shown upon which twelve letters appear.

On a second card the subject must tell which letters are in the same position as before; none really are. Large, medium-sized, and small squares are next presented, the subject being asked to find one of a size equal to one previously shown. The assumption here is that the suggestible person will tend to select a square toward the middle of the series on the board from which the selection is being made. Suggestions by leading questions after observation of a picture, and suggestions as to objects seen in an ink blot follow.

It will be noted that the tests up to this point do not deviate much from the ideo-motor type. A new factor is introduced in the following: A series of judgments is required of the subject, instructions being given in each case that "most people underestimate" or "most people overestimate"—the same instructions being given to alternate subjects. The size-weight illusion and the Müller-Lyer illusion are next used. The subject is told in the former that most people judge the large weight to be much lighter, etc.; in the latter, he is asked to adjust the lengths without being told in which direction most people err. The illusion is reduced by learning of the ordinary error. When a white cord is suspended from a skylight and the distance must be gauged between a marker near the top and another near the bottom, the subject's responses, with and without suggestion, are compared. Learning that most people's estimate is too long or too short produced the expected compensatory effect, as it did also in estimating the weight of a jug of water. The same principle is applied to aesthetic preferences. When adjusting length and width of a rectangle, the subject is told, for example, that most persons prefer to have one side more than twice as long as the other, or, in another case, that most persons prefer the rectangle to be approximately a square. Similar suggestions are given with regard to what most people prefer as to the shape of triangles, and the proportions of a cross. Efforts were also made to influence preference for colors, tones, and tone combinations.

The most striking thing about the results from this elaborate array of material is the low correlations between the scores on different tests. Individual differences are not sufficiently conspicuous to justify calling one person "very suggestible" and another "not suggestible." Rank difference correlations of all tests with each other are mostly positive but low. There is, to be sure, some common element running through this series of responses, pointing to the conclusion that, in the long run, the fact of one person's being very suggestible in one situation would justify us in saying that he would be slightly more likely to be suggestible than non-suggestible in another test. Yet the actual amount of correlation is so slight that such a guess will be right only a little more often than wrong.

Sex differences exist, if by this statement one means that after all the data are massed together, suggestibility scores are more likely to be high in women than in men. Out of the 26 tests, 13 reveal a clear difference, and in twelve of these thirteen cases the average woman is more suggestible than the average man. In three other tests there are slight but fairly reliable differences, the women again being more suggestible. Qualitative consideration of this statement is, however, probably more to the point. Women are more suggestible in tests involving imagined sensation, in the series of progressive changes, in the distortion of memory, and in the estimation of magnitudes. Tests with illusions give no clear difference, while tests on aesthetic judgments give contradictory or indecisive results. "Wherever written directions are used which give rise to false anticipations, or which contain statements concerning the usual course of most persons, these directions will prove more misleading to women students than to men."

Clearly, then, a qualitative comparison of the scores of the two sexes on different tests gives confirmation of the generalization that "suggestibility in general" is hard to define. Conclusions regarding sex differences are less easily drawn. If a sex difference in the sense of a fundamental biological trend predisposing to a more uncritical attitude in women does exist, it seems surprising that it should not make itself clear throughout the entire set of tests. If it exists, it can exist only in the sense that, despite its being masked by hundreds of other cognitive and emotional factors, it pops out in the long run more frequently in women than in men wherever the experimental conditions permit it. This really reduces itself to saying that some emotional or cognitive difference—whatever its origin—exists between women and men which will show itself in some situations involving ideo-motor action, but not in others. One of the controls needed, in this type of experiment, is that of the sex of the experimenter.

One technique by which suggestibility has recently been studied is that of extent of body sway under direct suggestion. The subject stands blindfolded, and his sway movements are recorded on a kymograph connected by means of a thread to a pin which has been placed, without his knowledge, in his clothing. Normal amount of sway (i.e., independent of suggestion) is determined by observing the initial degree of standing steadiness before the introduction of direct suggestion. Then, to quote one experimenter, the subject is told "over and over, in a quiet, confident tone, that she is swaying forward"; suggestion is continued for a standard length of time, e.g., five minutes, or until the subject falls over. It was found, in this experiment, that the amount of time required before responding to the suggestion was an utterly unreliable measure, but that the correlation between amounts of sway on two successive experiments was .78 (the subjects were 56 student nurses). There was, however, no reliable correlation between any of six measures of body-sway suggestibility and seven ratings of personality characteristics, including suggestibility.

The past few years have seen considerable work on suggestibility under hypnosis. In one series of such experiments four tests of suggestibility were used: time taken to respond to suggestion of postural sway, the Binet progressive lines test, the Binet progressive weights test, and response to unheated coils after four presentations of the same coils when heated. All these tests were repeated at least four times in both the waking and trance states. The experimenter presents only group results, but we have calculated intercorrelations for fourteen subjects for whom data are provided. The rank order correlations between mean scores in each of these measures in the waking state and the same scores in the trance state are .87, .88, .62, and .87, respectively, for the four tests mentioned above. Granting that individuals vary in degree of suggestibility to any particular situation (the author finds, in general, increased suggestibility in the trance state), these subjects tend to maintain characteristic individual degrees of suggestibility to three of these four particular situations. But no significant interrelationships appear among the four measures, in cither the waking or the trance state, except between the Binet lines and the Binet weights tests; these coefficients are .59 and .48, respectively, in the waking and trance states. Half of the remaining coefficients indicate negative relationships (i.e., contrary to the expected direction), though all are unreliable.

It thus becomes abundantly clear that we may not profitably consider suggestibility as a personality trait; it cannot be said that one person is definitely suggestible and another definitely non-suggestible, nor can an individual be placed with any confidence at all at a given point between the two extremes. And this, moreover, is precisely what we have expected, in view of the nature of suggestion, particularly those forms of it which are commonly referred to as "ideo-motor." (See pages 181-182.) The continuance of the term "suggestion," in view of the mass of experimental data pointing to its vagueness, is rather remarkable—the more so as Binet pointed out, nearly forty years ago, the nature of such confusion and the experimental path of escape from it.

Space does not permit describing at length the methods of personality measurement devised for immediate practical use in industry, but a sample study may be offered. Seven tasks offering opportunity for either care or haste were chosen as measures of *recklessness*. Both time and accuracy were measured for each of the seven, which were as follows: pouring water into a beaker to a designated level; walking a maze, with difficult hurdles as short-cuts; balancing copper disks on small steel rods; placing nuts on screws; placing a light weight on a platform suspended on springs so as to cause minimum vibration; tracing an electric contact maze, with the shorter routes narrower; and balancing a steel rod so as to make it stay upright as long as possible. Intercorrelations of these various measures ranged from .02 to .67. A "criterion" was constructed from ratings by fraternity brothers, the 21 subjects all being members of the same group. The correlation between the pooled ratings (the reliability of which was .86) and the optimum weighting of the laboratory tests was .61. Factor analysis revealed a dominant factor of haste, which had a range of correlations with the seven test scores from .33 to .81, the median being .53. It seems to us far more important to know that these tests are all measuring some aspect of a characteristic in respect to which there are fairly stable individual differences than to know that they can be weighted in such a way as to correlate highly with pooled ratings. The latter included such diverse "behaviors" as automobile driving, betting, handling money, "appearance of room," school work, and emotional stability. Just as we pointed out in our discussion of introversion-extroversion (indeed, recklessness as defined by these ratings is almost synonymous with several aspects of extroversion), so here also we could hardly expect such a wide range of behaviors, with their even wider range of social determinants, to correlate highly with single laboratory tests. There seems to us to be no good reason for considering the ratings as a criterion for the tests, and hence no reason for weighting the latter in such manner as to relate closely to the ratings. We should reason rather in the opposite direction: those behaviors (for example, automobile driving), the ratings of which correlate highly with the tests, may be presumed to represent behaviors which are not much altered by training and experience, whereas those situations for which ratings bear little relationship to the test scores (e.g., handling money) probably reflect behaviors which have been largely modified by accidents such as those of upbringing and economic status. For the chief value of the laboratory testing of personality traits is not to find agreement with ratings or self-report measures— the latter are far easier to obtain. Its value lies rather in the possibility it offers of determining objectively what are the characteristics in regard to which individuals show stable and accurately observable differences; and in the clues that may be forthcoming as to just what related behaviors are subject to modification by what types of experience, and to what degree.

Howells has not only shown the nature of at least one of the characteristics associated with willingness to "take a chance," but appears to have found laboratory measures with a higher degree of intercorrelation than that of the preceding measures of recklessness. The trait, which he labels "persistence," might seem to be more accurately styled "willingness to endure pain," were it not for the fact that all of the tasks were performed under strongly competitive motivation. The method thus resembles that of measuring drive in rats by the amount of electric shock to which they are willing to submit in order to get at food, a mate, etc. Howells arranged such harrowing situations as resting a wooden peg, under constantly increasing pressure, on the palm; exposing the hand to an electric toaster; pressing an edged instrument against the thumb; and transmitting an electric current between the thumb and middle finger. Several calculations of the odd-even reliability of the total battery of ten tests showed it to be at or about .90 (corrected by the Spearman-Brown formula). The intercorrelations among the tests ranged from .31 to .72, the median intercorrelation being .50.

Following the completion of the tests noted above, the 97 subjects were given the opportunity to raise their scores by successfully drawing a metal stylus through a highly charged metal groove, and again by touching an electrode known to be highly charged. Those who elected these opportunities to raise their scores had reliably higher scores in persistence than those who refused the opportunities, in each case. But (among those who refused to touch the electrode) there was no difference in persistence score between those who were willing to touch one of two, or one of three, identical electrodes, only one of which was charged, and those who refused to do so even under these conditions. And when it came to sheer gambling, as in the opportunity to raise or lower scores by the toss of a coin, the non-gamblers had a *higher* mean persistence score than the gamblers, by a reliable difference.

Persistence, as thus measured, is but slightly correlated with intelligence, but its correlation with university grades is .44, and the multiple correlation of grades with intelligence is .64. It is also of interest to note that the mean intelligence of subjects who attempted to raise their scores by guessing which electrode was charged was reliably lower than that of the remaining subjects. Similarly those who chose to gamble on the toss of a coin had a lower mean score in intelligence than those who refused to gamble. Persistence thus characterizes those who are willing to endure pain if there is a certain reward, but are unwilling to gamble for it, whereas those who are willing to gamble for it are characterized by somewhat lower intelligence. It is also of some interest that there was a correlation of

.44 (for 47 subjects) between the Allport ascendance score and persistence, and that the more persistent subjects tended to hold more radical religious views (see pages 933 ff.).

Several of the trait studies just reviewed, though they have made use of exceedingly accurate methods, have failed to demonstrate with complete satisfaction that the measures used were reliable. A revealing study of the reliability of one type of physiological measure took its start from the discovery that the reliability of scores on the steadiness test of the Minnesota mechanical ability battery was not raised as the number of trials increased. It has been commonly assumed, on theoretical grounds, that the reliability of scores obtained at different experimental sessions could be "stepped up" by the Spearman-Brown formula so as to indicate the "true" reliability of the performance at all sessions combined. Careful analysis of data obtained at repeated sittings led Paulsen to conclude that the test itself was not at fault, but rather that there were actual changes in the individual's ability from time to time, as a result of factors which were constant for a particular sitting, but variable from one sitting to another. Increasingly reliable scores for a given sitting may, of course, be obtained by increasing the length of that sitting; but this merely emphasizes the errors constant for that sitting, if the scores are combined with those obtained at other sessions. Hence, he concludes, the Spearman-Brown formula, based upon odd-even reliability coefficients, is not applicable with reference to retest reliabilities. Factors of day-to-day variability such as those operating here are undoubtedly responsible for many of the low reliabilities reported in other similar work. The same factors undoubtedly account for low relationships between laboratory scores and various personality characteristics, as reported in so many experiments, since the former are actually less reliable than they are made to seem. Apparently we must reconcile ourselves to the fact of individual variability. This, of course, is equivalent to saying that reliable differences of a stable nature simply do not exist in regard to all the characteristics for which the imaginative psychologist can devise "measures." It suggests also that, as found in studies of blood chemistry (pages 773-774), variability of such scores may be a more useful measure than their means.

Some aspects of humor make ideal material for the measurement of single-situation traits, though the laboratory situation presumably raises the humor thresholds of various individuals to different and unknown degrees. The experimental analysis of laughter and humor is, of course, a matter partly for general, partly for individual, psychology. Laughing from sheer good spirits, at least in the case of a little child, may, perhaps, approach that theoretical limit of completely non-social behavior to which we have referred (page 23), while the laughter of superiority usually represents behavior almost purely within the realm of social psychology. We shall put the physiological studies of laughter to one side, giving them the barest mention, and shall give chief emphasis to the social situations in which laughter or humor appears, and the psychological analysis of such behavior.

The problem may be approached through the study of group differences in humor. It is relatively simple to demonstrate, as in the following study, that age differences exist. The incidents mentioned by ten kindergarten children who were asked to tell the funniest things they knew, were based on the elements of superiority or surprise. Twenty girls, aged seven to ten, also included such items, but supplemented them with others classified under the headings of incongruity and debasement of dignity. All of the foregoing were mentioned by 82 college women, and to them were added the following classifications: play on words, vulgar, and sex. Certain elements thus appeared only at the college age, others had largely disappeared by this age (e.g., surprise), and the element of superiority had become still more frequent than among kindergarten children. Although the selection of a single incident or joke scarcely indicates stable characteristics in regard to the appreciation of humor, it is evident that there are individual differences even within age groups. No significant group differences dependent upon sex or social status appear to have been demonstrated.

Since the element of superiority has so frequently been found to be a major one in contributing to humor, one might expect to find group differences among racial or economic groups between whom there is conflict. This has been put to the test, the experimental hypothesis being that "the disparagement of an unaffiliated object is . . . one type of accessory pattern of humor stimuli." Sixteen jokes, half of them disparaging to Jews, were presented (both on a moving screen, one word at a time, and in typewritten form) to six Jewish and to nine gentile subjects. Responses were recorded in terms of actual measurement of laughter movements of the face (from moving pictures) and of appraisal by observers (both during the experiment and, later, from the films) of the "expressive action response" of the subjects. In addition to this, subjects rated each joke, both instantaneously, during the experiment, and deliberately, following it. The control jokes were equally appraised by Jews and gentiles, according to both observations and subjects' ratings. But measurements of laughter in response to the Jewish jokes were greater for gentiles than for Jews, and the same racial distinction appeared from the subjects' ratings, the differences being reliable. The deliberate judgments showed this difference most conspicuously. While the Jewish jokes were considered less funny by most of the subjects than the control jokes, the margin of difference was greater for all Jewish subjects than for all but two gentiles. All of the eight jokes rated funnier by gentiles than by Jews were Jewish jokes. Precisely the same results were later obtained when Scotch jokes were submitted to Jewish and to gentile subjects, leading the authors to conclude that Jews tend to "affiliate themselves mentally with Scots." The experiment thus contributes both to the theory of humor and to our knowledge of group differences.

Few of the investigations of humor reveal much concerning individual differences, particularly regarding their stability, though one investigator appears to have found humor types. The most extensive study of individual differences appears to be one in which seven categories of humor were included among one hundred jokes, some within each category having previously been rated as good, some poor, and some very poor. The one hundred jokes were presented to 124 college men, to 554 college women, and to 112 delinquent women of comparable age. Each joke was rated on a five-point scale; subjects also classified each joke as belonging to one of the seven categories, definitions being supplied. Correlation methods showed no reliable relationship, for any group, between total humor score and introversion, or intelligence, nor (for the delinquent group) between total humor score and Thurstone neurotic score, Pressey X-O score, suggestibility (Hull's test) or maze-learning. Within some of the categories, however, certain differences appear. For example, introverts tended to classify jokes into the repression category, and to value highly those so classified, whereas extroverts showed the same tendencies with regard to the "truth" category— i.e., hinging upon unrevealed thoughts, etc. Individuals of high intelligence preferred jokes which they classified as being based upon truth and incongruity more frequently than did those of less intelligence. Both the more and the less intelligent rated highly those classified as based upon superiority, though they differed as to which jokes were thus classified. Men made higher total humor scores than women, the difference being reliable for all categories except those of incongruity and superiority. (Even if this is because the jokes were originally selected by men, which the authors mention as a possible explanation, it still reveals a sex difference.) Delinquent girls did not appear to show consistent differences from college girls.

It appears probable that simple linear measurements, even though based upon refined categorizing, will not serve to reveal stable individual differences in the appreciation of humor. The few relationships indicated above are based upon small correlations. More complex measures, both of humor and of other personality characteristics, seem to be demanded. Factors both of past experience and of present motivation, neither of which can very well be tapped in trait measurements, point to the necessity of methods of the "total personality" type for light upon the problem. Unfortunately, such methods appear not to have been applied to the study of individual differences in humor.

There are, of course, grave defects in the policy of inferring distinctly social traits from rather non-social laboratory conditions. A few investigators have addressed themselves to the problem of measuring social traits in their native habitat, i.e., under actual social conditions. Some of these have been miniature social conditions created in the laboratory, and some have been simply behavior observations in whatever life situations seemed to offer the most likely opportunity of finding the particular behavior in question. An example of the latter sort of investigation (almost unique in respect to the age of the subjects) is measurement of degree of "emotional reaction" on the gymnasium floor. The subjects were college freshmen majoring in physical education who were observed by their squad leaders, maturer students who had been given training in the techniques of observing and recording the particular behaviors involved. Recording consisted simply of checking, soon after each gymnasium period, the presence of any of fourteen behaviors noted in each subject. From these records total scores were obtained for each subject, in terms of the sum of checks for all behaviors expressed as a percentage of the total number of hours during which he was observed. Observations were made twice weekly during a period of one month.

These data were later supplemented by both associates' and self-ratings, on a five-point scale of frequency, of the same behaviors; by scores on the Thurstone Personality Schedule; and by repeated observations, eight months later, of the same behaviors by different observers. Even with so great an interval of time, and in spite of the use of different observers, the reliability of the observations was .55 ± .07. Among these four scores thus obtained for all subjects, only two reliable intercorrelations were obtained. That between self-rating on emotional reactions and Thurstone score was .41 ± .06. The product-moment correlation between associates' rating and observers' score was .32 ± .07; but eta, the coefficient of correlation computed from data having a curvilinear relationship, was .62 ± .05. In view of the difficulties of obtaining and quantifying such observations, both the reliability and the validity of the observers' score are unexpectedly high. In spite of the rather heterogeneous list of behaviors which together constitute the trait (those most "diagnostic" of total score were, in the order mentioned, arguing, swearing, controllability, egotism, fighting, and breaking rules), individuals do appear to show something like characteristic degrees of behavior commonly regarded as emotional. The trait is not related to Thurstone score, to general athletic proficiency (ratings of which were also obtained), or to subjects' insight into their own degree of emotional behavior, as indicated by self-ratings. Perhaps we shall know, eventually, to what degree the same behaviors are shown in other situations, and with what other personality characteristics they are associated.

It is difficult to tell as yet to what extent the "behavior methods" can be used in the laboratory to measure the more complicated social characteristics; but one of the bolder attempts, that of Henning, ought at least to be described for the sake of the promise which it seems to give. This is similar to one of the studies of service which the Character Education Inquiry used, but unfortunately abandoned (the cooperativeness of boys was studied by their willingness to participate in group activities, such as making wooden ducks and automobile models). Henning has audaciously ventured to study cooperativeness and various other social characteristics by putting two individuals together and measuring the degree of their helpfulness, honesty, revengefulness, or competitiveness, in situations in which they *believe* themselves to be tested for some quite different function. Twenty-five different experimental set-ups are described for "partner or two-person experiments." Two subjects may, for example, be asked to work in the shop making patterns. An automatic registering device makes it possible to tell, in all cases where two people turn out the same pattern, which one was the leader and which was the follower. In one experiment, one of the individuals is asked to help out by acting as experimenter—for example, in a tachistoscope study. Here the apparatus can be handled so as to make the task agreeable for the one who watches the tachistoscope, or by a little carelessness and inconsiderateness it can be so handled as to make the observer exceedingly uncomfortable. The subject who has been told that he is the experimenter thinks, of course, that the other person is the only "subject," but his own character traits as shown in the way he handles the apparatus are measured.

In other experiments, competitiveness and generosity are shown by asking two individuals in the same room to work on a common task, making use of heaped-up materials necessary for construction work. In this case the tendency to grab, to be sly, to be indifferent, to be actively helpful, can all be shown. Other experiments make use of the competitive and cooperative motives in group games. Henning regards personality as a social matter to such a large degree, and the social aspects of personality as dominant to such a great extent even in everyday activities of thought, attention, memory, association, etc., that he proposes to make use of a large number of standard laboratory methods, ordinarily used for the study of individuals in isolation, as ways of determining how these functions are shaped by social factors.

Henning's techniques have since been repeated and elaborated by others. At least one of these has made a special study of the problem of reliability. Does the individual who proved to be a "leader" in an experiment such as those described, continue that rôle in other experiments with the same partner? And is there a hierarchy of dominance, such as that found among hens (cf. page 769), when different combinations of the same partners are used? Not necessarily, according to an experimenter who subjected many of Henning's procedures to such tests. In the two-scissors experiment, for example, neither time nor quality was found to be at all constant upon repetition. The situation contained too many variables for reliable measurement. In another competitive experiment, three repetitions of all possible pairings of three subjects gave totally inconsistent results. In other experiments subject A excelled over subject B, who excelled over subject C, who in turn excelled over subject A.

This is important evidence, of course, but by no means does it invalidate the techniques. As measures of traits, they would be suspect, but they were not primarily intended as trait measurements. Their chief promise seems to us to lie in their possibility of yielding data concerning the interplay of personalities which constitute groups, in a fashion similar to that used by Moreno (see page 307). Cooperative and competitive behaviors, considered as traits, are only abstractions. They become meaningful only as they are considered to be cooperation (or competition) with this individual, or this kind of individual, or with a representative of this group, or this kind of group. The magnitude of the problem is disclosed by the consideration that such behaviors are functions not only of the individuals, but also of the task and the total situation. We look for the next important developments in personality measurement within this area of interrelationships with specific groups.

We are faced with precisely the same complexities with regard to the study of leadership. We are again confronted not only with the general problem of measuring individual differences, but also with the question as to the way in which the relationship of polarity between leader and follower is established. The study of leadership has been left for the most part to sociologists and to educational psychologists. Since the former are not primarily interested in the individual characteristics of leaders, and the latter deal chiefly with leadership among children and adolescents, we shall not include their studies here.

In one laboratory measurement of individual traits associated with leadership in adults, groups of about twenty "leaders" each were selected from a state penitentiary, an army encampment, and a university. These were contrasted with groups of "followers" of the same number and from the same sources. Reliabilities are not stated, but leaders from each of these institutions appear to make higher scores in tests of finality of judgment and of speed of decision, and to be rated higher in self-confidence, than followers. But the difficulties of establishing the existence of the traits measured are readily apparent. Even with groups of presumably extreme subjects (all leaders and all followers are grouped together in computing correlations), the average intercorrelation of three tests of speed of decision is only .375, about the same as their average correlation with the trait "finality of judgment." Certain temperamental qualities are undoubtedly associated with the fact of being elevated to positions of leadership, but the degree to which these qualities are the same for different individuals and different groups is still unknown. Although the experimenter just cited argues for the presence of some common factor, it is evidently overshadowed by the variable factors.

Two studies of leadership in university populations indicate that one of the common factors is related to vitality, or extroversion, or tendency-to-indulge-in-overt-behavior. One of these is a statistical study of 250 senior college women; all the extra-curricular activities in which each of these individuals participated were noted, and a certain "weight" was assigned to each, depending on its importance or the amount of time given to it. In general, the greater the *number* of activities, the more *intense* the participation in them. Participation in extra-curricular activities being reckoned in terms of what the experimenter calls student "points," it is perhaps a little surprising to find a positive correlation of .38 between the number of points and the grades attained. In other words, participation in extra-curricular activities and what one might call effective participation in college work do not appear to be likely to interfere with one another—unless, indeed, these students would have made even higher grades had they not been participating in other activities.

Another study confirms much of this, and goes beyond it. Student leaders of both sexes in various fields of activities were paired with non-leaders. The 125 prominent students were characterized by superior socio-economic status, higher scores in college aptitude tests, and higher scholastic attainment, as compared with the non-leaders. Women leaders rated themselves as reliably more extrovert (Heidbreder scale) than did women non-leaders, and this difference became even larger according to associates' ratings; no such tendencies appeared among men. Both men and women leaders rated themselves as having more inferiority feelings than did non-leaders, though not reliably so. But in the case of the women fewer inferiority feelings were attributed to them by associates than to non-leaders. Analysis of the type of position held by these leaders indicated that editors were bright, mildly introverted, and self-confident, but not distinguished scholastically. Men debaters were highly intelligent, and possessed marked inferiority feelings and introvert tendencies, though women debaters were extroverted and admitted only mild inferiority feelings. Campus politicians were of average ability, but of low scholastic attainment; they were markedly extroverted, although the three women included professed extreme feelings of inferiority. Leaders in dramatics were slightly superior in both ability and academic work, but showed average tendencies regarding introversion and inferiority. Leaders in women's activities were about average in ability, did creditable classroom work, and most of this group were definitely extroverted. Perhaps the most interesting feature of this work is the demonstration of the "halo" surrounding leaders, whereby their associates consider them as relatively extroverted and free from inferiority feelings. The investigator suggests the possibility that in many cases it is conflict over inferiority which leads, by way of compensation, to positions of prominence. We have here a faint shadow, at least, of the leader-follower polarity which constitutes the dynamics of our problem, a polarity more or less specific for each group.

This completes our survey of single-trait measurements. We shall attempt to assess the results of the trait approach after presenting some examples of more ambitious programs of studying personality. We may stop briefly, however, to note some comparisons between the two methods of measuring traits, as they have been presented in this and the preceding section.

Our comparison has to do chiefly with the kinds of traits investigated. Some five or six of the traits which we have discussed have been studied both as response tendencies and as single-situation traits, and by far the greatest amount of work has been done with two of them: introversion-extroversion, and neuroticism, or emotional instability. Correlational studies indicate, however, that in spite of the labels, the existing measures of such traits frequently bear but little resemblance to one another. We have already indicated what we believe to be the chief reason for this: the inclusiveness, the excessive range of items appearing in the measures of the traits conceived as response tendencies. This, of course, is tantamount to saying that these traits, as amounts of some one attribute, do not exist. If, as is probable, introversion-extroversion is a quality permeating the entire personality, rather than a single dimension of it, it is as absurd to try to measure it on a single continuum as thus to measure the total personality. The same may be said of neuroticism: the most widely diverse personalities become neurotic, and the qualitative differences among them remain, so that "total neurotic score" may obscure more than it reveals. Single-situation traits obviously cannot cover so much ground; hence the relationships are low.

It is obvious that certain traits may readily be measured in one manner, but lend themselves to the other approach only with considerable difficulty. Thus, one can scarcely conceive a single situation in which a measurement of ascendancy would be considered valid for other situations in general. For everyone is ascendant in some situations and toward some persons; if this trait has any meaning it is only as an algebraic sum of plus and minus reactions, from which the probabilities of ascendant behavior in any given situation may be deduced. With some other traits the situation is reversed: perseveration, for example, can be tested only by observing and recording responses to carefully controlled stimuli. The problem of the generality of such traits must be solved by repeated testing in different situations, since impressions, by self or by others (which if usable, would quickly sample a variety of situations) are not a possible means of getting at this trait.

The question whether traits can be measured better by one method or the other is thus irrelevant; a trait conceived as a response tendency is simply not the same kind of thing as a trait conceived as a degree of reactivity to a particular situation. The question is, rather, which kinds of traits can best be measured in either of the two ways. A simple distinction will, we believe, go far toward making clear what each method can and cannot do. If the behavior of most individuals, for the trait in question, varies widely with environmental changes, the trait can have no meaning other than that of an abstraction from many response tendencies. And this is the more true as the environmental fluctuations involve principally social situations with their immense range of subtle yet all-important *nuances*. If, on the other hand, the trait represents a fairly stable characteristic, then degree of reactivity in any particular situation will offer a reliable measurement of it. To this distinction must be added, of course, the factor of the practical applicability of each method. Thus suggestibility and perseveration probably demand laboratory techniques, whereas no adequate laboratory method of measuring emotionality, if there is such a trait, has been discovered. These two criteria may, of course, conflict. This is probably why, for example, suggestibility as a trait has not been successfully measured: because of wide situational variations it *should* be studied as a response tendency, but ratings and methods of self-report are simply not applicable. (Nonprestige suggestibility might conceivably have some meaning in terms of degree of reactivity to a particular situation, but apart from age and intelligence differences, present indications are that even this is not a stable characteristic.)

Finally, we may venture a statement as to the significance of either kind of trait. If degrees of reactivity to more than one situation are reliably measured and closely related to each other, as demonstrated by their application to different populations, the trait may be said to be established. Such a trait would either have some organic basis, or correspond to some habit system which has been subject, so to speak, to unilateral influence, such as cultural pressure toward behavior in a certain direction. One would not ordinarily, therefore, attempt such methods of trait measurement without reasonable assurance that either organic or cultural influences have resulted in a considerable degree of stability. But response tendencies, varying with the situation (except under one condition mentioned below), correspond to traits only in the sense of being more frequently in one direction than in the other. They do not represent traits in the sense of including behaviors which are known to be coherent, so that one can be predicted from the other. The exception to this is the measurement of trait by responses *known to be associated*, so that they form a kind of syndrome; they hang together by necessity. These conditions, except for the beginnings described on page 795), have not been complied with, so far as we know, in the filtering out of any such trait. Nor are we at all sure (for reasons explained in the previous section) that it can ever be done. Apart from this, "situational" traits exist only in the rather diluted sense of preponderances (not consistencies) of behavior direction in run-of-the-mine situations. This preponderance can probably best be discovered, for many traits, by means of judgments of observers, rather than by statistical analysis of self-reports via questionnaire items. But at any rate, most social behavior is affected by so many variables that personality measurement will probably remain largely a matter of preponderances, with a few underlying stable characteristics around which response tendencies revolve.

"Total Personality" Measurements

We have from time to time hinted at methods of studying personality which are more totalitarian than those we have so far discussed. The phrase, of course, is not to be taken literally. It serves as a protest against what are regarded as atomistic approaches rather than accurate description. The degree to which the phrase is justified will appear as we proceed.

Although there is, in general, the widest discrepancy between methods used in trait and in total personality approaches, the methods described previously have, in a few cases, been applied in such manner as to yield, after a fashion, cross-section pictures of personality. Even ratings, when several traits may be seen in relation to each other, may serve such a purpose. The questionnaire technique also has been adapted for such purposes. Thus "temperament" has been so measured; in the investigation now to be described it was conceived not as a single trait, nor as composed of several traits scored by differential weighting of the same item responses (as in the Bernreuter inventory), but in terms of Rosanoff's theory of personality. The theory is derived from psychiatric experience, and assumes that each of the major psychiatric syndromes may be found, in greater or less degree, in all individuals. A given personality will thus be best understood in terms of the one or more syndromes revealed to a conspicuous degree. It is not an all-or-none question of possessing this or that syndrome; the degree of possession of each is measured by questions validated for that particular syndrome. The validation procedure consisted of submitting 450 yes-no questionnaire items to five groups of hospitalized mental patients (manic cycloids, depressed cycloids, autistic schizophrenics, paranoid schizophrenics, and epileptics), to carefully selected "normals," and to a group of "habitual criminals" in a state prison (chosen as presenting hysteroid tendencies). There were 436 subjects altogether in these seven groups. Item analysis revealed that the percentage of "yes" and "no" responses was reliably different, for one group or another, for 318 of the 450 items. The "purity" of the syndrome scores was tested by correlating, for each group of subjects, scores in their own component (i.e., syndrome tendency) with those in all other components. Fifth-order partial correlations (all other components being held constant) showed that the various components were, with one exception, relatively distinct. Seven of these 21 coefficients fell above .29; they are reproduced below:

Fifth-order partial correlations higher than .29

Epileptoid...........................40 (with paranoid schizophrenic)
Paranoid schizophrenic..............45 (with autistic schizophrenic)
                                   .42 (with hysteroid)
Autistic schizophrenic..............49 (with hysteroid)
                                   .45 (with depressed cycloid)
Manic cycloid.......................53 (with normal)
                                   .84 (with depressed cycloid)

Score distributions of each group in its own component, as compared with those of all other groups in the same component, were not only reliably different as to their means, but showed little and in some cases no overlapping. The reliability coefficients for the various components range from .70 (paranoid schizophrenic) to .88 (autistic schizophrenic and depressed cycloid). As we have so often had occasion to remark, such procedures are of unknown validity for purposes of detecting syndrome tendencies in non-psychotic populations. But it seems to us far in advance of the use of total score on a psychoneurotic inventory. If methods of clinical validation for "normal" subjects can be applied, it seems promising not only for the diagnosing of maladjustment (within the limits of self-report methods) but also as a method of measuring fundamental personality dimensions.

Dominant interests, or values, have been studied in quite similar fashion by Allport and Vernon—similar in that several personality trends are simultaneously measured by a questionnaire method, and the personality is evaluated in terms of their relative prominence. The six values for which scores are computed are those presented by Spranger, whose view is that evaluative attitudes present the best clue to fundamental personality differences. Sample items are reproduced below; the alternatives are to be ranked in order of preference, and we have inserted in parentheses the respective values represented by each alternative:

Do you think that a good government should aim chiefly at—
(social)   a. more aid for the poor, sick, and old
(economic) b. the development of manufacturing and trade
(religious)   c. introducing more ethical principles into its politics and diplomacy
(political)   d. establishing a position of prestige and respect among nations

In your opinion, can a man who works in business for his living all the week best spend Sunday in—
(theoretical) a. trying to educate himself by reading serious books
(political)   b. trying to win at golf, or racing
(aesthetic)   c. going to an orchestral concert
(religious)   d. hearing a really good sermon

The various items are validated by internal consistency methods. A split-half reliability coefficient of .72 is reported for the entire test; in view of the authors' insistence that it measures only the *relative* strength of the six evaluative attitudes, reliability coefficients for single-value scores lose their significance. The validity of the instrument may best be seen by the degree to which it distinguishes groups having known interests. Though there is considerable individual overlapping of scores, such group differences as the following indicate the merits of the test:

Group Tested	Values in Which High Average Scores Obtained	Values in Which Low Average Scores Obtained
10 psychologists	theoretical; aesthetic	economic; political; religious
26 students of science and medicine	theoretical	
13 students for the ministry	social; religious	theoretical; economic; political
17 business men in a Catholic club	political; religious	theoretical; aesthetic; social
64 students of engineering	economic	
43 students of economics and business	economic	religious
14 students of language and literature	aesthetic	social
26 Boy Scout leaders	social	aesthetic
18 students of law and politics	political	

Profiles may be used for the simultaneous presentation of all the scores. Opinions will differ as to how far into the depths of personality this instrument penetrates; such neat distinctions among vocational groups as those which appear in the preceding table might plausibly be explained in terms of acquired interests rather than in terms of fundamental personality dispositions which seem to be assumed. Certainly it would be difficult to maintain the thesis that these individuals entered these vocations primarily because of the personality "type" to which they had previously belonged. But at any rate, the instrument seems to us a more useful one for personality measurement (as contrasted with the aim of vocational prediction) than the more time-hallowed interest tests which are standardized on the differential responses of various adult occupational groups.

Among the less objective methods of obtaining polydimensional views of personality, the case history, as a means of recording conduct, has certain advantages. This method has several forms. One of these is the study of biographies, autobiographies, and letters. An example of one of the best of these is Thomas and Znaniecki's study of changes in personality and social organization of peasants coming from Poland to the United States. An historical background of Polish life is followed by a large collection of letters which show the process of disintegration of the Polish social organization and attitude toward life, and by an autobiography of one who himself went through the long process of acculturation. Sociologists have done vastly more than psychologists in recent years with letters, diaries and case studies in the attempt to show the life history of individuals in relation to a changing social *milieu*. One might almost say that the attempt to study changes in personality which result from social causes has been the legitimate prey of sociologists; and that, except for the contribution made by psychiatry, psychology has, for the most part, kept its hands off until recently. Of late, however, it has shown a rapidly increasing interest.

Both case histories and more literary forms of biography have frequently entirely omitted material which might serve to show the relationship between life development and cultural *milieu*. A recent attempt to introduce both systematization and cultural sophistication into the study of biography may therefore be adduced. A series of "criteria for the life history" is proposed, as follows:

1. The subject must be viewed as a specimen in a cultural series.
2. The organic motors of action ascribed must be socially relevant.
3. The peculiar rôle of the family group in transmitting the culture must be recognized.
4. The specific method of elaboration of organic materials into social behavior must be shown.
5. The continuous related character of experience from childhood through adulthood must be stressed.
6. The "social situation" must be carefully and continuously specified as a factor.
7. The life history material itself must be organized and conceptualized.

With these criteria in mind, six published life studies (biographical, autobiographical, and psychiatric) were examined. If to the reader all this seems to be elaborating the obvious, let him be assured that adequate attention to the criteria, even by those skilled in psychiatry and other disciplines, is extremely rare.

The problem of life history research has been greatly clarified by this endeavor to set up definite criteria for the life history. The life history, Dollard maintains, must be seen in terms of the cultural whole in which the personality develops. Culture must not be a disembodied set of forces. The forces must be personal forces, and they must act directly upon the organism. The organism must be not a plastic wax, but a bundle of strivings. The strivings must be stated in such a way that their social objectives and directing tendencies must be defined in a biologically meaningful way and biologically defined in a socially meaningful way. The physiology of hunger is one thing; the socialization of hunger through a process of mother-child interactions is another. "The organic motors must be socially relevant."

Yet a word of reserve about Dollard's approach is needed. His analysis is decidedly a step forward. Unfortunately, however, the organic motors are assumed to be alike, both quantitatively and qualitatively, from one person to the next. We are assumed to be born with the same drives, with the same thresholds for each of the drives, with the same capacity to repress or inhibit a specific drive, with the same potentialities for integrating drives. Our central nervous systems are assumed to be only slightly variable, our autonomic nervous systems not variable at all. The difference between your fear and my fear is a difference based upon the intensity or frequency of subjection to fear stimulation. This is definitely a step ahead of those sociologies which start with formless or unorganized human nature; but it is a step behind that conception of personality growth which stresses the ultimate and ceaseless interaction between organism and social world. Just as there is no hereditary trait which functions in social life without having been modified by social life, so there is no social response which does not concretely reflect the full individuality of the person. We all talk English, but with a tempo, pitch, emphasis, nasality or abruptness which springs in part from the biology of the individual's speech organs, central nervous structures and autonomic thresholds. The life history, then, is a life history of individual biological progression, the distinction between biological and cultural being arbitrary, since the biological has become social and nothing but the biological can become social. For some purposes the social scientist may regard us as all alike. If we wish to vote for President, we have to vote on the first Tuesday after the first Monday in November; we cannot reflect individuality by voting in April. To make ourselves understood, we must talk English. Institutionalized though our behavior may be, there is some individuality of a deep biological sort even in such acts; and with respect to a great deal of our institutional behavior the personal idiom is never lost.

A large number of German psychologists have made use of the *diary* method of studying change in attitudes and personality traits. The work of William Stern and Charlotte Bühler and their many pupils should be specially mentioned. In particular, students of the psychology of religion have in recent years laid a good deal of stress upon such diary material, usually with a view to studying the upheavals in religious belief and attitude which seem so common in adolescence. Much has also been written about the seclusiveness, negativism, loneliness, and sensitiveness of the early adolescent years.

It seems to us that certain weaknesses invalidate much of this material. For example, no one seems to have ascertained what proportion of adolescents in various countries and in various socioeconomic groups keep diaries. Diaries which are used to support a number of generalizations regarding adolescence seem to us to be worth but little unless there is some way of telling to what extent the adolescents who keep diaries are representative of those who do not—the latter must surely be the vast majority. There are, in fact, many reasons for believing that among those who keep diaries there are an undue proportion whose contacts are unsatisfactory and whose need to "talk out" their emotional problems can be satisfied in no other way. There are, to be sure, a few diaries of matter-of-fact youngsters who simply tell what they had to eat and whether they went to the movies or went roller skating; but they are few, and they would without doubt be immediately regarded by most students of diaries as unsatisfactory for psychological analysis.

For these reasons it seems to us that the *controlled* diary, with continuous record of one's own activities, comes much nearer to scientific requirements. But since, in most cases, this very element of control has restricted the nature of the entries made to a single type of behavior, the controlled diary has brought forth trait studies rather than total personality pictures. We shall pass directly, therefore, to a consideration of case history methods.

Just as the spontaneous diary has tended to be crowded out (for scientific purposes) by the controlled diary, so the whole case method has tended to take on a flavor of "control." Though case studies are still plentiful (biographies and autobiographies extending all the way from a page or two up to elaborate documents of hundreds of pages), and though they are often of great clinical value, the collection of more and more material has inevitably led to *statistical treatment of comparable data* and to the attempt to define and measure each of the items of behavior which appear in the life history. It is only in this way that causal relationships between what happens at one age and what happens at a later age can be defined. The intuitive use of the case method tends, therefore, to be crowded out by other methods in which items in one life history are compared with those in other life histories in order to determine whether necessary sequences actually appear. To explain an adult maladjustment as due to a childhood mother fixation is a convenient habit; and if one finds that among a hundred nail-biters twenty-eight have mother fixations, one may, and frequently does, *naïvely* conclude that about 28 per cent of nail biting is due to mother fixation. The use of control groups, however, has shown more and more clearly that statistics of the type described are of no value. Mother fixations, for example, may appear in 35 per cent of *non*-nail-biters, so that statistical comparisons become meaningless unless the presence of one trait bears *more than a chance relation* to the presence of another.

One of the most elaborate and carefully controlled of such attempts is a study of "experience variables." Dozens of adult personality traits of each individual are compared with items in the environment—personality of father, mother, brothers and sisters, religious and social activities of the individual as a child and in the early teens. In this way certain striking relations appear between the characteristics of the home and of the individual at the time of this inventory. With the data from nearly three hundred persons, the relation, for example, between present sex adjustment and the incidence of parental threats and punishments for sex practices is so striking that a causal relation between such threats and present maladjustment is "absolutely" certain (the Pearson method not being applicable, Yule's Q is used for such determinations). Similarly, social adjustment appears to be much better among those coming from homes where affection is freely expressed than those in which undemonstrativeness is the rule. Intimacy with the father appears in the case of both men and women to be a very important factor in present social adjustment. These data, being based upon self-estimates and memories, fail, of course, to obtain the objectivity of a contemporaneous behavior record. This represents, nevertheless, one of the most extensive and systematic quantitative "techniques of biography" for the discovery of hypotheses regarding causal relations in the growth of personality.

Thus the gradual merging of the case study method and the quantitative record of personality traits has engendered the bold hope of an actual *science of biography*. Among the most outspoken of the advocates of a systematic *biographical technique*, which will make biographical psychology as exact a science as psychophysics, is Lasswell. Starting with the psychiatric and psychoanalytic procedures, he undertakes to subject each individual to a series of physiological and psychological experiments, including continuous record of variations in blood pressure, respiration, galvanic reflex, etc. The interview is recorded verbatim, and when the records can be studied at leisure after the termination of the session, an attempt is made to find what physiological changes have accompanied the strain and stress of the interview, and to ascertain the physiological correlates of substitution, rationalization, compensation, and the like. Early reports on this work concern subjects' behavior while free associations directly concerned the psychoanalyst. At such times, when considerable tension was apparent, the subjects showed quite uniformly increased pulse rate and decreased rate of speaking. This, of course, tells us little in itself as to individual differences in personality. But it seems to us enormously important by way of laying groundwork. For by such methods life histories can be studied in terms of their significance for the individual. A great variety of other psychiatric and psychological methods are suggested, including "master inventories" of character and independent diagnoses by psychiatrists of different persuasions.

This belief in the possibility of a science of biography has even appeared in the writings of those whose life work has been primarily experimental. "I would rather," says J. B. Watson, "see the behavior of one white rat observed carefully from the moment of birth until death than to see a large volume of accurate statistical data on how two thousand rats learn to open a puzzle-box."

The interview has in recent years tended more and more to become an exact method. We find the "standardized" interview developing among social case workers, personnel officers, and psychiatrists, with variations characteristic of the different fields, but with the common purpose of avoiding those irregularities which make the usual interview data so difficult to subject to systematic quantitative treatment. A technique has been devised, for example, for the reporting of both verbal and non-verbal behavior in brief interviews, data being recorded on a standard chart. It appears from these data that such tensions and distractions as show themselves in change of posture, for example, offer a useful supplement to the verbal record. It is made clear that while actual difficulties in remembering what is said during a short interview are not serious, the development of a technique to record all that is really important in the interview is complex and difficult. Other attempts to put interview data on a more exact basis have involved the obtaining of the same information by two interviewers at about the same time, together with independent predictions as to the probable "success" of the interviewee, and the checking of interview results against other data. Questionnaires as guides to be followed in interviewing are also commonly used; the questionnaire as a standard form for organization of material while in the presence of the interviewer is, of course, quite a different thing from the one filled out in isolation or aloofness from all personal contacts.

The highly personal nature of the interview situation is itself full of problems for social psychology. Never has this been more clearly shown than in G. V. Hamilton's *Research in Marriage*. Hamilton, in interviewing two hundred married persons with regard to a wide range of topics having to do with success or failure in the marriage relation, found it necessary to standardize his procedure to a degree which might at first appear preposterous. The questions (over 300 in number) were typed on cards which the interviewee read and answered, Hamilton recording the replies verbatim. Having discovered that the sheer distance between the subject and the interviewer is an important variable, he tied the subject's chair to the wall so that this element could be held constant. Obviously there are many cases, even so, in which Hamilton's psychiatric interview is not standardized; he points out that some of his typewritten sentences acted as "leading questions," and that the element of personal suggestion was not eliminated. Furthermore, he allowed the subject to skip a question at a given time and to come back to it later, so that there must have been a piling up of unpleasant or "tense" questions at the end. But this work, together with certain other similar studies, appears to justify the conviction that even in such a complicated and delicate problem of inquiry, a genuinely scientific planning of the interview procedure may minimize those personal elements which distort accuracy of report, and may bring out in a definite form certain important elements in life histories which could not possibly be secured in any other way. Such inquiries point toward a *biographical technique*, a method of studying relations between past experiences and present adjustments.

Thus, when experimental method is not at hand, the systematic study of factors appearing in personality at various ages points the way to the determination of causes, and, when taken in conjunction with objective physiological and psychological tests and a study of heredity, should make it ultimately possible to compare the relative importance of a wide variety of interacting forces in the structure of personality. The *naïve* assumption that personality is determined by heredity alone, and the equally *naïve* but at present far more widespread idea that somehow all temperamental and emotional differences are imposed by the environment upon otherwise identical organisms, are at last giving way to a somewhat more critical quantitative approach.

We turn now to methods of measurement which are no less objective than those applied to the measurement of single traits. They might, indeed, be considered as simultaneous measurement of single traits. But the results now to be presented have consistently been offered with a totally different interpretation. The "unique trait" hypothesis has, as a matter of fact, often been specifically repudiated. The point of view represented by most of this work is perhaps typified by the "personalistic" position of Stern. Stern distinguishes (as translated by Allport and Vernon) between "vertical" and "horizontal" relationships among personality factors. The former are those "in which significance is sought in the depths of personality," whereas the latter represent single factors (regarded as on the periphery of personality) as related to other single factors. Stern insists, in common with most other German students of personality and character, that the individual's specific characteristics are of little significance, considered either singly or in relation to each other, unless each of them is related to the central conative drives, values, and emotional *penchants*. These not only give meaning to the specific traits, but actually control and guide them. To study single traits apart from central determinants is about as successful as the attempt to read purpose or meaning into the random flutterings of a chicken whose head has just been severed by the axe.

All this has been cogently stated by Vernon, together with illustrations of methods best adapted to personality research proceeding from such assumptions. It is not surprising to find that matching methods are presented as most suitable, since various angles of viewing the personality-as-a-whole can thus be compared. Several experiments, his own and others', are cited to show that interpretative sketches, or "structured impressions," yielded more accurate and more readily identifiable representations of individual personalities, and with more agreement among themselves, than schematic devices and ratings on specific traits. For example, twenty-five student subjects were observed by three experimenters during the administration of various performance tests. Their impressions were embodied in interpretative sketches and also in ratings of intelligence, quickness, extroversion, and emotional stability. Attempts by the experimenters to match the sketches with their recollected impressions of the subjects were successful in 23.3 per cent of the cases (equivalent to a contingency coefficient of .72 ± .06). Matching on the basis of ratings was much less successful, the comparable coefficient being only .27 ± .04. There seems to be little doubt that, for purposes of *identifying individuals*, such "whole" methods are more successful. We shall later consider the question as to their merits with regard to other aims in personality measurement.

"Expressive activities" have, logically enough, received a major share of the attention of experimentally minded adherents of this school of thought. For if personality does flow from certain inner springs, it should be objectively discernible through characteristic modes of expression, such as voice, gait, and handwriting. These offer avenues of investigation without making any concessions to trait ideology.

We have already seen (page 783) that certain personality traits may be matched with voices of unseen speakers with a limited degree of success. In a further experiment Allport and Cantril had each of three 50-word personality sketches read by each of three speakers, whom the sketches described. The percentage of correct matchings was reliably greater than chance, with six sets of three speakers. Altogether, 54.5 per cent of the matchings were correct, though only one-third of them would be so by chance. Again the percentage of correct matchings of the total personality sketches exceeds that of single characteristics.

Handwriting as an index to personality has been regarded both as an open sesame and as a cheap form of charlatanism. It has without question been exploited. Though for some time a small amount of honest and careful study has been devoted to it, only recently has it become the object of investigation by true experimental methods. It is only fair to add that most psychologists, remembering its unsavory past and witnessing the quack methods to which it is still largely a prey, have exhibited a certain cultural lag in their attitudes toward the more careful recent work. To say this is not to maintain that the interpretation of character by handwriting is a science; its most devoted adherents would make no such claims. It is to be used, rather, in the manner described in connection with the Rorschach test, as a source of reasonably dependable clues which demand considerable experience and insight before they are of much value.

Some criteria are obviously demanded if the merits of handwriting are to be assessed. The Allport-Vernon Test of Values was used in one attempt to determine the degree to which dominant interests could be judged by a graphologist. Fifty subjects took this test, receiving scores for each of the six values. They then wrote a given sample of prose with their own pens, "in natural manner," on paper of uniform size. From these samples an expert graphologist, who knew nothing concerning the subjects except their sex and their handedness, assigned to each of them a score for five of the six values. The two sets of scores were then correlated, with the following results:

Value	Correlation
Aesthetic	.40 ± .08
Economic	.29 ± .09
Theoretic	.25 ± .09
Political	.07 ± .10
Religious	−.06 ± .10

These correlations were then combined by considering the 250 scores as a single series; the resulting coefficient was .21 ± .04. Something more than chance is at work here, and this becomes the more certain when we consider the limitations of the test which was used. The reliability coefficients of the several values range between .54 and .84. Graphologists, moreover, are quick to point out the wide divergence between interests, as thus measured by questionnaire methods, and the fundamental characterological dispositions which are the object of graphological inquiry. In particular, it is maintained that any such test of interests is bound to sweep into its dragnet much that is of passing and superficial importance, whereas graphological methods attempt to plumb the underlying depths of stable personality features.

In view of these and other limitations, the foregoing experiment was continued. Six individuals were selected as being dominant in one, and only one, of each of the six values, according to *both* test scores and graphological diagnosis. These six individuals then rewrote the same letter on uniform paper, signing fictitious names. The letters were then photostated and sent to thirty-one graphologists, together with brief descriptions of Spranger's six types (to which the six values are intended to correspond). They were asked to match the scripts with the types, of which relatively "pure" representatives had written the scripts. As a control device, twenty-six "educated adults" of both sexes who were unacquainted with graphology, duplicated this procedure. Four or more of the matchings of seventeen of the twenty-six graphologists were correct, but not a single layman achieved so high a degree of success. The probability of the degree of accuracy achieved by the graphologists is about one in a million chances; of that of the laymen, one in 1.18.

Another experiment will afford a glimpse at graphological methods. The Allport Ascendance-Submission Test and the Thurstone Personality Schedule were given to fifty college women, who then wrote a 139-word selection of prose in the same room at the same time. These samples of writing were then judged by twenty-six objective graphological measures. Of these, only four yielded consistently reliable correlations (or nearly so). These, together with two multiple correlations, are as follows:

	Correlations of Graphological Scores with	
Graphological Measures	Thurstone P.S.	Allport A.S.
(a) capital height........................	−.46	.16
(b) capital ratio..........................	−.68	.46
(c) loopiness.............................	.55	−.24
(d) line-overlap..........................	.45	−.41
(c) and (d) multiple correlation............	.64	−.44
(b), (c) and (d) multiple correlation........	.84	−.56

The reliability coefficients of the various measures, most of which were obtained with the aid of microscope and calipers, ranged between .4 and .8, the median coefficient for the direct measures being .77, and for the ratio measures, .71. The reliability test, however, was a rigorous one, being obtained from a comparison of two samples of script written at different times under quite dissimilar circumstances. The factor of height seemed to be the most consistent of the several types of measures used; seven of them, all involving height, had an average intercorrelation of .54. The average intercorrelation of three measures involving spacing was .33. These results demonstrate, at the very least, that certain features of handwriting are fairly stable characteristics of the individual under some cultural conditions. Although most of the single measures show little relationship to neurotic and ascendant traits, the multiple correlations resulting from their optimum combination is striking.

Such procedures, while more satisfying to the objective-minded psychologist, are felt by many graphologists to be almost a prostitution of their art. Personality is acknowledged to be only one of the factors which determine handwriting. Hence no particular feature alone may be expected to be a reliable and definite indication of a personality trait. It is the "syndrome" that counts—the coexistence of parallel or contradictory features. Thus no great degree of correspondence between graphological and objective methods of portraying personality may be expected—or desired. At any rate, such experiments as we have quoted permit us to state the following reasons why careful graphological methods may no longer be ignored by the student of personality:

1. They can be made reasonably objective, both in the sense that retest reliabilities of single measurements have been found which compare favorably with those of other methods, and in the sense that a considerable number of graphologists have been found to agree fairly well with each other as to the total personality picture which emerges from their study.

2. Characteristics revealed by them (at their best) do correspond to some degree with those divulged by other methods. While this is true of single measurements to only a slight degree, graphological "syndromes" are fully as indicative trends as other forms of expressive activity.

To this may be added that the limitations of these methods (even at their best) are essentially the same as of those applied to other expressive activities. These will be discussed on a later page.

The inspiration for most of the experimental work on expressive activities has come from theories of personality which are native to German soil. The great majority of experiments have consequently emanated from German laboratories. But in spite of this, we present, as the most exhaustive research in this field, work from an American laboratory. Its sponsors would be the first to admit their debt to their German predecessors. We choose it in preference to the pioneering experiments because of the more careful attention that has been given in the Harvard laboratories to problems of reliability, and because the wide range of behaviors studied permits vastly greater insight into the interrelationships of different forms of expression.

In *Studies in Expressive Movement*, G. W. Allport and P. E. Vernon present the results of submitting twenty-five male subjects, ranging in age from 18 to 50, to an elaborate series of laboratory measurements. These included muscular pressures in writing and muscular tonus in the relaxed state; speed of reading aloud, of walking and strolling, of arranging cubes, of drawing various figures, of handwriting, and of tapping with fingers, hands, and legs; degree of over- or under-estimation of size of coins and dollar bills, of distance from the body, of angle of freely rotating arm, and of heaviness of weights; of tendency to space, closely or widely, cubes, drawn figures, and handwriting; and of tendency toward expansiveness of stride, of handwriting, and of drawn figures. Subjects were observed individually in three experimental sessions at four-week intervals. Motor tests were in most cases administered at least twice, and at different sessions. Two observers were always present, and their measurements were supplemented by qualitative observations and ratings.

From the mass of statistical material yielded by these data, two questions primarily concern us. If expressive movements have significance for personality they must, in the first place, permit of reliable measurement. If this test is passed, we shall then inquire into their interrelationships. The data, of course, are complex, and certain statistical questions bob up to render uncertain their interpretation at several points.

Most of the correlations based upon repetitions of single measurements suggest a considerable degree of individual variability. But since most of the measures are based upon very brief samples of behavior (the average period was about 30 seconds) the authors seem to be justified in supplementing the "raw" coefficients with those predicted by the Spearman-Brown formula for the scores based upon performance at both (or all three) sessions. Thus "stepped up," most of the speed tests show reliability coefficients between .8 and .9. These are uniformly a few points higher if computed from scores obtained at the same experimental session, than if from sessions separated by an interval of weeks. The retest reliabilities of the single measures of pressures and tensions, accuracy of estimation, spacing, and expansiveness were less satisfactory, most of them ranging between .6 and .8 (corrected). Composite scores, however, built up of similar or related tasks and "stepped up" according to the number of measures included, result in several "factors" whose reliabilities are in the neighborhood of .8. Individual scores in most of the single measurements, in other words, were not very reliable, but stable differences were found by combining scores.

The reader will have noted that, once composite scores are substituted for single measurements, the problem of reliability includes that of the interrelationship of measures. And here we find many surprises; often totally disparate measures are closely related, while almost identical ones are not. Thus, speeds of walking and of strolling yield a correlation of —.07; of length of walking and of strolling strides (corrected for height), .02; whereas extent of cubes (spread out at will upon the table) and overestimation of distance with the legs are correlated to the extent of .59. But *averages* of series of correlations are uniformly positive, and in most cases high enough to suggest that habits of gesture are reasonably stable characteristics of the individual. Thus the average retest reliability (uncorrected) of all measures is .684. Intercorrelations of similar tasks for different muscle groups are fully as high as repeat correlations for the same muscle groups; the latter are .75 for tasks separated by a few minutes, and .64 for those separated by a period of weeks.

The 45 speed measures are reduced to 14 composite measures, whose respective reliabilities (stepped up according to the number of single measures included) range from .74 to .96. But the average intercorrelation of the 14 measures is only .17. Clearly, there is no general speed factor present. (The authors quote several other investigations, all of which present average speed intercorrelations of about .45; these they believe to be spuriously high, because of "constancy of set" on the part of subjects, and the similarity of the tasks included.) Hence speed is separated into three factors, each measured by similar tasks found to be positively intercorrelated. Surveying the intercorrelations of all their tests, they discover three hard *psychological factors* (not "group factors" in the usual sense, yet psychologically coherent general ways of behaving which enter into and determine scores in individual tests). The factors are *area* (tendency to fill up space, whatever the movement and however made); *emphasis* (tendency to accept and throw into relief certain phases of expression); and *centrifugality* (tendency to move "out" rather than "in"). The nature of these factors, the average intercorrelations of the measures of which they are composed, and their own intercorrelations, are given in the following table:

Factor	Number of Component Measures	Average Intercorrelation among Component Measures (Uncorrected)	Internal Consistency (Corrected)	Correlation with Preceding Factors in Order Listed
Verbal speed.......	8	.46	.77	
Drawing speed.....	9	.58	.77	.61
Rhythmic speed....	9	.76	.90	.07; .19
Area..............	9	.33	.82	−.33; −.52; −.30
Centrifugality.....	7	.30	.75	.34; .07; −.03; −.03
Emphasis.........	13	.25	.82	−.38; −.20; .07; .25; −.22

If the evidence stopped here our conclusions would be mainly negative. There is clearly no general speed factor permeating all these forms of expression. Nor is there a "general psychomotor" factor expressing strength or vitality (the median intercorrelation of 24 variables presumably measuring this is .05). Physical pressure or tension appears not to be an individual constant; it is "significant only as part of a wider and more psychological tendency to make emphatic movements." Statistically speaking, the chief positive results of the experiment seem to us to be that certain specific expressive activities represent relatively constant individual variations. That general factors have been tapped would seem to be demonstrated by the second column of the above table, but two considerations render it less impressive than these coefficients would indicate: (1) in almost every case certain measures which on *a priori* grounds should be included in the composites are omitted because they show little relationship to the others; and hence (2) until these average interrelationships have been confirmed by the use of other subjects, these factors will smack of the accidental, the opportunistic. Nor are we impressed by the very respectable size of the corrected coefficients in the third column. The authors hesitate to "step up" 14 speed variables having an average intercorrelation of .168 to an internal consistency of .72; "here is a case where the use of corrections, however legitimate statistically, seems to distort and misrepresent the psychological situation." It seems to us that precisely the same might be said for its application to these factors. Their only significance, beyond that of the second column, lies in their applications for the reliability of the composite scores, and this could be more dependably presented in terms of simple correlations between composite scores as obtained from repeated tests.

But to present only this statistical material would give an untrue picture of the authors' position regarding both methods and results. Vernon's insistence on *congruence* of *vertical* measures rather than *correspondence* between *horizontal* ones has already been suggested (page 846). While the authors believe that their several factors represent, to a degree, vertical relationships, they are subject to all the shortcomings that inhere in statistical indices. Hence their supplementary methods must at least be hinted at. The thesis defended by this material is that "measures which do not correspond statistically may nevertheless be congruent psychologically."

"Case studies" of four of the experimental subjects are therefore presented. One of these was a vocational counselor for business executives who gave the impression of being vigorous, brisk, pleasing, and "go-getting." In all of the ten traits (voice loudness, speech connectedness, movement during idleness, gesticulation while speaking, freedom of movement, smoothness of movement, natural tempo, neatness of personal appearance, consistency of neatness, forcefulness of personality) he was rated in the top quartile, and at the very top in speed and forcefulness. As for the objective measurements, his mean score on the 24 variables was second highest, and he was next to the most consistent. He scored highest in the emphatic group factor, seventh in the areal, and thirteenth in the centrifugal group factor. Certain contradictions, however, appeared; he was slow in verbal, drawing, and strolling speeds; low in size of handwriting, size of check-marks, and length of strolling stride. The authors then proceed to show that these contradictions are actually contradictory only in the light of *a priori* logic, that they disappear when studied as aspects of a total personality. Thus, "although aggressive and self-confident, the subject has developed caution, precision, and the capacity for delay; when committing himself he must be certain. . . . His reading and speaking are slow because [?] his enunciation is exceptionally distinct and precise. The reduction in size of his handwriting . . . seems to indicate the same quality. The striking difference between his speeds of walking and strolling shows this same tendency of modifying any headstrong impulses at will. . . . There are, in short, no measurements in this case which might definitely contradict a subjective interpretation of this man's personality."

One further experiment is illuminating. Samples of the pressure curves (writing, and drawing parallel lines) of four subjects, and specimens of their handwriting—they were reproduced exactly for the judges' use—were presented to 32 judges, together with thumbnail sketches of the personalities of the same four subjects. These were as follows:

A. Highly artistic, hyperactive, generous and cheerful, "Bohemian."

B. Colorless, quiet, agreeable, and dependable student.

C. Immature, self-asserting, extravagant, unstable sophomore.

D. Forceful, active, efficient business man, but cautious and exact.

After the technique of obtaining the curves was explained to the judges, they were asked to match them with the scripts. By chance each script would be matched with each set of curves 6.25 per cent of the time; actually the correct incidence was obtained in 14 per cent of the judgments for subject D, and in 18.7 per cent for subject B. Subjects A and C were mistaken for each other with almost exactly the same frequency, correct matchings for these subjects being no more frequent than would occur by chance. Altogether, 43 per cent of the matchings were correct, as against 25 per cent by chance; this is equivalent to a biserial r of .63. It is quite rightly pointed out that these subjects were exceptionally heterogeneous; but the authors maintain that, nevertheless, the uniformity of judgments, which was much greater than the accuracy, points to a considerable congruence among very diverse expressive activities.

We have devoted considerable space to experiments with expressive activities. Their contribution may be evaluated as to methods, and as to the theory of personality toward which they point. Their most significant contribution to methodology appears to be the matching device. Its limitations are fairly obvious; chief among them is the practical impossibility of distinguishing among individuals who are not particularly heterogeneous. "Pure" and extreme types can often be identified by such means, but most individuals, particularly in large groups, do not become distinctively delineated. It is a rough instrument, but it cuts deep. If other instruments are more refined, this one is at least not limited to the probing of single symptoms. Within limits, it is capable of laying bare those elemental forces, whatever they are and however wide their influence, which lend to personality whatever degree of unity it has.

But precisely at this point we have to deal with an unknown quantity. If it is assumed that personality, being more unified than the flutterings of a decapitated fowl, has some focal point or points, are they alike, or at least commensurable, for different individuals? Are these foci native, or the result of cultural experience, or both? And do their radii become more or less extended with the cultural impress? Such questions suggest the extreme audacity of these methods of measurement. They also reveal a further weakness of the matching device. For whether it be voice, handwriting, gait, or pressure curves which are to be matched with each other, with single traits, or with personality sketches, a considerable subjective factor on the part of the matcher is involved. So far as we know, every investigator has found a greater degree of uniformity than of accuracy when matching techniques were employed. Success depends, in other words, upon the utilization of stereotypes. We are inclined to agree with Allport and Vernon that the stereotypes are in the right direction but exaggerated. The moral to the story is, then, that while we have learned something about the *general organization* of personality from these experiments, the best that can be said in individual diagnosis is that they are somewhat more likely to be right than wrong. For stereotypes notoriously fail with individuals who are an exception to the rule.

The concept of congruence among personality characteristics we hold to be an important one. Statistical investigation has thus far failed to reveal any deep-lying growth centers for such congruences among fundamental traits. The evidence for their existence is almost entirely based upon judgments. This is inevitably so, in our judgment, since personality characteristics (at least those of greatest social significance) are themselves cultural percepts, and not perceptually independent entities. This is not to say that they cannot be more closely approximated by exclusively objective means. But this will await a far better understanding than we now possess of the possible significance of various aspects of culture. For many aspects of personality may almost be defined in terms of the uses to which bits of the culture complex are put by individuals.

So much has been claimed for the Rorschach test by some of its proponents that appraisal of precisely what it can do, and how well, has become extremely difficult. The materials for the test are simple, and its conception is ingenious. It consists of ten irregular but symmetrical ink blots, five of them in blacks and grays, and five partially in colors, on a white background. Administration and scoring of the test, however, are elaborate and, at some points, highly subjective. The nature of these difficulties, as well as the inclusiveness of personality aspects which the test attempts to probe, will be shown by the following classification of responses which must be recorded. (The list is not complete, nor is there unanimity regarding methods of scoring.)

1. Mode of apperception:
   as a whole
   detail first, then fitted into whole
   part or detail

   unusual detail
   white detail
   detail, where whole very common
   most frequent sequence of above responses
   apperception type, based on all of above
2. Quality of response:
   form or shape (good or poor)
   movement
   judged wholly by color
   judged primarily by color, secondarily by form
   judged primarily by form, secondarily by color
   chiaroscuro
   total color score
   proportions of color and movement
3. Content and originality:
   original (good or poor)
   common
   animal
   involving humans
4. Total number of responses

We can indicate for only a few of these the significance for personality often ascribed to them. Whole responses represent a synthetic type of thought; detail responses, meticulous or analytic thought; too great preponderance of the former reveals unpracticability and carelessness of detail. An invariable sequence of part and whole responses shows compulsion and stereotypy, whereas too loose a sequence reflects an illogical and disordered mind. Two or more white details suggest opposition and obstinacy, since most subjects perceive the white as background. A moderately high proportion of good form responses indicates intelligence, but too high a proportion shows a formal and pedantic mentality. Movement responses reveal the degree of intra-psychic creativity; they are numerous in the artistic and the highly intelligent, whereas peasants, imbeciles, and the materially minded give few or no such responses. Color responses are unrelated to intelligence, but represent affectivity, fluidity of emotion. Pedants and depressives fail to give color responses, but they are frequent among the nervous, high-strung, and artists. Responses wholly in terms of color mean impulsiveness, and a preponderance of color over form responses reflects sensitivity or suggestibility. Chiaroscuro responses reveal anxious, cautious, un-free affective adaptability. Too large a proportion of original re-sponses shows fantasy rather than intelligence, but too low a propor-tion indicates either feeble-mindedness or poverty of imagination. Common responses reflect stereotypy or low intelligence. Animal responses, being the commonest, are frequent among the feeble-minded, but rare among artists. In general, the "apperception type," as determined by part and whole responses, is symptomatic of the intellectual life, as the movement-color responses reveal the affective life.

The reader must not conclude that Rorschach test results are cur-rently interpreted by the sheer addition of scores according to these indices. Both the strengths and the weaknesses of the method, as at present used, lie in this flexible interpretation of responses in a clinical manner. From any objective standards, there is much to be desired by way of standardization of the test. The following criti-cisms are offered by one who has used the test widely in this country, as applicable to European Rorschach work generally (the test has been used far more widely in Europe than here): (1) norms are based on few cases, or missing entirely, and usually presented with-out measures of dispersion; (2) the methods of interpretation are essentially those of the artist—judgments are qualitative or subjec-tive, even intuitive; (3) liberties are frequently taken with method, there is inconstancy in scoring, and no hard and fast normative cri-teria exist. Doubtful responses, for example, are sometimes classified *after* the test is concluded, in conformity with the modal tendency of the subject. To this it may be added that the reliability of the test is most uncertain, although recent improvements in the standardiza-tion of scoring have resulted in some fairly satisfactory reliabilities.

Attempts to use only objective scores of Rorschach responses have been somewhat disappointing. According to one study, twenty "healthy adults" made a reliably greater total number of responses than twenty-three non-hospitalized mental patients, but the ratios of various types of response were about the same for the two groups. The unstable subjects showed, however, a greater variability from picture to picture in number of responses than the stable group. Most investigators have found little or no relationship between

Rorschach's alleged criteria of levels of intelligence and scores of adults on intelligence tests.

Considered as a device for eliciting symptoms which are to be seen in relation to each other, much as a physician sizes up coexisting symptoms in making a diagnosis, the Rorschach test has been enthusiastically received in many quarters. Rorschach himself is reported to have compared notes with a psychoanalyst concerning a subject studied by both methods, with striking agreement. The analyst is said to have been able to add only content derived from the patient's history. Diagnosis of mental disease by Rorschach methods has in many cases been clinically confirmed. Bearing in mind the conditions under which the usefulness seems to have been demonstrated (these conditions may be labeled as psycho-diagnostic rather than objective), the testimony of one who is also familiar with more objective methods is of considerable interest: "I am unable to call to mind any other test of personality or temperamental traits which will tell me as much about my subjects in so short a time as does the Rorschach test." Since the test is being widely and gratefully used by many clinicians (and by many students of normal adolescents and children), and since its results are at present being compared extensively with life history documents with apparent mutual illumination, it is almost certainly more valuable and more promising than can be indicated by existing quantitative results. The reader will recall its usefulness in conjunction with other methods of appraising total personality in childhood (pages 287 ff.).

A thoroughgoing experimental approach has been applied by Luria to a host of personality problems. While his concern has been primarily theoretical, his work is a beautiful example of theory leading to experiment, which in turn leads to revisions of theory and further experiment. His basic method is as follows: the subject is given a word stimulus which must be responded to simultaneously by speaking a word and by pressing with the right hand a pneumatic bulb to which a kymograph is attached. The left hand, about which nothing is said to the subject, remains throughout the experiment resting upon a sensitive plate, also attached to the kymograph, so that involuntary tremors or more overt movements are continuously recorded. In some of the experiments pulse rate and galvanic skin reflex were also recorded, but they proved to be of little significance. Simple measures of reaction time and intensity of motor response were made, but interpretations are drawn chiefly from (1) shape and regularity of the voluntary muscle response curves; (2) their relationship to the time of the verbal response and to the nature of the verbal stimulus; and (3) the nature of the verbal response. In particular, the degree of *organization* which emerges from the sum total of behavior is scrutinized.

Luria's work leads him to postulate two types of persons, the "reactive-stable" and the "reactive-labile." The former are characterized by "complete coordination and relative regularity" of work, by absence of fluctuations in time of speech responses, and by accurate synchronizing of speech and motor responses. Their behavior is characterized, in short, by "an obvious regulating process." This rôle of regulation Luria conceives to be played by a "functional barrier" by means of which conflict is kept in the higher cortical centers until motor outlets are found through which the whole organism can be integrated. Conversely, therefore, the reactive-labile type is primarily characterized by disorganization. There are "marked and unequal delays" of the speech reactions, contrasting with spontaneous and uncontrolled motor responses of considerable irregularity. "Every excitation . . . at once passes over without any obstruction to the motor sphere." As in all type dichotomies, a fair proportion of subjects fell at or near the border lines, or between the two types. From a group of one hundred students tested, Luria reports 24 as being reactive-stable (with only "normal" deviations from regularity), and 31 as reactive-labile, their motor reactions being clearly irregular and uncoordinated.

It is a reasonable hypothesis that degree of disorganization is a function of the difficulty of the task for the subject. Hence variations in difficulty were introduced, both by using subjects of widely diverse abilities (children, feeble-minded adults, peasants, university students), and by restricting the type of verbal response required so that it became very simple or almost impossibly difficult as the case required. In general, the hypothesis was verified; the "functional barrier" was least operative in children and the feeble-minded, and under conditions of fatigue and extreme difficulty.

But many subjects of presumably good ability showed extreme disorganization in making even simple associative responses. Luria's primary concern was with behavior under conditions of affect. Hence most of his situations were so constructed as to involve conflict. By experimental means of great ingenuity he was able to demonstrate that differences in degree of organization of behavior, among subjects of about the same capacity, were directly traceable to conflicts known to be present. In some cases (e.g., neurotics) this was a relatively widespread and permanent state of conflict which was shown by irregular response to any and all verbal stimuli. Other cases involved temporary conflicts, such as those of students prior to an all-important examination, or of suspected criminals; in some subjects conflicts were experimentally produced under hypnosis. This latter technique was a particularly valuable one because "normal" behavior before the introduction of the conflict, and after its removal, could be compared with the behavior while the conflicts were acutely felt. All these data give impressive evidence that characteristically disorganized individuals may be detected by these means, and that conflicts known to exist in normal subjects may also be "spotted."

Fascinating as much of this material proves to be, our present problem is that of individual differences. What kinds of personality are associated with these differences in degree of integration? And are these differences stable, characteristic ones? It might be suspected, for example, that among the students facing examination, those who had reason to expect failure would show a greater degree of disorganization than those thoroughly prepared; but control experiments indicated that this factor played no part. The clinical symptoms found among the 31 reactive-labile students in this group included fatigue, anemia, affective instability, hyperthyroidism, neurasthenia, depression, "constitutional neuropath," hysteria, irritability, headaches, and excitability. One or more of these was found in all but four of this group, whereas similar diagnoses were made for only four of the reactive-stable group. The percentages are given below:

Clinical Classification	Reactively Labile	Reactively Stable
Normal, healthy...................................	13%	64%
Neuropathic symptoms (psychasthenia, hysteria, etc.).....	61%	16%
Somatic defects....................................	13%	20%
Undiagnosed......................................	13%	0

Following up this clue, a group of neurotic patients was intensively studied by the same methods. Twenty-five hysterical and neurasthenic subjects were found to be sharply differentiated from normals, in that their reactions were diffuse, and excitations found immediate motor outlet; they were, in short, unable "to keep the conflict isolated from the motor area." Luria states that among these twenty-five clinically verified neurotics there was not a single case of "the complete regulation of the movements and control of the equalized reactions."

Luria's methods have not only been systematically pursued by a large group of Russian investigators (an example of scientific cooperation rarely seen in this country on such a scale) but they are beginning to be applied here also. One comparison has been made of Luria's techniques with those of the "lie-detector," the galvanic skin reflex, and the association test. Fifty psychoneurotics and fifty normal controls were used as subjects. Their behavior, tabulated according to several of Luria's measures, is analyzed below:

	Reaction Time in Seconds			Percentage of Disturbance		
	Neutral Stimuli	Critical Stimuli	Post-critical Stimuli	Speech	Motor Local	General
Controls...........	1.9	2.7	2.1	19	17	8
Psychoneurotics.....	2.5	4.8	3.1	35	35	26
24 anxiety cases.....	2.7	5.4	3.4	41	33	30
19 hysteria cases....	2.3	4.1	2.9	31	36	21
7 obsessive-compulsive cases......	2.2	4.1	2.7	29	43	25

It will be seen that although the group data distinguish neurotics from controls, it would be unsafe to diagnose an individual as neurotic by these methods, and quite impossible to make a specific diagnosis according to present nomenclature. The authors' conclusion is that Luria's method seems to be more effective in the study of emotions than the other methods mentioned, and that "association-motor studies have a definite place in the investigation and treatment of the psychoneuroses."

Luria's work might conceivably have been discussed in the section dealing with traits measured in single situations. But the inspiration for his work has been so totally foreign to such a concept, and his interpretations so much more inclusive, that it quite definitely seems to belong with other total-personality investigations. For Luria is concerned, not with the trait of neuroticism, but with personality organization. If, incidentally, he has developed a usable measure of what others have conceived of as a trait, certainly the relationships in which he is interested are, in Stern's terminology, vertical rather than horizontal. A first-hand perusal of his data will convince the reader, far better than our brief presentation, that the disorganization of which he speaks is characteristic of more than a single kind of behavior; it is something central, and influences manner, speech, and muscular tensions. To have been able, in so many cases, experimentally to demonstrate the origin as well as the symptomatology of this disorganization is a psychological feat of the first importance. And the hand-in-glove fitting of first-rate experimental work to important theoretical developments is so rare as to render this work almost epoch-making.

We are now in a position to assemble our data. Two final questions remain. The first of them concerns the nature of personality organization. In so far as there are stable physiological foundations for the varying behaviors which distinguish individuals, we may expect to find general factors permeating much or all of any given personality. In so far as the individual is subjected to a constant stream of homogeneous cultural impacts, we may expect still other general factors to be acquired. But to the degree that personality is dependent upon varying segments of culture, to the degree that it is a group variable, or a person-to-person variable, it will be characterized by specific factors. We have considered in these pages measurements of single traits and of the total personality. Just how single are the traits, and how total the personality?

The answers depend, of course, upon the methods of measurement; and a comparative evaluation of them constitutes our final problem. The evidence seems at first to be overwhelmingly in favor of the specificity of behavior. For not only do these measures (with very few exceptions) show little or no relationship to other personality characteristics, but in general different laboratory measurements of the same trait show extremely low relationships. Witness the low intercorrelations among perseveration tests (around .3); the failure to find any two single laboratory measures which agree in diagnosing emotional stability; the notorious failure of introversion-extroversion tests to agree with one another; the complete absence of correlation among tests of suggestibility; the extreme variability even of repetitions of the same tests of competition and cooperation; and Allport and Vernon's demonstration of the non-existence of a general speed factor. Even the retest reliabilities of most of these are disappointing. Among the laboratory tests, only Howells' measures of persistence appear to pass the two tests of reliability and interconsistency.

But the argument proves too much; indeed, it is a boomerang. If laboratory measures reveal only specific behaviors, the laboratory as used has but demonstrated its own limitations for the study of personality, limitations which reach the point of almost total uselessness as far as the *organization* of personality is concerned. One of the reasons for this is that such personality variations as seem important enough to investigate fluctuate with precisely those *nuances* of social situation which the laboratory usually ignores or deliberately attempts to hold artificially constant. (Luria's work seems to us a glorious exception to this generalization; these very factors of social situation were, in most instances, the heart of his experiments.) If, as seems probable, whatever general factors there are in personality are those of adaptation to these subtly variable social situations, then it is no wonder that only specificities come through the laboratory sieve; the mesh is too small. And if, as also seems probable, that with which this adaptation is in conformity is uniquely determined by the peculiar experiences of the individual, the wonder becomes still less; what never got into the hopper cannot come through the sieve. If a personality, to change the figure, is an orchestra, most of its reeds and strings vibrate in response to social rhythms; its distinctiveness from other orchestras is determined not by its component instruments but by their fusing in accordance with the training and experience of its composite membership.

But what of single traits considered as broad response tendencies not varying with the situation? The various measuring devices which have been applied to these may be roughly classified either as ratings or as questionnaires, and the two must be considered separately. We do not include self-ratings under the former heading, for the fundamental distinction between the two methods seems to us to be the process by which the trait is singled out as a unit. The distinction, more simply put, is that between self-description viewed as behavior, and description of others, viewed as inherently "valid." On first appearance the questionnaire traits strongly suggest a considerable degree of generality. They are designed to include a multiplicity of situations, and many of them show high reliability. But their internal consistency, in spite of the tests to which the more carefully constructed ones have been subjected, seems to us to provide foundations for only very shaky conclusions regarding the generality of the traits in question. Item analysis of the same questions (e.g., by Thurstone, Harvey, and Willoughby) submitted to different populations has resulted in wide discrepancies as to which questions most clearly "hang together." Only when items involving widely differing situations have been shown to be related to each other by incidence of response reliably greater than chance among several populations can it be said that the trait is a general one. But this has so far not been done. It is easy to demonstrate that high odd-even reliability coefficients give little indication of internal consistency, particularly with large numbers of items. In so far as questionnaire scores on such traits as introversion, neurotic tendency, ascendance, etc., are of value, then, it is not because generalized traits have been validly measured, but because *preponderance* of reaction tendency—not *consistency* of reaction tendency—provides useful information. They make use of a kind of blunderbuss technique: "If this question doesn't catch 'em the next one will." Even if response to one item has almost no predictive value for response to other items (indicating the absence of generality of the trait) it may nevertheless be of value to know whether many or few responses regarded as similar in significance are made. Thus an individual who reports that he is subject to nightmares may or may not report that he blushes whenever embarrassed. But if he does, and also responds to a large number of other items in a manner regarded as "neurotic," the probability is that his behavior in still other situations (not included in the questionnaire) will frequently be of a similar nature. And this, of course, is generality of a sort. But it seems to us an attenuated sort. This is not to say that a greater degree of generality than this does not exist, but merely to point out that the statistical-treatment-of-questionnaire-response technique really yields very little information as to how generalized personality trends actually are.

The other method of obtaining quantitative statements of response tendency is that of ratings. The mere fact that different raters commonly show a considerable degree of unanimity regarding general traits might be interpreted as evidence for the generality of character dispositions. The halo bias which inheres in ratings need not trouble us too much; granted sufficient number and variety of raters, either the halos involved will differ, and thus tend to correct each other, or they will agree and carry their own weight of evidence for validity. Ratings are not, of course, "objective" in any laboratory sense. But the question of generality hinges upon validity (genuineness of observations) as well as upon objectivity (degree of agreement among observers). And on both of these counts, it seems to us, ratings provide more suitable source material for estimating the degree of generality of social behavior than do responses to questionnaires now in use. The evidence may be assembled as follows:

Objectivity: Defined as agreement among several observers, methods of self-report obviously cannot conform to this criterion; there can be but one observer, the subject himself. If questionnaire responses could be regarded as behavior to be studied quite apart from their "truthfulness" in view of the content of the questions, this consideration would, of course, be quite immaterial. But at the present stage this seems to us little short of an absurdity. Questionnaire items are still couched in terms so replete with "values" as to preclude the possibility of their being made in automatic, reflex-like manner.

Validity: Assuming then, that verisimilitude of self-reports must be considered, the multiplicity of variables in the questionnaire situation raises several serious questions. To put identical forms simultaneously into the hands of two subjects sitting side by side does not mean that response differences between them may be attributed to personality differences *of the type ostensibly measured.* Attitudes, varying with individuals, toward the conditions under which the questionnaire is administered, connotations and interpretations of the language of the questions, notions as to what is to be gained or lost by complete frankness, degree of insight into oneself, even the haste with which responses are made—all these variables, and others, are also being measured. The result is uncertain and irrelevantly determined responses by each individual and, what is worse, responses determined by different factors for different individuals. Traits thus measured are loaded with varying amounts of an unknown number of other traits.

The superiority of ratings, as data from which to study the problem of generality of social behavior, lies in the possibility which they provide of avoiding these very weaknesses of questionnaire methods. In the first place, any number of raters may be obtained for a single subject, and their differing angles of vision may serve to supplement each other until an all-round view is approximated. And secondly, in spite of the foibles and eccentricities with which human beings judge each other, it appears to us that only through the mediation of one human being can the behavior of another be so related to the almost infinite situational variables as to become meaningful. Just so, clinicians have found it necessary, for the most accurate measurement of intelligence, to employ individual examiners who can evaluate responses in terms of the conditions under which they are made. Personality traits are far more complex in their manifestations than intelligence; so much greater is their need for interpretations via the rater. If general factors persist in spite of these constantly shifting externals; if, as we have assumed, the general factors are primarily such as to be conceptualized only in terms of relationship of individual-to-situation, then they are surely more likely to be discovered through rating methods than through statistical analysis of questionnaire responses.

What, then, have rating methods revealed concerning the degree of generality in personality? Simply this: that certain traits are very widely generalized for certain individuals, whereas other traits are highly specific for the same individuals. Some individuals seem almost to be organized around easily definable traits, so that practically any behavior reflects their presence. Others, who seem to show little of such close-knit organization, must be interpreted either in terms of a multiplicity of traits of varying "strengths" and degrees of generalization, or in terms of more obscure but widely generalized characteristics. This, of course, is nothing more than a most probable present hypothesis. But to the extent that we proceed upon such a hypothesis, so much the less can we rely upon the methods of statistical analysis of questionnaire replies, a method built upon the assumption that a given trait is equally pertinent to all subjects who differ only in their degree of manifesting it. Our present conclusion is rather that the *pertinence of the trait to the individual* is the primary consideration. Behavior may be considered either to be episodic, unrelated to other behavior—in which case it defies study; or to be related to certain more or less generalized tendencies, which thus become the proper study of mankind.

Just as single-situation measurements tend to prejudge the question of specificity by their methods, so do those of total personality measurement. Just as "segmental methods can yield only segmental results," so also can total personality methods yield only patterned results—or nothing. How convincing, then, is the evidence of the latter for generality? That there are some factors common to many kinds of social behavior is beyond any doubt. The experiments of matching voice, gait, handwriting, trait scores, and personality sketches indicate, however, that the central forces are greatly deflected, and diversely so, as they influence the various behaviors. Common cores of personality seem to have been more successfully seen in terms of certain conceptualized organizational trends than as all-permeating traits of objectively measurable type. Thus a personality can be more completely "understood" through Luria's concept of degree of integration, or through a pattern of dominant

motives (compare, for example, Adler's "style of life") as gleaned
from case history material, than from single and more objective
measurements such as personal tempo or behavior syndrome. In so
far as reliability means fixity of response, we thus appear to be confronted with a kind of Heisenberg principle, to the effect that one
cannot have both significant and reliable information about a person
at the same time. If so, it is because personality is so largely a social
affair, and a complex society permits varying significance to be attached to similar behaviors, and similar significance to diverse behaviors. Thus, as in our preceding discussion of trait measures, we
conclude that, for the present and with present methods, general
factors in character are found to the degree that human insight is
permitted to organize raw observations, whether this organizing precedes or follows the recording of quantities.

The Limitations of "Personality Traits"

In view of the conclusions to which we have been forced, we must
refer again to our original distinction (page 781) between traits
which appear *regardless of situation* and traits which have to be defined in *terms of situation*. We have found that in the adult there
are some traits which seem so deeply ingrained that we can find
them wherever we look. Most traits, however, are of the situational
sort, and in measuring them some further reflections as to basic
assumptions and methods seem requisite.

The measurement of traits or dimensions of personality as defined
in the preceding pages involves necessarily an abstraction from the
unified free flow of activity in the whole organism. Attempts to
define traits of this kind in terms of deep-seated stigmata of the
personality have led to a bewildering complexity of names. There
are exactly as many fundamental traits as one wishes to define. Any
single question about one's conduct may involve a great many habitual modes of response. One's enjoyment of games of chance may
involve an interest in social gatherings, a desire to escape from hard
work, a desire to win prestige, or prestige and money together, and
a great many other habitual interests. Each single question in a

questionnaire may cut across several different tendencies within the person. The high internal consistency of a questionnaire based on correlating odd and even items or on retests shows nothing about the composition of the trait which the whole scale is supposed to measure. As we have pointed out, social traits of the type studied by questionnaires exist only as more or less useful abstractions.

This fact is usually regarded as a disadvantage. There is, however, much to be said for investigating and using these abstractions. Even if the feeling of dominance, for example, is an abstraction from feeling states which involve many other aspects besides dominance, and even if the feeling of dominance should ultimately turn out to be a composite of several different ingredients, there is a value in noting the relation between different particular abstractions and various other aspects of social life which are also abstractions. Predicting how the person will behave in campus politics, in hunting for a job, in making love, or in disagreeing with his neighbors is worth while. Indeed, we should go further and point out that the social patterns to which the individual must accommodate himself are usually of the type not to be characterized by the sheer psychology of drives. The situation "trying to play golf against a superior player on a muddy course with a poor set of clubs" is a highly specific situation, but one which should not be expected to call forth one specific psychological trait, residing like a birthmark in the tissues of the individual. If, from the man's behavior in seeking a job and in standing up against a reprimand from his boss, we can say something about the way in which he will behave when his investments fail and his small son refuses to obey, the prediction depends upon a knowledge both of the psychology of the man and of the character of the social situation to be met. If organisms were equipped to do ten simple definite things in response to ten simple definite stimuli, traits might be psychologically simple. If the stimulus patterns are actually very complicated, involving every degree of overlap from one to another, and if action patterns are even more complex, we should expect to find some value in simple abstractions like the existing traits. It must be noted, however, that the trait may disappear when the individual confronts an unwonted situation for which his previous habits have not prepared him, and that cultural changes may produce in a whole population the disappearance of deep-seated traits and the development of new ones.

An Interpretation of Personality in the Light of Quantitative Data

In an effort to define personality as it appears through analysis of the quantitative data given in this chapter and in earlier chapters in the book, the research implications of the following data must be considered:

1. Some reliably measured personality traits in pre-school children show marked changes when observed in an altered social situation. (Arrington, Jersild.)

2. The personality traits of nursery-school children vary strikingly in accordance with the personality traits of those with whom they are experimentally placed. (Harold Anderson.)

3. Sympathy scores which yield reliabilities from .94 to .99 appear among children whose responses change dramatically with variations in the child's security or other variations in the situation. (L. B. Murphy.)

4. Female delinquents treated as "bad" girls and "bad" women remain measurably and predictably "bad" (S. and E. Glueck) but, treated as human beings, behave as such. (Morse, Moreno.)

5. Not only conduct but the process of perceiving is profoundly altered by the social situation and altered in different ways for different persons. (Sherif.)

Evidence of this sort suggests that in most respects personality is not a stable entity capable of being pinned to a table and analyzed (in the manner of some psychiatrists and makers of personality tests), but that it interacts constantly with situations in such a way as to make it difficult to talk about personality traits as inherent only in the organism. What is really inherent in the organism is rather a wide range of *potentialities* more or less unique for each person. We know these potentialities only when we test them. But here a paradox arises, for the test situation is itself a social situation, responded to in very different ways by different persons. Just as the physicists' instruments for studying atomic structure alter the structure, so the psychologists' method of studying the potentialities of a personality changes the personality. If this is so, we need more reserve when discussing stable traits of organisms, for we never deal directly with an organism but only with an organism-in-an-environment.

The biologist knows this, and many psychological students of the growth process know it; but many students of personality, even if they know it, seem to forget it when they apply their research instruments.

There will be space to consider only one concrete illustration of the practical difference between the concept of personality traits as entities and the present view. Let us put the present formulation to an empirical quantitative test. This test relates to the normal curves supposedly attained whenever we measure personality traits. A normal curve arises from the operation of a large number of uncorrelated chance factors, and since most measurable traits of an organism come under this head we expect to obtain normal curves indicating imperceptible gradations from low to high amounts of each "trait." If personality is simply organism, measurement of personality will give normal curves.

Let us consider, however, the hypothesis that personality as known is not simply organism but organism in a situation. Here it is evident that the variations from one social situation to another frequently represent sharp transitions, all-or-none shifts in attitude or behavior, rather than variations in degree of a "trait" along a continuum. We are all familiar with such all-or-none shifts in daily social relations. In the midst of a congenial conversation a new inflection of a friend's voice changes the attitude from *receptiveness* to a *suspicion* that he is razzing us. The insecurity of a child when a large active dog enters the situation may change behavior from serenity to a sudden demand for protection. Shifts of a discontinuous kind occur constantly in the relations of organisms to their environments.

These discontinuities actually appear not only in quantitative analysis of the relation of a single individual to successive situations but also in quantitative analysis of measured behavior of groups of individuals; for if an experimental situation is anything like a life situation it will produce discontinuity of response, and our experimental data will show clear signs of bimodality or multi-modality as different *organism-in-environment fields* are set up (J. F. Brown).

If the tests are highly reliable and show the distribution clearly, aside from test errors, bimodality and multi-modality are very evident indeed. Thus, the trait "suggestibility," which appears at first sight to be normally distributed, has been shown by Aveling and Hargreaves and also by Estabrooks to yield bimodality. That is, many subjects are definitely suggestible, many others completely resistive to suggestion. So, too, we might expect a normal distribution of the rate of establishing a conditioned response; but Razran has found that among adult subjects there are three well-defined types of learners who reflect three distinct attitudes toward the experimental situation. One group is *naïvely* conditioned in the manner of Pavlov's dogs; the second group is indifferent and will not condition; the third group is negativistic and shows reliably less salivary flow in response to the conditioned stimulus than during the control sessions. As Razran remarks, the second and third group "catch on."

Day-by-day ratings of extroversion and pencil-and-paper tests of neurotic tendency analyzed by L. M. Hanks and S. Diamond seem at first to give normal curves; but when the data are more closely analyzed and chi square applied to the extremes, bimodality and multi-modality are evident. Here again, there seems to be a factor of "catching on" or awareness of the intent of the test in some subjects which makes the test situation for these subjects quite different from what it is for "*naïve*" subjects.

Another field from which concurrent evidence is at hand regarding the bimodality or, indeed, the all-or-none character of social responses is the psychology of propaganda. When normal curves were obtained for attitude toward war, some methods of propaganda moved the whole distribution to the right, causing reliable differences in means but no change in the general shape of the curve. Other methods of propaganda, however, caused both positive and negative shifts. We might at first sight guess that the result would be another normal curve but one flattened out in a smooth consistent way. Actually, however, the curves show that the propaganda which was delivered over the radio, so that the speaker was not visible, produced a marked favorable shift in many of the subjects, a marked unfavorable shift in others. The results show a "mesa" or table-top type of distribution, relatively few persons remaining indifferent to the issues, the tendency being to side with the speaker or against him. He puts his appeal over to the hearer, or if he fails by a hair's breadth, he may fail altogether and create against his position feelings which he never suspected.

Again, in the elaborate survey of adolescent attitudes toward the current social scene, Rundquist and Sletto report that attitudes toward remote "intellectual" issues are distributed normally, whereas in issues which come near home and arouse personal feeling, clear bimodality appears.

These quantitative findings are what we should expect if we follow through the implications of the thesis that a personality, even in a paper-and-pencil test situation, must be regarded not as organism only but as a focus of interaction between organism and social situation.

In some cases studied by L. B. Murphy, when two children interact, each calls forth potentialities in the other which were previously not known, so that the manifest personalities are different from what they were before. It would therefore be a mistake to say that "the personalities interact"; it would be nearer the truth to say that personality is being redefined from one situation to another. Some kinds of personalities appear only in certain kinds of groups constituted for particular work or play purposes. Let the group situation disappear; the personalities which appear in them go out like a candle. The present formulation does not deny that some aspects of personality, in some persons, are more rigid and unresponsive to alterations in the social environment than other aspects. This holds both for some traits which we highly value, like heroism in the face of persecution, and for some traits which we value negatively, such as catatonia.

The problem of organismic inflexibility is, however, an empirical one, to be clarified only after the organism has been exposed to wide variations in the environment. Even the total number of variations confronted by a person living in one culture is too limited to give us a clear picture of the actual potentialities of the person. Studies dealing with the general properties of personality as it appears in one culture are utterly inadequate to tell us what the potentialities of human nature in another culture might be. Sustained analysis of personality in other cultures, both primitive and advanced, occidental and oriental, capitalist and communist, is a necessary preliminary to any pronouncements regarding the potentialities of human nature in general or of individual persons in particular.

These figures are intended to suggest three ways of looking at personality. We think No. 1 is the conventional way.

O is an organism being stimulated by Situation S.

No. 1

The situation elicits traits already present in O but which now come to the surface; the traits reflect both heredity and old conditionings which are now warmed over, so to speak. The situation merely liberates a trait inherent in the organism.

In No. 2 a form of social stimulation is shown which sets up a field of interaction which constitutes the personality. The behavior is not a fragment of O just become visible but the resultant of the interaction of S and O. From the present point of view, such fields are what we study when we study personality.

No. 2

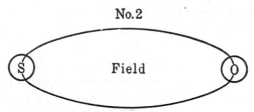

In No. 3 we have diagrammed what Harold Anderson and L. B. Murphy have found.

No. 3

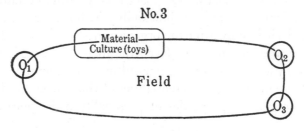

O_1, in the presence of toys and playmates, may set going in O_2 a form of social response which alters the subsequent behavior of O_1 and O_3, and from this time on the personalities of the three are developed by the developing situation. A fight, or a fit of the giggles, or a boasting contest not only expresses but alters the personalities. Not only do the personalities make the situation, but the situation does much to make the personalities.[1] Unless personality had the kind of relative fluidity which such a scheme implies, it is a little hard to see how social psychology could exist.

It would be easy to conclude, quite erroneously, that the present conception is environmentalistic, or that it gives cultural forces greater weight than biological forces in the formation of personality. From the present point of view, the relative importance of the two groups of forces in causing observed variance in personality is not under discussion at all. A statistical inquiry like the Burks and Freeman investigations might happen to proceed from premises of this sort; but we are not for the present concerned with them. Our interest is only to show that we are dealing with a bipolar situation, and that nothing fruitful about personality can be said except in terms of a field in which the two poles exist and must be considered.

The use of the term *field* in the foregoing discussion might easily be misleading. The ring or ellipse is drawn to include a part or aspect of the organism and a part or aspect of the stimulus situation. There is, of course, no intended implication that the physical space between the organism and the situation is always a dynamic part of the field. The vital thing about the concept of field is that reciprocal relations obtaining between the organism and the field are the actual data of personality study.

With equal emphasis we must stress that each organism accents, selects from, and makes use of, the environment in its own way, so that the same external environment may be functionally ten different environments for ten different organisms. (This, as far as we can see, is a refutation of any straightforward situationism.) At the same time, the environment acts selectively on each organism— accents, organizes, and selects from each organism in a way which no

---

[1] The field need not be homogeneous. Biological and social research is needed in each case to show empirically how the field is constituted.

other situation could do. (This, as far as one can see, is a refutation of any sheer nativism.) The two are mutually interdependent, each one selecting from a vast range of potentialities and making just one working reality.

To be put into a situation is to find something in yourself which could not be liberated by any other situation. To be psychoanalyzed, for example, by a Freudian, may mean to be set free and aided in the growth of certain important latent tendencies in yourself which could not possibly be liberated in any other way. To be analyzed with equal thoroughness by a practitioner of another persuasion might reveal and liberate aspects of personality not capable of being liberated by a Freudian. To function in a new social group; to participate in a new political movement; to find oneself living in a new economic world; to find oneself, after five years as the only child, a big brother having a little sister—these and all other new experiences do more than bring about "transfer" from previous similar situations. They all involve the liberation of what was only a potentiality. It may well be objected that nothing can be liberated unless it is already a potentiality; but since the number of potentialities is so very large, and by definition known only after the emergence of actualities, this does not help practically in defining the personality.

If one wishes to use the term personality to mean the potentialities lying within the organism at a given time—that is, the part of O lying *within the ellipse* in No. 2 above—there is no objection, provided that one does not predict from personality so defined as if he were predicting from personality as actually seen in social reactions. Theoretically, all the material in O could be included if all the possible social situations could be sampled. We should then know what the potentialities of O would be if we met any situation of a kind already considered. The whole trouble, however, is in telling how closely one situation must resemble another to justify our considering the two functionally equivalent. What may seem to be minute differences between different O's, and what seem to be equally minute differences between different S's, constantly cause in practice utterly different types of observable personality responses.

We may appear to reach an *impasse* at this point because of the apparent *infinity* of functionally real possibilities. Here, however, a sudden turn in our reasoning seems to be forced upon us. Unessentials being disregarded, persons can be classified empirically for many purposes into a few simple, clear types—typical ranchmen, stevedores, auctioneers. How can this possibly be true?

From the point of view of the organism, we may be dealing with a threshold, such that for one person a situation is above, for another below, the critical point. Thresholds of given individuals differ so widely that one man's meat may be another man's poison, one man's delight another man's boredom. At the same time, the social fields are mostly disjunctive—one takes the job or rejects it; one marries or declines to marry; one takes a chance skating on thin ice or one stays ashore; one starts a wild new venture at fifty or plods along familiar trails. Not universally, yet generally, life forces us into molds, each one distinct and unmistakable. There lies within each individual, by virtue of thresholds, the necessary raw material out of which these disjunctive social situations can make discrete and unquestioned types of response.

Moreover, as life goes on, a hardening process occurs so that the external molds are less necessary than they used to be. The structure, as Sherif would say, has been "interiorized." The field relations of personality still hold, but more and more attention must be paid to the internal structure of the person, the words and values which interplay and give what is called—quite correctly—firmness or even rigidity of character. Such character is still an interaction, still an aspect of a field; but to speak statistically for once, variation in fields produces less variation in response than it could during the period of immaturity.

One might use the analogy of the gyroscope, which whirls upright no matter how the train sways. The gyroscope may even keep the ocean-going vessel upright in the storm, but—it need hardly be said—sometimes with disastrous consequences to the sides of the ship. The gyroscopic type of personality is known to us. He builds the Great Pyramid, draws his circle in the sand though soldiers are coming to hale him to prison, attacks the invader at Orléans or, single-handed, forces a backward nation to set up institutions for the insane and feeble-minded in all its self-governing commonwealths. Previous fields of interaction, previous standards and patterns of inner reality, have become the core of the structure, so that the present external world becomes a relatively small part of the total field of interacting forces. The discovery of the degree of firmness of each such internal structure is one of the most pressing problems of personality research.

It may rightly be argued that whatever the outside world may once have done, certainly at the present time these traits are well established within the individual organism. They are as much within the organism as the heart or liver. They may happen to be given a new twist by a new environmental situation, but they are much more powerful in *changing* the environment than they are *responsive* to it. In fact, the person of strong character is one who defies any number of environments and who lives on in terms of an inner world of resolution and conviction.

We wish to concede and to stress this point. At the same time, we must emphasize that the environment over which a strong character exerts command is a specific environment; that the kind, intensity and duration of control exercised over it depend as much upon the environment as upon the strong character; that the supposed inner inflexibility could only mean, if taken literally, the utter ignoring of the world which is to be molded. Unless those features of the environment which are repugnant to the individual are grasped and reacted to with intensity and conviction, there is no meaningful expression for the personality. The question whether the person dominates or is dominated by the environment is meaningless in the present connection. The important thing is that the world, in order to be dominated, must be reacted to concretely, and therefore that each concrete response to the environment is different from every other such concrete response. Personality, in other words, is not simply the inner core, the fixed keystone of a stable structure; it is also an interplay with other persons and situations, an interplay depending always upon the concrete forces both without and within.

Finally, it may be objected that, whereas the separate aspects of personality may be defined in bipolar fashion, the *organizing principle*, the thing which holds the material in a dynamic system, must be within the organism. To this we must reply that there are organizing principles both within and without. To consider a simple illustration, we perceive animals as wholes; we do not perceptually combine the hind legs of a dog and the fore legs of a nearby cat. The organized character of the stimulus field is partly responsible for the organic wholeness of the organism-environment relation. Moreover, where the things to be perceived are socially important wholes involving groups of persons, the organized behavior of other individuals forming coacting groups (e.g., sheep-like followers surrounding a leader) shows how the social organization of the perceived pattern is fundamental for an understanding of the organized nature of the personality of each spectator or participant.

The emphasis on wholeness of personality is very salutary in so far as the emphasis falls upon the integration of responses in a biologically unified pattern. It is clear, however, that at this point a serious danger arises, namely, that the aesthetic satisfaction of envisaging the organism as a whole should interfere with the discovery of the confused, inchoate and incomplete phases of the person. The modern biographer, like the modern psychiatrist, has given so much emphasis to unity that the actual discord and confusion of human personality tend to be forgotten. Relatively little of personality, as Stern well remarks, is *Gestalt*; a large part is *ungestalt*.

We should add, however, what we consider an even more serious limitation in the existing methods of biographers and clinicians. The attempt to see the organism as a whole is based upon forgetting that the only wholeness which it ever enjoys is a phase of reciprocity with the external world. Just as Henderson has shown that the exquisite balance of the blood system is not the balance of gases contained within a fixed medium (arterial, venous and capillary blood) but a balance involving air both in the lungs and in the region outside the body, so the student of personality discovers that the unity of the person is not a unity which can be circumscribed by the psychologist, but a unity involving a flow of influences between a given individual and phases of the culture.

There is, as we have seen, a progressive establishment of inner principles of organization. The man as he grows older becomes more and more of a "gyroscope"; but he never achieves genuine detachment from the social world. The biographer, on the other hand, or the psychoanalyst is concerned concretely with a given organism.

Therapeutically what you wish to help is the person; the world of the person is relatively inaccessible. The person is defined as that which walks into your office. The field which is actually sick is known to you through only one of its phases. The biographer has an even more serious difficulty. His purposes are literary, his goal ultimately aesthetic. For his own satisfaction and for that of his reader it is necessary to conceive the personality as an integrated whole in its own right. The sketches of Walter Pater or Emil Ludwig derive most of their charm from the completeness and definiteness with which the personality is crammed into a few vivid lines. We see Leonardo asking questions of Nature, communing with a teacher who insists on communicating her knowledge in fragments and in the language of oracles. Draw a ring around Leonardo—you have the essence of science caught within the circumference. The older, more chronologically minded biographer would protest, and rightly. The man's life is partly the world in which his lines were cast. Exactly the same movement which has forced the painter of landscapes to subordinate mountains and trees to the purposes of pure design has forced the biographer to discount the vital reality of actual social living in favor of the ultra-clear and simple aesthetic unity of the person. This is not to be regretted if one maintains one's perspective regarding the history of the arts. It is seriously to be regretted if research upon personality is to prosper. The attempt to lift concepts of personality from contemporary biography into the psychological laboratory has, in fact, been partly responsible for the more serious errors in the personality-testing movement, in particular, the tendency to regard personality trends as entities residing within the tissues of the living being.

This organic relation between subject and object, between person and world, necessitates a term which will unambiguously define the functional entity with which the student of personality actually deals. This entity is clearly not simply "the organism as a whole." Not all aspects of the organism enter into the field, and not all aspects of the environment, either. From the broad potentialities of the organism by way of response, and from the broad potentialities of the situation in arousing the responses of varied organisms, one concrete stimulus-response relation is actualized. The term field, whatever its advantages, seems likely soon to fall on evil days—if it has not already done so—simply because it involves the notion of a homogeneous or undifferentiated area or supply of energy, or what not. We think the current phrase, "organism-in-environment," is better.

As a research tool this conception is valuable only in so far as it defines areas of research which cannot easily be defined with other concepts. An example of such definition appears in answering the question, What is the possible range of behavior of which human nature is capable in response to the social world? We are not here concerned with the theoretically infinite potentialities of human nature or with the theoretically infinite range of social situations. Concretely, the response of all members of the New York Stock Exchange is virtually the same when disaster suddenly closes the French Bourse; in fact, one could scarcely be a stock exchange member except in terms of functioning in a clear-cut and definable way in such a catastrophe. There are great personal differences among the individuals who have seats on the exchange; but the response, in terms of deciding to close the Wall Street exchange, is historically a matter of clear definition of what a person functioning in a given social situation must do. All members of the National Child Labor Committee must do about the same thing when child labor legislation in Alabama is nullified by resort to legal technicalities. In many other life situations there are alternatives; there are two or three, or a dozen specific and distinct things that might be done, but the number is not infinite, and the distinct patterns of conduct cannot be blended or confused. A child must decide between studying and going to the movies; a college teacher must decide between giving a grade which will result in a diploma or in failure; a woman must decide between two suitors. Everyone who participates in the economic or political scene must vote yes or no, or indicate which one of a series of definite alternatives is to be followed. Here are cases in which the social situation is so defined that the number of possible responses is finite; in fact, looking closely at the structure of the social world, we see that the very fact that it has structure means that social responses do not arise from the pooling of a large number of internal factors in such a way as to give normal distribution curves, but to give a series of discrete and qualitatively recognizable alternatives. Social situations are discrete and discontinuous.

Now, looking at the organism, we find that its responses are likewise discontinuous. We see that practically every response, or pattern of responses, can be thrown into action if—and only if—a certain threshold value is achieved by the stimulus. One puts up with a joke at one's own expense up to a certain point, then winces; one tolerates a real or supposed slight to one's racial group up to that critical point at which participation in mob frenzy is possible; one remains a pre-medical student, despite one's father's encouragement to go into law, up to the critical moment when one's friend paints a glowing account of the satisfaction in a legal career, and then is tumbled suddenly from a "pre-medical" to a "pre-law" decision. The factors which operate to produce the change may be many or slight. The effects may indeed be cumulative or may conform to the notion of the environment as an infinite series of uni-dimensional and measurable social influences; but even if this conception were universally sound, the organism, because of the fundamental nature of its thresholds, must at critical points be thrown from one mode of adjustment to another. Just as the little child laughs up to a certain point, then suddenly cries, the adult maintains a given attitude through thick and thin until, with the last straw, he finds himself in another world. Paul the persecutor becomes Paul the apostle. This is one more illustration, we believe, of the discontinuity mentioned in surveying the work on biological dominance (page 165): The addition of a stimulus biologically dominant over an older pattern may dislocate the older pattern so profoundly as to cause it to yield up its energy to the new pattern which has displaced it. The conception of organism-in-environment therefore illustrates discontinuity of response as much from the point of view of the organism as from that of the social world.

Now, putting the two together, we see that the transition from one response to another may depend upon changes, however slight, in the component factors playing within the organism, or in changes, however slight, in the component factors in the social environment. We refuse here to resort to any vague definition of the organism as a whole or of the environment as a whole, and persist in using the term "structure" to define the actual interrelation of component parts, whether of organism or of environment. We must note, however, that changes in components, as long as they remain above the threshold, may cause no change in response. Even a large change in a single component may, under some conditions, leave the response unaffected; whereas, if we are near a threshold value, a very slight change in one component may force a different mode of response. Experimental work on the equivalence of stimuli shows clearly that the magnitude of the absolute change in a stimulus may be a question of slight import unless we are near a critical point. One stimulus may be the equivalent of another; but a critical point can be found at which another slight change in the stimulus means that stimulation is no longer equivalent. It is clear, then, that the transition from one response to another depends literally on quantitative relations between factors that work within the organism and factors that work in the environment; and that, with one's eye either on organism or on environment, one notes that change in response arises at critical points and not at all points alike.

It follows from this analysis, if sound, that the number of organism-in-environment realities in a given society is not infinite but very limited. Neither environmental stimulation nor inner potentiality conforms to the statistically convenient conception of continuous variables. Here the research job of the social psychologist is to look straight at the situations which are actually well structured and defined in a given society, and to see under what conditions what organism responds this way or that to them; then looking at the organisms and defining in terms of thresholds, to see what it is that enables the organism to make response No. 1, No. 10, or No. 50. The number of kinds of organisms-in-environment possible in an environment is much greater than the number possible for a single individual, but it is still finite, for all that; in fact, we believe that for most persons in our own society the number of crucial decisions made in life is not very large, and the number of possible kinds of life open to us at any given time, very few. As a matter of fact, we should suggest that on any theory whatever regarding the will (or spontaneous activity) the choice is not between all the things that life offers, but between very few. Indeed, on general biological

grounds, it seems quite likely that, with a system of thresholds prevailing at a given time and place, a given organism finds itself
coerced to "choose" among limited avenues defined by the social
situation.

The empirical task of describing and cataloguing the real social
situations that are of importance and between which organisms must
decide would include analysis in terms of types of work and play;
objects of friendship, adoration and love; places in which to live;
methods of preventing sickness or accident, and similar classifications offered by the student of society.

For most persons, most of the time, the classification most useful
is that which is given in terms of getting a living. Whether the decision is made by one's parents or by oneself, or forced upon one
by dire necessity, the economic way of life is definitely organism-in-
environment in such a way as to make, even out of homogeneous
human material, definite classes of people. The son of a small re-
tailer in Middletown has before him today three real economic
possibilities (1, dependent on a wealthy family; 2, small merchant;
3, worker), not an infinite number. Negro boys growing up in Dollard's Alabama town have only a choice between two (merchant,
worker). To a large degree, the "personality" of the man, as the
term is used here, is defined in organism-in-environment terms. It is
important to note that this is not quite the same as the Marxist conception that the work makes the man, so that the members of a
given economic class must see life in terms of a class code. Since
from the present point of view the *properties of the organism* have
played some part in the original decision as to the class in which one
will function, the native intelligence and the habits of thrift may
partly determine what the farm migrant to Middletown will
do with the economic opportunities there. Still, in large part, personality types are defined in terms of the recurrent and recognizable
patterns which the situation permits. Granted that Babbitt is a caricature (as is any character that is "true to life"), the caricature is
as recognizable as is that of Theodore Roosevelt. It must have some
basis in social experience to serve even as a caricature. Indeed, the
stereotypes of the stage are successful in "placing" people because, in large part, there must be a group of related traits defined

by the social world before we can begin to deal intelligently with large groups of people whom we do not personally know. We believe that the student of personality, far from rejecting the sociologist's rough classification of classes on the grounds that these minimize individual differences, *must* recognize group differences in personality and give them psychologically a prominent place in order that the rôle of true individual differences in each class may be clearly perceived and adequately analyzed.

We have argued earlier (pages 198 and 837) that the best classification of personality at present is in terms of values; and we believe that this is, in fact, the only classification which fits the research problem which we have just defined. For the values of social classes differ markedly. There are central values without which a person does not find himself at home in his group. Without them, he is so much out of place that his own conception of himself and the conception of himself forced upon him by his associates are at variance; and he must give up either the values of his group or his own deep-seated and well-established self-evaluation. Such mavericks are as unhappy as they are rare. Other values, less central with reference to the economic needs of each class, may vary considerably. One's tastes, one's hobbies and, within limits, one's friends may vary within a fairly wide range. Since this is so, the psychology of personality, in so far as it is a problem in social psychology rather than one in genetics, is largely the psychology of the whole value system of each person, taking into account, to be sure, the economic class and position, but also taking into account some dozens and perhaps hundreds of other values which can function well enough within the personality provided they are articulated with the values which the economic situation defines.

Such an analysis is always bipolar; the genetic facts and the several idiosyncrasies of development interact constantly with broad situational factors at each level of personality growth. We know the man or woman in the situation, and we can seldom dissociate "personal" and "situational" factors; but in those cases where a person is suddenly thrust from one station in life to another, we can begin to guess at the true "stability of traits." The I. Q. is constant in a given environment, less so in a changing environment. Most personality traits owe their constancy in a large (but unmeasurable) degree to a constancy in situations. In the child and in the adult, many traits are so well defined that they insistently impose themselves upon all researchers, regardless of situation; but many of them reflect at any given moment both the inner make-up and the social world in which the person functions in such a way as to make the two logically (and experimentally) inseparable.

Chapter XIII

SOCIAL ATTITUDES AND THEIR MEASUREMENT

Problems of Method and Validity

Perhaps no single concept within the whole realm of social psychology occupies a more nearly central position than that of attitudes. The increasing concern with this topic, especially in recent years, has been paralleled by a constantly widening disparity in the use of the term. G. W. Allport, after a careful survey of the various senses in which it has been used, proposes the following definition: "An attitude is a mental and neural state of readiness, organized through experience, exerting a directive or dynamic influence upon the individual's response to all objects and situations with which it is related." The significant aspects of this definition seem to us to be those of *threshold* and of *object*; attitudes are more or less favorable, or more or less unfavorable, to particular customs, persons, events, etc. The attitude is primarily a way of being "set" toward or against certain things. Both the response and the situations are in most cases of verbal nature—almost exclusively so in so far as attitudes lend themselves to measurement. Hence we shall regard attitudes, in conformity with general usage in their *experimental* literature, as verbalized or verbalizable tendencies, dispositions, or adjustments toward certain acts. The question of our certainty as to the existence of a "tendency," particularly in the absence of "overt" behavior, will concern us later.

Allport also points out that while attitudes may be either individual or common—e.g., an attitude toward a past event in one's life, as opposed to an attitude toward labor unions—only the latter are susceptible to measurement, since "measurement requires a scale and there is no scale which does not depend upon the central tendencies and dispersions of opinions expressed by *many* people." Hence our

889

discussion will be limited to "common" attitudes, or, more accurately perhaps, to common issues toward which almost everyone has some attitude. Within these limits the term must be used broadly enough to include opinions and beliefs as the tangible and verbalized expressions of attitudes conceived, as in Allport's definition, in a more implicit sense. In a more behavioristic sense (pending our discussion of the "merely verbal" nature of attitudes on page 911), the terms attitude, opinion, and belief may be used almost synonymously as long as we are dealing with their measurement.

The various approaches to the study of attitudes may be classified either according to the method of ascertaining the attitude, or according to the nature of the variables whose relationship to the attitude is being examined. These variables may be sociological, having to do with such phenomena as size of community or the nature of various affiliated groups of people. Or they may be primarily psychological, either those of a genetic nature, as when individual experiences are studied, or those which are treated as existing characteristics of the individual, such as personality traits. All these variables are considered in later pages; our concern here is with methods, especially the more objective and quantitative methods.

Methods, also, may be considered as psychological rather than sociological, whenever individuals, rather than groups, are studied. There is, of course, no sharp line to demarcate the two types of methods, and we shall draw freely from both kinds of studies throughout this chapter. But in general it may be said that the characteristic psychological method is that of obtaining, in some manner, an individual score regarding the attitude in question, whereas the specifically sociological method is that of measuring the attitude in terms of pertinent group data of the census type. Attitudes measured by psychological methods may, of course, be related to sociological variables; but measures obtained by sociological means can usually be related only to sociological variables, since information concerning individuals is not commonly available under these conditions. It is for this reason, doubtless, that the great preponderance of attitude research has made use of psychological methods of measurement. This chapter, consequently, will deal primarily with psychological methods. Let the reader not conclude from this, however, that psychological variables are necessarily the most powerful determinants of attitudes.

Examples of characteristically sociological methods of measuring attitudes may be briefly cited. In one such study, the five most radical and the five most conservative counties of North Dakota were compared, radicalism being calculated according to degree of support of the Non-Partisan League. The conclusions were such that radicalism was definitely related to soil and windfall, that it was strongest in the newer and less settled communities, and in those in which a larger percentage of immigrants and new population was suffering under economic disadvantage. Similar data were obtained for Minnesota. Here, then, is a quantitative analysis of social causes of radicalism. Yet we do not see the individual farmer, or hear what he has to say. For this kind of information we must turn to psychological methods.

Sociological methods have been extensively used by H. Hart in the attempt to ascertain widespread attitudinal changes which have occurred in America during the past generation. His data are "based almost entirely upon statistical analyses of interests and opinions expressed in leading general magazines, supplemented by analyses of certain book and newspaper indices." Vast quantities of reading matter, ranging from the *Christian Science Monitor* to "periodicals devoting themselves to sensational fiction," were studied, and analyses made not only of their content and circulation, but of the frequencies with which endorsement of or opposition to certain topics was expressed. Comparison of these various sources with one another, and with certain objectively measurable social trends, led to considerable confidence in the reliability and validity of the findings concerning the outstanding trends in the United States since 1900. These may be summarized as follows: religious sanctions have been largely displaced by scientific sanctions; sexual irregularities, easy divorce, and sex freedom in general have recently been approved; opposition to prohibition has increased; there has been increased interest in international relations; discussion of economic and political institutions, unemployment, and business conditions has increased.

There is no pretense here of attempting to locate the *causes* of these attitude trends. The study differs in this respect from that previously cited, though it, too, uses characteristically sociological data. But even in the former study we do not know what were the selective forces which attracted certain farmers to the less hospitable regions of North Dakota and Minnesota, or the degree to which they were the heirs of "radical" traditions quite unrelated to present conditions making for economic security. Further data of a sociological nature together with the use of partial correlations would, of course, give some illumination regarding such obscurities. But such, in general, are the shortcomings of purely sociological approaches. Such data tell us little concerning the laws which govern attitudes. We need to know what rôle is played by many kinds of other factors which must be analyzed one at a time so that we may discover under what conditions each of them is related to any given attitude. We need, in other words, many kinds of information (including sociological information) about individuals if we are to discover the forces responsible for the development of attitudes.

Illustrative of the strengths and weaknesses of the large-scale survey methods are the careful investigations of the American Institute of Public Opinion. Getting under way in 1934, this Institute has sampled American opinion on all types of questions, from the three most pressing national problems to the question of human immortality. An extraordinary array of items has been put through the mill, yielding a far better idea of what people actually think than the newspaper or the wandering interviewer has ever been able to achieve. Of special note, of course, are the surveys on political topics, such as the prohibition question and the presidential candidates. The reason why such polls have on the whole been rather accurate and valuable in predicting actual election figures is that the various elements of the population, geographically and economically defined, have been represented by appropriate samples given appropriate weight. Where the Institute poll has failed, it has usually been in respect to sampling errors. Thus certain elements in the population respond to mail ballots more dependably than others. The Institute made many allowances for this fact, but even so, it did not make *enough* allowance for it in the 1936 presidential election; its only serious errors were in underweighting the elements which do not reply well to mail ballots. Follow-up interviewing is essential in this situation. This is expensive, but even more of it has to be done than has been done in the past.

When such surveys are intelligently conducted they help the psychologist in two ways: (1) they give him a preliminary view of the relative importance of many factors influencing opinion—age, education, sex, occupation, etc.; (2) at the same time they indicate drifts in opinion from month to month by which the efficacy of different types of propaganda or educational work can be gauged.

Another type of large-scale sampling of attitude is represented by studies such as those of the Psychological Corporation under the general name of "marketing research." In a broad sense, such research covers the psychology of the consumer of advertised products. Week-by-week analysis of the actual retail sales is compared with week-by-week sampling of dozens or hundreds of housewives' responses to interview questions about household commodities. Such questions relate partly to familiarity with trade names and slogans, their knowledge of the asserted advantages of the various products, and their preference for individual brands. In this way, for example, it has been possible to show the relative importance of various types of appeal frequently made in the press, over the radio or in outdoor advertising. While such interviewing is usually more personal and more revealing than the dragnet results of opinion polls, it still leaves the reasons for remembering slogans and preferring specific brands rather vague. This vagueness is not entirely removed by the preparation of well-controlled experimental programs of advertising in which, for example, one specific aspect of the appeal is inserted in some magazines and omitted from similar advertisements published in other magazines. It must be conceded, however, that such comparisons of market analysis and individual interviewing come to the very door of experimental social psychology in the strict sense, and within a short time will certainly have proved the right to enter. What clearly remains to be done is to rely more on experimental control and less on gross statistics; to discover, for example, why 71 per cent of the St. Louis housewives remember the claims of Lifebuoy Soap whereas only 31 per cent recall those of Heinz Ketchup. Presumably laws can be discovered and stated in quantitative form which will relate to the American consumer in general, and a second set of equally important laws can be formulated which relate to individual differences in consumer attitudes and reasons for the appearance of these individual differences.

Turning now to more distinctly psychological methods, we see that further classifications are readily apparent. Individuals' attitudes may be *inferred* from various overt behaviors. Joining the American Association for the Advancement of Atheism, for example, is an act so indicative of religious attitude as to render testing procedures quite superfluous. *Verbal* methods, however, are much more frequently used, as it is often desirable to discover the attitudes of individuals not identified with such attitude-revealing organizations. While in the vast majority of instances verbal methods are *direct*— i.e., the subject is asked point-blank to react to certain statements of attitudes—they may also be *indirect*, in that subjects are not aware that their verbal reactions are to be analyzed for revelations of attitudes.

One example of such *indirect verbal methods* is the use of conjectures concerning the future. It is probably safe to say that attitudes relate not primarily to the past, nor even primarily to the present, but as a rule to the future. "Do you believe in —?" is likely to mean, "Would you like to have so-and-so happen?" In one of several investigations along this line subjects were asked to state the factors most likely to be operative in the "decline of the west." The order of the ten items most frequently mentioned was: overpopulation, war, political corruption . . . unemployment, too much luxury, and exhaustion of natural resources. It seems reasonable to conclude that all of these are objects of unfavorable attitudes, and perhaps some relative degrees of unfavorableness may be deduced from the order in which the factors were ranked. These methods are often revealing as to modal tendencies of groups, but are of such questionable reliability as to be of little value for diagnosing individual attitudes. Their chief service seems to be that of suggesting problems to be investigated by more accurate methods. The validity of the method is no greater than the inevitably subjective and inferential process of interpreting the results.

Attitudes of prejudice have, in particular, been examined by indirect methods—necessarily so, since few, presumably, would deliberately indicate it. G. B. Watson, for example, has made ingenious use of inconsistency as a measure of prejudice. In one part of his test Watson included fifteen statements describing varying types of situations, with opportunity to approve or disapprove the act cited. Each of the fifteen instances is paralleled by one or more others of similar nature, but involving groups toward which attitudes are likely to be just the reverse. For example, in one instance, an unwarranted search of suspected radical headquarters is described; this is paralleled by another situation (though separated from it by several others) in which a similar procedure is carried out with a big business corporation suspected of dishonesty. To approve either of these acts while disapproving the other, Watson reasons, is to reveal prejudice. Such methods as this are chiefly valuable where, as in the case of prejudice, attitudes cannot be directly approached. They may also prove to be of increasing value where anonymity, as a means of insuring sincere responses, is impossible. But, in general, indirect approaches to attitudes will have to become less cumbersome and more fool-proof before they will be widely used.

What, then, of the more direct, verbal methods of measuring attitudes? The simplest of them is the questionnaire, consisting either of a list of statements to be accepted or rejected, or on which degrees of agreement or disagreement are to be indicated, or of multiple choice responses representing widely varying attitudes. Two questions arise concerning the validity of these methods. The first has to do with internal consistency: how can one be sure that the various items belong together, that they all get at the same attitude? The second concerns the scoring of responses: what certainty is there that a given response represents favorable rather than unfavorable attitude toward the issue involved, and how heavily shall it be weighted? All manner of care and sophistication is to be found in various attitude questionnaires, from those which answer all these questions by arbitrary assumptions, to those which are based upon elaborate statistical procedures. Those of the former group are legion. They are of little worth, even though they be buttressed by high odd-even reliability coefficients; for large numbers of items, even though possessing only a modicum of internal consistency, will in most cases pass this test of reliability.

A common method of evaluating each item response, particularly among the numerous questionnaires involving "conservatism" and "liberalism," is to employ the aid of "judges." Harper's Social Study, which has come into such general use as an indicator of "liberal" attitudes, is a good illustration. He constructed scales upon which each response was to be classified by judges as being (1) extremely conservative, (2) conservative, (3) liberal, (4) radical, or (5) extremely radical. Typical items, to which either a Yes or a No response is to be given, are: "In teaching the vital problems of citizenship, teachers should so impress on the students the approved opinions in these matters that life's later experiences can never unsettle or modify the opinions given"; "If our people were willing to try the experiment fairly, the government ownership of railroads would be for the best interests of the country." A large number of judges was asked to decide whether the Yes answer to each question was to be classified as tending toward the conservative or the nonconservative end of the five-point scale. Very high agreement was found, and the scoring of item responses was thus determined.[1]

Statistical methods of determining internal consistency of items are now commonly applied. This means, in effect, the use of a large preliminary group of subjects as "judges," instead of a small number of "experts." Scores are first designated in arbitrary fashion; either mean or standard scores for each item are then correlated with total scores for all items. If the resulting correlation is negative, the item is scored in the opposite direction; if low, the item is discarded as not measuring what the other items measure; otherwise the item is

---

[1] The terms "liberalism" and "conservatism" (in particular as measured by Harper's test) will be met so frequently in these pages that some comment concerning the validity of the type of measure just described is demanded. The type of liberalism which Harper attempted to measure must, of course, be interpreted in its space-time context. Its locus is that peculiar complex of issues which were held to be controversial and important by a group composed chiefly of professional urban educators a decade or more ago. Its content was largely determined by the preferences, within these controversial areas, of this culturally rather homogeneous group. Its value and its limitations inhere in these circumstances. Applied and interpreted as it was by Harper, it probably represents what did constitute "liberalism" as understood by such groups at that time. Its application to other groups, or after the lapse of sufficient time to produce cultural changes of importance in these areas (as is surely the case now), is more open to question.

retained. One investigator who has carefully described such a method found by its use that a single list of items actually contained two groups of items, each of which showed greater internal than inter-group consistency. Consequently two different attitudes, labeled "imperialist" and "internationalist," were distinguished, with distinct items for each; their correlation was .63.

The concept of attitudes involves, as we have seen, the notion of two extremes between which individuals vary—extremes of favoring or opposing something. That attitudes should be measured by some sort of *scale*, therefore, is a most logical consequence. The term, unfortunately, has been applied to the most diverse types of attitude measures, but our present concern is with the applicability of the rigorous scale technique to the measurement of attitudes. One of the first things to do in constructing a real attitude scale is to make sure of an order in which attitudes can be arranged from one point to another. No scale can really be called a scale unless one can tell from a given attitude that an individual will maintain *every* attitude falling to the right or to the left of that point (depending on how the scale is constructed). No one could use a ruler on which he could not tell whether the point marked 7 would fall between 6 and 8 or whether it would have a capricious preference for some other point on the instrument. If we have a genuine scale of attitudes toward compulsory military service, it is necessary to assume that every person favoring compulsory military service should also favor military service for persons conscientiously opposed to such service; the former proposition includes the latter. In the same way, a person who favors three years or more of military service ought certainly to favor two years of service if the choice is between that and no service at all. The question really is: what groups of attitudes are there, if any, which actually fall into a scale arrangement? Unless we arbitrarily define attitudes in such a way that, like the victims of Procrustes, they simply must fit themselves into a linear scale, our task is to find whether there are any attitudes for whose measurement really valid scales can be constructed, and if so, which ones.

As a matter of fact there is every reason to believe that none of the rather complex social attitudes which we are primarily discussing will ever conform to such rigorous measurement. Everyone

who has had occasion to score attitude tests is familiar with the
glaring inconsistencies (at least, so it appears) which appear in the
replies even of such groups as graduate students. Nor is this merely
due to carelessness, insincerity, or lack of discrimination. The notion
of consistency inevitably carries with it, in these areas, *some particular standard* of consistency. Very few individuals exist, it is safe to
say, whose attitudes concerning more than a few issues are so precise,
so neatly crystallized, as to lend themselves to the sort of scale
measurement which we have described. Attitude scales may seldom
be used like tape measures. Yet some of them do appear to have
resulted in fairly accurate measurements, and it will be part of our
problem to see why and how this is possible.

There have been wide variations and rapid changes in the use of
scales. One of the earliest attempts to use a scaling device for attitude measurement was the "social distance" method of Bogardus,
which has been widely used both in its original form and in later
modifications by himself and by others. Its original form is reproduced here:

DIRECTIONS: According to my first feeling reactions I would willingly
admit members of each race (as a class, and not the best I have known,
nor the worst members) to one or more of the classifications which
I have circled.

	To close kinship by marriage	To my club as personal chums	To my street as neighbors	To employment in my occupation in my country	To citizenship in my country	As visitors only to my country	Would exclude from my country
Canadians......	1	2	3	4	5	6	7
Chinese........	1	2	3	4	5	6	7
English........	1	2	3	4	5	6	7
French.........	1	2	3	4	5	6	7
Germans.......	1	2	3	4	5	6	7
Hindus........	1	2	3	4	5	6	7

(etc.)

Bogardus has from time to time presented the results of applying
the test to various groups. He has, for example, accompanied some
of his data with case material, as in the comparison of attitudes of
southern whites toward Negroes with those of whites in the Southwest toward Mexicans. Such material not only lends confidence in

the validity of the method, but helps to make intelligible the variations and the changes in attitudes which are also reported. Sectional differences, as well as sex and age variations, also are considered.

The careful student of Bogardus's data will find that the test is not a true scale of measurement in the sense defined above; in many cases steps on the test are skipped. Thus, for example, an individual may indicate willingness to admit members of a given group to his street as neighbors but not to employment in his occupation. In certain instances as many as two or three steps are skipped in the same manner. In general, however, Bogardus's own data reveal the kind of steady progression which suggests definite degrees, whether equal or not, of social distance. As evidence for this, we cite below the results of one of his investigations, in which 1725 native-born white Americans from all over the United States were studied. Since such group preferences are largely determined by the ancestry of the subjects, it is important to know that the great majority of these individuals were of north European descent. Most of them were, or had been, students in college or high school. The choices made by this group, which are given in percentages, suggest that for most

	To close kinship by marriage	To my club as personal chums	To my street as neighbors	To employment in my occupation in my country	To citizenship in my country	As visitors only to my country	Would exclude from my country	
English.....	94	97	97	95	96	2	0	
American (native white)....	90	92	93	92	91	1	0	*Note the decreases*
Canadians..	87	93	96	96	96	2	0	*following the*
Scotch......	78	89	91	93	93	2	0	*ing the*
Scotch-Irish.	73	82	88	89	92	17	0	*vertical*
Irish.......	70	83	86	90	91	4	1	*arrow,*
French.....	68	85	88	90	93	4	1	*and*
Welsh......	61	72	80	81	86	5	0	*increases following the*
....								*horizon-*
Spaniards...	28	50	55	58	82	8	2	*tal*
Armenians.. ↓	9	15	28	46	58	18	5	*arrows.*
Japanese....	2	12	13	27	29	39	3	

subjects this test does function rather well as a scale. Moreover, perusal of these and other similar data leads to the conclusion that, if not for all individuals, then for *large samples*, at least, it remains true that if a given group is not accepted in a given rôle, it will be refused in all "nearer" rôles.

Comparisons with the results of other investigations, using other methods, give considerable support to the validity of the social distance test. The application of Thurstone's paired comparisons method (cf. pages 901-905) has in several cases produced results almost identical with those of Bogardus. Such findings as that Negroes, Turks, mulattos, Japanese and Hindus invariably are recipients of the greatest amount of antipathy; and that social distance is exceedingly small wherever the subjects were closely related or believed themselves closely related to the groups in question, emerge with considerable certainty.

Over and above the specific "distances" revealed is a broad factor of distance toward out-groups in general. The names of twenty-one national groups being used, the split-half reliability of the Bogardus measure as a whole proved to be .94 in one student group, .95 in another. If one drew out of a hat the names of eleven nations, he could predict almost perfectly from the total Bogardus response to them the total amount of social distance to be discovered in relation to the next ten nations. The total Bogardus score as a measure of "general tolerance" also correlates .40 or better with various measures of "radicalism."

Our next problem is to see what can be done to make such tests of attitude into scales with equal step-intervals. This problem has been systematically attacked by Thurstone and his collaborators. His method is a simple adaptation of that of psychophysics, the method employed in investigating individuals' abilities to respond to large or small differences as, for example, in the lifting of weights. It is well known that two weights which differ by three grams will be correctly distinguished (as compared with objective measurements) by a larger percentage of subjects than two weights of the same magnitude which differ by only one gram. If they differ sufficiently, practically every judgment will be correct; if they differ scarcely at all, one will be judged the heavier about as frequently as the other. Thurstone presented not weights, but statements regarding a given attitude, to large numbers of subjects. But in the weight-discrimination experiment, the objective weights are known by the experimenter in advance; hence Thurstone simply reasons in the reverse direction: the "true" linear distance between any two attitude stimuli (which is not known in advance) is equivalent to the *percentage of judges who can perceive the difference*. The "absolute" difference between any pair of statements is, of course, immaterial; it can be stated in any convenient quantity. But by such means it becomes possible to determine objectively that two differences on a given attitude scale bear a definite mathematical relationship to each other, and hence a "true" scale may be built.

The method was first applied to the measurement of opinion regarding the seriousness of crimes. Scale values were assigned on the basis of the judgments of 200 students who were asked to compare each of twenty offenses with each of the others. By this method of *paired comparisons* the techniques of psychophysics could be readily applied, since the frequency with which every offense was considered more, or less, serious than every other could easily be ascertained. If, for example, the percentage of subjects judging murder to be more serious than arson is equivalent to the percentage of those who believe burglary to be more serious than vagrancy, the two distances may be said to be equal. Similarly, the scale distance between arson and burglary may be expressed as a certain fraction of the other distances. Precisely the same methods have been used by Thurstone to determine attitudes of student groups toward various races and nationalities. When applied to large student populations, this technique, though mathematically more precise than that of Bogardus (cf. page 898), has resulted in relative degrees of preference for social groups which are almost identical with those reported by Bogardus.

The paired comparisons method, simple though it is, when discriminations among offenses or national groups are desired, is not so readily adapted to the judging of long lists of statements regarding particular issues. The work involved, for example, in the comparison of each of 100 statements concerning prohibition (and this is a very modest initial number of items) with every other one would

be too onerous. The procedure for the scaling of attitude statements therefore represents a modification of the paired comparisons
method. It is known as the method of equal-appearing intervals. A
collection of from 100 to 150 statements concerning the issue involved, ranging from extreme hostility to extreme favorableness,
is obtained from various sources. The statements are then classified
by large numbers of subjects (Thurstone and Chave report the use
of 300 subjects at this stage) into eleven piles, the first of which
includes the most strongly favorable statements, the sixth pile those
most nearly neutral, while the most extremely hostile statements
are put into the eleventh pile. Degree of "ambiguity" of the statements is measured in terms of the inter-quartile range, those statements receiving widely divergent judgments being discarded. Scale
values are then assigned to the remainder of the statements in terms
of the median position assigned by the judges. The scale value assigned to any statement, in other words, is such that half of the
judges consider it more favorable and half less favorable than that
particular position on the eleven-point scale. Thus, for example,
if the median position assigned to statement A is 7.0 and that for
statement B is 8.0, the two statements are separated, according to the
judgment of the total group, by one "just noticeable difference." It
is this just noticeable difference which becomes the unit of the scale,
so that it becomes possible to say that the difference between statements A and B is just half of that between statements B and C when
C has been assigned a scale value of 10.0. The resulting scale values
rarely turn out to be whole numbers, of course, nor are adjacent
statements, when arranged in scale order, necessarily equidistant.
It is not necessary that they should be, since their mathematical relationship is known. The actual selection of statements for the final
scale (following the discarding of ambiguous items) is determined
by two considerations: (1) the requirements of statistical reliability
(most of the published Thurstone scales contain 20 or more items
in each of two equivalent forms); (2) the inclusion of statements
ranging between the two extremes (a typical scale of 20 items ranging from scale values of approximately 1.0 to approximately 11.0
thus contains 19 scale intervals averaging about 0.5 point each).
Validation procedures similar to those described elsewhere in this

chapter are then applied. Scales covering a wide variety of issues have now been published by Thurstone and his collaborators.

An extension of Thurstone's methods in the direction of mass production has recently been introduced. Master scales were prepared by the same methods, but the statements were so worded that they could be applied to any institution, any defined group, any practice, any occupation, etc. Their odd-even reliability coefficients, when filled out for various specific attitudes, were almost or quite as satisfactory as those of comparable Thurstone scales (but the latter contain fewer items). Scores on these generalized scales, moreover, correlated highly, in general, with scores for identical attitudes according to Thurstone scales. The advantages of generalized scales are those of time-saving (i.e., in construction); a wider range in scores (several groups of subjects showed wider dispersions in the generalized scales than in comparable Thurstone scales); and wider applicability, since a very few master scales permit the measurement of almost any attitude. Another advantage which has impressed us is the simple wording of most of the statements. This, though not inherent in the method, is of peculiar importance in view of the great need of investigating the attitudes of wide groups of relatively uneducated adults.

The generalized scales, however, are subject to one disadvantage which in the case of many attitudes seems bound to outweigh these advantages. This is the danger of obtaining responses, not to the actual content of the attitude in question, but to symbols which indirectly suggest it. To the extent that this occurs, the scores of various subjects are not truly comparable: each is reacting to his own individual connotations which happen to be associated with the name of the attitude inserted in the generalized scale. Many such labels serve as stereotypes, setting off highly emotionalized responses. This danger is nicely illustrated in an investigation of attitudes toward "Fascism." That this particular word does serve as a stereotype is indicated by the fact that 73 per cent of the subjects "strongly disapproved" of Fascist Germany, though many of the same subjects made very favorable scores on a questionnaire which had been carefully prepared to include the actual components of Fascism without using the actual term. If, as Stagner suggests, one were to carry the generalizing process to its logical extremity, one would develop a scale composed of such items as the following: I think ———— is lovely; I think ———— is terrible. The published generalized scales are, of course, more refined than that. But every attitude of importance is to a greater or lesser extent the result of considerations peculiar to itself; and to limit scale statements to those which can be applied to all attitudes of a class is to sacrifice needed refinement to ease of obtaining data.

The same criticisms, incidentally, may be leveled against most of the published Thurstone scales; i.e., nearly every statement repeats such labels as "the Church," "Communism," etc. This, however, is a remediable fault for singly constructed scales, whereas it is inherent in the method of generalized scales.

One might anticipate that opinions of individual judges would influence considerably their assignment of scale positions. There are, of course, individual variations in scaling, but it has been clearly shown that, for two of the Thurstone scales at least, they are not related to opinions held by student groups concerning the issues involved.

Another weakness of the method, as so far applied, must, however, be seriously heeded. The indictment has been phrased as follows:

The difficulties of building scales similar to Thurstone's and of applying them to the measurement of attitudes of social groups, become increasingly difficult once we leave the classroom, the discussion club, and the other small, comparatively infrequent and highly selected groups that enjoy having experiments tried upon them. Such groups already have developed ways of making their attitudes articulate. It is the more numerous workaday groupings of society, which are inaccessible to his controlled measurements, about whose attitudes the social scientist is in the most need of information. Students may be required, good-natured academicians may be cajoled, and sundry needy persons may be paid to sort cards containing propositions into eleven piles. But it is difficult to imagine securing comparable judgments or satisfactory measurements in the final application from bricklayers, business men, Italian-Americans, nuns, stevedores, or seamstresses. And, unless the scale itself is based upon equal-seeming differences to a random sample of the group which is to be measured, its validity—the degree to which it measures that which it purports to measure—becomes open to question.

That attitude studies have so frequently been limited to students is a misfortune that we shall have many occasions to lament. But that attitude measures based solely upon student judgments should be used with totally different types of subjects, such as those described above, is a matter of grave concern, and one, moreover, that appears to be inherent in the method. A further limitation of the method, as thus far applied, is that disappointingly low reliability coefficients, as measured by correlating scores on equivalent forms, have been widely reported.

These considerations, together with that of the arduousness of the method, have led Likert to propose a simpler alternative to the Thurstone method of compiling and scoring attitude statements. His research had clearly shown that degree-of-agreement responses (e.g., strongly agree, agree, uncertain, disagree, and strongly disagree) to attitude statements could be scored by simply assigning values of 1 to 5, with fully as much accuracy as when all responses were scored in terms of sigma values. His two scoring methods, indeed, yielded correlation coefficients of .99 and higher, and their reliability coefficients were almost identical. The simple scoring method was therefore applied to scaled attitude statements. Ten of Thurstone's attitude scales were filled out by various student groups, all groups using both forms of the scales given them. Directions were changed so that one of five degrees of agreement was indicated for each statement. The scales were scored first by the Thurstone method, and then by Likert's simple method. It proved necessary, incidentally, to ignore a few of the scaled statements in scoring by the latter method, as it was found impossible to assign positive or negative values to the "agree" responses. Fewer statements were thus used for the Likert method of scoring than for the Thurstone method. But in spite of this, reliability coefficients proved consistently higher by the Likert method. Altogether, 27 comparable coefficients are presented (several groups having taken more than one scale). Of these the median reliability by the Thurstone scoring was .76, and for the Likert scoring, .85. The median correlation between the two methods of scoring was .88 so that, with this degree of reliability, there is no question as to their actually measuring the same attitudes. Very likely reliability of the Thurstone scales, as scored by Likert's method, is increased by the presence of statements covering the entire range from favorable to unfavorable attitude. But this can evidently be fully as well done without the laborious judging process; the median of 24 reliability coefficients for Likert's own "scales," constructed without benefit of judges, was .85, precisely the same as for Thurstone's scales as scored by Likert's method.

Present evidence, therefore, indicates that the method of scaled attitude statements yields less reliable results than those which have been obtained by other methods. It is based upon an assumption that is never realized in practice, namely, that acceptance of a given scale position implies acceptance of all positions less extreme and in the same direction from the neutral position. Its validity is open to doubt except when it is given to the academically sophisticated, by whom the initial judgments must almost necessarily be made. To these more serious indictments, it may be added that despite the laboriousness of the method, the currently used scales probably elicit, to a considerable degree, responses to labels and stereotypes rather than to meanings which are constant for all subjects. All this has no bearing, of course, upon the conception of attitude scaling by the paired comparisons method as such. This is a particularly valuable approach to attitudes toward some problems. For example, when the item is a *single word* (the name of a race or of a crime) rather than a *proposition*, no equally accurate method seems to have been proposed.

Some indirect light on validity is shed by supplementing paper-and-pencil tests by other tests in which, though the *response* is verbal, the stimulus is non-verbal. Thus attempts have been made to compare verbal responses on the conventional questionnaire with verbal responses to pictorial material or, in particular, to motion pictures. Students' responses to a five-minute motion picture scene of a race riot, ascertained on a six-point questionnaire after seeing the film, and similar responses to a motion picture scene of an attempted lynching, correlated from .40 to .50 with a general verbal scale of attitude toward the Negro. This compares favorably with the correlation of single items on a questionnaire with the sum of all the remaining questionnaire items. It means that the motion pictures could, if necessary, be used as elements in a larger battery. A short motion picture, however, is necessarily specific and would take the place of a single item or, at most, of two or three items, not of a whole battery.

Still pictures may be as good as movies. Photographs from current news services showing economic conflict, e.g., the struggle between miners and deputy sheriffs and between strikers and the police, again showed fair correlation with conventional questionnaire material. With 21 cases, an r of .66 appeared between economic radicalism and degree of sympathy with strikers shown in nine photographs of strike conflict situations. There is undoubtedly a future for photographic and similar methods of attitude testing to supplement exclusively verbal methods. Yet it must be remembered that such methods are time-consuming, that they are likely to replace single elements on the scales rather than whole scales, and that, even if the stimulus is non-verbal, in the last analysis reaction to the material has to be verbal.

An exception to this last stricture may be urged in view of the possibility of applying the galvanic-skin-reflex techniques and similar methods to persons whose attitudes are deeply aroused. At best, however, these methods would supplement what has now come to be called attitude measurement; and the physiological indices become supplementary data regarding the background of attitude, and not substitutes for the verbally expressed attitudes themselves. In view of the highly verbalized nature of so much social behavior, we are inclined to think that the tendency to substitute other methods for verbal methods can be overdone. An integration of the various methods suggested, rather than the disparagement of one to the advantage of another, is more appropriate.

Regardless of the form of the measuring instrument, questions of validity arise and demand to be answered. What assurance is there, beyond the precautions taken during the construction of attitude tests, that they are actually measuring what they are supposed to measure? One method of validation is nicely illustrated by a study of attitudes toward prohibition, which merits detailed description.

The purpose of the experiment was to compare a *statistical* and a *case history* method of attitude research. The subjects were 238 students who took a test of attitudes toward prohibition which had been constructed according to Thurstone's method. The students also wrote anonymous accounts of their experiences, feelings, and opinions with respect to prohibition laws and to drinking liquor, from childhood to the time of writing. Each account was about a thousand words long. The case histories were read by four judges working independently, and were rated on a five-inch graphic rating scale to show the extent to which the attitudes were favorable or unfavorable toward prohibition laws. The judges were selected by a committee of the faculty of the Department of Sociology on the bases "of knowledge of the theoretical literature on attitudes, of experience in interpreting case materials, and of insight into human experience." They were told to use "whatever concepts of attitudes on prohibition they chose, to set their own standards of favorable or unfavorable, and to try to judge all papers by the same standards." The average of the six intercorrelations of ratings of each judge with ratings of each other judge was $+.87$, the range being from $+.83$ to $+.89$. The ratings by each judge were expressed in standard scores (deviations from the mean of his rating, divided by the standard deviation).

The validity coefficient, measuring the extent to which scores on the Smith test were correlated with composite standard scores on the case history ratings by four judges, was $+.81$, which became $+.86$ when corrected for attenuation. The validity coefficient of $+.86$ was checked in several ways, all of which tended to confirm the apparent fact that attitudes as measured by the test and attitudes as measured by the case history ratings are quantitatively much the same.

First, the students rated their own attitudes toward prohibition laws on a graphic rating scale similar to that employed by the judges. They rated themselves twice, with two days intervening, and the two ratings were combined, equal weight being given to each. The correlation of the self-ratings with the Smith test scores was +.80. The correlation of the self-ratings with the composite ratings of the four judges on the case histories was the same, +.80. "Unless spurious factors entered to account for the agreement between the findings of the statistical and case history method, one would seem justified in concluding that, whatever it may be that the two methods were measuring, each measured substantially the same thing."

The judges asserted that they used the same general definition of attitude that is used by the layman when he discusses "so and so's attitude about prohibition." The likelihood that the concepts of attitude of the judges corresponded closely to a common-sense usage tends to be confirmed by the fact that the ratings on a sample of 99 papers by two laymen, the superintendent of the Illinois Anti-Saloon League and the secretary and director of the Illinois Association Opposed to Prohibition, yielded about as high correlations with the ratings of the four judges and with each other as did the correlations of the four judges among themselves. The author sums up as follows: "(1) The validity coefficient of .86, in conjunction with the test reliability of .94, lends confidence in the Thurstone method of measuring attitudes. (2) The validity coefficient of .86, in conjunction with the case history ratings' reliability of .96, lends confidence in the objectivity of the case history method."

The most common validating devices are the use of ratings and of overt behavior as criteria. A particularly good illustration of the use of these methods is offered in a study entitled *Student Opinion on War*. A thousand students indicated on a five-point scale the degree of their agreement or disagreement with each of about 150 brief statements about war, such as, "War is always wrong"; "In case of war, those who continue to oppose it should be imprisoned"; "War is justified when its purpose is defensive"; "Armaments are the only sure guarantee of peace"; "Modern wars have been caused more by moral principles than by commercial questions." The questionnaire covered Alleged Causes of War; Alleged Results of War; Eliminating War; The Right or Wrong of War; Patriotism and Conscience; and American Action in the Immediate Future.

"For the purpose of standardization, 100 validation tests were obtained from persons whose position on questions involved was overt, and on which, in each case, from three to thirteen ratings by acquaintances had been secured on a scale of o to 10 (extreme pacifism to extreme militarism). Validation tests were used only if ratings agreed within a span of three steps on the scale of eleven." These 100 individuals now took the test, and (after items which did not appear to be of value in differentiating attitudes were thrown out) the score to be assigned to any given attitude is the *average rating received by all the individuals who held that attitude*. A large number of college groups show "normal distributions" of attitude toward war, the mode lying at the mid-point on the scale in the great majority of the groups. Three denominational colleges make a modal response slightly toward the pacifist end of the scale; a state university R.O.T.C. class made a modal response slightly inclined toward the militarist end, but none of the variations are at all striking. A group of adult reserve officers make a distinctively high "militarist" score, and a group of conscientious objectors and student pacifist leaders make a definitely "pacifist" score. All the lines of evidence appear to converge and to justify the belief that the scale does actually indicate the amount of reaction against war.

Preliminary validation, in other words, was later verified by applying the measure to individuals whose commitment regarding the issue was overt. This latter device, as opposed to the mere use of ratings alone for validating purposes, is meeting with increasing favor. The advantages of the method are obvious; probably its chief disadvantage is the fact that, while it is relatively easy to make use of individuals who stand at opposite extremes in regard to any given attitude, it is not always possible to determine just what kind of overt commitment represents an intermediate stand.

One or two other instances of validation by information concerning overt commitments may be cited. Thus a test of international attitudes was given to forty persons definitely identified with movements or activities of a genuinely international character, such as business men doing a large volume of business overseas, members of the Communist party, and leaders in international religious movements. It was found not only that attitude scores agreed with overt conduct, as inferred from their business and group affiliations, but that there was *not a single exception* to this agreement with predicted answers.

Again, church attendance and activity have been compared with scores of attitude toward the Church. In one such report the mean scores of 90 students who describe themselves as having "active" church relations was 2.06; of 83 whose church relations were "nominal," 3.38; and of 43 with no church relations, 3.85. The following comparison of scores with frequency of church attendance for the same students is even more striking (low scores indicate favorable attitude toward the Church):

Number of Subjects	Frequency of Church Attendance	Mean Score
68	regularly	1.91
57	frequently	2.48
58	occasionally	3.50
31	seldom	4.95
5	never	6.75

Another frequently alleged shortcoming of attitude tests is more difficult to deal with. Most attitude tests have *not* been validated in terms of either ratings or overt behavior; are they in general incapable of "validation"? After all, attitudes as here defined are verbal behavior or, to be exact, paper-and-pencil behavior with reference to verbal statement stimuli. What guarantee is there that attitudes represent any more than that? In many other areas we are skeptical of mere repeated verbalization and demand "action" as evidence of good faith. Have attitude testers been overcredulous?

The "merely verbal" aspect of attitude measurement has seemed to so many critics to be its Achilles' heel that we must take careful note of the conditions under which its "more than verbal" aspect can be demonstrated. Objective information concerning "overt" behavior, other than that supplied by knowledge of affiliated groups and asserted activities, is extremely rare. It is, almost of necessity, limited to a few individuals whose very overtness has made them conspicuous. The vast majority, who occupy middle positions regarding any attitude, simply fail to show behavior which clearly identifies them with any given attitude—except, perhaps, that of indifference. If we only *knew* that this middle majority were those failing to show such behavior, this in itself would be important.

validating evidence. But such negative evidence is almost impossible to obtain; we merely know that we do not have it; we do *not* know that it is not there to be had. The problem, in other words, must be "solved" by other than statistical means. Or perhaps we should say that statistical means are of use provided only that the logic of the situation is clearly formulated.

Actions are no more inherently "valid," in the first place, than words. The following remarks seem to us patently true: "Actions are frequently designed to distort or conceal 'true' attitude quite as fully as verbal behavior. . . . *All* behavior is subject to modification in the process of execution from considerations of courtesy, expediency, or other social pressures." And it is furthermore apparent that when verbal behavior is used to distort or conceal the "true" attitudes, the distortion commonly *conforms to everyday behavior*. The reasons for concealing "true" attitudes are the same for both verbal and "overt" behavior. If conditions of secrecy, and preferably of anonymity, are observed, there is more reason to expect free and complete expression of attitudes through words, thus freed from social pressures, than from behaviors which are open to all beholders. There are other methods, both psychological and sociological, for measuring what people *do*; here we are discussing attitudes, and observable behavior presents a weaker case for validity than "merely verbal" behavior, under proper safeguards. And, finally, it may be observed that a man's categorical agreement or disagreement with a rather strongly stated opinion about the Chinese, or Jews, or Rotarians, or Communists, is in everyday life regarded (if the man is sincere) as a *significant* part of his behavior. There seems to be no reason why this behavior should suddenly become *nonsignificant* when it is made the subject of careful inquiry, particularly if motives for insincerity are reduced to a minimum.

ATTITUDES AND INDIVIDUAL CHARACTERISTICS

Attitudes, like other social-psychological phenomena, may be related to either psychological or sociological variables. Before presenting the results of the more definitely psychological investigations, we may pause to examine, on *a priori* grounds, the nature and degree of relationships which may be anticipated between attitudes and characteristics with regard to which there are measurable individual differences. We need not expect, in the first place, that *any* invariable or highly consistent relationships will be found, since public attitudes, in any event, are borrowed, selected, or adapted from those various currents of social influences in which individuals are diversely immersed. The relationship, such as it is, will thus necessarily be that of a particular personality characteristic, in a particular segment of culture, to a particular attitude. For example, age differences in attitudes, with which we shall presently deal, are a function not only of mental growth and glandular changes, but of the rate of cultural change. Much depends on how free one is to change, because of such factors as parental domination and economic insecurity. One might, indeed, conceive of a freedom-to-change age which, in relation to the current stimuli-to-change, would go far toward "explaining" a particular individual's attitudes in any given time and place. Such a concept, at any rate, would show more direct relationships to attitudes than any simple variable such as chronological age.

What relationships we may expect to find depend, in the second place, upon the nature of the personality variables with which we start. If we conceive of personality as an aggregate of traits, the relationship of attitudes to any one of them would be subject to cultural pulls like those suggested in the foregoing discussion of age differences. Thus individuals characterized by social extroversion may be presumed to be "conservative" or "liberal" according to the nature of the predominant community influences to which they have been subject. The difficulties of predicting, or even of interpreting, any individual's attitudes from knowledge of his several trait scores become formidable indeed if each of the latter must first be put through the sieve of culture. One might therefore anticipate a greater degree of success in interrelating attitudes and other personality characteristics if a more "organismic" approach to the latter were taken. But, unfortunately, little exact attitude research has been undertaken except in this country; and American psychologists have not, until recently perhaps, been hospitable even to the more objective methods of "total personality" study. At any rate, there are few investigations in which data concerning both attitudes and "total personality" are to be found—except those, useless for our purposes, in which each has been inferred in circular fashion from the other.

We shall present such information as is available concerning the relationship of attitudes, first, to sex and age differences, then to differences revealed by test scores and laboratory measurements, together with some meager gleanings from total personality measurements. The relationship of various attitudes to individual characteristics, as reported by large numbers of investigators, is by and large very slight. Contradictory findings have often been reported; but, contradictory or not, such relationships have usually been by-products of investigations designed for other purposes. There has been extremely little research directed at these problems.

Sex differences are a case in point. Though there are areas in which sex differences are more consistently found, studies of attitude toward war present almost a typical situation. No differences whatever are reported in some studies, and in no case do differences appear to be completely reliable. One comprehensive set of data (cf. page 916) indicates that while differences are statistically significant only for a total group of "fathers and mothers," females are slightly more pacifistic than males in all classifications of age, socio-economic status, and religious affiliation. Judging from a large sample of Italian school children, sex differences of similar degree with regard to attitude toward war are not limited to this country.

Considerable evidence is at hand regarding sex differences in racial attitudes, but no generalizations whatever are warranted. Both men and women, according to various investigations, have been found to be "reliably" more favorable toward the Negro, while no differences at all are reported in still others. Nothing short of a comparison of males and females from the same homes can give us authentic information on this point, and we know of no such evidence.

When cultural pressures react differently on boys and girls, some attitude differences should be expected. Thus in regard to superstitious belief clear-cut sex differences have been reported year after year. Girls have not only heard more and reported themselves to be influenced by more false beliefs than boys, but actually believe more, though according to one report the last of these differences is not reliable in the case of rural children and college students. It has been suggested that superstitiousness is more acceptable among women than among men in many cultural areas, and this seems plausible. As supporting evidence for this interpretation is cited the fact that a group of men subjects had dropped about half of the superstitions held at some previous time, whereas women reported dropping only one-sixth of theirs.

Rather consistent sex differences have also been reported in the general realm of attitudes toward morals, the Church and religious belief. The comprehensive survey of attitudes made at Syracuse University reveals sharp sex differences among the 1406 students in the Liberals Arts College, which is about equally divided between the sexes. Belief in God was indicated by checking one of seven brief paragraph statements ranging from belief in a personal creator who answers prayer, to dogmatic atheism. Positions ranging from agnosticism to atheism were taken by 15 per cent of the women and 29 per cent of the men. "As the pressure of uniform group teaching diminishes, individual differences in background and personality assert themselves; . . . the differences between the sexes increase as the degree of orthodoxy diminishes." This interpretation, of course, reflects F. H. Allport's theory of institutional attitudes, which is discussed elsewhere (page 990). Whatever the merits of the interpretation, this sex difference in religious belief has been widely found.

The same report contains striking differences with respect to moral standards also. In regard to the "double moral standard," for example, half the men and 69 per cent of the women "believed in moral requirements equal for the two sexes." The percentages of those of both sexes who consider some acts worse for women are as follows: drinking, 74 per cent; illicit sex behavior, 71 per cent; telling obscene stories, 61 per cent; cursing, 58 per cent; smoking, 41 per cent; gambling, 39 per cent; murder, 18 per cent. The authors, of course, make no pretense that a universal sex difference in standards is here represented, though several other studies regarding the "double moral standard" are in general agreement. It had been pointed out earlier that on questions involving their own sex, women students are likely to be more "radical" than men, although the female subjects upon whom this observation was based were more conservative on political, economic, and religious questions than the males. All this is consistent with the findings of the Syracuse study.

This distinction in standards does not, however, mean that there are large sex differences in moral attitudes in general. This is shown, for example, in a series of rankings of the seriousness of transgressions obtained from professional men and women, from housewives, from manual laborers, from industrial workers, and from students. Among all these groups sex differences in estimation of the seriousness of crimes are but slight. Similar data have been gathered over a period of years by another investigator, for whom students in successive years and in various university centers ranked a list of offenses in order of "badness." Results from all groups are remarkably consistent, men agreeing closely with women in spite of the fact that sex offenses were included in the list. Correlations as high as .98 between men's and women's rankings of the offenses are presented.

Sex differences in attitude toward the Church have been commonly reported. Perhaps the most representative sample to be reported included 548 families with one or more "children" and one or both parents. Children's ages ranged from 14 to 38, and those of parents from 34 to 82. Mean scores on the Thurstone-Chave scale of attitude toward the Church were compiled for classifications according to age, sex, religious affiliation, and occupational status. While male and female scores are not reliably different in all classifications, in all of twenty-seven classifications females are more favorable to the Church than males. The differences, however, varied with both age and occupational level, being most pronounced at the lowest occupational levels, and for children of 17 years and younger, and least pronounced for parents whose ages were 56 and over. The considerable sex difference at the lowest age level is interpreted as due to the fact that boys break away from parents' attitudes at earlier ages than girls.

Still other factors appear in this study when males and females *of the same families* are compared, thus holding constant a host of other variables. Thus, among the younger group of parents (fathers under 50) husband-wife differences are almost twice as great where fathers are five or more years older than mothers, as where they are four years older or less. For the older group of parents, although a marked sex difference exists, this factor of age difference, in families where fathers are older, is not a distinguishing one; and in families where the father is not older than the mother the sex difference almost disappears. Similar factors appear to be operative in comparing siblings of opposite sex: in families where brothers are older by four years or more, the sex difference is twice as great as where the age difference is under four years, and in families where sisters are older, there are almost no sex differences at all.

Turning to the field of political attitudes, we find that questionnaire replies from 8419 men and women in thirty-seven states, received just prior to the 1932 presidential election, suggest similar conclusions regarding sex differences. Replies from these "voters of known occupations" were gathered in sealed envelopes personally by solicitors under the auspices of the League of Women Voters. Besides the query, "For whom will you vote?" the questionnaire contained two statements on each of twelve issues. These statements, to which either the "yes," the "no," or the "doubtful" answer was to be checked, were largely in politicians' or parties' wordings; naturally some of them were ambiguous. Replies are classified as to sex, preferred presidential candidate, and occupation. There are many sex differences; but the significant fact is that few of them are found in all occupational classes, or in all three groups as classified according to preferred candidate. For example, the statement that the United States should reduce its army and navy was favored by more women than men, *except in the lower occupational groups.* The statement that the railroads, power companies, and banks should be owned by the government was favored by more women than men, *except among the Thomas supporters and factory workers.*

Are females generally more "conservative" than males? It is often difficult to apply the term to a particular attitude, but even apart from this difficulty the results of many studies are conflicting. The answer is certainly in the negative with respect to pacifism, if anti-pacificism has been the generally accepted position in the past, and may therefore be considered conservative. Neither is there convincing evidence to the contrary. Does the placing of higher value upon public than upon private employment represent an attachment to things as they were? Then women are conservative in that field, as shown by L. D. White's polling of 7168 adults in eleven scattered cities (cf. page 987). Among this group, 21.3 per cent of the women and 14.4 per cent of the men revealed themselves as favoring public over private employment, and the results are similar for over 4000 Chicago adults in a previous study of the same kind. Is a favorable attitude toward prohibition evidence of conservatism? Perhaps it was in 1933, when one group of senior college women was found to be more favorably disposed than a comparable group of men. If satisfaction with job and employer is a criterion of conservatism, then women score again in that direction according to a study of 410 women factory employees who were more favorably inclined, by a difference of six times its S.D., than 2878 men. Or is some measure of conservatism-in-general preferred, such as the Harper Social Study? Then no conclusions at all may be drawn, for the most diverse and conflicting results have been obtained by the use of such measures.

Clearly, then, the question is not whether males are more "conservative" or "liberal" than females. It is not, primarily, whether the sexes differ even in more specific attitudes. It is far more complicated than that. It is patent that whatever differences have as yet been found are the result, not of biological but of cultural factors. The question of sex differences must therefore be at least as complex as are cultural variations within our civilization. This means that sex differences will be a function not only of age, economic status, geographical section, political and religious affiliation, etc., but also of the time at which the investigation happens to be made. It is fully as important to know these detailed circumstances as to know, for example, that in general women are more favorably disposed to the Church than men; these circumstances are, of course, *more* important as sources for clues to all the fundamental questions as to why such differences appear.

The problem of age differences presents us with a like situation. The question will be considered, in a rather oblique fashion, under the topic of educational influences as shown by attitudes at successive school levels (page 980). It is there suggested (though the point is almost incapable of verification because of the practical impossibility of obtaining controls) that many of these differences are undoubtedly the result of added years of living in a certain culture. These cumulative modifications we are accustomed to refer to as age differences; but we must eschew the implication, inherent in so much psychological discussion, that they represent simply "maturation," as if this meant the unfolding of latent dispositions.

One of the pitfalls in this type of research is illustrated by a simple and direct attempt to answer the question: When age differences are found, do they reflect primarily changes in mores and standards from one generation to another? Multiple choice tests of attitudes were given to thirty college men and thirty college women, and also to a large proportion of their parents and grandparents, whose participation was obtained at social gatherings. The questionnaire consisted of fifteen behavior situations, for each of which subjects were asked, not what they would do, but what *standard* they believed would govern their conduct. The four possible standards were: right as opposed to wrong; prudence, or intelligent judgment; public opinion; and aesthetic standards. It appears clearly, from their replies, that grandparents tend to rely upon absolute standards of right and wrong, whereas students believe themselves to be governed to a far greater extent by considerations of prudence and judgment. The difference in mean scores for the "right and wrong" criterion for these two groups is a reliable one. The group of parents, in general, occupy positions intermediate between the other two groups, parents resembling grandparents somewhat more closely than they do students. Such evidence, of course, is subjective and "merely verbal," but it suggests the background against which age differences must be seen.

The Lynds have made one of the few attempts of which we are aware, to study these changes of standards among adults. Mothers in their own homes were asked to indicate which of several habits they emphasized most and least in training their children. Each one was then asked to make a similar rating of the same list "as her own home training led her to believe her mother would have rated it thirty years ago when she was a child." Ratings were thus obtained for 37 "business-class" mothers and 34 of their mothers, and for 104 "working-class" mothers and 67 of their mothers. As the Lynds have occasion to point out on many other occasions, changes in the business class are much more rapid than those in the working class. Mothers of the first group report marked changes with respect to nine of the fifteen habits. They emphasize more than did their mothers concentration, social-mindedness, knowledge of sex hygiene, patriotism and independence. Strict obedience, loyalty to the Church, good manners, and getting good grades in school are emphasized less by this group than by their mothers. In the working class only two clear differences are shown, both in the direction of more emphasis by present-day mothers: appreciation of art, music, and poetry, and knowledge of sex hygiene. The authors comment that differences between generations are probably minimized here, because both of inclusion of what should be rather than what actually was emphasized by themselves, and of tendencies to assume that they were about like their mothers.

Very recently there have appeared some reports of student changes in attitudes over periods of a few years. In one of these, evidence is taken from an analysis of the responses of about a thousand college undergraduates to the Pressey X-O test in 1923, as compared to those of a similar number just ten years later. Changes during this period were very slight as regards total number of anxieties and of interests underlined, but there was a sharp decline in the number of *ethical disapprovals* in response to the names of various forms of conduct. In these the percentage of decline was, for a large proportion of items, as large as 20, and is considered by the author as evidence of "distinct liberalization of opinion." An analysis of the particular items showing the greatest change revealed certain patterns, of which the following are the most conspicuous:

such "milder vices" as smoking and betting; such sex-connoting words as flirting and divorce; the use of slang; debt and socialism— all these are less disapproved than formerly. The only item in which there was a marked increase in disapproval was "war." The most marked changes in interests were reflected in less frequent underlining of such words as business, salesman, and banker. Thus in many respects these changes are the epitome of an epoch. Perhaps another kind of change is reflected in the fact that the decline in disapprovals (particularly for men) was most marked in the under-class groups, suggesting that this particular symptom of maturity now appears at earlier ages than formerly.

In view of such changes of modal tendency of response, even within a brief term of years, it becomes clear that "age differences" must be interpreted with extreme caution. What the so-called age differences do not represent is inevitable or automatic changes in attitude which accompany mere organic maturation. What they probably do represent, to a very considerable degree, is twofold: different institutions, groups, and symbols toward which loyalty is felt; and differing ability to shift one's loyalty from one set of institutions, groups, and symbols to another of different nature. The hypothesis that the majority of individuals fix these loyalties during early maturity, and that only a minority change them, would account for most of the age differences in attitudes so far observed.

Turning now to the data concerning the comparative attitudes of various contemporary age groups, one of the areas in which we may expect to find age differences is in attitude toward the Church. The most complete data of which we know include replies of 778 children (including many sets of siblings) and 1159 of their parents to the Thurstone-Chave scale of attitude toward the Church. Slight but highly consistent age differences are shown. Between the ages of 17 and 30 there is a steady decrease in favorable attitude toward the Church, particularly by females, but the basis of selection at the age levels represented renders the differences questionable. Differences among parents, however, are clearly noticeable, and there is little evidence of age selection among them. Both fathers and mothers increase steadily in favorable attitude with advancing age. Precisely the same differences are shown when occupational classifications are made; the differences are least noticeable for children at the lowest occupational levels, and most noticeable for parents at the same levels.

A clue as to the process by which these age changes occur is to be seen in further comparisons, by age classifications, of children's attitudes with those of their own parents. Since exactly the same process appears to be at work with regard to another attitude for which scores are available from the same subjects, viz., toward Communism, comparisons are made below for both attitudes. (Low scores are favorable to the Church; high scores, to Communism.)

Attitude toward Church

Age group	Children's Mean	Parents' Mean	Difference
17 and under	4.27 (N 213)	4.23 (N 312)	.04
18 to 21	4.39 (N 304)	3.99 (N 491)	.40
22 and over	4.69 (N 261)	4.16 (N 356)	.53

Attitude toward Communism

Age group	Children's Mean	Parents' Mean	Difference
17 and under	4.89 (N 203)	4.87 (N 298)	.02
18 to 21	4.97 (N 290)	4.72 (N 472)	.25
22 and over	5.14 (N 252)	4.71 (N 340)	.43

Assuming that age differences for children are not entirely due to selection, it appears that children are gradually being molded by education and by a changing *Zeitgeist* away from their parents' attitudes with which they were in general conformity to begin with, whereas any given parent tends to remain stationary; hence the disparity. This suggests, as do certain other studies, that the older subjects retain their earlier group and institutional loyalties, whereas the younger ones are shifting their allegiances—the younger subjects, in the foregoing study, being largely selected on the basis of subjection to educational influences.

One suspects quite a different kind of process at work in L. D. White's report of age differences in the prestige value of public employment, both in his Chicago study of over 4000 adults and in a later one involving more than 7000 men and women in eleven scattered cities. These individuals were interviewed by house-to-house canvassers in various parts of the cities represented, and were asked to indicate, among such pairs of occupations as the following, for which they had "the higher esteem": stenographer, treasurer's office, Equitable Insurance Company, or stenographer, treasurer's office, City of Chicago; janitor, First National Bank, or janitor, City Hall Building, etc. Answers were classified as (1) showing greater esteem for city employment; (2) "doubtful, no difference, or unable to answer"; and (3) showing less esteem for city employment. Interviewers were careful to point out that all other considerations, such as salary, convenience, difficulty of work, etc., were to be assumed to be alike. Attempts were also made to investigate attitudes toward city employees. For this purpose association test techniques were used, in which relevant words were presented one at a time, the subjects being asked to reply with the first word that came to mind. Direct questions were also included, such as, "Do you get more courteous attention in dealing with city employees than in dealing with employees of private corporations?"

From all this material a "prestige index" was worked out, representing the difference between the sum of the prestige items for city employment minus the sum of prestige items for private employment. The relationship of this prestige index to age is clear: it is highest among the age group 15 to 19, and falls steadily with increasing age. Many other variables are also related to it; it is highest among unskilled workers, those of low socio-economic status, the foreign-born, and those of limited education. The author has not attempted to disentangle the effects of these obviously interrelated variables. We are content, for present purposes, to point out the age differences so clearly demonstrated.

Here, as in the case of attitude toward the Church, we have age differences as the result of (or at least closely associated with) increasing experience, educational and other. But the specificity with which these age changes occur may be noted from the different nature of the age curves with respect to these two attitudes. The curve of attitude toward public employment declines steadily from the teens to late maturity. The curve of attitude toward the Church, on the other hand, appears to decline from the teens to the late twenties, but to rise from then on to late maturity. These latter changes may be interpreted easily enough in terms of adolescent dependence upon parents, merging into youthful independence and individualism, which in turn gives way to increasing appreciation of socially approved values with increasing family and community responsibility. But no such pattern will fit the age curve described by White for attitudes toward public employment. Perhaps the latter pattern is to be understood partly as a compound of the small boy's desire to be either policeman or president, and of the less than realistic teaching in most of our homes and schools regarding municipal and civic affairs. The result of this could scarcely be other than gradual disillusionment. We suspect that the differences between these age curves are primarily due to the fact that adult beliefs concerning the Church are willingly inculcated in the young, who are, on the other hand, commonly protected against what are regarded by their elders as the sordid facts of political life. These are highly speculative interpretations, of course, but it is evident that qualitative analysis of the specific factors related to change, both for individual subjects and for particular attitudes, is needed.

Data from two age groups which are unusually well "equated" in other respects are supplied by two questionnaires concerning pacifism and certain economic issues (cf. page 1007). Replies were received from 1100 theological seminary students in 1931, and from nearly 1500 in 1934, approximately 3000 and 6000 questionnaires having been sent out in those respective years. These student replies are directly comparable with those of nearly 20,000 practising clergymen in 1931, and from about the same number in 1934. Percentages of pacifistic and of economically liberal replies are given in the accompanying table.

	Students (1931)	Clergymen (1931)	Students (1934)	Clergymen (1934)
Mean percentage of pacifistic replies to seven questions	74	58	73	63
Mean percentage of liberal replies to seven questions concerning economic issues	..	..	71	59

(The items concerning economic issues appeared only in the 1934 questionnaire.) Students answer more pacifistically to every one of the first group of questions, and more liberally to every one of the second group, than do clergymen. A comparison of the replies to the first group of questions for the two different years, moreover, is revealing. If these samples are assumed to be reasonably adequate, it is evident that the differences were greater in 1931; this is true, indeed, for each of the seven questions. Students made no significant changes during this three-year period, whereas clergymen had become slightly more pacifistic. The 1931-34 differences for clergymen, though small, are consistent, and the exceptions are limited to two of ten denominations, and to two questions. The following interpretation is suggested: Both students and clergymen are being influenced by a certain *Zeitgeist* within the American religious world. But students, being in centers where there is greater opportunity to become familiar with more recent trends of thought, are influenced by the forces of the hour more quickly. They are simply somewhat in advance of their elders; they have been caught in the current earlier. What appear to be age differences is the result of subjection to different influences in the immediate past. The age differences do exist, but they are, as we have so often suspected, results of particular cultural influences and not of an inevitable maturing process.

Once it is granted that prejudice against races is not a native trait there must, of course, be age differences in racial attitudes, since attitudes develop during some period of time. The only question is: How early and how rapidly do they develop? Some evidence has been gathered in studies by E. and R. Horowitz, to which we have already referred in another connection (pages 239-241), which indicates that anti-Negro prejudice develops extremely early, even among northern children. Subjects—boys ranging from kindergarten age to the eighth grade—were obtained in New York City, and in both urban and rural southern communities. Results must be understood in the light of the testing methods employed, methods simple, objective, and realistic. The "ranks" test consisted of a series of photographs of faces of four white and eight Negro boys, the latter being so selected as to represent various degrees of skin color, and as to be judged both racially typical and pleasant by several adults. Subjects were simply asked to "pick out the one you like best, . . . next best, . . . next best," etc. The same faces were used for the "show-me" test, in which subjects selected companions for a variety of imagined situations, such as occupying the same seat in a street car, or playing in the same game of ball; there was no limit to the number which could be chosen. Photographs of groups of boys in posed situations, such as playing marbles, listening to the radio, and eating around a table, were used for the "social situations" test. Each such situation was photographed twice, posed first by four white boys, and then with Negroes substituting for one or more of the white boys. Subjects were asked whether they wanted to "join in with them and do what they're doing along with them," responses being classified as affirmative, negative, or intermediate.

Results are, in the main, very definite. Preference for whites is present even in the kindergarten. No consistent age differences of any sort appeared for the ranks test. For the show-me test there was no reliable increase in prejudice after the first-grade level, though kindergarten groups were markedly below all other groups in prejudice. The relatively high correlations between "ranks" and "show-me" is due, in part at least, to the identity of the stimulus materials of the two tests. Only for the social situations test was there steady increase, with increasing grade level, from very little to very definite prejudice; and even in this test the increase (though the slope of the curve is reliable) was slight and irregular. The northern subjects, moreover, differed only very slightly from those from southern areas.

Two considerations, however, impress us as not being in conformity with the view that anti-Negro prejudice develops early in life, with but slight increase thereafter. The first is the fact that both reliabilities of the three tests and intercorrelations among them increase with age. Some of the intercorrelations are presented here-

INTERCORRELATIONS AMONG THREE TESTS FOR
TWO HIGHEST AND TWO LOWEST GRADES

Grade	N	Ranks and Show-me	Ranks and Social Situations	Show-me and Social Situations
Kindergarten	51	.53	.13	.01
1 B	45	.48	− .06	− .04
....	..	...	.....	.....
7 B	40	.76	.19	.28
8 B	35	.61	.24	.29

with. The other consideration has to do with the difference among the three growth curves in relation to the nature of the three tests selected. The "social situations" test, which impresses us as being far more realistic than the other two, i.e., corresponding more directly to the conditions under which children would or not manifest prejudice, yields results different from the other two in two respects: (1) A much smaller degree of absolute prejudice is revealed by it; prejudice, according to this test, is very slight in the kindergarten, first and fifth grades, and actually negative in the third and fourth grades. And (2) there is more definite growth in prejudice according to this test than according to the other two, as suggested by the curves appearing in his figure. The three tests thus appear to possess different degrees of sensitivity, in the sense that finer degrees of prejudice are registered by some of them than by others. They are measuring types of prejudice with different thresholds. We surmise that the first two tests (and, in particular, the first of them) are so extremely sensitive that even a relatively mild preference for whites over Negroes goes the limit of the scale and becomes registered almost as an all-or-none affair. The thresholds of prejudice, so measured, are so low as to render questionable the use of the term prejudice, as it is commonly used. On the other hand, the third test, which seems to us to have greater *a priori* validity, reveals the gradual type of growth in prejudice that other considerations would lead us to expect.

Most studies of racial attitudes, however, have been made with adult groups, and the majority of them have dealt with attitudes toward the Negro. One of these may be briefly cited. Two southern groups and two from New York City were studied; one group from each section was composed of students, and the other of adults of varying economic status, obtained through two Protestant churches. By comparing northern students with northern adults, and southern students with southern adults, age differences, if they existed, would presumably appear, even though the numbers of subjects are small. But few such differences appear. The most conspicuous exception to the general uniformity of response is in answer to the question, "Do you consider the Negro more than half the white man's equal intellectually?" While 29 of 62 northern students and only two of 39 northern adults answer this question affirmatively, 14 of 39 southern students and no southern adults do so. With most other questions, however, no "age" differences, or unreliable ones appear. The above question is, of the entire list, the one to which responses would presumably be most affected by university education, so that the apparent age difference must almost certainly be put down to educational influence rather than to any influences necessarily associated with age. Certainly no generalizations regarding age differences can be drawn from these data.

Not only do we know of no direct evidence of age differences among adults in regard to attitude toward the Negro, but all evidence of indirect nature points to their non-existence. Our hypotheses concerning the development of racial attitudes, moreover, argue in the same direction. For the identity of the groups to which allegiance is owed is, for most individuals, largely determined during or prior to early adulthood. And the pressures which are so subtly applied by such groups have been effectively applied long since, by the time that age is reached. Unless and until such social forces are operative as can influence primary groups to which young people belong, without similarly influencing those of their elders, we need not expect to find age differences among adults in this area.

Our conclusions regarding age differences are much like those involving sex differences. In such particular attitudes, and under such particular circumstances as they are found, they reflect susceptibility to different sets of cultural influences. Not even the commonly assumed increasing conservatism of age has been clearly demonstrated, nor is this due merely to the ambiguities of the term. If it be defined as continued identification of one's own attitudes with those of given groups or institutions, then almost the whole world is either conservative or reactionary, Communists and devotees of modern music included. If, on the other hand, we define it in terms of a given belief at a given time, there is ample evidence that a fair proportion of mature and elderly persons is able to adapt specific beliefs *pari passu* with institutional changes made necessary by the ravages of time. Older people seem more conservative (and often are, by the second definition) because the groups and institutions with which they are identified are more likely to date from a previous generation. For with increasing age, somewhat relenting economic pressure and social competition render the average adult less sensitive to changing structures of society, so that less attitudinal adaptation takes place. Those in whom the fewest changes occur are, other things equal, those upon whom changing structures impinge least urgently. The "other things equal" refers principally to considerations of personality factors, to which we now turn.

Are there not, in spite of all the emphasis we have put upon cultural factors as determinants of attitudes, some fundamental dispositions, perhaps native, upon which specific attitudes are built? Thus G. W. Allport pleads for the recognition of innate patterns or groups of dispositions which may reveal themselves in specific kinds of personality, on the one hand, or in specific groups of attitudes, on the other. One cannot, in fact, understand his approach to attitudes without considering sympathetically why he rejects the conditioned-response explanation of social habits. Despite the powerful influence of the environment, he regards personality as something deeper than habit, which expresses itself through the social *milieu*. It is easy to see, then, why radicalism and conservatism, ascendance and submission, extroversion and introversion, etc., seem to him basic expressions of personality, not fragments somehow attached to the growing organism. We have mentioned G. W. Allport because his writings are so explicit; he is, as a matter of fact, spokesman for a countless number whose views are just as dependent upon type theories of personality, though their language sometimes makes the fact obscure.

Among the first of the "native" characteristics which springs to mind is that of intelligence. Is there any demonstrated relationship between scores on intelligence tests and those on attitude questionnaires? So stated, of course, the problem has almost no bearing upon the thesis which we have identified with the name of G. W. Allport, for a single quantitative score can represent no more than an abstraction of a single one of many personality dimensions, each of which is a function of all the others. Fundamentally similar "sorts of persons," moreover, may presumably have a wide range of scores on intelligence tests, though not, perhaps, covering the entire range. There would seem to be little indication, on the other hand, that the impact of cultural influences in producing personal attitudes should have a clear relation to degree of intelligence. We may expect, then, that intelligence will bear little relationship to attitudes.

Examination of the evidence, however, does not entirely confirm such speculation. One of the earliest of such studies indicated that supporters of La Follette, during the 1924 presidential campaign, were characterized by decidedly higher average intelligence test scores than the supporters of Coolidge and Davis. The *extreme* religious radicals studied by Howells were reliably more intelligent, as we shall see, than the extreme conservatives. Few such decided relationships have since been shown, but the trend of the evidence is fairly consistent. Measures purporting to measure liberalism-in-general have almost invariably been reported to show low but positive correlations with intelligence test scores, and "international-mindedness" scores have often shown about the same degree and direction of relationship to intelligence. Zero or near-zero correlations with intelligence have repeatedly been reported for such diverse attitudes as those toward prohibition, pacifism, the Negro, and superstition. Totally unreliable correlations have also quite consistently been noted between intelligence and susceptibility to propaganda.

One study in which a "constant positive relation in all groups between liberal religious thinking and mental ability" is reported, is of interest for another reason. It was found that such correlations were larger in groups from liberal than in those from conservative communities. The coefficients range, for the former groups, from .42 to .55, and from the latter groups, from .13 to .29. Evidently degree of conservatism of family background operated, for a majority of these subjects, to determine the way in which intelligence could work. Intelligence plays a part in the determination of religious belief, presumably by way of "doing one's own thinking," only provided that the inertia of community traditions, etc., is not too great.

Somewhat higher correlations are the rule between scholarship and attitudes. The following rather striking results are reproduced, in part, from one study (percentages of "conservative," "neutral," and "liberal" responses are omitted):

Scholarship Level	Per Cent of Actual Choices, of Possible Choices	
	Reactionary	Radical
A students..........	0	52.6
B students..........	11.1	17.6
C students..........	12.5	5.9
D students..........	12.9	3.9

Among some hundreds of adolescents and young adults tested in Minneapolis in 1936, economic conservatism was negatively correlated with intelligence test scores and with high school grades. In nine university groups given the Murphy-Likert Survey of Opinions, college grades correlated consistently from .40 to .50 with "internationalism" and with "total radicalism."

Further light is thrown upon such relationships as these by another study in which a correlation of .45 between intelligence test scores and scores on Harper's Social Study was found for 112 students. Between intelligence and classroom grades in sociology, however, the correlation for the same group was .73. These facts, taken together, render it highly possible that brighter students were simply more adept at indicating both right answers and "right" attitudes, particularly since many of the replies were signed by students in this case. The subjective nature of grades given by teachers who themselves have attitudes is too well known. The dangers here are like those involved in tests of ethical attitude: either subjects know what responses are desirable, or the "experts" who evaluate the responses themselves introduce, unwittingly, the element of intelligence, or both.

Our initial surmise concerning the rôle of intelligence in attitude formation was not entirely correct. Religious and political radicalism, at least as measured by numerous experimenters, and social and economic liberalism as measured, for example, by Harper's test, do show consistent though usually low positive correlations with the common measures of intelligence. If groups had been more heterogeneous (through the inclusion of non-college subjects) the increased dispersion of scores would almost certainly have resulted in a higher relationship. At what points, then, was our hypothesis in error? Is intelligence, after all, one determiner of the "fundamental personality"? Or are intelligent persons really bombarded by a different set of cultural influences? We lean toward the second alternative.

While similar cultural influences surround individuals of varying intelligence, those influences which are effective for any individual follow a selective process, conscious or unconscious, by that individual. And selective range is limited by capacity. Cultural phenomena which are beyond one's ken are not, for such a person, cultural phenomena at all. This is not to say, of course, that lack of comprehension is necessarily the handmaiden of conservatism in the fields of politics and religion. But among large groups during the recent past, so far as our present evidence shows, the majority of those who adopt more radical positions on certain issues are at least *capable* of better understanding the complicated social fabric than most of their more conservative contemporaries. This may mean no more than that those with greater capacities are more sensitive to currents moving in a particular place and time. If so, it is equally probable that in other times and places the more intelligent individuals would be the more "conservative." But to whatever degree this is true, the fact remains that interests are in part selected by capacities, and that interests provide the soil without which attitudes do not develop.

Confirmatory evidence for such a view is found in the fact that among nine university groups no correlation was discovered between intelligence (however tested) and degree of radicalism on Internationalism, Imperialism, the Negro, and Economic issues, though there was consistently a positive correlation of the order of .40 to .50 between college grades and Internationalism, and between college grades and "total radicalism" as thus measured. Perhaps the more reflective or "bookish" student exposes himself more consistently to the printed page than his associate with the same "intelligence" but with less reflective or bookish habits; and the same habit exposes him to the whole post-war world of literature with its doubt and disquietude, its protest and rebellion. To be bookish today is to be radical. To be bookish in another age (say, the age of Johnson) would have led to quite contrary results.

We turn now to a consideration of non-intellectual characteristics as related to attitudes. The experimental approach to the problem made by Howells seems to point toward the views which we have attributed to G. W. Allport. Religious radicals and conservatives emerge from his laboratory as quite definite and distinct "sorts of persons." From an original group of 542 students, 51 extreme radicals and 50 extreme conservatives were selected on the basis of self-ratings regarding religious belief. The extremeness of opinion of these two groups was further ascertained by a questionnaire containing many items concerning religious belief. Twelve judges classified the responses of the 101 experimental subjects as being either radical, conservative, or doubtful. A few of them were thus classified as "doubtful," but not one in the original radical group was classified by the judges as conservative, or vice versa.

An extensive battery of laboratory tests was then applied to the 101 subjects. It included measures of visual discrimination, weight discrimination, auditory functions, threshold of sensation for electrical shock, simple reaction time, rate of tapping, muscular steadiness, and muscular coordination. The two experimental groups showed only slight differences with regard to the simple sensory and motor functions, with the single exception of muscle coordination as measured by ability to keep a metal stylus in contact with a moving metallic button. The radical group was superior in this capacity by an almost completely reliable difference—a difference such that the chances of its remaining with larger samples were 99 out of 100.

Surprisingly consistent differences appear between the two experimental groups in regard to the other tests. Thus a constantly increasing electric current, turned off at the subject's request, was endured by the radicals for a reliably greater period of time. Again, under conditions of strong incentive for maximum achievement (e.g., the further a metal stylus was moved down a narrowing metal groove before contact was made, the less severe the shock), the conservatives made enormous improvement over previous records achieved with no such incentive. The differences between radicals and conservatives were completely reliable in both of these experiments.

Differences were also striking when various tests of suggestion were applied. As measured by the Aussage technique ("leading" questions concerning objects appropriate to but not actually appearing in a picture seen just previously), the conservatives were more suggestible by a difference which would be assured in 98 cases out of 100 with larger samples. In another experiment, a slight electric current was passed through the hand, with instructions to report the first sensation of increase in current. Actually, the current did not increase at all, but it had been increased during the experiment just preceding. The conservatives reported an increase in the strength of the current with a reliably greater frequency than did the radicals. A similar result was obtained by informing subjects that they would probably feel an electric shock when the arm of a certain apparatus reached a certain point, though no shock was actually given. The conservative group was far more susceptible to this kind of suggestion than the radicals and, again, reliably so.

Howells also attempted to discover intellectual differences between the two groups by tests of memory, association, imagination, and rational judgment. The most definite of the resulting differences were those in scores on the Thorndike Examination (intelligence test), and the Iowa Comprehension Test. Composite scores based on these two tests proved to be higher for the radical group by a difference 6.1 times its probable error. Such a finding suggests, of course, that many of the other differences may have been determined by the single factor of intelligence, particularly in view of the known relation between intelligence and resistance to many forms of suggestion. Unfortunately, no partial correlations are reported, so that the bases for these astoundingly consistent differences remain in doubt.

For some of the factors involved, however, we do not need to resort to speculation. The two groups differ in respect to religious training and parental religious attitudes. The conservative group contained about equal numbers of Catholics and Protestants, whereas there were no Catholics among the radicals, several of whom had had no religious training at all. There was, moreover, a larger percentage of women in the conservative than in the radical group. The two groups did not differ in respect to urban or rural background, father's occupational status, nationality of parents, number of children in the family, or position in the family. It is not improbable that certain personality differences between the two groups may have been the result of different types of parental training associated with their differences in religious background. But it is improbable that the two factors of which we are certain—namely, sex and intelligence—can alone account for the whole series of psychophysical differences between the two groups.

In a recent publication Howells has reported upon more intensive experimentation with one of the traits mentioned above, persistence. Elaborate situations were devised, most of them involving careful measurements of the amount of pain willingly endured. Subjects were selected in this case, however, quite independently of religious belief, although this was later measured. The correlation (for 54 subjects) between religious radicalism and persistence was .37, and between intelligence and persistence (for 93 subjects), .10. The author believes his earlier investigations to be thus confirmed. If the relationship of radicalism and persistence seems less striking than before, it is perhaps of even greater value because run-of-the-line instead of extreme subjects were studied.

Such findings as these are, of course, notoriously dependent upon the nature of the questions asked, the method of scoring responses, and the particular manner of measuring the traits. Other experiments might be cited, some of which confirm and some of which contradict Howells' findings concerning religious belief and suggestibility though we know of no contradictory evidence concerning persistence.

Somewhat similar procedures had previously been used by H. T. Moore in an attempt to discover "innate" factors associated with radicalism and conservatism. Subjects were selected on the basis of twenty Yes-No questions dealing with domestic politics, industrial problems, international relations, etc. His two groups were composed, respectively, of those who gave fourteen or more, and those who gave seven or less, radical answers. Experimental procedures were then applied on the basis of five hypothetical distinctions between the two groups, as follows:

1. Susceptibility to majority influence, measured by changes in choices between paired statements, the subjects being informed as to majority opinion following their first indication of preferences. Only

18 of a possible 147 reversals were made by the radicals, while the conservatives made 34 of 109 possible reversals.

2. Ability to break long-established habits, measured by degree of success in mirror-drawing. Radicals excelled in this ability.
3. Speed of reaction time, in which radicals were somewhat superior.
4. Tendency to sacrifice accuracy to speed, as determined by the Münsterberg card-sorting test. Radicals were considerably superior in speed, but no more accurate than conservatives.
5. Ability to think in unusual terms, judged by responses to the Kent-Rosanoff word association test. Radicals gave fewer common responses than conservatives.

Here, then, there seemed to be a surprising degree of confirmation of a whole series of hypotheses. Yet the experimental groups were so small, the curves of radicals and conservatives mostly so skewed, as to make the results statistically very confusing. Similar experiments were soon undertaken at Vassar College. These later results turned out not to confirm those of Moore. Aside from statistical considerations, at least three considerations are relevant in comparing the divergent results: (1) the possibility of a sex difference, subjects in the former experiment having been male, and in the latter one, female; (2) the two groups at Vassar were distinguished by somewhat more lenient standards, since extreme conservatives, as defined by Moore, were very few there; (3) the dependence of the relationship between radicalism and personality upon the cultural atmosphere of the community. It may be that the temperamental make-up which would go with a moderately "conservative" set of attitudes at Yale or Dartmouth might go with a moderately "liberal" set of attitudes at Vassar. A person who is a middle-of-the-road conformist might be more or less radical after exposure to one environment, and more or less conservative after exposure to the other, without having undergone any real temperamental change.

Despite all this, there seems to be good reason in Howells' work for concluding that Moore is right in pointing to some fundamental relationships between personality and social attitudes. Not, of course, that they would hold for all groups or for all attitudes to which the terms "radical" or "conservative" may be applied. It is highly improbable, indeed, that the particular constellation of issues included in Moore's questionnaire would, in most times and places, constitute an attitude entity at all. But such is our present poverty that, provided it follows upon a reasonable hypothesis, any established relationship between almost any social attitude and any objectively measured personality characteristic in any group, is to be received with open arms.

But even if attitudes are related to basic traits, are the traits investigated by Moore, for example, really "innate"? Moore's statement of his problem seems to us to beg the question. One may perhaps grant that susceptibility to majority influence, ability to break long-established habits, and habits of speed and of thinking in unusual terms are deep-lying characteristics, perhaps dating from early years and relatively permanent. Yet they may all be simply established habits. They may, moreover, be very specific habits, to be found in one area and not in another. Nevertheless, if certain attitudes are found to be associated with certain personality characteristics *as measured by a given method*, this in itself is worth knowing. If it also turns out that there are clusters of personal characteristics (and there is abundant evidence in that direction), and that, as G. W. Allport holds, these characteristics are related to specified attitudes, so much the better for our understanding of them. We are as yet in no position to say in what respects "personality" is innate. The first question is whether there are important characteristics which determine that individuals subject to very similar cultural influences shall develop very different attitudes.

We turn now to paper-and-pencil methods of investigating much the same sort of personality characteristics, again avoiding the question of innateness. One of the few such investigations from which any clear conclusions emerge is a study of liberal religious belief. The 612 subjects were largely students, selected as coming from one of ten communities, half of which were "liberal" and half "conservative" in respect to general religious atmosphere. All sections of this country were represented, and one of the groups was Canadian. The measure used was the Watson Test of Religious Thinking, which includes sections concerning God, Jesus, prayer, the Church, immortality, Sabbath observance, other religions, etc.

A low negative correlation ($-.14 \pm .04$) was found between the number of things considered wrong according to the Pressey X-O test and the score of liberal religious belief. There was a positive correlation of similar magnitude between the number of things worried about and liberal belief. It should be added that, for the various groupings, most of the correlations were higher than these, which are computed from scores of all subjects. Neither the Allport Ascendance-Submission test nor the Bernreuter Personal Inventory showed any relationship between total scores and religious liberalism. There were, however, reliable differences between those answering "Yes" and those answering "No" to several of the Bernreuter items, and it is these which are of particular interest.

In general, these most distinguishing items suggested certain introverted tendencies on the part of the liberals. Thus, "prefer books to companionship," "understand a problem better by studying than by discussing," and several other items of similar nature to which the liberals tend to reply in like fashion, represent the self-sufficient aspect of introversion. None of the neurotic aspects of introversion, on the other hand, appear to characterize the liberals. Such responses as "not touchy on certain subjects," "do not sometimes feel just miserable," and "do not blush easily," which also reliably distinguish liberals from conservatives, would suggest greater degrees of certain neurotic tendencies in the latter group. One of the most highly differentiating items shows the same characteristic that Howells (page 933) found by experimental methods, namely, the liberals' more frequent affirmative response to "take a chance alone in a situation of doubtful outcome."

Some other items distinguished liberals from conservatives within liberal or conservative communities, but not from both. In conservative communities the liberals reported themselves "uncomfortable when considered different or unconventional," whereas in liberal communities liberals gave the opposite response by an equal margin of greater frequency than did the conservatives. Such an attempt to relate personality test responses to ecological factors is all too exceptional. It suggests, once more, that the relationship between personality and attitudes must be understood not alone as a problem in individual psychology, but also in relation to community forces.

Several investigators have pursued the hypothesis that liberals should make more unusual emotional reactions than conservatives. For this purpose the Pressey X-O test is almost ideal, since one of the scores which it yields is labeled "idiosyncrasy." (The test is described on page 799.) But with at least one measure of liberal attitudes its correlation has been variously found to be fairly high, barely reliable, and quite unreliable. These contradictory results may be attributed largely to the manner in which the items composing the attitude questionnaire were selected. These particular items, covering political, economic, international, and other issues, may represent an attitude entity among the group in whose cultural setting they were selected, and for whom their correlation with idiosyncrasy score was $.55 \pm .04$. But for other groups, whose attitudes toward such diverse issues are formed under different conditions, they may well seem but a jumbled assortment.

The factors associated with the holding of "typical" and "atypical" opinions have also been analyzed. A collection of students' spontaneously written statements concerning such issues as prohibition, the League of Nations, and the distribution of wealth was perused by six judges who arranged the opinions in scale fashion, from one extreme to the other in regard to each issue. Students were then asked to indicate their own positions on each of these scales, and also to state the degree of their confidence in each opinion. The most interesting finding has to do with the relation between extremeness of opinion and degree of certainty. Those holding extreme opinions were, in general, more confident than those taking intermediate positions. The conclusion was natural that individuals who recognize that their own opinions are those of a minority need some emotional support; this is found by the strengthening of opinion into conviction. Certain psychiatric theories have long pointed to this as a probable state of affairs, and it is an extremely important finding if further research proves to verify it.

Assuming tentatively that this is the case, one would expect to find little relationship between certainty of opinion and information. Something on this point is contributed in one rather elaborate statistical analysis of the association between belief and certain intellectual and emotional factors. Four different responses were obtained to each of thirty propositions, such as, "Is democracy the best form of government?" "Does death end personal existence?" "Does two plus two equal four?" These four responses, the first three of which were made on a scale in which +10 represented one extreme and −10 the other, were as follows: degree of *belief*, degree of *certainty*, degree of *desirability* (i.e., that it should be true), and *availability of evidence*. Subjects were 243 students from Columbia College, Barnard College, and the University of Nebraska.

The results indicate that for these propositions belief is closely associated with desire; the correlation, in fact, was .81 for the total group. One group of 31 students showed a similar relationship when a totally different set of propositions was used. Other coefficients of about the same magnitude between these two variables are presented, some being based upon group scores for the individual propositions, and some upon individual scores for all propositions.

The correlations between belief and evidence (except for one group whose coefficient was .69) are much lower, as are those between evidence and certainty. These considerations suggest that while desire might conceivably be either an antecedent or a consequent of belief, the former relationship is the more probable one. A further question which was put to two groups brought revealing responses. Asked to rate the relative importance of seven factors which influenced "the average college student" in arriving at his opinions, and to rate the same factors as to their influence upon their own opinions, most subjects regarded their fellows as swayed more by "teaching and training" than they themselves were, but themselves as influenced more by "personal reasoning" and "personal experience." Such evidence of rationalization further betrays the intimacy of emotion and belief.

Both of the last-mentioned studies have suggested that certainty of opinion is a function not of information, but of desire. Somewhat different conclusions are suggested by another report on the relation between information and certainty. The opinions of 357 students regarding candidates Hoover and Smith were obtained during the presidential campaign of 1928, together with an indication of the degree of certainty of each opinion. The students were also given an information test based on rather detailed questions concerning the personal and political history and characteristics of the two candidates. Comparisons of the several college classes showed that while information scores increased with each succeeding class, there was little change in degree of certainty. Although a coefficient of +.21 was obtained between certainty and information for all subjects, the relation was not a simple linear one. Those lowest in information were, in general, those who showed least certainty, but those who were best informed were also low in certainty, though not at the bottom. A correlation of +.28 between intelligence and information is also reported, but no partial correlations are given. On the basis of such evidence as this, we may at least challenge the assumption that certainty is simply an easy device for covering a lack of rational justification for one's views.

One of the theories according to which certain attitudes are assumed to spring from certain personality characteristics is identified with psychoanalysis. If there is any validity to the Oedipus theory, one might reasonably anticipate that political and economic radicalism would offer a convenient vehicle for revolt against parents. Such theories have rarely been put to the objective test, but one attempt to do so is of some interest. Seventy male students were given a questionnaire scored for frequency of extremely radical replies concerning a variety of public issues. Another questionnaire was designed to reveal degree of antagonism toward one's father. Items on this list had to do with fantasies for revenge, degree of suffering under paternal discipline, feelings of affection or of fear, etc., at various periods of childhood and adolescence. The final measure of paternal antagonism was arrived at by three judges who, with these latter replies in hand, assigned scores to each subject. The correlation between father antagonism and extreme radicalism proved to be .60 ± .05. This, of course, can scarcely be construed as a verification of the Oedipus theory, but such an interesting lead should by all means be pursued.

At least one attempt has been made to confirm these findings, though under somewhat modified conditions. Seventy subjects (cf. page 916), one or both of whose parents had filled out identical attitude scales, were given a test of parental antagonism. Twenty items were included concerning remembered degree of conflict, and twenty concerning present antagonism; each item was filled out for each parent separately, and the reliability coefficient for either parent proved to be .92. These scores were correlated with *difference* from parents' scores in attitudes toward the Church and toward Communism, both algebraic and arithmetic differences—i.e., difference in a given direction as well as difference regardless of direction —being computed. Not a single one of the resulting coefficients, however, whether computed separately for sons-fathers and for daughters-mothers, or for each child and each parent, turned out to be as high as .30. The difference between the previous results and these may be attributed in part to the heterogeneity of the latter group of subjects, and in part to the difference in measuring instruments, beyond the obvious consideration that a different time and place were involved.

We see no reason, however, to doubt that for the particular students involved in the earlier study, father-son relationships were intimately related to the growth of radical attitudes. This is posited upon the view that the measure of father-son antagonism used in that study was not so much an indication of what happened to the subjects at the hands of their fathers, as a personality measure. We have no reason to conclude that paternal treatment caused the attitudes. We know only that, whatever the associated personality traits, the more they remembered unhappy paternal relationships, the more they tended to embrace radical ideas. We suspect that in some cases paternal treatment did justify the memories, and at the same time created certain personality characteristics. We also suspect that in other cases totally extraneous forces led to the establishment of the personality characteristics, which in turn led to later selection among memories. This point of view may be summarized by saying that, in a given culture center, certain personality patterns will be associated with certain attitude patterns with much greater than chance expectancy, but that the personality patterns may stem from diverse sources and may assume greater or less degrees of prominence in the total personalities of the individuals. It is this latter consideration which renders so extremely difficult an intelligible view of the relationship between personality and attitudes.

Many type theories of personality have much to say, by implication at least, concerning attitudes. Chief among these is Spranger's six-fold classification of personality types. Upon this is based the Allport-Vernon "Study of Values" test, which gives the subject opportunity to indicate in many concrete choices the relative appeal which each of six values has for him. One study is available which includes scores on this test as well as on four of the Thurstone attitude scales; subjects were 187 students of educational psychology. Correlations between each of the six value scores and each of the four attitude scores are presented in the table below.

| | | Attitudes Measured | | |
| | Church | Prohibition | War | Negro |
Value	(low score favorable)	(high score favorable)	(low score favorable)	(high score favorable)
Theoretical	.41	−.27	.28	.35
Economic	.02	−.14	−.43	−.28
Aesthetic	.28	.06	.33	.23
Social	−.01	.28	.16	.08
Political	.28	−.36	−.26	−.31
Religious	−.78	.36	−.10	−.19

If each of the value types does represent a "sort of person," do these data indicate that the types have some reference to attitudes as currently measured? While only one of these coefficients is higher than .43 (and that one religious value with attitude toward the Church), the median (arithmetic) coefficient is .28 ± .045, and all but seven of the 24 equal more than four times their probable errors. There is no reason, moreover, why each of the value scores should be related to *all* of the attitude scores. There seems to be some justification in concluding, for example, that the "theoretical type" of person tends not only to differ from those low in this value with respect to these attitudes, but to differ in the expected directions: that is, in atypical or radical fashion. The "social type" does not differ much from those low in that value; perhaps he is the "sort of person" who is on the whole indifferent to such matters. Those high in religious value, again, show slightly more conservative tendencies in all attitudes than those low in religious value. There is some comfort here for those to whom, like G. W. Allport, attitudes are but one plumbing of the depths of personality, i.e., they must be understood in relation to those fundamental aspects of personality which the "Study of Values" is designed to measure.

It is rather remarkable that so little has been learned concerning the relationship between attitudes and objective measures of personality. The paucity of information which has resulted from the few studies that have been made is due to such considerations as the dependence of such relationships upon the peculiar content of the measures used; the inadequacy of our present measures of personality (as discussed in the preceding chapter); and the difficulties of holding "constant" such cultural conditions as parental attitudes and institutional allegiances. But even when these limitations are granted, there has been extremely little work done in this area. This is the more surprising in view of the frequency with which various attitudes have been "explained" in terms of emotional dispositions. Such personality equations as that which identifies "radicalism" with emotional maladjustment are commonly asserted but rarely investigated.

It may easily be pointed out, of course, that the correlation method is poorly adapted to reveal such intra-personality relationships as actually exist. And this would still be true even if the difficulties just mentioned could be surmounted. For there is no *a priori* reason why *extremeness* of attitude should be closely related to *extremeness* of the personality characteristics in question. The relationships, whatever they are, may develop in threshold fashion. It is altogether conceivable that there are certain critical points for various characteristics, below which the latter have little influence upon the development of attitudes, and above which they have a considerable influence.

It may not be unfair to conclude, therefore, that for the present more is to be learned concerning the niche which attitudes occupy in the personality structure by the study of individuals than by statistical methods. One such approach may be cited. The Watson Test of Public Opinion was given to 50 male and 50 female college students in several southwestern states. Other measures included an intelligence test, a word-association test, the Pressey X-O test, and the Woodworth-House personal inventory. Only the first of these measures yielded a correlation with total prejudice score ($-.24 \pm .06$). Relationships to *direction* of prejudice are more definite. Thus the seven subjects making the highest scores in religious radicalism give fewer responses suggesting maladjustment, and more suggesting self-sufficiency, than do the seven who were most conservative in religion scores, who were characterized by responses indicating fears and feelings of inferiority. Similar differences were noted between economic radicals and conservatives, and between "moral" radicals and conservatives. But numbers of subjects are small, and in every instance certain individuals proved exceptions to these generalizations.

Thirty cases were therefore studied individually, being selected as extreme in one or more of these fields (i.e., economic, religious, moral) and as being also either highly prejudiced or very nearly unprejudiced. The most significant findings seem to be certain distinctions between the "prejudiced" and the "impartial" subjects whose actual radicalism scores are similar. Thus, while all economic radicals are relatively "independent," those "without prejudice" reveal happier family relationships and fewer personal conflicts, and apparently have had to do less struggling for their independence than the "prejudiced" radicals. By an analysis both of total scores and of item responses, individual cases of prejudice can in almost every instance be related to the particular type of personality maladjustment revealed by the individual in question.

Thus a very radical student showing considerable prejudice responds in highly symptomatic manner to the personal inventory, gives many "unpleasant" associations to the stimulus words, and indicates that a large number of words in the Pressey test are unpleasant to her. She indicates a long history of physical ailments, and reveals strong tendencies toward suspiciousness, hypersensitiveness, and feelings of inferiority. The following interpretation is offered: "She has projected . . . her own personal situation upon the existing politico-economic organization. The result is a rationalization of her own thwartings, from which she derives support for the will to live. The external projection of her personal problems gives her, at the same time, a plausible moral justification for expressing a sadistic bitterness directed against those who are rich and happy" (our translation).

This individual may be contrasted with another, equally radical, who shows little prejudice. Her scores on the personality tests indicate a minimum of conflicts, frustrations, and dislikes, though there is some indication of a lack of self-confidence and of uneasiness concerning sex problems. Her radicalism is interpreted as follows: "A kindly spirit, well informed, thanks to unusual opportunities for acquainting herself with the significant trends of contemporary society. The little prejudice which she does show may be a compensation for her feelings of inadequacy." We cite such material, with these frankly subjective interpretations (though based upon "objective" data), not because the interpretations are considered as necessarily "correct" either by us or by the author, but because such dynamics as these are surely operative among many individuals, whether or not they are for these particular subjects. Similar attitudes (or at least those which by present measures are quantitatively similar) may be arrived at by very different avenues. "Each specific trait, each type of personal maladjustment, is found to be associated with contradictory sets of attitudes, impartial or prejudiced. Different individuals respond differently to a given situation. For each of them the important thing is the significance of the situation *for him*."

Such are the obstacles in the path of a quantitative analysis of the relationship of attitudes to other personality characteristics. They are not to be construed as insurmountable in any final sense. Their removal depends largely, we believe, upon two feats of social-psychological engineering. The first is the development of much better tools with which to examine the cultural zero point from which the individual's attitudes may be said to take their start. The second is the translation into some language of quantity, whether it be a language of scale degrees or of discrete units, of those forces which work within the individual in such fashion as to deflect his allegiances away from the known zero point.

The Experimental Modification of Attitudes

Some hints concerning the nature of the process by which values are crystallized into attitudes may be obtained from an examination of investigations in which attitudes have been measured before and after the introduction of some experience presumed to modify them.

While the method here is essentially experimental, it should be pointed out that in most cases there are a host of factors which are not controlled. Only the use of carefully equated control groups can render such investigations truly "experimental."

A large proportion of the investigations of attitude changes have had to do with some phase or duration of schooling. On pages 948-951 there appears a list of such studies. We shall comment in particular on only a few of them.

One of the experiments (Schlorff, chart, page 950) may be mentioned by way of illustrating the most careful procedure where the modification of attitudes is deliberately sought through curricular material. The measuring instrument was a social-distance scale involving ten personal relationships drawn from the everyday life of children of high school age. Paired comparisons, according to Thurstone's method, were then made for each of twenty nationalities by 425 high school students selected at random; the resulting proportions of judgment were converted into sigma units. Two ninth-grade civics classes were equated for age, national background, mental age, and emotional stability; one of these served as a control. The other was exposed to a modified curriculum "to increase tolerance toward the Negro," this prepared material occupying fifteen 45-minute periods at weekly intervals during a single semester. The modified curricular content included these topics: the Negro's origin and history, his contributions, and prejudice against him. The Negro had originally occupied the lowest place on the scale in both groups, and, for the control group, maintained the same place at the end of the experiment. But the mean position assigned to the Negro by the experimental group at this time was above those of Portuguese, Greeks, Russians, and Hungarians. In terms of the situations included in the scale, this was at the level of acceptability as neighbor, and almost at that of employer. Statistically expressed, this was a change by the experimental group of 1.23 units, equivalent to 3.5 times its S.D.

It will be noted that a considerable number of these investigations of changes deal with attitudes toward some race or nationality, and certain conclusions may be drawn from the entire group of studies. The principal variables apparent are age of subjects, method of in-

SOME EXPERIMENTAL STUDIES IN

AUTHOR	SUBJECTS	ATTITUDE
Caldwell and Lundeen	High school class in biology.	Unfounded beliefs.
Campbell and Stover	1. 40 high school students, paired controls.	1. International (Neumann-Kulp-Davidson, Thurstone scales).
	2. 24 9th-grade girls, paired controls.	2. Negro (Bogardus, Hinckley, Newman-Kulp-Davidson).
	3. 14 9th-grade boys paired in two groups.	3. Various races (Bogardus).
Cherrington	11 different groups, students and adults; controls for some groups.	War, international relations.
Droba	30 college students.	Negro (Hinckley A & B).
Gardiner	1. 581 7th- and 8th-grade pupils, and 180 controls.	1. War (Peterson-Thurstone).
	2. 247 8-th grade pupils.	2. War (Peterson-Thurstone).
	3. 228 college freshmen.	3. Prohibition (Smith-Thurstone).
Hedrick	48 parents.	Self-reliance of children.
Hurd	760 high school pupils in science.	"Appreciational concepts" in science.
Kornhauser	400 college students of economics.	Economic.
Kroll	183 senior boys in 6 high school classes.	Social (Harper).

CLASSROOM MODIFICATION OF ATTITUDE

EXPERIMENTAL FACTOR	RESULTS
Unit of instruction in unfounded beliefs, in science.	Decrease in unfounded belief; increase in factual knowledge; former change greater.
1. 18 wks.' teaching of geography, emphasizing respect for Germans and Chinese, and opposition to war. 2. Use of "opaque projector"; both groups study about Negroes. 3. Instruction, with pictures, concerning 10 race groups; 10 other races for 2nd group.	1. No reliable difference between experimentals and controls. 2. Experimentals reliably more favorable on Bogardus test, not on Hinckley scale. 3. 1st group showed reliable gain over 2nd for races studied; no reliable gain for 2nd group.
Various: single lecture; student conferences; college courses; summer at Geneva, Switzerland; 2-yr. series of lecture discussions, etc.	Few reliable changes; but shifts in direction of internationalism and of opposing war by almost all groups. In general, groups which did most intensive studying made least change in total score, and showed most uncertainty, while "single exposure" groups changed most and showed least uncertainty.
Course on the Negro.	No reliable gain.
1. Lecture, story, and chalk-talk against war presented at weekly intervals, each followed by test. 2. Combination of pro- and anti-war appeals at weekly intervals. 3. 2 pro-prohibition appeals at weekly intervals, each followed by test.	1. Steady and marked increase in opposition to war; no change by controls. 2. No change from week to week. 3. Steady increase from week to week in favorable attitude.
6 weekly classes in parental education.	Increase in favorable attitude equivalent to critical ratio of 3.41.
4 mos.' instruction, some attention to concepts.	Significant gains in mean scores.
Year's survey course in economics.	Less uniformity, undecidedness, extremeness, more liberalism; less than changes in information.
1 semester's instruction in English or History, by 1 of 3 radical or 1 of 3 conservative teachers.	Slight but not reliable gain in conservatism under conservative teachers; very great loss in conservatism under radical teachers.

SOME EXPERIMENTAL STUDIES IN

AUTHOR	SUBJECTS	ATTITUDE
Lichtenstein	11 classes, grades 4 to 6, controls.	1. Out-of-doors. 2. Scientific.
Longstreet	250 high school pupils in 4 schools.	Patriotism, constitution, war, law.
Manske	661 pupils in 22 9th- to 12th-grade classes, controls.	Negro (Hinckley).
Salmer and Remmers	112 college juniors and seniors.	Social (Harper).
Schlorff	425 high school students, controls.	Negro (paired comparison of 20 races).
Telford	4 college classes.	Treatment of criminals (Thurstone scale).
Weller	180 6th-grade pupils, controls for 30 of them.	Scientific.
D. Young	450 college students.	Race and nationality.

CLASSROOM MODIFICATION OF ATTITUDE (*Continued*)

EXPERIMENTAL FACTOR	RESULTS
Emphasis on desired attitudes through 1 semester's teaching (scientific) and 1 yr.'s teaching (out-of-doors).	1. No reliable gain. 2. Experimentals show great decrease, controls none, in superstitious belief; no experimental-control difference in prejudice or scientific attitude, though both gain significantly.
Year's course in American history.	Reliable changes only in class of teacher aware of experiment, and in attitude toward law in one other school.
10 "non-indoctrinating" lessons, by 1 of 16 teachers, ranging from "very liberal" to "prejudiced."	8 of 22 classes show slight changes *opposed* to teachers' attitudes; 2 change reliably in direction of teachers' attitudes.
Semester's course in sociology.	Reliably more "liberal" at end of semester.
Modified curriculum in civics classes, 15 periods at weekly intervals.	Considerable raise in rank assigned by experimentals; reliable gain.
Semester's study in psychology or sociology.	Increased leniency in all groups. Unreliable only for general psychology; huge for criminology.
2 units of science, emphasis on desired attitudes.	Reliable superiority over controls in each of 2 attitude tests.
Course in race problems.	No change in ranking of relative inborn ability of various races.

struction, and type of test. In neither of the experiments where subjects were college students was any change effected, although varying degrees of change in attitude toward the Negro are to be seen in the experiments involving high school pupils. Turning to the second variable, we find that neither of the two "regular" college courses produced reliable changes, whereas the experimental changes at the high school level followed the introduction of additional material designed to modify attitudes. Regarding the third variable, reliable changes are found in terms of social distance, but not in terms of score on tests of the scaled-statements type (note, in particular, the third experiment listed in the table, in which both types of measure were applied to the same group). Judging from these experiments only, we might arrive at some such hypothesis as the following: instruction regarding a single race does not significantly change attitudes as measured on a scale involving that race only, nor does instruction regarding several races produce changes in the rank positions assigned to those races; but instruction concerning one race may significantly change the rank position of that race among others.

Several of the experiments in the summary table deal with rather broad social and economic attitudes, and it will be seen that reliable changes are frequently reported. These changes, generally in the direction of "liberalism," commonly accompany both high school and college experience. They seem to be a concomitant, in particular, of the study of the social sciences, though it must not be forgotten that certain selective factors (e.g., "readiness for change") determine enrollment in such courses.

Another experiment (Kroll, chart, page 948), though atypical in that it deals with the effect not of particular courses but of particular teachers, is of more than ordinary interest. Subjects were boys in the senior class of a large high school; all of them had completed one year's study of European history and were currently studying American history and economics. Each of 183 boys was in a class of one (and only one) of six teachers, selected as follows: two conservative and two radical teachers of history, and one radical and one conservative teacher of English. The radical or conservative positions of the teachers were determined by the experimenter, the high school principal, the two departmental chairmen involved, and four fellow teachers in the same departments who had known them ten years or longer; these judges were unanimous in their labeling of each of the six teachers as radical or conservative. The teachers' scores on Harper's test (the measure used for the subjects also) further corroborated these labels. The test was given at the beginning and end of the spring semester in all six classes. The somewhat surprising finding is that while the boys taught by the conservative teachers made slight but unreliable changes in the direction of conservatism, those in the radical teachers' classes made tremendous leaps in the radical direction. The radical teachers differed among themselves in influence, as the gains in their respective groups are 4.67, 8.18, and 11.81 times their probable errors. For all the 92 boys taught by radical teachers the gain equals 12.89 times its P.E. While there were no control groups tested at the same time, the fact that the two sets of teachers influenced the boys in opposite directions indicates that the changes were really due to teaching, except in the improbable instance that teachers were chosen by the subjects on the basis of attitudinal position. The experiment is marred, however, by our uncertainty as to the degree to which the subjects were influenced by their teachers' knowledge of their test scores. Apart from this, however, the experiment is noteworthy and deserves repetition at the college level; teacher influence may vary considerably at different age levels. If this study should be confirmed by the use of anonymous questionnaires, it would suggest that the "liberalizing" influence of the social sciences may be due largely to the kind of teachers likely to be found in those fields, rather than to the subject matter itself.

One further question arises in connection with these experiments which make use of educational procedures. Granted that changes in attitude occur, how wide a range do they cover? Are they limited narrowly to the fields in which instruction is given? This, it will be noted, is one of the phases of the problem commonly referred to as that of "transfer." In one approach to the problem (Telford, chart, page 950), forms A and B, respectively, of the Thurstone scale of attitude toward the treatment of criminals were administered to members of four college classes at the beginning and end of the semester. Changes, all in the direction of increased leniency, were as follows (expressed in terms of difference divided by the probable error of the difference):

General psychology.............. 1.6　　Introduction to sociology.......... 4.0
Educational psychology........... 3.5　　Criminology.................... 8.5
　　　　　　　All four classes................. 8.5

The varying degrees of change are interpreted in terms of the degree to which the topic of the treatment of criminals (or allied topics) had been treated in each of the four classes. General psychology, as taught at this particular university, did not deal with human relationships, whereas educational psychology did, though criminology was not specifically considered.

The results of a series of experiments regarding international attitudes (Cherrington, page 948) have a bearing upon this problem. The attitudes of nine different groups were measured before and after experiences of various kinds and of varying duration. These included a three-day conference; a summer of concentrated activities in Geneva, Switzerland; a summer school course; and a series of lecture discussions lasting nearly two years. For all groups, responses were tabulated separately for "general" items and for "specific" items which represented concrete applications of the general principle. Thus a general question makes use of the phrase, "humanity in general," and a specific one refers to the possible loss of foreign investments. It was found, in every group, that "international" responses were more commonly made to the general than to the specific statements; the averages of the percentages for all groups were, respectively, 84 and 63 at the beginning of the experiments, and 89 and 72 at the end. There appeared to be little consistency of response to the specific items. The experimenter speaks of the "limited ability of most group members to recognize the connection between propositions or situations which are related, unless they are stated in the same way"; but there was "definite improvement in the ability to recognize the implications of accepted generalizations following instruction, with all groups except one. . . . This improvement, in the main, comes on items included in the subject matter of instruction." Even where such "improvement" is noted, however, it is slight. If it may be measured in terms of decreasing discrepancy between responses to general and to specific items, the responses of the group showing the greatest improvement may be summarized as in the accompanying table:

	Percentage of "International" Responses by One Group		
	General Items	Specific Items	Difference
Pre-test............	94	72	22
Post-test..........	96	84	12

These results are in general agreement with such other rather meager findings as are available regarding the degree of transfer of attitudes. No one imagines that modifications of verbally expressed attitudes will be limited to the exact words employed in the modifying experience. Neither is it to be supposed that totally unrelated attitudes will be affected by a given experience. It is, then, a question of the interrelatedness of the attitudes involved—a matter more fully discussed in a later section. Meanwhile we may come to some tentative conclusions. It has been concluded, for example (page 960), that propaganda has both a specific and a general effect, since statements not mentioned in propaganda speeches are apparently affected by them. Similarly, in the experiment in modifying parents' attitudes toward the self-reliance of children (see Hedrick, page 948), almost as great changes were found for those phases of behavior which had not been mentioned in the teaching as for those specifically taught. But such degrees of spread as this are so slight as scarcely to be considered transfer. The very fact that the statements specifically mentioned in the modifying experience were included in both of these experiments, together with others not previously referred to at all, as items purporting to measure a *single attitude*, suggests that no transfer from one attitude to another is involved. The general picture emerging from all the experiments known to us resembles closely that of "identical elements" so long familiar to psychologists. In other words, transfer may be expected to the degree that the different attitudes have identical subject matter or identical associations. (Need we remind the reader that, if transfer is being aimed at, the less the two areas have in common, the more pointed and concrete must be the attempts to show what the common elements are?) If we may anticipate some of the evidence to be presented later, the common ele-

SOME EXPERIMENTAL STUDIES OF THE

AUTHOR	SUBJECTS	ATTITUDE MEASURED
Annis and Meier	183 psychology students, 63 controls.	Previously unknown individual.
Biddle	350 high school and college freshmen students, controls.	Susceptibility to propaganda.
Bird	326 college students, 161 controls.	Material remembered from lecture.
Chen	519 college students, 143 controls.	Chinese and Japanese.
Cherrington and Miller	216 college students, 71 controls.	War.
Hartmann	Several city voting wards.	Socialist party.
Knower	1000 college students; controls.	Prohibition.
Kulp	343 graduate students, in 6 groups, including control.	Social (Harper).
Lorge	100 adults.	Economic.
Marple	300 high school seniors, 300 college seniors, 300 adults.	Miscellaneous controversial issues.
Millson	Several hundred students and adults.	Unemployment insurance.

INFLUENCE OF EXTRA-SCHOOL EXPERIENCES

EXPERIMENTAL FACTOR	RESULTS
Reading matter inserted in college paper, half favorable, half unfavorable.	Reliable difference between favorable and unfavorable groups, and between both of them and controls.
Reading of pamphlets on techniques of propaganda.	Experimental group more resistant to propaganda by huge differences.
Reading of distorted newspaper account of class lecture.	Those who had not read newspaper account much more accurate.
Pro-Chinese, pro-Japanese, and "neutral" oral propaganda.	Reliable changes in direction of propaganda heard.
Lecture or reading on abolition of war.	Both lecture and reading groups show great immediate change; reliable change remains after 6 months.
"Emotional" and "rational" political pamphlets.	Three times expected increase in Socialist vote in "emotional" wards; increase greater in "rational" than in control wards.
"Emotional" or "rational" speeches, heard or read.	Reliable changes by all groups hearing speeches, and by most groups reading them; little difference between "emotional" and "rational" appeals.
1. Prestige of various groups. 2. Prepared responses to questionnaire items.	All groups, except control and group for whom responses were conservatively marked, made reliable changes in direction of liberalism, regardless of authority to whom responses were attributed, and even when no authority was cited.
Information as to authorship of statements.	Statements approved to reliably greater extent if credited to name liked better than previously supposed author; otherwise, little change.
Majority and expert opinion.	Majority opinion caused more than half, and expert opinion nearly half, of all possible changes to be made.
"Academic," "exhibitionistic," and "conversational" modes of debate.	Little difference among 3 modes; little change in % of affirmative votes, but many more negative and fewer undecided after debate.

SOME EXPERIMENTAL STUDIES OF THE

AUTHOR	SUBJECTS	ATTITUDE MEASURED
Robinson	419 adults in small groups, controls.	Unemployment.
Rosenthal	100 college students, 100 student controls.	Political, economic, industrial.
Saadi and Farnsworth	3 groups of college students.	Miscellaneous controversial statements.
Smith, F. T.	46 graduate students, 46 paired controls.	Negro.
Thurstone and collaborators	Many groups, involving several thousand children.	Various.
Wilke	341 college students in 12 classes.	War, distribution of wealth, birth control, God. Each group experimental for one topic, control for another.

INFLUENCE OF EXTRA-SCHOOL EXPERIENCES (*Continued*)

EXPERIMENTAL FACTOR	RESULTS
4 consecutive weekly radio addresses, liberal and conservative.	No change in "liberality"; experimentals suggest more "solutions," and more uniformly than before; rate fewer statements "doubtful" and more "absolutely true" than before. Similar, lesser changes by controls.
Radical motion picture propaganda.	Experimentals reliably more radical on items related to propaganda, little change on remote items.
Association of each statement, in one of 3 groups, with a liked, a disliked, and a neutral name.	Most statements most generally accepted when linked with liked name, and least accepted with disliked name.
2 week-ends in Harlem, involving parties, teas, home visits, personal contacts, speeches.	Large gain for experimentals in total score and reliable for each separate test. Gain still reliable 11 mos. later.
Motion pictures.	All films produce changes in mean attitude score, many of them reliable, even for single films; in general 2 films more effective than 1, and 3 more so than 2; etc.; most groups maintain large % of change after interval of several mos.
10-min. speech, 10-min. radio address; same material in mimeographed form.	Experimental-control difference reliable only for personally addressed group among those neutral on pre-test, and only for radio group among those most conservative on pre-test; latter shift, if at all, to radical rather than to neutral position.

ments are most likely to be those associated with some stereotype, or some prestige-endowed individual or institution. The degree to which a given set of stimuli may influence other than the most directly related attitudes, in short, is less a matter of logical relevance than of the interlacing, within a given individual's peculiar experiences, of various bonds of allegiances and antagonisms. Transfer occurs primarily according to experientially acquired foci of likes and dislikes, and only secondarily by logic.

There are many difficulties in the use of a phase or a period of schooling as the experimental factor, and some of the most illuminating experiments have employed other kinds of experiences. Several such investigations are noted on pages 956-959, to which the reader is referred for the main outlines of the experiments. The deliberate introduction of propaganda material, for example, offers more clear-cut opportunity to study changes in attitudes than the supposedly unbiased lecture halls of our colleges. In one of these (Chen, chart, page 956) the experimenter took advantage of the conflict between China and Japan over Manchuria during the months following September, 1931, to test the influence of oral propaganda. Ten statements favorable to each country were chosen from a longer list, as distinguishing the more extreme supporters of the two points of view, and as being acceptable "almost without exception" to students from Japan and from China alike. Three control groups in widely separated sections of the country were asked twice (at two-week intervals) to state the degree of their agreement or disagreement with these statements. Propaganda material was presented orally to each of six experimental groups (totaling 519 students) from two New York City universities immediately before their second testing. Two of these groups received pro-Chinese and two pro-Japanese propaganda, prepared largely from public declarations of representatives of those countries; the remaining two groups were "propagandized" with "neutral" material prepared by the Foreign Policy Association. None of the control groups made reliable changes during the intervening weeks, though the difference in the case of one of them approaches significance. (The author reminds us that the newspapers almost daily at this time contained references, in prominent positions, to Manchuria. While this, of course, represents an uncontrolled factor, it is highly improbable that the very positive results can be attributed to it.)

One of the most interesting findings is the fact that even neutral "propaganda" had a noticeable effect. The differences in mean score, for the two groups to whom neutral material was given, were, respectively, 1.28 and 4.28 times their S.D.'s. Of course this would not have been possible if all groups had not been strongly pro-Chinese to begin with. The changes in the other four experimental groups were all in the direction of the propaganda to which they had listened, the differences ranging between 5.96 and 7.59 times their respective S.D.'s. Fortunately, the precaution was taken of reversing the rôles of the two instructors involved in the latter four groups; each presented pro-Chinese material in one group and pro-Japanese in the other, so that the changes are clearly due to the propaganda and not to the personalities of the instructors. Altogether the author's summary statement seems justified: "A few minutes of vigorous propaganda given orally in the classroom may, under these conditions, produce large and measurable results."

The study by Annis and Meier (cf. chart on page 956), though not presented by its authors as a study in propaganda, is instructive as to the conditions under which one-sided appeals may be effective. By collaboration with the printers, several editorials were "planted" in a university daily, i.e., they did not appear in the regularly circulated issues. These editorials, half of them derogatory and half laudatory, involved the Hon. W. Morris Hughes, Prime Minister of Australia from 1915 to 1922. Half of 75 subjects read one of each type of editorial at fifteen successive meetings of the same class. The same procedure was followed in another class of 63, except that there were only seven of each type of editorial. An information test before the experiment began indicated that Mr. Hughes was "entirely unknown," and a control group of 65, given the same opinion test that was taken by the experimental groups following the planted editorials, revealed that there had not been sufficient campus gossip to create any definite opinions concerning him.

The authors interpret their results, which show significant differences between the groups reading the favorable and those reading the unfavorable material, both immediately and four months afterwards, as follows: "Opinion can be induced by means of judiciously selected selections in as short a time as seven issues of a newspaper *even when* the person, institution, or question may be quite unknown at the inception of the series" (our italics). It seems to us that the italicized words should read "provided that." On most questions of importance almost everyone has both some information and some attitudes. A comparison of newspaper exhortations during political campaigns with election returns for the corresponding periods will give eloquent testimony to the futility of seventy times seven issues of a newspaper, with or without conflicting exhortations from other newspapers, when their influence is counteracted by stronger forces.

All this is nicely demonstrated by the series of experiments on international attitudes described on page 954. The only reliable changes in attitude toward war were made by two groups which were subjected, respectively, to a single lecture and to the reading of a single pamphlet. The largest change in international attitudes was that in a group who spent a relatively small proportion of a ten-day conference in the consideration of international problems. A smaller group attending the same conference, and not differing from them in initial attitude, made an intensive study of international problems; the latter group made a much *smaller change*, and indicated much *greater uncertainty* at the end of the conference. The failure of the group who spent most of a summer in Geneva to show changes in attitude is even more convincing. This group attended forums, lectures, and seminars; they attended sessions of the League of Nations; and most of the rest of their days were spent in informal discussion with a wide variety of "experts." Yet the only noticeable change in their attitudes was that of increased uncertainty. This is attributed by the experimenter to the "sudden immersion in the intricacies of international affairs . . . on the part of students whose international attitudes heretofore had been based upon altruistic feeling and purely academic instruction."

The effectiveness of "propaganda" is thus seen to depend upon how clear a field it has. Such, indeed, is the fundamental axiom of the propaganda-centered régimes which are currently labeled Fascist. Propaganda, if its effectiveness is to be guaranteed, must not be opposed by counter-propaganda. When such opposition is met, individuals will be diversely affected by the counterblasts, in accordance with other predetermining influences; and while individual changes may be worked, the average net result from the point of view of the propagandist may be a near-zero one.

All these points are simultaneously illustrated in Wilke's investigation. Four scales of attitude on social issues were administered to psychology students, but to each individual student only two issues were presented. By means of a rotation technique, each individual took one attitude scale on which he was to be retested for control purposes, and one attitude scale on which his scores were to be experimentally altered by propaganda. The four issues were the existence of God, the necessity for war, the justification of birth control, and the necessity for equalization of the distribution of wealth. The three methods by which the propaganda was to be presented were the public address in person, the address through the radio loudspeaker, and the printed page. With four issues and three methods, twelve groups of data were taken, each permitting the study of experimental shifts as contrasted with control shifts. The reliabilities under control conditions were never much above or below .90. The resulting curves indicated the amount of shift produced, respectively, by personal address, radio, and printed page. It was found that the personal address is by far the most effective, the printed page only slightly effective. The shifts are without exception in the expected direction, and those produced by personal address are considerable.

It will be noted that in one instance the control shift is not negligible but very considerable. This is the result of campus events occurring during the two-week interval between the first and second testing. Anti-War Week at Washington Square College witnessed some very intense anti-war propaganda activities, some of which increased the anti-war feeling of a large number of students. At the same time, the same activities produced a *negative* reaction on the part of a considerable body of students who, in terms of the scale used, moved in the anti-anti-war—that is, the "militaristic"—direction. This boomerang effect of propaganda, which has often been noted, proved to be easily measurable. The effect is clearly related to the general factor of bimodality in response to prestige suggestion, as pointed out above, page 875. The only thing one can possibly do when acted upon powerfully is to take sides, either with or against the influence at work. Neutrality becomes unpleasant or impossible.

Identically the same thing occurs in connection with the use of the radio throughout the study just described. In the case of all four issues, the radio address produced its propaganda effect, but also produced a negative effect, giving curves with a tendency to bimodality, table-top (platykurtic) curves which represent a potential bimodality. These curves can be statistically resolved into two independent curves, both normal, with means and sigmas of their own.

Strongly worded appeals, whether oral or printed, may, then, be of considerable effect upon attitudes under certain conditions. But what of the relative effectiveness of different types of appeal? In one comparison of oral with written exhortation (Cherrington and Miller, page 956), 170 students filled out Form A of Thurstone's Scale of Attitude Toward War three days before hearing a vigorous denunciation of war by a widely known pacifist. On the next day, and again in six months, they filled out Form B of the same scale. Another group of 46 students who, like the first group, were excused from class for the purpose, read a pamphlet, by the same man, entitled "The Abolition of War," but did not hear the lecture. This group also took Form B of the scale the next day and again in six months. A control group of 71 took the two forms at the same times as the experimental groups, but neither heard the lecture nor read the pamphlet. The reliability of the scales, as determined by correlating the control group's scores on the two forms, was only .69, so that the following results are less trustworthy than could be desired.

The lecture group became more pacifistic by a difference equaling 10.28 times its P.E. Six months later the 85 subjects still available showed a difference from their Form A scores of 4.18 times its P.E. (The authors compare these 85 with the 85 not available for follow-up study, concluding that there were no known selective factors in the determination of the former group.) The reading group was as much influenced as the lecture group; its gain in pacifism score just after the reading equaled 10.18 times its P.E. After six months the difference from the original scores was still

5.06 times its P.E. for the 22 cases available, and the before and just-after difference for these 22 was 7.02 times its P.E. Such permanence of change was scarcely to have been expected, though we are not justified in concluding that the six-months' change is to be attributed to a single lecture or a single pamphlet. One would need to know (and we suspect this to be crucial) just what the effect was on the whole campus just after the lecture, and what the subjects heard and read in the intervening six months. It is also to be regretted that the control group was not retested six months later.

An extremely elaborate attempt has been made, in another experiment (Knower, chart, page 956), to compare the effects of various hortatory methods. The attitude selected for study was that toward prohibition during the years 1930, 1931, and 1932, just prior to the repeal of the Eighteenth Amendment. Nearly one thousand students were used as experimental subjects, besides 300 others who served as controls. The main experimental factors were those of logical versus emotional appeal, the comparison being made for reading as well as listening to the speeches, the material being identical. Thus, there were four speeches which were both read and heard by different groups: a dry-logical, a dry-persuasive, a wet-logical, and a wet-persuasive. In every case initially "dry" subjects were subjected to "wet" appeals, and vice versa. After the experimental group had taken the initial test, it was so subdivided into subgroups that other experimental factors could also be controlled, such as sex of speaker, hearing or reading the speech alone as compared with a group situation, strength of initial attitude, etc. The measure used was the Smith-Thurstone Scale of Attitude Toward Prohibition; its split-half reliability proved to be .88.

Since our present interest is comparing various types of appeal, we shall omit most of the other findings of this investigation. The directly pertinent results appear below:

CRITICAL RATIOS OF CHANGE IN ATTITUDE

	Oral Presentation	Written Presentation
All initially dry subjects.............	6.66	3.14
All initially wet subjects.............	9.38	5.58
Logical appeal to dry subjects.........	5.47	2.73
Persuasive appeal to dry subjects......	4.00	1.33
Logical appeal to wet subjects.........	6.27	3.81
Persuasive appeal to wet subjects......	7.37	4.23

While there is little difference between the effectiveness of the logical and persuasive appeals for all groups, the oral presentations in every case produce greater changes in attitude than the written. The author's analysis of the relationship of initial attitude to degree and direction of change is also worth noting. Those whose initial attitude was more or less neutral showed the greatest change, and those initially neither neutral nor extreme changed their attitudes the least. This latter group of moderates, in fact, showed a relatively large percentage of negative changes, i.e., in the direction opposite to that of the appeal. Since those who were initially extreme in attitude tended to regress toward moderate positions on the same side of the neutral position, the implication to be applied by those interested in the changing of attitudes by such means is fairly clear; the most significant changes are likely to be made by those whose present position is near the middle of the scale. While we are not aware that similar results have been published for other attitudes than that toward prohibition, our present best guess is that this would hold for other attitudes of a similarly controversial nature.

As a sort of supplement to this experiment, 107 subjects read two speeches, one of which defended their previous attitudes, the other opposing them. While group changes, under this double bombardment, were not reliable, more subjects changed in the direction of intensifying their previous attitudes than in the opposite direction. This procedure closely resembles what happens during a debate, and the results are precisely what they are commonly supposed to be under debate conditions.

In one of the few objective studies of attitude changes following debates (Millson, chart, page 956), the attempt was made to compare the relative effectiveness of different modes of presentation styled, respectively, academic, exhibitionistic, and conversational. Several audiences filled out an opinion ballot, both prior to and following the debates, indicating an affirmative, negative, or undecided attitude toward the subject of unemployment insurance. But no reliable differences among the three modes appear to exist. Regardless of the mode of presentation, the percentage of affirmative votes after the debates was, in every case, almost identical with that previously expressed, and the percentage of negative votes was greatly increased, as shown in the following table:

| | Per Cent of Votes | | | | | |
| | Affirmative | | Negative | | Undecided | |
Size of Group	Before	After	Before	After	Before	After
217	35	34	16	49	49	17
177	41	42	16	41	43	17
380	34	35	25	41	41	24
317	33	29	17	55	50	16
240	38	40	16	42	46	18

We do not, of course, see individual shifts of opinion in this experiment. If there were changes toward the affirmative, they were far more than balanced by those in the opposite direction. The chief significance of the experiment lies in its further demonstration that those initially undecided are those in whom effective changes can be produced.

The foregoing experiments have relied primarily upon emphatic statement and presentation of evidence in their attempts to modify attitudes. But more than once the suspicion has arisen that certain other factors, not controlled in the majority of instances, may also have been operative. What about the personality of the experimenter, for example, and what institutional allegiances are stirred up by the various forms of exhortation that we have examined? We may suspect, in other words, that the factor of prestige must be of considerable importance. Several direct attacks have been made upon the problem.

For most subjects, evidently, the prestige may be that of either majority opinion or of "experts." In one experiment (Marple, chart, page 956) subjects were three groups of 100 each at each of three age levels, distributed as shown in the accompanying table:

SEX AND AGE DISTRIBUTION OF SUBJECTS

	Median Age	S. D. of Age	Per Cent Males
High school seniors	18	.83	40
College seniors	22	1.9	50
"Representative" adults	39	14.0	31

All the 900 subjects were retested after one month, Group A at the retest being informed of majority opinions concerning each item of the test, Group B being similarly presented with "experts'" opinions, and Group C serving as control. All three age levels were of course represented in each of these groups. The test itself involved 75 "specific problems on controversial topics or situations" to be answered by Yes or No; for example, "Good oil is made and not found," and "Installment buying has had a detrimental effect on the stability of American economic life." Results, which are summarized in the following table, reveal not only the usual age differences in suggestibility, but also a slight advantage of majority opinion over expert opinion, though the effect of each is marked.

MEAN PER CENT OF CHANGES IN PROPORTION TO TOTAL NUMBER OF
POSSIBLE CHANGES

	Controls	Majority Opinion	Expert Opinion
High school seniors	17	64	51
College seniors	16	55	45
Adults	14	40	34

Another experiment, more elaborately planned (Kulp, chart, page 956), suggests also that the prestige of majorities and of "experts" is about equally effective, even with graduate students. Two groups of 54 subjects each were selected as being equated for scores on Harper's Social Study. The same test was submitted one week later, but this time each of the 71 items in the test had already been marked in "liberal" fashion. The forms handed out to Section I were preceded by the statement that a large number of "lay citizens selected to represent typical voters" had shown 98 per cent agreement with the responses indicated on the questionnaire, and to Section II the same statement was made regarding a group of well-known social scientists. The scores made under these conditions showed a marked reduction in the number of conservative responses by both groups, the shifts from initial scores being equivalent to 10.94 and 11.13 times the S.D.'s of their respective differences. The test was later repeated with these two groups after another interval of eight weeks. Though some regression toward initial scores took place, final scores were less conservative than initial scores by differences of 7.61 and 9.12 times their respective S.D.'s. Unfortunately, no control group was tested at the end of the nine-week period.

The same procedure was used, except for the later retest, with a third group of 60 subjects. Almost identical results were achieved, the prestige group in their case being "a very carefully selected group of graduate educators of maturity and experience." Although the interval between first and second testings was in this case four weeks, the reduction in the number of conservative responses was equal to a critical ratio of 10.91.

Two further variations of this experiment, however, reveal the necessity of caution in the interpretation of results. A fourth group of 73 subjects, after an initial test one week earlier, was given questionnaires prepared in exactly the same manner as those given to the three preceding groups, but with no statement whatever concerning the meaning of the already marked responses. This group made a greater shift in a liberal direction than any of the other groups; it was equivalent to a critical ratio of 13.18. With a fifth group the same technique was used, except that all items were *conservatively* marked; again, no statement was made. Even this group made a gain in liberal score, though an unreliable one. Whether or not we accept the experimenter's suggestion that the responses, as prepared for this group, were to them absurd, it is clear that this group concluded fairly early in the game that whatever the criterion by which responses had been prepared, it was not to be trusted. It seems fair to us to conclude that a similar process was at work for the fourth section: whoever prepared these responses, they must have felt, was to be trusted in general, just as were the social scientists and educators to whom the liberal responses were credited in the second and third sections. In the same manner the opinion of "lay citizens" proved effective with the first section of graduate students not so much because it was believed to be majority opinion as because it appeared to be in tune with judgments of groups in whom they did have confidence. Since the same kind of influence seemed to be at work here whether or not a prestige group was named, provided it was influence *in the "right" direction*, it may be assumed that, where no prestige group was mentioned, it was supplied by the subjects themselves. It is evident that the results of this experiment presuppose a considerable degree of readiness for "liberal" attitudes on the part of these subjects. One might almost conclude that it is necessary only to present *some* attitude position to such a group; whether it is in agreement with or in opposition to this readiness, the group's own prestige loyalties will be aroused, so that the direction, if not the amount, of the effect is the same in either case.

Strikingly similar conclusions emerge from another experiment of quite different nature (Lorge, chart, page 956). Three sets of attitude responses were obtained from one hundred adult subjects. After securing information regarding their degree of respect for a large group of well-known persons, organizations, and publications, the experimenter had them indicate one of five degrees of agreement or disagreement with two sets of statements regarding economic issues. Each statement in the first set was accompanied by *two* names, one of which was to be chosen as the more probable author. In the second set (which followed the first by an interval of from two to four weeks) the same quotations were again checked for agreement or disagreement, but this time the name of the true author alone was appended. The prestige value of any name was determined from discrepancies in rating the two sets of identical quotations. That is, authorship, in the first rating of the statements, is inferred from the nature of the statement, rather than vice versa, and hence no prestige operates in this first rating. The prestige value of any name, therefore, equals the second rating (where prestige does operate) of statements by that author less first rating of the same statements. There were three possibilities in the selection of authors of statements in the first set: they might be attributed to better-liked names (i.e., better than the true author); to less-liked names; or to the correct names (or others equally well liked). Results for each of these possibilities were as follows: for all statements for which the correct name, or one equally well liked, was assigned in the first set, the mean degree of acceptance was essentially the same in the second set where the true author was known. The mean degree of acceptance of statements assigned in the first set to authors regarded *more* highly than the true authority, was slightly but not reliably higher than acceptance of the same statements in the second set where the true (and less respected) source was known. But under opposite conditions, large and reliable differences appeared: statements attributed in the first set to authorities *less* highly regarded than their true authors were accepted to a far less degree than when their true source was revealed in the second set. "An increase in esteem for the true author over that in which the presumed author is held will result in higher ratings of the quotations, regardless of the merit of the quotation." The effect of positive prestige was considerable, but little "negative" prestige appeared.

Findings are interpreted in terms of "settled" and "tentative" attitudes. The former are those definitely associated with known persons, publications, and organizations; and the latter, those unsubstantiated by any authority. This experiment deals with only a single issue, but it speaks volumes for the potency of prestige carried by persons or institutions with whom one tends to identify oneself. It is, of course, unsafe to assume that the second rating of the statements represented "true" attitudes whereas the first did not. But assuming that the subjects were equally sincere on both occasions, the fact that there were many changes, overwhelmingly in the direction of respected persons and institutions, indicates that such affiliation (reflected in attitudes expressed at the second rating) took precedence over what had previously (at the first rating) been considered as the subject's "own" attitudes.

Such experiments leave us dissatisfied at many points when it comes to applying them to our present problem. How far will people go in subscribing to statements of attitudes invested with the prestige of authorities, majorities, or trusted groups? Would they actually subscribe to conflicting statements if identified with symbols of equal prestige? And if so, could such fickleness be said to represent any genuine attitudes? Here is the troublesome question of validity again. We have little evidence concerning the permanence of the influence of such experimentally induced prestige; presumptions, indeed, are against it, since the forces responsible for the original attitudes probably remain. But "real life" prestige is no such transitory affair; and our tentative conclusion, lacking further experimental data, is that attitudes are determined largely by such recipients of prestige as families and churches, majorities and experts, and favorably regarded individuals.

After becoming accustomed to the barely significant changes in attitudes so often following experimental procedures, one is forcibly reminded of how unreal most of these procedures are. We give lip service to the fact that attitudes of importance are deep-laid in the fundamental needs of life as molded by group patterns, and then we proceed to experiment with the use of an opaque projector! Experimental ingenuity can surely be expended along the lines of our most important hypotheses.

The experiment of F. T. Smith in modifying attitudes toward the Negro (page 958) is almost uniquely satisfying, in view of the common defects just mentioned. Forty-six graduate students in education, whose mean age was 33, accepted invitations mailed to all the 354 students in six classes. They were invited to spend two consecutive week-ends in Harlem. The events scheduled there included addresses by a prominent Negro editor, a surgeon, and a novelist; tea with Negro college groups, and lunch at a Negro social workers' club. They visited churches, a hospital, and cooperative apartments. They attended a party at a "distinguished Negro home" where they met a well-known Negro poet, an artist, and a musician. The forty-six subjects, two of whom were southern, paid their own expenses, including carfare and meals.

Four attitude tests were used: Forms A and B of the Hinckley Scale of Attitude Toward the Negro; the Negro items from Murphy and Likert's "Survey of Opinion"; a 51-item social distance scale, of the most-many-some-few-no type, prepared by the experimenter; and a list of statements, also by himself, of the degree-of-agreement type. Split-half reliabilities were, respectively, .68 and .70, .83, .89, .81, and for the whole battery, .92. The control group of forty-six was matched for original scores, age, sex, and geographic origin. All members of all six classes were retested ten days after the second Harlem week-end, and forty of the original experimental-control pairs were retested after a further lapse of eleven months. The experimenter actually located forty-five of the forty-six experimental subjects at this time; the other was abroad.

At the first retest the controls showed no change, and the difference between their mean score and that of the experimentals was equal to 7.36 times its S.D. Differences were significant also for each of the four tests, the lowest critical ratio being 2.89. Forty of the forty-six subjects revealed more favorable attitudes following the experience. There was no significant relationship between initial scores of the total group of 354 and age or intelligence test scores, though an almost reliable sex difference appeared, men's scores being more favorable. Within the experimental group the younger subjects, those with least favorable initial scores, and women gained slightly more than the others; there was little relationship between change in scores and geographical residence in youth. At the follow-up test eleven months later, the forty available experimental-control pairs showed a difference in total score equal to 4.74 times its S.D., the difference still being reliable in three of the four tests. The losses (as compared to the first retest) were concentrated in a few subjects. Of the forty who had shown a gain in favorable attitude at the first retest, eight showed further gain, seventeen held the earlier gain, eight fell less than halfway back to the original score, two fell more than halfway, four returned to the initial score, and one fell considerably below this point. Altogether, twenty-five held their gains or increased them. Of the five subjects who failed to gain at the first retest, two made later gains, two remained stationary, and one made a further drop in favorable score.

Since the experimental subjects were self-selected, the question arises as to whether they were predisposed to become more favorable toward Negroes. They were, of course, equated as to original attitude; but, even so, the fact of accepting the invitation may have revealed some willingness to change not characteristic of the others. Twenty-three of the invited students who accepted but were at the last moment unable to go to Harlem constituted a suitable "interested control group" for the purposes of this question. The experimental group gained more in favorable attitude, compared to these twenty-three, than compared to the paired control group, so that the changes were clearly related to the experience rather than to the fact of having accepted the invitation.

A whole series of "life-situation" experiments has for some years been carried on by Thurstone and his collaborators. These concern the effect of motion pictures upon the attitudes of children, chiefly of high school age. The results of seeing five movies by as many school groups may be taken as typical. These five films were chosen as being (1) favorable to the Chinese; (2) unfavorable to the Chinese; (3) favorable to the Germans (this was a war picture, so that a scale of attitude toward war was also included); (4) unfavorable to gambling; and (5) unfavorable to bootlegging. Groups of children numbering between 133 and 254 from high schools (in one case the junior high school was included) were taken to the local theater, or shown the film in the school auditorium. All the schools were in small towns not far from Chicago whose population varied between 1200 and 4000. Large proportions of the school populations were included. All groups were tested a few days before and immediately after seeing the film. The paired comparisons method of testing was used in the case of attitudes toward bootlegging and toward the German people, and Thurstone scales were used for attitudes toward the Chinese, toward the Germans, and toward prohibition.

All the films had the expected influence, with the exception of the one involving bootlegging; neither the paired comparisons nor the scaled statements showed reliable changes in attitudes following this film. The one involving gambling led to ranking that offense considerably more seriously. The paired comparisons test, before seeing the film, resulted in the following ranking: ————— pickpocket, petty thief, gambler, drunkard —————; afterward the ranking was: ————— bootlegger, gambler, pickpocket, petty thief —————. There was no significant change in the rank positions of other offenses. The film thought to be favorable to the German people resulted in a change in mean score, in favor of the Germans, equal to 5.37 times the P.E. of its difference, as well as in a considerable shift according to the paired comparisons. The ranking before was: English, Irish, French, Swede, German, Scotch —————; and afterward: English, German, Irish, French, Swede, Norwegian —————. No other nationality group made any considerable shift. Of the two films involving the Chinese, the one thought to be favorable resulted in a mean change, according to the scaled statements, equaling 16.98 times the P.E. of its difference, in favor of the Chinese. The film which had been criticized by Chinese resulted in a change unfavorable to the Chinese, but the difference was equivalent to only 2.22 times its P.E.

These films involve so many variables that it is impossible to tell just why some of them produce significant changes while others fail to do so. The previous attitudes of the particular groups involved, moreover, must be an important factor. The group which saw the favorable Chinese film, for example, was to begin with more un-friendly to the Chinese than the group which saw the unfavorable film, by an amount almost as great as the amount of change shown by the former group. If each group had seen the other film, there might have been a reliable change against the Chinese and none in their favor. There is also the factor of previous familiarity with the issues involved. It is easily possible, for example, that the children who saw the bootlegging film had already heard endless discussion of prohibition, whereas those who saw the gambling film were perhaps being presented with a relatively new issue. It will be remembered that there was a reliable change after seeing the latter movie, but very little after the former.

The effects of two or more films presumably having an influence upon the same attitude were later studied. About 750 children in Grades 6 to 12 in a children's institution were divided into five sub-groups, A, B, C, D, and E, each a cross section of the total popula-tion. Procedure was as follows:

Date	Groups	Procedure
July 8	All	Took scale of attitude toward war.
July 20	B, C	Saw war film X.
July 21	B	Took scale of attitude toward war.
July 21	C, D, E,	Saw war film Y.
July 22	C, D, A	Took scale of attitude toward war.
July 22	E	Saw war film X.
July 23	E	Took scale of attitude toward war.

The results of the experiment were as follows (a high score indi-cates favorable attitude toward war):

Group	Experimental Factor	Mean Score Pre-test	Mean Score Post-test	Mean Score Difference
A	Control (no film)	5.04	4.92	.12
B	Film X	5.05	4.56	.49
C	Films X and Y	4.95	4.46	.49
D	Film Y	4.91	4.58	.33
E	Films Y and X	5.06	4.52	.54

A similar experiment with three movies dealing with criminals is summarized by the authors as follows (low scores indicate attitude of leniency):

Group	Experimental Factor	Mean Score Pre-test	Mean Score Post-test	Mean Score Difference
A	Films X, Y, and Z..............	5.22	4.83	−.39
B	Films X and Y................	5.23	5.03	−.20
C	Film X......................	5.14	5.13	−.01
C	Films X and Z................	5.14	4.97	−.17
D	Film Y......................	5.23	5.27	.04
D	Films Y and Z................	5.23	4.95	−.28
E	Three weeks' interval (control)...	4.95	4.98	.03

It is evident that degree of change is specific to the attitude measured. War film X alone is as effective as X and Y together; war film Y, though somewhat less effective than both, produces a noticeable change. None of the three criminal films, on the other hand, has any effect alone; any two of them are more effective than any one, and all three produce greater results than any two. Either the particular war films used chanced to be more effective than the particular criminal films, or (as seems more probable) the latter attitude is more firmly fixed, and more experiences are needed to influence it.

Follow-up studies of the experiments already described were also made. The following table summarizes the findings regarding the persistence of attitude changes among several populations:

Place	Films Involved	Number of Subjects	Interval	Per Cent of Immediate Change Remaining
L	Criminal film Z...........	257	2½ months	87
L	Criminal film Z...........	195	9 "	78
M	Chinese film X...........	117	5 "	62
M	Chinese film X...........	76	19 "	60
N	Negro film...............	350	5 "	62
O	War film Z...............	87	6 "	123
P	War film X...............	138	8 "	opposite direction
Q	War films X and Y.......	572	2 "	52
Q	War films X and Y.......	571	4 "	22
Q	Criminal films X, Y, and Z.	559	2 "	100
Q	Criminal films X, Y, and Z.	549	4 "	111

These experiments are commendable not only for their excellent technique, but also for their long-range planning. One wonders, of course, to what extent control groups in these follow-up studies would have shown parallel changes, as functions either of trends of the times or of further education and maturity. And one can but speculate as to the influence of the same films upon adults. Experimental difficulties in this area are, of course, enormous, but presumably not insurmountable.

One further experiment (Hartmann, see page 956) is note worthy in that it not only deals with a life situation, but itself played an actual part in a current activity of some importance. The experimenter, who was himself a Socialist candidate for a political position, attempted to compare the efficacy of a logical exposition of the case for Socialism with that of a more emotional approach. The first of the leaflets prepared for the purpose presented seven brief statements, for each of which the word "agree" or "disagree" was to be checked. A sample statement reads, "All banks and insurance companies should be run on a non-profit basis like the school." Following the seven statements appeared a few sentences, of which the following are most important: "Now go back and count the number of sentences with which you AGREED. Then count the number with which you DISAGREED. *If the number of agreements is larger than the number of disagreements, you are at heart a Socialist*—whether you know it or not. . . . *Why don't you try voting for the things you actually want?* . . . VOTE SOCIALIST!" The more persuasive appeal consisted of a letter addressed to "Dear Father and Mother," and signed "Your Sons and Daughters." Heartstrings are pulled, the sadnesses of depression days outlined, the imminence of war and the prevalence of poverty described as inevitable prospects unless the young people of the land can introduce Socialism. "Our generation cannot enjoy the beauty and justice of the *New America* if you block our highest desires. There was a time when you were young like us. We beg you in the name of those early memories and springtime hopes to *support the Socialist ticket in the coming elections*! . . . VOTE SOCIALIST!"

The city of Allentown, Pennsylvania, was selected for the experiment; its nineteen wards were so divided that every family in three wards received the emotional appeal, and every family in four other wards the rational appeal, while the remaining twelve wards received neither, serving as controls. Although perfect equating of the emotional and rational wards was by no means possible, the distribution of incomes in them was very nearly alike.

The leaflets were distributed by interested party members. About half of them were handed to the recipients, the other half being left under the doors, in their absence. The results, taken from the voting-machine totals, are somewhat complicated by the fact that the total vote in the city increased in the experimental year, 1935, over that of 1934. The essential data are reproduced in the accompanying table.

	Actual Vote 1934	1935	Expected Increase	Actual Increase[a]	Per Cent of Increase
Republican: Total.......	10233	12258	1708	2025	19.79
Emotional wards......	1218	1467	203	249	20.44
Rational wards.......	1490	1848	249	358	24.03
Control wards........	7525	8943	1256	1418	15.86
Democratic: Total.......	10801	12216	1802	1415	13.10
Emotional wards......	2303	2489	384	186	8.08
Rational wards.......	1553	1787	259	234	15.07
Control wards.........	6945	7940	1159	995	14.33
Socialist: Total..........	499	653	83	154	30.86
Emotional wards......	110	165	18	55	50.00
Rational wards.......	48	65	8	17	35.42
Control wards........	341	423	57	82	24.05
Entire city..............	21533	25127	3594	3594	16.69

[a] The "expected increase" column is obtained by multiplying the 1934 vote by the coefficient of increase of public participation, 16.69.

The actual number of votes represented in the experiment proper is, of course, small. Other factors must have entered, moreover, to influence the size of the vote in both sets of wards, as the author points out—factors possibly more important than the leaflets. Thus, for example, the 1934 Socialist vote was nearly twice as great a proportion of the total vote in the emotional wards as in the rational wards. But it is difficult to imagine just what forces should increase the Socialist vote by 50 per cent within one year in precisely the areas covered by the emotional appeal, while affecting the other areas to a much lesser degree. This was a percentage of increase more than twice that found in the control areas. And even if we grant that the small number of votes involved makes such an increase far easier to obtain, it is no mean feat to increase that vote from 3.03 per cent (in 1934) of the total vote of a certain area to 4.00 per cent in 1935—particularly when the comparable growth of the Socialist vote in the control areas was only from 2.30 to 2.44 per cent of the total vote in those sections. It is not "news," of course, that an emotional appeal is more effective than a rational one. But it is a scientific event of significance when such a common assumption is put to the test of a deliberately devised experiment having to do with realistic behavior of run-of-the-mine adults in a complex social situation.

A brief summary may be ventured of the methods which appear most effective in the experimental modification of attitudes. The method, in the first place, should involve vivid experience. Experiments seem to indicate that, other things being equal, experiences which are novel, emotionally charged, and realistic (as opposed to laboratory-like) are most effective. If, in the second place, it is desired to modify the attitudes of whole groups in a given direction, it is important that there should be neither strong counter-influences nor opportunity to become familiar with the complexities of or the objections to the point of view being advanced. While certain predisposed individuals may react even more strongly to such negative stimuli, this will not be true of unselected groups as a whole. The third conclusion emerges even more clearly from the experimental literature: the method should make use of individuals, groups, institutions, or symbols thereof, which have prestige value for those whose attitudes are to be affected. "So-and-so is the author of this statement"; "members of the Blank organization will perceive that this position is a logical outgrowth of their ideals"; or, even better, face-to-face contact with individual adherents of some position who are intimately known, greatly respected, or much in the public eye— such are the forces which few can resist. The experiment in modifying attitudes toward the Negro (page 958), for example, employs all of these devices. While the conditions here outlined are not invariably associated with marked changes of attitude, nor the absence of those conditions necessarily with failure to change, these appear to be the major factors. We may further state, in tentative fashion, that deviations from the general rules are in most cases associated with subtle factors of prestige which experimenters either do not or cannot control, and which, therefore, are rarely reported upon.

ATTITUDES AS DETERMINED BY LIFE EXPERIENCES

It is evident that attitudes may be modified by certain kinds of experiences. Some results of experimentally devised situations as attitude modifiers have been cited. But what of the more "normal" everyday kinds of experiences? Some of them are relatively constant for most individuals, some episodic in character; but either kind may prove to be of importance in the genesis or modification of certain attitudes. Such experiences are, by definition, not readily subject to the most precise kind of investigation, the scientific experiment, but certain other methods are nevertheless available.

One of the kinds of experiences which, in our society, may be presumed to have wide influence upon various attitudes is that of education, and a host of studies of this sort has been made. The method most frequently followed is that of simultaneously testing subjects at different educational levels. This procedure is completely valid only upon the assumption that the to-be-compared educational levels are within the same community, and that the sampling at one level is as representative as at another. The latter condition is, of course, never actually found, largely because of the retarding and eliminating effects of educational "standards"; and the former one is frequently violated, often from necessity, as in the comparison of high school and college populations. A more serious methodological difficulty lies in the practical impossibility of obtaining adequate controls. One is often left wondering whether attitude changes coincident with a given period of education are not simply consequences of additional months or years of living in a particular cultural environment, rather than results of the school experience itself. There exists no comparable group lacking the school experience at elementary school levels; and at higher levels such a group would be exceedingly difficult to find.

A brief compilation appears in the chart, pages 982 ff., of studies which in general follow this method of sampling successive educational levels. The list is not complete, but includes most of the investigations known to us in which numbers of subjects and reliability of measuring instruments seem to warrant some conclusions. Since the same problem, as approached by more careful experimental methods, has been discussed in earlier pages, we shall not discuss these studies at length.

The largest group of these investigations deals with a widespread group of issues to which the terms "liberal" and "conservative" are often applied. It is evident, from a perusal of the summary table, that a "trend toward liberalism with increasing exposure to academic influences" is the general rule at the college level. This seems to be true concerning such diverse issues as moral judgments, religious belief, social and economic opinions, and superstitious belief. Such effects seem to be more pronounced, as might be anticipated, among students from rural and small-town backgrounds, and among those enrolled in social science courses. Attitudes toward war, on the other hand, and toward occupations, appear to shift only slightly, if at all, under the influence of the total college experience, under contemporary American conditions.

Further insight into the process by which attitudes change with increasing age—and the change is almost certainly effected largely by school experience—is afforded by two investigations concerning attitudes toward certain disapproved actions. In one of these (Clem and Smith, page 982), 1172 pupils in Grades 7 to 12 of a city school system were asked to rank 14 such behaviors in order of their "badness." Results are presented below in terms of the critical ratios of seventh- and twelfth-grade mean ranks; a plus sign preceding the critical ratio indicates that the twelfth grade ranks the action as worse than the seventh grade, and a minus sign the reverse. The behaviors are presented in the order of the seventh-grade ranking, the "worst" appearing first.

Stealing	2.05	Cards on Sunday	−6.02
Gambling	−6.30	Selfishness	5.06
Drinking	−3.57	Conceit	4.73
Cheating	5.86	Smoking	−3.07
Lying	5.06	Gossip	7.84
Swearing	−3.95	Extravagance	2.82
Vulgar talk	3.79	Dancing	−2.76

SOME STUDIES OF ATTITUDES AT DIFFERENT EDU-

AUTHOR	SUBJECTS	ATTITUDE
Anderson	673 men college students, all 4 classes.	Occupations.
Boldt and Stroud	738 college students, all 4 classes.	Social (Harper).
Brameld	857 students in 9 eastern colleges, all 4 classes.	Social and economic.
Clem and Smith	1172 pupils, grades 7 to 12.	Disapproved actions (14) to be ranked for "badness."
Downing	2500 pupils, grades 8 to 12.	Scientific.
Droba	1000 university students, all 4 classes, graduates.	War.
Dudycha	College freshmen and seniors in 8 colleges.	Morals, religion, evolution, superstitions.
Eckert and Mills	458 high chool pupils, 2 schools.	International (Neumann).
Garrison and Burch	163 college students, 4 classes (South).	Negro.
Garrison and Mann	258 college men.	Social, economic, religious (25 statements).
Green	Children, ages 7 to 16.	National and race prejudice.
Haag	98 high school and college students.	Race (Bogardus, Watson).
Harris, Remmers, and Ellison	307 men and women college students.	Religion.
Jones	250 college freshmen, 75 upper-classmen.	Social, moral, economic (25 statements).

CATIONAL LEVELS OR IN DIFFERENT COURSES

RESULTS

No differences in order of ranking.

Steady increase in liberalism with higher classes, reliable even for adjacent classes; direct relationship between number of social science courses pursued and liberalism scores.

Most "conservative" statements ranked higher by freshmen than by seniors; reverse holds for "liberal" statements; other classes intermediate.

All 14 show quite or almost reliable changes between 7th and 12th grades; general tendency by older group toward greater leniency in interpreting violations of codes.

Gradual and uniform in % of "correct" answers; no relationship to amount of science studied.

Slight trend toward pacifism at higher class levels; differences reliable only for graduates compared to undergraduates.

Small but consistent differences; seniors accept fewer conservative moral and religious beliefs, believe fewer superstitions and more in evolution.

Those who have had 2 or 3 social science courses no different from those with only 1; highest quartile in international attitude score elect social science courses no more frequently than lowest quartile.

"Seniors somewhat more lenient," but few statements show consistent change through all 4 classes; conventional prejudices show general decrease; liberal (not extreme) statements, general increase.

Freshmen show more contradictions than seniors, no differences in certainty or extremeness; seniors more liberal in religion, less uncertain on social and economic questions.

Prejudices already fixed at age of 7; no age differences except in ingenuity of defending opinions.

High school students show less clearly defined race attitudes than college students, whose responses on Watson test more liberal and more extreme.

79 state they have less religious faith than when entering; 49 report more; former group slightly (not reliably) less conservative on Harper test.

Seniors and freshmen alike in % of "reactionary" responses; seniors more conservative on economic, less on religious questions.

SOME STUDIES OF ATTITUDES AT DIFFERENT EDU-

AUTHOR	SUBJECTS	ATTITUDE
Katz and Allport	1406 liberal arts students, all 4 classes.	Religion, church.
Kolstad	500 graduate and undergraduate students of education.	International (Harper).
Lundeen and Caldwell	718 high school seniors, 264 college students.	200 unfounded beliefs.
Maller and Lundeen	Grades 7 to 12.	Superstitions.
Matthews	644 students, grade 9 to college seniors.	Academic honesty (20 concrete situations).
Minard	1352 pupils, grades 7 to 12.	Race (32 life situations).
Moore and Garrison	210 college undergraduates.	Social and political (Vetter).
Symington	1. 190 high school seniors and college freshmen; 216 college juniors, seniors, graduate students (from east). 2. 57 college freshmen, sophomores, juniors; 41 seniors and graduate students (from west).	Religious beliefs (Watson).
Symonds	8th grade to college seniors.	Social, religious, economic liberalism.
Vetter and Green	350 members of Amer. Assn. for Advancement of Atheism.	Atheism.
White, L. D.	7168 persons interviewed in 11 cities.	Public employment.

CATIONAL LEVELS OR IN DIFFERENT COURSES (*Continued*)

RESULTS

Upperclassmen show reliably less belief in personal God and prayer, more in impersonal God, than underclassmen. Majority maintain same belief as when entering. Orthodox most likely, liberal theists and atheists least likely, to change. Less belief in miracles, more in ethics alone as satisfactory, than on entrance. More critical of church and of institutional practices than at entrance, but little change in "need for religion" or "interest in church."

Consistent rise in "internationalism" with higher degrees; "M.A." versus "no degree" difference statistically reliable; history group most, household arts and nursing groups least favorable.

College students have heard more, but believe less and state that they are less influenced by unfounded beliefs, than high school seniors; all differences reliable.

Negative correlation between age and superstitious belief.

Steady increase in % considered unjustified, through college sophomore level; college upperclassmen believe reliably fewer situations unjustified than underclassmen.

Consistent increase in agreement with "experts" as to desirable behavior, up to 10th grade; consistent drop in freedom from prejudice in terms of personal practice from 7th to 12th grades. Differences reliable with grade separations of 2-3 yrs.

Slight but consistent decrease, from freshmen to seniors, in % making reactionary and conservative responses; similar increase in % making neutral, liberal, and radical responses.

More advanced groups more "liberal" in both cases; critical ratio 12.2 for eastern group and 7.2 for western group.

Slight trend toward liberalism with increasing age, especially regarding government control and benevolence; information increases much greater.

% who had high school training exceeds by 29% those in total population with equal education; 39% have had 4 yrs. or more of college or professional training.

Groups with less schooling more favorable to public (as compared to private) employment than those with more.

The constellation gambling-drinking-smoking-dancing-cards on Sunday is clearly distinguished from that of gossip-conceit-selfishness-cheating-lying, the latter being considered more serious by the older group. The authors report, from other data, a general trend with increasing age toward leniency in interpreting violations of codes.

The study involving academic honesty (Matthews, chart, page 984) is comparable; relevant situations were presented, to be checked as justified, unjustified, or doubtful. Increase in school level was paralleled by increase in percentage of "unjustified" responses up to and including the college sophomore level; but there was a slight decrease in such responses above this level. The junior-senior scores were reliably lower than those of freshmen and sophomores. It is of interest to note that the total percentage of "unjustified" responses by 46 of the college faculty was 93, as compared to 77 for college seniors, 81 for college sophomores, and 52 for the ninth grade. This study may be thought of as a continuation of one aspect of the previous one, into the college level. The picture presented by both is that of codes, at first rather uncritically accepted from adults. Such codes gradually give way under the twin influences of the necessity for new codes under new conditions of life—e.g., academic honesty—and of increasing observation of the fact that the world at large does not apply the codes too seriously. Such development must, of course, be thought of as an outgrowth of the sum total of life experiences in a community (chiefly the school or academic community, in the case of academic honesty, at least) rather than as representing the effects of education, narrowly conceived.

The investigation concerning race attitudes at succeeding school levels (Minard, chart, page 984) seems also to reflect the existence of codes. The subjects, 1352 pupils in Grades 7 to 12 from five Iowa towns and cities, were presented with 32 "life situations," each followed by five possible courses of action. One of five degrees of response to each alternative was to be checked, the degrees ranging from "certainly" to "certainly not." Sample situations were: a Jewish family moving into the Gentile section of town; the presence of a Mexican boy on a basket-ball team. Questionnaires were scored in three ways: (A) freedom from prejudice, on *a priori* grounds; (B) most desirable behavior (agreement with "experts"); (C) personal practice, derived from questions stated in the second person. The A and B scores were correlated to the extent of .93, while their odd-even reliabilities were .90 or higher, so that it is difficult to see that A and B scores are in any way distinct. Their correlations with C score are, respectively, .79 and .68. The A and B scores show slight but consistent *increase* in freedom from prejudice, up to and including the tenth grade, whereas the C score shows continuous *decrease* in freedom from prejudice from the seventh grade on. The differences are reliable with grade separations of two or three years. The divergent trends of these scores raise serious questions, of course, regarding their validity. But the merit of this work lies precisely in the fact that it does distinguish between the two kinds of attitudes; the distinction is not unlike that made elsewhere between public and private attitudes. It appears to us to be not a question of one valid and one invalid measurement of race attitudes, but rather a reflection of what the psychoanalysts call ambivalence. Most of us are, as a matter of fact, subject to pulls from different if not opposite directions, and our "true" attitudes in one situation may be quite different from those in another. The "poles" between which we vacillate are presumably groups and their codes—in this instance the teacher-Sunday school-textbook versus home and play group codes.

One method of studying the relationship of education to attitudes, quite different from the foregoing, should also be noted. It is that of analyzing the educational backgrounds of groups selected on the basis of present attitudes. One of the best examples of this method is to be seen in the analysis of 350 replies received from 600 members of the American Association for the Advancement of Atheism to whom questionnaires were sent (Vetter and Green, page 984). The percentage of the 350 who were high school graduates exceeded by 29 per cent the percentage of the total population with equivalent schooling, and 39 per cent had had four or more years of college or professional school training. Similarly, L. D. White, in his investigation of the prestige value of public employment (cf. page 984), found a clear-cut relationship to level of education, individuals at the higher levels being uniformly less favorable to public as compared to private employment. It would be absurd, of course, to maintain that either of these attitudes is the "result" of education.

White found a very definite relationship, for example, between attitudes and socio-economic status, which is known to parallel closely educational level. The previous investigation, on the other hand, revealed no important relationship between atheism and occupation or income, but findings elsewhere reported concerning the relationship of religious radicalism and intelligence test scores (cf. page 934) suggest that the latter factor may have a good deal to do with the relatively favored educational background of the atheists. Whatever factors, such as economic status and intelligence, are under present conditions almost necessary correlatives of advanced education, will always appear to distort whatever "purely educative" influences may be operative. Selective forces are inescapable, and so far neither adequate controls nor partial correlation methods have served to disentangle them.

In spite of these and other shortcomings of present-day attitude experiments, at least a few conclusions concerning educational influences may be asserted with considerable confidence. This is true, in particular, of those findings which have emerged both from simultaneous measurement at different educational levels and from better-controlled experimental procedures. It has been shown, for example, by both methods, that more "liberal" attitudes tend to follow college courses in social studies, that little or no change in attitudes may accompany considerable increase in information directly related to those attitudes, and that steady decrease in superstitious belief usually accompanies increasing education. There are exceptions, of course, to this general agreement, and there are few cases of truly comparable studies. But there is sufficient uniformity of results to indicate that selective factors in the simultaneous testing procedure are far from being the major influence.

Before we leave the topic of the influence of education, we may mention one or two particular aspects of it whose effects upon attitudes have aroused wide interest. One of these is military training. The effects of the Reserve Officers' Training Corps experience upon students' war attitudes have been investigated in such manner as almost to remove any question of the selection of subjects. With the aid of several students, questionnaire replies were obtained from ten eastern colleges and universities in which there were R.O.T.C.

units; in some of them military training was compulsory, in others elective. In some cases whole R.O.T.C. classes filled out questionnaires with the permission of their military instructors. Other subjects, including many students not electing military training, were simply approached in unselected manner in their rooms or while walking across the campus, and asked to fill out the form on the spot. Only two individuals thus accosted refused to comply. In all, there were 400 replies (half from elementary and half from advanced military students) from institutions where R.O.T.C. work was compulsory; 496 (again, half elementary) from students electing it; and 254 replies from those not electing it in the same institutions.

The difficulties here are obvious: there can be no control group where the course is compulsory; where it is elective, pre-existing attitudes must have a great deal to do with its election. Thus, for example, in colleges where the course was optional, there were two and a half times as many of those previously attending military schools who elected R.O.T.C. work as who did not. In spite of all this, however, certain effects clearly attributable to R.O.T.C. training emerge. Of all R.O.T.C. men, 55 per cent reported that the experience had altered their attitude toward the army favorably, and 8 per cent unfavorably. The presence of the R.O.T.C. on the campus had little effect, in this respect, upon those not taking the course; 11 per cent reported a favorable and 11 per cent an unfavorable change, in answer to the same question. Where the course was compulsory the advanced students expected war sooner than elementary students, and anticipated a longer period before wars should cease; both differences are reliable. Where the course was optional, those who elected it expected war sooner, and expected wars to cease later than did those not electing it; again the differences are reliable.

There is considerable evidence, of rather indirect nature, of influence by "indoctrination." Thus in one college class eleven (14 per cent) of the advanced group stated that war accelerates scientific progress, whereas only ten students in all other colleges mentioned this. In another college every student stated that military training develops leadership. Indeed, belief in such supposed by-products of military training is perhaps its most conspicuous effect. The more R.O.T.C. training these students had had, the more they believed that it trains in character, self-confidence, and leadership. The majority of the R.O.T.C. students believed that the training develops patriotism. The following table alone would seem to justify the author's comment that "either the R.O.T.C. is instilling obedience to an unthinking kind of patriotism, or the R.O.T.C. selects and holds men already having this kind of patriotism":

PER CENT OF STUDENTS IN COLLEGES WHERE R.O.T.C. IS ELECTIVE WHO WOULD VOLUNTEER AND WHO WOULD EVADE SERVICE IN CASE OF WAR

	Offensive War			Defensive War		
	Advanced	Elementary	Control	Advanced	Elementary	Control
Would volunteer	44	25	18	87	69	49
Would evade service.......	8	21	40	0	6	8

Altogether, two-thirds of the men were convinced of the futility of war; only one-quarter of those who believed that good is to be derived from war specified what good they had in mind, and "where a specific good was stated there was a piling up of the same answer in a single institution, strongly suggesting the result of indoctrination." Reference to the earlier discussion of education as a means of changing attitudes (page 980) will suggest to the reader that either selective forces are more strongly at work here, or academic influences are in most instances less influential than military ones.

The experience of college fraternity life is one of such warm loyalties that it would not be surprising to find that certain attitudes had been influenced by it. Katz and Allport (cf. page 984), who have compared fraternity with non-fraternity members (the term is used to include sororities also) in one university, report some attitude differences between the two groups. The probabilities of selective determination of these differences are so great, however, that we shall comment only on certain intra-fraternity differences. The total fraternity group is divided into those who take "institutional" and those who take "individualistic" positions in regard to fraternities. The first group includes more than two-thirds of the entire membership; they conceive of the institution as having a pseudo-independent existence, transcending the lives of its individual members, upon whom its standards are imposed. The smaller group views things more realistically: fraternities exist only in their members, who themselves determine standards, largely for purposes of serving their own interests. These two groups are rather consistently distinguished in attitudes of various kinds. For example, in response to a question concerning their willingness to admit members of thirty specific groups to fraternity membership, the individualists are consistently more tolerant, and most of the differences are reliable. The individualists, moreover, vary in the direction of the attitudes of non-fraternity members, to whom the same question had been put regarding their rooming houses. Individualists resemble non-fraternity members more closely than they do their institutional brothers and sisters. While the authors are aware that fraternities may select rather than create exclusivists, they incline to the conclusion that the "group fiction" serves as a convenient rationalization. "The notion of the superior reality of a fraternity, whose reputation must be upheld, is a device which enables those who hold it to release, with a clear conscience, certain racial and group prejudices which might otherwise not be given expression."

Certain other patterns of attitudes characterize the institutionalists as distinguished from the individualists; the former believed more strongly in the importance of all kinds of institutions. They showed greater willingness to permit group control of individual behavior, and more confidence in the manner in which university functions were being administered. Thus, the institutionalists were more inclined than the individualists to believe that repeated athletic losses would detract from the merit (as distinguished from the reputation) of the university; they believed to a lesser degree in the importance of academic freedom and in the competence of students to supervise their own moral conduct; and they were more willing to have administrative supervision of the student newspaper. Whatever the personality factors associated with becoming an institutionalist, in this sense, there seems to be little doubt that those individuals in whom they are operative are, in the fraternity situation, exposed to a train of influences of considerable power to modify attitudes—influences to which a minority (the individualists) are relatively immune, and with which others (non-members) never come in contact.

We should like to be able to indicate what happens to various attitudes, among particular groups at particular times, merely as the result of additional years of living. Do given groups, under given conditions, tend to remain fairly stable, to change in parallel fashion so that individuals retain about the same relative positions, or to be affected with considerable diversity?

The stability of attitudes in the late adolescent and early adult periods is not known. Retest reliability on standard attitude tests on international and economic issues are of the general order of .90, but the time intervals have usually been at the most a period of a few weeks. One five-year retest has been completed, the first test having been given in December, 1929, the second in November, 1934. Students from the University of Michigan and from Columbia were followed up. It happened that those who agreed to take the retest proved an almost exact run-of-the-mill from the original distributions. The Columbia group, over half of whom were employed, most of the remainder being in law or medical school, had moved strongly in the radical direction on the four groups of questions utilized, dealing, respectively, with Internationalism, Imperialism, the Negro, and Economic Issues. The shift was larger on the economic issues than on the others, but was substantial throughout. Indeed, it amounted to one sigma of the 1929 distribution for total radicalism. The Michigan group also moved reliably in the radical direction on Imperialism, the Negro and Economic Issues, but did not alter its position on the Internationalism scale. An attempt to discover the reasons for the radical shifts yielded bizarre results, e.g., a man who had in fact moved far in the radical direction told solemnly why he had become so much more conservative; another who had become conservative told us that practical experience in life had made him much more radical than when he was in college. Individual analysis of the students' own reports made it clear that this kind of self-evaluation was at best only of suggestive value. On the other hand, there were some group trends which were definitely meaningful. We do not know to what extent the depression caused the increased radicalism; but students constantly referred to corruption, confusion and disorganization in business and in public life, implying that what they read and observed about them was often more important than the personal economic hardships to which they were subjected. There was no evidence whatever of a relation between economic success and amount of radical shift, but there was a definite and general trend to disparage the economic organization of a country unable to employ its population, and a tendency to protest in intense terms against the doings of war-mongers and propagandists.

One of the most important problems within the field of race and nationality attitudes has to do with the effects of familiarity and contact, and objective data here are rather easily obtainable. In the most direct approach that had been made to this problem, the experimenter states his problem as follows: "To what extent does greater familiarity with individuals from various national groups affect opinions regarding these groups?" His subjects were 87 foreign students and 24 American students in International House in New York City, 25 students at Columbia University, 73 students at Indiana University, and 78 students at Occidental College, Los Angeles. The students living at International House were reached in person. Those at Columbia University received a circular letter; those at Indiana and Occidental College were reached through a classroom experiment. The task assigned to the subjects was to rate each of ten national groups—Chinese, French, Greek, Japanese, Russian, English, German, Hindu, Norwegian, American—in respect to the following attributes: (1) Art (including painting, music and sculpture); (2) Industrial progressiveness; (3) Personal preference of the subject, considering such factors as meeting members of these groups socially, having them as friends and companions; (4) How well the subject would like to live in a neighborhood in which all families were of this nationality. After ranking the ten groups in respect to these four characteristics, the subjects recorded their own sex, nationality, and the countries which they had visited or lived in (stating the length of such visit or residence); the groups of which they knew at least three native-born members ("in the sense of having seen them on the street . . . or knowing them well enough to speak to . . ."); the national groups of whom three or more individuals were *intimately* known to the subject (well enough to "talk to them often and know their personal characteristics"). The merit of the method lies in the fact that every national group must be assigned a definite rank. It is impossible, on grounds of general "humanitarianism" or general "nationalism," to rate all groups high or all groups low. It is now possible to compare the above data with regard to *personal experience* of foreign peoples with the ranking in respect to the various questions. Counting 1 as the most preferred and 10 as the least preferred group, the following figures appear with reference to the influence of travel in foreign countries. Comparison is made with the answers to question (3), which is the one about personal preference. Each group had to rate *all ten* groups.

Travel in Foreign Countries	No Travel	Less Than One Week	One Week to Six Months	Six Months or More
Foreign students.	6.17	5.50	5.10	4.70
International House Americans.	6.44	4.75	4.87	4.21

Whatever the causal relations may be, there is a fairly clear tendency to rate a group higher, the longer one has been in contact with the group on its own soil. The result is even more striking when we compare the *number of intimate acquaintances* with the relative standing of the groups. The average position of all those groups among whom the given subject has no intimate acquaintance is 6.14; for those among whom there is one acquaintance, 5.07; two acquaintances, 4.50; three acquaintances, 3.19; four acquaintances, 2.65 (figures relate to *entire* group of subjects). This progression appears equally clearly among the foreign students, among the International House Americans, and among the Indiana and Occidental College students. These data may also be regarded as a measure of neighborliness, since the correlation between the group standings in reference to questions (3) and (4) is +.95 ±.02.

This work is unfortunately impaired, as the author points out, by the inclusion of self-ratings, or, rather, the ratings of one's own group. Fortunately the outlines of his results are not disturbed by this consideration; a case might have been made, perhaps, for the importance of using ratings of one's own group in comparison with others, but the data should, of course, be disentangled. That a striking result remains even after the removal of this possible source of error is shown by the fact that the rank difference correlation between *preference* and *familiarity* (familiarity measured by assigning a certain weight to intimate acquaintances, slight acquaintances, travel, and familiarity with foreign languages) is +.82 ±.07. It may be of incidental interest to know how the ten groups stand in the eyes of two groups of American students. For the Columbia University group, the preference ranking is (1) American, (2) English, (3) French, (4) German, (5) Norwegian, (6) Russian, (7) Greek, (8) and (9) Japanese and Chinese tied, (10) Hindu. For the Indiana group, the first seven are identical with those given by the Columbia group, followed by (8) Japanese, (9) Hindu, (10) Chinese.

No analysis of selective factors is made in the preceding study. Perhaps "friendliness brings contact" is just as true as "contact brings friendliness." At any rate, several lines of evidence do point toward the close association of familiarity and favorable attitude under some conditions. Such a simple solution to problems of racial antagonism would, of course, be only too welcome. But it is a far more reasonable hypothesis that contact *of a friendly sort* brings friendliness, while contact *under conditions of conflict* brings antagonism.

Several bits of evidence concerning attitudes toward the Negro readily lend themselves to this latter interpretation. Thus, for example, in one experiment attitudes of northern students in a southern university became steadily more unfavorable until by the third or fourth year they approximated the attitudes of southern-born students. We do not imply, of course, that such changes were solely the result of these students' own experiences with Negroes. The authors, indeed, believe them to be largely borrowed from university associates. But their experiences, whether direct or indirect, were surely very different from earlier ones in their northern communities, where less Negro discrimination is to be found. Replies received in connection with another inquiry suggest, similarly, that the different attitudes of northern and of southern whites toward Negroes are functions of their differing kinds of contact with them. Replies to the following two questions appear below:

"Is there a Negro whom you would regard as a friend?" and "Do you consider the Negro 100, 75, 50, or 25 per cent the white man's equal intellectually?" In spite of the fact that recent evidence re-

	Per Cent Answering "Yes"	Per Cent Rating not over 25 Per Cent as Intelligent
Columbia College...........	31	19
Northern adults.............	36	44
University of North Carolina.	72	30
Southern adults.............	77	63

garding intelligence test scores gives little or no support for assigning Negroes lesser degrees of native capacity than whites, we find here that southern groups, having greater familiarity with Negroes, allow their judgments to be warped more than do comparable northern groups. Such extreme opinions as those reflected by the statement that the Negro is not more than 25 per cent the white man's equal intellectually are assuredly the aftermath and not the forerunner of firmly held attitudes.

The experimental situation arranged by F. T. Smith (cf. page 958) may be mentioned in contrast to the conditions reflected by the preceding studies. The vivid and thoroughly pleasant experiences to which his subjects were submitted were followed by striking changes toward more favorable attitudes, most of which still remained after a lapse of one year. It should be noted, in passing, that a considerable degree of the "pleasantness" of their experiences was attributable to the prestige of the eminent Negroes whom they met.

Familiarity, as such, thus appears to bear no necessary relationship to favorableness of interracial attitudes. This is not to say, of course, that experiences with the members of other groups do not affect attitudes toward them. It is simply a reminder that the particular nature of the experience must be known. At certain cultural and economic levels, as, for example, those characterized by students at International House, friendly types of experience may predominate. It is easy to point out, on the other hand, that anti-Negro prejudice has increased in the North *pari passu* with increasing numbers of Negroes migrating from the South. The relevant consideration here is not simply that northern whites have had increasingly frequent contacts with Negroes, but rather that they have had more contacts characterized by economic and other types of friction. The nature of these Negro-white contacts in the North was predestined in view of the conditions of their importation in many cases, the living quarters available for them, and the industrial competition which, even without the injection of the race issue, was already severe. Too little research on Negro-white attitudes has taken adequate account of the cultural conditions under which the subjects had lived or the types of experience which had characterized previous contacts.

The kinds of experience, whatever they are, which lead to the possession of information may be similar to the kinds of experience involved in familiarity and contact. Is there any known relation between attitudes and relevant information? In the chart, pages 998-999, are included the results of a few studies bearing on the problem. Most of them, it will be noted, deal with attitudes toward races and nationalities.

By far the most startling relationship shown is that appearing in a study (Watson, chart, page 998) prepared for the Research Committee of the American Group, Institute of Pacific Relations, before the 1927 Conference of this Institute, in Honolulu. An elaborate questionnaire was prepared, with the aid of both oriental and occidental students, on the interracial attitudes prevailing between Americans and Pacific peoples. Some of the questions have to do with "How you feel," the subject checking, among a number of phrases, that one which most adequately expressed his first response to a stimulus phrase. The phrase, *Japanese Exclusion Act*, for instance, is followed by the choice of responses: (1) Insult; (2) Unfortunate; (3) Necessary; (4) Desirable; (5) Doesn't go far enough; (6) Must be undone. Another section of the inquiry begins with the phrase, "What you think," the subject responding to each of a series of sentences by checking symbols standing for "true"; "probably or partly true"; "in doubt" ("divided," "open question"); "probably or partly false"; "false." The subject must characterize by one of these symbols the sentences, *Japan is preparing to fight the United States;* or *an American doing business in China ought to be willing to abide by Chinese law, even though he con-*

SOME STUDIES OF THE RELATIONSHIP

AUTHOR	SUBJECTS	ATTITUDE MEASURED
Biddle	200 high school seniors and college freshmen.	International (Pacific problems).
Bolton	70 college freshmen and sophomores; controls.	Negro.
Carlson	357 college students.	Certainty of opinions concerning facts about presidential candidates in 1928.
Chen	519 students in several colleges.	Chinese and Japanese rights in Manchuria.
Hedrick	49 parents.	Self-reliance of children.
Kornhauser	400 college students of economics.	Economic.
Manry	Several hundred college students.	"World citizenship."
Reckless and Bringen	246 graduates and undergraduates from 6 colleges.	Negro.
Symonds	431 students from 8th grade to college seniors.	Social, political, and economic liberalism.
Uhrbrock	96 clerical workers in 12 firms.	Their own employment.
Watson	Over 3000 adults and students.	Chinese and Japanese.
Wrightstone	412 pupils, grades 9 to 12.	Economic liberalism.

OF INFORMATION TO ATTITUDES

INFORMATION CONCERNING	RELATIONSHIP
Foreign countries bordering on Pacific.	r of prejudice and information = $-.357 \pm .04$ for total scores; $-.027$, $-.207$, and $-.266$ for Philippines, China, and Japan, respectively.
Negro.	No reliable correlation for controls, or for experimental group either before or after gain in knowledge.
Presidential candidates.	$r = +.21$; those best informed below average, though not at bottom, in certainty.
Manchuria.	Those best informed offer greatest resistance to Japanese propaganda, but reverse not true.
Child development.	Gain in knowledge equals critical ratio of 4.73; gain in attitude change equals critical ratio of 3.41.
Economics.	Consistent improvement in information, for each quarter of year. Considerably less change in attitudes, which became somewhat less extreme and more liberal.
International affairs.	$r = +.69$.
Negro.	$r = .64 \pm .025$ for all subjects; r's range from .30 to .88 for various groups; rho of medians for 16 groupings = .96.
Similar items.	$r = +.28$; information increases steadily with increasing age, but little change in attitude with age.
Their own firms and products.	$r = -.01$.
Same.	$r = .82 \pm .04$ for Japanese; $.70 \pm .06$ for Chinese nationalism.
Historical knowledge.	rho (computed from rank order) = .58.

siders it inferior to that of his own country, etc. Some of the issues deal with missions, disarmament, and other matters not exclusively associated with oriental-white relations. The questionnaire also gathers information as to age, sex, race, occupation, schooling, church membership, reading habits, and other important personal data applying to those who answer the questions.

Ten thousand copies were sent out, and about one-third of them were returned. In some groups, such as high school classes, 100 per cent of those given the questionnaire filled it out, whereas in some of the others, such as farmer groups, the number responding was very small, so that the factor of selection seriously jeopardizes the results. The amazing range of social groups studied is indicated by a few samples: University of Chicago class in European history; students of naval science, University of Washington; Methodist Young People, Oak Park, Illinois; business girls, Houston, Texas; Palo Alto (California) Kiwanis Club; Ohio clothing workers; Richmond (Virginia) business men; New York Urban League (for Negroes); Farmington (Missouri) housewives; prisoners, Bridewell Jail, Chicago; Methodist Episcopal Church, Waterloo, Iowa.

Some of the items in the questionnaire had to do with matters of information. In general, information scores on relevant issues were associated with favorable attitudes toward the Japanese ($r = +.82 \pm .04$) and toward Chinese nationalism ($r = +.70 \pm .06$). The influence of information—or perhaps we should say familiarity —is shown rather dramatically in the fact that a favorable response toward *chow-mein* is correlated $+.67$ with the total favorable reaction to all questions relating to China (the correlation is based upon lumping together ten groups of very diverse questions so that the figure probably ought to be reduced slightly). As Watson points out, this "sounds too journalistic to be a matter of sober fact." Here, as elsewhere in the problem as to the relation between information and attitude, we are dealing not with a simple and obvious causal relation but with the dependence of both of our correlated variables upon a variable (or a group of variables) which is not directly measured.

Other results must, in general, be regarded as confirming these findings concerning international attitudes and information, though correlations are, of course, somewhat lower where subjects are homogeneous groups of students. It is interesting to note that in several of these studies positive and reliable correlations are presented between intelligence and *both* information and favorable attitude. Partial correlations are nowhere offered, but many lines of evidence suggest that certain independent factors influence simultaneously both of the variables measured. It is, of course, not impossible that increasing information in itself leads to changes of attitudes under some circumstances; but it seems more probable that such university influences as those of instructors and associates act in parallel fashion upon both information and opinion. The evidence cited on pages 939 ff. concerning the emotional determinants of belief lends strength to this interpretation.

Altogether, our rather meager present evidence suggests that those who know most about other races and peoples tend to have favorable attitudes about them, particularly in the case of more distant peoples and probably less so in the case of those more frequently met, such as Negroes in this country. And the conclusion also seems justified that "liberal" attitudes tend to be found among those most adequately informed on relevant issues. Both of these conclusions must be regarded as highly tentative, however; our present understanding of the whole problem is colored by the particular type of information which is related to attitudes, and by the peculiarly selected nature of most of the groups which have been studied.

We have been led repeatedly, in perusing these investigations, to the threshold of home and family as, in all probability, a major determiner of attitudes, though the previous attitude studies have not approached the matter directly. What, after all, is known about the effect upon attitudes of the continued experiences of association with a particular family?

One approach to the measurement of family influence upon religious attitudes is getting a general picture of home emphases and practices during childhood. One of the first objective studies of this type made use of 60 sophomore students as subjects. Religious attitudes were measured in terms of both *interest* and *belief*, by the method of degree of acceptance of questionnaire statements. Degree of present religious *practice* was ascertained by similar methods. These variables were then related to scores representing amount of religious *training*, measured by subjects' ratings of their own homes in six different respects. (In spite of the small number of items, a reliability coefficient of .92 was obtained.) From these data it appeared that amount of religious training bore little relationship to present interest or belief in religion, though barely reliable positive correlations are reported. When all the data are summarized concerning present attitude toward religion and degree to which religion was emphasized at home, no consistent or reliable relationship between them is demonstrated, but the correlation between home emphasis and present practice is definite—approximately .4. This discrepancy between present belief and practice, incidentally, is typical of the discrepancies which have led to skepticism in some quarters regarding the validity of verbal measurements of attitudes. We need only remark that, in the first place, the measure of practice was in this case also verbal, and secondly (as we pointed out on page 912), that freely expressed statements of belief may be "truer" than behavior which is subject to conformity-enforcing pressures. Apart from questions of validity, the discrepancy may be set down as an example of the lag of folkways behind changes in folklore, so often reported by the anthropologist.

A more comprehensive study along similar lines has recently been made. Anonymous replies were obtained to an elaborate questionnaire, the 384 subjects being adults, half of whom were men. Most of them were Protestant church members, but had a wide range of religious belief. Many different scores were obtained from the questionnaires, classified as follows: conservatism of religious belief (odd-even reliability, .914), prayer habits, "religious values," early religious influences, child-parent relations, and "life patterns," or certain personality traits. The last of these were obtained from self-ratings supplemented by ratings of two associates of each subject. The only clearly significant correlations with conservatism of belief are the following: childhood Sunday school attendance, .43; parents' church attendance, .39; and parents' "positive religious influence," .39. Another group of factors labeled "adult religious life" shows correlations with various early religious influences rang-ing between .28 and .50. All this, of course, is not in the least sur-prising. But these low positive correlations supplement a consider-able array of other evidence to show that adults subjected in childhood to strong religious influences are likely to maintain more than the average degree of religious belief and practice, though with many individual defections.

Nothing, of course, is more characteristic of our civilization than the fact of being brought up in a family. One of the most ele-mental questions, therefore, is that of the relationship of family members with respect to various attitudes. We have in mind not the effects of particular types of training, as in the last two studies, but simply the question of what relationships actually exist in unselected families.

The problem seems almost to have been ignored. One report is available concerning a special study of 331 pairs of siblings of senior high school age who were given the Newman-Kulp-Davidson In-ternational Attitudes test. Correlations were as follows: for 91 pairs of brothers, .29; for 85 pairs of sisters, .41; for 155 brother-sister pairs, .30; and for all pairs, .32. Other data (cf. page 916) for 346 pairs of siblings covering a much wider age range result in the following correlations: attitude toward Church, .60; toward war, .37; and toward Communism, .48. These coefficients, of course, do not tell us *what* family influences are responsible; we know only that the sum total of experiences shared by the children of any given family but varying among families, results in a certain intra-family community of attitude. As to why resemblances are not greater, it is clear that age is not a factor in either of these studies. Sex plays a very slight rôle when such factors as socio-economic status and political and religious affiliation of parents are held con-stant. Neither is the amount of education a differentiating factor. We are forced to conclude that two sets of forces are responsible for the rather wide variations among siblings: personality differences, including child-parent and sibling relationships; and those com-plicated chains of events which result in different circles of acquaint-ances and different spheres of influence among members of the same family.

Below is reproduced a table of parent-child correlations in three attitudes. (The manner in which the data were collected is described on page 916.) All possible pairs among 548 families are included in the zero order correlations; the partial correlations, based only upon 190 families of two parents, indicate the relationship to one parent where the influence of the other parent has been held constant.

PARENT-CHILD CORRELATIONS IN ATTITUDE

	Church		War		Communism	
	Zero	Partial	Zero	Partial	Zero	Partial
Mothers-sons..............	.575	.243	.454	.316	.580	.502
Mothers-daughters.........	.691	.460	.430	.330	.493	.238
Fathers-sons...............	.642	.284	.457	.265	.542	.080
Fathers-daughters..........	.648	.210	.434	.304	.621	.467
All siblings................	.599		.369		.475	
Mothers-fathers............	.757		.434		.578	

Children are thus as closely related to their parents, in two of these attitudes, as parents are to each other, in spite of the age difference of an entire generation. Only in attitude toward the Church is the father-mother relationship closer. Children resemble their parents more closely than their siblings by slight margins. This may, perhaps, be explained in the following way: siblings diverge not only from their parents, but they also tend to diverge from each other (cf. the evidence cited on page 917). They start, however, from a common point, so that sibling correlations, though lower than those for parents and children, are positive. This suggests that the personal relationships among siblings may be fully as important as those between parents and children.

The surprising differences among the four parent-child partial correlations in attitude toward Communism may, of course, be the result of some unknown selective factors, though numbers of subjects and consistency of other findings argue against it. If it be true that attitude toward Communism has, in recent years, been a likely field for the expression of parental antagonisms, and if one subscribes to the Oedipus theory of personality, he might find evidence in these data for relating the two phenomena. We shall content ourselves with pointing out the distinct differences in partial correlations between attitudes toward Communism and toward the

Church. Psychoanalytic theories may well be relevant in one area and not in the other, or in entirely different ways.

That other than personality factors enter into parent-child relationships in attitude is also evident from data presented in the same study. Coefficients based upon all parent-child relationships, and classified according to religious affiliation, age of children, socio-economic status, and parent-child age difference are offered. The last of these plays no rôle whatever, as the coefficients are constant for all groups. Coefficients are rather low for Protestant and Catholic groups, and high for those with no religious affiliation, the latter group being, of course, far less homogeneous than the other two. The relative influence of age and of socio-economic status is best shown in the following table, in which parent-child correlations are presented at each of three occupational levels, and in each of three age groupings. While the numbers of cases involved in the various classifications are not large, certain trends appear which would otherwise remain concealed. Chief among these is the fact

PARENT-CHILD CORRELATIONS IN ATTITUDE

	Occupational Level		
	I-II[a]	III	IV, V, VI
Church:			
Age 19 and under	.500 (72)[b]	.707 (212)	.760 (175)
Age 20 to 23	.476 (50)	.543 (114)	.624 (93)
Age 24 and over	.624 (57)	.551 (79)	.858 (53)
War:			
Age 19 and under	.243 (71)	.452 (210)	.660 (169)
Age 20 to 23	.262 (61)	.214 (115)	.537 (90)
Age 24 and over	.267 (56)	.397 (74)	.317 (52)
Communism:			
Age 19 and under	.710 (68)	.578 (210)	.553 (158)
Age 20 to 23	.167 (60)	.509 (111)	.574 (82)
Age 24 and over	.253 (57)	.378 (74)	.768 (52)

[a]I indicates the highest level, and VI the lowest.
[b]Figures in parentheses indicate the number of subjects.

that parent-child relationships vary more definitely and more consistently with socio-economic status than with age. With but one exception (attitude toward Communism at the lowest age level) the coefficients are higher at the lowest occupational level than at the highest, and are, in general, intermediate between the two at the middle occupational levels. The rather surprisingly high correlations at age 24 and above are undoubtedly due to the fact that subjects of those ages were partially selected as still living with or within easy reach of their parents. If we allow for this, correlation declines slightly with increasing age, as might be foreseen.

To the question, then, "How largely is one's development of attitudes dependent upon those held by one's parents?" the answer will be somewhat as follows: At the present time parental influence upon some attitudes appears to be considerable, particularly at the lower occupational levels; the degree of such influence declines slightly but inconsistently with increasing age; and is to an unknown extent dependent upon personal relationships to both parents and siblings.

So much for the family institution. What about religious institutions? We have frequently spoken of groups to which allegiance is owed as particularly potent forces in the growth of attitudes. Unfortunately, little evidence has been gathered concerning adults, among whom allegiance to church bodies is certainly stronger than among contemporary college students from whom most of the available data have been obtained. Mean scores according to Thurstone and Chave's scale of attitude toward the church are presented below according to religious affiliation. The three sources quoted resemble closely the results reported by several others. It is apparent from these data not only that widely separated student groups are very similar with respect to this attitude, and very similar to one group of adults, but that there are characteristic differences for each group of religious affiliates, as well as characteristic age and sex differences within each group. (Low scores, in this table, indicate favorable attitude toward the church.)

MEAN SCORES IN ATTITUDE TOWARD THE CHURCH

	Protestant	Catholic	Jews	Unaffiliated
Sons...............	3.99 (141)[a]	2.83 (122)	5.60 (95)	6.41 (76)
Daughters..........	3.35 (172)	2.74 (114)	4.74 (93)	6.02 (70)
Mothers...........	2.79 (175)	2.58 (113)	4.56 (84)	5.89 (67)
Fathers...........	3.22 (138)	2.94 (123)	4.90 (109)	7.11 (79)
Students (A)........	3.00 (172)	1.75 (30)	6.50 (8)	6.50 (9)
Students (B)........	3.97 (463)	2.90 (72)	5.44 (176)	

[a]Figures in parentheses refer to number of subjects.

By far the most complete data concerning church affiliations are to be found in a comparison of Protestant denominations. Early in 1931, 50,000 questionnaires concerning militarism and pacifism were sent to clergymen all over this country; of these, more than 18,000 were returned. Three years later nearly 100,000 questionnaires containing identical items (as well as some others) were mailed to clergymen of the same denominations, about 19,500 being returned. Denominational differences in responses are readily apparent, and the large number of respondents lends confidence in their reliability, despite the rather small percentage of ballots returned. The fact, moreover, that the rank orders of percentages of pacifistic responses of the several denominations are almost identical in 1931 and 1934 indicates that we have at least an approximation to characteristic replies from each denomination. The second questionnaire included, in addition to the previous seven questions regarding pacifism, seven others concerning economic liberalism. Below are given the percentages of pacifistic and of economically liberal replies to two representative questions. The order of denominations is from most to least pacifistic, and from most to least economically liberal (1934 data), according to *total* scores.

PER CENT OF "NO" REPLIES TO THE QUESTION, "DO YOU FAVOR MILITARY TRAINING IN OUR PUBLIC HIGH SCHOOLS AND UNIVERSITIES?"

Methodist Episcopal	91	United Brethren	86
Evangelical Synod	90	Unitarian, Universalist	82
Disciples of Christ	84	Baptist	81
Congregational	83	Presbyterian	78
Reformed	88	Protestant Episcopal	56

PER CENT OF "YES" REPLIES TO THE QUESTION, "DO YOU FAVOR A SYSTEM OF COMPULSORY UNEMPLOYMENT INSURANCE UNDER GOVERNMENT ADMINISTRATION?"

Jewish Rabbis	95	Protestant Episcopal	69
Congregational	71	Presbyterian	61
Methodist Episcopal	65	Baptist	60
Unitarian, Universalist	76	United Brethren	49
Evangelical	67	Church of the Brethren	37
Disciples of Christ	63	Lutheran	51
Reformed	68	Miscellaneous	51

That characteristic attitudes regarding both pacifism and economic attitudes should be found within these Protestant groups, whereas equally significant differences have not elsewhere been reported, may simply be due to the enormous number of respondents. It is probable, however, that these clergymen have been more influenced by institutional points of view than have laymen, who have been the subjects in other studies. This explanation would reinforce our thesis concerning the importance of organized groups in the development of attitudes.

Many comparisons have been made among many religious groupings in this country in respect to various attitudes. According to one study, for example, Christian students are reliably less pacifistic than either Jews or those with no religious affiliation. The same investigator enlisted the aid of thirty judges who rated each of ten church groups (those most frequently represented by his students) for conservatism "in general religious life, such as belief, rituals, and activities." The rank order correlation between these pooled ratings of conservatism and militarism scores of students in the same church groups was .54. In another study the attitudes of 215 university seniors were measured toward prohibition, the reality of God, war, Communism, and birth control. "Jewish undergraduates were the most liberal or radical . . . and Catholics the most conservative, except toward prohibition. Protestants were intermediate except toward prohibition, in regard to which they were the most conservative. The differences are consistent and in most instances are large enough to be statistically significant. . . . Religious affiliation of a student is an important factor in the determination of attitudes on these social questions." It is, the author continues, a factor more important than that of sex or of school training.

A totally different kind of investigation may be cited as a final example of the influence of religious bodies. After preliminary work with a considerably longer scale, a five-step test of social distance was so devised as to be reliable, unambiguous in wording, and equidistant between adjacent steps, which were as follows:

A. If I wanted to marry, I would marry one of them.
B. I would be willing to have as a guest for a meal.
C. I prefer to have merely as an acquaintance to whom one talks on meeting in the street.
D. I do not enjoy the companionship of these people.
E. I wish someone would kill all these individuals.
F. I know nothing about this group; I cannot express an attitude.

The test was given twice, with a one-month interval, to 170 freshmen at the American University of Beirut, Syria. The groups for whom it was filled out included 15 national and 11 religious groups, as well as 3 educational and 5 economic groupings, arbitrarily designated. The group of subjects was so extremely heterogeneous in origin that there were no less than 90 different intergroup distances for nationality, 66 for religion, and 15 for economic status. (By intergroup distance is meant the degree of acceptance of a Turk by an Armenian, for example, or that of a Moslem by a Jew.) Since replies were anonymous, retest reliability coefficients could not be computed from individual scores, but the reliabilities for intergroup distances proved to be .91, .70, and .96 for religious, national, and economic groups, respectively. That the instrument possessed a considerable degree of validity is suggested by the fact that the two intergroup distances which were expected to be greatest, viz., that of Armenians for Turks and of Palestinian Arabs for Jews, actually were so.

Some exceedingly interesting generalizations emerge. It was found, for example, that the distance indicated by any majority group toward any minority group (i.e., in their home community) was large. All groups showed various degrees of favor toward some others, and various degrees of disfavor to still others, so that their averages were nearly constant; but each group tended to be regarded with a characteristic degree of favor, ranging from very high to distinctly low, by all others. As far as attitudes among nationality groups are concerned, it is clear that neither geographic proximity nor abundance of contacts has much to do with them. "Definite acts of a benevolent or malevolent sort" come much closer to explaining the highly variable distances among nationalities. Thus, that of Armenians toward Americans is very low, as is that of Iraqis for British; recent historical incidents have laid a basis for these favorable attitudes. As for educational groupings, the distances are all "horizontal," i.e., all groups desire to rise, being more friendly to those of greater than to those of lesser education. Economic group distances show this same desire to rise, but only within rather definite limits. As the author expresses it, they would "prefer to stay in their familiar in-groups rather than to become too intimate with a very different out-group; . . . they would rather go down one level than up two levels."

But to return to our immediate concern, it was found that the greatest variations in distances were those among religious groups. Attitudes associated with religious affiliations toward those of other faiths seemed, indeed, to transcend in strength those identified with all other groupings. The dominance of religious forces in the Near East is pointed out: residences, schools, legal codes, even political representation, all are likely to be on the basis of religious affiliation. All this, of course, is radically different from what we have found about religious groupings in this country, and reminds us once more that we can speak with any certainty of the influence of such institutions upon attitudes only within a given culture, and even then provided only that it is a relatively stable culture. If religious affiliations are associated with a variety of attitudes far more intimately in the Near East than in contemporary America it is because there, to a far greater extent than here, the dominant interests of individuals are, partially in supposition and partially in fact, directly linked up with their status as members of religious groups.

Such findings as these might suggest that whatever it is in a given community that determines the economic status of a group will be found to be closely related to many of the attitudes of that group. This, of course, is one fruitful hypothesis, but it is not to be pursued to the exclusion of all others. The reader will not have failed to note that some of the attitudes associated with religious affiliation in this country must surely be in part functions of the different economic status of the various groups. For example, members of the Protestant Episcopal Church represent a different economic sampling from those of the Methodist Episcopal Church, from whom they differ greatly in attitude toward military training (cf. page 1007). But such factors of more immediate origin are hopelessly intertwined with those of more historic nature. Thus, members of the body of Friends are much like the Protestant Episcopal group in economic status, but like the Methodists in attitude toward military training. Such considerations do not, in our opinion, render any less useful the hypothesis that economic status must have an important influence upon attitudes. They simply serve as a warning of the necessity of examining, in every case, the historic reasons for the relationship of particular groups to particular attitudes, and of the further necessity of inquiring precisely how, in any given case, economic status is related to membership in any given group. Economic status may be a determinant or a consequent of institutional affiliation, but institutions are more potently modifiers of attitudes than selectors of those individuals who already possess "the right" attitudes.

Another secondary grouping, presumably of importance in affecting attitudes, is that of racial or national background. One effective demonstration of the rôle of ancestry in determining racial preferences may be cited. Paired comparisons for fifteen races were made by 1096 students from seven colleges, the range of subjects from the various colleges being from 62 to 211. The odd-even reliability, as measured by frequency of choice of each race, ranged from .967 to .9995. The intercorrelations for six of the colleges, in order of preference for the various races, ranged from .975 to .991, indicating a startling degree of conformity. The six colleges were in six different states, one eastern, one far-western, one southern, and three middle-western. The seventh college was New York University, 71 per cent of these subjects being of Jewish parentage. Correlations of order of preference between the first six and the seventh colleges ranged from .843 to .894. The range of individual preference scores, moreover, was smaller at New York University than at any of the other colleges. All this shows, precisely as we might expect, that racial background has much to do with racial preferences. But as a matter of fact, this effect is surprising small. The correlation between order of preference for the six colleges and the seventh is .866 *when* Jews are included as one of the races; if they are omitted, the correlation rises to .938 (our calculations).

The relationship between ancestry and racial preference is further shown by correlation methods. Ancestry from one or more of fifteen races was mentioned by 65 per cent of the subjects, and twelve of them were mentioned frequently enough to be included in the calculations. The correlation between number of grandparents among one or more of these twelve races and scale value for the same races turns out to be .814. It is also shown that the highly uniform order of preference is largely determined by the actual racial composition of our population. Using as one variable the foreign-born population of each nationality from 1890 to 1910 (one generation ago) and the scale values for the same races as the other, we find a correlation between them of .656. Though numbers of cases in these calculations are small, the study is important, not only as showing widespread conformity in racial preferences, but as showing at least some of the reasons for the particular order of preference—as well as for exceptions to that order.

One of the world's great laboratories for the study of racial attitudes is to be found in Hawaii, where both racial amalgamation and the coexistence of more or less insulated racial groups are to be found. Information was obtained, in one study, as to the racial preferences of 190 adult "first-generation" Japanese in Hawaii, and of 1088 "second-generation" Japanese from the second grade to advanced university status. Adults were asked to indicate degree of preference for each of eleven racial groups as playmates for their children. The younger subjects simply ranked the same groups in order of preference as companions. The resulting orders of preference were almost identical for the two age groups. No significant urban-rural differences appeared, nor was physiognomic appearance related to degree of acceptance. Thus Koreans were ranked lower than "other Caucasians," and Filipinos were ranked only above Puerto Ricans. The single determining factor appeared to be social and economic status. The order of preference, indeed, was very close to that resulting from the ranking, by another large group of adults, of the same eleven groups for "highest status." Thus the "other Caucasians" group, preferred above all others except the Japanese themselves, is financially and politically dominant in the islands. The three least preferred groups are Spanish, Puerto Ricans, and Filipinos; all of these are minority groups with little cohesion, and the last of them, having only recently arrived, has the lowest occupational status of all groups. Many social psychologists have long maintained that, under such conditions, race prejudice is largely composed of caste prejudice, but most of them have not had such clear-cut quantitative data as evidence.

Another occupational attitude apparently related to national background is that toward public employment. L. D. White's work has been previously described (page 987); he found the prestige value of public employment to be highest among the foreign-born, and to decrease steadily with length of residence in this country. Here, again, we have no "purely racial" characteristics, but almost certainly a reflection of the fact that in countries from which these people emigrated public employees enjoyed both higher status and standards of living than they themselves—perhaps beyond anything to which they dared aspire—whereas in this country public employment is not necessarily beyond their reach, and perhaps even less desirable than positions they hold after a few years of advancement. Whatever the reasons, certain occupational attitudes are definitely related to a certain racial and national ancestry.

Still other attitudes have, in a few studies, been found to be related to national background. One group of students of American parentage is reported to be more favorable to war, by a difference equal to 2.27 times its S.D., than those of foreign parentage. The same investigator also found, curiously enough, that children of like parents (i.e., both American, or both German) were consistently more favorable to war than those of unlike parentage, and the difference is reliable. According to another study, however, students of foreign-born parents or grandparents made *lower* internationalist scores than those whose parents were of American birth, by an almost reliable difference. Just how comparable these two groups of students are is unknown. But in spite of the reputed tendency in children of immigrants to "Americanize" themselves posthaste, the national groups from which they spring have widespread influence upon some of their attitudes.

One of the *bêtes noires* of attitude research is the constantly recurring suspicion that two or more groups being compared may differ partly because of differing socio-economic status. Just what is known about variation of attitudes with economic or occupational level? Some bits of information are at hand concerning occupational attitudes. Thus L. D. White's subjects of lower status (cf. page 922) were distinctly more favorable to public employment than were those of a more favored level. A considerable number of the former, however, were undoubtedly of foreign birth, and the failure of the others to prefer private employment may have been simply a reflection of the fact that their own status was lower than what they supposed to be that of public employees. According to an investigation already mentioned (page 918), mean score in attitude toward employment was higher for foremen than for workers in each of twelve factories; the critical ratio for 400 foremen and 3934 workers was 20.7. The 96 clerical workers occupied a position midway between these two groups, and differed from each of them by reliable margins.

Most of the attitude studies in which socio-economic status has been considered have dealt with some phase of "liberalism" or "conservatism"; we shall cite one of them. After a careful perusal of literature concerning Fascist Italy and Nazi Germany, a list of 35 statements, all favorable to "Fascist" doctrines, was drawn up. The concepts originally included were the following: nationalism (versus internationalism), racial antagonism, anti-radicalism, middle-class consciousness ("superior attitude toward the working class"), imperialism, militarism, and "benevolent despot or strong-man philosophy of government." An item analysis of the responses of over 200 students resulted in the selection of 18 statements clearly distinguishing those with highest from those with lowest scores. These 18 statements indicated that the last three of the seven concepts were not closely related to the first four, for those subjects. The briefer list, when submitted to about 400 adults representing Minnesota farmers and all occupational levels from Chicago, yielded satisfactory reliability coefficients (.84 and .88, respectively, for two groups of 60 and 80). The following variations with occupational level are shown: the income group from $1000 to $5000 showed less Fascist attitudes than those above and those below that income range. The most Fascist occupational groups were office workers, business men, and "high-class professionals"; manual workers, farmers, and less privileged professional groups were least so. The business group made higher Fascist scores than the professional group by a reliable margin. Members of labor organizations were decidedly less Fascist than others, the critical ratio being 3.58. The author is carefully tentative about the Fascist label as applied to the attitudes measured, but they are clearly related to those commonly designated as economic and international conservatism.

Such findings may be considered representative within the area of "radical" attitudes, though measures of more distinctly "liberal" attitudes (e.g., Harper's Social Study) have frequently been found to yield the highest scores for professional groups. If such a distinction may be made on the basis of the degree to which "class" concepts enter into the attitude, then the following summary may be offered regarding occupational status and radicalism: in general, if sex and age classifications are ignored, the groups representing unskilled labor and slightly skilled personal and public service are most conservative, but the professional and business group, as a whole, is only slightly less so. The middle groups, comprising skilled and semi-skilled trades, clerical, and minor managerial positions, are consistently least conservative, according to present evidence.

A methodological note is in order, finally. While many investigations include data on socio-economic status, most of them reveal no significant variations with attitude. It is probable that, in most cases, this is not because no such relationship exists, but rather that they have been concealed, in fact, doubly cloaked. Most of the measures of socio-economic status, in the first place, are based upon income, though such other considerations as occupational security, status, degree of organization, etc., are much more closely related to the processes by which attitudes are formed. The classifications, in other words, are artificial for this purpose. Other equally important factors, in the second place, are often concealed by the form in which the data are presented. In view of the complicated network of influences responsible for attitude formation, it seems positively *naïve* to expect to find simple correlations between socio-economic status and a particular attitude. Future research into this problem must include sufficient numbers of subjects so that such factors as age, sex, religious affiliation, intelligence, and even certain personality traits may each be held constant while the effect of socio-economic status is studied.

To what extent are groups in certain types of communities or certain geographic areas characterized by the possession of particular attitudes? We should like to be able to answer this question regarding widely different cultural areas in different parts of the world; but linguistic difficulties and an unfortunate divergence of interests and methods of procedure among social psychologists in various countries have resulted in an almost total absence of comparable data. The most noteworthy exception to this lamentable situation is Lapiere's study of interracial attitudes. He managed to obtain information, apparently without revealing the fact that he was collecting data, from hundreds of individuals in France and England concerning their attitudes toward colored people. Whenever a suitable occasion presented itself in the course of his travels in France, he asked the simple question, "Would you let a good Negro live at your home?" Replies were classified as in the accompanying table. The classification of economic status is made, because any possible better method was lacking, in terms of the places where the interviewees were met, such as cheap café or first-class railway carriage.

	Number of Cases	With Prejudice	Doubtful	Without Prejudice
Rural	227	8 (4%)	38 (17%)	181 (79%)
Urban	201	37 (18%)	58 (29%)	106 (53%)
Upper class	36	24 (67%)	9 (25%)	3 (8%)
Middle class	147	11 (7%)	60 (41%)	76 (52%)
Lower class	257	10 (4%)	27 (10%)	220 (86%)

Certain cultural and historic circumstances are cited as contributing to the striking increase of prejudice in successively higher economic levels, as well as to the less well-marked urban-rural differences. The latter are in part explained, for example, by traditions associated with labor conflicts in seaboard cities.

As for the relative freedom from prejudice among the total French group—a condition almost incredible to Americans—Lapiere obtained further corroborative evidence. Hotel managers and innkeepers were interrogated as to their willingness to admit Negroes.

Twenty-four of thirty-one thus interviewed expressed complete willingness; the seven managers who were doubtful or expressed unwillingness to entertain Negroes were, with one or two exceptions, those whose guests included many Americans. Since admission to a hotel is dependent to a far larger degree upon community opinion than upon the personal preference of the manager, the testimony even of so few hotel managers as this speaks volumes for the differences in attitude toward Negroes among French and Americans.

Lapiere then continued his investigations in England. Seizing, as before, upon opportunities to introduce the question in a natural and unobtrusive manner, he asked in several sections of the country, "Would you let children associate with those of good colored people?" The different form of the question was evidently in anticipation of finding greater degrees of prejudice than in France. This, at any rate, turned out to be the case, as seen in the accompanying table where responses are classified in the same manner as before. The contrast between the two countries is great, not only

	Number of Cases	With Prejudice	Doubtful	Without Prejudice
Upper class......	44	32 (73%)	7 (16%)	5 (11%)
Middle class.....	174	135 (78%)	31 (17%)	8 (5%)
Lower class......	97	87 (90%)	9 (9%)	1 (1%)

in respect to the much larger degree of prejudice in England, but also in respect to the class differences which, though slight, are in the reverse direction from those found in France. Sixteen of twenty hotel managers interviewed indicated that they would exclude both Negroes and natives of India. Attitudes toward these two groups were in general much alike. Lapiere is unable to find satisfactory explanations for the origins of these national differences in racial attitudes. They must certainly be imbedded deep in the cultural traditions of the two countries, and probably nothing short of an analysis of the interplay of imperialistic ventures with public opinion in both countries will serve to disclose them.

Another opportunity for comparison of this with another country is afforded by a report of the occupational attitudes of children in the government schools of Russia. Hand labor, even at unskilled levels such as that of digging ditches, is rated higher than such

occupations as banking and the law. This, perhaps, is only tantamount to saying that the intensive educational program of the
Russians regarding workers as a class has been highly successful.
The responses of these children must not, however, be regarded as
mere parrot-like repetitions of what they had been taught. The
question had to do with the *contributions* made by individuals of
various occupations, not with the attractiveness of those occupations.
The latter question was put by another investigator to more
than a thousand Russian children, most of whom were sons and
daughters of farmers and manual workers. The overwhelming majority indicated a preference for various types of intellectual work
rather than for such occupations as farming and housework. This
discrimination between attractiveness and contribution of occupations is particularly illuminating in view of certain findings concerning occupational attitudes of American college men (cf. Anderson, chart, page 982), who tended to equate the contribution of occupations with the incomes to be derived through them.

Within this country, attitude comparisons have frequently been
made of rural and urban groups. A comparison of three widely differing types of student bodies may be considered as fairly typical,
within the area of "liberal" attitudes. Vetter's attitude scale was
used; it covers seven groups of issues—political, sex and family,
individual freedom, economic, religious, international, and interracial, and gives five opportunities for response to each statement.
Replies, which are classified as reactionary, conservative, neutral,
liberal, or radical, are summarized below. The bearing of these

	New York University	Washington University	North Carolina State College
Reactionary and conservative..	1316	1664	1855
Liberal and radical..........	1776	1428	1261

results upon our immediate problem is somewhat distorted by the
fact that the New York University group was 80 per cent Jewish,
thus introducing an extraneous factor. At North Carolina State College 32 per cent of the subjects were sons of farmers, and the Washington University group lay somewhere between the other two in
the percentage of urbanites. In so far as such terms as "conservatism"
and "reaction" have any meaning when applied to so many diverse

issues at once, those characteristics are more frequent among rural than among urban students in these samples. Unfortunately, racial and sectional influences cannot be separated in these data, and definite conclusions regarding the problem await further research.

As to superstitious belief, rural-urban differences are well authenticated. In one study 373 "large-city" boys are compared with 153 "small-town" boys, and 205 "large-city" girls with 187 "small-town" girls. For each sex there are highly reliable town-city differences in number of superstitions heard, and in number of superstitions confessed to be an influence, the number being greater for the "small-town" children. As to number *believed*, no differences appeared for girls, but town boys believed more than city boys by a barely reliable difference.

It would be surprising if there were not variations in race attitudes with size of community, in view of the widely differing degrees of opportunity for contact and familiarity. No significant rural-urban differences in attitude toward the Negro have been reported among southern subjects, among whom opportunity for contact may be considered a constant factor. From a northern source, however, are reported differences that appear really startling. The measure of prejudice is based upon questions of the form, "What would you do?" These differences, all of which are reliable except at the tenth grade, are presented in the following table (high score indicates

MEAN "C-SCORE" OF FREEDOM FROM PREJUDICE

	Small Towns	Large Towns and Cities
Grade 7	33.14 (66)[a]	26.32 (147)
Grade 8	32.57 (82)	20.10 (140)
Grade 9	24.56 (53)	22.48 (117)
Grade 10	28.64 (86)	20.14 (210)
Grade 11	33.85 (65)	12.64 (185)
Grade 12	25.97 (64)	8.13 (118)

[a]Figures in parentheses refer to numbers of subjects.

"freedom from attitude of prejudice"). These data seem to indicate just the opposite of the generalization that "contact means friendliness," discussed on pages 995 ff. It is probably safe to assume that these urban Iowa children had had more contact with members of other races than had their small-town contemporaries. But were these contacts predominantly in situations involving friction? Or did the urban children's attitudes reflect relatively frequent conflict situations in which their parents had been involved, as contrasted with the rural children's parents? In either case we may conclude that if rural and urban communities provide different kinds and amounts of contacts with another race, then rural and urban attitudes toward that race will differ—whether the contacts be direct or indirect. Many studies have shown that the child acquires his attitude chiefly from his own primary group, not from personal contacts with the out-group.

Do attitudes vary more with sections of this country than with size of the community? The Hinckley Scale of Attitude Toward the Negro has been given to both northern and southern groups of college students, in one of the few direct attacks upon this problem. The mean score of the northern group is more favorable to Negroes, by a difference equaling 21 times its P.E., than that of the southern students from southern homes. What is far more impressive, however, is the fact that a third group of students, themselves northern but attending a southern university, is intermediate in score between the other two groups; the differences between their mean score and those of both other groups are highly reliable. This, of course, might be due to the probability that only unfavorably inclined northern students migrate to the South to study. But comparative scores for the several classes of all three groups indicate that such is not the case. These scores are given in the accompanying table. There is a steady decrease in favorable attitude for the North-in-South group, the difference between mean scores of freshmen and juniors-seniors equaling 7 times its P.E., whereas class differences for the other two groups are small or non-existent. The migrating students enter the South as freshmen with attitudes like those of the northern group, but by the time they are juniors or seniors they resemble

RELATION BETWEEN YEAR IN COLLEGE AND MEAN ATTITUDE FOR THREE GROUPS OF COLLEGE STUDENTS

	Northern		North-in-South		Southern	
	N	Mean	N	Mean	N	Mean
Freshmen	42	6.4	59	6.2	57	5.0
Sophomores	23	6.7	29	5.8	56	4.9
Juniors and seniors	31	6.8	25	5.2	44	5.0

closely the southern group. The authors incline to the explanation that the change registered by this group is largely due to susceptibility to majority influence.

The preceding study, though informing as to the process of attitude formation, must not be interpreted as indicating that there are wide or consistent differences between Northerners and Southerners in attitude toward the Negro, as currently measured. Mean scores, it is true, are invariably more favorable for northern groups, but wide individual variations are nearly always found among both groups.

We know of no conclusive evidence of sectional differences in "liberalism" as defined, for example, by Harper's Social Study. A survey, by means of this test, of 647 school superintendents in all sections of this country reveals some differences among this professional group. Though no computations of the reliability of the differences is made, those from the South appear to give definitely more "conservative" replies than those from New England or the Middle Atlantic States. The latter two areas, in turn, respond more "conservatively" than those from the West and Middle West. On the whole, the various sections show considerable uniformity. Modal response to all but 13 of the 71 items is the same for all sections, and variation from the modal response occurs in one section only for 9 of these 13 items. That section, in almost every case, is the Middle West, responses from which are distinctly less "conservative" to items concerning such issues as wealth distribution and public ownership. Responses from the same area, however, are more "conservative" to items involving educational issues, such as Latin versus music, arts, or home-making, or literature versus social studies. This, of course, illustrates the dangers of lumping together such diverse issues under the general heading of "conservatism" without reference to the specific content of the issues included by the measure which has been used.

Evidence could easily be multiplied to show that no sectional differences are so far apparent in such a variety of attitudes as order of preference for racial groups, superstitious belief, status assigned to occupations, attitude toward the Church and toward war. Evidently similar forces of major importance which influence chiefly, we believe, the primary groups to which people feel they belong, are distributed widely throughout the land. The implications drawn from the Orient-Occident study (cf. page 997) seem to be pertinent for many attitudes other than those toward Oriental peoples: "California business men are not clearly different from those of the East"; "California labor is more like Ohio labor than it is like the business men of California."

Our investigation of "natural" experiences as they affect attitudes may now be summarized. Three major types of experiences have been considered. Those which are more or less individual, rather than being associated with a particular group or a particular locality, have, in general, been shown to be of rather uncertain effect. Thus, opportunity for contact with members of other races or nationalities may result in more favorable attitudes toward those groups, but this appears to depend upon the nature of the contact. Again, devout religious upbringing is often followed by a considerable degree of adult religious belief, but loss of such belief is also common, personality characteristics being, perhaps, the determining factor. Few if any generalizations may be made regarding such experiences.

In the second place, experiences which are regularly associated with family, race, or church groups have more predictable relationships with attitudes. It can almost be said that close family relationships in attitudes remain by and large, regardless of all other variables. The degree of the relationship, of course, is more or less dependent upon these variables, but in any unselected group it appears to remain a close one. Religious affiliation, among some groups, apparently determines whole clusters of attitudes; religious ties in general are strongest among conservative bodies, and hence these attitudes are characteristically conservative. Racial bonds, too, are strong. Nationality of ancestors has much to do with racial preferences, and is closely related, among Jews in this country at any rate, to choice of occupation. Immigrant ancestry is related to attitudes toward public employment and toward war. There are countless reasons, of course, why the family should be the most influential of these primary groups: attitudes associated with Church and with race are mediated largely through families; personal ties are stronger; particular experiences are often shared by whole families; and so, also, are countless other neighborhood and community conditions.

The third classification of experiences, those shared by larger communities, geographic in their delineation, has proved to be little more than a will-o'-the-wisp as far as attitude research can show. Clear-cut urban-rural differences have thus far been shown only among children in regard to attitudes of racial prejudice, and in the field of superstitious belief. (We suspect that this is not because they do not exist, but because college students have in most instances been used as subjects. The crying need here is for unselected subjects, preferably adults.) Sectional differences within this country have almost entirely failed to appear, save in regard to Negroes and Orientals. It scarcely needs to be said, though there is little research to substantiate it, that there must be great differences in almost any conceivable attitude among unselected inhabitants of, for example, India, Italy, Russia, and the United States—so great, in fact, as to make the gathering of comparable data from such diverse sources an almost impossible feat. If and when such data have been gathered, however, our problem, in so far as we remain social psychologists rather than anthropologists, will be that of discovering what individual and group factors differ with variations in attitude. It is a more complicated problem, but not essentially different from that pursued, largely on the basis of American data, in these pages.

One final question remains, regarding the interplay of these various kinds of experiences. Some attitudes, apparently, are the result of commonly shared experiences, to the virtual exclusion of those which are unique to the individual. Not only are they much alike, for almost all *groups*, in various sections of this country, but they seem to transcend nearly all other classifications. This is true, in particular, of order of race preference, order of seriousness of misdemeanors, and order of status assigned to occupations. Nor is this uniformity, regarding race preferences at least, limited to the United States: one study reports a correlation of .98 between scale values assigned to the same list of races and nationalities by two groups of students, one American and one Canadian.

What, then, is responsible for such high degrees of uniformity as this? And why is it found for some attitudes, and not for others? It is, of course, a statistical truism that the larger and more homogeneous the groups whose average judgments are compared, the more nearly identical they will be; and the reader should beware of concluding that there are no individual differences in such judgments. But our present task is to distinguish those areas in which attitudes differ as a result of experience variables from those in which they appear to differ little.

The existence of certain attitudes which are highly uniform among diverse groups is simply a reflection of the fact that certain social relationships in our society are stabilized by custom—legal, economic and moral. This points the way to one of the keys to the intricately patterned lock behind which the process of attitude formation is to be seen. For any attitude (that is, any of the common attitudes which we are discussing) represents, fundamentally, a degree of liking or disliking of some custom. In any stable society, order of seriousness of offenses is, by definition, commonly accepted. Within any stable economic system—and ours has been thus considered until recently—the relative economic returns of various occupations (and hence, in our society, their prestige) are pretty much taken for granted. And in any community of fixed racial proportions the status of any given race (whatever are the antecedent reasons for that status) is freely observed and accepted by the great majority except, perhaps, members of that race. Uniform attitudes, in so far as they exist (and they have been measured chiefly among white American students), reflect uniform customs. And such uniformity may be expected only where some institution—governmental, religious, economic—has exerted powerful influence.

But where attitudes vary, as most of them do among families and among racial and religious groups, it is precisely because these primary groups which, after all, serve as mediators between the larger institution and the individual, exert a previous, a stronger, and a conflicting influence. These groups, particularly the family, thrive or suffer together. Some of them prosper under existing conditions and some do not, and hence they tend to accept or reject the custom toward which the attitude is directed. The family is, in our society, the guardian *par excellence* of custom. Hence its importance for attitudes.

The other "key" is that of personality differences. Without them there would be few intra-family variations in attitudes. But personality variations themselves are dually dependent upon family influences: in so far as personality characteristics are biologically determined there are, of course, hereditary resemblances within a given family. And in so far as they are conditioned by early social relationships—and this is very far indeed—they are peculiarly dependent upon such relationships within the family. The two "keys" function in opposite directions with respect to attitudes. Institutions tend to render them uniform, and personality variations tend to make them diverse. But both sets of influences are filtered through the funnel which we label family. Attitudes of rejecting certain customs may, if associated with certain personality characteristics, be in agreement with similar attitudes shared by other members of the family; or, with other personality characteristics, they may be in opposition to typical family attitudes.

The respective influences of these two kinds of factors, toward conformity and toward variation, have been set forth at some length by F. H. Allport. He is primarily concerned, however, with objectively observable behaviors rather than with what might be considered more valid expressions of attitudes actually possessed. That private or actually possessed attitudes may differ from public ones (e.g., as expressed in observable behavior) has been clearly shown by one of his collaborators. Allport's rather tautological hypothesis is that "in any field of conforming behavior"—i.e., by definition, where at least half of the individuals involved perform according to prescribed or "proper" rules for accomplishing a given purpose—"the distribution of measurable variations of that behavior . . . is in the form of a steep, unimodal, double-J curve." Under such conditions, in other words, some individuals (determined by relevant personality characteristics) will over-conform, though only a few will do so to any great degree, and others will fail to conform in various degrees. Total failure to conform is also limited to a few individuals, this group also being selected primarily on the basis of personality traits. Allport's data relate to such custom-ridden behaviors as stopping an automobile at a red light, arriving at place of work on time, and performing appropriate ritualistic acts on entering a place of worship. His only incursion into the field of attitudes proper concerns the distribution of beliefs concerning the nature of the deity among male Catholic students at one university in 1926. The mode of this distribution is at the most conservative position, representing "an Old Testament conception of the deity as personal creator and ruler." It seems reasonable to assume, with Allport, that this view "fulfills more adequately than any other view presented the purpose of the Catholic doctrine approved for members of the faith."

Our thesis, as applied to attitudes, is somewhat different. Granted that it is somewhat difficult to judge what constitutes over-conformity, it appears to us that the most extreme attitudes represent neither over-conformity, on the one hand, nor, on the other, mere breaking away from some code according to the compulsions of certain personality variations. Thus, as measured by attitude scales in present use, extreme positions with regard to many attitudes are precisely those "prescribed" by certain institutions which take positions in regard to those attitudes. For example, the two most extreme statements (as measured by scale values) from each of two of the scales published by Thurstone and his collaborators are as follows:

War is ennobling and stimulating of our highest and best qualities.
There is no progress without war.
The whole world must be converted to Communism.
Communism should be established by force if necessary.

One could easily cite chapter and verse to show that these are "official" doctrines actually being promulgated by organized groups whose interests are identified with these doctrines. Allport himself would doubtless point out that attitudes toward war and toward Communism do not represent "fields of conforming behavior" as defined by him; perhaps no attitudes as measured by questionnaire methods would be included in that definition. In that case his hypothesis simply does not apply to most common attitudes as currently measured.

We do not deny that personality characteristics may be decisive in adopting these extreme positions. We simply maintain that the latter represent conformity to attitudes prescribed by certain groups, not over-conformity to those of less extreme groups. They must be thought of, not in negative terms of violating prescribed attitudes, but in positive terms of being influenced by other groups with their own doctrine of "correct" attitudes. The rôle of personality factors is that of determining whether or not allegiance to "inherited" groups shall be continued, and, if not, to what groups it shall be shifted.

Unimodal distributions of attitudes, then, may reflect the influence of some conformity-enforcing agency, with variations due to personality factors. Where the modes or means of such distributions are highly similar for diverse groups, we may assume that some one institution (or more than one of like influence) has exerted strong pressures. But most attitudes are subject to pulls from conflicting groups. Except where measured by order-of-preference methods, the kind of piling up at one position demanded by F. H. Allport's hypothesis is apparently not found, and it is therefore not applicable to the realm of attitudes. Personality variations have much to do with shifts of loyalty from one group to another. But it is to face-to-face groups and the forces which cause them to be groups of value to particular individuals that we must look for our most direct information concerning the genesis of attitudes.

The Interrelationship of Attitudes

We have had more than one occasion, in these pages, to refer to the problem of "generality" versus "specificity" of attitudes. The matter is of interest not only as concerning the coexistence of various attitudes, but also as bearing upon our general theory.

The question of specificity of attitude hinges somewhat, of course, upon how narrowly we define the term. If one distinguishes between attitudes toward the current Italian and German brands of Fascism, for example, or between attitudes toward the prohibition of wines and beers and of beverages of high alcoholic content, then he may scarcely expect to find a high degree of specificity among attitudes. One investigator, for example, speaks of clusters of attitudes toward the Negro, pointing out that attitudes toward the Jim Crow car and toward a Negro's buying a home are closely linked. Specificity of this degree is primarily a problem of statistical reliability which has been discussed in earlier pages. Certainly no one possesses, in any meaningful sense, a stock of hundreds or thousands of disparate attitudes. The question is, which attitude responses are so closely knit as to be considered a statistically reliable unit? Only after such information is at hand may we investigate the relationship of these units. Wherever we have referred in these pages to an attitude as an entity, we have attempted to assure ourselves of a reasonable degree of reliability of the measuring instruments.

Interesting questions of this sort are raised by a recent series of papers concerning attitude toward Fascism. (See page 1014 for a description of the procedure involved.) The fact of immediate pertinence is that statements representing all seven of the concepts (though principally four of them) originally believed to be included in the doctrines of Fascism remained after an item analysis of internal consistency. As few as eighteen statements, which remained following the item analysis, yielded split-half reliability coefficients, with two adult groups, of .84 and .88. "Attitude toward Fascism" thus, by our definition, is entitled to independent status as an entity, though it is composed of seven "attitudes," most of which have also been separately measured. What is the difference, then, between "an attitude" reliably measured, and a closely related cluster of different attitudes? The answer to the question serves as a needed caution. The eighteen statements reflect "an attitude" *because they were selected to do so.* The criterion of their selection was the sum total of concepts originally surmised to constitute Fascism, and those statements which did not "hang together" were discarded. Those discarded were not necessarily less valid indicators of attitudes toward imperialism, nationalism, etc.; they were simply those which did not fit the *a priori* pattern. Other investigators, using independent measures for some of the same attitudes, have not found such high interrelationships among them. This is not to say that the phrase "Fascist attitudes" does not represent something genuine. The four more specific attitudes represented by the terms "nationalism," "racial antagonism," "anti-radicalism," and "middle-class consciousness" evidently do hang together in the minds of large numbers of contemporary Americans. The sum total, characterized by the author to be in essence the attitude of class superiority, is probably better labeled by the term "Fascism" than by any other. There is, moreover, every reason why such a common cluster should be referred to as "an attitude." The needed caution is simply that *no* attitudes as measured are genuine entities in the sense that there is anything "absolute" about them. For practical purposes any set of verbal responses which is statistically reliable may be considered an entity and given an appropriate name. Any measured attitude, no matter how reliable, might conceivably be broken down into two or more different attitudes with slightly different labels. A single label implies nothing concerning singleness of attitude. Indeed, the concept of singleness has meaning only in regard to the object of reference. If the attitude measured has reference to a custom, person, or institution commonly accepted as an isolable phenomenon and is reliably measured, it may be regarded as an entity. Hence attitude toward Fascism may be "measured" (not absolutely, but by a particular set of items) and considered as a unit. Its various components may also be separately measured (again not absolutely, but by some *a priori* criterion) and if closely related they may be considered a cluster. Whether or not various attitudes turn out to be closely interrelated, then, depends on the nature and the inclusiveness of the concept around which the items constituting the measure are constructed.

This matter of inclusiveness refers not only to the *range* of specific issues to which questionnaire items refer, but also to the generality with which the items are phrased. Thus, a measure of international attitudes might be composed of items of either of the following types: "Some form of international government is inevitable," or "Non-members should recognize and acquiesce in a League of Nations blockade." There is no justification for assuming that the kinds of attitudes measured by such different kinds of items are the same, or that individuals would make the same scores on two such different questionnaires. As a matter of fact, the statements just quoted are taken from an actual questionnaire, and responses to the general and to the specific items contained in it have been separately calculated. The average percentages of "international" replies made by eleven groups of subjects to the "general" items in this questionnaire ranged from 73 to 94; for the "specific" items the range was from 51 to 74. (These figures represent responses prior to the introduction of various types of learning experiences, for experimental purposes. At the end of these experiments the comparable ranges were 72 to 96 for general and 49 to 84 for specific items.) There is, of course, some relationship between these group averages of response to specific and to general statements, but the degree to which this is true of individual responses does not appear from the data presented. Our point is simply that the two scores are different, and that relationships among attitudes depend, to an unknown extent, upon the degree to which statements are worded in general terms.

Most of the postulated attitude groups have had to do with such concepts as radicalism and conservatism, nationalism and internationalism, etc. Many tests and scales have been constructed upon the sheer assumption that the various attitudes to which these terms may be applied together constitute an entity. Such tendencies-in-general may, of course, exist, but it is a matter requiring empirical determination. Do those individuals who are, for example, radical on one issue also reveal radicalism regarding many other issues? Unless most of them are shown to do so, the term should be applied with careful safeguards of specificity.

Both empirical and theoretical evidence has at various times been adduced in support of the theory of attitude types. Thus, for example, the fact is cited that some individuals do actually make large scores in radicalism on questionnaires covering a wide variety of issues. Such evidence, however, is unimpressive for two reasons. A certain number of people, in the first place, would make such scores quite by chance; any random collection of items would result in certain individuals' making extreme scores, and it has rarely been shown that extreme radicalism scores, on such types of questionnaires, represent anything more than this. Neither, in the second place, does a fairly high split-half reliability coefficient prove anything by way of homogeneity of items contained in the questionnaire when, as is usually the case, the same number of items pertaining to religion, to sex, to pacifism, etc., appear in the two halves which are correlated. The kind of empirical evidence which is demanded is intercorrelations among scores on separate questionnaires, each of which has shown adequate reliability.

The theoretical defense of the theory of attitude types is best illustrated by the writings of G. W. Allport. It is difficult to quarrel with his basic assumption that attitudes, being related to fundamental personality dispositions of which they are simply one form of expression, cannot be regarded as single and isolable phenomena, and must therefore be conceived in such clusters as correspond to general traits. His own data, however, are in general subject to the criticisms just made. But to meet him on his own theoretical ground, his conclusions regarding attitudes seem to us no inevitable consequence of his initial theories concerning the nature of personality organization. The crux of the matter lies in the influence of the intricate cross-currents of our contemporary culture. The respective rôles played in the formation of attitudes by cultural forces and by personality are discussed on pages 912 ff. The position there formulated is that even the most apparently contradictory attitudes may actually perform similar personality functions. Such is the dependence of attitudes upon the influence of individuals and groups of prestige value, and so great is the rôle of chance (i.e., of irrelevantly determined influences) in our society, that even the most nearly identical personalities may develop widely divergent social attitudes. And most individuals are simultaneously swept by various cultural cross-currents to such an extent that almost any conceivable combination of attitudes may result. One may grant, with Allport, that coexisting attiudes must be "congruent," i.e., they must fit into a pattern for the individual, without granting that they need have any ideological consistency.

Evidence abounds, as a matter of fact, to suggest that the most freakish assortments of opinions and beliefs are commonly held by single individuals. The prevalence of irrational beliefs, even among those at college levels, has more than once been amply demonstrated. Belief in various tokens and omens, particularly those portending "bad luck," is admitted even by those who make high scores in tests of information in various fields of science. "Rational" and "irrational" ideas may evidently be the best of bedfellows.

Quite apart from beliefs usually regarded as superstitious, rather startling degrees of inconsistency have again and again been reported. More than one observer has noted the checking, by many subjects, of the most contradictory statements included in attitude scales. One student of this matter reports, for example, that opinions were "undigested and contradictory," revealing uncritical acceptance of clichés, slogans, and stereotypes of the most diverse nature. (Would it not be more accurate to conclude that such individuals simply had no attitudes in these fields? We are reminded of a similar finding in the field of personality ratings, i.e., that certain traits were plainly irrelevant for certain individuals.) Perhaps this is just what is to be expected in view of simultaneous bombardment, through the press and other sources of publicity, from the various interest groups representing the several points of view included in many contemporary measures of attitudes. But the net effect is almost as if each individual's attitudes had no more pattern than that resulting from the several lines of fire that happened his way.

Such extreme disorganization, however, is far from characterizing all individuals in regard to all attitudes. The problem thus becomes that of discovering under what conditions attitudes are patterned, and under what conditions inchoate. One set of conditions is indicated by the study last referred to. The items used in this questionnaire had been selected as reflecting one of several economic and political interests currently competing for public favor, and were labeled as follows:

Pollyanna: believe present government is true democracy run for the good of most people.

Individualist: *laissez faire;* the only difficulty encountered by intelligent men is that of governmental interference.

Fascist: capitalism should be maintained by force of government.

Socialist: social justice; governmental control of socially shared goods.

While, in general, the greatest confusion was found among these undergraduate students, those who showed the fewest contradictions were those who accepted a large number of the statements classified as "Socialist." This corresponds closely to one of Harper's discoveries. The interdependence of his statements having been carefully established by a group of "expert" judges, he tabulated the average number of *inconsistencies* made by those of varying degrees of "liberalism" according to total score. The relation was striking, as shown in the accompanying table. Factors of both personality and

Those Making a Liberalism Score of	Average Number of Inconsistencies
40	10.5
50	7.5
60	6.0
70	3.4

institutional pressure are revealed in both these studies. Those whose scores are least conservative are, on the, one hand, likely to be characterized by somewhat higher intelligence (cf. page 931) and by more critical habits of thinking. On the other hand they are, by and large, those whose opinions have been formed by selective group affiliations, rather than, as in the case of those taking more conservative positions, by influences from relatively unselected groups which represent the *status quo*.

The same two factors apparently are responsible for the finding that correlations among related attitudes tend to increase with increased exposure to academic influences. This is illustrated by the following correlations between scores in attitudes toward internationalism and toward economic radicalism. Identical scales were given to identical students in two successive years. Whatever selec-

CORRELATIONS BETWEEN INTERNATIONALISM AND ECONOMIC RADICALISM

Group	N	1935	1936
Freshmen (in 1935)	55	.28	.53
Sophomores-juniors (in 1935)	63	.56	.73

tive forces operate to prevent dropping out of college, together with the particular attitudinal emphases at this particular institution, conspire toward the increased patterning of such attitudes.

Inter-attitude correlations, classified for a large group of heterogeneous subjects according to age, sex, occupational status, and religious affiliation, are presented in one investigation. Only in respect to the last of these classifications, however, do any consistent differences in intercorrelation appear. All other groupings, cutting across lines of religious affiliation, show similar degrees of relationship among the three attitudes. The coefficients for the religious groupings are presented in the accompanying table. They show, after a fashion, the degree of interrelationship among these three attitudes, with the factor of religious affiliation held constant. It is clear that there is no characteristic clustering of these three attitudes associated with these major types of religious affiliation, or with age, sex, or occupational level. It is equally clear that religious affiliation does

ATTITUDE INTERCORRELATIONS

	Church and War	Church and Communism	War and Communism
Protestants (N 595).........	.028	.300	−.084
Catholics (N 318)...........	.025	.254	−.053
Jews (N 317)...............	−.148	.377	−.326
No affiliation (N 274).......	−.242	.477	−.277
All subjects................	−.230	.449	−.263

influence relationship of attitudes, whereas age, sex, and occupational status do not. For inter-attitude correlations are significant when all religious groups are included, but are, with a single exception, much lower when each one is considered alone. Coefficients for age, sex, and occupational groupings, on the other hand, are as high for each group singly as for all groups together.

The reader must beware of concluding from the above table that there is no clustering of these attitudes within these religious affiliations. The coefficients are very low, but the uniformity of scores within these groups is so great that the slight variations in attitudes which do appear are little related to each other. The situation is analogous to the relationship of height and weight among three different age groups of children: the correlation would be low at any one age, but would be much higher for all groups together. There is a "typical" height and weight at each age level, and the two variables are related. Just so, there is a "typical" attitude position (cf. mean scores, page 1006) for each of these religious groups, and the attitudes are not totally independent of each other. Our point is simply that membership in any of these groups tends to carry with it characteristic positions with regard to *all* of these attitudes. Whether or not there are reliable correlations within the groups is of less significance for our present problem.

The dependence of inter-attitude relationships upon institutional affiliation is shown more clearly by further analysis of the same data. From the entire group of Catholics and Jews were selected all those who were extremely favorable to the Church, and those whose scores were on the unfavorable side of the median position for all subjects. Those very favorable included 39 per cent of all Catholics and 9 per cent of all Jews; those opposed, 13 per cent of all Catholics and 54 per cent of all Jews. These four groups were compared in attitude toward Communism, as in the accompanying table (low

Attitude Toward Church	Mean Attitude Toward Communism				
	Catholics	Jews	Difference	S.D.$_{diff.}$	C.R.
2.4 and below......	4.10 (123)^a	5.28 (35)	1.18	.25	4.7
4.5 and above......	4.91 (48)	5.86 (172)	.95	.21	4.5
Difference..........	.81	.54			
S.D.$_{diff.}$...........	.21	.25			
C.R...............	3.9	2.2			

^{a}Numbers of subjects are indicated in parentheses.

scores are favorable to the Church and unfavorable to Communism). Jews and Catholics whose scores on the church scale are the same are seen to differ widely in attitude toward Communism. It further appears that the difference in attitude toward Communism is greater between Jews and Catholics *whose church attitudes are the same* than between Jews opposed to or strongly favoring the Church, or between Catholics opposed to or strongly favoring the Church. The difference between the two Catholic groups in church score equals a critical ratio of 25.3, and the comparable critical ratio for the two Jewish groups is 39.6. And yet the two Jewish groups (and the two Catholic groups) resemble each other *more* closely in attitude toward Communism than do Jews and Catholics whose scores in attitude toward the Church are alike. Thus potent is the influence of whatever cultural influences are associated with membership in these two religious bodies.

Does parental influence provide another of the conditions under which patterning of attitudes occurs? That is, if certain children are found to resemble their parents closely in one attitude, will they tend to resemble them also in other attitudes? The above data have also been analyzed in the attempt to answer this question. Thus one group of families was selected (by inspection) on the basis of a very high parent-child correlation in scores of attitude toward the Church, and the parent-child correlations in attitudes toward war and toward Communism were calculated. Another group was similarly selected for high correlation in attitude toward Communism, and the other two relationships were calculated. The results appear in the accompanying table.

PARENT-CHILD CORRELATIONS

	Church	War	Communism
Group selected to correlate highly in attitude toward the Church (N 220)......	.960	.409	.623
Group selected to correlate highly in attitude toward Communism (N 227)....	.741	.351	.927
All cases, unselected (N 1090)..........	.626	.435	.564

A similar question might be stated as follows: will children of parents who show a high correlation between two attitudes, themselves reveal higher correlations between the same two attitudes than do unselected subjects? From the same source families were selected in which each of two parents showed close relationship of the same kind between the two attitudes, i.e., families in which both parents favored the Church and disapproved of Communism, or showed the reverse attitudes, or in which both were more or less neutral regarding each attitude. These are families, in other words, in which a definite and uniform cluster influence might be expected to be felt. There is the barest indication, as will be noted in the accompanying table, that children of such parents tend to share in the cluster. What might be called a cluster effect is thus passed from

INTER-ATTITUDE CORRELATIONS

	Families Selected for High Correlation of Parents' Attitudes Toward Church and Communism	All Cases, Unselected
Church and Communism (parents)....	.962 (N 136)	.481 (N 778)
Church and Communism (children)....	.600 (N 102)	.430 (N 850)
Church and war (children)..........	.312 (N 102)	.255 (N 866)

parents to children to the extent of the difference between the co-efficients .600 and .430.

The selective process was now carried one step further. From the same group of families, selected for high Church-Communism correlation among both parents, 56 children were selected whose Church scores correlated very highly with those of their parents (.963). The Church and Communism scores of these 56 children were then correlated, the resulting coefficient being .746. That is, in families where parents agree closely and where their Church and Communism scores are closely correlated, their children show a reliably higher Church-Communism correlation than do unselected children. The children of these same parents who agree closely with them in church attitudes yield a much higher Church-Communism correlation than do unselected children. (The three Church-Communism correlations for these groups of children are, in the order named, .600 and .746, as compared with .430 for the unselected group.) Only under such conditions, apparently, is there a noticeable family cluster influence.

Attitude patterning, then, is somewhat less noticeable as a result of family influence than might have been foreseen, even when the attitudes in question are those toward Communism and the Church. For the relationship between these two is presumably about as close as one can ever expect to find. Favorable attitude toward each of them is represented by conspicuous and organized groups, each of which, with minor exceptions, is vociferously antagonistic to the other. The reasons for this less than expected degree of family patterning influence must be sought in the realm of personality characteristics which have, as we have seen, a diversifying rather than a unifying effect. Institutional influences tend to be shared by families, and hence intra-family relationships in regard to any one relevant attitude tend to be close. But families mediate the influences of many institutions, and the relative degrees of these several influences upon various members of the same family are determined, in large measure, by personality characteristics.

We have seen that greater or less degrees of patterning develop under the influence of various institutional forces, and in accordance with certain personality characteristics. But patterning must not be thought of as a static affair, or necessarily as a gradual development. Relatively brief experiences may bring about quite new relationships in attitudes, judging from one comparison of employed and unemployed professional engineers. There were 300 men in each of the groups, which were matched for age, normal earning power, education, state licensing, nativity, and marital status. Three scales were used, measuring attitude toward religion, attitude toward employers, and "occupational morale." The experience of unemployment evidently affects all three attitudes. The unemployed have poorer "morale" than the employed, and are, quite naturally, more critical of employers; both differences are large and reliable. The groups do not differ, however, in respect to "radicalism" (as measured by a fourth scale) or in attitude toward religion. The author shows that "morale" decreases steadily with lessened economic security among both groups, as well as with length of unemployment.

The evidence for new patterning of attitudes is drawn from 21 of those in *extreme* financial straits who are compared with three other small samples chosen at random. The intercorrelations among three attitudes are presented in the accompanying table. This evi-

INTERCORRELATIONS OF ATTITUDES

Attitudes Toward	Random Samples	Group in Extreme Financial Straits
Religion, employers..............	.35 to .60	.68
Religion, occupational morale.......	.26 to .53	.71
Employers, occupational morale.....	.35 to .69	.79

dence, if the number of cases entitles it to a hearing at all, speaks in loud terms. We do not know, of course, how or to what extent the men in the financially straitened group suffered changes in personality. But the patterning which is apparent here did not automatically appear, whether with certain types of personality or not. The chief shortcoming of such an experiment as this, of course, is the unanswerable question of selection of subjects; to what extent such attitudes as that labeled "occupational morale" preceded dismissal from employment, and how much they had to do with it, we do not know. But even if it be maintained that the patterning was "potentially" present before the experience of unemployment, certainly it did not exist until "brought out" by the experience.

We venture one further hypothesis concerning the conditions under which patterning of attitudes is to be found: we suspect that the closest relationships are to be found among those who hold the *most extreme* positions. A single illustrative case is the student who made the highest scores, among 650 individuals, on all three attitudes measured (favoring the Negro, favoring friendly international relations, and opposing imperialism). The thesis would imply that those who hold more or less neutral positions with respect to one attitude are likely to show a wide range in respect to other attitudes. This, if true, is one reason why little relationship among various attitudes has been found in most unselected groups, the majority of whom do not hold extreme positions.

We have attempted to put this hypothesis to the test. As a group showing a wide range of attitudes, 258 individuals who reported "no religious affiliation" were selected. They were divided into three subgroups, as follows: those strongly favoring, those strongly opposing, and those more or less neutral toward the Church. Their attitude scores toward Communism were then tabulated, and means and sigmas were calculated. The same individuals were then similarly classified in three subgroups according to attitude toward Communism, and means and sigmas of attitude toward the Church were calculated for each subgroup. Results are given in the accompanying table (low scores indicate favorable attitude toward the Church and unfavorable attitude toward Communism). The correlation between

Attitude Toward Church	N	Attitude Toward Communism	
		mean	sigma
3.9 and below...........	45	4.72	.91
4.0 to 6.9.............	90	5.23	1.41
7.0 and above...........	123	6.37	1.50

Attitude Toward Communism	N	Attitude Toward the Church	
		mean	sigma
4.4 and below...........	75	5.59	2.05
4.5 to 6.9.............	125	6.10	2.34
7.0 and above...........	62	8.36	1.10

the two attitudes, for the entire group, is .477; within any of the subgroups the correlation would, of course, be very low.

Our hypothesis concerning closeness of relationship has not been fully confirmed by these data, since both those who are unfavorable to the Church and who are unfavorable to Communism reveal quite as wide dispersions in attitudes toward Communism and toward the Church, respectively, as do those who are neutral regarding each issue. We are thus led to revise the hypothesis: relationships of attitudes appear to be relatively close in the case, not of all those who take extreme positions in regard to one of them, but in the case of those who *strongly favor* one of them. Or perhaps this should be qualified: in the case of those who strongly favor an attitude promulgated by some organized group. For strongly favorable attitudes related to institutions are probably formed to a considerable extent by those institutions; and other issues toward which those institutions take a position are reflected in relatively predictable fashion in the attitudes of individual members thereof. Attitudes strongly opposed to a given institution, on the other hand, are probably fomented not by one but by many other antagonistic institutions, and hence other attitudes held by those opposing the given institution will vary widely and be far less predictable.

Another clue to the conditions under which attitude patterns exist is to be found in the rapidly increasing experimental literature regarding stereotypes. Our attitudes toward races, flags, nations, and national anthems, and toward the words which crystallize generally accepted values such as freedom, honor, and democracy, tend to be imprinted upon us in more or less *standardized* form. When we hear of patriots or Bolsheviks, we can scarcely stop to consider the individual attributes of all the individual persons thus designated. A stereotype of a patriot or of a Bolshevik, loosely regarded as serving to describe all members of the species, also serves the purpose of all but the most sophisticated and careful forms of thought. It serves, as Lippmann long since pointed out, not only as a laborsaver, but also as a defense, since the stereotype invariably acts to enhance the desirable attributes of one's own group.

The existence of stereotyped attitudes, as we shall see, has been amply demonstrated. Our query, however, has to do primarily with their *inclusiveness*. As a method of attitude research the study of stereotypes has the great additional advantage of being disguised; attitudes are only indirectly ascertained, and subjects are not tempted to be on their guard or to appear in the best possible light.

One of the pioneer studies in the field, and one which set the pattern for many later experiments, is an analysis of the function of stereotypes in relation to nine photographs taken from the Boston *Herald*. These represented Herriot (then French Premier), Duncan (vice-president of the American Federation of Labor), Krassin (Soviet ambassador to France), Agel (a bootlegger), Schwab (steel magnate), Heinz (of the 57 Varieties), Pepper (United States Senator), and others. These photographs were shown to nearly 150 students, together with a list of terms such as "premier," "labor leader," "Bolshevik," "financier." Individuals had to pick out the right word for each man. The stereotyping tendency to agree that a certain kind of picture goes with a certain appellation is perfectly clear-cut, not only where the designation is right but where it widely misses the mark. There is, in other words, a tendency to a stereotyped conception of what a labor leader or a financier looks like, and this, even in the case of mistaken identifications, produces a converging of judgments. In the case of Krassin, a winged collar, a Vandyke beard, and a mustache led to "fifty-nine identifications as the United States Senator, in comparison with nine as a Bolshevik and none as a labor leader." A similar experiment was tried on twenty-five members of a farmers' grange with very similar results; in fact, the rank correlation between farmers' and students' judgments was + .84.

After this experiment was terminated, three groups of students graded the nine individuals on the two traits, *intelligence* and *craftiness*, the latter being defined as "that characteristic, the possession of which would lead to the taking of an unfair advantage in a business negotiation." The first group of students did not at the time know the identity of the men whose pictures were shown. The second group were given false identifications based upon the stereotypes already discovered. The third group was informed of the real identities. The ratings on intelligence and craftiness are in the direction expected. Disclosure of the true identities led to changes of rating in the same direction among both students and grange members in the case of seven out of the nine individuals rated.

This experiment is in agreement with all others known to us, that while "guesses" from photos, voices, etc., are more often right than expected by chance, they are more uniform than right. In our attempt to discover the conditions under which stereotypes are built up we need therefore to ask, whence the "extra"? i.e., why are they more uniform than right? A likely hypothesis is that it is likes and dislikes around which these spurious uniformities tend to accumulate. Stereotypes, in other words, should be most definite, other things being equal, when they are associated with strongly favorable or strongly antagonistic attitudes.

Some pertinent evidence is available at this point in the replies of 100 college students who chose, from a list of 84 traits, those which they regarded as most characteristic of each of ten racial groups. Following this, each subject checked five traits as being "most typical" of each race. Degree of agreement was measured by the least number of traits, of the five checked, which had to be included to find 50 per cent of the 500 checks by all subjects. That is, with perfect agreement two and one-half traits would receive 250 checks, and with maximum disagreement one-half of eighty-four, or forty-two. Definiteness of stereotype, as thus measured, was as follows for the various groups:

Negroes	4.6 traits	Irish	8.5 traits
Germans	5.0 "	Americans	8.8 "
Jews	5.5 "	Japanese	10.9 "
Italians	6.9 "	Chinese	12.0 "
English	7.0 "	Turks	15.9 "

The authors suggest that, according to these data, definiteness of stereotype is unrelated to degree of prejudice; for Negroes and Turks, whose stereotypes are, respectively, most and least definite, have quite uniformly been shown to be the objects of most prejudice in this country. Americans, similarly, who are presumed to be most favorably regarded of all these groups, occupy not an extreme position, but a middle one. The data may, however, serve to point to quite other conclusions. These ten groups are far from being equally familiar to these eastern American students, and the definiteness of stereotype appears to be directly related to this factor of familiarity—not necessarily meaning first-hand contact by these students themselves, but rather by the various groupings which they represent. The relationship, as it appears from these data, is as follows: stereotypes are most definite toward groups with whom their own groups are, or have recently been in conflict; least definite for distant and unfamiliar peoples; and intermediate for their own and related groups. Our initial hypothesis must thus be partially revised: highly uniform stereotypes tend to gather around strongly *disliked* attitudes, but not necessarily around those which are strongly favored. Whether or not this would apply to stereotypes other than those regarding races and nationalities, we are uncertain. But in that area it is fairly obvious that the emotions which accompany favorable attitudes are more congenial to discriminations than are those which characterize antagonisms—and where stereotypes exist, there discrimination is not.

But is it true, as we have implied, that stereotypes are almost inevitably surrounded by halos of such inclusiveness as to carry connotations, favorable or unfavorable, for numerous attitudes? Is there an interrelationship of stereotypes, all radiating from some all-enveloping aura? Are there, to state it differently, points of reference about which several attitudes revolve? A considerable body of experimental evidence, though most of it is only indirectly relevant, indicates an affirmative answer. The aura, or the stereotype-in-chief, is one form or another of prestige—authority, expert opinion, or a well-known name. If the history of recent advertising in this country may be cited as experimental evidence—and in a sense it is just that—then it is abundantly evident that prestige gained in one field, e.g., tennis or "society," is of considerable potency in affecting widespread attitudes regarding purchasing. Certain news commentators, certain publications, certain religious officials—many such individuals or groups endowed with great prestige are presumed to exert great influence in several directions at once, among their respective audiences.

More objective evidence, however, is not lacking. Several experiments involving prestige suggestion and attitudes have already been cited (pages 967 ff.). The majority of these experiments, from which it became evident that prestige-endowed individuals, groups, and institutions have much to do with the formation of attitudes, involved a wide range of issues. In one procedure, for example, attitudes of graduate students of education, as measured by the Harper test, were greatly modified by the mere presentation of responses to the test as attributed to "expert" educators. In this experiment *the prestige-endowed group was the same* for all the diverse issues included in the test, many of them not dealing with education at all. The differences in score were so huge that most if not all of the several issues involved must singly have shown considerable differences. In such experiments as this the halo surrounding a respected group is shown to be reflected in many directions.

Halos attached to names are not indefinitely elastic, however, judging from another experiment. From a long list submitted to several groups of students, ten names were chosen as uniformly "liked," and ten others as "disliked." The former group included Lindbergh, Aristotle, Einstein, and Mark Twain; the latter, Capone, Aimée Semple McPherson, and Hearst. Thirty controversial statements were then presented to three other groups, each statement being attributed to a liked name for one group, to a disliked name for another group, and with no name attached for a third group. With few exceptions statements were most accepted when associated with a liked name, and least accepted when associated with a disliked name. The single reliable exception involved a statement having to do with American politics, which was more widely accepted when attributed to a discredited American politician than when followed (in 1932) by Einstein's name. Unfortunately, the statements are not reproduced, so that it is difficult to judge into how wide or how varied fields the prestige of these names carried. It is clear, however, that their influence was by no means limited to the fields in which their eminence had been achieved.

The final condition, then, under which patterning of attitudes seems to have been demonstrated is that the individual has been subjected to the influence of some prestige-endowed group whose positions with regard to several attitudes are known to the individual. Such patterning may or may not be crystallized into stereotypes, but it is probable that the coexistence of several stereotypes, with the easy indifference to the actual complexities of life which the stereotype makes possible, leads to a more neatly structured pattern than that which is found without them. Certainly the interrelationship of attitudes is more powerfully influenced by the nature of individuals, groups and individuals which are of prestige value, than by considerations of intellectual consistency. Patterning exists, by and large, according to prestige rather than by reason.

The conditions under which patterning is found thus appear to be almost exactly the same as those which determine the holding of almost any "single" attitude. The interrelationship found among attitudes depends, in the first place, upon the particular issues involved. If, as in the case of attitudes toward internationalism and imperialism, there is considerable ground common to both areas measured, a close relationship is to be expected, and there may be good reason to refer to the sum total as a single attitude. Such relationships we are inclined to attribute less to sheer intellectual consistency than to influence from certain groups which have taken definite positions regarding both or all attitudes involved. Affiliation with such groups is the second major factor in determining interrelationship of attitudes, and in many cases at least it actually includes the previously mentioned factor. The third concerns individual personality characteristics. We have seen that even within the same family some children share their parents' clusters of attitudes whereas others do not. It is not necessarily native characteristics, of course, which thus distinguish siblings: different associates and different experiences with their consequent diversifying influences upon interests are certainly not without their effects upon what we commonly call personality. Intelligence appears to be a factor, though it may function in different cases in opposite directions. We have presented some evidence indicating that more *consistent* patterns of attitudes characterize those of higher intelligence. Other things equal, however, individuals of low intelligence may be presumed to borrow ready-made attitude stereotypes most freely.

All in all, we are led to reiterate our conclusions regarding the determinants of "single" attitudes. Interrelated attitudes are rarely individual affairs, but are largely borrowed from groups to which we owe strongest allegiance. Individual variations such as age, sex, and various personality characteristics have much to do with the nature of the groups with which one becomes affiliated, and with the degree and permanence of such affiliations. Individual experiences, whether of accidental or occasional nature, on the one hand, or those occasioned by family membership or residential community, on the other, are also instrumental in determining group membership. This is by no means to deny the importance of purely psychological factors. But such experimental evidence as is available has led us to the conclusion that the latter are effective largely through their power to select this rather than that group affiliation, to react to it with greater or less intensity and, to some extent, perhaps, to modify it. The social psychology of attitudes is the sociology of attitudes illuminated by an understanding of the psychological factors which determine individual susceptibility to group influences.

REFERENCES

References are given by page, paragraph, and line. The number following each proper name is the number of the item in the bibliography. When a statement extends through several lines, the conclusion of a sentence is ordinarily chosen as the reference line.

Paragraph one indicates the opening lines on a page, even when these are the continuation of a paragraph beginning on a previous page.

Darwin, in the fourth reference, is not given a reference by line; this is because the reference is to the same line as the reference to Spencer; etc.

CHAPTER I

4	1	3	Bain (48)
		6	Steinthal and Lazarus (930)
		10	Spencer (918)
			Darwin (240)
			Bagehot (47)
	2	3	Braid (119)
		4	Bernheim (85)
		5	Binet and Féré (92)
	3	2	Tarde (963)
		3	Le Bon (590)
5	3	11	Fabre (298)
6	3	13	Dashiell (242)
8	2	7	Moede (713)
			Allport (10)
	3	1	Allport (10)
			Moore (720)
9	2	20	Triplett (989)
		25	Moss (727)
			Warden (1026)
			Richter (839)
14	1	3	Piaget (804)
		7	Lewin (616)
		12	Sherif (888)
15	3	23	Brown (139)
18	2	14	Lewin (615: p. 23)
19	1	14	Kroeber (562)
	2	5	Jennings (489)
	3	6	Alverdes (23)
20	1	3	Scott (875)
		13	Conradi (227)
	2	5	Warden (1027)

CHAPTER II

27	2	4	Child (212)
28	2	13	Henderson (439)
30	1	2	Burks (161)
			Burks and Kelley (164)
31	1	8	Wright (1098)
	2	8	Hanks (411)
		13	Allport (17)
36	3	3	Tallman (962)
			Wingfield and Sandiford (1084)
	4	6	Barrett and Koch (58)
37	1	8	Hildreth (450)
	3	3	Burks (163)
42	2	4	Freeman, Holzinger and Mitchell (326)
	3	1	Leahy (588)
43	2	3	Burks and Kelley (164)
			Burks (161)
	4	5	Newman, Freeman and Holzinger (761)
46	2	4	Yerkes (1103)
		10	Collins (221)
			Kempf and Collins (537)
		12	Goodenough (378)
		13	Jones (506)
	4	5	Furfey (337)
47	1	6	Furfey and Muehlenbein (340)
		8	Goodenough (378)
		10	Goodenough (378)
	2	4	Collins (221)

1047

52 2 6 Terman (965)
54 2 9 Mead (692)
    16 Lévy-Bruhl (614)
    19 Boas (102)
       Sutherland (950)
    24 Boas (102)
    25 Garth, Lovelady and Smith (349)
       Garth and Garrett (348)
55 1 4 Ferguson (305)
   2 4 Peterson, Lanier and Walker (800)
     8 Peterson, Lanier and Walker (800)
    12 Peterson and Lanier (799)
   3 2 Peterson and Lanier, (799. pp. 15–17)
64 3 2 Klineberg (545)
65 1 8 Klineberg (545)
   3 3 Murdock (736)
66 1 2 Darsie (239)
69 2 9 Franzblau (324)
   4 7 Hattori (427)
70 3 4 Murdock (736)
71 3 13 Anastasi (24)
   4 4 Goodenough (370)
     5 Goodenough (370)
       Allen (6)
       Anastasi (24)
74 1 3 Thomson (974)
       Anastasi (24)
   2 9 Terman and Miles (967)
    12 Mead (695)
   3 4 McQueen-Williams (691)
   4 6 Mead (692)

CHAPTER III

79 2 2 Allen (7)
     6 Thorek (975)
90 2 4 Craig (233) (234)
   4 5 Cannon (183)
       Cannon and Washburn (184)
     6 Wada (1016)
       Richter (839)
91 1 2 Wada (1016)
   2 3 Richter (839)
       Wang (1023)
92 2 12 Moss (727)
    16 Warden (1026)

     23 Warden (1026)
     28 Warden (1026: pp. 119–178)
95 1 1 Bühler (154)
    10 Bühler (153)
96 1 5 Dashiell (242)
       Kempf (535)
99 3 6 McQueen-Williams (691)
   4 5 Freud (330)
101 2 3 Holt (454)
104 3 7 Diamond (259)
105 1 14 Freud (330)
107 3 3 Watson (1044: pp. 219–222)
   4 2 Sherman (889)
       Sherman and Sherman (893)
108 2 2 Sherman (890)
   3 9 Gray and Klein (383)
109 1 5 Blanton (98)
     7 Blanton (98)
   3 3 Pratt, Nelson and Sun (819)
111 2 14 Gesell (357)
112 1 3 Carmichael (193)
    13 Stone (942)
   2 4 Avery (45)
   3 5 Tilney (985)
113 1 1 Coghill (220)
   2 5 Minkowski (708)
   3 3 Shirley (897)
134 1 4 Kuo (568)
     5 Avery (46)
   3 4 Jones (519: p. 583)
135 3 4 Lewin (616)
136 2 2 Barker, Dembo and Lewin (54)
137 2 25 Murray (745)
138 note 1 20 Thorndike (976: pp. 170 ff.)
139 1 4 Goodenough (372)
   3 6 Landis (576)
152 3 6 Landis and Hunt (577)
       Hunt (469)
153 5 3 Klineberg (548)
     6 Efron and Foley (286)
154 2 4 Brown (133)

CHAPTER IV

155 1 2 Conradi (227)
157 1 3 Watson (1044: pp. 231–235)
   2 5 English (291)
   3 2 Jones (518: pp. 42–43)

158	2	5	Hunter (471)
		12	Tinklepaugh (987)
159	3	2	Novikova (765)
	4	3	Munroe (732)
162	1	5	Razran (826)
165	3	3	Erofeeva (292)
		16	Razran (829)
166	2	3	Jones (516)
167	3	3	Razran (826) (827)
170	3	6	Whipple (1061)
	4	2	Triplett (990)
171	3	3	James (487)
172	1	14	Myers (748)
	2	5	Farnsworth and Beaumont (300)
	3	5	Binet (91: pp. 83–208)
173	2	2	Binet (91: pp. 83–208)
174	3	3	Vitale (1013)
			Binet and Henri (93)
		5	Binet and Vaschide (94)
	4	3	Giroud (366)
175	1	2	Aveling and Hargreaves (44)
			Estabrooks (293)
176	2	1	Aveling and Hargreaves (44)
178	2	2	Estabrooks (293)
180	3	5	Tarde (963)
182	1	14	Fulton (333)
183	4	7	Allport (12: pp. 183–186)
184	2	4	Novakovsky (764)
185	3	3	Starch (926)
187	2	8	Köhler (556)
188	3	11	Freud (330)
190	1	2	Dudycha and Dudycha (277)
191	1	29	Janet (488)
193	1	11	Anderson and Goodenough (30)
	2	2	McDougall (687)
		3	Freud (327: p. 453) (328)
194	2	7	Giddings (361)
		11	Whitman (1068)
197	3	3	Holt (454: pp. 91 ff.)
203	3	1	De Sanctis (255)
204	3	4	Hart (418)
205	2	11	Guthrie (399)
	3	8	Stofflet (937)
206	1	12	Levy (612)
207	3	20	Shinn (895)
208	1	3	Piaget (806)
		11	Piaget (806)

209	2	4	Köhler (556)
	3	2	Cooley (229)
210	1	4	Freud (327: pp. 33 ff.)
	3	6	Stratton (945)
211	1	26	Lewin (615: p. 175)
212	1	7	Hoppe (459)
	2	8	Stearns (927)
215	1	3	Piaget (806)
		23	Max (676)
216	2	5	Koffka (555)
	3	3	Löwenfeld (636)
		4	Bühler (159)
217	2	3	Bühler (155)
		7	Bühler (159)
		10	Bühler (159)
218	2	1	Calley (174)
219	1	2	Ansbacher (34)
	2	2	Razran (827)
220	1	1	Sherif (887) (888)
		10	Malinowski (653: pp. 87–92)
220	3	11	Sherif (888: pp. 25–42)
221	1	2	Sherif (884)
		9	Sherif (888)
	2	3	Sherif (887: pp. 113–142)
	3	5	Sherif (887: pp. 50 f.)
		6	Sherif (885)
		16	Sherif (886)
222	2	3	Bartlett (60)
223	2	3	Bartlett (60 pp. 206 ff.)
224	note 1	2	Murphy and Likert (738)
225	4	5	Cannon (182)
226	2	2	Steinberg (928)
	3	5	Levy (610)
228	3	8	Schiller (868)
			Kelley (532)
229	1	4	Bryan (145)
		11	Asch (43)
		21	Garrett, Bryan and Perl (344)
	2	2	Jung (524)
		3	Lecky (591)
231	2	8	Zawadzki and Lazarsfeld (1108)
234	2	3	Allport and Vernon (20)
	5	8	Allport (12: pp. 222–230)
235	1	3	Guilford (390)
	2	24	Dunlap (279)
236	3	6	Gates (352)
		8	Klineberg (548)

366 2 3 Hartshorne and May (424)
4 1 Murphy, L. B. (unpublished study)
371 3 2 Horowitz and Horowitz (460)
373 2 1 Murphy and Murphy (742)

CHAPTER VII

379 2 16 Maslow (669) (670)
18 Hattwick (429)
3 3 Jersild (493)
5 Caille (171)
380 1 10 Bathurst (62)
Murphy (740)
382 1 8 Bridges (128)
383 2 5 Burks, B. S. from (mimeographed *Memorandum on Research in Competition and Cooperation*, Soc. Sci. Res. Counc., 1937)
3 1 Dawe (248)
Jersild (493)
4 1 Bridges (128)
384 1 5 Jersild (493)
385 1 10 Jersild (493)
Murphy (740)
4 1 Sewall (880)
388 4 8 Smalley (908)
389 2 1 Foster (315)
390 1 5 Levy and Tulchin (607)
2 1 Reynolds (833)
391 2 1 Nelson (752)
3 4 Tilson (986)
4 2 Goodenough (371)
393 2 1 Rust (860)
394 2 1 Goodenough (371)
397 3 2 Jack (486)
401 2 1 Page (785)
404 1 1 Conrad (225)
Ezekiel (297)
Jersild (493)
2 4 Walker (1019)
405 1 6 Koch (553)
2 12 Kumin (567)
407 1 1 Fite, M. D. (unpublished study)
412 1 3 Goodenough (369)
Isaacs (484)
415 3 1 Klineberg (546)

416 2 2 Goodenough (369)
417 1 15 Levy (606)
419 1 9 Mowrer (728)
2 3 Hattwick (429)
420 2 1 Ginsburg (365)
421 3 2 Fite, M. D. (unpublished study)
425 2 6 Childers (213)
433 1 1 Piaget (805)
434 2 1 Piaget (805)
Lerner, E. (unpublished study)
3 Jack (486)
Page (785)
4 Moreno (725)
3 1 Updegraff and Keister (997)
437 1 2 Maslow (unpublished study)
440 1 7 Eisenberg (288)
2 2 Hoppe (456)
441 1 1 Frank (317)
443 2 4 Asch (42)
447 2 3 Binet and Féré (92)
452 3 3 Shirley (896)
Washburn (1036)
5 7 Jersild, Markey, and Jersild (494)
501 3 3 Forlano and Axelrod (312)
503 1 18 Fromm, E. (unpublished study)
1 19 Maslow, A. H. (unpublished study)

CHAPTER VIII

509 2 6 Challman (199)
Williams (1081)
510 1 1 Piaget (803)
Murphy (740)
2 1 Freud (330)
Isaacs (484)
511 3 1 Alberty (5)
Beeson (73)
513 2 1 Seagoe (876)
514 4 6 Freud (330)
12 De Sanctis (255)
15 Horney (458)
515 3 1 Parten (789)
517 2 1 Parten (789)
519 2 1 Doroschenko (268)
520 5 1 Moreno (725)

521 1 13 Partridge (791)
523 1 20 Arrington (40)
        Jersild (493)
        Murphy (740)
524 3 4 Partridge (791)
525 3 1 Bellingrath (76)
526 2 3 Anderson (27)
527 3 2 Pigors (808)
528 3 1 Washburne (1038)
531 3 2 Horney (457)
532 2 13 Murphy (470)
     22 Mead (693)
542 5 1 Piaget (806)
543 3 3 Piaget (804)
    4 2 Piaget (806)
546 1 1 Harrower (417)
    2 1 Lerner (unpublished study)

CHAPTER IX

553 1 21 Canestrini (181)
555 3 16 Jones (519)
556 1 5 Jones (519)
    6 Bühler (155)
    7 Shirley (896)
557 2 1 Washburn (1036)
559 4 1 Bühler and Hetzer (158)
562 2 1 Sherman (889)
    3 2 Jones (519)
    4 1 Valentine (998)
563 3 6 Hetzer and Tudor-Hart
        (448)
    7 Löwenfeld (636)
566 4 1 Washburn (1036)
567 3 1 Valentine (998)
    4 1 Jones (518)
568 2 1 Bühler (153)
    19 Hunter (471)
569 2 11 Hetzer (445)
570 2 2 Valentine (999)
571 2 4 Gesell (358)
    3 3 Dennis (252)
    5 1 Bühler (152)
574 2 3 Bühler and Hetzer (158)
575 1 8 Piaget (803)
    10 Freud (330)
577 2 2 Fries (332)
579 2 3 Washburn (1036)
        Shirley (896)

    3 2 Bridges (125)
        Shirley (896)
        Bühler (157)
        Washburn (1036)
580 4 8 Bateman (61)
581 2 2 Descœudres (256)
    5 1 Semenova-Boltunova (879)
582 2 1 Piaget (805)
    4 1 Rugg, Krueger and Sonder-
        gard (858)
583 2 2 McCarthy (684)
591 2 2 Berne (84)
592 1 1 Berne (84)
    2 5 Hall (405)
    7 Piaget (805)
595 1 6 Freud (331)
596 1 6 Mead (694)
601 2 3 Foster and Anderson (314)
616 2 16 McGraw (690)
        Gesell and Thompson (360)

CHAPTER X

621 1 2 Lynd and Lynd (647)
629 2 1 Svensen (951)
631 2 13 Reininger (831)
    15 Reininger (831)
    20 Moreno (725)
632 1 11 Moreno (725)
    14 Caldwell and Wellman (193)
    16 Reininger (831)
    20 Reininger (831)
    23 Moreno (725)
    26 Challman (199)
        Williams (1075)
        Caldwell and Wellman (173)
639 6 8 Frank (321)
642 3 1 Cameron (175)
644 3 5 Horney (458)
        Hurlock and Klein (479)
        Hurlock and Sender (481)
645 3 1 Zachry, C. (unpublished
        study)
650 1 7 Moreno (725)
    2 8 Piaget (806)
        Lerner, E. (unpublished
        study)
657 2 1 Cf. Wickman (1070)
659 1 3 Burks, B. S. (unpublished
        study)

660 3 12 Hartshorne and May (422)
Hartshorne, May and Maller
(423)
Hartshorne, May and Shut-
tleworth (424)
661 3 3 Hartshorne and May (422)
666 2 1 Hartshorne, May and Maller
(423)
671 4 1 Hartshorne, May and Maller
(423)
674 2 11 Meltzer (699)
676 2 4 Schaefer (866)
3 1 Macaulay and Watkins (649)
677 2 2 McGrath (689)
678 2 3 Muth (747)
679 3 3 Lockhart (628)

CHAPTER XI

688 3 3 Lange (581)
689 2 6 Clark (215)
691 2 2 Münsterberg (733)
3 2 Moore (720)
692 3 4 Allport (12: pp. 274–278)
693 2 4 Moore (721)
3 2 Landis and Burtt (580)
694 2 2 Landis (575)
695 2 2 Allport (10)
697 3 7 Weston and English (1060)
13 Farnsworth (299)
698 2 8 Laird (569)
699 3 11 Hamilton (408)
700 3 4 Gates (353)
701 2 4 Allport (9)
6 Moede (712: pp. 79–172)
3 3 Travis (988)
702 2 3 Whittemore (1069)
703 2 14 Moede (712: pp. 150 ff.)
3 2 Riddle (842)
706 2 8 Dashiell (241)
710 3 2 Knight (550)
711 4 6 Farnsworth and Williams
(301)
5 2 Gordon (381)
713 2 3 Wells (1059)
714 2 5 Bartlett (60: pp. 118–185)
715 2 2 South (915)
716 1 1 Bechterev and Lange (69)
719 2 1 Shaw (883)
730 3 1 Watson (1039)

738 4 3 Carr (194)
740 1 5 Mead (693)
3 2 Lynd and Lynd (647) (648)
741 1 13 Dollard (266)
743 1 5 Piaget (806)
747 3 7 Benedict (79: p. 106)
748 2 3 Steinberg (929)
14 Freud (327: pp. 30–59)
760 2 2 Duprat (280)
8 Tarde (963)
Ross (857)
13 Ross (857: p. 78)
761 2 12 Smith (909)
Marshall (666)
764 2 15 Kroeber (562)
Mac Iver (650)

CHAPTER XII

769 2 2 Schjelderup-Ebbe (869)
770 1 10 Maslow (669)
13 Murchison (735)
771 1 2 May (677)
3 3 Wechsler (1049)
773 3 2 Hammett (409)
4 4 Rich (836)
774 1 5 Goldstein (368)
775 1 2 Omwake, Dexter and Lewis
(783)
Patrick and Rowles (794)
7 Larson and Haney (583)
2 15 Wechsler (1048)
776 1 4 Landis (574)
2 7 Kretschmer (561)
778 1 5 May (678)
782 3 9 Pintner (812)
Anderson (31)
Uhrbrock (995)
783 3 5 Allport and Cantril (18)
784 2 8 Paterson (793)
15 Perrin (798)
785 2 3 Vernon (1007)
786 2 19 Adler (4)
21 Heidbreder (437)
3 5 Cogan, Conklin and Hollingworth (219)
9 Conrad (224)
787 2 2 Bradshaw (118)
788 2 16 Sears (878)

789 1 5 Cogan, Conklin and Holling-
          worth (219)
      2 6 Kinder (540)
      3 5 Trow and Pu (992)
      4 2 Luh and Sailer (638)
790 2 6 Heidbreder (438)
      3 2 Bernreuter (87)
791 2 4 Franz (323)
       12 Thurstone and Thurstone
          (984)
       17 Chambers (200)
792 2 5 Marshall (667)
        8 Landis and Katz (578)
      3 3 Hanna (412)
793 2 9 Habbe (401)
794 2 11 Harvey (425)
      3 1 Willoughby (1083)
795 2 4 Heidbreder (436)
        7 Gilliland and Morgan (364)
796 2 6 Guilford and Braly (393)
       10 Guthrie (398)
       15 Gilliland (363)
      3 1 Guilford (389)
          Guilford and Guilford (394)
797 3 2 Allport (16)
       10 Wang (1022)
      4 6 Beckman (72)
798 3 2 Bernreuter (86)
799 1 1 Flanagan (310)
      2 2 Pressey (820)
800 1 12 Chambers (200)
       16 Deutsch (258)
801 1 1 Kambouropoulou (525)
      2 8 Meltzer (698)
          Gates (351)
803 3 3 Ball (51)
804 1 11 Landis (573)
      2 4 Line and Griffin (621)
          Line, Griffin and Anderson
          (622)
805 2 7 Darrow and Heath (238)
807 1 3 Davis and Rulon (245)
        6 Guthrie (398)
      2 5 Weber (1047)
        7 Oliver (768)
       12 Schwegler (874)
809 1 6 Page (785)
          Jack (486)
      2 3 Eisenberg (287)

811 1 8 Washburn, Keeler, New, and
          Parshall (1034)
          Washburn, Hughes, Stewart
          and Sligh (1033)
      2 2 McDougall (685)
       14 Washburn, Keeler, New and
          Parshall (1034)
          Washburn, Hughes, Stewart
          and Sligh (1033)
       16 Ewen (296)
812 1 4 Guilford and Braly (392)
          Guilford and Hunt (395)
813 1 1 Stephenson (933)
      2 8 Stephenson (933)
          Pinard (809)
      3 4 Pinard (810)
814 2 8 Pinard (809) (810)
       22 Pinard (810)
          Cattell (197)
      3 3 Cattell (196)
815 2 9 Stephenson (934)
          Pinard (809) (810)
          Cattell (198)
       13 Stephenson (935)
816 1 2 Stephenson (932)
      2 13 Baumgartner (64)
817 1 1 Brown (141)
820 2 11 Baumgartner (64)
      3 6 Williams (1075)
821 3 3 Burtt and Frey (166)
822 2 4 Howells (463)
824 2 7 Paulsen (795)
825 2 3 Hester (444)
826 1 1 Wolff, Smith and Murray
          (1093)
      2 3 Kambouropoulou (525)
        7 Landis and Ross (579)
828 1 2 Scherer (867)
829 2 5 Henning (442)
830 2 9 Djerks (264)
831 2 4 Cowley (232)
      3 4 Chapin (202)
832 2 1 Sward (953)
836 1 11 Humm and Wadsworth (468)
837 2 4 Vernon and Allport (1009)
        7 Spranger (920)
838 1 4 Allport and Vernon (21)
839 1 2 Thomas and Znaniecki (971)
      2 5 Dollard (267)

842 3 2 Chassell (205)
843 2 6 Lasswell (584)
    16 Lasswell (585)
844 2 6 Watson (1045)
  3 9 Queen (823)
    19 Clark (214)
       Bingham (96)
       Moore (715)
845 1 2 Hamilton (407)
846 2 8 Allport and Vernon (20)
  3 3 Vernon (1007)
       Cantril (185)
847 3 5 Allport and Cantril (18)
848 2 4 Cantril, Rand and Allport (187)
  3 2 Cantril and Rand (186)
849 2 2 Harvey (426)
851 2 3 Allport and Vernon (20)
858 2 2 Vernon (1008)
859 2 7 Beck (70)
    19 Hertz (443)
  3 5 Line and Griffin (621)
860 2 16 Vernon (1008)
  3 2 Luria (646)
863 3 6 Barnacle, Ebaugh and Lemere (56)
875 1 2 Wilke (1073)
  2 2 Rundquist and Sletto (859)

CHAPTER XIII

889 1 6 Allport (14)
891 2 5 Lundberg (641)
  3 3 Hart (419)
894 3 7 Israeli (485)
895 1 2 Watson (1041)
896 1 5 Harper (415)
897 1 4 Lickert (619)
898 2 5 Bogardus (103)
899 2 11 Bogardus (103)
900 3 10 Murphy and Likert (738)
  4 3 Thurstone (980)
901 2 2 Thurstone (979)
    15 Thurstone (977)
    19 Bogardus (104)
902 1 8 Thurstone and Chave (981)
903 2 2 Remmers (832)
  3 11 Stagner (922)
904 3 6 Hinckley (452)
       Ferguson (306)

905 1 2 Rice (835)
  2 9 Bolton (108)
       Cherrington and Miller (209)
  3 3 Likert (619)
    11 Likert, Roslow and Murphy (620)
       Miller (705)
908 2 2 Stouffer (943)
909 3 4 Porter (815)
910 3 7 Neumann (754)
911 2 5 Telford (964)
912 2 6 Lundberg (644)
914 3 9 Newcomb and Svehla (747)
  3 11 De Feo (251)
915 1 4 Lundeen and Caldwell (645)
    7 Wagner (1017)
  2 6 Katz and Allport (529)
916 1 6 Lundberg (643)
  2 6 White (1064) (1065)
    10 Brogan (132)
  3 4 Newcomb and Svehla (757)
917 2 4 Robinson (847)
918 1 9 White (1064)
    16 Carlson (190)
    19 Uhrbrock (994)
919 3 4 Anderson and Dvorak (26)
920 1 2 Lynd and Lynd (647: p. 325)
  2 5 Buck (148)
921 3 6 Newcomb and Svehla (757)
922 3 5 White (1064)
924 2 3 Page (784)
925 2 8 Horowitz (459)
927 2 3 Hunter (470)
929 2 4 Allport (14) (15)
930 2 5 Moore (722)
    7 Howells (462)
    13 Symonds (959)
       Carlson (190)
       Eckert and Mills (285)
       Kolstad (557)
  3 3 Symington (956)
  4 4 Moore and Garrison (718)
931 2 3 Rundquist and Sletto (859)
    6 Murphy and Likert (738)
  3 4 Salmer and Remmers (863)
932 2 6 Murphy and Likert (738)
933 1 2 Howells (462)
935 2 2 Howells (463)
  4 3 Moore (722)

936 2 5 Washburn, Kepler, Mc-Broom, Pritchard and Reimer (1035)
937 3 4 Symington (956)
939 1 7 George (356)
      Murphy and Murphy (739)
    2 2 Allport and Hartmann (13)
    3 5 Lund (640)
940 4 4 Carlson (191)
941 2 7 Klein (543)
    3 2 Newcomb (756)
943 1 7 Pintner (811)
944 3 4 Bone (109)
955 2 3 Lichtenstein (618)
     11 Chen (206)
962 1 8 Lundberg (642)
980 3 20 Corey (230)
988 3 6 Rogers (850)
990 2 3 Katz and Allport (529)
992 2 6 Murphy and Likert (738)
993 2 7 Diggins (260)
995 3 6 Simms and Patrick (901)
     15 Hunter (470)
1001 4 3 Shuttleworth (899)
1002 2 2 Woodward (1096)
1003 3 4 Kulp and Davidson (566)
     9 Newcomb and Svehla (757)
      Telford (964)
      Thurstone and Chave (981)
1006 3 Table Newcomb and Svehla (757)
      Telford (964)
      Thurstone and Chave (981)
1007 1 2 Page (784)
1008 2 4 Droba (273) (275)
    3 2 Dodd (265)
1011 2 4 Guilford (391)
1012 2 4 Masuoka (673)
1013 3 4 Droba (273) (275)
     11 Kolstad (557)
1014 2 3 Stagner (922)

1015 2 4 Arnett (38)
      Robinson (846)
     14 Rosenthal (854)
1016 2 9 Lapiere (582)
1017 3 3 Davis (246)
1018 1 10 Arkhangelskii (36)
    2 4 Moore and Garrison (718)
1019 2 2 Lundeen and Caldwell (645)
    3 7 Minard (707)
1020 2 4 Simms and Patrick (901)
1021 3 5 Bair (49)
1022 3 13 Sward (952)
      Sparling (917)
1023 3 11 Chant and Freedman (201)
1025 3 3 Allport (11)
    8 Allport (14)
      Allport and Schanck (19)
1028 1 2 Likert (619)
    2 3 Stagner (922)
1030 1 1 Cherrington (208)
1031 1 2 Vetter (1011)
    2 2 Allport (14)
      Allport and Schanck (19)
    3 5 Lundeen and Caldwell (645)
      Whitelaw and Laslett (1067)
      Caldwell and Lundeen (172)
      Downing (271)
1032 2 4 Miller (705)
    8 Gundlach (397)
1033 1 3 Harper (415)
    2 5 Newcomb (756)
    3 3 Newcomb and Svehla (757)
1038 1 2 Hall (406)
1039 1 4 Likert (619: p. 32)
    2 3 Newcomb and Svehla (757)
1040 2 12 Lippman (624)
1041 1 3 Rice (834)
    3 3 Allport and Cantril (18)
      Gahagan (341)
      Litterer (627)
1042 2 2 Katz and Braly (530)
1043 3 9 Kulp (565)
1044 2 2 Saadi and Farnsworth (862)

BIBLIOGRAPHY

1.—Ackerson, J., On a correlation analysis of children's behavior problems (Abstract), *Proc. and Papers Ninth Internat. Cong. Psychol.*, 1929, Psychol. Rev. Co., 1930, pp. 53-54.

2.—Ackerson, L., Children's behavior problems: I. Incidence, genetic and intellectual factors, *Behavior Res. Monog.*, 1931.

3.—Adler, A., *The pattern of life*, 1931.

4.—Adler, A., A study of organ inferiority and its psychical compensation, *Nerv. & Ment. Dis. Monog.*, 1917, No. 24 (German original, 1907).

5.—Alberty, H. B., The permanence of the vocational choices of high school pupils, *Indus. Art. Mag.*, 1925, **14**, 203-207.

6.—Allen, C. N., Studies in sex differences, *Psychol. Bull.*, 1927, **24**, 294-304; Recent studies in sex differences, *Psychol. Bull.*, 1930, **27**, 394-407.

7.—Allen, E., *Sex and internal secretions*, 1932.

8.—Allen, E., and Doisy, E. A., The induction of a sexually mature condition in immature females by injection of the ovarian follicular hormone, *Amer. J. Physiol.*, 1924, **69**, 577-588.

9.—Allport, F. H., [Editorial comment], *J. Abn. & Soc. Psychol.*, 1924, **18**, 342-344.

10.—Allport, F. H., The influence of the group upon association and thought, *J. Exper. Psychol.*, 1920, **3**, 159-182; see also his *Social psychology*, 1924, 260-291.

11.—Allport, F. H., The J-curve hypothesis of conforming behavior, *J. Soc. Psychol.*, 1934, **5**, 141-183.

12.—Allport, F. H., *Social psychology*, 1924.

13.—Allport, F. H., and Hartman, D. A., The measurement and motivation of atypical opinion in a certain group, *Amer. Pol. Sci. Rev.*, 1925, **19**, No. 4, 753-763.

14.—Allport, G. W., Attitudes, in Murchison, C., *A handbook of social psychology*, 1935.

15.—Allport, G. W., The composition of political attitudes, *Amer. J. Sociol.*, 1929, **35**, 220-238.

16.—Cf. Allport, G. W., A test for ascendance-submission, *J. Abn. & Soc. Psychol.*, 1928, **23**, 118-136.

17.—Allport, G. W., What is a trait of personality? *J. Abn. & Soc. Psychol.*, 1931, **25**, 368-372.

18.—Allport, G. W., and Cantril, H., Judging personality from voice, *J. Soc. Psychol.*, 1934, **5**, 37-55.

19.—Allport, G. W., and Schanck, R. L., Are attitudes biological or cultural in origin? *Char. & Pers.*, 1936, **4**, 195-205.

20.—Allport, G. W., and Vernon, P. E., *Studies in expressive movement*, 1933.

21.—Allport, G. W., and Vernon, P. E., *A study of values*, 1931.

22.—Allport, G. W., and Vernon, P. E., A test for personal values, *J. Abn. & Soc. Psychol.*, 1931, 26, 231-248.

23.—Alverdes, F., *Social life in the animal world*, 1927.

24.—Anastasi, A., *Differential psychology*, 1937.

25.—Anastasi, A., and Foley, J. P., Jr., An analysis of spontaneous drawings by children in different cultures, *J. Appl. Psychol.*, 1936, 20, 689-726.

26.—Anderson, A., and Dvorak, B., Differences between college students and their elders in standards of conduct, *J. Abn. & Soc. Psychol.*, 1928, 23, 286-292.

27.—Anderson, H. H., Domination and integration in the social behavior of young children in an experimental play situation (Paper read at Christmas meeting of the Society for Research in Child Development), 1936.

28.—Anderson, H. H., Motivation of young children: Further studies in success and failure, praise and blame, *Child Devel.*, 1936, 7, No. 2, 125-143.

29.—Anderson, H. H., and Smith, R. S., Motivation of young children: The constancy of certain behavior patterns, *J. Exper. Educ.*, 1933, 2, 138-160.

30.—Anderson, J. E., Child development and the interpretation of behavior, *Science*, 1936, 83, 245-252.

31.—Anderson, L. D., Estimating intelligence by means of printed photographs, *J. Appl. Psychol.*, 1921, 5, 152-155.

32.—Anderson, W. A., The occupational attitudes of college men, *J. Soc. Psychol.*, 1934, 5, 435-466.

33.—Annis, A. D., and Meier, N. C., The induction of opinion through suggestion by means of planted content, *J. Soc. Psychol.*, 1934, 5, 65-81.

34.—Ansbacher, H., Perception of number as affected by the monetary value of the objects: A critical study of the method used in extended constancy phenomenon, *Arch. Psychol.*, 1937, No. 215.

35.—Antipoff, H., Observations sur la compassion et le sens de la justice chez l'enfant, *Arch. de Psychol.*, 1928, 21, 208-214.

36.—Arkhangelskii, A., (The village child and labor), *Psikhologia*, 1928, 2, 110-132.

37.—Armstrong, C. P., Delinquency and primogeniture, *Psychol. Clin.*, 1933, 22, 48-52.

38.—Arnett, C. E., *Social beliefs and attitudes of American school board members*, 1932.

39.—Arps, G. F., Work with knowledge of results vs. work without knowledge of results, *Psychol. Monog.*, 1920, 28, No. 3.

40.—Arrington, R. E., Interrelations in the behavior of young children, *Child Devel. Monog.*, 1932, No. 8.

41.—Arthur, G., The relation of I.Q. to position in family, *J. Educ. Psychol.*, 1926, 17, 541-550.

42.—Asch, S. E., Personality development of Hopi children. (Unpublished study.)

43.—Asch, S. E., A study of change in mental organization, *Arch. Psychol.*, 1936, No. 195.

44.—Aveling, F., and Hargreaves, H. L., Suggestibility with and without prestige in children, *Brit. J. Psychol.*, 1921, 18, 362-388.

45.—Avery, G. T., The congenital behavior of the guinea pig, Thesis in the Stanford University Library, 1924.

46.—Avery, G. T., Responses of foetal guinea pigs prematurely delivered, *Genet. Psychol. Monog.*, 1928, **3**, 247-331.

47.—Bagehot, W., *Physics and politics*, 1869.

48.—Bain, A., *The senses and the intellect*, 1855; *The emotions and the will*, 1859.

49.—Bair, F. H., The social understandings of the superintendents of schools, *Teach. Coll. Contrib. Educ.*, 1934, No. 625.

50.—Baker, H. J., Decker, F. J., and Hill, A. S., A study of juvenile theft, *J. Educ. Res.*, 1929, **20**, 81-87.

51.—Ball, R. J., An objective measure of emotional stability, *J. Appl. Psychol.*, 1929, **13**, 226-256.

52.—Ballow, A., *History of the Hopedale Community*, 1897.

53.—Barker, M., A preliminary report on the social-material activities of children, *Child Devel. Monog.*, 1930, No. 3.

54.—Barker, R., Dembo, T., and Lewin, K., (Paper read at the Christmas meeting of the "Dynamic Psychologists"), 1936.

55.—Barker, R., Dembo, T., and Lewin, K., Experiments on frustration and regression in children, *Proc. 45th Ann. Mtg. Amer. Psychol. Assn.*, 1937.

56.—Barnacle, C. H., Ebaugh, F. G., and Lemere, F., Association-motor investigation of the psychoneuroses, *Amer. J. Psychiat.*, 1935, **91**, 925-937.

57.—Barnes, E., Punishment as seen by children, *Ped. Sem.*, 1894-1896, **3**, 235-245.

58.—Barrett, H. E., and Koch, H. L., The effect of nursery-school training upon the mental-test performance of a group of orphanage children, *J. Genet. Psychol.*, 1930, **37**, 102-122.

59.—Barry, H., Jr., A test for negativism and compliance, *J. Abn. & Soc. Psychol.*, 1931, **25**, 373-381.

60.—Bartlett, F. C., *Remembering*, 1932.

61.—Bateman, W. G., The language status of three children at the same ages, *Ped. Sem.*, 1916, **23**, 211-241.

62.—Bathurst, J. E., A study in sympathy and resistance (negativism) among children, *Psychol. Bull.*, 1933, **30**, 625-626.

63.—Baumgarten, F., Reaktionstypen der Kinder und Jugendlicher in sozialen Verhalten, *Zsch. f. päd. Psychol.*, 1926, **27**, 537-556.

64.—Baumgartner, M., The correlation of direct suggestibility with certain character traits, *J. Appl. Psychol.*, 1931, **15**, 1-15.

65.—Bayley, N., Mental growth during the first three years, *Genet. Psychol. Monog.*, 1933, **14**, 1-92.

66.—Bayley, N., A study of the crying of infants during mental and physical tests, *J. Genet. Psychol.*, 1932, **40**, 306-329.

67.—Beaver, A. P., The initiation of social contacts by pre-school children: A study of technique in recording social behavior, *Child Devel. Monog.*, 1932, No. 7.

68.—Beaver, A. P., A preliminary report on a study of a pre-school "gang," *Child Devel. Monog.*, 1932, No. 7.

69.—Bechterev, W., and Lange, M., Die Ergebnisse des Experiments auf dem Gebiete der kollektiven Reflexologie (The results of the experiments in the field of collective reflexology), *Zsch. f. angew. Psychol.*, 1924, **24**, 224-254.

70.—Beck, S. J., Problems of further research in the Rorschach test, *Amer. J. Orthopsychiat.*, 1935, **5**, 100-115.

71.—Beck, S. J., The Rorschach method and personality organization: III. The psychological and the social personality, *Amer. J. Orthopsychiat.*, 1934, **4**, 290-297.

72.—Beckman, R. O., Ascendance-submission test—revised, *Person. J.*, 1933, **11**, 387-392.

73.—Beeson, F., A study of vocational preferences of high school students, *Voc. Guid. Mag.*, 1928, **7**, 115-119.

74.—Belcher, E. L., A technique for diary analysis, *Child Devel.*, 1932, **3**, 53-56.

75.—Bellerose, D., Behavior problems of children, Master's essay, Smith College School for Social Work, 1927.

76.—Bellingrath, G. C., Qualities associated with leadership in the extra-curricular activities of the high school, *Teach. Coll. Contrib. Educ.*, 1930, No. 399.

77.—Bender, I. E., Ascendance-submission in relation to certain other factors in personality, *J. Abn. & Soc. Psychol.*, 1928, **23**, 137-143.

78.—Bender, L., and Schilder, P., Aggressiveness in children, *Genet. Psychol. Monog.*, 1936, **18**, pp. 410-425, from Bender, L., Keiser, S., and Schilder, P., Studies in aggressiveness, Nos. 5-6.

79.—Benedict, R., *Patterns of culture*, 1934.

80.—Benjamin, H., Age and sex differences in the toy preferences of young children, *J. Genet. Psychol.*, 1932, **41**, 417-429.

81.—Benton, A. L., Influence of incentives upon intelligence test scores of school children, *J. Genet. Psychol.*, 1936, **49**, 494-497.

82.—Berman, H. H., Order of birth in manic-depressive reactions, *Psychiat. Quar.*, 1933, **7**, 430-435.

83.—Berne, E. V. C., An experimental investigation of social behavior patterns in young children, *Univ. Iowa Stud.: Stud. Child Welfare*, 1930, **4**, No. 2.

84.—Berne, E. V. C., An experimental investigation of social behavior patterns in young children, *Univ. Iowa Stud.: Stud. Child Welfare*, 1930, **4**, No. 3.

85.—Bernheim, H., *De la suggestion dans l'état hypnotique et dans l'état de veille*, 1884.

86.—Bernreuter, R. G., *The personality inventory*, 1931.

87.—Bernreuter, R. G., Validity of the personality inventory, *Person. J.*, 1933, **11**, 383-386.

88.—Bernstein, S., A study of the social development and behavior of infants between the ages of five and twelve months, Cooperative M.A. thesis, Columbia University, 1934. (See Budnick.)

89.—Biddle, W. W., Propaganda and education, *Teach. Coll. Contrib. Educ.*, 1932, No. 531.

90.—Biddle, W. W., The relationship between knowledge and a measure of autistic thinking on certain international problems, *J. Soc. Psychol.*, 1931, **2**, 493-496.

91.—Binet, A., *La suggestibilité*, 1900.

92.—Binet, A., and Féré, C., *Le magnétisme animal*, 1887.

93.—Binet, A., and Henri, V. (See Binet, *La suggestibilité*, 1900, 62.)

94.—Binet, A., and Vaschide, N. (See Binet, *La suggestibilité*, 1900, 24.)

95.—Binet, A., and Vaschide, N., Expériences des forces musculaires et de fond chez les jeunes garçons, *Ann. Psychol.*, 1897, **4**, 15-63.

96.—Bingham, W. V., The personal interview studied by means of analysis and experiment, *Soc. Forces*, 1929, **7**, 530-533.

97.—Bird, C., The influence of the press upon the accuracy of report, *J. Abn. & Soc. Psychol.*, 1927, **22**, 123-129.

98.—Blanton, M. G., The behavior of the human infant during the first thirty days of life, *Psychol. Rev.*, 1917, **24**, 456-483.

99.—Blatz, W. E., and Bott, E. A., Studies in mental hygiene of children: I. Behavior of public school children—A description of method, *J. Genet. Psychol.*, 1927, **34**, 552-582.

100.—Blatz, W. E., and Ringland, M. C., The study of tics in pre-school children, *Univ. Toronto Stud., Child Devel. Ser.*, 1935, No. 3.

101.—Blonsky, P. P., Das einzige Kind in seinem ersten Schuljahr, *Zsch. f. päd. Psychol.*, 1930, **31**, 84-97.

102.—Boas, F., *The mind of primitive man*, 1911.

103.—Bogardus, E. S., *Immigration and race attitudes*, 1928.

104.—Cf. Bogardus, E. S., A social distance scale, *Sociol. & Soc. Res.*, 1933, **17**, 265-271, for a revision in which a scale composed of seven equidistant steps is presented.

105.—Boggess, V., Some factors accounting for the variation in the social adjustment of children living in a tenement area, *Smith Coll. Stud. Soc. Work*, 1936, **6**, 324-359.

106.—Bohannon, E. W., The only child in a family, *Ped. Sem.*, 1898, **5**, 475-496.

107.—Boldt, W. J., and Stroud, J. B., Changes in the attitudes of college students, *J. Educ. Psychol.*, 1934, **25**, 611-619.

108.—Bolton, E. B., Effect of knowledge upon attitudes toward the Negro, *J. Soc. Psychol.*, 1935, **6**, 68-90.

109.—Bone, H., *Le prejuge*, 1935.

110.—Book, W. F., and Norvell, L., The will to learn, *Ped. Sem.*, 1922, **29**, 305-362.

111.—Bott, E. A., Blatz, W. E., Chant, N., and Bott, H., Observation and training of the fundamental habits in young children, *Genet. Psychol. Monog.*, 1928, **4**, No. 162.

112.—Bott, H. M., Observations of play activities in a nursery school, *Genet. Psychol. Monog.*, 1928, **4**, 44-88.

113.—Bott, H. M., Personality development in young children, *Univ. of Toronto Stud., Child Devel. Ser.*, 1934, No. 2.

114.—Boynton, P. L., Dugger, H., and Turner, M., The emotional stability of teachers and children, *J. Juv. Res.*, 1934, **18**, 223-232.

115.—Boynton, P. L., and Ford, F. A., The relationship between play and intelligence, *J. Appl. Psychol.*, 1933, **17**, 294-301.

116.—Boynton, P. L., and McGaw, B. H., The characteristics of problem children, *J. Juv. Res.*, 1934, **18**, 215-222.

117.—Brackett, C. W., Laughing and crying of pre-school children, *J. Exper. Educ.*, 1933, **2**, 119-126; also, *Child Devel. Monog.*, 1934, No. 14.

118.—Bradshaw, F. F., American Council on Education rating scale: its reliability, validity, and use, *Arch. Psychol.*, 1930, No. 119.

119.—Braid, J., *Neurypnology*, 1843.

120.—Brameld, T. B., College students react to social issues, *Soc. Frontier*, 1934, **1**, 21-26.

121.—Breckenridge, S. P., and Abbott, E., *The delinquent child and the home*, 1912.

122.—Bregman, E. O., An attempt to modify the emotional attitudes of infants by the conditioned response technique, *J. Genet. Psychol.*, 1934, **45**, 169-198.

123.—Brenner, B., Effect of immediate and delayed praise and blame upon learning and recall, *Teach. Coll. Contrib. Educ.*, 1934, No. 620.

124.—Bridges, K. M. B., Occupational interests of three-year-old children, *J. Genet. Psychol.*, 1929, **36**, 551-570.

125.—Bridges, K. M. B., Emotional development in early infancy, *Child Devel.*, 1932, **3**, 324-341.

126.—Bridges, K. M. B., Measuring emotionality in infants, A tentative experiment, *Child Devel.*, 1934, **5**, 36-40.

127.—Bridges, K. M. B., The occupational interests and attention of four-year-old children, *Ped. Sem.*, 1928, **36**, 551-570.

128.—Bridges, K. M. B., *The social and emotional development of the pre-school child*, 1931.

129.—Briggs, T. H., Praise and censure as incentives, *School & Soc.*, 1927, **26**, 596-598.

130.—Briggs, T. H., Sarcasm, *School Rev.*, 1928, **36**, 685-695.

131.—Brigham, C. C., *A study of American intelligence*, 1923.

132.—Brogan, A. P., A study in statistical ethics, *Int. J. Eth.*, 1923, **33**, 119-134.

133.—Brown, A. R., *The Andaman Islanders, a study in social anthropology*, 1922.

134.—Brown, F., A comparative study of the influence of race and locale upon emotional stability of children, *J. Genet. Psychol.*, 1936, **49**, 325-342.

135.—Brown, F., A comparative study of stability and maturity of non-delinquent, pre-delinquent, and delinquent boys, *Proc. 45th Ann. Mtg. Amer. Psychol. Assn.*, 1937.

136.—Brown, F., A psychoneurotic inventory for children between 9 and 14 years of age, *J. Appl. Psychol.*, 1934, **18**, 566-577.

137.—Brown, F. J., Knowledge of results as an incentive in schoolroom practice, *J. Educ. Psychol.*, 1932, **23**, 532-552.

138.—Brown, J. F., Über die dynamischen Eigenschaften der Realitäts- und Irrealitätschichten, *Psychol. Forsch.*, 1933, **18**, 2-26.

139.—Brown, L. G., *Social psychology*, 1934.

140.—Brown, M., Leadership among high school pupils, *Teach. Coll. Contrib. Educ.*, 1933, No. 559.

141.—Brown, W., Individual and sex differences in suggestibility, *Univ. of California Publns. in Psychol.*, 1916, **2**, No. 6, 291-430.

142.—Brückner, G. H., *Untersuchungen zur Tiersoziologie, insbesondere zur Auflösung der Familie*, 1933.

143.—Brugger, C., Die Vererbung des Schwachsinns, *Fortschr. Neurol. Psychiat.*, 1937, **9**, 93-102.

144.—Brunk, C., The effects of maternal over-protection on the early development and habits of children, *Smith Coll. Stud. Soc. Work*, 1931, **2**, 261-273.

145.—Bryan, A. I., Organization of memory in young children, *Arch. Psychol.*, 1934, No. 162.

146.—Bryan, E. S., Variation in the responses of infants during first ten days of post-natal life, *Child Devel.*, 1931, 1, 56-77.

147.—Bryn, D., The problem of human types, *Char. & Pers.*, 1936, 5, 48-60.

148.—Buck, W., A measurement of changes in attitudes and interests of university students over a ten-year period, *J. Abn. & Soc. Psychol.*, 1936, 31, 12-19.

149.—Budnick, F., A study of the relationship between the personality and the family history of infants in the second half year of life, Cooperative M.A. thesis, Columbia University, 1934. (See Bernstein.)

150.—Bühler, C., The child and its activity with practical material, *Brit. J. Educ. Psychol.*, 1933, 3, 27-41.

151.—Bühler, C., The curve of life as studied in biographies, *J. Appl. Psychol.*, 1935, 19, 405-409.

152.—Bühler, C., Die ersten sozialen Verhaltungweisen des Kindes, In *Soziologische Studien über das erste Lebensjahr*, 1927.

153.—Bühler, C., *The first year of life*, 1930.

154.—Bühler, C., *From birth to maturity*, 1935.

155.—Bühler, C., *Kindheit und Jugend*, 1931.

156.—Bühler, C., The social behavior of the child, In *Handbook of child psychology*, 1931, pp. 392-431.

157.—Bühler, C., The social behavior of children, In *Handbook of child psychology* (2nd ed. rev.), 1933, pp. 374-416.

158.—Bühler, C., and Hetzer, H., Inventar der Verhaltungsweisen des ersten Lebensjahres, (*Quell. u. Stud. z. Jugendk.*, No. 5.), 1927, pp. 125-250; also in *The first year of life*, 1930, pp. 63-64.

159.—Bühler, C., Hetzer, H., and Tudor-Hart, B., *Soziologische und psychologische Studien über das erste Lebensjahr*, 1927.

160.—Burgess, E. W. [ed.], *The adolescent in the family*, 1934.

161.—Burks, B. S., Needed evidence, *Amer. Natur.*, 1933, 67, 206-221.

162.—Burks, B. S., On the inadequacy of the partial and multiple correlation technique, *J. Educ. Psychol.*, 1926, 17, 532-540, 625-630.

163.—Burks, B. S., The relative influence of nature and nurture upon mental development; a comparative study of foster-parent foster-child resemblance and true-parent true-child resemblance, *27th Yrbk. of the National Society for the Study of Education*, 1928, 219-316.

164.—Burks, B. S., and Kelley, T. L., Statistical hazards in nature-nurture investigations, *27th Yrbk. of the National Society for the Study of Education*, 1928, 9-38.

165.—Burt, C., The young delinquent, 1925.

166.—Burtt, H., E., and Frey, O. C., Suggestions for measuring recklessness, *Person. J.*, 1934, 13, 39-46.

167.—Busemann, A., Bruder und Schwester, *Zsch. f. Sex.-wiss. u. Sex.-pol.*, 1929, 16, 392-400.

168.—Busemann, A., Die Familie als Erlebnis-milieu des Kindes, *Zsch. f. Kinderforsch.*, 1928, 36, 17-82.

169.—Busemann, A., Geschwisterschaft, Schultuchtigkeit und Charakter, *Zsch. f. Kinderforsch.*, 1928, 34, 1-52.

170.—Buttgereit, H., Führergestalten in der Schulklasse, *Zsch. f. angew. Psychol.*, 1932, **43**, 369-413.

171.—Caille, R. K., Resistant behavior of pre-school children, *Child Devel. Monog.*, 1933, No. 11.

172.—Caldwell, O., and Lundeen, G. E., Changing unfounded beliefs—a unit in biology, *School Sci. & Math.*, 1933, **33**, 394-413.

173.—Caldwell, O., and Wellman, B., Characteristics of school leaders, *J. Educ. Res.*, 1926, **14**, 1-13.

174.—Calley, D. M., (Unpublished study).

175.—Cameron, W. J., The interests of club-aged boys and girls (Paper presented at the annual meeting of California 4-H Club leaders), January, 1936.

176.—Campbell, A. A., Personality adjustments of only children, *Psychol. Bull.*, 1934, **31**, 193-203.

177.—Campbell, A. A., A study of the personality adjustments of only and intermediate children, *J. Genet. Psychol.*, 1933, **43**, 197-206.

178.—Campbell, D. W., and Stover, G. F., Teaching international-mindedness in the social studies, *J. Educ. Sociol.*, 1933, **7**, 244-248.

179.—Campbell, E. H., The effect of nursery-school training upon the later food habits of the child, *Child Devel.*, 1933, **4**, 329-345.

180.—Campbell, E. H., and Breckenridge, M. E., An experiment in the study of individual development, *Child Devel.*, 1936, **7**, 37-39.

181.—Canestrini, S., *Ueber das Sinnesleben der Neugeborenen*, 1913.

182.—Cannon, W. B., *Bodily changes in pain, hunger, fear, and rage*, 1929, 256-257.

183.—Cannon, W. B., *The mechanical factors of digestion*, 1911.

184.—Cannon, W. B., and Washburn, A. L., An explanation of hunger, *Amer. J. Physiol.*, 1912, **29**, 441-454.

185.—Cantril, H., General and specific attitudes, *Psychol. Monog.*, 1932, **42**, No. 5.

186.—Cantril, H., and Rand, H. A., An additional study of the determination of personal interests by psychological and graphological methods, *Char. & Pers.*, 1934, **3**, 72-78.

187.—Cantril, H., Rand, H. A., and Allport, G. W., The determination of personal interests by psychological and graphological methods, *Char. & Pers.*, 1933, **2**, 134-143.

188.—Carlson, A. J., *Control of hunger in health and disease*, 1916.

189.—Carlson, A. J., and Ginsburg, H., Contributions to the physiology of the stomach: XXIV. The tonus and hunger contractions of the stomach of the new-born, *Amer. J. Physiol.*, 1915, **38**, 29-32.

190.—Carlson, H. B., Attitudes of undergraduate students, *J. Soc. Psychol.*, 1934, **5**, 202-213.

191.—Carlson, H. S., Information as a factor producing certainty of opinion, Master's essay in Graduate College, State University of Iowa, 1929.

192.—Carman, A., Pain and strength measurements of 1507 school children in Saginaw, Michigan, *Amer. J. Psychol.*, 1899, **10**, 392-398.

193.—Carmichael, L., The development of behavior in vertebrates experimentally removed from the influence of external stimulation, *Psychol. Rev.*, 1926, **33**, 51-58.

194.—Carr, L. J., Experimental sociology: a preliminary note on theory and method, *Soc. Forces*, 1929, **8**, 63-74.

195.—Carter, H. D., Twin similarities in personality traits, *J. Genet. Psychol.*, 1933, **43**, 312-321.

196.—Cattell, R. B., Perseveration and personality: Some experiments and a hypothesis, *J. Ment. Sci.*, 1935, **81**, 151-167.

197.—Cattell, R. B., Temperament tests: I, Temperament, *Brit. J. Psychol.*, 1933, **23**, 308-329.

198.—Cattell, R. B., Temperament tests: II, Tests, *Brit. J. Psychol.*, 1933, **24**, 20-49.

199.—Challman, R. C., Factors influencing friendships among pre-school children, *Child Devel.*, 1932, **3**, 146-158.

200.—Cf. Chambers, O. R., Character trait tests and the prognosis of college achievement, *J. Abn. & Soc. Psychol.*, 1925, **20**, 303-311; A method of measuring the emotional maturity of children, *Ped. Sem.*, 1925, **32**, 637-647.

201.—Chant, S. N. F., and Freedman, S. S., A quantitative comparison of the nationality preferences of two groups, *J. Soc. Psychol.*, 1934, **5**, 116-120.

202.—Chapin, F. S., Measuring the volume of social stimuli: a study in social psychology, *Soc. Forces*, 1926, **4**, 479-495.

203.—Chapman, J. C., and Feder, R. B., The effect of external incentives on improvement, *J. Educ. Psychol.*, 1917, **8**, 469-474.

204.—Chase, L. E., Motivation of young children: An experimental study of the influence of certain types of external incentives upon the performance of a task, *Univ. Iowa Stud.: Stud. Child Welfare*, 1932, **5**, No. 3.

205.—Chassell, J. O., *The experience variables*, 1928.

206.—Chen, W. K. C., The influence of oral propaganda material upon students' attitudes, *Arch. Psychol.*, 1933, **23**, No. 150.

207.—Cherkassova, A., [On the question of studying experimentally the collective creativity of the child], *Dyetskii kollektiv i rebenok*, 1926, 138-196.

208.—Cherrington, B. M., Methods of education in international attitudes, *Teach. Coll. Contrib. Educ.*, 1934, No. 595.

209.—Cherrington, B. M., and Miller, L. W., Changes in attitude as the result of a lecture and reading similar materials, *J. Soc. Psychol.*, 1933, **4**, 479-484.

210.—Chevaleva-Ianovskaia, E., and Sylla, D., Essai d'une étude sur les enfants meneurs, *J. de Psychol.*, 1929, **26**, 604-612.

211.—Chevaleva-Ianovskaia, E., Les groupements spontanés d'enfants à l'âge préscolaire, *Arch. de Psychol.*, 1927, **20**, 219-233.

212.—Child, C. M., *Physiological foundations of behavior*, 1924, 121-127 ff.

213.—Childers, A. T., Hyperactivity in children having behavior disorders, *Amer. J. Orthopsychiat.*, 1935, **5**, 227-243.

214.—Cf. Clark, E. L., Value of student interviews, *J. Pers. Res.*, 1926, **5**, 204-207.

215.—Clark, H., The crowd, *Psychol. Monog.*, 1916, **21**, No. 92, 26-36.

216.—Clem, O. M., and Smith, M., Grade differences in attitudinal reactions of six-year secondary school pupils, *J. Educ. Psychol.*, 1934, **25**, 297-309.

217.—Coburn, C. A., Heredity of wildness and savageness in mice, *Behav. Monog.*, 1922, **4**, No. 5.

218.—Cockrell, D. L., A study of the play of children of pre-school age by an unobserved observer, *Genet. Psychol. Monog.*, 1935, **17**, No. 6.

219.—Cf. Cogan, L. C., Conklin, A. M., and Hollingworth, H. L., An experimental study of self-analysis, estimates of associates, and the results of tests, *School & Soc.*, 1915, **2**, 171-179.

220.—Coghill, G. E., Correlated anatomical and physiological studies of the growth of the nervous system in amphibia: VI. The mechanism of integration in amblystoma punctatum, *J. Comp. Neur.*, 1926, **41**, 95-152.

221.—Collins, J. E., The intelligence of school children and paternal occupation, *J. Educ. Res.*, 1928, **17**, 157-169.

222.—Collmann, R. D., The psychogalvanic reactions of exceptional and normal school children, *Teach. Coll. Contrib. Educ.*, 1931, No. 469.

223.—Conrad, H. S., *The California Behavior Inventory for Nursery School Children*, Institute of Child Welfare, University of California, 1933.

224.—Conrad, H. S., The personal equation in ratings: I. An experimental determination, *Ped. Sem. & J. Genet. Psychol.*, 1932, **41**, 267-293.

225.—Conrad, H. S., A statistical study of ratings on the California Behavior Inventory for Nursery School Children, *Genet. Psychol. Monog.*, 1934, **16**, 1-78.

226.—Conrad, H. S., The validity of personality ratings of nursery-school children, *J. Educ. Psychol.*, 1932, **23**, 671-680.

227.—Conradi, E., Song and call-notes of English sparrows when reared by canaries, *Amer. J. Psychol.*, 1905, **16**, 190-199.

228.—Cook, M. N., and Thomas, M., Family relationship in ascendance-submission, *Publ. Univ. Calif. L. A. Educ., Phil., Psychol.*, 1924, **1**, 189-192.

229.—Cooley, C. H., *Human nature and the social order*, 1910.

230.—Corey, S. M., Attitude differences between college classes: a summary and criticism, *J. Educ. Psychol.*, 1936, **27**, 321-330.

231.—Cowan, E. A., McClellan, M. C., Pratt, B. M., and Skaer, M., An adolescent personality schedule, *Child Devel.*, 1935, **6**, 77-87.

232.—Cowley, W. H., The traits of face-to-face leaders, *J. Abn. & Soc. Psychol.*, 1931, **26**, 304-313.

233.—Craig, W., Appetites and aversions as constituents of instincts, *Biol. Bull.*, 1918, **34**, 91-107.

234.—Craig, W., Male doves reared in isolation, *J. Animal Behav.*, 1914, **4**, 121-133.

235.—Crawford, A. B., Effect of scholarships: A study in motivation, *J. Person. Res.*, 1926, **4**, 391-404.

236.—Cressey, P. G., and Thrasher, F. M., *Boys, movies and the city streets*, 1933.

237.—Cushing, H. M., A tentative report of the influence of nursery-school training upon kindergarten adjustment as reported by kindergarten teachers, *Child Devel.*, 1934, **5**, 304-314.

238.—Darrow, C. W., and Heath, L. L., Reaction tendencies relating to personality, in Lashley, K. S., *et al.*, *Studies in the dynamics of behavior*, 1932.

239.—Darsie, M. L., The mental capacity of American-born Japanese children, *Comp. Psychol. Monog.*, 1926, **3**, Ser. No. 15, 89.

240.—Darwin, C., *The descent of man*, 1871.

241.—Dashiell, J. F., An experimental analysis of some group effects, *J. Abn. & Soc. Psychol.*, 1930, **25**, 190-199.

242.—Dashiell, J. F., *Fundamentals of general psychology*, 1937.

243.—Dashiell, J. F., A quantitative demonstration of animal drive, *J. Comp. Psychol.*, 1925, **5**, 205-208.

244.—Davis, A. J., Personality, parent intelligence, and "scatter" on the Stanford-Binet, *J. Juv. Res.*, 1934, **18**, 175-178.

245.—Davis, F. B., and Rulon, P. J., Gossip and the introvert, *J. Abn. & Soc. Psychol.*, 1935, **30**, 17-21.

246.—Davis, J., Testing the social attitudes of children in the government schools in Russia, *Amer. J. Sociol.*, 1927, **32**, 947-952.

247.—Dawe, H. C., An analysis of two hundred quarrels of pre-school children, *Child Devel.*, 1934, **5**, 139-157.

248.—Dawe, H. C., The influence of size of kindergarten group upon performance, *Child Devel.*, 1934, **5**, 295-303.

249.—Dawson, W. M., Inheritance of wildness and tameness in mice, *Genetics*, 1932, **17**, 296-326.

250.—Dayton, N. A., Influence of size of family upon the characteristics of the mentally deficient: Survey of 20,473 retarded children in the public schools of Massachusetts, *Amer. J. Psychiat.*, 1935, **91**, 799-832.

251.—De Feo, G., Les impressions des jeunes sur les films de guerre, *Revue Internationale du Cinéma Éducational*, 1932, **4**, 43-53, 141-150, 235-243, 322-330, 419-432.

252.—Dennis, W., An experimental test of two theories of social smiling in infants, *J. Soc. Psychol.*, 1935, **6**, 214-223.

253.—Denworth, K. M., The effect of length of school attendance upon mental and educational ages, *27th Yrbk. of the National Society for the Study of Education*, Part II, 1928, 67-91.

254.—Deputy, E. C., Knowledge of success as a motivating factor in college work, *J. Educ. Res.*, 1929, **20**, 327-334.

255.—De Sanctis, S., *La conversione religiosa, studio biopsicologico*, 1924.

256.—Descœudres, A., La mesure du langage de l'enfant, *J. de Psychol.*, 1924, **21**, 43-54.

257.—Detroit Teachers' College, *How children choose friends*, 1929.

258.—Deutsch, G. F., Conformity in human behavior with a test for its measurement, Master's essay in Columbia University Library, 1923.

259.—Diamond, S., A neglected aspect of motivation (to appear in *Sociometry*, 1938).

260.—Diggins, E., A statistical study of national prejudices, Master's essay in Columbia University Library, 1927.

261.—Dimock, H. S., A research in adolescence: I. Pubescence and physical growth, *Child Devel.*, 1935, **6**, 177-195.

262.—Dimock, H. S., A research in adolescence: II. The social world of the adolescent, *Child Devel.*, 1935, **6**, 285-302.

263.—Diserens, C. M., and Vaughn, J., The experimental psychology of motivation, *Psychol. Bull.*, 1931, **28**, 15-65.

264.—Djerks, H., Experimentelle Untersuchungen des sozialen Verhaltens, *Zsch. f. angew. Psychol.*, 1932, **43**, 193-270.

265.—Dodd, S. C., A social distance test in the Near East, *Amer. J. Sociol.*, 1935, **41**, 194-204.

266.—Dollard, J., *Caste and class in a southern town,* 1937.

267.—Dollard, J., *Criteria for the life history,* 1935.

268.—Doroschenko, O., Der Einfluss des Milieus auf den Inhalt und Aufbau frei entstehender Kollektive im vorschulpflichtigen Alter, *Zsch. f. angew. Psychol.,* 1928, **30**, 150-167.

269.—Dow, M. L., An observational study in a playground situation of differences in artistic personality at the child level, *Proc. Ia. Acad. Sci.,* 1933, **40**, 197.

270.—Dow, M. L., Playground behavior differentiation, artistic from non-artistic children, *Psychol. Monog.,* 1933, **45**, 82-94.

271.—Downing, E. R., Does science teach scientific thinking? *Sci. Educ.,* 1933, **17**, 87-89.

272.—Driscoll, G. P., The developmental status of the pre-school child as a prognosis of future development, *Child Devel. Monog.,* 1933, No. 13.

273.—Droba, D. D., Churches and war attitudes, *Social. & Soc. Res.,* 1931, **16**, 547-552.

274.—Droba, D. D., Education and Negro attitudes, *Sociol. & Soc. Res.,* 1932, **17**, 137-141.

275.—Droba, D. D., Effect of various factors on militarism-pacificism, *J. Abn. & Soc. Psychol.,* 1931, **26**, 141-153.

276.—Dudycha, G. J., The social beliefs of college seniors, *Amer. J. Sociol.,* 1932, **37**, 775-780; Moral beliefs of college students, *Int. J. Ethics,* 1933, **43**, 194-204; The religious beliefs of college students, *J. Appl. Psychol.,* 1933, **17**, 585-603; The beliefs of college students concerning evolution, *J. Appl. Psychol.,* 1934, **28**, 85-96; The superstitious beliefs of college students, *J. Abn. & Soc. Psychol.,* 1933, **27**, 457-464.

277.—Dudycha, G. J., and Dudycha, M. M., Adolescents' memories of preschool experiences, *J. Genet. Psychol.,* 1933, **42**, 468-480; Some factors and characteristics of childhood memories, *Child Devel.,* 1933, **4**, 265-278.

278.—Duffy, E., Tensions and emotional factors in reaction, *Genet. Psychol. Monog.,* 1930, **7**, No. 1.

279.—Dunlap, K., The rôle of eye-muscles and mouth-muscles in the expression of the emotions, *Genet. Psychol. Monog.,* 1927, **2**, No. 3, 199-233.

280.—Duprat, G.-L., *La psychologie sociale,* 1920.

281.—Durost, W. N., Children's collecting activity related to social factors, *Teach. Coll. Contrib. Educ.,* 1932, No. 535.

282.—Dybowski, M., Opór Dziecka i perseweracja, *Kwart. psychol.,* 1935, **7**, 139-156.

283.—Dybowski, M. (Perseveration as a measure of negativism, and its estimation by means of photographs), *Kwart. psychol.,* 1935, **6**, 221-236.

284.—Eaton, M. T., The effect of praise, reproof and exercise upon muscular steadiness, *J. Exper. Educ.,* 1933, **2**, 44-59.

285.—Eckert, R. E., and Mills, H. C., International attitudes and related academic and social factors, *J. Educ. Psychol.,* 1935, **9**, 142-153.

286.—Efron, D., and Foley, J. P., Jr., A comparative investigation of gestural behavior patterns in Italian and Jewish groups living under different as well as similar environmental conditions, *Zsch. f. Sozialforsch.,* 1937, **6**, 151-159.

287.—Eisenberg, P., Expressive movements related to feelings of dominance, *Arch. Psychol.,* 1937, No. 211.

288.—Eisenberg, P., Factors related to feeling of dominance (Paper delivered at Ann. Mtg., Eastern Branch, Amer. Psychol. Assn.), 1937.

289.—Eliot, A. A., Eating habits in relation to personality development of two- and three-year-old children, *Genet. Psychol. Monog.*, 1933, **13**, No. 5.

290.—Ellis, H., *A study of British genius* (new ed.), 1927.

291.—English, H. B., Three cases of the "conditioned fear response," *J. Abn. & Soc. Psychol.*, 1929, **24**, 221-225.

292.—Erofeeva, M., (Electrical stimulation of the skin of the dog as a conditioned salivary stimulus), Thesis, St. Petersburg (Pavlov's lab.), 1912.

293.—Estabrooks, G. H., Experimental studies in suggestion, *J. Genet. Psychol.*, 1929, **36**, 120-139.

294.—Etzion, M., A method of studying the character traits of the pre-school child, *J. Genet. Psychol.*, 1933, **42**, 184-205.

295.—Everetov, I., (Observations on the appearance of sociality in early childhood), *Metody obyektivnogo izuchenya rebyenka*, 1924, 104-110.

296.—Ewen, J. H., The psychological estimation of the effects of certain drugs upon the syntonic and schizophrenic psychoses, *J. Ment. Sci.*, 1931, **77**, 742-766.

297.—Ezekiel, L. F., Changes in egocentricity of nursery-school children, *Child Devel.*, 1931, **2**, 74-75.

298.—Fabre, J. H., *Social life in the insect world*, 1913.

299.—Farnsworth, P. R., Concerning so-called group effects, *J. Genet. Psychol.*, 1928, **35**, 587-594.

300.—Farnsworth, P. R., and Beaumont, H., Suggestion in pictures, *J. Gen. Psychol.*, 1929, **2**, 362-366.

301.—Farnsworth, P. R., and Williams, M. F., The accuracy of the median and mean of a group of judgments, *J. Soc. Psychol.*, 1936, **7**, 237-239.

302.—Farwell, L., Reactions of kindergarten, first- and second-grade children to constructive play materials, *Genet. Psychol. Monog.*, 1930, **8**, Nos. 5 and 6.

303.—Feleky, A. M., The expression of the emotions, *Psychol. Rev.*, 1914, **21**, 33-41; The influence of the emotions on respiration, *J. Exper. Psychol.*, 1916, **1**, 218-241.

304.—Fenton, N., The only child, *J. Genet. Psychol.*, 1928, **35**, 546-556.

305.—Ferguson, G., The psychology of the Negro, *Arch. Psychol.*, 1916, No. 36.

306.—Ferguson, L. W., The influence of individual attitudes on construction of an attitude scale, *J. Soc. Psychol.*, 1935, **6**, 115-117.

307.—Fisher, M. L., Measured differences between problem and non-problem children in a public school system, *J. Educ. Sociol.*, 1934, **7**, 343-364.

308.—Fisher, M. S., Language patterns of pre-school children, *Child Develop. Monog.*, 1934, No. 15.

309.—Fitz-Simons, M. J., Some parent-child relationships as shown in clinical case studies, *J. Exper. Educ.*, 1933, **2**, 170-196.

310.—Flanagan, J. C., *Factor analysis in the study of personality*, 1935.

311.—Forlano, G. (for a committee), An experiment in cooperation, *J. Educ. Res.*, 1932, **25**, 128-131.

312.—Forlano, G., and Axelrod, H. C., The effect of repeated praise or blame on the performance of introverts and extroverts, *J. Educ. Psychol.*, 1937, **28**, 92-100.

313.—Fortes, M., The influence of position in sibship in juvenile delinquency, *Economica*, 1933, 301-308.

314.—Foster, J. C., and Anderson, J. E., *The young child and his parents*, 1927.

315.—Foster, S., A study of the personality make-up and social setting of fifty jealous children, *Ment. Hyg.*, 1927, **11**, 53-77.

316.—Francis, K. V., and Fillmore, E., The influence of environment upon the personality of children, *Univ. Iowa Stud.: Stud. Child Welfare*, 1934, 9, No. 71.

317.—Frank, J. D., Individual differences in certain aspects of the level of aspiration, *Amer. J. Psychol.*, 1935, **47**, 119-128.

318.—Frank, J. D., The influence of the level of performance in one task on the level of aspiration in another, *J. Exper. Psychol.*, 1935, **18**, 159-171.

319.—Frank, J. D., Some psychological determinants of the level of aspiration, *Amer. J. Psychol.*, 1935, **47**, 285-293.

320.—Frank, L. K., The management of tensions, *Amer. J. Sociol.*, 1928, **33**, 705-736.

321.—Frank, L. K., Personality and rank order, *Amer. J. Sociol.*, 1929, **35**, 177-186.

322.—Frank, L. K., The problem of child development, *Child Devel.*, 1935, **6**, 7-18.

323.—Franz, S. I., *Handbook of mental examination methods*, 2nd ed., 1919, 171-176.

324.—Franzblau, R. N., Race differences in mental and physical traits, *Arch. Psychol.*, 1935, No. 177.

325.—Frazier, E. F., Certain aspects of conflict in the Negro family, *Soc. Forces*, 1931-1932, **10**, 76-84.

326.—Freeman, F. N., Holzinger, K. J., and Mitchell, B. C., The influence of environment on the intelligence, school achievement, and conduct of foster children, *27th Yrbk. of the National Society for the Study of Education*, 1928, 103-218.

327.—Freud, S., *Collected papers*, 4, 1925.

328.—Freud, S., *A general introduction to psychoanalysis*, 1920, 236 ff.

329.—Freud, S., Libidinal types, *Int. J. Psychoanal.*, 1932, **13**, 277-280.

330.—Freud, S., *New introductory lectures on psychoanalysis*, 1933.

331.—Freud, S., *Totem and taboo*, 1927.

332.—Fries, M. E., Factors in character development, neuroses, psychoses, and delinquency, *Amer. J. Orthopsychiat.*, 1937, **7**, 142-181.

333.—Fulton, B. B., Sound perception by insects, *Scient. Mo.*, 1928, **27**, 552-556.

334.—Furfey, P .H., The measurement of developmental age, *Cath. Univ. Amer., Educ. Res. Bull.*, 1928, **2**, No. 10.

335.—Furfey, P. H., A note on the relative development age scores of urban and rural boys, *Child Devel.*, 1935, **6**, 88-90.

336.—Furfey, P. H., Pubescence and play behavior, *Amer. J. Psychol.*, 1929, **41**, 109-111.

337.—Furfey, P. H., The relation between socio-economic status and intelligence of young infants as measured by the Linfert-Hierholzer scale, *J. Genet. Psychol.*, 1928, **35**, 478-480.

338.—Furfey, P. H., Social and physical factors in developmental age, *Nat'l Research Council, Univ. of Chicago*, 1933.

339.—Furfey, P. H., Some factors influencing the selection of boys' chums, *J. Appl. Psychol.*, 1927, 11, 47-61.

340.—Furfey, P. H., and Muehlenbein, J., The validity of infant intelligence tests, *J. Genet. Psychol.*, 1932, 40, 219-223.

341.—Gahagan, L., Judgments of occupations from printed photographs, *J. Soc. Psychol.*, 1933, 4, 128-134.

342.—Gardiner, I. C., Effect of a group of social stimuli upon attitudes, *J. Educ. Psychol.*, 1935, 26, 471-479.

343.—Garrett, H. E., Personality as "habit organization," *J. Abn. & Soc. Psychol.*, 1926, 21, 250-255.

344.—Garrett, H. E., Bryan, A. I., and Perl, R. E., The age factor in mental organization, *Arch. Psychol.*, 1935, No. 176.

345.—Garrison, K. C., and Burch, V. S., A study of racial attitudes of college students, *J. Soc. Psychol.*, 1933, 4, 230-235.

346.—Garrison, K. C., and Mann, M., A study of the opinions of college students, *J. Soc. Psychol.*, 1931, 2, 168-178.

347.—Garth, T. R., The intelligence and achievement of mixed-blood Indians, *J. Soc. Psychol.*, 1933, 4, 134-137.

348.—Garth, T. H., and Garrett, J. E., A comparative study of Indians in United States Indian schools and in the public or common schools, *School & Soc.*, 1928, 27, 178-184.

349.—Garth, T. R., Lovelady, B. E., and Smith, H. W., The intelligence and achievement of southern Negro children, *School & Soc.*, 1930, 32, 431-434.

350.—Gates, G. S., An experimental study of the growth of social perception, *J. Educ. Psychol.*, 1923, 14, 449-462.

351.—Gates, G. S., An observational study of anger, *J. Exper. Psychol.*, 1926, 9, 325-336.

352.—Gates, G. S., The rôle of the auditory element in the interpretation of emotion, *Psychol. Bull.*, 1927, 24, p. 175.

353.—Gates, G. S., The effect of an audience upon performance, *J. Abn. & Soc. Psychol.*, 1924, 18, 334-342.

354.—Gates, G. S., and Rissland, L. Q., The effect of encouragement and of discouragement upon performance, *J. Educ. Psychol.*, 1923, 14, 21-26.

355.—Gatewood, M. C., and Weiss, A. P., Race and sex differences in newborn infants, *J. Genet. Psychol.*, 1930, 38, 31-49.

356.—George, R. W., A comparison of Pressey X-O scores with liberal-conservative attitudes, Master's essay in Columbia University library, 1925.

357.—Gesell, A., *Infancy and human growth*, 1928.

358.—Gesell, A., *The mental growth of the pre-school child*, 1925.

359.—Gesell, A. L., and Lord, E. E., A psychological comparison of nursery-school children from homes of low and high economic status, *Ped. Sem.*, 1927, 34, 339-356.

360.—Gesell, A., and Thompson, H., Learning and growth in identical infant twins: an experimental study by the method of co-twin control, *Genet. Psychol. Monog.*, 1929, 6, No. 1.

361.—Giddings, F. H., Stimulation ranges and reaction areas, *Psychol. Rev.*, 1924, **31**, 449-455.

362.—Gilchrist, E. P., The extent to which praise and reproof affect a pupil's work, *School & Soc.*, 1916, **4**, 872-874.

363.—Gilliland, A. R., What do introversion-extroversion tests measure? *J. Abn. & Soc. Psychol.*, 1934, **28**, 407-412.

364.—Gilliland, A. R., and Morgan, J. J. B., An objective measure of introversion-extroversion, *J. Abn. & Soc. Psychol.*, 1931, **26**, 296-303.

365.—Ginsburg, E. L., Factors associated with variations in the intensity of hyperkinesis in children, *Smith Coll. Stud. Soc. Work*, 1932-33, **3**, 207.

366.—Giroud, A., La suggestibilité chez les enfants d'école, *Ann. Psychol.*, 1911, **8**, 362-388.

367.—Glover, K., and Dewey, E., *Children of the new day*, 1934.

368.—Goldstein, H., The biochemical variability of the individual in relation to personality and intelligence, *J. Exper. Psychol.*, 1935, **18**, 348-371.

369.—Goodenough, F. L., *Anger in young children*, 1931.

370.—Goodenough, F. L., The consistency of sex differences in mental traits at various ages, *Psychol. Rev.*, 1927, **34**, 440-462.

371.—Goodenough, F. L., The emotional behavior of young children during mental tests, *J. Juv. Res.*, 1929, **13**, 204-219.

372.—Goodenough, F. L., Expression of the emotions in a blind-deaf child, *J. Abn. & Soc. Psychol.*, 1932, **27**, 328-333.

373.—Goodenough, F. L., The expression of the emotions in infancy, *Child Devel.*, 1931, **2**, 96-101.

374.—Goodenough, F. L., Interrelationships in the behavior of young children, *Child Devel.*, 1930, **1**, 29-47.

375.—Goodenough, F. L., *The Kuhlmann-Binet tests for children of pre-school ages; a critical study and evaluation*, 1928.

376.—Goodenough, F. L., Measuring behavior traits by means of repeated short samples, *J. Juv. Res.*, 1928, **12**, 230-235.

377.—Goodenough, F. L., A preliminary report on the effect of nursery-school training upon the intelligence test scores of young children, *27th Yrbk. National Society Studies in Education, Part I*, 1928, 361-369.

378.—Goodenough, F. L., The relation of the intelligence of pre-school children to the occupation of their fathers, *Amer. J. Psychol.*, 1928, **40**, 284-294.

379.—Goodenough, F. L., and Anderson, J. E., *Experimental child study*, 1931.

380.—Goodenough, F. L., and Leahy, A. M., The effect of certain family relationships upon the development of personality, *J. Genet. Psychol.*, 1927, **34**, 45-72.

381.—Gordon, K., Group judgments in the field of lifted weights, *J. Exper. Psychol.*, 1924, **7**, 398-400; A study of esthetic judgments, *J. Exper. Psychol.*, 1923, **6**, 36-43.

382.—Graves, E. A., The effect of competition and reward on the motor performance of pre-school children, Master's essay, University Minnesota Library, 1934.

383.—Gray, C. T., and Klein, D. B., (unpublished study).

384.—Green, E. H., Friendships and quarrels among pre-school children, *Child Devel.*, 1933, **4**, 237-252. (Green, E. H., 1933 a.)

385.—Green, E. H., Group play and quarreling among pre-school children, *Child Devel.*, 1933, **4**, 302-307. (Green, E. H., 1933 b.)

386.—Green, G. H., Have Children a national bias? *Discovery*, 1932, **13**, 44-46.

387.—Greenberg, P. J., Competition in children: an experimental study, *Amer. J. Psychol.*, 1932, **44**, 221-248.

388.—Guernsey, M., Eine genetische Studie über Nachahmung, summarized in Bühler, C., *Kindheit und Jugend*, 28-39.

389.—Guilford, J. P., An examination of a typical test of introversion-extroversion by means of the method of similar reactions, *J. Soc. Psychol.*, 1933, **4**, 430-443.

390.—Guilford, J. P., An experiment in learning to read facial expression, *J. Abn. & Soc. Psychol.*, 1929, **24**, 191-202.

391.—Guilford, J. P., Racial preferences of 1000 university students, *J. Soc. Psychol.*, 1931, **2**, 179-204.

392.—Guilford, J. P., and Braly, K. W., An experimental test of McDougall's theory of introversion-extroversion, *J. Abn. & Soc. Psychol.*, 1931, **25**, 382-389.

393.—Guilford, J. P., and Braly, K. W., Extroversion and introversion, *Psychol. Bull.*, 1930, **27**, 96-107.

394.—Guilford, J. P., and Guilford, R. B., An analysis of the factors in a typical test of introversion-extroversion, *J. Abn. & Soc. Psychol.*, 1934, **28**, 377-399.

395.—Guilford, J. P., and Hunt, J. M., Some further experimental tests of McDougall's theory of introversion-extroversion, *J. Abn. & Soc. Psychol.*, 1931, **26**, 324-332.

396.—Guilford, R. B., and Worcester, D. A., A comparative study of the only and non-only children, *J. Genet. Psychol.*, 1930, **38**, 411-426.

397.—Gundlach, R. H., Confusion in political and economic ideas among undergraduates, *Psychol. Bull.*, 1935, **32**, 748-749 (abstract).

398.—Guthrie, E. R., Measuring introversion and extroversion, *J. Abn. & Soc. Psychol.*, 1927, **22**, 82-88.

399.—Guthrie, E. R., (Unpublished study).

400.—Haag, H. L., Study of racial attitudes of high school and university students, Master's thesis, library of University of Michigan, 1930.

401.—Habbe, S., The selection of student nurses, *J. Appl. Psychol.*, 1933, **17**, 564-580.

402.—Haggerty, M. E., and Nash, H. B., Mental capacity of children and paternal occupation, *J. Educ. Psychol.*, 1924, **15**, 559-573.

403.—Haggerty, M. E., Olson, W. C., and Wickman, E. K., *Haggerty-Olson-Wickman Behavior Rating Schedules*, 1930.

404.—Haggerty, W. E., The incidence of undesirable behavior in public school children, *J. Educ. Res.*, 1925, **12**, 102-125.

405.—Hall, G. S., in *Ped. Sem.*, 1891, *et seq.*

406.—Hall, O. M., Attitudes and unemployment, *Arch. Psychol.*, 1934, No. 165.

407.—Hamilton, G. V., *A research in marriage*, 1929.

408.—Hamilton, G. V., A study of trial and error reactions in mammals, *J. Animal Behavior*, 1911, **1**, 33-66; A study of perseverance reactions in primates and rodents, *Behavior Monog.*, 1916, **3**, No. 2, ser. no. 13.

409.—Hammett, F. S., Observations on the relation between emotional and metabolic stability, *Amer. J. Physiol.*, 1921, 53, 307-311.

410.—Hanfmann, E., Social structure of a group of kindergarten children, *Amer. J. Orthopsychiat.*, 1935, 5, 407-410.

411.—Hanks, L. M., Prediction from case material to personality test data, a methodological study, *Arch. Psychol.*, 1936, No. 207.

412.—Hanna, J. V., Clinical procedure as a method of validating a measure of psychoneurotic tendency, *J. Abn. & Soc. Psychol.*, 1934, 28, 435-445.

413.—Hardy, M. C., An appraisal of social adjustments of elementary school pupils, *Psychol. Bull.*, 1933, 30, 694, 695.

414.—Hardy, M. C., The out-of-school activities of well-adjusted and poorly adjusted elementary school pupils, *J. Educ. Psychol.*, 1935, 26, 455-467.

415.—Harper, M. H., Social beliefs and attitudes of American educators, *Teach. Coll. Contrib. Educ.*, 1927, No. 294.

416.—Harris, A. J., Remmers, H. H., and Ellison, C. E., The relation between liberal and conservative attitudes in college students, and other factors, *J. Soc. Psychol.*, 1932, 3, 320-335.

417.—Harrower, M. R., Social status and the moral development of the child, *Brit. J. Educ. Psychol.*, 1934, 4, 75-95.

418.—Hart, B., *The psychology of insanity*, 1916.

419.—Hart, H., Changing social attitudes and interests, in *Recent social trends in the United States: Report of the President's research committee on social trends*, 1933.

420.—Hart, H., and Hart, E. B., *Personality and the family*, 1935.

421.—Hartmann, G. W., A field experiment on the comparative effectiveness of "emotional" and "rational" political leaflets in determining election results, *J. Abn. & Soc. Psychol.*, 1936, 31, 99-114.

422.—Hartshorne, H., and May, M. A., *Studies in deceit*, 1928.

423.—Hartshorne, H., May, M. A., and Maller, J. B., *Studies in service and self-control*, 1929.

424.—Hartshorne, H., May, M. A., and Shuttleworth, F. K., *Studies in the organization of character*, 1930.

425.—Harvey, O. L., Concerning the Thurstone "Personality Schedule," *J. Soc. Psychol.*, 1932, 3, 240-251.

426.—Harvey, O. L., The measurement of handwriting considered as a form of expressive movement, *Char. & Pers.*, 1934, 2, 310-321.

427.—Hattori, F. S., Aesthetic judgment: an experimental study of the differences between the Japanese and the occidental people in respect to Japanese and occidental pictures, Master's essay in the Columbia University library, 1927.

428.—Hattwick, B. W., The influence of nursery-school attendance upon the behavior and personality of the pre-school child, *J. Exper. Educ.*, 1936, 5, 180-190. (Hattwick, B. W., 1936 a.)

429.—Hattwick, B. W., Interrelations between the pre-school child's behavior and certain factors in the home, *Child Devel.*, 1936, 7, 200-226. (Hattwick, B. W., 1936 b.)

430.—Hawthorne, J. W., A group test for the measurement of cruelty-compassion, *J. Soc. Psychol.*, 1932, 3, 189-211.

431.—Hayes, M., A scale for evaluating adolescent personality, *J. Genet. Psychol.*, 1934, **44**, 206-222.

432.—Hayward, R. S., The child's report of psychological factors in the family, *Arch. Psychol.*, 1935, No. 189.

433.—Healy, W., and Bronner, A. F., *Judge Baker Foundation case studies,* Series I, 1923.

434.—Healy, W., Bronner, A. F., Baylor, M. H., and Murphy, J. P., *Reconstructing behavior in youth; a study of problem children in foster homes,* 1929.

435.—Hedrick, B. E., The effectiveness of a program of learning designed to change parental attitudes toward self-reliance, *Iowa Univ. Stud.: Stud. Child Welfare,* 1934, **10**, 249-267.

436.—Heidbreder, E., Measuring introversion and extroversion, *J. Abn. & Soc. Psychol.*, 1927, **21**, 120-134.

437.—Heidbreder, E., The normal inferiority complex, *J. Abn. & Soc. Psychol.*, 1927, **22**, 243-258.

438.—Heidbreder, E., Self-ratings and preferences, *J. Abn. & Soc. Psychol.*, 1930, **25**, 62-74.

439.—Henderson, L. G., *Blood, a study in general physiology,* 1928.

440.—Hendrick, I., Ego development and certain character problems, *Psychoanal. Quart.*, 1936, **5**, 320-346.

441.—Hendrickson, G., and Huskey, J. F., Extroversion as a factor conditioning achievement in the fifth and sixth grades of an elementary school, *J. Educ. Res.*, 1932, **25**, 6-13.

442.—Henning, H., Charaktertests, *Indus. Psychotech.*, 1927, **4**, 270-273.

443.—Cf. Hertz, M. R., The reliability of the Rorschach ink-blot test, *J. Appl. Psychol.*, 1934, **18**, 461-477.

444.—Hester, M. St. C., Variation in sense of humor according to age and mental condition, Master's essay in Columbia University Library, 1924.

445.—Hetzer, H., Das volkstümliche Kinderspiel, *Deutscher Verlag. f. Jugend u. Volk,* 1927.

446.—Hetzer, H., Entwicklungsbedingte Erziehungsschwierigkeiten, *Zsch. f. päd. Psychol.*, 1928, **29**, 77-85.

447.—Hetzer, H., *Kindheit und Armut,* 1929.

448.—Hetzer, H., and Tudor-Hart, B., Die frühesten Reaktionen auf die menschliche Stimme, *Quell. u. Stud. z. Jugendk.*, 1927, No. 5.

449.—Hicks, J. A., and Hayes, M., The verbal responses of junior high school pupils in classroom discussions, *Child Devel.*, 1933, **4**, 176-182.

450.—Hildreth, G. H., The resemblance of siblings in intelligence and achievement, *Teach. Coll. Contrib. Educ.*, 1925, No. 186.

451.—Hilgard, J. R., Learning and maturation in pre-school children, *J. Genet. Psychol.*, 1932, **41**, 36-56.

452.—Cf. Hinckley, E. D., The influence of individual opinion on construction of an attitude scale, *J. Soc. Psychol.*, 1932, **3**, 283-296.

453.—Hion, V., Zur Aetiologie, Symptomatologie und Pathogenese des Stotterns, *Folia Neuro-Esthon.*, 1932, **12**, 190-195. (*See Psychol. Abst.*, 1935, 9, No. 3386.)

454.—Holt, E. B., *Animal drive and the learning process,* 1931.

455.—Hooker, H. F., The study of the only child at school, *J. Genet. Psychol.*, 1931, **39**, 122-126.

456.—Hoppe, F., Erfolg und Misserfolg, *Psychol. Forsch.*, 1930, **14**, 1-62.

457.—Horney, K., *The neurotic personality of our time*, 1937.

458.—Horney, K., Personality changes in female adolescents, *Amer. J. Orthopsychiat.*, 1935, **5**, 19-26.

459.—Horowitz, E. L., The development of attitude toward the Negro, *Arch. Psychol.*, 1936, No. 194.

460.—Horowitz, E. L., and Horowitz, R., (Unpublished study).

461.—Hoskins, R. G., Studies on vigor: II. The effect of castration on voluntary activity, *Amer. J. Physiol.*, 1925, **72**, 324-330.

462.—Howells, T. H., A comparative study of those who accept as against those who reject religious authority, *Univ. of Iowa Stud.: Stud. Char.*, 1930, **2**, No. 3.

463.—Howells, T. H., An experimental study of persistence, *J. Abn. & Soc. Psychol.*, 1933, **28**, 14-29.

464.—Hsia, J., A study of the sociability of elementary school children, *Teach. Coll. Contrib. Educ.*, 1928, No. 322.

465.—Hsiao, H. H., The status of the first-born with special reference to intelligence, *Genet. Psychol. Monog.*, 1931, **9**, Nos. 1-2.

466.—Hulson, E. L., An analysis of the free play of ten four-year-old children through consecutive observations, *J. Juv. Res.*, 1930, **14**, 188-208.

467.—Hulson, E. L., Block constructions of four-year-old children, *J. Juv. Res.*, 1930, **14**, 209-222.

468.—Humm, D. G., and Wadsworth, G. W. J., The Humm-Wadsworth Temperament Scale, *Amer. J. Psychiat.*, 1935, **92**, 163-200.

469.—Hunt, W. A., Studies of the startle pattern, *J. Psychol.*, 1936, **2**, 201-206.

470.—Hunter, C. W., A comparative study of the relationship existing between the white race and the Negro race in the State of North Carolina and in the City of New York, Master's essay in Columbia University Library, 1927.

471.—Hunter, W. S., The delayed reaction in animals and children, *Behavior Monog.*, 1913, **2**, No. 1; The delayed reaction in a child, *Psychol. Rev.*, 1917, **24**, 74-87.

472.—Hurd, A. W., Appreciation objectives in science teaching, *School & Soc.*, 1933, **37**, 124-126.

473.—Hurlock, E. B., The effect of incentives upon the constancy of the I.Q., *Ped. Sem.*, 1925, **32**, 422-434.

474.—Hurlock, E. B., An evaluation of certain incentives used in school work, *J. Educ. Psychol.*, 1925, **16**, 145-159.

475.—Hurlock, E. B., The psychology of incentives, *J. Soc. Psychol.*, 1931, **2**, 261-290.

476.—Hurlock, E. B., The use of group rivalry as an incentive, *J. Abn. & Soc. Psychol.*, 1927, **22**, 278-290.

477.—Hurlock, E. B., The value of praise and reproof as incentives for children, *Arch. Psychol.*, 1924, No. 71.

478.—Hurlock, E. B., and Burstein, M., The imaginary playmate: A questionnaire study, *J. Genet. Psychol.*, 1932, **41**, 380-392.

479.—Hurlock, E. B., and Klein, E. R., Adolescent "crushes," *Child Devel.*, 1934, **5**, 63-80.

480.—Hurlock, E. B., and McDonald, L. C., Undesirable behavior traits in junior high school students, *Child Devel.*, 1934, **5**, 278-290.

481.—Hurlock, E. B., and Sender, S., The "negative phase" in relation to the behavior of pubescent girls, *Child Devel.*, 1930, **1**, 325-340.

482.—Irwin, O. C., The amount and nature of activities of newborn infants under constant external stimulating conditions during the first ten days of life, *Genet. Psychol. Monog.*, 1930, **8**, 1-92.

483.—Irwin, O. C., Weiss, L. A., and Stubbs, E. M., Studies in infant behavior: I. *Univ. Iowa Stud.: Stud. Child Welfare*, 1934, **9**, No. 4.

484.—Isaacs, S., *Social development in young children*, 1933.

485.—Israeli, N., Attitudes to the decline of the west, *J. Soc. Psychol.*, 1933, **4**, 92-101.

486.—Jack, L. M., An experimental study of ascendent behavior in pre-school children, *Univ. Iowa Stud.: Stud. Child Welfare*, 1934, **9**, No. 3.

487.—James, W., *Principles of psychology*, II, 1890.

488.—Janet, P., *Psychological healing*, 1925, I, 682 ff.

489.—Jennings, H. S., *The behavior of the lower organisms*, 1906.

490.—Jensen, K., Differential reactions to taste and temperature stimuli in newborn infants, *Genet. Psychol. Monog.*, 1932, **12**, 361-476.

491.—Jersild, A. T., Training and growth in the development of children: a study of the relative influence of learning and maturation, *Child Devel. Monog.*, 1932, No. 10.

492.—Jersild, A. T., and Fite, M. D., The influence of nursery-school experience on children's social adjustments, *45th Ann. Mtg. Amer. Psychol. Assn.*, 1937.

493.—Jersild, A. T., and Markey, F. V., Conflicts between pre-school children, *Child Devel. Monog.*, 1935, No. 21.

494.—Jersild, A. T., Markey, F. V., and Jersild, C. L., Children's fears, dreams, wishes, daydreams, likes, dislikes, pleasant and unpleasant memories, *Child Devel. Monog.*, 1933, No. 12.

495.—Joël, W., Behavior maturity of children of nursery-school age, *Child Devel.*, 1936, **7**, 189-199.

496.—Johnson, B., Changes in muscular tension in coordinated hand movements, *J. Exper. Psychol.*, 1928, **5**, 329-341.

497.—Johnson, B., Emotional instability in children, *Ungraded*, 1920, **5**, 73-79.

498.—Johnson, M. W., The effect on behavior of variation in the amount of play equipment, *Child Devel.*, 1935, **6**, 56-68.

499.—Johnson, M. W., The influence of verbal directions on behavior, *Child Devel.*, 1935, **6**, 196-204.

500.—Jones, A. M., An analytical study of one hundred twenty superior children, *Psychol. Clin.*, 1925, **16**, 19-75.

501.—Jones, D. C., and Carr-Saunders, A. M., The relation between intelligence and social status among orphan children, *Brit. J. Psychol.*, 1927, **17**, 343-364.

502.—Jones, E. S., Opinions of college students, *J. Appl. Psychol.*, 1926, **10**, 427-436.

503.—Jones, H. E., A first study of parent-child resemblance in intelligence, *27th Yrbk. of the National Society for the Study of Education*, 1928.

504.—Jones, H. E., The galvanic skin reflex as related to overt emotional expression, *Amer. J. Psychol.*, 1935, **47**, 241-251.

505.—Jones, H. E., The galvanic skin reflex in infancy, *Child. Devel.*, 1930, 1, 106-110.

506.—Jones, H. E., Homogamy in intellectual abilities, *Amer. J. Sociol.*, 1929, 35, 369-382.

507.—Jones, H. E., The influence of motion pictures upon the social attitudes of children, *J. Amer. Asso. Univ. Women*, 1934, 27, 221-226.

508.—Jones, H. E., Order of birth, In *Handbook of Child Psychology* (2nd ed., rev.), 1933, pp. 551-589.

509.—Jones, H. E., The relationship of overt and "implicit" emotional response, *Psychol. Bull.*, 1932, 29, 590.

510.—Jones, H. E., Relationships in physical and mental development, *Rev. Educ. Res.*, 1933, 3, 150-162, 177-181.

511.—Jones, H. E., The personality study of adolescence, In *Nat. Res. Council, Comm. on Child Devel.*, 1933.

512.—Jones, H. E., and Hsiao, H. H., A preliminary study of intelligence as a function of birth order, *J. Genet. Psychol.*, 1928, 35, 428-433.

513.—Jones, H. E., and Jones, M. C., Genetic studies of emotions, *Psychol. Bull.*, 1930, 27, 40-64.

514.—Jones, H. E., and Jones, M. C., A study of fear, *Childhood Educ.*, 1928, 5, 136-143.

515.—Jones, H. E., and Wilson, P. T., Reputation differences in like-sex twins, *J. Exper. Educ.*, 1932-1933, 1, 86-91.

516.—Jones, M. C., The case of Peter, *Ped. Sem.*, 1924, 31, 308-318.

517.—Jones, M. C., The conditioning of children's emotions, In *Handbook of child psychology*, 1931, pp. 71-93.

518.—Jones, M. C., The development of basic emotions, *The child's emotions* (symposium), 1930.

519.—Jones, M. C., The development of early behavior patterns in young children, *Ped. Sem.*, 1926, 33, 537-585.

520.—Jones, M. C., The elimination of children's fears, *J. Exper. Psychol.*, 1924, 7, 382-390.

521.—Jones, V., Children's morals, In *Handbook of child psychology*, 1931, pp. 432-479.

522.—Jordon, A. M., Children's interests in books and magazines, *J. Genet. Psychol.*, 1925, 32, 455-469.

523.—Judd, C. H., Practice without knowledge of results, *Psychol. Monog.*, 1905, 7, 185-199.

524.—Jung, C. G., *Studies in word-association*, 1919, 350 ff.

525.—Kambouropoulou, P., Individual differences in the sense of humor and their relation to temperamental differences, *Arch. Psychol.*, 1930, No. 121.

526.—Kasanin, M. S., and Veo, L., A study of the school adjustments of children who later in life became psychotic, *Amer. J. Orthopsychiat.*, 1932, 2, 212-230.

527.—Kasatkin, N. I., and Levikova, A. M., The formation of visual conditioned reflexes and their differentiation in infants, *J. Gen. Psychol.*, 1935, 12, 416-435. (Kasatkin, N. I., and Levikova, A. M., 1935 a.)

528.—Kasatkin, N. I., and Levikova, A. M., On the development of early conditioned reflexes and differentiations of auditory stimuli in infants, *J. Exper. Psychol.*, 1935, 18, 1-19. (Kasatkin, N. I., and Levikova, A. M., 1935 b.)

529.—Katz, D., and Allport, F. H., *Students' attitudes: a report of the Syracuse University Reaction Study*, 1931.

530.—Katz, D., and Braly, K., Racial stereotypes of 100 college students, *J. Abn. & Soc. Psychol.*, 1933, **28**, 280-290.

531.—Katz, S. E., The family constellation as a predisposing factor in psychosis, *Psychiat. Quar.*, 1934, **8**, 121-128.

532.—Kelley, T. L., *Crossroads in the mind of man*, 1928.

533.—Kellogg, W. N., and Kellogg, L. A., The ape and the child: a study of environmental influence upon early behavior, 1933.

534.—Kelting, L. S., An investigation of the feeding, sleeping, crying, and social behavior of infants, *J. Exper. Educ.*, 1934, **3**, 97-106.

535.—Kempf, E. J., Autonomic functions and the personality, *Nerv. and Ment. Dis. Monog.*, 1918, No. 28.

536.—Kempf, E. J., The autonomic functions and the personality, 1921.

537.—Kempf, G. A., and Collins, S. D., A study of the relations between mental and physical status of children in two counties of Illinois, *U. S. Pub. Health Reports*, 1929, **44**, No. 29, 1743-1789.

538.—Kenderdine, M., Laughter in the pre-school child, *Child Devel.*, 1931, **2**, 228-230.

539.—Kerr, M., The Rorschach test applied to children, *Brit. J. Psychol.*, 1934, **25**, 170-185.

540.—Kinder, J. S., Through our own looking-glass, *School & Soc.*, 1925, **22**, 533-536.

541.—Kirby, T. J., Practice in the case of school children, *Teach. Coll. Contrib. Educ.*, 1913, No. 58.

542.—Kirkpatrick, M. E., Delinquency in Cleveland and Cuyaholga County during the depression period, *Amer. J. Orthopsychiat.*, 1935, **5**, 43-48.

543.—Klein, E., The relation between one's attitude to his father and his social attitudes, Master's essay in Columbia University Library, 1925.

544.—Klein, M., *The psychoanalysis of children* (trans. by A. Strachey), 1932.

545.—Klineberg, O., *Negro intelligence and selective migration*, 1935.

546.—Klineberg, O., *Race differences*, 1935.

547.—Klineberg, O., A study of psychological differences between racial and national groups in Europe, *Arch. Psychol.*, 1931, No. 132.

548.—Klineberg, O., (Unpublished study).

549.—Klineberg, O., Fjeld, H., and Foley, J. P., Jr., An experimental study of personality differences among constitutional, "racial," and cultural groups, (unpublished study), Summary from Anastasi, A., *Differential Psychology;* (see above).

550.—Knight, H. C., A comparison of the reliability of group and individual judgments, Master's essay in Columbia University Library, 1921.

551.—Knower, F. H., Experimental studies in changes in attitudes: I. A study of the effect of oral argument on changes of attitude, *J. Soc. Psychol.*, 1935, **6**, 315-347; II, A study of the effect of printed argument on changes in attitude, *J. Abn. & Soc. Psychol.*, 1936, **30**, 522-532; III, Some incidence of attitude changes, *J. Appl. Psychol.*, 1936, **20**, 114-127.

552.—Koch, H. L., An analysis of certain forms of so-called "nervous habits" in young children, *J. Genet. Psychol.*, 1935, **46**, 139-170.

553.—Koch, H. L., Popularity in pre-school children: some related factors and a technique for its measurement, *Child Devel.*, 1933, 5, 164-175.

554.—Koch, H. L., and Street, H., A study in rating technique with special reference to activity in pre-school children, *J. Genet Psychol.*, 1932, 41, 330-355.

555.—Koffka, K., *The growth of the mind*, 1928.

556.—Köhler, W., *Mentality of apes*, 1925.

557.—Kolstad, A., A study of opinions on some international problems, *Teach. Coll. Contrib. Educ.*, 1933, No. 555.

558.—Korn, E. M. F., The relationship existing between order of birth, intelligence, and temperament, Master's Essay in Columbia University Library, 1923.

559.—Kornhauser, A. W., Changes in information and attitudes of students in an economics course, *J. Educ. Res.*, 1930, 22, 288-298.

560.—Koshuk, R. P., Problems for sociological research (Paper presented at Christmas meeting of the Society for Research in Child Development), 1936.

561.—Kretschmer, E., *Physique and character*, 1925.

562.—Kroeber, A. L., The superorganic, *Amer. Anthrop.*, 1917, N. S., 19, 163-213.

563.—Kroll, A., The teacher's influence upon the social attitude of boys in the twelfth grade, *J. Educ. Psychol.*, 1934, 25, 274-280.

564.—Krout, M. H., Autistic gestures: an experimental study in symbolic movement, *Psychol. Rev. Monog.*, 1934-35, 46, No. 208.

565.—Kulp, D. H., II, Prestige as measured by single experience changes and their permanency, *J. Educ. Res.*, 1934, 27, 663-672.

566.—Kulp, D. H., II, and Davidson, H. H., Sibling resemblance in social attitudes, *J. Educ. Sociol.*, 1933, 7, 133-140.

567.—Kumin, E., The conflicts and resistant behavior of eighteen children in a nursery school, Master's essay in Columbia University Library, 1933.

568.—Kuo, Z. Y., Ontogeny of embryonic behavior in Aves: V. The reflex concept in the light of embryonic behavior in birds, *Psychol. Rev.*, 1932, 39, 499-515; Ontogeny of embryonic behavior in Aves: IV, The influence of embryonic movements on behavior after hatching, *J. Comp. Psychol.*, 1932, 14, 109-122.

569.—Laird, D. A., Changes in motor control and individual variations under the influence of "razzing," *J. Exper. Psychol.*, 1923, 6, 236-246. (Laird, D. A., 1923 c.)

570.—Laird, D. A., How the college student responds to different incentives to work, *Ped. Sem.*, 1923, 30, 366-370. (Laird, D. A., 1923 b.)

571.—Laird, D. A., How the high school student responds to different incentives to work, *Ped. Sem.*, 1923, 30, 358-365. (Laird, D. A., 1923 a.)

572.—Lambeth, M., and Lanier, L. H., Race differences in speed of reaction, *J. Genet. Psychol.*, 1933, 42, 255-297.

573.—Landis, C., An attempt to measure emotional traits in juvenile delinquency, in Lashley, K., *Studies in the dynamics of behavior*, 1932.

574.—Landis, C., Electrical phenomena of the skin, *Psychol. Bull.*, 1932, 29, 693-752.

575.—Landis, C., National differences in conversations, *J. Abn. & Soc. Psychol.*, 1927, 21, 354-357.

576.—Landis, C., Studies of emotional reactions: II. General behavior and facial expression, *J. Comp. Psychol.*, 1924, 4, 447-509. (This is one of a long series.)

577.—Landis, C., and Hunt, W. A., Studies of the startle pattern: III, Facial pattern, *J. Psychol.*, 1936, 2, 215-220.

578.—Landis, C., and Katz, S. E., The validity of certain questions which purport to measure neurotic tendencies, *J. Appl. Psychol.*, 1934, 18, 343-356.

579.—Landis, C., and Ross, J. W. H., Humor and its relation to other personality traits, *J. Soc. Psychol.*, 1933, 4, 156-175.

580.—Landis, M. H., and Burtt, H. E., A study of conversation, *J. Comp. Psychol.*, 1924, 4, 81-90.

581.—Lange, F. E., A statistical study of crowd laughter, Master's essay in Columbia University Library, 1923.

582.—Lapiere, R. T., Race prejudice: France and England, *Soc. Forces*, 1928, 7, 102-111.

583.—Larson, J. A., and Haney, G. W., Cardio-respiratory variations in personality studies, *Amer. J. Psychiat.*, 1932, 11, 1035-1081.

584.—Lasswell, H. D., *Psychopathology and politics*, 1930; The problem of adequate personality records: a proposal, *Amer. J. Psychiat.*, 1929, 8, 1057-1066.

585.—Lasswell, H. D., Verbal references and physiological changes during psychoanalytic interview: a preliminary communication, *Psychoanal. Rev.*, 1935, 22, 10-24.

586.—Laws, G., Parent-child relationships; a study of the attitudes and practices of parents concerning social adjustment of children, *Teach. Coll. Contrib. Educ.*, 1927, No. 283.

587.—Laycock, S. R., Adjustments of superior and inferior school children, *J. Soc. Psychol.*, 1933, 4, 353-366.

588.—Leahy, A. M., Nature-nurture and intelligence, *Genet. Psychol. Monog.*, 1935, 17, 235-308.

589.—Leal, M. A., *Physiological maturity in relation to certain characteristics of boys and girls*, 1929.

590.—Le Bon, G., *La foule*, 1895.

591.—Lecky, P., The theory of self-consistency in personal problems, *Rep. ann. Mtg. Amer. Coll. Person. Assn.*, 1935, 12-19.

592.—Lee, M. A. M., A study of emotional instability in nursery school children, *Child Devel.*, 1932, 3, 142-145.

593.—Lehman, H. C., Motivation: College males and the fraternity pledge, *J. Appl. Psychol.*, 1935, 19, 9-28.

594.—Lehman, H. C., and Witty, P. A., Periodicity and play behavior, *J. Educ. Psychol.*, 1927, 18, 115-118.

595.—Lehman, H. C., and Witty, P. A., *The psychology of play activities*, 1927.

596.—Lehman, H. C., and Witty, P. A., A study of play in relation to pubescence, *J. Soc. Psychol.*, 1930, 1, 510-523.

597.—Lerner, E., New techniques for tracing cultural factors in children's personality organization (Paper presented at Christmas meeting of the Society for Research in Child Development), 1936.

598.—Lerner, E., The problem of perspective in moral reasoning (unpublished study).

599.—Leuba, C., An experimental study of rivalry in young children. *J. Comp. Psychol.*, 1933, 16, 367-378.

600.—Leuba, C. J., The measurement of incentives and their effect, etc., *J. Soc. Psychol.*, 1932, 3, 107-114.

601.—Leuba, C. J., A preliminary analysis of the nature and effects of incentives, *Psychol. Rev.*, 1930, 37, 429-440.

602.—Leuba, C. J., A preliminary experiment to quantify an incentive and its effects, *J. Abn. & Soc. Psychol.*, 1930, 25, 275-288.

603.—Levy, D. M., Aggressive-submissive behavior and the Fröhlich syndrome, *Arch. Neurol. & Psychiat.*, 1936, 36, 991-1020.

604.—Levy, D. M., Experiments on the sucking reflex and social behavior in dogs, *Amer. J. Orthopsychiat.*, 1934, 4, 203-224.

605.—Levy, D. M., Hostility patterns in sibling rivalry experiments, *Amer. J. Orthopsychiat.*, 1936, 6, 183-257.

606.—Levy, D. M., Maternal overprotection and rejection, *Arch. Neurol. & Psychiat.*, 1931, 25, 886-889.

607.—Levy, D. M., and Tulchin, S. H., The resistance of infants and children during mental tests, *J. Exper. Psychol.*, 1923, 6, 304-322.

608.—Levy, D. M., and Tulchin, S. H., The resistant behavior of infants and children, *J. Exper. Psychol.*, 1925, 8, 209-224.

609.—Levy, J., A quantitative study of behavior problems in relation to family constellation, *Amer. J. Psychiat.*, 1931, 10, 637-654.

610.—Levy, J., A quantitative study of the relationship between basal metabolic rate and children's behavior problems, *Amer. J. Orthopsychiat.*, 1930, 31, 298-310.

611.—Levy, J., A quantitative study of the relationship between intelligence and economic status as factors in the etiology of children's behavior problems, *Amer. J. Orthopsychiat.*, 1931, 1, 152-162.

612.—Levy, J., Conflicts of culture and children's maladjustment, *Ment. Hyg.*, 1933, 17, 41-50.

613.—Levy, J., The impact of cultural forces upon children's behavior, *Ment. Hyg.*, 1932, 16, 208-220.

614.—Lévy-Bruhl, L., *Primitive mentality*, 1923.

615.—Lewin, K. A., *A dynamic theory of personality*, 1935.

616.—Lewin, K., Environmental forces, in Murchison, C., *Handbook of child psychology*, 1933, 2nd ed., 590-625.

617.—Lewin, K., [Psychological situation attending reward and punishment], *Stud. in Psychol. and Educ.*, 1933, 31-76.

618.—Lichtenstein, A., Can attitudes be taught? *Johns Hopkins Univ. Stud. Educ.*, 1934, No. 21.

619.—Likert, R., A technique for the measurement of attitudes, *Arch. Psychol.*, 1932, No. 140.

620.—Likert, R., Roslow, S., and Murphy, G., A simple and reliable method of scoring the Thurstone attitude scales, *J. Soc. Psychol.*, 1934, 5, 228-238.

621.—Line, W., and Griffin, J. D. M., The objective determination of factors underlying mental health, *Amer. J. Psychiat.*, 1935, 91, 833-842.

622.—Line, W., Griffin, J. D. M., and Anderson, G. W., The objective measurement of mental stability, *J. Ment. Sci.*, 1935, 81, 61-106.

623.—Lippmann, H. S., Certain behavior responses in early infancy, *J. Genet. Psychol.*, 1927, 34, 424-440.

624.—Lippmann, W., *Public opinion*, 1922, especially pp. 81-122.

625.—Liss, E., Play techniques in child analysis, *Amer. J. Orthopsychiat.*, 1936, **6**, 17-22.

626.—Lithaeur, D. B., and Klineberg, O., A study of the variation in I.Q. of a group of dependent children in institution and foster home, *J. Genet. Psychol.*, 1933, **42**, 236-242.

627.—Litterer, O. F., Stereotypes, *J. Soc. Psychol.*, 1933, **4**, 59-69.

628.—Lockhart, E. G., The attitudes of children towards law, *Univ. Iowa Stud.: Stud. Char.*, 1930, **3**, No. 1.

629.—Longstreet, R. J., An experiment with the Thurstone attitude scales, *School Rev.*, 1935, **43**, 202-208.

630.—Loomis, A. M., A preliminary study of the physical contacts of nursery-school children, in Thomas, D. S., *Some new techniques for studying social behavior*, 1929.

631.—Loomis, A. M., A technique for observing the social behavior of nursery school children, *Child Devel. Monog.*, 1931, No. 5.

632.—Cf. Lorge, I., Personality traits by fiat: I. The analyses of the total trait scores of the Bernreuter personality inventory, *J. Educ. Psychol.*, 1935, **26**, 273-278.

633.—Lorge, I., Personality traits by fiat: II. A correction, *J. Educ. Psychol.*, 1935, **26**, 652-654.

634.—Lorge, I., Prestige, suggestions and attitudes (unpublished manuscript), *Psychol. Bull.*, 1935, **32**, 750. (Abstract.)

635.—Lorge, I., Bernholz, E., and Sells, S. B., Personality traits by fiat: II, The consistency of the Bernreuter personality inventory by the Bernreuter and Flanagan keys, *J. Educ. Psychol.*, 1935, **26**, 427-434.

636.—Löwenfeld, B., Systematisches Studium der Säuglinge auf Klange und Geräusche (Systematic study of the reactions of babies to tones and noises), *Zsch. f. Psychol.*, 1927, **104**, 62-96.

637.—Lowrie, F. T., *A study of some effects of punishment on 1st grade children*, (Unpublished study).

638.—Luh, C. W., and Sailer, R. C., Self-estimation of Chinese students, *J. Soc. Psychol.*, 1933, **4**, 245-249.

639.—Luithlen, W. F., Zur Psychologie der Initiative und der Führereigenschaften, *Zsch. f. angew. Psychol.*, 1931, **39**, 56-122.

640.—Lund, F. H., The psychology of belief, *J. Abn. & Soc. Psychol.*, 1925, **20**, 63-81.

641.—Lundberg, G. A., The demographic and economic basis of political radicalism and conservatism, *Amer. J. Sociol.*, 1927, **32**, 719-732.

642.—Lundberg, G. A., The newspaper and public opinion, *Soc. Forces*, 1925, **4**, 709-715.

643.—Lundberg, G. A., Sex differences on social questions, *School & Soc.*, 1926, **23**, 595-600.

644.—Lundberg, G. A., *Social research*, 1929.

645.—Lundeen, G. E., and Caldwell, O. W., A study of unfounded beliefs among high school seniors, *J. Educ. Res.*, 1930, **22**, 257-273.

646.—Luria, A. R., *The nature of human conflicts*, 1932.

647.—Lynd, R. S., and Lynd, H. M., *Middletown*, 1929.

648.—Lynd, R. S., and Lynd, H. M., *Middletown in transition*, 1937.

649.—Macaulay, E., and Watkins, S. H., An investigation into the development of the moral conceptions of children, *Forum Educ.*, 1926, **4**, 13-33, 92-108.

650.—MacIver, R. M., *Society: a textbook of sociology* (rev. ed.), 1937.

651.—MacKaye, L., The interview with the behavior-problem child, *Univ. Hosp. Bull.*, Ann Arbor, Michigan, 1936, **2**, 9-10.

652.—Maier, N. R. F., Reasoning in children, *J. Comp. Psychol.*, 1936, **21**, 357-366.

653.—Malinowski, B., *The father in primitive psychology*, 1927.

654.—Maller, J. B., Character and personality tests, *Psychol. Bull.*, 1934, **31**, 501-524.

655.—Maller, J. B., Size of family and personality of offspring, *J. Soc. Psychol.*, 1931, **2**, 3-27.

656.—Maller, J. B., Cooperation and competition: An experimental study in motivation, *Teach. Coll. Contrib. Educ.*, 1929.

657.—Maller, J. B., Measurement of conflict between honesty and group loyalty, *J. Educ. Psychol.*, 1932, **23**, 187-191.

658.—Maller, J. B., and Lundeen, G. E., Sources of superstitious beliefs, *J. Educ. Res.*, 1933, **26**, 321-343.

659.—Maller, J. B., and Zubin, J., The effect of motivation upon intelligence test scores, *Ped. Sem.*, 1932, **41**, 136-151.

660.—Manry, C., World citizenship, *Univ. of Iowa Stud.: Stud. Char.*, 1927, **1**, No. 1.

661.—Manske, A. J., The reflection of teachers' attitudes in the attitudes of their pupils, Doctoral dissertation in the Library of Teachers College, Columbia University, 1935.

662.—Manwell, E. M., and Mengert, I. G., A study of the development of two- and three-year-old children with respect to play activities, *Univ. Iowa Stud.: Stud. Child Welfare*, 1934, **9**, No. 3, 67-111.

663.—Markey, F. V., The mental hygiene problems of school attendants, *Psychol. Clin.*, 1934, **4**, 277-280.

664.—Marple, C. H., The comparative suggestibility of three age levels to the suggestion of groups vs. expert opinion, *J. Soc. Psychol.*, 1933, **4**, 176-186.

665.—Marquis, D. P., Can conditioned responses be established in the newborn infant? *J. Genet. Psychol.*, 1931, **39**, 479-492.

666.—Marshall, A., *Elements of economics of industry*, 1892.

667.—Marshall, H., Clinical applications of the Bernreuter Personality Inventory, *Psychol. Bull.*, 1933, **30**, 601-602 (abstract).

668.—Marston, L. R., The emotions of young children: an experimental study in introversion and extroversion, *Univ. Iowa Stud.: Stud. Child Welfare*, 1925, **3**, No. 3.

669.—Maslow, A. H., The rôle of dominance in the sexual behavior of infra-human primates: IV. The determination of hierarchy in pairs and in groups, *J. Genet. Psychol.*, 1936, **49**, 161-198. (This is one of a series of studies.)

670.—Maslow, A. H., The rôle of dominance in the social and sexual behavior of infra-human primates: I. Observations at Vilas Park Zoo, *J. Genet. Psychol.*, 1936, **48**, 261-277.

671.—Maslow, A. H., and Flanzbaum, S., The rôle of dominance in the social and sexual behavior of infra-human primates: II. An experimental determination of the behavior syndrome of dominance, *J. Genet. Psychol.*, 1936, **48**, 278-309.

672.—Mason, S. H., A comparative study of four pairs of twins examined in kindergarten and in junior high school, with special reference to personality, *Smith Coll. Stud. Soc. Work*, 1933-1934, **4**, 197-286.

673.—Masuoka, J., Race preference in Hawaii, *Amer. J. Sociol.*, 1936, **41**, 635-641.

674.—Mathews, S. M., The effect of mother's out-of-home employment upon children's ideas and attitudes, *J. Appl. Psychol.*, 1934, **18**, 116-136.

675.—Matthews, C. O., The honor system, *J. Higher Educ.*, 1932, **3**, 411-415.

676.—Max, L. W., An experimental study of motor theory of consciousness: II. Method and apparatus, *J. Genet. Psychol.*, 1935, **13**, 159-175.

677.—May, M. A., The adult in the community, in Murchison, C., *Foundations of experimental psychology*, 1929, 738-785.

678.—May, M. A., The foundations of personality, in *Psychology at work*, 1932, 81-101.

679.—Mayer, A., Über Einzel- und Gesamtleistung des Schulkindes, *Arch. f. d. ges. Psychol.*, 1903, **1**, 276-416.

680.—Mayer, B. A., Negativistic reactions of pre-school children on the new revision of the Stanford Binet, *J. Genet. Psychol.*, 1935, **46**, 311-334.

681.—McCallum, G., The play activities of fifth-grade children in three communities, *Smith Coll. Stud. Soc. Work*, 1932-1933, **3**, 206.

682.—McCarthy, D., A comparison of children's language in different situations and in its relation to personality traits, *J. Genet. Psychol.*, 1929, **36**, 583-591.

683.—McCarthy, D., Language development, in *Handbook of child psychology* (2nd ed. rev.), 1933, pp. 329-373.

684.—McCarthy, D., *The language development of the pre-school child*, 1930.

685.—McDougall, W., A chemical theory of temperament applied to introversion and extraversion, *J. Abn. & Soc. Psychol.*, 1929, **24**, 293-309.

686.—McDougall, W., *An introduction to social psychology*, 1st ed., 1908.

687.—McDougall, W., *An introduction to social psychology*, 12th ed., 1917, 121 ff.

688.—McFie, B. S., Behavior and personality difficulties in school children, *Brit. J. Educ. Psychol.*, 1934, **4**, 30-46.

689.—McGrath, M., Some moral concepts of young children, *Cath. Educ. Rev.*, 1933, **31**, 477-487.

690.—McGraw, M. B., *Growth, A study of Johnny and Jimmy*, 1935.

691.—McQueen-Williams, M., Maternal behavior in male rats, *Science*, 1935, **82**, 67-68.

692.—Mead, M., *Coming of age in Samoa*, 1928.

693.—Mead, M., *Cooperation and competition among primitive peoples*, 1937.

694.—Mead, M., *Growing up in New Guinea*, 1930.

695.—Mead, M., *Sex and temperament in three primitive societies*, 1935.

696.—Meltzer, H., Children's attitudes to parents, *Amer. J. Orthopsychiat.*, 1935, **5**, 244-266.

697.—Meltzer, H., Personification of ideals and stereotypes in problem children, *Amer. J. Orthopsychiat.*, 1932, **2**, 384-399.

698.—Meltzer, H., Students' adjustments in anger, *J. Soc. Psychol.*, 1933, 4, 285-309.

699.—Meltzer, H., Talkativeness about, in relation to knowledge of social concepts in children, *Ped. Sem.*, 1926, 33, 497-507.

700.—Mengert, I. G., A preliminary study of the reactions of two-year-old children to each other when paired in a semi-controlled situation, *J. Genet. Psychol.*, 1931, 39, 393-398.

701.—Menzies, R., Conditioned vasomotor responses in human subjects, *J. Psychol.*, 1937, 4, 75-120.

702.—Merriman, C., The intellectual resemblance of twins, *Psychol. Monog.*, 1924, 33, No. 152.

703.—Meyers, M. R., and Cushing, H. M., Types and incidence of behavior problems in relation to cultural background, *Amer. J. Orthopsychiat.*, 1936, 6, 110-117.

704.—Miller, E., Temperamental differences in the behavior disorders of children, *Brit. J. Educ. Psychol.*, 1933, 3, 22-236.

705.—Miller, L. W., A critical analysis of the Peterson-Thurstone war attitude scale, *J. Educ. Psychol.*, 1934, 25, 662-668.

706.—Millson, W. A. D., Problems in measuring audience reaction, *Quart. J. Speech*, 1932, 18, 621-637.

707.—Minard, R. D., Race attitudes of Iowa children, *Univ. Iowa Stud.: Stud. Char.*, 1931, 4, No. 2.

708.—Minkowski, M., Sur les mouvements, les réflexes, les réactions musculaires du fœtus humain de 2 à 5 mois et leurs relations avec le système nerveux fœtal, *Rev. neur.*, 1921, 37, 1105-1235.

709.—Mirenva, A. N., Psychomotor education and the general development of pre-school children: experiments with twin controls, *J. Genet. Psychol.*, 1935, 46, 433-454.

710.—Mirk, M., The differences of emotional stability in girls of different ages, *Australasian J. Psychol.*, 1930, 8, 229-232.

711.—Mittelmann, B., A neurologic and psychopathologic study of juvenile adiposogenital dystrophy, *Arch. Neurol. & Psychiat.*, 1936, 36, 205-206.

712.—Moede, W., *Experimentelle Massenpsychologie*, 1920.

713.—Moede, W., Der Wetteifer, seine Struktur und sein Ausmass, *Zsch. f. päd. Psychol.*, 1914, 15, 353-368.

714.—Montelli, A. K., [Research in the sphere of social interests of secondary school pupils], *Pedologia*, 1930, 1, 107-118.

715.—Moore, B. V., The interview in social industrial research, *Soc. Forces*, 1929, 7, 445-452.

716.—Moore, E. S., The development of mental health in a group of young children, *Univ. Iowa Stud.: Stud. Child Welfare*, 1931, 4, No. 6.

717.—Moore, E. S., The development of mental health in a group of young children, *Univ. Iowa Stud.: Stud. Child Welfare*, 1931, 4, No. 6.

718.—Moore, G., and Garrison, K. C., A comparative study of social and political attitudes of college students, *J. Abn. & Soc. Psychol.*, 1932, 27, 195-208.

719.—Moore, H. K., Is the problem boy a weakling? *J. Juv. Res.*, 1934, 18, 79-89.

720.—Moore, H. T., The comparative influence of majority and expert opinion, *Amer. J. Psychol.*, 1921, **32**, 16-20.

721.—Moore, H. T., Further data concerning sex differences, *J. Abn. & Soc. Psychol.*, 1922, **17**, 210-214.

722.—Moore, H. T., Innate factors in radicalism and conservatism, *J. Abn. & Soc. Psychol.*, 1929, **35**, 220-238.

723.—Moore, H. T., and Gilliland, A. R., The measurement of aggressiveness, *J. Appl. Psychol.*, 1921, **5**, 97-118.

724.—Moragues, J., Esquema de l'evolucio sexual de l'enfant, *Rev. Psicol. Pedag.*, 1934, **2**, 117-119.

725.—Moreno, J. L., *Who shall survive? A new approach to the problem of human interrelations*, 1934.

726.—Morgan, C. L., and Morgan, L. V., Effects of immediate awareness of success and failure upon objective examination scores, *J. Exper. Educ.*, 1936, **4**, 63-66.

727.—Moss, F. A., Study of animal drives, *J. Exper. Psychol.*, 1924, **7**, 165-185.

728.—Mowrer, H. R., Study of marital adjustment as a background for research in child behavior, (Paper presented at the Christmas Meeting of the Soc. for Res. in Child Devel.), 1936.

729.—Mueller, R., The effect of encouragement and discouragement upon introverts, ambiverts and extroverts in mirror-drawing, Master's Essay, School of Educ., Univ. of Michigan, 1932.

730.—Muller, H. J., Mental traits and heredity, *J. Heredity*, 1925, **16**, 433-448.

731.—Muller, J., Versuch über die Einwirkung von Motiven auf Körperliche und Geistige Leistungen bei Schulkindern, *Zsch. f. angew. Psychol.*, 1924, **24**, 81-128.

732.—Munroe, R. L., (Unpublished study).

733.—Münsterberg, H., *Grundzüge der Psychotechnik*, 1914, 266-271.

734.—Murchison, C., *Social psychology: the psychology of political domination*, 1928.

735.—Murchison, C., Pomerat, C. M., and Zarrow, M. X., The experimental measurement of a social hierarchy in gallus domesticus; V. The post-mortem measurement of anatomical features, *J. Soc. Psychol.*, 1935, **6**, 172-181.

736.—Murdock, K. M., A study of differences found between races in intellect and morality, *School and Soc.*, 1925, **22**, I, 628-632, II, 659-664; Racial differences found in two American cities, *Indus. Psychol.*, 1926, **1**, 99-104.

737.—Murphy, G., *General psychology*, 1933.

738.—Murphy, G., and Likert, R., Public opinion and the individual, (Unpublished study).

739.—Murphy, G., and Murphy, L. B., *Experimental social psychology*, 1931, p. 664.

740.—Murphy, L. B., *Social behavior and child personality*, 1937.

741.—Murphy, L. B., and Biber, B., (Unpublished study).

742.—Murphy, L. B., and Murphy, G., The influence of social situations upon the behavior of children, in Murchison, C. (ed.), *A handbook of social psychology*, 1935.

743.—Murray, A., Facts which support the concept of need or drive, *J. Psychol.*, 1936, **3**, 27-42.

744.—Murray, H. A., Basic concepts for a psychology of personality, *J. Gen. Psychol.*, 1936, **16**, 241-268.

745.—Murray, H. A., (Oral comment on paper presented in No. 54).

746.—Murray, H. A., Techniques for a systematic investigation of fantasy, *J. Psychol.*, 1936, **3**, 115-143.

747.—Muth, L. C., *Children's opinions on what makes a thing good or bad*, Master's essay in Columbia University Library, 1928.

748.—Myers, G. C., Control of conduct by suggestion: an experiment in Americanization, *J. Appl. Psychol.*, 1921, **5**, 26-31.

749.—Myers, G. C., The social problem of the gifted child, *J. Except. Child.*, 1935, **2**, 39-43.

750.—Myers, T. R., Intra-family relationships and pupil adjustment, *Teach. Coll. Contrib. Educ.*, 1935, No. 651.

751.—Nathan, M., *The attitudes of the Jewish student in the colleges and universities toward his religion*, 1932.

752.—Nelson, J. F., Personality and intelligence, *Child Devel. Monog.*, No. 4, 1931.

753.—Nelson, J. F., Preliminary report on some uses of the psychological test situation for studying personality differences, in Thomas, D. S., Some new techniques for studying social behavior, *Child Devel. Monog.*, 1929, No. 1, 118-149.

754.—Neumann, G. B., A study of international attitudes of high school students, *Teach. Coll. Contrib. Educ.*, 1927, No. 239.

755.—Newcomb, T. M., The consistency of certain extrovert-introvert behavior patterns in 51 problem boys, *Teach. Coll. Contrib. Educ.*, 1929, No. 382.

756.—Newcomb, T. M., (Unpublished data).

757.—Newcomb, T. M., and Svehla, G., Intra-family relationships in attitude, (published in *Sociometry*, 1937).

758.—Newell, H. W., Family attitudes as revealed by the psychiatric examinations of 107 juvenile delinquents, *Amer. J. Orthopsychiat.*, 1932, **2**, 377-383.

759.—Newell, H. W., A further study of maternal rejection, *Amer. J. Orthopsychiat.*, 1936, **6**, 576-607.

760.—Newell, H. W., Psycho-dynamics of maternal rejection, *Amer. J. Orthopsychiat.*, 1934, **4**, 387-402.

761.—Newman, H. H., Freeman, F. N., and Holzinger, K. J., *Twins: A Study of heredity and environment*, 1937.

762.—Nissen, H. W., The effects of gonadectomy, vasotomy, and injections of placental and orchic extracts on the sex behavior of the white rat, *Genet. Psychol. Monog.*, 1929, **5**, No. 6, 451-550.

763.—Nissen, H. W., Machover, S., and Kinder, E. F., A study of performance tests given to a group of native African Negro children, *Brit. J. Psychol.*, 1935, **25**, 308-355.

764.—Novakovsky, S., Arctic or Siberian hysteria as a reflex of the geographic environment, *Ecology*, 1924, **5**, 113-127.

765.—Novikova, A. A., (Conditioned inhibition and conditioned reflexes of higher order in children), *Medikobiologicheski Zhurnal*, 1929, No. 1, 120-131.

766.—Nutting, L. R., Some characteristics of leadership, *School & Soc.*, 1923, 18, 387-390.

767.—Ojemann, R. H., The modifiability of attitude and its significance for research in child development, (Paper read at Christmas Meeting of the Soc. for Research in Child Development), 1936.

768.—Oliver, R. A. C., The traits of extroverts and introverts, *J. Soc. Psychol.*, 1930, 1, 345-366.

769.—Olson, W. C., Behavior problems of school children, *J. Mich. State Med. Soc.*, 1931, 38, 428-431.

770.—Olson, W. C., Birthplace and occupation of father as factors in nervous habits in children, *J. Genet. Psychol.*, 1932, 40, 214-219.

771.—Olson, W. C., Child-teacher relations, *The Nation's Schools*, 1936, 17, 20-21.

772.—Olson, W. C., The clinical use of behavior rating schedules, *J. Juv. Res.*, 1931, 15, 237-245.

773.—Olson, W. C., The diagnosis and treatment of behavior disorders of children; Emotional and social factors in learning, *In 34th Yrbk. of the National Society for the Study of Education*, 1935.

774.—Olson, W. C., *The measurement of nervous habits in normal children*, 1929.

775.—Olson, W. C., A Method for observational measurement, In Scientific method in supervision, *2nd Yrbk. Nat. Conf. of Supervisors and Directors of Instruction*, 1929.

776.—Olson, W. C., The prediction of delinquency from early behavior, *Proc. 45th Ann. Mtg. Amer. Psychol. Assn.*, 1937.

777.—Olson, W. C., *Problem tendencies in children; a method for their measurement and description*, 1930.

778.—Olson, W. C., Progress in measurement by direct observation, *Elem. School J.*, 1933, 33, 633-635.

779.—Olson, W. C., The quantification of direct observation, *Proc. & Papers 9th Internat. Cong. Psychol.*, 1930.

780.—Olson, W. C., A study of classroom behavior, *J. Educ. Psychol.*, 1931, 22, 449-454.

781.—Olson, W. C., and Cunningham, E. M., Time-sampling techniques, *Child Devel.*, 1934, 5, 41-58.

782.—Olson, W. C., and Wilkinson, M. M., The measurement of child behavior in terms of its social stimulus value, *J. Exper. Educ.*, 1932, 1, 92-95.

783.—Cf. Omwake, K. T., Dexter, E. S., and Lewis, L. W., The interrelations of certain physiological measurements and aspects of personality, *Char. & Pers.*, 1934, 3, 64-71.

784.—Page, K., 19,000 clergymen on war and peace, *World Tomorrow*, 1931, 14, 138-154.

785.—Page, M. L., The modification of ascendant behavior in pre-school children, *Univ. Iowa Stud.: Stud. Child Welfare*, 1936, 12, No. 3.

786.—Panlasigui, I., and Knight, F. B., The effect of awareness of success or failure, *29th Yrbk. of the National Society for the Study of Education, Pt. II*, 1930, 611-621.

787.—Parsley, M., The delinquent girl in Chicago: The influence of ordinal position and size of family, *Smith Coll. Stud. Soc. Work*, 1933, 3, 274-283.

788.—Parten, M. B., Leadership among pre-school children, *J. Abn. & Soc. Psychol.*, 1933, 27, 430-440.

789.—Parten, M. B., Social participation among pre-school children, *J. Abn. & Soc. Psychol.*, 1932, 27, 243-269.

790.—Parten, M. B., Social play among pre-school children, *J. Abn. & Soc. Psychol.*, 1933, 28, 136-147.

791.—Partridge, E. D., Ability in leadership among adolescent boys, *School Rev.*, 1932, 40, 526-531.

792.—Partridge, E. D., Leadership among adolescent boys, *Teach. Coll. Contrib. Educ.*, 1934, No. 608.

793.—Paterson, D. G., *Physique and intellect*, 1930.

794.—Patrick, J. R., and Rowles, E., Intercorrelations among metabolic rate, vital capacity, blood pressure, intelligence, scholarship, personality, and other measures of university women, *J. Appl. Psychol.*, 1933, 17, 507-521.

795.—Paulsen, G. B., The reliability and consistency of individual differences in motor control, *J. Appl. Psychol.*, 1935, 19, 29-42, 166-179.

796.—Paynter, R. H., and Blanchard, P., A study of educational achievement of problem children, *Commonwealth Fund, Div. Publ.*, 1929.

797.—Peck, L., Teachers' reports of the problems of unadjusted school children, *J. Educ. Psychol.*, 1935, 16, 123-138.

798.—Perrin, F. A. C., Physical attractiveness and repulsiveness, *J. Exper. Psychol.*, 1921, 4, 203-217.

799.—Peterson, J., and Lanier, L. H., Studies in the comparative abilities of whites and Negroes, *Ment. Meas. Monog.*, 1929, Ser. No. 5.

800.—Peterson, J., Lanier, L. H., and Walker, H. M., Comparisons of white and Negro children in certain ingenuity and speed tests, *J. Comp. Psychol.*, 1925, 5, 271-283.

801.—Peterson, R. C., and Thurstone, L. L., *The effect of motion pictures on the social attitudes of high school children*, 1933.

802.—Phillips, H. C., An analysis of the social contacts of junior and senior high school students in a rural community, Ph.D. thesis, Univ. of Iowa, 1934.

803.—Piaget, J., *The child's conception of the world*, 1929.

804.—Piaget, J., in *Factors determining human behavior, Harvard Terc. Publn.*, 1937, 32-48.

805.—Piaget, J., *The language and thought of the child*, 1926.

806.—Piaget, J., *The moral judgment of the child*, 1932.

807.—Pigors, P., Leadership and domination among children, *Sociologus*, 1933, 9, 140-157.

808.—Pigors, P., *Leadership or domination*, 1935.

809.—Pinard, J. W., Tests of perseveration: I. Their relation to character, *Brit. J. Psychol.*, 1932, 23, 5-19.

810.—Pinard, J. W., Tests of perseveration: II. Their relation to certain psychopathic conditions and to introversion, *Brit. J. Psychol.*, 1932, 23, 114-126.

811.—Pintner, R., A comparison of interest, abilities, and attitudes, *J. Abn. & Soc. Psychol.*, 1933, 27, 351-357.

812.—Pintner, R., Intelligence as estimated from photographs, *Psychol. Rev.*, 1918, **25**, 286-296.

813.—Pintner, R., *Intelligence testing: Methods and results*, rev. ed., 1931.

814.—Pintner, R., Maller, J. B., Forlano, G., and Axelrod, H., The measurement of pupil adjustment, *J. Educ. Res.*, 1935, **28**, 334-346.

815.—Porter, E., Student opinion on war, Ph.D. thesis in University of Chicago Library, 1926.

816.—Porteus, S. D., and Babcock, M. E., *Temperament and race*, 1926.

817.—Portneier, L. G., The "problem child" at the pre-school level, *J. Appl. Psychol.*, 1935, **19**, 93-100.

818.—Pratt, K. C., A note upon the relation of activity to sex and race in young infants, *J. Soc. Psychol.*, 1932, **3**, 118-120.

819.—Pratt, K. C., Nelson, A. K., and Sun, K. H., The behavior of the newborn infant, *Ohio State Univ. Contrib. in Psychol.*, No. 10, 1930.

820.—Pressey, S. L., A group scale for investigating the emotions, *J. Abn. & Soc. Psychol.*, 1921, **16**, 55-64.

821.—Pressey, S. L., and Pressey, L. C., A comparison of the emotional development of Indians belonging to different tribes, *J. Appl. Psychol.*, 1933, **17**, 535-541.

822.—Pressey, S. L., and Pressey, L. C., Development of the interest-attitude tests, *J. Appl. Psychol.*, 1933, **17**, 1-16.

823.—Queen, S. A., Social interaction in the interview: an experiment, *Soc. Forces*, 1928, **6**, 545-558.

824.—Radina, S. I., (A pedagogical study of children entering kindergarten), *Pedologia*, 1930, **4**, 468-476.

825.—Rauth, J. E., and Furfey, P. H., The maturational factor in adolescent conduct, *Child Devel.*, 1933, **4**, 90-91.

826.—Razran, G. H. S., Attitudinal control of human conditioning, *J. Psychol.*, 1936, **2**, 327-337.

827.—Razran, G. H. S., Conditioned responses, *Arch. Psychol.*, 1935, No. 191.

828.—Razran, G. H. S., Salivating and thinking in different languages, *J. Psychol.*, 1936, **1**, 145-151.

829.—Razran, G. H. S., Theory of conditioning and related phenomena, *Psychol. Rev.*, 1930, **27**, 1-12.

830.—Reckless, W. C., and Bringen, H. L., Racial attitudes and information about the Negro, *J. Negro Educ.*, 1933, **2**, 128-138.

831.—Reininger, K., Das soziale Verhalten von Schulneulingen, *Wien Arb. z. päd. Psychol.*, 1927, **7**, 14. (See Pigors, P., Leadership and domination among children, *Sociologus*, 1933, **9**, 140-157.)

832.—Remmers, H. H., Studies in attitudes, *Bull. Purdue Univ.*, 1934, **35**, No. 4.

833.—Reynolds M. M., Negativism of pre-school children, *Teach. Coll. Contrib. Educ.*, 1928, No. 288.

834.—Rice, S. A., *Quantitative methods in politics*, 1928, 51-70.

835.—Rice, S. A., Statistical studies of social attitudes and public opinion, in Rice, S. A., *Statistics in social studies*, 1930, 190-191.

836.—Rich, G. J., A biochemical approach to the study of personality, *J. Abn. & Soc. Psychol.*, 1928, **23**, 158-175.

837.—Richards, E. L., The origin of conduct problems in school children, *Bull. State Univ. Iowa*, 1934, N. S. No. 751.

838.—Richards, T. W., The importance of hunger in the bodily activity of the neonate, *Psychol. Bull.*, 1936, 33, 817-835.

839.—Richter, C. P., Animal behavior and internal drives, *Quar. Rev. Biol.*, 1927, 2, 307-343.

840.—Richter, C. P., Biological foundation of personality differences, *Amer. J. Orthopsychiat.*, 1932, 2, 345-362.

841.—Ricketts, A. F., A study of the behavior of young children in anger, *Univ. Iowa Stud.: Stud. Child Welfare*, 1934, 9, No. 3, 159-171.

842.—Riddle, E. M., Aggressive behavior in a small social group, *Arch. Psychol.*, 1925, No. 78.

843.—Riddle, O., Bates, R. W., and Lahr, E. L., Prolactin induces broodiness in fowl, *Amer. J. Physiol.*, 1935, 111, 352-360.

844.—Rieffel, M., Goûts professionnels de la jeunnesse ouvrière de l'U. S. S. R., *Bull. Inst. Nat. Orient. Prof.*, 1932, 4, 49-57.

845.—Roberts, M. P., A study of children's play in the home environment, *Univ. Iowa Stud.: Stud. Child. Welfare*, 1934, 8, 33-98.

846.—Robinson, E. S., Are radio fans influenced? *Survey*, 1932, 68, 546-547.

847.—Robinson, E. S., Trends of the voter's mind, *J. Soc. Psychol.*, 1933, 4, 265-284.

848.—Robinson, E. W., and Conrad, H. S., The reliability of observations of talkativeness and social contact among nursery-school children by the "short time sample" technique, *J. Exper. Educ.*, 1922, 2, 161-165.

849.—Rogers, C. R., Measuring personality adjustment in children nine to thirteen years of age, *Teach. Coll. Contrib. Educ.*, 1931, No. 458.

850.—Rogers, H. W., Some attitudes of students in the R. O. T. C., *J. Educ. Psychol.*, 1935, 26, 291-306.

851.—Rombach, J., Das soziale Verhalten des siebenjährigen, *Zsch. f. angew. Psychol.*, 1928, 38, 369-429.

852.—Rorschach, H., *Psychodiagnostik*, 2 vols., 1932.

853.—Rosenow, C., The incidence of first-born among problem children, *J. Genet. Psychol.*, 1930, 37, 145-151.

854.—Rosenthal, S. P., Changes of socio-economic attitudes under radical motion picture propaganda, *Arch. Psychol.*, 1934, No. 166.

855.—Ross, B. M., Some traits associated with sibling jealousy in problem children, *Smith. Coll. Stud. Soc. Work*, 1931, 1, 364-378.

856.—Ross, C. C., The influence upon achievement of a knowledge of progress, *J. Educ. Psychol.*, 1933, 24, 609-619.

857.—Ross, E. A., *Social psychology*, 1917.

858.—Rugg, H., Krueger, L., and Sondergaard, A., Studies in child personality: I. A study of the language of kindergarten children, *J. Educ. Psychol.*, 1929, 20, 1-18.

859.—Rundquist, E. A., and Sletto, R. F., *Personality in the depression*, 1936.

860.—Rust, M. M., The effect of resistance on intelligence test scores of young children, *Child Devel. Monog.*, 1931, No. 6.

861.—Rybnikov, N., Die Ideologie des russischen Schulkindes der Gegenwart, *Zsch. f. angew. Psychol.*, 1929, 32, 213-219.

862.—Saadi, M., and Farnsworth, P. R., The degrees of acceptance of dogmatic statements and preferences for their supposed makers, *J. Abn. & Soc. Psychol.*, 1934, **29**, 143-150.

863.—Salmer, E., and Remmers, H. H., Affective selectivity and liberalizing influence of college courses, *J. Appl. Psychol.*, 1933, **17**, 349-354.

864.—Salusky, A. S., Collective behavior of children at a pre-school age, *J. Soc. Psychol.*, 1930, **1**, 367-378.

865.—Saudek, R., A British pair of twins reared apart, *Char. & Pers.*, 1934, **3**, 17-19.

866.—Schaefer, M., Elemente zur moral-psychologischen Beurteilung Jugendlicher, *Zsch. f. päd. Psychol.*, 1913, **14**, 47-59, 90-98.

867.—Scherer, I. W., An investigation of a method of measuring emotional reactions in gymnasium situations, Master's essay in New York University Library, 1934.

868.—Schiller, B., Verbal, numerical and spatial abilities of young children, *Arch. Psychol.*, 1934, No. 161.

869.—Schjelderup-Ebbe, T., Beiträge zur Sozialpsychologie des Haushuhns, *Zsch. f. Psychol.*, 1922, **88**, 225-252.

870.—Schlorff, P. W., An experiment in the measurement and modification of racial attitudes in school children, Doctoral dissertation in New York University Library, 1930.

871.—Schmideberg, M., The play analysis of a three-year-old girl, *Int. J. Psychoanal.*, 1934, **15**, 245-264.

872.—Schneckenburger, H., Das soziale Verständnis des Arbeiterkindes, *Zsch. f. päd. Psychol.*, 1933, **34**, 374-385.

873.—Schuler, E. A., A study of the consistency of dominant and submissive behavior in adolescent boys, *J. Genet. Psychol.*, 1934, **46**, 403-432.

874.—Schwegler, R. A., A study of introvert-extrovert responses to certain test situations, *Teach. Coll. Contrib. Educ.*, 1929, No. 361.

875.—Scott, W. E. D., Data on song in birds, *Science*, 1901, N. S. **14**, 522-526.

876.—Seagoe, M. V., Factors influencing the selection of associates, *J. Educ. Res.*, 1933, **27**, 32-40.

877.—Searl, M. N., Play, reality and aggression, *Int. J. Psychoanal.*, 1933, **14**, 310-320.

878.—Sears, R. R., Experimental studies of projection: I. Attribution of traits, *J. Soc. Psychol.*, 1936, **7**, 151-163.

879.—Semenova-Boltunova, A. P., (Speech of the contemporary Russian proletarian and peasant child of primary school age according to data of an experimental-psychological investigation), *Pedologia*, 1928, **2**, 47-60.

880.—Sewall, M., Some causes of jealousy in young children, *Smith Coll. Stud. Soc. Work*, 1930, **1**, 6-22.

881.—Shallit, R., The dramatic play of ten nursery-school children, *Child Devel.*, 1932, **3**, 359-362.

882.—Shaw, C. R., et al., Delinquency areas: A study of the geographic distribution of school truants, juvenile delinquents, and adult offenders in Chicago, *Behav. Res. Monog.*, 1931.

883.—Shaw, M. E., A comparison of individuals and small groups in the rational solution of complex problems, Master's essay in Columbia University Library,

1930; also A comparison of individuals and small groups in the rational solution of complex problems, *Amer. J. Psychol.*, 1932, 44, 491-504.

884.—Sherif, M., Experimental determination of an attitude, (to appear in *Sociometry*, 1937).

885.—Sherif, M., An experimental study of stereotypes, *J. Abn. & Soc. Psychol.*, 1935, 29, 371-375.

886.—Sherif, M., Psychology of slogans, (to appear in *J. Abn. & Soc. Psychol.*).

887.—Sherif, M., *The psychology of social norms*, 1936.

888.—Sherif, M., A study of some social factors in perception, *Arch. Psychol.*, 1935, No. 187.

889.—Sherman, M., The differentiation of emotional responses in infants: I. Judgments of emotional responses from motion picture views and from actual observation, *J. Comp. Psychol.*, 1927, 7, 265-284.

890.—Sherman, M., The differentiation of emotional responses in infants: II. The ability of observers to judge the emotional characteristics of the crying of infants and the voice of an adult, *J. Comp. Psychol.*, 1927, 7, 335-352.

891.—Sherman, M., Phantasy types: Their relation to conflicts and hallucinations, *Ninth International Congress of Psychology, Proceedings and papers* (1929, publ. 1930), 392-393.

892.—Sherman, M., and Key, C. B., The intelligence of isolated mountain children, *Child Devel.*, 1932, 3, 279-290.

893.—Sherman, M., and Sherman, I. C., *The process of human behavior*, 1929, 128-135.

894.—Shevaleva, E. N., and Silla, D. D., (An attempt at experimental study of child leadership), see No. 211.

895.—Shinn, M. W., *The biography of a baby*, 1900.

896.—Shirley, M., *The first two years*, 3 vols., 1931, 1933.

897.—Shirley, M., A motor sequence favors the maturation theory, *Thirty-eighth Meeting of the American Psychological Association*, 1930, 12-13.

898.—Shirley, M., Studies of activity: I, Consistency of the revolving drum method of measuring the activity of the rat, *J. Comp. Psychol.*, 1928, 8, 23-38; Studies of activity: II, Activity rhythms, age and activity, activity after rest, *J. Comp. Psychol.*, 1928, 8, 159-186; Studies of activity: III, The relation of activity to maze-learning and to brain weight, *J. Comp. Psychol.*, 1928, 8, 187-195.

899.—Shuttleworth, F. K., The influence of early religious home training on college sophomore men, *Rel. Educ.*, 1927, 2, 57-60.

900.—Silverman, B., The behavior of children from broken homes, *Amer. J. Orthopsychiat.*, 1935, 5, 11-18.

901.—Simms, V. F., and Patrick, J. R., Attitude toward the Negro of northern and southern college students, *J. Soc. Psychol.*, 1936, 7, 192-204.

902.—Simpson, M., Parent preferences of young children, *Teach. Coll. Contrib. Educ.*, 1935, No. 652.

903.—Sims, V. M., *The measurement of socio-economic status*, 1928.

904.—Sims, V. M., The relative influence of two types of motivation on improvement, *J. Educ. Psychol.*, 1928, 19, 480-484.

905.—Skinner, B. F., Drive and reflex strength, *J. Gen. Psychol.*, 1932, 6, 22-37, 38-48.

906.—Slawson, J., *The delinquent boy*, 1926.

907.—Sletto, R. F., Sibling position and juvenile delinquency, *Amer. J. Sociol.*, 1934, **39**, 657-669.

908.—Smalley, R. E., The influence of differences in age, sex, and intelligence in determining the attitudes of siblings toward each other, *Smith Coll. Stud. Soc. Work*, 1930, **I**, 23-39.

909.—Smith, A., *Inquiry into the nature and causes of the wealth of nations*, 1801.

910.—Smith, F. T., An experiment in modifying attitudes toward the Negro, Ph.D. thesis in the Library of Teachers College, Columbia University, 1933.

911.—Smith, M. E., The pre-school child's use of criticism, *Child Devel.*, 1932, **3**, 137-141.

912.—Smith, M. E., A study of factors influencing the development of the sentence in pre-school children, *J. Genet. Psychol.*, 1935, **46**, 182-212.

913.—Sontag, L. W., and Nelson, V. L., Monozygotic dichorionic triplets, Part II. Behavior of a set of identical triplets, *J. Genet. Psychol.*, 1933, **42**, 406-422.

914.—Sorokin, P. A., with Tanquist, M., Parten, M., and Zimmerman, C. C., An experimental study of efficiency of work under various specified conditions, *Amer. J. Sociol.*, 1930, **35**, 765-782.

915.—South, E. B., Some psychological aspects of committee work, *J. Appl. Psychol.*, 1927, **II**, 348-368, 437-464.

916.—Sowards, G. S., A study of the war attitudes of college students, *J. Abn. & Soc. Psychol.*, 1934, **29**, 328-333.

917.—Sparling, E., Do college students choose vocations wisely? *Teach. Coll. Contrib. Educ.*, 1933, No. 561.

918.—Spencer, H., *Principles of sociology*, 1880-1896.

919.—Spencer, L. T., The effects of practice without knowledge of results, *Amer. J. Psychol.*, 1923, **34**, 107-111.

920.—Spranger, E., *Types of men*, 1928.

921.—Stagner, R., Economic status and personality, *School & Soc.*, 1935, **42**, 551-552.

922.—Stagner, R., Fascist attitudes: General and economic determinants, Abstract reference in *Psychol. Bull.*, 1935. (We are indebted to the author for the loan of the manuscript.)

923.—Stagner, R., and Drought, N., Measuring children's attitudes toward their parents, *J. Educ. Psychol.*, 1935, **26**, 169-176.

924.—Stagner, R., and Katzoff, E. T., Personality as related to birth order and family size, *J. Appl. Psychol.*, 1936, **20**, 340-346.

925.—Stalnaker, E., Language of the pre-school child, *Child Devel.*, 1933, **4**, 229-236.

926.—Starch, D., Unconscious imitation in handwriting, *Psychol. Rev.*, 1911, **18**, 223-228.

927.—Stearns, A. W., Homicide in Massachusetts, *Amer. J. Psychiat.*, 1925, **4**, 725-749.

928.—Steinberg, J., The relation between basal metabolism and mental speed, *Arch. Psychol.*, 1934, No. 172.

929.—Steinberg, W., *Die seelische Eingliederung in die Gesellschaft*, 1933.

930.—Steinthal, H., and Lazarus, M., *Zeitschrift für Völkerpsychologie und Sprachwissenschaft*, 1860-1890.

931.—Stemsrud, A. L., and Wardwell, S., A comparative study of fourteen socially well-adjusted children with their maladjusted siblings, *Smith. Coll. Stud. Soc. Work*, 1933-1934, 4, 165-166.

932.—Stephenson, W., Perseveration and character, *Char. & Pers.*, 1935, 4, 44-52.

933.—Stephenson, W., Studies in experimental psychiatry: I. A case of general inertia, *J. Ment. Sci.*, 1931, 77, 723-741.

934.—Cf. Stephenson, W., Studies in experimental psychiatry: II. Some contact of p-factor with psychiatry, *J. Ment. Sci.*, 1932, 78, 315-330.

935.—Stephenson, W., Studies in experimental psychiatry: III. p-score and inhibition for high-p praecox cases, *J. Ment. Sci.*, 1932, 78, 908-928; also, Perseveration and character, *Char. & Pers.*, 1935, 4, 44-52.

936.—Cf. Stern, W., Anfänge der Reifezeit, *Ein Knabentagebuch in psychologischer Bearbeitung*, 2nd ed., 1929.

937.—Stofflet, E. H., A study of national and cultural differences in criminal tendency, *Arch. Psychol.*, 1931, No. 185.

938.—Stolz, H. R., Jones, M. C., and Chaffey, J., The junior high school age, *Univ. High School J.*, 1937, 15, 63-72.

939.—Stone, C. P., The congenital sexual behavior of the young male albino rat, *J. Comp. Psychol.*, 1922, 2, 95-153.

940.—Stone, C. P., Further study of sensory functions in the activation of sexual behavior in the young male albino rat, *J. Comp. Psychol.*, 1923, 3, 469-473.

941.—Stone, C. P., The initial copulatory response of female rats reared in isolation from the age of twenty days to the age of puberty, *J. Comp. Psychol.*, 1926, 6, 73-83.

942.—See Stone, C. P., Recent contributions to the experimental literature on native or congenital behavior, *Psychol. Bull.*, 1927, 24, p. 40.

943.—Stouffer, S. A., An experimental comparison of statistical and case history methods of attitude research, Ph.D. thesis in University of Chicago Library, 1930.

944.—Stratton, G. M., Anger and fear: Their probable relation to each other, to intellectual work, and to primogeniture, *Amer. J. Psychol.*, 1927, 39, 125-140.

945.—Stratton, G. M., An experience during danger and the wider functions of emotion, in *Problems of personality, Studies presented to Dr. Morton Prince*, 1925, 47-62.

946.—Stratton, G. M., The relation of emotion to sex, primogeniture, and disease, *Amer. J. Psychol.*, 1934, 46, 590-595.

947.—Stuart, J. C., Data on the alleged psychopathology of the only child, *J. Abn. & Soc. Psychol.*, 1926, 20, 441.

948.—Sullivan, C., A scale for measuring developmental age in girls, *Stud. Psychol. & Psychiat.*, 1934, No. 4.

949.—Sullivan, E. B., Attitude in relation to learning, *Psychol. Monog.*, 1927, 36, No. 169.

950.—Sutherland, I. L. G., The study of Maori mind, *Ninth International Congress of Psychology, Proceedings and papers* (1929, publ. 1930), 419-421.

951.—Svendson, M., Children's imaginary companions, *Arch. Neur. & Psychiat.*, 1934, 32, 985-999.

952.—Sward, K., Jewish musicality, *Psychol. Bull.*, 1933, 30, 716.

953.—Sward, K., Temperament and direction of achievement, *J. Soc. Psychol.*, 1933, **4**, 406-429.

954.—Sweet, L., cf. Hartshorne, May and Shuttleworth, *Studies in the organization of character*, 1930, p. 284.

955.—Swinton, R. S., Analysis of child behavior by intermittent photography, *Child Devel.*, 1934, **5**, 292-293.

956.—Symington, T. A., Religious liberals and conservatives, *Teach. Coll. Contrib. Educ.*, 1935, No. 640.

957.—Symonds, P. M., *Diagnosing personality and conduct*, 1931.

958.—Symonds, P. M., The relation of child behavior to rejection by parents, *45th Ann. Mtg. Amer. Psychol. Assn.*, 1937.

959.—Symonds, P. M., A social attitudes questionnaire, *J. Educ. Psychol.*, 1925, **16**, 316-322.

960.—Symonds, P. M., and Chase, D. H., Practice vs. motivation, *J. Educ. Psychol.*, 1929, **20**, 19-35.

961.—Symonds, P. M., and Jackson, C. E., *Measurement of the personality adjustments of high school pupils*, 1935.

962.—Tallman, G. G., A comparative study of identical and non-identical twins with respect to intelligence resemblances, *27th Yrbk. of the National Society for the Study of Education*, 1928, 83-88.

963.—Tarde, G., *Les lois de l'imitation*, 1890.

964.—Telford, C. W., An experimental study of some factors influencing the social attitudes of college students, *J. Soc. Psychol.*, 1934, **5**, 421-428.

965.—Terman, L. M., *Genetic studies of genius*, I. *Mental and physical traits of a thousand gifted children*, 1925.

966.—Terman, L. M., *The measurement of intelligence*, 1916.

967.—Terman, L. M., and Miles, C. C., *Sex and personality*, 1936.

968.—Terry, G. C., A study of psycho-dynamic patterns, *Amer. J. Psychiat.*, 1929, **8**, 881-899.

969.—Thomas, D. S., *et al.*, *Observational studies of social behavior*, 1933.

970.—Thomas, D. S., *et al.*, Some new techniques for studying social behavior, *Child Devel. Monog.*, No. 1, 1929.

971.—Thomas, W. I., and Znaniecki, F., *The Polish peasant in Europe and America*, 2nd ed., 2 vols., 1927.

972.—Thompson, H., The growth and significance of daily variations in infant behavior, *J. Genet. Psychol.*, 1932, **40**, 16-36.

973.—Thompson, H., Research approaches to longitudinal studies of development, (Paper read at Christmas meetings of the Society for Research in Child Development), 1936.

974.—Thomson, H. B., *The mental traits of sex*, 1903.

975.—Thorek, M., Experimental investigations of the rôle of the Leydig, seminiferous, and Sertoli cells and effects of testicular transplantation, *Endocrinology*, 1924, **8**, 61-90.

976.—Thorndike, E. L., *The original nature of man*, 1913.

977.—Thurstone, L. L., An experimental study of nationality preferences, *J. Gen. Psychol.*, 1928, **1**, 405-425.

978.—Thurstone, L. L., The measurement of change in social attitudes, *J. Soc. Psychol.*, 1931, **2**, 230-235; Influence of motion pictures on children's attitudes,

J. Soc. Psychol., 1931, **2**, 291-305; The effect of a motion picture film upon children's attitude toward the Germans, *J. Educ. Psychol.*, 1932, **23**, 241-246.

979.—Thurstone, L. L., The method of paired comparisons for social values, *J. Abn. & Soc. Psychol.*, 1927, **21**, 384-400.

980.—Thurstone, L. L., Theory of attitude measurement, *Psychol. Rev.*, 1929, **36**, 222-241.

981.—Thurstone, L. L., and Chave, E. J., *The measurement of attitude*, 1930.

982.—Thurstone, L. L., and Jenkins, R. L., Birth order and intelligence, *J. Educ. Psychol.*, 1929, **20**, 641-651.

983.—Thurstone, L. L., and Jenkins, R. L., Order of birth, parent-age, and intelligence, *Behav. Res. Fund Monog.*, 1931.

984.—Thurstone, L. L., and Thurstone, T. G., A neurotic inventory, *J. Soc. Psychol.*, 1930, **1**, 3-30.

985.—Tilney, F., Behavior in its relation to the development of the brain, Part II, Correlation between the development of the brain and behavior in the albino rat from embryonic stages to maturity, *Bull. Neur. Inst. New York*, 1933, **3**, 352-358.

986.—Tilson, M. A., Problems of pre-school children, *Teach. Coll. Contrib. Educ.*, 1929, No. 356.

987.—Tinklepaugh, O. L., The multiple delayed reaction with chimpanzees and monkeys, *J. Comp. Psychol.*, 1932, **13**, 207-243.

988.—Travis, L. E., The effect of a small audience upon eye-hand coordination, *J. Abn. & Soc. Psychol.*, 1925, **20**, 142-146.

989.—Triplett, N., The dynamogenic factors in pacemaking and competition, *Amer. J. Psychol.*, 1898, **2**, 507-533.

990.—Triplett, N., The psychology of conjuring deceptions, *Amer. J. Psychol.*, 1900, **11**, 439-510.

991.—Trotter, W., *Instincts of the herd in peace and war*, 1916.

992.—Trow, W. C., and Pu, A. S. T., Self-ratings of the Chinese, *School & Soc.*, 1927, **26**, 213-216.

993.—Tulchin, S. H., Emotional factors in reading disabilities in school children, *J. Educ. Psychol.*, 1935, **26**, 443-454.

994.—Uhrbrock, R. S., Attitudes of 4430 employees, *J. Soc., Psychol.*, 1934, **5**, 365-377.

995.—Uhrbrock, R. S., Estimating intelligence from photographs, *Ninth International Congress of Psychology, Proceedings and Papers* (1929, publ. 1930), 451-452.

996.—Updegraff, R., and Herbst, E. K., An experimental study of the social behavior stimulated in young children by certain play materials, *J. Genet. Psychol.*, 1933, **42**, 372-391.

997.—Updegraff, R., and Keister, M. E., A study of children's reactions to failure and an experimental attempt to modify them, *Univ. Iowa Stud.: Stud. Child Welfare*, 1937, **13**, No. 4.

998.—Valentine, C. W., The innate bases of fear, *J. Genet. Psychol.*, 1930, **37**, 394-420.

999.—Valentine, C. W., The psychology of imitation with special reference to early childhood, *Brit. J. Psychol.*, 1930, **21**, 105-132.

1000.—Van Alstyne, D., The environment of three-year-old children, *Teach. Coll. Contrib. Educ.*, 1929, No. 366.

1001.—Van Alstyne, D., *Play behavior and choice of play materials of school children*, 1932.

1002.—Vance, T. F., and McCall, L. T., Children's preferences among play materials as determined by the method of paired comparisons of pictures, *Child Devel.*, 1934, **5**, 267-277.

1003.—Vance, T. F., *et al.*, The development of children in the home management houses of the Iowa state college, *J. Exper. Educ.*, 1933, **2**, 166-169.

1004.—Vaughn, J., An experimental study of competition, *J. Appl. Psychol.*, 1936, **20**, 1-15.

1005.—Veblen, T., *Instinct of workmanship and the state of the industrial arts*, 1914.

1006.—Vernon, P. E., The biosocial nature of the personality trait, *Psychol. Rev.* 1933, **40**, 533-548.

1007.—Vernon, P. E., Can the "total personality" be studied objectively? *Char. & Pers.*, 1935, **4**, 1-10.

1008.—Vernon, P. E., The Rorschach ink-blot test, *Brit. J. Med. Psychol.*, 1933, **13**, 89-118, 179-205, 271-295.

1009.—Vernon, P. E., and Allport, G. W., A test for personal values, *J. Abn. & Soc. Psychol.*, 1931, **26**, 231-248.

1010.—Verry, E. E., A study of mental and social attitudes in the free play of pre-school children, Master's essay, State Univ. Iowa, 1923.

1011.—Vetter, G. B., The measurement of social and political attitudes and the related personality factors, *J. Abn. & Soc. Psychol.*, 1930, **25**, 149-189.

1012.—Vetter, G. B., and Green, M., Personality and group factors in the making of atheists, *J. Abn. & Soc. Psychol.*, 1932, **27**, 179-194.

1013.—Vitali, V., *Studi anthropologichi in servizio della pedagogia*, 1896.

1014.—Voelker, P. F., The function of ideals and attitudes in social education, *Teach. Coll. Contrib. Educ.*, 1921, No. 112.

1015.—Von Bracken, H., Mutual intimacy in twins, *Char. & Pers.*, 1934, **2**, 293-309.

1016.—Wada, T., An experimental study of hunger in its relation to activity, *Arch. Psychol.*, 1922, No. 57.

1017.—Wagner, M. E., Superstitions and their social and psychological correlatives among college students, *J. Educ. Sociol.*, 1928, **2**, 26-36.

1018.—Walcott, E., Daydreamers: a study of their adjustment in adolescence, *Smith Coll. Stud. Soc. Work*, 1932, **2**, 283-335.

1019.—Walker, C., A qualitative study of the consistency of dominance in children, Master's thesis in Columbia University Library, 1937.

1020.—Walker, M. J., Social interaction in young children with special reference to domination and subordination of the individual child, (Unpublished study).

1021.—Walsh, M. E., The relation of nursery-school training to the development of certain personality traits, *Child Devel.*, 1931, **2**, 72-73.

1022.—Wang, C. K. A., The internal consistency of the Allports' ascendance-submission test (form for men), *J. Abn. & Soc. Psychol.*, 1931, **26**, 154-161.

1023.—Wang, G. H., The relation between "spontaneous" activity and œstrous cycle in the white rat, *Comp. Psychol. Monog.*, 1923, **2**, No. 6.

1024.—Wannamaker, C., The relation of the individual problem child to recreation, *The Playground*, 1925, **19**, 204. See also, Methods of recreational adjustment as a form of social case treatment, *Ment. Hyg.*, 1923, **7**, 744-754.

1025.—Ward, A., A study of one hundred only children referred to a child guidance clinic, *Smith Coll. Stud. Soc. Work*, 1930, **1**, 41-86.

1026.—Warden, C. J., *Animal motivation, Experimental studies on the albino rat*, 1931.

1027.—Warden, C. J., *The emergence of human culture*, 1936.

1028.—Warden, C. J., and Cohen, A., A study of certain incentives applied under schoolroom conditions, *Ped. Sem.*, 1931, **39**, 320-327.

1029.—Waring, E. B., A guide for studying the personality of a young child, *J. Exper. Educ.*, 1932, **1**, 96-109.

1030.—Warner, L. H., A study of hunger behavior in the white rat by means of the obstruction method, *J. Comp. Psychol.*, 1928, **8**, 273-299. (Also in Warden, C. J., *Animal motivation studies*, 1931, 56-80.)

1031.—Warner, L. H., A study of sex behavior in the white rat by means of the obstruction method, *Comp. Psychol. Monog.*, 1927, **4**, No. 22. (Also in Warden, C. J., *Animal motivation studies*, 1931, 119-178.)

1032.—Washburn, M. F., *The animal mind*, 3rd ed., 1927.

1033.—Washburn, M. F., Hughes, E., Stewart, C., and Sligh, G., Reaction time, flicker, and affective sensitiveness as tests of extroversion and introversion, *Amer. J. Psychol.*, 1930, **42**, 412-413.

1034.—Washburn, M. F., Keeler, K., New, K. B., and Parshall, F. M., Experiments on the relation of reaction time, cube fluctuation, and mirror drawing to temperamental differences, *Amer. J. Psychol.*, 1929, **41**, 112-117.

1035.—Washburn, M. F., Kepler, H., McBloom, N., Pritchard, W., and Reimer, I., The Moore tests of radical and conservative temperaments, *Amer. J. Psychol.*, 1927, **38**, 449-452.

1036.—Washburn, R. W., A study of the smiling and laughing of infants in the first year of life, *Genet. Psychol. Monog.*, 1929, **6**, 397-537.

1037.—Washburne, J. N., The impulsions of adolescents as revealed by written wishes, *J. Juv. Res.*, 1932, **16**, 193-212.

1038.—Washburne, J. N., A test of social adjustment, *J. Appl. Psychol.*, 1935, **19**, 125-144.

1039.—Watson, G. B., Do groups think more efficiently than individuals? *J. Abn. & Soc. Psychol.*, 1928, **23**, 328-336.

1040.—Watson, G. B., Happiness among adult students of education, *J. Educ. Psychol.*, 1930, **21**, 79-109.

1041.—Watson, G. B., The measurement of fair-mindedness, *Teach. Coll. Contrib. Educ.*, 1925, No. 176.

1042.—Watson, G. B., *Orient and Occident: an opinion study*. (Unpublished work on file at Inst. of Pacific Relations, 129 E. 52nd St., N. Y. City. A digest of a part of this study appeared under the same title in *Rel. Educ.*, 1929, **24**, 322-328.)

1043.—Watson, J. B., *Behaviorism*, 2nd ed., 1930.

1044.—Watson, J. B., *Psychology from the standpoint of a behaviorist*, 2nd ed., 1924.

1045.—Watson, J. B., Review of Hamilton, G. V., *A research in marriage*

(1929), and of Hamilton, G. V., and Macgowan, K., What is wrong with marriage? (1929), *J. Soc. Psychol.*, 1930, **1**, p. 182.

1046.—Watson, J. B., and Raynor, R., Conditioned emotional reactions, *J. Exper. Psychol.*, 1920, **3**, 1-14.

1047.—Weber, C. O., The experimental differentia of introversion and extroversion, *J. Genet. Psychol.*, 1929, **36**, 571-580.

1048.—Wechsler, D., The measurement of emotional reactions: researches on psychogalvanic reflex, *Arch. Psychol.*, 1925, No. 76.

1049.—Wechsler, D., *The range of human capacities*, 1935.

1050.—Wechsler, D., Crabbs, L. M., and Freeman, R. G., Jr., Galvanic responses of pre-school children, *J. Genet. Psychol.*, 1930, **28**, 203-222.

1051.—de Weerdt, E. H., A study of the improvability of fifth-grade children in certain mental functions, *J. Educ. Psychol.*, 1927, **18**, 547-557.

1052.—Weill, B. B., *The behavior of young children of the same family*, 1928.

1053.—Weiss, A. P., The measurement of infant behavior, *Psychol. Rev.*, 1929, **36**, 453-471.

1054.—Weiss, L. A., An experimental investigation of certain factors involved in the pre-school child's compliance with commands, Master's thesis, State Univ. Iowa, 1931.

1055.—Weiss, L. A., An experimental investigation of certain factors involved in the pre-school child's compliance with commands, *Univ. Iowa Stud.: Stud. Child Welfare*, 1934, **9**, No. 3, 129-157.

1056.—Weller, F., Attitudes and skills in elementary science, *Sci. Educ.*, 1933, **17**, 90-97.

1057.—Wellman, B. L., Growth in intelligence under differing school environments, *J. Exper. Educ.*, 1934, **3**, 59-83.

1058.—Wellman, B., The school child's choice of companions, *J. Educ. Res.*, 1926, **14**, 126-132.

1059.—Wells, F. L., On the variability of individual judgment, in *Essays philosophical and psychological in honor of William James*, 1908, 511-549.

1060.—Weston, S. B., and English, H. B., The influence of the group on psychological test scores, *Amer. J. Psychol.*, 1926, **37**, 600-601.

1061.—Whipple, G. M., *Manual of mental and physical tests*, part 2, 3rd ed., 1921, 222 ff.

1062.—White, K. B., A clinical study of twenty-six pairs of twins, *Psychol. Clinic*, 1932-1933, **21**, 243-252.

1063.—White, L. D., Further contributions to the prestige value of public employment, *Univ. Chicago Soc. Sci. Stud.*, 1932.

1064.—White, L. D., The prestige value of public employment in Chicago, *Univ. Chicago Soc. Sci. Stud.*, 1929.

1065.—White, R. E., Penal law and public opinion, Master's essay in Columbia University Library, 1927.

1066.—White House Conference, *The adolescent in the family*, 1934.

1067.—Whitelaw, H., and Laslett, H. R. A., A further study of the acceptance of popular misbeliefs among college students, *Kadelpian Rev.*, 1932, **11**, 297-300.

1068.—Whitman, C., The behavior of pigeons, ed. by Carr, H. A., Carnegie Inst. Washington, 1919, *Publ. 257*, **3**.

1069.—Whittemore, I. C., Influence of competition on performance: an experimental study, *J. Abn. & Soc. Psychol.*, 1924, **19**, 236-253; The competitive consciousness, *J. Abn. & Soc. Psychol.*, 1925, **20**, 17-33.

1070.—Wickman, E. K., *Children's behavior and teachers' attitudes*, 1928.

1071.—Wile, I. S., Neary, L., Mace, L., and Davis, R., The continuity of the neurotic processes, *Amer. J. Orthopsychiat.*, 1934, **4**, 49-72.

1072.—Wile, I. S., and Noetzel, E., A study of birth order and behavior, *J. Soc. Psychol.*, 1931, **2**, 52-71.

1073.—Wilke, W. H., An experimental comparison of the speech, the radio, and the printed page as propaganda devices, *Arch. Psychol.*, 1934, No. 169.

1074.—Wilker, M., and Waring, E. B., Book I, *The behavior of young children*, 1929; Book II, *The behavior of children with materials*, 1930; Book III, *The behavior of children with other children*, 1932.

1075.—Williams, G. W., Suggestibility in the normal and hypnotic states, *Arch. Psychol.*, 1930, No. 122.

1076.—Williams, G. W., and Chamberlain, F., An evaluation of the use of the Allport Ascendance-Submission Test with high school girls, *J. Genet. Psychol.*, 1936, **49**, 363-375.

1077.—Williams, H. D., A survey of pre-delinquent school children of ten midwestern cities, *J. Educ. Sociol.*, 1934, **7**, 365-370.

1078.—Williams, H. M., A factor analysis of Berne's "Social behavior patterns in young children," *J. Exper. Educ.*, 1936, **4**, 142-146.

1079.—Williams, J. H., Hereditary nomadism and delinquency, *J. Delinq.*, 1916, **1**, 209-230.

1080.—Williams, J. H., The intelligence of the delinquent boy, *J. Delinq. Monog.*, 1919, No. 1.

1081.—Williams, P. E., A study of adolescent friendships, *Ped. Sem.*, 1923, **30**, 342-346.

1082.—Willoughby, R. R., A sampling of student opinion, *J. Soc. Psychol.*, 1930, **1**, 164-169.

1083.—Willoughby, R. R., Some properties of the Thurstone Personality Schedule and a suggested revision, *J. Soc. Psychol.*, 1932, **3**, 401-424.

1084.—Wingfield, A. H., and Sandiford, P., Twins and orphans, *J. Educ. Psychol.*, 1928, **19**, 410-423.

1085.—Winter, L., *Mass. State Hosp. Bull.*, 1897, 463.

1086.—Witmer, H. L., The later social adjustment of problem children. A report of thirteen follow-up investigations, *Smith Coll. Stud. Soc. Work*, 1935, **6**, 1-98.

1087.—Witmer, H. L., Parental behavior as an index to the probable outcome of treatment in a child guidance clinic, *Amer. J. Orthopsychiat.*, 1933, **3**, 431-444.

1088.—Witmer, H. L., et al., The childhood personality and parent-child relationships of dementia praecox and manic-depressive patients, *Smith Coll. Stud. Soc. Work*, 1934, **4**, 289-377.

1089.—Witty, P. A., The only child of five, *Psychol. Clinic*, 1933, **22**, 73-87.

1090.—Witty, P. A., "Only" and "intermediate" children of high school ages, *Psychol. Bull.*, 1934, **31**, 734.

1091.—Witty, P. A., and Lehman, H. C., Sex differences: collecting interests, *J. Educ. Psychol.*, 1931, **22**, 221-228.

1092.—Wolf, R., and Murray, H. A., An experiment in judging personalities, *J. Psychol.*, 1936, **3**, 345-365.

1093.—Wolff, H. A., Smith C. E., and Murray, H. A., The psychology of humor, *J. Abn. & Soc. Psychol.*, 1934, **28**, 341-365.

1094.—Wood, T. W., The effect of approbation and reproof on the mastery of nonsense syllables, *J. Appl. Psychol.*, 1934, **18**, 657-664.

1095.—Woodrow, H., and Bemmels, V., Overstatement as a test of general character in pre-school children, *J. Educ. Psychol.*, 1927, **18**, 239-246.

1096.—Woodward, L. E., Relations of religious training and life patterns to the adult religious life, *Teach. Coll. Contrib. Educ.*, 1932, No. 527.

1097.—Woodworth, R. S., *Dynamic psychology*, 1918.

1098.—Wright, S., The method of path coefficients, *Ann. Math. Statist.*, 1934, **5**, 161-215.

1099.—Wright, W. L., Some effects of incentives on work and fatigue, *Psychol. Rev.*, 1906, **13**, 23-24.

1100.—Wrightstone, J. W., Civic beliefs and correlated intellectual and social forces, *School Rev.*, 1934, **42**, 53-58.

1101.—Wülker, L., Das einzige Kind, *Zsch. f. päd. Psychol.*, 1934, **35**, 324-326.

1102.—Yerkes, R. M., The heredity of wildness and savageness in rats, *J. Animal Behavior*, 1913, **3**, 286-296.

1103.—Yerkes, R. M., Psychological examining in the U. S. army, *Memoirs Nat. Acad. Sci.*, 1921.

1104.—Young, D., Some effects of a course in American race problems on the race prejudice of 450 undergraduates at the University of Pennsylvania, *J. Abn. & Soc. Psychol.*, 1927, **22**, 235-242.

1105.—Zaluzhni, A. S., (The character of the interaction between children of pre-school age), *Ukrainski vestnik eksperimentalnoe pedagogiki i refleksologi*, 1927, **2**, 5. In *Psychol. Abst.*, 1928, **2**, No. 3294.

1106.—Zaluzhni, A. S., Collective behavior of children at a pre-school age, *J. Soc. Psychol.*, 1930, **1**, 367-378.

1107.—Zaluzhni, A. S., *Formirovanie socialnich navikov u detey preddoshkolnogo vosrasta*, 1928. See Murphy and Murphy, pp. 282-283.

1108.—Zawadzki, B., and Lazarsfeld, P., The psychological consequences of unemployment, *J. Soc. Psychol.*, 1935, **6**, 224-251.

1109.—Zillig, M., Experimentelle Untersuchungen über die Glaubwürdigkeit von Kindern, *Zsch. f. Psychol.*, 1931, **119**, 311-371.

1110.—Zubin, J., Some effects of incentives: A study of individual differences in rivalry, *Teach. Coll. Contrib. Educ.*, 1932, No. 532.

1111.—Zulliger, H., Schwierige Schüler, *Zsch. psychoanal, Päd.*, 1935, **9**, 138-147.

AUTHOR INDEX

SUBJECT INDEX

Activity, levels of, 380
Activity drives, 94-95, 193
Adequate stimulus, 191, 197-199
Adience, 100-105, 188, 194, 210, 218
Adjustment, 210, 326
Adolescence, 374, 511.
   See also California Adolescent
   Study.
Aesthetic drives, 94-95, 193
Aesthetic preferences, 69-70, 690-692
Affect. *See* Emotion.
Affection, 195, 207, 237-238, 263-
   264, 324, 515, 630.
   See also Love.
Age, effect of, on suggestion, 174; in
   relation to social behavior, 324.
   See also Age levels; Development;
   Maturation.
Aggressiveness, 82-83, 285, 324, 330,
   332, 342, 352-353, 376, 508, 703-
   706.
   See also Conflict; Dominance, so-
   cial.
Ammassalik Eskimo, 754
Andaman Islander, 154
Anger, 107, 109-111, 138, 225, 402-
   403, 426-427, 801
Animism, 595-596.
   See also Egocentrism; Realism.
Anthropology, 54, 337, 739-757
Anxiety, 373-532
Approach-withdrawal, 300
Arapesh, 745-746, 750, 757
Arctic hysteria, 184
Artificialism, 595.
   See also Egocentrism.
Ascendance-submission, 257, 300, 324,
   330, 348-349, 397-404, 454-455,

460-461, 464-465, 633-636, 783,
   797-798, 824.
   See also Aggressiveness; Dominance, social.
Aspiration level, 212, 221, 426-429,
   441-442, 450, 504.
   See also Ego level; Reality level.
Association, 160-161, 170-172, 180.
   See also Conditioned response;
   Learning.
Attention, 180.
   See also Selective response.
Attitudes, 172, 179-180, 201, 206, 209,
   219, 223-224, 238, 248-250, 279,
   298-299, 304, 312, 325-326, 364-
   366, 371-373, 404-411, 421-425,
   619, 648-649, 686, 706-709, 749-
   757, 875, 888-1046; age in relation
   to, 919-929; economic and political,
   360-361, 514, 891-892, 930, 950-
   951, 954-959, 982-985, 992, 1007,
   1033-1040; modification of, 172,
   946-980; racial and national, 239-
   241, 283, 371-372, 514, 898-901,
   925-928, 948-952, 972, 982-985,
   992-1000, 1042; religious and ethical, 911, 915, 920, 933, 1001-1011,
   1034, 1038; sex, 312-313
Audience, influence of, 700-702
Authority, 180, 208, 238, 277, 335,
   339, 503-508, 545, 600, 647
Autism, 200, 223-224, 582
Autobiography, 288
Auto-competition, 702-703.
   See also Competition; Knowledge
   of results.
Auto-suggestion, 171-172.
   See also Suggestion.

V

U